CASEWORK
A Psychosocial Therapy

CASEWORK

A Psychosocial Therapy

FIFTH EDITION

Mary E. Woods
and
Florence Hollis

Boston   Burr Ridge, IL   Dubuque, IA   Madison, WI   New York   San Francisco   St. Louis
Bangkok   Bogotá   Caracas   Lisbon   London   Madrid
Mexico City   Milan   New Delhi   Seoul   Singapore   Sydney   Taipei   Toronto

McGraw-Hill Higher Education

*A Division of The **McGraw-Hill** Companies*

CASEWORK: A PSYCHOSOCIAL THERAPY

This book is printed on acid-free paper.

1 2 3 4 5 6 7 8 9 0 DOC/DOC 9 0 9 8 7 6 5 4 3 2 1 0 9

ISBN 0-07-290179-9

Editorial director: *Phillip A. Butcher*
Senior sponsoring editor: *Alan McClare*
Marketing manager: *Leslie A. Kraham*
Project editor: *Paula M. Krauza*
Production supervisor: *Debra R. Benson*
Freelance design coordinator: *Laurie J. Entringer*
Supplement coordinator: *Mark Sienicki*
Compositor: *Shepherd, Incorporated*
Typeface: *10 / 12 New Century Schoolbook*
Printer: *R. R. Donnelley & Sons Company*

Library of Congress Cataloging-in-Publication Data

Woods, Mary E. (1930)–
    Casework, a psychosocial therapy / Mary E. Woods and Florence
Hollis. — 5th ed.
      p.   cm.
    Includes bibliographical references.
    ISBN 0–07–290179–9
    1. Social case work. 2. Psychotherapy—Social aspects.
I. Hollis, Florence. II. Title.
HV43.W64 2000
361.3'2—dc21   99–28076
                                      CIP

http://www.mhhe.com

BRIEF CONTENTS

CONTENTS

PREFACE

This fifth edition of *Casework: A Psychosocial Therapy* is designed to give a clear presentation of the theory and techniques of the psychosocial approach to casework treatment. It deals with the "whys" and "hows" of clinical social work practice in the prevention and treatment of psychological, interpersonal, and social problems. Its methodology and its applicability address clients' concrete practical needs, environmental deficits and pressures, as well as personal and relationship crises or quandaries. Of course, new challenges arising from changing times and different types of difficulty call for variations in emphases and techniques, but, as the text explains, *the central principles of the psychosocial approach apply across the board* and can be adapted to assist clients facing a wide range of dilemmas.

The psychosocial perspective described and illustrated in this book prepares the way for *multilevel* and *multisystem assessments* of biological factors, internal psychological and emotional processes, relationship patterns, environmental conditions and pressures, and the interplay among these systems that impact the "person-in-situation," a casework term that represents the inseparability of all these influences on individuals and families.

Millions of Americans are receiving some sort of counseling or therapy, and caseworkers and clinical social workers are the *chief providers* of these services. Also, a majority of social work students are interested in careers in clinical practice. In our view, a "generic" approach to social work training does not adequately equip students with the theory and tools that are required for on-line clinicians. This edition of *Casework,* like the previous ones, has endeavored to provide its readers with a grounding in the basic knowledge, theory, and principles of practice fundamental to psychosocial casework and clinical practice.

READERS OF *CASEWORK*

From the information we have received, *Casework* is used as a basic text by many instructors in graduate schools of social work, often but not exclusively in casework or clinical social work departments. It is frequently assigned in clinical practice courses; some casework departments have required all master's students concentrating on direct or clinical practice to read the book in the first year so that they can refer to it throughout their graduate training. Specific chapters of the book are used in courses focusing on a specific area of clinical work, such as brief therapy and crisis intervention, environmental treatment, or conjoint therapy. We have also learned that the four chapters on family and couple therapy have formed the basis of courses in master's and doctoral programs designed to teach these modalities.

Undergraduate students, especially those majoring in social work and working toward a BSW, are also often assigned *Casework,* or portions of it, in various classes devoted to casework theory and practice.

We have been gratified to ascertain that many practicing clinicians, including some from other helping professions, refer to this book over the course of their professional lives to refresh or clarify their thinking and approaches to clinical practice. Agencies and organizations often make the book available to social workers and others who provide direct services. Students, educators, and researchers turn to *Casework* for detailed descriptions of Florence Hollis's classification of treatment procedures and client–worker communications. The book's value to social workers with various specializations, at all stages of their careers, has been repeatedly documented.

FEATURES OF THE FIFTH EDITION
Organization

Part One: "The Theoretical Framework" Part One sets the stage for further elaboration and illustrations of the psychosocial approach to casework in subsequent chapters of the text.

Chapter 1 discusses recent social trends and modifications in practice and a brief history of the development of the psychosocial approach from "diagnostic" or "differential" casework. The principles on which diagnostic casework was founded continue to be basic to psychosocial casework, but their interpretation and application in casework have changed in many ways and have been greatly expanded. Introduced in this early chapter, and fundamental to discussions throughout the book, casework's values and long-standing commitments are explained: to protect the rights of individuals, to attempt to alleviate injustice of all kinds, to serve the poor and the forgotten, to help people gain access to opportunities, and to try to eliminate obstacles to self-fulfillment. Chapter 1 includes comments on education for clinical social work specialization. Research issues, past and present, are remarked upon; we emphasize the importance of involvement of clinicians in the study of casework processes and outcomes.

Chapter 2 outlines the personality theories on which psychosocial casework operates, including modifications and adaptations of psychoanalytic, ego psychology, cognitive, object relations, and self-psychology concepts. Other ideas basic to the framework are discussed, especially systems and ecological theories; family therapy concepts; communication and role theories; knowledge gained from studies on culture, ethnicity, and gender; plus other pertinent social science and philosophical concepts. Readers are referred to this overview of the theoretical framework throughout the text. From the outset, the reader is helped to understand the dual focus of psychosocial casework: on people and their environments and on the interactions and "fit" between them. Also, in this chapter and later, we emphasize that in practice, over and over again, we find that modifications of the client's environment can result in emotional and behavioral changes and, conversely, personal growth can often give people the strength required to alter their external situations. Thus, we illustrate in various ways how clinicians may *concentrate on those systems most accessible to change, not necessarily the most "dysfunctional" ones.* In almost every chapter, including Chapter 2, we endeavor to demonstrate that the personality itself is a system, and that systems and ecological concepts can and must be integrated with psychodynamic theory.

Chapter 3 includes case examples designed to demonstrate the use of the concepts described in Chapter 2 in actual practice; the role that theory plays in guiding choices of techniques and treatment directions is illustrated.

Chapter 4 introduces Florence Hollis's research in identifying and classifying treatment procedures and client–worker communications; her typology is at the heart of *Casework*. The evolution of her classification is briefly recounted here; the procedures are summarized. The ongoing value of the Hollis topology for research and theory building is discussed. (Chapter 21, previously Chapter 9, elaborates on the methods Hollis developed to study and work with the classification, methods that can be informally utilized by clinicians to study their own cases.)

Part Two: "Treatment: Analysis of Procedures" Chapters 5 through 8 describe in greater detail, with many illustrations, the treatment procedures outlined in Chapter 4, including environmental interventions. Their applicability to practice with individuals, couples, families, and collaterals is illustrated in these chapters as well as throughout the text. Thus, because people's inner and outer lives are intertwined, sometimes interventions are aimed at modifying the environment; at other times individuals and families are helped to maximize opportunities and to develop creative means to cope with or find alternatives to (*not* adjust to) damaging external conditions before societal changes can be effected.

Chapter 9 discusses the profound significance and complexities of the client–worker relationship. We emphasize the fact that research and practice experience have consistently confirmed that *no other treatment variable is as important as the quality of the client–worker relationship;* positive therapeutic relationships and favorable treatment outcomes are closely associated. "Core conditions"—essential clinician characteristics and attitudes—are described. The rights of clients to self-direction and to confidentiality are stressed; mutuality, collaboration, and equality in the client–worker relationship are emphasized. Some of the meanings and uses of transference and countertransference in the therapeutic relationship are discussed. Issues related to worker burnout and worker self-disclosure are addressed. Throughout the text, and in this chapter, readers are encouraged to review the descriptions of treatment procedures and the discussions of the treatment relationship covered in Part Two.

Part Three: "Diagnostic Understanding and the Treatment Process" Chapter 10 is devoted to a discussion of principles and techniques that bear upon initial interviews and the psychosocial study. The material presented in Part Two on treatment procedures and on the client–worker relationship is further elaborated upon and explained with case examples.

Chapters 11, 12, and 13 describe in detail factors involved in arriving at assessments and diagnostic understanding. Processes pertaining to the selection of treatment objectives and procedures are explained and illustrated. These chapters emphasize the importance of mutuality between worker and client in arriving at the evaluation of a problem and in making choices about how to resolve it.

Chapters 14 through 17 concentrate on family and couple therapies. Even though discussions and case examples in earlier chapters describe multiple-person interviewing, these four chapters elaborate upon and discuss in greater detail some of the theory and practice techniques that have informed conjoint modalities. We have endeavored to explain complex concepts, illustrated with clinical examples, in a clear and helpful manner. The applicability of psychosocial theory and the Hollis treatment procedures to these modalities is explained.

Chapter 18 on crisis intervention and brief treatment expands upon earlier discussions of these modalities. Although there are examples of short-term treatment throughout the book, this chapter provides further information about the theoretical underpinnings and practice principles of these important approaches.

Chapter 19 discusses terminations between workers and clients and emphasizes the importance of individualizing clients and following their leads; worker sensitivity and self-awareness are stressed. Factors influencing the diverse courses endings take are discussed.

Chapter 20, which presents four detailed case examples, attempts to further enhance the reader's understanding of the methods of psychosocial study, diagnosis, and treatment and to illustrate just how choices about goals and treatment procedures are made.

Content Changes

Although alterations in chapter order and organization are minimal, there are changes in content and in emphasis throughout the new edition. Every topic and chapter has been reviewed for content, presentation, and language with particular attention given to whether the discussions are clear, thorough, and up-to-date. More headings, highlights, and bullets are used to make the text easier to read.

Psychosocial Casework's Roots   Even more than earlier, this edition emphasizes the importance of understanding the history of casework and its knowledge and traditions, especially in Chapter 1. Knowledge of the past and a sense of continuity illuminate the present; when we know where we have been, we can better evaluate where we are now and where we want to go. From awareness of the missions, perspectives, and struggles of our predecessors, we can learn from their achievements and from their mistakes as we continue to build on the ever-growing foundation of knowledge. Recurrent swings of the social work pendulum between preoccupation with the influences of personality on the one hand or with social forces on the other are more likely to be avoided when we ground our thinking in the balanced "person-in-situation" formulations of those who came before us. Furthermore, as we see it, knowledge of history is important because too often we come up with what we believe to be a new perspective on theory or practice, only to find that it is an old idea expressed in new terms or language.

Integration of New Perspectives and Knowledge with Established Principles Several chapters discuss in greater detail than previously recent ideas and perspectives that are comfortably assimilated by the psychosocial framework. These include even greater emphasis on describing and illustrating the value of the strengths and empowerment perspectives. We indicate how the constructivist and narrative approaches, among others, are consonant with the humanistic values that underlie psychosocial methods. As these perspectives have been elaborated upon, they play an important role in underscoring psychosocial casework's established commitment to collaboration and equality between worker and client. Along similar lines, perhaps this edition emphasizes even more strongly than before that respect for the individual is most effectively demonstrated by our humility, by listening keenly to our clients, and by conveying to them that *they* are *the* experts on their lives and visions and the meanings of these, and that their unique attributes and worldviews are important and understood. New knowledge and perspectives about family theory and practice have also been incorporated in this fifth edition. Discussions of single-parent, step-, and three-generation families have been expanded; more is included regarding gay couples and families headed by same-sex partners.

Diversity Chapter 2 and other chapters discuss in greater detail than previously the importance of understanding the influences of race, ethnicity, spirituality, class, gender, and sexual orientation on personality, family patterns, and casework treatment itself. Issues related to differences between worker and client are discussed and illustrated with case examples. The importance of individualizing clients is stressed, as is the need to avoid stereotyping; above all, the text accentuates how crucial it is for us to learn from our clients the meanings of their backgrounds and identities to *them;* the danger of operating on preconceptions is emphasized.

Assessment Chapter 11 on assessment and diagnostic understanding has been expanded in several ways. For example, guidelines for the assessment of strengths, of particular emotional or personality features or conditions, and of problems with substance abuse, among others, have been elaborated upon. Some of the hazards of clinical diagnosis and "pathologizing" clients are discussed. Chapter 8 includes more detail than formerly about the process of assessing environmental resources and deficits.

Short-Term Treatment   Because of the recent surge of interest in mastering short-term treatment approaches, Chapter 18 on crisis intervention and brief treatment has been expanded. Ethical concerns and policy issues related to managed care are addressed. We view it as very distressing that at the very time we have developed more sophisticated methods for working with clients with personality disorders and developmental deficits, among others, the constraints of managed care have made long-term treatment less readily available. Along similar lines, just when social workers are emphasizing more than ever the importance of client empowerment, third parties are given the power to make decisions about the type and length of treatment that will be allowed, decisions that used to be based on private discussions between client and worker.

Case Illustrations: Greater Variety of Clients, Cases, Settings and Services, and Types of Problems Presented   The number of detailed case examples, short illustrations, and vignettes in several chapters of this fifth edition has increased. Cases of voluntary and involuntary clients from many backgrounds, with a wide range of concerns and dilemmas, seen in a variety of settings, have been included. The examples are intended to demonstrate how psychosocial theory and principles of practice can be applied to clinical work with individuals, couples, families, and collaterals. Chapter 8, on environmental treatment, includes three examples of innovative, coordinated practice initiated by agencies and individual practitioners that have resulted in creative, accessible, multifaceted services designed to respond to special needs of special groups and/or to increase availability of casework help.

Chapter Notes and Bibliography   Notes and references have been radically updated. Many previous suggested readings have been eliminated, replaced by current references. But there are "classic" articles and books that we still recommend, not only because they illuminate casework history, but also because they have stood the test of time and are still relevant to today's perspectives and practice. The fact that chapter notes and the bibliography include references spanning several decades attests to both the continuity and the changes in direct casework practice, a practice that now serves more people than ever. As comprehensive and thorough as we hope *Casework* is, in the chapter notes we encourage readers to seek further elaborations on our discussions; we also often urge them to read about perspectives that are different from our own.

This fifth edition documents one more step in the growth of an approach to casework practice that has been developing for many years. We continue to be impressed by the soundness of psychosocial casework as a theoretical system. It is obviously an open system, constantly incorporating new ideas as well as corrections of old ideas, constantly expanding. While the system has a "skin" permeable enough to take in some of the new, it is resistant to ideas that have not been tested in practice or that are incompatible with its theoretical principles or value base. Change is therefore gradual, through assimilation rather than through assault. Comparison of the previous four editions of this book will clearly demonstrate this process.

ACKNOWLEDGMENTS

It may not have taken a village to produce this revision, but it certainly took the help and generosity of many people whom I am eager to acknowledge.

My most profound appreciation goes to Florence Hollis for inviting me to share in the writing of the third edition and entrusting me with future editions. I am glad that before her death I was able to convey to her how much this opportunity meant to me.

My part in this book, started by Florence Hollis in 1964, is the culmination of many influences in my life, professional and personal. It is not possible to acknowledge—or even to identify in my own mind—each person who has touched me or helped to shape my ideas. However, apart from my family, the hundreds of clients I have seen over the years—the many courageous people through whom I learned so much about painful human conditions and about imaginative ways that can be found to struggle against personal miseries and environmental assaults—have taught me the most, including about the resilience of the human spirit. Above all, my clients taught me the value of true listening, of mutuality, of self-direction, of tailoring each piece of work to the uniqueness of the person and his or her circumstances, and of humility. The very "demanding" or "recalcitrant" clients often taught me the most.

I am also indebted to those students and supervisees whose fresh ideas, optimism, deep concern for people's suffering, and eagerness to find ever better ways to help challenged me to explore further, to look at old and new problems in new ways. I was most fortunate to have the opportunity to learn along with them. Colleagues at Hunter College School of Social Work were very important to me in the revisions of *Casework*. Particular thanks go to Florence Vigilante. Harold Lewis, Mildred Mailick, Elaine Marshack, Maria Rosenbloom, and Robert Salmon were most generous in their own special ways.

Again, as I revised this fifth edition, my very good friend and colleague, Dorothy Kitchell, carefully went over every chapter and offered important suggestions and invaluable encouragement; I am grateful beyond words for the hours she spent reading and responding. With extraordinary generosity, Linda Kurtz volunteered to reread, from cover to cover, the fourth edition; her suggestions were very useful for this revision. I am indebted to Luis Zayas for his assistance in the literature search, for case materials, and for recommendations for the new edition. Mary Ann Jones's kindness and priceless assistance in the section on social work research are deeply appreciated. My thanks go to Fran Davidson who, with competence and speed, produced the Bibliography from sometimes almost illegible 5×8 index cards; her assistance in the review of page proofs was invaluable.

I am particularly grateful to Beth Chase, Sally Eaton, and Linda Robbins for case materials and for their firsthand information about innovative casework services and settings. Mary Ellen Noonan offered extremely useful suggestions, particularly about the environmental and brief treatment chapters. Ann Marie Garran graciously reviewed and commented upon some of the new text. I want to thank Howard Robinson for his thoughtfulness and encouragement. Words cannot adequately express my gratitude to all of these friends and colleagues.

The comments of anonymous reviewers were extremely helpful; I am sure they will find that many of their recommendations were taken to heart. And, finally, I am grateful to Nancy Blaine, former sponsoring social work editor at McGraw-Hill, for her support and competent help; I also want to thank her assistants, Heather Moss and Miriam Buyer, for their cheerfulness, patience, and assistance. The involvement of Alan McClare and Paula Krauza was essential to the final phases of the production of this 5th edition. Once again, the leadership of Phil Butcher, editorial director of the Social Sciences and Humanities Program at McGraw-Hill, has been greatly appreciated.

TRIBUTE TO FLORENCE HOLLIS
JANUARY 30, 1907–
JULY 3, 1987

A native of Philadelphia, Florence Hollis did her undergraduate work at Wellesley College and received her master's degree from Smith College School of Social Work in 1931 and her doctorate from Bryn Mawr School of Social Work and Social Research in 1947. Her social work career began while she was an undergraduate and, after her graduation from Smith, she was immediately assigned to a leadership position at the Family Society in Philadelphia. Through the Depression years, she worked at family agencies in Philadelphia and also in Cleveland, where she taught part-time at Western Reserve University. For five years during the 1940s, Dr. Hollis was editor of the *Journal of Social Casework*. In 1947, she joined the faculty at the Columbia University School of Social Work, where she was a highly esteemed professor of casework in the master's and doctoral programs until her retirement in 1972. While at Columbia, she developed her typology of casework procedures, which became the basis for ongoing and rigorous research into worker–client communication and the casework process; her classification and the research based upon it have been at the core of all editions of this widely used text, which has been translated into several languages. During her years on the faculty of Columbia, she also taught many summer sessions at Smith and frequently conducted seminars and institutes in this country and abroad. She was active on academic committees and professional councils, including the Council on Social Work Education. Over the course of her career, she published three books and over 40 articles on casework. As part of her very busy life, Florence Hollis saw clients on a regular basis; she considered this essential to the successful performance of her other professional roles.

I first met Florence Hollis when I was a student, in the early 1960s. Because she was interested, as I was, in an exchange of our sometimes divergent points of view, we had lunch and good conversations from time to time over the next several years. It was not until 1977, however, when she invited me to collaborate on the third edition of this book, that I spent extended amounts of time with her. From then on, until a few weeks before her death, I visited her several times a year at her lovely retirement home, Crosslands, at Kennett Square, Pennsylvania, and was in frequent contact with her by telephone. As her student, colleague, and coauthor, and as a friend to Flo Hollis, I feel most privileged to have known her.

When I was a student, Flo's interest in studying the relationship between casework and social class led her to urge her students— perhaps especially those of us with outlooks that were somewhat different from her own—to bring their thinking and casework experiences to the subject. She absorbed our suggestions and included many of them in her important paper published in *Social Casework* in October 1965, making sure to credit us with our contributions. As all who were taught by her know, she regularly sought and took seriously her students' ideas and reactions to her thinking.

As colleagues and coauthors of the third edition, we worked together closely for over two intense years. Always challenged, often exhilarated, occasionally frustrated, we hammered out our perspective and shared our ideas—surprised and pleased at how a meeting of the minds or new realizations often emerged from initially different slants on a particular question. We worked together also on the plans for revisions and additions to the fourth edition until her illness made this impossible.

Flo brought a spirit of mutuality and openness to our joint endeavors. Despite her revered position in the field, she was modest, always eager to search for and consider new ideas and strategies that might enhance casework practice, *if these were grounded in real experience.* The accumulation of abstract knowledge had little meaning to her if it could not be used on behalf of distressed people who turn to caseworkers for help. With Immanuel Kant, she firmly believed "Experience without theory is blind, but theory without experience is mere intellectual play."

In fact, Flo chose me to help to revise her text because of my strong background in clinical work in general, and also because of my special interest, training, and experience in family and marital treatment, modalities with which she herself had little experience. Just a few months before her death, as we discussed the fourth edition and our plans to include two new chapters on couple treatment, she said that she wanted me to remark on the changes that had evolved in her thinking since the publication of her well-known *Women in Marital Conflict* in 1949. It was important to her that students and others who would be reading the new book recognize the need to be ever open to consonant new ideas, data, and theory as these emerge. Thus, while Florence Hollis strongly urged us to preserve and protect the years of knowledge derived from day-in, day-out casework experiences with clients—knowledge that has proved its value—for 50 years she was also in the forefront of those who had developed the psychosocial approach that was *specifically designed* to assimilate new information.

To the end, Florence Hollis took a serious interest in social and political matters. She was very disturbed by the cutbacks in federal funding of social programs that occurred during the Reagan administration. She was deeply concerned about what she saw as the deterioration of standards and values in the country and the world, particularly when people's health and well-being were directly affected. She abhorred poverty, war, and injustice of all kinds. From her sickbed she spoke often of the hideous conditions endured by growing numbers of homeless individuals and families. As all who knew her well can attest, she never hesitated to stand up and be counted for her strong convictions, even when these were unpopular. In her personal relationships, in her pioneering role in the development of casework, and in her worldview, she was uncompromisingly ethical. She was dedicated to seeking means to bring out the best in people and their situations, and to right the wrongs when she could.

For 8 years she knew that she had lymphoma; she was indignant when the doctors told her—at age 72—that she would be lucky to have 10 more years. She wanted to reach the 90s, hers and the 20th century's. Her mother had lived to 91. When it became apparent in the last year that she would succumb sooner than she had hoped, she faced the facts squarely, complained very little, and made the best of the time she had left, letting go of life only after the price was too high and the rewards too few. Flo had an extraordinary religious faith that not only guided her through life but comforted her in her final years and days. From close friends who tended her daily in the Crosslands infirmary where she lived for several months, we learned that she died peacefully and willingly.

As a practitioner, educator, researcher, and author and, equally important, as a woman of integrity and caring, Florence Hollis made a contribution to modern clinical social work that is beyond measure. I am among hundreds who are grateful to her. She will endure in the memories of those who knew her; her wisdom will be passed on to many others through her writings.

I did not know just how much I would miss her. The revision of the book has been far lonelier without her. But I am fortunate to have gotten to know the many facets of Florence Hollis over her final decade. It means a lot to me to tell the readers even these few things about her. I hope to have conveyed how much she deserves to be remembered.

Mary E. Woods
August 1987

Without a doubt, Florence Hollis would be delighted to know that a fifth edition of the book she began in 1964 is now being published in the 21st century. Her research, her experience, her wisdom, her integrity, and her commitment to excellence—qualities that distinguished her—continue to be woven into the fabric of *Casework*. Despite revisions, expansions, and incorporation of new knowledge and perspectives, her spirit remains an important part of this edition; hence, *we* is used throughout the text in more than an editorial sense: it symbolizes the ongoing Woods–Hollis collaboration. I still miss her actual presence, but I am grateful for the many gifts she left behind. We are all richer because of them.

Mary E. Woods
October 1998

PART ONE

THE THEORETICAL FRAMEWORK

CHAPTER 1

CASEWORK: THEN AND NOW

The concern of this book is the description and analysis of the psychosocial approach to casework. Its ultimate purpose is to contribute to the improvement of the quality of casework or clinical social work treatment offered to individuals and families facing personal and social dilemmas with which they are not fully able to cope or which they are having difficulty resolving. These dilemmas have to do with the situations in which they live, their interpersonal relationships, their physical health, their individual functioning, their psychological and emotional lives, or some combination of these elements. We will try to clearly present the essential principles underlying treatment procedures so readers can enhance their skills.

The psychosocial framework described in this book is an open system of thought. It has assimilated much of the knowledge and practices of earlier years. The increase of the range of knowledge creates a large learning task for all casework practitioners,

those with experience and those just entering the field. Relatively little that the worker knew and used 50 years ago has become obsolete. Instead, the knowledge base has been expanded, built upon, and enriched, so that there is much more to learn than in earlier years and a wide range of approaches to study before the worker finds his or her own treatment emphases and preferences for specialization in practice.

The psychosocial approach includes in its methodology and in its applicability help with concrete practical problems, with environmental deficits and pressures, and with interpersonal and intrapersonal difficulties. Naturally, different types of difficulty call for different emphases and techniques, *but the central principles apply across the board.* The typology of treatment procedures described in this book is appropriate to *any* clientele, even if it is applied in different ways to suit various client situations. The psychosocial approach was developed in work with clients who either voluntarily sought help or who, if reached out to or referred by others, became clients when they recognized that the caseworker was offering a service that might be helpful. Over the years, more efforts have been made to provide services to involuntary clients, to those who do not necessarily recognize a need for help as perceived by others, or to those who do not trust the caseworker as a potential helper.

We will endeavor throughout to demonstrate the operational meanings of concepts by references to actual cases and clients (whose identities have been disguised, of course) ranging from brief illustrations to detailed case summaries. A broad range of voluntary and involuntary clients has been included. Such concrete illustrations enhance understanding of how principles and concepts are applied and suggest ways in which casework can be skillfully practiced.

We begin this chapter with a discussion of terminogy and overlapping concepts. Diverse approaches to casework are mentioned. This is followed by a brief presentation of relevant historical background, designed to give the reader an understanding of some of casework's roots, specifically of the context from which the psychosocial approach emerged and evolved. We then discuss recent developments in psychosocial casework knowledge and practice. Brief remarks about education for specialization in clinical social work follow. A final section considers the empirical base of casework on which theory is built and treatment processes and results may be studied; various research methods are mentioned.

TERMINOLOGY AND OVERLAPPING CONCEPTS

Terminology

A few comments about some of the words frequently used in this text are necessary. Because of its long history as the designation for service to individuals and families

by social workers, we have chosen to keep *casework* as part of the title of this book. While some others use *casework* to describe a service rendered by those who have not had any formal social work education, we use the term to refer to practice engaged in by workers with at least a bachelor's or master's degree in casework.

We also use the term *clinical social work.* This more recently developed term may be preferred by the reader, but at present the field also defines *clinical social workers* in various ways. We prefer to use this designation to refer to workers who have had a concentration in graduate school in the *study of direct treatment of individuals and families,* including substantial work in emotional and interpersonal problems, and who have subsequently had years of professionally supervised practice in direct service and often postgraduate training. These workers contrast with *generalists* or *generic social work practitioners* who have opted for broader training and who have not had sufficient time to acquire a high degree of skill in direct or clinical treatment. Similarly, those with only undergraduate professional training have just started to study casework and could not yet have mastered the complexities of clinical knowledge and practice. In this book, we use the term *clinical social work* to refer to that more complicated part of casework for which generic and undergraduate training can only begin to prepare.[1]

The psychosocial approach represents a set of principles that can be followed by caseworkers at various levels of competence. In clinical social work practice, full use can be made of the entire system. Naturally, advanced skill and knowledge can be reached only by years of both practice and study. All aspects of the approach cannot be mastered at once. Fundamentals of psychosocial practice are being taught in many schools at the undergraduate level, and also in the preparation of generalists at the graduate level.

Different terms are also used in referring to the casework and clinical social work processes: *treatment, the helping process, service, therapy,* and *intervention.* Each has its own claim to appropriateness, although they are often used interchangeably. We use the word *treatment* in its general dictionary sense of "dealing with" or "acting or behaving toward another person in some specified way." The word has a sufficiently broad meaning to cover most casework activities. Some social workers object to this term because it implies an emphasis on sickness or pathology rather than on health or because it seems to put the blame for any distress or dilemma on the client rather than on dynamic interactions and systemic processes. When the term *treatment* is used in this book, it is not intended to carry any such connotations. *Helping* or the *helping process* or *service* are used even more broadly than *treatment* to cover all forms of casework practice, including specific acts of practical help. We have used *therapy* in this text and in its title to refer to work in which social and psychological means are employed to enable individuals (singly or in families or in formed groups) to cope with environmental, interpersonal, and/or intrapsychic dilemmas—and the interactions among these—that are causing personal distress. The term *intervention* is preferred by some as a rather general term. It is commonly, but far from exclusively, used by family therapists in work with formed groups, in the behavior modification approach, in environmental work, and often in research. It is also preferred by others to whom the terms *treatment* and *therapy* seem to imply disease in the client or the idea that in some way clients are mainly responsible for their own unhappiness. The term *intervention* may seem to suggest a somewhat mechanistic or intrusive process, but we have employed it as an alternative general term because of its wide use in the field.

The term *client* is used in this book to refer to an individual, a couple, or a family. In parent–child situations, in dilemmas about aging people, or when people have catastrophic illnesses or severe physical or mental disabilities, *client* may actually refer to family members who must make decisions for others as well as to the individual with the obvious or presenting problem. The term *family* has been expanded in recent years (by many mental health practitioners, among others, but not by the U.S. Bureau of the Census) and is used in this book to refer to various constellations of two or more individuals who have some kind of commitment or bond, who may or may not be related by blood, legally married, or adopted; the "family unit" may or may not include minor children. Generally, when we speak of a "family," the members share some practical tasks required for living and some type of emotional connection.

Although the terms *collateral* (a person in a client's environment or network who affects or can be enlisted to affect the situation) and *collateral sources* (case histories, documents, reports, or psychological tests, for example) may strike some people as old-fashioned, we see no need to coin a new word when the old one can convey the idea. Similarly, we have not discarded terms such as *environmental work* or *environmental modification.* When interventions or procedures used by caseworkers focus on people or social or physical conditions *outside of the client* (individual or family) these activities can be referred to by these terms.

Interpenetrating Concepts

We want to emphasize that *divisions or chapter headings in this book are artificial and imply boundaries that exist only in theory.* To describe and manage the material we present, we have to break it down into separate parts; this is also necessary for assessment and intervention in actual practice.

For example, as we will repeatedly stress, environmental influences are always part of the assessment of *any* situation addressed by caseworkers. In a given case, decisions about where to intervene—*which is often different from the location of the problem or dysfunction*—may require information about an individual's health or personality system, the capacity for resilience, a family system, a social service system, or some aspect of the larger environmental system. If a person is mentally disabled, for example, the caseworker's efforts may be directed to the location of resources rather than to intrapsychic explorations; inner anxiety may be relieved by finding a job; individuals who have repeatedly been victimized by crime in their neighborhood may choose to seek better protection of their home, a new place to live, or a course in karate. Whether the problem seems to stem from inner, outer, or interactional forces, all aspects require consideration. When working with individuals, various systems and environmental concepts may be central to effective treatment. In family therapy, knowledge about personality may be as important as interactional theory.

Along the same lines, while there are four separate chapters on family and couple treatment, systems concepts and conjoint interviewing are discussed throughout the book. The treatment procedures we describe apply to individual and to conjoint treatment. While we include a chapter on the psychosocial study and initial interviews, treatment (the subject of other chapters) begins with the very first contact. Thus, material presented in each chapter interpenetrates all the others; divisions and headings are for convenience and manageability only.

DIVERSE APPROACHES

It is beyond the scope of this book to offer a comparative discussion of diverse points of view and approaches in casework and clini-

cal social work.[2] A rich array of theories or models of social work treatment have emerged over the past half century; these attest to the fact that social work practitioners are in touch with other therapeutic fields and with new developments in the social sciences and research and are formulating their own ideas based on trained observation and practice experience. Many practitioners do not routinely follow accepted methodology without incorporating new findings and theories. As will become clear later in this chapter, some new ideas or approaches do not constitute a *comprehensive* theory of clinical treatment, but rather supplement the various theoretical and practice perspectives in existence. Proponents of traditional theories, of which psychosocial theory is one, need never be threatened by new ideas; rather, new concepts should be welcomed and evaluated on their own merit and usefulness. Each new idea or theory throws additional light on some aspect of the helping process.

There are overlaps in practice between workers who follow different approaches, with each group often borrowing ideas and techniques from the others. This may account in part for the observation that differences in practice among workers are often not as great as differences in the theories they supposedly follow. However, distinct differences between some theories make them truly incompatible. To make informed choices about the use of diverse approaches, one needs to be clear about these incompatibilities.

Theories vary in many ways. They differ greatly, for instance, in the emphasis on the client–worker relationship: its nature and its importance in treatment. Some theories refer often to such concepts as acceptance, caring, sympathy, empathy, and respect. Others, even when not necessarily opposing such ideas, seem to give them very low priority in treatment. Some approaches rely heavily on giving directives and advice; others encourage clients to arrive at their own understandings and decisions. The concept of self-determination is also widely accepted, but there are great variations in the degree to which this quality is emphasized or adhered to in practice. The notions of mutuality and collaboration are interpreted differently, depending on the point of view. In the chapters on family treatment we point out that among family therapists there are variations of opinion concerning the expression of emotion, the use of past history, the development of self-awareness, the sharing of impressions and interpretations by the therapist, the need for assessing individual personality dynamics, and so on. As we indicated, some of the points of view involving these issues are not compatible with the psychosocial point of view for ethical as well as practical reasons.

Obviously, too, current approaches are based on differing perspectives on personality development and dynamics. Some personality theories have many common elements; others are far apart on such matters as the influence of past experiences on present behavior and the question of the unconscious. Ego psychology, its knowledge of ego functions and defenses, is not included in some theories. There are also great variations in concepts about the ways in which people can best be helped. As will become clear from reading this book, psychosocial caseworkers do not restrict themselves to cognitive measures or to educational and behavioral techniques, for example, as some others tend to do, although the psychosocial approach is richer because it has incorporated some of these ideas and methods into its broader framework.

Theories differ also in their definitions of the "problem to be worked on." This aspect of practice ranges from those who would deal only with the presenting problems and symptoms to those who feel that in many cases there should be some exploration at the outset for the possible existence of other related problems for which casework could be helpful. Some would limit work to the "interface" of interacting systems; others would limit their concerns to intrapsychic phenomena; still others would see a much more inclusive gestalt of dynamic, interlocking factors.

When reading about various points of view, it is important to note that some writers have insufficient or inaccurate knowledge of the viewpoints of others. There are authors, for instance, who write as if psychosocial casework were tied to a narrow linear type of causation that relies largely on past events. Some seem not to be aware of the relationships between psychosocial concepts of causation and systems theory. We hope that in this edition we make the connections between these clearer than ever. Some people still believe that psychosocial casework is merely a watered-down version of psychoanalytic theory and practice. This text should dispel such misconceptions. When mentioning other points of view in this book, we have made every effort to represent them accurately; we welcome corrections from the proponents of any theory who believe we have misunderstood their ideas.

A BRIEF HISTORICAL BACKGROUND

This short overview of the historical development of casework is presented here because, in our opinion, knowledge of the past illuminates the present. A sense of continuity provides us with rich understanding of where we have been, where we are, and where we want to go. Too often we come up with what we believe is a new perspective on theory or practice, only to find that it is an old idea (even if expressed in new terms or language). By learning about the missions, visions, and struggles of our predecessors, we learn from their achievements and from their mistakes.

Mary Richmond: Pioneer

Mary Richmond's first book, *Friendly Visiting among the Poor: A Handbook for Charity Workers,*[3] appeared in 1899, heralding the advent of modern casework theory and practice. American social work had roots in the charity organization society movements of North America and England in the 19th century,[4] but it was not until the astute and persevering Mary Richmond undertook the task of formulating and examining treatment principles and techniques that the casework profession as we think of it today was conceived.

Critical Analysis of Casework Practice
Early in the 20th century, Richmond and associates began a process that continued for many years: the systematic and detailed examination of case records from various practice settings. This scrutiny of case materials, from which a body of knowledge and new theories evolved, established the basis for the first *scientific* approach to casework treatment. New concepts were constantly evaluated and modified as new data were uncovered. Richmond's 1917 book, *Social Diagnosis,*[5] was based on cases drawn from children's agencies, medical settings, and the family field. It reflected her many years of study, discussion, and teaching. In this, her most famous work, and others that followed,[6] Richmond outlined procedures for collecting "social evidence" (obtained from the client, the family, and outside sources); from this information, inferences were drawn, leading to "social diagnosis and thence to the shaping of social treatment."[7] Thus, the *social study, diagnosis,* and *treatment planning* processes, still fundamental

to psychosocial practice, came into being. Beginning as early as 1905, Richmond and those who worked with her produced teaching materials based on the practice concepts they were developing. From 1910 through 1922, one-month summer institutes, led by Richmond, for secretaries (as workers were then called) and other paid workers were a principal source of leadership in casework practice. *Social Diagnosis,* widely used in schools and agencies during the 1920s, provided practitioners with knowedge about evolving treatment theories and methods.

Old Notions Are Challenged: New Perspectives on Treatment Develop
It was a major contribution to modern casework when Mary Richmond contested the prevalent view of her time that poverty and other difficulties facing clients (family unhappiness, alcoholism, and unemployment, among others) were the result of innate character defects, weak wills, or indolence. She stressed the *influences of surroundings and social relationships,* past and present, on individuals and their problems; she emphasized the need to study thoroughly environmental factors in order to understand a case. In part, her point of view reflected the new developments in sociology of her period, which saw personality as shaped primarily by the social experiences of the individual.

From this line of thinking, Richmond realized that treatment of the individual alone was not always effective. As will be mentioned in the family chapters of this text, she urged that whenever possible the individual should be seen in the context of the family and home environment. She was also convinced of a "fundamental truth" that "mass betterment and individual betterment are interdependent," with "social reform and social case work of necessity progressing together."[8] Years before systems concepts were introduced into psychosocial theory, Richmond's writings revealed her sophisticated comprehension of *interactional* factors. Although not expressed by the same term, the *person-in-situation* concept, about which much will be said in this book, was conceived by Richmond.

As practice theory was developing, it was apparent to Richmond that good intentions were not enough; "friendly visitors," usually well-to-do volunteers attempting to teach self-control and good habits to those they visited, were not trained caseworkers. Rather, agencies would have to be staffed by trained, supervised, paid, accountable professionals.

Treatment Strategies Evolve On the basis of her recognition of the importance of environmental factors and her ongoing methodical study of casework practice, Richmond identified two major treatment methods: (1) *Indirect treatment,* as it came to be known, consisted of interventions in the client's environment. *Social Diagnosis* presented and discussed many illustrations of inventive work in the environment designed to lessen pressure on the family or individual, to increase opportunities, to locate resources, and to cooperate with every possible source of assistance and influence. (2) *Direct treatment,* the influence of "mind upon mind,"[9] stressed the development of a strong, trusting relationship through which a worker could influence a client toward activities and decisions that would be in his or her best interest. Suggestion and persuasion were predominant techniques, but Richmond also discussed the need for frankness and honesty in the relationship; the client's participation in decision making was mentioned, which seems to suggest rational discussion, though this term was not used. Mutuality, an important concept in today's psychosocial practice, certainly was

not fully developed despite indications that the client's point of view about his or her problem and its solution was considered. Richmond's efforts nevertheless represented the first standardized typology of treatment procedures, upon which others later elaborated in greater detail.

Clients and Treatment Are Individualized "Differential treatment based on differential diagnosis," a principle put forth by Richmond (and expressed the same way today) was intended to convey the fallacy of generalization. She wrote about evaluating couples "one by one"; there are, she wrote, many variations in the personalities and environmental factors that influence "deserters" and "inebriates" and urged that they receive "individualized social treatment." Richmond's admonition is still relevant today: "*It is more important to understand the main drift of their lives than the one incident which brings them to our attention . . .*"[10] [Emphasis ours] She added that "like many other social disabilities" they

> are not so much separate entities as outcroppings of more intimate aspects of the individual's personal and social life. Diagnosis must lay a solid foundation for their treatment, therefore, by pushing beyond such "presenting symptoms" to the complex of causes farther back.[11]

As we will say often in this text, it is still necessary for us to caution ourselves against making assumptions about or stereotyping clients on the basis of a single piece of information, such as cultural or racial background, sexual orientation, gender, age, clinical diagnosis, the presenting problem or symptom, and so on. Richmond's wisdom deserves to be extended to the present: Each person and family is unique; the past is intertwined with the present; in and of itself, a symptom may not reveal a specific underlying difficulty; and every client needs to be listened to and understood individually, with all relevant information considered.

Perhaps it will become even clearer to the reader, as we proceed, why we are so committed to preserving and passing on the pioneering Mary Richmond's outstanding contributions to the development of casework theory and practice. Many of the empirically based, carefully honed fundamental concepts and principles she developed created a foundation upon which practice knowledge has been built; many of her basic ideas still apply. If Richmond's balanced "person-in-situation" perspective had remained in the forefront of theory through the years, the tendency for social work's pendulum to swing from one extreme to another might have been avoided. As we shall see, during some periods that followed, personality theory was emphasized; during others, socioeconomic forces were the major focus. But despite extreme shifts in attention, caseworkers never totally ignored either the social or the psychological side of their perspective on clients and their dilemmas; nevertheless, to this day, there are times when these inseparable, interacting influences on human behavior are not sufficiently integrated during the assessment and treatment processes.

Psychology and Psychiatry Make Their Mark

Social Influences Downplayed   The decade following the publication of *Social Diagnosis* was one in which psychology was flourishing. The major impetus to social work's turn to psychological theories came from the association of social workers with psychiatrists during World War I, followed by the establishment of the specialty in psychiatric social work at the Smith College School of Social Work, the special department of mental hygiene at the New York School of Social Work, and the course in social psychiatry at the Pennsylvania School of Social Work.[12] During most of the 1920s, a variety of psychological theories of that period were introduced into social work at different times and in different places. These new ideas about personality and emotional development and the importance of childhood influences on psychological growth partially overshadowed Mary Richmond's emphasis on the impact of the environment. Of this period, Virginia Robinson wrote, "These various and often conflicting viewpoints are frequently used indiscriminately, and nowhere has there been any attempt by a caseworker to organize or originate any psychological principles of interpretation."[13] In other words, social work was in a period of examination and ferment; often haphazardly, social workers were latching onto bits and pieces of knowledge without an orderly effort to determine just how the new notions might best inform practice with clients. They were eager for greater understanding of the complexity of personality than Richmond had been able to provide when social influences, heredity, physical makeup, and variations in intelligence were the main explanatory variables offered by psychology and psychiatry. However, it was not until the 1930s that social work began to incorporate knowledge about personality more systematically.

The "Functional" and "Diagnostic" Schools of Social Casework   In 1930, with the publication of Robinson's book, Otto Rank entered the field as a strong new influence. Throughout the 1930s, under the leadership of Robinson and Jessie Taft and associates at the Pennsylvania School of Social Work, *functionalism* influenced by Rank's will theory,[14] was becoming a focused, distinctive approach to social casework. Functionalism not only brought Rankian psychology into the field but also was in strong disagreement with the approach of Richmond and her successors. For the functionalist, past history was considered irrelevant and diagnosis was de-emphasized. The client's right to self-determination was strongly endorsed. Briefly stated, it was believed that the client's will and capacity to act upon his or her problems, currently or in the future, were stimulated by agency function, including limitations on time. The terms *functional, Rankian,* and *Pennsylvania School* were used to refer to this point of view.[15]

Meanwhile, Adler and Jung were also commanding some attention from social workers, but Freudian ideas became far more influential. Social work schools, especially the leading eastern schools—Smith, Simmons, New York, and Cleveland—and practitioners in agencies affiliated with them, were moving toward adopting Freud's explanations of personality and his contributions to treatment methodology.[16] Social workers who followed his views and incorporated psychoanalytic theory felt equipped with rich concepts that illuminated clients' inner lives; underlying—often unconscious—forces, conflicts, and motives helped to explain their clients' behaviors, emotions, and personality development. This approach, like Richmond's, required careful gathering of relevant data, often in great detail, from clients and others, including information about the past. This continued to be called a social study, although it had already become distinctly *psycho*social; based upon the information collected, diagnosis and a tentative treatment plan could be formulated. Often taught and guided by psychiatrists, caseworkers with a Freudian orientation were viewed by some as an elite (or elitist) group; psychiatric social work was sometimes more highly regarded than other specialties. Unfortunately, to some extent reflecting individualistic thinking of this period, the social side of people's dilemmas was often given scant attention; even during the Great Depression, unemployment and other conditions stemming from the breakdown of the economy were sometimes attributed to psychological conflict or inadequacy. Social workers with a psychoanalytic point of view were referred to as belonging to the "diagnostic," "differential," or "Freudian" school of thought.

The Right to Self-Determination   Concurrently with the development of the functional and diagnostic schools of thought, the concept of self-determination was widely discussed, and John Dewey's theories of education were receiving increased acceptance. Both approaches emphasized this important principle. Gordon Hamilton, for many years the leading exponent of the diagnostic approach, stressed in her writings the individual's "right to be himself," the uniqueness of the client's goals and objectives, and the movement away from authority and manipulation, as early as 1937.[17] In her 1940 book, *Theory and Practice of Case Work,*[18] widely used as a text in all parts of the country, she reiterated these points. Hollis, another early representative of the diagnostic school, wrote in 1939:

> The final choice of the pattern he (the client) wants his life to take in matters large and small is his and not the worker's to make . . . This principle is one of the most widely held in the field of casework. Its acceptance was greatly accelerated by its defense in Virginia P. Robinson's *A Changing Psychology in Social Case Work;* under the name of the client's right of "self-determination" it was also discussed by Bertha C. Reynolds in *Between Client and Community;* it is either stated explicitly or implied in almost all the writings by caseworkers listed in the Bibliography.[19]

This bibliography included writings of about 40 of the leading diagnostic caseworkers of the day. Thus, both functional and diagnostic schools departed from earlier directiveness or advice giving and from the assumption that the worker would know what was best for clients in the management of their lives.

The Diagnostic School Prevails During the 1930s, debates between the two schools were at times acrimonious but always vigorous, with each side staunchly defending its point of view. Until the middle l950s, there were no other generally recognized points of view in casework. Well into the 1950s, the diagnostic (soon to be called the psychosocial) approach became more widely accepted as the main body of casework thought. Some functionalist ideas that seemed compatible with the diagnostic point of view were assimilated along the way.[20]

Gradually, the diagnostic point of view developed beyond its Richmond predecessor. To a fault, however, the social side of data collection became less extensive and environmental interventions were discussed in a rather cursory fashion in much of the literature of the 1940s and 1950s; nevertheless, family influences were still believed to be very important.[21] As we said, the old directive techniques still common in the 1920s gave way to efforts to help individuals think for themselves and base decisions on their own judgment. The nature of history taking changed markedly with the recognition that treatment begins immediately and that facts should be gathered and observed more selectively and less formally than Richmond had advised. Diagnostic thinking changed radically in response to increased understanding of personality. Yet, the ideas about individualizing each client and recognizing that current functioning is influenced by past as well as by

present events continued to be regarded as basic to diagnostic treatment. Richmond's two major treatment modes—treatment through change or use of the environment and treatment through direct work with the client—were carried over into this point of view. Although often not given equal attention, they were considered, as Richmond considered them, interlocking components in treatment.

Once Freudian psychology was widely accepted as the most useful basis for understanding personality, the major theoretical task of the 40s was to define ways in which psychoanalytic understanding could be best used by caseworkers. Efforts were made to determine what factors distinguished casework treatment from psychoanalysis. Social work thinkers were trying to identify different kinds of work with clients within the broad methodology of differential casework; various classifications of treatment methods or techniques were proposed during this period (see Chapter 4). The further problem of developing guiding principles for the relationship of diagnosis to treatment emerged. These issues will be explored in later chapters.

Despite the many advances in thinking during this period, the casework field paid an unnecessary price as it assimilated psychoanalytic theory. Too often, it appears, caseworkers deferred to psychiatrists, with the result that their unique professional identity—years of experience, broad body of knowledge, and expertise—was somewhat eclipsed by the authority they invested in psychiatry.

The 1950s and 1960s Theories of ego psychology, many of which were being assimilated by the diagnostic school during the 1950s, resulted in a sudden spurt of growth in the diagnostic school of casework, in both theory and practice. Still based on psychoanalytic thinking, new perspectives on the ego modified some of the deterministic features of Freud's thinking, with the result that people were viewed as more self-directed and not so powerfully controlled by unconscious forces. The ego was seen as an important resource for change. Functions of the ego, now thought to be independent of unconscious sexual and aggressive drives, could be worked with—strengthened or modified—*directly; treatment,* therefore, did not rely so heavily on inference or on interpretation of unconscious motives or conflicts. Many of the concepts derived from ego psychology will be discussed in Chapter 2.

As we said, until the mid-50s, the only major approaches to casework were the functional and diagnostic, with the diagnostic school being more widely followed. In the late 1950s, several efforts were made to bridge diagnostic and functional thinking.[22] Out of these, Helen Harris Perlman's "problem-solving" approach developed. Conjoint, rather than individual, treatment of marital problems increased. More methods and approaches came into being in the early 1960s, including family therapy, crisis, planned short-term, and task-oriented treatment. The usefulness for our field of other theoretical positions were (and in some circles continue to be) explored and/or followed: Horney and Sullivan have been influential, the Rogerian approach (later called the client-centered system) has been favored by some, and behavior modification has many adherents. Other points of view came under study following this period, some of which we shall discuss later in this chapter and in Chapter 2.

In 1964, when the first edition of this book went to press, a number of these new approaches had been introduced. Many of them seemed to be variations in emphasis and elaborations on the diagnostic approach, with little or no basic incompatibil-

ity with that point of view. When the term *psychosocial* was first used by Hollis in the subtitle of this book, it was a descriptive term, chosen to emphasize that the diagnostic approach was characterized by concern for both social and psychological aspects of life. Hamilton had used the term as early as 1941 in stressing that all problems are to a degree both emotional and social.[23] The term was originally suggested in 1930 by Hankins, a sociologist, then teaching at the Smith School for Social Work.[24]

In the first edition of this text, Hollis, who firmly believed that the psychodynamic and social components of individual and family functioning were inseparable, was determined to restore the importance of environmental treatment:

> Not since Mary Richmond's time have we given the same attention to indirect as to direct work. This neglect has tended to downgrade environmental treatment in the worker's mind, as though it were something one learned to do with one's left hand, something unworthy of serious analysis. We have furthermore tended to think of direct work as psychological and indirect as non-psychological, or "social." This is an absolutely false assumption. Environmental work also takes place with people and through psychological means.[25]

In 1969, a symposium was held in memory of Charlotte Towle to secure clear statements about the approaches then used in the casework field. Functional, problem-solving, behavioral modification, and "psychosocial" were chosen as four "general" approaches; family group treatment, crisis-oriented brief treatment, and adult socialization were viewed as "middle-range" approaches addressed to specific groups in the general client population but having utility for wider application. In the publication of *Theories of Social Casework,* based on this series of discussions, the term *psychosocial casework* was used to designate the approach represented by the diagnostic point of view.[26]

Since then, *psychosocial* has been widely used as the designation for an approach described by many writers as well as in this book. In both theory and practice, this point of view has expanded considerably beyond the diagnostic approach on which it was based. Many elements now included in the psychosocial approach are not exclusive to it. Examining likenesses and differences between points of view reveals considerable agreement among most approaches regarding certain fundamental points that comprise a common core of casework practice.[27] In this book, we include both this common core of casework practice and concepts that are specifically components of the psychosocial approach.

The 1960s began a period of social protest. Student demonstrations opposing many social and political conditions became common; riots in the inner cities were more frequent; organizations demanding civil rights for many persecuted groups were mobilized; and the peace movement, with its resistance to the Vietnam war, grew. Social work was strongly influenced by these developments, and casework in particular was criticized for concentrating on problems of individuals and families when social forces were so powerful in oppressing them. Psychosocial caseworkers are now, as they were then, committed to fighting all forms of discrimination, injustice, and social abuse. However, we have believed all along that concurrently we must do all we can to help people improve the quality of their lives *now,* before or as social changes occur. It is this writer's (Woods's) opinion that Hollis's conviction about the indivisibility of social and psychological forces averted a radical swing of the pendulum in psychosocial casework during these years when

many social workers were convinced that clinical work was, at best, ineffective in the face of societal evils and ills. We will say more about this as we go on.

RECENT DEVELOPMENTS

Clinical Practice and the Social Context

Since the original publication of this book in 1964 and this fifth edition, social trends and client requirements have significantly affected every aspect of casework. Problems that come to the attention of social and health agencies have expanded. Many individuals and families are affected by teenage pregnancy, drug and alcohol problems, teenage suicide, AIDS, violence and unsafe neighborhoods, homelessness exacerbated by housing shortages and inadequate services for the deinstitutionalized mentally ill, severe economic problems facing farmers and rural communities, widespread substandard education, chronic poverty, family violence, and child neglect. There are huge gaps in income and employment opportunities between "minority" groups and whites; generally, women are still paid less than men for the same work. One child in four lives in poverty in America; millions of infants and toddlers are deprived of medical care, loving attention, adequate supervision, and intellectual stimulation. Beginning in the early 1980s (the Reagan years), the income of the poorest fifth of the population has declined, while the wealthy have become even more affluent.[28] There are indications that people in the lower socioeconomic half of society are almost six times more likely to experience emotional and psychological distress than those in the upper half.[29]

Clinical social workers alone cannot stem these tides or bring about systemic change. However, they can add their voices to others engaging in social action and advocating for programs that can bring relief, support, dignity, and opportunities to those who have been deprived and oppressed. To be as helpful as possible, practitioners need to be familiar with the conditions under which so many clients or potential clients struggle to survive.

Veterans of war and victims of rape and other crimes have brought attention to the phenomenon of post-traumatic stress. Tensions between various racial and ethnic groups have increased in some areas of the country. Many legal and illegal immigrants and refugees experience a broad range of difficulties. Only in recent years has the extent of incest and sexual abuse of children, and the toll these take on personality development and on future relationships, been so widely recognized. Casework practice has been stimulated—sometimes challenged and prodded—by the women's, gay and lesbian, and civil rights movements that continue to mature and to shape our attitudes and thought. The high divorce rate, the increase in single-parent families and stepfamilies, the large number of women in the work force, and the need for child care have all influenced recent approaches to casework practice. Changing family roles and structure have placed particularly heavy burdens on women. In all walks of life, the importance of clear communication has increased; value is placed on the open expression of feelings and ideas among people who are living or working closely together. Far more often than even a few years ago, the realities of terminal illness and death are frankly discussed; the dying patient and those who survive are freer to share grief with each other.[30]

More people than ever are seeking some kind of therapy for predictable life crises and transitions. While large numbers of clients have deep-seated family or emotional troubles or have to cope with noxious social conditions or catastrophic events, many other individuals and families view treatment as a means of prevention or as an opportunity for personal growth. Decreased support from family, church, and stable neighborhoods has given impetus to a search for new self-understanding and social opportunities. With growing social acceptance of a wide range of lifestyles, casework help is frequently sought to consider new kinds of choices. Some clients want to learn how to be more effectively assertive or self-directed. Probably more than ever, caseworkers concern themselves with the development of conditions and capacities for health rather than only with the amelioration of pathology. As this book will illustrate over and over again, *more often than not, casework interventions are not directed at "sickness," but are fashioned to promote strengths and growth.*[31] Practice continues to evolve to meet constantly changing needs and attitudes. Many of these areas will be discussed in this text.

Recent years have also seen positive shifts in general attitudes toward family and mental health services. Some people and groups who avoided treatment now seek it more readily; more men, more poor people, and more individuals and families from certain ethnic backgrounds who in the past tended to shy away from social or psychological services are now voluntarily on the caseloads of social workers and other mental health professionals. Many millions of people in the United States are receiving professional psychotherapy or counseling. Plus, social workers have numerous clients in institutional settings, such as hospitals, nursing homes, schools, and day care centers.

The division of labor among helping professionals has shifted remarkably in a single decade. In 1975, there were 26,000 psychiatrists and 25,000 social workers providing psychotherapy in the United States. By 1985, clinical social workers outnumbered psychiatrists almost two to one, with 60,000 social workers and 38,000 psychiatrists offering psychotherapy. Of all mental health practitioners, clinical social workers, many of whom are in part- or full-time private practice, provide the most psychotherapeutic services.[32] Undoubtedly the ratio continues to change, with more and more psychiatrists specializing in psychopharmacology and consultation rather than in ongoing direct practice. Most states now license social workers, making them eligible for third-party reimbursement; this development has also contributed to the setting of standards for advanced or independent practice. Elsewhere in this book, particularly in Chapter 18, we have discussed the advent of managed care and the constraints and difficulties this development has imposed on mental health providers; we strongly believe that social workers have a responsibility to respond to this development.

Social work salaries continue to be low, sometimes lower than those of other "female-dominated" professions, such as nursing and teaching. A study conducted by the National Association of Social Workers suggested several reasons, including social work's association with "disliked segments of the population"; difficulty demonstrating effectiveness; too little attention to marketing and public relations that would counteract misperceptions about social workers and what they do; lack of a fight for better pay; and shortage of public and private funding available for social services. As in many other occupations, men were found to be "disproportionately represented at the higher end of the salary range."[33]

Private Practice

Despite the impact of managed care on independent and agency-based clinical practice, the number of clinical social workers in private practice has continued to increase. Whether this trend will continue may depend on the course the American health care system takes. However, at the time of this writing, a substantial percentage of social workers are engaged and hope to continue in part- or full-time private practice.[34]

For many years private practice of clinical social work was resisted on the grounds that we should primarily serve people who cannot afford private fees and we should not take strength away from agencies set up for that purpose. We differ from this point of view and believe that the increasing recognition and professional sanction of private practice constitutes a positive step. In our opinion, the ideal of private practice should be to divide one's time between agency practice and independent work, thus ensuring that all experienced practitioners will devote part of their time to consultation, training, field instruction, or direct service with nonpaying or low-fee-paying clients. We hope that most private practitioners will continue to divide their time this way. We also hope that those who decide to engage in private practice will offer sliding fee scales to accommodate lower-income clients. Despite those who complain that private practice excludes the poor, we know a number of private practitioners whose clientele ranges from the well-to-do to the economically disadvantaged. Those independent workers who have the will to do so can be available to referrals from many sources, including those agencies—children's and geriatric services, the courts, the schools, and many more—that are seeking high-quality clinical services for clients who cannot pay much, if anything. It is consonant with our professional values to devote a percentage of our private practice hours to such individuals and families. Ironically, independent clinicians, who often have lower overhead expenses than agencies, can sometimes absorb nonpaying clients more comfortably than those organizations that struggle with inadequate budgets and therefore have to charge fees that are as high as or higher than those set by private practitioners. In our experience, agencies seeking referral sources are grateful to have collaborative relationships with experienced and skilled independent workers.

A further advantage of the spread of private practice for social work is that, as we become better known as independent clinicians, our profession will be more widely recognized as the challenging and personally rewarding work that it really is. This, in turn, will attract a greater number of well-qualified candidates to professional study. It will also mean that as social work becomes more and more valued as a profession by society, it will have a better chance of being heard when it speaks out for human rights and against social injustice. Members of other professions and their societies, such as those of the medical and legal professions, have brought pressure to bear (certainly not always in ways that we wish they would!) because of the status and respect they enjoy. If social work is going to influence broad social policies, it must become better known as a vital profession based on strength and high principles.

A justified concern about private practice has been that independent practitioners may have fewer supports than those employed in agencies, where various types of in-service training and consultation can be readily available and where the agency vouches for the competence of its workers. People served by private practitioners deserve the equivalent of this protection. Through licensing and other standard-setting measures, including competency exams, reexaminations, and peer review, taken by government bodies and profes-

sional societies, it can be expected and required that caseworkers qualifying for independent practice have advanced training and experience in clinical social work, are continuing their education, and are using peer consultation.

Practice Trends in Changing Times

In recent years, there have been many new trends in theories and practices in clinical social work. Treatment methods that were more or less experimental 35 years ago have matured and are now widely used. Some of these have developed into approaches that are alternatives or adjuncts to psychosocial casework. Others are expansions of the psychosocial approach itself. They provide workers with many new tools to help individuals and families cope with their concerns and dilemmas and move forward toward their goals.

Family and Couple Therapy Chief among these is family and couple treatment. Social workers have made substantial contributions to the family therapy movement. In the early 1960s, when the first edition of this book was being written, casework with clients was primarily limited to individual interviews.

At that time, we referred to joint interviews of married couples and family interviewing as "promising new trends" not covered by the data on which the book was based. Over the years it has become clear that conjoint treatment is a powerful tool for developing understanding of intrafamilial relationships and for bringing about change in these relationships, which often leads to intrapsychic change in individuals. Sometimes an entire contact consists of family interviews. Often, both individual and group interviewing are used in the same family, each form having its own purpose and value. Two chapters, introduced in the third edition of the text in 1981, have since been expanded and include discussion of psychosocial family therapy and of how family concepts and concepts derived from the psychodynamic study of the individual can be integrated in theory and in practice.

Marital problems continue to be a major focus of treatment, with gender roles changing in various degrees, depending on many factors including ethnicity, geography, and family tradition. As has been true for many years, improvement in the marriage is not the only acceptable goal; couples seek help to explore whether to try to improve the relationship or to separate. When divorce or separation is decided upon, often individuals seek help in recovering from the loss and in rearranging their lives. Cross-cultural couples are frequently seen by caseworkers. Second marriages often require complex adjustments, especially when children are involved. Same-sex couples, with and without children in their households, are bringing their relationship problems to treatment. Unmarried couples also ask for help in living together and sometimes in deciding whether or not to live together. Premarital counseling has become increasingly popular. Two chapters on couple treatment, first added to the fourth edition in 1990, include updated discussions of these issues.

Despite research that suggests family and couple therapies are often more effective than individual treatment, and are also more cost effective, currently there are some pressures to return to individually oriented practice.[35] Generally, for example, managed care does not approve conjoint treatment. As will be clear in the four chapters on family and couple therapy, we believe that many dilemmas are often best resolved in family-centered treatment; family members frequently become positive resources for one another.

Crisis and Short-Term Treatment   Crisis treatment, task-centered, planned time-limited, and agency-limited services have been used extensively by social workers in recent years. Historically, brief services have comprised a large portion of casework practice. Budget problems, rising costs, increased concern with accountability, and client preference have given added impetus to setting time limits on services and clearly defining goals of treatment that can be achieved in short periods. Managed care has pressured clinical workers and agencies to provide help quickly. While it is our view that the short-term treatment approach is not the best choice for many clients, for large numbers of others it has helped to keep treatment focused and eliminate aimless "drifting" or unnecessarily exhaustive interviews with clients. Similarly, the "contract," which makes explicit the mutual working agreement between client and worker, when flexibly implemented, helps maintain a clear direction in treatment. These matters are discussed in detail in the chapter on crisis and brief treatment and elsewhere in the text.

Constructivist Practice   Recent years have seen a proliferation of literature in the social sciences and other fields on the "postmodern movement" in its various aspects, including contructivism, the narrative approach, and social constructionism; many contributions to these subjects have been written by social workers and others in the mental health and family therapy fields. Some of the discussions have seemed esoteric and difficult to relate to clinical work; others have concentrated on arguing against "traditional" treatment and current research approaches. Increasingly, however, interesting illustrations of how these points of view can be applied in practice are appearing. Many of the ideas being suggested underscore our strong commitment to *collaboration* between worker and client, in contrast to a hierarchical relationship that places the worker in the role of "expert" rather than as an equal. We welcome this emphasis.

Some differences exist among thinkers, but generally, from the constructivist point of view, a "not-knowing" stance of clinicians prevents them from leading clients in a direction that the workers think is right; rather, the worker's task is to help clients find their own truths. Meanings for clients derive from *their* interpretations of their experiences and how these have affected *them;* they do not derive from the worker's theories or "expert" understanding. They are "co-constructed" in the dialogue between client and worker, assisted by the worker's encouragement and careful listening to clients' stories.

Although many of these ideas match our views, we do not fully agree with other features, at least as we understand them. For example, some constructivist practitioners downplay diagnosis or assessment and treatment planning on the basis that these imply there is an "expert" who knows more about the client than the client does. As this book will mention many times, in most cases (except when clients have serious mental disabilities or are dangerous to themselves or others), we believe that assessments should be arrived at *jointly,* with the worker offering tentative ideas about these and about treatment planning that are *always* open to modification or rejection by the client. But we do believe that it is important for client and worker together to arrive at an evaluation (assessment) and an organized view (and plan) of how to proceed. In our opinion, the effort to define the nature of clients' concerns and goals requires a clear and distinct picture of what is "wrong" (which may shift over time) and

what strengths, opportunities, and ideas can be mobilized to achieve the ends the clients seek. The constructivist approach amplifies notions that have been part of quality clinical practice, as our discussion of casework history illustrates. While constructivism may not seem to represent a radical departure from psychosocial theory and practice, it commands our attention and infuses our thinking with essential reminders and practical suggestions about how to apply our basic values of collaboration, mutuality, and self-determination to our work. We will discuss these issues further later in this text.[36]

The Strengths Perspective   Interest has increased recently in emphasizing clients' strengths in contrast to "pathology," "weakness," or "deficits." We applaud the increased attention being given to reinforcing positive capacities, to locating strengths and resiliencies; the many case illustrations in this book reflect our strong endorsement of accentuating strengths. As will become clear to the reader, interventions are often most effective when they do *not* target the troubled spots, but rather the solid or healthy aspects of the individual, family, and environmental systems.[37]

Empowerment   Closely related to the strengths perspective and, in many respects, to constructivism and the narrative approach is the recent emphasis on empowerment. Caseworkers, along with other social workers, continue to be outspoken advocates of the poor, the elderly, African Americans, Hispanics, Native Americans, Asian Americans, women, gays and lesbians, and many others who are discriminated against and deprived of rights and power. New emphases on helping clients become empowered apply to clients across the board, but they take on particular importance when working with individuals and families who have been subject to societal inequities and prejudices.

Empowerment involves supporting people in their search for ways to ameliorate a repressive environment. In many cases, it also involves helping clients to examine and revise internalized negative self-definitions that derive from living under oppressive conditions while encouraging them to build on their strengths, their capacities for healthy self-esteem, competence, and mastery.

The aspirations and needs of people trapped and debilitated by ghetto and slum life are more widely understood than formerly, although most caseworkers learned long ago how destructive it is to "blame the victim" of social injustice. Oversimplified concepts of the past about the "culture of poverty" or the "underclass" have been discarded by social work thinkers. The great variations in both personality and circumstance among people who live in poverty are being stressed. The possibility of individualizing service to persons and families in this heterogeneous group is thereby increased. It is our responsibility to support and encourage client empowerment *within* the client–worker relationship.[38]

Group Treatment The use of the small group as a means of treatment by clinical social workers continues to grow steadily in importance. Discussion of work with groups has not been included in this text simply because—as much as we might like it to be—this cannot be an "everything" book! Work with groups is an extremely effective modality and should be part of every caseworker's experience and training. The theory and practice of group treatment varies just as widely as work with individuals and families. Clinical social workers seeking an approach to group therapy compatible with psychosocial theory

can find it in writings of others who are experts in practice with formed groups.[39]

The Improvement of Human Services
Despite frustrating and unpredictable funding problems, greater attention than ever is being paid to the need to link people with institutional resources, services, and opportunities. Systems and ecological theories, to be discussed in the next chapter and throughout the text, have directed attention to the complexity of agency and other institutional operations, the interlocking of policy, administration, and staff personalities; these perspectives have helped caseworkers modify and humanize institutional functioning and services to clients. There is increased recognition of the importance of locating caseworkers in institutions and agencies where they can make themselves available in imaginative ways—in prenatal clinics, day care centers, communities of older people, hospitals and hospices, and so on—thus becoming enablers in the client's immediate "life space." Employee assistance programs often employ and/or refer to clinical social workers, offering convenient opportunities for workers to seek help with personal, job-related, or family problems. Some of these issues are discussed in Chapter 8.

Worker burnout continues to be a matter of concern. Obviously when workers are overworked, underpaid, handling large caseloads of clients with recalcitrant problems and seemingly few solutions, and given little recognition and support, or for various other reasons are exhausted and have poor morale, their effectiveness is seriously impaired. The identification and alleviation of systemic and other problems that contribute to burnout in social service professionals should be a prime concern of workers, supervisors, and administrators of social agencies. This subject is addressed in Chapter 9.

Knowledge from Other Disciplines

The following areas of knowledge that have come from other fields will be addressed in various parts of the text.

Systems and Ecological Theories In many disciplines, the approach to knowledge known as systems theory has proved a useful tool for helping the mind deal with the complexities of modern knowledge. Increasingly over the years, psychosocial casework has found this mode of thought helpful for dealing conceptually with the many psychological, familial, and social forces at work in the human situation. Closely related to concepts from general systems theory are concepts derived from the ecological perspective in sociology, which deals especially with the interdependence of people and their institutions. In our psychosocial approach, systems, ecological, and psychodynamic perspectives have become inseparable. These theories will be discussed in greater detail in Chapter 2 and in several other chapters in this book, including Chapters 8 and 14.

Communication Theory Theory about communication continues to be of great interest to clinicans working with individuals, groups, families, and collaterals. In many ways, as this book emphasizes, it contributes to the understanding of barriers that often prevent effective discussion between individuals. This important subject will also be discussed further in Chapter 2, in the family and couple chapters, as well as in other parts of the text.

Racial, Cultural, Gender Variations; Cultural Sensitivity and Competence Understanding of racial, cultural, gender, religious, and other differences, among clients and between clients and workers, continues to be recognized as critically important to assessment and treatment. Wider and more sophisticated use of knowledge from the social sciences and feminist thinkers has revealed how these may affect personality and social functioning. Cultural sensitivity and competence require us to be respectful of and eager to learn about our clients' lives, traditions, values, and attitudes about spirituality; it also helps us to be aware that certain behavioral, emotional, or thought patterns may not be "maladaptive" or "pathological" simply because they are different from our own. Chapter 2 in particular will address these issues, but they will also be included in other discussions throughout the text.

Knowledge Contributed by Psychiatry and Psychology New understanding also continually comes into the field from psychology, psychiatry, and other branches of medicine. Recent studies and clinical observations of individuals have led to new understandings of the diagnosis and treatment of clients with borderline and other personality disorders. *Self-psychology,* a term and theory developed by Heinz Kohut, among others, has also added to advances in personality theory; these will be commented upon in Chapter 2. New approaches to schizophrenia, spurred on in part by advances in psychopharmacology and by the return to the community of many mentally ill patients, have affected casework treatment over the past 20 years. The psychoeducational approach, used more and more by caseworkers in recent years, has incorporated educational and behavioral techniques to help the mentally ill and their families.

There is increasing evidence that many personality problems, clinical symptoms, and mood disorders have a physiological base that can be, or in the future will be, modifiable with medications. Depression, bipolar disorders, obsessive-compulsive conditions as well as schizophrenia are now responsive to drug therapies, often being used in conjunction with psychotherapy; not long ago these conditions were treated primarily with psychotherapeutic procedures. In discussions and case illustrations in this book, we will refer to some of these matters.

Editions of the *Diagnostic and Statistical Manual of Mental Disorders* (DSM) of the American Psychiatric Association have had a significant impact on caseworkers' approaches to clinical diagnosis. Our view of the advantages and limitations or hazards of this diagnostic system will be discussed in Chapter 11.

The Incorporation of New Knowledge

Fundamental to an understanding of all these new developments and changing needs is a *solid foundation in the basic knowledge and theory of casework practice.* Evaluating the new emphases and enlarging the knowledge and understanding of caseworkers so that they can use them in practice may seem formidable. However, many new trends or ideas represent additions to well-established casework treatment methods. Rather than tearing down an existing frame of reference, the caseworker's task is to expand the framework with new or underemphasized methods and procedures.

A clear understanding of fundamental principles is never more needed than when theory is being expanded, and choices must be made between what is to be retained and what discarded. It is, therefore, timely for caseworkers to formulate as clearly as possible their basic frame of reference. Treatment will become more effective only when what is potentially sound and useful in the new is admitted to the main body of principles whose value has already been demonstrated. Knowledge building should be a cooperative enterprise in which one reformulates, refines, and adds to existing knowledge and theory, accrediting the value of what has gone before in the certain realization that in due time others will have their turn at reshaping what now seems clear to us.

EDUCATION FOR CLINICAL SOCIAL WORK SPECIALIZATION

Space does not allow for an in-depth discussion of educational issues.[40] However, a few comments are called for here. We have already mentioned that many millions of people are receiving some form of professional psychotherapy or counseling and that, in terms of numbers, clinical social workers are the chief providers of these services. Also, a majority of social work students seem to be interested in careers in clinical practice. At some point, many of these will probably go into independent or private practice. Yet, in recent years, a significant number of graduate schools of social work have not provided master's students with adequate training for specialization in clinical work, preferring a more "generic" curriculum instead. Generally, the curricula of doctoral programs have focused on administration, social policy, theory-building, and research. To acquire advanced training and competence as clinicians, social workers have had to seek further education in institutes and Ph.D. programs directed by professions other than social work. In our view, a great contribution can be made to the quality of casework practice by the clinical doctorate. At last, a few—but still too few—clinical social work doctoral programs have emerged.

Unfortunately, some prospective social workers probably apply to graduate schools looking for "passports" to clinical careers, oblivious to the heritage and mission and the complex range of knowledge, visions, humanistic values, experience, creativity, and artistry that have combined to make social work—and clinical social work as a specialization—the profession that it is and all that we perennially strive to make it become. In our view it is as counterproductive to criticize the students who want to become direct practitioners as it is to ignore the ongoing interest in clinical specialization. Rather, we should provide our master's and doctoral students with the theory, the tools, and the experience that adequately prepares them for effective "on-line" clinical careers.

First, we must teach both the psychodynamic and the social content that social work history has repeatedly demonstrated is necessary to work with individuals, families, and groups. There is an enormous amount of relevant theory, knowledge, and technical skill to be absorbed by students going into direct services; a "generic" education is too broad to do the material justice. Equally important, caseworkers must be firmly grounded in social work's unique base of knowledge, its traditions and ethics. While there are overlaps in coverage, important issues distinguish social work practitioners from other clinicians. Historically, caseworkers have served every group in society, always with special concern for the problems of the poor and the dislocated; they have demanded social reforms for the benefit of forgotten people whom no other helping profession has so consistently championed. Social work practitioners have been in the forefront of human services; as mentioned earlier, despite the capriciousness of funding sources, the populations served and the settings in which social workers can be found have expanded dramatically over recent decades. Our vehement stands for self-determination and decent opportunities for every person and family and our identification with all who struggle for betterment and self-fulfillment derive from direct experience, not just from lofty ideals. Because of their familiarity with the needs of a broad range of people in a variety of situations and dilemmas, social workers have always been innovators of programs, of approaches, and of techniques.[41]

More than any other profession, social workers have used their firsthand knowledge about environmental influences on human suffering; the provision of concrete services and the creative development and utilization of resources have been part of the caseworker's special stock in trade from the beginning. Casework training, therefore, must require students to become familiar and comfortable with providing or locating resources, with making home visits, and with developing outreach programs. Psychosocial clinicians have not just borrowed a little of this and a little of that from other disciplines; over and over again they have broken new ground in hopes of better serving individuals and families from all walks of life. Knowledge about the history of casework, and all of the practice approaches that have derived directly from it, must be an important part of the education of the clinical social work specialist.

In recent years we have been alarmed by a trend that affects a significant number of schools of social work. As these schools have affiliated with academic institutions and funding problems have modified administrative policies, the teaching of direct practice by accomplished practitioner/scholars has declined. Public grants are usually awarded for research rather than for professional training. Ann Hartman has described the situation:

> What has been the result of the "academizing" of schools of social work? First, the faculty profile is changing . . . "Publish or perish" has become the name of the game, and faculty members whose major interests are in practice, teaching practice, and in field work are having difficulty earning tenure and surviving in the system.

This does not necessarily mean that faculty who are interested in practice are not interested in knowledge development or in publishing their work. However, the time demands of managing a full-time university appointment, meeting norms for scholarly activity and publication, and staying close to the world of practice, hopefully through actually practicing, are overwhelming . . .

In order to survive, other junior faculty, even if they are strongly interested in practice, are putting that interest "on the back burner" while they immerse themselves in research projects. But with the demands of academia, will practice ever be taken *off* the back burner?[42]

The pressure to publish and engage in research and the drastic reduction of faculty experienced in clinical practice have threatened the quality of clinical training in many schools. Teachers of practice courses are often adjuncts or very junior faculty with little influence on school policy; administrators are often busy securing research grants and promoting research publication rather than striving for excellence in training students for direct practice. Furthermore, in many schools the traditional involvement of seasoned faculty in arranging field placements and in field advisement has become a low priority because of the time these activities require; too often, therefore, there is little interchange between the agencies where students are placed and the faculty at the schools. Under these circumstances, social workers at the agencies have little opportunity to keep faculty informed of the realities of the world of practice and the instructors cannot keep agency staff up to date on what is being taught in the classroom.

There are still many schools of social work that continue to place as high a value on quality training for clinical practice as on research, despite the pull to "academize" or to become absorbed in securing large research grants. Perhaps the administrators and faculty from these schools could provide leadership to the entire field of social work education by proposing guidelines for training students for direct and clinical practice. Once again, all professional social workers are challenged to become advocates. Directors and supervisors of fieldwork agencies can put pressure on school administrators by demanding that students be properly prepared for direct services. Professional organizations could add their influence to try to reverse these worrisome trends. Social work journals and other publications can be encouraged to emphasize articles on clinical practice. And graduate students, so many of whom are seeking to become competent in direct services, could use their clout (since the schools cannot survive without their enrollment) by insisting that they be taught by seasoned teachers well grounded in clinical experience and knowledge.

THE EMPIRICAL BASE*

Early History

Psychosocial casework is, as we have already said, a blend of concepts derived from psychiatry, psychology, and the social sciences with a substantial body of empirical knowledge developed within the casework field itself. The direct empirical basis of the approach rests on the continued systematic study of treatment, focusing upon client response to the procedures employed.

From the time of Mary Richmond, social workers recognized that they could not claim respect for their efforts "based on good intentions alone"; we should, Richmond

---

*The author is deeply indebted to Dr. Mary Ann Jones, Ehrenkranz School of Social Work, New York University, for her wise advice and generous contributions to this section.

wrote, encourage social workers to "measure their work by the best standards supplied by experience."[43] The term *practice wisdom,* sometimes used to describe the empirical basis, does not sufficiently convey the continuous study process through which practice was observed and examined in the early years before more sophisticated research methods were developed. Practice theory was built upon widely debated premises derived from *scrutiny by practicing social workers of actual experience.*

The first step in the development of any body of knowledge or theory is close observation of the phenomena under study. This usually begins informally and proceeds to the collection of data based on increasingly systematic study. Formulation of concepts and hypotheses and testing of these are usually the next steps in the development of theory. Of course, such testing is only as informative as the accuracy of the observed data.

This is how the psychosocial approach was built. Many early reports analyzed a single case. A number of others were based on the study of a few cases, and a few were derived from systematic study of 50 to 100 or more cases.[44] For the most part, they were studies and articles based on practice designed to build, confirm, or demonstrate theory. They described, examined, but did not formally test or attempt to prove either theory or practice. Control groups were almost never used. Practice concepts were constantly modified, as well as expanded, as new evidence appeared. Later chapters will refer to some of these changes in both practice and theory.

In "How It *Really* Was" Hollis described how, in the early days of casework, "practice wisdom" was built through the study of detailed process recordings, collegial group thinking and exchange, and ongoing efforts to identify and examine approaches, procedures, and principles.[45] It was important

then, as we believe it is now, for caseworkers to *participate actively* in the search for empirically based guidelines to treatment to determine which methods or treatment procedures are most successful in bringing about the particular changes that clients are seeking. Ongoing involvement in the evaluation of our work is the only avenue to ethical and effective treatment.

Practitioners and Researchers Search for Answers

The Effectiveness of Casework Treatment　Beginning in the 1950s and continuing to this day, social work and other mental health professions have become more and more concerned with developing methods for empirically validating effective treatment. By the 1970s outcome testing was strongly emphasized.[46] These evaluative studies attempted to determine if a particular form of treatment was either better than no treatment or better than a second form of treatment. Although there were controversies among social workers and others in the helping professions during these years about how best to evaluate treatment outcomes, many important advances were made in the systematic study of the effectiveness of casework and psychotherapy.[47] However, an unfortunate by-product of these developments was that practitioners involved themselves less in research endeavors than they had in the early years. There was more separation and less collaboration between clinicians and researchers than had been hoped as new approaches to the systematic study of practice were being devised.

In any event, many lessons were learned from the research of this period about research methodology itself. Perhaps most important of all, research writers along with clinicians began to warn against the *dangers of overgeneralizing* from a specific, often small, experiment or demonstration to casework as a whole. Psychology, where research has played an important role, also experienced a drive to develop more effective methods to study treatment outcome. In 1977, Smith and Glass published a classic paper, "Meta-Analysis of Psychotherapy Outcome Studies," reporting on nearly 400 controlled evaluations of psychotherapy and counseling. By compiling the results of many evaluations, methodological shortcomings of individual studies could be overcome and the patterns or trends across studies could be identified; the risks of overgeneralizing the findings of a single study were thereby reduced. The authors concluded: "The findings provide convincing evidence of the efficacy of psychotherapy. On the average, the typical therapy client is better off than 75 percent of untreated individuals."[48]

Another important development in research was adding the views of clients (whose satisfaction with treatment is of paramount importance) and of clinical social workers. The extraordinarily comprehensive and important 1973 Beck and Jones follow-up study of over 3,500 cases from family agencies, *Progress on Family Problems,* using such data, produced many significant findings. Client and worker evaluations of casework services showed far more favorable outcomes than some earlier studies had suggested. Eighty percent of clients participating in the study reported that services were "helpful" or "very helpful." Although the study of effectiveness was highly important to social workers then, as it is now, this research also contributed to knowledge building by identifying factors associated with positive outcomes. *A very strong, highly significant association was found to exist between good worker–client relationships and positive treatment outcomes.* Those relationships

rated by clients and workers as "unsatisfactory" resulted in far less change in treatment than those rated "very satisfactory." Consistent and substantial increases in client gains were found as ratings of the relationship moved along the scale from negative to positive. No other client or service characteristic analyzed in this study was found to be as important to good outcome as the worker–client relationship.[49] As we shall discuss in Chapter 9, other studies also point to the critical importance of the quality of the therapeutic relationship.

Recent Validation of the Benefits of Casework and Personal Therapy
A meta-analysis by Gorey of 88 (1990 to 1994) independent studies of social work interventions concluded: "Overall, social work interventions are effective; three-quarters of the clients who participate in social work interventions do better than the average client who does not."[50]

In 1994, *Consumer Reports* asked readers to respond to a questionnaire inquiring about their experiences in psychotherapy.[51] Of the 2,900 who had seen a mental health professional (22 percent of whom were social workers), the vast majority reported that they felt better, no matter how poorly they felt at the start of therapy. Not only did the respondents feel they benefited very substantially, but the indications were that *those in long-term treatment did better than those in short-term treatment.* The responses suggested that psychologists, psychiatrists, and social workers were equally effective in helping respondents with their *presenting* problems; many also reported *changes in other areas of their lives:* productivity at work, interpersonal relations, insight, self-confidence, and enjoyment of life, among others. As Seligman, a consultant to the research, wrote, *"Consumer Reports* has provided empirical validation of the effectiveness of psychotherapy."[52]

Focus on the effectiveness of casework and clinical services appears now to have moved on from a general question of "are they effective?" to more specific questions such as "what kinds of treatments are effective?" and "what works best for whom?" Positive findings from outcome studies in related disciplines as well as social work itself have bolstered confidence in the effectiveness of psychotherapy; family, marital, and brief therapies; behavioral treatments; and more.[53]

Current Research Issues

Most clinical social workers concerned about delivering ethical and effective services see systematic research as being more important than ever. Perhaps in part because of encouragement from researchers and demands from funding sources for accountability, they are attuned to becoming more focused and purposeful and more realistic in trying to determine what they do and do not accomplish. Information that research provides about what approaches may be best suited to particular problems is vitally important to social work clinicians. There are various, although not necessarily conflicting, points of view about the preferred methods for empirically validating effective treatment.

The Single-Subject Design   The single-subject, single-case, or single-system design, which attempts to measure change in a single case at various times over the course of treatment, has been advocated by many for about two decades as the research model most appropriate for evaluation of clinical practice. Research courses in graduate schools of social work typically include instruction in this design. Introduced by the fields of behaviorism and behavior modification, this type of research can be adapted to the study of various casework approaches, including psychodynamic treatment.[54] Some people see it as a refinement of the case evaluation approach, mentioned earlier, but more methodical. Three influential books on the single-system research design (by Bloom, et al; Blythe, et al; and Fischer and Corcoran) have received attention from social work clinicians and researchers.[55] These well-respected researchers/authors advocate a *scientist-practitioner* model; that is, they strongly recommend that practitioners regularly select and assess indicators of outcome at various points during treatment to monitor their clients' symptoms and to evaluate progress. Fischer and Corcoran offer an array of standardized measures they believe can be applied in various clinical situations. The measures consist of clients' responses to a series of questions related to their initial symptom or complaint (argumentativeness, compulsiveness, loneliness, self-consciousness, and many more) that are scored for an overall rating of the quality being measured. Clinicians can devise their own measures tailored to evaluate change in individual cases. In this model, the roles of clinician and researcher merge; and treatment sessions provide the setting for conducting scientific research.

In contrast to group designs, the single-system approach avoids the danger of reliance on outcome measures that are only tangentially relevant to the problems of the client and the purposes of treatment. The practitioner-evaluator selects measurable indicators of target problems to be addressed and tracks changes in these indicators. Specific and real goals (sometimes only one), mutually arrived at by client and worker at the outset of treatment, can be identified for each case, with results examined in relation to the goals. Not only does the single-subject design assist the clinician and client in measuring progress in a particular case, but it also identifies at the case level issues that might then be generalized and examined through group designs. Although there are critics of this research method,[56] it has been viewed by many as casework's best answer to questions about how to demonstrate effectiveness; not only is the study relevant to the client's actual situation, but the single-subject design also makes it possible for clinicians to examine and evaluate their own work.

To the clinician's study of *outcome* (change) in a single case (using the single-subject design) can be added the study of the *dynamics of worker–client communications* (process). Thus, information about *whether* clients are making progress can be combined with identification of *what* occurred in treatment (for example, did the worker make supportive comments, give advice, encourage reflection? How frequently were various procedures used? What kinds of client communications followed?) One is then able to identify worker techniques and client responses that are associated with progress (or lack of it). Chapter 21 describes how practitioners can informally use Hollis's method of studying worker procedures and client communications to appraise their own work.

Clients' Right to Effective Treatment

Without a doubt, clinicians and researchers agree on the value of delivering effective services and on our clients' right to receive these. Strong and persuasive arguments are made for social workers to be "ethically bound" to provide empirically validated treatments to clients. There are different points of view, however, about how to define *empirically validated* and *effective* treatment that go far beyond the scope of this discussion.[57] The important point is that the ongoing commitment of clinicians

and researchers to working together is required to identify demonstrably useful therapeutic methods.

Other Trends in Social Work Research

For the reader interested in exploring current research issues in greater detail, researchers and practitioners have written much about the merits and limitations of various methodologies. Even though adherents of a particular approach or philosphy can sometimes be adamantly partial, it seems to us that in most cases one need not take an "either–or" stand. Different emphases need not be incompatible: Each has its own value. We will mention only a few additional issues here.[58]

Some social workers are urging the return to the *case study* approach as a *supplement* to other research methods. In a recommended article, Gilgun encourages clinicians to become interested in conducting in-depth, intensive studies of single "units" of their practice, such as individuals, families, or segments of treatment sessions. She argues that the case study, which evaluates many dimensions and variables of a case, "has potential for building social work knowledge for assessment, intervention, and outcome." Practitioners are offered guidelines for developing and interpreting case studies. In her view "generalizing is analytic rather than statistical and probabilistic." In other words: "In analytic generalization, findings extracted from a single case are tested for their fit with other cases and with patterns predicted by theory or with previous research and theory."[59]

Two contrasting approaches to the study of clinical practice are (1) *experimental* and (2) *naturalistic*. The *experimental* approach is highly controlled in terms of selecting individuals to be included in the study. Once selected, the subjects to be studied are assigned to one or more types of treatment or to no treatment. Some experimental research designs are controlled to the point of limiting the treatments under study to a prepared or "manualized" treatment protocol. One well-known, carefully designed study compared four different approaches to treating depressed patients. Treatment providers were monitored to assure they were adhering to their particular protocol so that a clear picture could emerge about which treatments rendered the most (or least) favorable outcomes.[60] However, some social workers are concerned about research designs in which a specific treatment protocol is prescribed and must be adhered to throughout the treatment in order to determine whether it is less, equally, or more effective than another treatment. It is argued that such designs do not reflect the real world of therapy or casework service where goals shift and techniques that are not working with a particular client are replaced with others, including involving family members in sessions or intervening in the environment. Generally, practitioners do not confine themselves to one prescribed intervention or set of interventions; rather they do, and in our view should, use different techniques based on the needs and reactions of particular clients at different times. Some conclude, therefore, that highly controlled, manualized therapy cannot be employed to study treatment as it actually occurs between clinician and client.

In contrast to the highly controlled design, the *naturalist* approach to research tries to capture the process and outcomes of the *actual experience* of clients in therapy as it naturally occurs, without attempting to control it. Seligman puts forth a naturalist view that is similar to that of many clinical social workers: "Psychotherapy in the field is almost always concerned with *improvement in the general functioning* of patients, as well as amelioration of a disorder

and relief of specific, presenting symptoms. Efficacy [highly controlled, experimental] studies usually focus only on specific symptom reduction and whether the disorder ends."[61] [Emphasis in original] He and others believe that research has to address a range of questions rather than focus on measures of change in one particular area.

Howard Goldstein is concerned that the rush to achieve scientific respectability has led to the downgrading of common sense, intuition, and practice wisdom in favor of detached objectivity. He and others also emphasize the role of the client as "co-expert" (with the social worker); the client "remains the expert about his or her reality, which includes the beliefs, values, culture, goals, and other subjective factors that give life meaning and purpose. In effect, these 'experts' . . . join in a collaborative endeavor within a life in process to unravel awareness and the means of confronting certain problems of living."[62]

As will be emphasized many times in this book, from the psychosocial point of view, the client is considered to be a "co-expert" throughout treatment. His or her participation in treatment planning and evaluation of the process and benefits of casework services are regularly elicited. As we see it, it follows that research that explores clients' views of services received or progress made (whether in the present or retrospectively) should be highly valued. It is disconcerting that some researchers report that when they inquire of clients how they fared in treatment and how they felt about the services they received, some clients indicate that no one ever asked them such questions before.[63] Clearly, there is a message there for practitioners; without input from clients, one cannot have a complete picture of how the work is going.

There has been a recent surge of interest in some social work circles in qualitative research methodology. In-depth interviewing, observation, and qualitative analysis of process recording of individual worker–client sessions and other documents appeal to some as the ideal approach to studying the complexities of practice. Even though some practitioners may feel more comfortable with this type of qualitative research, since some of its methods seem familiar and similar to the therapeutic process, Padgett believes that its purposes are quite different from and in some ways incompatible with clinical work. She strongly recommends that research and therapy not be engaged in simultaneously by the clinician who is already treating a client; there are others, however, who do not agree with her.[64]

Research Moves into the 21st Century

As already suggested, the growth of knowledge, the status of social work, and the improvement of clinical treatment require a spirit of *collaboration* between clinicians and researchers. Each has much to learn from the knowledge, perspectives, and skills of the other. It is critically important that a climate of mutual respect be nurtured.

There are very good reasons graduate students preparing to become clinical social workers are required to take one or preferably two courses on research methods. The more familiar practitioners are with research methods, the more they can understand them, and the more they can contribute, even bring initiative, to their application to clinical practice. When the expertise of researchers and clinicians combine, the best routes to the study of practice will be developed, including which research approaches are most useful and informative under what types of circumstances. Intelligent decisions will be made based on the kinds of clients, problems, treatment objectives, theoretical

orientations of the practitioners, and many other variables. With increased sophistication, it should become possible to design and select research strategies on the basis of the kinds of knowledge we are seeking and the practicality of implementation rather than on the basis of rigid adherence to a particular method or point of view.[65]

NOTES

1. For further discussion, see Cooper (1980), Ewalt (1980), and Eda Goldstein (1996). See also Lukton and Bro (1988) who discuss the fact that master's degree programs do not provide adequate training for clinical practice and describe an innovative clinical doctoral program.
2. See Turner (1996) and Dorfman (1988), both edited volumes, with chapters describing a wide range of theoretical orientations and approaches to social work treatment.
3. Richmond (1899).
4. See Woodroofe (1962).
5. Richmond (1917).
6. Richmond (1922, 1930).
7. Richmond (1917), p. 38.
8. Ibid., p. 25.
9. Richmond (1922), pp. 101–2.
10. Richmond (1917), pp. 146–47.
11. Ibid., p. 158.
12. Robinson (1930), p. 54.
13. Ibid., p. 81.
14. See Robinson (1930), Taft (1937), and Rank (1936).
15. See also Smalley (1970) and Dunlap (1996) for summaries of functional theory and applications to practice.
16. Contrary to popular opinion, psychoanalysis was not a major force in casework in the 1920s. Hellenbrand (1965) in her careful study of this period found very little mention of Freudian thinking in the literature or teaching materials of that period. Rather, it was gradually assimilated during the 1930s and by the end of that decade was a major component of the diagnostic or differential position.
17. Hamilton (1937).

18. Hamilton (1940).
19. Hollis (1939), p. 5.
20. Dore (1990), in an interesting article, argues that basic concepts of the Pennsylvania School's functional model have become an integral part of social work theory and practice "often without real awareness of their origins" (p. 369). Among these are: the client's right to self-determination, understanding of individual differences, starting where the client is, the evolving nature of assessment, the important role played by the helping relationship, and time as an organizing component in the intervention process.
21. See Kasius (1950, 1962). For the most part, the articles by major leaders of casework in these compilations indicate that during the 1940s and 1950s there was far more focus on psychodynamic aspects of theory and practice than on environmental influences or resources, even though family-oriented casework was increasingly discussed, especially in the 1950s.
22. See Aptekar (1955) and Perlman (1957).
23. Hamilton (1941).
24. Hankins (1930).
25. Hollis (1964), p. 5.
26. Roberts and Nee (1970).
27. Turner (1996) in the concluding chapter, "An Interlocking Perspective for Treatment," deals with this issue. Additional readings on casework's roots and evolution include Kendall (1982) and Hollis (1983).
28. For resources, see Bronfenbrenner, et al. (1996) and Family Service of America, *The State of Families* (1991, 1995). They contain not only a wealth of information, facts and figures, about economic and other conditions and trends in the United States but also many policy recommendations. See also Jiminez (1990) for an excellent discussion on changing conditions that place new and increased demands on the human services professions. In a recommended and thoughtful article, Hartman (1995) urges social workers to involve themselves and take action to help shape humane family policy. The June 1990 issue of *Families in Society* is devoted to challenges to families as work patterns change.

29. In their important book Mirowsky and Ross (1989), sociologists, discuss their criticisms of the idea that life changes and stressors necessarily cause psychological distress. However, they link many social factors and deprivations to the alarming differences between the less fortunate and the more privileged in the emotional pain they experience. See also Williams (1994). The November 1993 issue of *Families in Society* is devoted to articles on poverty. Chapter 8, note 12 includes more information on poverty and its implications.
30. Many of these matters will be discussed in this text. A review of professional journals of the last decade, especially *Families in Society, Social Work, Clinical Social Work Journal, Smith College Studies in Social Work,* and *Social Service Review,* will reveal many articles and references related to these issues.
31. See one of Weick's (1986) articles elaborating on this important emphasis. See also note 37 of this chapter.
32. See the *New York Times,* April 30, 1985, pp. C2 and C9. See Eda Goldstein (1996).
33. *NASW News* 43 (March 1998), pp. 1 and 12. See also Ozawa (1993) for a discussion of the comparison of social workers' earnings to those of other professional groups.
34. See Gibelman and Schervish (1996) and Eda Goldstein (1996). Strom (1992 and 1994) discusses some of the issues related to choices to go into private practice (because of bureaucratic constraints in agency work, for example); she also points to reasons workers choose to remain in agency practice (including managed care constraints, security, larger cross section of clients, and more opportunities to fulfill the professional mission).
35. In a very good article, Anderson (1995) expresses concern about a trend that threatens a shift in social work from family-centered to individually oriented practice; she urges that schools of social work develop more curricula in family theory and practice. In a very useful and interesting article, Cole (1995) reports on "fragile" and limited initiatives in child welfare agencies to change from being "child rescuers" to make "efforts to preserve

families, make foster care more family friendly, reunify children separated by foster care, and place more children for adoption" (p. 163); she urges early-intervention and family-support services and the continuation of family-preservation services.

36. The June 1996 issue of *Families in Society* is devoted to constructivism in social work practice. See the volume edited by Franklin and Nurius (1998) with very useful and informative chapters on constructivism written for social workers by social workers and others; many are helpful in linking theory to practice. Other readings on constructivism and related issues such as the narrative approach to therapy include Atherton (1993), Carpenter (1996), Dean (1993), Dean and Rhodes (1998), Focht and Beardsley (1996), Horner (1995), Kelley (1996), Larner (1996), Lee (1996), Nye (1994), Franklin (1995), Sands (1996), and Strickland (1994). Readers may be interested in an article by Pozatek (1994) who asserts: "Social workers should not expect to know in advance what the outcome of clinical interactions will be" (p. 397). In Pozatek's view, a position of uncertainty helps the worker to try to understand the client's experience rather than make assumptions about it.

37. Very worthwhile readings on the strengths perspective and related issues include Howard Goldstein (1990b), Jones and Kilpatrick (1996), a book and an article by Saleebey (both 1996), Hwang and Cowger (1998), and Weick, et al. (1989).

38. For excellent references on empowerment, see Judith Lee (1994, 1996) and Kondrat (1995). We recommend Pinderhughes's article (1995) that emphasizes that effective empowerment interventions require workers with cultural competence. See also Browne (1995) who discusses empowerment in work with older women. Hegar (1989) urges empowerment-based practice with children: "Children can successfully adopt a worldview that involves feelings of internal control and acknowledgement of external responsibility for many aspects of their lives" (p. 378). Cohen (1998) conducted a study on percep-

tions of power in client–worker relationships; she interviewed men and women living in residential settings who had histories of homelessness and psychiatric hospitalization; the clients were "clear about their distaste for authoritarian relationships" (p. 440). Cohen raises the question whether goals of shared power, mutuality, and collaboration are truly realizable when client–worker relationships are embedded in a hierarchical structure. Gitterman (1989) discusses the issue of professional authority in an interesting article that includes a case example of a young boy in residential treatment. Chapter 9 will discuss mutuality and collaboration in much greater detail. Orlinsky, et al. (1994), in their review of process-outcome research, indicate that, particularly from the patient's point of view, interactive collaboration was important to outcome.

39. See Northen (1976, 1995), who is highly regarded as a social work specialist in small groups. See also Garvin (1997), Yalom (1985), Hepworth, et al. (1997), Chapter 17, and Shulman (1992), Part IV. Dean (1998) discusses a narrative approach to groups. Feit, et al. (1995) edited a volume of 15 papers from the 13th Annual Symposium of Social Work with Groups on "Capturing the Power of Diversity"; while they derive from the branch of social work known as group work, several of the chapters are very interesting and useful to caseworkers, more of whom are taking an interest in working with various types of groups.

40. See Woods (1983) and Hollis (1980) for the authors' views on education for clinical practice that, in our view, pertain to today's conditions and requirements. See also Lukton and Bro (1988). Three still relevant—now historic—papers expressing concern about the quality of education for clinical social work practice appear in *Clinical Social Work Journal* 5 (Winter 1977): Helen Pinkus, et al., Shirley Cooper, and John D. Minor. See also note 1 of this chapter.

41. See Levy (1979) and Lewis (1982, 1987) for discussions of social work knowledge, traditions, values, and ethics.

42. Quoted from Hartman's (1990) recommended article on education for direct practice, p. 41. See also Eda Goldstein (1996). We recommend Witkin's (1998b) thought-provoking editorial urging an appreciation of the benefits of divergent perspectives of agencies and academics; he suggests creative approaches to using the tensions between them to work more effectively together.

43. Richmond (1917), p. 25.

44. It may be useful to cite a few illustrations. Among the small studies ranging from 9 to 12 cases, in chronological order, are Lewis (1937), Reynolds and Siegle (1959), Geist and Gerber (1960), Jolesch (1962), Prodie, et al. (1967). Among the larger studies, ranging from 75 to several hundred cases, are Hamilton (1947), Hollis (1949), Ripple, et al. (1964), Young (1964), Bailey (1968), Bitterman (1968), Cohen and Krause (1969).

45. Hollis (1983). Although from somewhat different angles, DeRoos (1990) and Howard Goldstein (1992) both believe that "practice wisdom" emanates from practice experience, working with and listening to clients.

46. Eysenck's (1952) evaluation of 24 treatment studies of 7,000 treatment patients led him to conclude that psychotherapies in use were largely ineffective, sparking deep concern in the mental health professions about the benefits of therapy. Nathan (1998) gives a brief history of subsequent efforts, especially in the field of psychology, to identify empirically supported treatments. In social work, Fischer (1973) and Wood (1978) were among those who reviewed studies of casework practice and raised questions about the effectiveness of casework treatment.

47. For discussions of research methodology and outcome evaluations during this period, see Hollis (1976), Geismer (1972), and Crane (1972). The authors urged methodological improvements and held out hope that casework was more effective than some critics had suggested.

48. Smith and Glass (1977), p. 752. They add: "Few important differences in effectiveness could be established among many quite different types of psychotherapy."

49. Beck and Jones (1973).

50. Gorey (1996), p. 119. He recommends research in which disinterested, external evaluators' ratings of social work effectiveness accompany internal evaluations by workers and clients. See also Yedeka-Sherman (1988).

51. "Mental Health: Does Therapy Help?" *Consumer Reports,* November 1995, pp. 734–39.

52. Seligman (1995), p. 974.

53. See Orlinsky, et al. (1994) for a review of process-outcome studies, in which outcomes were analyzed not just to determine whether results were positive or negative but also to identify the components of therapy that related to outcome; once again, they reported that "the strongest evidence linking process to outcome concerns the *therapeutic bond*" (p. 360). Readers interested in research studies of outcomes and process of a broad range of treatment will want to look over Bergin and Garfield (1994). See also Thomlinson (1984) and Gurman and Kinskern (1981) on family therapy outcome research.

54. See for example, Dean and Reinherz (1986) and Nelsen (1990) for elaborations on this point.

55. Bloom, et al. (1995), Blythe, et al. (1994), and Fischer and Corcoran (1994).

56. For example, Epstein (1996), Meyer (1996), Slonim-Nevo (1997), and Wakefield and Kirk (1996). MacEachron and Gustavsson (1997) recommend reframing the model in which the role of the practitioner is "practitioner-scientist" rather than "scientist-practitioner"; the scientist role should be subordinate, they believe; they also recommend including qualitative methods "to capture the social work contexts and complexities" (p. 654).

57. For further discussion see Myers and Thyer (1997) and responses from Raw (1998) and Witkin (1998a). See also Geismer and Wood (1982) and Ivanoff, et al. (1987).

58. In addition to other references cited in this section, see Reid (1994) for an excellent discussion and overview of the empirical practice movement from its beginnings in the early 1960s.

59. Gilgun (1994). See also Berlin (1983).
60. See Elkin, et al. (1989). The authors report on the National Institute of Mental Health study of 250 depressed patients who were randomly assigned to four types of 16-week treatment: interpersonal therapy, cognitive behavior therapy, medication plus clinical management (support, encouragement, and direct advice if necessary), and a placebo plus clinical management. The report concluded: "Significant differences among treatments were present only for the subgroup of patients who were more severely depressed and functionally impaired; here there was some evidence of the effectiveness of interpersonal therapy with these patients and strong evidence of the effectiveness of imipramine [medication] plus clinical management. In contrast, there were no significant differences among treatments, including placebo plus clinical management for the less severely impaired patients" (p. 971).
61. Seligman (1995), p. 967.
62. Howard Goldstein (1990a), p. 38.
63. For example, see Festinger (1983).
64. See Padgett (1998). Smith (1998) also argues that qualitative research is relevant for evaluating practice and, in contrast to Padgett, believes that practitioners can use qualitative methods to study their own cases and caseloads. See also Franklin and Jordan (1995) who favor qualitative techniques for clinical assessment; in their article they review five methods, illustrating them with case materials.
65. Jones (1991) has written an interesting and informative chapter on measuring outcomes in family preservation services. Taynor (1990) suggests a scale to evaluate treatment outcome for families. See Atherton (1993) who summarizes and strongly recommends an end to the heated arguments between empiricists and social constructionists.

CHAPTER 2

THE PSYCHOSOCIAL FRAME OF REFERENCE: AN OVERVIEW

In this chapter we sketch the frame of reference upon which psychosocial casework rests. The reader may find this overview helpful as a reference to return to when reading subsequent chapters.

BASIC VALUES

Certain basic values of casework form the first component of the psychosocial framework. Psychosocial casework is characterized by its direct concern for the *well-being* of the individual. Its purpose is not to bring the individual into conformity with society and thus rid society of the social hazard presented by the discontented, unsatisfied, rebellious individual. On the contrary, casework came into being as a response to the needs of human beings for protection against social and natural deprivations and catastrophes. Historically, it represents a turning away from the laissez-faire doctrines that followed the unhappy combina-

tion of Malthusian thinking with Darwin's emphasis on the development of strength through the survival of the fittest. From its inception, casework has stressed the value of the individual, and for the past 60 years it has consistently advocated the right of each person to live in a unique way, provided he or she does not infringe unduly upon the rights of others. Traditionally, caseworkers have been committed to doing all they can to help people to gain access to opportunities that promote maximum realization of their potentials and aspirations and to reduce obstacles to self-fulfillment.[1]

This emphasis upon the innate worth of the individual is an extremely important, fundamental characteristic of casework. It is the ingredient that makes it possible to establish the relationship of trust that is so essential for effective treatment. From it grow the two essential characteristics of the caseworker's attitude toward a person coming for help: first, *acceptance,* and second, respect for the client's right to make his or her own decisions—often referred to as *self-determination.*

Acceptance

By acceptance we mean the maintaining of an attitude of warm goodwill toward the client, whether or not his or her way of behaving is "socially acceptable" and whether or not it is to the worker's personal liking. This is without doubt the main ingredient in the development of a therapeutic or helping relationship. At the beginning of treatment, the client is often distrustful of the worker's interest and desire to help and may also have feelings of helplessness and lack of self-esteem or fear of criticism. Uncritical acceptance by the worker lessens these fears and begins the building of a client–worker relationship in which the client feels support and can talk freely. In actual practice, we may have to confront our own negative reactions to clients whose behavior is hostile, cold, destructive, or otherwise objectively or subjectively distasteful; the ideal of warm goodwill sometimes takes deliberate effort to try to achieve. When meeting with families—especially if one is caught in the crossfire between angry, blaming family members—it can be difficult, but nevertheless important, to maintain an attitude of acceptance and impartiality.

Empathy and Acceptance Acceptance goes beyond objectivity. It requires more than intellectual understanding of a person's behavior and plight. Mere tolerance is not enough. Acceptance of our clients—liking and feeling warmly toward them whether or not we like how they appear or what they do—requires an additional and essential element: empathy. We define *empathy* as *the capacity to enter into and grasp the inner feelings or subjective state of another person.*

Perhaps even more than many others in the helping professions, caseworkers encounter people who are severely disabled, physically, emotionally, and mentally. Many of our clients have literally or figuratively been battered by life circumstances, by economic deprivation, by bigotry. Some have answered violence with violence. Others have learned to cope with life passively, unable or unwilling to seek alternatives to present circumstances. Still others respond to misfortune by deteriorating, emotionally or physically, by caring for themselves poorly, or by neglecting or abusing family members. Acceptance and understanding require caseworkers to *feel with* a broad range of excruciatingly painful experiences of others. We need to recognize the desperation that lies behind reactions to these experiences. Obviously, the more accurately we are able to empathize, the greater the likelihood that we can use our understanding in constructive interactions with our clients. Empathy is often the critical ingredient to maintaining a constant caring feeling.[2]

Acceptance and Evaluation Acceptance is not to be confused with refraining from evaluating or questioning the appropriateness or usefulness of the client's ways of functioning. For example, one might ask a father who frequently demeans his timid son's lack of athleticism whether he thinks this supports their relationship or the boy's potential interest in sports. But even accurate and perceptive evaluation is of little value if it is accompanied by feelings of condemnation, hostility, or revulsion toward the client.

Self-Determination

From the psychosocial perspective, self-determination[3] is a fundamental principle and a highly valued attribute of the individual.

When we speak of the right to self-determination or to self-direction, we refer to the right to make one's own choices. The more that clients exercise autonomy, making decisions and directing their own lives, the better; and the less the caseworker tries to take on these responsibilities, the better. In Chapter 1 we mentioned the long history of this concept in social work, with its early beginnings found in the writings of Mary Richmond.

In the Client–Worker Relationship
Even though the principle of self-determination has remained central to social work thought, there have certainly been compromises in practice. For example, based on the clinician's "urge to rescue," or on the belief that professional training arms one with knowledge that can help determine what is "best," it can be tempting to try to lead the client to follow the worker's ideas about what course should be taken. The influences of the constructivist and narrative approaches to social work, mentioned in Chapter 1, are important because we need to continually re-emphasize the value and the ethical imperative of collaboration and mutuality in the treatment relationship. "In a professional relationship," wrote Weick and Pope, "in which 'knowledge' by virtue of training is characteristically lodged with the practitioner, the act of subverting client choice in favor of professional judgment is too easily accomplished."[4]

To make sound decisions, the client sometimes simply requires new information; often, help is needed from the caseworker in exploring and understanding various aspects of a dilemma. In some cases, the client's ego is to varying degrees impaired in its capacity for accurate perception or judgment, or its functioning is distorted by the operation of mechanisms of defense, so that the problem becomes one of

strengthening the capacity for decision making. *The objective of such work is to increase the ability to make decisions, not to make them for the client.* In extreme situations, where there is danger of real harm to self or to others, or where the client or client's family is incapable of carrying this responsibility, the caseworker may have to take over and make decisions for the client. But this is done *only* where the necessity for such action is absolutely clear.[5]

A belief in the value of self-determination does not mean that the caseworker plays a passive role with clients. On the contrary, change is promoted in clients' functioning when it is believed that this will enable them to meet their needs more effectively. A worker may encourage a client to take a high school equivalency test to be eligible for a better job *the client wants*. The means a worker chooses to bring about change must be consistent with the goal of increasing the client's capacity for self-direction: his or her autonomy. On an ongoing basis, the goals of the treatment must be shared and reviewed by worker and client together; self-direction by the client requires a casework relationship that fosters *mutuality*. Thus, the relationship is consistently an honest one; the worker shows respect for the wishes and goals of the client and sometimes offers suggestions or advice—not, however, as directives but as opinions that the client is free to accept or reject. Over and over again, workers may raise questions such as: "Would it help if . . . ?" "Does it make sense to you to consider . . . ?" "Do you think that idea will work out in practice?" Even these inquiries are designed to help clients become experts on making decisions that seem best to *them;* they are not intended to persuade them to take a particular action.

A worker sometimes offers suggestions about *how* to reach a goal that a client or family desires. Obviously, this is different from becoming directive about *what* goal or decision is to be chosen. In reaching decisions and moving toward the realization of an objective, the worker's role is to help clients clarify thinking. In other words, whenever possible—and this is most of the time—clients are helped to reason things through for themselves, to correct their own misconceptions, and to accept the maximum responsibility of which they are capable for formulating their own ideas. Where more active guidance is needed, either because of lack of knowledge, as is sometimes true in child-rearing problems, or because of limitations in education or in intellectual capacity, more active guidance may need to be given. But even in these circumstances, every effort is made to promote the client's self-directive ability. Techniques for drawing out the client's own reasoning and decision-making capacities are emphasized.

Limits on Self-Determination   The value of self-determination or self-realization is a relative concept; it is subject to many conditions, constraints, and moral dilemmas. Many clients of social workers are so physically, socially, or economically handicapped that they have very few choices.[6] It is our responsibility, as individual workers and as members of our profession, to do all we can to maximize opportunities for everybody, but in many cases the options of disadvantaged clients are extremely limited. Furthermore, people constantly have to weigh their own preferences or desires against conflicting needs or wishes of others. A woman client, for example, may want very much to work full time but decide against it because of the lack of quality child-care resources for her preschool child. For career reasons, a man may want to relocate to another state, but chooses not to because his aging mother

and father who live nearby are becoming increasingly dependent and isolated; he forfeits his opportunity out of feelings of duty and love for his parents.[7]

THE PERSON-IN-SITUATION

Psychosocial casework has always been concerned with the improvement of interpersonal relationships and life situations. Despite shifting emphases over the years, it has consistently recognized the importance of internal psychological processes, external social and physical conditions, and the interplay among them. As we said in Chapter 1, throughout its history, in its endeavor to enable individuals to meet their needs and function adequately in their lives and social relationships, psychosocial thought has drawn continuously from other scientific fields as they uncovered data and developed theory that promised to throw light on the psychological, social, and interactional aspects of human problems. Psychology and psychiatry; cultural anthropology and studies in ethnicity; sociology, including theories on role and gender, communication, family and group dynamics; and systems and ecological theories all have contributed, and continue to contribute, essential knowledge to the field of psychosocial casework.

Gordon Hamilton's concept, "the person-in-his-situation," is central to casework theory and refers to the threefold configuration consisting of the person, the situation, and the interaction between them.[8] The terms *internal pressure* and *external pressure* have often been used to describe forces within the individual and forces within the environment as they impinge upon or interact with each other. External pressure is sometimes referred to as *press* and internal pressure as *stress*.

The person–situation interaction is highly complex. External press is immediately modified by the way in which the individual perceives it. Depending upon their individual natures, needs, or internal stress, individuals will react to their perceptions of press in their own particular ways. Because the term *situation* often implies a human situation—family, friends, employer, teacher, and so on—or intricate social and physical environmental forces, the situation is at least as complicated as the "person" who confronts it. The individual's family is usually seen as a fundamental component of the "situation," and the interactions occurring in the family system in both past and present are of high salience. When a person overtly reacts to an external press, this reaction becomes a press upon some other human being, who then responds with his or her own perceptions and needs. Hence, the individual and the environment can only be understood within the framework of their inextricable interdependence on one another.

Fundamental purposes of casework, and social work as a whole, include resolution or reduction of problems *arising out of disequilibrium between people and their environments*. Sometimes personalities or families are truly "pathological," "dysfunctional," or "inadequate" in the sense that they defeat their *own* purposes and/or harm others. At other times, these same assessments can be applied to aspects of the world around the client. In addition to relatives and friends, these environments include other people, physical surroundings, cultural attitudes, organizations or institutions, even communities and larger social systems. When one or more of these are unhealthy or substandard (an ill spouse, lack of housing, discrimination, a tight job market, etc.), the client is directly affected. Problems may also be created by dysfunctional transactions *among* various systems in a client's milieu (take, for example, the stress a child feels when his or her foster parents, natural par-

ents, and child welfare worker are in conflict or are pulling in different directions). Certainly many client difficulties are the consequence of dysfunctional interactions *between* a client and one or more aspects of the environment (spouse, in-laws, employer, or neighbors, for example).

Often, understanding the person-in-situation requires an understanding of the psychology of the people involved in the *gestalt*. Gestalt is a term we use to describe a configuration of phenomena that is so well integrated that the *sum cannot be defined by its parts alone*. Equally often, it requires an analysis of environmental forces impinging on the person or family with whom one is working. There are also many instances, as this text will illustrate, when a worker's focus is on the interactions or reciprocal influences between people and their situations, rather than on the individual or the environment as such. As caseworkers, we aim to promote positive adaptations by supporting strengths and/or by correcting or preventing maladaptive interactions.[9]

SYSTEMS THEORY AND THE ECOLOGICAL PERSPECTIVE

An Overview

As mentioned in Chapter 1, systems theory has proved extremely useful to psychosocial casework as an aid to conceptually understanding the many psychological, familial, and environmental forces at work in people's lives. It has helped to identify and describe various aspects or systems within the person–situation gestalt.[10] As early as 1941, Gordon Hamilton,[11] in a major paper, used the term *organismic* to characterize the psychosocial approach and referred to its use in 1938 by Henry A. Murray in *Explorations in Personality*. Murray, in describing an organism, said:

"The organism is from the beginning a whole, from which the parts are derived by self-differentiation. The whole and its parts are mutually related; the whole being as essential to an understanding of the parts as the parts are to an understanding of the whole."[12] He also referred to human beings as adapting, integrating, and differentiating "within a changing environmental matrix." Systems theory adds to Murray's early conception the *transactional concept of the interlocking relationships between individuals and their environments*. When viewed from a systems perspective, the "case" of an individual or family includes the situation and is seen as a system of interrelated, reciprocal forces that dovetail and reinforce one another.

The closely related ecological perspective, also focusing attention on the intertwining of the person, family, and environments, was introduced into casework by Germain and Gitterman in 1976.[13] This aspect of ecology both parallels and contributes to the increased understanding of the nature of person–situation interactions and to the place of the environment in treatment, as these have been developing from the psychosocial point of view.

Throughout this text, we attempt to demonstrate that in both theory and practice, systems and ecological concepts can and should be integrated with theories about personality and individual functioning. It is our hope that the day is past when a caseworker is torn between the two perspectives that together, in our view, provide greater understanding and more opportunites for helping than were previously available to us. From the psychosocial perspective, the combination of closely related systems and ecological concepts on the one hand and knowledge about psychodynamics on the other are themselves interdependent.

Applications to Practice

A primary characteristic of any system is that all its parts are in transaction, so that whatever affects one part of the system to some degree affects all parts. Change in one aspect *requires* changes in the others. *Adaptation* is defined as a transactional process, an action-oriented process, in which people influence and shape their environments and, in turn, are influenced and shaped by them. People and their environments are constantly changing. As Germaine wrote: "Adaptations may be directed to changing oneself in order to meet environmental opportunities or demands, or they may be directed to changing the environment so that physical and social settings will be more responsive to human needs, rights, goals, and capacities."[14] Thus, assessment requires simultaneous attention to features of the person and to features of the environment.

Circular Causality Transactional relationships imply *circular causality* in contrast to *linear causality*. For example, if a teacher reprimands one student, that student may cry; the same kind of scolding may stimulate anger in another pupil. The responses to these two incidents will evoke different reactions from the teacher who might, for example, regret her behavior toward the first student and apologize, but trade irate remarks with the second. If one brought linear thinking to these incidents, one might say the teacher "caused" the first youngster to cry and "caused" the second one to become angry. But, as this simple illustration demonstrates, in most transactions, linear or simple cause-and-effect explanations do not tell the whole story because each person (or other feature of the environment) is influenced in the process. Furthermore, as just indicated, a reaction does not usually stop with one event, but triggers another consequence. To take the illustration one step further, suppose the teacher became so annoyed with the second student that she called in the parent or suspended the youngster from school; the circle becomes larger as additional events occur, which can then become both cause and effect of yet further processes. Assessments of far more complex transactions are commonly required in practice.

From these assessments, interventive approaches are then designed. Individuals are in constant interaction, or transaction, with members of their immediate family; with other relatives; with networks of friends and acquaintances; with employment, health, welfare, and a multitude of other systems, including value systems that are shaped by the interactions, past and present, with one's family, culture, and society. Through a spouse or a child there may be either direct or indirect interaction with other systems, such as the school or hospital system. In casework, the focus of attention—for assessment, treatment planning, and intervention—goes beyond the individual or family to include those systems that appear to be of salient importance to the resolution of problems for which help is sought.

The Person–Environment "Fit"   Recently, caseworkers have been more attuned than ever to the need to assess the match or fit between individuals and their environments. Rather than blaming a mother for an imperfect bond with a child, it is understood that characteristics or temperaments of youngsters as well as those of parents can have profound implications for the parent–child relationship: the quality of the "fit." Opportunities for resolution can be examined less defensively when it is clear that the problem is defined in terms of

difference rather than inadequacy. Without ascribing pathology to an individual or to a workplace, assessing the "fit" between the employee and the job can provide guidelines for casework intervention. Vigilante gives examples: "The workplace that requires privacy may be experienced by some workers as isolation. On the other hand, the workplace that requires personal interaction may be experienced by a worker as invasion . . . An authoritarian administration may make some workers feel controlled and powerless and make others secure and certain about expectations and performance."[15] An individual's temperament, needs, and preferences and the available opportunities can be evaluated and, whenever possible, matched to better suit both sides. This perspective contributes to a "no-fault" approach to reducing person–situation disequilibrium.

The Interdependence of Systems: An Example   The interrelationship of systems and their components—of the person and the environment—becomes apparent in every situation that comes to the attention of social workers. If a young daughter in a family becomes seriously ill, for example, this is certain to affect both father and mother in some manner: worry over the child, direct involvement in the child's care, time and attention required by the child's condition. These changes then may influence many other systems in which each member is involved, such as the extended family, employment, and educational systems. For instance, if the mother is now unable to make customary weekly visits to her elderly father, she may not only disappoint him but also may interfere with plans made by her sister, with whom the father lives, to enjoy time freed by the expected visit. If the mother's value system requires her to give attention to elderly relatives, guilt at being unable to do so may create additional strain on her and those around her. The child's illness may worry her father so much that he becomes irritable or distracted at work, potentially contributing to tensions with fellow workers or superiors. Feeling harassed at the job, this man may then begin to place demands on his already overburdened wife, creating problems in the marital system that had previously been a source of comfort to both spouses. The sick girl may learn that, because of her absence, a classmate is being given a role in the school play that had originally been assigned to her. This disappointment may retard her recovery, which, in turn, reverberates in all of the other interdependent systems just mentioned.

This situation provides another illustration of *circular causality*. When two or more systems are in interaction because they have a common member, occurrences in one system will affect other systems. This may be referred to as *input* from one system to another or as *transactions* between or among systems. If the illness of the child described above continues, there may be repetitions of that input from the nuclear family system to the other systems and various additional *feedback* processes that occur among them. The mother's sister may pressure her to resume regular visits, which may ultimately add to the already considerable tensions between husband and wife. The father's supervisor may be increasingly annoyed with him and cause worry about whether the job and security are in jeopardy. Mounting pressures and marital distress may then trigger angry interactions between parents and the other children in the family. These children may subsequently develop problems in school, which in turn add further to the strain between husband and wife.

Obviously, the possible cycle of events is endless, and the individuals being influenced by many forces at the same time undoubtedly will have to arrive at some resolution. Decisions may be made to effect some positive change in the environment: by locating a baby-sitter for the child or a home health worker for the aging father to reduce pressures on the caretakers, by the mother's talking problems over with her sister, by the father's taking vacation time or explaining his unusual behavior to his supervisor, and so on. The couple, concerned about any or all of the escalating negative events in their lives, may agree to seek help in problem solving from a social worker. Even if only one parent evaluates his or her own behavior toward the other and takes steps to improve the quality of the marital interactions, very possibly all the impinging relationships will improve. Just as one event—in this illustration, the child's illness—can precipitate many mounting negative transactions, so *one positive change can be the beginning of a reversal of the downward spiral*. Not only are all aspects of the system involved in the problem, but also the actions of *any* member can contribute to the solution.

When individuals attempt to cope with or modify their situations or their relationships to others, or seek a better "fit" between themselves (their needs and aspirations) and their environment, they have to make some inner changes; at the very least, a new adaptation requires thought and initiative to improve external circumstances or to locate opportunities. However, often more changes from within are necessary. For example, a person may be ambivalent about the steps required to modify circumstances, or be fearful of making a desired change. *The personality is itself a system with various and sometimes conflicting forces within.* In personal relationships, every action is shaped by these internal forces as well as by the presses and gratifications (either experienced or anticipated) from others with whom the individual is in interaction. As we shall see later in this chapter, sometimes a small shift in the balance of the personality system can trigger significant changes in the individual and, subsequently, in the quality of transactions with other people or systems.

This realization that human beings are themselves systems of a very complicated and subtle nature radically modifies the application of systems theory to human transactions. If this fact is overlooked, the use of systems and ecological concepts becomes simplistic. From the psychosocial perspective, only by combining these extremely useful concepts with adequate knowledge of the nature of human personality can we productively understand the person–situation gestalt.

PERSONALITY AND SOCIAL FUNCTIONING

A major emphasis of this book is on psychosocial procedures used by clinical social workers (see Chapters 4 through 8) to bring about change in the social functioning of individuals and families, in their interpersonal relationships, and in their interactions with various aspects of their environment. The data on which this book is based are derived from family, medical, mental health, and child welfare agencies, and various innovative settings, among others; a relatively small amount of case material has come from the private practices of clinicians. Nevertheless, the principles are applicable to all settings and all populations.

Before we can comprehend the dynamics of psychosocial treatment, we must have a clear picture of what the caseworker understands by personality and its social functioning. Social functioning represents the interplay between the two major variables, the social environment and individual, each

of which, in turn, is a composite of various forces. The environment offers opportunities and gratifications, frustrations and deprivations. It consists not only of concrete realities—such as the availability of food, clothing, shelter, medical care, employment opportunities, physical safety, and educational and recreational opportunities—but also of sociopsychological realities expressed through interpersonal relationships. Human beings need social relationships as much as they need food and shelter. Studies and theories, of Spitz and Bowlby among others, about early attachment, separation, and loss illuminate the crucial and far-reaching role that nurturing relationships, or lack of them, have on personality development.[16] Studies of young chimpanzees have demonstrated that even they are profoundly affected by the absence of warm care by the mother chimp.[17] An individual must rely on the environment to provide opportunities for social relationships of all sorts: with parents, brothers and sisters, extended family relationships, marriage partners, lovers, friends, and acquaintances. The quality of these relationships is to no small degree determined by forces independent of the individual's own efforts and choices.

Socially influenced psychological realities also exert profound pressures, particularly in values and perceptions. Ethnic, class, race, regional, and role factors contribute to standards of behavior, aspirations, and perceptions of others and of self. At first these influences are transmitted primarily through parents or caretakers and later through other social institutions and relationships. When individuals are oppressed or discriminated against, personality development is powerfully affected. The total environment as experienced by any individual is a complex set of interacting forces *impinging upon* the person simultaneously from many different directions and interacting with an equally complex set of forces *within* his or her own personality.

THE PERSONALITY SYSTEM

Freudian Theory Modified by Systems and Ego Theories

Although Freud did not use modern systems theory, recent thinkers in our field have applied this framework to his concepts about personality. As we shall describe later in this chapter, it is very useful to conceptualize the personality as a system made up of components that are in constant interaction and in which the balance of forces can be significantly shifted even when minor changes are introduced.

For years, psychosocial workers have found some of the ideas developed by Freud extremely valuable.[18] However, theories of ego psychology, which began to be assimilated by "diagnostic" caseworkers in the late 1940s and 1950s, resulted in modifications of Freudian or psychoanalytic theory that proved to be enormously beneficial to clinical practice. Anna Freud, Hartman, Kris, Loewenstein, Rapaport, Jacobson, White, and many others made significant contributions to this development. Chief among these was the revision of Freud's deterministic thinking about instinctual sexual and aggressive drives. With the advent of the new ideas, ego functions, including defenses, were viewed as independent of these unconscious drives. Thus, rather than being ruled by unconscious forces, ego capacities could be worked with directly: Clients could be helped to mobilize, strengthen, or restore these capacities in order to adapt, cope, and actively solve problems. Ego functions were viewed as potent resources for bringing about change, for enabling people to take charge of their

lives. These concepts about the ego were useful in helping clients effectively influence transactions with the environment and mediate various components within the personality. There was new optimism about people's ability to change and grow, to be self-directed, to take responsibility for influencing the course of their lives even under difficult circumstances. Although it was still believed that significant feelings and thoughts are sometimes outside of a person's awareness, it was no longer thought that major intrapsychic work or the improvement of social functioning could take place only through the analysis of unconscious material. These perspectives continue to be advanced by psychosocial caseworkers.

Erikson, another ego psychologist, gave special attention to environmental and cultural influences, further increasing our understanding of the critical importance of the ego to individual adaptation and functioning; his thinking was therefore also appealing to psychosocial caseworkers. A number of other psychoanalytically oriented writers and practitioners have also built on some of Freud's basic tenets. Writers known as attachment, developmental, and object relations theorists, including Spitz, Bowlby, Mahler, Fairbairn, Winnicott, and Guntrip, who were also grounded in psychoanalytic theory, added considerably to our understanding of psychological and social development, further expanding ego theory. More recently, Kohut, who is known for his theory of self-psychology, and others, Kernberg among them, contributed to our knowledge of the origins and treatment of severe personality disorders resulting from developmental deficits and deprivations.[19] We will not attempt a detailed review of the accumulated, evolving knowledge incorporated by our psychosocial framework, but we will summarize certain features that have been particularly useful to the practice of casework.

The Id

New Concepts Modify Freud's Theories on the Id and Instincts   Freud postulated a *tripartite personality or psychic structure* composed of the *id,* the *ego,* and the *superego.* The id can be thought of as a set of drives or instincts that are present from birth, in various degrees of strength, in all individuals. "Pure" Freudians would describe these drives as libidinal and aggressive in nature. In short, Freud believed that the individual's behavior is guided by the drives of the id to seek pleasure and avoid "unpleasure"; this idea is referred to as the *pleasure principle.* Modification of the pleasure principle is achieved as the individual matures and the ego begins to operate on the *reality principle.* Some theorists have dispensed with or drastically altered Freud's view of drives. Modern thinkers, who have focused on object relations and self-psychology, teach that the infant's needs and strivings (or drives) are for affirmation, admiration, stimulation, and dependence on or merger with the caretaker, followed by an equally important need for "optimal frustration" and the development of a sense of self. As we shall soon elaborate, the goal of the early ego is to seek "objects"—other people—and, with maturity, to strive for a feeling of well-being, for *autonomy* and *satisfying interpersonal relations.* Some theorists suggest that not only children, but also people of all ages, have inborn drives or strivings for assertion and curiosity, for health, for competence, and for creativity.[20] We find these ideas far more encouraging about the human potential and more useful in practice than Freud's narrow notions about the unconscious determinants of behavior.

Many of these differences between Freud and the later thinkers are more often than not a matter of emphasis; newer theories have been extremely important to psychosocial casework because of the light they throw on social functioning. Furthermore, by focusing on how early, especially family, relationships (more precisely, representations of relationships) are internalized by the psyche of young children, these newer ideas have also provided important conceptual links between intrapsychic and family treatment, in which healing of family connections often can be promoted. Later chapters of this book will illustrate these points.

The Id and Primary Process   In any event, the id can be conceptualized as the agency of the psychological structure that contains raw, chaotic, undifferentiated energies that are largely unconscious. The term *primary process* describes an unconscious process, a primitive way of thinking and being, that originates in early childhood before the development of logical, rational thinking. Wishes are imbued with magical power. Hence, when a child wishes that a parent or sibling would get hurt, and some mishap subsequently occurs, the child may feel that he or she has actually caused it and fear retaliation. When someone close has died, the child may regard this as an act of purposeful abandonment and resent it accordingly. Children cannot always distinguish their own thoughts and feelings from those of others; when angry, a child may believe others are angry at *him* or *her.* Contradictory ideas exist side by side in the mind, and no need is felt to reconcile them. When crossed, a young child may feel anger that is not tempered by the good things experienced from the same source that is now frustrating. The child generalizes indiscriminately, often experiencing all grown-up men to be like Father, all women like Mother. Certain individuals with developmental deficits or personality disorders can be inordinately ruled by primary process. In relatively mature adults, primary process usually becomes most apparent in dreams or in the compelling urge to take action *without thinking:* it refers to the primitive level of organization of innate drives or needs and the tendency of individuals to seek immediate and free discharge of excitation.[21]

The Ego

The Ego and Secondary Process   Ego psychologists elaborated on Freud's first conceptualization of the ego. From birth onward the personality includes a set of adaptive and growth-producing qualities, known in composite as the *ego.* As the child's ego develops, so does the *secondary process,* the function of which is to begin to bring order, memory, reason, and regulation to the drives and demands placed upon the individual by the id. The components of the ego, some of which are conscious and others unconscious, like the energies of the id, vary in strength and quality in different individuals and are subject to hereditary as well as environmental influences. In early Freudian theory, the ego was thought to develop out of the id and for that reason dependent on the development of drives.

Ego Theory and the Strengths Perspective   As indicated, later theory sees the ego as independent and potentially much stronger than was formerly believed in its ability to deal with and move toward goals of its own selection. Thus, the development of ego psychology gave a better theoretical underpinning for the positive results that could be achieved by those caseworkers who stressed working with the "strengths" of the personality rather than focusing primarily on "pathology" or being unduly pre-occupied with early causative factors. Combined with crisis theory (to be discussed in Chapter 18), modern ego theory led to the development of shorter treatment methods for certain types of difficulties. It also threw light upon various forms of personality disorders, to be discussed later in this text.

The Development of the Ego   While the ego system organizes, controls, and regulates the energies of the id, it also mediates stimuli and pressures placed upon it by the physical and social environment, and by the superego/ego ideal, to be described shortly. Commencing very early in a baby's life, the ego increasingly finds means for dealing with chaotic emotion, internalized expectations, external dangers and opportunities. At young ages we can see children begin to remember and think about positive and negative consequences of previous actions (a smile brought an adoring hug; a finger on the hot stove resulted in a burn or a spanking). As time goes on, youngsters use the capacity of reason to anticipate events that they have not yet experienced and learn to solve increasingly complicated problems. The totally dependent newborn becomes more and more autonomous, a process of development that we shall briefly discuss later in this chapter.

Specific Ego Functions   Bellak and his collaborators described and studied 12 functions of the ego as they are assessed "in schizophrenics, neurotics, and normals." These are discussed in detail in their comprehensive report and are summarized in Eda Goldstein's recommended book.[22] Some that are very important in casework assessment and treatment will be mentioned now. There may be variations in the degree to which ego functions have matured and serve the person's needs; some capacities may be much stronger or more fully developed than others. It is important to try to evaluate whether apparent disturbances in ego functions are temporary responses to stress or chronically deficient in some way.

Reality testing is a principal ego function. When intact, it enables a person to distinguish between—and accurately perceive and interpret—internal and external stimuli or events. *Judgment* allows an individual to anticipate probable consequences of behaviors and to act accordingly and appropriately on the basis of awareness of these probable consequences.

Regulation and control of drives, affects, and impulses is another important ego function. This capacity includes the ability—under relatively normal circumstances and when required—to postpone expressing emotion or acting on impulse and the general capacity to endure strong feelings without becoming overwhelmed or flooded. *Under*control sometimes leads to serious interpersonal problems. *Over*control, on the other hand, may result in turning negative feelings against oneself or may prevent expression of softer or passionate feelings that enhance intimate relationships.

Object relations, as a function of the ego, refers to the quality of interpersonal connectedness. It depends on the degree and kind of relatedness to others. When this function is well developed, the individual has the capacity for loving feelings, autonomy, mutuality and reciprocity, empathy, intimacy, trust, and the ability to maintain a sense of being related to others over time, even in their absence.

Thought processes include the ability to remember, concentrate, and conceptualize, using either concrete or abstract thinking, depending on which is most appropriate to a particular situation. These functions of thought reflect the shift from primary to secondary process.

Autonomous functioning refers to the ego's capacity to function relatively independently of pressures from the id, such as anxiety or conflict, or from demands of the environment. Thus, reality testing and judgment, for example, are not seriously disturbed by stresses arising from inner or outer forces. It is possible to manage stress in some areas of one's life more successfully than in others. For example, a person may be more devastated by internal self-criticism after making a mistake than by a close friend moving away; another person might have the opposite reaction.

Synthetic-integrative functioning refers to the capacity of the ego to organize and synthesize all aspects of one's personality (cognitive and affective), including behavior, even those that are contradictory or in conflict; when this capacity is not well developed, the personality and behavior will be chaotic or fragmented.

Mastery-competence is extremely important to casework assessment and refers to how competent a person feels and is in mastering developmental tasks or in affecting and interacting with essential aspects of his or her environment. People's performances and efforts at mastering themselves and their surroundings have to be evaluated in conjunction with the responsiveness or recalcitrance of the environment, including other people in it. If the *actual* competence is significantly greater or less than the individual's *sense* of competence, disabling underachievement or grandiosity may follow.

All ego functioning must be evaluated in terms of the life circumstances of the person in question. Assessment of performance and capacity also has to take into account the level of functioning that is considered age-appropriate in the context of a person's life and reference group.

Ego Defenses The important defensive functions of the ego require special attention. Mechanisms of defense are necessary to development and start to evolve in the very young child as a way of protecting the fragile, budding personality from being overwhelmed. Certain defenses normally begin to arise in infancy while others develop as the youngster grows older. Defenses are usually to one degree or another unconscious (or at least outside of one's immediate awareness); nevertheless, in our experience, people often have some intellectual awareness of the fact that they are defending against unwelcome material. Broadly speaking, the ego attempts to ward off anxiety or conflict stemming from internal impulses and from the individual's reactions to real occurrences. Unacceptable urges or painful emotions are held at bay. A woman who has been taught that angry thoughts and feelings are "bad," for example, may protect herself against becoming aware of them. People sometimes restrain themselves from crying, for fear that their sadness will overwhelm them. A man who has been told that he has a fatal illness may—at first or throughout the illness—ignore or twist the facts to avoid the terror and sadness of the truth. Adult personality traits are strongly influenced by which combinations of defenses characteristically predominate when the individual experiences inner or outer pressures.

Defenses can be adaptive or maladaptive. By definition, they distort the actual internal or external situation to one degree or another. Defenses that operate on a temporary basis and yet are flexible may give the ego a chance to assimilate an overload of information or internal pressure; the man mentioned above may need a little time to take in the full implications of his catastrophic illness. In an emergency, defenses allow us to take necessary action before fully registering the danger of the situation. These defensive functions are essential to maintaining a sense of balance and well-being.

On the other hand, the woman who persistently cannot permit herself to feel anger may remain aloof from other people to avoid the dreaded feelings and by doing so never enjoy close personal relationships. A person may develop somatic responses or symptoms that derive from diverting or choking off from awareness conflicts or emotions—jealousy, sadness, affection, anger, etc. If a man cannot risk the anxiety of confronting his wife with negative feelings, he may direct his anger at his son, thereby adding to rather than alleviating family distress. A person who lost a parent as a child may defend against tender feelings for fear of being bereaved again, with the result that his or her relationships lack intimacy.

Unaware that they are using defenses that originated in childhood, adults may erroneously feel as vulnerable as they were when they were totally dependent on others and too immature to protect themselves adequately against real or feared threats, such as abandonment, rejection, and humiliation. Recognition that some of their predominant defense mechanisms are now "out of date" and dysfunctional, and no longer essential to survival, can be an important milestone for some people in casework treatment, especially treatment in which individuals seek to make changes within themselves to improve their social functioning or life situations.

In many cases, for people to feel and function better, or to make the changes they want to make in therapy, defenses need to be *relaxed*. In other cases, defenses need to be *bolstered* rather than mollified. For example, defenses required to fend off chaotic drives of the id may be too weak to prevent primitive affects (or emotions) from flooding a person's thought processes; or when a person is severely stressed over a period of time by situational pressures, defensive functioning may unravel, creating intense anxiety. As we shall discuss further, careful assessment of the individual is required before efforts are made to modify defenses.

Common Defenses A number of defenses are frequently and usefully employed by adults and, increasingly as they mature, by children from the beginnings of latency (age five or six) on.

Sublimation, for example, is a process whereby inner drives are altered and directed toward socially productive or creative activities; unacceptable aggressive impulses are often converted into enthusiasm for sports or into advocacy for social change. Frightening urges or feelings can be sublimated into acceptable endeavors. Feared or unwelcome sexual desires may be transformed into religious fervor. Or an individual who is fascinated by fire may actually reverse a drive to commit arson and become a firefighter! Tender feelings for others also are often sublimated and converted into loving attachments to animals or interest in romantic literature; of course, if *all* of a person's desires for relationships are channeled elsewhere, the result may be loneliness and disappointment.

Altruism is another often valuable defense; by recognizing the emotional gratifications of serving the needs of others, one's instinctual energies may then be channeled into generous, even self-sacrificing, activities. This defense becomes problematic when the urge to give is compulsive (say, when one insists on giving to others who do not require or want the gifts or services), or when one consistently repudiates one's *own* needs or aspirations and totally focuses on those of others.

Humor, too, can serve a very constructive defensive function; when selectively employed, humor allows us to put personal shortcomings or stressful circumstances into a perspective that makes them more tolerable and more easily confronted or accepted.

Repression is probably the most pervasive defense of all. Anxiety-producing thoughts, feelings, and memories are forgotten or never experienced; they are pushed or drawn into the unconscious. This unconscious content, especially of early childhood, is the center of attention in psychoanalysis; when inner drives or feelings are extensively repressed, personality conflicts and distortions arise. Although repressed material is a major pivot of neurotic distress, it is also true that everyone has repressed matter that will not and need not ever surface and does not appreciably interfere with functioning. Primitive primary process functioning, for example, is necessarily repressed to make way for the development of a more orderly secondary process, thereby enhancing the individual's growth to a higher level of functioning. Sometimes the memory of a catastrophic event and the feelings surrounding it are permanently repressed; forgetting may serve a protective and adaptive function.

Suppressed material is more likely than repressed material to be accessible through procedures used by clinical social workers. In this mechanism, the anxiety-arousing mental content is pushed, at times consciously, only partly below the surface of the mind to the preconscious rather than to the unconscious. It is a commonly used and sometimes useful mechanism whereby a painful matter is put aside: "After a good night's sleep I'll forget all about it." Or: "I'll worry about that later—when I can do something about it."[23] Chapter 7 further discusses conscious, preconcious, and unconscious material and the mechanisms of repression and suppression.

Avoidance is a common—sometimes socially useful, sometimes self-destructive—defense. Efforts are made by the individual to avoid a feeling or situation that is potentially disturbing. As with suppression, avoidance can be a partly conscious or preconscious mechanism: Often, for example, people will say, "I'm afraid to even think about that time of my life because of the painful feelings that might get stirred up." Like the other defenses already mentioned, depending on its pervasiveness and purpose, avoidance can be helpful or harmful to the person who uses it.

Isolation as a defense is used to separate different parts of a person's experience, especially events or memories and the feelings associated with them, so that matters that are actually interrelated appear not to affect one another. For example, an adult may be aware of general feelings of anger but may not relate these to clearly remembered experiences of childhood abuse.

Intellectualization is frequently employed to fend off unacceptable affects, as is the case when one talks or thinks about potentially highly charged or disturbing issues in one's life without allowing the accompanying emotions to be fully experienced. Sometimes this defense is used constructively to enable people to make sense out of difficult situations or distressing feelings or to get through a crisis; but overuse can cramp one's capacity for experiencing and expressing emotion, including positive or pleasurable emotion.

Rationalization is used by everyone at times and can be closely related to intellectualization, such as when people explain unhappy events with: "It's all for the best." Or it can be used to explain away behavior that one would otherwise not condone, such as an affair with a married man: "His wife doesn't understand him." Or it may be used to justify a decision: A woman who cannot give herself permission to have a vacation may justify doing so by persuading herself that her husband and children need a holi-

day. Excessive use of intellectualization and rationalization is often associated with obsessive-compulsive personality characteristics; but it is important not to generalize without sufficient data about the individual and his or her internal stress and external pressures.

Reaction formation is another common defense of the ego. It involves the substitution of one unwanted emotion or attitude for another, more or less opposite, feeling or response. To try to endure intolerable oppression, rather than becoming enraged, people sometimes become detached, passive, or placating in their manner. Or one may defensively claim: "Of course I don't love him; in fact, I hate him."

Turning against the self occurs particularly in relation to unwelcome anger. When using this defense, a person becomes angry at the self when the logic of the situation would seem to require anger at another. If realization of this outwardly turned anger would cause too much anxiety or guilt, or if its expression would result in frightening reactions from others, the emotion may be experienced as feelings of self-criticism or depression: that is, as anger turned against the self. Sometimes when people are being or have been abused, this defense is employed.

Identification with the aggressor is a mechanism that also may occur when one has been victimized. In contrast to reaction formation, aggression from others may result in the victim taking on or even taking in (incorporating) similar aggressive qualities to allay fears of being destroyed. Victims of oppression may take on hostile and aggressive characteristics of the victimizers. Victims of childhood physical or sexual abuse may identify with qualities of their abusers to avoid anxiety or feelings of helplessness.

Projection is a mechanism that can be observed in all people from time to time, but when it is pervasive and not accessible to correction by the facts, it becomes extremely dysfunctional. In projection, the individual's unacknowledged thoughts and feelings are attributed to others. We may, for example, falsely see our own unacceptable motives, anger, loving feelings, or any number of fears or wishes in someone else. A man who is sexually stimulated by his pubescent daughter may angrily accuse her of being a "whore" rather than allowing awareness of his own unacceptable impulses. In severe cases, when negative projective mechanisms are used extensively, people sometimes see rejection or danger all around them and become overly suspicious, combative, or withdrawn, even though these responses are not warranted by the circumstances.

Displacement is another common defense that may or may not be problematic depending on the extent to which it is used. In displacement, feelings and thoughts that refer to one person are transferred to another. Sometimes this occurs because it seems less threatening to express feelings to the substituted person; it may feel safer to show anger to a child than to a spouse, for example. Displacement may result from superficial similarities between two people or because both occupy the same role in relation to the person doing the displacing. Fear one has for one's father, for instance, may be displaced onto other men in authority.

Denial, another frequently used defense, occurs when a person refuses to recognize the existence of an anxiety-provoking emotion, thought, internal conflict, or event. Denial, like avoidance, intellectualization, and some of the other defenses already mentioned, can be adaptive under some circumstances but is most problematic when the person's perceptions are permanently distorted. A seven-year-old child replied: "He's not dead," when told his beloved older brother had been killed in an accident. In

the short run, the defense helped the boy's young ego to pace the assimilation of the tragic event. Had he continued to deny the facts, however, the result would have had serious psychological implications.

Regression refers to returning to an earlier stage of development to avoid an anxiety-producing situation. In the face of illness, loss, or unhappy relationships, adults may revert to childlike demanding or dependent behaviors. Regression sometimes occurs in response to anxieties about the approach of a new life cycle stage, such as going away to college or retiring. A child who has become appropriately independent may go back to clinging or whining after learning his parents are planning to divorce. Often the regressive reactions are temporary and adaptive, but sometimes the person then becomes dysfunctionally "fixated" or "stuck" at a particular level of maturity.

Recently Emphasized Defenses Additional defensive mechanisms have taken on particular importance in theoretical developments about individuals with certain developmental deficits or borderline personality disorders. These defenses are believed to originate in very early childhood.

Splitting is one such mechanism. To ward off anxiety, the person divides his or her self-concept and image of others into all "good" and all "bad," with no balance or middle ground; self and others are alternately viewed as all-powerful or as needing to be devalued. To illustrate: A person who has a sense of being magically omnipotent "flips"—for little or no apparent reason— into a feeling of helplessness and despair. A man who is angry at his wife over a minor matter is so consumed by negativity that he is unable to remember that only moments before he had idolized her. "All or nothing" feelings can lead a client to view a clinician as thoroughly trustworthy at one point and totally untrustworthy at another. Because of the split, there can be no synthesis of the opposite experiences. Presumably, by avoiding the integration of contradictory feelings and thoughts—from the unconscious point of view of the person using the defense—the "good" is saved from being contaminated or overwhelmed by the "bad."

Primitive idealization, the tendency to see others as totally "good," also protects positive attitudes from being spoiled by the negative.

Devaluation refers to the pervasive inclination to attribute exaggerated "bad" qualities to self or others.

Projective identification, a term with several meanings which can be confusing, is sometimes used to describe a defense— similar to projection as described earlier—in which a person projects onto others aspects of his or her own unacceptable impulses or self-image. Once externalized, these feared attitudes or feelings that originated from within are seen in others, especially others with whom one is closely related; then, for reasons of self-preservation, the individual believes that the other people and their attributes need to be controlled or attacked. For example, a man who is consciously or unconsciously frightened by his own homosexual impulses may project these onto his son and then castigate the boy and restrict his associations with male friends. In projective identification, there is often a true inability to distinguish self from other. Some definitions of this concept further expand on the usual notions about projection by including the idea that the individual using the defense invokes behaviors in others that serve to confirm his or her distortions. For instance, a mother who has pervasive feelings of inferiority, may project her sense of inadequacy—her image of herself—onto her daughter and then, unconsciously, find means to induce the child to fail.[24]

Classification of Defense Mechanisms

Defenses are classified by some writers according to the developmental phases in which they originated. As we said earlier, some defenses arise in very young childhood, while others are erected as the youngster grows older. *Very* roughly speaking, the above listing of some of the common defenses begins with the most "mature" and ends with the most "primitive."[25]

As already indicated, in adults, many of the more "mature" defenses (such as sublimation, altruism, and humor) can serve healthy, adaptive psychological purposes; they may also be utilized in a very socially productive manner. At the other end of the continuum, sometimes an adult person's *predominant* and *pervasive* defenses (such as splitting and projective identification) originated at a very immature stage and have not been replaced by more mature defenses. Or some individuals habitually and severely regress in the face of internal or external demands. When defensive patterns are extremely immature, we often find that general functioning is— at least to some degree in some areas of the person's life—impaired and dysfunctional, especially under stress. It is not uncommon for a particular individual to manifest defenses deriving from various developmental phases, not just from one; the level of maturity will depend in part on which level of defensive functioning dominates.

In our view, a classification of defenses based on levels of maturity has its shortcomings and can be misleading. For example, denial is sometimes seen as a "low-level" or "immature" defense. However, as previously noted, sometimes denial serves very healthy purposes and enables people to maintain equilibrium under threatening circumstances. At the other extreme, suppression is considered by some to be among the most "mature" defenses. Yet, if it is used excessively it may impede a person from taking necessary action. Repression is a defense that is often associated with neurosis, and yet it is also essential to mature development. It is important, then, not to jump to conclusions about a person's pathology or level of development on the basis of the manifestation of a particular defense; misuse of a classification may lead us to assume lesser (or greater) overall maturity than is actually the case and lead us to generalizations that cannot be substantiated. Furthermore, we repeat: *the pervasiveness, chronicity, and rigidity of a defense—not its mere presence— is critical in the assessment of a person's level of "maturity."* The constructive or destructive effect of a particular defensive style can also be appraised by determining whether it promotes healthy coping with life's pressures or whether it impedes rational behavior and decisions. Caseworkers and clients *together* frequently evaluate whether defenses are enhancing or interfering with functioning and gratifying interpersonal relationships. Finally, one cannot accurately evaluate how functional or dysfunctional defenses are without an overall understanding of external circumstances that may have triggered the protective mechanisms.

Summary The individual's perception of the external world is a combination in varying degrees of what is actually there and what is perceived or expected to be there. We often do not see what we do not look for, but we create for ourselves what we seek to find. People who anticipate hostility may read belligerence into others' behavior whether or not it exists and by their own responses may give rise to hostility in the others. In so doing, to a high degree people create their own environments, a form of *self-fulfilling prophecy.*

Because defenses are employed by all people in varying degrees, caseworkers need to recognize and understand them. Defenses allow individuals to manage anxiety and to adjust to developmental, interpersonal, and environmental demands. But defenses that served us well in childhood often have outlived their usefulness and interfere with current functioning. As we said, whether defenses are adaptive or maladaptive, it is important to remember that they have been developed as protection and, hence, should not be casually or impetuously challenged. Special attention is required, especially when defenses are rigid. Even if a client's goals point to the need to modify defenses or even if disabling symptoms seem to derive from defensive patterns, care and accurate and *mutual* assessment of the individual's tolerance for change must guide the worker's interventions. Fortunately, as we shall see in later chapters, clients can often be helped to become aware of maladaptive ego functioning, sometimes in individual instances and sometimes as patterns of behavior. Such awareness can then lead to positive changes.

The Superego/Ego Ideal

The concepts of superego and ego ideal, like the ego, refer to both conscious and unconscious functions. They represent the individual's *conscience* and are comprised of internalized parental prohibitions and values, as well as ideals and social and moral standards derived from the world around the individual. The superego/ego ideal contains the "dos and don'ts," the ethical views and aspirations of the individual's personality. It can be destructively self-critical and guilt-inducing; it can be idealistic and self-approving. Generally, the *superego* represents that part of the conscience that is absorbed primarily from the parents: by parental dictation or by identification with parents in early childhood. Other significant adults or caretakers can be influential, especially when parents are absent. When the superego is overly severe, it is not always functional because the harshness can lead to intense self-hate, self-punishment, and even to virtual immobilization of various ego functions. When it is underdeveloped in an individual, the result can be antisocial behavior and lack of feeling for others. The *ego ideal* is generally thought of as a later development, representing identifications with nonparental figures as well as with later perceptions of parents. It contains goals and ideals of later childhood, adolescence, and maturity. In contrast to some aspects of the superego, it is more apt to be consciously acquired and subject to ego evaluation.

Personality Development

The many advances made over recent decades in ego psychology and object relations theory, among others, have added to our understanding of child development and have been extremely valuable to casework practice. In particular, on the basis of observation of and clinical experience with parents and children, attention has been paid to concepts relevant to the development of the relatively *autonomous, self-reliant, well-related personality*. Optimal circumstances, including "good-enough" parenting[26] and environmental conditions, for the child include the following:

1. Fairly consistent parental availability, responsiveness, and support *and* the child's ability to bond with the parent and receive the attentions.
2. Parental encouragement of the child's independence and self-direction, appropriately timed to the child's age *and* the child's ability to assimilate that encouragement.
3. Parents who take some sense of pleasure or delight in the child and in the child's accomplishments *and* the child's ability to absorb the approval.

4. Environmental conditions that are secure and supportive enough for the child's caretakers so that they are free to provide the child with the stability required for "good-enough" parenting.

Ideally, as the child proceeds through the separation-individuation process described by Mahler,[27] he or she begins to internalize an integrated sense of self and other; "good" and "bad" images that were "split" from one another in early infancy become consolidated around the age of two or even earlier. By the time children reach about three years of age, they can maintain a stable, independent concept of significant people even in their absence (referred to as *object constancy*) and a realistic sense of ability and capacity for taking care of themselves at age-appropriate levels. A balanced but essentially positive memory of the parent (which earlier had been split into "good" or "bad" images) provides the youngster with a sense of continuity: There is the realization that even when he or she is alone, a parent will eventually return, and it will be possible to manage until then. When the child's capacity for object constancy and some sense of his own identity has been attained, unless external changes reverse or retard growth, the child has the ego foundation on which to continue to mature.

Problems may ensue when family and environmental conditions do not provide these fundamentals. Developmental failures may result when:

1. Parents overprotect their children and therefore do not foster individuality. Children who are not expected to take care of their own needs in age-appropriate ways and are not challenged by conditions providing "optimal frustration" often fail to master essential developmental tasks. Along the same lines, children who are always the center of attention in their

families or can "do no wrong" in their parents' eyes often do not develop inner resources and self-assurance; without a realistic measuring stick, their judgment about themselves may be faulty and they may not learn to discriminate between socially acceptable and unacceptable behavior, or they may not develop a balanced view of their strengths and shortcomings.

2. Parents prematurely and too frequently leave their children to their own devices. Deprived of the minimal guidance, support, and encouragement required for healthy growth, many children become depressed, "pseudo-independent," or develop some type of personality disturbance.

3. Parents are grossly inconsistent in their caretaking. Children who cannot count on fairly regular positive attention to their needs may not develop object constancy, self-esteem, mastery, and an adequate sense of competence. Dysfunctional personality traits and severe emotional disabilities may be the outcome.

4. Children for constitutional reasons, or because they are in some way incompatible with their caretakers, cannot get the benefit of even "good-enough" nurturance.

5. Environmental conditions are inhumane, unpredictable, or assaultive. Many families try to raise children under impossible circumstances of poverty, homelessness, or extreme racial or ethnic discrimination. Inadequate resources, inconsistency, and violence in the larger world can render it almost impossible for parents to provide children with the minimal or basic conditions required for healthy development.

As the individual grows and matures, the importance of age-appropriate "good-enough" conditions for personality development continues. Erik Erikson's seminal contributions to theory include his view of the growth of the healthy personality as it moves through developmental stages and crises and masters life's outer and inner challenges and dangers. If circumstances have allowed it, by adolescence the child has achieved, in successive steps, trust (versus distrust), autonomy (versus shame and doubt), initiative (versus guilt), and industry (versus inferiority).[28] Each stage of development depends on the quality of the resolution of the one before it. Failure to master one essential challenge impairs successful handling of the next.

INTERACTIONS BETWEEN INDIVIDUALS AND THEIR ENVIRONMENTS

Because Freud and some of his followers elaborated more upon the intrapsychic needs and responses of the individual than upon the impact of social interactions and the larger environment, it is sometimes assumed that psychoanalytic theory disregarded environmental influences. But Freud strongly emphasized the influences of both intra- and extra-familial life experiences. His theory rested upon social as well as intrapsychic factors. One of Freud's major departures from predecessors such as Janet and Charcot, who regarded neurosis as a manifestation of constitutional weakness, was to see neurosis in terms of human relationships. The person with a hysterical paralysis, for example, in psychoanalytic theory was believed to be using this symptom as protection from something feared in relationships with other people. Although Freud saw neurosis as a way of resolving conflicts among inner drives (the id), the superego, and the ego, he also recognized that such conflicts emerge from the interactions between the child and parents or other caretaking figures. The later thinkers, some of whom we have mentioned in this chapter

and in Chapter 1, both corrected and enriched many of Freud's concepts and gave
much more attention to the *interactive* aspects of personality development and functioning. As we described, these theories
greatly enhanced psychosocial casework and
are part of a total frame of reference that includes whatever data the social sciences can
provide to illuminate the nature of the environment and the social forces with which
the individual interacts.

This dual orientation lends itself very
well to systematizing casework findings.
Since the social worker's laboratory is the
common everyday world, there is ample
opportunity to observe the interplay between inner and outer forces. Social workers have repeatedly seen people change for
the better and for the worse under the impact of beneficent and traumatic environments. Psychosocial casework theory
stoutly maintains that human beings are
not merely products of their environments,
clay upon which social influences leave
their print. It insists, and rightly, that individuals make their own demands upon
their environments. They are not only affected by their surroundings but they also
participate in creating them. Ego psychology underscores the capacity of the individual's ego to make changes in the environment, rather than just passively
adjusting to it.

The foregoing may seem highly theoretical
but, as discussed in earlier sections
on the person-in-situation concept and on
systems and ecological perspectives, it has
major practical implications. It emphasizes
reciprocal *interactions* between people and
their environments, including other people.
In cases of marital unhappiness, in individual or conjoint meetings, it guards the
worker against seeing one partner as merely
a victim of the other. In parent–child disorders, it leads to a balanced examination of

both what the parent is "doing to" and
expecting of the child and what the child is
"doing to" and demanding of the parent. In
general, it leads to the assumption that each
individual can almost always do *something*
about an interpersonal problem and that the
worker's task is to enable clients to develop
greater capacity to do so. Concurrently,
recognition is given to the pressures stemming from the client's environment and to
the problems of "fit" discussed earlier. It is
always the responsibility of the caseworker
to work with and for the client to try to ameliorate noxious conditions as well as to try to
find ways to shape aspects of the environment so that they better suit the needs and
goals of the particular individual or family
affected.

Contributions of Sociology and Anthropology

Casework's understanding of the interactions between the individual and the environment came not only from observation
and case-by-case direct experience but
also from the fields of sociology and cultural anthropology. These have been
drawn upon extensively over the years to
describe and explain the nature of the influences of one upon the other. Beginning
with the work of Benedict and Mead,[29] the
field was alerted in the 1930s to the great
differences between cultures and to the
extent to which even such central matters
as child rearing, marriage, and sexual behavior not only differ among cultures but
also are regulated by customs. Kardiner's
work studying cultural influences on behavior was a "bridging" contribution between culture and personality theory.[30]
Casework writers such as Boie and de la
Fontaine[31] demonstrated the use of these
concepts in the understanding of family
and personality problems.

During and following the Depression of the 1930s, studies of the social effects of unemployment on individuals and families gave social workers new understanding of the pressures created by this periodically widespread social condition.[32] As marriage counseling developed in family agencies in the 1940s, studies of marriage and divorce from a social and psychological standpoint became important.[33]

The 1950s and 1960s saw the burgeoning of the family therapy movement, which, as the chapters on family treatment will discuss, was influenced by several of the social sciences. This period also advanced our understanding of the strong effects on personality and behavior of the "opportunity structure." When legitimate opportunities for social recognition, education, employment, and recreation are not available, illegitimate means may be sought, such as membership in criminally oriented gangs, participation in drug traffic, prostitution, and delinquent or antisocial behavior of various sorts.[34] Sociological facts and theories about poverty and political powerlessness, the deterioration of the inner city, broken homes, child neglect, unmarried parenthood, racial discrimination, and many other social issues were widely studied in the 1950s and 1960s by social workers who were thinking more deeply than ever about integrating knowledge of the person and the environment in order to improve services and opportunities for clients.[35]

During the same period, studies of differentials in the treatment of psychiatric patients in both hospitals and clinics demonstrated the neglect and discrimination suffered by the poor in general and by African Americans and other minorities in particular. We learned the extent to which mental health practitioners brought a negative bias to the diagnosis and treatment of patients from minority and lower socioeconomic groups. Most disturbing of all were subsequent research findings that pointed to vulnerable areas of social work itself, a profession that has prided itself on its advocacy of social justice and equal opportunity for all. Clinical judgments by caseworkers, too, could be adversely affected by sociocultural factors; idealistic caseworkers discovered that differences between worker and client were important variables in treatment and needed to be addressed.[36]

The concept of social role, expanded upon in the 1960s, became an important link between social influences and personality development. Its contribution to casework practice will be discussed in the next section of this chapter and also in the chapters on family and couple treatment.

More recently, knowledge about single-parent families, stepfamilies, unmarried mothers, same-sex relationships, alcoholism and substance abuse, child and spouse abuse, incest, and many other social phenomena has been incorporated by casework, influencing its approaches to treatment. The social effects of changes in marriage and divorce have been of particular interest to caseworkers. Many of these matters will be referred to over the course of this text.

Diversity: Culture, Class, Religion, Gender, Sexuality

As the years went on, social workers increasingly emphasized the need to understand the influences of race, ethnicity, spirituality, socioeconomic factors, gender, and sexual orientation on personality, family patterns, and on casework treatment itself. Information and clinical experiences related to African American, Hispanic, Asian, and Native American cultures, among others, were more prominent in social work curricula and journals and continue to be.[37] The women's movement stimulated studies on the traditional and unevenly changing roles of women and power differentials between men and women; the influence of gender in marriage, in family life, and in the workplace drew attention.[38] Literature on the theory and practice of clinical work with gay men and lesbians burgeoned, and interest in these areas continues to increase.[39] While focus on the damaging effects of racism, sexism, and prejudice of every kind continued, more and more emphasis has been placed on the positive traditions, belief systems, and influences of background on individual and family pride and on identity formation.

Differences between Worker and Client The emphasis social workers were placing on becoming informed seemed all the more urgent because of the fast growth of diversity in North America; a greater variety of clients from many backgrounds were seeking social and mental health services. Increasingly, women were demanding that their voices be heard. Larger numbers of those with a same-sex orientation were "out" and going to clinicians to resolve a wide range of dilemmas. Caseworkers seeing clients who were different from themselves, or whose backgrounds were different from their own, realized the necessity of becoming more knowledgeable.

As social workers became increasingly aware of the importance of understanding the characteristics, patterns, values, traditions, family and child-rearing styles, and attitudes toward help-seeking of various groups, it seemed more and more imperative for them to achieve "cultural literacy," "cultural sensitivity," and "cultural competence." Male workers were encouraged to look at their approach to therapy through a feminist "lens." Heterosexuals felt impelled to become better informed about gay and lesbian issues.

We applaud the abounding knowledge related to diversity found among various groups. Data and clinical theories about "special groups" of all kinds have raised our consciousness and improved our practice. Each group brings its special *strengths* and *vulnerabilities.* Members of various groups may be subject to very different *stresses.* For example, the African American, Greek, and Vietnamese teenager may each have entirely different experiences with teachers, doctors, employers, and others whom they encounter. Certain people have experienced repeated and traumatic events only because they are members of a certain group. No caseworker can become an expert on every group, but we should all become familiar with general information available about the people with whom we work most closely. It is also our responsibility as caseworkers to understand how our own identities or social position may affect our perceptions, our prejudices, our clinical strengths, and the ways we listen to clients whose backgrounds, traditions, social positions, and sexuality are different from our own.

A Few Words of Caution As committed as we are to the addition of new information, we are equally committed to *avoiding the misuse of information.* Sometimes, it seems, we are so eager to become familiar with and sensitive to dissimilarities that we may actually create barriers to understanding. There are several overlapping matters to be considered as we strive to become more knowledgeable about differences among groups:

1. Every Culture Is Fluid and Within Itself Diverse Ethnic and other group values and traditions are not static, but ever-evolving. For example, when we emphasize the impact of a particular ethnic background on attitudes, family structure, roles, child rearing, and so on, it is important to recognize that these change in accordance with the times, class factors, how long ago individuals or families immigrated, the context in which people are living, and much more. The Asian American may come from one of several countries, a city or a rural area, and so on. Sometimes the sociologists and others who study or write about ethnicity disagree, so often there are differences in emphasis in what they believe is to be expected when interviewing clients from a particular background.

Moreover, unique personalities and widely diverse family dynamics exist *within* cultures, and these profoundly influence how people conduct their business, live their lives, and face challenges. Individual differences can be even greater than those between cultures. And, as we all know, even people from the same family can have very divergent attitudes and values.

2. Expertise on Culture Is Not Always Possible Because of the wide and growing range of ethnic groups in this country, it is impossible for the student of ethnicity or the practitioner to become adequately informed about many cultures; the number and diversity of newly arrived immigrants, for example, has increased considerably in recent years, and little specific information about some of the groups is available to guide clinicians.

3. Gender Differences Are Often Oversimplified For the past decade or more, a number of popular, best-selling books have been written about the so-called different languages men and women speak. Many people have felt helped by reading them. Gender roles certainly do shape the ways people express themselves. But it is not our experience or that of many others we know—in life or as clinicians—that women

are necessarily better than men at expressing vulnerabilities and emotion. Not all men focus on power, control, and status. Women are not always more nurturing or more concerned with intimacy than men. It is often the other way around. In couple therapy, men frequently speak from their hearts about their longings, sorrows, and joys; their tender sides are often not as hidden as is sometimes thought. Several cases described in this text illustrate these points.

4. Preconceptions Can Lead to Stereotyping Relying on partial data about differences among people or generalizations about groups can be misleading at best and seriously countertherapeutic at worst. With all clients, we must not fall into the trap of treating statistics: ("single parents are . . . ," "incest survivors need . . . ," "adult children of alcoholics require . . ."). When a client comes for help, he or she must be viewed not as a "culture carrier" ("African American men feel . . . " "Italian mothers think . . ."), but as an individual with particular idiosyncratic characteristics who may or may not evidence qualities often found in his or her particular category. In our wish to help those who seek our services, we must be sure that we are not replacing old stereotypes with new ones. (Even members of the *same* group can overgeneralize about one another.)

Preconceptions can misdirect our professional efforts. African American inner-city residents, for example, are sometimes assumed to require concrete services primarily, because of the great adversities they face. But if we see problem-solving skills, self-awareness, or resolution of relationship problems relevant only to the more affluent, we discriminate. In fact, no people are more in need of searching for creative alternatives to their circumstances than those most severely deprived and embattled.

Cases described in this book demonstrate how casework can help people feel better about themselves and harness their energies to try to beat the odds they face, no matter how unfair those odds.

5. Many Human Needs Are Universal
Sometimes we can complicate our work by assuming differences that do not exist. For example, in therapy with gay men or lesbians, more often than not, their needs, their personal and family dilemmas, and their relationship problems are more similar than different from those of heterosexuals. The notion that they are very different has been imposed on them by others, with the result that many have suffered alienation, discrimination, and abuse. Along the same lines, a mother—whether she is Peruvian Catholic or white American-born Protestant—may experience very similar heartbreak upon learning that an adolescent son has been diagnosed with schizophrenia. In our experience, the issues people come to social workers with often do not derive from group norms per se, but rather from a disjunction between their needs and the fulfillment of these. Broadly speaking, people's requirements are very much the same; it is their opportunities, depending in large part on their place in society, that are not. Despite variations in experience or cultural tradition, many of the dilemmas, the needs, and the emotions that bring people to treatment can be remarkably alike. The Chin couple, soon to be described, illustrates this point.

Learning from Our Clients   When we rely too heavily on our knowledge about various groups, we not only risk being very wrong in our assumptions, but we also deprive ourselves and our clients of the opportuinity to let them teach *us* the relevance of their culture, gender, sexuality, or spiritual

beliefs from *their* points of view. Even when we belong to the same group as our clients, we must find out how *they* believe their culture, identity, or orientation affects them and their current needs or problems. It can't be said too often: *We never know the special meanings of our clients' experiences until we hear directly from them.* As discussed in Chapter 1, the ideas coming from constructivist theory and practice and the narrative approach have accentuated what we believe to be an imperative component of casework treatment: a collaborative, non-hierarchical relationship in which the "not-knowing" clinician respectfully and with great interest attempts to elicit from clients the meanings of their lives and experiences. This model is essential to understanding clients' unique sense of who they are and how who they are matters to them. Sometimes such inquiries also result in helping people to clarify the nature of their connection to the groups to which they belong or to the roots from which they have come. In a highly recommended article, Dyche and Zayas write: "We argue that one should begin cross-cultural therapy with minimal assumptions, and that one way to learn about culture is from the client." They advocate two therapist attitudes: "cultural naïveté" and "respectful curiosity":

> We define naïveté as a state of openness and receptivity. Curiosity is defined as an activity that flows from naïveté and is composed of both the impulse to look beyond assumptions and the love of surprise . . . [T]he work of emotional healing with clients whose backgrounds are different from therapists' will proceed well when therapists develop the discipline to acknowledge their inevitable naïveté about another person's life and to use the compass of a respectful curiosity.[40]

When the emphasis is on learning from our clients rather than on making assessments based on our preconceived notions, we are less likely to misuse theoretical concepts and assume that pathology or dysfunction exists when it does not. For example, notions about "age-appropriate autonomy" in children or "enmeshment" (to be discussed in Chapter 14) have to be understood in the context of the clients' traditions and preferences, not in abstract terms. We will say more about this point in discussions about assessment.

A Case Illustration Mr. and Mrs. Chin, both in their late 30s, were referred to a clinical social worker by the Employee's Assistance Program connected to the hospital in which they both worked as laboratory technicians. The event that precipitated their current situation was the tragic death of their 16-year-old son, the oldest of two boys, three months earlier. The young man hung himself, either by intending suicide or by engaging in an autoerotic experiment. From the beginning of the first session, it appeared that Mrs. Chin was in deep mourning and that Mr. Chin was very angry with his wife.

With the help of relatives who lived in a large Eastern metropolitan city, the couple had come from China about two years previously; neither spoke much English, although Mr. Chin was a little more at ease with the language than his wife was, but with some effort (and some nonverbal communication) the couple and the worker were able to convey their meanings. The white, Pennsylvania-born woman social worker was 62 years old, spoke no Chinese, and, although she had some friends who originally came from China, she considered herself to be uninformed about Chinese culture. Mr. Chin volunteered very early in the first meeting that he came from Taiwan and his wife came from the mainland; they met when Mr. Chin was in the military stationed near his wife's rural town. He indicated that part of the problem they were having (which had not yet been elaborated upon) was because he and his wife were raised very differently. What, the worker inquired with genuine interest, were the differences and how had these affected them? Mr. and Mrs. Chin both seemed to relax when the worker shared her lack of cultural knowledge and her eagerness to learn from them. Both participated in explaining that in Taiwan people were "tougher"; where Mrs. Chin grew up, more emotion was expressed. They agreed with each other on this perspective, which actually was offered by the couple in greater detail than described in this summary.

Once they shared this information, it seemed easier for them to begin to talk about their son's death and its meanings to them. Mrs. Chin led by saying that her husband was angry at her for crying so much; he blamed her for neglecting their 13-year-old son because of her unhappiness. She said it was very hurtful that, as she saw it, he had no sympathy for her sorrow; it disappointed her also that he didn't seem to feel very deeply about the loss of their boy. By the end of this first session and during the next one, Mr. Chin was not blaming his wife as much as he had, but it was still not clear to the worker or to Mrs. Chin just how the tragedy had affected him. With gentleness and patience, the worker helped him express his reactions. His wife was wrong, he said. Of course he felt terrible about his son's death, made even worse by the fact that they did not know what really happened; he thought about the boy all the time. Why, his wife asked, are you so angry with me? Suddenly, his rage burst forth. In essence, he said that his wife would never be grieving like this if it had been *he* who had died. Although shocked by the accusation, after four sessions Mrs. Chin was able to reassure her husband that, indeed, she would be lost without him. Once she understood what was behind his bitter attitude toward her, and knew that he, too, mourned their son, she felt closer to him again. Although their mourning would continue, each was now able to share sorrow with the other rather than feeling alone and alienated.

The Chin case was selected for this discussion for four reasons: First, it illustrates how welcoming and reassuring it can be to clients when the worker asks to be taught about their lives and the meanings these have for them; not only did the worker learn the Chins' perspectives on their backgrounds and culture, but also her authentic and respectful interest and involvement engaged them. Second, despite the language difficulty and the possibility of a culture gap, this brief cross-cultural therapy was very successful. (From a follow-up call two months later, the worker learned that even though they were still shattered by their loss, they were getting along with and supportive of each other.) Third, the dynamics between Mr. and Mrs. Chin could have occurred in a couple from *any* ethnic group; the Chin case demonstrates the universality of many of the basics of the human condition, including the need to feel understood and cared about. Finally, had the worker assumed that the Chins would be reluctant to seek help outside their family or that they would tend to somatize their emotional problems, qualities that can be found in some Chinese people,[41] she might have injected these expectations into her approach in ways that would have diverted her from exploring the couple's perspectives and feelings.

A Question of Policy As consciousness has been raised by members of so-called minorities, by gays and lesbians, and by women, social workers have wondered whether heterosexuals could understand gays, whether whites could help African Americans, whether men and women are able to communicate effectively. When possible, clients are often offered opportunities to seek services rendered by members of their own groups. Nevertheless, in many settings, African Americans often have to turn to whites, gays to straights, and so on. In our eagerness to provide relevant, accessible services to the underserved, we have tried to recruit African American and Hispanic workers (of which there are still too few) to work in the inner cities with "minority" clients while white workers often work primarily with white clients in other areas. We may want to ask ourselves about the messages this situation sends. Are we promoting de facto segregated services? Should we move toward encouraging an ethnic mix of workers in *all* agencies?

There are no easy answers to these questions, but we believe they should be faced. Research suggests and it is our experience that white, heterosexual social workers—those with empathy, skill, and breadth—can and do help people from all backgrounds and same-sex orientations.[42] This was true in the Chin case. There is no doubt that African American, Hispanic, and social workers from other cultures can and should be working *regularly* with white clients in those agencies that now, at best, have only token "minority" professionals on staff. The overall "fit" of the worker to the person or group may be far more important than the matching of ethnicity, gender, or sexual orientation. People from different groups can learn much from each other. There *is* richness in diversity. If we aim to assign clientele primarily to workers with similar backgrounds, we may inadvertently be reinforcing separation, distrust, and alienation among people who have already been too sharply divided by bigotry, fear, and unequal opportunity.

Role Theory

Roles and Social Expectations Especially helpful in understanding the interplay of person and situation is role theory.[43] Ideas that were originally introduced by sociologists and anthropologists in the 1930s were widely incorporated by social workers by the 1960s. A number of role concepts are particularly useful in understanding how the superego and ego ideal are shaped by social influences and the part played by such influences in the judgment and decisions of the ego. Role theory points out that the individuals and groups surrounding the child from birth onward hold certain behavioral expectations. Role expectations may derive from beliefs shared by society at large, from the traditions of particular ethnic or socioeconomic groups, or from the mores of geographic regions; on the other hand, they may be based on idiosyncratic family or individual preferences.

Specific ways of behaving are commonly accepted as appropriate or necessary for individuals in certain areas of functioning—as parents, as husbands or wives, as employees—and they are perceived in terms of the way role performances conform, or fail to conform, to the norms held by the group. For instance, a man's perception of whether or not his wife loves him can depend upon quite different cues in different groups. In some cultures, the wife's housekeeping tasks are deemed so important that the husband would be likely to see her subordination of them to interest in a job as personal neglect and evidence of lack of love. This perception might be reinforced by the opinions of his friends, before whom he could be disgraced. Similarly, a parent's view of a child usually depends greatly

upon the extent to which the child behaves according to group-influenced expectations. The ways in which an adult is expected to fulfill obligations to elderly parents, teacher–pupil relationships, interracial relationships, the roles of priests, rabbi or pastor, and congregational member—all of these are in part culturally defined. The same person is also expected to act differently under different circumstances. Norms of behavior acceptable at a political rally or a football game are usually considered highly inappropriate in professional situations. Similarly, one person functions in a multitude of roles: as mother, as wife or partner, as daughter and caretaker to aging parents, as employee, as PTA member, as loving friend, and many more.

Role and Status Status, or one's position in life, influences social expectations of behavior. Status may be ascribed by age, gender, ethnic, or socioeconomic group into which one is born; or it may be achieved by getting married, by learning a trade or profession, and so on. In any culture a child is expected to act in many specific respects quite differently from an adult, an employer from an employee, a member of the upper classes from a poor farmer, and so on. In some groups or families, the elderly are revered and looked to for wise counsel; in others, they lose status as they age. The important influence of role designations in families is discussed in the chapters on family therapy.

Role Complementarity Roles may be complementary or noncomplementary. Successful role performance on the part of one person may require reciprocal performance by another. If one fails, the other is frustrated. A priest cannot act as a confessor if the parishioner does not come to confession. A wife who defines her role behavior as including management of the budget is frustrated in carrying out this role if her husband, disagreeing with this definition, independently makes important financial decisions. Lack of complementarity may arise from lack of knowledge about expected role behavior (such as when one travels to an unfamiliar country), from lack of communication between role partners, or from disagreement about desirable roles (about which parents and teenagers often argue).

Thus, many role expectations, even those that are widespread, are by no means held identically by everyone. Sometimes this fact provides the basis for interpersonal tension or misunderstanding. A particular individual may expect another to behave in a certain way because of his or her status while the second person defines the role behavior required in a different way. One elderly man is gratified when a young woman offers him a seat in a crowded bus; another man of the same age with different expectations of roles feels humiliated and angered by the offer.

Changing Role Definitions   Recent years have witnessed rapid changes in many culturally determined role expectations in all types of interpersonal relations. Conflict in marriage may derive in part from changing roles of men and women. This can be particularly true when different definitions exist concerning decision making in general, or child care and distribution of household tasks, especially when a woman is working outside the home. In some cases it may be easier for a woman to claim her own expanded role than to be comfortable with a man's equally logical desire to be freed of some of the responsibilities he had accepted when he saw himself as head of the family and sole wage earner. Changing role definitions can cause inner turmoil for a young person. Many young

women, for example, are torn between either early marriage and raising a family immediately or taking many years first to establish themselves in a career. A young man, too, may be conflicted between becoming a "family man" or an independent single person. Not much more than a generation ago, these and many other role behaviors were more specifically defined; in general, deviance from "traditional" roles drew more attention than it does now.

Client–Worker Roles   Clients' expectations of how they should behave or how the caseworker will act will vary according to personal and social experience. Some casework clients assume that they must agree with and be directed by the worker, even though the worker is ethically and professionally bound to a process of mutuality and exchange between them. A man who has been trained to view women in very particular ways may have difficulty being comfortable with or taking seriously a female social worker.

For workers to convey the same impression of goodwill, objectivity, and competence to clients of varying backgrounds, life experiences, or personality styles, they need to become as aware as possible of their clients' preconceptions and interpretations of workers' actions. Every effort should be made to bring divergent expectations out in the open and to agree on a common ground for working. A worker learns that to be effective one needs to be more "friendly," outgoing, or casual with some clients, more "professional" or formal with others. With some involuntary or "hard-to-reach" clients, much generous and active help may be necessary to overcome the stereotype of the caseworker as an interfering or hostile "do-gooder," or as an indifferent bureaucrat. Not only is role theory important in assessing clients' life situations, but it also is equally important to understanding what is required to establish a successful, complementary working relationship.

Communication Concepts

Theories developed by scholars and researchers from various fields of the social sciences and by clinicians have advanced our understanding of the processes of communication and of the various ways in which misunderstandings can arise.[44] Some of the findings especially pertinent to clinical social work will be discussed in later chapters, but brief references to the communication factor are needed here.

Faulty perceptions or distortions by the ego—which may derive from group opinion, misunderstood personal experiences, prejudice, or actual ego impairment—are viewed as major components in faulty communication among different members of a family or members of any other social system. Assumptions and preconceptions can cause people not to listen to each other or to hear something different from what has been said. Ego defenses such as projection and displacement interfere with many efforts to communicate. If a son-in-law expects the same negative reaction from a father-in-law that he got from his own father, his comment to the father-in-law may be aggressively asserted and then viewed by the latter as an expression of dislike rather than the fear it actually is. Of course, the father-in-law's provoked response may then sound angry or sarcastic and belie his underlying warm feelings for his son-in-law. Two men who want to be close nevertheless become increasingly alienated and wary of one another.

As seen in this illustration, distortions of the ego's perceptions resulting from earlier experiences and from the ego's patterned defenses against anxiety are among the *internal factors* accounting for inaccurate assessments of others and failures in realistic reception of communications. Internal elaborations and attributions of intent by the receiver can cause endless misunderstandings. Distortions in the way intonation is heard also can make great differences in interpretation of meaning. Fortunately, as will be illustrated throughout this book, sometimes misunderstandings arise from a simple lack of knowledge about the intent of another person, in which case straightforward explanations can clear up the matter quickly. In other instances, however, distrust is great for various reasons, and understanding takes more time and effort to achieve.

When working with clients, we frequently find that communications are transmitted unclearly because people are afraid of being direct about what they mean. Some people do not communicate complaints or negative feelings lucidly for fear of "rocking the boat"; some are reluctant to state beliefs and preferences because they feel unentitled to do so or assume that their assertions will not be accepted; others share tender feelings tentatively or not at all for fear of being rejected. It is often possible to assist people to express their thoughts and feelings clearly and without attacking others. To minimize misinterpretations and for problems to be resolved and relationships to thrive, straightforward communication is usually essential.

There are equally important factors that have to do with other aspects of the communication process. Most communication occurs through symbols, both verbal and non-verbal. For accurate communication, these symbols must be commonly understood by sender and receiver. The meaning of gestures, posture, intonation, and even words of the same language can differ markedly among people of different educational backgrounds, social classes, and ethnic groups. Symbols of courtesy and discourtesy that are so basic to interpersonal relationships are particularly vulnerable to misperceptions.

INTERACTING SOURCES OF DISTRESS

Major Factors

When clients come to a clinical social worker for assistance because there has been a breakdown in social adjustment, this breakdown has three possible *interacting* factors:

1. Current life situations that exert excessive pressure or that fail to provide essential opportunities for satisfactory personal and social functioning.
2. Faulty ego and superego functioning that derive from hereditary factors and/or developmental deficits and flaws; when these functions are unevenly developed or underdeveloped, the individual often manifests emotional volatility and/or makes excessive demands on others to gratify immature or unfulfillable needs.
3. Overly restrictive or rigid ego defense mechanisms and/or superego functions.

The degree to which each of these is present varies with different people at different times. Sometimes all three substantially contribute to a client's dilemma.

Current Life Pressures Common among these are economic deprivation, lack of opportunities for employment, marginal working conditions, poor housing, dangerous neighborhoods, homelessness, substandard educational opportunities, racial and ethnic hostility, illness, and loss of love by death and separation. To these must be added innumerable individual life experiences that arouse frustration, anger, feelings of inadequacy, guilt, and so on. Pressures may occur, among other places, in family relationships when the needs of one individual conflict in a major way with those of another.

The need to care for a retarded child or chronically ill family member, for example, may conflict with the vocational aspirations of a woman who is tied to the home by these circumstances. Such stresses also exist when employment and living conditions are realistically very irritating and demanding, even though not substandard. And they certainly occur when general social conditions, such as racial discrimination or bias against homosexuality, create constant environmental pressure of overshadowing proportions.

Frustration with other people and situations is frequently a major component in a circle of deteriorating interaction. It can set up circular responses both in the situational interaction and within the personality. Externally, expression of the individual's anger and other behavior often further alienate sources of satisfaction in a reverberating pattern. Internally, the deprivation may increase the need for love or appreciation, or self-expression, and may increase feelings of lack of worth. These, in turn, increase the need for reassurance and gratification in the external world where these are already lacking or where antagonism has developed in reaction to the individual's negative attitudes or behavior.

Immature or Inadequate Ego and Superego Functioning In varying degrees, these deficits can lead people to have exaggerated narcissistic needs, make excessive childlike demands upon the world, and feel inordinately dependent on or hostile toward others. Fear of separation, with resulting anxiety or timidity, often causes individuals to require excessive protection and prevents them from assuming adult responsibilities, from operating independently, or from engaging in reciprocal and loving adult relationships. Extreme fluctuations of mood are common. Although it is sometimes possible for people with immature needs and uneven ego development to find social situations in which their needs are gratified, for the most part this does not occur. Rather, the individual is usually left with a constant sense of frustration or emptiness and characteristically behaves in ways that create antagonism in the social environment, thereby cutting off the very gratifications they crave and that might otherwise be available.

Faulty ego functioning also can include distorted perception of either the outside world or the self, poor judgment, excessive anxiety, difficulty managing impulses or behavior, poor reality testing, immature uses of ego defenses, and an unstable self-image. When superego and ego ideal functioning are extremely inadequate, it can mean that the individual has not incorporated much in the way of standards of "right and wrong" and has few ethical views or personal aspirations. The superego or conscience can be primitively harsh and literal. Usually when functioning is faulty, standards and self-requirements are unevenly developed rather than absent.

Sometimes, because of cultural or idiosyncratic factors that existed in a person's background, standards of conduct that may seem flawed to others are actually out of harmony in the context of the current environment rather than underdeveloped as such. A pair of twins, for example, who were raised to do and share almost everything as a unit were discovered talking together during an examination at college; both young men, who actually had very firm ethical beliefs and would not have

"cheated" in other ways, were amazed by the consternation their behavior provoked. In any case, dissension with the outside world can be the result.

Faulty ego and superego functioning almost always add substantially to environmental pressures felt by the individual. If the ego misperceives pressures, stress experienced in response to the distorted version of reality may be more severe than would have been appropriate to the actual life events. Faulty perceptions and judgments can also lead to actions that are self-defeating or unnecessarily self-depriving. If, for example, a woman perceives a co-worker as jealous of or competitive with her when this is not the case, she may behave in a hostile manner toward that person, with the result that she is treated negatively in return. The woman with the misperception then may seek associates who are willing to confirm her distortions, thus reinforcing the tendency to faulty reality testing.

Restrictive or Rigid Ego Defenses and Superego Functions   These often lie behind difficulties clients bring to caseworkers. When the experience and/or expression of feelings, thoughts, conflicts, and behavior have been severely restrained, or when standards for self and others are impossibly unbending and perfectionistic, individuals may become symptomatic. When important aspects of one's emotional or intellectual life have been cast outside of awareness, a person can experience considerable tension and distress. Often people with these qualities are productive and conscientious, but they may never feel satisfaction in their accomplishments. The capacity for joy or the ability to relax is seriously compromised. If individuals have buried their feelings or opinions, they sometimes feel at the mercy of other people's ideas or behaviors toward them, yet do not know how to define their own positions. In contrast to those with immature functioning, where help often takes the form of encouraging people to *build* on their capacities and to mobilize their strengths, those with overly restrictive egos and superegos usually get relief from *uncovering* and *expressing* disowned feelings and thoughts or from *relaxing* and *softening* inner demands.

Often some aspects of a person are underdeveloped while other functions are overly restrained or demanding, in which case a combination of these approaches may be considered. Cases discussed in the next chapter will demonstrate the interplay of all three elements in personal difficulties.

Ameliorating Person-in-Situation Stresses

Environmental Intervention When a major cause of a client's discomfort is in reaction to the environment, it is sometimes possible for the caseworker to modify the pressure or deficiency directly; location of an apartment, a job, or medical services may be all that is required. In some instances, a referral by the caseworker to a resource may be more effective than the client's self-referral. Sometimes attitudes of individuals who are creating difficulties for the client can be altered through casework contact; when such modification is required, so-called environmental intervention with collaterals actually becomes *psychological* in nature. Some services—child placement is a prime example—can be extremely complicated in the treatment required. Chapter 8 deals in detail with environmental procedures.

Worker–Client Collaboration and the Environment Environmental services rarely stand alone. They are often accompanied by work directly with the client, in

which his or her reactions become a focus of attention. The court-mandated adult client of a child protective agency understandably resents being investigated yet has to endure the process to resolve issues related to the children. Out of fear or misunderstanding, the hospital patient may be unwilling to undergo recommended medical procedures. The child may be reluctant to use educational or recreational services that have become available. Empathic understanding of clients' responses is essential, as is a concerted effort to elicit their perspectives about the matter and their participation in the resolution. Preparation involving *both* the resource and the client may be necessary. Often the assessment and improvement of the "fit" between the resource and the client are required before presenting difficulties can be resolved.

Instead of relieving environmental pressures directly, often the worker helps clients to bring about the necessary changes themselves, thereby reinforcing their feelings of competence. Obviously, environmental changes brought about solely for removing unusual pressures or deficiencies need not involve an individual's effort to make personal changes as such. At times, however, improvement requires that client and worker address an ego problem, such as misinterpretations of events in the environment, dysfunctional reactions to pressures that do exist, or lack of confidence in the ability to initiate external changes.

Inseparability of Inner and Outer Phenomena A person may function more comfortably as a result of external change; in fact, outer changes can produce permanent shifts in the inner balance. If a person previously deprived is less frustrated and more gratified, energies may be released for psychological development that had previously been stunted; *at all stages of an individual's life, the ego has amazing innate powers of maturation and resiliency.*

Sometimes it can be very difficult to differentiate between an individual's inner life and the world outside, particularly when aspects of the environment impinge directly on a person's situation. As Loewenstein pointed out in her important article, so-called "impulse-ridden youth with 'weak superegos' are quite able to obey rigid rules established by the gang to which they belong."[45] The psychology of people changes according to the context in which they are interacting. In practice, over and over again, we find that modifications of a client's external situation can result in emotional or behavioral changes, just as emotional growth can often give the individual the strength required to fully utilize or make changes in the environment. *The caseworker may concentrate, therefore, on that system or those systems that seem most accessible to change, not necessarily the most dysfunctional ones.*

It may be necessary to help a client find personal alternatives to an unjust external condition; even serious economic or political injustice may require individual initiative to find new adaptations. At other times, internalized emotional disturbance may best be treated by altering the environment. For example, it may be more efficient and caring to help a man, victimized by unemployment, to retrain or relocate than it would be to wait until pressure can bring about changes in the unhealthy economic situation. As unfair as it may seem, individuals are constantly having to make new adaptations to counteract external assaults. On the other hand, a person with a severe or chronic psychiatric disorder may respond better to a supportive milieu than to therapy aimed directly at the intrapsychic disturbance or deficit. A symptomatic child

may be quickly relieved by improvement in marital relations of the parents. Paradoxically, then, the caseworker's focus for intervention may be the seemingly "healthiest" aspect of the person–situation configuration, when this is the one most amenable to influence and change. The psychosocial approach to problems in or with the environment, therefore, requires an understanding of the people involved, the impinging environments, and the interactions among these, in order to evaluate which of them are likely to be modifiable.

Lasting Personality Changes As just mentioned, radical modification of the environment can bring about *enduring personality change.* Sometimes a change of jobs will bring about a better fit between work and personality, leading to greater personal comfort, improved functioning, and enhanced self-esteem. A woman may become less tense, less hostile, and more able to give love to her children when she is working outside the home and having others care for her children during the day than when she devotes her full time to their care. If the woman arrives at this decision and, perhaps with the caseworker's help, makes practical arrangements so that she can take a job, there may be marked improvements in her feelings of well-being, her functioning, and her relationships, all of which may endure even if at some point she gives up her outside work. Lasting personality change can result when a particularly fortunate choice of a marriage partner leads to a long period of satisfying living that seems to undo the effects of earlier misfortune and brings about a reorientation to life. A good marriage can be one of the best therapies! Women labeled as "dependent personalities" have often become autonomous and self-directed when exposed to the women's movement or to other influences in their lives. The phenomenon of religious conversion also can effect major personality change.

With children, enduring changes often occur readily in response to shifts in the environment, and this is a major method of casework treatment used with children. Significant personality changes in the child, particularly the young child, can often be brought about by various forms of substitute parental care: adoption, foster care, or day care centers. Less extensive changes may be promoted by modifications in the school environment or by provision of recreational and other group experiences such as camping, bringing a "big brother" or other interested person into the situation, and so on. Because children's personalities are still so fluid, environmental changes profoundly affect their views of the world and their ego and emotional development; even when "good-enough parenting" was not available earlier on, corrections can sometimes occur quite rapidly when youngsters are exposed to healing situations.

Often, we try to bring about changes in parents' attitudes and behavior. Family treatment (see Chapters 14 and 15) can be one of the most effective means of altering a child's environment and also of promoting personality changes. In a case where a mother may be encouraging her son's babyishness and excessive dependence on her, in family therapy it may be revealed that her overinvolvement in her son's life is a compensation for her husband's remoteness; the boy's development may be further retarded by the fact that the father has been displacing his unexpressed anger at his wife onto his son. If changes in the marriage can be effected that result in greater satisfactions in the relationship between husband and wife, the family environment will more likely support the boy's age-appropriate independence. When environmental changes are impossible or are not

sufficiently effective, direct casework with the child may either accompany environmental modification or become the major form of treatment.[46]

Direct Work with the Individual

To whatever extent the three interacting sources of distress described above contribute to a client's problem, change in the *person* frequently becomes an important goal of treatment. Such treatment may range from attempts to bring about lasting changes in the client's personality or way of functioning to temporary adjustments of behavior during a period of stress. These changes, as we have said, may be made by direct or indirect interventions. When *direct* work is decided upon, casework uses the client's current reactions and behavior and sometimes memories that are either immediately accessible to consciousness or suppressed, unverbalized, or uncomprehended. Truly repressed material that is so remote from consciousness that only such means as free association, hypnosis, or therapy under drugs can bring them to the surface is obviously not available for use in most casework practice. Sometimes in the face of a family crisis or dilemma, the entire family is worked with directly; in the Chin case described earlier, the couple worked together to be able to share their grief about the death of their son.

Casework Techniques and the Therapeutic Relationship Psychosocial casework is a form of treatment that relies heavily upon reflective, cognitive procedures embodied in the matrix of a sound, helping or therapeutic relationship. Whether the emphasis is on thinking things through, uncovering suppressed material, modifying rigidities in personality, building ego strengths, or planning action that will bring about environmental changes, the client is helped to define his or her own goals and needs. Casework seeks to engage the client's ego—the capacity to think, to reflect, to understand—in a reevaluation of internal and interactional issues. By engaging clients as fully as possible in their own treatment, caseworkers endeavor not only to preserve but also to enhance self-reliance, encouraging them to make decisions about themselves and their lives. In some cases the treatment process is extremely intense; sometimes it can take many months or more to achieve the desired results. At the other extreme are instances when just having a caseworker truly interested in understanding, someone to whom one can safely get things "off one's chest," can provide sufficient relief and clarity for the person to go on without help from there.

As indicated earlier, casework does make use of directive techniques such as suggestion, advice, and persuasion when diagnosis indicates that the client is unlikely to respond to measures that rely upon his or her own active thinking. This may be the case when one is temporarily overwhelmed by pressing life circumstances, such as illness, death, or desertion. Advice sometimes is given about such matters as child rearing, job hunting, or how a client might achieve a goal, but it is almost always accompanied by explanations that supply understanding of the advice given. Directive procedures are *never* used in isolation from cognitive measures and are employed *only* when the client is not ready or able to use reflective procedures. Psychosocial casework therefore differs markedly from truly directive therapies in which the therapist takes a very active part in advising the client, relying primarily upon the weight of "professional authority" and upon the positive relationship to modify the client's, or patient's, responses. Chapters 4 through 8

describe psychosocial treatment procedures used with individuals, families, or people in clients' environments.

THE BALANCE OF FORCES

Understanding the Balance

To understand how work can be effective that does not reach the "deeper" (repressed) layers of personality or does not substantially modify environmental influences, we must appreciate the various ways in which the personality system and its interactions with the environment constitute a balance, sometimes a very delicate balance, of forces.

We have already referred to the Freudian concept of the personality as consisting of id, ego, and superego/ego ideal. It is also useful to consider the balance of forces *within* as well as *between* each of these components, as seen from the vantage point of social functioning. For example, the primary process of the id—the raw, chaotic, undifferentiated emotion—can be counterbalanced by needs and drives that have been organized and regulated by the ego. Thus, immature energies can be counterpoised by drives that are more harmonious with the needs of others. For the individual, then, impulses can be postponed or the capacity for giving and receiving love can be accentuated without actually relating to the unconscious material of the id.

The ego and superego are also a balance of socially functional and dysfunctional tendencies. The ego does not always perceive and understand realistically. Certain defenses may obscure or distort the events of life. Self-confidence may be weak, guilt may be overbearing, general lack of ego integration may impede constructive action. An individual may function satisfactorily until some even minor external event provokes ill-considered and damaging action. The early and restrictive superego may still be so harsh that certain actions or feelings are inhibited in unnecessary and harmful ways. On the other hand, any of these weaknesses may be offset by other tendencies in the personality that promote personal growth and socially realistic, gratifying functioning. These include the capacity to function autonomously rather than only reactively, to feel competent, to make accurate appraisals of others, of the self, and of the external world; these and other ego functions are likely to result in responses that bring gratifications for the individual, contribute to meeting the needs of associates, and enhance harmonious functioning of the social systems of which the individual is a part.

In a sense, opposing tendencies (whether within or between personality components) struggle with each other at any given moment, and the resultant action often depends on *whether strengths or weaknesses predominate.* When certain reactions or inner drives push the individual toward self-destructive behavior, or into actions that hurt others, the healthy parts of the personality say no. When the ego distorts reality by projection or magical beliefs, or when other unconscious or primitive processes cause distortions, the healthy parts of the ego correct these and keep the irrational tendencies in check. It is often nip and tuck as to which side will win, depending upon the relative power the two sets of forces bring to bear in any particular situation. "If my wife had said just one more thing, I would have thrown the hammer at her." That is, "If I had been just a little more angry, nothing my ego was telling me would have been enough to keep me in control."

An important aspect of this balance of forces is that while the decision to act may hang upon a hair's weight of difference—either in the opposing intrapsychic forces

or in the nature and force of external pressures—the action that this slight difference triggers may be of major proportions and have extensive consequences. If the wife just mentioned had in fact said "one more thing," and the man did not call upon ego functions of judgment and impulse control to regulate his reaction, he might have seriously hurt the woman and ended up in jail.

Anger left over from the family fight might then tip the scales in this man's decision to respond to criticism from his employer by throwing down his tools and walking off his job. The reverberations of this action in his personal and family life obviously could exacerbate the already desperate situation, but the action itself—walking off the job—resulted from only slight changes in the man's ego capacity to manage his anger. A series of such transactions can combine and interact to create a pattern of considerable, perhaps disastrous, significance. But, looking at the situation from another perspective, if crowded housing conditions for this couple were relieved (even if nothing else changed), the balance of forces might shift enough so that the same marital interaction might not lead the man to such drastic action.

Modifying the Balance of Forces

A Small Change Tips the Balance It is, as we have just illustrated, not the strength of a drive or the degree of a tendency toward distortion alone that determines whether a person takes action. These may be opposed by an equally strong counterforce, in the form of capacity for reality testing and ability to control impulses or of a positive change in external circumstances.

When the opposing strengths are almost equally balanced, a relatively small amount of improvement in ego functioning may be enough to enable the individual to make significant changes in social functioning, which in turn may increase the sense of confidence and self-esteem, which can then promote enduring change in the person's behavior and feelings of well-being.

This is one answer to the oft-repeated question: "When immature demands and distortions are not directly modified, how can there be any real change?" Although the demands and distortions may not be addressed directly by casework treatment, the person may handle them differently. If certain ego functions are strengthened or external pressure is alleviated, sometimes immature qualities may even be permanently modified. It is the belief in the positive capacities of the human being for change and growth that provides the main incentive for the treatment process.

A Hypothetical Example   All formative influences do not occur in early childhood, nor are they all unconscious. Consider, for example, a young daughter (whom some might describe as having "unresolved oedipal rivalries") who, through projection, incorrectly believes her mother is hostile toward her because she has a "special" relationship with her father. The daughter's assumption may be reinforced by experiencing actual hostility from her mother as she grows older. Or, conversely, her belief may be lessened by experiences of an opposite nature. In the latter instance, not only is the original tendency not reinforced, but the ego also is given a means by which to counteract the effect of the original distortion. In the former instance, when the mother's later behavior reinforces the daughter's belief that enmity must exist between them—a belief that may affect her attitude toward other women—there are several possible modes of treatment that need not involve an effort to uncover and

correct the *original,* possibly unconscious, material derived from early childhood.

Alternative Treatment Approaches   In one approach, the client is encouraged to *ventilate* feelings about the events she spontaneously remembers or can recall. For a person who has not previously been able to express her anger toward her mother, eliciting it may have a useful cathartic effect, which can reduce the amount of suppressed hostility pressing for displacement on current female figures in the client's life. If there has been guilt over the angry feelings, the worker's acceptance of them as natural may reduce the guilt and subsequent need to use defenses such as projection or turning against the self.

Another approach is to provide the client with an opportunity for a *"corrective relationship."*[47] By allowing a relationship to develop in which the client regards the worker in some respects as a nurturing parental figure, it may be possible to counteract the earlier disappointing mother–daughter experience by enabling the client to see, through the new experience, that the characteristics of her relationship with her mother need not apply to all relationships with women. This may also tend to undo some of the attitudes about herself, men, marriage and sex, child raising, and so on, that she acquired in her early relationship with her parents.

Another choice is for the client and worker to look carefully at current problematic and emotionally upsetting personal interactions in which the woman's unconscious attitudes have contributed to her unrealistic responses. Details of interactions can be examined to see if the responses were warranted by what the other person actually did, correcting unnecessary or dysfunctional responses bit by bit. If the anger has been displaced onto a female child or other adult women, it may be possible to enable the client through *reflection* to examine patterns of belief and behavior and test them against the realities of the situations. With new awareness, she may be able to recognize and refrain from behavior that provokes counterhostility and causes her to experience constant repetitions of her original unhappy experience with a woman. This process can actually strengthen the person's overall ability to correct misperceptions and restrain impulsive actions should other situations arise.

Still another approach is to enable the client to review her conscious and preconscious or near-conscious early memories of experiences, including her fear that because she was "daddy's little girl," her mother resented her. A worker might first *reassure* her that such worries are common in children. Then, by seeing and *reflecting* upon the effects of early memories on her personality and on her current reactions to life, she may free herself from childhood and adolescent reinforcements of her (possibly "oedipal") distortions and, in turn, reduce the degree of distortion with which her adult ego must deal. Along with this reduction of the force of childhood experiences, she may then be helped to recognize her tendency to carry over feelings from childhood to current relationships; with this understanding, she may be able to improve these relationships by careful testing of her own reactions against the realities of other people's behavior.

In actual practice, as will be discussed in later chapters, all of the above approaches are used, sometimes even in the same interview. Characteristically, several are continuously used together.

Even when individual treatment is the treatment of choice, additional joint interviews can often be effective. In the case just described, meetings with the woman and her mother or both of her parents might be arranged. By correcting distortions and improving *current* relationships with parents, often negative childhood influences and/or distortions can be significantly dissipated. A "corrective relationship" with one's actual family can sometimes be more far-reaching than one provided by the caseworker. Even when the family relationships never become what the client might wish, family meetings can provide the opportunity for some sort of resolution that is often more difficult to achieve when clients simply talk about the people who have significantly influenced their lives.

A Case Example: The Balance Shifts

Over and over again we witness how small shifts in the balance of a family and the personalities within it can create significant and lasting changes. The following case of the Smith family illustrates this point.

Joan, a 13-year-old African American girl, was referred by her junior high school guidance counselor to a family agency because she appeared morose and recently had begun to underachieve. Family sessions that included Joan and her mother and stepfather, Mr. and Mrs. Smith, who had been married for six years, were arranged. Mrs. Smith had become critical of her daughter's blossoming interest in boys in part because she, the mother, had made a "mistake" and become pregnant many years ago and projected feelings that her daughter would do the same. Furthermore, the mother, who tended to be extremely anxious and compulsive, was particularly stressed for fear she would have to give up her job—upon which she depended for discharge of her high energies, approval, and a sense of competence—to supervise her daughter more closely. Her concern about not being able to work prompted even more anxiety and irritation with the girl. Joan, who had been afraid to challenge or reassure her mother, believing her mother would discount whatever she said, had become increasingly silent, which further contributed to the mother's escalating apprehensions. Mrs. Smith reported that she was unable to sleep well or concentrate at work; she had always been nervous, she said, but now she feared she was "going crazy."

Even though he had confidence in his stepdaughter and had a more comfortable relationship with Joan than his wife did, Mr. Smith had been reluctant to interfere or express his opinion, partly because he tended to be reserved and partly because he was not sure he had the "right" to be involved because he was not the girl's "real" father. With only a little encouragement from the caseworker, however, in a couple session, he did tell his wife that he did not think her anger and criticisms were helpful to Joan and, furthermore, that *he* trusted the child.

This single change on the part of the stepfather triggered immediate and resounding shifts in the balance of the family system and the personalities of all of the members. Mrs. Smith's anxiety diminished almost immediately because "at last" her husband was willing to talk about and share the family burdens (which turned out to include more issues than concern about Joan). Feeling her stepfather's support and her mother's relaxation, Joan became more forthcoming; she was able to tell her mother convincingly that concerns about becoming sexually active were unwarranted; she also said that she wanted to become involved in some afterschool art and drama programs, which she had been afraid to discuss because she feared her mother would disapprove. Actually, Mrs. Smith was relieved because these were supervised activities of which she thoroughly approved. As a result of feeling less fearful, the

mother's criticisms of Joan abated. When she realized she need not quit her job, she began sleeping better and was no longer frightened about her mental state. Mr. and Mrs. Smith became more open with each other and, after a short time, felt closer. Joan, who had internalized feelings in reaction to her mother that she was somehow "bad," began to look better, smile more, and get good grades in school again.

Gently, the worker had encouraged Mr. Smith to assert himself with his wife. In turn, Mrs. Smith was comforted by his increased participation; her harsh superego, which had contributed to her anxiety about herself as well as to her criticisms of Joan, softened. Almost immediately, Joan appeared and said she felt more confident and cheerful; she was enjoying school and new activities. Four family sessions, two marital sessions, and one individual session with Joan were sufficient to shift the balance of forces and create positive changes. In a follow-up interview six months after termination, it was revealed that the improvements had endured: Joan had become more competent and independent; Mr. and Mrs. Smith were getting along and working together much better than before.

Experience in individual and family treatment has demonstrated that even in adulthood, the ego is often readily open to influence and capable of growth and modification. In systems terms, we have learned that families and personalities are "open systems" that constantly shift in response to exchanges with the outside world, including situational changes and changes that can be brought about by interaction and collaboration with the caseworker in the process of treatment.

In summary, when casework is employed to help clients achieve better social functioning, it can become a form of psychosocial therapy. In addition to improvements in the environment and external functioning, treatment can bring about such *internalized modifications* as: improvement of the ego's perception and reality-testing ability; improved self-acceptance and self-esteem; better integration of all aspects of the personality; shifts in the uses or rigidities of defenses; changes in the demands, or in the reactions to demands, of the superego; lasting reductions in the strength of destructive character traits such as chronic dependency or hostility; reduction of oppressive influences of parental ties; and maturation that not only consolidates capabilities, but also reduces self-defeating, driven behaviors. Such modifications are built into the personality and enable individuals to function better even when confronted by circumstances identical or essentially similar to those under which functioning was previously impaired. It is reasonable to expect that such changes will continue after treatment has ended.

Psychosocial treatment relies mainly on reflective procedures, sometimes augmented by methods of direct influence or suggestion, and by direct efforts by the caseworker and/or the client to bring about environmental changes when their mutual assessment suggests that these will be effective. Of paramount importance in such treatment is the relationship upon which it is based. The worker's acceptance of the client and wish to respond to the client's need is constant; this worker attitude is expressed in varying ways, depending upon the client's wishes and needs but always characterized by honesty, basic supportiveness, and a spirit of collaboration. Often, when clients feel valued and when their strengths are affirmed, they become better able to value themselves and others and thereby respond differently in relationships. Focus is always upon the person-situation gestalt, which is seen as an interacting balance of forces between the needs

of the person and the influences upon him or her of the environment. Individual functioning is the end result of a complicated series of interactions between different parts of the personality highly susceptible to outside influences. In psychosocial therapy, focus is on either the environment, including the family environment, or the personality or both. When it is directed toward the personality, it can reduce the force of destructive trends in the individual by decreasing the force of earlier life experiences and by increasing the capacities of the ego and superego to handle current life experiences more capably and realistically. Thus, the work strengthens clients in their ability to achieve goals they set for themselves. The remaining chapters in this book attempt to explain and illustrate the process of psychosocial therapy in greater detail.

NOTES

1. For fuller discussions of casework values and also of ethical issues, dilemmas, and challenges, excellent references include Abramson (1996), Chernot (1998), Grossman and Rhodes (1992), Reamer (1990), and Rhodes (1992). As usual, Howard Goldstein (1998) writes a thought-provoking article, this one on ethical issues in education and practice. The May–June 1998 issue of *Families in Society* has several articles on ethical challenges. See also Lewis (1982, 1987) and Levy (1976). The National Association of Social Workers *Code of Ethics* (1996) is also an important reference.

2. Two very useful books on empathy with clinical illustrations are Margulies (1989) and Rowe (1989). In a recommended article by Raines (1990), he differentiates empathy from sympathy, insight, identification, and intuition. See also Keefe (1980) and Berger (1987).

3. An excellent group of still relevant articles on self-determination can be found in McDermott (1975). See a thoughtful, recommended

article by Weick and Pope (1988) who write that each person "carries within her or himself the capacity and the power to develop in a uniquely personal way" (p. 14). In a small exploratory study it was found that there were enormous variations in the application of self-determination; see Kassel and Kane (1980). See Tower (1994) on "consumer-centered" practice and self-determination.

4. Weick and Pope (1988), p. 12.
5. Abramson (1989) interviewed 30 workers in adult protective services and concluded that when safety and freedom conflict, "paternalistic beneficence" is favored by the workers over client autonomy.
6. Berger (1986) makes this point in his article and takes a critical view of the psychosocial and other models of social work that claim to espouse abstract values that cannot be realized in practice. In our view, it is still our professional obligation to do all we can to eliminate obstacles to self-realization, even though we often fall short of helping clients achieve their ideal goals.
7. See Howard Goldstein (1987) who discusses complex personal and professional issues involved in helping clients deal with moral dilemmas.
8. Hamilton (1951). See a very interesting article by Dean (1994).
9. See Germain's recommended text (1991). See also DeHoyos (1989) for an interesting discussion of the person-in-environment that has some similarities to the psychosocial perspective; she describes a tri-level model (the personality, interactional, and sociocultural system) that she believes helps guide the worker in making decisions about interventions.
10. Bertalanffy (1968) is a classic reference on systems theory. Lazlo's book (1972), published during the period when systems theory was being incorporated by various thinkers, is a compilation of excellent articles that discuss the relevance of general systems theory to various disciplines. For a social work reference on systems theory, see Andreae (1996). See also Gyarfas (1980) for a discussion of a systems approach to clinical social work diagnosis.
11. Hamilton (1941).
12. Murray (1938), pp. 38–39.
13. For references on the ecological approach in addition to Germain (1991), see Allen-Meares and Lane (1987), Germain and Gitterman (1996), and Gitterman (1996).
14. Germain (1991), p. 17.
15. Vigilante (1982), p. 297.
16. For a comprehensive review of the findings concerning the effects of maternal deprivation, see Spitz (1946), Bowlby (1952, 1980, 1988), Ainsworth (1962), and Ainsworth and Bowlby (1991). See McMillen (1992) for a summary of attachment theory and the effects of early loss; implications for practice are discussed. See also Sable (1992) for a very useful discussion of the application of attachment theory to clinical practice with adults. For other relevant references, see Chapter 5, note 19, and Chapter 14, note 46.
17. van Lawick-Goodall (1971).
18. For comments on this, see Garrett (1958), Hamilton (1958), Weisberger (1967), and Wood (1971). See also Phillips (1993) who discusses new thinking about psychoanalytic theory, beyond ego psychology, and recommends integration of several theories and approaches to help to bridge traditional theory and clinical social work; he indicates that some psychoanalytic theorists are challenging the notion that interpretations are the crucial agent of change.
19. Eda Goldstein's recommended volume (1995) provides an up-to-date and thorough discussion of concepts from ego psychology and their usefulness to social work practice.

Seminal works by ego psychology theorists include Anna Freud (1946), Hartmann (1958), Hartmann, Kris, and Loewenstein (1946), Kris (1950), Erikson (1959), Rapaport (1951), and White (1963).

For background on casework's integration of ego psychology, see Parad (1958), Parad and Miller (1963) and Stamm (1959).

There are many readings on object relations theories. We include here works by some of the major theorists: Fairbairn (1954), Guntrip (1961), Mahler et al. (1975), and Winnicott (1958, 1986a). See also Buckley's

(1986) compilation of papers on object relations theories and on their modifications of Freudian theory on instinct. We also recommend Blanck and Blanck (1986).

See Kernberg (1975) and Kohut (1977).

20. See Elson (1986), especially pp. 8–10; we recommend this excellent book on self-psychology in clinical social work. See also Donner (1988) who summarizes some features of self-psychology theory and believes that, in contrast to psychoanalytic theory, it has the potential for enhancing person-in-environment treatment.

21. Ways of thinking and feeling characteristic of the young child were vividly portrayed in the studies of Jean Piaget and Susan Isaacs (1937). For less detailed but useful descriptions, see Erikson (1950) and Fraiberg (1959).

22. See Bellak et al. (1973). See also Eda Goldstein (1995).

23. Eda Goldstein (1995, pp. 75–76) discusses an interesting distinction between defense mechanisms and coping mechanisms. From this point of view, suppression could be considered a conscious or preconscious coping mechanism rather than an unconscious defense. In any event, in our discussion, defense mechanisms can be viewed as adaptive or maladaptive means of coping depending on the circumstances and the positive or negative value to the individuals using them.

24. Anna Freud's classic work (1946) was the first comprehensive study of ego defenses. See Goldstein (1995), chapter 4.

For a discussion of some of the more "primitive" defenses, see Kernberg (1975) and Kernberg (1986).

25. Discussions of classifications of defense mechanisms can be found in Meissner (1985), especially pp. 388–90; and Yalliant (1977).

26. The term *good-enough mother* was introduced by Winnicott to describe the part played by the mother (or substitute parent) in creating an environment that facilitates healthy psychological development of the infant. The good-enough mother "starts off with an almost complete adaptation to her infant's needs, and as time proceeds she adapts less and less completely, gradually, according to the infant's growing ability to deal with her failure." See Winnicott (1986b), p. 265.

27. See Mahler (1975).

28. See Erikson (1959), chapter 8.

29. Benedict (1934) and Mead (1935).

30. Kardiner (1939).

31. Boie (1937) and de la Fontaine (1940).

32. See especially Angell (1936), Cavan and Ranck (1938), and Komarovsky (1940).

33. See for example, Bergler (1946), Burgess and Cottrell (1939), Hollis (1949), Terman (1938), and Waller (1930).

34. Two of the classic articles that influenced casework thought during this period: Bateson, Jackson, Haley, and Weakland (1956) and Cloward (1959).

35. See Cohen (1964), Ferman (1965), Lewis (1967), and Maas (1955).

36. See Hollingshead and Redlich (1958). The Hollingshead-Redlich study on the greater prevalence of certain types of mental illness in lower socioeconomic classes aroused great interest and led to examination of the question of how prevalence was related to class-related differences in the formulation of diagnostic opinion and treatment. For two influential casework articles from this period see Hellenbrand (1961) and Meier (1959).

37. There is a rich literature that addresses issues of race, ethnicity, and class that are pertinent to the social worker's understanding of how these influence person–situation interactions. Some of these we include here; most are written by social workers. There are several important volumes that are very useful as references. The second edition of *Ethnicity and Family Therapy* (1996), edited by Monica McGoldrick et al., is a compilation of chapters discussing 47 different ethnic groups. McGoldrick's edited volume, *Revisioning Family Therapy* (1998), has chapters on various issues related to race, culture, and gender as these pertain to clinical practice. Comas-Diaz and Griffith (1988) have edited a book with an array of chapters on ethnosociocultural factors that affect cross-

cultural treatment; there are also discussions of issues related to mental health services for special ethnic groups. A book by Elaine Pinderhughes (1989) is devoted to the understanding of race, ethnicity, and power; it also addresses cross-cultural problems in social and mental health services. We recommend Boyd-Franklin's (1989) book on therapy with black families. See also Alex Gitterman's (1991) book on vulnerable populations. With these and other readings on culture and ethnicity, as we emphasize in the text, it is critically important to beware of stereotyping.

The following readings cover a range of issues about several ethnic groups, including some commonly found characteristics, strengths and vulnerabilities, acculturation, immigration, help-seeking attitudes, intragroup diversity, cross-cultural treatment, and research.

Recommended references on African Americans and other people of color include: Boyd-Franklin and Shenouda (1990), Brown (1995), Carter (1997), Chatters and Taylor (1989), Cochran (1997), Cooper and Lesser (1997), Daly et al. (1995), Dillon (1994), Thrasher and Anderson (1988), Gray and Nybell (1990), Gutierrez (1990), Harvey (1995), King (1993), Robinson (1989), Sewell-Coker et al. (1985), Swigonski (1996), Taylor et al. (1989), Wade (1994), Williams (1992), and Wright and Anderson (1998).

Recommended references on Hispanics and Latinos include Castex (1994), Dyche and Zayas (1995), Zayas et al. (1997), Zayas (1994), Zayas and Bryant (1984), Zayas and Dyche (1995), and Zayas and Palleja (1988).

Recommended readings on Asians, Pacific Islanders, and Hawaiians include: Agbayani-Siewert (1994), Browne and Broderick (1994), Ching et al. (1995), Crystal (1989), Ewalt and Mokuau (1995), Marsella (1993), Mokuau (1990), Mokuau and Browne (1994), Ryan (1985), Segal (1991), Tung (1991), and Yamashiro and Matsuoka (1997).

We suggest the following on Native Americans: Dubray (1985), Horejsi et al. (1992), and Williams and Ellison (1996).

See Gibbs and Moskowitz-Sweet (1991) for an interesting study of biracial and bicultural adolescents.

On immigration, migration, and resettlement see: Drachman et al. (1996), Hulewat (1996), and Streier (1996).

Rosenbloom's article (1983) is a classic on the implications of the Holocaust for social work. See Linzer (1984) on the Jewish family.

Additional useful references related to diversity, cross-cultural treatment, and cultural sensitivity include Comas-Diaz (1992), Congress (1994), Dore (1990), Dore and Dumois (1990), Dungee-Anderson and Beckett (1995), Falicov (1995), Freed (1988), Greene et al. (1996), Lee (1996), Newhill (1990), Rogler et al. (1987), Rose and Meezan (1996), Saleebey (1994), and Shapiro (1996).

For papers on ethnicity and on socioeconomic class, see Turner (1995), chapters 95 through 101. Chapter 103 addresses spirituality. Further references will be found in the chapters in this book on the client–worker relationship and on family and couple treatment.

For a useful article on spirituality and on the importance of learning from our clients how their spiritual beliefs shape their experiences, see Cascio (1998).

38. See especially *The Invisible Web* (1988) by four outstanding women leaders in family therapy—Marianne Walters, Betty Carter, Peggy Papp, and Olga Silverstein—who pioneered in bringing a feminist perspective to family theory and practice that, for the most part, had been dominated by men. See also Carter and McGoldrick (1988), especially Chapter 2 by McGoldrick on "Women and the Family Life Cycle," and excellent papers in the volume on women in families edited by McGoldrick et al. (1989). Additional references can be found in the chapters in this book on family and couple treatment.

39. For recent references on issues related to gay men and lesbians, including on "coming out," on homophobia and heterosexism of clinicians, on gay and lesbian families, on research, and on various treatment issues, see Ben-Ari (1995), Berkman and Zinberg

(1997), Cain (1991), Caron and Ulin (1997), Cornett (1997), Faroa (1994), Eda Goldstein (1997), Green (1996), Hare (1994), Hartman and Laird (1998), Jones & Gabriel (1999), Levy (1992), Long (1996), and Morrow (1993). Further references appear in Chapter 16, notes 52 through 66.

40. Dyche and Zayas (1995), p. 390.

41. See Lee (1995).

42. See Beck (1988, p. 60) who found that satisfaction for Hispanic clients was somewhat greater when matched with Hispanic counselors, but blacks showed insignificant differences in outcome whether seen by a white or a black counselor. For white clients, those seen by white counselors showed only a modest difference from those who were non-matched. She also found that there was "no consistent support for sex matching" (p. 52). See Sue (1994, pp. 790–91) whose review of relatively sparse studies suggests that whether clients were ethnically matched or not, outcomes did not seem to be affected. There is no doubt in our minds that sensitivity and respectful curiosity on the part of workers in cross-cultural or cross-gender treatment strongly influence client satisfaction and success.

43. See Davis (1995) and Perlman (1968).

44. See Greene (1996). We recommend Nelsen (1980) and Knapp (1980). See also Satir's excellent book (1983), especially Part Two, and the classic by Watzlawick, Beavin, and Jackson (1967). See also Chapter 9, notes 13 and 14. Additional references will be found in the family and couple chapters.

45. Loewenstein (1979) in a highly recommended article that has stood the test of time, pp. 23–24.

46. Direct individual treatment of children is not a subject covered by this text. See especially Mishne (1983), Singer (1993), and a volume edited by Webb (1991) with chapters on children who have witnessed family violence, have been victims of sexual abuse, who have experienced losses, and have been subjected to other crises and catastrophes. Garvin et al. (1991) discuss preventive intervention for children of divorce. Silvern and Kaersvang (1989) urge immediate intervention for children of violent marriages. See also Baker et al. (1992) and Christ et al. (1991), Norris-Shortle et al. (1993), and Siegel et al. (1990) on childhood bereavement. Ryan-Wenger (1992) reviewed studies on children's strategies for coping with stress and located 15 ego-related strategies. Other references on assessment and treatment of children include Coker and Thyer (1990), Connors et al. (1997), Freeman and Dyer (1993), Kates et al. (1991), Loewenstein (1995), and Lucco (1991). Jackson (1995) discusses the importance of assessing preadolescent suicide. Muir and Thorlaksdottir (1994) describe interventions with mothers and children in day care.

47. Lucille Austin (1948) introduced this term to casework. Blanck and Blanck (1979) refer to the *reparative* experience: The therapist provides a therapeutic "climate" for the patient that fosters ego building and healthy development.

CHAPTER 3

EXAMPLES OF CLINICAL SOCIAL WORK PRACTICE

Before we proceed with further discussion of the principles of psychosocial casework, some case illustrations may be of value in demonstrating the practical use of the concepts presented in the previous chapter. By introducing real case situations now, cases that will be referred to from time to time throughout the text, we hope to provide the basis for a beginning understanding of how the theory guides treatment. The six case examples that follow illustrate situations in which serious breakdowns in social adjustment led the clients to seek or to be referred for clinical social work assistance.

These cases were selected to show competent casework practice and treatment that resulted in significant gains for the clients. Even the most experienced worker sometimes must face the fact that a particular piece of work was not as helpful as hoped. But these cases are representative of many in which workers and clients together are able to ameliorate person–situation disturbances.

Each case illustration includes a discussion of the three interacting factors, discussed in Chapter 2, that contributed to the clients' difficulties: (1) What current life or environmental situations were exerting excessive pressure or failing to provide opportunities necessary for satisfactory client functioning? (2) To what extent did immature or faulty ego-superego functioning and developmental deficits affect the clients' problems? (3) Which ego or superego functions were excessively restrictive or rigid and therefore maladaptive? *Particular attention is given to appraising the clients' personality strengths and environmental supports.*

While studying the case material, it may be helpful for the reader to try to identify the ways in which these factors interacted to affect the clients and their problems: Specifically, how did casework intervention help to shift the balance of forces within the individual or family, or between the personality of the individual and the pressures from the environmental or interpersonal situation? Was the change in balance achieved by strengthening or modifiying a specific aspect of the person–situation configuration, or did treatment address all three contributing factors? On the basis of the preliminary discussion in Chapter 2 of treatment procedures or techniques (further elaborated upon in Chapters 4 through 8), what interventions did the worker choose and why?

In general, the quality of the *relationship between worker and client* is seen by psychosocial caseworkers as crucial to the effectiveness of treatment. Basic to a good therapeutic alliance is the positive attitude of the worker toward the client. In these case presentations, attention is given to the treatment relationship and how it varies according to the needs and personalities of the clients. Occasional mention is made of the concept of *transference*. This phenomenon will be examined in greater detail in Chapter 9; suffice it to say for now that when we use this term here we are referring to feelings and attitudes (positive or negative) that the client brings to the worker from other (often early family) experiences in relationships. When the client develops a strong positive transference to the worker, trust and treatment are often enhanced, providing the client with temporary supports needed to mobilize inner and outer resources sufficiently to cope with or resolve difficulties. On the other hand, negative transference reactions, when discussed openly, can be important in helping a client develop self-understanding. As the reader will see, for some clients, transference reactions have little bearing on treatment; this is true when the worker is viewed for the most part realistically: primarily as an expert in treating problems of social functioning.

Psychosocial clinicians believe that choices about the nature, focus, and length of therapy should be made on the basis of clients' needs or goals and the worker's assessment. Ideally, agency or other constraints (imposed by managed care organizations, governmental programs, etc.) should not determine the direction the work takes or the number of sessions required to achieve satisfactory results. From our point of view, it behooves all social workers to advocate on every possible front for the availability of quality services based on *need* for service, rather than on cost-saving or bureaucratic policies. We discuss these issues in greater detail in Chapter 18.

As we shall see, for some difficulties, long-term treatment may be the only means of ameliorating distress. But often, with relatively little help, clients may quickly see their present situation in a new light and then take steps toward improvement; the cases of the Chin couple and of Joan in Chapter 2 illustrate this point. Modifications in the environment can also tip the balance of forces, resulting in emotional or behavioral changes. In a brief period, clients themselves often discover they can adjust their reactions or behavior or can change their environment, or both. In these cases, there may be no need to explore longstanding patterns of behavior or the roots of the difficulties. Often enough, after a period of exploration and brief treatment, clients and workers agree that significant gains have been made and that therapy can be terminated, at least for the time being; when possible, the door is often left open for the client to return to consider new issues or to further consolidate the gains made in treatment.[1]

The case illustrations that follow have been arranged on a continuum according to the length of treatment; the first cases describe successful brief therapies, followed by examples of longer-term work that was required because of complicated situational pressures and/or the need for fundamental psychological change.

THOUGHTS OF SUICIDE

Mrs. Perez* (who indicated in the first session she preferred to be called Esperanza), age 40, was referred by a friend to a male social worker of Puerto Rican descent employed at a mental health clinic. With intense emotion conveying a sense of urgency, she immediately and forthrightly explained that she wanted help because she was very depressed and had persistent, uninvited thoughts about jumping from the window of a tall building. She also felt anxious constantly, did not sleep well, had lost her former sense of fun, took no pleasure in her family life, and could not concentrate well at work; on top of everything else, she was afraid she might lose her job. She worked as a clerk at a law office in a high-rise building; it was there especially that she found herself preoccupied with ideas about jumping. She had always been a rather "nervous" person, but she had never been this depressed in her life; she could not understand her present condition. In answer to the worker's question, she said that she never before had even a thought about killing herself. Although it was not yet clear to the worker just what she meant, she added that she was feeling isolated and humiliated.

Esperanza reported that she had recently seen another therapist for four sessions, a Latino woman whom she liked very much; however, she complained, the therapist tried to persuade her that her difficulties stemmed from "unconscious anger at my mother." In response to the worker's inquiries, she said she had not felt any sus-

tained anger at her mother and, anyway, she could not understand what anger at her mother had to do with her present misery.

The worker asked the distraught woman what she thought had led up to her present unhappiness. "What has happened recently?" he asked. Haltingly and tearfully, yet making every effort to think about this question, Esperanza described several events of the past year. She gave birth to her second daughter ten months ago. (Her other daughter just turned nine; Esperanza recently had her 10-year wedding anniversary.) During her pregnancy, her mother, who lived nearby, had suffered a severe depression that required an extended hospitalization. As the youngest of two daughters of a traditional Ecuadorean family, she was expected to take major responsibility for her mother. Several weeks after her mother was in the hospital, while preparing to do laundry at home, Esperanza accidently found a love letter written to her husband, Juan, by one of his co-workers; from what she read, it was apparent that they were having an affair. Never before had she suspected him of being unfaithful; when she confronted him, he denied any sexual involvement with the woman who wrote the letter.

Esperanza said it was at this point that the depression began to come over her. About two months after the birth of her child, her friendship with a lawyer at work evolved into a sexual relationship. Over the three months that she was seeing this man, she realized that she was being driven by feelings of revenge toward her husband, not by loving feelings for her co-worker; yet, the affair had provided a temporary respite from depression. One day, her lover told her he was worried she might give him a sexually transmitted disease. Esperanza was crushed by this remark and ended the affair. Feelings of despair and shame became unbearable. After this, about two months

---

*All case material in this book is disguised, and fictitious names are used throughout.

before seeing the present social worker, she thought more and more about killing herself and sought help from the first therapist.

Esperanza showed some signs of relief after detailing, with much feeling, the events of the past year. She appeared to be reassured by the worker's understanding comments as she spoke, particularly when he said it seemed to him that she had gone through an awful lot of difficult situations, many of which had been out of her control. He summarized the series of circumstances: the pregnancy, her mother's depression, her sense of responsibility for her mother, her husband's affair, her daughter's birth, her own sexual relationship at work, and the humiliating remark made by her lover. Almost anyone would be affected by such a stressful string of events, he said. At this point, Esperanza confided that she thought she must be going "crazy" to feel so bad and to have such thoughts. "What's happening to you has nothing to do with being 'crazy,'" the worker assured her. "It has to do with you being overwhelmed and depressed."

Esperanza asked the worker whether he thought anger at her mother had anything to do with her problem. He said it seemed to him that, with or without anger at her mother, she had plenty of reasons for feeling upset; from his point of view, only she could know for sure what her feelings toward her mother really were. Being given this "permission" to rely on her own feelings and beliefs—rather than on anyone else's—seemed to unburden her further. Probably, the worker sensed, it helped her to feel more in control when so much had happened that had made her feel powerless. The worker thought to himself he saw some very hopeful signs: Esperanza related quickly to the worker; she was motivated to try to figure herself out in order to feel better; she was able to get emotional relief

from expressing her many feelings about the facts of her recent life; she got immediate benefit from the worker's understanding and his belief that the cumulative effects of the stresses in her life surely would be difficult for anyone; and she could accept reassurance that she was not "crazy," which she clearly was not.

Nevertheless, before ending the first meeting, in a sensitive but direct manner the worker asked Esperanza some questions about her suicidal thoughts. First, he said he wanted her to think carefully before answering: Did she think she would actually take her own life? "I know I wouldn't do that. I just don't want to even *think* about jumping any more," she thoughtfully replied. "I could not do that to my children or my mother." The worker asked: "How big a part of *you* wants to end your life now— aside from the effects on your family?" Weeping gently, Esperanza answered: "I want to live." The worker's belief that she was not truly suicidal seemed confirmed, but he was taking no chances: "I definitely hear that you have too much good in your life to cut it short. But, *if* by any chance you find yourself thinking that you might do something hurtful to yourself, will you call me?" Esperanza's promise to do so seemed genuine. "I feel more hope already," she added. The worker shared with her some of the strengths he had observed; these, he said, made her chances of feeling better look good. For the first time, the worker saw this woman truly smile. They made an appointment for three days away, a plan that clearly pleased her. She said she looked forward to coming back. The worker suggested that at the next meeting they could discuss the possibility of her seeing a psychopharmacologist for medication that might ease her symptoms. Although the worker was not seriously alarmed about what she might do to herself, he was glad that he introduced an informal "contract" with her to contact him if she experienced self-destructive impulses.

Had the worker thought that this client's life was at risk, he would have made an immediate referral for psychiatric consultation. However, Esperanza was straightforward, expressive, and capable of self-awareness; his initial assessment led him to believe that essentially she had good reality-testing as well as other well-developed ego functions, even though she may not have exercised the best judgment by becoming involved in an apparently empty and ultimately painful affair. Of utmost importance when it comes to suicidal thoughts is the assessment of impulse control, which, in general, Esperanza seemed to have. From her reactions to their first meeting, she demonstrated rather remarkable flexibility and balance. She was looking to the future. He felt confident that she was not in immediate danger.[2] Furthermore, whatever fears she had been harboring about going "crazy" (which she said she had never shared with her previous therapist) might be reinforced if he urged her to see a psychiatrist right away. It was also important for her, the worker believed, to have a say about the referral for medication; the more control she regained, the stronger she would feel, he was certain.

Esperanza returned saying she was very much relieved that her depression had a reasonable explanation, based on the many unhappy things that had happened to her. Without the worker asking, she said that even though she was feeling better, she wanted to try medication if there was a chance (the worker could not promise) that it would help her feel less depressed.

For the next eight weeks, Esperanza and the worker met weekly. Without a doubt, within about two weeks, the medication relieved her depression considerably. However, in the worker's opinion, drugs alone would not have sufficed.[3] A strong working alliance was quickly built between Esperanza and the worker in which, together, they methodically reviewed the events of the previous year, examining the meaning each had in her life. Without much discussion of her relationship with her mother, it was clear that she was feeling less pressured by her mother's needs; she was able to be helpful to her without experiencing the heavy burden she had previously felt. It was disappointing to her that she had found it hard to enjoy her infant daughter, but she accepted the fact that she had been very preoccupied during the pregnancy and after the birth. She said she could forgive herself and looked forward to many good times with both daughters. Some of her guilt about her retaliatory affair lingered but was greatly reduced by her ability to understand that she had simply found "the wrong way" to try to take care of her heartbreak and anger about her husband's unfaithfulness. She became proud that at least *she* ended her affair; she was able to recognize that the comment made by the man she became involved with had nothing to do with her and, therefore, was no cause for shame or humiliation.

Esperanza grew to think that much of her desperation stemmed from her relationship with her husband; in many ways they were strangers. Perhaps, she realized, he had the affair because he, too, felt isolated; that thought helped her feel more sympathy for him than she had. She definitely would not leave her marriage; she really loved Juan, she said. Apparently, he was no longer involved with his former lover, but the marriage was still distant. She and the worker discussed some ways she might open up conversations with her husband. At the worker's suggestion, Esperanza told her husband she was talking with a social worker and invited him to join her; he was a "proud man," she said, and could not bring himself to come with her, but he seemed pleased that she wanted to improve their relationship. In a short time, Esperanza's efforts to get closer to him and to talk more were succeeding, she said; she no longer felt so lonely and estranged and he seemed happier, but she knew she had to keep working at it.

In view of her steady improvement, it was no surprise to the worker that after 10 sessions, Esperanza said she felt very much better; she was hardly depressed. She had learned a lot in a short time, she gratefully told the worker. She told him she knew she couldn't have made so much progress without him. Although she was a little concerned about not having the worker to talk things over with, she decided to discontinue weekly meetings, at least for now. She would continue taking medication and seeing the psychopharmacologist (with whom the worker worked closely) once every six weeks. Throughout this termination discussion, client and worker reviewed in detail the changes she had made. The worker gave her much credit for the work she had done; he reiterated the many strengths they both learned she had, strengths that would surely help her through new developments in her life.

The worker's confidence in Esperanza and the hopeful, caring attitudes he conveyed were undoubtedly essential in this brief, successful treatment. His willingness to listen and understand expressions of strong emotion had a healing effect. Her mother's illness and consequent demands and the distance in her marriage had left her without strong emotional supports; now that both of these relationships had improved, the connection to the worker was less vital. Certainly, the transference was a very positive one; without her capacity to readily trust the worker, the therapy would

not have been so successful. She was not unduly dependent, however; she was now able to call upon her characteristic self-reliance and decide to "go it alone," with the understanding that she was welcome to return if she felt the need.

In this case, the pressures faced by Esperanza had compounded to overwhelm her. Without major emotional supports, her judgment may have failed her briefly but, generally speaking, ego and superego functions were neither underdeveloped nor rigid. Because she was so able to benefit from reflecting on her current situation, the nature of her reactions and behaviors, and changes she could make, there was almost no need to explore long-standing emotional or behavioral patterns; developmental influences (other than occasional references to cultural expectations) were barely mentioned. She discovered that changes she initiated resulted in significant improvement in her marriage. Her many strengths were mobilized, effecting gratifying changes in her emotional and situational life. In fact, from the psychopharmacologist and a call from Esperanza herself, six months after treatment ended, the worker learned that she was doing well and coping with new challenges as they arose.

A MARITAL CRISIS

The case of Dick and Susan Jones illustrates how clinical social work can sometimes help clients bring about substantial changes very quickly. The worker's understanding of individual and interpersonal dynamics and the couple's motivation for change led to an improved marital relationship in 11 joint therapy sessions held over three months.

Susan Jones, age 30, telephoned a family service agency stating that her marriage of seven years was at the "crossroads." She was afraid of her husband, who, she said, had become an "angry man." They were arguing constantly. Although reluctantly, her husband Dick, age 32, was willing to participate in marital counseling.

During the first meeting, the caseworker learned that the open conflict was precipitated a month earlier when Dick discovered that Susan was having an affair with her boss. Although the very short affair ended before marital therapy began, Dick was still enraged, distrustful, and frightened that he would lose Susan, despite Susan's reassurances that she wanted their marriage to work. They reported that they had considered terminating the marriage, but they wanted to keep the family together for the sake of their three "delightful" and "normal" children: Charles, age six, and twins Ann and Andy, age five.

Both Dick and Susan were from large, stable, two-parent working-class families. Dick's parents were characterized as more rigid and emotionally aloof than Susan's, whom they portrayed as warmer and more communicative. Although Dick was black and Protestant and Susan was white and Jewish, neither of their families had strongly disapproved of their courtship and marriage. Both sets of grandparents enjoyed their grandchildren and visited with the Joneses quite regularly; they were close but not intrusive and good in-law relationships had been established early in the marriage.

Since high school graduation, Dick had worked for the electric company as a mechanic. Susan worked for several years before her marriage and, a year before her affair, had taken a secretarial job. Although the extra income was important, Susan's motivation to work again was in large part based on feeling trapped, bored, and isolated from adults when she was at home all day with the children. They lived in a rural area with very few opportunities for casual socializing, and Susan was afraid of becoming "nothing more than a housewife"; she spoke of needing to find her own "identity." Since Dick worked the evening shift, he had agreed to take on many of the child care and household functions. Although the division of roles was worked out comfortably between them, as treatment progressed, it became clear that he had been afraid from the beginning that Susan would find the outside world so attractive she would lose interest in him and in their home. He did not, however, resent sharing the duties (he even took pride in their vegetable garden and in doing canning and preserving), and he knew that she, like he, thoroughly enjoyed the children.

Neither Dick nor Susan evidenced severe personality difficulties. However, although Dick was conscientious in work, fond of his home, and caring in his relationships with the children, he tended to be passive and emotionally remote with Susan; generally, he let her take the lead. Susan, on the other hand, was a more expressive person who in many ways had been the pursuer of the relationship with her husband. Nevertheless, over the years she had not confronted Dick with her disappointment about the fact that he rarely initiated affectionate moments or sexual relations between them. By the same token, she had not encouraged him to share his dissatisfactions with her. Instead, she slowly but steadily began to withdraw. Although aware of the distance that was developing between them, Dick, too, took no steps to rekindle the intimacy they had enjoyed early in marriage. When Susan went back to work, she was flattered by her employer's attentions and briefly, albeit guiltily, yielded to them. Her remorse, she said, would not have allowed the affair to continue very long even if Dick had not discovered it.

Although it was Susan who initiated treatment, Dick joined the first session with more apparent motivation for self-understanding than she did. He was concerned about his inability to control his temper since discovering Susan's unfaithfulness to him; he found himself shouting at her on the slightest provocation. Furthermore, he disliked his distrust of Susan when his "reasonable mind" believed the affair was over. He said he wanted to make changes in himself and recognized that these would be important to the marriage. Susan, on the other hand, insisted that now that she was no longer involved with her boss, the rest of the problem was up to Dick. She had tried over the years to bring excitement to their life together, but nothing "set a fire under Dick." Contrary to Susan's expectations, however, Dick was quickly able to recognize the roots of the passivity about which she complained. As the youngest of seven children, with four older sisters who catered to him and yet dominated him, he had little chance to take the initiative in his relationship with them. He began to understand how he had carried this pattern of unassertiveness to his marriage.

By the third session, they were arguing less. Dick recognized that his anger had been in reaction to the blow to his self-respect and his feelings of helplessness in the face of Susan's betrayal. Tentatively at first, he began to take the initiative in moving closer to Susan. Now it was Susan who maintained an aloof reserve; she was barely responsive to Dick. At first she explained this by saying that she was still afraid of his temper and felt safer at arm's length from him. As the worker pressed her to explore her feelings further, Susan acknowledged that because she had been angry with Dick for such a long time she now felt like "giving him a taste of his own medicine." Beyond that, and more to the point in the long run, she was keeping her tender feelings for him in check for fear that she would "fall" for his overtures, after which

she expected he would revert to his remote and passive ways. Fortunately, Dick was not deterred and continued to risk being affectionate and open with Susan, with the result that Susan recognized the need to examine her own reactions.

As Susan developed greater awareness of the part she played in the problem, she explored some of the roots of her behavior. She was the second of four daughters and believed that her father preferred her older sister, Anita. As hard as Susan tried to please him, her father always seemed to find Anita smarter, prettier, and more talented than she. When she realized that much of her current resignation and anger at Dick were displaced feelings about her father, she began to take the chance and accept the changes Dick was making. Within a few weeks, their relationship grew warmer and more trusting, more like it used to be, they both said.

When treatment began, the caseworker and the couple had "contracted" for 10 sessions with the understanding that the therapy could be extended, if necessary, after an evaluation at that time. During the 10th session they reported that they were feeling much more hopeful about their marriage, and both Dick and Susan had maintained an awareness of how each had participated in bringing about the crisis that had developed between them. They rarely resorted to blaming each other, but each took responsibility for working to make the relationship better. They decided to come for a final, 11th meeting in which they were able to summarize and reinforce the good work they had done. Almost a year later they sent a Christmas card to the caseworker on which Susan wrote, "We are recommending marriage counseling to all our friends! We learned a lot and everything is going well."

What were the factors that contributed to threatening this marriage? In most respects,

Dick and Susan were psychologically healthy. Yet both brought to their relationship some unresolved emotional issues and personality features that played into the difficulties. Dick's lack of assertiveness in personal relationships was, in part, derived from his childhood experiences with his older sisters who were managerial and indulgent. Since they had expected little in return for their love—except compliance—Dick did not learn well enough how to take the initiative to get what he wanted when it was not naturally forthcoming. Also, he was not used to expressing openly his deeper feelings about anything. Therefore, when faced with the threat of losing Susan, he withdrew, feeling helpless and angry. Susan, for different reasons, also tended to despair in the face of withdrawn affection; since she felt she had never been fully appreciated and loved by her father, even though she came from a warm, essentially nurturing family, she could easily lose hope about ever having a man who truly treasured her.

In this case, some unfulfilled childhood needs and ego weaknesses interfered with adult adjustment. However, for both Dick and Susan, the damage was not pervasive and the deficiencies were less disabling than they are for many clients. In this marriage, each partner was able to bring good reality testing and an "observing ego" (objective self-awareness) to the situation; both had the capacity to reflect on the aspects of their own personalities that led to the difficulties. They both functioned well in most areas, were able to take pride in their accomplishments, and were capable of enjoying life. Each was able to be empathic. Dick had the capacity to understand how his passivity had contributed to Susan's sense of isolation and subsequent willingness to engage in an extramarital affair. Because he was determined to save the marriage, he quickly learned to take initiative. Susan's

sense of values (ego ideal and superego) helped her to recognize that her sexual relationship with her boss was no solution to her problems; her capacity for reality testing enabled her to understand that unless they worked on their marriage it would continue to deteriorate. She realized that by withdrawing from Dick she, too, had taken a passive role in the marital interaction.

The marital problems that the Jones couple experienced were not simply a product of the weaknesses of each. In interaction with one another, their separate vulnerabilities were aggravated and reinforced, resulting—as often occurs in marital and family relationships—in a sort of negative complementarity. As discussed in Chapter 2, one primary characteristic of a system is that the parts transact: acting and reacting one upon the other. The marital treatment, therefore, focused not only on the personalities of each partner, but also on the reciprocal dynamics, the circular interactions, between Dick and Susan. As their actions and reactions changed, the climate of the relationship improved and the unhappiness each was experiencing was alleviated. Because each brought many strengths, and because the marriage had been gratifying earlier, it took relatively little work or time to resume a positive balance and achieve renewed satisfaction.[4]

The therapeutic relationship was important in that the worker's competence, objectivity, and wish to help enabled Dick and Susan to trust her and reveal themselves. But, in contrast to many clinical cases, the worker did not need to make extensive use of supportive or sustaining procedures. Relatively little time was required for ventilation of feeling. The transference aspects of the treatment were negligible; primarily, the worker helped Dick and Susan to reflect on their situation, on their patterns of interaction, and on some aspects of their past lives that contributed to their marital problems. Once they understood the dynamics, between sessions they were able to bring about many improvements in their situation.

Although of relatively minor importance, it is worth noting that environmental influences, beyond those of the marital system itself, played a part in this couple's situation. In a general atmosphere in which women's issues were coming to the forefront, in which many women were pressing for equality at home and in the workplace and advocating greater assertiveness, Susan's eagerness to have a life outside her home was supported. Unlike many marital pairs, Dick and Susan had the flexibility to redefine "male" and "female" roles to accommodate Susan's wish. Also, again in contrast to many other couples, the Joneses had a supportive extended family network in which the in-laws showed interest but did not interfere or take sides. This was especially impressive since the marriage was interracial. With a minimum of outside pressure, efforts to resolve the marital difficulties were enhanced.

SOME PROBLEMS OF AGING[5]

Clients often come to social workers at a time of crisis: when there has been an illness, the loss of a loved one, a change in employment or financial circumstances, or when new living arrangements are needed. Sometimes, as in the Jones case, a crisis occurs in reaction to a problem that has erupted in a family relationship. Any of these events can affect a person's self-esteem or sense of well-being. For the aged, who constitute a greater proportion of our population than ever before, disruptions in their lives are practically inevitable. It is often at these times that casework intervention is sought.

The needs of older people have much in common with those of every age group. For the elderly as well as for the young, certain essentials are required in order to live with full dignity: an acceptable home, economic security, social status and recognition, a meaningful purpose in life. As difficult as it is for many people of all ages to fulfill the conditions necessary for optimum adjustment, the aged often have the hardest time of all.

Sometimes, when working with aged clients, there is a tendency to think in terms of "limited goals." In some cases where there has been extreme physical or mental deterioration, the caseworker's efforts may have to be circumscribed. But there are large numbers of older people, starting with those in their 60s, who may have 10, 20, or even 30 fulfilling years ahead of them. For clients in this group, substantial gains are often possible. In the case illustration that follows, the aim of therapy was to help the client, Mr. Kennedy, to reduce the impact of changes in his circumstances and to aid him to find satisfactory replacements for several losses he had endured. Had the young caseworker viewed Mr. Kennedy solely as an old man whose best years were behind him, she would have overlooked the possibilities for helping him as she did, in which case her client might well have rapidly declined into a state of hopelessness, poor health, and dependency.

Miss Kennedy, age 27, was referred by her psychiatrist to the geriatric service of an outpatient mental health clinic; she was seeking help for her 67-year-old father. An elementary school teacher, she had lived with her father until recently. Her mother had died of alcoholism 13 years before. Mr. Kennedy, a construction worker, had been retired for two years and was maintaining himself with social security benefits and odd jobs as a handyman. His daughter portrayed him as a man who had always been active and an independent thinker; for many years he was an officer in his union local. He had lived in his neighborhood for 30 years, was well known, and was considered something of a "street-corner politician," devoting much time to agitating for social causes.

Six months earlier, Miss Kennedy had moved to an apartment of her own, against her father's wishes. Since then Mr. Kennedy had become depressed and had given up his part-time work. He was blaming his daughter for leaving him alone in the apartment they had shared, with the entire rent to pay. He had two sons who lived at a distance and from whom, for all intents and purposes, he was estranged. Miss Kennedy said he had always been domineering and possessive of her. Leaving him had not been easy, but she felt she had to take this step for the sake of her own "sanity." She knew that if she stayed, her father would interfere in her relationship with a man in whom she was interested. She felt guilty when he accused her of betraying him; she confided that sometimes she wet her bed after an explosive argument with him.

The worker explored the possibility of joint meetings between father and daughter, but Miss Kennedy adamantly refused. She further indicated that her psychiatrist, with whom she was in intensive treatment, had encouraged her to minimize her contacts with her father at this time. Since Miss Kennedy's therapy was expensive, she was not in a position to offer her father much financial help, even though she had recently given him a little money after he angrily demanded it. Miss Kennedy had spoken with her father about the clinic and believed he would be willing to meet with the worker, but she herself preferred no further involvement.

Even before contacting him, the worker began thinking about Mr. Kennedy. With the incomplete information she had, she made some tentative efforts to understand and "feel with" her new client and to get a sense of his current predicament.[6] Assumptions and predictions based on anticipatory preparation are always subject to revision. Nevertheless, she considered possible aspects of his objective and subjective situation: He is probably worried about money, she thought. Apparently he had been very dependent on his daughter for emotional as well as financial support, so it seemed likely that he would now feel profoundly bereft. She anticipated meeting a man who was not only lonely, but also very frightened, angry, and depressed. He might have little motivation at this point to help or take care of himself; if this turned out to be true, the worker imagined that he might require considerable support and encouragement. Yet, he was described as a man who always did things "his way," so Mr. Kennedy would probably need reassurance that he would be in charge of whatever decisions were made. She also wondered how he would respond to a woman worker about the same age as his daughter. Would he transfer his anger onto the worker? Would he want to cling? Or would it be comforting for him to work with a young woman? Finally, the worker reflected on some of her own reactions that might be provoked by Mr. Kennedy and his situation. She had a recently widowed father who was finding it difficult to adjust; she realized she would have to guard against identifying too closely with Miss Kennedy and against becoming countertherapeutically reactive to Mr. Kennedy's possible dependency.

When the worker telephoned Mr. Kennedy, he readily agreed to come in to speak with her. He spent much of the first session berating his mother (who had left his father when he was a child); his wife, who had been a heavy drinker for many years; the Catholic Church, toward which he felt very bitter for various reasons; and, above all, his daughter. They had all mistreated him—"a good man"—and, in his view, the result would be an "early grave" for him. He had loved and cherished his daughter, he said, and now she was treating him like this: leaving him sick and penniless. He did not care whether he ate or worked. Actually his physical health was good, but he felt ill and listless. If only his daughter could come back to share the rent and keep him company, he was sure he would be all right again. Nothing else would help.

Without exploring alternatives at first, the worker recognized his loneliness and made evident her interest in helping. She expressed understanding of how difficult the recent changes had been for him. She voiced her confidence that, together, they might be able to find some answers.

Fortunately, Mr. Kennedy took to the worker quickly, and there were several long interviews within a period of a month. They began to talk over steps he might take to improve his situation. Usually the worker followed the client's lead, but occasionally she offered some suggestions of her own. Gradually but consistently, Mr. Kennedy's feelings of hopelessness diffused and he began taking on new or renewed interests: He became attached to a puppy a neighbor gave him and took it with him everywhere he went. He solved a complex oil burner problem for his landlord for which he was paid. He began visiting with friends again. He resumed his interest in political affairs. Sometimes between meetings he would call the worker and tell her about the things he was doing.

It is important to note that in an early session with Mr. Kennedy, the worker (who was placed as a graduate student at the clinic) informed him that they would be working together for only a three-month period, after which she would be leaving the service. In view of Mr. Kennedy's strong reaction to losing the companionship of his daughter, it was especially important for the worker to give him as much advance notice of her plans as possible. She also reassured him that, if necessary, another worker (her supervisor) would be available to him after she left. Initially annoyed and unsettled by the worker's impending departure, he nevertheless was able to talk about his feelings easily; he asked about her plans, some of which she explained to him. He said he thought it was good that she was "bettering herself" by getting more training and added that he was proud his daughter had gotten a better education than either he or his wife had had.

Often an important indicator of a client's strengths (or weaknesses) can be found in the quality of the therapeutic relationship he or she is able to establish. The basic soundness of the personalities of Dick and Susan Jones was evidenced by the way they realistically related to their caseworker and quickly utilized her expertise to help them resolve their difficulties. Mr. Kennedy, who was feeling so bereft, needed the worker temporarily to fill a place that his daughter had left by moving out. By keeping in close touch with the worker, he was able to find the help his daughter no longer provided; he could become dependent (although certainly not blindly compliant!) until he was able to remobilize his own inner resources. Another area of strength was perceived immediately by the worker: Although he was clearly depressed and shaken, in the first meeting he had come in fighting; he was neither withdrawn nor totally dispirited. With the worker's help, Mr. Kennedy was able to redirect his belligerent energies and utilize them in the service of more satisfying ends.

In their next-to-last session, the worker asked her supervisor, who would be the new worker available to Mr. Kennedy, to join them. While talking over his situation, the supervisor offered information about a nearby apartment building in need of a superintendent. He applied immediately and was accepted; in return for services, he was given a rent-free apartment. On several counts, it was fortunate that the agency could direct him to this opportunity. Since it was the supervisor who gave him the information, the transition to the new worker was facilitated. Furthermore, since one of the most profound but frequent insults to the aged is the loss of feelings of usefulness and respect, the job reestablished these. Also highly important was the financial relief the job provided.

In the final meeting with the worker, Mr. Kennedy reported that his daughter was planning marriage, adding, "It's about time!" He was able to say that it had meant a lot to have someone to talk to, but that he was doing much better now. He wasn't sure he would need frequent appointments any more, but he liked the supervisor and would keep in touch with her. He concluded by wishing the worker good luck in her career and, interestingly, advised her to get married and have children because he was sure she would make a good mother! Before the worker left, Miss Kennedy telephoned to thank her and say that, although she still felt guilty about leaving her father, he was no longer blaming her. He seemed more like his "old self" again.

With older clients, as with every client, it is important to take an individualized approach. One cannot generalize about "good planning." In this case, the worker was optimally helpful because she assessed the family situation, Mr. Kennedy's many strengths, and the resources available to him. For example, by knowing even as little

as she did about Miss Kennedy's complicated involvement with her father, it was evident that he (unlike some elderly clients) would not be able to solve his problem by living with her. Eventually, the worker realized, he would have to accept this. Also, it was clear that Mr. Kennedy was not a man for whom hobbies, or many of the activities provided by the local senior citizens center, would have sufficed; he would have seen them as "busy work," an indication of his loss of status. What he needed was the very personal interest of the worker and an opportunity to feel purposeful and economically secure.

The effect of the worker–client relationship was by no means the only dynamic in treatment but, temporarily, it played a large part. This worker was really "there" for Mr. Kennedy when he was feeling rejected and needed someone to understand. The fact that it was a warm, yet very professional, relationship permitted the remarkably easy shift to the new worker.

Some people might refer to this kind of treatment as a "transference cure." When a strong therapeutic relationship is used to make suggestions as a way of directly removing symptomatic behavior, it is extremely likely that a new symptom will arise. It may even be a more harmful symptom than the one originally "chosen" by the client. If, however, the transference relationship is used to remove or lessen the effect of the factors contributing to distress, as it was for Mr. Kennedy, it is entirely different. By design, the worker gave him practically no advice; had the worker used her influence directly to induce her client to make specific choices, this would have been "symptomatic" treatment. Very likely the improvement would then have been only temporary; experience would lead us to believe that when the worker left the clinic, he might have reverted to looking to his daughter to provide emotional supplies, as he had for so many years, and fallen into despair when she refused him. Instead, the relationship with the worker provided Mr. Kennedy with the support he needed to mobilize his many strengths, seek his own solutions, make his own decisions, and benefit from environmental resources and opportunities. In short, in the context of the therapeutic alliance, he regained his capacity for autonomous functioning. He visited the new worker only a few times over a period of months and gains he made were maintained.

Finally, it is important to note that in the treatment of Mr. Kennedy, a principle of economy was followed. That is, although the worker surmised that many of the difficulties he was experiencing had their roots in the traumas of his childhood, or in past family relationships, practically no attention was paid to this material in the actual treatment. His relationship with his daughter, for example, may well have been a reflection of earlier unfilled needs or grief over his unhappy marriage. When viewed in the framework of psychoanalytic theory, it is conceivable that there were unresolved oedipal issues. But, wisely, the worker made no effort to explore these more remote matters when it became clear that positive results could be achieved in the context of the present.

The reader might well ask at this point what the outcome of casework treatment would have been if Mr. Kennedy had been too ill to work or had not had so many well-developed ego functions on which to build. Under such circumstances, would he have been able to regain his self-esteem? Suppose he was forced to accept financial aid or had to be moved to a health-related facility? Many elderly clients face these situations. Sometimes, it is true, solutions are at best compromises. But the case of Mr. Kennedy illustrates the fact that older clients in crisis

are not necessarily on an irreversible downhill road. Even caseworkers can sometimes lose sight of the fact that many aging clients, including some who evidence a degree of physical or mental deterioration, *can* make changes and enjoy a dignified style of life.

A THREE-GENERATION "MULTIPROBLEM" FAMILY

This case and the one to follow illustrate the complexity of skills required for successful intervention in clients' environments. As discussed in Chapter 2, and as illustrated in the case of Mr. Kennedy, assessment of the client's milieu is as essential as evaluation of personality; the "fit" or interface between the two is often the focus of casework attention. Direct work with the environment—with people who are part of the client's world or with people who can be introduced as helpful resources—is part of the total treatment process in many cases. Often a complex blend of environmental activities and direct work with clients is crucial to the success of casework treatment. A worker who fails to apply basic understanding and skills to work in the environment is seriously handicapped in efforts to help clients with intra- or interpersonal problems, as well as with clients who are oppressed by noxious social conditions.

People of all circumstances and class, educational, and ethnic backgrounds can require work with various systems that impinge upon them. The family we will describe now, the Wests, lived in a middle-class suburban community; the parents and grandparents were college-educated and trained for professions; they were white, of English-Scotch origins; their religious affiliation was Episcopalian. As we shall see, the ethnic and socioeconomic circumstances of the next family to be presented, the Stones, were quite different. Yet both families had multiple problems. In this connection, we caution against the lumping together of "multiproblem," "hard-to-reach," and poverty families.[7] These terms do not connote diagnostic entities; valid generalizations cannot be made on the basis of labels about family structure, individual personalities, or sociological characteristics. Many multiproblem families are not poor, many poor are not hard to reach, and many well-to-do families tenaciously resist change.

A 44-year-old widower, Mr. West, living with his ailing mother of 77 and his 14-year-old daughter, applied for help at a community mental health agency. He had been referred by a guidance counselor at the high school because his daughter Ellen was failing her major subjects, skipping school, and associating with a disruptive group of classmates. She had been suspended several times, and the counselor's efforts to guide her had failed. Very early in the initial interview, Mr. West also discussed other problems: He had been depressed since the death of his wife three years before. He was concerned about his pattern of periodic heavy drinking. Employed as an inspector for a government agency where he had worked for 20 years, he was not in jeopardy of losing his job because he could take sick leave when his drinking became incapacitating. Every few months he would sign himself into the hospital to "dry out" and then function well until he started drinking again. A further concern was his mother's rapidly failing health. When his wife died, Mr. West decided to move with Ellen and his son John (at the time of intake living away from home with a friend) into his mother's comfortable home in order to provide supervision and companionship for the children. Since then, however, the elder Mrs. West had become almost blind and hard of hearing, and she had developed a serious heart

condition; her arthritis had become so severe that sometimes she could not walk downstairs without help. She seemed dispirited and hopeless, Mr. West told the worker. For the most part, Ellen fended for herself, and she and her grandmother were more irritating than helpful to one another.

Home visits by the worker and several meetings with all three family members resulted in a group decision to search for a live-in housekeeper. Although there were several reasons for arriving at this plan, the need seemed all the more pressing because Mr. West's work required him to be out many evenings, leaving Ellen and his infirm mother alone. The family income was limited, but as they talked it over with the worker, they realized that by cutting down on certain expenses they could afford a modest wage.

Fortunately, as it turned out, also on the worker's caseload was Mrs. Wilson, a 72-year-old retired domestic worker and food caterer who had recently become depressed after the death of her sister, with whom she had lived for many years. She had considered doing day work but thought this too grueling for her at her age. Yet she was lonely and disliked being idle. When it occurred to the worker that this client also might be helped by taking a job with the West family, she assessed the entire situation *very* carefully. It was important that she consider any aspects that might cause the arrangement to fail. Mrs. Wilson was a capable, dependable person who was interested in other people. At various times she had been active on church service committees, and she had taken care of her ill sister at home for many months before the latter died. She had a sense of humor and seemed to get along with young people, as evidenced by the fact that two teenage great-nieces visited her often. And she had housekeeping skills; she had earned her living in related areas for most of her life. There were no apparent reasons why the West family would not find Mrs. Wilson a very pleasant and suitable housekeeper. The worker's major concern was that Mrs. Wilson, who tended at times to be overaccommodating to others, might feel obliged to take the job even if she did not really want to, either to please the worker or because she would consider it a duty to help people in trouble. Therefore, without any pressure, the worker fully explained the West family situation to her, adding that she might not be interested since the family had many problems. The worker urged Mrs. Wilson not to consider it unless she thought it would be of benefit to her. She assured her that the Wests could find a solution if she was not interested. The worker watched closely for any signs that might betray a negative reaction to the idea. But Mrs. Wilson seemed genuinely enthusiastic and said she wanted to meet the Wests.

(Before sharing information about the family's circumstances and needs with Mrs. Wilson, the worker obtained permission to do so from each member of the West family. It was not necessary to take the same precautions about confidentiality in connection with Mrs. Wilson, because the worker did not reveal to the Wests that she was her client; the worker simply indicated that she could highly recommend Mrs. Wilson. Of course, if *she* wanted to confide that information to the family, there was no reason she should not.)

When they were introduced, Mrs. Wilson liked the West family immediately. She was delighted that the worker had suggested the idea. She agreed to the wage offered since, because of her age, her social security benefits would not be jeopardized. After she left, Ellen, at that time not given to expressing positive feelings about anything, exclaimed: "What a lady!" Mr. West and his mother concurred.

Within a short time, this motherly, very competent woman was able to bring both warmth and organization to the West home. The family was eating regular meals together instead of haphazardly grabbing snacks as they had; Mrs. Wilson was able to enlist Ellen's help with many household tasks too difficult for both older women. Ellen told the worker that she enjoyed coming home from school to the aroma of Mrs. Wilson's cakes and cookies baking in the oven.

The adults, too, seemed heartened to have a home life again. When Mrs. Wilson went home for two days each week, both Ellen and her grandmother were impatient for her return. Mrs. Wilson herself reported that she had gained a "new lease on life" now that she felt needed and her days had a sense of purpose. John, who had moved out of the home a year before, after an angry argument with his father, returned to live in the household. A few family group meetings, which often included Mrs. Wilson, were held with the worker, in which the discussions ranged from practical housekeeping matters, to difficulties that arose among them, to sharing of some intense feelings of grief over the loss of the younger Mrs. West, which had deeply affected all the family members.

The worker arranged for a public health nurse to visit Mr. West's mother twice weekly to give her baths and nursing care. Ellen stopped the truancy and, slowly, her academic work improved. The worker and Ellen met with the high school guidance counselor to make changes Ellen wanted in her course program. Learning that Ellen had an interest in the theater (her mother had been an actress), the worker located a drama class at the YWCA that the girl enjoyed and where she made friends. By the time Mrs. Wilson had been in the home for a year, no significant school problems remained for Ellen; Mrs. West, despite her infirmities, was more cheerful and comfortable; and the sullen, irritable relationships that had characterized the Wests' family life were replaced by greater affection and cooperation among them. Mr. West, however, continued his pattern of excessive, periodic drinking. In between bouts with alcohol, which were a little less frequent but just as intense, he felt better than he had. The family physician, to whom Mr. West turned for hospitalization when his drinking became incapacitating, warned him of the damage he was doing to his body. The worker explored his willingness to join Alcoholics Anonymous, but Mr. West staunchly refused. He disliked the organization's religious emphasis and, even more to the point, he could not bear the humiliation of sharing his private "weakness" with strangers.

Mr. West, who was the only family member who still had regular weekly treatment sessions after the first few months, began to realize that the onset of a period of drinking usually followed a disappointment in a relationship with a woman. For many reasons he had repeatedly failed in his attempts to find a loving sexual companion, and after each letdown he would become depressed and take "one drink," which would start the cycle all over again. A case that had begun with the need for considerable environmental intervention now became one in which direct treatment of Mr. West was the primary focus. Mr. West remained in treatment for a few more months, exploring long-standing emotional patterns and problems, derived from his early life, that related to his drinking and interfered with his developing a satisfying love relationship. When he terminated with the worker, he felt he had made some important changes. Ambivalently, he then decided to join a group for "problem drinkers" (he preferred

this term to "alcoholics") at a nearby clinic that specialized in alcohol-related issues.

As this family's case illustrates, environmental intervention requires skilled and intricate work, coupled with sensitive understanding of individual and family dynamics. An unusual aspect of the case was that while Mrs. Wilson served as a resource for the family, the Wests were an equally important resource for Mrs. Wilson, who no longer required individual treatment after she began to work again. Relatively small adjustments of external conditions triggered significant shifts in the inner lives for all the individuals involved. In addition to relieving some of the acute distress each person had been suffering, treatment in this case certainly served a *preventive* function. There was substantial evidence that, as the quality of life improved for the clients, feelings of well-being, relatedness, and self-esteem were nurtured. Without intervention, these likely would have continued to decline for each individual, as they had before referral to the mental health agency.

A FAMILY IN CRISIS: AGENCIES COLLABORATE TO HELP

In contrast to the West family, the family we present now was African American, originally from the rural South, and had moved to a ghetto neighborhood in a medium-sized northern city six years earlier. None of the adults had completed high school. By tradition, the family members were Baptists. A crucial factor that the two situations had in common, however, was the worker's focus on external conditions and opportunities; once again, the assessment of the environment was as important as the understanding of individual and family dynamics.

Mrs. Stone, a 30-year-old woman receiving public assistance for herself and five children, ranging in age from 14 to 2 years, was reported by a neighbor to child protective services. It was alleged that she was severely beating one of the children with a belt. Although the protective worker investigating the case determined that the report was unfounded, because of the many problems the family was facing, he decided to refer Mrs. Stone to a newly formed, publicly funded family service agency that worked closely with the child welfare department. The oldest child, Doreen, was staying out late at night, was truant from school, and did not help around the house. Of even greater concern to the worker were his observations of Brian, age nine, who appeared withdrawn and depressed; the worker heard this child talk only when he muttered to himself. And, most pressing of all, the protective worker learned that the family was to be evicted because the landlord intended to use their apartment for a member of his own family—his right, according to city law.

The family services worker made a home visit and found Mrs. Stone to be an attractive, intelligent woman who seemed depressed, almost listless. When the worker told Mrs. Stone she knew of the impending eviction and wanted to help, Mrs. Stone hardly responded. She had asked the landlord for time but he was adamant; the city marshal would put the Stones out if they did not move within the next month. Mrs. Stone agreed to allow the worker to speak with the landlord, although neither she nor the worker felt hopeful about influencing him. Mrs. Stone said she felt sure nobody would want to rent to a "welfare family" with five children. Knowing of the acute housing shortage and widespread discrimination in the city, the worker agreed that finding another apartment would be very difficult.

On this first visit, three of the five children were in school. The youngest, Michael, age two, an apparently placid baby, seemed well cared for and healthy. Brian, age nine, was lying in the bedroom staring (vacantly, the worker thought) at the ceiling with his thumb in his mouth. When the worker asked whether Brian was ill, she learned that he was not but that his teacher said he was not learning, even though he was smart. He was not to return to school until he was tested. Describing Brian as a good boy, "quiet and very deep," Mrs. Stone said she did not understand why the teacher was having trouble with him. She was more worried about her oldest child, Doreen, who had a "loud mouth," did not mind, and was always in trouble. As much as she yelled at Doreen, nothing helped.

Most of Mrs. Stone's relatives lived in the south. She had one brother, Robert, age 21, who lived in another part of the city and attended a training program in carpentry. She and Robert were close. Mrs. Stone married when she was 15 and Mr. Stone, the father of the four oldest children, had left the household permanently three years before, after several previous separations. He was a heavy drinker, a sometimes violent man who did not keep in touch with the children or send money to the family. On the other hand, Michael's father visited often and voluntarily contributed to his child's support.

The worker later telephoned the landlord, who maintained he had been more than patient because Mrs. Stone was a "nice woman." But with so many children, she could hardly be called an ideal tenant. Although not totally unsympathetic to the difficulty the family would have finding other housing, he planned to give the apartment to his son, and nothing would change his mind. The worker then called Mr. Beck of the Legal Aid Society, who said that perhaps action could be stalled, but eventually the landlord would be allowed to evict. The lawyer agreed to meet with Mrs. Stone.

The next home visit was scheduled when all of the children would be at home. When the worker arrived, Doreen was just leaving after a screaming exchange with her mother. Quietly, but angrily, Mrs. Stone said, "Sometimes I could kill her." Raymond, age 12, and Cynthia, age 6, were playing good-humoredly. Pointing to Raymond, Mrs. Stone said bitterly, "That's the one I was accused of beating." The worker said she could understand how upsetting it was to have been investigated. Mrs. Stone did not know who to be madder at, the person who had lied about her or the man who came to the house to "snoop." As she listened, the worker realized that it might take time for this client to trust her too.

Mr. Beck, the lawyer, was able to get a 45-day extension from the court to give the family time to find housing. Mrs. Stone spoke to her minister, who headed the Housing Action Council, a grassroots group that worked for tenants' rights, but he was unable to find a suitable apartment. Those that were available were in deplorable condition. The worker met with the welfare housing consultant, who had little to offer but his pessimism. After exerting considerable pressure on the welfare commissioner's office, the supervisor got "broker's approval," which meant that Mrs. Stone was authorized to pay a Realtor fee to locate an apartment.

Appearing unexpectedly at the family service agency late one afternoon, Mrs. Stone, close to tears, told the worker that the psychologist from the Board of Education thought Brian should go into the hospital. The more she talked, the angrier she became. She asked whether anything could be done. The worker, who had immediately sensed that Brian was emotionally disturbed, realized that Mrs. Stone was still determined to believe her child was not in trouble. While the mother was there the worker telephoned the psychologist, who

told her that Brian's intelligence was above average, but that he was severely emotionally damaged; the boy was hallucinating and his fantasies were filled with violence. He had witnessed his father's brutally attacking his mother when he was six. The psychiatrist, who had also seen Brian, was strongly recommending hospitalization for observation; even long-term inpatient treatment might be necessary.

Mrs. Stone was furious, insisting, "He's *not* crazy." The supervisor, whom the worker had asked to sit in, pointed out that if, after observation, it was believed that Brian was not in danger of hurting himself or anyone else, by law he could not be kept in the hospital without Mrs. Stone's consent. Noting that the mother was listening now and not arguing, the supervisor added that since the psychologist seemed worried about Brian it might be best to have him checked and settle the matter one way or the other. When Mrs. Stone asked whether she had a choice, the supervisor admitted that she was not sure but told Mrs. Stone she could ask.

Reluctantly, Mrs. Stone allowed Brian to be admitted to the children's psychiatric unit of the city hospital. After three weeks, the doctor told her that the boy was definitely not suited for a regular classroom or even for a class for the emotionally disturbed within the school system. He was not likely, however, to be destructive to himself or others. Angrily, Mrs. Stone retorted that she could have told him that. Later, after talking with the hospital psychiatrist, the worker, at the suggestion of her supervisor, told Mrs. Stone about a new special day school program for children diagnosed as having a psychotic disorder, administered by the state hospital. Although the psychiatrist had recommended further hospitalization, he, too, was aware of how strongly Mrs. Stone opposed this. Also,

Brian wanted to go home. The referral to the day school was made and, fortunately, Brian was accepted almost immediately.

Two days before the stay of eviction had expired, Mrs. Stone had not yet found an apartment. She pleaded with the worker to help. The supervisor had a good working relationship with the city marshal and was able to persuade him to delay the final action, but only for a few days. The following afternoon, Mrs. Stone, who had been following every lead, located a large, attractive apartment in a two-family brownstone. The rent, however, was $100 over the amount allowed by the Welfare Department's regulations, and efforts by the supervisor to secure an "exception" from the commissioner's office met with failure. From the lawyer, Mr. Beck, Mrs. Stone learned that she had a right to a fair hearing from the state to determine whether the rent guidelines could be exceeded, and a petition was filed for a state review. The lawyer also filed for another stay of eviction. Mrs. Stone was aware, however, that these processes would take time, and that the particular apartment she had found surely would be rented before the decisions were handed down.

The next morning Mrs. Stone and her brother Robert, whom the worker had not met before, were waiting at the family services office when the worker arrived. Robert, it turned out, had agreed to move with his sister to the new apartment if they could get approval for having his contribution cover the excess rent. After a series of calls to the welfare office, the worker was able to get this plan accepted. Robert said he was looking forward to living with his sister and helping to fix up the new apartment. Mrs. Stone learned that the landlord was slow to make repairs, and the worker offered information about a tenant education class on home maintenance given by the state university.

The worker gave a lot of credit to Mrs. Stone, as she had throughout their work together, for taking the initiative, despite her understandable discouragement about the problems she faced. She had fought hard to hurdle what seemed to be almost impossible obstacles, and her work had paid off: Now she had an apartment that she liked and Brian was adjusting very well to the day school. Before leaving, Mrs. Stone asked whether the worker would stop in and see her when she got settled. To herself, the worker wondered whether now that some of the crises were over, Mrs. Stone would want to work on her still contentious relationship with Doreen.

The complexity of environmental treatment, combined with direct work with clients, is well demonstrated by this case. Despite the many factors mitigating against effective work (not the least of which was the fact that the family services worker was simultaneously carrying a hundred families on her caseload, some with comparable emergencies), the worker and her supervisor were in contact with over a dozen collaterals and agencies up to the point that this part of the summary of the Stone case ends. They were able to establish an excellent, mutually respectful relationship with the lawyer, one that would facilitate work for other clients in the future. This was particularly important because Mr. Beck had had less cooperative contacts with some members of the public assistance staff previously. Patience, tact, persistence, and optimism were all qualities the family services worker had—and needed to have—to gain Mrs. Stone's trust and to succeed as she did, with client and collaterals. On the other hand, cynicism, indifference, "burnout," and prejudice—characteristics often (sometimes unjustifiably) attributed to public agency workers—might well have led to the demoralization of the Stone family. Clearly,

Mrs. Stone became more hopeful and active when she had others who gave support and shared in her efforts. The worker and her supervisor functioned in a broad range of roles in their endeavor to provide and locate resources and to interpret, mediate, and intervene in this family's environment. Together, they sought to bring about changes within the agency as well. Even when stymied by restrictive policies and laws, they, along with Mrs. Stone, found workable alternatives.

Given the commitment of worker and supervisor, this case illustrates that effective casework *is* possible in a publicly supported agency, even in a dense urban area. Such commitment is most likely, we believe, where there is strong social work involvement. In this case, the supervisor had an MSW and years of experience and the worker had had one year of advanced training. We would add that, although similar work might have been possible in a private agency, the workers there probably would not have had the same access to or influence with public officials within and outside the welfare system; it is unlikely that they would have been able to bring about the modifications of rules and policies so important to the work with Mrs. Stone. On the other hand, when caseloads are large, as they were in this agency, some clients will not get the services they need. When asked about caseload management, the supervisor interviewed about this case frankly admitted that often those clients and situations most accessible to change receive the most attention. There are many other clients referred to family services whose emotional, physical, and situational difficulties are so recalcitrant and of such long standing that only small caseloads and, more likely, major social changes could begin to remedy them.

As we have said, it is sometimes difficult to assess where the effects of environmental pressures leave off and emotional relationship problems begin. As in the West case, once the critical issues facing the Stones were handled, the worker and family then could address other areas, including the angry relationship between Doreen and her mother; the need for special help for six-year-old Cynthia, who had a learning disability; and the location of a day care program for Michael so that Mrs. Stone, who had long wanted a high school diploma, could attend a course to prepare for the equivalency examination. By remaining active with the family for six months after the Stones moved into the new apartment, the worker was then able to help with these and other matters.

An important matter that had not been fully addressed during the height of the family crises related to Brian's difficulties; shortly after the boy began attending the special day program, the director had upset Mrs. Stone considerably by offhandedly referring to Brian as "deeply disturbed." At Mrs. Stone's request, the worker accompanied her to a conference about Brian at the school in which it was clear that the director had little sympathy for Mrs. Stone's "denial" of the severity of Brian's condition. In a skillful, nonconfrontational way, the worker was able to say to the school personnel that often in her experience, especially when a child is quiet and causes no problems, it is hard to believe that he is troubled. When bombarded with many urgent problems as Mrs. Stone had been and when information and explanations are meager, even the most well-intentioned parent often fails to see the gravity of an underlying psychiatric disorder. This intervention on the worker's part was very meaningful to Mrs. Stone; she later told the worker that she always had "special feelings" for Brian and maybe it was true that she had not wanted to see his unhappiness. As it turned out, a better rapport between the director and Mrs. Stone was established, which undoubtedly benefited Brian as well as his mother. As the supervisor of this case pointed out, "When a family can't find a decent place to live, it hardly has the stamina to attend to much else, no matter how important."

EARLY DEPRIVATION

Some people need more extended and intensive treatment than was required by the clients thus far described in this chapter. Donna Zimmer, whose case we will now discuss, was in therapy for four years. In the view of the writers and the worker who treated her, a brief casework contact would have been, at best, of minimal value. As we have said, clinical experience has repeatedly demonstrated that when developmental deficits have been severe and healthy ego organization has been significantly interrupted, improved adjustment usually takes considerable time to achieve. This case is representative of many cases seen by clinical social workers for which such long-term treatment is necessary. It also illustrates the three interacting sources of distress mentioned on pages 66–68, and the complexity of the interactions among these factors. Treatment that addressed life history, early needs and deprivations, ego development, and current environmental pressures was vital to the successful outcome.[8]

Referred by her physician, Mrs. Zimmer, age 33, applied to a family service agency. She had numerous somatic complaints that her doctor believed were primarily psychogenic. During her first appointment, she sobbed continually, said her stomach ached unbearably, and complained about being unfairly treated by her mother, her ex-husband, and others. Over and over she said she might as well die, that she was "good for nothing." Although she was an at-

tractive woman—petite, casually but tastefully dressed—her face was contorted, there were dark circles under her eyes, and during much of the interview she hugged her knees to her chest and rocked as she wept. In this initial meeting, and in many that followed, she evidenced intensive, pervasive anxiety and despair; she wanted help because she was afraid of "falling apart."

Mrs. Zimmer was seen at least once and often twice weekly during her four years of therapy. From time to time there were family meetings with her and her children. There were also several sessions held jointly with her mother. In early sessions with the worker, Mrs. Zimmer was able to provide relevant information freely about her current situation and background. In contrast to her chaotic emotional condition, her approach to factual material was thoughtful and well organized.

Mrs. Zimmer was clearly frightened about the extreme rage she often felt toward her children—Sonia, age 11, and Michael, age 8—since her recent separation from her husband. Although she had ended her tempestuous marriage, she was reacting with strong feelings of anger and depression, as if she had been the one rejected and abandoned. Easily set off by even minor external pressures, she described herself as numb or empty when not in the grip of torment or rage. She characterized her husband as an angry man, otherwise emotionally remote, who could not fulfill his responsibilities. During their 12 years of marriage, he had worked only now and then and provided sporadic financial support for the children.

After her separation, Mrs. Zimmer had enrolled in a secretarial school. Despite her emotional distress, she was able to concentrate enough to complete an accelerated course. But she was worried about finding a job during an economic recession and afraid she could not earn enough money to support herself and her children. Although her mother lived in the same city, she could not give financial help. Furthermore, Mrs. Zimmer felt her mother had little else to offer; frequently, she would make promises to drop by and then cancel at the last minute. No other relative lived within visiting distance.

The current situational pressures on Mrs. Zimmer were obvious. She was having to take full responsibility for the care of her children. She had few friends or people to whom she could turn. She was forced to try to enter a tight labor market with newly acquired skills and no previous work experience. Furthermore, the children were reacting negatively to the breakup of the marriage and were more likely to vent their anger at her than at their father for fear that even his occasional visits would end. Much of Mrs. Zimmer's distress, then, was realistically based.

But what unfulfilled infantile needs and flaws in ego development did Mrs. Zimmer bring to her already troubled circumstances? The oldest of five children in a Jewish lower-middle-class upwardly mobile family, she was placed at age three in a children's home for several weeks while her mother was hospitalized for postpartum depression. Mrs. Zimmer remembered this event vividly, and with intense fury; for her, it symbolized a general feeling of abandonment by her mother (a gentle, listless, guilt-ridden, self-effacing woman who seemed ineffectual and indecisive to her daughter). In addition to this separation from her family, when she was an infant Mrs. Zimmer herself was hospitalized several times for operations to correct a malformed eyelid. There were, then, many breaks in her early nurturing.

Furthermore, Mrs. Zimmer believed that by the age of seven or eight her mother had

depended on her, the only girl, to be the "little mother" to her brothers. Her needs came last, she said. As she saw it, any wish of hers was met with guilt-provoking responses that led her to feel undeserving. If she got what she wanted, other family members reacted with jealousy and anger. The worker surmised that Mrs. Zimmer's experience with early relationships had led her to believe that she would either be abandoned or "used" in the service of the needs of others. She never felt that she was loved freely for being herself.

Mrs. Zimmer still raged at her mother about the fact that on the same day she graduated from high school (at age 16 with honors), one of her brothers was graduating from elementary school and her parents attended his ceremony and not hers. She recalled that when she complained, her father told her that education was much more important for boys than for girls. As she saw it, like the man she married, her father was an angry, critical person who could not express loving feelings; her timid mother, she said, cowered and cringed in the face of his dominating personality. At the time her father died when she was 17, Mrs. Zimmer felt she had to take over as head of the household until she "escaped into marriage" at 21.

During the first year of treatment, the extreme oscillations in her view of herself and others were striking. At times she railed at her parents and her husband, seeing them as "all bad" and herself as the "good" one who had been unappreciated and victimized by them. Then, abruptly, often within the same treatment session, she would shift to the opposite view and become convinced that she was the "bad" one, and she would see this as the reason for having been treated so "shabbily" by her family. When she experienced these negative feelings toward others or herself, her hostility would consume her. She would often act impulsively. Angry feelings would then be displaced onto her children, particularly her son Michael, whom she came close to abusing physically and whom she was afraid one day she would "kill in anger." Her long-standing rage, which the worker saw as deriving from early emotional deprivation, reinforced by later experiences, was often aimed at Michael because she felt he ridiculed her as her father had. All of her personal relationships were fraught with conflict and vacillation; her behavior toward her mother and various men in her life was impulsive and erratic. On several occasions, Mrs. Zimmer had explosive encounters with friends when she felt that they were trying to take advantage of her or that they were unsympathetic to her problems. A flood of emotion would lead directly to uncontrolled action: Rage led her to strike out aimlessly; when she felt lonely or despairing, she became clinging or demanding.

In considering the effects of Mrs. Zimmer's early experiences, it is important to avoid the simplistic view that her parents' inadequacies or the early separations had "caused" her adult difficulties. To do so would overlook the contributions of her inborn temperament, of her experiences in interaction with her family and the wider world, and of the ways in which she used later events both to compound and to correct the effects of unfulfilled early needs. This point leads us to a discussion of the interplay of her drives, her ego development, and her current life circumstances.

Faulty ego functioning was apparent in her frequently distorted evaluation of herself and others: as "all good" or "all bad." Since anything less than "perfect" was judged by her to be "terrible," her "all bad" reactions predominated. Her ego's ability to regulate and control infantile impulses was seriously impaired, causing her to create

more environmental pressures on herself. Her intellect, good judgment, and reality testing—evident in the less emotional aspects of her life—were very vulnerable when strong impulses were stimulated. Flawed ego organization was evident in her inability to balance positive and negative feelings. In effect, the memory of a pleasurable feeling could not be retained when negative ones (despair, rage, fear) arose; good and bad experiences could not be integrated; she often had difficulty differentiating one feeling from another. Her defensive functioning—her heavy reliance on projection and denial and her "splitting"—provided evidence of the depth of her difficulties and also contributed to many of her interpersonal problems. During the early months of treatment, only rarely could she admit that her negativism and provocative behavior created difficulties for her.

Apparently, her parents had taken little delight in her accomplishments and therefore she, too, could not realistically appraise or enjoy them. Nor could she take pride in the achievements of her children. Superego development was apparent in her conscientiousness, ethical values, and consistent ability to deal honestly with others in practical matters; on the other hand, her superego was severe and, for the most part, unforgiving. When self-critical (for example, about her frequent anger at her son), she became overwhelmed with such remorse that she had little energy for self-understanding. To rid herself of these self-hating feelings, she would seek reasons to place blame on others.

Some ego functions were far better developed than others. On the positive side, she functioned competently (but rarely without anxiety) in the routine aspects of her life. She learned and could master new skills quickly. She consistently attended to the physical, educational, and even cultural development of her children. Her strengths and her good intelligence were of primary importance to her motivation for therapy and to its successful outcome. (It was not until the final months of therapy, however, that Mrs. Zimmer could say that she had kept coming to sessions because she had some hope that she could "get well." To have admitted that earlier, she said, would have made her feel vulnerable: afraid that the worker would try to "take away" her belief in herself, as she felt her parents had tried to do. But the regularity with which she kept appointments and participated in them gave evidence to the worker that there was a healthy part of Mrs. Zimmer that wanted change.)

The aim of treatment, then, was to help her to repair the damage while affirming her adaptive qualities. Specifically, the worker's treatment approach for the first year was in large measure supportive. During this time, Mrs. Zimmer poured out a great deal of rage, hopelessness, and despair. Alternately, she idolized and furiously distrusted her worker; on some occasions, she would try to cling to her physically and see her as her only "lifeboat"; at other times, often in an abrupt switch, she would accuse her of condemning her and wanting to be rid of her. Patiently and kindly, over and over again the worker conveyed her understanding of how deprived of genuine caring Mrs. Zimmer felt she had always been and acknowledged that, indeed, some early experiences had been hurtful to her. At the same time, she expressed confidence that now that Mrs. Zimmer was an adult—although it would probably take time—there was every reason to believe that she could grow to feel better and improve her life. When Mrs. Zimmer begged the worker to hold and rock her or to prolong the treatment hour, the worker assured her that she recognized that these re-

quests stemmed from deep unhappiness but gently yet firmly explained the realities of what she could and could not do.

It would have been futile for the worker to make early efforts to help Mrs. Zimmer deal directly with her problems of impulse control, even though these were contributing to her many difficulties. For example, advice about how to handle her impulsivity would probably have been ineffective; in the worker's view, Mrs. Zimmer's ego controls were not yet sufficiently developed to change her reactions to stress. Efforts to persuade her to act differently when she could not might have reinforced her profound feelings of failure. On the other hand, when Mrs. Zimmer occasionally did complain about her inability to control her temper, the worker caringly agreed that her intense hostility *did* create many problems for her, working against her own wish to be a good parent, to have friends, and to have a better relationship with her mother. False reassurance could have played into Mrs. Zimmer's tendency to blame others for her troubles. In general, however, the worker's approach at this stage was not to press Mrs. Zimmer to examine her behavior per se but rather to encourage her to try to understand the feelings that stimulated it.

After about a year of therapy, Mrs. Zimmer was feeling slightly better and realized, at least intellectually, that her caseworker would not abandon her. Her security about this was undoubtedly enhanced by the fact that the worker saw to it that the agency fee was adjusted during periods in which Mrs. Zimmer was financially pressed, and sometimes extra appointments and telephone reassurance were offered when Mrs. Zimmer was in acute distress. During the worker's summer vacation, she sent Mrs. Zimmer weekly postcards as a reminder of her ongoing interest, since separations to this client were synonymous with abandonment. All of this was indisputable proof of the worker's caring, difficult for Mrs. Zimmer to deny, even when she felt distrustful. Beyond this, the worker's ability to accept and remain unprovoked by Mrs. Zimmer's negative feelings, including those toward the worker herself, served to reduce them, relieve her anxiety, and foster greater trust. Negative responses the worker sometimes felt in the face of angry outbursts or of clinging, demanding behavior were tempered by her empathy and awareness of the depth of Mrs. Zimmer's pain and unhappiness.

Although a very experienced clinician who had treated many people with uneven ego development and enduring emotional troubles, the worker belonged to a peer support group in which clinical social workers shared difficult cases; in addition to talking over assessments and interventions, the group often focused on subjective, countertherapeutic reactions to clients that can be induced in their therapists.[9]

From the onset, and throughout treatment, the worker avoided being drawn into debates with Mrs. Zimmer. The importance of this approach was demonstrated by an event that occurred after about 18 months of therapy: Mrs. Zimmer telephoned to say she wanted to stop coming. The worker, although surprised by this sudden move, did not argue. Rather, she said that perhaps a vacation from therapy might have some value but suggested that they meet at least once again. Mrs. Zimmer agreed. As they discussed her wish to terminate, without pressure the worker asked whether Mrs. Zimmer thought she might not make further progress if she continued. On the other hand, the worker went on, perhaps Mrs. Zimmer's wish to conclude therapy was an indication of her wish to "try her wings on her own" for a while, an indication of how far she had come. Taken aback but apparently relieved, Mrs. Zimmer said that she

really *did* want to continue her sessions. She explained that she had been afraid the worker would insist that she stay, and that expectation had made her feel "used," as she felt she had been used by her family, to whom she felt acceptable only if she did things the way they wanted her to.

As it developed, this session was a turning point for Mrs. Zimmer; she had asserted her independence: in and of itself a sign of growth. Furthermore, the worker supported her in this by not arguing or holding on to her, attitudes early experiences had led Mrs. Zimmer to anticipate from others. Rather than assuming that Mrs. Zimmer was just being hostile or resistant, the worker believed her move also reflected healthy strivings to grow up (self-assertion was replacing regressed anger and feelings of helplessness). And, of utmost importance, this session firmly established for Mrs. Zimmer that it was *her* motivation that brought her to sessions, *not* the worker's need to possess or manipulate her. From this point on, Mrs. Zimmer became increasingly aware of the ways in which she distorted reality to conform to old expectations, thereby depriving herself of opportunities available to her in the present. Needless to say, the handling of Mrs. Zimmer's request to terminate required skill and delicacy, without which the client might have interpreted the worker's response as a rejection.

Now that a solid relationship had been established, the worker was able to confront Mrs. Zimmer and help her reflect on the contradictions between her feelings and her intellect and between her values and her behavior. To have done so earlier would probably have angered or frightened Mrs. Zimmer and might have jeopardized the therapeutic relationship. But when it was possible, together they explored sudden reversals, such as when Mrs. Zimmer shifted from idealizing her children, her friends, and her caseworker to disparaging them. The worker challenged her unwillingness to entertain any other attitude than hatred toward her mother; Mrs. Zimmer was helped to tap other feelings, including sadness, longing, affection, and empathy. (Her mother's kindness as well as her blandness and dependency were apparent in joint therapy sessions, which gave the worker an opportunity to help Mrs. Zimmer take a more balanced and realistic view.) Similarly, when the client raged about how she wished her son had never been born, the worker expressed understanding of anger at his disobedience but wondered whether Mrs. Zimmer could remember that she had just spoken lovingly about him during the previous session. Asking her to think about this encouraged continuity of feeling and synthesis of "good" and "bad" feelings and experiences.

Mrs. Zimmer (and many clients with significant ego deficits) often expressed her feelings in global terms: that is, it was hard for her to differentiate one feeling from another. Therefore, when she said she felt "awful," the worker urged her to get a better sense of what was wrong: Was she feeling lonely, self-critical and guilty, hurt, abused, or just what? Often this was hard for her, but it was one of the important techniques employed by the worker that, over time, undoubtedly led to better ego functioning and self-awareness.

Similarly, it was necessary for Mrs. Zimmer to learn to distinguish feelings from thoughts. Sometimes when she was flooded by emotion—usually amorphous feelings of pain or rage—she did not use her intellect to bring reality or perspective to her reactions. If she had angry feelings toward a person, for example, she *believed* as well as *felt* that that person must be "bad." Increasingly, in no way discounting what she was feeling, the worker helped her to realize

that her fury was often out of proportion to minor events that triggered it. Primary process functioning, described in Chapter 2, gradually yielded to rational review. Intellectual and emotional processes became much better integrated.

By the time Mrs. Zimmer had been in treatment for two years, improvement in all of her relationships could be noticed. Most of the time she was able to relate civilly to her ex-husband about the children and financial support. To her surprise, Mr. Zimmer became somewhat more consistent in sending payments and in visiting the children, and she could recognize that some of his hostile attitudes had been provoked by hers. Although at times she was still impulsive, her verbal abuse of the children was less extreme and less frequent; she no longer felt in danger of physically attacking her son Michael. More often than before, she began to take what she called "the middle road" in regard to her feelings and behavior; her emotions were no longer "all-or-nothing." When she was angry with someone, she was also able to maintain some awareness of her warm feelings. She was less likely either to idolize or to denigrate her worker; more frequently, she saw her as a helpful person who was also human.

During the third year of treatment, Mrs. Zimmer worked to achieve further stability within herself and in her relationships. Her improvement was strongly tested by Sonia, who by this time was 14 and in angry rebellion most of the time. (During this period, Sonia was seen by another clinical social worker for about six months.) Despite repeated fluctuations and regressions, Mrs. Zimmer was able to maintain a balance of feeling and behavior toward her daughter, recognizing that she, too, was having "growing pains." In other relationships she was able to react more appropriately, tactfully, and warmly than she had. She saw it as a milestone in her therapy when, during a session with her mother, she was able to hug her and tell her that she very much wanted them to become closer than they had been; with occasional backsliding, their relationship improved substantially because Mrs. Zimmer had grown to accept her love for her mother, even though she disliked certain of her mother's qualities. Opposite feelings could now coexist.

But she was still having difficulty reaching out for new friends, even though she very much wanted them. She was afraid of rebuff and of her own volatility. During this period of loneliness, the worker's constant interest and confidence in the changes that had occurred and in the possibilities for more were very supportive. Mrs. Zimmer was afraid that the worker (like her mother, who tended to be suspicious of outsiders) would try to discourage her from friendships. Instead, without pressure, the worker shared some ideas about how Mrs. Zimmer might meet new people and was helpful to her by talking over the ways she was handling new relationships. By the end of this third year of work, Mrs. Zimmer had made several women friends on her job and at her temple.

With little direct help from the worker, Mrs. Zimmer established herself vocationally. Once she completed her secretarial course, she located a job with a small firm, where she was immediatelysuccessful; she then returned to school part time to take bookkeeping, for which she had a natural aptitude. Within six months of completing her course, she was given a promotion and, by the time treatment ended, she had advanced to the position of full-charge bookkeeper. She was now better able than before to value her abilities and, by doing so, to bolster her self-esteem.

The final year of treatment focused intensively on her relationships with men. She had always been afraid of her sexual feelings (which, as she recalled, her father had directly discouraged); she realized she had married her husband partly because she was not attracted to him. Her sexuality was as frightening to her as her angry and tender feelings had been. After separation from her husband, her only sexual encounters were those she called "vindictive"; she would have relations once with a man for whom she had contempt and then refuse to see him again, delighting in the fantasy that she had punished him for "taking advantage" of her. Here again, the worker helped Mrs. Zimmer examine contradictions. For example, the worker asked whether expending so much energy "getting back"—through these men—at the people who had deprived her so long ago served her present wish to have positive relationships. The worker's attitude toward sex, as a natural and potentially rewarding adult experience, undoubtedly also gave Mrs. Zimmer "permission" to be less frightened and guilty about the possibility of enjoying it.

As she used defenses of "splitting," projection, and denial less persistently, good feelings became more available to her; slowly and tentatively, she reached the point of wanting "a person of my own to love." She began to date men she respected. She delayed becoming sexually involved until she grew to care deeply for one man whom she dated for several months during this phase of treatment. Before terminating therapy, she brought him to a session for the worker's "approval"; they were discussing marriage but neither she nor he wanted to rush into it.

The termination phase required careful handling by the worker.[10] The thought of leaving treatment excited Mrs. Zimmer but also stimulated old feelings of fear and anger. On the one hand, she was able to take justifiable pride in her hard-earned attainment of greater maturity and stability; on the other hand, she would sometimes feel outraged by the fact that she had had to work so hard to overcome the deprivations of her early years while, as she saw it, "normal" people could simply "sail" through life. Thoughts that perhaps the worker had wanted to get rid of her all along were activated as they talked about ending their work together. Separation fears were profound as Mrs. Zimmer began to say goodbye to her worker, who had nurtured her through tumultuous times. Never before had Mrs. Zimmer experienced an intimate relationship in which her growth toward independence and adulthood was unambivalently encouraged. Although she was realistically grateful for this, the final phase of therapy also stirred a sense of loss associated with her childhood. When the worker helped her to examine and sort out her reactions, Mrs. Zimmer was able to distinguish which were projections or old feelings about herself as a "bad" person and which were genuine feelings of sadness aroused by termination. In the final session, Mrs. Zimmer presented the worker with a Hummel figurine of a smiling, robust child that symbolized for her the "second chance" she had been given to grow up "the right way."

In analyzing the case of Mrs. Zimmer, we see that treatment was slow, turbulent, marked by periods of stalemate and regression. Mrs. Zimmer's conflicted, vacillating relationship with her worker tended to replicate old relationships, reflecting inner turmoil and ego deficiencies. The worker's acceptance, patience, consistency, caring, and optimism were important dynamics of treatment. Fortunately, she neither retaliated when Mrs. Zimmer denounced her nor was countertransferentially seduced by excessive praise. Instead, Mrs. Zimmer was provided with a sustained experience of closeness without being hurt, "used," or abandoned.

However, the relationship was more than "corrective" (in the sense of providing parental support that she had not had). When the timing was right—always gently, sometimes firmly—the worker prodded her to reflect on distortions, contradictions, and oscillations; repeated discussions of current realities and of her feelings and behavior helped to strengthen ego functions of perception, judgment, synthetic functioning, and impulse control.

Previously dissociated feeling states became better integrated as ego functions consolidated and healed. For some clients who have excessively suppressed emotions, relaxation of restrictive defenses may be required. In Mrs. Zimmer's case, on the other hand, treatment was designed to provide the opportunity for her underdeveloped personality structure and defensive functioning to mature. Efforts to "uncover" feelings that were so raw and undifferentiated would have been countertherapeutic.

When she attained success in one area of her life, her increased self-esteem helped her make further gains. On the basis of the worker's diagnosis, little attempt was made to explore directly very early life experiences that had contributed to this client's difficulties; many of these had occurred before there could be any memory of them. But treatment that worked with the residuals, later memories, and current issues—in the context of a positive relationship—resulted in significant personality change and improved functioning for Mrs. Zimmer.

In conclusion, we add that it was fortunate that Mrs. Zimmer was referred to an agency that had the flexibility to accommodate long-term, often twice-a-week therapy. We believe that efforts to abbreviate treatment would probably have failed, might have been experienced by Mrs. Zimmer as rejection, and perhaps would have discouraged her from seeking other therapy.

Furthermore, when extended therapy is not made available, too often clients with severe personality deficits—in contrast to many others who *are* helped in brief treatment—only get "band-aid" assistance during crises. Each episode of treatment is too short to internalize lasting changes and to develop necessary self-awareness.

The six cases presented in this chapter illustrate clinical social work practice approached from the psychosocial point of view. In the chapters to follow, the theory and dynamics of the treatment process will be discussed in further detail. Additional case illustrations can be found in Chapter 20.

NOTES

1. See references on brief treatment in the notes of Chapter 18 of this book.
2. For readings on treatment of suicidal behavior see Klugman et al. (1995) and, for a cognitive approach, see Freeman and White (1989).
3. Research indicates that depressed clients often show greater symptom reduction with a combination of psychotherapy and medication than with either treatment alone. See Klerman et al. (1994), especially pp. 760–61. See also the report of Elkin et al. (1989) discussed in note 60, Chapter 1. For a reference on psychopharmacology and clinical social work, see Willinger (1996) who urges social workers to deepen their knowledge about medications to be able to identify situations in which medical consultation might be helpful.
4. See the notes to Chapters 16 and 17 on couple therapy for readings on marital treatment.
5. For a useful discussion of clinical practice with the elderly, see Barlam and Soares (1997). For a good article that addresses countertherapeutic worker reactions to working with older clients—such as burnout, overinvolvement, and detachment—see Sprung (1989) who urges the development of worker self-awareness and the

encouragement of client self-determination. See also Burstein (1988) who discusses ethical and practice issues related to the fact that the elderly are sometimes involuntary clients. For other helpful readings on various aspects of the needs of the elderly and treatment approaches see Barry (1988), Goldmeier and Fandetti (1992), Ivry (1995), Parsons and Cox (1989), Florence Stafford (1988), and Stevens (1992). See Smallen (1995) who discusses the devastating effect job displacement can have on older people. Chatters and Taylor (1989) discuss difficulties and coping strategies of older adults of color. See also Francis J. Turner's edited volume (1995), chapters 6, 7, and 8 for additional references.

6. See Germain and Gitterman (1996) and Kadushin and Kadushin (1997). Both books emphasize the value of "anticipatory empathy."
7. See Hollis (1965) who made this point many years ago and cautioned against generalizing about very diverse groups of clients. We will emphasize this point throughout the text. Davidson (1990) has written a relevant article that stresses the importance of finding innovative ways to help families with multiple stressors; she cautions against stigmatizing them as "multiproblem," "underorganized," "hard-to-reach," etc.
8. See notes to Chapter 2, especially notes 16, 26, and 27 on maternal deprivation, attachment theory, and related matters. See also discussions on personality development and environmental influences in the text of Chapter 2.
9. Mrs. Zimmer's clinical condition was diagnosed as "borderline personality disorder" by the worker who treated her. There are many readings on this phenomenon and on other personality disorders, including theoretical discussions of faulty ego development and implications for practice. Many writers share some common views but have definite differences in emphasis. Especially recommended is Eda Goldstein's (1990) volume: a "must" for all social workers working with people with borderline disorders.

Additional references include: Beck and Freeman (1990) on cognitive therapy and personality disorders; ego psychologists Blanck and Blanck (1979); Dungee-Anderson (1992) who discusses a cognitive-behavioral approach in treatment of borderline conditions, as do Heller and Northcut (1996); Eckrich (1985) wrote on the identification and treatment of borderline disorders. Freed (1980 and 1984) published two very good and relevent articles. Readers will also be interested in Graziano (1986).

See also Harriette Johnson's chapter on borderline disorders (1999). Theodore Millon (1996) has written a very comprehensive, scholarly, and thorough volume on personality disorders. Palumbo (1983) wrote on borderline conditions from a self-psychology perspective. Woods (1999) has a chapter on the diagnosis and treatment of several of the personality disorders other than the borderline condition.

Recommended authors who were among those who broke ground in the study of and theory-building about borderline and personality disorders and developmental deficits are: Giovacchini (1986), Kernberg (1975, 1984, and 1986), Kohut (1977), and Masterson (1976).

In an interesting article, Corwin (1996) discusses high-risk behavior and high attrition rates of young adult clients with borderline disorders; she recommends early intervention strategies and brief treatment approaches. There is no question that sometimes short-term treatment with clients with borderline conditions can be helpful, but in our experience—as Mrs. Zimmer's treatment illustrates—it can sometimes take many months or years for such clients to make fundamental changes. Meyer (1993) writes an excellent defense of long-term treatment, especially for the many troubled clients who have difficult developmental histories and whose backgrounds were "riddled with abuse, neglect, and deprivation"; he mourns the "vanishing holding environment"; in his view, the numbers of clients who have had damaging early experiences are growing at the very time social workers are being pressured to provide brief services.

10. The importance of careful and sensitive handling of the termination of treatment is discussed in Chapter 19 of this book.

CHAPTER 4

THE HOLLIS CLASSIFICATION OF CASEWORK TREATMENT

Logic might dictate that we move into a detailed discussion of the casework process first through chapters on initial interviews and psychosocial study, then on assessment, diagnosis and treatment planning, and finally on treatment procedures. But to understand what information we should seek in the psychosocial study and what types of assessments and diagnoses will be useful in treatment planning, we must begin with further understanding of the nature of treatment itself as it has evolved in psychosocial casework.

Treatment is a *goal-directed* process. Different means are used by various approaches to bring about an intended effect. There are many ways of classifying these means. We have found it useful to base classification on the *dynamics* of treatment. In other words, we want to describe what we, as clinical social workers, actually do. What processes or *procedures* do we use? How and what do we communicate? To cap-

ture a full picture of what occurs in treatment, we must be able to classify *client communications* in the treatment process, not just the worker's.

Consider the situation of Vanessa (who prefers to be called by her first name), a 19-year-old single mother of two children, ages four and two; she is dependent on her modest salary as a supermarket cashier to support her family. She was referred to a social service agency by the hospital social worker because she requires immediate surgery but is terrified of it. She is frightened partly because she is too sick to figure out financial arrangements or plan for the care of her children during her absence from home and her recuperation. She is anxious partly because she is going to a strange doctor and is uncertain about the outcome of the operation. And, her caseworker suspects, she may also be fearful partly because unconsciously she anticipates punishment for her hostile attitudes toward her mother who became permanently handicapped after an operation that Vanessa erroneously assumes was similar to the one she is about to undergo. Many different procedures can be employed by the worker to help this woman reduce her anxiety:

1. Environmental Intervention   Milieu work is one alternative that probably would be considered. With Vanessa's consent, the worker can arrange for temporary financial assistance and care of the children. This help can have a double effect: It will relieve the client of that part of her anxiety related to realistic concern about finances and her children's needs; it will also demonstrate that others care for her welfare and are ready to assist her when she is weakened and unable to manage her own affairs. Serious illness sometimes leads to regression and to intense dependence. It is extremely important at such a time for the patient to feel that someone with strength will take care of her and her responsibilities. The way in which plans for the children are made will be of particular importance. If relatives or friends toward whom Vanessa has warm feelings can care for them, so much the better. When appropriate, family meetings may provide opportunities for making plans. If agency care for the children must be sought, the degree of relief from anxiety will vary with the amount of confidence the mother and family members have in the goodwill and competence of the caseworker who makes the arrangement. Often, when trusted family members are part of the planning process, the patient feels less pressure—partly because others are taking over the responsibilities, and partly because the relatives feel they have some control over the process and do not then convey, intentionally or otherwise, doubts about the quality of the children's care to the mother.

2. Encouragement of Expression of Feelings   Vanessa and other family members, including the older child, can be helped to express emotional reactions, particularly apprehensions and fears, about the operation; the caseworker shows understanding of anxieties, indicating that these are natural reactions for all concerned under the circumstances. When possible, *reassurance* is given by the worker to the patient as well as to her relatives that the doctors are interested and skillful. If the operation is not a dangerous one, this reality can also be used to allay fears in everyone *once they have been expressed.* Reduced anxiety in the patient can contribute to the success of medical procedures. When family members feel reassured about what is happening, they are less likely inadvertently to reinforce undue apprehension in the patient.

3. Increased Understanding of the Facts   Vanessa's anxiety and that of family members may be reduced if they have more information about the operation. The caseworker may arrange for them to talk in detail, together or separately, with the doctor. Sometimes they may need to go over the facts with the caseworker, clarifying their understanding of what the doctor said. Again, when family members feel informed, they are less likely to transfer their anxiety to the patient.

4. Increased Understanding of Feelings   This alternative may or may not be necessary. Vanessa may seek understanding of the relationship between her hostility to her mother, her mother's illness, and the possibility that her present fears about her own illness are related in part to her guilt about this hostility. The use of this alternative depends on the client's need and/or her interest in *exploring earlier feelings* and *making connections* between these and current fears about the operation.

These procedures all have a common aim: to reduce anxiety; but the dynamics involved in each are different. In one instance, some of the stimuli for anxiety are removed by environmental meaures. In another, expression of fears is encouraged and reassurance is given, procedures that depend for their effectiveness on confidence in the worker. In the third, the patient and family are encouraged to understand the situation more realistically. And, in the fourth, the patient may be helped to understand prior emotions involving interpersonal relationships and their connection to current reactions. In all of these procedures, the worker must be keenly aware of how Vanessa's situation is significantly affected by *environmental, family,* and *personality systems* and how these *interplay*. The repertoire of treatment procedures used by the worker in this example addressed each of these systems at one point or another; by doing so, Vanessa, her children, and other family members would more likely be relaxed during this stressful time than if the worker treated only Vanessa herself.

It was in an effort to seek a more orderly understanding of diagnostic casework, from which the psychosocial approach developed (as noted in Chapter 1), that Hollis developed the classification of treatment procedures used in the first edition of this book. Before discussing the typology, we will touch upon some historical developments in classifications in diagnostic (or psychosocial) theory.

EARLY CLASSIFICATIONS

A Brief History

Over the years, a number of classifications of casework treatment methods were suggested. As noted earlier, as far back as 1922, Mary Richmond made the very simple distinction between "direct" and "indirect"

treatment. By the former, she meant those processes that take place directly between the client and the worker—"the influence of mind upon mind." By the latter, she meant changes the worker brings about in the client's human and physical environment.[1]

Despite many changes that occurred in casework in the 1930s, it was not until 1947 that new classifications began to appear, reflecting the preceding years of growth in understanding of what Mary Richmond had called *direct treatment*. By then, psychoanalytic concepts had not only been found useful in understanding psychological and emotional elements in personal problems but had also contributed to the interviewing processes. It was clear, of course, that caseworkers were not conducting psychoanalyses and that there was a large part of casework that was only tangentially touched by psychoanalysis. However, because certain techniques had been borrowed from psychoanalytic methodology, it was important for caseworkers to define in what specific ways the two treatment methods did or did not overlap. As discussed in Chapter 1, in the 1940s and 1950s, tentative boundaries between casework and psychoanalysis were drawn, holding that casework does not reach deeply unconscious material but may deal with content that, though not conscious, is relatively accessible. These efforts set in motion further interest in examining more closely the dynamics of the casework process.[2] Changes in classifications reflected the expansion of knowledge in diagnostic theory and practice. Thus, the impetus for studying the casework process was twofold: first, to differentiate casework practice from psychoanalysis and, second, to expand and organize understanding of the components and dynamics of casework treatment.

Each new typology was built upon former ones and attempted to define the scope of casework treatment.[3] Partially developed from earlier typologies and partially based on the study of a series of cases from family service agencies, in 1953 a committee of the Family Service Association of America (FSAA) proposed a simple classification of casework into two types *based on the aim of treatment.* It designated type A, or *supportive casework,* as "treatment aimed at maintaining adaptive patterns," and type B, or *clarification,* as "treatment aimed at modification of adaptive patterns." The first type of treatment was described as resting upon such techniques as environmental modification, "reassurance, persuasion, direct advice and guidance, suggestion, logical discussion, exercise of professional authority and immediate influence."[4] The second was characterized mainly by its use of techniques designed to help clients separate objective reality from distortions of the external world, in addition to other techniques. Surprising as it is to us now, the committee reported that it had decided not to include a category corresponding to insight development or insight therapy included in preceding classifications because it found that this type of treatment was used in very few agencies. Five years later, in 1958, this classification was further developed by a committee of the Community Service Society, which described in more detail the techniques used in the "supportive treatment method" and the "modifying treatment methods," limiting the latter to modification of "selected ego mechanisms of defense."[5]

These two reports played an important part in illuminating several issues concerning casework treatment. Their specificity was a distinct improvement over earlier efforts. Three issues were identified and spelled out in a way that led to further study:

1. To what extent is "insight therapy" undertaken by caseworkers?

2. Are changes in adaptive patterns dependent upon the use of clarification as a predominant treatment technique?
3. Is casework correctly conceptualized as a dichotomous process having two distinct treatment modes, one in which clarification is the predominant technique and one in which this technique either is absent or plays a minor role?

Personality Changes and Treatment Techniques

The Relationship between Changes in Adaptive Patterns and Treatment Methods The first of these issues to be examined systematically was that of the relationship between changes in adaptive patterns and treatment methods. The FSAA report mentioned above was challenged on this question.[6] Adaptive patterns, some believed, could be changed with little use or no use of clarification. This was an important point because there was a tendency for caseworkers to belittle work other than clarification as "just" supportive, when experience suggested that supportive techniques were capable of bringing about changes in adaptive patterns.

What is actually meant by a "change in adaptive patterns"? Such a change is *internalized,* built into the personality. It results in improvement in functioning that cannot be fully accounted for by improved circumstances, passing of a crisis, or influence of the worker during the period of treatment; rather, it constitutes *a change in the client's way of functioning that will enable him or her to respond differently even when the external situation has not changed and when the worker is not part of the client's current life.* The individual will have learned to act differently and will respond to the same or similar life events more constructively than before treatment.

Improvement in Functioning without a Change in Adaptive Patterns This might occur in situations such as the following:

- A widow, depressed by the loss of her husband, is unable to give good care to her children. She receives casework help during this period of grief and, as the grief subsides, she is once again available to her children.
- A husband has been quarreling with his wife because of anxiety at work. In discussions with the worker, he realizes the source of his irritability and transfers to another, less pressured job. Subsequently, he is less argumentative at home.
- A construction worker loses a leg in an accident and is told he will no longer be able to continue in his line of work. He loses interest in life, does not try to obtain a prosthesis, and retreats to dependent, whining behavior. After a good deal of skillful work, including development of some understanding of his current responses, he regains his former stability and finds another kind of employment to which he adjusts well.

In none of these cases have "new adaptive patterns" necessarily been established. Improvements in functioning often occurred in response to supportive treatment methods and constituted a very important type of recovery from a period of strain or disaster that might otherwise result in permanent impairment of functioning. But could the other type of improved functioning, which *does* rest upon *modification of habitual patterns* of behavior and responses, be brought about without treatment using clarification techniques?

In 1956 Hollis addressed this question by conducting a small study of nine cases from a family service agency. It appeared that *it was possible to bring about changes in adaptive patterns using supportive procedures,* the point at issue. A brief description of three of these cases illustrates this point:

- Mrs. Knight, an immature young woman in her teens, was married to a man old enough to be her father. At first he enjoyed her dependence, but soon became irritated by her inability to manage the home and be an adequate mother to the two children of his former marriage. Mrs. Knight sought help "in growing up" from the caseworker. The approach was one of *guidance* and *support,* with reliance on elements in the *relationship,* on considerable *logical discussion,* and on *environmental supports,* such as the extensive use of a visiting housekeeper and of a nurse who educated the client concerning her own and the children's health. With the ego strengthened by increased knowledge and skill, maturation that had been arrested when Mrs. Knight was so overwhelmed began again to occur. Now that she could handle demands that previously seemed beyond her, there was marked improvement in her functioning as a wife and mother. There was every reason to believe that the improvement in adaptive patterns had been internalized and would be lasting.
- Mrs. Landers, the mother of five children, was driven by a strong need to succeed, which showed itself in the form of perfectionistic demands upon the children and excessive self-criticism when difficulties arose in relationship with them. The worker became the "good mother," and on the basis of this *supportive relationship* Mrs. Landers was able to *think through* ways of handling the children more realistically, reducing the demands of her superego upon the children and herself. She became able to set up more lenient goals for her family and to see that she was overreacting in holding herself so completely

responsible for their behavior. Once again, a nurse was used for discussion of health problems; better housing plans were worked out; camp opportunities were provided for the children. Mrs. Landers learned new ways of handling her children and incorporated less demanding standards for herself and her family through the supportive approach of the worker.

- Mr. Ingersol, a married man of 35, was repeatedly in trouble at work and with his wife because of impulsive behavior. His difficulties were compounded by periodic heavy drinking. At first, he denied that drinking was a problem or that his own behavior contributed to quarrels with his wife. After treatment had advanced to a point where Mr. Ingersol trusted the caseworker, he was finally able to realize and admit that after a certain number of drinks he said things he would not otherwise have said, thereby precipitating negative responses from his wife. Once he could face this, he made a real effort to control his drinking and succeeded in markedly reducing it. A pattern of greater control was established, not by bringing suppressed material to consciousness or by seeking causative understanding of his drinking beyond current provocations, but by the effect of *close examination of present realities*.

Another factor at work in Mr. Ingersol's progress was the *client–worker relationship* itself. A dependent man who greatly admired his father, he developed similar feelings toward his caseworker, whom he wanted to please as he had wanted to please his father. The worker did not interpret the transference but made use of it by giving him *encouragement*: credit and appreciation when he showed understanding of the effects of his behavior and when he tried to modify it. His efforts to change were further fortified by the satisfaction he secured during periods of a better relationship with his wife. *Logical discussion, advice, approval,* and *encouragement* were all used in an effort to enable him to improve the quality and strength of his ego controls. At several points in this case *clarification* was briefly used, but it was not the predominant technique. Considerable *improvement in adaptive patterns* seems to have occurred in this case, although one could not be wholly optimistic about the permanence of the new patterns.

In each of these cases, it appeared that changes in adaptive patterns occurred in response to techniques defined as primarily "supportive." This gave further substance to the belief that the response to treatment was more fluid than the FSAA dichotomizing hypothesis maintained.

Diverse Approaches to Changes in Personality

Why are we so concerned about the question of how changes in adaptive patterns can be accomplished? A change in adaptive patterns makes it more possible that whatever improvement in functioning has occurred will continue not only in the immediate circumstances but in other vicissitudes the individual may meet. A better method of functioning will have been learned and become part of the personality. What, then, are some ways to achieve changes in adaptive patterns?

1. First, there is the basic personality change, often called "structural change" in psychoanalytic terminology. This includes and goes beyond changes in adaptive patterns. It occurs when some of the decisive formative experiences of life are reached and relived in treatment and undergo reevaluation. From the psychoanalytic point of view, this involves bringing to consciousness and understanding

material that was previously unconscious or repressed, such as memories, thoughts, or fantasies representing infantile destructive and sexual impulses and wishes, and reactions and distortions growing out of very early life experiences and deprivations. Many of the early feelings are thought to be revived in the transference in which the patient temporarily regresses to childhood. Structural change can be brought about by psychoanalysis and sometimes by less extensive psychotherapy carried on by therapists trained in psychoanalysis.

2. Second, as was earlier pointed out, irrational and inappropriate responses are also often based on *preconscious* influences, on events that at most have been *suppressed* rather than repressed and, hence, can be brought to the surface of the mind by the type of interviewing techniques used in casework. Many early influences are not even suppressed. Sometimes they are well remembered, but the client needs to recognize the connection between these childhood experiences and his or her current responses in order to see their irrationality. Experiences of adolescence and early adulthood may also be of great importance. The ego defenses, in particular, often operate on a preconscious level. Not infrequently, a person can become aware of and will modify defense patterns on seeing their irrationality or their harmfulness without needing to look back to factors that influenced the development of such patterns. That is, the dynamic may be understood independently of origins. Recognizing the influence of conscious and preconscious early life experiences and becoming aware of defenses are both forms of *clarification* in the FSAA use of the term and constitute a second way in which adaptational patterns can be modified.

3. A third way of bringing about changes in adaptive patterns consists of helping the individual to deal more effectively with current life relationships and problems. Better understanding of other people, thoughtfulness about the effects of one's ways of relating to others, and fuller awareness of one's feelings and actions and of the effect of others on oneself will lead first to better functioning in the immediate current life, or at least a sector of current life. As individual life events pile up, the adaptive patterns themselves may be modified, even though they have not been discussed as such. This form of change parallels natural life experience. Without the help of any type of therapy, the relatively healthy individual repeatedly learns from experiences as he or she seeks to develop more effective ways of mastering the vicissitudes of life. A similar process occurs in treatment, but the individual's efforts are augmented by professional help.

4. A fourth way in which change occurs in adaptive patterns is in the context of a strong positive relationship to another person who is accorded a leadership or pattern-setting role in some area of living. In such a relationship, the individual either identifies with and imitates the worker, or subscribes to the worker's values, or accepts his or her assessment, suggestions, and advice. Again, treatment parallels a process common in natural life experience.

5. A fifth way in which adaptive patterns can change is in response to more favorable life experiences. These are relatively easy to arrange for children. Adults can often be helped to make such changes for themselves: a new marriage, a better or more suitable job, completion of educational plans, and so on. Again, similar processes occur in natural life.

6. A sixth way in which personality change comes about is through the positive reinforcement that results from more effective and satisfying functioning. Sometimes this reinforcement is in the form of verbal or nonverbal communications from the worker. More often, it arises in subsequent life experiences. When temporary change in functioning is rewarded by positive experiences in interpersonal relationships or in other important areas of functioning such as work, a powerful incentive is given to continue the new ways until they constitute a new adaptive pattern. This also commonly occurs in life.

Several of these ways of bringing about change usually occur together in work with one individual or family. It appears that *treatment is actually a blend of many influences that in combination are designed to bring about more effective and satisfying functioning*. In the opinions of many experienced practitioners, casework is not best conceptualized as a dichotomous process leading to two different outcomes. Rather, a more fluid model must be sought that would readily permit us to think in terms of a blend of procedures flexibly adapted to the complex set of needs brought by individuals and families.

DEVELOPING A TYPOLOGY

What sort of classification would be useful in relation to this revised understanding of the casework process? In 1958, Hollis began devising a *classification of treatment procedures in which the means by which treatment is carried out would be separated from treatment goals*. This would permit workers and researchers to examine what procedures were actually used when changes occurred. It might also result in clearer thinking about the essential nature—the dynamics—of treatment procedures.

When work on such a classification, or typology, was begun, it was soon discovered that it is no simple matter to formulate a logical and useful classification of casework treatment, especially if this formulation was to be rich enough in its dimensions to make conceptually worthwhile distinctions, and yet not so elaborate as to be impractical.

It was important also to think about what purpose would be served by a treatment classification. Would it merely enable us to describe casework in a more orderly way in writing and teaching? This is one important use of classification; the very need for such clarity constitutes a strong impetus toward developing one. Would it provide agencies with a systematic way of grouping cases for reports of accountability, work distribution, evaluation, and the like?

Yes, but there was a more fundamental purpose: that of *studying casework itself*. Many questions needed to be answered to use casework effectively. For what configuration of personality tendencies and problems and what sorts of social problems is a particular treatment method or technique appropriate? What other factors—the client's wishes and responses, time available, worker skill, agency function, and so on—influence treatment choices? What is the result of using this or that technique under such and such circumstances? What alternative means are available to the end that client and worker have in mind? Under what circumstances is one means more likely to serve the purpose than another?

Before answers could be found to these questions, the numerous variables involved would have to be separated. In the end, ways would have to be found to identify and classify not only treatment procedures but also personality characteristics, types of problems and situational factors, outcomes, and relationships among these variables. Treatment procedures would be a good starting point.

It was particularly important that the *aim* of treatment and the *methods used* be examined as *separate variables.* Only by so doing could we hope to test the relationship of one to the other and examine the conditions under which specific techniques can lead to specific results.

Several intensive case studies and line-by-line examination of interviews, beginning in 1958, provided the basis for Hollis's early typology of treatment procedures and communications that could then be tested in a larger, more rigorous study. (See Chapter 21 for details.) Concurrently, input from students in master's and doctoral programs and from colleagues helped in refining the classification.

Value of the Typology

The typology that finally emerged dealt primarily with the interviewing process.[7] It is essentially a *classification of communications* that take place between client and worker, or collateral and worker. The typology has demonstrated its value in a number of research projects; some of these are described in Chapter 21. The classification, which provides a framework for the discussion of treatment in this book, has been particularly useful as a tool for clarifying what goes on in psychosocial casework. It is not the empirical base upon which psychosocial casework rests. Rather, it is a tool for studying this approach and for describing it. It allows us to follow the flow of each interview and can be used either in informal analysis or in more rigorous research.

As had been hoped, the classification makes possible examination of the *dynamics* of treatment and exploration of such questions as: In what way does a given procedure affect a client? What are the relationships of client personality factors to choice of treatment method? What is the re-

lationship between problem and treatment steps? What factors in the client's response in a particular interview indicate the advisability of using a particular procedure? What procedures in early interviews are most likely to encourage the client to remain in treatment?

As pointed out earlier in the case of Vanessa, anxiety can be reduced in different ways: A given result can be achieved by a variety of procedures, ranging from direct reassurance to full understanding of the intrapsychic cause of the anxiety. Under different circumstances and with different individuals, one approach will be more effective than another. Determining which means is usually most useful under particular conditions is central to any study seeking to understand and improve casework methodology and is therefore an especially valuable feature of the Hollis classification.

The classification also distinguishes sharply between the *means* or *procedures* employed and the actual *effect.* For example, the caseworker's expression of interest in and appreciation of an individual or family's situation or feelings is a means generally thought to promote perception of the worker as someone who is interested and capable of understanding. This strengthens the feeling that there is someone who will help. By this means, it is hoped, anxiety will be lessened and, consequently, functioning will be improved. A person with a paranoid disorder, however, may interpret this kind of response by the caseworker as a kind of magic mind reading, an effort to bring the person under some obscure influence, and the technique will not have the desired effect. Nevertheless, in the Hollis typology, if a worker, however unwisely, used this technique it would be classified as a *sustaining procedure,* the term for this type of *potentially* reassuring technique. Such a *separation of the means employed from the outcome* puts us in a position to examine the actual effect of a treatment step, to study the circumstances under which it does not have the desired effect, and thereafter to use it more appropriately. Or, if by research we find it rarely has the effect we theoretically thought it should have, we can correct our theory. A classification of this sort is not static. It can be modified as research and study constantly correct our theories. It can also lend itself well to expansion as new techniques are developed.

THE MAIN DIVISIONS OF THE HOLLIS CLASSIFICATION

With these preliminaries, we may proceed to a brief description of the classification. Detailed discussion of the specific technical procedures included under the main divisions of the classification will be found in chapters immediately following. The major dimensions of the classification are presented in this chapter, together with specific illustrations used only to clarify the meaning of the main categories; thus, we will be able to discuss certain general theoretical questions before going extensively into details of procedures.

Client–Worker Communications

For the moment, let us set aside the question of treatment through the environment, Richmond's indirect treatment, and deal only with those procedures that take place directly between worker and client, Richmond's direct treatment. When working directly with clients—whether singly, in pairs, or in family group treatment—it was found that the caseworkers' techniques can be placed in six major groupings. The first two of these derive their force or influence from the *relationship* that exists between client and worker, from the way in which the

client regards the worker and the degree of influence the client accords the worker or permits in his or her life. The third draws its strength from *ventilation,* the *description* of stressful events, and the *expression of feelings* that are causing distress. The fourth, fifth, and sixth groups rest primarily upon various kinds of *reflective considerations promoted within the client.* Brief descriptions of the six major categories follow:

1. Sustainment This group of procedures includes such activities by the worker as demonstration of interest, desire to help, understanding, expressions of confidence in the client's abilities or competence, and reassurance concerning matters about which the client has anxiety or guilt.

Sustaining techniques are used in varying degrees in all cases. Much of this type of communication occurs through nonverbal means: nods, smiles, an attentive posture, murmurings. In the early interviews, no matter what else is done, the worker usually tries, by listening carefully and sympathetically and by using other sustaining techniques, to lessen anxiety and give clients the feeling that they are in a place where help will be forthcoming. Subsequently, cases vary in the extent to which sustaining techniques are needed, with fluctuations from time to time in the same case. Remarks such as "I can understand how difficult that must have been," "Such feelings are natural," or "You have obviously given a lot of thought to what this situation means to you and your family" are illustrative.

2. Direct Influence This category includes a range of techniques among which suggestion and advice are most frequently used. They involve in one form or another the expression of the worker's opinion about the kind of action a client should take, with such comments as "It might be better to do this rather than that," "Perhaps you ought to ____," or "No, I don't think that will work; you had better ____," and so on.

Procedures of direct influence are far less universally used in pschosocial casework than sustaining techniques, but, particularly in their more tentative forms (questions such as "What do you think?" or "How does this idea strike you?") constitute a recognized part of treatment. Their effectiveness depends to a high degree upon the existence of a strong positive relationship between client and worker, which in turn is promoted by sustaining procedures. As we have said, whenever possible, it is far more respectful and supportive of clients' sense of competence to foster their reflective consideration about what *they* might plan to do than it is for the worker to give them directions.

3. Exploration, Description, and Ventilation This group of worker–client communications is designed to draw out descriptive and explanatory material from the client and to encourage the pouring out of pent-up feelings and descriptions of emotionally charged events. This material helps the worker to understand clients and their concerns. In addition, this outpouring often relieves tension felt by the client. Frequently, the relief obtained by verbalization is supported by sustaining procedures that further reduce the accompanying anxiety or guilt. At other times, the content of the ventilation process is picked up to promote reflective consideration of it: "Yes, tell me more about it," "Yes, yes—go on," or "What about your job? How do things go there?"

4. Person–Situation Reflection This grouping consists of communications designed to draw clients into reflective consideration of their situations and of their functioning within them. Here we refer to reflection upon current and relatively recent

events, exclusive of early life material. This broad category can be subdivided into six areas of understanding. Specifically, clients' attention may turn to consideration of (1) others, their own health, or any aspect of the outside world; (2) their own behavior in terms of its actual or potential outcome or its effect on others or themselves; (3) the nature of their own behavior, thoughts, and feelings; (4) causative aspects of their own behavior or responses when in interaction with others or provoked by external circumstances; (5) some aspect of their own behavior, self-image, concepts of right and wrong, values, or principles from an evaluative stance; and (6) feelings about the worker and the treatment process.

In the first of these subdivisions, attention is directed outward; in the second it is partly outward and partly inward; and in the last four it is directed inward to some aspect of the person's own feelings, thoughts, or actions: that is, toward a form of self-understanding that depends entirely upon reflection about specific interactions and reactions in the person–situation gestalt. To illustrate: (1) "Can you think of anything else that might be making your wife so nervous lately?" (2) "When you say things like that to Bud, what reaction do you get?" (3) "You sound as though you were very frightened; is that true?" (4) "What actually happened that could have made you so angry? What do you think it was?" (5) "You sound as though you feel very uncomfortable about the choice you made; is that so?" (6) "Are you still concerned that I will take John's side?"

It is impossible to imagine a case in which some of these types of person–situation reflection would not be used. The type of problem brought by the client is one important determinant of where the emphasis will be. The more realistic and external the problem, the greater the likelihood that interviews will emphasize procedures from the first two subdivisions; the greater the subjective involvement in the problem, the more likely the third, fourth, and fifth subdivisions. The sixth subdivision is extremely important; in almost every case the client must be encouraged to express reactions to the worker and the treatment process; only in this way can the worker truly know whether the client is finding the worker interested and fair and the process safe and helpful. These procedures of person–situation reflection are combined in varying degrees with sustaining techniques and may be accompanied to some degree also by direct influence. They are techniques that are also always an important part of the treatment process when other types of reflective consideration are in action.

5. Pattern-Dynamic Reflection This treatment category also relies upon reflective discussion. It consists of procedures for encouraging clients to think about the psychological patterns involved in their behavior or responses and the dynamics of these patterns and tendencies. The client is helped to reflect upon some of the internal reasons for responses and actions and encouraged to look at the dynamics of his or her behavior by studying the relationship between one aspect of behavior or response and another. The client goes beyond thinking about a specific distortion of reality or inappropriate reaction toward consideration of the operations of the intrapsychic component itself: "I wonder whether you don't often think other people dislike you when underneath you are critical of them" or "Does it seem to you that you often take it out on Linda when you're really angry at your wife?"

6. Developmental Reflection This treatment category, also a type of reflective discussion, includes procedures of encouraging the client to think about the development of his or her psychological patterns or tendencies; again, this is a subjective area. Clients are helped to deal with early life experiences that are important because, although they occurred in the past, they have been internalized to such a degree that they are now part of their responses to current situations. As in pattern-dynamic reflection, treatment revolves around consideration of the relationship of one facet of behavior, one reaction, to another; this time, however, in historical terms: "You always talk about how wonderful your father was . . . sort of a superman. I would think that would be hard to live up to . . . How was it?" and later, "Do you think that has something to do with your underrating yourself now?" Or, in another case: "Is it possible that your reluctance to commit yourself to Ron, even though you love him so much, has anything to do with a fear of being hurt since your father's disappearance when you were young was so very painful for you?"

These six major categories of client–worker communications will be discussed in detail in Chapters 5, 6, and 7.

Person-in-Situation or Environmental Interventions

In the years following the Great Depression of the 1930s until the development of poverty programs in the 1960s, social work did not give the same quality of attention to "indirect" treatment of the environment as to "direct" treatment of individuals. Even family group treatment, one form of environmental intervention, was not common. This neglect tended to downgrade so-called environmental modification in the worker's mind, as though it were something simple to do and unworthy of serious analysis. Furthermore, social workers tended to think of direct work as psychological and indirect as nonpsychological or "social." This is, of course, a false assumption. *In actuality, environmental work is extremely complex and takes place with people through psychological means.* We cannot physically make a landlord, teacher, or anyone else—even the representative of a social agency—do something for the benefit of our clients. We have to talk with *people* about the clients' needs and desires, and in the process we must use psychological procedures of one sort or another. We also have to enlist our clients in reflections about what kinds of changes in their lives they are seeking. Even when the worker and/or client advocates for improvement of social conditions in a neighborhood, for example, changes come only when one works effectively with people who are in a position to help bring them about.

Furthermore, to improve environmental conditions and opportunities, it is necessary to assess the particular needs, aspirations, and limitations of the clients we serve as well as the potential for change in the systems that surround them. *It is casework's purpose to assist in providing the best possible fit or adaptation between person and situation.* The complexities of both sides of the match must therefore be evaluated.

One can think in terms of treatment *through* the environment and modification *of* the environment. The former uses resources or opportunities that exist, are potentially available, or can be developed for the benefit of the client in the total situation. The latter deals with modifications that are needed in a situation to lessen pressures or increase opportunities and gratifications. A clear example of treatment through the environment would be a worker's enlisting the help of a warm, friendly relative to provide companionship and practical assistance for a woman experiencing postoperative depression. Work upon the environment is illustrated by a worker's

intervening to change a situation where a child is badly suited to a school placement or a landlord is failing to make necessary repairs. Examples of both kinds of treatment can be found in the Kennedy, West, and Stone cases described in Chapter 3.

Increased appreciation of the complexities involved in bringing about changes in the interactions between people and their environments led Hollis to suggest a classification of casework activities not developed in her original typology study. In the third edition of this book, she introduced new categories of environmental procedures, recognizing the need to bring greater specificity to previously vague conceptualizations about "indirect" casework. She proposed classifying and examining environmental procedures in three general ways: by *type of communication,* by *type of role,* and by *type of resource,* each having its own values and uses. Some modifications in the classification have evolved since then. A brief discussion of categories of environmental work follows. These will be elaborated upon in greater detail in Chapter 8.

Type of Communication One can analyze environmental or milieu work from the viewpoint of types of communications used. All milieu work takes place through some form of communication, regardless of whether it is verbal. Nonverbal communication is often of great importance. *The type of classification presented in the preceding section on worker–client communications in "direct work" is also of value in studying communication between worker and collateral.* Environmental treatment uses the first four groups of procedures described for direct work with clients but does not use the fifth and sixth (*pattern-dynamic* and *developmental reflection*). One does not discuss with *any* collateral—be it teacher, minister, doctor, landlord, friend, or relative—the dynamics of that collateral's *own* attitude, behavior, or development. It is only when a relative, "significant other," or friend subsequently enters treatment that these types of reflection would become appropriate.

On the other hand, each of the other four types of communication *is* used in environmental work. There are times when the techniques of *sustainment* are important in building the relationships necessary to involve collaterals constructively, or less destructively, in clients' affairs. One does sometimes use *direct influence* by giving suggestions or advice (in a manner that does not prompt defensiveness). *Exploration, description, and ventilation* are of great importance. Encouragement of ventilation is often the key to a relationship that will permit cooperative work. The fourth group of communication procedures, *person–situation reflection,* almost always occurs in collateral work as workers describe clients and their needs (again, except in preventive work, always with the client's permission); or, quite often, the collateral offers helpful information or perspectives about clients' situations. Through discussion, a worker frequently hopes to modify or enlarge collaterals' understanding of clients and their needs, or the worker may seek assistance and even suggestions from collaterals in order to best understand and assist clients. These four categories of communication can be very useful in analyzing samples of interactions with collaterals. Reasons for the success or failure of efforts to help the client through the milieu can often be identified thereby.

Type of Role   Environmental work can also be classified by type of role: that is, in terms of the role a worker may be assuming when working with an agency or a collateral individual on behalf of clients. Five possible roles are identified in the Hollis typology: (1) The worker may be a *provider* of a resource.

This is true, for example, when he or she is the representative through which one's own agency's services are given. (2) As a *locater,* the worker seeks and finds a resource—agency or individual—that gives promise of meeting a client's need. (3) When it is believed that it would be necessary or helpful, the worker may be an *interpreter* of a client's need to an agency or collateral, especially when for various reasons clients are unable to do so for themselves or when client and worker together decide that the worker's involvement would be beneficial. (4) In more difficult situations, the worker may become a *mediator* for the client with an unresponsive or abusive agency or collateral. (5) In extreme situations, where an agency is clearly failing to carry out its responsibilities or is misusing clients, or when an individual is violating clients' rights, the worker may need to take on a role characterized by *aggressive intervention.* This role often includes *advocacy,* when workers engage in activities—when possible, in concert with clients—designed to secure services to which clients are entitled, but which they are unjustly denied or unable to secure by their own efforts. The fourth and fifth roles just described are often assumed when clients do not receive needed services such as public assistance, medical care, housing, safe shelters for the homeless or for battered and abused women and children, appropriate educational opportunities, or helpful police protection, among others. These roles are also taken on by workers—again, whenever possible, together with clients—when discrimination on the basis of race, ethnicity, gender, sexual orientation, or handicap is impeding clients' goals or threatening their physical or psychological well-being, as prejudice almost always does.

Type of Resource   It can be useful for social workers to organize their thinking about milieu work in terms of four subcategories of the kind of resource involved in providing service or assistance to clients:

1. A primary source of such help is the organization where the worker helping the client is employed. One thinks immediately of the family service agency or the child-placing agency where workers are responsible for making resources of the agency available, such as foster and adoptive homes. This subgroup also includes organizations with caseworkers on staff or that have a social work department; examples include schools, courts, or hospitals where social services are offered to the client.

2. An important type of resource is the agency where the worker helping the client is *not* a staff member but with which the worker must interact and, perhaps, try to influence on the client's behalf. This subcategory includes social service agencies, institutions that employ social workers, and non-social work organizations of all kinds.

3. Independent social work practitioners represent a kind of resource to whom, for example, a hospital social worker might refer a client who is being discharged. Or, a clinical social worker treating a client may locate a private practitioner who specializes in group therapy that would supplement individual work; collaboration (with the client's permission, of course) between two workers involved with the same client is not uncommon.

4. The final subcategory includes individuals or *collaterals* in the milieu: *(a)* those who clearly have an *instrumental* or *task-oriented* relationship to the client, such as employers and landlords; *(b)* those who have an *expressive* or *feeling-oriented* relationship, such as relatives, friends, close neighbors;and *(c)* those independent professionals or others *ethically committed* to

being of help to the client; this group includes mental health practitioners, doctors, teachers, lawyers, and religious leaders who may fall between the instrumental and expressive categories: that is, they are more closely connected to the client than the former, but usually less personally or emotionally involved than the latter. Many charge fees for their services but maintain a professional, helpful, and caring attitude toward clients and their well-being. These people often can be important resources for social workers to contact on behalf of clients.

Summary

This chapter offers a classification of treatment procedures that starts with Richmond's suggestion of separating casework into direct work with clients and indirect work with the environment on their behalf. The Hollis typology picked up some components of subsequent classifications, finally arriving at an arrangement that uses as its logical foundation the major dynamics employed by clinical social work in its effort to enable clients—individuals and families—to move toward their goals.

Accordingly, six categories of direct treatment and three types of environmental procedures are delineated.

Six Categories of Client–Worker Communications:

A. Sustainment.
B. Direct influence.
C. Exploration, description, ventilation.
D. Person–situation reflection concerning:
   1. Others, client's own health, and outside world in general.
   2. Effects of clients' behavior on themselves and others.
   3. Nature of clients' own behavior, thoughts, and feelings.

4. Causative factors of clients' interactions or behavior when in interactions with others or other situational provocations.
5. Clients' self-evaluation.
6. Worker and treatment process.

E. Pattern-dynamic reflection (discussion of dynamics of response patterns and tendencies).

F. Developmental reflection (discussion of developmental or historical aspects of response patterns and tendencies).

Three Types of Environmental Procedures:

A. Type of communication (parallel to first four client–worker categories).

B. Type of role.
  1. Provider of resources.
  2. Locator of resources.
  3. Interpreter of client to milieu person.
  4. Mediator between client and milieu agency or collateral.
  5. Aggressive intervenor between client and milieu organization or collateral or advocate on client's behalf.

C. Type of resource.
  1. The agency where the worker helping the client is employed.
  2. An organization where the worker is not employed.
  3. Independent social work practitioners.
  4. Individuals (collaterals) who are:
     a. In an instrumental relationship with the client.
     b. In an expressive relationship to client.
     c. Independent professionals or others who have a commitment to the client's well-being and goals.

According to this system, the casework treatment of any case as a whole is seen as a *constantly changing blend of some or all of these treatment procedures.* The nature of the blend will vary with the needs of the case and with the nature of the client's personality, his or her dilemma or problem, and a number of other variables.

Chapters 5, 6, and 7 will discuss in detail the first half of this typology, communications between client and worker. A more detailed description of the research of Hollis and others relating to worker–client process and procedures can be found in Chapter 21. Chapter 8 will elaborate on environmental issues and procedures in psychosocial casework.

NOTES

1. Richmond (1922), p. 102. Other references of historical interest are Virginia P. Robinson (1921); and *Social Casework, Generic and Specific: An Outline: A Report of the Milford Conference* (New York: American Association of Social Workers, 1929).

2. See Grete L. Bibring (1947). Dr. Bibring, a psychiatrist who worked closely with caseworkers in Boston, developed a classification of treatment procedures; it was her opinion that caseworkers did not usually interpret unconscious material as psychoanalysts did.

   For references to the classifications of treatment techniques that were being developed in the 1940s and 1950s, and to discussions of distinctions being made between casework and psychoanalysis, see Florence Hollis (1947 and 1949); and two articles by Lucille Austin (1948 and 1956).

3. For those interested in more detailed discussion of the early development of classifications, refer to previous editions of this text.

4. Family Service Association of America (1953), p. 19.

5. See Family Service Association of America (1958), p. 15.

6. Sidney Berkowitz (1955) was the first writer to raise questions about this issue.

7. Florence Hollis (1968). This publication was a reprint of four articles published in 1967 and 1968 issues of *Social Casework.*

PART TWO

TREATMENT: AN ANALYSIS OF PROCEDURES

CHAPTER 5

SUSTAINMENT, DIRECT INFLUENCE, AND EXPLORATION– DESCRIPTION– VENTILATION

Having discussed the skeletal outline of the Hollis classification of casework treatment, we shall try in this and the following chapters to put flesh on its bare bones.

Although in the reality of treatment there is a fluid mixture of procedures as interviews proceed, to understand their nature one has to pull them apart and examine them separately. From time to time, nevertheless, we will have to shift from discussion of one to another in order to see some of the relationships among them.

SUSTAINMENT

Sustaining procedures are those designed to reduce feelings of anxiety or lack of self-esteem or self-confidence by a direct expression of the worker's confidence or esteem for the client, or confidence that some external threat is not as dangerous as it seems, or— by demonstration of interest in the client— acceptance of the person and desire to help.

In such work, the relief comes not from self-understanding but from the worker's implied assurance to the client who has placed confidence in him or her that it is not necessary to be so worried. The dynamic is not one of reasoning but of faith, dependent upon the client's confidence in the worker's knowledge and goodwill.

Sustaining procedures are perhaps the most basic and essential of all psychosocial casework activities; without them it would be extremely difficult even to explore the nature of the client's difficulties. When an individual, a couple, or a family seeks assistance from someone else, *discomfort* and *anxiety* frequently arise. People are admitting that there is difficulty in managing some aspect of life and that outside help is necessary. There is uncertainty about revealing oneself, often in intimate detail, to an unknown person. Questions arise: Have I (we) come to the right place? What will the caseworker think of me (us)? Is the worker going to prefer another member of the family over me? Will the worker want me (us) to do something I (we) don't want to do? Is the worker competent, truly interested, and ready to help? Will the worker be honest and sincere? Will this stranger be critical or judgmental? Even when people seek help with practical or environmental concerns only, some of these questions may occur. A number of people turn to clinical social workers wanting a sounding board to sort out issues related to important life decisions or to explore avenues for personal growth or richer family relationships; these prospective clients, too, usually harbor apprehensions about what reactions they will encounter when they come for help. Experience has repeatedly shown that clients will be able to give more complete and less distorted information if initial tension is relieved and they feel safe enough to discuss their situations candidly.

In problems that involve interpersonal adjustment, some anxiety typically continues—although with varying levels—throughout the whole treatment. Often, anxiety itself can be a major problem in individual or family adjustment. Sometimes it derives from a general sense of failure or inability to function adequately; sometimes it reflects acute concern about some external situation confronting the clients: an operation, a new and challenging job, a plan for an elderly relative to move into the household. Anxiety may come from a traumatic threat, such as a serious medical diagnosis, an impending eviction, destructive behavior of an adolescent family member, or the possible breakup of a marriage; sometimes there is fear of impulsivity, one's own or a family member's; some people seek treatment because of consuming feelings of guilt.

In general, *the greater the clients' anxiety or lack of self-confidence either initially or during treatment, the more need there will*

be for sustaining techniques. Chief among these is interested, sympathetic, and careful listening, which conveys to clients the worker's concern for their well-being. This skill comes naturally to most caseworkers, for it is an interest in people and their affairs that has brought them into social work in the first place. Nevertheless, workers do vary in their ways of showing it. *Receptiveness* can be indicated by a subtle set of techniques, often not adequately recorded, because the attitude is frequently expressed by the worker's overall behavior and demeanor; some of the most powerful sustaining procedures are not conveyed by specific words at all. Facial expression, eye contact, tone of voice, even a way of sitting as one listens convey the worker's interest, revealing certain underlying attitudes that tend to relieve anxiety and also increase clients' self-respect and self-confidence.

Clients are not seeking avid curiosity, oversolicitude, or effusive expressions of sympathy, but they also do not want cold detachment.[1] Furthermore, as we shall illustrate throughout this text, *clients differ in the amount of sustainment they require or feel comfortable with.* A specific show of concern or sympathy by a worker may be very soothing to one client, while another reacts self-consciously to a similar communication. But in every case, an *attitude of interest is essential throughout treatment.* Specific pains must be taken to communicate it to clients whenever their anxiety is high unless, as we shall see later, there is some therapeutic reason for allowing tension to remain unrelieved.

Another component in the atmosphere between client and worker that can have sustaining value is the sense of *mutuality.* Meetings with individuals and families are not authoritative encounters in which superiors relate, however benevolently, to weak inferiors. Psychosocial casework is an undertaking—a *collaboration*—in which two or more people will work together on a problem. They have mutual respect and mutual interest in improving client well-being. In individual and family meetings, the worker's *frankness and openness* contribute to a feeling of mutuality: "I'm really sorry a more convenient time for our meeting wasn't possible. I'll do my best to work out something better." "Let me be sure I understand you clearly. Are you saying . . . ?" "I hope you will feel free to speak up with any ideas or questions that may come to you as we talk." "I imagine it must be hard for you to talk about this so soon after the accident." "If you find yourself confused or upset by anything I say, please let me know." Ideally, the worker immediately brings the spirit of openness to the task. For some clients it cannot exist right away, but grows as the work proceeds. These issues will be discussed further in Chapter 9 on the worker–client relationship and in Chapter 10 on initial interviews.

Acceptance

A sustaining procedure that goes beyond expressing the basic attitude of interest, concern, and mutuality is that of conveying acceptance to a client.[2] This is a *constant component* of all treatment. It is particularly important that this positive, understanding attitude be conveyed to a person feeling guilt or shame, anger or fear. As explained in Chapter 2, *acceptance* refers to the worker's *continuing goodwill toward the client, whether or not the worker approves of the client's opinions and actions*. A worker may be deeply disturbed by antisocial behavior that can be permanently damaging to its victims, such as physical assaultiveness or incest. Yet it is not only possible but necessary for the worker to communicate

an attitude of acceptance even while stating clearly that the client's behavior has been harmful to others.[3] Acceptance is not an expression of opinion about an act but an expression of goodwill toward the actor.

As difficult as it may seem to maintain an attitude of acceptance toward a client who has violently abused others, it can be equally challenging for a worker to maintain goodwill in the face of hostile or "demanding" behavior. Yet acceptance is of utmost importance when working with individuals (such as Mrs. Zimmer, discussed in Chapter 3) who have severe developmental deficits or difficult personality traits. As we will examine more closely in Chapter 9, *acceptance and empathy go hand in hand*. When we realize that behavior sometimes pejoratively described as "manipulative," "guilt-provoking," or "self-centered" often derives from feelings of desperation, or from crucial needs left unattended during childhood, it becomes possible for us to function in a more understanding and healing manner.[4]

Reassurance

A further step in the sustaining process consists of reassurance about anxiety and guilt. For example, a mother who has great difficulty recognizing her own feelings of hostility may during treatment become aware of strong anger toward her child. The worker may seek to reassure her by expressing *understanding of the feeling and recognition of the provocation*. This technique must be used with delicacy and discrimination. *It can sometimes be tempting to overuse reassurance* in an effort to build up a relationship or because the worker cannot endure the client's anxiety. Yielding to the urge to offer too much support, however, may merely leave the client with the feeling that the worker does not fully comprehend the reasons for guilt or anxiety, or that the worker is deficient in moral discrimination and therefore is not a person whose judgment matters. Moreover, when the client is ready to explore the reasons for actions, the worker needs to be particularly careful not to give reassurance so readily that the client becomes completely comfortable and feels no need to understand troublesome behavior and its effects. *Reassurance must be justified by reality,* or the client will almost always sense falseness or at best feel temporary comfort.

In the illustration in the previous paragraph, it was important to reassure the mother at first because she had unusually high guilt and could acknowledge her feelings only with great reluctance. But after time, when she became better able to talk about her angry feelings toward her child, the worker no longer needed to be reassuring; instead, she agreed that the feelings were unusually strong and, shifting to procedures for developing understanding (*reflective procedures*), suggested seeking out some sources of her extraordinary irritation.

Similarly, it certainly does no good to tell a man or his family that there is no need to fear an exploratory operation that is being performed to determine whether there is cancer. Instead, one may want to go into procedures for *reflective discussion* of the fears in light of the real situation. This too would lessen anxiety, but by a dynamic different from that of *sustainment.* If there is panic about the operation, the worker's calm consideration of its possible outcomes will probably be reassuring. If the clients are overreacting—either by anticipating cancer when this possibility is not realistically justified, or by ignoring the possibility of medical help if a malignancy is revealed— reflective discussion combined with reassurance may clarify the situation. The anxiety of the patient and family members may be reduced by bringing attention to the reality

of a possible positive outcome of the operation and the fact that cure may be possible even if cancer is found. If the worker already has the clients' confidence, further reassurance could be offered by an expression of confidence in the doctors, when this is justified, to increase trust in them.

If clients are afraid of their own impulses or those of family members, reassurance is sometimes helpful, but *only* if the worker has a factual basis for believing that the clients are really able to handle destructive feelings and want to do so.

> Parents, unable to convince their 14-year-old boy to join them for a family session, came for an initial visit to a caseworker, reporting that they were terrified that their son was going to seriously hurt his younger sister. The worker assumed that the parents were overreacting since the boy had never physically harmed his sister, or even threatened to do so, even though he frequently verbally abused her. Unfortunately, the well-meaning worker, who wanted to allay the parents' fears, gave them undue reassurance by reminding them that adolescents are often hostile. As it turned out, a few days later, the boy did push his sister off of a bicycle, causing her to break an arm. Not surprisingly, the family found another therapist.

In this case, never having met the boy, the worker simply did not have enough information to go on. In other situations, when the person involved is present, sometimes reassurance can help if accompanied by other procedures, especially forms of *reflection,* where the dynamic is increased knowledge and understanding; in this way the client may have reason to believe that greater control can be achieved and is worth achieving. The worker can refer to similar situations in which the client has been able to exercise control. Sometimes the worker addresses the dynamics of behavior, pointing out that an acknowledged impulse can be more easily held in check than a hidden one; or, the client may be helped to consider some of the unrealistic factors contributing to the urge to act on certain feelings. Had the teenager in the above case been able to reflect on what was behind his abuse of his sister, he might have been helped to see his relationship with her differently or to find other ways of dealing with his feelings. In family meetings the relationships among family members, and the possible dynamics contributing to the boy's behavior, could be reflected upon by everyone present. All these procedures can be strengthened by concurrent sustaining communications that convey the worker's understanding of the emotion and acceptance of the individual, even when the effort is to help the client reconsider destructive behaviors.

Obviously, except at the very beginning, sustaining procedures are usually preceded by *exploration, description,* and *ventilation.* One can scarcely react in a sustaining way until the clients have talked about the matters that are causing feelings of inadequacy, anger, or anxiety. Sometimes, however, people are so anxious or so guilty that they are blocked from talking about these things. Then the worker's verbal and nonverbal indications of interest, concern, and desire to help are of value in overcoming the hesitation. The case of Jed Cooper (Chapter 20) exemplifies this point.

Encouragement

A similar process occurs when a worker expresses confidence in clients' abilities, recognizes achievements, and shows pleasure in their successes. Encouragement is especially important in work with children, and it is also especially effective with adults who generally lack self-confidence, are faced with especially difficult tasks, or are going

through a period of anxiety in which their normal self-confidence is weakened. Almost everyone can benefit from genuine encouragement. There is a great difference, of course, between honest appreciation and flattery. The very fact that people are insecure often makes them extremely sensitive to hollow insincerity, and their trust in the worker evaporates if they suspect encouraging comments are merely a technique meant to inject courage into their personalities.

When expressing confidence in clients' abilities to handle specific tasks or situations, it is important that the worker be realistic about clients' capacities. It is equally important to be sensitive to *clients' own perceptions* of their abilities.[5] Too ready assurance, even when realistically justified, can cause the client to bottle up anxiety, which may then reappear in full force the very moment that self-confidence is most needed. If lack of self-confidence is very great, other procedures in addition to sustainment may be called for. Initial *ventilation* followed by *reflective consideration* of the situation causing so much self-doubt or fear may be required. Encouragement is often the effect of identifying and reflecting upon past successes with similar tasks. A woman afraid to speak up to her child's teacher may recall how she was able to defend herself against false accusations made by a landlord. Recognition of the strength it has taken to confront discrimination or abusive treatment of any kind—situations that are part of so many people's lives—can encourage clients to see that past successes may bode well for future efforts. But *over*encouragement can boomerang if the client does not have the capacity, or is not yet ready, to follow a particular plan of action; self-doubt will be fostered rather than alleviated.

Another caution concerning procedures of encouragement: They tend to arouse in clients the feeling that they should live up to the worker's expectations. Particularly if there is the possibility that the client will not succeed, it is important to deal in advance with the anxiety this may create by making it clear—in words or in actions—that the worker will not be upset by failure, will continue to feel interest and confidence in the client, and will help the client to deal with disappointment and to find another solution. Other sustaining techniques of conveying acceptance and reassurance often need to accompany encouragement.[6]

Reaching Out

At times an individual or family's need for sustainment is so strong and distrust or anxiety so great that something *more concrete than words* is needed to demonstrate the worker's concern and wish to help. We are most familiar with the use of such techniques with children who, it has long been recognized by practitioners, may need concrete evidence of the worker's goodwill. Small gifts and snacks have been used to build a positive relationship with children, especially young children. It is customary for a worker to express fondness directly and, with small children, to convey it physically—by holding a child on one's lap or by putting a protective arm around an upset youngster.

A comparable process is sometimes needed with adults. The early literature on the "hard to reach" emphasized the importance of winning clients' confidence partly by doing concrete things for their benefit, offering *environmental help:* working out difficult situations with a landlord or the department of welfare, arranging camp for children, or finding a volunteer to take children to busy clinics when a parent cannot do this. Advocacy and linkage to resources combined with nonjudgmental respect and flexibility are all often essential to effectively engage and assist individuals with se-

rious difficulties who usually do not seek help for themselves.[7] Outreach to homeless persons who often need services or protection of one kind or another can be critical to engaging them. Genuine *acceptance*—in contrast to the disdain often expressed toward them—and *concrete assistance* such as food, clothes, and medical or financial assistance may begin to demonstrate the worker's personal interest in homeless individuals and families.[8] These are *important services in their own right, but they also symbolize the worker's concern and thus act as emotionally sustaining factors.* Offering concrete assistance is not only useful to work with the socioeconomically disadvantaged. The elderly, the physically or mentally disabled, those experiencing difficult life events, and many others who simply have not received a fair share of personal attention are often supported by the worker's special efforts to reach out to them.[9]

Sometimes when the contact with clients has usually been in the office, the "reaching out" is a visit to them at home at a time of stress; sometimes it is arranging for an extra session or merely giving extra time in a regular interview. A telephone call, note, or attendance at a funeral can mean a great deal when there has been a death in a family. Securing information or making a phone call about available resources can be supportive. *Whenever the worker's action is designed especially to convey to clients a desire to help, it represents this form of sustaining work.* Again, it would not be the only procedure employed, but it might accompany or be a necessary prelude to other techniques. In work with adults, such concrete demonstrations are not universally needed, and in any case they must be used with great discrimination based on sound diagnostic thinking. They should not grow out of the worker's enjoyment of gratitude or need to encourage dependent relationships.

Nonverbal Sustainment

As already noted, much sustainment is given nonverbally. Workers do not listen to clients impassively. Rather, sympathetic "umms," facial and bodily expressions of complete listening, facial changes and gestures respond to, and sometimes mirror, what the client is saying or feeling. Brief verbal comments such as "yes," "I know," "I see," and a repetition of the last word or two of a client's sentence are all used to show continuing attentiveness. The very way in which a client is received in an office can have either a reassuring effect or the opposite. Is the receptionist courteous? Is the waiting room pleasant? How does the worker greet the client? Is the worker prompt? Interaction begins at once.

Workers differ in their nonverbal expressiveness. Through the use of one-way mirrors, films, and videotapes, we can study this elusive quality and its bearing upon successful work.

Secondary Sustainment

After some experience with the Hollis typology in teaching and in research, it became clear that there is both direct and indirect— or secondary—sustainment. In other words, *sustainment can be a by-product of procedures used primarily for the encouragement of reflection or even of exploration or direct influence.* For instance, we sometimes do not understand what a client is trying to say. One may then simply make comments such as, "I don't quite know what you mean," and ask for further explanation until the communication is clear. This procedure is primarily a part of the process of *exploration* or *ventilation,* but it can also communicate the worker's interest and constant attentiveness. In this sense, it is a secondary type of sustainment.[10]

Workers differ greatly in the extent to which they insert sustaining words and phrases into their reflective communications when there is a possibility that these communications may arouse anxiety. Further research would be required to determine whether the smaller *quantity* of sustaining statements offered by some workers is compensated for by the *quality* of the overall support they provide, a matter that is difficult to measure directly. To study this question, client ratings of a worker's supportiveness and interest could be contrasted with the actual frequency of sustaining words and phrases.[11]

Sustainment and Conjoint Interviews

The use of sustaining procedures in *joint or family interviews* is just as important as in individual work, but special care is required because they have to be seen in the light of the effect they will have on everyone present. A communication that is accepting, encouraging, or reassuring to one person may be interpreted differently by another. Worker *impartiality* is essential in all conjoint work, with the worker clearly establishing a "no-fault" climate in which blame is not cast (at least by the worker) and solutions are worked on by all involved. Otherwise, for example, sympathy with the hurt feelings of a wife may convey disapproval to the husband, whom the wife is already blaming for "causing" the suffering. Or, sustainment of one marital partner may arouse jealousy in the other. The use of the Hollis procedures in family and couple treatment will be discussed further in Chapters 15 and 17.

DIRECT INFLUENCE

The second set of procedures, those designated direct influence, includes the various ways in which the worker tries by the force—in various degrees—of his or her opinion to promote a specific kind of behavior by the client. For example, a worker may give advice or make suggestions about dealing more advantageously with an employer, consulting a doctor, going through with a medical recommendation, handling the children, or improving interpersonal communication skills.

For many years, this type of activity has been suspect in casework. In the days of innocence, before the 1930s, when workers were universally thought to be wiser and better informed than clients, advice was one of the "friendly visitor's" chief stocks in trade. Through bitter experience, caseworkers gradually learned that the wife who took the worker's advice and separated from her alcoholic husband more often than not took him back again, despite her fear of the visitor's disapproval; that the mother who let herself be guided by the visitor's child-rearing theories somehow managed to demonstrate that they did not work with her Johnnie; and that the homemaker who let herself be taught how to make up a set of budget envelopes did not simultaneously learn how to keep her fingers out of the wrong envelope when the bill collector came to the door. From such experiences came considerable reluctance to tell clients how to run their lives. Nevertheless, it has been generally recognized in casework practice that at some times, for some clients, there is need for carefully considered direct influence.

There is some evidence—and we would expect this to be so—that in parent–child problems workers are more likely to give advice than in marital work.[12] It has also been thought by some that clients with little education, members of lower-income groups, or those from particular cultures come to agencies seeking advice and are dissatisfied with the worker who gives little

or none.[13] In most cases, *mutual assessment by client and worker is required to determine what kind of advice—if any—a particular client is seeking and can use:* decisions always have to be made on the basis of the person's or family's need, rather than on assumptions about requirements of people with particular educational, economic, or ethnic backgrounds. It is true, however (as we shall discuss in Chapter 18), that in *crisis treatment,* when people are often very overwhelmed, decisive interventions, including strong suggestions or advice from the worker, may be necessary. When a situation is dangerous—such as in cases of physical abuse or incest within a family—the worker may have to be directive, but even in these cases the best results usually come from joint efforts on the part of worker and clients to consider what options best suit the circumstances.

There are many aspects to the question of determining how much advice is helpful: To what extent, when advice is given, is it used? To what extent has advice proved beneficial in the situation for which it was given? Then there is the hardest question of all to answer: In the long run, is it more helpful for the client to follow advice or to be helped to think things through without being given specific suggestions or opinions?

It is probably apparent to the reader by now that on ethical and practical grounds we, the authors, prefer to help clients—through *reflective discussion—to make their own decisions* about what changes they want to make and what steps they want to take to make them. Certainly psychosocial casework's commitment to the value of *self-direction* is better served thereby. In our experience, also, there is *more positive carry-through into other aspects of their lives* when clients participate in learning how to make their own choices rather than when they blindly follow the lead of the worker.

Yet, as we have said, under some circumstances, direction from the worker is not only sought by clients but also is useful to them. It becomes our responsibility to make the best determinations we can, on an ongoing basis, about when advice giving is indicated and when it may impede self-reliance. The discussions that follow suggest some broad guidelines.

Degrees of Directiveness

Direct influence consists of a graduated set of techniques of varying degrees of directiveness. As one works with these procedures, one discovers that they constitute a range of processes that form a *continuum*. If some kind of guidance is to be given, in most situations, *preference should be given to the most gentle form of influence that can be employed successfully.*

1. Giving Advice or Stating an Opinion Taking a stand concerning actions that the worker thinks the client should take is placed in the middle of the continuum. The worker may point out to a child's mother that Lydia knows her way to school, is careful about crossing streets, and will have more chance to play with other children if her mother does not accompany her. Or the worker may comment to a client, Mr. Ruiz, who is hesitating to ask for a seemingly deserved raise, that several other people in his office have been given a raise, and that the only way to find out whether he can get one is to ask for it.

2. Making a Suggestion This is a less forceful way of presenting these same ideas. The worker might comment to Lydia's mother, "It's only two blocks to the school. My guess is that Lydia is old enough now to go that far with her friends." Or, one might say to Mr. Ruiz, "Sometimes people just ask

for a raise." The solution is raised in the client's mind in a way that conveys the worker's inclination toward it, but leaves the client with the alternative of rejecting the idea without feeling that he or she is being contrary to the worker's definite opinion. Furthermore, the client usually has more information than the worker, such as about the safety of the neighborhood for Lydia or about the boss's particular attitude toward Mr. Ruiz.

3. Underlining A still milder form of influence is that of simply emphasizing a course of action the client is already contemplating. The mother thinks it might be a good idea to let six-year-old Lydia walk to school alone; the worker agrees it might be worth trying. Or Mr. Ruiz says he is thinking of asking the boss for a raise, and the worker nods approvingly. Even if this client eventually decides against the step, there is little likelihood that he will feel he has opposed the worker's opinion because it was his own idea in the first place. When the client does go ahead with an idea and it works, the client takes the credit; if it fails, the edge may be taken off the failure, since the worker also made the mistake of thinking it would work.

4. Urging or Insisting Putting forcefulness behind the advice that is offered is toward the other end of the continuum. A worker tells a mother that it is essential for her to take Johanna to school, even though the child is frightened. Such pressure is sometimes necessary in treatment of school phobia, especially when the mother's own need to keep the child close may be contributing to the difficulty. In such situations, treatment of the child cannot wait upon a slow change in the mother's attitude, which might take months to bring about; in the interim, problems may be added to the initial phobia to such a degree that a permanent learning or social difficulty may ensue. Also, Johanna's fears may snowball dangerously if she does not return to school immediately.[14]

5. Strongly Cautioning   This is toward the very directive end of the continuum. A worker might warn Mr. Ruiz that it would be *very unwise* for him to ask for a raise when he is on such bad terms with his boss, that such action might result in his being fired. When there is a possibility of severe consequences of an impulsive, ill-considered action, or when sufficient time is not available to help the client think a matter through rationally, such active persuasion may be worth trying. But if the client does not take the advice and suffers the predicted result, the worker must avoid anything that can be construed as an "I told you so" attitude. Properly handled, the client is able to express disappointment and to feel that the worker, too, feels regret; the failure may even open the way to reflective consideration of what was involved and possibly ward off a repetition. If the client's decision worked out, it is a wonderful opportunity for the worker to say something encouraging like: "You really had a better understanding of the situation than I did, didn't you?"

6. Actually Intervening in the Client's Life   Most extreme of all directive techniques is taking such measures as removing from a home a child subjected to cruelty or to a high degree of neglect, or accompanying a psychotic or suicidal client to the hospital, or arranging for an elderly woman living alone, at risk of harming herself, to be moved to a protective facility. Such forceful interventions must rest on two conditions: First, one must be convinced that the step is fully justified and not motivated by some overreaction of one's own; second, one must have thorough knowledge of the community resources involved in the plan of action, of their level of care, and of the extent to which they will support the intervention. In some situations the court may become involved, and it will be important for the worker to be well informed about the conditions under which it would uphold the action taken. Obviously, if the effort fails, one may have lost constructive contact with the client and made the situation worse. When this technique *is* employed, the worker's confidence, firmness, and kindness—and the absence of punitive motivation—are essential for the client to feel the worker's strength and therefore reject the temptation to test it. The worker must also be convinced that the solution is preferable to the problem that inspired it.

At the outset, if at all possible, *the involvement of the client's family or close social network* is critically important in cases in which decisions against a person's or family's will may have to be made. Options and decisions then can be considered that may make it *less necessary for the worker or agency to take sole responsibility for finding solutions.* Relatives may want to offer their own ideas or services that would negate the need for immediate drastic action. For example, parents accused of neglect may be more willing to have their children stay with family members than in a shelter or foster home; a father charged with sexually assaulting his daughter may be willing to leave the home rather than requiring the girl to adjust to some new living arrangement; adult children of the elderly may decide to provide backup services or a place in their home or make their own arrangements for protective care of their parents; family meetings to consider the best action to help severely emotionally distraught individuals may open new possibilities.

Because family dynamics can be so complicated, the worker *must resist taking sides* with anyone involved. If the worker and agency believe that some protective measures must be taken, then that position must be stated clearly: "At least until matters are sorted out, Doreen and you [the father charged with incest] cannot live in the same household." "Now that your [elderly] mother has been found wandering the streets at night several times, and is obviously not eating properly, a new arrangement has to be found." In a climate of neutrality, the worker can then invite all interested people to participate in considering plans that respond to the problem.

There are situations in which techniques of influence are necessary. Sometimes workers have more information—for example, about resources, about child rearing, or about interpersonal communication skills. For various reasons, there are clients who have such strong expectations that the worker will give advice that the worker's reluctance to do so would be misinterpreted as indifference or incompetence. Some clients are simply not yet ready to think things through—either because they are overwhelmed by a traumatic event or oppressive living conditions; are seriously anxious, depressed, or dependent; or have severe psychiatric conditions, such as schizophrenia or an acute borderline disorder.[15] In as many cases as possible, it is the goal of psychosocial clinicians to supplant advice giving with methods that rest on *reflection*—sometimes very early in the contact, at other times gradually.

As long as the worker is philosophically committed to the value of *self-direction,* reasonably conscious of his or her own reactions to the client's need for dependence, and alert to every possibility of encouraging clients to think for themselves, wise use can be made of these procedures.

Risks in Advice Giving: Moving to Reflection

Direct influence has many pitfalls. The most obvious is that *one may give the wrong advice.* Hence, the worker must be reasonably sure of knowing enough about what is best for the client to warrant advice. Especially on important decisions, the worker rarely has enough information to justify influencing other people. For instance, in a decision about whether to break up a marriage, a third person cannot be aware of the subtleties or of the subjective feelings and needs involved to weigh them adequately; this is true even when the objective realities seem to point toward the wisdom of separation. By the same token, despite our general commitment to gender equality, advice related to shifting an apparent imbalance of power in a marital relationship is not called for, especially when this issue is not being raised by the clients. Even if a wife comments, "My husband never lets me write checks or look at our bank balance," it is not the worker's role to react with horror, thereby conveying a strong opinion—verbally or nonverbally. Rather, under some circumstances, one might turn to procedures of *exploration* or *reflection* and ask, in a *neutral* tone, "Why is that?" or "Is that all right with you?" Idiosyncratic personality requirements or cultural tradition may result in marital arrangements that can seem unjust to the socially conscious social worker with different views about gender roles.

Recommended Safeguards

Measures that can be taken to guard against giving the wrong advice or preempting the client's decision-making abilities include:

1. Explore Clients' Expectations   If clients are seeking advice, is it because they are so distraught or bewildered that they truly cannot think clearly? Because of the clients' personalities or cultural backgrounds, are they assuming that guidance and advice are the major functions of a social worker? Are they feeling desperate—realistically or otherwise—for immediate answers? Are they trying to please the worker? If possible, help clients to express their expectations with no more prompting than necessary.

2. Do Not Abruptly Refuse to Give Advice; Give Explanations At the beginning of the contact and sometimes again later, it is necessary to let clients know your reasons for not telling them what to do. Depending on the client and the situation, one might say: "I'd give you advice if I thought it would help, but really *you* are the only one who can know what you want to do. Talking and thinking it out often helps. Let's work together and see whether you can come to a decision that seems right to you." Or, with a different client: "It would be arrogant of me and insulting to you for me to assume I know better what is good for you than you do yourself." See the brief case illustration of Miss Clay on page 249 for another response to appeals for advice.

3. Be Sure the Need for Advice Rests in the Client and Not in the Worker It can be tempting to tell people what to do. It may bolster the worker's self-esteem to be called upon for professional advice. All negative connotations of the word *authority* can be removed simply by putting *professional* in front of it, transforming "authoritativeness" into "strength the client can lean on." That there is such a thing as professional expertise is not to be denied, and under certain circumstances it can be put to good use.[16] However, the need to see oneself as an authority is not sufficient reason for invoking that role.

4. Turn to Reflective Discussion Clients sometimes press the worker into thinking advice is necessary when it is not. Some people like to be told what to do because passive or dependent traits interfere with their ability to think things out for themselves; sometimes later, if things go wrong, they blame others. Anxiety-ridden people with little confidence and people who want very much to please others often ask for more direction than they need. People with obsessive-compulsive traits often seek a great deal of advice because they can be very ambivalent, tending to find initial relief in being told what to do; yet their ambivalence and often harsh superegos can result in a kind of negativism that leads them to then have to prove that the advice given will not work.

In the early stages of the treatment relationship, it may occasionally be wise to accede to a client's request for advice by making *tentative* suggestions. Ideally, however, from the outset the worker finds ways to encourage clients to think things through independently, to consider both subjective and objective factors in their situations, to define their goals, and to enable them to reach solutions for themselves. If necessary, the worker may then affirm the client's decision by expressing agreement, but even this amount of influence is best used very sparingly. Rather, when authentic, the worker may want to reinforce the client's capacity for problem solving: "You really put a lot of good thought into a very complicated problem. What do you think about the decision you have made?" Or, "It must be a real relief to know that you actually had the answer all along, but hadn't been quite aware of it."

5. When Possible, Ask Questions Rather Than Make Statements Instead of giving even gentle advice, it is often preferable to direct a question: "What is it that worries you about Lydia walking to school on her own?" Or, more specifically: "Do you think Lydia would have more friends if you didn't walk her to school every day?" "Is there some safety or other problem that makes you concerned about her going on her own?" Or, to Mr. Ruiz who wants a raise: "What exactly is your hesitation about asking your boss for a raise?" With inquiries such as these, the client is *induced to reflect* on the situation and pull together information that the worker cannot be fully privy to. Not only is independent thinking encouraged, but also because of the client's familiarity with the complexities of the situation, decisions will usually be better informed than if the worker jumps in with advice.

Sometimes direct influence is a *secondary* feature of other worker communications. As we indicated earlier in this chapter, there can be a secondary form of sustainment; so there can also be *secondary directiveness*. Often questions provide clients with guidance about a possibly fruitful avenue of reflection and, in that way, may be offering an opinion or a course of action the client might take. For example, a worker may say to parents who have "grounded" their teenage son for several weeks because of failing grades: "Has his schoolwork improved?" Or, to a father who frequently spanks his apparently hyperactive child ("My parents spanked me and it kept me on the straight and narrow"), a worker might ask: "Do you find the boy is calmer as a result?" In these cases, if the parents' efforts to modify their children's behavior have not been successful, the worker may then wonder aloud, saying something like: "Do you think it would be worthwhile for us to put our heads together and see if there is some other way of helping your son?" Indirectly, the worker is giv-

ing direction, even as she is encouraging the parents to reflect upon their methods and seek other alternatives. Or, a worker may ask a woman who has said she wants to improve her relationship with her husband whether she thinks she will achieve her purpose by so consistently attacking or belittling him. By implication, the worker is advising the client to change her behavior toward her husband to achieve her goal of a better marriage.

Since we believe in the importance of *self-direction,* we need to be very careful in reflective work about exerting secondary direct influence, by being acutely aware that phrasing questions in a certain manner may lead toward a certain answer.

6. Avoid Giving Advice about Major Decisions or Goals Almost always, advice about *how* to implement a decision or reach a goal *set by the client* is more appropriate than advice about *what* objectives should be chosen. For example, a worker might suggest that a client bring a tape recorder to treatment sessions; experience indicates that certain clients with extreme anxiety or those who have difficulty remembering can benefit from reviewing material covered in treatment sessions. Workers frequently make recommendations in individual and conjoint meetings about means for improving communication patterns. It is also common for workers to urge clients to bring in a spouse or other family member to address interpersonal problems or to discuss situations that affect people close to them. In the Russo family interview (see Chapter 15), the worker set down some ground rules or recommendations for family members to follow. In all of these instances, workers usually *explain explicitly the connection between their suggestions and the clients' goals.*

Sustainment and Direct Influence

A close relationship exists between sustaining procedures and direct influence. Procedures of direct influence, except for active intervention, are *effective only in proportion to the client's trust in the worker*. The client will come to the worker with certain preconceptions growing out of past experience with, or knowledge of, other social workers. Also, certain expectations are inherent in the worker's position: that is, they are *ascribed* to anyone functioning in this particular role. Immediately upon contact, the worker has to begin to *achieve* the reputation of a person to be trusted by virtue of his or her own ways of acting with the client. The client's trust in the worker will be made up mainly of two components: respect for the worker's competence and belief in the worker's goodwill. The latter is built up largely through sustaining processes.

Both direct influence and sustainment draw upon the client's *dependence on the worker,* which must be kept in mind both in using these techniques and subsequently in helping the client regain or strengthen the ability to be *self-reliant.*

EXPLORATION–DESCRIPTION–VENTILATION

The third major division of the typology includes two related but different concepts: exploration–description and ventilation. To *explore* is to *inquire*. To *describe* is simply *to give the facts* as one sees them. To *ventilate* is to *bring out feelings associated with the facts. Exploration–description* is a part of the *psychosocial study,* an effort to secure from clients descriptions of themselves, their situations, and the interactions involved in their dilemmas. *Factual descriptions are rarely either neutral or emotionless.* Sometimes the worker takes the lead

and *explores* or *inquires* as the client explains or spells out the particulars in his or her words.[17] Or, as often happens, individuals or families spontaneously *"tell their stories,"* and the worker listens, injecting questions or occasional comments. In any event, the psychosocial study is a *collaborative inquiry,* a mutual effort to construct a cohesive story in which the *perceptions* of the clients are of primary importance, even though the worker actively assists in the quest for information and coherence. The reciprocal process of exploration–description occurs not only in beginning interviews when the initial picture is emerging but also in each subsequent interview, as the most recent events are gone over and bring to mind other connected events and their *meanings* from the client's perspective.[18] Of course, clients' interpretations of the facts are usually *strongly affected by family and cultural attitudes* that can be important to understanding.

Naturally, clients frequently experience and sometimes express strong feelings on reviewing the facts as they see them. The distinction between *experiencing* and *expressing* emotion is an important one, and it is the chief reason that exploration–description and ventilation are placed together. Clients often experience feelings, even strongly, without showing them. Less strong feelings are often not overtly expressed. Yet, a picture of the client's situation cannot be fully developed unless both cognitive and affective components of the client's circumstances are sought. The worker, therefore, needs to be alert throughout the exploration–description process to feelings—feelings that might have been expected but have not been revealed—and to emotional reactions that may be specific to a particular client.

These procedures are also interlocked with those of *reflection.* In the latter, one often helps a client become aware of feelings that have been suppressed. This is done commonly by encouraging clients to recognize emerging emotions (no matter how slight or transitory) as events are discussed. When such emotions are reflected upon, a great deal of *ventilation* may ensue. This release can bring considerable relief and may also be an important way of demystifying, or making less frightening, feelings that are ambiguous or hard for the client to understand. Furthermore, *insight* or self-knowledge, not just emotional release, may occur when exploration–description and ventilation occur in the context of a comfortable *relationship*. Thoughts about oneself, about others, or about specific events can change as they are described and feelings about them articulated, often leading the client to new perspectives.

Anger, Hatred, and Ventilation

Feelings of anger and hatred are especially likely to lose some of their intensity if they can be given adequate verbal expression. This is particularly true for clients who have difficulty accepting negative or aggressive emotion. Frequently, ventilation makes it possible later to move to *reflective discussion* of the circumstances and the provocations of the anger. Eventually, the client may be able to reach greater understanding of such matters as: other people involved in the problem, faulty communication, or ways of preventing the anger-arousing situations. It is often important that such ventilation be accompanied by *sustainment,* particularly *acceptance.*

Angry feelings are not always relieved through ventilation, however. As we shall describe shortly, sometimes expressions of anger are actually a *defense against other, "softer" feelings,* which some clients find more difficult to face or admit. Also, anger

is often a natural reaction to feeling helpless, trapped, or victimized; although the emotions must be thoroughly understood and acknowledged by the worker, ultimately the *anger is not likely to diffuse until the people no longer feel powerless and have gained some sense of control over their lives, even in the face of difficult life events.* Treatment, therefore, will often include *reflective procedures* aimed at finding ways to modify the constraining situation and/or the person's attitudes about it so that changes can be made. It often seems unfair that clients have to be the ones to find new ways to manage when their distress is so closely related to unjust external assaults or oppression.

Grief Reactions

The importance of enabling people to mourn has long been recognized in casework. Some individuals, either for cultural reasons or because they place an especially high value on being stoical or "strong," are embarrassed to show their sorrow. *Ventilation* plays an important role in bringing these feelings of grief to expression in a sympathetic atmosphere. With a person who is depressed after the loss of a loved one—whether through death or through separation of any other kind—it can be of special value to feel that here is a place where it is all right to cry and where the grief is understood.[19]

Similarly, expression of feeling can bring relief to a person who has a permanent disabling illness or injury, or had disfiguring surgery, or is facing death or the diagnosis of a fatal illness. Relatives, friends, and sometimes medical personnel may praise patients for their courage in maintaining a calm exterior when their greatest need is really to "let go," to be heard and understood.

As is true in the use of any treatment procedure, *timing* is important. When helping a client to bring out grief reactions, one must be sensitive to defenses holding back the discharge of emotion and wait until the client is sufficiently comfortable to express the feelings.

Not infrequently, where we would expect grief, the underlying emotion is a different one, such as *anger* or *fear*. Reactions to loss may occur in stages. *Guilt* or *shame* may be felt, for example, by a client who has lost a breast through surgery or who has had a colostomy. It is *critically important that the worker does not push for an emotion that the client is not experiencing or unwittingly cut off expression of a feeling because the worker is not expecting it.*

For the terminally ill, there are often periods of *denial* or, occasionally, refusal to believe that death is imminent. Such denial temporarily precludes the expression of feelings associated with it. In all these instances, *ventilation does not occur until after awareness of the deeper emotions.* Thus, a form of *reflection* will need to precede and make possible the ventilation of emotion. Here, again, the worker must respect defenses and proceed with gentleness. Feelings about impending death should be approached when the client shows some sign of wanting to talk about them, not just when the worker thinks it would be good for the person to do so. In the case of Mrs. Stasio (see Chapter 20), denial was unusually mild and ventilation was an ongoing emphasis in treatment.

Mourning is not always confined to recent events. Often, for example, while recounting history, clients bring up memories—sometimes long forgotten—about early losses and deprivations or neglect and abuse. Any traumatic event can stir up strong emotional reactions of sorrow and loss that may or may not have been previously expressed.

Guilt Feelings

In the ventilation of guilt feelings, the interplay between *ventilation* and *sustainment* is particularly close. Alleviation of feelings of guilt requires more than mere expression, although expression may be the first step. It is the worker's attitude toward guilt that is of primary importance. If the guilt is an appropriate response to events in the client's life, the worker's continued *acceptance* of the person after the guilt has been articulated is of great value in reducing the intensity of these feelings. An accepting gesture is sometimes enough. Expressing sympathy about these guilt feelings often helps: "Yes, it is hard to find you have been wrong." "We all do things sometimes that we later wish we hadn't." "Yes, I know, it's terribly painful to face it."

Guilt feelings are also often inappropriate: One may blame oneself too much, for too long, or for no reason. Too often, guilt derived from a *harsh, punitive superego can be immobilizing and destructive to self-esteem.* This can be the case with individuals who appear to have *avoidant, obsessive-compulsive,* or *dependent* personality traits and many individuals with *anxiety problems,* including panic disorders and generalized anxiety. Ventilation should usually be followed by either *sustainment* or *reflective discussion* of these overreactions, or both, in an effort to help the client assess the feelings more realistically.

Thirty-seven-year-old Alejandro came to a family agency with symptoms of depression following the death of his mother in Guatemala. When the loss of his mother, who had had a long illness, was *explored,* he expressed guilt for not having been at her bedside "as a good son should." For years, he had worked to support his mother and developmentally disabled brother, both living in Guatemala, leaving Alejandro with just enough resources to maintain himself, his wife, and two daughers in the United States. Trips to Guatemala, therefore, were too costly and would have drained him financially. Alejandro was helped to reduce his guilt, through *sustainment, ventilation,* and *reflection:* The worker's accepting, sympathetic stance toward Alejandro's reactions was bolstered by acknowledging the culturally influenced sense of obligation he felt toward his mother. Alejandro could then express feelings of regret that were deeper than even he had realized. Consideration of the realistic facts about his financial situation that had prevented him from traveling to be with his mother, and his recognition that he would have been with her if he could have been, helped Alejandro to regain the self-esteem he had always enjoyed through his role as family provider.

Although helpful to Alejandro, assisting clients to relieve guilt immediately is not always the most helpful intervention. *Realistic guilt* can be constructive. Critical self-evaluation that helps individuals reflect on the disparity between their behavior and the ways they want to act, or feel they should act, or the kind of persons they wish to be can lead to productive changes. Constructive guilt can be preventive. Clients who have gaps in superego development (*superego lacunae*) or whose ego functioning is not adequate to help them regulate their impulses or have empathy for others—characteristics sometimes associated with *antisocial* or *borderline* personality disorders—may lack remorse about their actions. When concern about the effects of their behavior on others begins to evolve, it can be viewed as an important sign of growth. This may be accompanied by mild feelings of guilt when an interim stage has been reached, in which actions are still primarily at an immature, self-gratifying stage, but regret (sometimes a more useful emotion than guilt) is beginning to be felt about harm done to others.

Frequently, people simply do not realize the extent to which they are hurting other people. In these cases, the problem is not lack of concern, but lack of awareness of the impact they have. When they do begin to recognize the effects of their behavior on others—family members, friends, or associates—they may experience guilt or distress over what they have been doing. In family and in individual sessions, we often hear clients say, in effect: "I had no idea that what I said or did made such a difference or caused so much pain. I feel terrible about it." When they lead to change, such reactions promote the growth of *self-awareness* and *ego controls*. Greater understanding and sensitivity to others often follow. When clients realize that their actions have powerful effects on others and they then develop more effective ways of interacting, not only do relationships usually improve, but *self-esteem* and the sense of *mastery* are often enhanced as well.

Many clinical social workers treat clients who have committed serious crimes or have physically battered or sexually molested others. Even in these cases, guilt is not useful unless it helps people to reflect on their behavior and then make amends and modify behavior patterns. *Excessive and self-debasing guilt may only make matters worse.* Many destructive acts are perpetrated by people whose self-esteem is minimal and who have little confidence that they can change or that they can be valued by others. When one is working with such clients, many sustaining procedures may be required to help them gain enough self-acceptance to be able to reflect on themselves and the meanings of their actions. *Too much attention given to the ventilation of guilt may actually defeat the purposes of treatment.*

Anxiety

Feelings of anxiety may be acute and primarily related to a particular event or situational stress, including that of coming to a professional for help. On the other hand, some clients experience chronic or repeated states of anxiety and have little knowledge of their causes. In both instances, such feelings often can be relieved during the *exploratory phase.* As the anxious client relates the facts that precipitated the distress or describes aspects of present or past life, there is almost always discharge of some emotion associated with these. The fact that the worker is calm can be reassuring and help the client deal with underlying issues contributing to the anxiety, once it is expressed. Here, again, *ventilation* is followed by *sustainment* or *reflection* or both. Often, the worker's realistic confidence that the client has the strength to bear the anxiety and that he or she can find ways of reducing it contributes to the client's ability to do so.

Sometimes anxiety is not directly expressed, but the worker can be alert to its signs. For example, a client may become restless or "block" when certain material is discussed or may perspire or tremble. Under these circumstances, sometimes a sustaining word from the worker (e.g., "You seem to be having difficulty talking about this") can help the client *ventilate* the discomfort enough to allow further *exploration* of the trouble. Or, the worker may address the anxiety-related material through the use of *pattern-dynamic reflection,* such as: "Have you noticed that when we start talking about your husband, you often change the topic?" Of course, there are times when anxiety is so keen that it is necessary for

the worker to postpone exploration of a particular subject until the client can approach it with less apprehension.

Contraindications for Ventilation

Although a certain amount of emotional release is of value in all cases, there are some circumstances when *ventilation* is *not* encouraged. Occasionally, so much anxiety, anger, or other emotion is ventilated that it seems to be *"feeding on itself."* Talking does not bring the client relief and a reduction of feeling, but instead deeper engrossment in it. If this seems to be occurring, the expression of such emotion is not helpful. The worker may discourage it by turning the client's attention to less emotionally laden content or to the question of what can be done to modify the situation or the feelings about which the client has been talking. Often, it is even more helpful to address the matter directly, by bringing the client's attention to it with remarks such as: "Does it seem to you that the more you talk about this, the more agitated you become? I wonder if it might work better if we put our heads together and try to find other ways to gain relief and improve your situation."

Occasionally, especially for people with psychotic or near-psychotic disorders, *ventilation* may lead to the production of increasingly bizarre material, or it may become a stimulus to irrational actions. Accurate diagnostic assessment of the presence of psychotic trends alerts a worker to this possibility. In these cases, it may be more helpful to explore areas that will *strengthen realistic, coherent thinking* rather than to encourage ventilation that may evoke material that in less seriously disturbed people would remain unconscious or would be better organized by the synthesizing ego functions. Again, it is usually respectful and therapeutic to comment directly, as suggested above, thus enlisting the client in a *mutual effort* to find new ways of dealing with feelings and with life situations. This is not to say that all ventilation by people with psychotic disorders should be discouraged. For example, such clients can feel—sometimes very justifiably—that they and their feelings are not taken seriously by others who have labeled them "crazy." In such situations, it can be extremely important for the worker to elicit and acknowledge hurt or anger about this, as was the case with Mrs. Barry (see Chapter 20). Furthermore, in contrast to some others with serious disturbance, ventilation of emotion related to present and past events was of utmost importance to Mrs. Barry's treatment.

For some clients, the *expression of one emotion keeps another hidden.* For example, a client may defend against feelings of anger by excessively venting reactions of grief. Similarly, we often find that intense anger masks "softer" feelings such as sadness, fear, or tenderness. Thus, when we put value on the "open" expression of feeling, it is important to be sure that the expression is of the basic emotion and not just of its "cover." A worker who is alert to this will listen for clues to the underlying feeling and turn from *ventilation* to *pattern-dynamic reflection;* the client can then become aware of the tendency to use this form of protection against exposing a particular emotion and of the reasons for feeling this is necessary.

Occasionally, a worker may observe that a client is deriving marked gratification from *talking freely about himself or herself but seems to be making no effort to use the interviews to move toward any change or improvement,* either in dealing with inner problems or in coping with the situation. Sometimes the client is trying to enlist the worker's sympathy. At other times, the client's complaints function only to post-

pone making essential changes; or they can be a way of putting all the blame on others. Talking may provide temporary narcissistic satisfaction; it may serve a tendency to be self-punishing. None of these help people to better their plight. Once it becomes clear that the client's talk is not leading to any productive discussion or action, it behooves the worker to find a constructive way to lead the conversation elsewhere or, usually better yet, to raise the concern directly, often with questions or comments such as: "What would you like to gain from our talks together?" "Do you think reviewing the same material over again is helping?" "It seems to be difficult to put your finger on just what changes you might make that would improve your situation. Since you can't change your husband directly, do you think you might want to consider taking a different approach with him? Would it help to talk over what you might like to try, or why you are not feeling like trying at all?" In these ways, the idea is conveyed that if things are to get better, changes will be required that only the client can make; at the same time, the worker is offering support, direction, and a collaborative approach. The hope is that whatever reluctance the client has will be uncovered, if not immediately at least after a few such pointed efforts on the part of the worker. Successful treatment of this sort requires a client willing to change, but also a worker free of hostile counter-transference reactions that can be aroused by clients who use ventilation in nonproductive ways.

Ventilation in Joint and Family Interviews

As in sustainment, there is a difference in the ways in which ventilation of certain types can be used in individual and conjoint treatment. There is some evidence that there is less ventilation in joint interviews when compared to individual interviews.[20] Certainly many clients—out of consideration or because they are fearful—refrain from expressing negative emotion toward others present in sessions. In an individual meeting a father, frustrated by his son, may exclaim, "Sometimes I hate Joseph." In a family session, on his own or with the encouragement of the clinician, the father might express his anger more constructively by sharing his exasperation or worry about the boy's behavior, for example, rather than his momentary feelings of hatred. In couple treatment, when one or both people have been unable to express feelings of anger or hurt, the worker's support may enable them to do so in ways that are not destructive. More honest communication may then begin. Such expression can have a profound influence on a partner who has been unwittingly hurtful because of lack of awareness of the spouse's feelings. On the other hand, if emotions are bottled up, people can explode when the pressure becomes too great, or else they may find outlets that are destructive to themselves or others. In conjoint sessions, the extent to which ventilation of negative feelings is helpful depends upon its effect on others. Often, the worker can help family members to express feelings in a way that they are more readily heard, such as with "I" statements rather than with "you" statements ("I feel so frustrated/defeated/hurt/lonely when you ignore me" versus "You are so thoughtless and selfish"). But, when ventilation of negative feelings is not helpful, or relentlessly demeaning and vicious, this should be discussed with the clients; sometimes it is best to turn to individual interviews until a less destructive stage of the relationship can be reached. But, once again, anger or harsh complaints may be defending against risking "softer" feelings of disappointment,

loneliness, and the longing for affection. Frequently, when these are elicited in joint interviews, the extreme or hostile attacks subside. These matters will be discussed in detail in the chapters on family and couple treatment.

NOTES

1. See the well-known work of Truax and Carkuff (1967) whose research indicated that therapist characteristics associated with positive outcome in therapy were accurate empathy, nonpossessive warmth, and genuineness; these "core conditions" are discussed further in Chapter 9. Beutler et al. (1994) discuss supportive treatment in their chapter on therapist variables. See also Greenberg (1986) and Ornstein (1986) on issues related to supportive treatment.

2. The importance of this concept has been emphasized in social work since the 1930s. Annette Garrett's classic, widely read book on the principles and methods of social work interviewing that first came out in 1942 stressed acceptance; see the revised edition of the still very useful guide to interviewing: Garrett (1982).

3. For example, see Bookin and Dunkle (1985); Dougherty (1983); Lester (1982); Jacobson and Gottman (1998); and Williams (1992). See also Chapter 10, note 9.

4. Chapter 3, note 9 provides references on the treatment of borderline and other personality disorders that discuss the many ways in which these techniques are necessary to successful treatment. See discussions of countertransference in Chapter 9. Case examples, with various kinds of presenting difficulties, are to be found in Elson (1986); see also her discussion of this issue, pp. 5–7. Garrett (1982) also gives relevant case illustrations.

   Hepworth (1993) offers specific suggestions for managing clients' "manipulative" behavior in a warm but clear and firm manner.

5. Furstenberg and Rounds (1995) discuss the concept of self-efficacy: the individual's perceived (versus actual) ability to carry out a

particular task or action; of course, the greater the belief in one's ability, the greater the effort to perform the task. Using a behavioral approach, the authors suggest interventions to help increase self-efficacy. See Wachtel (1993), a book we recommend, Chapter 7, for discussions of building on strengths. See Chapter 1, note 37 for references on strengths.

6. For illustrations and discussion of sustaining techniques, see Chescheir (1985). See also Wachtel (1993), especially pp. 150–56. See Greene and Orman (1981) for an interesting discussion of supportive techniques used with the emotionally and economically deprived client.

7. See an excellent article by Klein and Cnaan (1995) on reaching out to high-risk clients with severe mental illness and secondary diagnoses such as substance abuse and AIDS. See Ivanoff, et al. (1994) who, from research, developed concepts and techniques for working with involuntary clients in a variety of settings, including child protective and criminal justice organizations. Schlosberg and Kagan (1998) offer practical and useful ideas for engaging chronic "multiproblem" families. See also Krumer-Nevo (1998) on working with mothers from "multiproblem" families, and a volume by Rooney (1992) on strategies for working with involuntary clients. Other references on providing services to reluctant, involuntary, "hard-to-reach," and "multiproblem" individuals and families can be found in Chapter 6, note 3; Chapter 8, note 19; Chapter 9, notes 3 and 4; and Chapter 10, note 5.

8. For readings on outreach to and practice with homeless persons, see Blankertz, et al. (1990); Lindsey (1996); Sheridan, et al. (1993); and Zeifert and Brown (1991).

9. Burstein (1988) discusses ethical and treatment issues involved in working with elderly clients who have not voluntarily sought services and may not want them. Jones and Kilpatrick (1996) apply "wellness theory" to work with clients with disabilities, urging emphasis on self-determination, strengths, and a nonblaming approach.

10. Boatman (1974).

11. Ehrenkranz (1967).

12. See Davis (1975).

13. Several studies were conducted in the 1960s and 1970s suggesting that clients from certain groups, classes, or cultures sought and preferred to be given direct advice. Among them were Reid and Shapiro (1969) and Mayer and Timms (1970) who reported that satisfied clients received more guidance than less satisfied clients (p. 93). On the other hand, Geismer, et al. (1972), after examining treatment outcomes reported: "The relatively more successful worker was found to have been supportive rather than directive . . . and to have greater client participation in treatment."

We have been unable to locate any recent studies that link clients' desire for advice with any particular group or background. Beutler, et al. (1994) report on a meta-analysis of 19 studies of short-term psychodynamic psychotherapy and conclude that "therapist directiveness was generally counterproductive to therapeutic outcomes in psychodynamic therapy" (p. 256).

14. School phobias were first identified by Klein (1945). There is considerable evidence that conditioning, essentially a form of direct influence, can be effective in removing symptoms and helping the child to return to school. See Lassers, et al. (1973). However, often the problem has very little to do with school (although this should be individually assessed), but represents a child's worry about a parent or other family member that leads the child to feel insecure and stay at home and even cling to that person; the longer the child refuses to go to school, the greater the probability of regression and withdrawal. As Lieberman points out (1979, pp. 173–76), crisis intervention to remove school phobia is important, but the underlying anxiety and other symptoms are likely to persist or increase without additional treatment. In our experience, family therapy can be helpful in identifying the dynamics of the situation and helping family members make the changes necessary to put the child at ease.

15. For illustrations and discussions, see Klugman, et al. (1995) on suicidal clients; Nelsen (1975a; and 1975b, reprinted in Turner's 1995 edited volume) on treatment of schizophrenia; Wegscheider (1981), especially Chapter 11, on the alcoholic family; Chapter 10, note 12 for readings on alcoholism; Chapter 20, note 5, for references on adult children of alcoholics; and Wetzel (1984) on treatment of depression.

16. See Gourse and Chescheir (1981) and Hutchison (1987) for discussions of the use of authority. Dworkin (1990) raises important issues in her discussion of conflicts experienced by practitioners in terms of their use of authority and power. See also Diorio (1992) who conducted a qualitative study of 13 parents receiving mandated protective services from child welfare workers; he determined that some parents felt the authority used was unjust and makes recommendations for workers to respect parents' reactions and perspectives and appreciate the extent to which any abuse of power can exacerbate parental fear and make matters worse. In an interesting study of power in client–worker relationships, Cohen (1998) found that in residences serving men and women who had histories of homelessness and psychiatric hospitalizations that the residents/clients "were very clear about their distaste for authoritarian relationships" (p. 440) and wanted to have input into plans and decisions that affected them.

17. See Wachtel, Chapter 6, aptly titled "Exploration, Not Interrogation."

18. See Chapter 1, note 36, for references on constructivism, all of which are relevant to this process of the client's evolving understanding of the meanings of his or her experience and situation. See the December 1996 issue of *Family Process* for articles on narrative therapy with children.

19. We especially recommend the volume edited by Walsh and McGoldrick (1991) with many very useful chapters on working with death in the family from a systems perspective. Shapiro (1994) takes a developmental and systemic view of the griever and the context in which the griever lives and functions; in another article (1996), she discusses cultural influences on bereavement. See also Baker (1992), Warmbrod (1986), and Woods (1982) for discussions of childhood bereavement and clinical treatment. Norris-Shortle et al. (1993) discuss grief in children three and under and recommend interventions.

For further useful references on mourning and loss, see Brunhofer (1997), Sable (1992), Prichard, et al. (1977), Rosen (1990), Schwartz-Borden (1986), and the classic by Kubler-Ross (1969). A good article by Pill and Zabin (1997) describes short-term therapeutic groups for women who lost their mothers at a young age. For other relevant readings see Chapter 2, note 16 and Chapter 14, note 46.

20. See Ehrenkranz (1967) and Hollis (1968).

CHAPTER 6

REFLECTIVE DISCUSSION OF THE PERSON–SITUATION CONFIGURATION

As is evident from the preceding chapters, psychosocial casework emphasizes drawing clients into *reflective consideration of their situations and of their functioning within them.* In Chapter 4 we suggested the usefulness of three major divisions of work of this kind:

1. *Person–situation reflection* in which consideration is given to the nature of the client's *situation,* his or her *responses,* to it, and the *interaction of situation and responses.*
2. *Pattern-dynamic reflection* in which response *patterns* or tendencies are considered.
3. *Developmental reflection* in which attention is centered on *developmental* factors in these patterns.

The first category of reflection, the subject of this chapter, is a form of treatment *universally used in casework.* In the psychosocial approach, the worker characteristically tries to help the client arrive at some form of *increased understanding,* no matter how much the reflective discussion may need to be buttressed by sustaining, directive, or ventilating work.[1]

The procedures used in person–situation reflection are comments, questions, explanations, and nonverbal communications that promote the client's reflecting primarily upon *current or recent events.* Person–situation reflection is distinguished from developmental reflection by the fact that the latter is concerned with early life experiences, those that occur when the individual would normally be living with parents, the years of growth to adulthood. Pertinent material located in time between the beginning of adulthood and the present is considered as part of person–situation reflection.

As discussed in Chapter 4, *person–situation reflection* can be divided into six subcategories: The clients' consideration of:

1. Others, their own physical health, or the situation.
2. Their own actions in terms of outcome, effects on others, or alternatives.
3. The *nature* of their own acts, thoughts, and feelings.
4. The external provocations or stimuli or the immediate inner reasons for their reactions and responses.
5. Their own acts, feelings, and thoughts from an evaluative stance.
6. Their reactions to the worker and the treatment process.

OTHER PEOPLE, HEALTH, AND THE SITUATION

The first of these subdivisions has to do with the client's thinking about the *situation,* or the external world, a form of reflection that might be called *extrareflection* (in contrast to *intrareflection*). Here we are dealing partly with *perception* and partly with a question of *knowledge.*

So often people see only a *distorted* or one-sided picture of the reality before them, either because they see or hear what they anticipate or because their feelings lead them to ignore or blot out important aspects of a situation. The father who is convinced that his son is retarded like his own brother may focus only on those activities in which his son has failed. Yet, without noticing it, he may reveal to the worker areas in which the son's learning has been unimpeded or even above average. The worker's first approach would usually be to call the father's attention to events that show the other side of the boy's capacities. In a situation such as this, workers sometimes err by rushing into a discussion of the distortion itself—in this

case, the displacement from brother to son—instead of seeing whether, when the client's attention is called to the reality picture, he or she is able by this procedure alone to modify earlier misconceptions. By testing the client's capacity to do this, one can measure the force of the need to distort.

There is a rule of parsimony in casework treatment as well as in science. If a person is able, with a little help, to perceive more realistically, it is not necessary to pursue the whys or wherefores of a previous failure to do so. If the distortion does not yield to a look at the facts, the diagnostic information and material from this preliminary effort can later be used to draw the client's attention to the discrepancy, between reality and his or her view of it. If the man mentioned above is perceptive and motivated—as many clients are—he may accept the cue and go on to talk about the matters that complicate his feelings toward his son, possibly his *patterns* of response or his *early life* experiences. Another person will need more prompting from the worker for treatment to move on from person–situation reflection to *pattern-dynamic* or *developmental reflection.*

A person's lack of understanding of a situation may be due not so much to distortion of or blindness to the facts as to actual *lack of knowledge* about normal reactions. Parents, unaware of the universal turmoil of adolescence, the need to assert independence that so often shows itself in negativism, the seeking of peer approval—whether in clothes, hair, language, or relationships with the opposite sex—sometimes mistake healthy reactions for alienation and revolt. In so doing, children may be driven toward the very associations the parents fear. Much of the turmoil of youth has to do with grave problems of our total society—racism, poverty, poor educational opportunities, inferior housing, and neighborhood violence—problems beyond casework's reach, although we must all bear responsibility for trying to modify them. But nothing is gained by the parent's misconstruing normal development as complete loss of a child or by overreacting in a way that alienates the young person at the very moment when communication most needs to be kept open. More understanding can lead to more patience, which furthers the chance of greater exchange of ideas between generations. This does not imply the suspension of parental thinking about wise and unwise activities. Nor should the worker infer that parental guidance should be evaded when reality demands it and the ability to influence the child effectively exists. But it does mean that parents can be helped to see their children more realistically and in better perspective, thereby coming to understand more fully what the young person is experiencing and what inner needs and outer pressures are contributing to the situation. Parents then are certainly in a better position to help rather than hurt their child.

In this connection, when relevant, it is important to help parents recognize that the *cultural or family traditions* of their generation—perhaps particularly if they have immigrated from another country— may be quite different from those the adolescent is exposed to in school and with peers. Different attitudes toward curfews, relationships with the opposite sex, dress and cosmetics, and even education may be contributing to the intergenerational difficulties. In these instances, it is important— once again—for the worker to maintain a stance of *neutrality;* it is rarely helpful to take a position about such specific matters as hairstyles, dating, and so on that are really a matter of taste and tradition. For the worker to try to persuade parents to relax standards or revise their outlook probably would not work and would likely result in them distrusting or leaving the worker. In

cases such as these, family meetings can be encouraged; in these the worker, who takes no sides, usually comments on the discrepant life experiences of the parents and their teenager. The parents may come to understand that the adolescent is strongly influenced by a set of standards and preferences to which he is exposed; at the same time, the teenager may become less angry and more aware of his parents' good intentions when recognizing the source of their rules. In a less combative climate, constructive communication and negotiation may then begin.

Harmful parental responses sometimes derive from commonly held prejudices and fears. A mother, for instance, may accept her son's report of being threatened by a child of another background—class, race, religion, or ethnicity—without inquiring for details of what actually happened. Thus, the mother cannot know whether the child might have misinterpreted or exaggerated the event or might even have provoked the incident. The caseworker, first demonstrating appreciation of the mother's concern, can go on to ask about the details of what occurred. This not only clarifies the reality for the mother but also indirectly demonstrates a way in which the mother could have handled the situation. The mother, too, needs first to comfort her son but then to help him see if his report of what happened was entirely accurate. If it was, then thought must be given to the next steps— the second form of person–situation reflection: What can the mother help the child to do? What might the mother herself do? If the report is *not* accurate, the mother can assist her son in seeing this particular episode in a truer light; furthermore, it can strengthen the child's overall ability to assess reality. If the boy's accusation against the child of another background was an expression of his parents' tendency to stereotype and blame other groups, the worker may be able to find a way to ask: "Do you think Kevin would have been so quick to blame a boy of his own background?" The worker is not lecturing on the perniciousness of prejudice, but indirectly is leading this mother to reflect on some of its innate evils.

Lack of awareness of another person's feelings and/or inability to understand the meaning of their behavior often generates hostility between people.

A husband intent on his own professional career failed to see that his wife was frustrated by her dead-end job that did not call on her special training. Nor did it occur to him that she was exhausted after eight hours at work and needed help in caring for the home and children. Because they had bought new appliances he thought that the problem was solved. He concluded his wife was either incompetent or stubborn because he did not realize the extent to which her feelings of frustration with the circumstances of her life were interfering with her functioning and general disposition. As it turned out, he *was* capable of understanding his wife's reactions and needs when she explained herself in couple sessions. Even before reflecting further on his family of origin's attitudes toward women or his own "sexist" sentiments, he began to perceive his wife's circumstances more accurately and fully. Without help, however, he had become increasingly more irritated and critical of his wife. She, too, was able to realize that her husband's annoyance and lack of consideration derived not from lack of love but, in part, from the fact that she had never before spoken directly to him about the extent of her unhappiness.

In this case as in many others, the very process of understanding another person more fully sets in motion a change in behavior. As we said, often people do not respond to actual situations but to their *perceptions* of them. Thus, when a distorted perception is corrected, the response often corrects itself.

Joint and family interviews offer excellent opportunities for increased understanding of one person by another. People, such as the woman described above, often reveal aspects of themselves in the relative safety of the treatment situation that they have not had the courage to show in the hostile or anxiety-ridden home situation. A worker can draw out a client's thoughts and feelings to enable another family member who is listening to understand the one who is speaking, thereby correcting misconceptions.

The process of understanding the external world takes place not only in relation to people but also in relation to life events. Clients sometimes need help in understanding financial matters, a work situation, medical recommendations, or the implications of their own or someone else's physical condition. The *psychoeducational approach* to working with people who have a mental illness and their families, among others, has helped all involved to better comprehend the significance of diagnoses, symptoms, and treatment options; psychosis can be far less frightening when everyone—the patient and those close to him or her—understands some of the expectations and requirements of the illness, which helps when inevitable day-to-day problems arise. The more fully clients can comprehend these points, the more appropriately they will handle them. *Reflective consideration is a more tedious process than advice giving, but it increases the client's competence in a way that directive procedures do not.*[2]

A worker has several ways to help clients to reflect upon their understanding of people and their situations. Some workers like to explain things to their clients in a more or less didactic way; others are skillful in leading people to think things through for themselves. Some workers might immediately explain the universality of sibling jealousy to a mother who does not understand the irritability of her three-year-old after the birth of a new baby. In the psychosocial approach, we believe it is usually more effective to ask the mother whether she has thought of any explanation for the older child's irritability. This approach offers the worker and mother an opportunity to understand what theory, if any, the mother holds about her child's actions or attitudes.[3] *People often form hypotheses about their own or someone else's behavior.* Sometimes explanations of human behavior are based on cultural beliefs, or on "family lore"; how often we hear a parent say that a child's conduct or temperament is *just* like father's or Aunt Carmen's.

If the mother just described does *not* have an explanation, one can still inquire whether she thinks the arrival of the new baby might be making Lisa feel left out. The more clients think for themselves, the more conviction they will have about answers they find. Usually, they will then become less dependent on the worker's theories and, at the same time, will be helped to develop or strengthen ego skills that can apply to other situations. Here too, the *psychoeducational approach*—with as much emphasis as possible on reflective thinking—can bolster the mother's understanding of her child's behavior.

One form of reflective consideration of the situation is that of telling the client about ways in which changes can be made through either *legal or social action.* For example, there are lawyers who are especially interested in problems of poverty and social injustice; resources may be available for those seeking legal help to meet certain external problems, but clients often do not know of

these. Straight information can increase clients' knowledge of resources within reach. Some areas may have women's centers providing advice and activities relevant to various concerns of women. There are organizations and neighborhood groups in which families can participate in group action to protest or improve adverse social conditions. It is just as important for workers to be informed about these resources as about those of health, education, employment, and recreation.

DECISIONS, CONSEQUENCES, AND ALTERNATIVES

The second type of person–situation reflection *lies between extrareflection and intrareflection* and *requires both.* It involves clients' *decisions* and *activities* and how these affect or are affected by people with whom the client lives or associates. It also entails consideration of *alternatives,* such as of available resources and opportunities, and the "fit" between these and clients' requirements. *The interaction of person and situation is the focus of this subdivision of treatment.* Over and over again, workers strive to help clients think about the consequences of their actions on others and/or on themselves. Consideration is often given to the response an action may provoke. Ego functions of *judgment* and *reality testing* (see Chapter 2) are called upon in this kind of reflection.

An action may involve a *practical decision,* such as the advisability of moving into a housing project, the pros and cons of changing jobs, or the wisdom of choosing training for one particular vocation over another. Or it may be a decision about a medical problem, such as whether or not to undergo recommended surgery.[4] Often, it involves a complicated *emotional or interpersonal decision,* such as whether or not to separate from a spouse or lover, to adopt a child, to place a baby for adoption, or to have an abortion. In any of these instances, *the client tries imaginatively to foresee what personal consequences a plan or decision may have and/or how it may affect other people whose lives are involved in the decision.* The client sometimes only needs help to focus on the subject at hand, using the worker as a "sounding board"; often, the worker contributes to the reflective discussion by raising questions about aspects of the situation and alternatives that may have been overlooked: "If you decide to take another sick day from your job to accompany your mother to the clinic, how will that affect your work situation?" "Are you afraid she won't get there otherwise? Can anyone else fill in?" "Is there a transportation service provided by the senior center?"

At other times, it is not a direct decision but *an understanding of the effects of the client's own behavior on someone else that is involved in the reflection.* A mother may not realize that when she hits her 14-year-old son in front of his friends, she is virtually compelling him to defy her in order to maintain the respect of his peers. A child may not realize that if he is a poor sport when losing at games, his friends go to play with someone else. A husband may not see that when he ridicules his wife about her weight, her angry reaction may actually deflect her efforts to diet. A mother who verbally abuses her children when they do not live up to her expectations can be helped to become aware of her unrealistic demands, as well as the negative consequences of her behavior. Conjoint treatment sometimes helps people hear firsthand the connection between actions and responses.

Here as elsewhere, psychosocial workers hold that the best procedure for the worker is not to "explain" the relationship between behavior and consequences, but to *lead the*

clients to see the sequence themselves: "What did Mike do when you hit him in front of the other fellows?" "What happened just before Jake left you to play with Mark?" "Does your wife eat less when you needle her about her weight?" "Do you find that the children behave better when you talk to them that way?" Many clients will draw appropriate conclusions, once the effects of the behavior are brought to their attention. If more help is needed, the worker may go on with, "Do you suppose that . . . ?" or "Have you noticed that . . . ?" or "Often boys of this age . . . ?" When a full explanation is really needed, the worker may give it, but not until an effort has been made to see whether the client can arrive at conclusions independently, so that he or she will gain experience in thinking in terms of consequences in general in addition to understanding the matter under consideration.

Discussion of decisions and future action is often linked with *situational understanding.* Greater *knowledge of another person or of resources* at one's command is naturally followed by consideration of what to do in light of this knowledge. "How can I talk with Ted about this?" "What should I say to Jean?" The worker could respond with advice, but again it is usually more helpful to encourage clients to think the answer out for themselves, since this will increase their capacity to respond to future situations without help. Similarly, when the use of a resource is at issue, clients should be led step by step to consider advantages and disadvantages rather than being advised to choose one alternative or another.

A more subtle sort of misunderstanding about consequences is that of *fearing reactions that need not occur.* A husband or wife may underestimate a spouse's ability to accept differences between them. A man may think that his wife will be angry if he takes a night to be with his friends when, in actuality, she might be glad for an evening alone. A wife may worry that if she chooses to read occasionally rather than watch television with her husband in the evening that his feelings will be hurt, when, in fact, he has no problem with this. Fear that differences in lifestyles, tastes, opinions, feelings, pastimes will necessarily bring withdrawal of love is common. Sometimes these do become a separating factor, but this is not a necessary consequence if thought is given to how differences actually affect a relationship. Often, for example, it is not the difference but the way in which the difference is asserted that makes the trouble. Or the fear of expressing differences can lead to a buildup of resentment that then strains the relationship. Detailed examination of interactions is a very important type of reflection about consequences. The worker can ask for details of the circumstances surrounding what appears to be a difference. "How did it come up?" "How did you put it?" "What did Julia actually say or do?" "Have you talked it over?" "Are you sure Daryl was that upset?" In this sort of situation, there is *a close interweaving of thinking about consequences and trying to understand other people and their needs.* Again, family and couple sessions provide an excellent opportunity for discussions of differences and the meanings these have to the particular people involved.

INWARDLY DIRECTED AWARENESS

The third subdivision of person–situation reflection, which parallels the procedure of helping the client look outward with greater perceptive accuracy, has to do with increasing the client's awareness of *the nature of his or her own responses, thoughts, and feelings.* This requires some form of *intrareflection,* sometimes involving recognition of so-called hidden feelings or reac-

tions. There are *many degrees of "hiddenness."* A client may be fully cognizant of reactions but may be afraid to speak of them because of shame or fear of ridicule or criticism. This may be the case, for example, with a father who knows he is very angry at one of his sons but is ashamed to admit it, or with a woman who expects disapproval if she tells the worker about a recent abortion and her mixed feelings about it. Or a client may have refrained from talking about feelings because of a lack of recognition of their significance: A man may know he is embarrassed at having had a "nervous breakdown," but may never speak of it to the worker because he does not realize the way in which this shame is related to his job failures. Or a client may be truly unaware of feelings because they are not part of conscious thought: A mother may not realize the degree of her dependency on her teenage son; a young adult may not have become conscious of a same-sex romantic attraction. We are talking here *not of early memories but of reactions to current life.* The uncovering of hidden *early* memories is part of *developmental reflection* rather than of the *current* person–situation gestalt.

When workers believe they can "read" a client's thoughts or feelings, it is a great temptation to do so out loud. This may seem necessary on some occasions: Sometimes a client is unable to bring these into the open but will be relieved if the worker does so; or there may be a therapeutic justification for bringing them out even though this may produce discomfort. (Of course, when a worker *does* decide to speak for people who have not yet spoken for themselves, it is essential to be open to corrections provided by the clients; our educated or intuitive hunches can miss the mark to one degree or another.) Far more often, rather than articulating hidden material, skill lies in finding ways of enabling clients to bring it out themselves. A low-key, broadly framed question such as, "Do you think you may have some negative reactions to your son?" is usually preferable to a pointed inquiry such as, "Do you think you are feeling very angry with your boy but are afraid to face those feelings?" But, in almost every case, even pointed questions are better than "mind reading" or interpretations such as, "Clearly, you are angry and aren't admitting it to yourself."

On those infrequent occasions when it *is* advisable to put the client's thoughts or feelings into words, this should still be done tentatively, making it possible for the client to make corrections or maintain defenses if needed: "I am not altogether sure about this, but it seems to me that maybe you are feeling quite angry with your boy. If so, it may really help to understand your feelings better." Also, it is important to safeguard clients from agreeing too readily to a possibly incorrect interpretation. When workers do offer direct, unqualified interpretations, they should be *very* sure of the ground on which the comment is based. In any event, whenever there are decisions to be made about bringing thoughts and feelings to the surface, workers should manage both their curiosity and their uneasiness about undisclosed matters so that choices are made only on the client's behalf.

As in the simpler process of spontaneous ventilation, when feelings are brought to the surface, the worker has several choices about the next step. It may be helpful to turn to *sustaining procedures,* trying immediately to allay a client's anxiety or guilt; one may seek to involve the client in further understanding of the *dynamics* or of *developmental aspects* of his or her reactions; at other times, it may not be necessary to do more than concentrate on the immediate consequences of these reactions in the client's current life.

When full awareness is present and clients feel secure in the worker's sustaining approach, they generally speak about relevant material without any specific prompting. If, however, it is obvious that the client is struggling with the question of whether to speak of something, the worker may want to comment on this hesitation directly: "It is difficult to speak freely, I know, but perhaps as you become more comfortable it will become easier." Or the worker may gently say, "I know it is hard to talk sometimes, but I can only help you with the things you can bring yourself to talk about." Or, "Can you tell me what it is that makes it hard for you to talk to me about this?" Or, "I have a feeling that you may be afraid I will criticize you. Is that true?" "Is there anything I've said that makes it difficult to go on?" "Perhaps it will be easier for you as we go along." Various types of sustaining comments can put the client at ease.

At other times, when the worker is fairly sure of what a client is reluctant to speak about, it may be possible to make comments that refer tangentially to the anticipated content, thus inviting the client to talk about it without facing him or her with it directly. For instance, one can *give reassurance or acceptance in advance of the client's communication:* "It isn't always possible, you know, to feel loving toward a difficult child." Or, "Sometimes parents, even though they try not to, do feel dislike for a child." Or, "It happens that people can be so unhappy about a pregnancy that they have to do something about it." Often, one can call the client's attention to discrepancies between fact and feeling, or overemphases, or inconsistencies, as these may point toward important feelings. At times, this can be done merely by repeating a revealing statement in a questioning tone. With an inflection of mild surprise, a worker might say to the sports-minded father of a son with no interest in athletics: "Are you saying that you *weren't* disappointed when Josh—once again—refused to go to the ball game with you?"

Closely related to helping a person to become aware of feelings and thoughts is encouraging the individual to recognize and consider *unusual or problem activities or irrational reactions*. The worker brings a mother's attention to the fact that she has several times called her daughter Carol "Linda," the name of the mother's sister. One might comment on the fact that a client continuously works overtime without extra compensation for a boss he says he hates, even though he could easily get another job. A worker expresses surprise when a man, who considers himself a pacifist, talks excitedly about violent scenes in a movie. When the client's attention is in one way or another directed to unproductive behavior or irrational reactions, if the individual is capable of it, he or she is very likely to go on to consider either the consequences of the behavior or the reasons for it. The worker who lacks patience omits this step and rushes on to explanations, depriving clients of the chance to seek these out for themselves. The risk of an inaccurate or inadequate understanding is always greater when trust is put in one's own "expert" insight instead of that of the client.

RESPONSES TO SITUATIONAL PROVOCATIONS AND STIMULI

A fourth form of reflection consists of the effort to understand some of the reasons for reactions: that is, the *external provocations and internal thought processes* that contribute to a reaction. A husband who is opposed to his wife's working looks at the possibility that he feels unloved because for him her managing their home symbolizes love. Or he considers the possibility that her

working seems to belittle his own place in the family. This type of causation lies in interactions with others or with external conditions, reasons for doing something that lie in the "outer" or in the person's own feeling about the "outer." The worker might comment: "You have talked about how upset you were to lose the baby. Do you think that has anything to do with your present anger at Kwesi?" Or, "Does it seem to you that when you think your supervisor might criticize you, you become anxious and then start making mistakes?" Or, "Do you think you are actually most likely to withdraw from Lisa when she is especially affectionate?" Or, "I get the impression that when the bus is a little late you get very upset even though there are no serious consequences from the delay. Is that true?" Or, simply, "You seem tense today. Has anything happened?"

SELF-EVALUATION

The fifth type of reflection has to do with self-evaluation. This may be related to the *superego,* ideas about right or wrong, or thoughts about self-image, principles, values, or preferences that have value implications. A worker may comment, "Do you think you are expecting too much of yourself?" Or, "Which means more to you, success in this competitive, demanding job or a closer relationship with Betty Mae?"

Another facet of this process comes into play when the worker helps a client to *use external realities to correct a distorted self-image.* A boy who is excessively fearful of a school examination is reminded of his successes in previous tests. A woman is helped to evaluate whether her image of herself as weak and helpless is justified by the facts. A girl who says she is not popular and has no one to invite to a party is encouraged to think over the several people she has previously said actually do like her. A man who feels unsure of his ability to perform on the job after absence due to serious illness is helped to reflect on capacities that remain intact despite current physical limitations. This type of reflection is closely related to reflection that develops a better understanding of external realities; the two processes often occur in rapid succession. *But consideration of external reality here is the means by which clients are helped to become aware of misperceptions about themselves;* it is not for the purpose of understanding another person. It is essentially *inwardly,* not *outwardly,* directed reflection.

REACTIONS TO THE WORKER AND TO TREATMENT

Psychosocial casework stresses the importance of a sixth form of person–situation reflection. This concerns clients' reactions to the worker, to treatment, or to agency rules and requirements. Just as clients may misperceive other aspects of a situation, so they may distort or fail to understand casework and the caseworker. Here, too, previous life experiences may lead a client to imagine hostility where it does not exist, to anticipate criticism, to fear domination, or to have unrealistic expectations of the help available. Or, for various reasons, including differences in background between people seeking help and those providing it, the client may simply lack knowledge of the nature of the casework "situation."

Whether the client approaches the caseworker with apprehension or lack of knowledge, and/or from a different cultural perspective, misconceptions can be greatly reduced if there is adequate discussion, preferably in the first interview, of the purpose or nature of the contact. A full understanding is required of *what the clients want,* of *how the worker will try to help,* of the fact that *caseworker and clients will be collabo-*

rating in an effort to lessen the difficulty or resolve the dilemma, and that the *relationship is not hierarchical but reciprocal.*

There is a tendency to think that there is something mysterious about the casework relationship, something that makes it fragile and untouchable except by the very expert. In fact, it is no more complicated than—but just as complicated as—any other relationship. In the type of reflective discussion considered here, attitudes and responses to the caseworker are handled in the same way as other attitudes and responses. Where distortions or misunderstandings exist, the clinical social worker tries to straighten them out by demonstrating the realities of his or her behavior toward the client and the actual nature of treatment. If a client who tends to be dependent accuses the worker of indifference because the worker is unwilling to prolong the interview, in a caring way the worker may explain that time has to be scheduled, that it is not a matter of lack of interest, and that they can go on with the same discussion when they meet again. If, on the other hand, there is a repeated attempt to complain about the requirements of time or to cling to the worker, it is well to suggest that there seems to be a problem, and that the client and worker should look at it in the next interview.

Reflection by clients on their reactions to the worker can be a very fruitful source of *understanding of similar reactions in other parts of their lives.* If a client thinks the worker is angry, it is important to find out what this conclusion is based on. If a remark has been misinterpreted, the worker can indicate what was really meant and reassure the client that there is no anger. (This assumes the worker is truly not angry. When, as occasionally happens, one *is* angry, it is usually best to admit it and either explain why or, when appropriate, apologize or do both.) If the client expects advice and is disappointed at not getting it, a simple explanation of why the worker doesn't think it will help may clear the air. (This point was elaborated upon in the previous chapter.) Clients do not need long and theoretical explanations of treatment processes, but when they ask for information or when misunderstandings arise, it is not only appropriate but also essential to discuss the nature of casework in order for it to become a constructive, participatory process. Participation in treatment is a role to which clients may be unaccustomed, and it may need to be explicitly defined. By reflecting on reactions to or expectations of the worker, often clients—sometimes spontaneously—see similarities to their responses to other people; they may move briefly to *pattern-dynamic reflection,* realizing a tendency to anticipate anger, to lean heavily on others for advice, or to assume a "one-down" position when dealing with professionals.

If a client is kept waiting, any annoyance about this should be elicited and acknowledged, usually with an explanation. If clients are dissatisfied with treatment and think it is a waste of time to come for interviews, the dissatisfaction should be brought out into the open so that the reasons for it can be discussed and misunderstandings—on the part of the worker or the clients—can be straightened out. If a client fantasizes that the worker is interested in a personal relationship, this, too, should be brought into open expression; full acceptance of the feelings is usually necessary to avoid the client's reactions of rejection or embarrassment.

Individuals and families who have immigrated from other countries may approach casework services in ways associated with the manner in which help is sought and received in their own cultures. Their view of the worker or agency can be very different from that of native-born clients, who often have at least some general notions about casework, counseling, or psychotherapy. Because of information obtained from school or the media, the more acculturated offspring of first-generation immigrants may be more familiar than their parents with the casework process. Even so, they may approach the caseworker with some worries or misconceptions.[5]

Differences in background—education, nationality, color, religion, class—may create a barrier to the development of a relationship of trust. Previous experiences with casework or with prejudice or reluctance to turn to a representative of another race, religion, or ethnic group for help may interfere with the client's confidence in the worker. It is almost always best from the beginning—and, if necessary, later on—to inquire how a client feels about having a worker from a different background or group and about the worker's approach to offering help. *Awareness of one's own cultural biases* and recognition that differences may affect the work are critically important. As discussed in Chapter 2, workers from every background need to challenge themselves to be culturally informed and sensitive. Being scrupulously careful not to stereotype, it is important to have knowledge of how a person of a different group *may* react and to be acutely aware of the negative experiences oppressed people and so-called minorities generally face on a regular basis. Without these understandings, thoughtless actions can lead to unintentional offenses that can be hurtful and very damaging to the client and to the treatment relationship. By heeding the possibility of misunderstanding, the worker can guard against behavior that will either precipitate or aggravate it. Above all, *the importance of being alert to differences between worker and client and aware of one's own attitudes about these differences cannot be overemphasized.*

It is equally important to let clients know that they are the experts on their own experiences and cultural traditions and what these mean to them. Furthermore, it is *their* requirements of casework that are important, and *their active involvement will be a major influence on the course treatment takes.* The worker's eagerness to receive honest feedback and information often gives clients permission to share their concerns and hopes. When clients are clearly apprehensive, honest discussion combined with sincere goodwill usually alleviates tension. It is important not to assume hostility exists where it does not or not to assume it is due to race, ethnic, or other differences when it has a different source.

When clients come to an agency because someone else insists—a school principal, employer, marital partner, or concerned person in the community—the worker can anticipate resistance, if not hostility. Although sustaining techniques are important, as noted earlier, reflective procedures are also essential. Clients must know why the worker is there and for what initial purpose. They must know that they will not be judged, pushed around, or manipulated. They must know that their resentment is both understood and respected and that the worker asks primarily for a chance to demonstrate caring and potential helpfulness. The worker need not say this in so many words, but the substance of these communications must get across, along with an opportunity for the client to express anger and fears about the intrusion. In these situations, it is particularly important for clients to know that the worker wants to understand the problem from *their* perspective, not just—or even primarily—from that of the referral source.

Experience has repeatedly shown the value of frank discussion of clients' reactions to workers, even in the most matter-of-fact, practical work. Psychosocial casework holds that all casework depends in part upon establishing and maintaining a sound relationship between client and worker. Obstacles to such a relationship can occur in any form of treatment and can best be removed by recognition and discussion. "Hard-to-reach" or involuntary clients, in particular, have often had very bad experiences with other social workers or with people whom they mistakenly thought were social workers, or their neighbors or friends have had such experiences. It is natural that they should expect and fear similar treatment from the current worker. Realistic discussion can be the first step in bringing distrust into the open. When possible, misconceptions can be corrected, thus creating the foundation for a constructive and respectful casework relationship.

The value of client feedback cannot be overemphasized; the worker may be operating under the misconception that the work is going well when the client has reservations about it. Only by making *genuine* inquiries can misunderstandings be straightened out and/or a new approach be initiated by the worker. These and other aspects of the client–worker relationship will be discussed in Chapter 9.[6]

It has taken many pages to describe the treatment processes involved in reflective discussion of the person–situation configuration. But, as we have seen, the type of understanding examined here is a *central* part of psychosocial treatment with all kinds of clients and problems.[7] In many cases, more extensive understanding is either unnecessary or inadvisable. Frequently, however, a certain amount of pattern-dynamic and developmental understanding is embedded in what is primarily person–situation understanding. Sometimes the worker sees an opportunity to deepen the client's understanding at crucial points. Interviews may flow back and forth with person–situation reflection forming the base to which, from time to time, dynamic or developmental understanding is added. In situations in which dynamic and developmental reflection are a *major* part of treatment, preliminary discussion of current realities can provide important diagnostic information for worker and client and serve as grounds from which to proceed to consideration of dynamic or developmental factors.

NOTES

1. Although the same term has not always been used, the importance of *reflective discussion* has been referred to in the literature of social work over the years. Sometimes terms such as *logical discussion, counseling,* or *confrontation* refer to processes that resemble reflective communications described in this chapter. Some techniques referred to as "cognitive" have much in common with reflective discussion. Like cognitive therapy, psychosocial therapy seeks to help clients gain cognitive understanding of themselves and their situations and correct distortions that negatively influence behavior and experience. Unlike some cognitive or cognitive-behavioral therapists, when appropriate, psychosocial clinicians emphasize uncovering (sometimes preconscious) material (thoughts, feelings, memories) that has been hidden from awareness by defense mechanisms to allay anxiety but that interferes with current functioning; from the psychosocial point of view, bringing the preconscious matters into consciousness allows them to be processed by the ego. Cognitive therapists generally believe that when dysfunctional ways of thinking are corrected, emotional and behavioral changes follow. For useful books describing cognitive theory and therapy written by some of the leaders in the field, see Beck and Freeman (1990); Epstein, et al. (1988); Freeman, et al. (1989); and Guidano and Liotti (1983). For a chapter on cognitive theory and social work treatment see Lantz (1996).

2. Except perhaps in very directive therapies, reflection is always part of the therapeutic process and is described in the literature that gives case examples and describes techniques. See, for example, Mirkin's (1985) very helpful edited volume on adolescents, family therapy, and the need for teenagers, their parents, and people in the larger systems to understand the dynamics, circumstances, and requirements involved in addressing the issues. See Moynihan, et al. (1988) for a discussion of issues that require reflection by people with AIDS. See Bernhein and Lehman (1985) for a clear presentation of the psychoeducational approach used when working with families of the mentally ill. Libassi (1988) has written a useful article that describes the use of reflection in direct work with the mentally ill.

3. The reader may find an article by Lesoff (1977) useful; the author discusses her own interesting approach to helping parents recognize and reflect on the consequences of their attitudes and actions on their children's behavior. Rooney (1988) recommends that when contracting with involuntary clients their views of the problem be elicited and addressed; if, for example, a parent who has been abusive blames the child's actions, worker and client can reflect together on how the child might be helped to change behavior without the use of physical punishment. For another good article on abused children, see McInnis-Dittrich (1996) who outlines a nonblaming approach and sees child maltreatment in context, as a function of individual, family, community, and cultural variables. Hoorwitz (1983) offers guidelines that involve reflection for treating father–daughter incest. Readings on reluctant, involuntary, and "hard-to-reach" clients will be found in Chapter 5, note 7; Chapter 8, note 19; Chapter 9, notes 3 and 4; and Chapter 10, note 5.

4. One of the best examples of this is found in Bender (1976). Here the person–situation procedure is combined with ventilation and developmental reflection, but the emphasis is on the fuller understanding of the surgery.

   The June 1993 issue of *Families in Society* is devoted to teenage pregnancy; the decisions and consequences related to sexual activity, birth control, and plans for a baby necessarily require reflection and are addressed in several of the articles. Rubenstein, et al. (1990) describe a pilot program in which well-functioning teen mothers were paid counselors to younger pregnant teenagers; the results were good, but must be viewed with caution because the study was small. Other readings related to teenage pregnancy and parenthood include Rains, et al. (1998), Cervera (1991) Dellman-Jenkins, et al. (1993), and a volume edited by Lerman and Ooms on young unwed fathers (1993).

5. The chapters in the volume edited by Mc-Goldrick, et al., on ethnicity (1996) usually address some of the help-seeking attitudes that may be found in individuals from various cultural or racial groups. See also a chapter by Sue, et al. (1994) that discusses research on psychotherapy with culturally diverse populations. See Chapter 2, note 37 for further readings on the traditions and attitudes of different ethnic groups.

6. See relevant readings on "resistance" to therapy and/or to the worker: Hartman and Reynolds (1987), Nelsen (1975), Rhodes (1979), and Howard Goldstein (1986). The concept of resistance is discussed in Chapter 12, with additional references in note 7 of that chapter.

7. In his interesting study of workers' and clients' perceptions of what helps, Maluccio (1979) found that both groups deemed reflective discussion between worker and client, in which workers are sensitive to clients' feelings, goals, etc., *the* most important process of successful treatment.

REFLECTIVE CONSIDERATION OF PATTERN-DYNAMIC AND DEVELOPMENTAL FACTORS

The two remaining forms of reflective communication are those that seek to promote dynamic and developmental understanding. Intrapsychic forces of which a person is not fully aware may so strongly influence behavior that it is not possible to perceive and act differently in response to person–situation reflection alone. It is sometimes helpful to turn such a person's attention briefly to the underlying dynamics of his or her personality or to early life experiences that are still unfavorably influencing current adjustment. Often, but not always, both types of understanding can be developed.

UNDERSTANDING AND INSIGHT: THE CONSCIOUS, PRECONSCIOUS, AND UNCONSCIOUS

We use the word *understanding* more often than *insight* in this text because the latter term has been given so many different meanings in various clinical circles. When we do use the term *insight* here, we are *not* using it as it is used in psychoanalysis: to refer specifically to the workings of the *unconscious*.[1] In psychosocial casework, the terms *dynamic* and *developmental reflection,* and the understanding to which these lead, refer primarily to *conscious* or *preconscious* material. Insight often involves: (1) *cognitive* or *intellectual* understanding, such as when a certain behavioral or emotional pattern is recognized to be related to or have an influence upon the dilemma at hand; or (2) *emotional* understanding, which often is deeply felt, sometimes suddenly bringing new awareness to one's own feelings or relationship patterns; emotional insight sometimes occurs when early feelings are uncovered and are linked to current feelings or circumstances. As we shall see, both kinds of insight or understanding lead to new levels of *self-awareness.*

It has long been recognized that certain technical procedures are employed by casework to keep the work on the conscious and preconscious rather than the unconscious level: Interviews are usually held with client and worker able to look directly at each other. Sessions are usually spaced farther apart than in analysis proper; most often interviews are held weekly, although sometimes a client is seen several times a week. And casework clients are not required to say everything that comes to mind; *they may choose which material they wish to bring forth.* In psychoanalysis, on the other hand, the patient is encouraged to bypass the censorship of the ego and engage in *free association,* thereby affording access to the unconscious.

Nevertheless, the line dividing *un*conscious (*repressed*) and *pre*conscious (*suppressed*) material—conflicts or memories—is not as clear as it once seemed to be. Both kinds of material are *not conscious.* While theoretically preconscious material is more accessible to the client, in practice it is often not available at will or by merely shifting attention to it.

> After many weeks of wondering about her childhood, which she had only vaguely remembered, a 35-year-old woman client arrived at a session, excitedly announcing to her worker: "Until we started talking about my family, I had completely forgotten how often my father came home drunk and started vicious, physical fights with my mother. And I also forget how frightened I was at those times. I guess I just couldn't face the pain. But now I can see these terrible brawls so clearly in my mind, as if they happened yesterday."

In this woman's case, the *emergence of hidden memories* (preconscious or unconscious) led to *understanding* or *insight* on several levels: She developed an *intellectual awareness* of a connection between early experiences and her current *pattern* of fear of conflict, confrontation, and self-assertion—the concerns that brought her to treatment. This cognitive understanding was joined by *emotional insight,* that is, by new awareness and experience of her feelings, past and present, that had previously been blocked, as the memories had. Thus, not only did she retrieve information about her early life, but she also achieved enormous relief from ventilation of feeling (sometimes referred to as *catharsis*) and deeper *understanding of emotional connections.* More often than not, from the psychosocial point of view, understanding and change of this type require both intellectual and emotional insight. The kind of revelation illustrated here is frequently accompanied by a sudden sense of penetrating self-awareness (sometimes called an "ah-ha" experience!) and a depth that may be akin to the surge of creativity felt by artists. An experience repressed or suppressed for years or decades may also be *spontaneously provoked* into consciousness by a current, often powerful, event. Buried memories of childhood sexual abuse, for example, may emerge in adulthood when current situations prompt them. (Here and in other parts of this book, however, we urge extreme caution against pressing for the recovery of buried memories of abuse when we are only assuming they are there and the client has no awareness of them.[2] See further discussion in Chapter 13.) Less dramatically but surely more frequently, a client—especially a client highly motivated to achieve self-understanding—may be reminded of long-forgotten incidents when simply asked about early memories.

Also, reflection on material that *derives from the unconscious,* such as the consideration of *dreams* or *"slips,"* may stimulate useful self-awareness. A client reported that he dreamed he was being pulled under by ocean waves when his caseworker (an older woman) jumped in to rescue him;

until discussing the dream with his worker, he did not realize how totally he was counting on the worker to save him from danger, external and internal. A mother referred to her son as her "husband"; only then did she begin to recognize her intense connection to and dependence on her son. It is important to emphasize that much of the material considered in pattern-dynamic and developmental reflection is *conscious* to begin with, but in the course of casework treatment is *viewed from a new perspective.*

A young father, George Poulos, knew that he was distant from his young son in ways that his now deceased immigrant father, who had worked two jobs for years, had been remote from him; and he knew he wished to be different but, he said, "something stops me." In therapy, he focused on painful childhood longings and on how deeply he regretted missing this second chance at a father–son connection. His deeper self-understanding combined with his commitment to being a conscientious parent, resulted in a strong determination to provide his son with a good early life experience. None of these matters had been hidden from him, but he had not viewed them so intensely and thoughtfully before. Having done so, he grew to be more involved and more openly tender with his son.

Chapter 2 discussed the *balance of forces* within and between the various parts of the personality. Psychosocial theory, supported by practice experience, maintains that dynamic and developmental reflection, even though these may not lead to insight into the unconscious, can in many instances bring enough modification in the balance between functional and dysfunctional aspects of the personality system (between strengths and deficits) to enhance the individual's ability to cope with the problems

for which social work assistance is sought. This is what occurred in the case of the father just mentioned.

REFLECTION CONCERNING DYNAMIC FACTORS

When we consider dynamic factors with a client, we are simply extending the process of *intrareflection* or self-exploration using procedures—comments, questions, occasionally explanations—whose content and timing are designed to help to pursue some intrapsychic reasons for his or her feelings, attitudes, and ways of acting, to understand the influence of one personality characteristic upon another: in other words, the way in which thoughts and emotions work. Here we go beyond the understanding of single interactions or even a series of interactions, as in the person–situation reflection (see Chapter 6), to *consideration of the intrapsychic pattern or tendency* that contributes to the interactions.

Often, a client is aware—sometimes clearly, sometimes vaguely—of unrealistic, destructive, or self-defeating behavior. The client may delve into the question of why without any prompting from the caseworker. At other times, the worker takes the first step by calling the inconsistency or inappropriateness to the client's attention: "Have you noticed that you don't have trouble being firm with Paula but seem to be afraid to be firm with Ed?"—to a mother who does not realize that her difficulty in disciplining her son probably springs from some hidden feelings or attitudes. *At this point, the worker is moving beyond one interpersonal event to raise a queston about a series of events, a pattern.* Probably, *individual instances* of difficulty in showing consistent firmness had been considered before, but without enabling this mother to act more effectively. The worker then suggests to the client that this may be part of a general tendency. Recognition of the pattern can turn the client's attention to the question of why. The answer may lie in displacement of some feelings from husband to son, in an underlying hostility to her son, in a desperate fear of losing her son's love, or in specific early life events—to name a few possibilities—or in some combination of these.

Similarly, in another situation, the worker says, "I wonder how it is that you can be so understanding of the children and yet seem reluctant to try to understand your husband," to a woman who is ordinarily very perceptive of other people's feelings. Only on reflection does she begin to realize that she does not want to lessen the conflict with her husband because she fears intimacy and is uncomfortable with their sexual relationship; for many years she had felt "safer" not to be on good terms with him.

In yet another case, a worker may ask a man, "What do you suppose makes you constantly insult people you say you want to be friends with?" The worker may sense that this man defends himself against his fear of rejection by first antagonizing others. Yet, *whenever possible, the worker encourages the client to seek the answer for himself rather than offering an interpretation.* This is true for two reasons: first, because the client's self-esteem, sense of achievement, and independent thinking are strengthened thereby; and, second, because the client's own understanding may vary—a little or a lot—from that of the worker and therefore feel more authentic and significant to him.

Sometimes the client does not recognize problem behavior; in other words, it is *ego-syntonic,* acceptable to the ego. For change to occur it must become *ego-alien* or *ego-dystonic,* unacceptable to the ego. Otherwise the client will not be motivated to try to understand and modify it. A mother who continually got into tempestuous fights at the

table with her son saw her reactions only in terms of his slow and sloppy eating habits, which she felt made such scenes inevitable. After a substantial period of exploration, patient listening, reflective discussion, and suggestions, the worker responded to the heated description of a stormy session with the comment: "You are like two children battling each other, aren't you?" The remark implied a value judgment; adults do not consider it a compliment to be told that they are behaving like children. It carried force with this client because a strong relationship had been established between her and her worker, which made her value the worker's opinion. The fact that the worker rarely took a position of this sort gave it added impact.

Sometimes a client, in response to a strong stimulus such as the one just described, begins to think about reasons for his or her reactions; *at other times, further comment is needed.* In this case, the worker later added: "There seems to be something between you and George [husband] that we need to understand; what thoughts come to you about it?" The client first realized that she prolonged scenes at the table for the relief she derived from hitting her son; subsequently, she discovered that she also had identified her son with her husband and was taking anger out on the boy she did not dare to express directly.

Thus, clients seek understanding of thoughts, feelings, or actions when dissatisfaction is felt: when they are recognized as ineffective, self-defeating, contrary to their values, interfering with relationships, or in some other ways are *ego-alien.* Until this attitude exists, dynamic interpretations will probably fall on deaf ears. When awareness does exist or emerges, the client will often be able to arrive at understandings with relatively little prompting or interpretation by the worker. Almost any aspect of the personality—conscious, preconscious, and even on occasion hitherto unconscious—may come under scrutiny.

Ego Defenses

Understanding is often sought in the area of the ego defenses, such as defensive hostility, projection, intellectualization, rationalization, altruism, denial, avoidance, projection, displacement, turning against the self, among others. (See Chapter 2 for a discussion of defense mechanisms.) The following are examples of worker communications designed to promote *pattern-dynamic reflection of ego defenses:*

- "Have you ever noticed that sometimes people get angry when they are scared? Do you think you might have been pretty edgy about having that talk with your brother-in-law and so hit out at him before he had a chance to attack you?" (*Defensive hostility.*)
- "Do you think your wife was really angry, or were you so furious yourself that you kind of expected she would be? What did she actually say at the beginning?" (*Projection.*)
- "Have you noticed how often you go off on this kind of theoretical discussion when I ask you about your own feelings toward Mary?" (*Intellectualization / rationalization.*)
- "When you told me that it might be better after all that you were assigned to me, a white worker, after specifically asking to see an African American clinician, do you think you were just trying to make the best of a disappointment? Or were you trying to protect my feelings rather than paying attention to your own? This is *your* treatment, you know." (*Rationalization / altruism.*)
- "When you say everything is 'fine,' do you think you are finding it hard to face

worrisome signs about your son's behavior?" (*Denial / avoidance.*)
- "Is it possible that you are expressing your frustrations about your boss when you become so easily annoyed by things your wife does?" (*Displacement.*)
- "Do you think that you are feeling depressed because you are really so mad at Fred but believe you can't let it out? Sometimes, you know, you can turn those angry feelings against yourself and then feel depressed." (*Turning against the self.*)

Questions and comments such as these can be as effective in *family and marital sessions as they are in individual treatment,* as Chapters 14 through 17 will illustrate.

Initially, *defense mechanisms often have to be explained to clients* because they may not be familiar with the way they work and cannot be expected to arrive at this kind of understanding on their own. Subsequently, however, *clients are frequently able to spot their own use of a particular defense* under various circumstances. One goal of this type of treatment is to enable them to do this for themselves.

Great care is necessary in work with defenses, however, for they are self-protective mechanisms used by the personality to ward off anxiety. *They should not be abruptly "broken through"; rather they should be "worked through," when evaluation and mutual discussion indicate the individual can bear the anxiety involved.* One important reason for *asking clients questions rather than giving interpretations* is that if the defenses feel vital to them, they are better able to reject the worker's ideas, however on target they may (or may not) be. And, for the most part, interpretations should be made tentatively and with an attitude of acceptance, which often needs to be put into words.[3]

Superego

Important as defense mechanisms are, they are by no means the only part of the personality under scrutiny in dynamic understanding. Often, superego characteristics need to be thought about, especially the *oversensitivity of the severe conscience.* A client who is too hard on herself may be helped by knowing that she is suffering from self-criticism rather than from too-high requirements of others, as she had thought. People who feel deeply hurt by the discovery of imperfections in themselves may be helped by recognizing that the demand for perfection is a function of their own personalities. "Have you noticed how upset you get whenever anyone makes the slightest criticism of your work?" "You hold very high standards for yourself, don't you?" "Do you think you demand even more of yourself than you do of others?" "You seem to be harder on yourself than anyone else would be, is that so?"[4]

One hazard of helping a person to become aware of superego severity is that the worker may appear to the client to be too lax in standards. It is extremely important to prevent this impression, and great care must be taken not to seem to be sponsoring antisocial behavior. If the client does react in this way, the reaction must be brought into the open and discussed: "I have the feeling that you are worried that I may be too easygoing. Let's talk about it." Once the client shares such concerns, it is important to clarify that the worker is not opposed to maintaining standards, but rather is wondering if the client could be suffering from a harmful, self-punishing conscience. Reflective discussion may follow, revealing that it is the client's pattern to judge others—sometimes including the worker—in a similar manner.

A client who illustrates this point is the African American mother of a child who had been referred for treatment because of school failures inconsistent with his intelligence. She was a very religious Protestant woman who set extremely high standards for herself and for her son. Initially, she found treatment difficult, probably because she feared that some flaw in herself might be contributing to her son's troubles; her faith in herself as a good mother seemed at risk. Every attempt by the worker at developing understanding, no matter how carefully worded, was taken as criticism from which she cringed. Furthermore, it became apparent that she was very angry at her son for underachieving, but felt guilty because she was unable to suppress her hostility toward him. When the worker tried to help her reduce her self-condemnation in favor of understanding of her feelings, the client accused the worker of trying to undermine her faith and principles.

One day she brought a Bible to the interview and seemed quite agitated. When the worker asked gently whether she had brought the Bible for a special reason, she opened it to the famous letter of Paul to the Corinthians on love, reading particularly the verse "When I was a child, I spoke as a child, I felt as a child, I thought as a child; now that I am a man I have put away childish things." She cried as she finished it. The worker said it was a beautiful letter and asked whether she had ever thought of why it was written. Did she think perhaps Paul might have observed that many people in fact did bring into adulthood feelings and thoughts from childhood?

As the client seemed confused, the worker put her thoughts in terms of gardening, a known interest of this client: "If you had a garden and weeds were choking out the good plants, you could cut off the tops of the weeds and the garden would look good for a while, but the roots would still be there. Wouldn't it be better to pull out the roots? It would be harder, but the results would be better. The same thing is true for human emotions. Many of us try to hide our feelings or difficulties and stamp them down, but this takes energy that could be used for better things. It seems worthwhile to try to uproot difficulties. The only method I know for uprooting them is to understand and face things that are painful and intolerable and to know that you have the strength to do so." The client was silent for several minutes and then said she was greatly relieved and that she had had no idea the caseworker had such deep understanding of her feelings.

Some clients whose self-confidence and control of impulses are more tenuous may have great anxiety about a sudden breakthrough of irrational behavior if strong, hidden desires are allowed to reach awareness. With such clients it is extremely important for the worker to *distinguish between recognizing an urge and carrying it out.* One can convey that this is not encouragement to act upon impulses but rather an expression of confidence that the client can be aware of them and still control them. Here, *the client's strengths as well as problematic patterns are reflected upon.*[5] It can also be pointed out that impulsive behaviors are sometimes more likely to occur when feelings or urges are stifled; in other words, impulses more readily break past the intellect when they are outside of awareness. If this type of approach is to be used, however, knowledge of the client and discussion between client and worker helps them determine whether the ego is able to handle strong urges. When danger of breakthrough does exist, it may be better not to disturb

defenses against it. Careful and collaborative diagnostic assessment, although always important, is essential to work in which the clients' understanding of emotional patterns is involved.

Ego Functioning

Along similar lines, clients may also be helped by understanding various ego functions when they contribute to personal problems or when they can be recognized as strengths that can be mobilized. (See Chapter 2 for descriptions of ego functions.) It can be helpful for some individuals to become aware of excessively *strong needs of the personality*—such as traits of great dependence, a high degree of self-absorption, or vindictiveness—and how these can cause trouble. *Persisting distortions in perception and unrealistic ideas about one's own tendencies and capacities* are also among the many ego areas in which help can be given. It is equally important to recognize *habitual patterns of handling situations that have been successful* for the client. In the following case, for instance, part of the difficulty lay in the client's unrealistic fear of being unable to control impulses, even though it was apparent that his conscience was strong and his judgment and capacity to regulate impulses were intact.

A retired man in his late 60s was extremely angry at his wife for pressuring him to locate to another part of the country, a move he did not want to make. She had taken several trips to explore retirement homes and he was becoming anxious and frustrated by her persistence. At the same time, he had not been able to state his position on the matter firmly, nor did he initiate a discussion with her of possible alternatives or compromises. He felt victimized and defeated. The day his wife was to fly home from one of her trips, he called his caseworker in a severely frightened state. He confided that he had momentarily wished that the plane would crash. The worker, whom he trusted, was able to help him reduce his fear by pointing out how often people have violent wishes and thoughts when they feel angry and frustrated. The breakthrough of deeply hostile feelings led this very controlled and passive man to believe that he would either become ungovernably violent ("I feel like a murderer," he said) or would break down emotionally. Knowing the man as well as she did, the caseworker was able to reassure him that his unbidden urge to see his wife dead in no way meant that he would act on his wish in any way. Once these suppressed feelings came to the surface, he was able to bring sound thinking to his reactions; he reflected on his lifelong pattern of suppressing his own desires for fear he would lose the love of people close to him. Furthermore, he began to recognize how his pent-up anger was based on feelings of helplessness in the face of his wife's tendency to dominate him. Finally, he was able to talk directly with her about *his* wishes for retirement. He found he actually could influence their plans and, as it turned out, his wife treated him more respectfully when he became less self-effacing.

An important step in dynamic understanding is the client's bringing reason and judgment—ego functions—or cognitive awareness to bear upon the personality characteristic and its functioning that have been brought to his or her attention. Exploration of this man's many strengths as well as his self-defeating patterns were essential to his changes. It was not enough for the religious mother to see that she was trying to handle her anger and fears of being flawed by suppressing them; she had to become aware of her own competence and capacities before she could use her good judgment to consider alternative ways of handling her feelings that would be more comfortable for her and more helpful to her son.

The *client's reactions to the worker* are also a fruitful source of dynamic understanding. As defense mechanisms or personality characteristics such as fear of criticism or excessive dependence come into play in the client–worker relationship, they can enable the clients to see the inner workings of their personalities in action. They can then use this understanding to recognize similar dynamics operating in other life experiences. These issues will be discussed in further detail in Chapter 9.

Pattern-dynamic communications are usually built upon previous person–situation reflection described in the last chapter. When discussing a current person–situation matter, a few comments or questions about the dynamics involved may enable the client to understand personality patterns more fully. For example, in a couple session: "Am I right that you tend to relate to both your wife and your woman boss by teasing them a lot? Do you find that you are likely to be that way with women more than with men?" When the teasing, which the wife found hurtful, was identified as a habitual way of relating to women in general, discussion could soon return to the person–situation realm: that is, the man's way of relating to his wife. (Recognition by the wife that her husband's behavior was a *pattern* of his helped her to take the teasing less personally.) Even in those cases where pattern-dynamic reflection is a major component in treatment, discussion never rests long in that realm exclusively. It is always accompanied by *sustaining measures* and may at times be supplemented by procedures of *direct influence. Exploration, description, and ventilation* remain essential ongoing processes. *Environmental interventions* often go hand in hand with intrareflection. Dynamic understanding is frequently achieved without discussing the roots or the development of the personality characteristic under discussion. In the case just described, the *origins* of the tendency to tease women were never explored.[6]

DEVELOPMENTAL UNDERSTANDING

Encouragement of reflection upon historical material is often undertaken in an episodic way in psychosocial casework, certain themes being explored as it becomes apparent that factors in the client's past are blocking improvement in current social adjustment. This procedure helps the client become aware of the way in which certain personality characteristics have been shaped by earlier life experiences and often helps to modify reactions to these experiences. Developmental reflection is sometimes necessary because certain dysfunctional characteristics cannot be overcome except by understanding of and becoming more emotionally connected to the experiences that contributed to their formation. The word *contributed* is used advisedly because one can never identify all determinants of a given phase of behavior or emotional pattern. Constitutional factors and early preverbal experiences that cannot be reached even by psychoanalysis are important in preparing an initial "personality set" that profoundly influences the way later infantile and childhood experiences are received by the individual. Even though preverbal experiences are not remembered, individuals who were apparently neglected, violated, or treated inconsistently during infancy often benefit considerably from *mak-*

ing inferences about early experiences and how these influenced later difficulties, such as problems trusting others, pessimism, wide emotional swings, and confusion in distinguishing feelings from thoughts. Mrs. Zimmer (see Chapter 3) was relieved when she realized that some of her distressing personal problems derived from early deprivation; this heightened awareness also helped her to begin to give herself more understanding and compassion than she felt she had received when she was young.[7]

In Chapter 2, we pointed out that *later reinforcement of earlier experiences* is extremely important in personality development. Harmful infantile experiences are sometimes overcome by health-inducing later ones. But often, unfortunately, repetitive hurtful events confirm and reinforce the child's misconceptions or distorted generalizations. When, for example, neglect at home fosters a child's pessimism, that child may react similarly in school even if the reality there does not justify such downheartedness. Or a person with little trust may interpret many new situations with suspicion and, by doing so, reinforce a distorted outlook. When people have lived in abusive families or violent communities or have been subjected to demeaning discrimination, for example, they will often continue to be fearful even when external conditions improve.

Again, the concept of a balance of forces in the personality comes into play. *Psychosocial casework theory holds that understanding of later reinforcements can lessen the strength of damaging tendencies in the personality and may enable healthier components to take the ascendancy in controlling and directing personality functioning.* This is often done by considering *positive* as well as detrimental early life experiences and personality features. The purpose of encouraging the client to reflect upon the past is to bring about a beneficial change in the personality system. In general, casework does not attempt to reach infantile experiences directly, but to examine later childhood and adolescent events that can be considered causal only in the sense that they are contributory developmental experiences.

Reflection versus Description-Ventilation

The worker cannot assume that every time clients talk about past life they are developing understanding of it. This is usually not the case. Often, the client is simply *describing* past experiences rather than reflecting upon them. At other times the client's talk about the past is for the purpose of *catharsis*. As we said earlier, a person may get considerable relief from telling the worker about painful life events and from expressing anger or grief about them. Or, clients often bring up the past to *justify* present feelings, attitudes, or behavior. They are not then really trying to gain understanding but instead trying to explain to the worker why this or that reaction or feeling is warranted, or why they should not be blamed for so reacting; in other words, *the past is used as a defense of a present position.*

- A husband repeatedly said in couple sessions: "Of course I'm sarcastic when I'm afraid I'll be criticized. When I was growing up, everyone in my family was like that." Only after persistent questioning by the worker was this man able to recognize that habits from the past, that could be modified, were interfering with his marital relationship.
- A woman repeatedly told her therapy group that unless the members or leader asked her questions she would rarely speak because her parents had never encouraged her to express herself; not until she was challenged over a period of many months did she indicate a wish to use this

understanding of the past to change her behavior or to increase her opportunities in the present.

This type of defense is sometimes of great importance to the client; it can protect against overly severe self-criticism. When this is so, care needs to be taken to ensure that it is not thoughtlessly or prematurely stripped away.

In other cases, clients can keep talking about the past to evade thinking about the present. And clients sometimes have the impression that the past is what the worker is interested in and talk about it to please the worker!

Movement into Developmental Reflection

Many clients can be helped greatly in understanding self-defeating or unprofitable ways of acting by becoming aware of historical sources. Some clients quickly and spontaneously seek this kind of understanding. Others need help from the caseworker before they are ready and able to do so. *Apparent readiness needs to be carefully distinguished from real readiness.* Sophistication about psychological matters and personality theories makes intellectualization about childhood events a particularly common form of defense.

Movement into consideration of developmental factors follows much the same path as that just described for moving into pattern-dynamic reflection. Attention is drawn—by client or worker—to self-defeating or inconsistent behavior or to feelings and attitudes that are painful or hurtful to others. Sometimes clients are aware of counterproductive habits and present the need for change as the matter to be worked on; motivated and self-aware clients often initiate discussions about the influence of past events on present troubles. With other clients, the worker takes the lead by asking questions about earlier life that might be relevant to current problems: "Have you had feelings like this before?" "Does this make you think at all of similar things that have happened to you?" Or, more specifically, to a mother who is distraught by her son's mediocre school report: "How was it for you in school?" Or, to a man who is extraordinarily upset when mentioning his brother's divorce: "You haven't told me much about your brother; what was he like?"

The client may then spontaneously move into developmental understanding by seeing connections; or the worker—on the basis of information already given by the client—may promote thinking with *tentative* suggestions, often put in the form of a question: "Have you wondered whether your neighbor's death has stirred up feelings about the early loss of your mother?" "Could it be that the humiliation you felt as a child about failing grades in school now affects your attitude toward Jimmy?" "Do you think you still feel responsible for your brother as you did when you were growing up?"

Developmental Reflection and Use of Conjoint Sessions In previous general exploration of the client's earlier life or as the client has talked about childhood for other reasons, the worker will have obtained clues to historical factors that may be of significance in understanding and modifying a particular reaction. These clues can then be used to expand or deepen the client's thinking. In many instances, more benefits can accrue from the new understandings when family members participate in the therapy.

Mrs. Segal, who was unduly resentful of what seemed to her neglect by her husband, had earlier mentioned to the worker that her father had paid very little attention to her as a child. When she complained at length about her husband's disregard of her, the worker responded by asking her more about her father. By simply thinking of the two parallel situations in juxtaposition, the client saw the similarity and asked whether she could be carrying some of her feeling toward her father over to her husband. Subsequently, her husband joined in the treatment and the contentiousness between them was minimized, in large part because the wife realized the source of much of her discontent and was able to share this with her husband.

Sometimes the worker must suggest the connection to the client:

Mrs. Robinson, a single mother of four, had been referred to a social worker by child protective services for abusive behavior toward her children. A few weeks after treatment began, she became uncontrollably angry with her 14-year-old daughter, Cheryl, for borrowing her costume jewelry without permission and came close to engaging in a physical fight with her. The worker was already aware of this woman's deep hostility to her mother and suspected that it was being displaced onto her daughter. She also knew that as an adolescent and later, this client had been required to carry much of the financial burden of the home, depriving her of many things she wanted. The worker asked, "Do you think Cheryl's taking your things arouses feelings like you had as a girl when your mother didn't let you get pretty things for yourself?" This question touched off an outburst of feeling from Mrs. Robinson about her deprived adolescence, followed by the realization that she had been taking out on her daughter stored-up feelings from her own childhood.

When subsequent family sessions were arranged, this mother was able to say that she thought she had been unfair to Cheryl, that her reactions stemmed from her own bitterness and had little to do with the jewelry incident. By sharing some of her early experiences, the mother helped her daughter to understand her. Cheryl began to feel less guilty and angry and, in turn, could get closer to her mother than she had been for some time. In this case, as so often happens, when one family member's reflection about the past resulted in changed behavior and more straightforward communication, the relationships of all involved improved. Mrs. Robinson and Cheryl became calmer and warmer with each other; the mother and other children got along better; and violence among the siblings subsided. The family climate was so much more tranquil, and relationships so much more positive, that the worker felt confident in recommending that the protective service withdraw from the case.

In the marital treatment of Dick and Susan Jones (see Chapter 3), both spouses reflected on some childhood experiences that had contributed to their current difficulties; this understanding helped them both to consider behavior changes that were relevant to their present circumstances. In the couple sessions, not only was self-understanding achieved but Susan and Dick were also able to realize that the problematic reactions of the other derived from early experiences and therefore need not be taken so personally. For the Jones couple and in the Segal and Robinson cases just described, the *value of family and conjoint sessions cannot be overstated.* As we say many times in this book, changes in one client seen in individual treatment can have powerful reverberations on interacting

systems, often the family system. However, when family members can understand the origins of the difficulties—those that can derive from developmental reflection—the capacity for empathy is enhanced and feelings of blame or self-blame often are reduced. While there may be reasons not to include family members in some situations, in many cases we recommend it. As Chapters 14 through 17 will further indicate, developmental reflection can actually be facilitated by conjoint treatment.

Reevaluation of Past Events   Often, as we have said, the recollection of an event and recognition of its influence in current life may not be enough. Rather, past history may need to be reevaluated so feelings about it are modified.

- A woman who was very resentful that her father did not provide adequately for his family was helped to realize that his failure was due to illness and a high unemployment rate rather than to lack of caring, weakness of character, or unwillingness to carry family responsibilities; this new understanding helped to reduce the amount of hostility she had displaced upon her husband, a hardworking man who did not earn as much as she wished he did.

- A young woman who had believed that her parents discriminated against her because she was a lesbian, by not letting her go to college, began to recognize that as a high school student she had not shown any interest in college; perhaps, the client began to think, her parents had been unaware of her interest in further education. She also realized that she might have misinterpreted her parents' seemingly cold attitudes toward her. Considering new ways of interpreting past events led to reduction of the client's hostility toward her parents (who, it turned out, had felt intimidated by their daughter), enabling her to have frank conversations with them that dramatically improved their current relationships. It also substantially reduced her feeling, which carried over to many of her adult relationships, that she was not loved and was somehow unworthy of love because of her sexual orientation.

Before moving into this reevaluation process, it is often necessary to allow considerable *ventilation* of initial hostile feelings. From this, the client obtains relief and also benefits from the worker's continued *acceptance* despite feelings about which the client may feel quite guilty or humiliated. Furthermore, there probably will not be readiness to reconsider attitudes about earlier relationships until there has been an opportunity for catharsis. If the worker attempts the reevaluation process prematurely, the client is likely to resent it, thinking that the worker is uncaring, critical, or more sympathetic to the person toward whom the client is hostile.

Obviously, *reevaluation is useful only when the client has really misconstrued the earlier situation.* Many times, early realities have been extremely painful, even traumatic. Under such circumstances, ventilation plus sympathetic acceptance by the worker and realization of ways in which early events are unnecessarily influencing current life often follow.

Developmental Reflection on Strengths

More often than clinicians seem to report, *reflection on one's early years can lead to self-affirmation and positive reinforcement.* Frequently a worker makes remarks such as: "You certainly handled your terribly unhappy family situation well by finding people—teachers, neighbors, friends—who provided support you so badly needed. Your creative way of reaching out when you

needed to still seems to stand you in good stead." Or, "What remarkable strength you were able to muster when your father left home and your mother became ill. Your capacity for resourcefulness seems to have lasted to this day." While these comments are, in part, *sustaining,* they also help clients *reflect* on, value, and validate creative responses developed in childhood, even under difficult conditions. Recognition of past strengths may be the key to bolstering present approaches to handling difficult situations.

One woman in her early 50s, who was grieving the tragic, accidental death of her teenage son, spontaneously began talking to her clinical social worker about her childhood. Her mother had died when she was eight. Her sadness never left her, she said, but she remembered her mother well as a loving, ethical person whose example the client consciously began to imitate at a very young age. And, she added, when she felt mistreated by her father she always remembered the devotion and support she had gotten from her mother: "I knew how much she had loved me and that saw me through." These reflections not only affirmed this client's strengths, but also helped her try to come to some kind of peace in her present grief by focusing on what a special boy her son was and how fortunate she had been to have him, even though the loss was devastating to her.

Degrees of Awareness

It should be apparent from our discussion and illustrations so far that sometimes a client is fully aware of relevant early experiences and little or no anxiety is involved in recalling them; the next step—in individual or conjoint sessions—is simply for the individual to reflect upon and experience more deeply the influence of the past on present concerns. At other times, the early feelings or experiences are to some degree hidden from view. Or there may be fear of criticism or shame about things that are perfectly well remembered; an event may not be regarded as significant or pertinent to the interview; or memories may have been suppressed or repressed because of their painfulness. Only as clients' stories unfold and worker and clients together examine the meanings of past events will they begin to shed light on the present and lead to changes that enhance current functioning and relationships.

Relationship with the Worker

As we shall discuss further in Chapter 9, the relationship with the worker can often be viewed as a source of developmental understanding. At times, clients are clearly reacting to the worker in terms of attitudes carried over from early life. In these cases, the worker should—if consideration of these factors seems appropriate *and* acceptable to the client—gently pursue the clues: "Do you think that you fear criticism from me as you did from your father?" "Is it possible that you want me to urge you to study just as your mother used to? Then, of course, you may be angry with me for 'nagging' as you used to be at your mother." Generally, questions or interpretations like these would be made only after a client has achieved some measure of understanding toward parents and has confidence in the worker's acceptance and competence.

Sometimes comments about *transference reactions* are necessary to straighten out the relationship with the worker so that treatment can proceed. They are also of great value in helping the client become aware of similar transferred reactions in other parts of current life. Because the worker is observing the client's reaction in a controlled situation, he or she is in an excellent position to make an accurate, convincing interpretation. (Of course, as we shall discuss more fully in Chapter 9, one must be very careful to determine that the client is not reacting *realistically* to the worker; for example, it is useful to point out the client's transferred expectation of being judged only if the worker is *not* feeling judgmental.)

A young African American woman, Ms. Cave, who had been seeing a white worker for several weeks for help in dealing with relationships on her job, said she felt comfortable with the worker; she felt she was making progress. Early on, when asked, Ms. Cave indicated that she had no objection to working with a white person: She had lived near and worked with many white people; she had a white stepfather of whom she was fond. However, when she arrived for one session, she seemed uncharacteristically reticent and ill at ease. She was aware of her change in attitude even though, she said, she could not put her finger on the reason. The worker knew that in high school this client was very attached to a white woman teacher who had subsequently shared an important confidence about Ms. Cave with another teacher; the thought of this betrayal still stirred up painful feelings. After she seemed blocked from understanding her present withdrawal, the worker said: "I don't know if there is anything to this, but do you think there may be some connection between the way you feel today and the way you felt when your teacher broke your trust?" For the first time in the worker's presence, this very poised woman sobbed without restraint. Finally, she said, "That's it. I think when I begin to feel really close to someone, especially an older woman, I am afraid that I will feel crushed again, as I did by that teacher." This recognition led to a more relaxed and trusting treatment relationship than ever. Subsequently, it also became clear that some of her difficulties with people at work derived from her fear of being let down if she became too friendly with co-workers; as a defense, she closed up, with the result that others probably thought she was unfriendly.

PERSONALITY DISORDERS AND REFLECTIVE PROCEDURES

In earlier years, caseworkers, particularly those engaged in intensive or long-term treatment, worked mostly with clients who seemed to be handicapped by neurotic symptoms or conflicts. More recently, large numbers of people in the caseloads of clinical social workers are diagnosed as having some type of personality disorder. Surprising as it may seem to us now, for some time it was generally believed that people in this group, in contrast to neurotic clients, were not capable of pattern-dynamic or developmental reflection. It was thought that their behavior was ego-syntonic (acceptable to the ego); the presence of underlying anxiety and pain was not fully recognized. Generally, it was believed that only person–situation reflection would be useful by helping such clients to see how they are really hurting or depriving themselves.

From clinical experience we now know that many clients with these conditions suffer terribly. Better understanding of the varieties of personality disorders and of their varying dynamics reveals that discomfort, pain, and anxiety are often immediately apparent or very close to the surface. Thus, socially dysfunctional behavior and self-defeating emotional patterns are often *only superficially ego-syntonic,* if at all. If the client has the capacity and motivation for establishing a working relationship, and

ego functions—especially reality testing and impulse control—are strong enough or can be strengthened sufficiently, tremendous benefits can come from intrareflection about personality dynamics and early life experiences that could result in some relief for the client and improvement in current functioning. Since the difficulties in which people suffering from personality disorders find themselves tend to result from rigidly repetitive emotional, attitudinal, and behavioral patterns, understanding of these—and of their historical development—can be important and even necessary in moving toward change. The treatment of Mrs. Zimmer in Chapter 3 is a clear example of this type of work.

Generally, the more severe the personality disorder, the more *sustainment* is necessary before turning to reflective procedures. While exploring inner dynamics and past influences, these clients may need particular support to help them through anxiety and depression that can accompany growing self-awareness. And if, for example, an adult survivor of early trauma, such as abandonment, violence, or sexual abuse, becomes emotionally overwhelmed, the worker can always return to discussions of the present and help the client strengthen cognitive understanding until further exploration is even considered. When given sufficient support, careful assistance, and structure as discomfort increases, these clients' motivation for treatment and change may increase dramatically.[8]

Periods of work on personality patterns or early life influences occur in many cases that are mainly focused on person–situation reflection. Only when discussion of the present does not lead to change are the procedures described in this chapter employed. They often push forward the person–situation understanding when this is temporarily blocked by intrapsychic influences. The way may then be cleared for better perception and handling of current affairs.

In reflective communications, the more clients can do on their own, the better. If the client sees connections without help, all the better. Otherwise, the more the worker can limit communications to starting the client off on a possibly fruitful train of thought—with a question, suggestion, or tentative comment—the more likely the client will think independently and develop skill in intrareflection. Interpretations, when they are necessary, should be made tentatively unless the worker is absolutely sure of their accuracy. In any case, the worker must convey that he or she wants to be challenged if the client thinks the worker's thoughts are not correct or helpful. In individual, couple, and family psychosocial therapy, *the ultimate understanding or insight comes from and belongs to the client.* While the worker's empathy, support, guidance, or well-educated guesses may coax the client to reflect along certain lines, room must always be there for clients to modify or discard the worker's ideas and come up with their own perspectives. True collaboration not only fosters autonomy but also helps clients move beyond superficial explanations on the one hand or the clinician's interpretations on the other.

Sustaining comments often provide the client with the necessary confidence in the worker's goodwill and competence, facilitating a climate of trust during difficult explorations. When anxiety mounts as a result of new awarenesses—or memories, feelings, and connections are uncovered—sustaining communications can help to carry the client through a difficult period of work. We must repeatedly emphasize that no more penetrating or intensive approach than is necessary or therapeutic should be considered.

The procedures discussed in this chapter are closely related to intrareflective proce-

dures described in Chapter 6. These can be skillfully used only when the worker has substantial psychological knowledge and understanding. To promote consideration of pattern-dynamic or developmental matters as a major part of treatment, the worker must, in addition to being skilled in all other casework processes, be thoroughly familiar with the workings of the personality—of unconscious as well as of conscious factors— and with the way in which the personality develops and early life events find continued expression in the adult personality. Although there is evidence that in the past intrareflection was only a small part of casework process,[9] from the literature and our own experience it seems that, when appropriate, intrareflective procedures are now more commonly used. From the psychosocial point of view, caseworkers engaged in treatment of disturbances in interpersonal relationships need a total repertory of casework procedures. Workers must be particularly sensitive to the nuances of the client's feelings, have considerable security when dealing with anxiety, and be aware of and able to control the flow of their own reactions. They must also be free of the need to probe into a client's life to secure vicarious satisfaction either out of their own curiosity or of an appetite for power, or for other narcissistic gratifications.

NOTES

1. Those interested in a historical glimpse into this matter are referred to Grete Bibring's classic paper (1947).
2. In recent years there has been a heated debate in the mental health professions about childhood sexual abuse recalled in adulthood. In the 1970s and 1980s, largely as a result of women's movements and efforts, incest and sexual abuse survivors demanded to be heard and clinicians began to listen. Since then, however, some believe that professionals have

too frequently assumed sexual abuse occurred when clients evidence repression and dissociation; or they advise skepticism when there is no corroboration to verify a memory and caution us about the power of suggestion and "false memories." At the other extreme are those who are deeply concerned that this questioning, or "backlash against sexual abuse survivors," is a profoundly destructive trend that results in blaming and negating the reality of the victims and catapults us into a state of denial. The details of the extreme points of view on this matter go beyond our discussion here, but clinicians working in this area should become familiar with the issues. However, to this extent we agree with Robbins (1995, p. 486) who writes: "It is imperative that we recognize the serious consequences for our clients and their families when our personal biases lead us to either underdiagnose or overdiagnose childhood sexual abuse. Further, we must remember that the imposition of our personal values and beliefs is antithetical to our deeply held value of client self-determination." See another point of view, expressed by Benatur (1995). Madden and Parody (1997) review some of the issues debated about traumatic amnesia; they also address legal concerns and make recommendations they believe are based on caution that will help clients but reduce the potential for legal problems. See Feld and Fetkewicz (1997) who discuss their reactions to Madden and Parody; among the several points they make is the importance of distinguishing between clients who recently recovered "memories" of incest and those who come into therapy with continuous memories of childhood abuse.

For additional readings on the subjects of adult survivors of childhood sexual abuse, repression and dissociation, recovered memories, and other related matters, see: Briere (1992), Joyce (1995), Liebman (1994), Lynn and Rhue's (1994) edited volume, Nelson (1991), Stocks (1998), Westerlund (1992), and Yapko (1994). Cornell (1991), Knight (1990), Maltas and Shay (1995), and Wartel (1991) discuss effects and clinical considerations for adults who were sexually or physically abused as children.

For a useful discussion of some factors involved for clients in making decisions about disclosure of childhood abuse to nonoffending significant people and about confronting the perpetrator, see Weingarten and Cobb (1995).

3. See Paul L. Wachtel (1993), especially Chapter 5, for a good discussion and examples of interpretations that can facilitate understanding without being accusatory. Garrett (1982, pp. 41–43), in her updated classic, makes good points about interpretation; verbatim interviews provide examples. See also a still useful discussion by Hammer (1968, pp. 31–42), as well as other useful chapters in Hammer's edited volume.

4. See Eda Goldstein (1990, p. 49) on the variations in superego pathology that occur in clients with borderline personality disorders; she writes that these clients "frequently have strict standards for their behavior and are persecuted by their superego if they do not live up to its unrelenting demands. Some therapeutic reactions reflect a deep-seated sense of guilt that does not permit them to enjoy life." See also Woods (1999), especially the discussion of individuals with obsessive-compulsive personality disorders who are often conscientious and perfectionistic to an extreme. Various distinctions have been made between guilt and shame: see Lewis (1992) and Nathanson's (1987) edited book on shame and its implications. We also recommend the very interesting book by Morrison (1989) on shame.

5. See Wachtel (1993), especially Chapter 7, "Building on the Patient's Strengths." For additional readings on strengths, see Chapter 1, note 37.

6. For readings on using narrative and related approaches to achieve self-understanding, see four highly recommended articles, some with case illustrations: Kopp (1989); McInnis-Dittrich (March 1996); Nye (1994), pp. 43–57; and Strickland (1994).

7. See Dungee-Anderson (1992) who illustrates how clients' recognition of patterns and developmental gaps helps them in the self-nurturing and healing process. Goldstein (1990) and Woods (1999) discuss in further detail work

with clients with developmental deficits. See Chapter 3, note 9 for many references on borderline and personality disorders.

8. Neurosis (a term no longer used by DSM because of its effort to be neutral with respect to theories of etiology) and personality disorders will be discussed in Chapter 11.

9. Studies reported by Mullen (1969) and Reid and Shyne (1969) found some workers avoided using either pattern-dynamic or developmental reflection even when it would have been appropriate to do so. Perhaps at that time there was insufficient understanding about how to use these procedures.

CHAPTER 8

PSYCHOSOCIAL THERAPY AND THE ENVIRONMENT

Psychosocial therapy, as the term implies, does not mean that every person–situation imbalance or disturbance requires that individuals must make changes from within. It is often the *situation* or *interactions* that must be treated, modified, changed. As discussed in Chapter 2, many problems experienced by the clients of clinical social workers do not stem from personality deficiencies; rather, they require analysis of *environmental deficits* or the *person–situation disequilibrium*. For instance, "deviance" of some sort may be an expected response to a closed or inadequate opportunity structure or to a lack of resources necessary to meet basic human needs. Myriad kinds of "pathology" may be the outcome of "mystifying" or "double-binding" communications (see Chapter 14 for definitions). "Acting out" may be the only apparent alternative to resignation and hopelessness in the face of noxious social conditions.[1]

As the psychosocial framework has incorporated systems and ecological perspectives, clinical social workers following this approach have become increasingly sophisticated in their conceptualizations of client–situation interplay, and this has contributed to more precise assessments of what is wrong or what is needed to improve a given situation. As we will demonstrate, a division between person and environment is artificial and is made only to analyze interpenetrating components of the person–situation gestalt.[2]

This chapter on environmental treatment is separated from other chapters for convenience only. "Direct" and "indirect" work are inevitably intertwined. Environmental interventions rarely stand alone. Caseworkers must work directly with their clients in making choices about external changes. Although we are always advocating the elimination of inhumane conditions and the enrichment of the general quality of people's lives, it is equally important to help our clients or potential clients determine just what improvements or services they require. It serves no purpose to urge opportunities upon people who do not wish or feel free to use them. Without consistently consulting the presumed beneficiaries of change or of social services, we can err badly by making unilateral judgments based on what *we* have decided is best. Opportunities that suit one person may be uninteresting, frightening, or even repugnant to another. Again, the assessment of the "fit" between the person and environment is crucial to successful intervention. *Mutuality* between worker and client is at the bedrock of *all* casework activity, including efforts to enhance the quality of our clients' environments.

It is also true, of course, that to utilize whatever opportunities are made available, people can be helped to acquire new adaptive or coping skills; increased competence and self-esteem may enable people to take advantage of opportunities that previously seemed beyond their reach. Sometimes a casework relationship can be the medium through which clients learn to develop or release capacities for change and growth. When clients' strengths are identified and autonomy supported, they are then in the best possible position to choose what kinds of environmental changes are important to them.

Since people's inner and outer lives are (as described in Chapter 2, especially on pages 38–44 and 68–70) inevitably intertwined, it can be difficult to differentiate the two. Thus, *sometimes environmental modifications result in enduring personality change.* This was true for both the West and Stone family members presented in Chapter 3; particularly at first, the workers and clients in these cases focused on environmental rather than personal changes. On the other hand, *personal changes or emotional growth may be required for the individual to maximize available opportunities;* this was true for Mr. Kennedy (Chapter 3) who could not take advantage of resources potentially available to him until—with the help of his relationship with his caseworker—he began to recover from the depression triggered by his daughter's departure from the home. In the face of racism or other unjust recalcitrant social conditions, individuals may first have to make personal changes to achieve desired improvements in their lives, to maximize available resources, or to find alternatives to their current circumstances. It follows, then, that after assessing people, their environments, and the interactions among these, *psychosocial workers usually focus their interventions on those systems most accessible to change, not necessarily the most "pathological" ones.*

Some social workers think it is reactionary and/or futile to attempt to assist individuals in the face of societal evils and ills that can so profoundly grind them down. As we see it, however, one need not support or be satisfied with the status quo of a grossly imperfect social system in order to attempt to help people improve the quality of their lives *now,* before more basic changes become possible.

In this connection, it is important to remind ourselves of what casework can and cannot do. Some professional modesty is called for. While as *social workers,* individually and through professional organizations, our heritage compels us to advocate for social change, to participate in movements, and to vigorously support legislation that challenges oppressive aspects of our social structure, our goals for change can far exceed our power. Yet we know what we, as *caseworkers,* can do. When working with victims of social injustice: We can be supportive, which includes trying to truly understand the many destructive effects of oppression. We can share with clients our distress with conditions and not (as we have sometimes been accused) try to "adjust" them to intolerable situations. We can develop techniques that are responsive to the needs of people living under miserable circumstances. We can assist people in their efforts to "negotiate the system." We can work together with clients to develop self-esteem and competence in the face of oppression, which in turn empowers them to find new alternatives and/or to work toward community and social change. We can offer concrete help in opening up opportunities in the client's environment. We can promote policies and approaches in agencies and institutions where we have influence and thereby try to make service delivery more humane, relevant, and accessible. We can participate in reflecting on ways in which clients themselves, or in concert with others, can induce environmental changes. From our own experiences with clients trapped in communities without decent resources—schools, police protection, housing, jobs, even a corner grocer—we can document the deprivation large numbers of citizens endure and advocate for social change. We can help to locate or create services or social networks for people who need or want them.

Over the years, despite fluctuations in public and private funding, social workers have struggled to provide resources *before* serious problems develop, by offering educational, therapeutic, facilitative services in clinics, schools, day care centers, to populations "at risk," thereby helping to contribute to the *prevention* of future life problems or personality disturbances. Outreach services and comprehensive programs for abused women, for the homeless, for people discharged from psychiatric facilities, for residents of single-room occupancy hotels,

for people with AIDS, for immigrants and migrant workers, among many others have been developed to link people to resources that will provide protection, opportunities, and comfort.[3] In this chapter we will discuss some of the casework principles and skills required for such environmental work. We will also give some examples of creative programs designed to offer services and opportunities to clients.

But the treatment we offer cannot "cure" the extraordinary problems that a large group of overwhelmed clients face.[4] We readily acknowledge that casework does not and cannot eradicate poverty, homelessness, unemployment, racism and all forms of discrimination, or the dehumanizing effects of a society that can place low priority on improving the quality of the lives of citizens increasingly beleaguered by the effects of urban conditions, rural poverty, political corruption, impersonal bureaucracies, and shortages of resources. But casework should not be discredited because it does not do everything we wish it could.[5]

Sometimes students and caseworkers make the mistake of assuming that environmental work is needed only by the poor and disadvantaged. This kind of casework is of great importance to many clients: children, the elderly, the physically and mentally ill or disabled, and many other individuals and families facing either "expectable" or extraordinary crises. Certainly those in poverty are particularly stressed by practical problems, but people from all income groups benefit from environmental interventions that help them through difficulties or improve their lives. Just as many poor or poorly educated clients with emotional or interpersonal problems have the capacity and motivation for introspection, so some well-to-do clients seek only "concrete" services. *The tendency to assume that social action and environmental work are relevant only to the poor and that psychotherapy is useful only to the financially comfortable sells both groups short.*

Environmental work is not simple. Yet, in some social work circles it is undervalued and delegated to volunteers and untrained workers. There is evidence that some psychodynamic social workers tend to underemphasize environmental and even interpersonal or family influences on clients' problems, choosing to see the locus of the difficulty as being primarily within the client's personality. In Beck's study, to our surprise, with the possible exception of treatment of complicated family relationship problems, counselors *without* significant graduate-level training were more effective in helping people with many of their difficulties than were those with professional education.[6] Untrained workers can certainly become experts in giving clients information on resources, in assisting access to services, on clients' rights, on community issues, and in providing various follow-up services. However, it is alarming to realize that many opportunities for change are being overlooked or undervalued by social workers whose attention is disproportionately focused on personality dynamics because they have not been well enough trained in the assessment and treatment of environmental influences or the person–situation interplay. As we often say, when our clients' situations improve, individual and family functioning is frequently enhanced.

As we see it, effective environmental work requires caseworkers with the most training, skill, and experience, workers who have knowledge about the inner and outer lives of people and about casework procedures and differential interviewing, workers who are interested in breaking new ground and developing increasingly sophisticated approaches. The most refined principles, skills, and techniques for effective

work in the environment will evolve from direct practice experience. When we rely heavily or almost exclusively on untrained personnel (whose effectiveness also should not be underrated)—as we too often do—we imply that work with the environment does not have the same value as casework that focuses on psychological or family dynamics; the fact is that change in external circumstances frequently enhances individual and family functioning.

ENVIRONMENTAL CHANGE BY CLIENT OR BY WORKER?

The general casework value of enabling the client to increase in competence has a direct bearing on the decision of how to deal with problems that either involve environmental etiology or depend upon environmental resources for their solution. We are always confronted by the question of whether to take action on the client's behalf or to encourage the client to attempt to tackle the milieu problems alone. By and large, the more one can do for oneself, the greater the increase in one's competence and in one's self-respect. But if this is to be the outcome, the change that is required must be one that the client is likely to be able to bring about. Some environmental factors are more responsive to the worker than to the client. As examples in this chapter will demonstrate, sometimes the worker, because of status, role, and experience, has more "clout" and can influence the environment or the people in it in a way that the client cannot. At other times, knowledge or skill in human relations may enable the worker to effect changes beyond the clients' capacities to achieve these by their own efforts. For example, the presence of a social worker at a school conference that is called to make determinations about the education of a child who has had adjustment problems in school may be instrumental in arriving at decisions in the best interest of the child.

The decision of when and when not to intervene in the environment rests upon the worker's assessment of the modifiability of the factors of the milieu, the client's capacity to handle them, and the agreement reached by worker and client *together* about what approach would be most effective. There are occasional instances when the worker intervenes with collaterals (i.e., people in clients' environments who affect or can be enlisted to affect their situations) even though the clients could do this as effectively on their own. When carefully assessed, it may be decided that the meaning such a move would have to a particular client—such as a demonstration of worker interest to a person who is distrustful—temporarily outweighs the importance of supporting the client's efforts to seek the change independently. As discussed in earlier chapters, so-called "hard-to-reach" clients, or those who are involuntary, are sometimes reassured by the worker's willingness to take action on their behalf. The worker's demonstration of interest in helping can strengthen a collaborative relationship.

Often, worker and client *together* may see a collateral person to explore opportunities or resources or to work toward desired changes in the client's environment. Such joint efforts have two advantages. First, the worker's knowledge and influence may contribute to a more successful result; second, the client has an opportunity to raise questions, express reactions, and perhaps learn through demonstration and experience how to handle certain situations. But we would add a note of caution here: There are times when a worker's presence can be a liability rather than an asset; for example, it may seem to the worker or the client that a collateral could interpret the worker's involvement as an intrusion or as a sign that the

clients are too weak or incapable to take care of their own affairs. Such interpretations might result in less willingness on the part of the collateral to take an interest than if the client made the contact independently. In one case, a young male worker and a Puerto Rican client family, who had been burned out of their home, decided together that the worker would accompany the single mother and her twin nine-year-old sons to look at an apartment that was advertised in the newspaper. The mother, a characteristically shy person who spoke only a little English, wanted the worker there as a support and interpreter. However, the social worker's presence was clearly an annoyance to the rental agent; rudely, he asked the client if she was hiding something and if that was the reason for bringing along a "bodyguard." Although the client did get the apartment, it was only after a great deal of effort on the part of the worker and the mother to persuade the agent (who, gratefully, did not live in the apartment complex!) that the worker had come only because of the client's concern about a language barrier. In retrospect, this event might have been less painful if the worker and client together talked about—or even rehearsed—the meeting with the agent ahead of time, then deciding that the mother and her boys might do better on their own.

Whenever possible, clients should become *active* participants in seeking resources or bringing about changes, although, in some cases, *extensive use of sustaining procedures and reflective discussion may be required before the client is prepared to act.* Even when caseworkers become advocates or "social brokers" for their clients and attempt to alleviate abhorrent environmental conditions or help them to "negotiate the system," the best results come when the worker carries out the functions *with* and not simply *for* individuals and families, thereby nurturing self-esteem and autonomy. Treatment that reinforces clients' growth and competence will render them better able to act on their own behalf when, inevitably, future difficulties arise. Furthermore, *direct involvement by clients can allay suspicion about what others are saying about or planning for them.*[7]

In previous chapters, we have considered forms of communication between worker and client. In Chapter 7, we saw that reflective discussion of dynamic and developmental factors is interwoven with all the other forms of client–worker communication. Cases vary: In some there is no work of this type; in others it occurs in a scattering of interviews; in still others it plays a major role. Similarly, some clients do not need environmental help, either because their problems do not involve the type of situational matters in which the worker can intervene directly or because the clients are able to act on their own behalf. (At times, nevertheless, clients may want to practice or even role-play an anticipated interview with a collateral or a planned action of any kind.) At the other extreme are cases in which a major part of the work consists of bringing about environmental changes through communications between worker and collateral, through joint efforts with the client to modify some aspect of the milieu, or through the location of needed services and resources. Again, the concept of a *blend* is useful. Environmental work is intertwined with other procedures. It also involves subtleties and complexities that must be understood if it is to be carried on with skill.[8] The Kennedy, West, and Stone cases in Chapter 3 illustrate these points.

As outlined in Chapter 4, milieu work can be viewed in at least three ways: (1) in terms of the types of *communication* between worker and collateral; (2) in terms of the *role* or function that the worker is car-

rying; and (3) in terms of the type of *resource* involved. A discussion of these categories follows.

TYPES OF COMMUNICATION WITH COLLATERALS
Confidentiality

In all communication with collaterals, the importance of *confidentiality* cannot be overemphasized. When the caseworker shares specific information about a client with another person or agency, permission to release such information *must* be obtained. Often this should be secured in writing (particularly when dealing with resources outside the family). Clients have a right to know with whom (within and outside the agency) information may be shared. It is also true that problems regarding legal liability of the worker or the employing agency are thereby minimized. But, above all, straightforward discussion with clients about these matters, and conscientious attention to obtaining consent when required, conveys respect for clients' ethical right to privacy and right to take charge of their own affairs.[9]

Discussions with Collaterals

The first four sets of communication procedures (sustainment; direct influence; exploration–description–ventilation; and person–situation reflection) are just as germane to environmental work as to direct work with the client. The use of these procedures with collaterals is very similar to their use with clients and requires an equal amount of skill.

Discussions with collaterals have many purposes. A worker may want to learn more about a client or about services or opportunities possibly available to the client. The worker may attempt to change or expand the collateral's understanding of clients and their circumstances, so that the collateral's attitude or actions will be tempered, or resources will be provided, or conditions over which the collateral has control or influence will be modified. But collaterals are often not free agents. They may be part of a system—school, business, court, police—with policies and regulations. Relatives may have pressures of their own or may be involved in disturbing interactions with the client, and therefore reluctant to participate in a discussion or take steps to help. Many influences in addition to the client's needs may enter into a collateral's decisions.

As with the client, the worker has to assess—often very quickly, sometimes during a telephone conversation—the collateral's attitudes and feelings toward the client, the degree of interest, and the willingness to get involved in the client's concerns or situation. In an interview, the worker has to be attuned to the collateral's subtle responses, including the facial expression and other nonverbal behavior, to evaluate accurately the person's receptivity.

Sustainment

In work with collaterals, contact and rapport have to be established, and sustaining procedures beyond common courtesy are often of great value. The client is not the only person who may be afraid of being blamed: so may the teacher, the public welfare worker, the nurse, the landlord, and the relative. They can be angry. They can be anxious. They have needs too. Their way of handling their feelings may be defensive hostility that leads them to attack either the worker or the client. Often they will respond better if workers show understanding of the problems they are up against, make it clear that they have not come to criticize, express interest in their point of view, and are willing to listen to the headaches the client has caused them. They, too, may need encouragement concerning efforts they have already made to deal with the situation.

Direct Influence

Reinforcement and suggestion, for example, along with other procedures of direct influence have an important part in environmental work, particularly when the worker is trying to modify the way in which a collateral is acting toward a client. Advice can sometimes be of value, with insistence or even coercion occasionally necessary. The administrator of a nursing home, pressured by a long waiting list, may have to be strongly encouraged to admit an elderly client in urgent need of immediate care. A busy public welfare worker may have to cut through red tape quickly to give aid and special consideration to a family burned out of its home by fire. Landlords who cannot be persuaded by other means may have to be told that violations in their buildings will be reported to the appropriate government agency unless immediate repairs are made.

It goes without saying that *when a worker attempts to persuade a collateral to adopt or change an attitude toward a client, careful evaluation of all pertinent aspects of the client–situation system is necessary.* In every instance, the caseworker must have confidence that the client wants and will benefit from the changes being promoted; to know this, *the worker must know the client.* If, for example, a caseworker helps to reinstate a student suspended for truancy without understanding what this behavior means, or if a worker helps a man whose job performance has been erratic to locate a job he will not hold, does not want, or is not qualified for, the probability is great that the result will be frustration for client and collateral alike. Past failures experienced by the client will only be reinforced if the caseworker's interventions are based on faulty or inadequate assessment. And the collateral who was encouraged to make a change will be reluctant if the worker tries to enlist his or her help again for another client, with the result that an important resource may then become unavailable.

Exploration–Description–Ventilation

Often the person being interviewed has a great deal of emotion about the client or about the situation in which the person and client are involved. Offering collaterals opportunities to ventilate frustrations or feelings of resentment can be critical to establishing a working relationship. The landlord resolved to evict an ill mother and her several active children may need to express aggravations experienced with this family before being ready to reconsider such drastic action. So, too, may the nurse or teacher who has had to put up with an "acting out" child or intrusive parent.

Sometimes collaterals vent feelings and express attitudes that are offensive to the worker. A landlord may complain that a building is being destroyed because the tenants are of a particular color or ethnic background. A white teacher may be prejudiced, incensed by actions of an African American student that would be tolerated in others. More often than we would wish, welfare workers make denigrating remarks about "those people" on their caseloads. In such instances, it requires particular discipline and skill to listen, to continue to be supportive, to respond uncritically, and at the same time to avoid seeming to agree with the point of view being expressed or arguing for one's own view when this will do no good. It is obviously important not to alien-

ate the very person from whom one is seeking help on behalf of a client; in many cases, direct confrontation would make matters worse rather than better. And often, once anger is expressed, the collateral may then be better prepared to listen to what the worker wants to say or ask; in some cases, as the worker presents the clients and their situations in a different light, the collateral may even be able to modify a bigoted reaction. When this does not happen, certainly a more aggressive approach may be necessary. But such a decision should be made only by worker and client together, and only after considering the risks and possible repercussions involved. This point will be discussed more fully later in the next section where worker roles are examined.

Reflection

As in direct work, experience has shown that procedures for *reflective discussion* are of great value with collaterals, particularly when trying to help one person to understand another. Often, such understanding is brought about simply by telling the person about some aspects of the client and his or her life. At times the worker may enter into the reflective process with the interviewee in much the same way as with a client, although the scope of the contact is more limited, frequently to a single interview. Often, worker and collateral—frequently with the participation of the client, too—are actually thinking together to arrive at a solution. Care must be taken to estimate the ability as well as the willingness of the collateral person to listen or engage in reflective discussion.

The worker is less likely in such contacts to use reflective procedures that involve thinking about consequences to the *self,* although this, too, can occasionally take place.

Sometimes, for example, collaterals will discover that the changes being sought will benefit them as well as the client. This kind of reflection may be extremely useful when the vested interests of the collaterals have made them resistant to understanding or responding to the needs of the client.

> In one situation, Tom, a teenage boy employed after school in a restaurant to supplement his family's modest income, was fired for stealing food. "That's not my problem," the employer told the school social worker who had explained the difficult conditions under which the boy and his single mother lived. The worker realized that efforts to expand the employer's view by giving information about the boy's background angered rather than appeased him; it was apparent that he needed to vent his feelings about Tom's actions. Therefore, the worker listened with understanding, making no attempts to deflect the anger. Then, only after the employer became calmer, Tom, who was present at the meeting, and the worker offered the idea that Tom could pay off his debt if he were allowed to work it off. Since Tom had been a good employee, the discussion of this suggestion led the employer to recognize the advantage to himself of giving the boy another chance.

In this example, it became clear that the employer was unwilling to be responsive to Tom's needs. Therefore, the worker used procedures of sustainment, encouraged ventilation, and only then made a direct suggestion. These procedures were followed by reflection in which the employer realized that his self-interest could be served by rehiring his youthful employee. The fact that Tom, who genuinely regretted what he had done, participated in the discussion—and offered a solution as well as apologies—may have

supported the employer's confidence that the boy would not steal from him again. This case also illustrates that the *extent* of the communication procedures differs, but the greater part of the *range* is common to work with collaterals and clients alike.

Reflective procedures may also be necessary to straighten out the relationship between the caseworker and the collateral. The worker's intent or attitudes may need to be clarified before effective work can proceed. Sometimes a simple explanation will suffice. In other instances, the worker may try to elicit a collateral's negative reactions about the worker and the purpose of the interview, so that misinterpretations can be cleared up. Naturally, the details of achieving this kind of understanding depend on the context in which they are being applied, the need for such discussion, and the willingness of the collateral to engage in it. But, whether or not the interviewee's reactions are brought out into the open, the worker must be sensitive to them and skillful in finding tactful ways of conveying his or her own true attitudes and role. This is true whether the collateral is an employer, teacher, landlord, or member of the client's family.

> Mrs. Davis, who was being seen by a clinical social worker, complained that her mother, who cared for Mrs. Davis's children during the day, was undermining Mrs. Davis's authority with the youngsters, with the result that they were becoming unmanageable. The grandmother disapproved of her daughter's therapy, yet reluctantly agreed to come to a joint interview with her. It was necessary for the worker to be accepting of the grandmother's view of her as an "interferer" and to realize that this woman was expecting to be criticized. By demonstrating a supportive manner and telling her that her help was needed to better understand

the children's problems, the worker conveyed her respect for the grandmother and the purpose for the meeting. Only then, and after giving the grandmother a good deal of credit for her conscientious care of the children, was the worker able to discuss with her the apparent effects the conflicts between the adults were having on the youngsters. As it turned out, the grandmother decided to come to subsequent meetings and, as the treatment evolved, Mrs. Davis and her mother were able to agree upon the latter's role as an experienced "consultant" to her daughter in the caretaking of the children. The tensions and competition between the two women were thereby virtually eliminated. The children's behavior improved in a short time in response to the changes made by the adults.

In summary, then, all that has been said about sustaining work, directive procedures, ventilation, and reflective discussion of the person–situation gestalt applies to work with people in the client's milieu as well as to contacts with the client: to indirect as well as direct treatment. On the other hand, it is extremely unlikely that collaterals will become involved in extensive intrapsychic reflection, especially dynamic or developmental aspects of their own reactions. When people in the client's milieu are sufficiently involved in the client's affairs to be willing to engage in gaining self-understanding (as Mrs. Davis's mother was), the situation is one of interpersonal adjustment in which they, too, become clients. This can occur when a client's family becomes engaged in ongoing family treatment.

TYPE OF ROLES

The role or function of the worker has many variations:[10] (1) provider, (2) locator,

or (3) creator of a resource; (4) interpreter; (5) mediator; and (6) aggressive intervenor. A worker often carries more than one role simultaneously when working with a client on various aspects of the milieu. The role may shift rapidly, and conflict between roles can exist. Yet each role has its own characteristics. Sometimes these roles are carried out in *collaboration* with workers from other agencies, with members of a team of which the worker is a member, or with various other professionals in the community.

Provider

One is a provider of a resource when one gives the resource through the agency in which one works or as a private practitioner. More of the intricacies of this role will be discussed in the next section on resources. Sometimes the worker's role as provider involves efforts to expand agency services or to make them more accessible. A caseworker in a mental health clinic, for example, may decide to organize a group for relatives of patients recently discharged from psychiatric hospitals; or a multiple family group for these patients and their families may be formed. Increased outreach efforts may be offered, such as through home visits or the establishment of "storefront" neighborhood services.

From the point of view of role, the worker represents the resource, and the client reacts as though the worker were directly responsible for both the positive and negative features of the service given or the service withheld. A client may feel very appreciative of the caseworker who describes the agency's homemaker service that can be enlisted in the care of an elderly relative. On the other hand, a client may blame the caseworker or make accusations of discrimination if her income is too high to enroll her child in the agency's day care center funded to serve children of impoverished families. In the first case, there may be positive effects on concomitant direct work with the client; in the second, direct work may be impeded by the client's anger. Thorough knowledge of agency policies, flexibility in their application, readiness to help clients decide whether they want the resource or want to qualify for it are all part of the administration of a resource. So also is working with clients' resentment and resistance when these occur. And so is listening to needs for service expressed by clients and working toward changes in agency programs. Direct and indirect work are here closely intertwined.

Independent clinical social workers are often providers of special resources. They may form groups for people with special needs, such as for clients with eating disorders, or those who are adult children of alcoholics, or who are survivors of childhood sexual abuse, among many others. Some workers in private practice offer parent education groups, new mothers' groups, and so on.

Locator

The role of locator of a resource is an extremely important one. Success in it depends not only on thorough knowedge of the local community, but also on an imaginative assessment—on the part of worker and client—of the client's need. The worker must display ingenuity in finding the resource in unexpected places and skill in getting individuals interested in making provisions for the client's special requirements. Assessing certain needs and locating some resources, such as the appropriate public welfare office or the state employment ser-

vice, may be simple enough. But sometimes clients' needs are less routine: Genetic counseling may be helpful to a newly married couple where one spouse has a family history of genetic problems; a clinic specializing in the treatment of headaches may be able to diagnose and bring relief to a suffering client; affordable fertility clinics or services are often difficult to find; a teacher of braille may be helpful to a man who has recently lost his eyesight; many children need but cannot afford tutors to help them with school subjects. Patience and much telephone work and some footwork may be required to locate the resources that can be most helpful to the client. In large urban areas where there are many agencies and services of all types, the caseworker may need to consult directories of social agencies and health facilities or seek guidance from organizations that specialize in information and referral services.

Creator

Just beyond the locator role comes that of creator of a resource. The same qualities and activities are involved in this as in the more difficult aspects of the locator role. If, for example, the resources mentioned in the above paragraph cannot be located in or near the client's community, the worker, often with the help of a supervisor or administrator, may attempt to influence a hospital to create specialty clinics for genetic counseling, headache treatment, or fertility problems; the worker may encourage a local school for blind children to offer classes for adults; a community action agency may be prevailed upon to start an after-school tutoring program that also provides a day care function for children of working parents; or teenage volunteers may be located to assist younger children with their studies. Volunteers can often provide or arrange for various kinds of services when organized resources are not available or when those available do not offer quite what the client needs. Transportion and escort services are frequently needed, for example, when parents—who are working or caring for other children— are unable to accompany their child to a clinic; the elderly and handicapped often need help getting to appointments. Churches and synagogues can sometimes be involved in hosting resources, as can service-oriented clubs of various kinds. For example, such organizations are frequently willing to sponsor Alcoholics Anonymous or other "12-step" programs where there are none, children's camps, activities for single parents, bus trips for the elderly, special interest groups, and many more. The wider the worker's network of associations in the community, the more likely he or she will be able to become a resource creator.

Interpreter

In the role of interpreter, the worker is helping someone else to understand or behave differently toward the client. *The accuracy and completeness of the worker's own understanding of the client are the obvious baseline.* As noted in the discussion of communication procedures with collaterals, it is essential also to be *attuned to the attitudes and feelings of the person to whom one is trying to explain the client.* Much of the time interpreting is no simple fact-giving process, but an interactional one in which information and opinions are exchanged and strong feelings come into play. Sometimes, the worker is apprised of previously unknown aspects of the client's situation or functioning that may then be-

come pertinent in direct work with the client. A teacher—to whom a worker is turning for help for a handicapped child— may let the worker know that the child often comes to school hungry and ill-clothed and is teased unmercifully; in direct work with the family, the worker may then be able to determine what they can work out together to improve the child's physical or social situation. In another case, a teacher may tell a worker about a child's special talents or personality qualities of which even the family may not be aware.

When acting as interpreter, the worker must be absolutely sure that the client is willing to have information shared. Even so, the information given should be only that which is pertinent to the objective of the contact. It is rarely relevant when trying to persuade a landlord to make repairs in a family's apartment to disclose that the couple is having marital problems, that the adult son is gay, or that the teenage daughter is pregnant; even if the family has given the worker *carte blanche,* sharing such information is no more constructive than is careless gossip. However, if one were referring this family to a family therapist, if permission has been given, some or all of these facts may be revealed (even though sometimes it serves clients better to leave the divulging to them, to do in their way when the time seems right to them). Particular care must be taken not to inadvertently give out information that might create difficulty for the client.

The nature of interpretive communications is strongly influenced by the type of collateral to whom information is being given. Other considerations being equal, the worker can share more freely with a fellow social worker or with a member of another helping profession. Beyond this, special care must be taken to be guided not only by the collateral's personality and attitude toward the client, but also by knowledge of the role played in the client's life; it is necessary to appraise the ways in which the collateral's self-interest, responsibilities, or limitations are involved. Occasionally, despite the greatest care, misuse is made of information. In one situation, which illustrates the need for extreme caution, a clinical social worker had seen a husband and wife for marital counseling. Several weeks after they terminated the counseling, the couple separated. Family court became involved and requested information about the agency contact. The worker obtained a written release from the wife and sent a summary of the treatment of the couple to the court, including some personal information about the husband, who later sued the agency and the worker for revealing confidential matters without consent. Sometimes, too, a client may think information has been misused even when it has not. The worker should be alert to the possibility of this in interviews with the client and should bring into the open any feelings on the client's part that the contact has misfired. As noted earlier, one way of minimizing suspicion is for clients to be participants in conferences with collaterals when practical.

Mediator

The roles of mediator and aggressive intervenor share some common features because they are two aspects of *case advocacy.* Both go further than interpretation. Both assume some strain or conflict in the relationship between client and collateral. They differ, however, in method. *Mediation* relies on the force of greater understanding of clients, and of their needs and rights, by the collateral. *Aggressive intervention,* to be described next, calls for the use of some type of force.[11]

Mediation involves both direct and indirect casework. In this type of work with the collateral, all that has been said about the role of interpreter holds for that of mediator, some of it with even greater vigor. Since this role usually applies when there has been tension between a client and another individual or representative of an institution, there is often anger or at best irritation or annoyance. When an organization or agency of some sort is involved, there is usually defensiveness about a decision already made or an action already taken. The possibility of client distortion—or at least of misunderstanding or misinterpretation—is high. The worker *must be ready to listen to the other side and be able to withhold judgment.* One must try to understand the collateral's point of view and sometimes must modify one's own. *Mediation is a two-way street.* When worker and client discuss an upcoming meeting with a collateral (whether the client is going to attend or not), it is important for both to recognize that to achieve results, it will be necessary to elicit from the collateral his or her opinions about what will be needed to improve the interpersonal situation. The interview with the collateral may lead the worker to expand a view of the client; it may become apparent that the client will have to change behavior or viewpoint if tension is to be reduced. It is the worker's responsibility to share such impressions with the client who, if in agreement and motivated, may then decide to try to alter his or her approach. Once worker and client are both convinced that their position is sufficiently persuasive, the right moment and the right words then need to be found to induce the collateral to reconsider actions or attitudes toward the client.

In terms of communication procedures, mediation requires ventilation and person–situation reflection, with timing and tact of utmost importance.

A 16-year-old boy, David, had been periodically suspended from school for cutting classes and for displaying a surly— at times menacing—attitude toward teachers. David disliked the academic program and wanted to be transferred to a special vocational program to train in automobile mechanics, for which he had a special gift. The school authorities, however, who were clearly angry, were unwilling to refer him to this program, which would cost the school district money; from David's behavior, they concluded that he would be a poor risk. After learning this, the worker was able to help David recognize that his attitude contributed to the school's unyielding position. Subsequently, a conference at the school was arranged by the worker. David participated and, with the worker's support, was able to speak for himself; he explained his unhappiness with his present program and apologized for his behavior. The worker's expression of confidence in David's seriousness about vocational training was instrumental in tipping the balance, and the transfer was approved. An intense period of direct work, in which the worker affirmed David's strengths and helped him reflect on his entire situation, preceded mediation with the school. Had the worker intervened prematurely, before David was willing to share responsibility for the problem, the effort would have backfired. In terms of communication procedures this success-

ful mediation, required *ventilation* and *person–situation reflection* with proper timing and tact.

The growth in destructive activities, especially by youths in their teens and young adults, has greatly complicated intervention on the client's behalf. On the one hand, fear and hysteria lead to unjustified punitiveness, to hasty accusations, and often to racial stereotyping. Terrible damage is done every day to young African American men, for example, who are frequently viewed with fear and hate even when they have done *absolutely nothing* to deserve these reactions. (Groups of males, especially young men of color simply walking down the street, often are viewed with apprehension and suspicion.) Whether on a case-by-case basis, as a spokesperson for an agency or professional organization, or as a member of a community, it is the social worker's responsibility to do all that is humanly possible to counter racist responses. As much as we wish it were not so, some police, school, and welfare personnel, among others in positions of power, jump to conclusions on the basis of race and ethnic background alone. In these instances, advocacy can play an important role. Too often our clients are treated with condescension, disdain, or abuse by people who should be trustworthy and protective of people's rights. Simply bemoaning bigotry is not enough; often it is possible to find effective ways of exploring and confronting the situation, as we do in all other forms of mediation.

On the other hand, some forms of youth aggression are truly dangerous, and individuals have a right to protect themselves and others in legitimate ways. Too many young people from all walks of life and ethnic or racial groups seem to have little hope or sense of purpose, perhaps for very different reasons. Some young people from middle- or upper-class families, who seem to lack direction and maturity, engage in unhealthy and/or destructive behaviors. "Today," Louis Gates reports, "one-third of all black Americans working full time live beneath the poverty line. Hope for a future has practically disappeared from the inner city."[12] Lack of opportunity and despair, racism and bigotry in all of its forms—including its often violent forms—have played a large part in the recent increase in crime and violence perpetrated by rageful youth.[13] In most respects, these social problems and disturbing trends are beyond the social worker's influence. For individual clients or members of client families who have been accused of crime, the caseworker cannot take on the lawyer's role, representing them in court whether they are guilty or innocent. The social worker is just as deeply concerned about clients' rights and well-being as the lawyer, but the worker's orientation and responsibility are to the larger community as well as to clients. Therefore, decisions about intervention call for careful evaluations of long-run as well as short-run effects. In the role of mediator, the worker's *over-* or *underprotection* of the client can be unrealistic and lead to further aggressive activities that help neither the client, the family, nor others. Direct work with some young clients may be invaluable in helping them recognize patterns that are destructive to themselves and have negative effects on others, as in the case of David, cited above.

Aggressive Intervenor

There are times when it is clear that a client's rights are being ignored, denied, or abrogated, and interpretation or mediation have not been successful in correcting the injustice. Here the worker must turn to the second type of advocacy: *aggressive intervention*. The worker may argue forcefully for the client, often going beyond the collat-

eral to a supervisor or a higher executive of an organization. When the worker is employed by an agency, the total system becomes pertinent to decisions about what means to use. Often, a higher level within the worker's own agency can bring pressure more effectively than the worker can alone, possibly even succeeding through mediation so that aggressive intervention is not needed. Community resources, individual or organizational, may be induced to bring further pressure to bear in the client's favor.

> The staff of a family service agency had obtained repeated evidence from clients and others that a large company in the city was refusing (sometimes blatantly, sometimes more covertly) to hire qualified black workers except on the maintenance staff. For the agency members who wanted to protest, the situation was complicated by the fact that one of the lay board members held a management position with the company. The board member was protective toward the firm and was also concerned, as were other board members, that the agency would alienate the company if it took a direct stand against it. Staff members, determined to take some kind of action, met with the board and persuasively argued that the local Commission on Human Rights should become involved. This public agency could assist several clients who had been discriminated against without revealing the agency's interest in the situation. A lengthy investigation by the commission resulted in an order to the company, backed up with the threat of penalty, to cease discriminating; as a result, the personnel practices of the firm were changed.

When the worker moves from persuasion to a form of pressure or exercise of power, new considerations come into focus. The use of power inevitably arouses hostility and resistance. If the worker uses it and loses, the client may be worse off than before because of the counterhostility that has been generated.

In the above example, had the agency taken direct aggressive action against the company that was discriminating against blacks, not only would it have lost an important board member, but of greater significance, the action also might have antagonized this powerful firm enough for it to attempt to use its influence with the United Way—the funding body on which the agency heavily depended—to retaliate against the agency. If the agency's finances had been jeopardized, the loss to many clients benefiting from its services would have been immeasurable. Referring the matter to a public agency with greater expertise and the authority to investigate eventually brought about the changes without causing any repercussions to the clients and without exposing the agency to attack.

Groups of lawyers and various activist organizations particularly interested in protecting the rights of people who are in poverty or subject to discrimination—including racial and ethnic groups, women, gays and lesbians, and people with handicaps, among others—have provided new and valuable resources upon which to call for case advocacy that go beyond what the social worker can do alone. Familiarity with such groups and, if possible, knowledge of particular individuals within them often prove to be very valuable to clients.

Aggressive intervention is a form of advocacy to be used only after other methods, including mediation, have failed; when one is quite sure that injustice is being done; and when the aggressive effort has some possibility of succeeding. When there is danger of backfire, the worker and clients

should discuss this, with clients determining whether they want to take the risk. Although the worker may help to weigh the pros and cons, the ultimate decision belongs to the client. If one is not extremely careful about this, actions that the worker takes and the results of these may negatively affect clients and relationships with them.

Professional goals and ethics are also involved in the use of aggressive intervention. The worker is still operating as a caseworker, and means that conflict with professional ethics are not justified by the ends they serve.[14] A caseworker should not, for example, wittingly misrepresent the facts, lie under oath, or blindly advocate violent conduct against adversaries of the client, no matter how unjust their actions might be.

Case Advocacy and Social Advocacy

A distinction is commonly made between *case advocacy* and the more general *social action* or *social advocacy*. The former refers to the worker's efforts to join with the client to remedy an immediate concrete injustice to which the individual client is being subjected. The latter refers to a more general attempt to participate in efforts or movements to change policies or practices that harm a whole group of clients or others in the community. In practice, the line between case advocacy and social action advocacy is sometimes blurred, as in the case of company discrimination described earlier.

Often, when clients gain self-confidence and become more self-directing, when they have some freedom from their own pressing concerns and greater knowledge of the effect of community conditions, they join groups in the general community through which they can participate in social action. If clients show interest in this, one frequently can assist them in a search for appropriate social action groups, just as one helps clients locate other resources. Of course, it is unethical to use the casework treatment relationship to *enlist* clients in causes or organizations, no matter how good these may be. To do so is similar in principle to steering clients into one's own religion or political party; it carries all the same hazards of any behavior that results in clients feeling impelled to please their workers upon whom they are dependent for social and psychological help.

With so much injustice and widespread indifference to the needs and rights of others prevailing today, the call for social action and advocacy is great. Poverty, inadequate public income assistance (often made worse by welfare "reform"), discrimination, poor housing, homelessness, unemployment, and inferior educational facilities have denied millions of citizens access to opportunities and comforts that many others take for granted. As an editorial in the *New York Times* states: "The yawning gaps between rich and poor and between blacks and whites are not going away soon."[15] For many of the elderly, sick, and disabled there are often no individual solutions. There must be massive reform even to touch upon the inhuman day-in-day-out realities of people trapped or neglected because of societal deficiencies.

Even though casework on its own cannot eradicate massive societal problems, caseworkers do have avenues through which to bring about significant social changes. Often, the worker's agency is already engaged in social action within its area of competence and effectiveness. It may be part of one's regular work to participate in this action. *The movement from case to cause is essential.* By collecting information about injustices and needed resources in individual cases, the worker can supply the data that can initiate social advocacy, giving evidence through which change can be accomplished.[16] Agencies carry a definite responsibility for providing ways in which such information can be used. If the agency is not active in areas in which it could be effective, the worker, as a staff member, can try to influence it to develop a social action program.

In 1951, Bertha Reynolds, a psychiatric social worker of great integrity, charged that social work:

> has tried to deny incurable poverty, illness, and social maladjustment, first by assuming that the solution lies in the treatment of unconscious conflict within the person, instead of in society itself. Then, in self-protection, social agencies have moved away from contact with cases in which poverty, illness, and friction were too obviously beyond the reach of a change in the clients' feelings.[17]

While there have been changes since 1951, when inordinate emphasis on psychoanalytic and other personality theories held sway in some social work circles, there are still indications that social work is not consistently serving those whom society has so cruelly shortchanged. Many social agencies are serving predominantly white, middle-class clients and are not reaching those who have too often been forgotten or ignored. To make matters worse, funding of social services and programs for the most deprived and oppressed are often frivolously cut back. Some believe that social work has abandoned its mission of social activism in favor of delivering psychotherapeutic services.[18]

The social worker also has a personal political life, professional associations, and opportunities for common action with groups of colleagues. Socially minded lawyers and social workers have also found that they have similar objectives and work collaboratively with great effectiveness. Some social workers particularly interested in championing human rights have sought additional

training in law. For psychosocial caseworkers, we see participation in social advocacy
of one type or another as a clear professional responsibility.

TYPES OF RESOURCES

Having described types of communication
and types of roles employed in environmental work, we turn now to variations in the
type of resource or collateral that the
worker is enlisting or attempting to enlist
on behalf of clients. At one time, it was possible to classify resources in clearer detail
than we can now; in recent years, the nature of many human service organizations
has changed. For example, many social
agencies—public and private—are now administered by men and women with backgrounds in business, not by trained social
workers as they often were in the past.
Mental health services are often staffed by
several disciplines, not primarily by social
workers; to qualify for third-party payments, some former family service agencies
have converted to or merged with clinics
with medical directors. Funding arrangements are constantly changing and have become far more complicated than they used
to be. Government involvement in agency
policies and fiscal matters is far more complex and pervasive. At the same time, the
number of independent or private practitioners of social work, particularly clinical
social work, has increased, sometimes in reaction to bureaucratization in addition to
the need for supplemental income. For
these reasons, we have altered our classification to better suit the changing circumstances. In Chapter 4, the following types of
resources were identified:

1. The organization where the worker helping the client is employed.
2. The organization where the social
   worker is *not* employed.

3. Independent social work practitioners.
4. Individuals who are
   a. In an instrumental (business or "task-
      oriented") relationship with the client.
   b. In an expressive ("feeling-oriented")
      relationship with the client.
   c. Independent professionals or others
      who are ethically committed to the
      client's well-being or goals.

Organization Where Worker Is Employed

This large category includes many kinds of
organizations, public and private, including
those still directed and/or staffed primarily
by social workers. It also includes organizations with caseworkers on staff or with a department that employs them but that are
primarily controlled by another profession:
for example, a hospital, school, or court.
Governmental agencies rendering various
social services (child welfare and family services, preventive and protective services for
children, protective and custodial services
for adults who because of age or disability
are unable to handle their affairs) fall under
this heading, as do agencies under the auspices of state departments of mental health.
(There have been significant changes in the
administration of public income assistance
programs; financial aid usually now is dispensed on a standardized, impersonal basis
with little direct connection with casework
services that were available in the past in
the best welfare agencies.) Because of
changes in funding and reduction of services
in recent years, non-MSW caseworkers,
paraprofessionals, or case aides have taken
over some positions previously held by social
workers with graduate degrees, although
sometimes there still may be trained workers in supervisory positions.

As already indicated in the section on
worker roles, in many resources, especially

those non–social work organizations that employ one or more social workers, the client often sees the worker not only as a caseworker but also as a representative of the hospital, school, or court. Client reactions to these services, including their weaknesses, must be handled. The probation worker must try to find the common meeting ground between the function of the court and the aspirations of the client. The worker must be responsive to the client's often angry feelings about the policies of the agency that the worker represents. (If the worker disagrees with important policies, some alternatives are possible, as described below under the heading, "Handling Harmful Policies.")

There are instances, especially when working with involuntary or mandated clients, when resentment of the organization is transferred to the worker; reactions can range from unyielding resistance to physical violence against workers. Yet in our experience and that of others, many involuntary clients *can* accept and do utilize casework services, especially when the worker takes seriously the clients' concerns and thoughts about what they need and conveys genuine respect for their wishes and goals.[19] It is often necessary for the worker to *mediate* between the client's needs and the agency or organization function; or a worker may locate resources that will be relevant to the help the clients want. (In the case of Mrs. Stone, described in Chapter 3, the mother accused of beating one of her children accepted a referral from the protective services worker to a family service division where help for many urgent needs was provided. See also the Carter case, described in Chapter 20.)

In addition to offering practical or therapeutic services to the client, the worker can facilitate the way in which the organization is being used as a resource by the client. The worker often *interprets* the agency services and philosophy to the client and de-velops methods for inviting client feedback. Caseworkers in hospitals, for example, may arrange group meetings of patients or of patients' relatives not only to screen for those who need special services or to give them an opportunity to share their feelings about illness, but also to express their reactions to the hospital services. Similarly, parent groups in day care centers are often organized to encourage parents to raise questions, to offer suggestions, and to get clarification about the operations of the program their children are attending.

The caseworker also helps other professions to understand the needs of the client better. Because the worker sees the client from a different vantage point and within a different professional frame of reference from the doctor, teacher, or judge, for example, he or she can contribute greatly to the quality of the other service. At times the worker may need to act as *mediator* between the service and the client, sometimes even as an *active advocate* on the client's behalf. Doctors may be reluctant to give adequate attention to certain patients because of their critical or hostile attitudes or their failure to understand or follow medical advice. The social worker can try to remedy this situation. (In the case of Mrs. Barry, Chapter 20, the caseworker tactfully but persistently advocated for her client's right to treatment beyond medication while in the hospital in conversations with the psychiatrist.) Or a teacher may take a dislike to a child. By acquainting her with the facts of the child's background, the social worker in the school system may be able to modify the teacher's reactions. Here again, thorough understanding of the organization as a system and of the ways of working, patterns of thought, and the values and mission of the other profession is essential if either *mediation* or active *advocacy* and *collaboration* are to be successful.

Fostering Organizational Change A worker who is employed by an agency, even a large one, is often able to promote improvements in service, both large and small. The direct worker's familiarity with the agency's orientation and the needs of clients and the community put him or her in an excellent position to assess what changes might be possible and beneficial. Workers or others outside the agency are not usually as knowledgeable as those who are involved in day-to-day functions of the organization; even some administrators or middle-management employees may not have as good a grasp of the need for innovation as the direct service worker does. While organizations are different, and administrative flexibility varies, efforts toward change often trigger organizational resistance for innumerable reasons: inertia, fears of all sorts, financial concerns, and others. Nevertheless, as Frey points out in his excellent and recommended article directed primarily to on-line workers, "Some organizations may not only encourage practitioners to identify organizational issues and problems that need to be changed, but may also have formal policies and procedures to initiate change. In such environments, the presumed resistance to change may be tempered by the philosophy and policies that promote change."[20] Agencies can and sometimes do provide effective channels for passing on the worker's observations and ideas so that policy can be a fluid instrument with room for experimentation rather than a set of relatively fixed administrative rulings. Experimentation with new ideas is essential if service is to be pertinent and effective. As Frey also explains, a specific *proposal* for change (not just a general or abstract *goal* for change) requires one systematically to assess factors related to recommendations for improvement.[21]

In every instance, social workers must have thorough knowledge of the systems within which they are working, its lines of responsibility, and its power structure. They must understand the "culture" of the other professions with which they are dealing, the attitudes of administrators, boards, and other social work colleagues. They must have infinite tact, a high degree of confidence in themselves and their profession, and the courage and zest to pursue aims despite exasperating discouragements.[22] The Stone case in Chapter 3 and the Barry case in Chapter 20 illustrate some complexities of interdisciplinary interaction.

Trained caseworkers, especially those employed by public agencies or other large, bureaucratic organizations, are often in the difficult position of being the representative of an agency but disagreeing with many of its policies. This may be particularly so when there are few other social workers on staff. Many hospital and school social work departments have been drastically cut back or are staffed mostly by untrained workers; clinical workers hired by prisons, courts, and police departments often have few social work colleagues. Even so, workers can influence procedures, program, or even policy. They have a responsibility to do everything possible to improve services and to use the available resources skillfully. Even in large organizations, or in facilities with few social workers, there is sometimes leeway in administrative policy and an opportunity for constructive change in response to pressure at the caseworker or supervisory level.

Handling Harmful Policies In agencies where undesirable policies that are destructive to individuals or families prevail, the workers face many complications in bringing the agency's resources to their clients. It is difficult enough when a necessary policy creates hardship. (This can happen, for example, when certain services target low-income clients, and those not eligible resent being excluded.) Then the path is fairly clear: Allow or even encourage the anger to be expressed, genuinely appreciate the hardship for the client, sometimes explain why the policy is necessary, and help the client adapt to it, perhaps by finding suitable alternatives. There is no basic conflict about carrying out the policy. But when the policy is either unfair, unwise, unnecessary, or damaging to the people who are supposedly being served, it is even more important for the client to express anger and to know that the worker recognizes the hardship and is genuinely distressed by it.

Three alternative courses are open to workers. One course is to express to clients personal disagreement with the policy and perhaps to tell of efforts that are being made to change it. At the same time workers may help clients to decide whether other options are available and, if they are not and if no legitimate way around it can be found, help them decide whether they want to comply with the agency policy and/or find ways to register their protests effectively. In some cases, the worker may be able to locate alternative resources that meet the clients' needs.

The second course is that taken by workers who stand strongly for better policy and stay within the system to work for it. Sometimes, as we said, they are able to improve policy and its administration. When supervisory or administrative staff can be enlisted to support flexible application of policy, the impact on the client can be modified considerably. (See the case of Mrs. Stone in Chapter 3 for an example of this kind of creative practice.) Too often, however, there is considerable resistance to changing administrative policies, even when these are harmful. Workers can and should bring up-

to-date research to the attention of reluctant administrators when advocating for change. By documenting in writing incidents of unfairness or abuse to clients, protests may carry more weight and *specific* proposals for improvement can be formulated. Workers can also advise clients of their rights and of possible actions that can be taken to register their complaints. Social work employees (sometimes joined by client activist groups) have used court action to challenge the legality of extreme policies.

The third course is for workers to decide they can no longer carry out policy with which they are in basic disagreement and leave the agency. This action is justified in some situations, but it is not a truly satisfactory solution. If all workers who disagree with bad policies leave the agency, no one is left to fight for better ones. Workers who leave are all too easily replaced by workers without any social work education, who may not find it so difficult to carry out destructive agency policies. This is not to say that every worker needs to feel duty-bound to work forever under impossible conditions. Eventually, one may feel that one has fought long enough and that someone else should take up the cudgels. (The subject of worker burnout is discussed in the next chapter.) Workers in public agencies who choose either the second or third course can also work through channels external to the agency to bring about better legislation that can improve the whole system.

Many people from all walks of life want and can use casework services. Individuals and families living below the poverty line, frequently dependent on public agencies for income assistance and for some services, often need the kind of help casework can give to deal with the many pressures in their lives.[23] They have a right to first-rate services from professionally trained workers as much as do those who can pay for them. Many of these services have to be operated under public auspices or, at least in part, publicly financed. In many instances, social work services are not eligible for reimbursement by private or public third-party payments. As welfare policies change and keep changing, we believe it is incumbent on us all, wherever we work, to make sure that quality services are available, readily accessible, sensitive, and relevant to client needs and circumstances.

Examples of Organizational Change Initiated by Workers In addition to being well informed about research relevant to delivery of services, clinical social workers must also use their own observations of the effects of current services on clients. Only then will they be in a position to initiate or contribute to procedural, program, or policy change in their organizations.

In one fairly small hospital, the director of social service learned from an audit of drug overdose patients that a number of them had not been referred for casework attention. She consulted with the nurses and discussed the importance of automatic notification of the social work department of all such cases at the time of admission. The nurses had not understood that casework services might be helpful to the families involved and had not made the referrals because frequently the patients were unconscious at the time of arrival! Similarly, this same director persuaded the hospital administration to institute changes in the admitting procedures so that certain information could be elicited (such as whether a patient lives alone or has small children); by reviewing the screening data on every patient (many of whom were elderly or single mothers), the social work department could then reach out to those who might need casework services. Also, after

this director had been employed at the hospital for less than one year (as the only social worker on staff), she designed a very detailed and persuasive proposal for adding three additional social workers to keep up with patients' needs; she presented her material and arguments to the lay board of the hospital and, after considerable resistance and debate among board members, permission to hire two workers was finally approved.

Systems theory observations concerning the importance of the *point of maximum reverberation** are fully confirmed in the role played by key persons in medical, nursing, and other hierarchies. As we have said, it is extremely important that pressure for change be exercised only after a sound assessment has been made.

A clinical social worker newly employed at an adult residential care facility for the frail elderly quickly noted that between meals most of the 65 residents either retreated to their small rooms or sat and slept or stared in the lounge area. Few participated in bingo games and other available activities. Social interaction was at a minimum. Deciding to explore residents' feelings about their leisure time, the worker developed a simple questionnaire, which she helped each person to fill out, inquiring about hobbies, recreations they used to enjoy, and activities they would like to have available at the residence. She wanted to find out whether their inactivity was a real choice or the result of a lack of appealing opportunities. In casual conversation, the residents

---

* According to systems theory, change applied to part of a system will reverberate in a differential way throughout the system. A point of maximum reverberation is the point at which change will have the greatest effect on the total system.

made such comments as: "What's an old woman to do? Sit. What else is there?" But when they were questioned more closely, it turned out that many of the residents were eager for cultural programs. As luck would have it, the social worker was a former English teacher and began a pilot poetry discussion group, which, by the fourth meeting, had become so popular that it had to be divided into two groups. The residents were primarily Jewish, African American, and Irish in background. This creative worker was able to introduce works written by poets from these cultures, making the experience even richer; residents enjoyed writings representing their own culture and those of their fellow residents. From this pilot project, an expanded recreational program developed. A multigenerational glee club, which brought in members of high school choruses and church choirs, was organized. With assistance from a volunteer journalist who lived near the facility, a newspaper by and for the residents was published. Residents were regularly canvassed for ideas about new projects.

In this example, even though there had been few innovations in programming for years before the worker's arrival, there was no resistance from the non–social work administration to the new approach to recreation. It was generally believed that the increased intellectual stimulation, socialization, and greater contact with the community at large would significantly promote the mental and emotional health of the elderly participants. A key to the success of the worker's approach was the residents' participation in planning the new programs. Persuasive evidence shows that when the elderly feel they have some control over their living situations, they become significantly less depressed and their lives are prolonged.[24]

Organizations Where Worker Is *Not* Employed

This large group of facilities in which the worker helping the client is *not* a staff member includes:

1. Social Agencies That Employ and Are Administered by Social Workers

This subcategory includes not only many family service agencies but also community centers or neighborhood houses where there are opportunities for group experiences, cultural activities, vocational training, tutoring, recreation, and social action through groups. Organizations such as homemaker services, day care centers, and employment counseling and vocational training services also fall into this category when they are administered by social workers.

When one is seeking cooperation from another agency on behalf of a client or clients, often collaboration is easier to achieve with fellow social workers than with other personnel. Common objectives, a common professional language and body of knowledge, and a common value system facilitate the effort. But no profession is completely homogeneous. Within a range, values, objectives, language, experience, and even knowledge differ. Idiosyncrasies and different points of view exist within as well as among professions. One must be sensitive to the reaction of the worker within the other agency; careful use of communication skills may be required. Social workers are people too: They can feel threatened, competitive, and under pressure at work or about personal affairs. Furthermore, social work agencies have their own agendas, depending on their particular mandate or mission; policies may constrain the worker employed elsewhere, making it difficult to be responsive to a request on behalf of clients. The more one has established friendly working relationships with social workers in community settings, the more likely efforts to assist clients will be given maximum consideration. When seeking help from another resource, there is great value in setting up person-to-person conferences between workers with clients attending, too, when indicated.

2. Organizations Not Administered by Social Workers That Have a Social Work Department or One or More Social Workers on Staff

Many schools and hospitals fit into this category. Falling under this heading also are group living or halfway houses, under many different names and auspices, that offer protection to patients released from psychiatric hospitals and to recovering substance abusers, among others. Mentally disabled adults often learn to function in the community when living in supportive group settings. In many areas, recreational and educational programs, including day care, are offered to the above groups and to elderly, ill, or physically handicapped people living in the general community. Some of these facilities are part of large state or federal departments and are often subject to the many restraints and regulations associated with large bureaucracies. Programs for the homeless, although still not pervasive or powerful enough to ameliorate the enormous problems of people living on the streets or in temporary shelters, may fall under this heading. Usually these resources are not administered by social workers, although some (too few) may employ them.

3. Organizations that Do Not Employ Social Workers

This type of organization includes legal aid or civil rights organizations, public housing agencies, visiting nurses associations, tutoring and vocational or employment services, as well as schools, hospitals, and group and nursing homes that do not have social workers on staff.

The greater the worker's knowledge about the other organization, the profession, or the personnel with which one is dealing, the better. Much exploratory work may need to be done before the proper help can be secured. Not only will clients' time be wasted if they are sent to inappropriate places, but also some clients may be discouraged from trying further. It may also reduce confidence in the worker's interest and competence, and it may have a negative effect on simultaneous direct work with clients. Both phone work and footwork may be necessary to prepare the way for a client's first contact. Ingenuity in locating appropriate resources and skill in interesting other organizations in a client are important in milieu work, whether one is seeking a social work resource or one that has no connection with social work.

A busy child welfare worker referred a woman client, with a marginal income, to the legal aid society to obtain advice about a custody suit that had been initiated by the client's divorced husband. After waiting weeks for an appointment, the client was then informed that she was not eligible on the basis of her income, as modest as it was. The worker then sought assistance from the local bar association, which advised that there was a panel of low-fee attorneys who could assist the woman. Precious time and frustration could have been saved had the worker explored the available resources before making the referral.

Independent Social Work Practitioners

Over recent years, as discussed in Chapter 1, the private practice of social work has achieved recognition and professional sanction as well as some criticism. In our view, independent practitioners have become an extremely important resource. Many have sliding fee scales and are committed to accommodating low-income clients, often devoting a percentage of private practice hours to individuals and clients who require low fees or who cannot afford any fee.[25] As we said, many private practitioners have developed specializations of one sort or another, work with couples and families, with children or adolescents, with the elderly and their families, or with substance abusers, among many others. Groups of all sorts are run by independent clinical workers. Collaborative relationships with experienced and skilled independent workers can be very valuable to agencies seeking referrals.

Sometimes organizations hire social workers as consultants to share their expertise on human social behavior with school personnel, lawyers, medical professionals, public housing officials, and the like. Some school systems, for example, hire experienced social workers in private practice to run seminars for teachers on such matters as family dynamics, cultural influences on personality and family life, and group dynamics. When social work positions or departments in various organizations or agencies have been downsized or eliminated, independent social workers are sometimes employed—often on a time-limited or per diem basis—as advisors or as leaders of in-service training or of conferences in areas in which they have expertise. These social work practitioners provide unique services.

Professional social work organizations issue registries of licensed or certified clinical social workers, usually including information on educational background, experience, and specializations. These directories are invaluable in efforts to locate private practitioners who can offer particular services the agencies or clients are seeking.

Individual Collaterals

The section on types of communication included illustrations of contacts with *individuals* on the client's behalf. The fourth and last type of resource involves three categories of individuals: those in an *instrumental* (business or *"task-oriented"*) relationship with the client; those *independent professionals and others* who have a commitment to the client's well-being and goals; and those in an *expressive* (or *"feeling-oriented"*) relationship with the person the worker is trying to help.

Instrumental Collaterals   This category includes employers, landlords, and others. With these task-oriented individuals, workers may be seeking such opportunities as jobs or better housing for the client; they may be intervening on behalf of clients in misunderstandings or clashes that create hardship. In each of these cases, the worker deals not with another profession or some type of service organization but with people who have their own interests at stake. They tend to be either indifferent to the client or hostile. Before meeting with such collaterals, the worker must be sure of facts or else be aware of the possibility that all the facts are not yet known. Overidentification with the client is a frequent cause of failure in this type of contact. As we have said, there is no benefit in persuading an employer to make special plans to hire a client by giving a false picture of the client's abilities or readiness for work. It will only end in embitterment on both sides. When liabilities are acknowledged and sympathetically interpreted, the collateral can then make a decision in which the risks are weighed and the realities understood. If the situation is such that the worker cannot be frank about liabilities, it is better for the client to make his own job contacts.

Similarly, when trying to modify attitudes or actions of an instrumental collateral, the worker has to listen with an open mind to the collateral's side of the story. For example, clients may complain that the landlord has not painted their apartment. On speaking with the landlord, however, the worker may be told that the tenants have abused the property and the landlord feels justified in refusing to paint. The worker must then judge whether to press for greater understanding of the clients' view by the collateral or perhaps to drain off some of the irritation followed by work with the clients to arrive at some mutual amelioration of the total situation.

Independent Professionals and Others Concerned about Clients' Welfare

These individuals have a commitment to the client's well-being and objectives even though they may charge fees for their services. Civil rights lawyers, religious leaders, tutors, teachers, educational consultants who diagnose learning disabilities, nurses, psychologists who specialize in various types of testing, and psychopharmacologists are among the ranks of professionals who generally have an ethical obligation to work with clients on their behalf, in contrast to instrumental collaterals. Service to clients is greatly enhanced if one is familiar with professionals in the community. It can be very helpful to meet with some; in this way, when clients need particular services, the worker can make informed decisions about referrals. Based on personal impressions and firsthand information, the worker assesses the "fit" between the client and the professional; the success rate of this kind of careful work is far higher than when one makes "blind" referrals that have a great possibility of being inadequate or inapproprate.

Expressive Collaterals This group includes those people who have a feeling-oriented relationship with the client. With these individuals the situation is quite different than with instrumental collaterals; an expressive relationship implies a personal, sometimes emotional investment in the client's welfare. This is true even when anger exists and the worker is intervening in the hope of improving interactions. In such relationships, anger is often a sign of caring or involvement. With caring, a new component enters. Relatives and even friends may believe that they know the client better than the worker does, and this may be true. Those collaterals who feel they have a stake in the situation may want the worker to change the client; an angry adult daughter, for example, may want the worker to "make" her elderly mother—the worker's client—move to a residential care facility. Rather than responding positively to the worker's efforts to mollify her relationship with her mother—so that a plan that might suit both could be formulated—this daughter may oppose all the worker's efforts. As we shall discuss further in the chapters on family therapy, family members can be threatened by any change in the balance of the family system. They may oppose change even though theoretically such change would benefit them as well as the client. In such situations it is important for the worker to maintain an attitude of *neutrality;* that is, he or she does not take sides (except under certain urgent conditions, such as when an elderly person is at immediate risk of danger), but rather—through *interpretation* and *mediation*—continues to try to help the client and collateral search for a solution that can be acceptable to both.

In work with expressive collaterals, we reach ground that is very close to work with the client. Sometimes it turns into direct work in which the collateral becomes a second client, either through individual interviews or through a shift to family or joint interviewing. Short of this, however, relatives and friends can become powerful allies in treatment. Sometimes it is sufficient to let them know they are needed. At other times, work must be done to help them understand how they can be of assistance. Simply helping relatives and friends to see their importance to the client and the ways in which they can help often motivates them to offer opportunities and psychological support. They may need assurance that a little involvement in the client's troubles will not result in their being left with greater responsibility than they want to assume. This is particularly true when the client is elderly or disabled or when help with child care is required. Needless to say, the question of whether to intervene directly with friends or relatives or to help the client to approach them is a delicate one, calling for careful assessment and discussion with the client.

Family Sessions on Behalf of Individual Treatment As the family therapy chapters describe, often the problems of an individual are the impetus for exploratory family therapy. When a family is in treatment, each family member is in some way committed to the therapy. But when an individual is in treatment and family members are invited for sessions, they are viewed as part of the individual's environment and related to as expressive collaterals. Besides providing the client with psychological support or practical help, the presence of family members in sessions can provide a powerful tool for freeing the client of internalized distortions that are interfering with functioning.

A 22-year-old secretary, Sally, living with her divorced mother, sought treatment at a mental health clinic during a crisis in her relationship with her fiancé with whom she was constantly arguing. She described her feelings toward her mother as "indifferent" or "mildly friendly." She was estranged from her father and had been angry with him since his separation from the family 10 years earlier. A few weeks after she began treatment, her mother announced that she planned to remarry; after hearing this Sally became seriously depressed and had suicidal thoughts. Although reluctant at first, she accepted the caseworker's suggestion to bring her mother to a session with her. In three meetings, mother and daughter shared some old pains and achieved an intimacy and openness they had not enjoyed in many years. Sally recognized that her mother truly cared about her and she allowed herself to care in return. Later on in treatment, a joint meeting was arranged with Sally and her father, who made a special trip from another state to attend the session. Her father was able to clarify his reasons for leaving the family and reassured Sally that these had nothing to do with her. To Sally's amazement, he said he was very much interested in rebuilding his relationship with her. Sally's early parental introjects (her internal images of an indifferent mother and a remote, punishing father) clearly had distorted her view of the current situation. She was able to share feelings and develop relationships with her parents that she never believed would be possible. Furthermore, she realized, she had been displacing and projecting some of these distortions onto her fiancé, and these had contributed heavily to the hostilities that had developed between them. During the latter part of the therapy, Sally's fiancé joined Sally for premarital counseling; in joint sessions, some of these issues became better understood by both.

Had the caseworker confined the treatment to individual meetings, Sally's myth about the hopelessness of deepening her relationships with her parents would have taken longer for her and the worker to recognize—whether through talk about her parents or through transference with the worker. Since her distortions had a direct bearing on her difficulties with her fiancé, this relationship (which originally motivated her to seek help) might have deteriorated to the point that it could not have been saved, had she not resolved the long-standing problems with her mother and father. And, of course, the direct participation of her fiancé further facilitated the treatment.

Network Therapy[26]   Sometimes the worker and client invite other people to help to accomplish psychological objectives identical with those sought in direct treatment. Relatives, friends, teachers, and doctors are sometimes in a far better position than social workers to give sustaining help to a client. Often they do so spontaneously, but the caseworker can also motivate them to take this type of responsibility. Particularly with extremely anxious or depressed people, it is sometimes most helpful to enlist the interest of friends or relatives who like the client and have a warm nature, a good deal of common sense, and a capacity for equanimity. It is surprising how often such people can be found if the worker is alert to the possibility and not so tied to a desk that he or she never makes contact with them.

Network therapy involves mobilizing feeling-oriented collaterals to provide a stable support group to a client in crisis and to prevent future difficulties.

Mrs. Antonini, a recently widowed 58-year-old housewife, whose children were grown and married, sought help at a community mental health clinic for depression. Her symptoms were so severe that it was feared that she could become suicidal and might have to be hospitalized, an idea Mrs. Antonini opposed. The clinical social worker encouraged her to join her in calling a meeting of her children and a neighbor. Several of her in-laws, with whom there had been some friction over decisions Mrs. Antonini had made about her husband's burial, were also invited. In a two-and-a-half-hour session, the worker introduced the problem of her client's depression and isolation and then turned to the assembled group for ideas about what could be done and how this "network" might be able to help. Mrs. Antonini's daughter, who took the most initiative during the meeting, suggested that a schedule could be worked out whereby family members and friends would alternate in being available for telephone or personal visits. Everyone agreed to this plan. Once the details of how each person in the network could be reached were worked out, it was decided that Mrs. Antonini would take the initiative for making the contacts when she needed or wanted them. It should be added that during this meeting the tensions with the in-laws were, in large part, relieved.

Slowly but surely, with the network as a consistent resource of support for Mrs. Antonini, combined with casework sessions and the location of some baby-sitting jobs, this client's depression lifted. Long after treatment ended, her network was available to her and, as it turned out, she was also able to provide support to other members when they faced difficulties in their own lives.

Similarly, in one family therapy case of a teenage boy, an only child in angry rebellion against his elderly parents, the therapist invited one of the boy's peers, a cousin, and a teacher to join a few sessions. The presence of network members was supportive to the entire family and helped to lend perspective to the boy and his parents, whose relationship had become so seriously polarized.

Artificial networks (in contrast to natural ones of relatives, friends, and others whom the client already knows) with mutual aid functions have long been utilized by Alcoholics Anonymous, weight-losers groups, and so on. More recently, various kinds of groups, organized formally and informally, provide support and a feeling of relatedness to single parents, lesbians and gay men, members of a particular ethnic group, and so on. Sometimes when family and friends are not available, artificial networks may have to be created. Social agencies, various organizations, and many independent clinical workers provide groups for widows and others who are bereaved; for parents of mentally and physically disabled or ill children; for people with AIDS and their families; and for children of alcoholics, incest survivors, and relatives of terminally ill patients. Group therapy itself can provide a network of peer supports.

PERSON–ENVIRONMENT GESTALT: ASSESSMENT AND INTERVENTION

Environmental Resources and Deficits

Availability or Lack of Availability
The assessment of the availability or lack of availability of essential (or important quality-of-life) resources is critical to designing interventions for change. We need to know what opportunities, services, relationships, and conditions currently exist in clients' world. Together, clients and worker

can evaluate the presence or absence of basic resources such as:

Food and good nutrition.
Adequate shelter.
Medical care.
Safety and protection.
Comfortable physical surroundings.
Education.
Family/social supports.
Recreation.
Opportunities to feel competent, effective, productive, and meaningfully engaged.
A sense of belonging and purpose (e.g., as part of a community, racial or ethnic group, religious or political organization, etc.).

We must also be concerned with the *quality* of these resources. When any of these are truly substandard, it is obvious to everyone. Quality can be assessed by clients, individuals, and families far more accurately than by a worker alone; clients know or can best try to discover the value or meaning of the opportunities and supports that are or should be available to them.

Arriving at an assessment of the *nature of the connections or transactions* between clients and resources requires careful study. When a child's school problems are presented, for example, it is not enough to help the family evaluate whether educational opportunities are "satisfactory" or "unsatisfactory," based on some general standard. It is important to determine how the particular child experiences school: Does she find it stressful, nurturing, interesting, etc.? In what ways? What is the quality of her peer relationships? Details are important. Are parents involved? What is their assessment? If the worker joins a school conference, what observations can he or she contribute to the assessment of the "fit" between the child and the school? Similarly, do clients find extended family and social relationships conflictual, strained, comforting? Do family members experience these connections similarly or differently? In these situations, too, the "fits" or transactions are assessed.

Readers are urged to study and learn to use the *eco-map* designed by Hartman and Laird.[27] It is an invaluable, visual tool—requiring only paper and pencil—that provides a picture of the connections between families (or individuals) and the various resource systems and relationships with which they transact. As worker and clients work together to complete the eco-map, they "identify conflicts to be mediated, bridges to be built, resources to be sought and mobilized."[28]

Guidelines for Resource Assessment

As worker and clients survey the person–situation gestalt, the following questions assist in the exploration of client–environment strengths and deprivations:

1. With what systems (resources, relationships, services) are clients currently involved?
2. Are these connections voluntary or involuntary? (For example, whether there are court involvements, social agency relationships, or family and social functions or rituals, is client involvement mandatory? Is it experienced as obligatory based on family or cultural expectations? Are these resources that clients chose and/or find valuable?)
3. What needs are being addressed by resources? How adequately are they being met? How responsive are resources to clients' requirements? Are resources flexible or seemingly inflexible?
4. What additional resources are necessary or desirable? Are they immediately available? Or must they be located, created, advocated for?

5. If needed resources are available but clients are not utilizing them, why not? Is there some problem with the quality of the "fit"? Are clients feeling apprehensions or concerns that require exploration?
6. Who should take responsibility to make resources available to clients or to improve the quality of transactions? What is the client's capacity to locate new resources or to initiate changes in their connections to resources and opportunities? Would worker initiatives facilitate access to resources? Or would it be more supportive to clients' ego functioning, especially competence and mastery, for them to make the necessary moves, either on their own or in collaboration with the worker?

Environmental Interventions

Successful milieu treatment depends in part on evaluation—by client and worker—of the *client's capacity in relation to the particular task*. It is essential that *the quality and responsiveness of the environment are simultaneously assessed*. Questions emerge, such as: Is the client intellectually able to deal with the particular resource or system in question? Does he or she have the necessary language ability, or is an interpreter needed? Are perception, judgment, control, and self-directive capacities sufficiently strong that, after talking over the situation, the client will be able to handle a problem, improve a relationship, or locate a needed resource independently? If assistance is required, would involvement of a family member rather than or in addition to the worker be supportive? If a whole family is affected by a situation, are family members supportive of one another, or, as a result of feeling frustrated or demoralized, are they blaming and working against each other? Is the individual or family immediately ready to make agreed upon moves, or are feelings so deeply involved that *ventilation* is needed as a prelude to taking further steps to improve the situation? Is self-confidence so low or anxiety so high that a large measure of *sustaining procedures* is required before client and worker can engage in *reflective discussion* of the situation and ways in which it can be changed?

Note that the personality or family is not being assessed in the abstract here. People may be capable of rational consideration of one type of dilemma, but not of another; self-confident in many situations but unsure in some; overwhelmed by anxiety under some circumstances, cool and collected in others that to someone else might seem just as threatening. These sample questions illustrate that *personality and environmental systems are inevitably intertwined* and that it is difficult to differentiate between the two; the people, the situation, and the nature of their transactions must all be considered.

Further questions arise: Should worker roles—such as locator, interpreter, mediator—be employed? Do workers and clients work together to create or advocate for needed resources? Or will some combination of these address the need for change? Should treatment focus on supporting clients' capacities—competence, confidence—to use or enhance resources and opportunities?

Occasionally, the decision of who should intervene is influenced by *timing.* For the benefit of a child it may be important for a teacher who has a negative attitude toward the youngster to be seen immediately, before the problem gets worse. Though it might seem better for the child's parents to make the contact, it might take weeks before they can feel comfortable enough to do so. In this situation, the parents and caseworker together may decide that it would be advisable for the worker to make the original contact

with the teacher. In another case, a young single mother with two children—who had demonstrated she had problems in judgment and a quick temper—realized that initiating an encounter with a hostile landlord could end in disaster. Because the apartment in which the client lived had many dangerous violations, it was decided that the worker should intervene—by threatening to report the landlord to the city housing department, if necessary—so that badly needed repairs would be made. In contrasting situations, sometimes competent but dependent or mildly depressed clients may look to others to "do for" them when taking steps on their own behalf can enhance autonomy and reduce feelings of helplessness; in these cases, even if the need for action is urgent, workers are usually best advised to encourage the client to intervene and explain why they are doing so.

In Chapter 2, we referred to the balance of forces in the personality system and pointed out that a small amount of change often tips the balance, resulting in considerable relief of distress or improvement of social functioning. For example, in the above illustration of the young woman for whom the caseworker intervened with the landlord, the caring evidenced by initiating the action satisfied some of the client's longings for someone to minister to her needs; the worker further hoped that the support would quell some of the woman's angry feelings. When less pressured by inner (id) drives, it is possible that adaptive (ego) functions can be freed, strengthened, and mobilized. These could help this client to begin to gain better mastery over other aspects of her life. On the other hand, when workers take initiatives that clients are capable of taking, dependency and low self-esteem can be reinforced, and ego functions of competence and mastery may be undermined. Often, with little direct treatment, helping discouraged, self-blaming clients find a new job, a better school, or a social resource can result in reduced self-criticism; when the superego is less punishing, adaptive ego functions are no longer immobilized, and the person is freed to meet life's challenges more successfully and enjoy life more fully. As these examples illustrate, when we make decisions about who takes responsibility for particular interventions, we need to analyze just what part of the ego needs strengthening and how the intrapsychic balance of the individual may be affected.

Again, even within the framework of oppressive conditions and unresponsive systems, some individuals and families *can* make changes to improve their lives rather than wait until their needs are met by hard-won social changes. Creative interventions may be devised. For example, a lonely elderly woman living on meager income assistance benefits may be healthy enough to be employed as a foster grandmother for neglected children. A man who is demoralized because he can no longer find employment in his own craft may be versatile enough to train for another, more employable trade. An intelligent student attending a second-rate high school may develop the confidence to prepare for and take a test to be admitted to a school designed to serve gifted young people. Each situation must be evaluated separately to determine whether a particular client can mobilize the capacity or motivation to circumvent, at least partially, the unhealthy social conditions that led to the difficulties.[29] When workers bring enthusiasm and optimism to difficult tasks, clients are often encouraged to surmount difficulties that they previously believed were beyond their ken or reach. Writing on the "strengths perspective," Saleebey makes the important point that "individuals are best served, from a health and competence standpoint, by creating belief and thinking around possibility and values, around accomplishment and renewal, rather than centering exclusively on risk factors and disease processes."[30]

CASE MANAGEMENT

Case management, a relatively recent and still emerging approach to service delivery, is introduced toward the end of the chapter on the environment because it requires sophisticated understanding of variations in types of roles, communication, and resources; assessment and interventions occur at the interface between people and their environments. Many of the functions described in this chapter may be carried out by case managers; sometimes clinical and case management functions are carried out by the same professional.

As a response to increasingly complex, bureaucratized, and fragmented health and social service delivery systems, case management has become a fairly prevalent effort to meet the needs of many, often very vulnerable, people, including chronic psychiatric patients, people with AIDS, the physically and mentally disabled, the frail elderly, severely disorganized families, seriously disturbed children, and many others. Even the healthiest and most capable clients sometimes need help finding their way around health and social service systems. But those who for various reasons are unable to make their needs known or to take initiatives on their own cannot possibly negotiate the confusing maze of a complicated service delivery system. A major impetus for the growth of case management was to prevent people, particularly those at risk, from "falling through the cracks" of uncoordinated human services systems.

Austin defines case management as "an intervention whereby a human service professional arranges and monitors an optimum package of long-term care services."[31] The case manager's functions commonly include: *coordinating* services for clients, *locating* needed resources and *linking* clients to them, *monitoring* how services are being provided, and *assessing* the quality of services provided. *Case advocacy* and *social action* are often required to address shortages of resources, bureaucratic resistance to change, and discrimination against certain clients, among other matters. Because case managers have access to information and their own experiences that document effectiveness and quality of service delivery, they are in an excellent position to inform policy development. To the extent of their abilities, clients should be part of the entire process of planning, negotiating for resources, and assessing services. *Coordination, cooperation,* and *collaboration* among agencies and collaterals are usually necessary because rarely can one organization provide all the resources and services required for clients with diverse and multiple needs. The most effective case managers are those who are resource specialists and have thorough knowledge of the communities in which they work as well as the clients they serve. Clearly, if one person—the case manager—or a case management team has full responsibility for overseeing and integrating comprehensive service delivery, there is less likelihood that individuals and families requiring various kinds of assistance will languish or deteriorate because of unmet needs.

Case management functions are performed from many perspectives, depending on many factors, including the type of setting, the needs of the clientele being served, the philosophical orientations of the agencies or organizations involved, fiscal and policy constraints, and many more. Nurses, paraprofessionals, as well as social workers and others assume case management functions; professional orientations,

therefore, can influence the way a program is carried out. Certainly social workers' commitment to—and often special training in—the person–environment perspective makes them ideal candidates for this practice specialization. As we have said before, work with people and their environments is intricate work that requires special skills and expertise. One cannot define the case management role or practice in a clear or single way; every case management program is different.

The above description of some of the core concepts of case management is based on an ideal picture. The actual case management situation, however, generally suffers from important limitations.[32] Included among them are the following: (1) A significant impetus behind the growth of case management has been to contain costs; unfortunately, the primary objective of improving the quality and delivery of service is often compromised by fiscal concerns. If case managers want to "buy" services from another agency—a homemaker service, for example—they may not be given authority to do so. (2) Case management can only be as effective as the quality and quantity of resources available or at least those that can be easily created; because case management was developed, in part, as a response to inadequate services to begin with, and in many areas services have been cut even more, the location and linkage of services are often more of a hope than a reality. (3) Although the definition of case management often includes systems intervention (such as advocacy for better services), the ability of case managers to create system changes is often seriously limited by lack of authority granted by organizations and funding sources; effecting major organizational changes is usually beyond a case manager's power. (4) Bureaucratic impasses and agency competition—

for funds or for prestige—can seriously impede coordination and cooperation among them. (5) The training and experience of case managers varies widely, with the result that people with little expertise are sometimes assigned tasks that are enormously complicated and require infinite knowledge and skill.

Thus, case management as it now stands certainly helps many clients who might be deprived of essential services otherwise. But it is no panacea and is an area that social workers as a group need to influence and work hard to improve.

EXAMPLES OF INNOVATIVE, COORDINATED PRACTICE

Despite—and sometimes because of—the increased bureaucratization of human services and the downsizing and cutbacks discussed above, initiatives by agencies and even by individual social workers have resulted in the creation of innovative, accessible, multifaceted services. Many new programs have been designed to respond to special needs of special groups; others originated in communities where quality clinical and other services and opportunities were not readily available. We are pleased to conclude this chapter with brief descriptions of three such initiatives, each illustrated with a case example.

Integration of Services for HIV-Positive and AIDS Patients

In the late 1980s, in a sizable, sprawling, populous, multi-ethnic metropolitan area, two large organizations joined to develop a far-reaching, comprehensive "Linkage Service," created to provide and coordinate a broad range of services to the then growing population of HIV-positive and AIDS-infected individuals. Services to families and close as-

sociates of patients were built into the program from the beginning. One organization is a highly regarded, nonsectarian, nonprofit family and children's agency founded many decades ago to provide casework and child guidance services, foster care programs, family education, and much more. This agency has many branches in various areas of the city. The second organization was founded in the mid-1980s when the AIDS crisis exploded, quickly expanding to offer innumerable services to people with AIDS and their families. Both agencies are well-endowed, have effective fund-raising campaigns, and receive various public and private grants; clinical services provided by the family agency are partially reimbursable by some medical insurance plans and by Medicare and Medicaid.

Two social work "linkage coordinators"— one from each organization—direct and supervise the assessment, management, and referral of HIV- and AIDS-afflicted clients for medical, psychotherapeutic, family treatment, legal, housing, financial assistance, and many other services.

Mr. and Mrs. Diaz, both age 30, were referred by a visiting nurse to the Linkage Service, located at the AIDS agency, for HIV testing. Mr. Diaz, an intravenous drug user for many years and still using, and his wife, who had never used drugs, both tested positive. Their two daughters, ages 10 and 7, tested negative. When they first came, it was apparent that many services would be required: The intake worker observed that Mr. Diaz seemed physically ill and that Mrs. Diaz in particular was very depressed. The worker also learned that the apartment building where the family was living had been condemned and they would have to move, but they had not found another place to live. In the first interview, arrangements were made for them to plan a move to "scattered site" supervised housing with an on-site case manager who would assist this family in various ways. For example, she contacted the AIDS division of the department of welfare for financial aid and arranged for the girls to transfer to schools near their new housing. Other resources were made immediately available: Both Mr. and Mrs. Diaz were referred for complete medical evaluations. With their consent, an appointment was made with a family therapist at one of the family agency's nearby satellite clinics. Mrs. Diaz was evaluated by a psychopharmacologist for possible medication. The older girl joined a group for children with HIV- or AIDS-afflicted parents. Mr. Diaz was referred to an intensive, outreach substance abuse service.

Only a few months after they first came to the service, Mr. Diaz became so ill that he was barely ambulatory. It was arranged for a "buddy" to visit him weekly (support groups for volunteer "buddies" to AIDS patients are conducted by the service on a regular basis). Just before Mr. Diaz died, after a few more months, Mrs. Diaz—now not physically well herself—was assigned a part-time homemaker. With the help of the family therapist, her mother, from whom she had been estranged, reconciled with Mrs. Diaz; she became a "care partner" (the name given to friends, relatives, and lovers of patients for whom the service also runs regular support groups). At the time of this writing, a year and a half after Mr. and Mrs. Diaz came to intake, family meetings are being held that include Mrs. Diaz's mother and sister, in addition to Mrs. Diaz and the girls. There are frank discussions about Mrs. Diaz's failing health and about arrangements for the girls to live with their aunt when their mother can no

longer care for them. The almost unbearable grief this family endures is shared, giving the girls an opportunity to feel a part of the process rather than being outsiders to it. Although there can be no satisfactory ending to the tragic story of the Diaz family, without such comprehensive, accessible, and well-integrated services, the parents' health needs and the children's fears and losses probably would have received "patchwork" attention, leaving many gaps as they shuttled from resource to resource.[33]

A Creative Linkage Program: One Social Worker's Initiative

Within a suburban city with a population of about 80,000, there is a community of about 2,000 people known as Lincolntown. Residents include African Americans who have lived there for generations and more recently settled Spanish-speaking (mostly Mexican, Puerto Rican, and Ecuadorean) residents. Many of those who work are earning low incomes, often living below the poverty line; most of the others are barely getting by on various financial assistance benefits. Lincolntown, a *de facto* segregated area of the city, is surrounded by homes lived in mostly by white, middle-class, and upper-middle-class families.

A part-time clinical social worker, who saw the need for a new program, was employed by the Family Counseling Center in the city; this agency has a staff of social workers and other mental health professionals providing individual, couple, and family therapy, crisis intervention, and family life education. The worker was concerned that the residents of Lincolntown, who lived at a distance from the counseling center, were rarely using clinical services offered by the agency. Having lived in the city for over 30 years, this worker was aware of the complex and unrelenting problems in Lincolntown related to poverty, to discrimination by and alienation from the larger community, and to language and cultural barriers that restricted opportunities.

On her own, but with the support of the counseling center's director, this energetic, dedicated worker established herself as a person to be trusted by Lincolntown residents. She participated in programs run by two other well-respected agencies in the area: the Community Action Program (CAP), which has many services including day care for preschool children, after-school recreation, surplus food distribution, and referral services; and the Lincolntown Housing Agency, which builds and manages low-income housing and also provides referral services, from time to time planning community programs and workshops for tenants. These organizations are not staffed with clinical social workers; both are within the Lincolntown community and primarily serve the residents there.

The worker was welcomed by the directors of both organizations, and in a short time, the Family Counseling Center launched "Project Outreach," receiving a grant from United Way and private contributions (some of which were directly solicited by the worker, who had many contacts in the city). With full cooperation of the directors of the other two agencies, Project Outreach was designed to target Lincolntown residents by providing on-site clinical services at the CAP and Housing agencies. Since the worker, who provided most of the casework services, had been participating as a consultant to various programs of these agencies on a regular basis, she was known not only to staff members, who made referrals to her, but also to children, adolescents, and adults who attended the agencies' various programs. Because they already knew her, it was easier for

them to consider seeking clinical social work help. At the time of this writing, after a year and a half, Project Outreach is expanding; it will employ a Spanish-speaking social worker, now has a social work volunteer, and plans to take on an MSW student. In addition to having clinical services that are now geographically accessible and staffed by a worker already respected by potential clients, there is flexibility in the way services are delivered: Walk-in clients are served as quickly as possible; wary potential clients who prefer it are met in informal settings, such as a pizza parlor, rather than in an office; rides are provided for those who cannot walk even short distances. And, of utmost importance, the highly regarded directors of CAP and of the Lincolntown Housing Agency have strongly endorsed Project Outreach, further enhancing the trust of residents of Lincolntown.

Malik, an 11-year-old African American youngster, was referred to the worker by the director of the after-school program at CAP. His disruptive behavior had become a problem to the operation of the program; he was loud, argumentative, and unwilling to follow rules or treat others with courtesy. At other times, he would withdraw, seem very sad, and refuse to participate; the director was worried about him. Malik complained that he had too much homework and no time for fun. From the program director, the worker learned that Malik, who had been living with his maternal aunt for two years, strongly disliked his mother's boyfriend and had asked to leave her home. His mother has shown very little interest in him; he rarely sees her or his younger brother who lives with her. His father abandoned the family several years ago; no one knows where he is. The worker got to know Malik at the after-school program and quickly recognized that he was not only profoundly depressed but also was articulating ideas about suicide.

However, Malik could not be seen in therapy until the worker got permission from his family. The program director at CAP was quite certain that the aunt would be uneasy about involvement in any clinical services, but he suggested that he speak with the aunt's brother (Malik's maternal uncle), whom he knew well and who he believed was viewed as the informal head of the family; he was the only one of his siblings who had attended college. After a conversation with the program director, Malik's uncle contacted the worker; once he understood the concerns about Malik, he encouraged the aunt to let the boy be seen by the worker. Before therapy began, however, the worker had a meeting with the aunt, explaining to her the worries the program director and she had about Malik. She asked the aunt for her ideas about her nephew: What did she think his distress might be about? How had she found he could best be reached? She wanted the aunt to know that the worker saw her as a primary consultant and as someone who could be an important part of the solution to Malik's unhappiness.

Malik took to the worker and his meetings with her "like a duck to water," as the worker put it. He was angry, especially at his mother; he hated and loved and missed her, he said. He talked sadly about not remembering his father. As he saw it, he had never really been *asked* how he felt before; people were "always telling, not asking," he complained. Quickly, ideas of suicide subsided. From time to time, the worker had meetings with the aunt, who was a resource for the worker and whom the worker helped to

view Malik's behavior differently. The aunt and also Malik's teacher, with whom the worker met several times, both became more sympathetic instead of critical of the boy and his behavior. Slowly, over six months, Malik's depression lifted considerably and his behavior improved, which led to better relationships with other young people and with adults, adding to greater satisfaction on his part. "He has turned into a regular guy," the program director at CAP reported. Had outreach services not been available, this youngster's depression probably would have deepened, with the result that he might have seriously "acted out," become self-destructive, or both.

Women Getting Ready for Work: A New Program Succeeds

In 1996, a social worker at a family service agency situated in a small, culturally diverse city (population about 35,000) initiated a job readiness and job search program for mothers receiving Aid to Families with Dependent Children (AFDC). State welfare reform measures were requiring that AFDC mothers find work after they received financial assistance for 21 months. Concerned about the implications of the new welfare policy, the worker submitted a grant proposal to the United Way asking for "seed" money for a pilot "welfare-to-work" project. The proposal was approved, and with the further cooperation and financial support of the department of welfare and from several local organizations and contributors, the family agency sponsored the experiment.

Five single mothers were the first to join the program. It was from these first recruits that the project coordinator—the trained social worker who had originated the plan—began to learn just what such an undertaking would require. The participants' ideas were elicited and incorporated as the program was developed. A 10-week course was designed to help the women achieve the goal that became this first group's slogan: "Get a job. Keep a job." During two-hour classes, held twice weekly, it became evident that important barriers to work for the women were: (1) preparing for and locating a job and (2) meeting child care needs. The coordinator helped the participants to consider just what is entailed in the search for employment, in dressing and interviewing for a job, and in conducting oneself at work. A significant part of the course was devoted to discussions about what the women should expect of a workplace, including their right not to be exploited or harassed, and the realistic demands that employers would make of them. Generally, self-confidence of the women, some of whom had never held a paying job, was low. The coordinator helped them to recognize and begin to draw upon skills and qualities they had but gave themselves little credit for—including the expertise they had acquired as mothers and as managers of limited finances. And, the coordinator pointed out, despite various kinds of discrimination, hardships, and heartaches they had endured, they had all bounced back, a fact that attested to their strength and tenacity. Support and encouragement among the women became an important benefit of the classes; when one woman would say to another, "I know you can do it," it carried special weight. For any of the participants who wanted it, individual and family therapy were provided at the family service agency; referrals to substance abuse programs and psychiatric evaluations for medication were available when necessary.

Practical help was also necessary for the program to succeed. Quality child care for young children and after-school programs for the older ones were located by the program coordinator to meet the unique needs of each family. Beginning training in computers was made available for two of the five participants who wanted it. The women were helped to search for jobs themselves during the 10-week course; sometimes the coordinator acted as a liaison with employers in the community, but, for the most part, the women found their own work. Help with clothing (work outfits) and transportation were provided when necessary.

All five women completed the course and secured jobs. Of utmost importance to the success of the program were weekly one-to-one meetings with a volunteer mentor for one year after the end of the course. In these meetings, the mentor encouraged and coached them, directed them to resources when necessary, and worked with them to overcome the inevitable hurdles that accompany the transition from welfare to work; together, mentors and new employees grappled with difficulties encountered on the job or with child care. Almost two years later, two of the women have remained at their original places of employment; the other three are also working but at different jobs.

Since the first successful pilot project, the welfare-to-work program has expanded, has more classes, always has a waiting list, and has hired a job consultant and a child care coordinator, and has acquired a volunteer mentor specialist. The coordinator is currently working with the department of public welfare to develop a postgraduate program for advanced training, such as in computers and office machines. Of the more than 60 graduates of the program since its beginning, *85 percent got a job and continued working.* Four program graduates are preparing to become mentors to new participants in the program.

Ms. Potofski, a 34-year-old mother of three children ranging in age from 3 to

12, was one of the original five graduates of the welfare-to-work program. According to the coordinator, this woman "had the lowest self-esteem of almost anyone I ever met." She had run away from what she described as an unhappy home several times as a teenager, never completed high school, had been arrested twice on drug and prostitution charges before she was 21, and when she entered the program she described herself as a "recovering alcoholic." Except for a short-lived, part-time job at a florist shop before she had children, she had never been in the work force.

Although she knew her AFDC benefits would be coming to an end, she said she had no belief in herself; she didn't think anyone would want to hire her, but even if she found a job, she was sure she would not be able to keep it. She repeatedly said she was very afraid of failing at anything she tried. The facts about her were quite different from the picture she had of herself: She was a woman with a ready and contagious smile, an ability to sympathize with others, a good head for arithmetic, and—above all—under difficult circumstances, with no partner and very little family support, she was raising three seemingly well-adusted children; the two attending school were doing average work.

Over and over again, the very caring coordinator and the other women reminded her of her accomplishments and her capabilities; gradually she began thinking about herself differently. In group meetings, she role-played job interviews until she felt more confident about speaking with a prospective employer. By faithfully reading the newspaper, Ms. Potofski located a job opening at a local manufacturing company; she was hired and, two years later, she still works

there. She has had to get up at 4:30 A.M. to get the children ready for school, make their lunches, walk them three blocks to the baby-sitter, and take public transportation to be at work by 7:00 A.M. The first few months on the job were difficult; when one of the children was ill, out of concern she stayed home rather than taking the child to the baby-sitter. She was reprimanded at work for her absences but, with the help of the mentor, she worked out arrangements for the children that made her more comfortable to leave them. Subsequently, her attendance at work was perfect. Some months later she was promoted from assembly line worker to product inspector, earning four dollars above minimum wage.

At the time this is being written, Ms. Potofski has just bought a car, has her first credit card, and, now that she has made long-awaited purchases for her children, she announced: "I'm finally going to outfit myself. I've worked for it."[34]

NOTES

1. See, for example, the classic papers: Cloward (1959), Bateson, et al. (1956), and Laing (1965). See other references pertinent to psychosocial therapy and the inseparability of the person and his or her environment: Gitterman (1996), Germain and Gitterman (1996), and Loewenstein (1979).
2. Germain (1991) used a colon in the representation of the person:environment "to signify a holistic or unitary system" (p. 19). In her view, hyphenating person-environment suggests a fractured connection.
3. There are many good articles that discuss this approach and describe programs designed to provide preventive services of various kinds at the times and places they may be needed. See, for example, Blazyk and Canavan (1985); Cornille, et al. (1996); Eber and Nelson (1997); Effron (1980); Friedman

and Friedman (1982); Kurzman (1980); Lightburn and Kemp (1994); Shepard (1997); Vincentia and Conrad (1980); and Webb (1981).

In addition to brief examples throughout this chapter, at the end of it we have included illustrations of three innovative programs that have proved to be very successful and show every sign of continuing despite the capriciousness of funding.

4. There have always been some social workers who have disparaged the casework approach, believing it puts the burden for change on the individual rather than on the society that deprives and oppresses. It is beyond the scope of this book to address this issue at length, but the reader may be interested in comments made by one social worker still well known for her years of dedication to advancing fundamental social changes. Writing during the Depression of the 1930s, Bertha Reynolds (1934) responded to those who believed that casework should be put aside until "a just and healthy social order is achieved" by asking, "Is there not a place also for the development of personality, individual by individual?" If, she went on, casework can free people "from crippling accumulations of fear and hate so that they may have energy to use what intelligence they possess; if it educates in the best sense of the word for the use of freedom of choice and for healthier social relationships, it becomes not a luxury but a necessity in a time of social change. For, after all, do we not know, when we are most thoughtful about it, that we are held back from a better social order not by the absence of some lucky change to set in motion the wheels of normal living, but rather because we are not ready, as a people, to think freely and maturely? If social case work itself can grow up to a maturity which will create the conditions of more abundant and responsible life in the individuals with whom it enters into relationship, then indeed it has a place in the cooperative commonwealth which is our only hope for the future."

5. See Hopps, et al. (1995) on clinical effectiveness with overwhelmed clients.

6. See Dorothy Fahs Beck (1988), especially pp. 35–48. These are some of the possible explanations offered by Beck for the unexpected findings: "Could it be that master's level preparation for counseling concentrates to such a degree on training for therapy focused on family relationship problems that it does not prepare graduates adequately for work on other problems, particularly those requiring a heavy component of case management, information giving, referrals, home visits (with related travel requirements), case advocacy, or the coordination of support services? A further possibility is that some graduate programs may encourage students to value skill in family therapy more highly than corresponding skill in counseling focused on support and linkage functions, thus encouraging a greater investment in the former. Students looking toward a future in private practice may also push faculty in this direction. Some graduates may even attempt insight therapy or modification of basic relationship patterns with clients who see their own needs solely in terms of concrete services and support, thus alienating them so that they drop out prematurely." As mentioned in Chapter 1, in the section on graduate education for clinical social workers, training in environmental work is as important as education about psychological matters.

See also Rosen and Livne (1992) who studied 176 social workers' responses to standardized intake summaries; workers were asked to formulate the locus of client problems. The researchers conclude: "In the present study, we demonstrated the existence of an overemphasis in the social workers' formulations of client problems that favors personal problems over interpersonal and environmental, and we showed that social workers' adoption of a psychodynamic theoretical orientation related positively to that bias. A systematic, planned, and evaluative approach to practice, in contrast, tended to be negatively associated with such overemphasis" (p. 95). From our psychosocial point of view, as we say frequently in this text, we do not take an either/or approach to psychological and situational influences: We look at both and at the ways in which these interact.

In a provocative but recommended book, Specht and Courtney (1994) assert that social work has abandoned its mission to promote social change and instead has embraced the practice of psychotherapy.

7. For an excellent article on the importance of helping clients develop their own skills to modify the environment, see Hashimi (1981). See also Pearlman and Edwards (1982) in which the authors describe a method used for helping clients become their own advocates and their own change agents.

8. In addition to other references cited in these notes, discussions of various aspects of the situational component of the person–situation gestalt can be found in the following recommended readings: Ambrosino (1979), Auslander and Litwin (1988), Beckett (1988), Denby, et al. (1998), Gray and Nybell (1990), Gutheil (1992), Lehman (1996), Padilla (1997), Reiner (1979), and Whitaker et al. (1986).

9. For a book essential to all social work practitioners, see Wilson (1978). See also Hepworth, et al. (1997, pp. 78–83) for a good, practical discussion of confidentiality; he cites additional readings.

10. Lest we forget! The social worker's role in reducing environmental pressures has long been recognized for many years. Wrote Mary Richmond (1930, p. 174): "Social casework may be defined as the art of doing different things for different people by cooperation with them to achieve at one and the same time their own and society's betterment."

See also Hollis (1936 and 1939) for discussions of providing environmental treatment based on clients' needs.

11. See a good article by Gibelman and Demone (1989) on social workers as mediators in the legal system. On the subject of advocacy, aggressive intervention, and social action, see Ezell (1994) and Sosin and Caulum (1983). See also Hepworth, et al. (1997, especially pp. 468–72) for a clear and helpful summary of the indications for and techniques of (case or cause) advocacy and social action.

Humphreys, et al. (1993) discuss the importance of linking clinical social work and social policy; they urge more thinking about how clinical social workers can introduce policy issues that are affecting their clients' lives into treatment without distorting their own objectivity or stimulating troublesome countertransference issues. They encourage clinicians to become active in shaping social policy recommendations since it is they who have firsthand knowledge of the conditions their clients are facing and the policies that require attention.

In an interesting article, Young (1994) thoughtfully argues that the self-psychology perspective helps us to understand how improvement of an individual or family's life can be achieved through modification of their human environments.

12. *New York Times,* February 10, 1998, p. C20.

Williams (1994) points out that, contrary to popular belief, most people living in poverty work. "Although single women and children make up the majority of the poor, recent statistics indicate that in more than 40% of families who are now falling into poverty, both parents are working" (p. 47). In Chicago, those living in poverty rose from 12% to 22% between 1960 and 1990.

According to a *New York Times* editorial, February 17, 1998, p. A18, the typical white family earned almost twice that of blacks and about "95 percent of black families own no stock or pension funds." Although poverty among black children has fallen, "at 40 percent the level remains horribly high. Unemployment among black men fell last year to 8.6 percent, the lowest in 23 years, but nevertheless twice the jobless rate of white men." No wonder hopelessness in urban ghetto communities in which people of color and "minorities" reside runs rampant. According to the *New York Times,* September 25, 1998, pp. A1 and A25, the U.S. Census Bureau reported that poverty rates dropped especially for blacks and Hispanics, while the poverty rate for white non-Hispanics remained unchanged. The number of people living in poverty in 1997 dropped to 35.6 million, 3.7 million fewer than in 1993. The trend may be positive, but the numbers are still overwhelming and we all pay a high price for them.

13. Safyer (1994) writes about the impact of inner-city living and exposure to chronic violence and deprivation of necessary resources on adolescent development; he urges more research and programs geared to prevention. Resnick and Burt's (1996) article addresses the many influences, including neighborhood, poverty, and family dysfunction, that contribute to young people's difficulties and behaviors; he discusses implications for service delivery. Temple (1997) discusses work with inner-city families of homicide victims. Zayas (1995) discusses some of the influences of culture and the impact of poverty, urban environmental stresses, and family difficulties on child rearing and development. King (1993) writes about the disproportionate percentage of African Americans who are incarcerated and the resultant financial and relational strains experienced by families; he urges community-based programs, social services for inmates and their families, and special training for social workers in this important area. Johnson (1996) reviews some of the social work and mental health literature about the impact of cultural, economic, and family factors on violent behavior, but points out that we have mostly overlooked the possible biological influences; she discusses implications for practice.

14. Two important, still pertinent, articles were written about this important matter in the 1970s: Levy (1974) and Gilbert and Specht (1976).

15. *New York Times,* February 17, 1998. See also note 12 in this chapter.

16. See Sunley (1970) and Grinnell and Kyte (1975).

17. Quoted on p. 223 of Lee (1994).

18. Specht and Courtney (1994).

19. See especially the excellent article by Ostbloom and Crase (1980). Using case examples of work with abusing parents, the writers discuss the importance of support, a meaningful worker–client relationship, and respect for client autonomy and decision making.

Magura (1982) reports on a study in which a majority of clients surveyed—who were receiving public protective services for abuse, neglect, and parent–child conflict—reported an improvement in self-confidence and an increased capacity to cope with feelings and life stresses: "There was a high degree of correspondence in how clients rated case improvement and satisfaction with their caseworker." The author concluded: "A good relationship is usually a necessary, though not sufficient, condition for case improvement." Empathy, genuineness, unconditional positive regard, and accessibility were the reasons given by clients for satisfaction with their caseworkers. "Dissatisfactions, which were infrequent, focused on unwanted advice, lack of skill, or inaccessibility." Confirming previous studies, the findings indicate that "training and competency in the conduct of relationships is essential to successful protective services casework" (pp. 529–31).

For additional references that have stood the test of time, see: Ehline and Tigue (1977), Goldberg (1975), Holmes (1981), a volume edited by Kempe and Helfer (1972), Oxley (1977), and Roth (1975).

From our personal experience and informal conversations with colleagues in child protective services in medium and large metropolitan areas, it seems that a significant proportion of clients voluntarily return to their workers, seeking help and referrals, even though casework services originally had been imposed upon them. In many such agencies, however, staff shortages and large caseloads have resulted in a diminished capacity to take the time to provide adequate service.

For additional references on involuntary and reluctant clients or others who require outreach, see Chapter 5, note 7; Chapter 6, note 3; Chapter 9, notes 3 and 4; and Chapter 10, note 5.

20. Frey (1990), p. 144. This highly recommended article presents a very useful framework to help direct service practitioners analyze potential organizational resistance to or support for change.

21. Ibid., p. 143.
22. For readings on some of the problems faced by social workers in various settings and suggestions about how changes may be initiated, see Dolgoff (1981), Jansson and Simmons (1986), Lee (1983), and Olmstead (1983). The following readings deal with issues related to some of the roles and needs of caseworkers in public welfare agencies, along with other issues relevant to public services: Gibelman and Schervish (1996); Ginsberg (1983); a volume edited by Laird and Hartman (1985) on child welfare; Lindsey, et al. (1987); and Vinokur-Kaplan (1987).

For research and discussions related to foster care, see: Fanschel and Shinn (1978) who report on a longitudinal study; Jones, Neuman, and Shyne (1976), a research report of a demonstration project in foster care designed to reduce or shorten placements away from home; Kates, et al. (1991) on assessment and treatment; and Sosin (1987) on permanency planning.

See also Jiminez (1990) on challenges of the human services professions based on changing needs.

23. The contention that casework is ineffective with the poor was contradicted by the findings of the Beck and Jones (1973) outstanding study of clients' and counselors' views on family agency services, based on 3,596 cases from 266 agencies. The researchers reported (p. 116): "The socioeconomic status of clients proved to be a relatively minor factor in outcomes," adding, "minimum differentials in outcomes were achieved in spite of the greater handicaps faced by lower status clients—more problems, more difficult problems, less adequate environmental supports, and less knowledge of when and where to go for help." As they pointed out, some earlier research had led to the opposite view: that the casework approach is not effective with low-income clients. "Perhaps," wrote Beck and Jones (p. 116), "the explanation [for their own findings] lies in the improved awareness of and accommodation to the needs and problems of the disadvantaged

that are inherent in the current multiservice approach of many agencies and in their increasing use of planned, short-term, crisis-focused service."

In a very interesting chapter by Lorion and Felner (1986) many aspects of treatment for the poor are discussed. One point among many that the authors make in their survey of relevant reseach is that often time-limited therapies are the most effective. It is suggested that assisting low-income clients to cope with or resist environmental demands and helping in the location of resources and social networks may increase commitment to treatment. Fortunately, the authors emphasize that the poor are not in any way a homogeneous group; obviously, generalizations about treatment of low-income clients cannot be made. Problems regarding treatment of clients different from their therapists may derive from bias among therapists as much as reluctance of clients to engage in treatment. Studies by Fischer and Miller (1973) and Franklin (1986) indicate that the attitudes of some clinical social workers, when reading case materials, can be biased solely by the social class variable. Recommendations about treatment differed according to socioeconomic status, even though case materials were identical except for social class.

See also Garfield (1994) whose review of relevant research suggests that social class is not related to treatment outcome (p. 206).

24. See *New York Times,* October 7, 1986, pp. C1 and C9. See also Cook (1980) and Wetzel (1980).
25. See Chapter 1, note 34 for references on private practice.
26. For readings on network intervention, see Auslander and Litwin (1987), McIntyre (1986), Rueveni (1979), and the volume edited by Whitaker and Gargarino (1983).
27. Hartman and Laird (1983), Chapters 8 and 9.
28. Ibid., p. 159.

Additional readings on resource assessment include: Gutheil (1992) who reminds us to consider the physical as well as the social environment; Mailick and Vigilante

(1997) who suggest the use of a family assessment wheel that is consistent with social
constructionism by stressing process and
emphasizing family experience, understanding, and client participation; Tracy and
Whittaker (1990) who suggest a social network map with specific suggestions about
how to interview to obtain useful information; Vigilante (1982) on the evaluation of
the "fit" between the individual and work environment; Vigilante and Mailick (1988) on
their earlier needs-resource evaluation
wheel; and Vosler (1995) on family access to
necessary resources.

29. On the need to understand the individual
client, Bertha Reynolds (1934, p. 12) wrote:
"Since human beings need all sorts of
things—ranging from food and shelter to
recreation, education, friendship—and since
attitudes play a part in their getting or not
getting all of these, there can be no such
thing as social case work that does not take
account of attitudes." She added: "But I am
equally sure that no case work can succeed
in isolating a person's attitudes and treating
them apart from the conditions of his life in
which they find expression."

30. Saleebey (1996), p. 301. His writings on the
strength perspective are highly recommended.

31. Austin (1993), p. 452. This article and a volume edited by Austin and McClelland (1995)
provide excellent background information on
the various dimensions and variations of the
practice of case management.

32. For additional references on case management, see: Johnson and Rubin (1983); Moore
(1992); O'Connor (1988); and Sullivan, et al.
(1992). A volume edited by Vourlekis and
Greene (1992) provides an excellent overview
of case management and its relationship to
social work practice; traditional values of
self-determination, mutuality, and dignity
are emphasized.

33. Relevant and useful readings on AIDS include: Cates, et al. (1990); a volume edited
by Dane and Levine (1994); Land and Harangody (1990); McDonell, et al. (1991); and
Moynihan (1988),

34. According to a news article in the *New York
Times,* May 27, 1998, p. A17, after several
large American corporations made systematic efforts to hire welfare recipients, execu-
tives were canvassed and reported "to their
surprise" that they retained a larger proportion of the former welfare recipients than
other entry-level employees; workers stayed
on the jobs longer, with less turnover, than
other employees.

CHAPTER 9

THE CLIENT–WORKER RELATIONSHIP

Basic to psychosocial casework treatment, and one of its most powerful tools, is the relationship between worker and client. Experience has demonstrated that successful treatment depends heavily on the quality of this relationship. Over and over again, research has validated social workers' observations about its singular significance to successful therapy. In a follow-up study of over 1,500 cases from family agencies, Beck reports: "Beyond all else, the findings confirm the critical importance of the counselor–client relationship." Clients' evaluation of a superior outcome of their counseling service was highly associated with a "very satisfactory" (the highest) rating of the counselor–client relationship.[1]

Research and years of observation of practice have identified many of the components or underpinnings of the positive therapeutic relationship. Some of these will be discussed in detail in this chapter. Therapist characteristics of *nonpossessive warmth and concern,* *genuineness, empathy,* and *nonjudgmental acceptance* have been found by studies—and are known by many clinicians—to appreciably enhance therapeutic interaction and client satisfaction. The worker's *optimism, objectivity, professional competence,* and capacity to communicate these play an important role in the treatment relationship. In every case, in order to foster a climate of comfort and mutual regard, the worker's *self-awareness* is crucial to effective casework.[2]

The client, too, participates in establishing a favorable relationship; he or she must be able to muster the hope and courage necessary to engage in treatment, and, with the worker's help, the client must develop motivation for action or change; beyond that, the person must be able to achieve some trust in the worker's desire to help and ability to do so.

Whether the treatment is centered around individual, interpersonal, or environmental problems, or some combination of these, and whether the contact is brief or long-term, an effective relationship requires that *the worker and client collaborate to arrive at some mutual agreement on the purpose of treatment and the objectives they jointly seek.* It is generally agreed that the "therapeutic alliance"—the working relationship between worker and client—is most successful when based on mutual respect and trust, as well as on a firm commitment to agreed-upon goals.

While every chapter of this book describes client–worker interaction in one way or another, this chapter will examine six particularly significant aspects of the treatment relationship. We will view it in terms of (1) realistic attitudes and responses of client and worker; (2) unrealistic attitudes and responses: transference and countertransference; (3) problems of communication between client and worker; (4) mutual agreement and collaboration; (5) worker self-disclosure; and (6) the client–worker relationship in the dynamics of treatment.

REALISTIC ATTITUDES AND RESPONSES

Client Reactions

Customarily, we think of two kinds of responses and attitudes between client and worker: realistic and unrealistic. First, we will discuss realistic reactions. It is important not to mistake these for unrealistic attitudes and responses that can occur in treatment relationships, particularly *transference and countertransference,* to be discussed in the next section.

Fears about Seeking Help As discussed in Chapter 5, it is common knowledge among clinicians that when people come for help, with personal, interpersonal, or even situational problems, they almost always experi-

ence some anxiety. This is partly so because they are usually aware that their problems, or at least the solutions, lie to some degree within themselves. Conscious or unconscious feelings of shame or self-blame or recognition that one may have to make personal changes can lead to intense and realistic discomfort. Such feelings are widespread, but the intensity with which they are experienced varies according to the significance of the treatment. Generally, when clients are consulting the worker about matters that are of vital interest or are emotionally laden there will be greater anxiety than when the consultation is about peripheral matters. For example, difficulties coping with children, unhappy family relationships, a serious medical diagnosis, or environmental threats can arouse deep apprehension.

People also experience discomfort about entering into relationships in which they expect to be dependent. Clients—individuals, couples, or families—applying for clinical social work help often express this uneasiness directly: "I was ashamed to ask for help," or "We wanted to solve it ourselves." To some clients, seeking help can signify weakness, even though recognizing the need for help and deciding to come for it require strength. To admit an inability to solve difficulties without outside assistance can evoke childlike feelings, feelings of failure. It can be a blow to self-esteem and feelings of competence. By seeking casework services, clients often feel that they are acknowledging that another person is wiser or stronger. They frequently expect to be criticized or judged. Taking the first step in allowing oneself to trust another unknown or little-known person can be very frightening.

Even when an individual, couple, or family has eagerly sought help, the desire to bring about change—internal changes, changes in behavior or attitude—may create considerable anxiety, depending on the nature of the anticipated changes. When there is satisfaction about present ways or when current modes that may need to be modified are deeply entrenched, uneasy feelings about getting help can be exacerbated. And, as will be discussed and illustrated in the chapters on family and couple therapy, when family members come together for help, each individual may expect to be discovered to be the "cause" of the difficulties.

Involuntary Clients If a client has been either overtly or subtly pressed to get help, there may be anger as well as anxiety. Clients may see referral for treatment as criticism of their abilities, as an intrusion on their independence, or as a reflection on their emotional balance. Adolescents can be angry about being required by their parents or others to see a clinical social worker particularly when, as is often the case, they see the problem as deriving from family or some kind of external difficulties that they cannot resolve on their own. For teenagers who are characteristically struggling with conflicts about dependence and independence and with developing a sense of personal identity, and who can be wary that clinicians will try to control them (as they often feel parents and other adults in authority do), there is realistic concern about engaging in a treatment relationship.[3]

Many elderly clients do not initiate getting help themselves but are pressed into accepting services, and even into making major changes in their lives, by family members; they, too, can feel trapped by the referral and frightened that they will be stripped of their independence. Families who are reported to child protective services, for example, naturally are fearful about the consequences of the action; they are usually realistically angry, distrustful, and/or expecting to be blamed. Outreach, including home visits, to such families may demonstrate social workers' willingness to extend themselves, but apprehension about exposure and invasion are common reactions by clients at least at first. The mandated client, on whom casework services have been imposed by an authoritative agency or court action, can be extremely resentful at being compelled to accept help. (See the Carter case in Chapter 20 and the Stone case in Chapter 3.) The involuntary referral of clients to a psychiatric in-service facility can be terrifying. (See the case of Mrs. Barry in Chapter 20.)[4]

Effects of Prior Knowledge What the client knows about clinical social work, family therapy, or psychotherapy will also affect initial attitudes. If the client has heard favorable reports about an agency or an individual worker, a welcoming reception and skillful help will probably be anticipated. On the other hand, previous bad experiences or negative reports by others may lead the client to expect the worker to be critical, hostile, or condescending.

Expectations Based on Differences between Client and Worker The section on "Diversity" in Chapter 2 discussed issues related to differences between client and worker. Here, we focus on client responses and expectations.

Attitudes toward social workers or a particular agency may be affected by *cultural or class factors*. As discussed in Chapters 2 and 6, individuals who have immigrated from other countries may have a different idea of the nature of the helping relationship, based on experiences in their countries of origin. Understandably, prospective clients who have experienced prejudice, social oppression, and deprivation of many kinds may approach the treatment process with apprehension and lack of confidence that their situations will be understood.

Racial and class differences between worker and client, in a society in which separation of people with divergent backgrounds is so often the rule, arouse realistic concern. Clients may worry that actual differences even within the same ethnic group—in terms of money, power, education, and life experience—are so great that there can be no meeting ground, no comprehension by the worker of the issues that matter the most. Trust itself is difficult enough to achieve, but it can be even more difficult to bridge the gap between people from vastly different backgrounds and life circumstances, particularly in a society in which racism and class biases prevail. Overtly or covertly, clients may view their caseworkers with fear, suspicion, or anger. (Again, see the Carter case in Chapter 20.) *It is critically important that such client reactions not be confused with transference.*

Sometimes *class differences,* including general education, may increase the confidence of the blue-collar client in the professional abilities of the caseworker, but they may also make him or her fearful of being looked down upon or misjudged. In some instances, the less educated client may feel (perhaps realistically) that life experiences have been better teachers than a young worker's books. At another extreme, professional or upper-class clients may believe that the social worker is not as "intellectual" or "cultivated" as they are; these clients may be doubtful about the caseworker's ability to help. But again, if clients have been referred by friends, relatives, or neighbors who have had positive experiences with a particular worker or agency, despite vast differences in background, the expectation of a caring and respectful approach from a competent professional is likely.

Concern about *religious differences* can lead a person to worry about being understood. It is not unusual for a client to say, "I guess you are not Catholic (Jewish, a Jehovah's Witness)"; this is often a way to evoke the worker's attitudes toward religion or to express concern that the difference may be an obstacle.

As soon as a client meets a clinical social worker, the latter's *age* and *physical appearance* set reactions in motion. A young worker may find an older adult distrustful of his or her skill, particularly if this is not counterbalanced by obvious superiority in education. On the other hand, this worker may be more trusted than an older worker by an adolescent, who may expect greater understanding from peers and near-peers than from older people.

Gender differences also arouse different realistic reactions. A man may find it initially difficult to turn to a woman for professional help; the extent of this attitude varies with people of different backgrounds. Sometimes men and women expect a woman worker to be more sympathetic and "nurturing." A particularly pretty, handsome, or vital worker may arouse feelings of sexual attraction, even though there is no seductiveness in the worker's actual manner. People may be skeptical about bringing marital or parent–child problems to an unmarried caseworker—male or female—with no children.

Gay or lesbian clients often anticipate negative or naive responses to their *sexual orientation;* some fear that the worker will try to change them.

Even the appearance of the worker's office and experiences in the waiting room will add to a client's reactions. All these responses occur independently of what the worker actually *does!*

While it can be useful to anticipate a particular reaction to differences, one has to be very careful not to make assumptions or to stereotype. Sometimes clients are far more engrossed in their troubles than in worker difference. Many people are open-minded and trusting enough to assume there will be competent, caring help unless their experiences prove otherwise. We discuss the matter of differences between worker and client in greater detail in Chapter 2. Many case illustrations throughout this text attest to the fact that differences need not defeat positive relationships and successful treatment outcomes. (See, for example, the Stone case in Chapter 3, the Chin case in Chapter 2, the Garcia case in Chapter 17, the Green case in Chapter 18, and the Carter case in Chapter 20, among others.)

But when distrust *is* evident, it may take a good deal of patience, empathy, and painstaking work to convey to the client—in words and in actions—that the worker's intent is not to intrude or to depreciate group pride or aspirations but to listen carefully, understand, and assist. When we convey to clients our eagerness to learn the meanings of their backgrounds, identities, and experiences from *them,* and we resist making assumptions, clients usually feel safe enough to engage in the relationship. We will say more later about the worker's responsibility for promoting a climate of mutual respect and trust. The possible responses reviewed here are all realistic from the client's point of view, in the sense that they are either appropriate reactions to the situation or else to reality as it is seen by some members of the client's group.[5]

The Worker's Manner What workers actually say and the way they act when saying it are the next reality factors affecting the client's realistic responses. Before concluding that a client is displaying transference reactions or subjectively conditioned resistance, the worker must make certain that he or she is not actually saying or doing something that is giving the client a realistic basis for negative responses. Workers *are*

sometimes hostile, or at least critical or uninterested. When overworked or distracted, they may not pay attention to basic courtesies that are essential for putting people at ease. Out of their own needs, some act in a superior, overly impersonal way. Some enjoy a subtle type of domination that puts the client in an unnecessarily dependent or inferior position. Others reveal their desire to be loved, or at least admired and appreciated. Some are late for appointments, forgetful about doing things they have promised, and so on. Even the best of caseworkers will exhibit occasional "untherapeutic" reactions, by which we mean responses that are not helpful or healing. Caseworkers, too, are affected by mood changes, health, events in work or private life, and factors outside the particular treatment situation. Who of us at some time—on a hot day or when short of sleep or under the influence of an antihistamine—has not yawned in a way that could not be concealed from the client?

Unfortunately, some caseworkers also stereotype or react anxiously to clients of particular racial, cultural, or class backgrounds. Or they may view some clients only as victims of oppression, failing to see them also as people with unique strengths, experiences, and personalities. There are also workers who have fixed attitudes toward clients of a particular sex, age, sexual orientation, lifestyle, or physical condition or toward those with certain intellectual or emotional disabilities. Sometimes workers are critical of certain personality characteristics. As we shall discuss more fully later in this chapter, the development of self-awareness about countertherapeutic reactions can be among the most challenging, yet essential, tasks for the clinical social worker to achieve. When these untherapeutic behaviors do occur and when clients react to them, they are responding realistically.

In most cases, as we repeatedly suggest in various ways throughout this text, *the client's reactions to the worker should be elicited and discussed and always welcomed with interest, understanding, and respect.* Clients can be reassured when their concerns are taken seriously, when told that these are not only realistic but also to be expected. And when, through words and actions, the worker consistently demonstrates empathic, nonjudgmental attitudes and a desire to listen intently and to help in every way possible, most worries and doubts can be dispelled. Future work is almost always enhanced by the openness encouraged by the worker.

Worker Reactions

The Worker's Training This brings us to the realistic aspects of the worker's part in the treatment relationship. The well-trained, self-aware worker's responses are not the natural reactions of one person on the street to another. The worker entering the field begins with such natural responses, but they are subject to other influences of purpose and training. Workers' perceptions of clients are not those of the average person; their attitudes about what they perceive and the overt behaviors that follow are usually very different. A person who is trained as a psychosocial clinician does not see a client's behavior as an isolated event. This worker has become attuned to the reasons for client responses, the kinds of life histories that lie behind different response tendencies, the defenses people use to cope with anxiety. The psychosocial therapist reacts not simply to the client's overt behavior but also to a complex of stimuli that includes possible reasons for the behavior and the knowledge that, even if they are not apparent, reasons do exist, whether in life experience or in

constitution. The stimulus, then, is different for the clinical worker than for the layperson. The perception—or, better, apperception—includes many elements that are part of the worker's experience and education. To the well-trained clinician, the cue "anger" under some circumstances may read "defensive hostility" or "anxiety" or a defense against "softer" feelings; the cue "defensive" may sometimes read "overly severe superego" and may express the client's fear of criticism. If the client's response is thus read, the worker's response is automatically different from what it would otherwise be.

Diagnostic Understanding Diagnostic thinking about the client helps the worker to understand and respond realistically to the meaning of the client's defenses. For example, a client with obsessive-compulsive traits may be fending off strong, frightening instinctual urges by intellectualization; a client with a histrionic disorder may relate seductively to a worker; a dependent, emotionally deprived client may bring anger or unrealistic expectations derived from past ungratifying relationships; a man with a diagnosis of schizophrenia may talk evasively out of fear of exposing deeper thoughts and feelings that humiliate him or that he fears will repel the worker. Similarly, the homosexual client may underplay strong feelings about sexual preference for fear the worker will look down on or try to change him or her. *Dislike of clients' qualities or behavior can be more easily overcome when they are understood as reactions to pain or fear.* In some social work graduate schools and field placement agencies, students are helped through role playing to get as close as possible to the inner feelings of the client. Putting oneself in the shoes of another, so to speak, can help to generate one's empathic responses.

Understanding of Suffering Workers' reactions are further modified by observation of a great deal of human suffering in their training and experience. They have lived with clients through disappointment, sorrow, physical suffering, death, crippling frustration, and hopelessness; they have been closely associated with the torture of mental illness; they have read and listened to life history after life history in which the distortions of the adult personality could be traced step by step to misfortunes, deprivations, mistreatment, mishandling, and misunderstandings in childhood. Unless they have remained untouched by these experiences, they cannot but respond with more spontaneous understanding and acceptance than would have been the case if they had not become caseworkers. Herein lies one of the answers to the question often put to therapists: "How can you be so unspontaneous? Don't you get worn out controlling, or concealing, your natural reaction?" The worker's natural, spontaneous reaction itself is different from that of the untrained person because both perception and judgment have been modified by training and experience. No worker ever reaches the perfection of understanding and acceptance just implied, but that fact does not modify our conviction that successful psychosocial caseworkers must always strive in that direction.

Countertherapeutic Responses Although genuine responses of the caseworker to the client usually do have a predominantly positive flavor of sympathizing, accepting, liking, and wanting to help, *worker responses that are not therapeutically useful, even though they may be realistic, nevertheless occur in varying degree.* There may be irritation at the client who is hostile and attacking or who is "resistive" and thwarts the worker's therapeutic intent

(or aspirations)! Workers may feel threatened by a client's anger or negative feelings toward them; they may be overly concerned about whether their clients like them. Despite training, there may be residues of dislike of or insensitivity to clients whose behavior runs counter to the customs or mores of the worker's own class or ethnic group. There may be particular resentment of the client who mistreats another person, child or adult. An especially attractive client may arouse erotic reactions. Commonly, there is realistic anxiety about ability to help: The client may be confronted by almost insoluble problems and may sometimes be so seriously disturbed that the problem is beyond the worker's skill. Threats of suicide especially arouse the worker's anxiety. Occasionally, a desperately angry, psychotic, or near-psychotic person arouses realistic fear of bodily harm.

Even when workers fail to achieve understanding and acceptance and instead feel hostility, aversion, or some other antitherapeutic emotion, they usually try to avoid translating it into speech or action. This is for two reasons: because the worker knows it will hurt the client and does not want to do this, and because the purpose in being with the client is a therapeutic one and to show feelings impulsively will defeat that purpose. Workers' training to become aware of their reactions helps them control their expression.

One sometimes hears the opinion that the worker should never refrain from spontaneous expression of reactions on the grounds that to refrain introduces insincerity into the relationship. In our view, this is at best a misleading half-truth. We certainly agree with the need for genuineness, frankness, and simplicity in the relationship, but to refrain from showing an emotion is not insincerity. Whether the feeling is one of anger, boredom, sexual attraction, or intense like or dislike, *the seasoned psychosocial worker makes every effort to guide the expression of personal feelings according to their value to the therapeutic work.* As we will soon point out, spontaneous or direct articulations of a worker's emotions, whether positive or negative, *can* sometimes benefit the client when they have a bearing on mutual goals. When this is so, the worker may choose to express them. But, as we see it, they are neither justified nor necessary when based on the worker's own need to be "open" or "natural." Objectivity and reserve about the expression of feelings do not preclude warmth and genuineness. The creative yet controlled "use of self" requires that the worker keep a constant and conscious balance between head and heart, distance and closeness. The therapeutic relationship can be intensely personal—indeed, it can be uniquely intimate—as the client lays bare inner feelings and dilemmas. But it is for this reason, above all, that it is critically important to take every precaution to protect clients from emotional reactions of the worker that are not truly in their behalf.

> With resistance, a man came with his wife to see a clinical social worker to discuss his wife's wish to begin marital counseling. A lighted cigarette dangled from his mouth. Upon entering the interviewing room, he could not miss the "thank you for not smoking" sign. He protested loudly, impulsively crushing his cigarette against the inside of the metal wastebasket. A few moments after the interview began, smoke started to rise from the basket, and the worker had to douse the smoldering contents before proceeding. She felt angry in the face of this man's seemingly rude behavior and the inconvenience it had caused her. At the same time, she recognized that his

> actions derived from his fear and anger at being "dragged" by his wife into treatment; she knew from his manner and a previous interview with his wife that he expected to be blamed for the marital problems. Rather than sharing her immediate emotional response to the incident, the worker was able to connect with her empathy for this man's anxiety. Once she had given herself time to put her anger into perspective, with a light touch she simply said, "Sometimes the smoke has to clear before we can get down to work."

Sharing Worker Reactions   There are special circumstances, however, in which it is highly therapeutic to allow clients to become aware of negative (or positive) reactions as part of the process of helping them to understand themselves or the effects they sometimes have on other people. Worker feedback can stimulate reflection about habitual patterns of behavior and about the meaning of recurrent feelings or thoughts. But the timing of this type of intervention is important; it must be diagnostically sound and geared to the client's readiness, not to the worker's need for spontaneity.

> Mrs. Glass, diagnosed as having a borderline personality disorder, periodically accused her worker of not being interested in her; she bitterly attacked the worker for not always being instantly available by telephone. These complaints did not annoy the worker since she saw them as an expression of the client's rage, rooted in early parental deprivation. However, during one phase of treatment Mrs. Glass began to stall at the end of each session; sometimes she would cling to the worker, begging to be hugged. This behavior became increasingly irritating to the worker, who often

had another client waiting; she was angered by Mrs. Glass's seeming lack of consideration. But whether the worker became firm or appealed to the client's reason, the latter persisted in trying to prolong the hour. After several weeks of this, the worker finally opened a session by sharing her feeling with Mrs. Glass. She told her that she had begun to resent being delayed; she pointed out that she was always prompt for Mrs. Glass's sessions and that she wanted to give the same courtesy to her other clients. When these reactions were shared with Mrs. Glass, with whom the worker had a solid relationship, the client was then able to work on her intense and ever present feeling of "never getting enough"; discussions that followed gave the worker an opportunity to help Mrs. Glass see how she was alienating other people by so persistently concentrating on what was lacking in a relationship rather than on the benefits available to her.

In another situation, a charming and attractive man, whose wife had recently deserted him, had a gift for recounting amusing stories to his worker that the latter found she thoroughly enjoyed. She gave the client credit for his intelligence and humor; she found herself tempted to sit back and be entertained. However, sensing that his behavior was defensive, she shared with the client the difficulty she was having directing their discussions to the problems that had brought him into treatment; she found herself easily diverted by his wit, she told him. When these reactions were brought to the client's attention, he was able to recognize that he was avoiding painful material by being entertaining. He also realized that he had a long-standing pattern of attempting to curry favor from others by being the center of attention and by making them laugh. As it turned out, reflection on these issues was far more pertinent to the therapy than the worker's ongoing appreciation of this client's talents for showmanship.

Worker Reactions as a Diagnostic Tool Sometimes a worker's subjective reactions to a client can be useful as a diagnostic tool. For example, if a worker feels depleted after an interview with a client it may be a signal that the client is depressed, is dependent, or has passive-aggressive qualities. A client who is or feels helpless, deprived, or needy may prompt the worker to feel inordinately protective or to have the "urge to rescue." Irritation, frustration, or guilt may be the reaction to clients whose behavior is demanding, "manipulative," intrusive, or excessively ingratiating. Feelings of anxiety and loss of confidence may be the effect of overt or subtle criticism or devaluing of the worker by a client. Narcissistic, emotionally detached, or obsessive client styles may result in boredom or daydreaming by the worker. Obviously, *each worker's response is unique,* but, with experience, one becomes familiar with one's own particular reactions that may give clues to a client's personality qualities or inner state. Just as we have to substantiate theoretical hunches about our clients and their situations, speculations about diagnoses deriving from our own subjective responses must be *very* carefully verified on the basis of other data before they become part of our overall evaluations.

Handling Countertherapeutic "Slips" Inevitably, a worker, however experienced or self-aware, will inadvertently or impulsively disclose countertherapeutic reactions to a client. Whether these are based realistically on the client's behavior or are caused by something within the worker, they may be expressed in a way that is not in the client's best interests. When this happens, such reactions can often be turned to therapeutic use. For example, if a client senses anger and asks about it the worker should not deny it (this would be insincerity) but handle the situation realistically, depending on whether the response was appropriate to the client's actions or an overreaction; the worker's honesty can help to strengthen the client's trust. When it becomes clear that the worker and the client are interacting in a counterproductive pattern, usually the question is not whether to bring this up but how and when to do so. By taking responsibility for his or her part in the problem, the worker realistically acknowledges being "human" and capable of making mistakes. Of course, whenever a worker has acted in a countertherapeutic manner, it is important that the client be encouraged to express his or her reactions to the incident. The feedback is important for the worker and can give the client a feeling of being listened to and understood. The worker is thus demonstrating that even though people and relationships are complex, *open exchanges about difficulties that arise can often lead to resolution and growth.* For many clients, fearful of sharing feelings or of being blamed, the worker–client relationship can serve as a model for handling problems that arise with other people in their lives.

Positive Feelings The worker's expressions of regard or admiration for clients' abilities, achievements, or personal characteristics can often be very supportive. Experienced workers are aware of how significant it can be for some clients—particularly those who never felt authentically responded to—to know that they have an impact on the clinician; such "affective authenticity" sometimes can have enduring

meaning and promote emotional growth.[6] All such expressions must be screened and modulated according to their value to the client, not to the worker's pleasure in conveying them. But sometimes workers are so fond of certain clients that they respond in ways that are not therapeutic. For example, a worker may lavish so much praise, such as about progress being made, that the client feels obligated to keep pleasing him or her, even if in disagreement about how the therapy is working. Or the client may wonder if the worker is being insincere or sees the client as weak and in need of excessive bolstering. In some cases, the client may be led to believe that the worker is seeking a social relationship. In other situations, the worker may be too worried, protective, or overhelpful, which can detract from the client's efforts to make decisions that are part of the need to struggle and grow. When workers realize they have been oversolicitous, it is important to be forthright about this: "Were you afraid I was displeased when you said you were going back to your husband since I had praised you for having courage to leave him?" Or, "I guess I was so excited about your great job opportunity that I started offering advice that you really don't need!" Simple "I" statements and straightforward explanations are supportive but also respectful.

UNREALISTIC ATTITUDES AND RESPONSES
Transference

Early Life Transference When we speak of a client's unrealistic or *transference* reactions, we usually mean that the client displaces onto the worker feelings or attitudes originally experienced during early childhood toward a family member— most often but not necessarily the mother or father[7]—and responds to the worker as if he or she were, at least in some respects, this person. Often the transference is an unconscious or preconscious process. However, the client may be aware that the reaction to the therapist is extraordinarily intense; the client may sense feeling unduly angry with, fearful of, or adoring of the therapist. Strong feelings of longing or dependency may be stimulated by the relationship with the worker. In some cases, particularly if clients are unable to maintain an "observing ego" when flooded with strong emotion (as occurred at times during the treatment of Mrs. Zimmer, described in Chapter 3), they are unaware that their reactions are unrealistic, based on earlier experiences in relationships or deprivations; they often assume they are natural responses to the worker's actual personality or behavior. When clients exhibit unrealistic reactions and when it is thought that treatment will be facilitated by bringing these into awareness, the worker seeks opportunities to do so.

When the timing is right, and when self-understanding is a goal of treatment, we often make comments such as: "When you expected I would judge you, do you think you were bringing feelings here that you had when your father criticized you?" Or, gently, usually with a client with whom a strong relationship has been established: "Were you hoping I would pick up the job of making those telephone calls for information, even though you are able to make them for yourself? Does that remind you of the way your relationship with your mother went?"

Displacement Reactions A similar phenomenon can occur with displacement from later important associates: "Are you looking to me for advice about whether or not you should leave your wife? Or are you expecting me to tell you what to do the way you say your wife does?" As with any other reflective communication, the worker offers these questions in a way that encourages the client to consider them, then modify or reject them.

Transferred Personality Styles Equally important but less specific phenomena, still considered transference reactions, are those idiosyncratic behaviors or ways of relating to people that are brought into treatment, also derived from early experiences. These have become a part of the personality, whether or not the client identifies the worker in a direct way with early family figures. For example, clients who were raised in families where hardships and sorrows were dealt with by joking, or where intrusiveness was a family style, or where expressions of anxiety were basic to the way family members related to each other, often bring this style into the treatment relationship. Again, when timely, the worker might ask: "Have you noticed that when you feel the saddest, you try to kid yourself out of it?" Or, "I've noticed that you often express worry about my health when in fact I am perfectly well. What do you make of that?"

Identificatory Transference Wachtel adds another interesting aspect to this subject, which he terms *identificatory transference*. In this process, the client responds to the worker in ways that central figures from early life responded to him or her. For example, a woman who was dominated by an intimidating father might start treating the worker in this manner, even though in many parts of her life she is dependent and conciliatory. Again, if the treatment would be advanced by bringing the observation out in the open, Wachtel might suggest a gentle intervention such as: "When you began telling me in such strong terms how you thought I should furnish my office or rearrange the waiting room, do you think you were trying to convey to me what you went through when your father bossed you around?"[8]

Working with Transference   Just as it is usually therapeutic to encourage clients to express openly their realistic feelings toward the worker, discussion of the client's transferred negative or positive feelings can play an important role in treatment. There are times when the feelings can complicate or even obstruct it; they can interfere with client–worker communication. They can bewilder worker and client alike. When they are brought out into the open, they often provide the client with one of the richest sources of dynamic and developmental understanding and can be among the most useful components of the treatment relationship. A later section of this chapter, "The Client–Worker Relationship in the Dynamics of Treatment," discusses in fuller detail many of the ways in which transference plays a significant part in the treatment process.[9]

Countertransference

The worker is also sometimes unrealistic in reactions to clients.[10] Workers may identify clients with early or later figures in their lives; or they may bring into the treatment relationship distorted ways of relating to people that are part of their own personalities. They displace feelings, attitudes, and fantasies onto some clients more than onto others, depending on their life experiences. Although a very important part of a worker's training involves the development of awareness of these tendencies in order to keep them at a minimum, they are never completely overcome and may be part of the reality to which the client is reacting. The term *countertransference* is rather broadly used to cover not only these unreal-

istic reactions of the worker but also realistic responses, such as those discussed earlier; they may be induced by the client but are *potentially countertherapeutic* when not carefully monitored.

The Importance of Worker Self-Awareness   Sometimes beginning students have even greater difficulty becoming aware of countertransference of displaced feelings than they have mastering casework theory and skills. Irrational reactions can interfere with the therapeutic relationship and the treatment process; when activated, the worker's responsiveness and understanding can be impaired. Supervision, consultation, and trusted groups of colleagues that meet regularly to discuss clinical issues and countertherapeutic reactions are important to advancing self-awareness and detecting one's own "Achilles' heels" in responses to clients. Personal therapy (which we would encourage every clinical social worker to consider) can increase understanding of one's own reactions, prejudices, and relationship patterns. It may significantly increase the worker's ability to be sensitive to inner feelings and attitudes catalyzed by clients. It may also enhance one's humility and empathy to have a firsthand experience of "walking in the shoes" of the client.[11]

In general terms, workers need to be alert to their own issues including:

1. Vulnerabilities derived from family-of-origin relationships.
2. "Triggers" related to sensitive current issues (e.g., loss of a loved one, divorce, problems with difficult teenagers, a failing or dependent elderly family member, etc.).
3. Prejudices and stereotypes of all kinds, including the tendency to use labels such as "borderline" or "manipulative" to describe the whole person rather

than a condition or trait, or to designate families as "multiproblem" without being specific about in what part of the system the difficulties lie, and without balancing the appraisal with an assessment of strengths.

4. An "urge to rescue" or to foster dependency.
5. A tendency to deny pain.
6. Overidentification with pain or "vicarious traumatization."
7. Intolerance of client's "symbiotic" or "urge-to-merge" transference.
8. Irrational fear of anger from clients, especially toward oneself.
9. Urge to impose one's own agenda.
10. Frustration or loss of interest when change is slow or not apparent.

Handling Countertherapeutic Reactions in Treatment In sessions with clients, when one becomes aware of a countertherapeutic inner experience, it is particularly important to choose words or phrases even more carefully than at other times. As one reflects on the work one does, one must continually ask oneself questions such as:

- What are my responses to the character or behavior of this particular client?
- What client characteristics trigger intense reactions within me?
- Are these reactions realistic or derived from other life experiences or personality qualities of my own?
- If they are realistic, in what way (and when) might it be therapeutic to share these with the client?
- If unrealistic (in which case we rarely choose to burden the client with them), to whom or what in my life am I reacting? For example, do I feel overly protective toward this woman because of my early experiences with a chronically ill sister? Does this man annoy me because he is in some ways like my husband, with whom I

am having problems? Or is his managerial manner reminiscent of my father?
- Does this client's "resistance" threaten my sense of competence?
- Am I trying to elicit praise or gratitude from my clients to serve my own needs?
- Does this client's "motherly" manner or strength evoke my longing to have someone to lean on?
- Because I am a member of a society that fosters racist attitudes and class and ethnic biases, am I feeling superior (or inferior) to this client? Or is my compassion for the "underdog" so keen that I fail to truly understand the uniqueness of the particular victim of injustice to whom I am relating?

While these discussions of transference and countertransference are adaptable to all modalities of treatment, Chapters 14 through 17 will discuss issues specifically related to transference and countertransference in family and couple treatment.

Worker Burnout

"Burnout" has been a subject of deep concern among social workers for over two decades. When used to describe a condition experienced by direct service workers, the term can refer to such symptoms as emotional exhaustion; lack of interest in or detachment from the needs, pains, and aspirations of clients; cynical, punitive, or blaming attitudes toward clients; a sense that one's work has no meaning; feelings of alienation and lack of support; and hopelessness. These responses often lead to low morale, absenteeism, and job turnover. Burnout has been found among child welfare, community mental health, and family service workers, although contributing influences may vary. Sometimes workers no longer want to endure the pains and sorrows of their particular line of social work, be it working with people with AIDS or other terminally ill clients, abused children, or the deteriorating elderly, among many others; if all else fails, in these instances, the worker may consider a job change.

However, it has become evident that numerous other factors–including agency procedures and policies, understaffed agencies and huge caseloads, constraints of government and managed care organizations, ever-increasing demands for paperwork and reports, community attitudes, and desperate and unyielding societal problems that afflict clients—interact to create the burnout phenomenon. In this connection, as others have pointed out, it is not the workers who should be held primarily responsible for burnout. While individuals may find relief in stress-management training or peer support groups, until organizational and systems factors are addressed, burnout will not be eradicated. As discussed in Chapter 8, in their agencies workers can try to identify, confront, and ameliorate conditions contributing to stress, but often broader political or social action and changes are required.

Clients often feel discouraged about problems that are even more overwhelming than the worker's, and they need reassurance that something can change. But when workers are feeling tired, hopeless, isolated, or angry, they are often unable to mobilize the energy or optimism to help others. In addition to doing whatever they can to try to humanize their agencies and promote social changes, workers still have to determine how they can best take care of themselves and their own lives. This is necessary to be professionally effective, to say nothing of personally content. Even when working under the most benign conditions, workers' intense daily involvement in other people's heartaches and despair requires that they take pains to bring positive balance into

their own lives, that they take care of their personal relationships, and that on a regular basis they seek gratifying opportunities for recreation and renewal.[12]

PROBLEMS OF COMMUNICATION BETWEEN CLIENT AND WORKER

Specific Barriers to Effective Communication

Irrational Attitudes   As is already apparent, the nature of the feelings and attitudes (realistic and unrealistic) that exist between worker and client profoundly affects communication between them. If the parent of a child with schizophrenia is trying to describe the child's unreachableness to a worker who has negative countertransference attitudes to mothers and blames them for their children's difficulties, the worker may fail to understand the parent's communication, interpret it as rejection of the child, and fail to be alerted to this and other danger signals that point to the child's serious illness. Compounding the problem, the mother may sense the worker's reaction (even if it has not been made explicit) and screen her communications to please the worker or evade her criticism.

If a client, on the other hand, has identified the worker with an insincere, manipulating mother, he or she may construe the worker's efforts to communicate acceptance and encouragement as flattery with an ulterior motive. This type of misinterpretation can sometimes be overcome by repeated demonstration of the worker's sincerity and lack of desire to manipulate, but the process ordinarily can be greatly accelerated by bringing the client's distrust into the open. Then it can be recognized as a factor in the relationship and reacted to by the worker and perhaps be understood by the client, in dynamic or developmental terms.

Symbols Another source of distortion in communication is the assignment of different meanings to symbols. All communication, verbal and nonverbal, uses symbols, but if the two people trying to communicate do not assign the same meaning to the symbols, the communication will be distorted. A most important example of such distortion is the misunderstanding that can occur when the client has only a partial understanding of English and the worker does not speak the client's native language. (However, in the case of Mr. and Mrs. Chin described in Chapter 2, effective treatment was possible despite language limitations.) More subtle are differences in choice of words, which may be dependent upon class, education, ethnic background, age, region, and other variables. Not only do workers need to understand the full significance of their clients' words, but they must also be able to express their own ideas in terms that will accurately communicate their meanings to clients. This does not require, however, that workers adopt their clients' vernacular; to do so introduces falseness that is antitherapeutic. The client whose background differs greatly from the worker's does not expect the worker to be like him or her and might not come for help if this were the case. But there is a middle ground in which words can be introduced that particularly express the worker's meaning in the client's language. With most people, simple nontechnical, nonjargonized language is the most likely to be clearly understood. If there is some doubt about whether the client grasps the worker's meanings, it is important to encourage the client to say so: "If anything I say is not clear, please let me know."

It is usually helpful to bring concern about possible misunderstandings into the open, particularly when there are differences in background or age between worker and client. A worker might say: "Since you and I have been trained in different languages, let's make extra sure that we understand each other. If you find that you have trouble with any words I use, please let me know. And suppose I ask you to explain if I find I do not quite understand what you are saying." If the client uses slang or colloquialisms that are unfamiliar to the worker, it is not only necessary but also often supportive for the worker to say good-humoredly: "I am going to need your help with what you just said." Or an older worker might say to a teenage client, "I guess I'm not quite up to date; the slang of my generation is somewhat different from yours. Would you mind if I asked you about an expression you may use if its meaning is not quite clear to me?" Not only is communication enhanced but also a spirit of equality can be fostered by asking clients to share their expertise in areas in which the worker is not well informed.

Professing one's ignorance—be it about language, cultural beliefs, customs, and traditions, or any other matter—in no way diminishes the clinician. The professional who admits to lack of knowledge and asks for the client's explanations not only avoids misunderstandings related to the current topic of conversation, but—the act of careful inquiring—also conveys interest, attentiveness, and an eagerness to learn from clients about matters that are important to them.

Nonverbal Communications Actions or nonverbal communications are symbolic of feelings and attitudes. Facial expression, tone of voice, inflection, posture, gestures, eye contact (or lack of it), all convey meaning.[13] When the worker and client are of different backgrounds, nonverbal messages require particular attention, as is true for verbal exchanges between them. But even when people are of similar cultures, class, and education, nonverbal communications can be easily misunderstood. Often, workers will take it for granted that by their actions they have conveyed a particular feeling or attitude when they have not, or they may assume they understand the significance of a client's gesture or facial expression without exploring it further. Accurate communication requires that the worker be alert to any tendency to rely on suppositions about nonverbal messages; such messages often need verbal clarification because they are open to divergent interpretations. But the worker who consistently fosters a climate of openness and a recognition of the importance of collaborating to ascertain meaning will find that clients will usually follow suit and ask for clarification of ambiguous nonverbal communications.

The Elusiveness of Language   Clear communication of every kind is difficult to achieve.[14] Clarifying and qualifying statements we make and checking the meanings of messages received require an understanding of the complexity of communication and of the many subtle ways in which communication can fail. The same word or phrase has different meanings for different people or in different contexts. A client may use the word *we* and mean himself, himself and his wife, his entire family, or his social or cultural group. Similarly, people often say *you* when they mean *I* (e.g., "You get angry when your kids act up in public"). The phrase "Take it easy" can imply "Don't be hard on me," "Take good care of yourself," or "I'll see you again."

Also, the subjective connotation of a particular word varies. Even simple but charged words such as *mothering, discipline,* and *responsibility* call upon the worker to make sure their full meanings in the context of the conversation are mutually understood. Many messages, particularly those that attempt to describe inner emotional experiences, are next to impossible to convey thoroughly with words. Even when clients say they are

"heartbroken," "pained," or "in love," or use other words of equal intensity, the depth or quality of the feeling is not transmitted by the words themselves. Questions such as, "Can you tell me more about how it was for you when your mother died?" encourage the client to express more fully the meaning of his or her experience. Similarly, if the worker says, "I understand," the client can only begin to know the level on which the worker means this: Does the worker understand the facts or the feelings? Is the worker recognizing the truth in what the client says? Is he or she expressing empathy and caring? Sometimes when words are accompanied by nonverbal expressions the communication becomes clearer. For example, a sympathetic nod or a facial expression signifying that the worker feels a client's pain may help to clarify what is meant by "I understand." Of course, the possibility of misinterpretation must still be considered.

Assumptions   In everyday life, as well as in treatment sessions, people tend to fill in unknowns about what another person is saying with assumptions. Sometimes these assumptions can be very accurate. But one primary failure in communication derives from incomplete messages: A sends only a partial message and B, rather than asking A to elaborate, inaccurately completes it and acts upon it. For example, a worker may end a session with, "Shall we meet again at this time next week?" The client may assume the worker is not really asking for an opinion, but that the worker wants another meeting. Or a client may say something like, "I always enjoy sex with my husband," and the worker may assume that the client enjoys orgasm. Unless the worker seeks clarification, it may be much later before he or she learns that the client enjoys closeness and affection with her husband and gets pleasure from pleasing him, but that she is also disappointed that she has never achieved sexual climax.

The worker must continually attempt to get feedback from the client about his or her understanding of the worker's message, such as "What are your thoughts about getting together next week?" By the same token, when the client makes an incomplete statement, such as "I always enjoy sex," the worker can ask, "What do you find particularly satisfying about your sexual life?" By seeking clarification and feedback, the worker is more likely to elicit mixed feelings, disappointments, and other concerns. Along the same lines, when the worker has a hunch about a client's reaction, it is best to check it out: "You sound as though you were hurt by your husband's remarks. Am I right?" To this, the client can respond with "Yes, that's right," or she can correct the worker's impression by saying, "No, it's not that I feel hurt; rather I feel inferior, like a child, when he speaks to me in that way."

Ambiguities, Evasions, and Contradictions   To complicate the matter, unclear or incomplete communications are sometimes, consciously or unconsciously, designed to evade certain issues. The worker who simply said, "Shall we meet again at this time next week?" may have hoped to avoid hearing that the client did not want to return, or that the client would prefer another time that was not as convenient to the worker. And the client who did not elaborate on her concerns about never achieving orgasms may have been embarrassed to bring it up, or she may have felt that exploring the problem would be too painful to face. This does not mean that the worker should insist that clients discuss issues before they are ready to do so. It does mean that if communication gets precise enough, the worker can then be alerted to areas that may require further exploration in the future.

Communication problems occur when people send ambiguous and contradictory messages: when a worker suggests an appointment change *he* wants but implies it would be better for the client; when he shows anger or boredom but denies it; or when he articulates warm interest in a client but keeps the client waiting for an appointment without explanation. When the client says, "I really love my wife" and stiffens or frowns, or when he says, "I am angry at my wife" and smiles, he is sending two opposing messages simultaneously. Along similar lines, when a mother volunteers, "I love all my children the same," she may be saying this to avoid admitting to herself, the therapist, or both, "but Malcolm makes me furious." It is the worker's responsibility to enhance worker–client communication by persistently attempting to clarify conflicting communications. Satir wrote:

> The therapist must . . . see himself as a *model of communication* . . . he must take care to be aware of his own prejudices and unconscious assumptions so as not to fall into the trap he warns others about, that of suiting reality to himself. His lack of fear in revealing himself may be the first experience the family has had with clear communication. In addition, the way he interprets and structures the action of therapy from the start is the first step in introducing the family to new techniques in communication.[15]

Worker Inattentiveness   Compton and Galaway[16] identify several worker barriers to effective communication with clients. One, mentioned only briefly in this chapter, is inattentiveness of the worker. If the worker's mind wanders (or if one is excessively fatigued, restless, preoccupied, or slips into daydreaming), it is impossible truly to listen and respond to the client.

When the worker has lost concentration, it is advisable to say something like, "I'm sorry, Mrs. Dawes, I was distracted for a moment." Under some circumstances, a further explanation may be given. In any case, one may add, "I wonder if you would be kind enough to go over for me again just how you learned about your son's problem in school." Again, by demonstrating one's honesty and wish to understand, negative reactions to the worker's momentary lapse are usually offset. As Compton and Galaway point out, barriers to communication will seriously affect the validity and reliability of information received from clients and on which treatment plans and goals are based.

MUTUAL AGREEMENT AND COLLABORATION

In recent years, the trend has been toward a more relaxed client–worker relationship. Generally, the climate now is freer, less formal and distant. But even among psychosocial workers, there are differences in the extent to which they follow this trend. There are also variations to be considered on the basis of the client's needs, as we will point out later in this chapter.

Nevertheless, the worker generally attempts to promote an environment of equality in which he or she and the client *search together for answers* to the problems at hand. *Worker and client are both experts in their own right; they both share responsibility for how the treatment progresses.* The worker is trained to assess people's strengths and difficulties, to understand "the-person-in-situation" concept, and to use that knowledge and those treatment procedures that can help people find their own meanings, make changes, function more effectively, and enjoy life more comfortably. It is only our clients, however, who can know how dissatisfied they are, how they think

their current circumstances came into being, what their dreams and ambitions are, what changes in their situations or emotional reactions they are looking for, and whether they find treatment helpful.

How Treatment Decisions Are Made
Some agencies provide certain types of services that the client chooses either to use or to reject. Under these circumstances, it is the agencies that make the choices, deciding both what services to offer and who is eligible for them. For example, clients are not given a foster home for a child just because they want one, nor are they allowed to choose the type of foster home their children are placed in. Some agencies or practitioners specializing in certain brief treatment methods give the client little or no choice about the length of therapy; others may offer well-structured courses of treatment, such as some behavior modification or substance abuse programs, in which the client has relatively little input.

Generally, however, in psychosocial treatment, it is not only inadvisable but also almost impossible to impose treatment or goals upon a client. Except in certain aspects of protective work, when a worker in an emergency may be doing something specific against the client's will—taking a seriously psychotic or suicidal person to a hospital, placing a child who is being badly mistreated, reporting a delinquent's parole violations to the court—treatment and goal setting *always* involve the client's participation. Not only does the client have every right to reject casework service as a whole, but also any particular goal of treatment a worker may espouse.

The client can and often does negate the worker's efforts. The worker can offer wholehearted reassurance, but it will not be reassuring to the client who is unwilling to accept it or to believe in it. The worker can suggest and advise, but it is the client who chooses whether or not to follow the advice. The worker may feel sure it would be best for a client to end a marriage, to spend money more carefully, to change jobs, to deal with a drinking or weight problem, but only the client can decide from his or her point of view whether these plans are best and whether he or she wants to work toward them. Workers may try to stimulate clients to think about their situations or themselves; only the clients can *do* it. Interpretations are futile unless clients are willing to consider their validity. When they are not consulted, clients may be unable or unwilling to use the kind of help that is offered; they may show that they want (or can better use) something else. Under these circumstances, workers usually have to change their approach or lose their clients.

Psychosocial treatment is a *mutual* affair. A worker may suggest a particular course, with an explanation of why the suggestion is being made. But clients are encouraged to bring ideas and reactions to the worker's proposal; they are not simply invited to accept or reject it, but to modify or build upon it. *The more the client has participated in developing a working definition of the problem, and in formulating goals and plans for achieving them, the greater the motivation for change.* For example, when a worker unilaterally decides that a woman client should learn to see her children's needs more clearly, the client is then in the position of being led by the worker to gain a new perspective. When the worker asks the client *her* views of the children's needs, the worker may learn new information from the client and—even if the ultimate mutual goal that comes from this discussion is similar to the worker's original thinking—the worker is not imposing ideas on the client but is urging the client to share in construction of a plan, a solution.

Not only must client and worker participate together in the treatment process, but they also must reach an *explicit* mutual agreement about the nature of the treatment and its goals.[17] Clinical observations and research indicate that therapeutic efforts often fail without such a common definition or where there is a clash of perspectives between worker and client.[18] Disappointments, frustrations, unfocused treatment, and early terminations are among the dangers when there are "hidden" or "double" agendas or when divergent assumptions are made by worker and client. Throughout treatment, expectations and goals must be openly communicated by the worker and regularly elicited from the client as they formulate and reformulate or expand them together. The *therapeutic alliance* develops as a result of a deepening understanding between both as they arrive at a shared approach to their work together.

As suggested numerous times in this book, it is often best if the worker's remarks are framed as questions (e.g., "Do you think Lonnie is reacting to the divorce or to something else?" "Do you think there may be another way to encourage your husband to join our sessions?"). Or, at the end of a comment or suggestion, one may add: "Does that sound true to you?" "How do you see it?" Treatment is enhanced if the worker offers ideas with a built-in opportunity for the client to refute or modify them. This is so for several interrelated reasons: Client autonomy is fostered by the worker's expectation that the client may have a different or better notion; the client is not encouraged to be dependent on the worker for the last word; the client is urged to search for understanding from within; worker–client collaboration is reinforced; the worker may be under a misapprehension that only the client can correct; and the tendency of some clients to get stuck in oppositional resistance is neutralized.

We must be ever careful not to label our clients "resistant" simply because their views of problems, goals, or solutions differ from ours. Rather, it is our job to facilitate an *open discussion* of the divergent ideas in the hope that through ongoing reflection an agreed upon approach, in which the client has fully participated, will evolve. (The concept of resistance will be elaborated upon in Chapter 12.)

Mutuality is as complex as it is necessary. For example, parents may apply for help for their seven-year-old son's behavior problem in school. The immediate goal for the parents is the improvement of the boy's conduct. However, during the exploratory phase, the worker may get the impression that the boy is acting out some of the marital strains between the parents. Although initially the worker and parents mutually agree on the latter's goals, if it seems clear that change for the boy is unlikely unless the parents address the marital difficulties, it is the worker's responsibility to share these views with the clients at an appropriate time. After doing so, it is still the parents' choice, first, *whether* and, second, *how* they want to resolve the marital conflict. Often, the worker has to assume leadership in advancing goals or new options, but it is still the client's prerogative to accept or reject these, to modify them, or to offer alternative proposals.

There are also times when the worker, for ethical or other reasons, cannot agree upon goals advanced by the client. An extreme example is that of the woman who asked a worker to tell her young son that he could be arrested if he continued to wet his bed, on the belief that this would frighten him and "teach him a lesson." The worker could not agree to participate in this plan, but it was the worker's responsibility to explain why she could not and then to suggest that they reflect on the situation further to arrive at an alternative on which both could agree.

In no way do we imply that mutual agreement means that the worker's role is a passive one; in no sense is the worker abdicating responsibility—to the contrary, the worker is defining it. By explicitly stating that it is the client's task to learn to make choices and decide on what life plans are suitable, the worker is freed to offer expert help in the pursuit of mutually understood goals. This function is manifold: The worker can provide information the client does not have. The worker can give feedback about distortions or contradictions in the client's outlook or behavior (such as by asking a man to consider whether he thinks he will get the response he wants from his wife by berating her). The worker can lend active guidance to the client in the selection of treatment aims. He or she can recommend procedures within treatment sessions (such as suggesting that a couple discuss a problem with each other or that they make "I" statements rather than "you" observations). The worker can share ideas about means that experience demonstrates have been effective in solving problems or bringing issues into focus. The worker can explain, in terms the client can understand, that self-direction and developing a sense of mastery over one's life can be crucial to resolving person–situation difficulties or emotional distress; in this way, the worker urges the client to take responsibility for participating actively in seeking solutions and in giving the worker feedback about the treatment. Workers who are secure in their skills can distinguish which areas of expertise are theirs, and which must be the client's, and take responsibility for holding both to their jobs.

Mutuality provides an opportunity for the client to strengthen ego functions such as reality testing, judgment, competence, and autonomy. The treatment process itself can be an arena in which clients develop powers; locate resources, from within and without; and gain experience in effectively taking charge of their lives. (Even the "involuntary" clients, such as those seen by protective or probation workers, will be most successfully engaged and motivated if the worker makes it clear that their needs, concerns, visions, and goals are the stuff on which successful treatment depends.) With clients who expect to be given advice about what to do or how to live, the worker must take a particularly active role in helping them to begin to think and function independently.

Miss Clay, a timid 44-year-old single woman who lived with her domineering mother, came to a clinical social worker because she had begun to cry frequently and uncontrollably. Her job as a receptionist was jeopardized because of her tearfulness. Her mother, her older brother, and her boss, she complained, tried to manage her every move; they often ridiculed her and treated her as though she were incompetent. She resented them but was afraid to take independent stands of her own. In the early phase of therapy, she continually asked the worker questions such as: "Do you think I should move?" "Would it help if I changed jobs?" "Should I learn to drive a car?" The worker warmly but clearly told her that she was not going to direct her in making these choices since she had too many people running her life already. She would, however, talk over various aspects of the options she was considering. At first, the worker had to keep reminding Miss Clay that their purpose together was to help her reach her own solutions. As time went on, however, this client not only began mak-

ing decisions for herself but also was able to recognize the important part she played in encouraging others to treat her like a child.

The Contract Perhaps a mention of the *contract* would be helpful here. When this term is used to describe the explicit, conscious agreement between worker and client concerning the nature and aims of treatment, we endorse the concept. Sometimes, however, the contract is viewed as a formal, rigid, or binding (sometimes written) agreement. In our opinion, particularly when problems are complicated, neither the client nor the worker can easily arrive at what treatment will entail, how their perceptions of the situation may change, or what new issues or goals may arise as treatment progresses. At the beginning of treatment, the contract may simply be a mutual recognition of the fact that it may take time to determine the length and objectives of therapy. In the case cited above, the worker and client agreed that only as they worked together would it become clear what steps Miss Clay would want to take to feel better about herself. On the other hand, there are times when a worker may offer a suggestion such as "Why don't we meet together for six sessions and then, together, evaluate where to go from there?" This kind of approach or proposed contract can be reassuring to clients who fear they will be snared into an interminable treatment process; in other situations, it may mean that the worker believes the problem can be resolved quickly. We see little need for the written contract in psychosocial treatment (except, perhaps, around such concrete matters as fees). As long as there is open communication between worker and client and an understanding that client participation is highly valued and essential, too much literal dependence on a contract can be distracting and can seriously hamper the flexibility necessary to effective treatment.

WORKER SELF-DISCLOSURE

The question of worker self-disclosure in treatment has created considerable interest and disagreement among social workers. There are also various definitions of this complex concept. In this discussion, we will consider *two major ways in which clinicians may make themselves known to their clients:* (1) The worker's reaction to the client and (2) the disclosure of personal information.

The Worker's Reactions to the Client

It should be apparent from the previous discussion and examples given throughout this book that *authenticity* on the part of the clinician is not only acceptable but also desirable. That is, direct responses to clients *within* the interviewing room, when sought by the client or considered useful to the treatment by the worker, can have very positive effects.

Expressions of Sympathy or Empathy These can be very therapeutic when conveyed in a relevant and heartfelt way, modulated depending on the depth of the client's feeling and the assessment of the client's style. (Some clients, for cultural or personal reasons, are more formal than others, in which case a more controlled expression is usually best.) "I am so sorry this has been such a difficult time for you," can be said with varying degrees of intensity and discloses to the client an emotional side of the worker, which can demonstrate caring and genuineness and thus can have a comforting or healing effect.

Personal/Professional Observations Even when negative, observations can be usefully shared when carefully timed and relevant to the treatment. For example, in a couple session, one might remark: "As I listen to the two of you say such hurtful things to each other, I find myself wondering how you handle so much pain. I must say, it would be hard for me."

Positive Reactions to Clients' Achievements or Progress When genuine, accurate, and not excessive, such reactions are often supportive: "I am delighted that you were able to bring up that difficult subject with your mother as you hoped you would." "I can't tell you how impressed I am by the changes you have made so quickly."

Negative Reactions and Feedback Sometimes these are not only helpful to clients but also necessary for treatment to proceed. In the case of Mrs. Glass (see pages 236–37) the worker shared her increasing resentment about this client's clinging and stalling at the end of sessions. This disclosure not only solved the worker's problem but also led Mrs. Glass to reflect on some related behavioral and emotional patterns.

Authentic, Reasonable Expressions of Many Kinds There are many ways in which these can make the worker seem more like a "real" person. Admitting a mistake, taking responsibility and apologizing for inadvertently hurting a client's feelings or causing inconvenience, being good-humoredly open to suggestion or correction: all are ways of letting the client know the kind of person the worker is. Frequently, clients ask actually or in effect: "How can I believe you really care and are not being nice just because it is your job?" Sharing one's personality qualities and feelings, when these are compatible with the goals of the treatment, can foster trust and sometimes openness in clients. In words and/or actions, the worker's forthrightness sends the message: "You can count on me to say what I think or mean."

Workers' Statements about Their Own Personal Matters or Past History

Some practitioners—perhaps those most concerned about contaminating transference reactions—might not fully endorse even the kind of openness just described, but it is generally agreed that sharing of one's personality and responses to the client that are relevant to the treatment process is different from revealing information about one's personal life. Some aspects of one's interests or life situation are incidentally revealed (by office furnishings, books, a wedding ring, family photographs, and so on). Other aspects are inadvertently disclosed (such as by a chance meeting at a community function or restaurant, or by the discovery that worker and client have a friend in common). Observations by the client or accidental out-of-the-office encounters require decisions about how to handle them on a case-by-case basis; usually, the worker brings up the matters in a matter-of-fact manner, giving emphasis to eliciting the client's reactions to the information they have gleaned.

Clients' Questions It is not unusual for clients to seek information about the worker. At the *beginning of treatment,* it is their "right to know" certain aspects of the worker's background, particularly educational preparation, years of professional experience, expertise in the particular problem the client is bringing, be it substance abuse, eating disorders, serious mental disorders, difficult family relationships, and so on. In most situations, it is best simply to

answer such questions, discuss the client's responses to the answers, and go on.

However, once the treatment is under way, other considerations are part of the worker's decisions. When clients inquire about the worker's personal life (such as "Do you have children?" or "Where are you going on vacation?"), it may be best to give a brief, unelaborated response: "Yes, I have three," or "To the West Coast." Sometimes the clients do not seek further information because the motive for the question is simply to show appropriate interest. On many other occasions, however, there is pressure from the client to know more about personal matters: "Have you gone through a divorce?" "Did your teenagers give you the heartache mine have? What were they like?" "Do you go to church regularly?" "Are you straight or gay?" In these cases, occasionally it may be respectful to answer briefly again; more often one might, with a light touch, say something like: "I wonder what makes you ask about this?" If the response is comparable to "I just get curious," and the client has no other ideas about what the question means, this may be the opportunity for the worker to remark: "This is your hour, and cluttering it with discussions about me certainly distracts us from our major focus, don't you think?" Or: "In my experience, it can be confusing to treatment to bring in extraneous facts about my life. Once information is shared it may divert us or muddy the waters of our work. So, generally, I make a practice of not talking a whole lot about my life outside this office, particularly when we need all the time we can get to grapple with your concerns." In our opinion, it is difficult to assess—for worker and client—what the outcome would be if workers revealed themselves in response to a client's questions. By answering, sometimes the worker is colluding with the client who wants to avoid difficult material. In other cases, the client may disapprove of the worker's life choices or become overly involved in thinking about specifics of the worker's life. And, almost always, if the worker is a competent, disciplined, talented professional, his or her life situation is irrelevant and distracts both client and worker from their joint endeavor. For these reasons, we recommend that *sharing of personal information be very sparing.*

Probably the most common trouble new social workers have with clients' personal questions is how to avoid seeming evasive or withholding and still explore what might be behind a client's inquiry. Each clinician has to develop an approach that is comfortable and consonant with his or her style. Abrupt, defensive replies from clinicians—induced by feeling pressured by the client—can be hurtful and/or provoke a power struggle. In our experience, when the worker comfortably gives explanations for not answering, such as those mentioned above, or says, when it is true, "I don't really mind giving you an answer, although it seems a little remote from our current focus, but I am unclear about what you are really asking. Do you have an idea of what the difference would be to you if you knew for sure whether I was married, divorced, or single?" Sometimes the ensuing discussion becomes enlightening to clients, and the interest in their questions dissipates. In cases where the worker simply does not want to reveal the information because it is too private or might be disconcerting to the client, one may openly say so: "I really don't think I'll share that kind of private information with you, but I also don't want to hurt your feelings when it probably took courage to ask me the question. So let's talk a little more about what the question means to you and how you feel about my decision not to answer it." This kind of respectful, nondefensive forthrightness can enhance the relationship and yet give the client realistic feedback about the worker's boundaries.

Similar Experiences   Sometimes a client will share a feeling or information that triggers the worker to think about a comparable personal matter. The death of a family member, a divorce, experiences with bigotry, and many other situations clients talk about may evoke powerful feelings and memories in the worker. Sometimes the worker has a strong urge to share these responses with the client, even believing that trust or intimacy would be enhanced by doing so. But, unless one is *absolutely* sure that such sharing *serves the needs of the client* (and, in our view, that is very rarely) *and not the worker,* it is best to refrain from it, however tempting it may be. Even a partial disclosure, such as "I know what that is like," or "I've been through some very similar situations" can deflect attention from the client's concerns and can sometimes be experienced as the worker's self-absorption or lack of empathy.

Summary on Worker Self-Disclosure

From the psychosocial point of view, in a relationship based on mutuality, it is impossible, unnecessary, and generally untherapeutic for workers to try to seem anonymous or devoid of human responses. The client is usually put at ease by the natural expressions or spontaneity of the worker when, but *only* when, such openness serves the purposes of treatment. With experience, the worker naturally or intuitively gets to know which feelings or perceptions to share and which to withhold.

On the other hand, we strongly believe that the sharing of personal information that is not directly pertinent and deemed useful to the client's concerns or to the treatment relationship is usually contraindicated. (If the worker is ill, pregnant, or has a death in the family and meeting arrangements have to be changed, some matter-of-fact explanation is usually given, but the client's reactions to these events are what require the attention.) In some cases, personal disclosures may lead clients to worry about the therapist's stability or ability to focus on clients' needs. Furthermore, we see no justification for *ever* allowing the focus of treatment to be shifted more than *very* briefly (and only when there is a clear reason to do so) to discussing any aspect of the worker's personal life. Research in the area of therapist self-revelation is sparse, sometimes contradictory, and inconclusive. Our experience leads us to believe that the only responsible and professional position we can take is this: *For the most part, less is better!*[19]

THE CLIENT–WORKER RELATIONSHIP IN THE DYNAMICS OF TREATMENT

Thus far, we have been considering the elements that go into the relationship between client and worker. Now we turn to a closer examination of what part these elements play in treatment.

The Basic Therapeutic Relationship

The basic relationship first must be distinguished from the special uses to which elements in the relationship can be put. No matter what the form of treatment, the worker's attitude must be a positive one, with concern for the client's well-being; the worker conveys liking, respect, positive affective involvement, acceptance of the client as an individual, and a wish for that person to be happier or at least more comfortable and better able to handle situations.

Research on attitudes and attributes of therapists conducted by social work and other disciplines has resulted in remarkably consistent findings. A now classic study by Ripple, Alexander, and Polemis[20] found an

attitude of *positive encouragement* in the worker was the primary factor in both continuance of treatment and favorable outcome. The initial work with those clients who continued in treatment was characterized "by warmly positive affect, efforts to relieve discomfort, assurance that the situations could be at least improved, and a plan to begin work on the problem." On the other hand, "a bland, seemingly uninvolved eliciting and appraisal of the client's situation, in which the worker appeared neutral in affect" was strongly associated with discontinuance and with an unfavorable outcome in those clients who did continue despite the worker's lack of encouragement. Current research backs up these findings. Client ratings of therapist warmth, respect, interest, encouragement, and so on have indicated that clients who evaluated their therapists in a positive light showed greater levels of improvement. "Collectively," writes Beutler et al., who summarized research on therapist variables, "the quality of the therapeutic relationship . . . has consistently been found to be a central contributor to therapeutic progress."[21]

The frequently cited research of Truax and Carkhuff also found that positive outcomes in psychotherapy depended heavily on the quality of the patient–therapist relationship; three characteristics of the therapist were found to be strongly associated with patient improvement: *accurate empathy, nonpossessive warmth,* and *genuineness.* Our experience strongly supports the importance of these *core conditions.* A study of nine major review articles on research that studied relationship variables concluded, "There are few things in the field of psychology for which the evidence is so strong" as that supporting the "necessity, if not sufficiency, of therapist conditions of accurate empathy, respect, or warmth, and therapeutic genuineness."[22]

Frank stressed the importance of the therapist's ability to convey *hope and confidence* to patients.[23] Beck found that the *counselor's sense of competence* appears to be related to the client's perception of change.[24] The *emotional well-being of therapists* has been found to be related to good treatment outcomes.[25] Of course, the worker's positive personality qualities are not enough; knowledge of theory, competence, and experience can play an important part in treatment outcomes. But the freer the worker is of countertherapeutic communications, the more likely it is that the client will sense that it is safe to trust the worker and engage in treatment.

To achieve successful treatment outcomes, the client will need to have enough capacity to perceive the worker as trustworthy and to participate in the ongoing process. Reviewing the research, Beutler states: "Current literature . . . clearly indicates that the therapeutic relationship is not a therapist quality but is a set of processes that are dependent on both therapist and client."[26] Sometimes, in the early weeks of treatment, the client keeps coming because of external influences or feelings of desperation. The first task of treatment is to find a way of communicating the real nature of the worker's attitudes so the client will gain confidence in the worker as a therapist, counselor, or simply "helper." With many clients there are periods when the realistic view of the worker as a person to be trusted is obscured by unrealistic reactions, but these clients are usually carried over such periods by a previous positive perception.

Treatment Procedures and the Therapeutic Relationship

Sustaining Procedures In large part, sustaining procedures demonstrate the worker's goodwill and warmth toward the client. Variations in the use of these techniques with different clients should not depend upon the extent of the worker's positive feelings; they should reflect the worker's assessment or diagnostic understanding of a particular client. Some clients consistently need to have the basic therapeutic attitude demonstrated to them more clearly than others do. A client seeking concrete services may need information primarily and require only a minimum of support. When a particular client is passing through a period of anxiety, he or she especially needs to be aware of the worker's goodwill. When the client has strong positive transference feelings toward the worker, sustaining procedures will usually promote the positive side of the transference; this may take on an added significance to the client: a feeling that reassurance and love are being received from someone who was important in early life.

Clients with severe personality or psychotic disorders, although often able to benefit from reflective procedures, frequently need more support than other clients do, particularly—but not only—during the early phase of treatment. They usually need ongoing acceptance, comfort, and affirmation of positive qualities and achievements. But for most clients, overemphasis on sustaining procedures can create excessive dependency in terms of the realistic relationship and the transference components. "Optimum frustration," discussed in Chapter 2, fosters self-reliant functioning. Too much support can result in clients losing confidence in their abilities; they may get the impression that the worker sees them as inadequate in some way, in need of extraordinary bolstering. Therefore, sometimes we help by *not* being always available to speak with clients on the telephone, by expecting certain courtesies or adult behaviors rather than indulging immature functioning, by not "doing for" people what they can do for themselves.

Procedures of Direct Influence   For effectiveness, these depend in considerable part upon the client's confidence in the worker as an expert or as a responsible person with authority, particularly when persuasion and active intervention are required. Workers using these techniques must also have this self-image if clients are to take them seriously. Young workers in foster care agencies sometimes run into difficulty when they try to give advice to older foster parents who are many years their senior and far more experienced with children; these workers realistically lack confidence in their own competence, and this is conveyed to the foster parents. In these situations, and also when the gaps in age and experience are not so wide, it is almost always the best approach to discuss issues with a spirit of collaboration, with worker and client together arriving at a plan or solution. In Hollis's research (see Chapter 21), there was evidence that *directive procedures are more often used to help the client learn how to utilize interviews and the therapeutic relationship than they are to give the client advice about personal decisions.*

Exploration and Ventilation   These often require support and acceptance that go beyond simple sustaining procedures. The worker's *empathy,* or ability to feel *as if* he or she were the client, to experience deeply the client's feelings (without, as Carl Rogers and others have cautioned, ever "losing the 'as if' condition"[27]), can be highly therapeutic. When, for example, a client is grieving the death of a loved one or is filled with anxiety, the worker's profound understanding of the pain or desperation can bring relief.

Person–Situation Reflection   This may be introduced to bring the treatment relationship into discussion. In the types of procedures just considered, the worker's attitude is *demonstrated* but not actually discussed. But now the client's reactions to the worker are brought into the open, and the client is invited to compare these with what the worker presents as the reality of the situation between them. In the process, the worker becomes better informed about the client's reactions and, in some instances, may get some useful feedback (for example, a client may say, "You seem a little less energetic than usual"). When the client's perception is accurate, the worker usually acknowledges the fact and, at times, offers an explanation ("You may be right; in hay fever season my allergies act up and can be a little draining, but I assure you I am paying close attention.") If, on the other hand, the client has misinterpreted or distorted the worker's attitude ("I almost didn't come back because I thought you were feeling impatient with me"), the worker has the opportunity to straighten out the matter ("I wasn't at all impatient with you; in fact, I think what you may have picked up was my enthusiasm about your plan to find new ways to talk things over with Peter. I'm surprised that seemed like impatience to you, but I'm glad you let me know.") In either case, the worker has an opportunity to clarify the matter and to build a therapeutically positive relationship through which the clients can learn a great deal about themselves, their reactions and ways of relating, and how straightforward discussion can strengthen a relationship.

The Corrective Relationship   The reparative or corrective relationship experience is of utmost importance in many treatments. The nature of the worker's activities in helping clients think reflectively about themselves and their situations often conveys to clients respect for and confidence in them. The fact that the worker refrains from excessive advice giving or from condemnation and demonstrates interest in clients' opinions may establish the worker as different from parents who have been critical or controlling. This may encourage strong positive feelings toward the worker, based on the reality of the relationship. Sometimes reflective discussions are buttressed by the worker's *sustaining attitudes* and by a *mild form of direct influence* that encourages pleasurable, psychologically healthy activities discouraged in the past by restrictive or angry parents.

This particular *combination of procedures* that are employed in a corrective relationship was referred to by Austin as "experiential" treatment. Usually the client has at first regarded the worker as a parent substitute, anticipating, because of transference reactions, that the worker will respond to verbalizations and behavior as the client's parent would have done. When the worker reacts differently, the effect of the early parental situation is partially corrected. Clients, responding to the worker as to a parent, are now accepted in ways they felt they were *not* by the true parent; one could say that the worker offers a *liberal emotional education* instead of the restrictive one originally experienced. The worker's consistently therapeutic attitude toward clients is realistic in enlightened terms, represents adult reactions (in the sense of both privileges and responsibilities), and is consistently accepting of clients and their needs. Although the second experience does not efface the first, it can do much to counteract it.[28]

In current clinical practice, clients are often diagnosed as having some type or types of personality disorder. (See Chapters 2 and 11 for further discussions of personality disorders.) In certain of these disorders, client difficulties may spring not from oversevere parenting but from inconsistent, neglectful, or even overindulgent parents. These clients, who in their early years were deprived of reliable nurturance and/or well-timed encouragement of independent functioning, are likely to manifest self-defeating traits or some kind of developmental disorder. In all of these, the realistic and transference relationships to the reliable, caring worker—the corrective experience—can facilitate the closing of developmental gaps and the resumption of the growth process that had been interrupted or distorted at some point.[29]

When the problem is one of "acting out," the corrective feature in the relationship may be that the worker comes to represent a pattern of stronger ego controls than the individual has previously experienced. Sometimes the main therapeutic task is helping clients to find ways to refrain from behavior that causes them trouble. In these corrective relationships, it is most important that clients see the therapist as someone who does not stand for an overly restrictive life and is not disapproving, but who is interested in helping clients find ways not to defeat *their own ends* by activities that inevitably boomerang.

As discussed on page 249, it was necessary for Miss Clay (who had traits of a dependent personality disorder) to experience a relationship in which her thoughts, feelings, and capacity for making her own decisions— in short, her independence—were valued rather than denigrated. For clients with borderline personality disorders, the corrective aspects of the relationship may involve the worker demonstrating consistent caring, optimism, patience, and the ability to handle hostility without either retaliating or withdrawing. The work with Mrs. Zimmer, discussed in Chapter 3, illustrates this kind of relationship.

An important facet of the corrective relationship is the effect it can have on the client's self-image. We know that children often see themselves as their parents see them. When clients have unrealistically dismal pictures of themselves and the worker holds a more optimistic view, this attitude can be conveyed to the client in many ways. In the context of a transference, such an attitude can powerfully affect the client's self-image. It can be even further strengthened if, through developmental reflection, clients become aware of the sources of their self-devaluation and understand how certain experiences gave them unrealistic pictures of themselves. Sometimes clients blame parents for their parts in the problem. Sooner or later these feelings may be dissipated, either by gaining understanding of why parents behaved the way they did or at least by realizing that the ways they were treated were never a reflection of their personal worth. Once a person's self-esteem is strengthened by these processes, he or she is far more likely to manage life's ups and downs and to find and maintain nurturing relationships outside the treatment situation.

Sometimes, as the chapters on environmental work and family therapy explain, corrective work can be facilitated by bringing the client's parents into treatment sessions. When it is possible for a client to get realistic reactions, acceptance, and support from parents themselves rather than indirectly through the positive relationship with the worker, the therapeutic work may be accelerated. One small sign of parental caring and encouragement may be as effective as many sessions with a supportive worker. The uncovering of misunderstandings or the sharing of regrets often can start healing between the generations.

The client's self-image is often affected in a special way by the worker's "therapeutic optimism." Although one can never know in advance the actual outcome of a phase of treatment, on the basis of training and experience, the worker does foresee the possibility that as a result of therapy the client will be more comfortable, more effective, or both; if there were not some hope of this, there would be no justification for continuing the contact. Such therapeutic optimism can have a corrective effect by being perceived by clients as meaning that someone believes in their possibilities and sees them more positively than they see themselves. (Even in the absence of the transference and life experience upon which the corrective relationship treatment is based, the worker's optimism affects the client's self-image and is an important element in treatment. The Jones marital case in Chapter 3 illustrates this point.)

The Client's Identification with the Worker

Another fairly frequent factor in successful treatment springs directly from positive reality feelings about the worker, often reinforced by a positive transference. Clients frequently say, in describing a difficult current happening in their lives, "I tried to think, 'What would____(the worker) do about that?' And then I said____." What they then say is often close to what the worker has said to them under similar circumstances. The phenomenon is sometimes referred to as the worker's "lending the strength of the ego" to the client. It is an imitative sort of learning, similar to a child's learning from copying the parent with whom he or she identifies, in ways that may then be incorporated in a lasting way into the client's personality.

It is often thought that this type of identification is accelerated by assigning a worker who is of the same sex, a similar age, has the same sexual orientation, and sometimes the same race or ethnic background as the client. In our experience, this may or may not always be necessary or even advisable. When there is too much similarity, the worker may have to work hard to guard against the possibility of overidentifying with the client and overusing the transference. For example, a young worker may become overly involved in struggles a young adult client is having separating from parents. Or a gay clinician may become excessively emotionally engrossed in life struggles or indignities reported by a gay client. A recently divorced practitioner may have unresolved bitterness that skews reactions to a client whose marriage is breaking up. While most trained workers will not blatantly try to impose their own feelings or values on a client, under these circumstances one must be especially alert to subtle communications derived from overidentification.

Diagnosis Factors

These factors can affect a client's transference reactions. For example, a man with an obsessive-compulsive disorder may be so eager to be a perfect client and please the worker that he takes on a deferential attitude. At the same time, his unconscious need to control may influence him to resist the strong positive involvement in the therapeutic relationship necessary for change to occur. Discussing these transference reactions can be central to helping him to reflect on his ambivalence toward treatment and on the conflict between his strong need to win favor and his anxiety about intimacy or loss of control. When the difficulty is a borderline disorder, the client may suddenly vacillate between seeing the worker as "all good" (the loving,

perfect parent) and "all bad" (depriving and uncaring). This kind of defensive "splitting" may lead the client alternately to cling to and distrust the worker. The quality of the transference not only helps in formulating the diagnosis but also becomes a useful tool in treatment. With Mrs. Zimmer (Chapter 3) the transference and subsequent reflection on the extreme reversals in the ways she experienced the worker were basic to her progress in integrating her "good" and "bad" feelings about herself and others.

Dynamic and Developmental Reflection and Transference Reactions

These often go hand in hand in the treatment process. As we have said, clinical social workers often use transference reactions to help their clients increase self-understanding of patterns of behavior or early life experiences. However, the therapist–client relationship in clinical social work, particularly in its transference aspects, differs from that in psychoanalysis. Repressed (in contrast to suppressed, preconscious) emotion and conflicts, for example, are not usually brought into consciousness although their derivatives often are. The cases of Mr. Kennedy in Chapter 3 and Jed Cooper in Chapter 20 illustrate this point.

Mrs. Zimmer's situation was somewhat different. The feelings she transferred to the worker were not repressed; rather they were raw, chaotic, undifferentiated emotion that emerged under stress or intensity because of flaws in early ego development. She was unaware of some of the specific sources of her emotional reactions because many of the inconsistencies in her upbringing occurred before she could speak or remember. For some time she did not realize she was displacing childhood feelings—such as rage, despair, terror—onto the worker. Ultimately, though, she became keenly aware of the vacillations in all her relationships, including the treatment relationship. In addition to the supportive, "ego-building," and corrective functions of the relationship, developmental reflection also provided her with the opportunity to understand the probable origins of the extremes within her and to work productively toward consolidating these.

Some clinicians are fearful of going too deeply into the transference, taking the position that transference reactions should not be interpreted for the purposes of aiding the client's self-understanding but discussed only as necessary for the maintenance, or restoration, of a positive relationship. (The reasons for this position are beyond the scope of this chapter, but for the most part relate to concern about uncovering repressed material.) In our opinion and experience, however, there is no more danger in touching on transference responses to the worker than in commenting on unrealistic reactions as these emerge in other areas of clients' lives.

Among the procedures used in reflective consideration of pattern-dynamic and developmental content are those that help the client to understand dynamically some of the transference and other unrealistic responses to the worker and the way in which these responses repeat earlier reactions to parents and other closely related people. The client can then put this self-understanding to use in recognizing similar reactions as they occur in current life situations outside of treatment. With these insights, the client is in a position to correct distortions and to respond to people more realistically. We deprive the client of a potent source of help in the struggle toward realistic living if we neglect to use the vivid "here-and-now" experiences that occur between client and caseworker.[30]

A FURTHER WORD ON CLIENT–WORKER MUTUALITY

The tendency in recent years to move toward greater informality and mutuality in the treatment relationship is regarded by the writers as a sound one. It is appropriately responsive to widespread distaste for anything that approaches authoritarianism. Of course, we do not favor a climate so casual that the client assumes the worker is encouraging a social relationship, in which case very obvious and realistic difficulties can ensue; the limits should always be made clear. But we do endorse a caring, professional relationship that avoids aloofness and that fosters as much equality as possible, a working alliance in which the client participates actively in the treatment process and in the selection of treatment objectives.

Very real questions arise, however, concerning the degree of informality and expressed warmth that is useful under different circumstances. This is particularly so when self-understanding is an aspect of treatment and in certain types of corrective relationships. For the most part, there is agreement among psychosocial workers that neither a cold, intellectual approach, on the one hand, nor a "hail fellow well met" stance, on the other, is appropriate. But some tend to favor a fairly formal relationship, especially for those clients who have difficulty becoming aware of negative feelings. These practitioners point out that a worker can be so "relaxed" or "kind" that the client is inhibited from expressing even those negatives of which he or she is keenly conscious. Similarly, they maintain, the client can see the informal worker as such a "real person" that transference fantasies or irrational feelings may not get a chance to come to the fore. The less giving, restrained relationship can help to intensify these, making it more possible for the client to become aware of them while attempting to develop self-understanding.

Other caseworkers lean toward a more relaxed relationship out of concern for those clients who require strong support and an easygoing manner to feel safe enough to share their feelings and fantasies. They point out that in some cases, when the worker is too formal, clients can be inhibited from sharing personal reactions for fear they will be criticized or misunderstood. Clients have been known to terminate treatment prematurely because they felt "put on the spot" by a worker's reserve.

These differences may not be as great as they seem on the surface. A middle ground between the two positions can be found, even though a worker's emphasis is necessarily influenced to some degree by his or her natural personality style. But, in our view, the approach should depend primarily on diagnostic assessment. For example, particularly in the first months, Mrs. Zimmer required a great deal of sustainment and open encouragement to trust the worker enough to engage in long-term treatment. A remote stance would probably have been so anxiety-producing that she would have discontinued therapy. Furthermore, she had no difficulty in becoming aware of strongly negative reactions to the worker, even in the face of the worker's warmly outgoing approach. An important aspect of the therapy involved helping Mrs. Zimmer to contrast her angry accusations about the worker's lack of interest with the worker's actual attitudes and behavior. Since this worker had been consistent in actively helping, in demonstrating that she cared, willing to be available by telephone in times of stress, and so on, it was possible

to confront Mrs. Zimmer with her distorted reactions. A more withholding approach might well have confirmed her skewed view that the worker was indifferent or hostile to her. Effective work in the Kennedy, West, and Stone cases (also in Chapter 3) and the Carter case (Chapter 20) required a worker with a warm, active, flexible approach to reach out to the clients and their family members. A rigid, subdued, or humorless worker probably would not have been able to engage or help these clients. On the other hand, there are many people who feel so guilty about angry, competitive, or "unkind" feelings of any sort toward the worker that they have difficulty expressing these in a climate of relaxed friendliness; they feel more "justified" in sharing them when the therapeutic relationship is less giving than it was in Mrs. Zimmer's case. Certainly, research in this area would be useful to refine our knowledge and help us to distinguish the conditions under which one or the other emphasis is most effective. But lacking that, as we see it, the choice should depend more on the client's personality and circumstances than on the worker's need for reserve or for camaraderie.

The question also arises as to whether it is accurate to say that a "corrective" relationship, in which the worker is in some measure seen as a "good parent," is truly "mutual" or "equal." For example, Mr. Kennedy (again, see Chapter 3) turned to the worker for nurturance or "mothering" before he could mobilize himself to begin to take constructive action. The temporary positive transference relationship, in which he was indeed dependent and in that sense unequal to the worker, gave him the support he needed to arrive at his own decisions. On the other hand, certainly mutuality was evidenced by the fact that at no time did the worker use the relationship to attempt to induce Mr. Kennedy to resolve his predicament in a particular way; the success of the treatment depended on the fact that he made his own choices and carved out his own directions. The objectives of treatment, to reduce his depression and to find satisfactory solutions to his situation, were mutually understood and agreed upon. In some instances, then, equality per se may be temporarily limited because of the client's need for dependence. The client may need to lean heavily on a worker, sometimes in an almost childlike manner. Yet even when this is so, the overall goal of any treatment is to help the client become as self-reliant and autonomous as possible. As we see it, mutuality—in the sense that worker and client come to a shared agreement about the course and purposes of treatment—must be carefully preserved in every therapeutic relationship.

NOTES

1. Beck (1988), p. 27; as she reports, practice experience and research findings agree on the critical importance to outcomes of the counselor–client relationship (p. 11). See also the Beck and Jones study (1973), pp. 128–29; Beutler, et al., (1994), pp. 243–44; Orlinsky, et al. (1994); and Lambert (1982).
2. Over the years, clinicians and research findings have identified therapist characteristics that are important to successful treatment relationships and positive outcomes. See Frank (1959 and 1968) and Smaldino (1975) on the role of hope. Keefe (1980) and Raines (1990) emphasize the importance of empathy (see Chapter 2, note 2 for more references on empathy). Truax and Carkuff (1967), especially pp. 176–89, identified accurate empathy, nonpossessive warmth, and genuineness as strongly associated with client improvement (see notes 20 through 25 and 27 in this chapter for additional references; the section on dynamics of treatment further discusses these issues).

Coady (1993) argues that despite emphasis on the importance of the worker–client relationship over the years, and despite research findings in psychology and psychiatry (several of which he cites) that confirm its role in treatment outcome, recently social work has given more attention to theoretical and technical aspects of practice than to relationship factors; Howard Goldstein (1990a) makes a similar point.

3. See two very good articles on engaging and treating adolescents: Mishne (1996) and Zayas and Katch (1989). See a succinct article by Rubenstein (1996) on adolescent development, behavior, and clinical intervention.
4. See especially Burstein (1988) who discusses ethical and practice issues related to involuntary aging clients. For references on elderly in institutions, see Cook (1980) and Wetzel (1980). Additional references on work with elderly clients can be found in Chapter 3, note 5.

   For further references on engaging reluctant or involuntary clients, see Chapter 5, note 7; Chapter 6, note 3; Chapter 8, note 19; and Chapter 10, note 5. References on home visits can be found in Chapter 10, note 14.

5. In an interesting article Comas-Diaz and Jacobsen (1987) discuss the use of "ethnocultural identification" as a therapeutic tool that can promote and consolidate the client's sense of identity. See also Dungee-Anderson and Beckett (1995) who discuss, with the aid of a case example, failed communication in cross-cultural work. See references on race ethnicity, gender, class, and same sex orientation in Chapter 2, notes 37, 38, and 39. See also Chapter 8, note 23.
6. See an excellent and recommended paper by Reiter (1995) who discusses the healing effects of the clinician's modulated "affective authenticity."
7. See an interesting and useful discussion by Coleman (1996) on sibling transference.
8. Wachtel (1993), pp. 99–103.
9. For readers who are engaged in clinical work, we highly recommend a book by Kahn (1991) on the therapeutic relationship. In this engaging volume, he gives background

on Freud's discovery of transference and discusses its development and use in treatment
by various psychotherapeutic approaches.
From a self-psychology perspective, Goldmeier and Fandetti (1992) discuss the use of
transference with elderly clients and include
case illustrations.

10. A book by Gorkin (1987) discusses the evolving
definitions of countertransference and has
chapters on some of its aspects, including: on
its use as a source of information, on sexualized
responses, on reactions to suicidal patients, on
its occurrence in cross-cultural relationships,
and on its appearance in supervision.

   We especially recommend two articles:
Comas-Diaz and Jacobsen (1991) and Perez
and Foster (1998) discuss important considerations of countertransference in cross-
cultural therapeutic relationships. See Grayer
and Sax (1986) on the diagnostic and therapeutic uses of countertransference. Gabriel
(1991) and Dunkel and Hatfield (1986) address countertransference reactions in working with persons with AIDS. See also Rhodes
(1979) who distinguishes countertransference
reactions from worker personality traits.
Schamess (1981) discusses countertransference and boundary issues. See Sprung (1989)
on transference and countertransference in
work with older adults. Teitelbaum (1991) addresses the potential for hurting clients with
countertransference reactions.

   See also Kahn (1991) on countertransference in Chapter 6; and Elson (1986), Chapter
6 on transference and countertransference.

11. Mackey and Mackey (1993) report on an interesting qualitative study of 15 experienced
social workers and 15 second-year graduate
students. All but one student indicated that
therapy had helped them as clinicians. The
findings suggest some indicators of how personal therapy may enhance practice. See
also Mackey and Mackey (1994).

12. For useful readings on burnout see Beck
(1987), Cournoyer (1988), Jayaratne and
Chess (1984), Keefe (1984), Oktay (1992),
Powell (1994), Ratliff (1988), Streepy (1981),
and Walsh (1987).

13. See essays by Birdwhistell (1970), a pioneer
in the study of nonverbal communication.

14. For a clear and very helpful summary of the
importance and some of the difficulties involved in achieving functional communication see Satir (1983), especially pp. 79–115.
See also Watzlawick (1978). For discussions
of communication between worker and
client, see Rumelhart (1984) and Seabury
(1980). For additional references on communication, see Chapter 2, note 44.

15. Satir (1983), pp. 125–26.

16. Compton and Galaway (1994), pp. 312–17.

17. The concept of the "contract" between
worker and client was first widely accepted
by social workers in the 1970s. See the classic article on this by Maluccio and Marlow
(1974). See also Sirles (1982).

18. This recognition also captured the interest of
social workers in the 1970s. See, for example, Maluccio (1979), Mayer and Timms
(1969), and Silverman (1970).

19. Every clinician is challenged to develop a point
of view about how to handle self-disclosure.
We highly recommend the following readings:
Anderson and Mandell (1989), on the basis of a
review of the literature, suggest guidelines for
use of self-disclosure; 365 clinical social workers surveyed indicated that self-disclosure has
gained acceptance over the years. See Eda
Goldstein (1994 and 1997) for interesting,
thoughtful, and helpful discussions with case
illustrations. In his balanced and useful article, Raines (1996) suggests six guidelines for
self-disclosure. Palumbo (1987) discusses spontaneous self-disclosure. Wachtel (1993) devotes
Chapter 11 to the prospects and pitfalls of self-
disclosure.

   Beutler, et al. (1994), pp. 256–57 think it
is possible that the dearth of research on
self-disclosure can be attributed to the complexity of the matter, such as how the information is disclosed and what is disclosed;
they do indicate that there are *tentative*
findings that some kinds of therapist self-
disclosure may have a positive effect on
clients' symptomatic improvement.

20. Ripple, et al. (1964).

21. Beutler, et al., p. 244 (1994). Social work researchers Beck and Jones (1973) and Beck (1988) came to similar conclusions.

22. Quoted by Beutler, et al., p. 243. See also Truax and Carkuff (1967), pp. 176–89. These studies and others suggested that therapists who are accurately empathic, genuine, and nonpossessively warm, regardless of training, modality used, or theoretical approach, are effective with a wide range of problems and client populations in a variety of treatment settings. Clearly, as is true of every aspect of research about treatment, further work is needed to ascertain under what special conditions improvement occurs. However, our clinical experience and that of many of our colleagues convince us of the therapeutic *and* humanistic value of these worker characteristics, although certainly they are explicitly expressed in varying degrees, depending on the needs of the client, the treatment situation, and the personality of the worker. Furthermore, as indicated in this chapter, we do not believe that these worker characteristics are *sufficient* conditions for successful treatment; competence of the worker and client motivation and perception of worker qualities and attitudes are among many other factors that must be considered. For further discussions of therapist relationship attitudes, see Beutler, et al. (1994); on client variables, see Garfield (1994).

23. Frank (1959 and 1968).

24. Beck (1988), pp. 33–34.

25. Beutler, et al. (1994), p. 238.

26. Ibid., p. 244.

27. Rogers (1966), p. 409. Rogers coined the familiar term *unconditional positive regard,* a concept generally accepted by social workers as a necessary attitude toward clients.

28. Austin (1948) developed theory and practice principles of the corrective relationship; Blanck and Blanck (1979) wrote about the reparative relationship. From a perspective of attachment theory, Sable (1992) discusses the safe, stable treatment relationship that provides a secure attachment, a climate in which clients can explore life experiences, especially those related to attachment, separation, and loss; Sable makes a clear distinction between attachment and dependency; her approach has much in common with the corrective or reparative experience. For additional readings on attachment and loss and related matters, see Chapter 2, note 16 and Chapter 14, note 46.

29. See Chapter 3, note 9 for references on personality disorders.

30. For additional readings relevent to the client–worker relationship, see the following: Abramson (1985), Duncan (1997), Edwards and Bess (1998), Elliott (1984), Fox (1993), Gitterman (1989), Goering and Stylianos (1988), Howard Goldstein (1990b), Kadushin and Kadushin (1997), Lammert (1986), Marziali (1988), Marziali and Alexander (1991), Perlman (1979), Proctor (1982), Sands (1998), Shulman (1992) and Siporin (1988 and 1993).

Biestek (1957) published a classic text on the casework relationship that is still being used. See his brief but very well expressed analysis of the relationship in the December 1994 issue of *Families in Society,* pp. 630–34.

We recommend an interesting compilation of papers edited by Gilligan and Price (1993) on therapeutic conversations.

PART THREE

DIAGNOSTIC UNDERSTANDING AND THE TREATMENT PROCESS

CHAPTER 10

INITIAL INTERVIEWS AND THE PSYCHOSOCIAL STUDY

Thus far we have considered the frame of reference upon which psychosocial casework treatment rests. We have discussed various means and procedures by which the worker endeavors to enable clients to improve their lives. The importance of the client–worker relationship to successful treatment has been emphasized. We must now turn to the more specific question of how treatment is related to a particular individual, couple, or family confronted by the need to cope with practical, personal, or interpersonal problems.

Treatment begins from the moment of the first contact, even when client and worker initially speak over the telephone or when an agency receptionist greets an individual or family. The subjects of this and the next three chapters—social study, diagnosis, selection of treatment objectives, and choice of treatment procedures—are inevitably intertwined. They are also always going on at the same time. Nevertheless, we

artificially try to separate them in order to analyze each of these aspects of the therapeutic process.

Psychosocial casework emphasizes the importance of trying to understand what an individual's or family's dilemmas are: above all, how does the client view the current situation? What does the client hope to achieve? What seems to be contributing to the troubles or concerns? In this way, worker and client together build the basis upon which treatment is tailored to ameliorate the problem(s) presented. This mutual understanding rests first upon an accurate and adequate factual base that is obtained primarily though not entirely in early interviews. It is called the *psychosocial study*.

It is extremely important to be clear about the difference between psychosocial study, a process of gathering facts, and diagnostic understanding. Psychosocial study involves careful listening, observation, and orderly arrangement of the *facts* about a client and his or her situation. Diagnostic understanding represents *the thinking about* the facts: the *inferences* drawn from them. It will be strongly influenced by the theoretical frame of reference used for guidance in understanding the meaning of the facts. Mary Richmond quoted Dr. Richard Cabot: "In social study you open your eyes and look, in diagnosis you close them and think."[1] While social study and diagnosis usually go on simultaneously, with open exchange of information and ideas between worker and client, these diverse processes should be kept separate in the worker's mind; otherwise, there is great danger of skewing the facts to fit the theory, asking questions in such a way that answers based on *a priori* assumptions are likely to emerge. Psychosocial casework emphasizes seeing understanding as a *collaborative effort,* not an analysis that is either implicitly or explicitly imposed by the worker upon the client.

From the beginning, client and worker decide upon the course treatment will take, depending primarily on the nature of the difficulties and on the client's goals. However, as the contact continues, clients often develop a different understanding of their troubles and become interested in addressing issues for which they did not at first have any motivation. Frequently clients' definitions of their concerns and salient issues evolve over time, simply by talking things out to someone or because the worker has enabled them to reflect on matters differently.

The worker's contribution to the course treatment takes depends upon knowledge of the nature of the individuals seeking treatment, of the current situation, of interactions within the person–situation system, and of the variety of factors that are involved in the clients' predicaments. This seeking of understanding is a continuous process, although it is emphasized especially in early interviews. It goes hand in hand with the treatment

process, and as treatment continues, new understandings emerge.

To the collaborative effort to achieve understanding and arrive at decisions about how to proceed, the worker brings a balance of: (1) professional knowledge and skills, including the determination to listen to and discern what matters to the particular client; (2) professional experience; (3) a broad range of life experiences; (4) self-awareness, as discussed in Chapter 9, that works to protect against countertherapeutic attitudes or reactions, including the urge to rescue or to impose meanings or goals upon clients; (5) personal endowments and talents, including an ability to relate to others empathically, to bring perspective and balance; (6) capacity for critical, analytical thinking; and (7) intuitive, creative faculties (which we will discuss shortly).

Clients' participation in the treatment depends, in part, on: (1) the capacity and willingness to explore themselves, their relationships, or their surroundings: the issues that relate to their present concerns; (2) the ability to begin to arrive at their *own meanings* and definitions of their circumstances; and (3) the growing motivation to take action that will modify or improve their current circumstances. Based on these, the worker and client will make choices about the duration and nature of treatment.

THE INITIAL INTERVIEW

Anticipatory Preparation

Even before meeting a client or family, there is often some information, however minimal, available to help the worker prepare for the initial interview. This anticipatory preparation can be of two kinds.[2]

Cognitive Preparation Cognitive preparation is based on thoughts the worker has about clients and their situations. If, for example, it is known that the home of a family one expects to see for the first time has burned down or a family had to move in with relatives because there was no heat or hot water, the worker might immediately consider possible resources for temporary housing. Or, if one is about to see a family in which the only child, described by the parents as "perfect" until now, has suddenly begun to underachieve and behave disruptively in school, one may consider the possibility of some change in the status of the parents' marriage, relationships with extended family, or other circumstances. One may also wonder whether something happened in the school situation to precipitate the child's uncharacteristic actions. Similarly, if a couple recently emigrated from Pakistan has applied for help, the worker unfamiliar with cultural patterns and traditions of that country is likely to seek information about these to try to better understand the people who are coming for an interview.

Affective or Empathic Preparation
This type of preparation involves the effort to put oneself in the other's shoes. What would it be like suddenly to lose one's home or try to live in below-freezing temperatures without heat? How might a heretofore "model" child feel upon losing the status of being an excellent and well-behaved student? How pressured must that child have felt to give up such a positive position at home and at school? What might it be like to be new to this country and among the very few Pakistani people living in the area?

It goes without saying that *anticipatory hunches and empathic feelings of the worker are tentative and are immediately modified on the basis of information and attitudes presented by the clients when they are actually seen.*

A mother of four children, ranging in age from 4 to 13, called a worker in private practice seeking help for her 11-year-old

daughter who, the mother said, was having difficulty making friends. The worker learned that the mother had been widowed two years earlier after her husband, who had been employed by a utility company, was electrocuted on the job. As the worker thought about the upcoming meeting with this woman, she wondered what it would be like to lose a spouse in such a sudden and tragic way. Once she met the new client and heard more of the details about her husband's death, the worker remarked, "What a terrible accident that was." Without any hesitation, the woman replied, "Yes, it was terrible. But imagine how much worse it would have been if I had loved him." There was no way to anticipate the client's reaction to the loss of her husband. It was fortunate (or, more accurately, borne of experience) that the worker did *not* impose her own expectation on the client by saying something like, "How very terrible that must have been for you"; instead, she simply followed the client's lead and commented on the accident itself, without presuming its meaning to her client.

Intuitive, Creative Processes Professional and life experiences lead the worker to develop a capacity for picking up "implicit" cues about people's feelings, personalities, or circumstances—*knowledge that is arrived at without rational thought or inference.* This capacity supplements "explicit" information we gather from clients. In an initial meeting, for example, a worker may sense that a client prefers formality or distance in the treatment relationship without this ever having been said. Accurate empathy, which we have already discussed, is in large part based on intuitive processes. When sitting with a family in treatment, it is sometimes helpful to suggest that the members talk to each other about the matter at hand. This gives the worker "space" to *think* about the family, and it also frees up creative processes that permit the worker to get a *feel* for the family's emotional style and dynamics. Sometimes slowly, sometimes with surprising suddenness, a new recognition evolves or a revelation bursts into consciousness. One cannot simply analyze one's way through complex or subtle situations; one also feels one's way through. (A comparable process occurs, for example, when one is blocked trying to write a term paper. Putting it on the "back burner" or "sleeping on it" often release creative processes, sometimes suddenly leading to a "Now I've got it!" experience.) Explicit and implicit faculties of cognition go hand in hand; they are different lenses through which the worker attempts to understand clients and their situations. *Just as hypotheses based on the analysis of a situation have to be validated for accuracy and relevance, so hunches stemming from intuition need to be confirmed, usually by the client.*[3]

The Meeting Begins

Getting Started   As mentioned in Chapters 5 and 9, it can be anticipated that clients will feel considerable anxiety when they come to a first meeting. Treatment issues relevant to clients' initial discomfort are discussed further in Chapter 13. In all cases, a warm welcome sets a tone for this first interview. When one meets clients for the first time, especially in one's own office, treating them as one would treat guests in one's own home can take the awkwardness or anxiety out of the beginning moments. For example, one can offer to take a coat or ask if one chair looks more comfortable than another. It can be an act of courtesy to inquire by what name a client wants to be called; for example: "You told me your name is Charlene Rice. How would you prefer that I address you?" Some new clients begin recounting their concerns—even their most personal ones—with little warmup or encouragement. Others start more slowly and cautiously. It is up to the worker to try to follow the client's rhythm. Those clients who are emotionally distraught need the worker to show understanding before probing for facts; those who are tentative need to know that the worker is keenly interested in what the client's concerns are but is also very patient and will not push.

Initial Decisions

In a first interview, two of the many questions to be answered are: (1) Is this the right place for the client to be helped? and (2) How long shall we decide to work together? We usually begin with the first of these: "How might I help you?" or "Can you tell me what prompted your call to the agency?" or "You seem concerned. Can you tell me more about it?" "It sounds like a difficult situation. Can you tell me more about what it is like for you?" Later in the first interview, perhaps: "Are there other troubles?" "Are there other things you are worrying about?" Or even, "I get the impression there are other things that may be worrying you. Is that right?" At some juncture, one may ask: "What do you think led up to the situation you find yourself in now?" And, as a way of affirming and locating clients' strengths: "How do you account for having managed so well under such trying circumstances?" At a later point, one often inquires: "How do you think we can help you?" or "Did you have something special in mind that you hoped we could do?" And, toward the end, it is important to elicit feedback, such as: "Can you tell me how you felt about our meeting today?" By word and by action, the concept of *mutual-*

ity is introduced. Tailored to the nature of the clients' requests—whether the first meeting is with an individual, a couple, or a family group—in some form these questions must be asked. Specific issues related to interviewing families and couples are discussed in the chapters describing these modalities.

Referral Sometimes the problem is not one with which the worker or the agency can help, and this has to be explained. Usually there is some other resource about which one can tell the client. When this is so, it has been demonstrated that "referral" is far more effective than simple "steering."[4] In referral, if the client consents, the worker contacts the other agency, sometimes arranging an appointment, and prepares the way for an easy reception. One must be certain that the clients *want* this assistance and that efforts to expedite matters are not seen as either rejection by the worker or railroading into an undesired contact. Sometimes there are questions to be asked about the other resource, and sometimes feelings need to be worked through about whether or not to pursue help at another place.

It often takes a lot of preparation and courage for clients to ask for help with problems, particularly when they are related to intimate or family matters. Some people, for personal or cultural reasons, find it particularly humiliating to talk about private issues to a stranger. Thus, extreme sensitivity is required of the worker when explaining to clients that they have come to the wrong agency and if they still want assistance they must start over.

Reaching Out Caseworkers frequently *offer* services to hospital patients and their families, students and their parents, and others. In these cases, more initiative has to be taken by the worker. One must first explain in nonthreatening terms the reasons for reaching out. One might say to certain potential clients: "Sometimes family members have concerns about the patient's condition and progress or want to talk over plans for future care." Or a school social worker might say to parents of a young child: "The teacher has noticed recently that Jennifer seems a little preoccupied, and we wondered whether you have noticed any changes yourselves. We thought we could be most helpful to her if we better understood what might be distracting her."

Involuntary or Reluctant Clients Some initial interviews occur with involuntary clients—those conducted by workers in court or protective settings, for example, or with clients who have been referred to other agencies by such services. (See the Carter case in Chapter 20.) Often adolescents are referred to treatment against their will.[5] One member of a couple may "drag" in the other. In these cases, the worker's questions take a somewhat different tack. It is essential to help clients express their negative or mixed feelings about the interview at the beginning. Once that is done, a worker may go on with, "Even though you did not want to have this meeting, do you think there are any matters that might be useful to talk over?" Sometimes an offer of practical assistance helps clients to feel more comfortable. Trust may be enhanced by assurances about confidentiality of information that is shared, when these assurances are realistically given. Certainly, it is essential for the worker to show warm interest as well as understanding of feelings of reluctance. It is rarely helpful to try to *convince* clients of the potential benefits of casework services, but it is necessary to convey that what matters to *them* is of prime interest to the worker, not the concerns of those who referred them.

Deciding on the Length of Treatment

If it appears that the client has come to the right place and wants to return, sometime during that first interview, usually toward the end, a preliminary estimate is made of how long the work will take. (Brief services will be discussed in Chapter 18.) Sometimes in the initial interview client and worker both believe that the client has received all the help needed or available. "Thank you, that's what I needed to know," from a client who was seeking homemaking services to help with the care of an elderly relative and was given information about resources. "I guess if that's the way it is, I'd better not try to find a job now," from a mother who has learned that there are no local day care facilities for her year-old baby. "I see, I hadn't thought of it that way; I think I can handle it better now," from a man seeking ideas on how to have a discussion about drugs and alcohol with his teenage son. "You really helped me see how the kids might be reacting this way as a result of the separation," from a woman who was having trouble managing her children after her abrupt decision to leave her husband.

In some cases, the worker may think that further meetings might be helpful even though the client believes the single interview is all that is needed. It may be appropriate then to indicate that, in the worker's experience, such matters are sometimes more complicated than they seem and it might be better to go a little more slowly: "Would it make sense to you to come back and talk a little further about this?" Or, "Do you think another meeting might help to make it all a little clearer than it is right now?" Or, "Do you want to try out what we

discussed and come back another time to talk over how or whether it worked?" If clients still feel satisfied with the help received, it is almost always counterproductive to try to prevail upon them to return; clients may think that the worker believes they are in greater difficulty than they are or that the worker has little confidence in their abilities to go forward on their own. It is far more respectful, for the worker to express pleasure in the fact that the clients feel helped, indicating that they are very welcome to return if the need arises.

Sometimes the agreement at this point is only for another interview so that client and worker can understand the dilemma better before deciding whether to continue. At other times a definite commitment can be made for a longer period. The worker usually suggests a time span. It may be, "I think we may need two or three meetings to think this through," or "I would suggest that we plan on weekly meetings for two (or some other number of) months and then evaluate the situation. What do you think?" Or, "It can take time to work these things through. As you said, it has been a long time that all of this has been building up. Why don't we plan to meet for six sessions and then decide whether you want to go further?"

The suggestion of an initial time span can be especially helpful with many reluctant clients or with others who fear they will be snagged into an interminable treatment process. With others, we might want to say: "It's hard to know yet how long we may want to meet. Let's decide that as we go along and know more about what is involved."

Under the best of circumstances, the decision is a mutual one between client and worker. The client may refuse or suggest a different time period. The worker may simply assent or else pursue the matter further if this seems appropriate. Also, agency constraints or third-party payers sometimes in-fluence decisions about the length of treat-ment. Clarifying time arrangements and arriving at agreement about these as well as about appointment times and, when rele-vant, fees are part of what is sometimes called the *contract.*

Locating the Problem

A second area in which mutual understand-ing is needed is that of ascertaining "the problem to be worked on." Sometimes this is simply and directly the problem the client brings. It may be concrete: housing, complications in receiving financial bene-fits, arrangements for day care for children, planning for discharge of a patient from the hospital, and so on. Or it may be both prac-tical and psychological: job difficulties, a child's school problem, a marital problem. Experience leads us to think, however, that one can never be sure of whether there are additional ramifications to the presenting problem without asking the client whether there are other troubles or without explor-ing factors that may be contributing to the difficulties that may also require considera-tion. For instance, it may develop that the housing problem is acute because neighbors object to poorly behaved children or loud ar-guments among adults. The housing situa-tion is still real and perhaps the most ur-gent part of the problem to be dealt with, but this problem is likely to repeat itself if it remains the sole focus of attention. Or it may be that a very elderly person has to move from a fourth-floor walk-up. The question then may arise: Is moving to an-other apartment the best solution? This may require much broader discussion than the housing question alone. Or a client may appear depressed. This needs to be com-mented on and, if the client is willing, talked about in terms of how long, what

precipitated the feelings, how deep the feel-ings of depression are (e.g., "How does it af-fect you? How is your appetite? Are you sleeping a lot, or having trouble sleeping? What do you do with your time? Do you see friends, relatives? What medicines are you taking?"). A barrage of questions is not ap-propriate, of course, but areas such as these should be covered as they appear relevant.

With a child's school problems, in addi-tion to getting specific details of the difficul-ties and prior school history, one would cer-tainly inquire about the child's behavior with other children and in the home. One would ask, too, how other children in the home are getting along and, *when the timing is right,* about relations between the parents or with others involved in the child's care. The latter can be explored by asking the parent present how the other parent (or an-other adult involved in caretaking) responds to the child or the problem. Obviously, joint meetings with the parents and family meet-ings give the worker the opportunity to ask and observe directly. To the parents one might say: "I imagine you sometimes find you are in disagreement about how to man-age Billy's problems with homework. Is that so?" The answers may help to uncover the inevitable differences, the conflict between parents, or the notion held by some parents that they have to bury disagreements rather than work to resolve them.

In psychosocial casework we explore out-wardly from the problem to areas that one theoretically expects will be related to it. For the child with the school problem, in addi-tion to those areas just mentioned, the ex-ploration may include questions about health, intellectual ability, learning difficul-ties, previous school history, sibling relation-ships, and information about the school it-self. Other leads may come from the content of the interview itself. Sometimes it is learned that illness in the family, financial or work problems, substance abuse, parental or intergenerational conflicts, experiences with discrimination, or even child sexual abuse are involved.

When the actual problems seem broader than or different from the presenting one, this needs to be commented on in a way that will bring possible complications to the client's attention. One must ascertain whether the clients are willing for these to become part of the treatment process along with the presenting problem. Sometimes one can be quite specific about this (e.g., "Do you think Alma is having trouble adjusting to the arrival of her baby brother, especially since he needed so much special attention during those first few months?"). At other times one may be more general: "These things all seem related, don't they?" or "You do seem troubled about a lot of things; do you think we might look at them and try to sort them out?" The important thing is that—*when the timing is right*—these possible additions to clients' original requests for help be brought to their attention; then the worker can find out whether they want to consider them.

In some casework approaches, this defining of the problem is a very specific process ending in a contract that specifies just what facets of the problems or behavior will be modified. In the psychosocial approach, while the problem or some aspects of it may be well defined, attention initially is broader, focusing on other potentially relevant parts of the gestalt, and the process is usually kept more open for greater understanding as the facts are revealed to both client and worker. Nevertheless, clients should become aware of what the focus or areas of work may be, insofar as these can be foreseen, so that the worker can elicit reactions to the expanded focus.

Sometimes several interviews are needed to help clients decide whether they want to continue and whether along broad or narrow lines. When the worker thinks it will be impossible to give help if discussion is limited to the restricted area of the presenting problem, this must be explained when the time is ripe. This might be the case, for example, if it appeared that a child's behavior problem was so directly related to serious strife between parents or other important adults in the child's life that it would be impossible to help the child without also working on the conflicts around him.

Precipitating Factors

It is important to ascertain the event or events that finally brought about the request for assistance and those that seem to have precipitated the emergence of the problem. These should be inquired about to the extent possible in the first interview, although it may take more meetings to uncover all such significant information. Facts about issues that may have triggered problems are often key to the diagnostic understanding of the dynamics of the dilemma. The client frequently will talk about these spontaneously. At other times one can ask: "What happened that you decided to come in just now?" Or, "Can you put your finger on just when you first became aware of this (or felt this way)?" Or, "Did anything special happen at that time?"

Sometimes clients have no awareness of the precipitating events, but by asking questions the worker can pinpoint and bring to their attention possible contributing factors to the problem. Information about events that occurred either at the same time or in proximity to the presenting difficulty may be obtained by the worker asking questions such as: "Did you say that your mother died shortly before your daughter began to refuse to go to school?" "Did you find yourself feeling depressed about the same time you moved to the new apartment?" "Am I right that your headaches began soon after your husband changed jobs?" A genogram, a tool that will be mentioned in the chapters on couple treatment, sometimes reveals to worker and clients alike data about family incidents that have influenced the present situation.

Identifying Strengths

Gathering facts about client strengths and inner resources, and about available interpersonal and environmental opportunities, is just as crucial as determining what the troubles or weaknesses are. When clients are in distress, sometimes their self-esteem is so low and their views of the situation are so pessimistic that they do not consider the many ways in which they have coped successfully before the current difficulties. Clinical social workers can be so focused on the problem and its ramifications that they neglect to inquire sufficiently into past achievements or potentials for growth and change.

For example, to a husband and wife who say that "recently everything has gone wrong with the marriage" that they want to save, a worker might say: "I know that you have become very irritated with each other recently, but can you tell me what made the marriage work for the 10 years before the trouble began? I get the impression that during that time, in spite of many challenges and sorrows, including your daughter's illness and loss of both of your mothers, you bounced back, coped very well, and drew strength from one another. Why don't we look at how you managed your relationship so effectively during those years?" In this way, the worker brings some optimism and balance when clients' perspectives are negative and confidence is low; the implication that the worker believes in the possibility for improvement can support clients' hopes, no matter how dim these are at the moment. Furthermore, as clients respond to these kinds of questions, they may gain the

self-assurance to consider their own strengths and abilities to find creative solutions to their current unhappiness. *Preoccupation on the part of worker or client with failure and deficits can paralyze imaginative thinking about the direction treatment can take.*[6]

Mrs. Lucia sought help for her nine-year-old daughter, Maria, an only child, who was fearful of going to school. It was learned in the first mother–daughter session that Mrs. Lucia's mother, to whom she and Maria had been extremely close, had died six months ago; that her husband was emotionally distant and also was away for days or weeks at a time as a long-distance truck driver; and that both mother and child seemed to be clinging to and worrying about one another. Rather than focusing on a "dysfunctional, overly dependent" view of their relationship, in the first session the worker said to Maria in Mrs. Lucia's presence: "It makes perfect sense to me that you two would want to stick together since you just lost grandma and daddy is away so much." By affirming the adaptation they had made—which was healthier than lonely withdrawal on both their parts—the worker freed them to consider other ways of addressing the child's school problem.

In a brief period of treatment (about two months), the teacher was enlisted to give support to the child, who was isolated and scapegoated by other children. Maria joined a time-limited latency-age group at school; within a few days her fear of going to school subsided. Mother and daughter had not directly shared their sadness about the loss of Mrs. Lucia's mother, who had been at the center of both of their lives; with the worker's encouragement, they talked together about their happy memories and their sadness.

Somewhat reluctantly, Mr. Lucia agreed to join his wife for three sessions, during which Mrs. Lucia told him how lonely she felt, having lost her mother and feeling so remote from him. Fortunately, Mr. Lucia was not only responsive but also made it clear that he had thought he was not as important to his wife as her mother had been and when he was at home he "felt like an outsider" because Mrs. Lucia and Maria were so close. Despite the distance and scant communication between them, they were both loyal and generous to each other (important facts about marital strengths gleaned in the social study); once they shared the meaning each had for the other, they were relieved and grew closer. By supporting the *strengths* in the family from the beginning, every member was soon able to participate in finding solutions that benefited them all.

Differences between Worker and Client

When seeing clients for the first time, the worker considers dissimilarities between interviewer and interviewee in ethnic or class background, age, gender, sexual orientation, and so on. This issue was discussed in detail in Chapter 2.[7] Sometimes it is necessary to address the differences almost immediately: "Are you finding any difficulty feeling comfortable speaking with a white (black, older, younger, male, female, etc.) social worker?" This question must be asked in a manner that makes it clear *the worker really wants a frank answer.* Often, this recognition and openness puts people at ease. Occasionally, worker and client together may decide to try to locate another worker who is more similar to the client, or is fluent in the client's native language, someone with whom he or she will feel more at ease. As we have said, when clients are particularly distraught

they may not be concerned about these matters, as long as they sense the worker is interested and knowledgeable about the problems of concern. In some cases, because of differences in background and life experience, it may be necessary to give detailed explanations of agency functions and casework services, while other clients are more familiar with this information.

From the first interview, workers need to be alert to personal reticence, distrust because of differences, marked dissimilarities in experience and values between client and worker, or difficulties in casting the worker in a therapeutic role. These are all obstacles to treatment. It is the worker's responsibility to make every effort to bridge the gap by becoming as familiar as possible with some of the generalizations about people at various stages of life or about a client's cultural traditions and patterns, class identifications, and so on. However, and even more important from our point of view, the worker must approach clients of different backgrounds—and all clients—with humility. *Our most important information about clients comes from clients themselves.* They are the experts on what the differences mean to *them.* They are also the most reliable resource on how cultural influences affect the problems they bring or the way they approach the worker and the treatment process.

People of similar origins or ages can be very different from one another, making it essential for the worker to seek specific data from clients themselves: "Is your distress over the abortion compounded by religious feelings?" "I am not very familiar with some of the traditions of the country in which you were raised. Can you tell me whether this matter has some special meaning to you that I might not know?" "Are there experiences you have had in your particular upbringing that you think pertain to this situation or that you think I need to understand?" When asked courteously, these questions convey respect, interest, and the worker's willingness to learn; they contribute to the climate of mutuality. Also, such inquiries sometimes can help clients feel better about themselves because recognition is being given to what *they know* rather than to ways in which they may feel at fault or inadequate.

Who Is to Be Seen?

There is also the question of whether to proceed with the new client alone or to suggest seeing others in the family. Sometimes this decision is made on the telephone, with the worker saying something like: "Would it be possible for you and your husband to come in together since you are both so involved in this matter?" "Why don't you bring the entire family in so we can get everyone's point of view about what the problems are and what can be done about them?" Often one family member has made the application (or has been referred) for help and yet it appears to the worker in the first interview that it would be advisable to include others. In recent years there has been greater willingness, among clients and workers, to have conjoint meetings. In the first interview with an individual client, help can be offered about how to tell other members about the treatment and how to invite them to join in without putting them on the defensive. For example, when a client tells other family members that their help is needed, it is far less threatening than announcing to them that "the social worker wants you to come because she thinks your behavior is causing the problem"!

Some therapists refuse to treat clients with family problems unless conjoint interviews can be arranged. Others (with whom we agree) would favor interviewing all persons involved (usually together), *when indicated,* but would not insist on it if the client

were strongly opposed or if the others were unwilling to participate. We do not push past defenses. Ordinarily, we explore the client's reluctance to having joint or family meetings. Sometimes clients have good reasons for their "resistance" and it is important to consider these. On the other hand, if indicated, one might say something like: "Do you think we could get a better idea of John's real feelings about this if we asked him to join us?" Or, "Since John knows that you are disturbed about your marriage, is it possible that he will be even more upset wondering what you are saying here about him than he would if he came to meetings? This could allow him the opportunity to know exactly what is on your mind and to discuss the situation from his point of view." If there is still reluctance, the worker may agree with or at least accede to the client's wishes; but when circumstances seem to call for it, he or she may press further. It is important to let clients know that *when one person makes changes in therapy, these changes can affect the quality of a relationship with someone who is closely involved but not participating;* therefore, it may be wiser and fairer to include that person in the treatment or at least offer him or her the option of being involved.

If conjoint interviews are handled as a routine expectation rather than as a major issue, the individual client usually accepts these as a natural procedure, unless there are special reasons for the interview to be regarded with concern. If there are such reasons—such as lack of trust, fear of consequences, a felt need for "something of my own"—it is important to understand them, for they often contribute important information to the social study and diagnostic understanding.

In some cases, it is best to plan individual interviews; in others, joint treatment of two or more people may be agreed upon; in still others, the whole family may become involved. Chapter 15 suggests some indications and contraindications for family therapy. During treatment, one can move back and forth from one mode to another as each seems to be called for. In the first interview one merely decides upon the immediate future, but it can be helpful to prepare clients for possibly including family members at some point. Whether or not ongoing conjoint interviews are decided upon, the social study often can be greatly facilitated by multiple-person or family interviews; one has the opportunity to observe in vivo the interactions among family members as well as to learn directly from as many people as possible their views of the situation.

Observation and Deduction

While all this is going on, the worker is observing how clients handle the first interview and relate to the worker. Is the client or family direct and open, relating naturally to the worker and explaining the situation in a fairly clear way? Or do clients appear anxious and fearful? Confused? Withdrawn? Hostile? Overly friendly? Are some ego defenses immediately apparent? (See Chapter 2.) What strengths can be located in the individual or family system? Is affect appropriate to the material being discussed? Is there depression? Is there reason to suspect any neurological illness? In family interviews, different members manifest different styles and reactions to the matters at hand. Are some family members better able than others to develop creative solutions? Such things are learned from observation and deduction within the interview as clients explain their concerns and talk about the present situation, related past events, and their own efforts to deal with the relationships and their dilemmas. It is particularly useful to ask clients what they have already tried to do to alleviate the troubles: What has

worked? What has failed? Answers to these questions not only provide important information but also can tell us about the client's ego capacities, areas of competence, ability to cope with challenges and ways of doing so. Also, such inquiries are often supportive, eliciting the clients' active participation and helping them to recognize the importance of their input to resolving their difficulties and of client–worker collaboration in the search for solutions.[8]

Gains in the First Interview

Progress can usually be made in the first interview, not only in defining the problem but also in securing information that will lead to understanding the factors that may be contributing to it. This not only helps the worker but also turns clients' minds toward issues that they may later want to think about more fully.

The worker's ways of warmly welcoming the client, mentioned above, convey respect, interest, and desire to help. Ideally, the interview is unhurried, with time and privacy protected so that it will not be interrupted, in surroundings that are attractive and professional. These are all *sustaining procedures* that, one hopes, result in clients leaving the first interview with some hope that there is someone who is competent to help and, at best, some readiness to take the first steps toward understanding and alleviating the problem. Most problems or dilemmas—personal, interpersonal, or environmental—touch off some emotion; thus clients typically experience relief in the first interview simply by talking about the situation and the feelings that go with it (*exploration-description-ventilation*) to a worker who is constantly attentive, empathic, accepting, and offering help. Sometimes suggestions (*procedures of direct influence*) are offered, such as: "It would probably be helpful to bring Allan with you to the next meeting, don't you think?" Or, "I would suggest you consider taking a look at the Oak Lane nursing facility before making the final decision about your mother; in my experience with it, it has some particularly good features to recommend it."

Sometimes when clients are part of the problem, it is difficult for them to come to even a beginning realization of this fact. With care and tact, often the worker can stimulate *reflection* by asking questions, such as: "Do you think the time and concern involved in taking such good care of your ill mother may make your daughter (husband, wife) feel you have lost some interest in her (him)?" "Do you sometimes try to be a good sport and go along with what others want but then find you resent this and suddenly explode over some small matter?" Treatment thus begins immediately.

A Case of Family Violence: Presenting Issues Evolve[9]

A woman client with some transient problems, a generous heart, and a forceful personality brought her neighbor, Mrs. Harris, to her own session with a clinical social worker at The Women's Center. The client, who was clearly indignant, said she wanted Mrs. Harris to use her hour: "Her husband beat her up. You've got to help her." The worker looked at Mrs. Harris, who had visible bruises about her face and arms and dark circles under her eyes. Gently, the worker asked, "Do you want to come into the office?" Timidly and without much comment, the woman indicated her willingness to follow the worker. A condensed version of the early part of the interview follows:

Worker: "How do you feel about your friend bringing you here?"
Mrs. H: "She wants to help, I guess."

Worker: "Will it help do you think?"
Mrs. H.: "I don't know."
Worker: "Does it seem that your friend is more outraged than you are?"
Mrs. H.: "Yes, I think so. I should be angry but I'm not."
Worker: "What are you then?"
Mrs. H.: "Confused."
Worker: "How so?"
Mrs. H. (sobbing gently): "This doesn't happen often. I love him so. The bruises don't matter."
Worker: "Your relationship is more important to you?"
Mrs. H: "Yes. Yes. He's a good man except when he drinks. He's hardworking and honest." (The worker registered the fact that Mrs. Harris did not use words such as *caring* or *kind*.)
Worker: "Then, from your point of view, there is no real problem or reason to be here. The occasional beatings aren't enough to talk about?"
Mrs. H.: "I guess that's right." (Pause. More tentatively.) "At least they [the beatings] are something."
Worker: "How do you mean ?"
Mrs. H. (crying harder now): "At least when he is angry I know he cares."
Worker: "Are you saying that this is one way you can be sure of his feeling for you?"
Mrs. H. (nodding, still crying): "Yes."
Worker: "Is this the only way you can tell if you are cared about?"
Mrs. H. (thoughtfully, crying more softly): "I think that is true. I never thought about it quite like that before."

This initial conversation demonstrates several basic principles of clinical practice, including:

1. "Starting Where the Client is" To be effective, clinicians need to make every effort to "read" the client's message and meanings, to regard clients as the ultimate experts on their own motives and goals, and to relate in terms of the clients' reality and interpretation of the facts.

2. Mutuality   Enlisting Mrs. Harris as a partner in assessing herself and her situation not only supported her self-determination but also bolstered self-esteem, competence, and creativity. Disowned or unrecognized parts of this client's understanding surfaced as the worker explored the meaning of the situation to *her;* Mrs Harris surprised herself with the realization that she had been willing to accept the physical violence in return for reassurance that her husband cared about her. Had the worker imposed her own reactions to violence or pressured the woman to express her outrage or to take some kind of action, these insights probably would not have come into Mrs. Harris's awareness.

3. Involved Impartiality   Maintaining a balance between (1) intense concern and a strong therapeutic connection and (2) neutrality (or unwillingness to take sides) is essential in individual as well as in conjoint treatment. Without a doubt, Mrs. Harris knew that the worker was warm and interested in helping. However, if she had said something like, "What kind of a man would do this to you?" Mrs. Harris might have retreated or become defensive. Instead, she was moving toward becoming an active participant; she began to reflect on the meaning of her situation to her. Among the forces that could have interfered with the worker's involved impartiality are: the "urge to rescue," overanxiousness or overprotectiveness, an impulse to impose her own values or view of reality, and countertransference reactions (such as anger at Mr. Harris).

4. The Evolving Contract   As already indicated, in clinical treatment, the contract is the explicit, frequently reviewed agreement between worker and client regarding goals and means of reaching them; a major benefit of the contract is that it elicits client participation. Even in the fragment of the first meeting with Mrs. Harris, it is apparent that her view of her situation was beginning to shift and that her role had moved from one characterized by passivity to more active reflection about herself and her situation. Only in this way could she even begin to consider her own objectives and options or know what kind of help she needed.[10]

(In Chapter 11, pages 311–12, there is a follow-up discussion of the subsequent treatment in the Harris case.)

THE EXPLORATORY PERIOD AND THE FACT-GATHERING PROCESS

The Social Study Continues

After the first interview, social study, diagnostic understanding, and treatment continue to go hand in hand. Each interview adds its increment as new aspects of the person and the person–situation gestalt emerge. The worker is dealing with a living, changing process. Meanings change, feelings change, new events constantly occur, people reveal themselves more fully as trust grows. One needs to be sensitive to clients' feelings and responses and the significance of new information throughout the contact, even though the main outlines of a psychosocial study are arrived at early. The length of time this takes and the amount of information secured are proportionate to the time span agreed on for treatment. Ideally, all of these are directly related to the complexity of the problem and the extent to which client and worker try to deal with these complexities, although too often time is limited by agency constraints or other circumstances. If it is decided that a very brief contact is appropriate or necessary, one sticks close to the "problem to be solved" in seeking information.

During the early exploratory period, clients usually gain further understanding of the trouble, benefit from the ventilation that occurs, and experience support from the worker. Often considerable progress can be made in working on and resolving practical problems. Intrareflection is usually encouraged, but often somewhat cautiously until the dimensions of the problem are clarified. (In the case of Mrs. Harris, however, she began to be intrareflective before describing hardly any facts about her life.) Clients' responses to all forms of reflective communications are among the most important sources of information and of diagnostic understanding. *The better clients are able to think clearly about themselves and their situations and the more flexibility they demonstrate, the more likely it is that they will be able to make necessary changes.*

As we have indicated, during the study process the worker will be reaching for diagnostic understanding. Preliminary formulations help in knowing what areas will probably need further exploration. Nevertheless, it is essential to guard against "contamination" of one by the other, making a clear distinction between facts and opinions.

Decisions about Explorations

How does the worker know what lines of inquiry to follow in a psychosocial study, and how does one go about it? Usually, people come to a clinical social worker with a specific problem. "My child is irritable, mopes, and pays no attention to what I say." Or,

"Since my husband died a year ago everything has gone wrong. Now the rent is going up. I don't want to be a burden to my children." Or, "We just can't understand each other anymore: every time I open my mouth she takes the other side." Always a person–person or a person–situation gestalt is involved. Or, to put it another way, certain systems are involved: the parent–child system, the husband–wife system, the family system, the health, school, community, or work systems. *A set of interacting forces is at work, and what goes on in one system inevitably affects what happens in another.* The worker listens to the client receptively but not passively. Knowledge of factors that often contribute to different kinds of dilemmas immediately suggests the various systems that may be pertinent. In a marital problem, for instance, the worker is concerned first with the interactions between the partners. Then the worker needs understanding of the major features of the two personality systems. Children may also be part of the picture. Since marital problems are so often complicated by interactions and histories with relatives, the worker is alert to references to members of the extended family, either in the present or earlier in life, and uses these to inquire about major relationships. Factors in the husband's or wife's employment system are often of significance. Friendships may be important. Crowded housing or other crises of living can seriously contribute to marital tension. Worries about health can upset a relationship.

A parent–child problem would involve some of these same systems plus additional ones, especially at school. In the case of an older person facing a decision about living arrangements or discharge from a medical facility, not only are immediate family relationships important but also the families of the children (especially if living with them is at issue), friends and neighbors, the client's health, and resources for alternative living arrangements. In parent–child situations, or dilemmas about aging people, or situations involving catastrophic illnesses or severe physical or mental disabilities, the term *client* may actually refer to relatives who must make decisions for others as well as to the individual with the obvious problem. Each type of difficulty that emerges in early interviews suggests avenues that may need to be explored.

The fact-gathering process receives its impetus and direction from two sources: (1) the client's desire to explain the difficulties and (2) the worker's desire to understand what they are, how they came about, and what motivation, capacities, and opportunities exist for dealing with them. Psychosocial casework uses *a fluid form of interviewing* that combines these two sets of interests. By encouraging clients to follow trends of thought related to the problem as these come naturally to their minds and leading them to develop them further, the worker gains access to the elaboration of significant matters with relative ease. At the same time, the worker often must fill the inevitable gaps in this type of exploration by directing the interview along lines that the client does not spontaneously introduce. The worker can do this easily when such matters are "adjacent" to subjects the client is discussing or flow logically from them, or they can be explored when the client has temporarily exhausted spontaneous productions and is ready to follow the therapist's lead. "You have never told me much about your father." "Set me straight on your schooling; where were you when you finished?" "You haven't said much about your work; what do you do and how do you like it?"

The caseworker needs to take a fairly active part in the gathering of *relevant* information. Clients cannot be expected to know completely what information is needed; furthermore, they cannot always free themselves without help from reluctance to discuss painful matters that may be pertinent to an understanding of their troubles. Sometimes, out of curiosity or overconscientiousness, a worker may inquire into areas of a client's life that are irrelevant to the difficulties at hand or so remote that the client may be offended or confused by the worker's probing. Although some agencies have intake outlines to guide the clinician, if they are used too rigidly, without regard to what kind of information is needed to understand the particular clients or their problems, their use can be diversionary and/or intrusive. Before asking, one must question one's own motives for making the inquiries. It is important that reasons for asking about anything be made clear so the client can understand the pertinence, especially when it comes to highly intimate or painful matters.

The Client's Involvement in the Problem

In areas in which a problem appears, it is necessary to inquire not only about the details of the problem but also about the client's participation in the difficulty. It is not enough for the client to say, "My wife is a spendthrift"; the worker needs to follow up with specific questions: "In what way?" "Can you help me to understand by giving me a recent example?" By getting detailed accounts of what happens in the client's household when there is a conflict over money, one can begin to evaluate to what extent—if at all—overspending actually seems to be occurring. Are attitudes about financial matters very different between husband and wife? Does the wife think she spends too much? What does she say? It may be revealed that the wife thinks the husband is "cheap." If it seems that the wife's spending is out of hand, other questions arise: What sorts of situations, within the wife's personality or in the marital interaction, touch it off? Is it possible that the husband's response plays a part in the repetitious, no-win struggle over money that goes on between them? The events or circumstances that precipitated the client's decision to come for help are usually significant, although they may be minor in and of themselves.

The best way to secure a clear picture of interaction is not simply to ask direct or specific questions but rather to encourage the client—or the clients if it is a joint or family interview—to describe things in detail. This can be done by saying, "Tell me more about that," or by asking other broad, open-ended questions, such as, "What actually happens between you when you find your wife has made purchases that you think are unnecessary?" This kind of approach tends to bring a good deal of ventilation and enables clients to relive the situation with details of what actually happened. Interviewing of this sort does not interrupt the natural flow of the clients' thoughts, yet it allows the worker to grasp the nature of the interplay (at least from the husband's perspective, if his wife is not present) and the degree of feeling about it. It is ideal to see husband and wife together to obtain the most accurate information about the specific issue and to explore the marital relationship difficulties intertwined with it.

If, in this case, initial evidence suggests there is little or no basis for the husband's accusations about his wife's spending, the worker looks for circumstances under which the client believes it to be true, what factors within the client or marital interaction might have touched it off, and what purpose his unrealistic reaction serves. Again, an important aspect of these explorations is their revelation of how the client tries to cope with whatever difficulty he is experiencing, knowledge that is especially useful in throwing light on strengths and deficits in ego functioning, problematical interactional patterns, or misinformation of some sort.

Reactions to the Worker

Throughout the initial phase, in individual or conjoint meetings, the worker continues to observe carefully and elicit clients' reactions in response to the treatment situation. What is being asked of the worker? Is there extreme sensitivity to anticipated blame or criticism? Is there fear that the worker will take the side of one family member over another? How accurately are they perceiving the worker and the worker's reactions? To what extent is there warmth, hostility, or remoteness toward the worker? These observations often throw light on the nature of the clients' demands and expectations of others, on ego and superego functioning, and on their relationship styles. It is important to be sure that negative client reactions are not specific, realistic responses to the attitudes of the worker, rather than indicative of the client's general personality or relationship patterns. Above all, as we have said, it is important to foster a climate of openness and encourage clients to share their reactions so that the worker can fully understand the clients' perspectives and feelings, and, if there are misunderstandings on either side, these can be straightened out.

Physical and Emotional Illness

Information about General Health and Physical Condition An important area of the social study that should not be neglected is the client's physical health. Caseworkers often refer to a "biopsychosocial" study. In most cases, questions about health and recent medical examinations are routinely asked. The psychosocial worker is alert not only to what the client says but also to other signs that might point to the possibility of illness. Appearance tells a good deal. Other indications of ill health that the client may not fully appreciate appear in references to poor appetite, tiredness, or sleep problems as well as to mild symptomatology such as pain, swelling, rashes, indigestion, and dizziness. Certain physical conditions have characteristic effects on personality functioning, and alertness to them will often help account for the client's reactions. Illness also is likely to play a significant part in interpersonal difficulties. It frequently causes pain or anxiety.[11] It often increases self-centeredness and provokes regression to greater dependence. It can be used as an escape from unpleasant responsibilities or interactions. It can change the self-image and distort relationships in family life.

The worker is also alert to the effect of bodily changes associated with different periods of life: the uneven growth rate and the genital and secondary sexual growth changes in adolescence, reactions to menopause or the climacteric, and to physical changes of old age. Experiences around menstruation and pregnancy are often relevant. Unusual physical features or disabilities also have direct bearing on social and emotional functioning.

Drug and Alcohol Use   When personal adjustment problems are involved, it is well to inquire about the use of drugs that have psychological effects. Legal drugs of this type are often prescribed by physicians, and supplies can sometimes be secured for self-dosage. Even when addiction is not a problem, such medications frequently contribute to troublesome moods or have other side effects. "Are you under a doctor's care? What has been prescribed?" Or, "Has your doctor given you anything to calm your nerves or to help you sleep? To the person who is not seeing a doctor (and one might ask the reasons for this): "Do you sometimes need to take something to keep your nerves quiet?"

Routine questions about illegal drug use or alcohol habits are usually necessary. Having witnessed the tragic effects on emotional, physical, and family life deriving from substance abuse in clients from all walks of life, clinical social workers are now more alert than ever to this possibility. Familiarity with physical changes and behavioral indicators associated with substance addiction is essential. The timing and way in which these inquiries are made are of crucial importance.

Clinicians are sometimes hesitant or anxious about asking clients questions related to drug and alcohol use. Some clients easily become defensive when asked about substance use. Usually, even in an initial interview, a matter-of-fact question in a nonjudgmental tone that comes across as a routine inquiry will not be felt as offensive. For example, while inquiring about health, as mentioned above, or about emotional symptoms, one can simply ask: "What about alcohol or drugs? Do you use them?" If the client replies in the affirmative, low-key follow-up questions such as "How much?" and "How often?" follow easily. On occasion, a client may say, "I have been a little concerned that I drink too much. I've been thinking about cutting down." This provides the opportunity for an open discussion of how the client wants to pursue this matter.

Clients, even those concerned about overuse of a substance, may not want to reveal the extent of their problem, especially early in the contact. Also, even though dependent on or becoming addicted to drugs or alcohol, a client may define himself or herself as one who uses illegal drugs "recreationally," as a "social drinker," or as one who "never drinks anything but beer" and therefore is not alcoholic; definitions of substance abuse vary. In these early interviews, it is not productive to challenge clients' responses or to antagonize or frighten them with insistent questions. One can, however, observe the ways they respond to the routine questions and later, after more trust has developed, find ways to bring the subject up again; the better one knows the client, the easier it may be to sense evasiveness, "denial," and so on. The longer we know a client, the more we will be able to recognize signs, which cannot be explained otherwise, that might suggest alcohol or drug dependency: uneven attendance at work or school, family violence, automobile accidents, reluctance to remove sunglasses, the smell of alcohol on the client, and others.

Also, when gathering information from clients, the worker should be alert to risk factors that may make them vulnerable to substance problems, such as family history, peer group practices, the culture at the job, and so on. When inquiring about family background, one can also routinely ask whether any family members have or had alcohol or drug problems. If the worker senses a further comment might be acceptable, one might add something like: "Because heredity plays a part in alcoholism and maybe even drug problems, those of us with substance abuse in our family background have to be attentive to our own use of substances; sometimes dependency can creep up on us."

In family interviews, matter-of-fact questions about drug and alcohol use often, but not always, yield immediate responses. If one family member is concerned with, or feels abused by, another member's use of substance and says so, at least the matter is out in the open, whether there are denials or not. In other cases, the family has a covert, or even overt, agreement to hide it. Again, as time goes on more signs will probably emerge.

As concerned as we may be about a client's drug use or drinking, like every other situation, we can demonstrate our interest in helping, our lack of condemnation, our empathy and sensitivity; we can provide information and locate resources; we can encourage the client to reflect on the personal, family, and social consequences of the problem; and we can help clients to consider the function substances play in their lives (perhaps as a sedative, as an escape, or as a comfort) and try to help them find new ways to deal with old issues in the hope that they will take charge and disengage from abusing themselves; but, of course, only the client can actually *do* something about the matter.[12]

Emotional Illness   The worker needs to be alert for indications of mental or emotional illness or symptomatology. Clients often refer to these tangentially or even describe them without realizing their significance. References to periods of "nervousness," "tiredness," "depression," or extreme boredom warrant inquiry. One may pick up clues that there is delusional thinking or that there have been hallucinations. References to periods of hospitalization or long absences from work may mean mental illness as well as substance abuse or physical illness. If the client mentions loss of memory or periods of "blanking out," further questions about these should be asked. Data that might point toward depersonalization should be followed up. Flight of ideas and substitution of associative thinking for logical thought should be noted if they occur. Problems with reality testing are often quickly revealed. Mood and affect appropriateness can be observed. Obsessiveness or compulsions usually reveal themselves or are mentioned by the client.

Early History

So far we have been mainly considering data from the present or recent past. To what extent does the psychosocial worker go into earlier history? Certainly, one wants to learn the clients' thoughts about when the present difficulty began. This may be in the recent past, some years earlier, or in early life. Sometimes clients will spontaneously associate current dilemmas with their childhood: "I often wonder whether my mother's prudish attitudes toward sex have anything to do with my sexual uneasiness now." At other times, however, clients do not see childhood or adolescent experiences as pertinent to their problems unless the worker suggests a possible connection. Exploration of early life should occur only when the timing is right and the worker (or the client) has specific reason to believe that this will throw light on the problem. When making inquiries, it is very important to refer to the possible relevance and to be open to the client's opinion about the pertinence of the questions. (After four meetings, Esperanza Perez, described in Chapter 3, discontinued with her first clinician who apparently had tried to convince Esperanza that her difficulties related to "unconscious anger" at her mother.)

To an involuntary client who has been referred for physically abusing her children, the worker might gently say: "I was wondering if your parents were physical with you in the way you have tended to be with your children." Or, to another client: "Is it possible that your recurring expectation that your needs will never be heard by others has anything to do with the fact that you came from such a large family and your

parents didn't have time to listen?" Or, "Do you think that your worries about displeasing people, making it hard for you to be firm with your children, stem from childhood fears you had of your parents? I think you mentioned that they were quite strict." Such exploration tends to be thematic rather than wide-ranging. As in these examples, generally we ask questions about early life that might reasonably be tied to current concerns. Sometimes the genogram can provide a useful means for workers and clients to gain perspective on personal and family history and patterns.

Unexplained gaps in a history are sometimes due to a period of trouble: mental or emotional illness, difficulty with the law, substance abuse, or periods of mental conflict and pain. One needs to be alert to the sequence of events, especially important happenings that preceded or coincided with periods of symptomatology or poor functioning. For instance, a child's regression may have followed the severe illness or death of a family member, especially if the child was kept in the dark about it and never helped to share in the mourning. New employment may change family patterns and perceptions, contributing to marked changes in family behavior and relationships. The same careful regard for details must attend the exploration of the client's past that accompanies the exploration of current events. It is not enough for the client to say, "My mother always preferred my older brother." The worker seeks out details, asking, "In what way?" "What makes you think so?" "Could you tell me more about that?" "What was that like for you?"

Additional Sources of Information

Conjoint Sessions   As we have said, and as the chapters on family and couple treatment will further explain, it is now widely accepted that in cases of children's problems or marital difficulty, conjoint interviews have significant advantages. Even individual meetings with family members of clients do not have the same value for social study as marital or family sessions. (Furthermore, except under very specific circumstances, it is more respectful to clients to have them present when members of their family speak with the worker.) Conjoint sessions are often more effective than individual meetings because a picture *is* worth a thousand words, not only to the worker who is trying to gather the facts but also to family members whose attention can be brought to interactional patterns *while they are in process*. Communication styles, relationship patterns and interactions, the emotional climate, and distortions and discrepancies in perceptions among family members become much more apparent in conjoint sessions.[13] Such interviews may include husband and wife, parent and child, or a whole family, even three generations.

Home Visits   Another possibly important source of information is the visit to the client's home.[14] Some clients for various reasons—health, transportation, unavailability of baby-sitters, and so on—actually cannot come to an agency office. There are people who are sensitive about home visits, however, fearing that the worker wants to "snoop" for information. Others may feel embarrassed about modest or inadequate homes. When there are such concerns, they must be taken seriously. Sometimes the client can be reassured by an explanation of how a visit might add to the worker's understanding and ability to help. But such a plan should be pursued *only* if and when the client is clearly willing for the worker to come (unless the worker is employed by the court or a protective service that requires home visits).

In some cases, the home visit makes possible important observations about family functioning, the family's pride in the home, and many personality characteristics of its occupants, including those whom the worker might not otherwise meet. Firsthand witnessing of parents' interactions with children in the natural setting of the home may provide especially significant data. (This was true in the Stone case; see Chapter 3.) In some cases, a worker can become more empathically attuned to housing or neighborhood conditions client families must endure. When certain types of situational problems are important or there is a need to reach out to a family, home visits are often essential. One may grasp a natural opportunity that arises for an interview in the home as a means of widening the scope of the social study. It is not, however, necessary in many cases.

Collaterals   In addition to interviews with the client and the immediate family, it is sometimes useful to consult other people who may be in a position to add to the worker's understanding of the client. This should be done only with the client's full knowledge and consent and on a very selective basis. This issue was discussed in detail in Chapter 8. When a child is involved it may be particularly useful to talk with the teacher. Contacts with doctors or nurses may yield valuable information. Occasionally a member of the clergy, employer, or friend can add to the understanding of a particular aspect of the client's problem. As we have said, it is always important before seeing collaterals to gauge the potential effect of the interview on the client and his or her relationship to the worker. Only under exceptional circumstances, principally of a protective nature, is it wise to seek information at the expense of arousing antitherapeutic reactions in the client. This is not to say that contacts with other people should never be made if the client is anxious about them. Mild anxiety frequently occurs, but discussions with the client before and after the meeting with the collateral provide opportunities to relieve uneasy feelings. As we said in Chapter 8, under some circumstances, one can lessen anxiety by suggesting that the client participate in contacts with collaterals if he or she wants to do so. This can also encourage the client's active involvement in the entire treatment process, bolstering confidence and competence.

Reports of medical or psychiatric diagnosis or treatment, psychological test results, and information about previous treatment may be pertinent to the social study. If the client is willing and the information seems relevant, these and other types of (usually) written material may be secured selectively during the study period as well as later in the contact.

In Conclusion

The psychosocial study starts with what the client sees as the problem and its antecedents, as well as what he or she has tried to do about it, and how these efforts have worked. It is important to elicit the client's thoughts about how the difficulties might be resolved; not only does this promote a spirit of collaboration early in the contact, but also the client almost always has knowledge of issues involved in the trouble that the worker does not have. Usually, the study can then move on to look for present and sometimes past factors that may be contributing to the current dilemma.

Throughout the exploration, one must be attuned to the anxieties of the client. One does not push through defenses. For example, clients who heavily use ego defenses (see Chapter 2), such as intellectualization

or avoidance, may be fearful of questions about emotionally laden or intimate material. When a client is reluctant to talk about something, *even though he or she recognizes its relevance,* one may comment gently on this reluctance. Perhaps the client can say why ("It is so upsetting to talk about that," or "It feels too personal"), and by doing so feel relief and become more comfortable. But perhaps he or she cannot explain or continues to feel uneasy about discussing a particular matter. The worker can say, "Maybe later on it will be easier for you to talk about this. It may help our understanding of your situation when you can bring yourself to it." If the worker thinks the reluctance to talk may be due to distrust or to the worker's attitudes, this too can be explored. "I know it is hard to talk about such things. You don't know me very well yet. Perhaps later you will trust me to understand." Or, "If there is anything that I can do that will make it easier for you, please let me know."

Although psychosocial workers do not follow a set pattern for social study interviews, and in many ways follow the client's lead (as in the case of Mrs. Harris), they do have definite ideas concerning the type of information they want to obtain, and they share their thoughts about this with their clients. A great deal of ineffectual drifting and failure to formulate suitable treatment approaches results when the caseworker is too passive in seeking specific information, especially in early interviews.

As the caseworkers learn about clients and their lives, they begin to form opinions about the nature of the difficulties. Often in trying to formulate diagnostic thinking, the worker recognizes gaps in a psychosocial study, areas of information about which further inquiry must be made for the client and worker to construct a clearer picture. It is important to guard against allowing speculation to substitute for facts. The best way to obtain an accurate picture is to enable clients to have sufficient confidence in the worker so that they can speak fully and frankly about the facts and the meanings these have for them.

NOTES

1. Richmond (1917), p. 347.
2. Germain and Gitterman (1996) and Kadushin and Kadushin (1997).
3. *Intuition* is defined by Webster as "the act or process of coming to direct knowledge or certainty without rational thought; revelation by insight or innate knowledge." The subject is rarely discussed in the literature on clinical treatment, but in a good article by Raines (1990) on empathy, he differentiates empathy from sympathy, insight, identification, and intuition. Cancro, et al., eds. (1974, p. 6) caution against reliance upon it: "We must be wary of the intuitive diagnosis in which we sense the presence of the thought disorder but cannot illustrate it with the patient's verbal productions." This admonition applies equally to the gathering of *any* data for the social study; we must be able to back up our intuitive understanding with facts, knowledge, and reason. See our discussions of empathy as a component in understanding, especially in Chapters 2 and 9.

    Among many interesting points made by Imre (1990) is her discussion of the importance of integrating thought and feeling rather than relying on one or the other.
4. In their broad study of family agency services, Beck and Jones (1993, pp. 6 and 67) report, "Advance contact by the counselor with the resource to which a client is referred was found to increase significantly the proportion of clients who follow through on referral."
5. References on engaging reluctant, involuntary, "hard-to-reach," and "multiproblem" individuals and families can be found in Chapter 5, note 7; Chapter 8, note 19; and Chapter 9, notes 3 and 4.

For additional references, see Cingolani (1984), Howard Goldstein (1986), Gourse and Chescheir (1981), Moore-Kirkland (1981), Oxley (1981), Schlosberg and Kagan (1988), and Weitzman (1985).
6. See especially McQuaide and Ehrenreich (1997) who summarize in detail characteristics that represent strengths; they recommend a self-report instrument that can help clients and their families recognize strengths of which they may not be aware; brief case illustrations are provided. See also DeJong and Miller (1995) for suggestions of interviewing questions designed to identify strengths related to clients' goals; conceptually, they combine the strengths perspective with a solution-focused approach. Cowger (1994), too, discusses the assessment of client strengths that will help in the exercise of personal and political power.

    See Hwang and Cowger (1998) for a report on their study of the extent to which social workers emphasize strengths in practice; they come up with some encouraging findings, although, as is apparent from their conclusions, more research will be required. Chapter 1, note 37 provides recommended readings on the strengths perspective.
7. For references, see Chapter 2 notes 37, 38, and 39; see also Chapter 8, note 23; and Chapter 9, note 5.
8. We recommend a succinct, useful essay by Pilseker (1994) on "starting where the client is." See also Duehn and Mayadas (1979) for an interesting study and discussion of the importance of empathically "hearing" the client's concerns and priorities in intake interviews; and Marziali (1988) on the first session. We also recommend Howard Goldstein (1983) for a very helpful discussion of the need to try to grasp the reality—the perceptions and individuality—of clients, rather than making assumptions based on our own expectations.

    For a valuable approach to initial interviews from the point of view of communication see a chapter in Nelsen (1980), pp. 43–65. Goldberg (1975) discusses breaking the communication barrier in the initial interview with an abusing parent; for other references to work with clients who have abused or have been accused of abusing children, see Chapter 8, note 19.

9. We have selected several references among many on victims and perpetrators of spouse abuse and family violence. See Gibbons, et al. (1994) whose interesting paper discusses the need to integrate two opposite responses to victims: by seeing them as vulnerable and innocent, but also as influential; by responding only to clients' vulnerability, the clinician may inadvertently collude with an ongoing sense of powerlessness and victimization. Hendricks-Matthews (1982) discusses the concept of "learned helplessness." Finn (1985), Horton and Johnson (1993), and Johnson (1992) also address issues related to battered women.

Douglas (1991), Neidig, et al. (1985), Taylor (1984), Weidman (1986), and Weitzman and Dreen (1982) discuss assessment and treatment of spousal abuse and couple violence. See Kerlin and Brandell (1997) and Holmes (1981) on family violence and clinical practice.

Saunders (1992) suggests a typology of three different types of men who batter. Williams (1992) offers a practical, culturally sensitive, and positive approach to work with African American men who batter. Sakai (1991) recomends group intervention with abusers before couple or family treatment. Gondolf (1995) discusses the complex relationship between alcohol abuse and wife assault; he argues that both types of abuse are manifestations of an underlying need for power and control related to gender-based distortions and insecurities. A book by Madanes (1995), a well-known family therapist, and her associates suggest treatment interventions with violent men. Dwyer, et al. (1995) discuss research on domestic violence, current theories, and practice issues. Again, we recommend the book by Jacobson and Gottman (1998) on wife battering. See also Turner (1995), Chapters 69, 70, and 71 for discussions of treatment in spouse abuse cases. See Chapter 15, note 32 for readings on physical and sexual abuse of children.

10. See discussions of the contract and mutuality in the text of Chapter 9 and references in notes 17 and 18 of that chapter.

11. Patterson, et al. (1998, pp. 52–53) make suggestions for assessment of biological factors. We recommend a thought-provoking article by Saleebey (1992) who points out that social work pays too little attention to the body, which is in constant interaction with the mind and the environment. See Part 2 of the volume edited by Turner (1995) for chapters related to physical and medical conditions.

12. We recommend an article by Gregoire (1995) who views some of the current responses to alcoholism as narrow and sterile and recommends that we give more thought to our commitment to self-determination and to our empowerment and strengths perspectives when considering approaches to helping clients overcome alcohol addiction. We, too, believe there is more than one way to address drinking problems and that approaches should be individualized. Amodeo and Jones (1997) very respectfully and usefully discuss the importance of taking into account cultural influences and belief systems related to alcohol and drug use; rather than working from generalizations, they urge individualized approaches.

Recommended also is a useful book by Kaufman (1994) on treatment of addiction; he favors an integration of psychodynamic, 12-step, and family therapy approaches.

For discussions related to 12-step programs and Alcoholics Anonymous see Davis and Jansen (1998) and Shulamith and Spiegel (1996).

Amodeo and Liftik (1990) suggest interventions to work with denial. Lester (1982) discusses special issues related to alcoholism in women; Leikin (1986) discusses the identification and treatment of alcoholism. Patterson, et al. (1998) suggest approaches to the assessment of substance abuse and include screening questionnaires. See also Chernus (1985), Levin (1987), and Zimberg (1978).

We also recommend the well-known book by Wegscheider (1981) on the "alcoholic family." See the volume edited by Hester and Miller (1989) with chapters that describe a range of treatment approaches for alcoholism. A comprehensive book by Nace (1987) provides theoretical and practical information related to clinical treatment of alcohol dependence and addiction.

13. See Chapters 14 and 15. Linda Anderson (1979) suggested that caseworkers' lack of knowledge and training for family-oriented interviewing has limited its use by them. On the basis of a survey designed to determine family, caseworker, and agency needs, specific training objectives were recommended to help caseworkers learn to understand family interaction and communication and become skilled at intervening. Unfortunately, Sandra Anderson (1995), 16 years later, has to urge us to resist the trend *away* from family-centered practice toward individually oriented practice. Without adequate training, the caseworker can be confounded by the vast amount of data derived from family interviews and thus be unable to use it meaningfully for social study purposes.

14. Although it has fallen into disrepute from time to time, over many years the home visit has been used for reaching out to reluctant or homebound clients and for social study, diagnosis, treatment, and research. Behrens and Ackerman (1956), pioneers in the family therapy movement, were among many family therapists who recommended the home visit.

For references on the home visit and home-based practice, see: Beder (1998); Hancock and Pelton (1989); Hodges and Blythe (1992); and Leonard Woods (1988).

CHAPTER 11

ASSESSMENT AND DIAGNOSTIC UNDERSTANDING

Understanding is central to psychosocial treatment. As we indicated in the previous chapter, much understanding is intuitive. One immediately senses anxiety, anger, grief. Common knowledge of causative factors quickly brings explanations to mind. But one cannot rely upon intuition alone. Common knowledge is notoriously undependable. These constitute only a first step in the process of understanding, providing *hypotheses* to be checked out against reality. Through the psychosocial study—the fact-gathering process—the worker seeks to come as close as possible to securing an accurate picture of clients' inner and outer situations and the interactions between them. In assessment and diagnosis, the worker attempts to understand—to give meaning to—the picture in order to answer the question "How can this individual or family be helped?"

The terms *diagnosis, assessment,* and *evaluation* are sometimes used inter-

changeably. *Assessment* is occasionally used to describe the process that we call the social study. For some social workers, the word *diagnosis* suggests adherence to a "medical model" of casework. The concern is that those who use the term are placing responsibility—or even blame—for difficulties on clients rather than on their situations, that they are focusing on people's weaknesses—"illness," "pathology," "dysfunction"—rather than on strengths and capacities to cope with and bounce back from difficulties. It is reasonably argued that concentration on deficits is not only disrespectful to clients but also hampers our ability to help them find solutions. Some are concerned that the use of labels stereotypes and stigmatizes people, thereby ignoring each individual's uniqueness. It is further feared that diagnoses of clients artificially separate them from the social contexts in which they live, that attention will not be paid to understanding

293

the imbalance between people and their environments, and that potential opportunities for social supports will be overlooked. *Diagnosis,* some believe, supports the notion that the clinician imposes evaluations without participation by clients.

Concerns such as these would be true if one sought diagnoses of clients and their deficits alone. It is *not* true if one seeks to assess strengths and weaknesses of the person or family, of the situation, and of the circular interactions that constantly recur between the various components of the systems of which the client is a part. As far back as 1917, pioneer social worker Mary Richmond proposed a "no-fault," multidimensional definition of the diagnostic process that took into account person–situation interdependence:

> Social diagnosis . . . may be described as the attempt to make as exact a definition as possible of the situation and personality of a human being in some social need—of his situation and personality, that is, in relation to other human beings upon whom he in any way depends or who depend on him, and in relation also to the social institutions of his community.[1]

Our approach to understanding person–situation dilemmas has become more sophisticated as we have incorporated systems and ecological concepts that identify the complex interactions between people and their environments and that assess the quality of the fit between them (see Chapters 2 and 8). In a recommended and persuasive essay, Turner urges us to preserve the term and concept of "diagnosis," pointing out that it

> does not mean, as some of our practice texts imply, the assigning of labels; it does not mean the identification of pathology; it is not unidimensional; it is not keyed exclusively to the "medical model"; and it is not a process

that by definition excludes the client from the helping process. Rather, for social workers, it suggests the conceptual act of formulating ongoing judgments for which we take professional responsibility and upon which we base our interventive activities with clients, be they individuals, couples, groups, families, or communities.[2]

With new information these judgments may shift, and as clients' own understandings evolve, new, mutually-arrived-at perspectives usually emerge.

Whatever terms are used, it is the point of view of this book that both the client and the situation are virtually always involved in the problem and must be understood, that it is in their interactions and interrelationships that many explanations can be found, and that the recognition of personal strengths and environmental opportunities is of paramount importance to diagnostic assessment.

CLIENT–WORKER PARTICIPATION

In the psychosocial approach, client and worker both participate in developing diagnostic understanding. Once clients understand the value of collaboratively searching for the reasons for feelings and behavior, they will often look for explanations and contributing factors. In individual or conjoint meetings, the worker also suggests lines of thought and often *tests hypotheses by asking for clients' reactions to them:* "From what you say, it seems as though Eric's bed-wetting began shortly after Julia broke her leg. I imagine Julia got extra attention during that time. Do you think there is a connection?" Or, "It sounds as if you were really furious at your mother for staying so long. Was it easier to take it out on Laurie?" Or, "Have you asked Frank to put the kids to bed or do you just wait for him to offer?" Or, "Do you think it is easier in this family to express anger than other feelings?" When the worker asks questions such as these, it is important to make room for clients' thoughtful responses; often they can either refine or modify the hypothesis or suggest another.

In each of these illustrations, the worker's thinking started out being ahead of the client's. This is not always the case. Many clients spontaneously seek explanations of behavior and express their own thinking, to which the worker reacts. These explanations often show considerable insight. A woman who was considering leaving her recovering alcoholic husband said: "We are a bad match. I used to think everything would be all right after he quit drinking. But now I realize that his willingness to let me boss him around brings out the worst in me and makes it hard for me to respect him." At other times, client explanations derive from misinformation or are rationalizations and intellectualizations (e.g., "Her father's temper has no connection to Lucille's school problems; she ignores him," or "He would be all right if he took his vitamins," or "I think he has an oedipal problem with his mother") to which the worker may listen in silence or, when the timing is right, indicate some doubt: "Perhaps, but I think there is more to it than that." Or, "Are you truly satisfied with that yourself?" Or, "Do you really think that John is the only one who needs to make changes for the marriage to improve?" Or, "You know, you've read a lot of psychology, and sometimes knowledge of that kind can get in the way of real understanding. Right now it is your feelings about the situation that are important. Can you try to let them come and not bother so much about reasons and explanations?"

Even though the client is the best expert on what he thinks and feels and wants, ordinarily, and particularly at the beginning of treatment, the worker can be expected to understand some of the points more quickly and fully than the client. This is so for several reasons:

1. In situations in which they are closely involved, people are often blind to what they are doing and reveal by behavior many things of which they are not aware.
2. People tend to see other people's contributions to problems more clearly than their own, in part because they fear being blamed or finding "flaws" in themselves.
3. Although every situation is different in detail from all others, it is also true that human beings have a great deal in common, react in similar ways, develop in similar ways, and are exposed to many similar life events. Working over and over again with clients caught in successive dilemmas, not identical but nevertheless similar, enables the clinical social worker to understand the problems of new clients more quickly and more fully than would be possible without prior experience.
4. Knowledge has been accumulated by social work, psychology, and the social sciences that can illuminate human problems and that is part of the social worker's education. This consists of knowledge of biological influences, of the dynamics of human behavior and of human development, of family functioning and the social and physical environment, and of the various ways in which interacting factors in both past and present can create problems of pressure, deprivation, or dysfunction.

Clients' own assessments of their situations are nevertheless enormously important on many levels. This issue will be discussed in further detail in a later section of this chapter.

THE ASSESSMENT PROCESS AND DYNAMIC UNDERSTANDING

How does the diagnostic assessment proceed? The total process consists of worker and client trying to understand:

1. What the trouble is.
2. What factors seem to be contributing to the trouble.
3. What can be changed and modified.

We evaluate *motivation* and *capacities* for growth within the *person* and *opportunities for change* in the social and physical *situation*.[3] Strengths as well as weaknesses in the person, situation, and *interactions* are prime considerations.

Diagnostic assessment occurs in two ways: First, as the worker listens in an interview to what clients are saying, he or she tries to answer the three questions just posed; in consultation with the client, what he or she does in the current interview will be determined by this understanding. Second, periodically during the total contact, the worker, with the client's participation, needs to look back over all that is known about the person–situation gestalt to answer these questions more fully in light of this total knowledge. When treatment is expected to continue beyond a few interviews, the first of these more extensive assessments usually occurs after four to six interviews. By that time, there is usually sufficient information gathered through the social study to arrive at a working basis for the major outlines of ongoing treatment, *subject to modification by later diagnostic reassessment.* The first diagnostic thinking is taken as a set of *working probabilities* to be constantly rechecked, extended, and modified, as additional information emerges during ongoing treatment and as the clients' feelings, attitudes, and circumstances change. *Treatment continually uncovers diagnosis.*

Dynamic Understanding   To understand what the trouble is, the worker begins by scanning all the facts brought out in the psychosocial study. The diagnostic process moves from delineating *what* the realities of the client situation are to *why* the problems exist. In *dynamic understanding,* we look at the data of the social study to see which of the observed features seem to be contributing to the client's difficulties.

Worker and client together seek to understand the dynamics of the client's dilemma in terms of both current interactions and the effects of prior events, recent or remote, on client functioning. Assessments of individuals, couples, or families and their situations go hand in hand. We continually try to determine to what extent clients' problems lie within the situations, including family situations, that confront them and to what extent and in what way they are products of unusual needs within the personality of individuals or of flawed or underdeveloped ego or superego functioning. *One must understand the pressures people are under before one can have any opinion about the adequacy or inadequacy of individual or family functioning.*

We then try to establish interrelationships among the various factors that combine to create clients' discomfort or problems in social functioning. We are particularly interested in looking at the *ways in which these components interact.* In this process, a systems approach is again useful because the problem usually does not lie in a given failure in the personality or a specific lack or condition in the milieu but in the way that various weaknesses or idiosyncrasies in the total system interplay and affect each other. Similarly, strengths and potentials for solutions almost always reside in the person, the situation, and at the interface of the two. Because every factor in a system affects every other factor in that system, the worker scans the field again, looking for interactions.

A Hypothetical Example   Suppose 10-year-old Steve is doing poorly in school despite normal intelligence, and we know that he and his teacher are in constant conflict. Is the teacher critical of Steve because he is disruptive? Because he has been placed in a class for which he is not suited? Because his mother criticized her? Because Steve is from a different ethnic group than his teacher? Because Steve is big for his age, does the teacher think he should behave in a more mature manner than he does? Is she critical because the principal is pressing her about the reading grade average of her class? Only by talking with the teacher as well as with Steve can we get hints of what lies behind the strain existing between them. And only as we come to understand the interplay of pertinent factors in the situation will we know what steps can realistically be taken to ease Steve's discomfort in school.

It is also possible, as problematic as the interactions between the teacher and Steve are, that some aspects of the problem may reflect difficulties within Steve's family. Perhaps Steve's father has been very critical of his son and the boy has an expectation of being belittled and then adopts a manner that results in a "self-fulfilling prophecy"; in other words, he may "act up," smirk, or cower, provoking (not "causing") negative treatment by the teacher. It is further possible that Steve's mother, who resents her husband's attitudes toward the boy, becomes extremely solicitous of her son when he is criticized, with the result that by exaggerating the teacher's behavior, he can induce special favors from his mother. Additional explanations may emerge as marital strains between the parents become apparent, or it is revealed that Steve's father was never praised by his own father.

The possibilities are endless, but as the worker seeks explanations, he or she is also *assessing what aspects of the various systems and influences are most accessible to change.* Will working with the teacher on Steve's behalf help? Would it be better for Steve if he were transferred to another class? Is concern for her students one of the teacher's strengths after all? What are the capacities for change and growth on the part of each family member? Can Steve begin to understand his part in the difficulty? Can the parents be helped to see the situation differently? Do they want to resolve differences between them about their way of handling Steve, or reduce the tensions in the marriage, or understand factors in their own personalities that perpetuate the family discord? Which or how many of these approaches are relevant and which would be most practical and influential?

In the end, we are concerned with the interactions and the "fit" between people and their situations; we are looking for the points at which therapeutic interventions would be most effective. But to understand these we may have to examine many of the elements separately.

What Is Needed for Clients to Engage in Treatment?

We have discussed in some detail in Chapters 2, 9, and 10 general requirements of the worker and the treatment process to produce effective interviewing and engagement. However, our assessment must be finely tuned to the needs of the particular clients we are seeing. Some clients require very little sustainment (such as the Jones couple in Chapter 3); others (Mrs. Zimmer also in Chapter 3 and Jed Cooper in Chapter 20, although with very different diagnoses) require a great deal in order to feel trusting and at ease enough to participate. Some clients like lively and even intense interactions with the worker; others prefer to maintain considerable space or even an aloof distance. Some clients, in individual and family sessions, find silences next to unbearable, yet others welcome quiet moments for reflecting or for getting centered. Some clients enjoy humor and find it gives them relief or perspective; others may find a light or jocular comment offensive. Often the worker intuitively senses the "comfort zones" of clients; in some instances, the optimal approach is not as apparent. But, in all cases, it is important for the worker to elicit feedback about the worker's approach. *Assessments of the clients and their situations are of little value unless we simultaneously evaluate what clients require in the treatment process in order to carry on their most effective work.*

One must also assess whether conditions of the agency suit clients' needs. The conditions to be considered include: the particular workers on staff, the availability of treatment hours, the frequency of appointments possible, the agency's flexibility in terms of long-term treatment or home visits, the fee schedule, and the location of the agency. If some conditions are not favorable, can changes be made to accommodate particular clients or should they be referred elsewhere?

Symptoms

In individuals, families, and societies, symptoms usually have a message value. They tell us that something is wrong somewhere. The symptom usually is not the ultimate problem, and often it is not or cannot be treated directly. Rather the symptom may serve as an SOS. Heart palpitations may indicate that one has heart disease, or anxiety, or that one has fallen in love! A fever usually tells us there is an infection somewhere in the body, but where or what kind needs to be determined; aspirin may lower temperature, but does not touch the underlying problem. A child's behavior difficulties may signal a learning disability, marital conflict, or family stress or dysfunction. Homelessness and drastic dips in the stock market point to serious social and economic dysfunction.

Traditional psychoanalytic thinkers viewed an individual's symptoms primarily as evidence of internal unconscious conflict, such as between drives or impulses (the id) and the ego or superego. More recently, family and systems theories have alerted us to interpersonal features of symptomatology. Inner and outer phenomena are much more intertwined than was previously recognized.[4] Frequently, as will be discussed more fully in the family and couple chapters, *"antisystem" symptoms* (i.e., symptoms that a particular family or social system cannot tolerate) are required in order to force change. In some families, for example, a child's lie may be sufficient to upset the family balance and press the family into treatment; in other families, auto theft by an adolescent may be accepted with a "boys will be boys" attitude and, *if* there is internal pressure for change, the young man may have to "find" a symptom that will be more convincing or troublesome to get across the message that something is wrong.

It has long been known that "symptomatic treatment"—the direct effort to "cure" a symptom—too often is followed by development of another, sometimes more disabling, symptom. A woman successfully treated for chronic headaches believed to be psychogenic in origin may develop a spastic colon, for example. There is strong evidence that treatment for depression with medication alone is not as effective or lasting as when it is combined with psychotherapy that addresses personal or situational stresses.[5] Similarly, in family treatment we have learned that if one symptomatic child improves, a sibling often begins to show signs of trouble. To the surprise of some people, it is not unusual for a spouse of an alcoholic to become depressed when the latter stops drinking. Along the same lines, a symptom often helps to maintain the balance of a relationship: A spouse may, consciously or unconsciously, pretend to be more dependent and helpless than he or she actually is to accommodate the other spouse's need to feel in control or superior; the relationship may be protected that way although at a price that compromises autonomy (which may result in other symptoms, such as depression). When symptoms are present, further exploration is required to understand underlying meanings and issues.

The Situation and Expectations

Average Expectable Environment, Negative Conditions, and Opportunities
In evaluating the various features of the situational component, one can use the concept of an *average expectable environment,* where the term *average expectable* signifies "within the range of normally healthy experience."[6] It is where the actual experiences vary to a substantial degree from these expectable ones, especially where they vary in the negative direction, that the worker and client examine external factors that contribute to the client's problem. Serious *external pressures and deprivations include:* an income below the poverty line; homelessness; inferior housing; dangerous neighborhoods; day-in-day-out prejudice because of race, sexual orientation, age, or gender; inadequate schooling and medical care; lack of employment opportunities; exploitive or abusive working conditions; and many more. Many clients seen by social workers are subject to such extraordinarily noxious external conditions that it is remarkable they survive as well as they often do.

Even when they are not presented by the client as a major problem, employment, housing, and neighborhood factors can be important contributing factors to parent–child or couple conflict. The realities of the school environment—the opportunities for learning and for socialization, the respect for students, and so on—are of great significance for children. As we well know, social institutions such as the courts and police have negative as well as remedial or protective impact on the problems that occur in many communities.

On the positive side, one looks for *opportunities:* new employment possibilities or programs that prepare and/or train people for work; availability of safe shelters or better housing; ability to transfer to another school, the strengths of a skilled teacher, or location of a community center tutoring class; programs that provide a broad range of services to people with AIDS or other serious medical problems; advocates for legal problems, for women, and for others oppressed by discrimination; and the availability of self-help or therapeutic groups, among many others. (Resources and innovative programs are described in Chapter 8.)

Family and Personal Relationships
Family connections that are reasonably satisfying and opportunities for friendships are components of an "average expectable environment" in the more personal realm. This does not mean these relationships are necessarily conflict-free, any more than "average" income is equated with affluence. These expectations vary according to cultural and other variables and must be viewed from the standpoint of general expectations and those of particular clients. An extremely authoritative husband may be "expectable" in Turkish culture, but he may be experienced as a distinct "pressure" by a woman brought up in this country or

even by a Turkish woman if she has lived here long enough to expect greater equality in marriage. If workers attempt to impose their own biases or try to promote equality, serious repercussions understandably may ensue. *The clients' own views of these factors is of paramount importance.* To what extent and in what way does each spouse experience stress?

Along similar lines, a teenage girl who recently immigrated with her parents from Puerto Rico may quickly be exposed to a peer group whose families have different values, are more lenient in certain expectations of behavior, and so on. When this creates intergenerational conflict in the girl's own family, it is not the worker's function to try to persuade one "side" or the other, but rather to help all family members understand the basis for dissension, to normalize (rather than to "pathologize") it, and to work on how to reach a solution that is respectful of parental concerns, of the teenager's struggles, and of each member's individuality.[7] Again, each family member must be assessed for his or her uniqueness and not viewed simply as a member of a particular ethnic group.

If parents are concerned about a child, the worker can assess the quality of the parents' functioning only in light of the realities of the child's behavior that confront the parents. What is living with this son or daughter like at the moment? Is the child so withdrawn that he or she is hard to reach? Is the youngster provocative in a hostile way, "expectably" arousing parental anger? Is the child's behavior publicly humiliating to the parents? If the child is ill, how much of a strain does caring for him or her cause? Are parents deprived of sleep? Are there constant demands? Any tendency to feel more sympathetic toward children than adults will be counterbalanced when one attempts to put oneself in the place of

each family member and carefully assess that person's circumstances and burdens.

In any sort of problem, the worker must evaluate the pressures to which clients are responding, as illustrated in the hypothetical case of Steve, discussed earlier. *An individual's problems never stand alone.* It is also the exception rather than the rule to find pressure in a single spot. As the chapters on family and couple treatment will describe, there are usually people in either the immediate or extended family systems who are part of the difficulty and are also part of the solution.

In response to stress in the family or personal arena, one again searches for *opportunities:* Within the family, who is able to give what is needed? Who can take leadership in resolving problems or finding creative solutions? Is there a relative or friend on whom a depressed adult or disabled person might depend? Is there a young adult in the family or friendship network who might help a troubled adolescent? Are there resources for socialization or social supports in the larger community? Peer groups? Church or neighborhood organizations that provide spiritual or recreational connections?

Whatever situational problems are within or outside the family, one must assess not only whether the pressures are relatively ordinary or extraordinary but also whether they are *transient* or *enduring.* When assessing the many multidimensional processes in the external situation in interaction with individuals and families, the worker and clients must try to determine which are the most salient influences and which are most accessible to intervention.

The Personality System

Motivation, Hope, and Capacity   In individual, couple, or family treatment, we almost always assess personality dynamics and characteristics as well as external pressures and opportunities. The more complex the treatment, the more we usually need to understand about the workings of the personalities. Among the important factors to evaluate is client *motivation.* How much interest is there in making changes or working toward certain goals? Usually there is motivation for some changes and not for others. Motivation is closely linked to the degree of *hope* that change is possible. The worker's role in both eliciting motivation and supporting realistic optimism is discussed in other chapters, especially Chapters 9, 12, and 13. It is important here to emphasize the significance of these in the overall assessment.

Capacity for "normal" or *optimal functioning* and for *change* must be evaluated. In many cases, the client's assessment is better informed than the worker's; in almost every situation, worker and clients together gauge these matters. For example, is the person employable? Retrainable if necessary? Does a high school student have the ability to go to college? Can an elderly woman function alone at home after discharge from the hospital? Does a husband have sufficient role flexibility to take on or share child care functions when his wife becomes ill or gets a full-time job? Some fairly well-functioning people want to make intrapsychic or behavioral changes or modify their situations but cannot seem to do so because of extreme rigidity. Others with more severe personality deficiencies but greater flexibility are sometimes better able to make substantial gains in treatment. The capacity for change, therefore, is not entirely contingent on the seriousness of the clinical diagnosis.[8]

Average Expectations   When assessing the personality system, it is again helpful to use the concept of "average expectations." Flexible norms that exist within every cultural group define expectations of how an individual with a "healthy" personality will act and react. These expectations create a theoretical frame of reference against which one can view the functioning of any individual. It is important to keep in mind that this is *theoretical.* It does not imply a *stereotype* of expectations of how a "healthy" individual will or should function. Wilson Bentley, who spent a lifetime studying snow crystals, took over 6,000 pictures of snowflakes. Out of this number of pictures, he was unable to discover two that were identical. In his discussion of Bentley's research, John Stewart Collis wrote: "The variety is inexhaustible, but very often (though it would be rash to say always) the foundation of a hexagonal shape is adhered to, so that each is a little star with six rays crossing at an angle of sixty degrees."[9] People are a bit more complicated than snowflakes, but they too have both infinite individuality and common patterns!

Personality is so complex that one has to view its functioning in a systematic way in order to understand and to assess its strengths, its weaknesses, its potential. Just as one scans the field of the client's milieu, the various systems of the person–situation gestalt, so one can assess the data of the social study that concerns the person. Psychoanalytic, ego psychology, and object relationship theories provide a picture of the "patterns," the basic structures and functions of personalities, from which individual variations grow. The worker is helped to recognize the patterns quickly and carefully by keeping in mind general knowledge of the major aspects of personality and its functioning. Rereading the overview of the personality system presented in Chapter 2 can be useful at this point.

The Tripartite Personality Structure
When assessing the personality system, inferences made about the qualities and

interactions of *id, ego,* and *superego/ego ideal* become important. We know that personality functioning must be evaluated in conjunction with situational circumstances because, as we have repeatedly said, *individual characteristics—strengths and deficits—cannot be accurately assessed without a full appreciation of the social context in which these are observed.* It is also always important to view personality in terms of developmental phases. Nevertheless, it is also true that many features of personality, particularly of adult personality, are enduring and have been with the person for many years, beginning in childhood.

Among the many questions one may ask when assessing personality are: Is there evidence of dysfunctional residues of primary process thinking, or have secondary process functions developed fairly successfully? Is the ego able to regulate and control impulses when necessary? Do emotions frequently "drown out" intellectual functioning? Does the person seem capable of mature, loving relationships in which there is tenderness and constancy? Is there the capacity for consideration and realistic trust of others? Is the person relatively consistent in his or her feelings, or is there an unusual amount of ambivalence or mood fluctuation? Are there unresolved hostilities or overly intense attachments to parents to the extent that these interfere with current family or other relationships? Is the person able to stand up to others when necessary and pursue goals with vigor, or is there extreme inhibition or destructive aggression?

An extremely important question is: Is the individual able to see things as they are, or is there constant distortion? Is the person generally able to test perceptions and plans for action against reality before coming to conclusions about them? Or is there a consistent tendency to distort or

make untested assumptions? How sound is the person's judgment? Is self-image fairly accurate or does the person over- or underestimate actual abilities? Does the person have adequate self-respect? To what extent is the individual clear about his or her identity? Can his or her own opinions, values, feelings, and sense of purpose hold up even in the face of criticism? Or does the person stubbornly maintain a point of view even in the face of information that disproves it? Mastery and competence are extremely important in assessing how well people can cope and get things done. How able are they in affecting or interacting with other people or functioning within the various systems with which they are involved? Are social skills poorly or well developed?

Is *intelligence* average? above? below? Is thinking overly concrete when abstract concepts are required? Are there gaps in the way thoughts are processed? Are memory and concentration on par with expectations? One must be especially careful in assessing intelligence because it is easy to confuse the results of educational level or cultural background with basic intelligence. Sometimes people with very limited education have been well schooled in life experience and demonstrate keen understanding of the world and human relationships. Functional intelligence is often diminished by depression, anxiety, distraction, and other emotional conditions. If assessing intelligence appears to be a problem, a more definitive evaluation can sometimes be made by psychological examinations as long as the well-known limitations and cultural biases of these are considered.

Assessing *ego defenses,* described in detail in Chapter 2, is *very* important. Which defenses does the person rely upon most? Are they functional or dysfunctional in terms of the person's relationships and life situation? Are they serving healthy or pathological psychological ends? Are they rigid and entrenched or flexible when circumstances require?

One sometimes hears the term *ego strength* used as if the ego were some kind of composite force that could be measured as a unit. Rather, as discussed in detail in Chapter 2, it is a series of functions and qualities of many different and interpenetrating dimensions. Perception is accurate or inaccurate, judgment is sound or unsound, self-image is appropriate or inappropriate. One may be highly competent or relatively incompetent, function more or less autonomously, have good or poor capacity for object relationships. Only the control functions of the ego may be strong or weak. One may say about the ego as a whole that it functions well or poorly, but this description is not as useful as a delineation of *which* aspects of the ego function well, which poorly, and when poorly in what way.

Superego–ego ideal qualities are also important. Is the person overridden with feelings of guilt or shame? Is the person overly critical and overly self-punishing for what most would think of as minor transgressions? Is there an extreme tendency toward embarrassment or humiliation? Are there lacunae, spots where standards would be expected but are absent? What is the quality of the person's self-standards? Are aspirations commensurate with background and life roles? Are they realistic and stable? Are there indications of inconsistencies, such as those sometimes characteristic of narcissistic or borderline personalities?

In evaluating the client's superego–ego ideal functioning, the worker considers both the general structure of the superego, its relative strength or weakness in the personality, and the quality of its demands, the level of its demands and the consistency of the standards it supports. Particularly in this aspect of the personality, assessment is

made in the light
class, education,
ual orientatior
Clients sometimes
groups from which ego
derived: They are exposed
culture, which upholds one set
tions, and to family and peer cultu
which may be quite different. Is there conflict among these demands?

The extent to which the worker needs to assess personality qualities and functioning varies a great deal with the predicament about which clients are seeking or willing to accept help. Assessments are arrived at by deductions from the picture described by clients about the problem, the situation, and themselves as well as from direct observations of the clients and their functioning in individual and conjoint interviews.

Variable Expectations Forming an opinion about whether or not a person's functioning is within the "average expectable" range or varies from it sufficiently to be problematic is not easy. As indicated in Chapter 2 in the discussion of role expectations, there is no single model of appropriate or realistic or healthy (or whatever term is chosen) functioning. This is influenced by many variables: age, sex, class, ethnic background, religion, educational level, geographic location, and social role, as well as idiosyncratic differences. Acceptable aggressiveness or assertiveness for a person of one background is defined as overaggressiveness for a person of another. People of different backgrounds normally emphasize different defenses and have different norms for expressing sexual feelings, tenderness, anger, and so on. Concepts of appropriate male and female ways of acting are very differently defined in different parts of the world. Even the level of psychosexual maturity expected of men and women varies among different cultures.[10]

...nately, in this country, recent years ...een some shifts in stereotyped expec- ...ns of male and female personality ...es. Heretofore, in general, men were dis- ...uraged from the expression of many of the "softer" feelings: sadness, fear, and to some degree even tenderness. Strong, sometimes disabling defenses (repression, intellectual- ization, etc.) were often required to subdue normal emotion. This is still true, but less pervasively so. Women, on the other hand, were, to one degree or another, warned against the demonstration of assertiveness, to say nothing of aggression. Sometimes women were taught to seek their ends by devious behaviors, through manipulation or seduction; often, however, these were either unacceptable or ineffective, and women sometimes developed depressive symptoms because opportunities for healthy assertion and achievements were blocked by social ex- pectations. Cultural background still plays an important part in gender expectations.[11]

The general atmosphere within which an individual is reacting and particular an- tecedent events are also significant to per- sonality assessment. In periods of turmoil, such as when students and others are en- raged by events such as unpopular wars, po- lice brutality, prejudice against various eth- nic groups, abuse of gays and lesbians, unbearable neighborhood conditions and the like, it would be a grave error to think that the passions unleashed indicated abnormal character traits of the participants. Campus and community rioting may sometimes at- tract people with poor impulse control or hitherto contained fury seeking release, but many normally well-balanced individuals also find themselves enraged beyond en- durance or may determine that aggressive action is essential to foster change. As can be seen, assessment of personality factors is far from simple. It requires not only knowl- edge of the general nature of personality but

also finely tuned judgments about the inter- acting influences of situational realities brought together in the social study.

Disentangling Interactions How does one assess complicated personality charac- teristics? One applies clinical judgment to knowledge of the ways in which clients in- teract with others, including the caseworker, and handle their own affairs. Again, it is im- possible to evaluate components of the per- sonality properly, except as they are seen in the context of an individual's situation. One must take into account the whole gestalt. For instance, one cannot judge whether a re- action of anger or anxiety is normal or exces- sive unless one knows the realities behind it. It is one thing to be plagued by the fear of losing a job in normal times when one's per- formance is adequate and quite another when there is a recession or one's perfor- mance is marginal. It is one thing for a client to accuse his wife of belittling him when in actuality she does constantly criti- cize and devalue him and quite another for him to distort her remarks, projecting onto them his own devalued self-image or experi- ences he has had with others in his life. Feelings of depression may be part of a par- ticular physical illness syndrome, a reaction to the loss of a valued friend, a response to a dysfunctional marital relationship, or, in the absence of any such provocations in reality, evidence of a bipolar or depressive disorder.

This disentangling of the reverberating interactions between external realities and the individual is a complicated task. Some- times, however, the worker can bring gen- eral knowledge to bear on the situation. For instance, the worker often knows what a given neighborhood is like, or how a partic- ular doctor reacts to patients, or what the eligibility procedures in the local public as- sistance agency are. General knowledge of this type, however, has to be used with caution. Sometimes the doctor, public assistance interviewer, or school principal has not acted in a specific instance in the way prior knowledge would lead one to expect. Direct observation is more certain. It is simplest when it has been possible in the social study to observe the interplay with the externals directly. Here lies the great advantage of the worker having direct contact during the social study with the principals in any interpersonal problem, and of the home visit, and of couple and family interviews from which so much can be learned. But even insights thus gained are not infallible and sometimes give the worker a false sense of certainty.[12] Things that have been "seen with my own eyes" and "heard with my own ears" carry great weight, but they are also subject to misinterpretation by the worker because of countertransference and other subjective judgments.

Another method of disentangling the objective from the subjective is to evaluate the circumstantial detail that the client uses to support opinions and reactions. Does the situation described bring the worker to the same conclusion? Insofar as the worker's own perceptions and judgments are realistic, he or she can then evaluate the client's reactions. One reason for emphasizing the importance of self-awareness in worker training is to reduce biases, or at least to bring them near enough to consciousness to alert one to possible sources of error in judgment.[13] As discussed in Chapter 9, a worker's own subjective responses to clients can sometimes provide useful information for personality assessment.

Repetitiveness provides another useful clue in assessing behavior, for if an individual has a tendency to over- or underreact, to distort, to deny, to intellectualize to excess, and so on, it will not occur in a single instance only but will show itself again and again. If the same type of seemingly unreal-

istic response arises several times, and particularly if in each instance it occurs in reaction to *different people,* the chance is very great that a dysfunctional personality factor is involved. This illustrates the special value of knowing the client's history when the nature of the problem requires particularly careful assessment of the personality. Since psychosocial workers believe that much of the personality structure is shaped in early life, it is expected that repetitive patterns will often show themselves clearly in the life history and in interactions with family of origin members. Specific symptoms or evidence of affective, personality, or psychotic disorders in the client's past are of great significance. Current or past substance abuse and experience with battering, incest, childhood sexual abuse, and so on also are important leads to understanding present personality functioning.

Family Systems Theory, Complementarity, and Communication

In problems of interpersonal adjustment, such as marital or parent–child problems, one person is in a sense the other person's situation, and vice versa. The term *complementarity* is sometimes used to describe these characteristic patterns.[14] As noted earlier, the action of one person upon another takes effect only in the form in which it is perceived by the other. For example, Susan may use a complaining tone because of fatigue, but if her husband Joe perceives the tone as anger, he reacts to it as such. Susan's response, in turn, may be silence, or martyrlike murmurings, or explosive retaliation, depending upon her personality, the earlier experiences of the day that have set a mood, her perception of Joe, her notion of the requirement of the role in which she is functioning, the pressures she is under, and a variety of other factors. Joe's next response is subject to similarly complicated influences.

If one studies a series of such transactions, one finds that similar patterns in interaction can characterize the behavior of whole families. In most cases in which there are problems of social functioning or even severe individual stress and symptomatology, dynamic diagnosis must include evaluation of interactions with family members and other significant people. This involves understanding of the way in which one person's attitudes and behavior set off or provoke certain responses in the other, the extent to which this is consciously or unconsciously purposeful, and the extent to which unrecognized complementary needs or defenses are being expressed in the process. In family and marital conflict, the worker may make serious treatment errors if he or she is not aware of complementarity in various relationships in the family. Some so-called father–daughter marriages or mother–son marriages, relationships in which there is inequality based on gender or other factors, "sadomasochistic" couples, adult children who continue to live with their parents in very dependent or "symbiotic" relationships, alcoholic families, and many other complementary relationships are complex and delicately balanced, requiring careful assessment before treatment goals are determined. Sometimes a worker may find that serious trouble has emerged in a family where a previously existing complementarity has been disturbed.[15] In some such cases, where there is the possibility that the upset balance may result in emotional breakdown or suicide, for example, serious consideration must be given to the possibility of helping to restore the previous balance. Family relationships are frequently the means by which individuals with rather serious handicaps in functioning are en-

abled through complementarity to function at a reasonable level of personal satisfaction, social effectiveness, and stability.

Just as individual behaviors and attitudes repeat themselves, so interactions among family members become patterned and entrenched. Particular behaviors are predictably followed by certain reactions, which foster other repetitive responses, and so on, in circular transactions. When these represent persistent dysfunctional family styles, a family member may become symptomatic or problems may arise between the family and systems that surround it, thus bringing the family to the attention of clinical social workers.

In any social or interpersonal system the quality of communication determines and, in turn, is affected by the nature of the relationships among the people involved.[16] When communication is dysfunctional— when people *persistently* send confusing, contradictory, or incomplete messages, for example, or inaccurately receive messages from others—this can be viewed as both cause and effect of problematic relationships. Communication and interaction are intertwined. In most cases in which there are personal or family adjustment problems, one needs to assess communication patterns and, if they are dysfunctional, try to determine what interferes with clear communication and what these patterns tell us about the relationship. We ask ourselves such questions as: Are certain ego defenses interfering with full expression of attitudes, desires, and reactions? Are defenses interfering in reception of these by another? Are nonverbal behaviors contradicting verbal statements? Do poor communication patterns reflect realistic or unrealistic fear of retaliation or abandonment? Is lack of autonomous functioning revealed by unclear statements made by family members to one another? Are either words or gestures being misinterpreted because of variations of meaning related to sociocultural factors?

The four chapters in this book devoted to family and couple treatment discuss assessment of interactional and communication patterns in greater detail.

Use of the Past

Previous life history, as we have said, often reveals repetitive patterns. These can be immensely valuable in helping the worker to understand "causation" in the developmental sense of how the person came to be the way he or she is. Knowledge of early family relationships is particularly helpful in understanding the level of psychosexual development and autonomous functioning and the nature of parental attachments, superego–ego ideal development, many qualities of the ego, and the basis for anxieties that give rise to ego defenses. Traumatic events in a child's early years—death of a parent, placement in an institution, and so on—or ongoing neglect or unavailability of "good enough" parenting sometimes adds to our understanding of certain developmental deficits and personality disorders. Family history can also help to explain intergenerational patterns of behavior and interaction; a genogram may reveal that alcoholism, depression and suicide, violence and abuse, incest, or other problems have recurred throughout the family system through the years. It is also important to evaluate sharp discrepancies in the way an individual functions at different times in life; these can provide excellent clues to the ways in which situational factors affect a particular person.

Psychosocial caseworkers always have thought in terms of *multiple* causation, recognizing the *circular effect* of interacting contributing factors in the present and those derived from the past. Transactions of the past are incorporated in present person-

alities and relationship patterns, thereby influencing the nature of the current interactions; the past thus lives on to modify the present. This systems point of view is in contrast to linear thinking, e.g.: "Jane is depressed because she was raised by a domineering mother." Rather, Jane's depression may be understood in part as her particular low-key personality's reactions to a controlling mother and alcoholic father from whom she felt little comfort and who discouraged independent development. Self-esteem was further influenced by the fact that she attended a small rural school with no girls her age to play with and received poor instruction from a teacher who lacked warmth or sensitivity to children. In order to get some relief, at age 16 she married Henry and moved to an urban manufacturing area where she knew no one and felt very out of place. Henry, like her father, developed a drinking problem. Her father died, and her mother discontinued any communication with her after Jane refused to leave her husband and go back to live with her mother and mentally handicapped brother. Jane had four children within five years. When the oldest child was seven, the factories in the area closed and Jane's husband was out of work for almost a year. For a few months, Jane had an extra-marital affair that she took few pains to conceal from her husband; when he discovered it, for the first time he beat her severely. Jane made several efforts to leave her increasingly destructive marital relationship; on one occasion she found adequate housing and received public assistance, but she returned to live with her husband because, she said, she felt sorry for him. A few months later her mother contacted her after many years of estrangement; Jane became clinically depressed and was briefly hospitalized.

This abbreviated case history can only be fully appreciated in "no-fault" systems terms, as a network of circular and evolving interactions over time in which the issues of cause and effect as such become irrelevant. All people in this tragic situation affected and were affected by past and present actions of others, which, in turn, were influenced by conditions in other impinging systems and every individual's reactions to these. Again, part of the assessment process requires a determination of where treatment interventions would be most effective. *Therapy is most successful when it addresses those aspects of the system that are most accessible to change, not necessarily those that seem to be the "sickest."* In the case just described, some short-term work with Jane's husband, who was quite shaken by his wife's depression and feared losing her, resulted in his making significant behavioral changes; Jane, in turn, became more optimistic about her marriage and after several months of couple treatment, the relationship improved. Jane continued to work on finding more loving ways of relating to her mother. As these interactions improved, her relationships with her husband and children were positively affected, in part because her internalization of her mother's interactions with her had afflicted her self-esteem and close relationships.

Often, by acquiring a different understanding of past experiences or different attitudes toward them, people begin to interact differently in the present and thereby help not only themselves but also others who are part of the same family or social system. Again, a change in one part of a system inevitably impacts the other parts.

The Client's Own Assessments

We want to reiterate that although the worker is trained to understand human behavior and relationships, he or she alone cannot properly assess the dilemmas people bring to treatment. The clients' own evaluations of their troubles are of utmost importance for many reasons:

First, clients are the ones who know what they think and feel, what the circumstances are like for *them,* what has helped or has not helped in the past, and so on. Over and over again, we ask: "What have you tried?" "Does this explanation seem accurate to you?" "What are you hoping to change?" *Understanding is based in large measure on the meaning of the situation to the client.* A worker may not want to see an adult daughter continue to live with and care for her aging parents instead of becoming more independent, but the assessment of the situation as well as the treatment goals are contingent on the *client's* preferences and values, not the worker's. The worker's respect for the value of self-determination is basic to the assessment process.

Second, client motivation and self-esteem are enhanced by the worker's confidence in clients' ideas and opinions: the expectation that understanding is within their reach, not something that is delivered from "on high" by the worker.

Third, it is important that clients become *experts on themselves* because this helps them to develop the tools to make changes, to make new choices, to relate differently to others, to find solutions. Thus, for both ethical and practical reasons, the spirit of mutuality is essential not only to establishing goals but to achieving the fullest understanding of what is wrong and why. Too often in mental health circles assessments are made by the therapist or in case conferences without sufficient input from clients. Or worse, the client's point of view is unappreciated or even ridiculed.

CLASSIFICATION

Another step in biopsychosocial diagnosis is classification or categorization, recognizing that a characteristic or set of characteristics belongs to a known grouping about which generalized knowledge exists. Three types of classification or categorization have so far been found by psychosocial workers to have particular value for treatment: health, problem, and clinical diagnosis.

Health

The *medical classification,* or diagnosis, often has implications for personal and social consequences, which are guideposts to casework treatment.[17] For instance, a childhood diabetic may need help with feelings that he or she is defective and with resentment at the deprivations of foods or activities that friends can enjoy. An adolescent athlete whose knee is permanently injured may consequently lose status as "star" of the high school team or have to give up a dream of making the major leagues. After a diagnosis of heart dysfunction, a successful businessman may have to limit his activities and give up strenuous interests and outlets, some of which he had engaged in to distance himself from his unsatisfying marriage. A person with multiple sclerosis is confronted with the certainty that physical functioning will become increasingly impaired over time, and this fact will have practical and emotional implications not only for the person but for all members of the family. The man who has had a serious stroke or certain kind of injury is placed in a regressive and dependent condition, requiring him to relearn previously automatic processes he had mastered as an infant, such as speaking and walking. Catastrophic illnesses—terminal cancer, kidney failure, AIDS, etc.—have tragic meanings to individuals and loved ones. Knowledge of the implications of various physical disorders and disabilities and the adjustments they require immediately provides the worker with information for the overall assessment once the medical diagnosis has been made.

Problem

A second type of classification refers to problems addressed by clinical social workers including: parent–child difficulties, homelessness, wife battering, sexual or physical abuse of children, delinquency, substance abuse, ambivalence about pregnancy, incest, terminal illness, suicidal ideation, various kinds of family dysfunction and marital conflict, situations involving adult children of alcoholics, adult survivors of sexual abuse, among many others. Each of these problem categories tells us something about the difficulty and can become the focal point for assembling data about the trouble; from there one can formulate hypotheses. The problem category informs the worker and suggests treatment steps that may have to be taken. To demonstrate how one problem category may aid the worker's assessment and suggest possible treatment approaches, we include the following example.

Wife Battering   In this discussion, we expand upon the category of spousal battering (95 percent of which is committed by men against women[18]) to include violence in unmarried and same-sex couples. When clients present battering as the difficulty or when it is uncovered in the exploration of other concerns, immediate decisions are required. The most critical questions have to come first: Does the woman who has been beaten require a safe house of some kind? If there seems to be serious risk, will the woman need to go to a relative, friend, or shelter? Are children in danger? Should a court order of protection be secured?

While these questions are among the most urgent, and may require prompt action or location of resources, simultaneously the worker must begin to assess the seriousness of the beating and determine whether there has been a history of battering. If so, for how long? How often? How severe? Are alcohol or drugs involved? If so, does the couple see substance abuse as a problem? Are there guns in the household or readily available? Does the batterer assume responsibility for his violence and indicate a wish to stop? Does he appear to have the capacity to be introspective and in touch with emotions other than anger? Does the wife want to save the marriage? Does she say she wants to separate but see herself as powerless? Does she believe she has any influence—positive or negative—on the marital interaction and the escalation to violence? Has the couple heretofore denied violence, to themselves and/or others?

What strengths can be assessed in each spouse and in the relationship? For example, are fairness, loyalty, and caring apparent despite the abuse? Is there stability in job performance, in caretaking of the children, and so on? Are there strong family, friendship, or community supports? Are there external pressures contributing to the situation, deriving from unemployment, poverty, extended family problems, repeated experiences of prejudice and hostility from others because of ethnicity, race, or (in a same-sex couple) sexual orientation? Did either or both of the spouses come from households where there was family violence?

Would this couple be willing and able (without out-of-control blaming and anger) to have conjoint sessions? Or is the situation so severe that couple treatment clearly will not work and might even endanger the woman? Even if the couple wants to work together on the marriage or on some kind of resolution (such as about children if they separate), it still may be wise to see each spouse separately at least once to get the most accurate account from both partners; otherwise, information and attitudes can often be drowned out by defensiveness, fear, blame, or anger. Would the husband be willing to join a group that helps batterers to find alternative responses to anger or panic,

to improve communication patterns, and so on? Would the wife consider a group that would provide support and help understanding her role in continuing in an abusive relationship, or aid her in the examination of difficulties with self-esteem, assertiveness, communication, and so on?

In cases of wife battering (which is far more prevalent than many realize), the worker has to pay special attention to *countertransference* (because the worker's capacity to participate effectively in the treatment relationship is an important part of the assessment). Physical violence is extremely distressing. It may seem difficult to feel empathy for a person who abuses others. Sometimes it is possible to get to underlying dynamics of the violent behavior (e.g., feelings of powerlessness, low self-esteem, unlovability, fear of losing love, difficulty expressing "softer" emotions, fear of intimacy), but such exploration is possible only if the batterer feels regard and caring from the worker. Often such men have particular difficulty with trust. One must also beware of countertransference reactions to couples in which change seems unlikely, which can be the case when patterns are deeply entrenched. It can be exasperating when the abuser is unable or unwilling to give up violent behavior. The worker may feel impatient with a wife who keeps returning to her battering partner, even though practical avenues for leaving are available. In any event, workers must assess and reassess their own countertherapeutic responses.

Some clinicians assert that conjoint sessions are contraindicated for couples experiencing violent behavior, that couple meetings imply an equality between the spouses. Some believe that a "no-fault" systems stance holds the victim as responsible as the perpetrator when, in fact, the physically stronger partner is usually the batterer, has more power and control over the relationship, and is the only one who can make changes that curb the violence.

However, we believe that cases of battering require *differential diagnoses,* just like all other interpersonal situations. It is true that some batterers will not change, even if they want to. It is also true that some batterers are out of control, and their wives are in incredible danger; in such cases it is obvious that conjoint work would be contraindicated and the goal of treatment would be to help the wife take all steps possible—legal and personal—to protect herself. As with all other situations described in this book, in our view it is never fruitful to blame or "pathologize" anyone in trouble; it *is* necessary, however, to assess realistically each situation, to elicit the clients' perspectives, and to share our opinions with them.

With some couples where physical abuse has occurred, it *is* possible to promote an open dialogue. In our experience, many such couples have a long history of failure to communicate with each other, to share personal meanings and emotions. However, the worker may need to establish ground rules, to remain sympathetic yet adopt a strong, firm leadership role. For progress to occur, *it is necessary for batterers to be held responsible for their behaviors.* The worker must indicate in a very definite and straightforward manner that *there is no real chance for change or for the marriage unless the violence stops.* Battered women, too, usually need to be helped to become aware of their options, of their strengths, of their own needs, and of their fears of taking stands for themselves. One does not necessarily deal with all the above dimensions in every case of battering, but each of them needs to be in the worker's mind as possible matters for consideration.

A similar type of tentative outline of dimensions for assessment and treatment possibilities can be made in relation to any problem category; in some situations, the outline for evaluation is even more complicated than the one just given, and in others it is far less complex. A given client or family may have several types of problems, each with its own diagnostic and treatment requirements.[19]

Postscript on Mrs. Harris, a Battered Woman It will surely be encouraging to the reader to learn that Mrs. Harris (whose initial interview appears in Chapter 10, pages 279–80) did return to see the worker. After three meetings, the contract evolved, and with some suggestions from the worker about how to approach her husband (e.g., without blame, asking for his help), Mrs. Harris invited him to join her in sessions. He came to the first meeting seemingly resentful and bitter. Before the beating had even been mentioned, he blamed his wife for being too easy with the children and spending too much time with friends; he complained that she let her mother strongly influence her. Was he, the worker asked, interested in working together with his wife to improve things? "I'm here, aren't I?" he responded. Deliberately, the worker waited to determine whether either the defensive Mr. Harris or the self-effacing Mrs. Harris would raise the question of the beating. Finally, as he seemed to feel a little more trusting, Mr. Harris said, rather sheepishly, "I guess my wife told you I hit her." (This, the worker thought to herself, could be a good prognostic sign.) The worker asked, "Have you thought about what led you to take such an action?" Mr. Harris responded with more blaming. The worker persisted: "Do you really believe that anyone could *make* you do something like that?" Mr. Harris shrugged but seemed to get the point. Shortly afterward, the worker added: "I get the sense that you did something against your better judgment because you have little confidence that you can get through to your wife any other way. Is that right?"

After Mr. Harris hesitatingly agreed, the worker went on: "Do you believe for a minute that she can get your true message that way?" Mr. Harris shook his head. The worker followed up with: "What would you like her to know about how you feel?"

During three months of once-a-week couple treatment, both were able to speak of their loneliness and hopelessness in the marriage. Mrs. Harris indicated that she never got the feeling that she mattered to her husband. Mr. Harris said he felt he always came last with his wife: after the children, her friends, and her mother. With difficulty and some help, Mr. Harris acknowledged that his abusive behavior, verbal and physical, was contrary to his idea of the person he wanted to be (his ego ideal). Mrs. Harris recognized that she did not show the same affection to her husband that she did to the children and to her friends. She explained that it was not because she did not love him, but she thought *he* did not love *her*. She said that she had come to realize that she had tolerated the beatings because somehow, at least at those times, she felt he cared.

When the couple terminated, there was much more openness and warmth between them. Both Mr. and Mrs. Harris believed that physical violence and avoidance of meaningful communication were now behind them. Six months after treatment ended, the worker made a follow-up call and learned from Mrs. Harris that, although the marriage was not always a "Hollywood romance," no further beatings occurred; when tensions mounted they talked problems out, and things were "better than I ever thought they could be."

Clinical Diagnosis

Social Work Use of DSM The *clinical* classification, or clinical diagnosis, is a combination of terms derived from psychiatry and used to designate certain major personality syndromes or configurations. In recent years, the revised editions of the *Diagnostic and Statistical Manual of Mental Disorders* (DSM), published by the American Psychiatric Association, have been used widely by social workers.[20] The DSM classifications reflect the "state of the art" as judged by respected clinicians and researchers. Although social workers have had broad experience with personality assessment and psychosocial evaluation, so far they have no typology that begins to compete with the DSM. Classifications in recent editions of the manual are based on more extensive field trials than those in earlier editions were; the systematic descriptions of various disorders and inclusion of diagnostic criteria undoubtedly have improved reliability.

Social workers often have responsibility for making diagnostic decisions and formulating treatment plans based on these. It has become essential, therefore, that they be familiar with the typologies and standards of current practice. As members of multidisciplinary treatment teams and when collaborating with other professionals, social workers need to be able to share in a common language about diagnosis so that they can communicate with colleagues. Increasingly, DSM has become the official reference manual in mental health facilities. Agreement on nomenclature is now far greater than before, resulting in less confusion about terms being used. Furthermore, social workers have had to familiarize themselves with the DSM system because managed care and insurance carriers generally require them to provide a DSM diagnosis to be eligible for reimbursement.

A Broader Person-in-Situation Classification Urged Unfortunately, social work lacks a systematic typology that classifies problems encountered by social workers, a system that simultanously grasps the complexities of the personalities in interaction with their situations. In a thought-provoking article, Kirk et al. strongly urge social workers to work toward the development of a classification system that suits their needs and reflects their mission and values. Instead, they point out, "Because DSM is so widely used in mental health practice, the American Psychiatric Association's system of naming and classifying mental disorders has *unofficially and by default* had significant effects on diagnosis in clinical social work."[21] [Emphasis ours.] Social workers, they believe, "do not need a new jargon that stereotypes clients."[22] Rather than the DSM medical model, they assert, social workers need to develop a system of assessment that ensures the systematic consideration of factors required to evaluate the problem and personality in the context of the situation. A classification based on research that could precisely identify information that clinicians need to understand the person–situation gestalt would be welcome and could lead to a far more illuminating method of assessment than the unidimensional DSM system.

DSM purposely takes a generally atheoretical and descriptive approach to clinical diagnosis with the intent of making the manual useful to clinicians of various theoretical orientations and to researchers. Its value is seriously curtailed for psychosocial workers, however, not only because the significance of interpersonal or other external influences is neglected, but also because psychodynamic and etiologic theories are ignored. Many social workers have not found DSM useful in treatment planning, in assessing family difficulties, or in reflecting the complexity of the problems clients present.[23] As illustrated in the case of Mrs. Zimmer in Chapter 3, we often view personality disorders in part as an outgrowth of early deprivation and flaws in ego development. The effects of the client's milieu on the diagnosis must be evaluated. For example, a woman with a dependent disorder may marry a domineering man, in which case the traits of both may be reinforced by marital complementarity.

Or paranoia may be aggravated by a sadistic family environment, by abusive discrimination, or by various sociocultural factors; if these are not considered, the clinician may recommend inappropriate treatment. For example, the belief that one is being persecuted could be absolutely true or based on realistic expectations; or the so-called paranoia could be based on a belief system common to the client's reference group; or, because of language or cultural differences, the clinician may misunderstand what the client really means and assume there are ideas of persecution when there are none.[24] Further concerns about DSM and clinical diagnosis in general will be discussed shortly.

Clinical Diagnosis May Be Unknown or Irrelevant Often, the caseworker does not have sufficiently extensive contacts with a client to make a clinical diagnosis with any degree of certainty (even though for administrative or reimbursement purposes the worker may be required to do so). In many situations, especially in brief treatment, if there is no indication of psychosis, further delineation of the clinical diagnosis is not needed in order to help the client with the particular problem that has brought him or her to the worker. Problems with family or other social systems often are not the function of clinical disorders. One need not be considered "disordered" to benefit from social work help.

Clinical Diagnosis in Conjunction with Consideration of Other Factors But, as we shall discuss further, when difficulties in the personality itself are the major focus of treatment, such a diagnosis—*along with the assessment of strengths, the situation, and interacting systems in the client's life*—may be useful in adding clarity to the overall evaluation and treatment.

In some ways, the clinical classification is more complicated than the problem classification. The client usually tells the worker what the problem is, but the clinical classification must be deduced from facts and observations of the social study and assessment. It depends in part upon the recognition of signs or symptoms that are generally known to be characteristic of particular neurotic, psychotic, or personality disorders. Hallucinations, delusions, severe depression or anxiety, obsessions, and phobias, for example, usually lead one to consider a category of mental disorder. The clinical diagnosis is an attempt to define or classify, or put into a category, *one* way in which the personality as a whole functions when substantial dysfunction or distress is indicated. The *functioning* or the *condition* is categorized by psychosocial workers, *not the person*. (One is not a "borderline," although one may have a borderline personality disorder.)

When personality diagnosis is called for, the worker first attempts to arrive at the *broadest discriminations*. Is the person apparently functioning adequately without serious distress or impairment? Or is there evidence of psychosis or some kind of neurosis or personality disorder?

Psychosis The extent to which clinical workers are familiar with psychoses depends on the settings in which they practice. In a psychiatric hospital or outpatient facility, the worker will be familiar with many types of mental disorders. Although psychosis is in many respects a medical condition, all practitioners should learn to recognize the major symptoms of schizo-phrenia and other psychotic conditions.[25] *Persistent* delusion—of persecution, of grandeur, of having one's thoughts controlled, of controlling thoughts of others, of being spoken to by the dead, of "thought broadcasting," (i.e., the notion that others can hear one's thoughts), of "thought insertion," (i.e., that thoughts of others are being inserted into one's mind), etc.—suggest the possibility of schizophrenia, although it is always necessary to consider any cultural basis for seemingly "bizarre" thoughts. Auditory, visual, or olfactory hallucinations; "thought disorders," including loose associations, constant jumping from one idea to another, and incoherence; flat or "inappropriate" affect (e.g., laughter in the face of sad events or unprovoked outburst of anger); and certain types of disturbed psychomotor activity, including extremely odd mannerisms and catatonia, are all characteristic of some schizophrenic disorders. For most individuals who are severely afflicted, there are confusions around identity, limited capacity to take reasonable care of oneself, and recurrent problems in interpersonal relationships. Often, but certainly not always, these disorders first appear in adolescence or early adulthood.

Sometimes family members or others report extraordinary changes in a teenager or young adult. For example, if a young person who was previously an outstanding student, an athlete, and respected by his peers suddenly starts failing in high school or college; becomes reclusive, elusive, or antisocial; or begins acting or speaking in a bizarre manner, shows extreme obsessiveness or ragefulness not previously manifested; or evidences any *radical* shift in behavior and attitudes, a psychiatrist—preferably an expert in schizophrenia—should be consulted. Adolescence is usually accompanied by turmoil, mood changes, and often rebellious attitudes, but changes that seem to permeate or transform the personality of the individual *may* be an indication of the early onset of schizophrenia.

There are people who have been diagnosed as having schizophrenia, yet they function quite well most of the time in many areas of life. Some people, probably relatively few, have an acute breakdown that never recurs. For others, episodes of severe psychotic symptomatology are years apart, with periods of remission in between. Often medication can prevent or minimize exacerbation of symptoms. Occasionally, remissions are spontaneous. Tragically, a substantial number of people are chronically disabled by schizophrenia and their functioning deteriorates over a period of years. Unfortunately there are no "cures." Even when severe episodes are alleviated by medication or various kinds of therapy (including family treatment) and other supportive services, many people with schizophrenia still become increasingly disabled over time. The long-term downhill course this disorder frequently follows is often compounded by the cumulative consequences of medications; although drugs assist patients in their ability to function, they often do so at a price. Accurate diagnosis of various forms of schizophrenia requires knowledge of the course the condition has taken; a full history from the patient and/or the family is therefore extremely important.

The bipolar (formally known as manic-depressive) disorders sometimes have and sometimes do not have psychotic features. Bipolar conditions are characterized by episodes of excited, often euphoric, sometimes grandiose thinking and behavior; at other times there may be episodes of depression, from mild to psychotic. These occurrences may alternate with periods of relatively "normal" moods, but clients are often either manic or depressed when they come to our attention. Whether psychosis is involved or not, a bipolar disorder frequently responds well to medication. Therefore, when a worker suspects a person has this condition, psychiatric consultation is definitely in order.

By being alert to any of the symptoms of psychosis and related disorders, it is then possible to determine which of one's clients should be referred for a psychiatric diagnosis and evaluation for possible medication or hospitalization. One need not arrive at a definitive diagnosis, but when there is evidence enough to suspect psychosis, a medical opinion should be sought. Where an organic factor is involved, caseworkers have very little diagnostic competence, but here too they need to have sufficient knowledge of symptomatology to recognize signs that can then be reported to a medical consultant.

Neuroses and Personality Disorders

When psychosis is not indicated, but the cause of the problem seems to lie sufficiently within the client to indicate some type of personality disturbance, the next distinction to be made is most frequently between some type of personality disorder (described in DSM Axis II) and neurosis. The term *neurosis* has been omitted from recent editions of DSM in an effort to maintain its atheoretical position and dissociate itself from Freudian or psychodynamic theories about etiology; nevertheless, some conditions in Axis I—especially the affective disorders—refer to syndromes that could be called "neurotic." We choose to preserve the term *because* of its implications about origin and intrapsychic dynamics.

Neuroses and neurotic symptoms are basically responses to internalized or intrapsychic conflicts, stress betweeen the ego, id, and superego. The stress can be significantly augmented by life events. From the psychoanalytic point of view, in neurosis, the

individual in childhood reached a fairly high
level of psychosexual development, although
the personality may have regressed from
this level as a result of recent serious pressures or trauma. Repression, suppression,
isolation, intellectualization, and rationalization (see Chapter 2) are common ego defenses. An extremely demanding or punishing superego, compulsive and perfectionistic
tendencies, depression, obsessions, excessive
fears, anxieties, and conversion symptoms
(i.e., specific physical symptoms that derive
solely from inner conflicts or needs) are
among the indicators that *may* lead to a diagnosis of neurosis. Obviously, cultural factors and current life circumstances must be
weighed before a definitive determination is
made. Many people with neurotic features
function extremely well even though they
may be painfully unhappy.

In *personality disorders,* psychological development has not been as fully reached as
in neuroses. The roots of the difficulties lie
in large part in the early formation of the
ego, the failure to develop a repertoire of ego
functions and defenses that operate adequately; ego synthesis is not fully achieved.
Anxiety in neurosis results from conflict between differentiated parts of the personality.
In severe personality disorders, especially
but not exclusively borderline and narcissistic conditions, anxiety may result from the
unevenly developed ego's effort to avoid regression to a very early stage—a stage characterized by strong feelings of helplessness—
and to stave off ego disorganization. Many
of the more "primitive" or "immature" ego
defenses described in Chapter 2—including
pervasive denial, regression, "splitting," projective identification, primitive idealization,
and devaluation—can be found in some people with serious personality disorders. Some
degree of impulsivity and failures of judgment and reality testing are not uncommon.
People whose intellectual functions are eas-

ily overwhelmed by emotion, who consistently have a very fragile sense of their own
well-being or the goodwill of others, who are
self-centered with little capacity for reciprocity, affectional attachment, or empathy in relationships, may be showing signs of personality disorder. As is true in all psychological
conditions, personality disorders fall along a
continuum from the relatively mild to the
very severe. Most of us have traits that are
associated with these disorders, especially
under stress. It is therefore important to get
an overview of the person's overall patterns
of functioning before arriving at a diagnosis.

In most cases in which long-term treatment of interpersonal maladjustment is
sought (and can be arranged despite pressure for short-term treatment), it is possible
for the experienced clinical worker to make
finer distinctions among the neuroses such
as: obsessive-compulsive, anxiety, phobic,
and depressive (dysthymic) neuroses. Similarly, distinctions among personality disorders are important; avoidant and schizoid
disorders have some similar features but
very important differences. Borderline, dependent, and histrionic personality disorders have some common but many distinctive features. Although space limitations
prohibit us from detailed descriptions of the
many neurotic and personality disorders,
clinical social workers dealing with intrapsychic and interpersonal problems need
to be familiar with the literature that elaborates on the assessment and treatment of
these conditions.[26]

In many settings, personality disorders
seem to be diagnosed more often than neurotic or affective disorders. Features of neuroses and personality disorders often appear together in the same person, however.
There are very few "pure" conditions or disorders. Clinical terms represent a cluster of
focal points on several different continua.
When individuals show features of more

than one disorder, all possibilities should be kept in mind with indication of where the greater emphasis lies *as it relates to the person's current concerns or treatment objectives.* Once again, emotional or personality difficulties can *never* be evaluated or accurately diagnosed without an understanding of the family and societal context in which people are living.

When intensive work on interpersonal problems is being undertaken with individuals suffering from any type of severe clinical disturbance, there is often value in psychiatric consultation. The more severe the dysfunction appears to be, the more important such consultation may be. Any physical symptoms also call for medical evaluation, even when in the worker's judgment these appear to be of psychological origin. Psychological problems in clients with serious psychosomatic disorders should be treated under medical auspices or in close coordination with medical treatment. If depression is present to any significant degree, psychiatric consultation is often helpful, partly because medication may be indicated and partly because it can be useful to have a medical opinion as to whether the severity of the depression or possibility of suicide makes medical supervision or even hospitalization advisable. Whether or not there is a biologic or genetic predisposition to particular clinical conditions (and opinions often differ about this), increasingly there are medications available that provide clients with relief from anxiety, depression, and obsessive-compulsive conditions; such medications work especially well when used in conjunction with psychotherapy. Problems with drug and alcohol abuse also often benefit from medical consultation that accompanies other treatment approaches.

The helpfulness of psychiatric consultation depends upon the quality of psychiatry available. Communities and settings differ enormously. There is much variation in the training and experience of psychiatrists. Consequently, the usefulness of consultations varies. If a patient interview with a psychiatrist is required, the advantages have to be weighed against the disadvantages of procedures and attitudes that the client will have to face in the medical diagnostic process. In these days when social workers are the primary providers of mental health services and often have far broader therapeutic experience than many psychiatrists, it may be discouraging to worker and client alike if consultation is required when there is no medical reason for it; among other things, the client may be led to believe that the worker is not certain of his or her own competence or judgment.

Value of Clinical Diagnosis

The value of clinical diagnosis is sometimes questioned, in the belief that the dynamic diagnosis is sufficient and subject to fewer risks. But the clinical diagnosis has an additional value of designating a cluster of factors—traits, behaviors, thought and feeling patterns—characteristically found together. For instance, the term *obsessive-compulsive disorder or neurosis,* when correctly applied, immediately conveys certain information about a client. From the psychoanalytic point of view, it signifies that the individual has reached the oedipal stage of development in relationship to parents but has not resolved all the conflicts of this period and has regressed to some degree to an earlier period of development. People with this diagnosis have severe superegos to which they may be overly submissive on the surface but which they are unconsciously fighting. They are often very sensitive to criticism and have strong dependency needs, even though these may be covered over. They sometimes want to please the worker and other "parent" figures but at other times can either be negative or subtly sabotage suggestions. Often perfectionism and ambivalence are present. Obsessions and/or compulsions can cause much distress, take up a great deal of time, and interfere with functioning. There is usually heavy use of such defenses as intellectualization, rationalization, isolation, and reaction formation. Parents with this condition may be strict in bringing up children, ambivalent in training them, or strict on the surface while unconsciously promoting them to act out. Not all these characteristics will be true of every person with an obsessive-compulsive disorder, but the presence of a few of them in the absence of contrary evidence will alert the worker to the probable diagnosis and to avenues to explore that will either confirm the diagnosis or contradict it.

A clinical diagnosis, then, suggests many qualities the person with a particular disorder *may* have even if they have not yet been observed or described by the client. If an individual is accurately diagnosed as having an avoidant personality disorder, we know there has been a long-term maladaptive pattern of functioning. We can also expect that the client will have extraordinary sensitivity to real or anticipated criticism, frequent and extreme feelings of anguish and humiliation when sensing even the slightest disapproval, painful shyness, deeply felt loneliness, severe self-criticism and self-doubt, and yet a strong desire for social relationships and affection (in contrast to a person with a schizoid personality disorder). Again, although the individual may not have all these characteristics, it is likely that many of them will be manifested to one degree or another.

Using the above example, there are immediate implications for treatment. For in-

stance, we know we must work cautiously, respecting the client's need for gentleness and distance, avoiding strong interpretations or confrontations. Even though the longing for social contact is strong, we would hesitate to make an early referral for any kind of group experience until it seemed likely that the client could tolerate the stress of intense social interaction without taking flight.

Thus, as it takes firm shape, the clinical diagnosis becomes a sort of index to many factors about the individual that have not yet become clear from what has been observed or said. It often enables the worker to anticipate reactions to contemplated treatment steps and to guide them accordingly. Such knowledge can also help greatly in the control of antitherapeutic countertransference reactions. Intellectualism that accompanies the obsessive-compulsive disorder, for example, can arouse feelings of frustration and dislike in the worker. If, however, the worker can recognize this trait as a defense against anxiety created by an oversevere conscience, knowing that the client feels in part like a child afraid of a harsh mother or father, negative feelings may well be displaced by empathy and the desire to help. In the borderline personality disorder, the worker will not be surprised by extreme oscillations of feeling about the self and others, including feelings about the worker. Splitting of others into "good" and "bad" often occurs. The use of projection and denial will be expected and understood as familiar components of the condition, making it easier to accept clients with this disorder and their sometimes provocative attitudes and behaviors.

An accurate diagnosis not only suggests some of the factors and patterns that may be present but also usually tells us something about the durability of the problems associated with it: A personality disorder points to long-term dysfunctional traits; dysthymia in an adult means that the person has been in a depressed mood for at least two years, and so on. Specific symptoms such as phobias, hysterical or conversion symptoms, obsessions, compulsions, evidences of depression, various defenses such as "splitting," delusional thinking, and so on, quickly alert the worker to *possible* diagnoses. Symptoms alone, however, do not establish a clinical diagnosis. There are always several possible explanations of any symptom. Only when a specific form of behavior can be shown to be part of a larger configuration characteristic of the disorder in question can any certainty be felt about the diagnosis.

One weakness of the *dynamic* diagnosis taken by itself is that it tends to see a little bit of this and a little bit of that in an individual without reaching a definite delineation. It is when one tries to say whether the difficulty is primarily a personality disorder or a neurosis; whether a borderline personality disorder, schizophrenia, or a major depressive episode; and so on, that incompleteness in the psychosocial study or lack of clear-cut evaluation of the facts often becomes apparent. This assumes that when a *clinical* diagnosis is arrived at, it is not a glib designation based on superficial impressions.[27]

Hazards and Misuse of Clinical Diagnosis

Several dangers are involved in the use of diagnostic categories. One is that of stereotyping, assuming that all people with the same condition are exactly alike. As noted earlier, each person has many individual qualities that make him or her unlike anyone else, despite the fact that in the rough outlines of a personality disturbance an individual may have much in common with others suffering from the same disorder. Another danger is careless categorization, assuming a person belongs in a given group because of superficial qualities or overlooking other qualities that point in another direction. Again, it is essential to be clear that we are not diagnosing *people* but *characteristics* of people and their situations that interfere with their coping and contentment.

The clinical diagnosis, by definition, focuses on pathology. Diagnosticians have not yet developed a systematic means for assessing positive qualities and traits that bear upon the way individuals handle themselves and their lives. For example, two individuals may be correctly diagnosed as having a schizoid personality disorder; some of the same etiological and psychodynamic factors may be similar, but the two people may lead very different lives. One may live marginally as a recluse or on the streets; the other may be a high-functioning forest ranger or researcher. Of course, the opportunity structure may play a crucial part in the very different lifestyles.

It also follows from this example that the second individual may have better developed thought processes, more useful defense mechanisms, a greater sense of mastery and competence, more capacity for autonomous functioning, and—as both cause and effect of these—greater self-esteem. The assessment of ego and superego–ego ideal functions may be more useful than the clinical diagnosis. Talents, sense of humor, values, flexibility, curiosity, and capacity for empathy and altruism all can have enormous significance for evaluation and treatment.

Diagnosis is admittedly a subjective process, despite the fact that it is an effort to increase the objectivity with which one views clients and their treatment needs. As a subjective process that often deals with impressionistic data, it is open to influence by suggestion. One prevalent form of suggestion is the currently popular diagnosis. Just as appendicitis was widely overdiagnosed in a recent period of medical history and before that tonsillectomies were far too widely performed, so in psychiatry schizophrenia has sometimes been too easily assumed to exist, and, especially today, borderline personality disorder may too often seem the appropriate designation. The subjectivity of diagnosis is illustrated by the fact that strong protest by gay rights and other concerned groups apparently was required to persuade the Board of Trustees of the American Psychiatric Association to vote in 1973 that homosexuality should not, after all, be classified as a mental disorder. This was one instance when the biases of those being diagnosed won out over the traditional prejudices of the diagnosticians!

Along the same lines, the "normal" personality in one culture, place, family, or period of history may be considered "disordered" in another. Behavior or traits acceptable in New York City's Greenwich Village might be viewed as bizarre in a small town in the Midwest or in a rural area of Canada. Hairstyles in the 1960s were often used as a measure of normality or disturbance!

Extremely disturbing are indications from research and from practical experience that lower-social-class clients tend to be diagnosed by mental health practitioners, including social work clinicians, more negatively than members of other socioeconomic classes.[28] To the extent that clinical judgments made about lower-class clients are more discouraging than those made about members of other classes, the likelihood is that poor people often will not be offered the best opportunities for treatment.

From the psychosocial perspective, the purely descriptive approach of DSM may be misleading. For example, it may be revealed after a period of treatment that hysterical features are a defense against a narcissistic personality structure; phobic symptoms may cover a borderline condition; compulsive traits may defend against a psychotic process; alcoholic problems may cover dependency, obsessional traits, physical pain, and so on.

Another danger is that of premature diagnosis. When definitive data are not available to make a clinical diagnosis, it is better to admit that we have not been able to establish one than to fix a label superficially. The rate of agreement among clinical diagnosticians is not as high as we would wish, although reliability has improved in recent years. The fact that a high degree of accuracy has not been achieved is not an argument against an effort to improve diagnostic skill. It *is* an argument against snap judgments and against *overreliance* on the clinical diagnosis. The greatest safety lies in building our understanding on many sources of information—the assessment and dynamic diagnosis, the problem classification, health, and the clinical classification—using all the knowledge that each of these can obtain for us.

Many generally well-functioning people seek social work help under stress. If a worker feels pressured to arrive at a clinical diagnosis, it may be a distorted one, describing the client's reactions only in the crisis state and not at other times. It is also imperative that we emphasize again that even severe clinical conditions are *significantly* affected, positively or negatively, by external circumstances and by the range of options available, including opportunities for decent work, housing, and fulfillment of interpersonal relationships.

Some diagnoses, such as schizophrenia or borderline personality, can seem so discouraging that there is danger that they may relegate the person to very superficial treatment or even to no treatment. This should not happen. A clinical diagnosis is never a pejorative. The diagnosis tells the worker something about what may help and what probably will not help, but it certainly should not be used as an excuse for not *trying* to help. Realization of the great variation among individuals given the same diagnosis precludes such stereotyping in treatment. The fact is that *the degree to which a person is dissatisfied with his or her condition may be more important than the diagnosed disorder*. The capacity for optimism can be a critical factor. Motivation for change relies heavily on discomfort with the status quo and hope that things can be better.

The person–situation gestalt concept puts the clinical diagnosis in perspective as only one of several aspects of the total diagnostic assessment. The reader will recall the work described in Chapter 3 with Mrs. Zimmer, who was diagnosed as having a borderline personality disorder. Over time this client made very significant changes in fundamental aspects of her personality. In Chapter 20, work with Mrs. Barry, who was suffering from paranoid schizophrenia, will be presented. Paranoid schizophrenia is often considered an especially discouraging diagnosis. Yet, Mrs. Barry was able to gain a good deal of understanding about herself and her relationship with her husband and was also able to recognize the importance of overcoming her reluctance to take medication. Subsequently, she was well enough to live fairly comfortably in the community, avoiding rehospitalization. In such cases, knowledge of the clinical diagnosis makes substantial difference in treatment, but the assessment of the client's individuality and strengths is of equal importance.[29]

THE TIME FACTOR

The degree to which one can arrive at an understanding of the person-in-situation varies with the fullness of the social study on which it depends. Even in a short contact of one to four interviews, one must understand enough of the interplay of inner and outer dynamics to enhance the client's ability to cope with the main problem (often the presenting one) in a way that either resolves it or diminishes its severity. Pressures that can be modified and opportunities or resources that can be located within the limits of time available are assessed. Even in brief contacts, one can get an impression of certain features of a client's ego: perceptive ability, coping powers, ways of handling anxiety, and so on. One sometimes also observes major defenses such as projection, turning against the self, reaction formation, rationalization, and intellectualization. Aspects of the superego may show themselves if it is unusually severe, lax, or inconsistent. Impulsiveness or rigidity is often immediately apparent. Usually, however, it will be difficult to assess the *degree* to which any of these characteristics exist.

Turning to the dynamic diagnosis, one certainly has to understand something of the dynamics of both inner and outer forces and of the interplay between them in all clinical social work whether the contact is brief or extensive. Without this, very little help can be given. In crisis treatment (to be discussed in Chapter 18), where former conflicts and problems may have been brought to the surface because of the present trauma, quick recognition of dynamic elements is required.

A clinical diagnosis, on the other hand, can rarely be arrived at in the first interview and usually only when there is a very serious disorder: psychosis, severe neurotic symptomatology, or personality dysfunction. Usually the clinical diagnosis will be established only very tentatively if at all in the entire brief contact. So little time is available in which help can be given that treatment occupies center stage very quickly. Because the factual basis is inevitably restricted, it is not only difficult but also sometimes risky to try to determine a clinical diagnosis; often it is not clear whether any such diagnosis is even appropriate.

In general, diagnostic understanding in very brief treatment will be limited to components of the person–situation gestalt that are close to the matters to be dealt with and close to the immediate treatment process.

In summary, diagnostic assessment involves a many-faceted but orderly understanding of the client–situation configuration. The caseworker tries to understand the nature of the interaction of the multiple factors contributing to the client's difficulties—internal and external factors, past sources of present aspects of the difficulties, and internal dynamics within the personality or among the environmental forces. In preparing for the treatment planning, all that is known, strengths as well as weaknesses, is reviewed and evaluated for the purpose of learning how best to help.

As the contact progresses, the fund of knowledge grows and the worker repeatedly refers to it in making the decisions that either modify or implement plans made at the outset of treatment. The more orderly the ongoing diagnostic process in which assessment is made and dynamic understanding grows, the more wisely will the worker decide what treatment to offer the client.

NOTES

1. Richmond (1917), p. 357.
2. Turner (1994), pp. 168–69; he makes distinctions between assessment and diagnosis that will interest the reader. Many of those concerned about diagnosis, labeling, and classifications are rightfully worried about misuse and abuses of these activities when they attribute blame and deficiency to individuals or do not individualize clients. The wide use by social workers of the classification of mental disorders by the American Psychiatric Association (1994), critics fear, is in sharp contrast to social work's traditional person-in-situation diagnosis of social functioning that considers the context in which clients' difficulties are experienced. See Kirk, et al. (1989), Gingerich, et al. (1982), and Kutchens and Kirk (1988). Later in this chapter we will discuss some hazards of clinical diagnoses, although we, like Turner, do not object to their use if they are not narrowly applied out of context, take into account client strengths, and are not used pejoratively.
3. See the classic, still important, work of Ripple, et al. (1964) on the interacting influences of client motivation, capacity, and opportunity.
4. Highly recommended readings on this subject include Framo (1982), Chapter 2 on symptoms; and Loewenstein (1979).
5. See Klerman, et al. (1994), especially pp. 760–62. See also Elkin (1989). Wetzel (1984) strongly recommends that depressed clients not be treated with medication alone, but with concurrent psychotherapy.
6. Hartmann (1958), p. 23.
7. We recommend Zayas and Bryant (1984), a respectful paper on culturally sensitive treatment of adolescent girls and their families that includes case examples.
8. See Woods (1999) on personality disorders in which this point is made.
9. Collis (1973), p. 81.
10. See early research on these variations by Margaret Mead (1935 and 1949). See also Skolnick and Skolnick (1977).

    As discussed in Chapter 2 and elsewhere, the sources of knowledge concerning these variations are myriad. Many useful references have been included in notes to several other chapters; see especially Chapter 2, notes 37 and 38.
11. See the volume edited by McGoldrick, et al. (1996) on ethnicity and also her edited volume (1998) with several chapters that address these issues.
12. The reader interested in the history of "evidence" gathered in social diagnosis will want to read Richmond (1917), Chapters 2, 3, and 4.

13. The text of Chapter 9 emphasizes the importance of worker self-awareness. See also Chapter 9, notes 10, 11, and 12. Lammert's (1986) article on self-awareness is recommended. Further discussion and references will be found in the family and couple chapters.

14. The concept of complementarity in marriage has been recognized in casework for many years; see Hollis (1949), p. 90. The early family therapists also utilized the same notion when assessing interactional marital patterns; see Ackerman (1954).

15. For an especially wonderful illustration of this point, see Pittman and Flomenhaft (1970).

16. There are many references on the important subject of communication. See Chapter 2, note 44 and Chapter 9, notes 13 and 14. Additional discussions and references will be found in the family and couple chapters. We especially urge the reader to become familiar with Nelsen (1980) and Satir (1983).

17. See Turner (1995), Part 2, for chapters related to physical and medical disorders. See also Chapter 10, note 11.

18. Douglas (1991), p. 525; this helpful article describes a "violence continuum" and suggests prognostic signs to assist in the assessment of specific cases; of course, all batterers are not alike. For references on battering and family violence, see Chapter 10, note 9.

19. See Turner (1995) for many chapters on an array of psychological, personal, and interpersonal presenting problems.

20. The American Psychiatric Association (1994). Since 1980, the DSMs have been used far more widely by mental health professionals, including social workers, than any of the earlier diagnostic manuals were. See Williams (1981), a social worker who has participated in the development of the manuals since 1980; she presents her viewpoint on the importance of social workers becoming familiar with the classification of mental disorders.

21. Kirk, et al. (1989), p. 295.

22 Ibid., p. 304. Of relevance here is the study by Rosen and Livne (1992) that indicated social workers tended to perceive problems as personal rather than interpersonal or environmental, a perspective that greatly influenced the workers' treatment approaches.

23. See, for example, Kutchens and Kirk (1988) in addition to other references cited in notes 2 and 28 in this chapter.

24. See an excellent, informative, and important paper by Newhill (1990) on the role of culture in the diagnosis or misdiagnosis of paranoid symptomatology.

See also Wachtel (1993), pp. 24–30, for an interesting discussion of what he terms "accomplices" in interactional patterns; other people in the client's life behave in ways that result in shaping or supporting the actions or difficulties of the individual. This concept is closely allied to notions about complementarity and circular interactions already discussed; in the family and couple chapters we deal in detail with these concepts and with the interpersonal influences of projection and projective identification, concepts also related to Wachtel's point.

A recommended article by Noonan (1998) on the "difficult" client points out that client characteristics and behavior sometimes "may be problematic but the degree of difficulty is also related to therapist expectations, affective responses and needs, and capacity for tolerance" (p. 129). A case illustration is used to explain the importance of a "dual person" perspective.

25. See Kaplan and Sadock (1985) for excellent chapters on a range of psychiatric disorders and conditions. For selected references that address issues relevant to the diagnosis and treatment of psychoses and chronic mental illness, see Arieti (1974), Bellak (1973), Klein and Cnaan (1995), Libassi (1988), Nelsen (February 1975, reprinted in Turner's 1995 edited volume; and March 1975), Walsh (1995 and 1999), and Zentner (1980). Drake, et al. (1996) discuss treatment of individuals with a dual diagnosis of substance disorder and severe mental illness. The March 1975 article by Nelsen was reprinted in the volume edited by Turner (1995), Chapter 48; see also Chapters 46 and 47 in the Turner book for more readings on schizophrenia.

26. On personality disorders, written by authors with various theoretical orientations, see Beck and Freeman (1990), Clark (1996), Freed (1984), Eda Goldstein (1995), Johnson (1999), Hartocollis (1998), Heller and Northcut (1996), Millon (1996), and Woods (1999). See also Elson (1986); and for further references, see Chapter 3, note 9.

    For readings on neurotic or affective disorders, see Fann, et al. (1979), Guidano and Liotti (1983), Palumbo (1976), Rauch, et al. (1991), Wetzel (1984), and Zentner and Zentner (1985). See also Turner (1999) for chapters on a range of disorders.

27. For additional selected references relevant to assessment and diagnosis and to personality development, see Fox (1993), especially Chapter 6; Gilgun (1996); Hellenbrand (1961); Litz (1968); Mischne (1986); Polansky, et al. (1995); and Pray (1991).

28. See Chapter 2, note 36 and Chapter 8, note 23.

    The danger of misuse of clinical diagnoses is conveyed by Kutchins and Kirk (1987) and other references in note 2 of this chapter; see Levy (1981) on the issue of labeling. Atwood (1982) discusses worker bias against the psychotic client; suggestions are offered to counteract this and to minimize diagnostic stereotyping.

29. See Cowger (1994), Howard Goldstein (1990b), Hwang and Cowger (1998), and McQuaide and Ehrenreich (1997) on assessing for strengths. See also Chapter 1, note 37 and Chapter 10, note 6. See an article by Kopp (1989) who recommends that clients be encouraged to play a significant role in assessment through self-observation.

    For articles from the narrative perspective relevant to assessment: Nye (1994) and Strickland (1994).

CHAPTER 12

CHOICE OF TREATMENT OBJECTIVES

We now move from diagnostic understanding to questions associated with treatment planning. This includes the clarification of the long-range objectives of treatment and of various subgoals that are sought as stations on the way to final goals. (We use the terms *goals* and *objectives* interchangeably.) In Chapter 13 we will discuss the choice of means—treatment procedures—by which objectives can be achieved.

Psychosocial caseworkers believe that *the final word on objectives is said by clients*. It is their lives that are being changed and, for the most part, they who will make the changes. However, at the outset, they may or may not be aware of what is needed or what can be done. Sometimes much *reflective discussion* is required for clients to define what they want to work on or achieve; at other times, their objectives are very clear from the beginning. Once goals are articulated, the worker and client together begin to formulate the various *subobjectives*

that will constitute steps toward the achievement of the client's long-term goals. Some are immediately apparent; others emerge gradually as treatment and further diagnostic understanding evolve.

In some instances, the worker may be the one who first envisages and suggests tentative goals of treatment, but never without seeking the client's thinking and feedback. Objectives are influenced not only by what types of changes might be considered desirable by the clients, but also by whether or not means for bringing about such changes exist, both in the client–situation gestalt and in the casework process. Sometimes, as we shall see, clarity about goals is not easily achieved. Client anxieties about seeking help or making changes, situational pressures, and other factors may slow down or interrupt the process.

Knowledge made available by the psychosocial study and diagnostic assessment is useful in two ways. First, it provides both client and worker with a basis for major decisions concerning the objectives and general direction of treatment and for details of its early stages. Second, it provides a fund of information that can be drawn upon throughout the entire treatment. Knowledge attained in the initial phases often gives shape to what comes later. As we have said, social study, diagnosis, and treatment go on simultaneously. As new information or new perspectives emerge, the treatment contract evolves, and goals are reinforced, modified, or substituted by new ones.

In this chapter we will consider: (1) ultimate or long-range objectives, (2) motivation and objectives, (3) resistance and objectives, (4) short-term or intermediate objectives, and (5) intervening variables affecting objectives. In the next chapter we will discuss treatment methodology and choice of procedures.

ULTIMATE OR LONG-RANGE OBJECTIVES

This section on long-range goals necessarily precedes our discussion of short-term (or intermediate) goals for obvious reasons: One cannot know what way stations will be required until we know what the *ultimate* aim of treatment is. For example, unless we know that a woman's ultimate goal is to separate from her husband, we cannot decide upon short-term goals such as locating a lawyer; making arrangements about housing, care for the children, and a job; dealing with feelings of loss; and so on.

Clients' Planned Changes Impact on Other Systems

The ultimate, mutually accepted objective of treatment is always some type of improvement in living conditions or personal-social life. Many clients seek improvement in their environments or within themselves or greater satisfaction in achievements or in interpersonal relationships. These types of improvements often go hand in hand, although the client may be primarily concerned with one more than with the others. External conditions often have repercussions on personal or family functioning. There is so much interplay between an individual and family members (or sometimes other people in a person's environment) that change in one individual's functioning usually significantly affects the other relationships. *Sometimes improvement in an individual's functioning is welcomed by others.* For example, the person may become easier to live with: more relaxed, freer, more giving with friends and loved ones, less hostile, more direct and clear in communications, more responsible, or able to avoid overuse of alcohol.

However, as we have pointed out elsewhere, *sometimes when an individual changes, the relationship is negatively affected;* other people close to that person may feel threatened. If, for example, a woman in individual treatment decides to pursue a career or to be more assertive with her husband who has tended to dominate her, serious marital problems may evolve. Or, a person with an alcohol problem gives up drinking but to his surprise—since he has been blamed and has blamed himself for family dissension—his wife may still be dissatisfied with the marriage; or other family members may manifest some new symptomatology, which affects family relationships. If possible, when individuals come into treatment, it is both ethical and effective to let the clients know that changes may not be wholeheartedly welcomed by other family members. Often, a worker will suggest including spouses or other involved people at some point, if not in ongoing conjoint therapy, so that changes can be incorporated more smoothly by the relationship system. In this way, each member can participate in the accommodation of the changes, ideally to the benefit of all.

Sometimes the problems seem to lie primarily in someone else, but even here interaction is involved and there is need for some change in the person seeking help. This was true in the case of Mrs. Harris (see pages 279–80) whose husband had beaten her. She had to decide what steps she wanted to take, whether she wanted to come back to see the social worker, whether she wanted her husband to join in the treatment, and so on. If a husband works long hours and is rarely home or is having extramarital affairs, the behavior may in some way reflect (but *not* be caused by!) problems in the marital relationship. If it is the wife who is coming for help, she will have to decide what to do. Does she want to try to engage him with her in therapy to try to improve the relationship? Does she still care about him and simply want to try to accommodate his behavior? Does she want to leave him? If so, is this realistic at this time?

Ultimate Goals Often Shift or Evolve

Frequently, location of a problem appears to be in one area at the outset of treatment but in another after a few interviews. The client may see the problem as difficulty with a child, while the worker, listening to the divergent ways in which the client and his wife handle the child, may locate the trouble as being also, or even primarily, tension between husband and wife. The worker may then need to find ways of helping the client make this connection so that he too will consider the objective of improving the marriage, at least as it contributes to the child's problems. We are repeatedly struck by how often children's symptoms subside when parents begin to address their

own difficulties. Or, as in the brief treatment of Esperanza Perez (Chapter 3), the initial goal of reducing depression and eliminating suicidal thoughts evolved into objectives related to her marital and family life.

Thus, as illustrated by the cases just mentioned, the *initial* long-range goal is usually related to the problem that clients are aware of at the beginning of the contact. However, objectives may shift as the client comes to redefine problems and needs. Sometimes clients have a broad awareness of the nature of the problem at the outset of treatment. In the very first interview, a mother may say, "I know there is something wrong with the way I am handling Tommie." She does not know all that lies behind the trouble, but she sees that she is involved as well as Tommie and either explicitly or implicitly recognizes that the goal of treatment requires that changes be made by her as well as by her son. Often, however, the client sees the trouble as residing only in the other person: child, husband, wife. Parents may see the problems of their teenage son as unrelated to their unhappy marriage although, in fact, he is reacting to his deep concern that they will divorce and is (often unconsciously) bringing attention to himself in hopes that they will unite in efforts to help him.[1]

Not only are initial goals often modified as treatment proceeds, but also other problems sometimes emerge; clients raise these problems for discussion, thus broadening the scope of treatment. Because of agency constraints or requirements of third-party payers for brief treatment, workers sometimes *prevent* an expansion of issues to be considered by keeping the focus narrow. In such cases, it is the agency or worker that *unilaterally* decides to limit treatment, often never letting the client know that more help might be beneficial. If additional problems become apparent and the worker cannot offer extended treatment, opportunities for appropriate referral should be vigorously sought. We do our clients and our profession a great disservice when we buckle under to the demands of bureaucracies or insurance companies, compromising our mission, without making every possible effort to locate the help for clients when we know they would use it. Upper-middle-class and affluent clients can always locate and pay for service; as discussed in Chapter 8, we need to make sure that agencies and independent practitioners are available to provide quality, affordable treatment to all others. (Issues surrounding managed care are discussed in greater detail in Chapter 18.) In the case of Mrs. Barry (Chapter 20), the worker in the psychiatric hospital attempted to refer her and her husband for marital treatment when it became apparent that Mrs. Barry's psychosis was only one of the issues that could be beneficially addressed.

External Pressures

In some cases where the problems derive almost exclusively from outside conditions, the goal is to promote changes in the external situation, either directly or by helping the client to do this. In others, the client may have to develop new ways of circumventing or adapting to the disturbing problems. For example, if a work or school situation is unsatisfactory or intolerable, client and worker together may search for new opportunities. If an elderly uncle joins a household, for example, and tensions develop, new means of coping with the situation may be found. Rather than just being irritated with the uncle's tendency to intrude on the handling of children or management of household matters, the parents may find ways to engage this older person as a "consultant." This role may provide him with a sense of effectiveness while au-

thority of the parents as managers of their home and family is not compromised. The more the clients actively engage in the search for solutions, generally the more successful the outcome; while the worker may offer support, encourage reflection, and make suggestions, it is the clients who will know best how to tailor their efforts to suit the circumstances with which they are far more familiar than is the worker. Once creative approaches to dealing with external pressures have proved effective, often when new problems occur in the future, clients are then better able to handle them without help. Thus, the achievement of specific objectives can lead to increased confidence and improved overall functioning.

Narrow and Broad Goals

Ultimate goals are sometimes quite limited and specific and at other times quite broad. The goal may be to enable an older person to arrange more suitable living arrangements, to work through a patient's fears about a necessary operation, or to help parents locate an appropriate resource for a child with special needs. On the other hand, as we have seen, it may be to bring about a better marital or parent–child relationship, or to help a client with chronic schizophrenia to make a better work and social adjustment, or to enable a person with a personality disorder to function more realistically and with greater personal satisfaction. Occasionally, worker and client simply cannot agree. For example, a client asked a worker to arrange for her seven-year-old son to be put in the local jail for a few days to impress him with the consequences of disobedience. Obviously, the worker could not comply. The only possible course was to accept the mother's desire to help her son behave differently and explain that the worker did not think jail was realistic, but that she would be glad to help her think about other ways of trying to influence the boy. If the client had insisted on her original goal (she did not!), worker and client would have reached an impasse.

MOTIVATION AND OBJECTIVES

No matter how accurate the worker's thinking about appropriate goals or subgoals may be, the force creating movement toward these objectives is dependent on the client's motivation.[2] This motivation, in turn, is dependent upon a variety of factors. One of these is the client's own *degree of discomfort* with things as they are. Have the clients come in on their own volition or have they been urged or even coerced into seeking help?

Reluctant Clients

If the referral was pressed upon people by relatives, by school, or by a supervisor at work because of personality or substance abuse problems, much will depend on the therapist's skill in helping the person to consider potential gain that might result from participating in treatment. With *support* from the worker, such clients may need to *ventilate* a good deal of feeling about the situation that precipitated the referral and about the person who urged it; they may blame others for their circumstances. Beyond that, they will need to be convinced of the worker's acceptance and interest in understanding and helping, *for their own sake* rather than to please others who are expressing dissatisfaction. Often, they expect the worker to judge them. Except in certain protective or court-mandated treatment, the client will need to know that the worker does not intend to impose services or change but is there to help, *only with the client's consent.* Helping clients to *explore* and *reflect* upon *their* concerns, to evaluate what if anything troubles *them* in their situation or in their relationships, can induce motivation. The worker must listen carefully and without bias or too many interruptions to clients' stories, to their interpretations and experiences; motivation to set goals derives from the elucidation of what is important to *them.* Guided by the client's objectives and motivation, worker and client arrive at some sort of "contract" about the purposes and nature of their work together.[3] The goals of the original contract, as described above, may be modified as treatment progresses.

Mandated Clients

The absence of motivation can make casework with mandated clients extremely difficult, although some of the above approaches can mobilize interest in the treatment process. Almost everyone who has been *ordered* to see a clinician has something to complain about, and the worker's understanding of the client's reactions can begin an engagement process. The Carter family case in Chapter 20 illustrates this point; even though involuntary clients do not have freedom to decide against casework contact, the worker can often devise techniques that induce incentive to consider goals that suit *their* needs and purposes. Sometimes clients are given "space" to choose to get help from the treatment process when the worker "joins the resistance" and says something like "I gather that you are not really interested in making any changes right now." When the client no longer feels that he or she must defy or react against the worker's efforts, motivation may emerge.[4]

The Influence of Hope

Motivation is very much affected by hope. It is easier to pursue a goal if one has faith that it can be achieved. Hope is partly influenced by the dilemma itself, which may be either stubbornly intransigent or one that can be remedied with relative ease. Most troubles, however, fall between these extremes. The worker's attitude, both expressed and unexpressed, can have considerable influence upon the degree of hope felt by the client. It is often helpful for the worker to put into words a belief that the client can achieve greater comfort or satisfaction through treatment, when the worker is confident that this is so.[5] Closely related to the influence of hope is the contagious effect of the worker's *enthusiasm* and *energy*. These can be expressed in various ways, including, with keen interest: "Let's see if we can't put our good heads together and find a way out of this difficulty," or "I'll bet if you and I really struggle to understand this, we can begin to arrive at solutions that will make a difference in how things work out."

Other Factors Affecting Motivation

We know that clients often enter treatment with much trepidation and often with underlying resentment at having to take what is in varying degrees a dependent position. This can be true even when clients come of their own volition, with favorable attitudes toward the agency and the nature of treatment. In a culture that values independence as much as ours does, it is not easy to admit that one cannot handle one's own problems, although increasing numbers of people seek some sort of counseling or psychotherapy. Fear of criticism or blame and fear of changes to which treatment may lead are often present, too. The resulting anxiety and discomfort may decrease motivation and make participation difficult.

On the other hand, *without some anxiety motivation may lag*. Anxiety is often the mobilizing force behind the request for help. The ideal therapeutic situation is one in which clients are anxious enough about their difficulties to want help and to keep coming for it but not so afraid that fear interferes with the ability to use help. When the circumstances that concern clients are—or, during the process of treatment, become—like "a thorn in the side," motivation is often high, even when there is considerable anxiety about the nature or the difficulty of the process required to make changes. People who are ordinarily very private about personal matters often will tolerate the discomfort of revealing themselves to the worker or to other family members when the problems seem severe enough to them to require this. In our experience, when threatened with the loss of their spouse or their employment, people with alcohol problems are more likely to seek help than when marriage and job—or something else of value—are not at risk.

Along the same lines, motivation is affected by the client's appreciation of the nature of a problem and its ramifications. Most individuals tend to minimize or to blind themselves to their difficulties. A husband may remember that he was irritable last night but does not fully appreciate the fact that last night was only one of many and that he is slowly becoming discouraged with his marriage, while his wife is becoming withdrawn and despondent. His motivation for treatment may be very low unless in the first few interviews he can come to realize that his marriage is really in trouble and that his wife, despite her defensive appearance of indifference, is deeply hurt because she still has a great deal of love for him. Often, when one partner's caring for the other comes to light during the exploratory period in joint interviews, the other will exclaim, "But I thought you didn't care anymore. Why haven't you told me this before?" Or, "How could I have been so blind?" After such realizations, motivation may come to life. Their occurrence at any stage of treatment may mark the turning point from resistance to full participation and may make possible intermediate goals quite different from those thought feasible before.

Motivation and Values

Motivation is closely related to values. Only if parents believe that a child should do well in school will they become interested in improving the child's school adjustment. Only if parents believe that a child should be happy and spontaneous will they be disturbed by the child's excessive anxiety and inhibitions. Only if a wife believes in an egalitarian marriage will she complain if her husband is dominating. Clearly, class and ethnic factors, as well as more individualized family and personal norms, enter into these values.[6]

The fact that a certain way of client functioning is the "mode" for a particular ethnic group or class is not sufficient to ensure that it is the most useful way of functioning if the client's goals appear to be impeded by it. Workers must *never* try to impose their own ways of doing things or introduce culturally foreign goals because of personal preference, but they should raise questions if it appears that social functioning and personal well-being will be enhanced if another perspective is considered. When cultural customs interfere with goals that interest clients, the worker may be able to offer a broader vision of choices. Men in some cultures are raised with the slogan "Men do not cry"; women from many parts of the country and world were taught that they should be deferential to their husbands; some children are still expected to be "seen and not heard." When individuals or families seek treatment for some problem or tragedy that has befallen them, and the worker believes that a culturally influenced

approach is hampering resolution, it is often necessary to sensitively question whether these particular traditions are serving the clients well *at this point*. Here we can see the value of encouraging *reflection; very rarely* in these instances would we recommend that the worker use *direct influence*.

Similarly, in a family in which a teenage son may be angry at his father's "old world" expectations and demands, the worker can help the father consider how hard it is for the son to make friends when he is so much more restricted than his peers are. The worker might ask the father about his own teenage experiences, his friendships outside of the family, and whether these were valued by him. Along with this, the son can be encouraged to realize the basis for his father's ideas and the differences between the old country and the new. The worker's major task here is—by promoting understanding—to reduce the animosity between father and son and perhaps to offer options, thereby helping them to reflect on whether and how they wish to resolve the conflict between them. Again, it is not the worker's role to impose or even recommend a specific solution or compromise.

It has long been recognized that workers' values, including those deriving from class and ethnic background, can enter into judgments concerning treatment goals. Like any other countertransference, the worker must be alert to the urge to translate *personal* values into goals for the client. There are times, however, when *professional* norms or values inevitably become a factor in the consideration of treatment objectives. In cases where parents use physical measures to chastise their children—even if their actions do not constitute abuse—it is usually appropriate to encourage more supportive means of responding to children's behavior; this can be true even when parents justify physical punishment, indicating that they were disciplined in this way and benefited from it. Current knowledge indicates that spanking often promotes aggression in children, and this information can be shared with clients. Or, when a mother complains about her adolescent daughter's attitudes, such as moodiness or negativity, the worker may point out that these are not unusual in teenagers and often reflect the young person's conflict between dependence and independence. The worker's response should include considerations of class and ethnic background that influence role expectations; these constitute part of any evaluation of norms. Under some circumstances, the worker may suggest a tentative objective of narrowing the gap between the initial problem as presented by a client and the worker's professional conception of socially and personally healthy functioning. Of course, such an objective is realizable only if the client also can see its value.

Many clients are extremely self-critical and have been trained that it is "only right" to be very harsh with themselves about any real or imagined shortcomings or mistakes. In these cases, the worker may recognize that their demanding superegos significantly impair ego functions that could enhance their lives and relationships. Workers often help clients realize, by educative techniques and by example, that a more compassionate and balanced view of themselves may ultimately lead to greater personal comfort and freedom. This type of evaluation leading to client–worker reflection is a constant part of the development of treatment themes and objectives.

RESISTANCE AND OBJECTIVES

Resistance may be defined as anything that clients do or feel, consciously or unconsciously, that interferes with the mutually agreed upon work and goals of therapy. As Nelsen points out in her now classic article: "Resistance is a most useful sign of something going awry, of a relationship or issue needing clarification."[7] In many respects, resistance and motivation are two sides of the same coin: to "reduce resistance" is often to "increase motivation." The term *resistance* is used pejoratively at times; it is occasionally implied that clients who evidence resistant behavior are doing so deliberately or out of stubbornness. Workers can talk about resistance in a way that implies they have "caught" the client at something. Occasionally, groups are unfairly characterized as "resistant" or "uncooperative": the poor, the uneducated, the "hard-to-reach," the adolescent, or people in the criminal justice system may be stereotyped as such when the worker simply may not have found ways to engage them or to determine what goals might interest them.

In most treatment situations, resistance is natural and should be expected to some degree. It can provide clients with opportunities for self-understanding. It can be a way of letting the worker know that something is amiss in the treatment relationship or process. To address resistance (which, with an eye on timing, we almost always should), we must first try to determine, *primarily through discussion with clients,* what clients are actually resisting. An individual or family may start missing appointments, changing the subject, seeming worried or uneasy during sessions, heavily using defenses of intellectualization or denial, or refusing to bring in family members who are involved in the problems. Treatment is usually impeded by such attitudes or behavior. Clients' reactions to the therapy process must be explored. Is there resistance to the worker's approach or style? Or is the worker's agenda different from the clients'? Are clients in disagreement with goals suggested by the worker but averse to saying so? Is there fear that the worker wants clients to change in ways that they do not want to? Is the client worried about worker criticism or blame? Is there (realistic or unrealistic) concern about repercussions of inviting an angry spouse to join sessions? Is there anxiety about facing painful material? Or does it represent natural hesitation about changing ways of thinking and behaving, even when the client sees this as necessary? Is there reluctance to modify long-standing relationship patterns even though the client realizes these are not now functional?

Sometimes clients, without prompting, explain unreadiness to proceed. Generally, however, *it is the worker's responsibility to anticipate resistance and to become attuned to signs of it.* One must then find ways to discuss it. The worker may inquire: "Are you finding it hard to understand why I am asking questions about this?" Or, one might say: "As we go along, you may find yourself dissatisfied with the way we are working on this, or you may feel upset by or in disagreement with something I say. It is important that you mention these feelings when they come up." When it appears that clients are concerned that they will be pressured into changes they do not want to make: "Let's go over the goals you have in mind in this situation; decisions about these will be entirely up to you, you know."

Acknowledgment that ambivalence is to be expected often helps: "With everything else you are having to do right now, it must be awfully hard to concentrate on this matter, even though you think it is important." Or, "I sense that it is just too hard right now to ask your husband to join us." Or, "Some subjects are painful to discuss. Do let me know when you find it hard to talk about something." Or, "As much as one may want to make things better, it can still be hard to change old habits." These comments

not only help to bring resistance out in the open but also protect the *mutuality* of the treatment, a critical issue discussed in detail in Chapter 9.

When a client is often late or is skipping sessions one might say, "Are you having some mixed feelings about our work together?" Or, when a client volunteers nothing about being appreciably late: "Did you have trouble getting here today?" This nonthreatening question leaves room for the client either to share information about something that caused a delay or to raise some other issues that suggest uneasiness about coming to the session. To a person who has the goal of "getting my life together" but is at the same time evading discussion of self-destructive behavior: "You have told me that you wish to get help to put your life in order, but I sense that some of the issues that relate to this goal seem almost too painful for you to look at." Or, "Have you noticed that when I suggest looking at other ways of dealing with your feelings, you quickly change the subject?" Or, to a heavy drinker, "When you keep saying that you wouldn't drink so much if Susan behaved differently, do you think you are finding it hard to take a look at your part in what is happening?" To a couple: "Do you think it is easier for you both to focus on your son's mischief than on the tension in your own relationship?" When the worker's nonjudgmental interest in the client is accompanied by bringing resistance out in the open, the treatment process is usually significantly enhanced. Of course, there must be a willingness to listen to negative comments from clients, even when they are about the worker or the therapy; worker self-awareness and professional discipline are required here, because sometimes it can be very uncomfortable to listen to unflattering remarks from clients. Yet, when resistance is not addressed, the result is often misunderstanding about objectives, client dropout, or ineffective drifting during sessions.

SHORT-TERM OR INTERMEDIATE OBJECTIVES

The short-term or intermediate goals of treatment are way stations on the road to the ultimate aim, means by which it is hoped the final objectives will be achieved. As long-range objectives are modified or substituted for others, these subgoals also change. For example, a client had an ultimate goal to separate from her husband but, after a period of treatment, she decided she wanted to try to see if the marriage could work after all. Intermediate goals had to be reevaluated to correspond to the new goal (e.g., moving from preparing for conjoint meetings with her husband to discuss custody of the children to planning couple meetings to explore the viability of the marriage.)

For guidelines to the formulation of subgoals, the worker relies upon insights gained in the diagnostic assessment. The strengths and weaknesses and the dynamics of the person–situation systems have now been at least partially clarified; there is some degree of understanding of the major factors that contribute to the problem. Again, the field is studied, this time to see where modification may be possible. What factors seem to be salient in bringing about the difficulty? Which are not likely to change or will change only with great difficulty? What weaknesses or idiosyncrasies exist in the client's personality, relationship patterns, or larger environment? Where are the personal strengths and external resources that can be brought to bear on the dilemma? Usually, worker and client go over these questions together.

Illustrations of various kinds of intermediate goals may be useful. We speak of encouraging a mother to send her child to camp or to help a husband share his thoughts and feelings more fully with his wife. Or we say that we will endeavor to reduce the severity of the superego or to strengthen a client's ability to assert needs or to modify a tendency to project. These are "shorthand" descriptions of what may be a lengthy process. The plan to encourage a mother to send her child to a camp he was eager to attend was a treatment objective for a woman who had been widowed a year earlier and knew she was overly dependent on her 14-year-old son. As a result, the son was being deprived of normal developmental experiences. The mother wanted her son to mature but found many reasons for not sending him to camp. It took many weeks of work to enable this mother to recognize her fears; to discuss her husband's death, her grief and resentment; to see that her dependence on her son was denying him companionship with boys his own age and that this was not good for him; and to realize that she was postponing getting on with her own life by keeping her son so closely tied to her.

Such short-term objectives are sought only because they are seen as necessary to achieve an ultimate goal of improved personal-social functioning. They are closely related to *procedures of treatment* (as described in Chapters 5 through 7) and are often articulated in combination with them. A worker may say he "hopes to reduce anxiety with *acceptance* and *reassurance* and by *suggesting* that the sister-in-law who lives nearby visit daily," or that he will "try to reduce hostility toward a child by *ventilation* of the parents' suppressed anger," or he will "help the mother to see that her failure to set limits on her young son is increasing the boy's anxiety," or he will "use a *corrective relationship* to help Mrs. George reduce her tensions about sex," or he will "try to help Mr. Juarez through *developmental reflection* to recognize that his anger at his son is related to underlying hostility toward his father," or he will "urge Mrs. Field to *reflect on the consequences* of her impulsiveness in an effort to help her to regulate it."

None of these objectives is an end in itself but a way station on the road to better personal-social functioning. *Each is a means to the client's overall objective.* The connection between these intermediate goals and the client's wishes is almost always discussed in detail with the client, in language that is nontechnical and understandable; often the client participates in the selection of subgoals. Such discussion has a double advantage for the client: (1) increasing motivation to participate in treatment steps toward the ultimate goal and (2) recognizing the value of similar ways of handling problems when they arise in the future.

The Presenting Problem and Intermediate Objectives

The Jones Couple   In the brief treatment case of Dick and Susan Jones discussed in Chapter 3, the presenting problem was the crisis in their marriage precipitated by Susan's affair. The ultimate goal agreed upon by husband and wife never really changed: They wanted to save their marriage. As it turned out, they not only prevented it from breaking up but also stabilized and improved it. The selection of several subgoals, *in consultation with Dick and Susan,* led to the successful outcome. These intermediate goals included: (1) to explore Dick and Susan's concern about Dick's temper; (2) to help Dick put into words his angry feelings of betrayal, his fears of losing his wife, his loss of trust; (3) to enlist Susan's participation by recognizing her part in the marital problem; (4) to help them both reflect on their patterns of interaction during their years together; (5) to en-courage Dick's reflection on the roots of his "passivity" and tendency to withdraw that both spouses believed had contributed to the buildup of marital problems; (6) to help Susan recognize the influence of her family-of-origin experiences, especially the feelings about her father that led to her feel hopeless about ever having a man who truly loved her; (7) to affirm and support the many personal strengths of both spouses, including their roles as caring parents and their dedication to the marriage despite their crisis; (8) to explore their role flexibility in view of Susan's wish to work outside the home; and (9) to offer realistic hope that they have the capacity to achieve their goal and even bring their marital relationship to a new level.

Subgoals in the Case of Mrs. Kord
Similar outlines of intermediate goals can be made in many other situations that confront clients. In the case of Mrs. Kord, a 65-year-old woman whose husband's mental and physical deterioration after several strokes appeared to require permanent institutional care, the worker proposed several subgoals. All of these were fully discussed with and contributed to by Mrs. Kord as they considered her situation: (1) to learn through a medical appraisal whether she was right in believing that institutional care was the best plan; (2) to help Mrs. Kord emotionally accept the inevitability of this step; (3) to the extent possible, to prepare Mr. Kord for this change; (4) to help Mrs. Kord work through her feelings of guilt over no longer being able to care for her husband; (5) to help Mrs. Kord work out the actual plans for her husband; (6) to involve close relatives who were concerned about Mr. Kord and who unrealistically brought pressure to bear on Mrs. Kord to continue to keep him at home when she was physically unable to do so; (7) to help Mrs. Kord begin

to resolve her guilt over the placement and her grief over the loss of her husband; and (8) to help Mrs. Kord resume former interests and pleasures.

The nature of the presenting problem is an important determinant of both long-range and intermediate goals. The subgoals and associated tasks are decided on the basis of many other factors, including the personalities, preferences, motivation, and capacities of the individuals involved and the availability of resources.

Intermediate Objectives and Systems Considerations

Dynamic Understanding   Intermediate goals are related to the dynamic understanding of factors contributing to the difficulty. It is not enough, however, simply to locate what appear to be salient contributing factors. A second question arises: *Which of these numerous factors lend themselves to modification?*

Unmodifiable Contributing Factors Sometimes the most prominent factor in the dynamics of the problem is not the most likely to yield to treatment. The most directly disturbing element in a family may be the presence of a severely retarded boy whose condition is not expected to improve. It is the other family members, particularly the parents, who have to determine how best to plan for the child. There may be disagreement: One parent may favor institutional placement and the other may prefer to keep the child at home. There may be no suitable place to send him within visiting distance that does not have a long waiting list. It may be possible to find a day care program for the boy so his needs do not dominate the household and deprive the other children of attention; this possible plan might also afford the boy opportunities

for social connections outside the family. On the other hand, problems arising with other children in the family, exhaustion of the parents, or reflective consideration by the parents may lead to shifts in perception that ultimately result in a decision to place the handicapped child.

Poor housing is often a factor that cannot be improved. High rents, a family's low income, and crowded conditions in the city may make it impossible to move to a better location, at least for the time being. Attention may have to be focused on resources for recreation, on the children's peer relationships, and on opportunities to strengthen these in the local community center; health care and income management may be of concern. Sometimes a marital and/or parent–child problem arises because of the physical deterioration of one parent—who has multiple sclerosis, for example—which is not yet serious enough to require hospitalization but does require substantial modification of family roles and relationships. Although the major cause of the problem cannot be remedied, the family develops new patterns to accommodate changing circumstances.

Sometimes the unmodifiable contributing factor lies *within the personality* of the client. An illustration of this occurred in the case of a very attractive young woman who was extremely dependent and desperately wanted a man to take care of her; this attitude led her to involve herself in unwise relationships with lovers who gave the appearance of strength but always turned out to have severe personality flaws that eventually caused her unhappiness and suffering. It became clear that her dependence was so strong and deep-seated that it was impossible for her to change it very much. However, the caseworker was able to help her to recognize her pattern and the consequences of her haste in trying to satisfy her needs;

together, they endeavored to strengthen her perception and judgment so this client would be better able to find a suitable person to lean on. As it turned out, she did meet a stable, kind, older man with many caretaking and other complementary qualities whom she eventually married and with whom she was able to be relatively content. Similarly, a man with a severe obsessive-compulsive personality disorder may never be able to experience much pleasure or spontaneity or to enjoy relationships fully, but, with casework treatment and medication, it may be possible for him to reduce his rigidity and tendency to procrastinate and to become less painfully perfectionistic.

One whole group of contributing factors can never be changed: *harmful developmental experiences.* The individual's *reactions* to these experiences may be modified, but not the experiences themselves. This was true, for example, of the woman described in Chapter 7 who harbored anger at her parents for not letting her go to college although, as she later came to see, she never let them know that college interested her. At other times, however, such as in cases of sexual and physical child abuse, or parental alcoholism, or neglect, or loss of a parent, reactions cannot be totally reversed; the pain and sorrow of these experiences generally last to some degree for a lifetime. However, once clients have had an opportunity to experience relief and understanding and become aware of how these early traumas have influenced current functioning, it is often possible to reduce the overwhelming intensity of the effects; from there, many are able to learn to build on personal strengths and seek opportunities for constructive, loving relationships that enrich their present lives. Sometimes the best "corrective" experiences are found in caring, reliable personal rather than professional relationships. The degree of modifiability of reactions and

the setting of realistic goals are related to assessment of strengths and weaknesses in the client's situation, to strengths of the various ego functions, and to motivation to engage in sometimes extended individual, family, and/or group treatment.

The Point of Intervention and Tipping the Balance By knowing that change in any element of a system has an effect on every other element, we know it is not necessary to work directly with all aspects of a problem. We discussed earlier how improvement in one part of a system can either bring improvement in another or can affect another part adversely. For instance, when the presenting problem is a teenage boy's hostility toward his mother, if this is accompanied by rivalry between father and son, encouraging a better mother–son relationship may result in increased father–son tension and husband–wife tension. In such a situation, other approaches, or intermediate objectives, may be both possible and preferable. A better husband–wife relationship may need to precede work on the son's problem. Or it may be best to work with the father, helping him with fear that he is less important to his wife than is the son. Or it may be better to work with the boy himself, helping him to build greater security outside the family. Frequently, the most effective approach would be to treat the total family problem in family interviews or to combine these with couple and individual interviews.

The *order* in which different aspects of a problem are best considered can be important. A pertinent illustration of this is found in the Russo case, described in Chapter 15, in which the father–daughter conflict was an initial focus in family treatment. This was so for two reasons: first, because it was one of the problems the family found easiest to discuss in early sessions and, second, because on assessment of the family system, it was predicted that an improved relationship between Mr. Russo and his daughter would diminish the force of the mother–daughter collusion against the father. Also, as mother and daughter became less dependent on one another, the treatment focus could then shift to the marital relationship.

In choosing which aspect of a dilemma to deal with, workers often use another characteristic of systems—each system usually has *a point of maximum reverberation.* This refers to a salient spot in a system at which change will bring about the greatest amount of modification in other elements. One member of a family may be a "key person." The case of Joan (see pages 74–75) illustrates how a single change in the stepfather triggered resounding changes in the balance of the family system and the personalities of all the members. In an employment problem, the key person may be the union representative rather than the supervisor, or it may be the client's wife or husband. Within the personality system, even a small amount of relaxation of the superego can help to free many ego functions that have been inhibited by harsh self-criticism. In Chapter 16 we will describe how seemingly intrapsychic phobic symptoms in women may be remarkably relieved when their husbands join them in treatment and become more intimately involved and self-revealing. In other words, by looking at the interrelationships within and among systems, the worker can judge where the point of greatest effectiveness lies and suggest intermediate treatment objectives that may begin to modify the balance of forces.

Clinical Diagnosis

As indicated in the previous chapter, the clinical diagnosis sometimes supplements dynamic understanding. When relevant, it

helps to clarify dynamics and increases sensitivity to elements that are likely to exist, even if they are not yet apparent. In this sense, it affects intermediate treatment goals in the same way that dynamic understanding does, with the additional value that it suggests some goals and provides information about what may or may not be acceptable or helpful to an individual.

Examples may help. Often a person suffering from a neurotic disorder is ready to understand and accept goals directed toward the well-being of another much sooner than, for instance, a person with a narcissistic personality disorder. Generally, when a narcissistic personality disorder is involved, because of intense self-centeredness, altruistic objectives are not realistic, at least not early in treatment. A client with an obsessive-compulsive personality disorder may accept a goal for the benefit of another person readily enough; but if efforts to achieve the goal fail, there is risk of impatient frustration or of increased guilt and reinforcement of an already too punishing superego unless care is taken to ward it off.

Neuroses   Broadly speaking, treatment objectives for neuroses often relate to reducing inner conflict, usually by facilitating a shift in the balance of the personality system. Rigid or harsh aspects of the person's psychological functioning, especially ego defenses and the superego, often need softening. Usually, this will free up already well-developed ego functions stifled by other elements of the personality. Sometimes, ego capacities, although relatively sound, require support and validation, especially when painful inner conflicts or external pressures have undermined confidence. Events, thoughts, feelings, and needs that have been buried or diverted may need to be brought into awareness. References to such concepts as *reduction, relaxation, affirma-*

tion, and *uncovering* are often included in treatment plans for clients diagnosed as having neurotic conditions: "to help Mr. Ortiz reduce guilt or self-criticism"; "to ease anxiety by 'giving' Mrs. Gray permission to explore her own needs and feelings"; "to help Mr. Noto relax his severely restrictive superego so that he is less driven by rigid 'shoulds' and 'oughts' "; "to affirm Mrs. Blye's capacity for good judgment about her handling of the children"; "to help Ms. Smith uncover and recall some childhood experiences and feelings that seem to relate to current fears and tensions in close relationships."

Personality Disorders   In contrast, people with personality disorders frequently need help in *building* and *integrating* capacities that have gaps or lack synthesis. Some or many of the ego functions and defenses often require *strengthening* rather than relaxing. Cognitive capacities often must be encouraged and reinforced. Many clients with personality disorders need help with *differentiation,* that is, with distinguishing one feeling from another, or thoughts from feelings, or thoughts and feelings from reality. In treatment, amorphous global feelings (such as rage and emptiness) sometimes can be matured into feelings that are more specific. The "split" between "good" and "bad" feelings about self and others may need to be bridged. When realistic, it is often necessary to support a sense of continuity—an "emotional memory"—that allows the individual to be aware that he or she will be all right, or that others will remain constant, even in the face of a minor setback or disagreement. Greater independent functioning— less reliance on others for direction or for filling basic emotional needs—may have to be fostered by the development of greater self-reliance and confidence. Many clients with serious personality disorders are se-

verely self-critical and unforgiving of themselves. They frequently need help appraising themselves more realistically; almost always they need to develop a greater capacity for "self-soothing." The superego and ego ideal may need to be better or more evenly developed in various ways.[8]

The following illustrate some treatment objectives that may be formulated for clients with personality disorders: "to help Mrs. Altman become aware of the relationship between her cutting criticisms of her husband and his withdrawal"; "to help Mr. James to make 'ego-alien' his urge to belittle his son"; "to encourage Mrs. D'Alia to distinguish between what she *perceives* her husband is doing and saying and what she *fears*"; "to help Mr. Barnes to recognize feelings of sadness and fear rather than only pervasive fury"; "to foster Ms. Klein's tolerance for her past behaviors and to develop greater compassion for herself"; "to heal the 'split' and encourage Mr. Allen to begin to recognize that 'good' and 'bad' feelings toward himself and others can coexist"; "to help Jane believe that even though she is receiving poor grades in college, her emotional well-being or her relationship with her father will not be permanently jeopardized"; "to help Mrs. Cabot realize that she has many worthwhile opinions of her own and need not rely so consistently on those of others"; "to help John begin to learn the good feelings he can enjoy through helping others"; "to promote a 'corrective' therapeutic relationship in order to facilitate the maturation and synthesis of ego functions."

Overlapping Conditions   As we said in Chapter 11, neurotic and personality disorders often overlap and are often observed in the same person. Some blend of both kinds of objectives may be necessary, always depending on and related to the client's reasons for seeking treatment.

Some of these objectives may be relevant when no clinical diagnosis is indicated but when a client's difficulties seem to arise in part from personality traits or behaviors that interfere with functioning or with the achievement of ultimate goals.

Psychosis With psychosis in general, treatment objectives are usually closely related to the development of a stronger and more accurate sense of reality, to coping with concrete problems, and to strengthening social and coping skills. With clients with schizophrenic disorders, often one important subgoal is to establish a steady, nonjudgmental, caring but—in many cases—not-too-close relationship. Although it is essential to convey acceptance and understanding, it is often also important to protect a client with schizophrenia from becoming frightened of engulfment by the worker; if the treatment relationship is experienced as warm or close, as much as this may be desired by the client, it may stir up great anxiety. As noted earlier, with clients with psychosis, it is often an intermediate objective of the worker—which clients may not at first share—to encourage an evaluation by a psychiatrist that includes consultation for medication.

INTERVENING VARIABLES

Thus far we have been discussing treatment goals from a client-centered perspective. A number of other factors must enter into the emergence of both intermediate and long-term goals.

Needs of Family Members and Others

It is the exception rather than the rule that the worker can be concerned with the welfare of the individual client alone. The total client–situation system usually includes other members of the client's family, or at least other individuals of significance to the client. The social worker always has an indirect responsibility to these other people. This constitutes another factor intervening between motivation and treatment goals. As we mention at various points in this book, the worker must consider the effect on others of changes sought by or for the individual who for the moment is the focus of attention. This does *not* mean the worker suggests that clients should sacrifice their interests to those of another. But it *does* mean that it is the worker's responsibility to bring to clients' awareness the complementarity that exists in family relationships: change in one member not only brings changes in others, but also results in counterreactions that affect the person who initiated the change. This is not an intrusion into the integrity of the treatment process, for neither worker nor client can wisely plan goals without giving full consideration to implications for others.[9] Earlier in this chapter we gave examples of positive and negative reactions by family members to changes made by an individual in treatment that had repercussions on the entire family system. As discussed in the family and couple chapters, ideally, significant family members participate in the treatment process to some degree.

Sometimes clients consider goals that could be hurtful, detrimental, or even hazardous to people with whom they are not intimate but with whom they are associated. For example, one woman client seriously discussed a plan for circulating negative rumors about a co-worker with whom she was competing for a promotion. In another case, a man resented the fact that a large family from an ethnic group different from his own had rented a home near his; this client was considering ways of harassing his prospective neighbors in a manner that would frighten them and pressure them to live elsewhere. In both cases, it was important for the worker to ask the clients about these intentions. To each of them she asked questions something like: "Are you surprised that you would consider taking actions that would create so much pain for others?" "Do you think you will have regrets if you follow through?" "Would you consider doing this to people you care more personally about?" "What would it be like for you if the situation was reversed?" Almost always, people who would seriously contemplate such antisocial behavior show signs of uneven superego–ego ideal development that affect other aspects of their lives. Questions such as these are designed to help people reflect on their own values and motives, on what kind of people they want to think of themselves as being; and, one would hope, they are helped to develop or get in touch with caring feelings for others. Often, when clients bring up such ideas in treatment they are feeling conflicted about them.

Sometimes when a client has little motivation for making personal changes, interest can be mustered to make changes that will benefit others. The following case illustrates the point. In her family and on her job, a woman habitually took on the role of "martyr" or "go-between," doing a lot for others, seldom asking for anything for herself, and yet resenting that others did not show her the consideration she showed them. Despite her irritation, awareness of this long-standing pattern did not result in her making significant changes. However, when she realized that by being the one to mediate between her teenage son and his father, from whom she was divorced, she was interfering with the father–son relationship and actually infantilizing and promoting fear in her son, only then did she make efforts to modify her habitual behavior.

Peripheral Factors

Before examining treatment procedures in the next chapter, we must consider a few additional variables that intervene between treatment and the ideal objective of modifying or removing some factors contributing to clients' difficulties.

Time   An obvious variable is time. If experience indicates that a certain type of change is likely to require a number of months of work and the client will be available for only a few interviews, it is usually contraindicated to embark upon a line of treatment that will have to be interrupted midway. A decision on time is sometimes influenced by the special function or orientation of the agency (as in certain crisis or hospital services where contact is limited to a short time span, or in an agency that offers only brief treatment); under these circumstances, referral to another agency or practitioner may become a major treatment objective. Clients' situations may also affect timing; the matter about which a client is coming for help may have to be settled within a few days or a few weeks. Even in long-term treatment, a client or family may have to move away. Themes may be emerging at this point about which treatment decisions must be made. If they cannot be developed profitably within the time available, they should be set aside rather than opened up and dealt with inadequately; in these cases, if clients feel that their short-term or long-term goals have not been achieved, referral possibilities should be discussed.

Agency Function   Another variable affecting the goals and nature of treatment may be the way in which agency function is defined. The course of a case in which there are both parent–child and marital problems may differ if the client applies to a child-oriented clinic rather than to a family service agency. A woman who is deciding whether to separate from her ill but very difficult husband may be offered very different treatment if she goes to the social service department of the psychiatric hospital where her husband is being treated rather than to a community mental health clinic. Treatment planning and formulation of treatment objectives may be significantly influenced by the role definition of the agency and the worker.

Agency Priorities and Resources   An agency's view of priorities in its function will often translate itself into other variables affecting the treatment process: offices that do or do not provide privacy or protection from interruption during interviews, caseloads that permit 45- to 60-minute interviews per week for each client who needs the time, or caseloads that are too large to permit interviews of this length or frequency, among others. Casework that has as its central objective a substantial change in individual functioning usually requires uninterrupted and regular interviewing time. Exceptions to this do occur. Crisis treatment often occurs in the midst of interruptions and unplanned interviews: in hospitals, schools, storefront facilities, or at the scene of disaster. The intensity of emotion aroused by the crisis may make concentration possible despite distractions, and the immediate availability of interviews may be more important than other considerations. The availability of medical, psychiatric, educational, or other kinds of consultation, depending on client need, may significantly influence treatment goals and procedures.

Skill   The clinical social worker's skill is another intervening factor of great importance.[10] Different themes, aims, and procedures call on various kinds of skill. Individual, couple, and family treatment each require particular abilities and talents. Work with children and adolescents has its special demands. Patients with catastrophic illnesses and their families usually do best with workers who have personal and professional experience and skill in this area. Treatment of chronically ill psychiatric patients calls for specific knowledge and ability.

The worker must define treatment objectives that lie within his or her range of competence and skill rather than venturing into a treatment for which he or she is unprepared and unsure. This requirement, however, must not be taken to mean that treatment skill is static and cannot be further developed in workers; but professional development is achieved by *gradually* reaching just beyond the border of one's present well-established ability, not by luring the client into deep and troubled waters to sink or swim along with the worker!

Ideally, the client's need should be met by whatever form of treatment will bring the greatest relief from discomfort; it is important for clinicians to be informed about (and even participate in) research that can throw light on what types of treatments may be effective with particular types of problems or personalities. This means either that the agency function should be sufficiently flexible to adapt to varying needs and new information or that, when necessary, transfers should be made to other agencies that offer the required treatment. It also means that within agencies clients should be referred to workers whose skill and experience are adequate to meet their particular needs. Similarly, a clinical worker in private practice needs to know other workers and agencies that specialize in areas that are not part of his or her own expertise.

The ultimate objectives of treatment are determined jointly by client and worker. The motivation of individuals and families is central to treatment. Intermediate goals are means to clients' ultimate objectives, sometimes formulated and suggested by the worker, sometimes devised by the client or by worker and client together. In any case, these short-term goals are always discussed in lay terms with clients to ensure that they are mutually acceptable; sometimes clients refine or modify subgoals to more closely suit their perspectives. Intermediate goals rest on the nature of the problems to be dealt with, on dynamic understanding, and on clinical diagnosis. They are guided also by the assessment of modifiability, of strengths, of weaknesses, and of points in the client's personality, family, or social system at which interventions are likely to be most effective. Several intervening variables require attention. The objectives of treatment must be thought of as fluid, altered as changes develop in clients' circumstances, in their understanding of their own needs, and in their motivation. Ideas about ultimate goals and subgoals also may shift as the worker's understanding of clients' situations, requirements, and capacities grows. Clients' responses to treatment and ability to use it are of major importance in these reformulations. Goals not only enable workers and clients to avoid drifting along in a friendly way but also make it possible to avoid blind alleys. Conscious treatment planning compels the clinician to think through the possibilities and consequences of a line of treatment before undertaking it and involving the client in fruitless effort. Collaborative, well-focused, well-thought-out therapy is likely to be effective therapy.

NOTES

1. See Satir (1983), especially Chapter 5, "Marital Disappointment and Its Consequences for the Child." Chapters 14 through 17 on family and marital therapy in this book discuss this important issue more fully.

2. Motivation is often discussed under the name of its opposite, that is, resistance, by which we mean any attitude or behavior of the client (of which he or she may be unaware) that interferes with the *mutually agreed upon* work of treatment. We will say more about resistance in this chapter. Perlman (1957) discusses motivation and related factors in Chapter 12 of her still useful text. See also Gold (1990) who writes about the importance of exploring issues related to client motivation. Smyth (1996) urges creative strategies in motivating persons with dual (psychiatric and substance-abuse) disorders.

3. As discussed previously (see especially Chapter 9), the term *contract* is generally used to describe the explicit common understanding of conditions and goals of treatment arrived at by client and worker. In psychosocial casework it is usually seen as an informal, ongoing process, with new agreements made as goals are modified or new goals emerge. On the general subject of client and worker goal-setting, see Compton and Galaway (1994), Chapter 10. For very useful readings on the contract, see Maluccio and Marlow (1974), Rothery (1980), and Rhodes (1977). Seabury (1976) discusses the uses, abuses, and limitations of the contract; while appreciating its value, he also cautions us about its shortcomings and possible dangers.

4. For references on reluctant or involuntary clients, see Chapter 5, note 7; Chapter 6, note 3; Chapter 8, note 19; and Chapter 9, notes 3 and 4.

   The idea of "joining the resistance" is not a new one, but it has taken a somewhat different turn in the last 20 or so years with the emergence of so-called paradoxical interventions. For the most part, we eschew paradoxical approaches. We do not like the seeming "trickiness" of them; many of the techniques do not strike us as being respectful to clients; as we see it, they tend to foster an "expert–idiot" model rather than a collaborative approach to treatment and the client–worker relationship. For ethical reasons, we prefer more straightforward communications; we believe that paradoxical interventions can be confusing and that clients generally do better when they understand how the changes they have made came about. Nevertheless, for those readers who are interested in exploring the notions upon which paradoxical treatment is based, we suggest two of the most responsible volumes on the subject: Papp (1983) and Weeks and L'Abate (1982).

5. In their well-known research report, Ripple, et al. (1964) dealt extensively with this issue in their study of the "discomfort-hope" balance in the client's use of treatment; for their conclusions, see pp. 198–206. Frank (1959 and 1968) was one of the first to emphasize the role of hope in treatment; see also Smaldino (1975) who wrote specifically about the importance of hope in the casework relationship. Subsequent research by Frank and others suggests that hope and related attitudes overcome demoralization; see Beutler, et al. (1994).

6. See Chapter 2, note 37 and Chapter 8, note 23. As always, it is important not to generalize, stereotype, or anticipate that clients will have particular attitudes on the basis of their class status or group identification.

7. Nelsen (1975c), p. 588. In addition to this excellent article, we recommend Anderson and Stewart (1983), Frankenstein (1982), Gitterman (1983), Howard Goldstein (1986), and Hartman and Reynolds (1987), and some very useful papers in the volume edited by Milman and Goldman (1987). In "Managing Opposition to Change," Hepworth (1997, pp. 568–75) offers clear ideas and suggestions.

8. See references on the treatment of personality disorders in Chapter 3, note 9 and Chapter 11, note 26.

9. In addition to numerous references on family and marital interaction and treatment cited elsewhere, see Leader (1979) in which he discusses the importance of helping family members to take responsibility for the effects of their communications and behavior on one another.

10. These issues were discussed in detail in Chapter 9 accompanied by many references in the notes on the skills, attitudes, and characteristics of the clinician that are most likely to lead to favorable treatment outcomes.

CHAPTER 13

CHOICE OF TREATMENT PROCEDURES

When we turn to the choice of treatment procedures (described in Chapters 5 through 8) by which we hope to move toward long-range and intermediate goals, we see that certain overall decisions about procedures are dictated by both objectives and diagnostic understanding. If one objective is to bring about environmental improvement, either *environmental treatment* or *extrareflection* is certain to be prominent. If there are problems of personal dysfunctioning and both diagnostic thinking and the client's motivation make self-understanding a reasonable objective, *intrareflection,* including, perhaps, *dynamic* and *developmental reflection,* will play a major role. Where the objective is improvement in interpersonal relationships, all aspects of current *person–situation reflection* will be in the forefront.

Not only does the broad initial diagnostic thinking guide the details of treatment, but also indispensable to the *immediate* choice

of procedures is continuous sensitive understanding. For instance, after an interview in which a client had ventilated much feeling about her husband's "TV addiction," as she called it, the worker anticipated that there would be an opportunity to encourage her client's beginning awareness that her intense annoyance at her husband's preoccupation with sports on TV paralleled a childhood reaction to her father's regular Saturday trips to the "Game," which always came before any family activity. However, as soon as the client entered the room for her next session, the worker noted her harassed expression and the recurrence of an eye twitch. The anticipated plan for the interview had to be set aside, and instead the worker sought to learn the cause of her client's present distress. Both basic diagnostic thinking and immediate perception of the client's need and readiness for one of these alternatives enter such decisions, decisions that must be made in a flash.

Each interview is a constantly moving encounter between a clinician and an individual, couple, or family—occasionally with a collateral person present when objectives require this—undertaking a common task. The worker's part in that task includes being continuously alert to clients' immediate feelings and attitudes, thinking, and reactions. In communication language, this is alertness to feedback, feedback that reveals how the interaction is proceeding and guides the worker's next procedures. Accurate reception of these communications requires not only close attention but also, even more important, empathy with the clients, a capacity to *feel with* each individual involved, at the same time one is *thinking* about what response will be most helpful. When one is unsure of exactly how clients are reacting, it is essential to seek as much information as possible through nonthreatening questioning rather than operating on guesswork.

ENVIRONMENTAL CHANGE

Many aspects of the relationships between diagnostic understanding and the procedures of treatment have been discussed in the chapters describing these procedures and their uses. The identification of factors contributing to a client's dilemma is the first indicator of whether environmental treatment is needed. Also, as we have pointed out many times, changes in the environment often have immediate effects on the inner life of an individual and on interpersonal relationships. A new job that is a better "fit" for a client may increase self-esteem, reduce anxiety, and contribute to a more satisfying marriage with little or no need for intrareflection. Locating a cheerful and competent homemaker may relieve a woman with young children enough to permit convalescence from major surgery without additional casework help. If a change in the external situation would seem to benefit a client, a second indi-

cator is the assessment of whether or not it is likely that the change can be brought about. If it appears that this might be possible, the next decision to be made is that of *how* to effect the change, through direct intervention by the worker or through helping clients to act for themselves.[1] Of course, the *general* preference of the psychosocial worker is to enable clients to do things for themselves whenever possible. So we must turn again to assessment: Is the client able or likely to become able to do this? Is the environment likely to respond to the effort? Will the worker's intervention be more effective than the client's? The dynamic diagnosis will be involved: How immediate is the need for the change? Is it urgent that change be made faster than the client is likely to be able to bring it about? One further diagnostic consideration: What is the state of the client's motivation and trust in the worker? Is it important for the worker to win the client's confidence by immediately doing something that will better his or her situation?

If direct environmental work is decided upon, the actual steps taken will again depend upon diagnostic thinking about collaterals as well as about the client. In work with people in the client's social environment, some impressions can be formed from what the client has said to the worker, but much of one's understanding is arrived at on the spot, as the person consulted responds to the worker's approaches. Since details of environmental work and of the issues involved were discussed in Chapter 8, we need not deal with them further here.

INTERPERSONAL RELATIONSHIPS, INTERNAL CHANGE, AND PERSON–SITUATION REFLECTION

When we turn to problems that primarily concern interpersonal relationships and internal change, we find that the nature of the problem and the opportunities for effective solution determine which procedures we select. As just mentioned, sometimes inner distress or dissatisfaction in relationships is efficiently addressed by modifying some aspect of the environment. Similarly, as the chapters on family and couple treatment will describe, there are times when apparently intrapsychic symptoms (e.g., depression or panic attacks) can best be relieved when changes are made in the family or marital balance.

In most cases, interpersonal and personal difficulties lead us to emphasize procedures designed to promote both outwardly directed and inwardly directed understanding.

Whether working with individuals, couples, or families, it is usual after the initial interviews for a predominance of worker communications to be of a reflective type, especially *person–situation reflection.*[2] (See Chapter 6 for a discussion of these reflective procedures and their uses.) The client, following the worker's lead, usually responds with a gradual increase in reflective communications. Sometimes, diagnostic observation indicates that a person is so depressed or that a family is so grief-stricken, so pressured by a crisis or health concerns that treatment at first is very heavily weighted with *sustainment, ventilation,* and some *direct influence* (see Chapter 5). In other cases, particularly with clients who are easily overwhelmed by their feelings, reflective procedures are blended heavily with sustainment. But in almost all cases, there is some movement into *thought* about themselves, their circumstances, and relationships; usually, there is also an effort to expand the *awareness of feelings* beyond anger, depression, or grief to other emotions.

As the worker listens to clients' discussions of interpersonal or other problems, the question constantly arises: Which thread of the communications should be picked up? This can be a particularly challenging issue in couple and family interviews. The worker seeks means to enable clients to gain the understanding needed to deal more effectively with the dilemma as rapidly as possible. However, it is important to avoid the possibility of overloading them with more new ways of looking at things than they can comfortably assimilate or are ready to take on. One should also go slowly and listen carefully to grasp rather than guess at clients' meanings and priorities. *To go too fast may be to lose clients.*

The Anxiety Factor in Early Interviews

A study by Hollis compared 15 clients with marital problems who continued in treatment with 15 who dropped out after the first or second interview. Those clients who dropped out were seen by workers who made markedly more lengthy interpretations and explanations in the initial interviews than did the workers whose clients continued.[3] Furthermore, it was found that these communications in many instances had a distinct potential for arousing anxiety. In contrast, in early interviews with clients who continued, anxiety-arousing comments had largely been avoided. This is not to say that reflective techniques, even *intrareflection,* can never be used in early interviews. Sometimes a worker can be straightforward, even incisive, yet nonthreatening. More often than not, reflective comments are put in question form (e.g., "Are you saying you think you acted more quickly than you wish you had?") so that clients do not feel pressured to accept the worker's interpretations.

If care is taken to assess the anxiety factor, introduction of some *person–situation reflection* into early interviews induces feedback that can aid diagnostic understanding and mutual clarification of early objectives of treatment. This also gives clients a sample of what the contact will be like, especially when there is an immediate treatment gain.

Mrs. Motley, a young single mother, was referred by a school psychologist to a family service agency because her eight-year-old son was daydreaming and crying in class. Projective tests revealed that he was consumed with rage and with fears that his family would abandon him. His father had died of AIDS two years earlier. In the first interview, the mother, who had had a very unstable childhood herself, wept and said that she saw history repeating itself. She had lived with a series of men, had moved frequently, and had been hospitalized for a "nervous stomach" three times over the past two years. She was sad, she said, that she had not given better care to her son than her alcoholic parents had given her. Expressing understanding of this woman's deep distress, the worker gently asked whether Mrs. Motley was perhaps asking for some help in stabilizing her own life as well as that of her son. Mrs. Motley, looking relieved, replied, "That's exactly what I want. I've been unhappy with myself for a long time." At the end of the first interview, it was clear that this client wanted to think introspectively about her own life and about her part in her son's problems. This young woman's openness to reflective thinking was a positive diagnostic sign and an indicator of her motivation for change.

When the worker can choose the sequence of issues to address, assessing the anxiety-arousing potential of each choice is highly pertinent. In the case of Mrs. Motley, who immediately indicated her concern about history repeating itself, the worker realized that *supportive comments* and *op-*

portunities for ventilation would *not* have been enough; because of the client's motivation for change, she might have been disappointed in the initial interview if the worker had not encouraged *reflection.* In other cases, as we have said, there is too much anxiety, sorrow, or other emotion to be able to focus right away on understanding the depth of the dilemma or to embark on a joint search for solutions.

When the worker recognizes tension and anger in family relationships, clients usually require adequate opportunity for expression of hurt and resentment. Questions or interpretations concerning how the *other* person feels or why the other person may act in a certain way are more likely to be accepted if they come later, unless diagnostic assessment reveals unusual openness to self-awareness and empathic feelings. Generally, it is more effective to help people speak about themselves and their own feelings before encouraging them to understand or feel for family members. When there is significant animosity, usually there is little readiness for appreciation of the way in which clients are hurting others, even a spouse or child; more often than not, they are not yet willing to look at how their behavior is provoking negative reactions, such as withdrawal or counterhostility. Assessment often indicates that not only client *ventilation* but also *acceptance* by the worker of feelings of hurt or desire to retaliate may be needed to prepare the way for clients to *reflect,* to understand others' needs, or to consider their own contribution to the troubles.

Personality Factors and Choice of Treatment Procedures

Factors within the personalities of clients will greatly influence readiness to try to understand themselves, their behavior, its effects on others, and the needs or feelings of people with whom they are involved. This point is well illustrated by two cases, carried by the same worker, of women in distress about their marriages.

A Study in Similarities and Contrasts: Two Case Studies   In the case of Mrs. Sonne, the worker was very active during early contacts in promoting the wife's *reflection* concerning her husband. In the case of Mrs. Lisov, emphasis was placed instead on the wife's expressions and *awareness of her own feelings.* The reasons for the difference in treatment lay not in the situations but in the worker's diagnostic understanding of the personalities of the two women. Both women were very afraid of not being loved, both were volatile women, both were of southern European background, both were belittling their husbands and putting all the blame for family unhappiness on them. Both were intelligent and motivated to seek help.

Mrs. Sonne, however, had no doubt of her love for her husband and had matured emotionally to the point that she was well related to other people and cared for their welfare as well as for her own. Clinically, one could say that her personality was relatively balanced and well developed, with evidence of some histrionic features. This client immediately responded with understanding to the worker's carefully worded questions about how her husband might feel, what her thoughts were about why he might be acting as he was, and what effect some of her impulsive hostility might be having on him. So it was possible for client and worker to proceed rapidly. Mrs. Lisov, clinically classified as having a narcissistic personality disorder, was a more dependent and self-centered person, preoccupied with her own anxieties; she clung to her husband but had difficulty feeling or demonstrating affection for him. She had little sponta-

neous interest in her husband's feelings or reasons for them. She wanted and needed to talk about herself and how he had hurt her. Her understanding of her *own* feelings toward her husband had to be given precedence over attempts to develop her understanding of him or the consequences of her own behavior.

Key Personality Factors   If we think of individuals as being on a continuum, falling into position at some point along the way, *guidelines for treatment* are often suggested. Among the key personality qualities to be considered and assessed are:

1. Self-Absorption versus the Capacity to Love   The quality of a person's capacity to love others—the ego's capacity for *object relationships*—is of primary importance in influencing readiness for *understanding others* and *reflecting on the effects of one's actions* upon others. Individuals greatly lacking in this quality usually are not sufficiently attuned to appreciate fully the feelings of others or to see ways in which they provoke and hurt them; generally this was true of Mrs. Lisov. Such people often lack motivation to look inward for the cause of difficulties; they may be unable to use treatment that requires much self-examination or *intrareflection,* especially in the early stages of treatment. There may be some introspection, but often of the narcissistic or self-pitying type. Sometimes such clients can be reached only to the extent that they feel the worker's strong *support* and genuine, nonjudgmental *acceptance.* Sometimes a client with this difficulty can be led to think of the effects of behavior on others *in the context of his or her own self-interest.* In the case of Mrs. Lisov, it took several weeks, and a great deal of *sustainment,* for her even to begin to *reflect* on her contributions to her marital problem and to her own unhappiness, a major one being her oblivion to the needs and feelings of her husband, who was increasingly withdrawn and unavailable to her. Generally, the greater the clients' capacity for affectional attachments, empathy, and reciprocity in relationships, the fewer *sustaining procedures* are required and the more quickly they can move into *reflective consideration* of themselves, others, and their relationships.

The willingness to engage in *reflection* can be significantly influenced by factors that seem to be *outside* of the personality. If there is a crisis or significant external pressure of any kind, self-understanding and understanding of others may be affected positively or negatively. Even a person who is generally very self-absorbed may be jolted into understanding the needs of another when, for example, a spouse threatens separation or a child develops severe psychological symptoms. On the other hand, if an individual becomes seriously ill or suffers a significant loss, there may be an increase in self-preoccupation and, at least temporarily, less concern for others. In other words, once again, *external events can bring about significant intrapsychic changes.*

2. Regulation of Emotion   The assessment of another ego function, the capacity to modulate feelings, guides decisions about the choice of treatment procedures. Some individuals are easily and frequently overwhelmed by emotion. *Ventilation* by such clients, and the worker's keen understanding of how the clients feel, is necessary; Mrs. Zimmer's worker (see Chapter 3) often had to acknowledge her feelings of unhappiness, about how she thought others had misused her, or about how her head and stomach ached. But, as we described in Chapter 5, too much expression of raw, undifferentiated emotion—rage, agony, or anxiety—may feed on itself and become counterproductive.

Those frequently flooded by feeling sometimes require *direct advice* or *suggestions* to encourage them to *think* more about their situations rather than only react emotionally. The development of *cognitive awareness,* an aspect of *reflection,* is of particular importance for those who have difficulty with regulation or differentiation of feelings and cannot separate feelings from thoughts.[4] In general, such problems require *reflective procedures* aimed at *building* upon ego capacities (e.g., "Do you think that sometimes your intense anger covers up feelings of sadness?" Or, "Is it that you *feel* like paying John back by having an affair, or do you *think* that is what you will do?")

Those people at the other end of the continuum, who have a pattern of *over*control of emotion, who may rely particularly heavily upon *intellectualization* as a defense, often require help of the opposite sort: *reflection* that results in *relaxation* of defenses and the *uncovering* of feelings (e.g., "I know you understand reasons for Diana's relapse with alcohol, but how did you *feel* about it happening the way it did?")

Experience has taught us that those who are easily overwhelmed by emotion are far better able to understand interpretations or *reflect* on themselves and their situations *when the intensity of feeling abates.* Those who are disconnected from their feelings or overregulate them are more likely to move beyond intellectual insight, into deeper emotional understanding, *when inner or outer pressures have upset the personality balance and emotions are intense.* Even though Dick Jones (Chapter 3) had the capacity for introspection, undoubtedly the crisis in his marriage accelerated self-understanding and access to his feeling life.

3. Thought Processes and Self-Understanding   The capacity for logical, reality-oriented thinking and the degree to which secondary rather than primary processes are dominant also strongly influence the extent to which *reflective procedures* can be used. The direction and pace at which work can proceed is guided by the extent of the client's capacity for clear thinking. Can the client make only rather simple connections, or is there capacity for more analytical and sophisticated thinking? Can the person be led to reason things through independently, or must the worker explain concretely step by step? How strong is the ability to concentrate? Some people know a good deal about psychological mechanisms long before they see a clinician. Others are psychologically naive and must have matters spelled out in detail. As noted earlier, greater intellectual knowledge sometimes leads to a superficial acquiescence or to a facile denial of the importance of an interpretation, even though it may be an accurate one. In our experience, although average intelligence facilitates reflection, superior intellectual ability or advanced education does not necessarily lead to readiness to be introspective or to understand others; the talent for these reflective processes seems to be a separate capacity.[5]

The need for a worker to distinguish between a client's sophistication about psychological theory and his or her capacity for *person–situation reflection* that leads to change is illustrated by the following contrasting examples:

One client, a brilliant chemist, often talked at length in treatment sessions about the "cause" of his anger with his wife, which he related to the influence of his "overprotective" and "seductive" mother. In his view, his early experiences resulted in his being wary of women, always fearful that they wanted to control him. Therefore, he would explain, when his wife made affectionate or sexual overtures, he would convert his fright into hostility. His appraisal of his difficulties had merit, but he seemed far better motivated to perfect his elaborate analysis of himself and his reactions than he was to make changes.

In contrast, Dick Jones (Chapter 3), who was seen in marital therapy with his wife, had no advanced education and little knowledge of psychological matters. Nevertheless, his capacity for introspection led to productive work in treatment far surpassing that of the chemist. Dick Jones's quickness in understanding the nature of his passivity, its effect on his wife, and the dysfunctional pattern of interaction that had developed between them was important to the marked improvement in the marital relationship that was achieved in brief treatment.

Often, behaviors similar to the sort that the worker is trying to help the client to understand are common in children and can be recognized in them. For example: "Look, have you ever noticed how when Verne is mad at Phil (older brother) he starts picking on Stella (little sister)?" If the client's response shows understanding—"What about that! He sure does; he just takes it out on her"—the client will probably be able to understand the same defense mechanism in her own displacement from husband to son.

For some people, however, this sort of reasoning and carryover from one situation to another are impossible, even when the interpersonal adjustment problem is acute. If the shortcoming in thought processes is not accompanied by general emotional immaturity or a severe thought disorder, progress can sometimes be made by *suggestion* and *advice*. But this is not likely to be effective unless a strong positive relationship has been established, so that the client has confidence in the worker's goodwill and competence.

As we all know from personal experience, thought processes, including the capacity to *reflect* on one's difficulties, can be temporarily impaired under stressful conditions. Sometimes the worker cannot make a definitive assessment of cognitive functions until some of the pressure is relieved. When overwhelmed by intense reactions during a crisis, a client may need the worker to take active leadership in guiding the person's thinking or suggesting steps that might be taken. (See Chapter 18 on crisis intervention.)

4. Superego and Ego Ideal In various sections of this book (see especially Chapters 2 and 11), we discussed how the *superego* (or *conscience*) in some people is underdeveloped, resulting in an inconsistent set of standards of "right and wrong," lapses in ethical conduct, or even a pervasive lack of social conscience and feeling for others. Understandably, such clients frequently provoke serious interpersonal problems. The superego can be harsh, self-hating, and literal. The *ego ideal* can be immature in the sense that the individual's aspirations and values have not been well-formulated. Motivation for change is often stimulated by external pressures: legal troubles, tragedies, or losses. A great deal of *sustainment* is usually required before moving on to *reflective procedures*. If a strong, *"corrective" treatment relationship* can be established, there is an especially good chance of helping clients to find new ways of thinking about themselves, others, and their situations and to develop a repertoire of moral standards that better serve them. In the context of such a relationship, the worker may "stand in" as a caring parental figure who guides the client into more mature, satisfying, and goal-directed attitudes and behavior. Often clients with inadequate superego and ego ideal functioning need help to develop *compassion* for themselves

and self-soothing skills to soften their punitive self-criticism. Realistic appraisal of one's *strengths,* and how these have been and/or can be mobilized to cope with difficulties and meet challenges, is as important as reflection on one's negative contributions to difficulties.

Other clients may be hampered by a restrictive superego that can seriously paralyze ego functions; they often place unrealistic expectations on themselves. Such individuals often do not need to build on superego and ego ideal functions; rather, they need help in *relaxing* inner demands and developing greater tolerance for themselves. They, too, can usually benefit from having a kinder attitude toward themselves and an appreciation of their positive qualities.

5. Clinical Diagnosis *Clinical diagnosis per se does not immediately lead us to the selection of treatment procedures.* People with similar diagnoses can be very different in ego capacities, in values, and in superego development; they also enjoy different degrees of social support and opportunity.

To be able to think about themselves and their situations, clients diagnosed with severe personality disorders and psychoses often require special gentleness and a large amount of *support:* acceptance, reassurance, encouragement, and active involvement from the worker. Other clients—with high anxiety or those in the throes of a crisis—may need just as much *sustainment.* For very disturbed people, *direct influence* may be necessary to promote trust or to provide structure if they are too disorganized to provide it for themselves. For others who are equally upset, advice may arouse suspicion or hostility. Although many clients need very few directive comments from the worker, others with or without serious personality problems seek and make good use of various kinds of advice. *Ventilation* is necessary and helpful for almost all clients, but for people who are extremely disturbed lengthy and intense emotional release can result in decompensation. For others, even some with mild neurotic disorders, ventilation may result in the emotions snowballing, frightening the clients rather than relieving them. The extent to which people usefully engage in *person–situation reflection* also depends on many factors other than the clinical diagnosis. As we shall illustrate in an upcoming section of this chapter, and as descriptions of cases throughout this book have illustrated, *pattern-dynamic* and *developmental reflection* is also useful to clients with a broad range of diagnoses.

Dynamic Assessment and Treatment Procedures

The *specific content* of any question, interpretation, or *reflective comment* by the worker is directly dependent on dynamic understanding. The worker who tries to help an individual see another person more clearly depends on an assessment of the meaning of the other person's actions. This understanding can be expected to be more accurate than the client's only to the extent that the worker: (1) has taken more factors into consideration than has the client, (2) has looked at the matter from the other person's point of view, (3) is more objective and is thus not hampered by distortions that may skew the client's perceptions, and (4) uses knowledge that the client does not usually have concerning the functioning of personalities and of interacting systems. Obviously, if the worker has met the others, especially in conjoint sessions in which interactional patterns become apparent, the worker's interpretations about the other people are more precise and can also be checked out with

them. For example, what appears to be hostility in another person often is actually fear or hurt, and recognition of this can make a difference in the client's attitude and reactions. In the Russo case, described in Chapter 15, and in other cases discussed in the family and couple chapters, family members were frequently helped in conjoint sessions to understand one another more clearly. In family and couple interviews, we shall see that one treatment procedure can have different meanings to different members; for example, a communication from the worker that is *sustaining* to one person may be *directive* or promote *reflection* for another.

Specifics of what the worker seeks to help the client to become aware of and understand will depend upon the ongoing assessment of the factors contributing to the difficulties and of which of these appear to be the most modifiable. Take the case of a man who has been depressed after being laid off from his job and to whom it seems unlikely that he will find similar work elsewhere because he is close to retirement age and the demand for his skills is shrinking. Does the worker promote *reflection* on the possibilities of seeking another kind of work or a retraining program? Does the client want to consider retiring a little earlier than he otherwise would have? Does he seem to need *reassurance* as well as appraisal of his worth to bolster his self-esteem? Does it seem likely that his depression is also affected by tension in his marriage and that couple counseling should be considered? Would it help to explore the idea of antidepressant medication? The possibilities are nearly endless. Procedures are modified constantly by the choices the client is interested in considering, what he or she can assimilate, and the goals and subgoals of treatment, as these may shift during joint discussions.

The choice of procedures *within* the various types of *person–situation reflection* (see Chapter 6) obviously hinges very strongly upon the kind of problem the client is trying to resolve and the worker's assessment of the factors contributing to the problem. In interpersonal problems, treatment themes usually include both outwardly and inwardly directed reflection concerning the *current* interactional gestalt. When family relationships are involved, only as the worker recognizes (and preferably witnesses in vivo) dysfunctional responses and understands the factors that touch off such responses can he or she enable the client to become aware of them. Again, the Russo case is a good example of dynamic assessment that led to selection of particular treatment procedures.

Situational and Ethnic Factors

As we have said elsewhere, when families are plagued with severe environmental problems, these sometimes dominate the whole picture so completely that reflection about relationship problems seems of little importance. Casework should then concentrate on the practical problems. Once these are alleviated, perhaps there will be motivation for tackling strain in other parts of the system, such as internal family stress.[6] This was the case in the Stone family described in Chapter 3. Family members can sometimes make progress toward learning to be mutually supportive in times of stress rather than taking frustrations out on each other. Family sessions are often the best way to move toward such a goal.

Ethnic factors are extremely divergent in their significance to choice of treatment procedures. Some cultures reinforce a strong aversion to discussing personal or family troubles with outsiders. In some, men especially regard the need for such help as a disgrace and a sign of weakness. Language differences can be a deterrent to the kind of communication necessary for complex, especially intrapsychic *reflection*. Yet in the Garcia (Chapter 17) and the Chin (Chapter 2) cases, despite lack of knowledge of Spanish or Chinese on the part of the workers, such reflection was possible and effective in promoting change. Differences between worker and client, as discussed especially in Chapters 2, 9, and 10, can create obstacles to treatment of any type and sometimes may be problematic when self-understanding is needed. The degree to which potential difficulties are prevented depends heavily on how the differences are handled by the worker. Many problems involving dissimilarities are surmountable.

PATTERN-DYNAMIC AND DEVELOPMENTAL REFLECTION

The decision about whether to lead clients to pattern-dynamic or developmental reflection (see discussions of these procedures in Chapter 7) or to expand on clients' own spontaneous moves in this direction is again guided by the worker's diagnostic understanding. These types of reflection about oneself are encouraged when the difficulty is one for which this kind of help is useful or seems necessary, and when clients are capable of and interested in participating in the process. Dynamic and developmental understanding can help clients see how and why they are reacting in unrealistic or dysfunctional ways, can strengthen their grasp of patterns and their origins, and can contribute to the ability to change them. Even when person–situation reflection predominates, as it often does, there may be occasional moments—initiated by client or worker—when there are brief discussions about repetitive patterns of behavior or responses or about the influences of early history. In many cases, however, successful treatment is achieved without much use of these types of reflection, as illustrated by the case of Esperanza Perez (see Chapter 3).

These types of reflection are also often very helpful in recognizing and supporting *patterns of strength:* many people fail to fully appreciate their capacities to cope successfully, even under severe stress or at an early age, with life's challenges. Awareness of successes often inspires optimism; current efforts to find solutions to dilemmas are reinforced.

Motivation

Some clients are highly motivated to develop self-understanding that goes beyond consideration of *current* behavior and responses. Such motivation often occurs when individuals are caught in a crisis or faced by developmental changes within themselves or within members of their families. Instances of the latter are the birth of a child, a wife's decision to work full-time, a husband's change to a radically different form of work, the departure of grown children from the home, retirement, and death in the family. These rather sudden changes may overtax the ego defense system or upset a longtime balance of intrapsychic or family forces. *Dynamic* or *developmental reflection* is not always needed, but in many instances it is exceedingly helpful in enabling clients to deal with new situations. Sometimes, clients consider long-standing patterns and early history to help the worker understand them more completely; being *deeply understood*—an experience many people feel they have been deprived of—can be healing and can lead to further self-understanding.

These procedures can also be particularly useful and interesting to clients when they

are dissatisfied with their ways of relating to others or with feelings about themselves or when they feel they are not living up to their abilities. In some cases, clients' motivation for developing *pattern-dynamic* and *developmental understanding* emerges only after they finally recognize that they *cannot change other people* but *can* change themselves. The procedures can be very helpful in many family or other relationship problems when current person–situation reflection is not sufficient to enable the person to change self-defeating ways of interrelating with others. Again, reflection on *patterns of strength* can bolster efforts to change those patterns that are creating difficulties.

Widespread Use

At one time, it was believed that efforts to help people understand the dynamics of their psychological functioning and its development should be limited to carefully selected clients, those who had few or no emotional difficulties. On closer examination of work done by skillful clinicians, it was determined that clients with a wide range of clinical diagnoses were benefiting from such reflective procedures. The assessment of various aspects of ego and superego functioning, ability to deal with anxiety, motivation, interpersonal and other situational factors, among others, turned out to be far more influential on a worker's choice to use such procedures.

The cases discussed in this book demonstrate how clients with a wide range of problems and clinical diagnoses were able to participate in *pattern-dynamic* and *developmental reflection*. These reflective procedures, combined with *person–situation reflection* and frequent use of *sustainment,* were, to varying degrees, components of the long-term treatment of Mrs. Zimmer (Chapter 3), diagnosed as having a borderline personality disorder. Dick and Susan Jones (Chapter 3), both basically sound psychologically, were able to be introspective about their personality patterns and their early life experiences as they worked to resolve their relationship difficulties. Mrs. Barry (Chapter 20), diagnosed as having paranoid schizophrenia, astonished the worker with her capacity for making connections between her present situation, her father's alcoholism, and her position as the overlooked "middle child." Mrs. Stasio (Chapter 20), faced with terminal cancer and an awareness of some of her neurotic patterns, used these types of intrareflection a number of times in her treatment experience. Although originally involuntary clients, both Mr. and Mrs. Carter (Chapter 20) were able to reflect on patterns of behavior that had interfered with their functioning and family life. Jed Cooper (Chapter 20), whose anxiety had many histrionic features, was able to make helpful connections between his current difficulties and his complicated ties to his parents. Mr. Russo (Chapter 15), although not characteristically given to introspection, was able to reflect movingly in family sessions on how the early death of his mother and frequent changes of foster homes when he was a boy had contributed to the depression he suffered at the time his older daughter moved away from home. Tom and Kathy Brent (Chapter 17) were both able to link the significant deprivations of their childhood with the dysfunctional interactional patterns of their marriage.

ANXIETY AND GUILT

Assessment of the degree of anxiety and understanding of the client's way of handling it are very important considerations in the choice of treatment procedures, and especially so in *intrareflection*. Although we have commented a number of times on the significance of this factor, further points remain to be considered and reemphasized. Anxiety and guilt may logically be discussed together, for guilt is one form of anxiety—in Anna Freud's words,[7] the ego's fear of the superego—and what is said about anxiety in general applies with equal force to guilt. Anna Freud also called attention to anxiety caused by the ego's fear of the instincts or drives: that is, fear that thoughts, feelings, and actions not approved by ego or superego will break through despite efforts to control them. This form of fear is especially prevalent in psychosis and in severe personality disorders.

Sensitivity to the existence of anxiety and to the degree to which it is present in the client at any one moment is essential, as is awareness of the extent to which the client is chronically anxious or is vulnerable to its arousal. What particular elements in the client's present or past provoke this anxiousness? How does this anxiety show itself, and how does the client handle it? Does anxiety impel the client to behavior that creates problems or that he or she later regrets? Does it result in increased psychological or somatic symptomatology? What defenses does the client use against it? Is the person immobilized? Will he or she run away from treatment? In what ways does the client try to get relief, and do they work?

Observation of Anxiety

To be alert to the presence of anxiety in the client, one must be aware of the ways it expresses itself. Occasionally, clients spontaneously say that they feel anxious. Sometimes, anxiety is shown physically, by trembling of body or voice, body tenseness, sweating or pallor, nervous gestures or excitement, and so on. Sometimes the client reveals it by posture, sitting on the edge of the chair or at a distance, wrapping a coat tightly or refusing to take it off. When a person has been seen at least a few times, the worker may be able to spot anxiety because the client's demeanor has changed in some way. Most often, anxiety shows itself in increased use of the client's characteristic defense mechanisms. The intellectual may go off into theoretical, often contentious discussions; defensive hostility erupts in the challenge that treatment is not helping, with the implication that the worker is incompetent; rationalization, reaction formation, denial—any of the mechanisms of defense—may be brought into play in their characteristic role of attempting to protect the individual from experiencing anxiety. Avoidance may finally result in the client's skipping interviews. If these signs of anxiety are recognized early enough, they can alert the worker to the presence of anxiety and the need to discuss the problem with the client. *Resistance* is often a manifestation of anxiety; ways of handling it are discussed in the previous chapter. Sensitivity to the presence of anxiety needs to be accompanied by awareness of the conditions under which anxiety tends to be high, both for clients in general and for the particular individual(s) with whom one is working.

Anxiety and the Treatment Process

We have already commented on the many ways in which anxiety can be aroused by the use of various treatment procedures. A brief review here will emphasize the importance of this factor in applying diagnostic understanding to the treatment process. *Reflective consideration* of intrapsychic content is by no means the only set of treatment procedures by which anxiety is aroused. Merely *describing,* as part of the application process, life events of which one

is ashamed may be a very painful, anxiety-provoking experience. *Ventilation* that involves the expression of emotions or desires of which the client is afraid may bring fear that talking will be a forerunner of acting. Guilt may very easily be aroused in a sensitive person by discussions that produce awareness for the first time of the harmful effects of his actions on others or even of needs of his child or wife to which he has been blind. The individual with a very severe superego will feel guilt very keenly whenever matters in which he or she appears to be even slightly in the wrong are raised. Even when the worker merely listens, such an individual anticipates criticism, often projecting his or her own self-condemnation onto the worker; the person then may fear loss of love or the worker's indifference and may in self-defense blame the worker or resort to denial or defensive hostility or even withdraw from treatment.

Even the giving of *suggestions* and *advice,* under certain conditions, can arouse anxiety.

In one case a worker was greatly concerned about the severity with which an impulsive mother disciplined her seven-year-old son. Early in the contact, the worker advised her against this and was gratified at the change in her client's handling of the child and his immediate improvement. Unfortunately, however, she had not made a careful diagnostic study of the mother or thought ahead to the possible consequences of her advice. The child had never been controlled in any other way. His initial reaction was to be very good, but, as might have been foreseen, he soon began to explore the limits of his new freedom and became increasingly defiant of his now disarmed mother.

In addition to being impulsive, the mother had a great deal of compulsiveness in her makeup. A more thorough assessment would have identified the clinical signs of this, which is usually accompanied by a severe conscience and a strong wish to please. Along with her impulsivity, then, this woman had a need, carried over from childhood, to win the approval of others, especially those in authority. She tried very hard to be a good mother along the lines the worker suggested. In fact, however, after the initial good news of improvement in the child, she found it very hard to let the worker know that things were not going so well. This also could have been foreseen. Eventually, one day "all hell let loose," and her anger against her son burst forth in a potentially dangerous way. Then, to justify herself, she had to condemn the child as uncontrollable by any other means and turned completely away from the worker and her advice.

Self-Understanding   On the whole, the development of understanding of oneself and one's own functioning, whether in discussion of the current person–situation interaction or of personality patterns, tends to arouse more anxiety than do other treatment processes. The reasons for this are several. These are types of self-examination. As the client becomes involved in such treatment, he or she may become more acutely aware than previously of his or her faulty functioning. This realization can cause discomfort and pain, particularly if the client has a severe superego. These discomforts, in turn, frequently stir up anger at the worker, the bearer of ill tidings, who causes the client still more discomfort.

Uneasiness may also arise when clients, in individual or conjoint treatment, develop enough self-awareness to realize the degree to which they have been attributing their emotional responses and behavior to the actions of others: "When he criticized me the other morning, I was too devastated to go to work." Or, "I will never be happy again now that my daughter plans to marry outside our faith." Or, "I can't tell my wife that I would like to go out in the evening with my friends occasionally, because she would get too angry with me." As will be discussed more fully in the family and couple chapters, very often in families where interactions are chronically dysfunctional, family members are hesitant to change well-established patterns—as a result of fear of abandonment, of being overwhelmed, of being disloyal, etc.—and become extremely anxious about the prospect of making changes even when it becomes evident that these could bring relief and satisfaction.

Preconscious Material and Veiled Memories   Anxiety can be great, too, when treatment involves the client bringing to consciousness memories and realizations that have been hidden, or at least that a person has not talked about with others. These matters would not be hidden if they were not painful. It may be the pain of sorrow or frustration. Or the superego may be affronted, for the client may be defying parental standards in producing particular memories or becoming aware of certain feelings and attitudes. Adults who were victims of incest or abuse as children sometimes have totally or partially blocked recollections of their painful experiences and the fears, guilt, and confusion attached to them; if memories begin to return, spontaneously or in the treatment process, a great deal of anxiety often accompanies them.

A note of caution: In recent years, as we have mentioned in previous chapters, efforts to encourage adult clients to "recover" presumed repressed or suppressed memories of sexual abuse have been prevalent in some mental health circles. There are clinicans and researchers who believe that victims of childhood abuse can be accurately identified by their symptomatology and personality profiles, *even when the supposed victims have no recollections of having been violated.* Sometimes, when a clinician who holds steadfastly to this point of view is convinced that a client has sexual abuse in his or her background, there may be a well-intended (although overzealous) effort to encourage— even urge—the client to recall experiences and feelings about these, even though they may never have occurred. Some people are referred for hypnosis or other special treatments when the clinician infers there are buried memories. From our point of view, unless clients actually recall such experiences or spontaneously get in touch with them, it is *extremely* risky to make assumptions. For people who are dependent, easily influenced by others, or eager to please the clinician, mental images of sexual violations may emerge and begin to seem real even if they never happened. When this occurs, not only is the client done a great disservice, but also family members may be falsely accused of perpetrating abuse, thus badly damaging relationships. In a review of research on recovered memory therapy and its techniques' Stocks's conclusions underscore our serious concerns:

> Although each of the techniques may lead to recovery of accurate memories, they can also result in the recovery of distorted or wholly constructed memories.
>
> Furthermore, there are no procedures that have been demonstrated to reliably distinguish confabulations from accurate memories. Similarly, no symptom cluster has been demonstrated to reliably identify individuals who have "repressed" memories of abuse. . . .
>
> Currently, the outcome research on use of recovered memories in therapy is thin. As of this writing, four studies were found that systematically evaluated outcomes of clients who had received recovered memory therapy.

None of them supported the notion that recovered memories had clinical utility. In fact, each study demonstrated deterioration for clients while in recovered memory therapy.[8]

Of course, *there are many who have been abused* who remember or come to remember what happened to them. It is not uncommon for clients to seek therapy to try to come to terms with their memories or the consequences of sexual abuse. Some adults who were sexually abused as children have profound problems with sexual relationships, self-esteem, and guilt. Some have recurrent flashbacks. Many clients have been helped by clinical social workers to achieve new understandings of their experiences, to learn to bring compassion to memories of the child who was so helpless, confused, or in pain. Anger and hurt about the injustice can often be dissipated through ventilation and feeling understood by a caring worker. Many clients who feel shame or have blamed themselves come to recognize that they were not responsible for having been misused. However, in view of the questions regarding validity about recovered memories, in some cases it may be important to inform clients that such memories are not always accurate. It might be particularly important to make this point if clients are preparing to confront those they believe abused them. In such cases, it is important for worker and client to discuss all aspects of the situation rather than impulsively take action first. Each situation must be individualized.

Painful early experiences have sometimes been so traumatic that extreme anxiety would be involved in reliving them. Strong resistance to reviewing or recalling experiences should serve as a *caution signal* to the worker. This can even be true for adults who, for example, suffered the extremes of persecution during the Holocaust or for men and women who witnessed or endured the atrocities of war. Some of these experiences were so difficult to assimilate that they could be surmounted only by being walled off by suppressions and repressions that it probably would be unwise to disturb. Unless or until the client wants to talk about this material in detail, and if client and worker agree that current difficulties are probably affected by the earlier experiences, the worker is usually best advised to be *extremely* careful about encouraging clients to uncover traumatic events.

On the whole, a past experience that arouses anxiety deriving from the pain of reliving the experience is more easily borne than one that also arouses guilt or humiliation. If, for instance, the memory involves actions or even feelings and wishes that the individual thinks are shameful or wrong, fear of the worker's disapproval may be very strong. Guilt is frequently associated with childhood hostilities toward parents and others in families in whom such high value was placed on surface amiability that all anger had to be hidden. It is also associated in many people in our culture with childhood sexuality, with masturbation, with homosexual thoughts or behavior, and with so-called sexual perversions of various sorts. Both individual and cultural values are strong determinants here. For one person, hostile feelings will be taboo and shameful; for another, lying; for still another, erotic responsiveness.

Other Sources   Even positive feelings in treatment can cause anxiety in some people. Some individuals who have been badly hurt in close relationships fear further suffering if they allow themselves to come too close to others; uneasiness may develop as they begin to experience warm feelings toward their worker. Others fear entrapment or engulfment. It is important that the worker try to assess consequences of expressions of

warmth or strongly supportive communications, avoiding them when they might be misinterpreted or frighten a client.

Fear of change itself is often present in any form of treatment having as its goal some degree of change in personality functioning or behavior. Even though present ways of functioning cause discomfort, they usually also have some secondary advantages. Anticipated changes may require greater self-control, less expression of hostility, less blame of others, and more altruistic and less self-centered behavior. The client may desire change but may also feel uneasy about it and reluctant to give up old ways because of fear, as we said earlier, or because in some respects these ways are comforting.

The client may wonder: "Just what will the change be like?" "Will my wife (husband, parent) be pleased or dismayed by the change?" Sometimes these concerns can be addressed in conjoint sessions.

This is not to say that *intrareflection* is universally anxiety-arousing. Certain themes, even when they are dynamically or developmentally explored, may be fairly low in their anxiety potential and therefore can safely be explored even in so-called fragile personalities.

An example is that of a woman diagnosed as having a schizophrenic disorder who was able to see that her suspicious expectation of a hostile attack from a woman in her current life was a displacement from childhood experiences in which she had been very badly treated by a harsh grandmother. Discussion of the circumstances not only did not arouse anxiety but actually allayed it. Talking about her memories of her grandmother's cruel behavior was not frightening because the worker did not attempt to explore whether the client was partly at "fault" but accepted the situation as having been extremely painful and a regrettable hardship. Recognition of the possibility of displacement also involved no blame for the client; instead, it gave her a rational explanation for some of her fears, so that she was able to look more realistically at the lack of evidence in the current situation to justify them.

Anxiety Reduction

Clients sometimes find great relief in talking about painful experiences in the presence of a sympathetic worker who is not overwhelmed by their *ventilation*. This process may help the ego to assimilate the memories, to be less afraid of them, to be more able to bear the pain involved, and to express the natural emotions of grief and anger associated with the experiences. Such verbal activity is similar to the play activities of children, in which they repeat painful and frightening experiences in an effort to assimilate them. When the happenings that are being aired are also responsible for some current reaction that is causing clients trouble, they may in the very same interview also experience a sense of relief from talking about them. For instance, a person who as a child had very critical parents, and consequent feelings of distrust in his or her abilities, may obtain almost immediate relief from talking about their unjust criticisms. By sensing the worker's confirmation that they were unjust, the client can experience some freeing from the earlier acceptance of the parents' views. *Reflective procedures* may also be used to help the client think about why the parents were harsh or punitive; realization that their behaviors were derived from pressures or unhappiness in their own lives, having little to do with the client as a young child, often produces not only relief but a reduction of internalized self-blame. If the parents are living and able to attend

conjoint sessions, acknowledgment and explanations from them usually can be more forceful than reassurances from the worker or speculations by the client.

The main reason that clients pursue understanding despite anxiety is the satisfaction gained from new realizations about themselves, their fears, their self-criticisms, and their inhibitions. A load is often lifted, and sometimes genuine excitement is felt as insight exposes an encumbering defense. Understanding gained about childhood sources of unhappiness or about parents' actions often results in significant relief.

There is much the worker can do in helping the client deal with anxiety. Of primary importance is the worker's continuous attitude of support and acceptance, which softens the impact of comments. When this is communicated to clients, they can find support in a basic security with the worker; whatever the exigencies of the moment, clients can then hold to a strong underlying conviction that the worker has positive feelings for them, respects them, and is endeavoring to help them. This conviction is inevitably obscured from time to time at difficult moments in treatment by transference elements and by projection of clients' own attitudes. Such distortions can be corrected only if the actual relationship is a positive one and is fundamentally perceived as such by the clients. To achieve this basic relationship and keep it alive, both direct and indirect sustainment are important.

Worker Style and Client Anxiety

What might be called the "form" or "style" of worker communications used in promoting reflective thinking also has direct bearing on clients' potential anxiety. Worker comments can vary, as we have seen, from direct interpretation or explanation to completely nonsuggestive questions or comments that merely draw the client's attention to something the worker would like the person to consider. An illustration of the latter is the repetition of the last phrase or so of something the client has said. In general, the more open-ended a worker comment is the less likely it is to arouse anxiety, since it can be ignored; if clients are not ready to follow the worker's lead, they can easily respond without any recognition of the matter to which the worker is trying to draw attention. More direct comments and questions push clients harder, and interpretations, of course, formulate an opinion with which the client must deal.

To illustrate these points: A worker might make one of the following comments to a woman whose father apparently sexualized his relationship with her when she was young: "Were there any other things about your experiences with your father that made you uneasy?" Or, "Is it possible that your father turned to you for some kind of affection or comfort since his relationship with your mother was so contentious?" Or, "It seems that there was a great deal of sexual tension between you and your father when you were a child." Other factors being equal, the more direct the comment the greater the possibility of stirring up anxiety.

A worker always searches for ways to express ideas that support rather than hurt, even though questions and comments may also generate anxiety. Based on an assessment of the right timing and of the client's personality, sometimes interpretations can be softened with a light touch; for example, to a very self-critical woman: "In addition to all those other things you blame yourself for, are you saying that you think it was also *your* fault that your parents divorced when you were two years old?" When clients have gained some understanding, the worker—who naturally is pleased—may

"reward" them. Sometimes this is put into words: "Even though it was hard, you've done a good job of thinking that through." Just as often, facial expression and tone of voice communicate the feeling that the client has taken a step forward.

Balancing Anxiety and Movement

When a basically secure relationship has been established, clients often make very good use of anxiety-provoking comments. It is sometimes necessary to refrain from reassuring and comforting remarks at specific points so the client will not ease up but will continue to pursue understanding of the issue at hand.

To illustrate: A woman who tends to be extremely critical of her husband tells the case-worker about an incident in which this tendency was prominent and half apologizes for her disparaging words. The worker may either make a reassuring remark about the distress she must have felt that prompted her to castigate her husband or comment more directly, if the basic relationship is a good one: "You *do* have a sharp tongue!" Or, with a light touch, "How did those cutting remarks affect your husband?" The latter procedures will not be very reassuring. They will increase rather than decrease the client's anxiety and, if the worker has correctly gauged her ego and superego qualities, will motivate her to reflect on her overreaction or her communication style. Great care must be exercised in finding the balance by which to give enough warmth and security to nourish progress and protect the client from excessive anxiety and at the same time to maintain a level of tension conducive to motivation toward self-understanding.

A worker sensitive to either the likelihood of anxiety or its actual presence can often help the client bring this into the open, thereby reducing it. "Perhaps it scares you a little to tell me about this." Or, "I guess that was a tough question." Or, during an anxiety-arousing interview, "Let me know if you think we're going too fast." Remarks such as these may not only provide relief but also promote feedback from the client as part of his or her responsibility for guiding the treatment. If it seems wise to go on, the worker can proceed in a number of ways. Sometimes it is possible to draw the client's attention to defensiveness. At other times, it may be necessary to work first on the personality characteristic that makes the individual respond so strongly: with clients with compulsive traits, for instance, the overly severe superego and perfectionism may need to be softened through a positive therapeutic relationship in which both *sustaining* and *reflective* procedures are employed.

At times it is necessary to have a period of relaxation in treatment, in which the worker says directly or in effect, "Perhaps later you will feel more able to talk about this." At other times, when the worker has good reason to think that the client is close to talking about certain experiences but is afraid to do so, ways can be found to frame a question or comment that will relieve anxiety before the frightening content is actually expressed. For example, depending on knowledge of the client, one might say: "Even though it seems hard, do you suppose that if you took the plunge you might actually feel some relief?" Or, "Do you think you expect criticism if you talk about this?"

After a difficult episode of self-understanding, the client in the next interview may stay on superficial material or take time to evaluate progress already made. This relaxation may be necessary. *A balance needs to be found between relaxing and sustaining measures on the one hand and procedures pressing toward self-understanding or change on the other.*

Despite the relief and growth that may come from *intrareflection,* it can sometimes be exhausting; it can even temporarily deflate self-esteem, for example, when clients recognize how their behaviors or patterns of response have negatively affected other people. One reason for helping clients to *recognize their strengths* is so that they can maintain a realistic perspective about themselves while struggling with dilemmas; too often people, because of their personal or relationship difficulties, view themselves negatively. Positive qualities in general—the capacity for empathy, talents, intelligence, sense of humor, among many others—call for acknowledgment in the course of exploration and reflection as these qualities become apparent to the worker. Many clients—even those who have faced terrible injustice or tragedy—demonstrate remarkable creativity and resilience in the ways they have coped with challenges and overcome obstacles. Realistic appreciation of these capacities and past successes can help clients find ways to grapple with current challenges.

When anxiety or guilt or shame is either chronically very high or aroused by coming to treatment, a good measure of sustaining procedures, including *indirect sustainment,* is valuable. For instance, the worker may draw a client out about experiences in which he or she has played an especially helpful or positive role. Or one may refer to the client's good motivation even when discussing an effort that misfired. In individual or conjoint sessions, the situation can be reframed: "You obviously meant to be helpful to Ivan even though he was frightened by being treated the same way your father treated you." Or, "You may have sounded quite angry at your wife even though you were trying to tell her how very hurt you were feeling." It is important that such supportive remarks be realistic.

If the client is unable or unwilling to deal with anxiety, one can refrain from pursuing anxiety-arousing content. It may be possible to reintroduce it later, when the client feels stronger, is more trusting of the worker, or is more motivated, or worker and client may agree that this particular content will remain untouched. Timing and sequence are always important. Continuous diagnostic assessment and sensitivity to the client's current moods and reactions can enable the worker to avoid explorations for which the client is not yet—or may never be—ready.

If treatment is kept close to the realities of life, if *person–situation reflection* is the central focus, the client who develops more understanding usually experiences improvement in interpersonal relationships. Whether treatment is individual or conjoint, often clients receive new responses from others as they change ways of handling matters.

If the worker is sensitively attuned to the client by means of accurate diagnostic assessment of both underlying personality patterns and nuances of feelings and reactions during interviews, casework is not basically painful. There are ups and downs from interview to interview. But if efforts to develop understanding of self and others are well paced, clients can experience satisfaction and even excitement in their greater grasp of their dilemmas and increased ability to cope with them. Self-esteem is often strengthened by the nourishing therapeutic relationship and by new achievements.

This chapter delineates ways in which the casework treatment procedures rest upon the worker's differential understanding of a wide range of characteristics of the client and the personal–social–environmental situation. Treatment is always an individualized blend of the objectives mutually arrived at by the client and worker, of the themes or subgoals in the service of these objectives, and of the procedures that develop these themes. The nature of the blend is not a matter of individual artistry or intuition, important as these may be. As this chapter has tried to illustrate, choice and emphasis of particular procedures rest upon a *careful and ongoing assessment of* the nature of the problems; external and internal etiological factors and their modifiability; availability of resources and opportunities; and clients' objectives, motivation, and pertinent personality factors, including their strengths and vulnerabilities. As treatment progresses, the choice of procedures varies in harmony with changes in the clients, in their goals, and in their circumstances.[9]

We emphasize that there should be familiarity with the nature, effects, and demands of the different types of casework procedures, as described in this chapter and in Chapters 5 through 8. The worker can then match clients' needs and capacities with a combination of procedures that will be of most value in enabling clients to overcome, or at least to lessen, their difficulties. As much as possible, treatment is a shared process in which client initiative and feedback are encouraged and strongly influence the course therapy takes.

We repeat here a point that will be further elaborated upon in the chapters on family and couple treatment. Conjoint interviews are more complex than individual treatment sessions. Nevertheless, *all of Hollis's six major categories of treatment procedures can be used in family and couple interviews as well as in one-to-one meetings.* As already indicated, the meaning of a particular worker communication may be different for every person who hears it, and therefore the worker must assess possible consequences of each intervention on *all* who are present.

NOTES

1. See Chapter 8, text and notes, for further discussion and references on environmental procedures.
2. See the Hollis (1968) study of marital counseling cases in which she found that from the second interview onward over 50 percent of the worker's communications were of the reflective type: predominantly person–situation reflection.
3. Ibid.
4. For comprehensive references on the theory and practice of cognitive therapy, and a brief discussion of it from the psychosocial point of view, see Chapter 6, note 1.
5. Gardner (1983) in his very interesting book argues persuasively that individuals have potential for a multiplicity of intelligences, including the capacity to understand themselves and others. See especially Chapter 10, "The Personal Intelligences," in which he writes about the capacity to access one's own feeling life, "one's range of affects or emotions: the capacity to effect discriminations among these feelings and, eventually, to label them, to enmesh them in symbolic codes, to draw upon them as a means of understanding and guiding one's behavior . . . At its most advanced level, intrapersonal knowledge allows one to detect and to symbolize complex and highly differentiated sets of feelings. One finds this form of intelligence developed in the novelist (like Proust) who can write introspectively about feelings, in the patient (or the therapist) who comes to attain a deep knowledge of his own feeling life, in the wise elder who draws upon his own wealth of inner experiences in order to advise members of his community" (p. 239).

6. For good discussions of related points, see Brennan, et al. (1986), Krystal, et al. (1983), and Ostbloom and Crase (1980).
7. Anna Freud (1946).
8. Stocks (1998), pp. 231–32. See also a book by Yapko (1994) that takes a balanced but cautious view of recovered memory therapies. See also Chapter 7, note 2 for related references.
9. As supplements to references already cited in this chapter and previous chapters on casework diagnosis and treatment, the following are relevant and represent various orientations or emphases. In addition to useful theoretical discussions, many of the readings provide clinical discussions and case illustrations: Ballen (1980), Blake-White and Kline (1985), Bonnefil (1979), Chernus (1979), Cohen (1983), Dean (1993), DeRoos (1990), Edward and Sanville (1996), Freed (1977), Sophie Freud (1998), Furstenberg and Rounds (1995), Giancarlo (1991), Howard Goldstein (1986), Hepworth (1993), Kelley (1996), Lee and Rosenthal (1983), Lieberman (1982), Loewenstein (1977), Middleman and Wood (1991), Miller (1977), Mufson (1993), Palumbo (1979), Parsons, et al. (1988), Ranan and Blodgett (1983), Siporin (1983), Specht and Specht (Parts I and II, 1986), Taylor (1984), Walsh (1981), and Young-Eisendrath (1982). See the edited volume by Turner (1999) with chapters on various types of adult psychopathology. See also Turner's (1995) edited volume, an excellent source of articles pertinent to the relationship between diagnosis and treatment; his prefaces to four editions are included and recommended.

CHAPTER 14

FAMILY THERAPY AND PSYCHOSOCIAL CASEWORK: A THEORETICAL SYNTHESIS

This chapter and the three that follow will discuss family and couple treatment. As we have indicated and illustrated along the way, all that has been written in preceding chapters is relevant to conjoint as well as to individual treatment. By the same token, concepts and techniques described in these four family and couple chapters can be extremely useful to *all* treatment modalities, including one-to-one interviews. Integrating this material into earlier chapters would have been cumbersome and difficult for the reader to assimilate before the psychosocial approach was explained in detail. It is our hope that by presenting additional concepts and treatment strategies that have emerged from family and couple practice at this juncture, the readers will gain further perspectives on treatment planning and intervention.

The psychosocial framework is able to accommodate and greatly benefit from the synthesis of psychodynamic and family systems concepts. In our view, these major features of psychosocial theory are not only exquisitely compatible with but also indispensable to effective clinical treatment.

THE CHANGING FAMILY

One distressing paradox of recent decades is that at the same time that the support of the family structure is needed the most, the turbulence of the larger social system has endangered it. Federal and state governments have cut back on aid and services to families and children, with the result that large numbers of people are left wanting for the most basic necessities. As American society has become more impersonal and bureaucratized, it has rendered people in ever greater need of the shelter and solace of family life. Concurrently, rapid social changes and widespread shifts in traditional values have had a disturbing effect on the quality of family relationships, often depriving the individual members of essential built-in supports.

The family is being challenged from within as well as from without. Families have given up some of their former functions: socialization of the very young and nursing care of the old and ailing, for example, are shared with the broader community. Although still discriminated against in the workplace, women are nevertheless more independent economically than ever before. In most marriages both spouses are employed. The vast majority of women work at paying jobs and do the bulk of the housework as well. Traditional sex-role relationships have been challenged and, to varying degrees, have changed. Many customary family patterns have died out with new lifestyles replacing them. Often families splinter and disperse. In three decades the divorce rate more than doubled. Many children live in single-parent homes, usually but not always headed by women. Homeless families try to survive in cities and towns where housing is unavailable and temporary shelters are inadequate at best and life-threatening at worst. When the family has been weakened or fractured, it may be unable to fulfill its ideal function as a haven of love and acceptance. Family violence, homicide, teenage suicide, and substance abuse are tragic indicators of how quality family life can buckle under the strain of internal and external assaults. With greater frequency than ever, we hear people denying any commitment to their families. Marriages are being delayed and large numbers of young people are choosing to remain unattached.[1] Concern about teenage pregnancy is on the increase in some sectors, while teenagers themselves have far greater tolerance for out-of-wedlock births than they did just two decades ago.[2] There are some who question whether the American family as an institution will survive the forces that threaten to undermine it.

In Chapter 1 we indicated that in recent years the term *family* has been expanded by many social workers and others (but not by the U.S. Census Bureau) to refer to *various constellations of two or more individuals who have some kind of ongoing commitment or bond, who may or may not be related by blood, legally married, or adopted; the "family unit" may or may not include minor children. Generally, when we speak of a "family," the members share some practical tasks required for living and some type of emotional connection.*

In our view, it is inevitable that some form of family life will endure. Most people search for loving and reliable personal relationships. No adequate substitute has been found for the nurturance and socialization of the young. The family has been central to molding personalities, to defining values and worldviews; the child's innermost emotional development is derived in large measure from experiences in the home. Family relationships cannot be compared to any other social connections in the depth and intensity of their effect upon individual members. And, as we learn from our clients every day, the family is the unit people of all ages often turn to, or else long for, in the face of personal unhappiness. Large numbers of those who were adopted go to great lengths to search for birth parents or siblings from whom they were separated. Many others try to locate their "roots," at home and abroad. Despite the many changes it has undergone and the diversity of lifestyles it encompasses, the modern family is still seen by many of its members at all stages of life as the primary place for comfort and refuge from the larger, unpredictable world. It still can be said that "most families, despite or because of changing structures and a frequently unfriendly environment, are performing their functions and meeting the needs of their members and society apparently better than society is meeting the needs of families."[3]

The failure of social institutions to provide adequate resources for families along with changing family structures and values, new gender definitions, and the increase of culturally diverse populations requiring clinical services have required social workers to examine and expand their approaches to practice.[4]

The psychosocial approach, with its commitment to understanding families, their larger environments, individual personalities, and the interactions among these, has been uniquely equipped not only to assimilate consonant principles from family therapy and family research but also to contribute to their synthesis.

FAMILY GROUP TREATMENT AND THE SOCIAL CASEWORK TRADITION

The family outlook is woven into the fabric of the social work tradition. From the earliest days of the profession, social workers have recognized the importance of family life to the healthy development and functioning of its individual members. The report of the first White House Conference on Child Welfare in 1909 defined home life as "the highest and finest product of civilization" and urged that homes not be broken up for reasons of poverty alone.[5]

In her groundbreaking work of 1917, *Social Diagnosis,* Mary Richmond was remarkably cognizant of the need to study the individual in interaction with the environment. Recognizing what we today may take for granted, the pioneering Miss Richmond pointed out that the individual must also be regarded in the context of the family group:

> Family caseworkers welcome the opportunity to see at the very beginning of intercourse several of the members of the family assembled in their own home environment, acting and reacting upon one another, each taking a share in the development of the client's story, each revealing in ways other than words social facts of real significance.[6]

In less quaint language, current family therapists, including those interested in home visits and nonverbal communication, share her approach to understanding the family.

Over 80 years later, Miss Richmond's advice reminds us that "the man should be seen," and that other relatives (now referred to as the "extended family") must not be overlooked. How modern her ideas seem to us as we read "The need of keeping the family in mind extends beyond the period of diagnosis, of course." Without a family view, "we would find that the good results of individual treatment crumble away." Miss Richmond had a prophetic grasp of the "drift of family life," as she called it, that heralded casework's understanding of the complexities of family interrelationships.[7]

Social casework continued to emphasize the interdependence of people and their environments. Even during the decades following World War I, when psychological and then psychoanalytic thinking began to inundate the field, resulting in intense fascination with the inner emotional life of individuals, social workers never abandoned understanding of the significance of family history and interaction. Caseworkers, vital contributors to the mental hygiene and child guidance movements of the 1920s and 1930s, realized that the behavioral and emotional problems of children as well as the mental disorders of adults were profoundly influenced by family relationships. Also, there was growing realization that family members needed treatment, too, if the problems of the individual (or, now, the "index client" or "identified patient") were to be resolved.

By the late 1930s, caseworkers in family welfare (now family service) agencies were also working "above the poverty line," ministering to the emotional and interpersonal disturbances of family life as well as to the financial and environmental aspects. Although frequently the individual was of major interest, family casework objectives of 60 years ago were broadened to include "remedial and preventive treatment of social and emotional difficulties that produce maladjustment in the family," "intrafamily harmony," and the development of "the capacities of all family members to the fullest."[8] In short, neither environmental assistance to the family nor treatment of the individual out of his milieu were deemed sufficiently helpful. Many caseworkers recognized that the family as a whole required attention.

Gordon Hamilton, in her classic introductory text on psychosocial casework, built on the earlier casework approach to the family as the "unit of work." Today's family therapists would have little quarrel with her view:

> Using "group process" in family life . . . locates and clarifies the problem through discussion; it permits expression of opinions; it dissipates anxiety for each child, because the situation is shared . . . and this participation releases ability to move toward action. Work with families inevitably includes children, adults, adolescents, young married couples, and the aged; *none of these can be treated as isolated problems, because of the nature of social relationships themselves.* [Italics ours]

She added, "There are considerations of family balance and behavior as a group as well as from the point of view of each individual member." In the ordinary course of the child's development, she said, "first through identification and then through increasing the psychological 'distance' between the self and the persons around him . . . [he] moves healthily out of the 'undifferentiated unity' . . . of the parent–child relationship."[9]

Hamilton's concepts preceded the family therapy movement, yet they had much in common with ideas that followed. Notions about "family homeostasis," "differentiation," and "individuation," which became central to many family thinkers, are elaborations and refinements of Hamilton's thinking. Others, including Hollis, were among those who took early steps to develop a family-centered approach to family and marital treatment.[10]

Modern family treatment, like casework, rests on a blend of knowledge, theory, and "practice wisdom" from various disciplines and sciences, with input from psychoanalytic concepts, systems and communication theories, ego psychology, and several of the social sciences. Social work professionals, although not always sufficiently credited with their contributions to the family therapy movement that began to burgeon in the 1950s and 1960s, can be proud of their place in its growth. They have not simply accepted and assimilated theory and interventive techniques; they have been in the forefront of their development. For years, social workers were viewed as *the* experts in family practice. In mental health and child guidance clinics, in hospitals, and in family service agencies, the individual whom we now refer to as the "identified patient" was often seen by a psychiatrist or psychologist, but parents, spouses, and family groups were routinely assigned to social workers.[11] A renowned trailblazer, Nathan Ackerman, credited much of his early work in family treatment to his association with the Jewish Family Service social work agency. Virginia Satir, Frances Scherz, Arthur Leader, Sanford Sherman, and Harry Aponte are among many others with social work backgrounds who, early in the family movement, made substantial contributions to the theory and practice of family therapy.[12]

CHANGE, STRESS, AND FAMILY ADAPTATION

Challenges to Families

Before presenting some key concepts relating to families and family treatment that have been incorporated by the psychosocial framework, we pause briefly here to consider the inevitable challenges faced by *all* families. Without exception, families are repeatedly required to adapt to stress and change. Over time, roles must be modified, positions shifted, and patterns of behavior adjusted. As the familiar means of meeting needs become outmoded, new ways must be discovered. *There are no "problem-free" families.* Pressures may result from:

1. A Life Cycle Transition of an Individual Member of the Nuclear or Extended Family When a child reaches adolescence, or a young adult leaves the family home for good, or a daughter challenges her parents' mores and chooses not to marry, or an elderly grandparent can no longer function independently, the family is required to adapt to new roles and rules and new patterns of interaction. Having a baby, however joyful, can create a crisis for a marriage. Each such change may be accompanied by a sense of loss, even a period of mourning and temporary regression on the part of at least one family member. Ideally, the struggle to adjust ultimately results in creative adaptation and growth.

2. Illness, Injury, or Impairment of a Family Member When one person becomes sick, emotionally distressed, or has an accident, or when a mentally or physically handicapped child is born, the special needs of the situation call for reassignment of family roles and functions. Whether the outcome is recovery, institutionalization, or death, adaptations and readaptations will be required.

3. External Stress on an Individual Member A crisis on the father's job, a change at a child's school, the death of a close friend of the mother's, or acts of racism or other discrimination encountered by any member, all reverberate upon the family system.

4. External Stress on the Entire Family When fire or flood destroys the family home, when a family suddenly becomes homeless and cannot locate another place to live, when neighborhood violence erupts, when the breadwinner loses a job, or when the economic situation compels a family to apply for public assistance, the whole family is directly affected, and mechanisms for coping must be activated. The addition to the household of a foster child, stepparent, or elderly relative requires adjustments in the system to enlarge family boundaries.[13]

Function and Dysfunction

As families inevitably face transitions and stresses such as these, they are usually confronted by conflict and pain. They fear change, yet need to change. Feelings of bereavement can be profound when familiar relationships and patterns have to be modified. A period of disorganization and confusion may follow. *For many families, the outcome is resolution, growth, and even revitalization.* Others, however, become chronically regressed, chaotic, or symptomatic. When as clinicians we meet with a family, we require a framework for analyzing and assessing the relationships, interactions, and patterns that operate within its structure. Specifically, we must try to evaluate whether the family style is *functional* or *dysfunctional as it relates to the requirements of the particular situation.* For example, one family may be extremely effective in mobilizing strengths and creative energies to locate new housing or new employment or to accommodate an elderly relative in the home; yet, when an adult child decides to marry outside her race or religion, that same family may be thrown into turmoil. We often hear families labeled as "functional" or "dysfunctional" (too often as "dysfunctional"!); however, *the overall functioning of the family should not be assessed as one or the other, but only in terms of the capacity to cope with current circumstances and challenges.*

Usually, when a family comes for treatment, one or more of its members feels the pressure of a problem. We then try to determine whether the difficulty relates to a transient phase of stress, a transition for which the family has the strengths to accommodate, or whether the family process in the face of the pressures involved is too dysfunctional or resourceless to regain its balance.

In family therapy, as in all other methods of clinical social work, we must be keenly sensitive to variations in style that are either culturally determined or idiosyncratic to a particular family group. Diverse family roles and relationship patterns exist in our society. However atypical, these family modes may be functional and adaptive. The extended "urban matriarchal" family, which can include grandmother, mother, children, and sometimes other relatives, often operates successfully and creatively whether or not all members live under the same roof; with roles well defined, basic functions, such as making a living and child rearing, can be effectively carried out. The sharing and cooperation that can occur in poor families with this structure often allows for a good balance of mutuality and independence. Single mothers or fathers—even though sometimes incredibly stressed—often are successful in providing a nurtur-

ing home for children. Male–female roles based on individual preference or family customs are often adaptive. For example, in some families the father takes on major aspects of homemaking and child rearing, while the mother is the breadwinner. In others, the father's patriarchal style, often based on cultural tradition, strongly influences family relationship and communication patterns to which other members accommodate relatively comfortably and/or do not want to change. (While the worker may cringe at the *idea* of some family role arrangements, especially those that place women in the subordinate position, as a clinician one cannot assess these arrangements as "dysfunctional" unless symptoms or family conflict seem to derive from them, as they sometimes do.) Many same-sex couples, who must develop special role definitions, competently and lovingly raise children and should *never* be diagnosed as dysfunctional on the grounds of sexual orientation alone. *The quality of family relationships and the capacity for adaptation and growth are far more significant as indicators of family functioning than are the facts of the family's structure, composition, or role designations.* We turn now to a summary of some central concepts that help us to assess family functioning.

BASIC CONCEPTS OF FAMILY TREATMENT

Concepts describing the internal workings of families provide us with guidelines for understanding and for fashioning interventions in a particular family situation. They help us to identify functional and dysfunctional family processes. They do not replace but augment our knowledge about personalities and social interaction. As we have said, family theories can be applied not only to conjoint work but to individual treatment as well.

We have found the concepts included here useful in our clinical practice. In some instances, the language of family theory is so abstruse that it can seem hard to apply to the real people who visit our offices. In our presentation, however, we have attempted to connect the concepts as closely as possible to the human beings they attempt to describe. Family theory has wide gaps, and the principles vary in their levels of abstraction and inclusiveness.

Ideas from various "schools" of family therapy often overlap; frequently a similar idea is expressed by different terms. The constructs that follow represent our effort to extract and integrate key concepts from some of the major family theories; we will also try to provide a basic framework and language with which to describe and expand our understanding of family life and functioning. In psychosocial casework, we do not endorse or "prefer" any particular model or theoretician of family therapy. In our view, the basic concepts are useful *only* to the degree that they can be accommodated by our theoretical framework. Although we may find a particular concept very helpful, it does not mean that we follow the total approach of the "school" that developed it. For example, as we shall discuss in greater detail later in the chapter, proponents of some major family treatment approaches do not see the relevance of assessing individual personalities; yet, concepts from these same models, relating to family structure and process, can be extremely helpful when *adapted to* and *blended with* psychodynamic and person-in-situation theories basic to the psychosocial framework. In other words, we have not imported family concepts "lock, stock, and barrel," but rather we have selectively chosen those that can be tailored to our needs and expand our perspective. For this reason, we have made no attempt either to summarize any particular school of thought or to systematically survey the array of approaches to family therapy.

The Family as a System

Despite differences, the various "schools" of family therapy have based their thinking at least in part on systems concepts. The systems perspective is the bedrock on which other concepts described here are built. As we have indicated throughout this book, ideas from systems theory have become increasingly important to the psychosocial approach in recent years. More precisely than before, we perceive family members as interacting, interdependent parts of an organic whole. The family unit, like an intricately coordinated clock, is greater than the sum of its parts because of the interactions and interrelationships within it. Without the interdependence, there is no family system, simply a cluster of individuals. Intrapsychic events alone cannot account for the movement and flow of the family system that develops its own patterns of behavior and affective expression, its unique rules and role expectations.

Family functioning is not simply the sum total of strengths or deficits of individual members, but the product of the family as an entity. The "identified patient" or "index client" (i.e., the individual who seeks treatment or is viewed by the family as the troubled member) often represents a family symptom through whom the family expresses its difficulties as a system. As Framo says, "Although all symptoms are not interpersonally determined, they always have interpersonal relationship consequences which will determine their nature, course, preservation, or removal."[14] When a family comes for treatment, the therapist's focus may not be on individual pathologies as such (even though these may be included in the overall assessment) but on the family system or interactions that produce or sustain troublesome symptoms. Experience has taught us that family members frequently become symptomatic in shifts, with individuals taking turns. Often we find that when a problem child improves, a sibling then develops difficulties, or else marital or intergenerational tensions are exposed. Even when the presenting problems relate to biological conditions, such as congenital birth defects, schizophrenia, or Alzheimer's disease, the ways family members interact with one another in connection with these conditions can vary greatly.

Systems theories are repeatedly demonstrated in practice: When one person makes significant changes, all those in close emotional connection with him or her are required to make compensatory changes. In families burdened by dysfunctional processes, if one member is hurting, we usually assume that others are also in pain. Family processes are regulated by corrective *"feedback mechanisms"* that work within the family's internal structure to maintain its stability.

> In one family treatment case, an adult son who was suffering from psychosomatic symptoms had unsuccessfully made attempts to move out of his parents' home. His presence was key to maintaining the balance of his parents' marriage; both mother and father were closer to him than they were to each other. Marital dissatisfactions remained hidden since the parents were united by their overinvolvement in their son's life. Moves the young man made toward independence were met with his parents' efforts to discourage him (feedback mechanisms) in order to maintain the status quo (or equilibrium) of the marital relationship.

Family Homeostasis This familiar term refers to the capacity of the family's internal environment to maintain a constancy or equilibrium, healthy or dysfunctional, by a continuous interplay of dynamic forces that restores it to its familiar state after disturbances in its balance. Such family equilibrium *does not imply a static condition but the balance of its dynamic components* comparable to the interacting factors that keep a bicycle balanced while in motion.

When literally applied from other sciences to family processes, this concept may limit our expectations and our appreciation of the capacities families have for adaptation, change, and choice. Human beings have faculties for making *deliberate* and *immediate* modifications; no other organisms or systems have the capacity to think of creative ways of solving problems and to institute life-enhancing innovations. Generally, families are *open systems.* They interact with and acquire information from the larger environment; however, they can shift from being more or less open, depending on the family's felt need for input from the outside or its perception of external danger. Sometimes family systems are so open that the family's separate identity is underdeveloped; or, if it is essentially closed, it functions in isolation and is deprived of outside social supports.

When we refer to the principle of "homeostasis," we intend it as Ackerman used it: to signify what he termed *controlled "instability."* Without "instability," he wrote, "there can be no growth, no adaptation, no learning, no creativity. But this is controlled 'instability,' controlled so as to offset a too rapid and destructive change. [We] envisage the homeostatic principle as a kind of shock barrier, both for body and mind, which enables *expansion of the organism while protecting its integrity.*"[15] [Emphasis ours] Although all families need to maintain stable properties—shared values, roles, a sense of continuity and coherence—*adaptation and innovation come more easily for families that can function with flexibility than for rigid family systems in which any change is experienced as a threat.* In some cases, a major gain in treatment is the family's recognition that change *is* possible (or necessary) and need not be feared.

The source of a disturbance to family balance can be internal or external. In the example on page 374, the son's attempt to separate from his family represented an internal disturbance that was followed by his parents' efforts to return the family system to its former steady state. Frequently, a change in the system is most possible when the homeostatic balance is upset. The notion that a family in crisis can be most accessible to growth-producing change derives from this principle. The entry of a therapist on the family scene can disturb the balance, and many family therapists recommend deliberately inducing an upset to make way for a new and healthier homeostasis. Just as is true of the personality system, *emphasis on building strengths in various components of the family system can contribute to surmounting former vulnerabilities or deficits.* For instance, in the example just cited, by supporting the positive aspects of the parents' marital relationship and simultaneously encouraging the son to articulate his own goals, the young man was able to pursue an independent course, and the quality of the parents' marriage improved appreciably. A new equilibrium was achieved.

Hartman and Laird described three of the ways in which change in families may be effected:

> First, change can occur as a result of new input or information from the world outside the family; second, change may emerge from the exchange of information among components within the system; and third, an au-tonomous or differentiated position taken by one member of the family system may become the spur to change. Clearly if change occurs in any one of these ways, it is likely to effect transformations in the others.[16]

Circular versus Linear Causality   As we have indicated in previous chapters and will illustrate further in case illustrations in chapters to come, one clarifying idea that emerged from systems theory is that there is no single cause of an action, a symptom, or a reaction. In the example on page 374, the young man did not "cause" his parents to delay examining their marriage any more than the couple "caused" their son to remain at home. Rather, the actions of the son stimulated reactions in the parents, which were followed by the son retreating from his resolve to take an independent stand, thereby temporarily reinstating the status quo. When interactive, circular patterns such as these are repeated again and again, they become entrenched and often require outside intervention to interrupt the dysfunctional cycle. One of the many advantages of this focus of the systems perspective is that clinicans are less likely to blame one family member for the problems of another; ideally, as we shall see, each member is helped to take positive initiative and responsibility for participating in finding solutions.

Antisystem Symptoms   As mentioned in Chapter 11 (see page 298), in families (as well as in individuals and social systems) symptoms often communicate a message that something has gone awry. Sometimes unconsciously, but nevertheless purposefully, a family member "chooses" a symptom that will frighten or worry others enough to take notice, in hopes there will be change in the family. In the case previously mentioned the eruption of the young man's psychosomatic symptoms was sufficient to arouse his parents' concern; they cared deeply for him and wanted him to be well. However, had he become reclusive, rarely spending time with peers, the parents might not have recognized this behavior as a sign of their son's distress because they were so dependent on him and wanted him to remain close to them. In the case of Joan (see pages, 74–75), her unhappiness and underachievement brought her to the school's attention; the mother's "nervousness" or the stepfather's "passivity" would not have been a powerful enough SOS for the family to seek treatment.

In this connection, practice experience and research findings lead us to believe that specific symptoms or psychiatric disorders in and of themselves do not reflect a particular kind of family dysfunction. In other words, whether a family member is depressed or alcoholic, has an anxiety disorder or schizophrenia, as Walsh says, "It is erroneous to type a family by the diagnosis of a dysfunctional member."[17] Rather, in every situation, family processes have to be assessed apart from the presenting problem. It is our hunch that specific symptomatology (particularly problems that are *not* essentially biologically based) depends heavily on whether or not the emotional or behavioral manifestations will be sufficient to jolt family members into taking notice. Symptoms can be viewed as a powerful stimulus for change.

Relatedness, Differentiation, and Boundaries

Central Assumptions   Central to family theory are two premises around which many of its principles can be organized:[18] First, it is believed that each human being strives for a sense of *relatedness and closeness in associations with others.* A particular relationship may not last a lifetime, but

the individual's need for sharing with others is ongoing. Second, and equally important, it is thought that every person seeks a sense of *personal identity, a self-definition,* that *differentiates* him or her from others, that has consistency and cohesion over time, despite emotional ups and downs or inevitable external pressures. Each new developmental phase will alter some aspects of an individual's self-definition.

On the basis of these assumptions, we can see that difficulties can arise when (1) the pursuit of interpersonal relationships drives a person to sacrifice or negate a sense of self, or conversely, (2) when an individual is so determined to maintain a sense of identity that the need to share his or her life intimately with others is forfeited.

Differentiation and Enmeshment   The student of family literature will repeatedly come across a group of more or less analogous terms such as *differentiation, individuation,* and *autonomy.* Equally prevalent are an assortment of words that express the opposite idea, including *enmeshment, fusion, undifferentiation,* and *symbiosis.* Generally, these terms (many of which can also be found in writings of psychoanalysts and ego psychologists) refer to *the degree to which individuals and subsystems within the family accept, or do not accept, themselves and each other as distinct, self-defined, and self-directing.* According to our assumptions, growth occurs when individuals experience themselves, their thoughts, their feelings, and their qualities as uniquely theirs and separate—or differentiated—from those of others; at the same time, they recognize the need for close relationships and can be intensely involved in the lives of others.

A family that *functions well* in these terms provides its members and subgroupings (such as the marital pair or sibling subsystem) with definite yet flexible boundaries and roles. In other words, one person or subsystem can operate independently and yet share intimately with other members.

In contrast, in the family that operates *dysfunctionally,* members tend to define themselves in relation to others and are often threatened by divergent or independent points of view or expectations. Often in families we see clinically, differences are resisted or denied. Making "I" statements ("I think," "I plan," "I stand for," "I want," "I feel") can seem risky to members of highly undifferentiated or enmeshed families because independent positions are believed to threaten the continuity of relationships. When family members are constantly agreeing with or trying to please others at the sacrifice of achieving their own satisfactions or goals, these behaviors are often guided by the notion that they will thereby make their relationships safe; thus, fears of disapproval or abandonment can preclude autonomous functioning. A father who has made his living in a craft that has been handed down for several generations may see his son's interest in becoming a musician as disloyal or as a challenge to his way of life and to his value as a father; he may, therefore, react with angry or rejecting behaviors. In many troubled families, separation threats are used as a means of control; such threats often effectively keep family members fearful of abandonment and therefore anxiously attached and dependent.[19] By the same token, change and spontaneity are often resisted for fear that these will result in the deterioration of the family relationships without which the members fear they cannot survive.

Sometimes family members explain their own feelings, actions, or sense of personal worth on the basis of the behavior of others. "If it weren't for you, I'd be happy" is a sentiment frequently expressed in family meetings. A husband may remark about his wife, "If she feels good, then I feel good." In some families it can be hard to discern whose feelings are whose; a mother may say in all seriousness, "We are not feeling well" when, it turns out, her son is upset about a girlfriend's rejection of *him.* Parents often believe that their children's successes are more important than their own, and therefore their happiness can depend on their youngsters' choices of career, lifestyle, or mate. A wife may measure her self-esteem by the degree or type of affection she receives from her husband rather than relying on her *own* evaluation of herself. Carried to its extreme, in enmeshed families, each member operates on the myth or delusion that he or she cannot live without the other(s) and, therefore, has no independent existence.

Even when family members refuse to have contact with other family members (such as when adult children "disown" or are "disowned" by their parents or when adult siblings cease speaking), generally *this* represents an effort to reduce the intensity of fused relationships with people with whom they continue to still be very emotionally involved; usually, these kinds of estrangements (or *"cut-offs"*) do not reflect differentiation. However, when family members drift apart, this may represent a genuine lack of interest or involvement with one another.

Closeness versus Enmeshment Sometimes clinicians fail to distinguish families in which there is a great deal of closeness among members and involvement in one another's lives from enmeshed families. For cultural or other reasons, many families are *intensely* connected with various family members: Adult children, for example, may be in daily contact with their parents or siblings. Before coming home to his nuclear family, a man may have dinner with his mother several times a week. Three or four generations may live together and be very closely involved emotionally and in sharing life's tasks. Teenagers may be required to be present at family gatherings, such as Sunday dinner or birthday parties for members of the extended family, even if they would rather be elsewhere with their peers; separation and independence may not be strongly encouraged. These traditions can be found in *some* Italian, Latino, or African American families, among many others, but certainly not in all. *Dysfunctional enmeshment is a different matter* and must be distinguished from family or cultural patterns and traditions that do not lead to severe distress or symptomatology. Each family must be assessed separately and carefully.

Self-Differentiation and the Individual
Bowen devised a scheme with which to assess the level of an individual's self-differentiation. His theory places people on a "differentiation of self" scale, according to their *ability to distinguish their subjective feeling processes from their objective thinking processes.* The higher on the scale (i.e., the higher the level of differentiation), the more the individual, even under stress, can distinguish between emotions and intellect, between feelings and facts.

Well-defined individuals can make rational decisions or plan actions in their own best interests *even if emotional reactions strongly urge them in another direction.* For example, even in the face of severe fear, a person can decide to make a speech to a large group, disagree appropriately with a formidable authority figure or parent, go on a difficult job interview, and so on. Although deeply angry, one can speak in a civil manner to one's boss when any other action could threaten a pay raise or promotion—or the job itself. Despite sadness and pain, one can still decide to visit a dying friend, go to a funeral, or explore difficult material in

therapy. When temporarily separated from a loved one, a person can derive comfort from knowing that there will be a reunion. Furthermore, the well-differentiated person can be intimate with others without fear of fusion and loss of a sense of self. Close relationships are formed on the basis of choice rather than compulsion and fear. The person's definition of "self" is not severely shaken by the disapproval of others, nor must there be constant approval to feel adequate; people's reactions may be considered but are screened by one's own attitudes and judgments. People who are on the high end of Bowen's scale are more flexible and better able to handle stress than those on the lower end. Complete differentiation or emotional maturity, in Bowen's terms, describes a degree of functioning that none of us actually achieves.[20]

Poorly differentiated individuals, on the other hand, especially when stressed or anxious, often cannot distinguish feeling from fact. The intellect is so *flooded by emotion* that decisions are based on what will temporarily reduce anxiety rather than on rational assessments or beliefs. Emotions and thoughts are so commingled that their lives are ruled by immediate, unreasoned reactions. In psychoanalytic terms, ego functioning (especially judgment and impulse control) is impaired or overridden in the face of powerful instinctual drives. These individuals depend on the feelings and opinions of others to define them and, as described previously, often cannot distinguish their own emotions from those of the people close to them, particularly those on whom they heavily rely.

Relationships are often marked by extreme dependency. When things go wrong, it is common for people who are not well differentiated to see their difficulties as rooted in the behaviors or "faults" of others. It may not be their intention to place "blame," as such; rather they imbue others with far more power than they themselves have and therefore try to induce *the others* to make changes; they often have little sense that modifications that *they* make will affect their relationships. When physically healthy, intelligent adults unrealistically see others rather than themselves as; essential to their well-being (or survival), they often place more burdens on relationships than are tolerable. Sometimes they are described as having a "bottomless pit" or never getting enough from the people around them; those who are so poorly self-defined do not know that they have themselves to rely on. Obviously, we are not referring here to individuals who are realistically victimized by others or by noxious social conditions and powerless to act to free themselves.

In Bowen's view, and also in that of many other family and individual therapists from various schools of thought,[21] *helping people to become aware of the difference between their intellectual processes and their emotional processes* can be critical to helping them become better able to solve problems and improve overall functioning. People can learn to monitor their own emotional reactivity and thereby use their mental faculties to make thoughtful choices. They need not (and should not) deny their feelings, but they also need not be ruled by emotion. Once feelings do not automatically dominate actions, people are then freed to use judgment and discrimination in relationships with others and in life decisions. The reader may see the similarity between these notions from family theory and some of our earlier discussions of the use of *reflective procedures,* particularly with those who have certain personality disorders; as we said, for such clients, differentiation of thoughts and feelings can be an important feature of treatment. These ideas and those of cognitive therapists also share some common ground.

Differentiation and Closeness Notions about differentiation are sometimes misunderstood. When we speak of independent, self-defined individuals, we do not imply that they operate exclusively in their own orbits or that they are necessarily self-absorbed, self-centered, or "selfish" in their relationships. To the contrary, as people learn to tolerate true intimacy (in contrast to enmeshment or "stuck-togetherness"), they can also be very responsive to the feelings and attitudes of others. Without sacrificing one's personal identity—one's values, one's goals, one's emotional life—one can also be altruistic. In our experience, those who can maintain a sense of themselves as uniquely special, separate, and self-directing people are better able to be thoughtful to others and giving and loving to those close to them than individuals who cannot function autonomously. The person who relies on others for self-definition, who operates out of fear and extreme dependency—whose *fundamental sense of self* "was acquired at the behest of the relationship system and . . . is negotiable in the relationship system"[22]—eventually harbors resentment toward those on whom he or she so thoroughly relies.

Bowen believed that marriages usually occur between two people of similar levels of self-differentiation. The lower the level of differentiation of family members, the greater the fusion or blending (or symbiotic dependency) with one another. For example, one spouse may appear to function more independently than the other. Close examination, however, reveals that the "strength" of one partner may be contingent on the "weakness" of another. In clinical practice, we frequently observe the rapid decline of the "strong" family member when the "fragile" or "sick" (e.g., spouse or adult child) separates or dies. The incompetence of one is required for the stability of the other. Bowen's concept of the "undifferentiated family ego mass"* describes the quality of fusion or "emotional oneness" that these kinds of family relationships evidence. Members of an undifferentiated family mass, particularly when under pressure, can become deeply involved in the feelings, thoughts, and fantasies of one another. Often the phase of extreme "we-ness," which can be overwhelmingly intense, is followed by a period of distance and even hostile rejection. We frequently see marital pairs, or families with adolescents, going through such cycles of profound dependence and angry repulsion.[23]

Boundaries   Important to theory about family structure are boundaries, the means by which individuals, subsystems, and generations protect their differentiation and maintain a sense of identity. As Minuchin conceives them, boundaries at one pole are very rigid, and the individuals and subgroups within the family are quite uninvolved with and disengaged from the others. At the other pole are those families with diffuse or loose inner boundaries; the family members and subsystems are enmeshed or fused with one another. Most families fall within a wide range between these extremes and have *clear yet penetrable boundaries* that permit both autonomy and close relationships among their members.[24]

The family system is subdivided into subsystems that have their own boundaries. For example, husband and wife or mother and child can be subsystems. Subsystems can be formed by generation, by gender, by interest, or by function or task. (For example, in a single-parent home, mother and grandmother may share child care and administrative functions while the older children are assigned to specific chores.) In-laws constitute subsystems and, along with other members of an extended family, often participate in the emotional and/or task-oriented life of a nuclear family, with or without two parents.

Experience has taught us that two-parent families (whether of the same sex or the opposite sex) usually operate optimally when the *spouse subsystem* has a boundary that can protect it from constant intrusion by other subsystems, particularly when children are small or aging parents have significantly prominent needs; the spouses need a refuge and stimulation, time for mutual support, and opportunity to engage in adult interests. The *parental subsystem,* comprising the same people as the spouse subsystem, is responsible for socialization of the children; the boundary should be permeable enough to provide children with access to *both* parents, while preventing them from assuming spouse functions. *Single parents,* too, have to establish similar boundaries that protect their adult interests and relationships, yet are penetrable enough to be available to children.

Minuchin writes that the *sibling subsystem* "is the first social laboratory in which children can experiment with peer relationships." They "support, isolate, scapegoat, and learn from each other . . . how to negotiate, cooperate, and compete . . . how to make friends and allies, how to save face while submitting, and how to achieve recognition of their skills."[25] When it works well, training acquired from sibling interactions prepares children in important social skills, an opportunity not available to only children. But when there is too much parental intrusion or when sibling activities and rela-

---

* Although Bowen discontinued using this phrase to describe a family's emotional fusion, it appears so frequently in the early family literature that we have chosen to include it.

tionships are diverted by personal or marital problems of the adults, the children's social development may be retarded.

Generally, family therapists believe that healthy family functioning requires individuals and subsystems to have clear boundaries. Within limits, the exact nature of the authority and responsibilities assigned to subsystems is not usually as important as the clarity with which these are defined. For example, a 16-year-old daughter may take considerable responsibility for younger children while her parent or parents work, but the limits and prerogatives of her power must be precisely delineated. An 11-year-old child may accompany a parent who does not speak English to a doctor's appointment to act as interpreter without compromising generational boundaries. In two-parent families, the adults should agree on the designation of responsibility to prevent dysfunctional alliances and blurring of parental boundaries. A grandmother may successfully carry out various functions for a family as long as these are primarily delegated by the parent(s) and are distinctly understood by all involved. Cultural and idiosyncratic family variations in family structure should not be deemed dysfunctional, as long as roles and rules are generally clear and parents maintain the ultimate executive authority in relation to major family policies and decisions. More will be said about this issue in the section on "Family Roles."

At various stages of a family's development, disengagement and enmeshment can coexist. For example, it is common to find a tendency toward enmeshment and diffusion of boundaries between a mother and her small children, while the father is more disengaged. A father and son, or mother and daughter, may become very close, enjoying an almost exclusive relationship when they avidly share a mutual interest in sports,

the arts, intellectual matters, and so on. Greater disengagement may occur, and boundaries may become firmer and less permeable, as adolescents and their families prepare for the natural separation often associated with this life phase. When associated with developmental phases, Minuchin's concepts of disengagement (rigid boundaries) and enmeshment (diffuse boundaries) do not in themselves represent functional or dysfunctional family styles.

Families that consistently operate at one pole or the other, however, can be dysfunctional. Thus, a family system with rigid inner personal or subsystem boundaries can accept a wide range of individual differences, but the disengagement can be so marked that support from the family group is called forth only when the system is severely stressed. Otherwise, family members operate independently, with minimum help from the others and little sense of belonging.

> The professional parents of an 11-year-old boy, both deeply immersed in their respective careers, were unaware that their youngster was being bullied and forced to hand over his carfare to older boys each day until a sensitive janitor alerted the school social worker. The boy, trained to be self-reliant, had been walking home from school and suffering the humiliation of his plight without feeling free to seek his parents' guidance and comfort.

Discussing a similar family process, in different terms, Pittman writes:

> Family tension is hard to describe, but it is palpable. It may be seen as a measure of the members' experience of one another. Tension can be so low that no one feels involved in anyone else's life. Adolescents can develop severe drug habits, young adults can have affairs, and older ones can deteriorate with Alzheimer's, before anyone is aware of anything unusual.[26]

In the extremely enmeshed, fused, or overly dependent family, the most minor event occurring to one member immediately creates a stir of activity among others. Boundaries are so diffuse that privacy is minimal and the feelings of one person seem indistinguishable from those of another. In Pittman's words, "The emotional tension is so intense that one person's emotions are felt instantly by other family members and seem owned by the reactor rather than the originator."[27] The tasks of one member may be absorbed by others, often arresting the development of the individual's sense of competence and autonomy.

A 17-year-old girl with recurrent headaches, for which no physical basis could be detected, was referred for treatment by her physician. In family sessions it was revealed that her mother, who had always thought of her daughter as "delicate," did a major portion of the girl's homework, recommended which friends she should or should not choose, and bought much of her clothing without consulting her about her preferences. The mother told the worker, "I know Alice's feelings better than Alice does." The father complained that his wife always put Alice's needs above his.

Caseworkers frequently meet families such as this one, in which one parent is in an "undifferentiated alliance," or a symbiotically dependent relationship, with one or more children. In these situations the marital relationship is often distant or hostile, and the child frequently becomes symptomatic. Similarly, when a parent has remained fused or excessively involved with his or her parents, the marital boundaries are sacrificed to hostile-dependent relationships with families of origin. Reverberations upon the entire system are inevitable.

A couple and their 16-year-old son (the youngest of four children and the only one living at home) were in family treatment because the boy, although extremely bright, was failing in school and was isolated from his peers. The mother's mother lived in an "in-law" apartment in the family home. Shortly before the boy's symptoms were exacerbated, his usually sullen and remote father, in a rage, pushed the grandmother against a wall, bruising her. Although the mother and grandmother argued frequently, it was clear that the mother kept trying to win her mother's rarely expressed approval. They spent many hours together during the day. Even after the father came home, the mother visited the grandmother for part of every evening. The boy "could do no wrong" in his grandmother's eyes, and she often allowed him privileges denied by one or both parents.

In this family system, the individual, marital, and generational boundaries were repeatedly violated. The grandmother, who had little other life of her own, was excessively involved with her daughter and her daughter's marriage; she also intruded on the parenting of the boy. Rather than confronting his wife directly for being more closely connected to her mother than to him, the father attacked the mother-in-law. At other times, he displaced his rage and became critical of his son. The wife was more deeply invested in her relationship with her mother than that with her husband or her son. The goals of family treatment were to help the marital pair to achieve a warmer, less hostile relationship; to assist the grandmother in developing some social group contacts that would bring her satisfaction and reduce her need to intrude on the life (or boundaries) of her daughter's family; and to support the boy in developing peer friendships as well as closer relationships with his older siblings, who could guide him in his efforts to differentiate from this complexly enmeshed family system. Family therapy progressed accordingly, and the boy became less burdened by the family pathology. Eventually, he was able to establish more comfortable relationships with every member of his family. His schoolwork improved and his friendships increased. When treatment terminated, every family member felt benefited by it.

Chapters 16 and 17 discuss cases that exemplify how members of undifferentiated families—in these illustrations, spouses—often carry psychic functions for and act out the expectations of others. When self-esteem is low and individual boundaries are diffuse introjected expectations may then be projected onto and assumed by others. For example, the father who believes that he is not worthy enough to produce a successful son may project this notion onto the boy with the result that the boy fails in the very areas his father anticipates he will. A mother, who was raised by a critical mother, may induce her daughter to find fault with or demean her in the ways her mother did. In both situations, the children are unconsciously accommodating the inner psychic functions of their parents.

Family Roles

Role Reciprocity, Functional and Dysfunctional   As Spiegel defined this concept important to family theory, a role is "a goal-directed pattern or sequence of acts tailored by the cultural process for the transactions a person may carry out in a social group or situation." Furthermore, *no role exists in isolation but is always patterned to gear in with the complementary or reciprocal role of a role partner."*[28] [Emphasis ours] Particular roles are specified in part by the cultural or subcultural values held by a family; thus, the larger society or community to which people belong defines certain aspects of the husband role or the mother–child role. Within the family, however, roles are additionally designated according to the family's particular needs or values. Sometimes an individual's role lasts the lifetime of the family: "the brain," "the loser," "the baby," and "the clown" are among many we see again and again. Over time, roles may be interchanged or substituted for new ones.

Roles are, functionally or dysfunctionally, assigned in families to accommodate real or assumed needs; they are patterns of behavior designed to fulfill family functions. "Breadwinner," "homemaker," "chief cook," "mechanic/carpenter," "money manager," and "mother's or father's special assistant" are among many other roles often assigned to one member. There are families in which roles are haphazardly allocated; when there is too much "underorganization," essential functions may not be carried out. In these cases, families may deteriorate unnoticed, or they may be referred to some kind of social service, where, it is hoped, they can get help establishing role expectations.[29]

Although all families designate roles, some are assigned to cloak a dysfunctional family balance.

A husband and wife came to treatment for severe marital problems. The husband was a heavy drinker at whom the wife self-righteously raged. After a brief period of treatment, the husband stopped drinking, and the wife, to her own amazement, became depressed. Her low self-esteem and deep-seated expectations of disappointment were masked by her husband's willingness to accept the "alcoholic" role. As long as she could rant about his behavior (taking on the reciprocal role as "nag" or "martyr"), she could maintain the illusion of superiority that protected her from facing her feelings of worthlessness and despair.

This case illustrates the complementary or reciprocal nature of roles. In no way do we mean to imply that the husband's drinking was "caused" by the wife's behavior. In a somewhat similar situation, over the course of treatment a wife stopped complaining to her husband about his drinking; soon afterward, the husband was fired from his job for stealing equipment. In therapy he began to recognize his stake in finding another way to provoke his wife to "scold" him; it was his effort to preserve their accustomed roles and the status quo of the system. Just as a change in one part of the system requires a shift in the other, *if one person modifies or drops a role, the role partner will be compelled to make compensatory changes.*

In families with dysfunctional role reciprocity, some member(s) may be labeled "dependent" or "helpless," with the apparent result that a role of "martyr," "hero," or "rescuer" must be taken on by another family member to get things done. In some families, *the underachievers become essential to the (albeit fragile) sense of well-being of the overdoers.*

Parentification   It is sometimes a child who is called upon to "rescue" parents who seem unable to fulfill family roles; we often refer to such a child as "parentified." As Boszormenyi-Nagy, et al. write about parentification:

> In a healthy family, to the extent a child supplements the parents' resources, this can be an avenue of growth and enrichment; for example, the child who comforts mother when mother has suffered a loss. Yet, when parents are set to draw heavily on a child's resources, the child can become captive to devoting his or her life to becoming a parental figure.[30]

When a young boy assumes the role of mother's "confidant" when she is in the throes of separation, or when a young girl acts as "mediator" during arguments between her parents or between her mother and grandmother, *and* these roles are consistently encouraged by the adults, the child—out of loyalty and/or fear—forfeits his or her own personal development to take care of parents who are having trouble taking care of themselves. On the other hand, when a young teenager is responsible for supervising her younger siblings as they prepare for school because the mother is working, ego capacities of self-reliance and competence may be strengthened. Those children who take on important family responsibilities may become less self-centered as adults than those who have been catered to, but when children are called upon *on a regular basis* to *take over for* rather than to *assist* their parent(s), important childhood needs and strivings are sacrificed. In some cases, the parentified child may gain in competence, but in many cases, when the undernurtured young person becomes an adult, relationship troubles will surface.

Irrational Role Assignments   These can derive from dysfunctional role reciprocity. Often symptoms develop in reaction to roles: A parentified child may become depressed to escape from burdens that are stifling or are beyond him or her. When rewards for being the "martyr" severely diminish, yet the person is too frightened to refuse the role allocated by the dysfunctional family system, he or she may develop psychosomatic symptoms. In Chapters 16 and 17, on couple treatment, we will discuss this process in further detail.

Role Satisfaction or Dissatisfaction   An evaluation of the level of *cooperation* or *contention* among family members when carrying out roles may provide vital information about family functioning and unexpressed feelings and attitudes; complaints about assigned duties *may* reflect relationship dissatisfactions, not problems about roles per se. For example, when a husband gives no recognition to his wife for the double burden she carries as homemaker and wage earner, he may be acting on "sexist" beliefs about family roles, or he may be expressing resentment about his wife's lack of affection toward him. Feeling overworked and unappreciated, the wife is not feeling warmly toward her husband at this point. This situation illustrates *circular causality*. Each spouse is reacting to the other in a repetitive manner: He withholds and she withdraws; when she withdraws he withholds more; they may then start arguing more often and more angrily, or they may become distantly hostile. The point is, they may not be protesting role designations as such, but rather the lack of emotional closeness and support between them. If the couple seeks therapy, particularly before such patterns become too entrenched, it may be possible to interrupt the troubled cycle and help the couple reinstate their loving connection; more often than not, once closeness is regained, any needed role adjustments will be easily achieved.

Role Flexibility   When meeting with families, it is also useful to assess role flexibility. As important as it is to have roles (and boundaries) fairly clearly defined, it is equally important that definitions be revised to meet new conditions. How does the role structure adapt under the stress of vicissitudes families inevitably face? Will a father take on responsibilities usually carried by his wife when she is ill? Or vice versa? Can the adolescent take care of the younger children if the mother has to go to work or care for an elderly relative? When there is role rigidity, it can be predicted that the family will have less capacity for coping with crisis than the family with role flexibility.

Scapegoating   In family therapy, the term *scapegoat* is frequently used to describe the individual—often the "identified patient"—who reflects the family pathology by becoming symptomatic. Hostility or unresolved disappointments between parents, for example, can be displaced onto a child who then "acts out." Frequently, clinicians view the "identified patient" as the scapegoated "victim" because his or her problems mask the problems among other family members. In reality, however, there is no single victim. Thus, the incorrigible child whose role is to obscure the marital tensions in the family may be "victimized" by carrying the burden of the parents' problems, but the rest of the family ultimately become the victim of the child's behavior. In this sense, *every* member is scapegoated by the hidden, often unconscious, issues that plague the family as a whole.

Although never fully accepting the view that the family is a system, Ackerman commented on the clinical situation in which one part of a family seems to "draw the breath of life at the expense of the other." Disturbed families, he hypothesized, threatened by differences among their members, create alliances that battle for dominance. A member or faction attacks, and the victim (scapegoat) finds family allies with whom to counterattack. Another member or faction, at times even the scapegoat, takes on the role of "healer." Thus the roles are fulfilled by particular members and, with the passage of time, by other members. Each is selected for the respective role by unconscious emotional processes within the family.[31]

Similarly, in families in which there is alcoholism, Wegscheider reported that in addition to the "alcoholic" (or "dependent") role, five other roles—"enabler," "hero," "scapegoat," "lost child," and "mascot"—are repeatedly, sometimes interchangeably, played out as an unhealthy way of "preserving the family system at whatever cost" (see the case of Jed Cooper in Chapter 20). Too frightened to confront their many practical and emotional problems, family members unconsciously adopt these roles, hiding their real feelings "behind an artificial behavior pattern." She sees each family member as carrying "a supporting role in the alcoholic drama, which seems to promise some kind of reward in a system that offers few . . . Each role grows out of its own kind of pain, has its own symptoms, offers its own payoffs for both the individual and the family, and ultimately exacts its own price."[32]

Triangles   As we mentioned earlier, an idea emphasized by many family therapists is that the human being simultaneously strives for close relationships and for a sense of personal identity. The balance between the two can be difficult to maintain. When, as we have already illustrated, a close relationship between two people becomes tense (out of a fear of intimacy, through overdependency, or as a result of any unresolved conflicts), the pair may involve a third person on whom the anxieties are displaced. A mother, for example, disappointed by her emotionally distant husband, may try to fill her unmet needs in her relationship with her young son. The father, equally dissatisfied, may vent his feelings by criticizing the boy. By "triangulating" or pulling in the child in this way, the tension between the parents is displaced and reduced, the balance of the relationship is resumed, and the issues between them remain obscured. Triangulation can also describe the process when two people pull in a family pet, the television set, alcohol, or an external event to evade problems between them and to stabilize the relationship. Numerous triangles exist simultaneously in a family, but, over time, the emotional forces within it can reside mostly in one triangle.

When this happens, the triangulated or "triadic" one, such as the boy in the example, takes on a role not unlike that of the scapegoat. The more undifferentiated the individuals, the more often triangulation will occur.

Minuchin identified three sets of conditions that produce dysfunctional triadic structures: (1) When each parent demands that the child side with him or her against the other parent. (2) When marital stresses are expressed through the child and the illusion of parental harmony is thereby maintained; unconsciously, the parents may reinforce any deviant or "sick" behavior of the child and then unite to protect the youngster. (3) When one parent establishes a coalition with a child against the other parent.[33]

A nine-year-old boy was in treatment for encopresis (soiling), which was interfering with peer relationships and creating general embarrassment for him. Meetings with the family, including a 15-year-old daughter, mother, and father, further revealed that the girl was a severe nail-biter and underachieved in school. Seating positions of the first sessions were the same. The boy sat close to and interacted mostly with his mother; the girl assumed a similar position vis-à-vis her father. The parents, although polite to one another, sat as far apart as the office chairs allowed. When they spoke together they talked almost exclusively about their concern for the children. After four meetings, the worker was convinced that there were some charged issues between the parents and arranged a session without the children. With considerable difficulty—and much support from the worker—they disclosed that the father, a diabetic, and the mother, a rather timid woman, had not had sexual relations for three years. They had never shared with each other their feelings about this, nor had they made any attempts to adapt their sexual practices to accommodate the father's potency problem (a common symptom of diabetes). As their relationship became more distant, each turned to a child for emotional support to bolster waning self-esteem. The children, unable to bear the strain of demands they could not meet, became symptomatic.

In this family, both children were "triangulated" (or one might say scapegoated) by the marital pair. And, as we frequently find, the children became the "passport" for the parents' marital treatment. The symptoms of both children subsided after more than a year of marital treatment. The daughter's symptoms cleared up more quickly than the son's, perhaps because the father had many outside interests that he had pursued more avidly after the deterioration of his marital relationship; he was not totally dependent on his daughter to fulfill his emotional needs. The mother–son dyad, on the other hand, was the most intense connection in the mother's life, and achieving greater differentiation required more time for her and her son.

Various writers on family therapy may approach the same or similar points of view but often by using different language. For example, triangulation is one form of scapegoating in which a third person is blamed, alienated, or "chosen" to be symptomatic in order to obfuscate the conflict or stress between two people. In psychological terms, both of these concepts involve the ego defense of displacement and sometimes of denial: that is, the strain between family members is denied and then displaced onto another.

Pseudomutuality   All family relationships and roles are by nature, in some form, complementary; compromises are required to achieve compatibility and smooth functioning. When there is *genuine* mutuality in

a family, divergent interests, opinions, and feelings are tolerated; flexible role behavior can add stimulation and vitality to family life. Pseudomutuality refers to the family's compulsive absorption with "fitting together" that, as Wynne describes it, creates "the illusion of a well integrated state even when that state is not supported by the emotional structures of the members."[34] Threatened by differences among its members, the family promotes the myth of harmony. To maintain it, the individual members must lock themselves into rigid roles and relinquish their personal identities. They must suppress or deny differences that they fear may destroy the family relationship. If sufficiently persistent, the resulting inhibition of self-expression can create severe personality disturbances in family members.

> Neighbors complained to the police about an 18-year-old man exposing himself in the courtyard of the housing project where he lived with his parents and three younger siblings. Placed on probation, he was referred to a mental health clinic for treatment. He related superficially to his young male worker but contended that he had no problems. Referred for family therapy, the parents insisted they had a "perfect family" and that the boy was framed by jealous neighbors whose testimony had convicted him. Both parents were cordial and, on the surface, cooperative. It was not until some relatives of the mother came from the West Indies to live in the household that the family became intolerably stressed. At this point, family tensions surfaced and hidden grievances between the parents were uncovered. Work with the family could then begin.

In this situation, the parents had been unwilling to recognize the serious implications of their son's behavior. They feared that giving up the illusion that all was well with him—or with the marriage—would threaten the family structure. After the family was engaged in treatment, it became evident that the denial of all differences and problems among the members had placed such a strain on the young man's internal psychological system that he became symptomatic. The younger children, too, were manifesting stressed reactions to the family mandate to conform: to think, feel, and behave in a prescribed manner. Wynne sees no real victims in pseudomutuality since all members of the family participate. In this case, the young man, as well as his parents, maintained that family life was ideal, despite the high prices he paid as an individual; he, too, promoted the myth of harmony. Had external forces not stressed the family beyond endurance, family meetings, a contingency of the young man's probation, might have gone on as meaningless exercises. In all likelihood, without therapy, even more disturbing personality problems would have developed in this family.

Family Myths and Secrets   Myths serve the function for families that defenses serve for individuals. To protect itself against conflict or ambivalent feelings and to maintain its balance, the family—or individuals within it—paints a picture of a situation or of relationships that are distorted or untrue. The myth may be shared by the family as a whole, or it may be promoted by one or more of its members. Role designations that misrepresent particular family members as "weak" or "bad" are myths. Myths may be perpetuated to avoid or to deny painful feelings of self-blame, as they often are in families that exclusively attribute their miseries or misfortunes to one family member. For example, the alcoholic in a family may be assigned the role of "culprit" to exonerate others of responsibility for family problems.

Families may protect themselves against intrusions or judgment of the outside world with myths, as with the myth of pseudomutuality just described. Incest and extramarital affairs are often well-kept secrets. In families in which there is incest, usually it is children who are misused and sacrificed—often sworn to silence—to protect adults from resolving their own personal or relational issues. In cases of infidelity, too, the secret almost always is an indirect means for handling unresolved individual and/or relational issues (see Chapter 16). Myths and secrets may also go hand in hand to cloak "unspeakable" events of the past, or a family tragedy.

A nine-year-old girl with an incessant and obsessive fear of snakes was referred for family therapy after a period of unsuccessful individual treatment. The parents appeared to enjoy a loving relationship with each other and with their only child, Deborah. Yet the family climate seemed unexplainably strained. Only after several sessions, in response to a random question, did the worker learn that the mother suffered from a heart condition, a fact the parents had not shared with Deborah. The worker sensed that the mother's illness was more serious than the parents were acknowledging and hypothesized that the child had picked up the tension about it, as the worker had. Not understanding its meaning, Deborah, the worker suspected, had displaced her feelings of dread onto snakes. After some careful and sensitive work in family therapy, the child (and the worker) learned that both parents feared the mother's illness could prove fatal. With the support of the worker, the relationships among the three became more open and intimate. As the underground anxieties surfaced, the family members could share their feelings of heartbreak and affection.

Deborah's fear of snakes all but disappeared. It was fortunate for the child that her symptoms were alarming enough to prompt her parents to seek outside help, because the mother died less than a year after treatment terminated. Had the family denial persisted, Deborah would have been left with guilt, lack of resolution about the loss of her mother, and—if she learned the truth—bitterness toward her parents for having promoted the myth that all was well in a household in which her mother was dying.[35]

In this family, the parents consciously kept the secret and perpetuated the "all-is-well" myth to "protect" Deborah. (The notion that children cannot tolerate tragedy is itself a myth.) The parents had been less aware of their *own* need to maintain the myth in order to obscure from themselves their feelings of terror and sadness.

Communication Concepts

Jackson, Haley, and Satir, among others, turned to communication theory to conceptualize the workings of the family system. In her highly recommended volume, *Conjoint Family Therapy* Satir summarized her view:

> A person who communicates in a functional way can:
>
> *a.* Firmly state his case
> *b.* yet at the same time clarify and qualify what he says,
> *c.* as well as ask for feedback
> *d.* and be receptive to feedback when he gets it.[36]

Work with family groups necessarily involves interventions by the therapist to focus and clarify the messages exchanged among members. Beyond this, the distortions and unexplored assumptions that generally pervade the communication process

of disturbed families become the grist for treatment. The myths and misapprehensions on which the family operates must be exposed and dispelled. In family therapy, members can learn to inquire about the thoughts and feelings of others and to share their own. Any tendency of family members to act on untested suppositions often can be revealed more quickly in family therapy than in individual treatment. The child who believes his behavior caused his parents' divorce and the woman who erroneously assumes her daughter-in-law hates her have opportunities to correct their distortions in family group meetings.

Principles of communication set forth by Jackson and his colleagues have become important in family assessment and treatment.

Relationships and interactions depend not only on *what* is communicated, but on *how* the message is sent. Thus, the *quality* of the communication can reveal more about the relationship than the *content*. For example, the manner in which we ask someone to pass the salt (i.e., our tone of voice, inflection, physical gestures, and so on) can define a peer or a superior–inferior kind of relationship. The content is similar, but the message about the relationship can be very different. A *metacommunication* (defined as a communication about a communication) qualifies the literal content of a message by means of a second verbal or nonverbal statement.

> In a family session a usually passive and agreeable husband turned to his wife and said with feeling, "You make me angry." Immediately after this statement he smiled, adding, "I was only kidding." His second message, the metacommunication— it was later revealed—masked his fear of his wife's retaliatory anger.

In Jackson's view, verbal communications reveal less about relationships than nonverbal messages. The latter, however, can be more ambiguous: tears, smiles, and frowns have many meanings. Furthermore, he points out, it is impossible *not* to communicate. Silence and withdrawal are strong messages. If a family comes for treatment and the teenage son sits silently, or the daughter sits outside the family circle, these are communications for the therapist to decipher and find ways to ask the family about.

Often in trying to appraise the nature of relationships in the family system, the therapist can learn as much or more from feeling tone and body language that accompany the intercommunications than from the message content itself. A man may say to his wife, "I want to hear what you have to say," at the same time turning his back to her. A woman may say to her husband, "I am sorry I hurt you," while simultaneously gritting her teeth. No message is simple. The family therapist is alert to an accompanying message that may deny or confirm the first. When the nonverbal communications are not clear, the clinician then seeks further information. In these illustrations, in a gentle and nonjudgmental way, one might ask the man: "Do you think you are a little concerned about what your wife wants to tell you?" To the woman: "Do you think you, too, are still feeling hurt?"

In some families faulty communication patterns derive primarily from lack of knowledge; if this is so, misunderstandings and difficulties may be cleared up fairly quickly. The clinical social worker may act as "coach" to family members who simply never learned to make "I" statements or to speak directly to one another rather than *through* or *about* a third person. For example, a mother who is angry with her husband may say to her young child: "Tell your father to let the cat out." Or, a father, referring to his wife who is in the same room, may say to his teenage son: "See how she is?" Examples of communications such as

these are common in family sessions. "Go-betweens" and triangulation interfere with functional exchanges. Some families can be taught the value of allowing disagreement, even about "taboo" subjects. By the same token, the worker may help family members to listen rather than to interrupt, distort, reinterpret, or make assumptions about what others are saying. Those who tend to speak in generalizations can be helped to become more specific.

Sometimes, families out of habit have not talked about certain subjects, but these can be elicited with just a little support and reassurance. However, in other families, poor communication may reflect lack of differentiation, fear of losing relationships, problems around boundaries and roles, and so on. Under these circumstances, more extensive treatment may be required to help family members become less frightened, more autonomous and self-defined, as well as more communicative.

The Double Bind   A classic article written by Bateson, Jackson, and colleagues describes the *double bind* as "a situation in which no matter what a person does, he cannot win."[37] The essential ingredients of this particular kind of communication situation are:

1. Two or more persons, one designated as "victim."
2. Repeated experience or a continuing condition.
3. A primary negative injunction such as "Do this or I will punish you."
4. A secondary injunction conflicting with the first at a more abstract level, enforced by punishments, threats to survival, or promise of a reward.
5. A situation in which the victim can neither leave the field nor comment on the discrepant messages.

The child whose mother accuses him of not loving her enough is in a "no-win" situation when he tries to kiss her and she anxiously recoils, as though to say "go away." If this condition is repeated, it is double binding. The boy needs his mother, so he cannot leave. If he comments on the contradiction, he will be scolded. Obedience to one message results in disobedience to the other.

The double bind can be perpetrated by one or more individuals:

A father constantly complained that he wanted his 21-year-old, unemployed son to get a job and "become a man." In words, the mother agreed, but whenever the young man found work, she told him it was either dangerous or "beneath" him. In a family session he told his mother he thought she was babying him. Both parents then called him "stupid."

In this case, if the son remained idle, his father belittled him. If he found a job, his mother disapproved. If he complained about the bind, his parents joined together to insult him. Unfortunately, this young man participated in the double-binding situation by defining himself as too weak to make a move without his parents' approval.

In a follow-up article, written in 1962, the same writers modified one aspect of this important theoretical contribution: "The most useful way to phrase double-bind description is not in terms of a binder and a victim but in terms of people caught up in an ongoing system which produces conflicting definitions of the relationship and consequent subjective distress."[38] As illustrated in the above example, the participation of the "victim" is as essential to the perpetuation of the bind as are parts played by the "binders." This modification is an important one for family therapists to remember when they find themselves feeling partisan to the "underdog" who, unless

he or she is a child or severely handicapped, has taken on the role and may (to the therapist's surprise) fight to protect it.

Clearly, in family situations where there is wife abuse, for example, the power of the victim often is not equal to the power of the abuser who is doing the "double-binding." Social factors do contribute to the actions of the perpetrator and to the weakened position of the abused woman. Nevertheless, from a family systems perspective, interventions would be designed to empower the wife and hold the husband absolutely responsible for his behavior, despite external factors that have contributed to the inequality between them.

Mystification   R. D. Laing coined the term *mystification* to describe an indirect means of handling differences or conflict. When A's perceptions contradict B's, for example, A may insist to B: "It's just your imagination" or "You must have dreamt it." Or, another example of mystification given by Laing: A child is playing noisily in the evening and his mother is tired. She could make a direct statement, such as "I am tired and I want you to go to bed." Or, a mystifying statement would be: "You are tired and should go to bed." Mystification becomes a serious matter when:

one person appears to have the *right* to determine the experience of another, or complementarily, when one person is under an *obligation* to the other(s) to experience, or not to experience, himself, them, his world or any aspect of it, in a particular way.[39]

Thus, the not necessarily tired boy in the above example may or may not be confused about his own feeling state, but he may feel obliged at some level to disclaim his subjective experience. In mystification, Laing says, some kind of conflict is present, but evaded. (Perhaps in the above example, the

interaction between them as discrete matters, casework has long recognized how each affects the others. As the concepts described in this chapter illustrate, internal and external phenomena are intertwined. *When changes occur in a family system, the behavior and inner lives of individual members shift. Conversely, individual changes reverberate on the family as a whole.* The actions of one individual are both cause and effect of the actions of others. In contrast to the single-cause, linear approach to understanding human behavior, the psychosocial orientation assesses the multidimensional, reciprocal influences of the personality, the family, and the larger social system, as each acts on and reacts to the others.

Freudian, ego-psychology, object relations, and other theories about personality have deepened our view of individual dynamics. The social sciences have advanced our understanding of the environment. More recently, the ideas that have emerged from the family therapy movement equip us with means for studying the transactions of individuals within the family environment; new information about the properties of the family as a system has become available. Family concepts have filled some real gaps in casework theory; the place for including them is provided by the psychosocial framework.

The Personality System

Freudian Concepts While some of Freud's ideas have been significantly revised over the years, others remain important to the psychosocial approach. Freud broke new ground with his proposition that personality is shaped by social as well as biological forces. Neurosis, he asserted, is an outgrowth of the individual's family experience and inborn drives. The intrapsychic oedipal conflict, as he described it, is grounded in early parental relationships. In

his well-known case of "Little Hans," Freud worked with the father, not with the boy himself. The successful treatment of the boy's horse phobia was achieved through interventions in the family system. Unfortunately, as psychoanalytic theory was passed down, some followers not only failed to expand on the interactional aspects of personality but also narrowed the theory to minimize the social side of Freud's thinking, which, although not fully developed, was there all along.[42]

In Chapter 2 and elsewhere, we discussed the Freudian concept of personality structure, consisting of the id, ego, and superego–ego ideal. As we have illustrated, systems concepts have been very useful in understanding intrapsychic dynamics. Just as occurs in a family system, a change in one part of the personality system affects the other parts. Relaxation of a strict superego can liberate ego functions that have been immobilized by self-criticisms and unrealistic expectations. When the drives of the id press for gratification, ego functions can organize or channel these in one direction or another, usually with some input from the superego. As in every system, the components of the personality system are dynamic and in constant interaction, acting on and reacting to one another.

Internalization and Introjection
These concepts derived from the study of personality direct us to some significant theoretical links between intrapsychic and family systems phenomena. As we know, the child's superego internalizes or introjects the commands, prohibitions, and ideals of the parents or other authority figures, with the result that the youngster learns to conform to their demands and values even in their absence. Yet our understanding of a particular client requires an additional, interactional perspective. Take,

for example, a man who feels hostile toward his mother, oppressed by demands he believes she makes on him. Often we discover that he is reacting to his *early mother introject*, which bears little resemblance to his mother of today; the demands, if she ever made them, *are no longer hers but his own.* Yet his negative attitude toward her may provoke angry or defensive responses from her that tend to reinforce his internalized representation of her. To see the total picture, we must understand the client's inner life, the interdependence of the past and the present, and the circular nature of the mother–son interactions. Joint or family sessions may be the most efficient approach to expose and correct internalized distortions as they are played out in interpersonal relationships.

In this case, it is also probable that this man's introjected expectations, derived from his past (possibly *always* distorted) image of his mother, are evident in other interactions; he may, for example, view his wife as "controlling," even when objective evidence does not support his perception. As some family therapists (those who recognize how the past affects the present) have emphasized, individuals emerge from their families of origin more or less "programmed" to reenact introjected roles and qualities that derive from family relationships and experiences as they assimilated them in childhood.[43]

Multigenerational Transmission Processes or Family Projection Processes

The process just described is often referred to as the intergenerational, multigenerational, or family projection process. (However, in the perspective of some proponents of these concepts, the processes go beyond conditioning, assimilation, or even introjection of past experience. Rather, family processes are believed to have come down through many generations; hence the value of genograms that diagram family patterns, styles, strengths, and vulnerabilities of one's predecessors.)[44] In marital treatment, the process becomes additionally complicated when *each* spouse brings his or her own internalizations of family history to the marital relationship. Marital and family-of-origin sessions may most efficiently expose and correct internalized distortions as these are played and replayed in present interpersonal relationships. Chapters 16 and 17 discuss these issues as they are revealed in couple therapy.

Externalization and Projection

Our understanding of these closely allied notions helps to bridge theories of individual dynamics and family relationships. These concepts refer to the act of attributing inner, subjective phenomena, including wishes, fears, conflicts, and thoughts, to the external world. We can see how such internal matters or aspects of one's self, once externalized, become part of an interactional process, particularly when they involve other people. For example, a client may tell us he is unhappily married but that he will not leave his wife for fear she will break down emotionally; in fact, however, he is externalizing his hidden concern about his own stability. Or a wife who says she wants to plan a vacation because her husband needs it may have difficulty giving *herself* permission for a holiday; furthermore, the husband may be counting on his wife to accommodate *his* difficulty planning pleasure on his own behalf. *Unacceptable dissociated inner expeiences*—in these examples, fears and wishes—once externalized *are no longer discrete internal events.* They affect and are affected by the interpersonal arena; interactional forces take on a life of their own above and beyond the individuals involved.

Projective Identification and Trading of Associations   *Projective identification,* described in Chapter 2 (page 52), refers to the often unconscious process—usually occurring in close relationships—in which person A perceives person B as if B contained (often feared or despised) elements of A's personality. A is able to induce B to behave in ways that conform to A's perceptions. Then A reacts by attacking the qualities in B that A disowned, projected, and induced. For example, A might have perceived (his own) cowardice in B, then found a way to elicit B's timidity, and then berated B for it. Thus, projective identification refers to intrapsychic *and* interpersonal phenomena.

Taking this process one step further, Wynne described the *trading of dissociations.* This concept refers to complementary or interlocking externalizations of intrapsychic dissociations. In other words, a man, unaware of a particular quality in himself, may see it located in the personality of his wife and believe his problem can only be relieved by changes in her. Similarly, the wife locates her own unacceptable qualities or ideas in her husband and sees her difficulties as a function of his personality. For example, a man may (accurately) view his wife as angry and bitter when he has suppressed his own violent feelings; the wife, on the other hand, may see her husband's dependence on her while disclaiming hers on him. The fixed view that the man has of his wife is unconsciously exchanged for the fixed view she holds of him. The purpose of the reciprocal and shared trading of dissociations is twofold: first, both individuals protect themselves from experiencing their dreaded feelings; yet, second, each is able to "retain these qualities within his purview, at a fixed distance from his ego."

A teenage daughter may perceive her mother's punitively moralistic qualities, while dissociating those same features in her own personality; the mother, unaware of dreaded ("bad") sexual impulses within herself, becomes keenly attuned to those of her daughter. Each sees the need for change in the other, since each perceives aspects of the other that are outside that person's awareness. By externalizing inner, unacceptable parts of themselves, they may each persecute the other for these qualities rather than enduring what would otherwise be very painful self-castigation. It is easy to see how complicated and futile the relationship between this mother and daughter could become. As Wynne explains: "The trading of dissociations means that each person deals most focally with that in the other which the other cannot acknowledge. Thus, there can be no 'meeting,' no confirmation, no mutuality, no shared validation of feelings or experience."[45] This process can be extended to involve every family member in a network of traded perceptions. The individuals involved, as Wynne points out, might be diagnosed as having ego-syntonic character disorders who may not be motivated for individual treatment.

Often, however, these same people become engaged in family therapy because they recognize the need for other family members to get help. In family sessions, intrapsychic, dissociated aspects of individuals that have been located in the personalities of others often can be identified and sorted out.

Separation and Individuation: Attachment and Loss   Individual and family thinking merge again when we examine the writings and research findings of Bowlby, Spitz, Mahler, and others from the psychoanalytic tradition on separation and individuation, who spearheaded theories about attachment and loss.[46] Many family therapists, too, have been keenly interested in these matters.

There is general agreement that the development of a relatively autonomous, self-reliant personality depends heavily on two conditions of the individual's childhood: (1) consistent parental availability, responsiveness, and support; and (2) parental encouragement of the child's independence and self-direction appropriately timed to the child's age. Absence of either of these conditions can contribute to lasting separation anxieties in the youngster. A mother (and/or a father, grandmother, or other key person to whom the child is attached), sensing her child's emerging independence, may be threatened by separation feelings and withdraw more completely and abruptly than the child, who still requires steady reassurance and support, can bear. Or the mother's anxiety may lead her to cling to the child; she may do this by overprotecting or "parentifying" the child (i.e., treating him or her as a parental substitute). In any case, the mother's separation and abandonment fears are transmitted to the child. Unwittingly, parents may pass on to their children the unfulfilled longings, or wishes to retaliate, that grow out of their own childhood experiences.

Thus, the adult who in early life was abandoned, literally or emotionally, may cling to a person or even a memory out of fear of feeling alone again. Or the individual may set up interpersonal situations in which the experience of abandonment is painfully repeated over and over again.

Some people who experienced childhood loss remain angry or depressed; some have become so distrusting that they disengage, defensively avoiding intimate connections with others, including spouses and children. These emotional responses affect the lives of those who try to interact with them. Family therapy is often an excellent vehicle for resolving past losses and connecting with people who can be available, who have not abandoned them.

Similarly, the adult who was steadily discouraged from functioning independently may hold on desperately to others to maintain a sense of belonging. In family treatment, we frequently see families in which the members, sometimes alternately, cling to or abandon their parents, their spouses, or their children. Such overdependency and estrangement among family members can often be traced to earlier separation-individuation disturbances. The longings, fears, and anger derived from old parent–child experiences are transferred to current family relationships. Leader believes that "in the majority of families seeking help, the intergenerational theme of abandonment flows deep like an underground stream."[47] Family myths, roles, and interactions are patterned to guard against conscious and unconscious separation fears. As we have already illustrated, often family members deny inevitable differences of opinions, thoughts, or feelings among them, for fear that these will lead to separation or estrangement. In these situations, each individual is deeply enmeshed in the larger family process. Symptoms and troubled feelings, although in part a function of the dynamics of the personality, cannot be appraised fully in isolation from this outer reality.

In summary, the selected illustrations included in this section support our view that the psychosocial framework can accommodate family concepts. Caseworkers can improve their treatment skills when they are equipped with specific information about the nature of the complex interplay of forces that prevail in a family system. "How," asked Ackerman shortly before his death, "can we choose between the family and the person? The person is a subsystem within the family, just as the family is a sub-system within the community and culture."[48] We agree with Minuchin: "Changes in a family structure contribute to changes in the behavior and the inner psychic process of the members of that system."[49] Repeatedly, in our clinical practice, we see how the moods and behavior of individuals change as their families change. However, with Ackerman, we would caution against a mechanistic approach to systems that tends to deny the force and integrity of the individual personality. Each family member has a private inner world, unique natural endowments, character structure, and personal identity that endure over time. The special qualities of the individual reverberate upon the family system as well. The greatest possible sophistication about the dynamics of the personality system and the family system, and the nature of the reciprocal influences between them, is required to understand the problems individuals and families bring to treatment. As Moultrup wrote: "A family therapist who ignores the individual will enjoy the same success or lack of success as an individual therapist who ignores the family."[50]

In the chapter that follows we will demonstrate how, as we broaden our knowledge base, we increase our choices of treatment methods, strategies, and goals.

NOTES

1. For useful information on changing family situations, see Family Service America (1991 and 1995).
2. See Bronfenbrenner et al. (1996), p. 6 in the section on youth. See also Chapter 4 on trends in American family life.
3. Zimmerman (1980), p. 204.

   In a wonderful and very readable book, Martin (1992), a philosopher of education, puts forth the idea of the "schoolhome"; in short, as family life changes, with the majority of women and mothers (and men and fathers) in the work force, she challenges us to rethink the functions and scope of our educational systems. She envisions schoolhomes as safe, nurturing environments, communities in which children can learn not only the three Rs but also social awareness and responsibility and enjoy a sense of connectedness and consistency that busy and preoccupied parents are often unable to provide.

4. See especially Froma Walsh (1996) who, in an excellent article, elaborates on the resiliency-based approach to family intervention, prevention, and research; resilience is an especially important concept that expands our understanding of family processes in the face of social change. In another paper, Walsh (1998) asserts that family beliefs and spirituality are important to resilience and meeting the challenges of adversity. We also recommend her (1993) very useful edited volume on normal family processes. See also Hawley and DeHaan (1996) on family resilience. See also useful discussions by Freed (1982) and Startz and Cohen (1980).
5. Quoted in Bruno (1957), p. 177.
6. See Richmond (1917), p. 137. For more on the roots of family treatment in social work history, see Montalvo (1982) and Siporin (1980). Braverman (1986) discusses social work's tendency to disregard early casework contributions to family therapy and offers possible explanations for this phenomenon.
7. Richmond (1917), pp. 134–59.
8. Greater detail on the history of the shifts in social work emphases can be found in Witmer (1942), especially Chapters 8 and 17; Fink (1942), especially Chapter 4; and Woodroofe (1962).
9. Hamilton (1951), pp. 95–97.
10. See Mudd (1951) and Hollis (1949).
11. Siporin (1980), p. 14. See also Gurman and Kniskern (1991), pp. 4–6, for a brief history of social work and family treatment.
12. See Ackerman (1958), a family therapy classic. See also Satir (1983), Scherz (1970), Leader (1969), Sherman (1967), and Aponte (1976).
13. See the excellent compilation of articles in the volume edited by Carter and McGoldrick (1988) on the changing life cycle. See also Parad's (1965) well-known volume on crisis intervention with very good articles that describe the impact of various crises and stressful events on family life; of particular relevance to this section are papers in Part 2, pp. 73–190. The ways in which family and individual developmental tasks necessarily run parallel are discussed more fully in

Scherz (1970). Again, see Froma Walsh (1993 and 1996).

14. Framo (1982) in his chapter "Symptoms from a Family Transactional Viewpoint," p. 53. See also his thorough and useful chapter, "Rationale and Techniques of Family Therapy."

   A study by Hadley et al. (1974) on the relationship between a family developmental crisis and the appearance of symptoms in a family member found a positive and significant relationship between the onset of symptoms and two types of family crisis: the addition of a family member and the loss of a family member.

   The early family research in the 1950s that led to some of the central principles guiding the family therapy movement focused primarily on the study of families in which a member was diagnosed as having schizophrenia; but as the movement began to take hold, it became apparent that many of the original concepts could be applied more broadly to families with various symptomatic members, or even to "normal" families. Ackerman (1958) and Bell (1961) were among the early pioneers who studied families of nonpsychotic clients. For an orientation to the rationale and history of the family therapy movement, see Zuk and Rubinstein (1965); the entire edited volume in which this chapter appears provides further insight into the development of the movement.

   For a recommended, very readable text that examines major theories and approaches to family treatment, see Goldenberg and Goldenberg (1991). Froma Walsh (1997) briefly summarizes some major approaches to family therapy.

15. Ackerman (1958), p. 71. Developed by Jackson (1968) and others as a family concept, the idea of homeostasis was elaborated on by Ackerman who described the homeostasis of the personality, of the family, and of the larger environment and the interdependence of the three. See also Jung (1983) and Moultrup (1981).

16. Hartman and Laird (1983), p. 95.

17. Walsh (1997), p. 135. See Walsh and Anderson (1988) on chronic disorders of the family. A study conducted by Friedmann, et al.

(1997) found that in general "the type of the patient's psychiatric illness did not predict significant differences in family functioning" (p. 357), but the presence of *any* acute psychiatric disorder was associated with poor family functioning.

18. See Wynne et al. (1968) and several chapters in the volume edited by Guerin (1976).

19. See Argles (1984).

20. Bowen (1978). See Green and Werner (1996) for a very interesting discussion of distinctions between enmeshment and closeness.

21. See Framo (1982), Pittman (1987), and Rogers (1961) for useful references on differentiation.

22. Bowen (1978), p. 366. See Innes (1996) who recognizes Bowen's contribution to family theory, but argues that in his insistence upon rigorous inquiry, Bowen based his theory on a natural science perspective, rather than also on knowledge specifically about human interaction and social organization. See also Freeman (1992) who discusses theory and practice of multigenerational family therapy based on many of Bowen's ideas.

23. For many years, social workers have been aware of the phenomenon of positive and negative "complementarity" (see Chapter 11 and note 14 to that chapter) in couple relationships and in interactional behavioral patterns of entire families. This concept, along with concepts about symbiosis and dependency, is closely related to some aspects of Bowen's theory and to notions about role reciprocity, which we shall discuss further in the next section on "Family Roles." Sometimes an unequal yet complementary relationship is so necessary to the functioning of the individuals involved that it can be dangerous to disturb the balance even though one believes the adaptation is pathological; for a reference to a case example, see Chapter 11, note 15.

   See two excellent articles on intergenerational dependency and separation anxiety: Shulman (1973) and Leader (1978).

24. Minuchin (1974).

25. Ibid., p. 59.

26. Pittman (1987), p. 21.

27. Ibid., p. 22.

28. Spiegel (1968), p. 393.

29. Aponte (1976).
30. Boszormenyi-Nagy, et al. (1991), p. 213. See also a book by Jurkovic (1997) on the parentified child. An article by Kabat (1996) discusses and provides case illustrations of situations in which the mother is not receiving emotional support or responsiveness from other adults and therefore relies on her daughter to fill these needs; needless to say, as the daughter becomes a young adult, separation efforts may be impeded.
31. See Ackerman (1969) and also an excellent paper by Vogel and Bell (1968).
32. Wegscheider (1981), pp. 84–86.
33. Minuchin (1974). See also Bowen's and Fogarty's discussions of triangles in Guerin (1976), pp. 75–78 and pp. 147–48; and Satir (1983), pp. 69–77. In an important paper, Falicov (1998) urges us to beware of automatically pathologizing triangles; they must be understood in the cultural and family context in which they exist.
34. Wynne, et al. (1968), p. 628.
35. This case is described in greater detail by Woods (1982). A highly recommended book edited by Imber-Black (1993) contains excellent chapters on a broad range of secrets kept by individuals and families. See also Ferreira (1963) and Stierlin (1973).
36. Satir (1983), p. 88. We encourage the reader to study Part 2 of Satir's book devoted to communication.

    See also Watzlawick (1978), Watzlawick, et al. (1967), and Birdwhistell (1970) on nonverbal communication.
37. Bateson, et al. (1956), pp. 251–64.
38. Bateson, et al. (1963), 154–61.
39. Laing (1965), p. 346. See also Laing and Esterson (1971); this book includes clinical studies of families of patients with schizophrenia and identifies mystification as an important aspect of the families' communication styles.
40. See, in particular, Haley (1987). Minuchin (1974), although to a lesser extent, also minimized the importance of diagnosis of the individual. See Gurman and Kniskern (1991), pp. 51–56, for a summary of how systems concepts are utilized by a range of models of family therapy, including the psychoanalytic, structural (Minuchin), Bowen, and strategic (Haley).
41. In addition to other references on the history and practice of social work already cited in this book, see Simon (1970). See also the chapters in Dorfman (1988) and in Turner (1996); despite many variations in orientation among casework theoreticians, the person-in-situation concept is recognized by most points of view.
42. Freud (1964), pp. 5–148. See also Ackerman (1958) for an interesting approach to the integration of psychoanalytic concepts and the influences of the family environment.
43. We recommend a practical book by Allen (1988) who uses concepts related to family relationships, past and present, to heal current personal difficulties and relationship problems.
44. See Friedman (1991). See also Bowen (1978) and Freeman (1992). The edited volume by Scharff (1989) and Scharff and Scharff (1987) help to conceptualize intergenerational therapy from an object relations perspective.

    The reader is encouraged to read the invaluable book by Framo (1992), written for clinicians, who summarizes his family-of-origin, intergenerational approach to therapy. See Bedrosian and Bozicas (1994) on the cognitive approach to family of origin problems.

    See McGoldrick and Gerson (1985) for their excellent book on how to understand and construct genograms.
45. Wynne (1965), pp. 297–300.
46. See Ainsworth (1962), Bowlby (1965), and Mahler, et al. (1975). See also Blanck and Blanck (1974), pp. 40–60, and Brunhofer (1997). For other relevant references, see Chapter 2, note 16 and Chapter 5, note 19.
47. Leader (1978), p. 141.
48. Ackerman (1972), p. 451.
49. Minuchin (1974), p. 9.
50. Moultrup (1981), p. 113. See also Scharff and Scharff (1987), p. 13, for a similar statement.

    For an excellent discussion of the merging of systems theory and psychodynamic concepts, see the very clear and readable chapter by Bentovim and Kinston (1991), which includes a case illustration.

CHAPTER 15

THE CLINICAL PRACTICE OF FAMILY THERAPY

From the point of view expressed in the preceding chapter, it follows that we cannot fully understand individuals without knowledge of the families to which they belong. Conversely, when we assess a family's system, structure, and dynamics, the total picture requires a grasp of the characteristics of the individual members. In some case situations, understanding of the biological and psychological qualities of the individual(s) is the most salient guide to treatment; in others, the properties and transactions of the family system are of greatest consequence. In still others, we must be particularly attuned to how individuals and families are influenced by and interact with the larger community and social system. We are alert to the economic, social, ethnic, and racial context of families who turn to us for help; the assessment of environmental opportunities and resources, as discussed in Chapter 8, may be particularly important. Respect for and under-

standing of family values and cultural beliefs are as essential to family as to individual assessment. And, as we have repeatedly indicated, by carefully listening, we attempt to elicit from clients *their* concerns, *their* views of the meaning of their current situation, *their* goals and visions.

All that we have written in previous chapters about acceptance, self-determination, initial interviews, social study, assessment of strengths as well as weaknesses, mutuality and goal-setting, and the fluid blending of treatment procedures applies to family therapy as well as to individual treatment. Here, we will emphasize family evaluation and intervention in particular; the reader may want to review concepts from earlier chapters upon which discussions in this chapter are built. The separate examination of therapy in the context of the family is necessary for manageability of discussion only; in reality, the psychosocial approach is grounded in the idea that people's behaviors occur in the context of many dynamic interacting systems. However, when larger social systems are not immediately accessible to change, the family and the individuals in it must mobilize strengths and find creative solutions to dilemmas that derive from oppressive or depriving conditions.

We need not choose among levels of conceptualization. Rather, as we collect the mass of information that clients bring, we must try to organize the germane data from as many perspectives as possible. After weighing the influence of the various levels (e.g., individual, family, sociocultural, and socioeconomic) on each other and on the problem at hand, and identifying accessible points of intervention, we are then in a position to consider approaches to treatment. To demonstrate the thinking that goes into arranging data and deciding whether or not to engage the whole family in treatment, we introduce the Russo case. This family will illustrate how basic family concepts incorporated by the psychosocial framework can be applied in practice.

AN INTAKE REQUEST: THE RUSSO FAMILY

Mrs. Russo telephoned the mental health clinic in her area, seeking an appointment for her husband, whom she described as depressed and withdrawn. He had not asked her to call and she had not told him she was doing so. She believed she could persuade him to keep the appointment, however. Since Mrs. Russo was making the application, the worker recommended that she come in with her husband so they could both speak to the concerns she was presenting. From the telephone conversation the worker learned that this couple, in their late 40s, had two daughters: Linda, age 22 (who moved with her husband from her parents' apartment building to Canada

three months before Mrs. Russo's call to the clinic), and Angela, age 17 (a senior in high school). At the time of intake, Angela was vacationing with her maternal grandmother, a widow for 20 years, who lived next door and to whom Angela had always been close.

During an extended interview with Mr. and Mrs. Russo, the worker found Mr. Russo to be quite severely depressed, self-blaming, and indecisive, yet still able to function on his job; he initiated very few comments and tended to defer to his wife, but, when the worker gently made inquiries, he answered questions cordially and thoughtfully. Mrs. Russo came across as a woman with managerial and perfectionistic traits; she talked at length, often on her husband's behalf. The only goal that either could articulate clearly was for Mr. Russo to recover from his depression. On the basis of this first contact, the worker ordered and weighed the information she gathered from four interpenetrating vantage points:

1. Mr. Russo's Biochemical Situation
The worker learned that during a previous depression Mr. Russo had responded favorably to antidepressant drugs. To help relieve his symptoms, one treatment option would be to refer him to a psychiatrist who could evaluate him for medication.

2. The Intrapsychic Level From the outset, it was apparent that Mr. Russo was a competent, conscientious man who cared about his family. However, he had very little emotional energy with which to rebound from his despair; the worker guessed that he was not generally accustomed to taking initiative on his own behalf. It was a positive sign that he could still perform on his job. The worker hypothesized that Mr. Russo's depression was in part rooted in early deprivation. His mother had died when he was three, after which he spent several years in a series of foster homes and institutions; he became tearful and was more emotionally expressive about this time of his life than he was about his current situation. He did say that his current depression developed shortly after his daughter Linda, with whom he had always had a warm relationship, moved to Canada. He retreated into a partial withdrawal and experienced a pervasive sense of "emptiness" and hopelessness; "nothing seems to matter," he said. The worker surmised that feelings of loss experienced in his young years had been reactivated. On the basis of her knowledge about early deprivation and depression, she tentatively concluded that Mr. Russo's tendency toward self-deprecation and low self-esteem were exacerbated when Linda left. Without Linda's kindness and interest in him, he felt abandoned and alone once again. Yet, unable to accept his anger at her, he turned it against himself.[1] The worker considered the option of individual treatment in which *sustainment,* some *direct advice,* and *reflection* could occur in the context of a *"corrective relationship."*

3. Current Family Relationships Various aspects of the family situation were revealed. Although Mrs. Russo was genuinely concerned about her husband, her tolerance for his morose dependency was strained and her anger poorly masked. The younger daughter, who was close to her mother, often ridiculed and demeaned her father. Fairly openly, the mother defended Angela's apparent contempt for Mr. Russo, blaming it on his apathetic and self-pitying manner. The worker guessed that Angela was voicing feelings her mother could not express directly. From her knowledge of family systems, the worker hypothesized that the mother–daughter collusion provided the mother with external support and gratifica-

tion (and probably gave the daughter some of the same), and the father had become the outsider, particularly now that the older daughter had moved away. Mr. Russo participated in the collusion and promoted his "odd man out" status by being so self-depreciating. Paradoxically, his pathetic demeanor also brought out the motherly side of Mrs. Russo, who was taking more and more responsibility for many areas of her husband's life. The tendencies for Mrs. Russo to overfunction in the family relationships and for Mr. Russo to defer were probably of long standing; this complementarity undoubtedly became more skewed after Mr. Russo became so depressed. Thus, although the price both paid was high, Mrs. Russo was protecting her husband from feeling totally alone. Family sessions, the worker considered, might foster a more mutually rewarding marital relationship, thus mollifying Mr. Russo's depression and providing greater gratification for Mrs. Russo. In turn, this might assuage her anger and reduce her need to ally herself with ("triangulate") Angela. Involving Angela in treatment, the worker suspected, could be preventive by helping her to individuate, to separate from her mother enough to begin to establish her own life and plan for her college years. Plus, without Angela's participation, she might work against progress made by her parents if her role in the family process continued.

Despite tension and feelings of discontent and despair that were manifest during this interview, the worker perceived that Mr. and Mrs. Russo cared about each other and about their daughters; they both spoke respectfully of Mrs. Russo's mother, even though she and Mrs. Russo undoubtedly participated in the "gang-up" against Mr. Russo. Basic values, such as fairness, concern for others, and family loyalties, were well-established if somewhat blurred at this point; even though Mrs. Russo's anger and

Mr. Russo's passivity pervaded their communications, the difficulties did not stem from intentional meanness or self-absorption. It seemed clear to the worker that *neither* Mr. nor Mrs. Russo felt truly "entitled" to speak for themselves, to take an "I" position, to assert their own thoughts and feelings; Mr. Russo tended to defer and/or withdraw and Mrs. Russo usually spoke for other family members but did not directly assert her own needs or aspirations.

4. The Socioeconomic and Sociocultural Systems The most salient feature that was revealed in the first interview related to Mr. Russo's work situation. He blamed his depression in large part on a recent shift in his job. As a receiving clerk, Mr. Russo had been in charge of two other men and had successfully organized his small department. His boss had often commended him for his reliability, his willingness to work overtime, and his pleasing manner. Two months before the intake meeting, the company for which he worked was taken over by a large concern. Although given a promotion in terms of job title and salary, he no longer supervised other people and he had little contact with his old boss. Because of new technology, his job no longer challenged his organizational talents and his work was duller and more routine. The impersonal climate of the new company provided little positive support for Mr. Russo. The worker speculated that referral to an employment service for vocational testing and placement in a smaller, more intimate establishment might better utilize his capabilities and fulfill his need for praise from others.

On the basis of the above facts about the past and the present reported by Mr. and Mrs. Russo, and her observation of the couple's behavior and interactions, the worker

evaluated the Russo case on these four interdependent conceptual levels. No single hypothesis or conclusion reached at any one level could be considered more intrinsically "true" or "right" than any other. As the worker studied the Russo case from each perspective, the overall assessment became richer and more complete. The question of choice came up only as she considered which treatment approach could most effectively relieve Mr. Russo's depression. It was clear that she could address more than one level at the same time. For example, she could arrange an evaluation for medication and then set up individual or family sessions. Or, in addition to other treatment approaches, she could refer him to an employment service. Of particular interest to us in this chapter are the criteria that helped the worker determine whether she should see Mr. Russo in individual treatment (with, perhaps, occasional family or couple meetings), or whether she should arrange to see the family as a unit.

INDICATIONS FOR CONSIDERING FAMILY TREATMENT

Although we will resume our account of the Russo family later in this chapter, we pause now to consider the conditions under which a worker might decide on family therapy as the treatment of choice. There are differences among practitioners and writers on the question of indications (and contraindications) for family therapy. Yet, we often must ask ourselves: Under what circumstances should we try to see the family as a group and when should we choose to work with individual members? Over the years, research has contrasted the outcomes of marital and family therapy with the effectiveness of individual treatment. There are indications, for example, that family therapy is often more effective than individual treatment, *even for difficulties that are not presented as interpersonal,* but rather seen by clients as individual or intrapsychic in nature. There is also evidence that including the father in family meetings "clearly improves the odds of good outcomes in many situations."[2] But there is not yet a solid body of research that specifically identifies the treatment of choice for many categories of presenting problems, family situations, or relationship styles. Of course, whether we see one person, a subgroup, or an entire family in treatment, we use family and systems perspectives as well as psychodynamic concepts to assess our clients' psychosocial situations.

A typology of criteria for selecting the family therapy approach must rest, therefore, on empirical evidence and clinical experience. The list that follows represents a blend of selected recommendations made by several authors in the field,[3] combined with our own views, on the conditions under which family therapy might be considered the treatment of choice:

1. At the Family's Request Sometimes the family, whether in crisis or handicapped by long-standing problems, asks to be seen as a group and defines its difficulties as affecting all family members. As family therapy has become known, more such requests are initiated by families.

2. The Presenting Problem Immediately Suggests a Relationship Difficulty A problem, or more than one, between family members such as marital or parent–child conflicts or problems with extended family members or strife among siblings may indicate the use of family therapy.

3. One Family Member Seeks Help for Another Fairly often, one member will make an appointment for another or wants to bring another in for help; in these cases, conjoint meetings may be advisable.

4. Children's Difficulties When children's unhappiness or symptomatology is the impetus for seeking treatment, exploration usually reveals that the child's symptoms are, at least in part, an expression of other difficulties in the family system. We agree with Sherman: "The child's boundaries are so fluid and interlaced with the little world outside himself—primarily his family—that, in important respects, we cannot be sure what is inside him and what is outside him."[4]

5. Adolescents or Poorly Differentiated Adults When teenage or adult children, particularly but not exclusively those living in their parents' home, either cling to or defensively disown their families, family therapy may be called for. In such situations, boundaries are either diffuse or rigid and impenetrable. In either case, the individuals have been unable to separate effectively. Whether a person is submissively tied or rebelliously acting out, usually similar problems can be found in other family members. Individuation of the identified patient or index client may be discouraged by the family situation. Furthermore, as Mitchell wrote: "The clinical evidence is overwhelming that the human being does not separate from what he needs but has never had, until he finds it or its equivalent."[5] Individuation is most successfully achieved when the family group supports the young person's (or immature adult's) growth and autonomy. Contrary to the view of some emerging adults (and, on occasion, their social workers), geographical distance from their families does not in and of itself foster differentiation. A change in the patterns of relationships, which allows both closeness and independence, often does.

6. Impaired Communication When family communication patterns appear to be distant, restrained, vague, or bizarre; or when messages are contradictory; or when members seem to be acting on faulty assumptions about one another, these patterns may be observed and addressed most incisively in the context of the family group. Bewildering symptoms can sometimes be understood when viewed as a reaction to the family communication style. Family members who have difficulty taking "I" positions that convey their meanings, their thoughts, and their feelings can often be helped to express themselves directly to other members in family meetings.

7. The Index Client Believes Others Are at Fault for Problems When the identified client believes that his or her distress or behavior is the function of the personality or personalities of *other* family members, it is often most efficient to try to sort out each person's involvement in family pain or tension in family meetings. Consistent projection or "trading of dissociations" (see pages 394–396) can respond to intervention aimed at the interpersonal aspects of these processes. Particularly since individuals who project in these ways are often not very amenable to intrareflection, family treatment may be preferred.

8. The Index Client Is Scapegoated When family members express feelings of distress but see them only as reactions to the symptoms or behavior of the identified client, the burden for the well-being of the entire family is unrealistically placed on the shoulders of the scapegoated (or "triangulated") one. Interventions that promote the sharing of responsibility for difficulties and their solutions call for the participation of the entire family in treatment.

9. Consistent Violation of Generational Boundaries When, for example, parents "parentify" children, they deprive them of needed nurturing and delegate roles or authority to them that they cannot manage. When dysfunctional intergenerational coalitions or triangles become a way of life for the family, as when one parent depends heavily on or attacks a child because of unresolved tensions in the marriage, or when two family members team up against a third (mother and son against father, grandmother and grandchild against mother, and so on), family therapy is often needed.

10. Distortions in Perception about Others or Myths and Secrets Are Apparent When these or understandings of the family value system and ideals appear to be faulty, exposure, clarification, and corrections are usually best achieved in the family context.

11. Intrafamily Relationships Do Not Provide Adequate Support When relationships within the family are impoverished, chaotic, or hostile, participation of all family members in treatment may be the most effective way to facilitate learning new, more nurturing and loving patterns.

12. A Family Member Is Receiving Inadequate Support Family meetings may be indicated when, for example, elderly or ill clients on our caseloads are estranged from or neglected by family members, are receiving inadequate physical or emotional support, or are poorly cared for, depressed, or lonely. Similarly, some psychiatrically ill or retarded individuals living at home, in halfway houses, or in institutions would benefit from family involvement. In some instances, it may not be possible or advisable, because of his or her condition, for the index client to be present at family sessions. Other members, however, often have conflicts and unresolved feelings about the client or among themselves that can be clarified in family group meetings, ideally resulting in more support for the neglected member. Sometimes the family as a unit becomes the client and engages in treatment. In any event, the potential for improving the presenting situation can be explored by calling together the relatives.

13. The Index Client Is Not Motivated for or Is Unable to Use Treatment
When clients have been urged to have therapy or have been mandated to do so, they sometimes have little motivation to become engaged, however hard the worker tries to find out what the client thinks might be helpful. Such individuals may need, at least temporarily, the support of being seen with family members. Sometimes spouses, adolescents, or the elderly, for example, are more amenable to couple or family treatment than to individual therapy.

14. The Worker Has Not Decided on a Treatment Modality
When it is unclear how to proceed, beginning with family meetings may reduce the possibility that an individual will be reluctant to share the worker with other family members if family therapy becomes the treatment of choice. By the same token, the family may be less likely to believe in the worker's neutrality if the worker has had a longer relationship with one member than with the others. Arranging family sessions at the outset also diminishes the possibility that the worker will become strongly identified with the index client and thus unable to maintain "involved impartiality" so important to family (or any other) therapy. Individual meetings can always be arranged later. This is not to say that individual treatment cannot comfortably evolve into family therapy as well as vice versa. (In

some situations, a phase of individual therapy, or concurrent individual treatment, may be necessary for one member. A severely scapegoated one, for example, may need extra support to relinquish this role.)

Even when one or more of the above conditions point to the selection of family therapy, other factors may interfere. First, the worker may not feel comfortable or competent enough to treat the family as a group. In this instance, if family treatment is indicated, the worker would be best advised to refer the family to another therapist or to invite a more experienced colleague to act as co-therapist.

Second, a small percentage of families cannot be persuaded to enter treatment as a group. Or, some family members may adamantly refuse to be involved, with the result that family meetings are incomplete. In these cases, the worker will have to work either with the index client alone or with part of the family. The worker need not, however, abandon the family orientation or efforts to understand the family system. The worker should be alert to changes in the index client that may have unsettling repercussions on the family. (Sometimes, as we shall discuss later in this chapter, changes made by the motivated member can result in positive changes in others in the family.)

Third, in some cases there are geographical obstacles. Often young adult clients, for example, live many miles away from their parents; even when family treatment would be helpful, it may be impossible to arrange. Also prisons, residential treatment centers, training schools, psychiatric hospitals, and institutions for the retarded are often located far from the family homes. Family treatment may be limited thereby, although not necessarily ruled out. In some facilities, increased efforts have been made to involve families even when they do not live near the institution.[6]

Sometimes, after a series of family meetings, the worker may decide to move into individual treatment with one or more of the family members. This may occur when there seems to be motivation to explore personal issues. However, in making the shift, it is important for the worker to utilize all the available knowledge about the workings of the particular family system. The worker must consider whether the family's dysfunctional equilibrium will be reactivated and militate against changes the individual is working toward.

A worker did not object when a family discontinued weekly sessions. He wanted to give individual support to a 23-year-old daughter, who wished to work on her relationships with men. But, the young woman's problems were so intertwined with those of her parents that, as soon as she made moves to individuate and live an adult life, her mother and father began to interfere by infantilizing her, as had been their lifelong pattern, thus drawing her back into a dependent role. The daughter allowed and unconsciously encouraged this out of years of familiarity with the pattern. Progress achieved earlier was reversed until the worker resumed family meetings.

In families such as this, one member's effort to grow up can seem like an abandonment threat to the others, and tendencies toward enmeshment are intensified. In this case, the worker had been "inducted" into the family system (i.e., drawn in on the side of the family's defensive resistance to change) in the hope that the young woman's efforts to individuate might be better served. It became clear, however, that the homeostatic family process was so powerful that the

daughter was unable to make changes from within herself when she was so pressured by the family from without. After a year of family work, including some marital treatment of the parents, the daughter was then able to make progress in individual treatment.

CONTRAINDICATIONS FOR FAMILY THERAPY

Under what conditions would we recommend against family group meetings? With Sherman, we agree that family therapy may "take" even under circumstances that seem to contraindicate it.[7] Nevertheless, we present a list of those situations that call for the exercise of particular caution as a worker considers the family therapy approach:

1. A Family Member Is in the Throes of a Psychotic Break   Usually, it is best to wait until there is some stabilization of the most acute symptoms. Depending on the clinician's assessment and the wishes of the family, some family meetings may be arranged without the client with mental illness present.[8]

2. A Family Member or Family Members Are Grossly Deceitful or Manifest Seriously Suspicious or "Psychopathic" Behavior   Under these circumstances, constructive family work is usually not possible.

3. Family Interactions Are Extremely Destructive   When the family process or some members are so destructive that the negative interactions have a snowball effect, effective family treatment may be precluded or at least postponed until harsh and abusive patterns are modified.

4. A Family Member Has a Severe Psychosomatic Illness   Sometimes such conditions can be life threatening; clinicians have reported that family therapy occasionally sets off dangerous somatic reactions in these cases. In such situations, before embarking on family (or individual) treatment, medical or psychiatric consultation is advisable.

5. The Family System or Its Members Seem Dysfunctionally Balanced or Fragile When a complementary relationship appears to be "pathological" yet stable (such as when a marriage has a "father–daughter" or "mother–son" format or a parent appears to be infantilizing an adult child), careful assessment is required to determine whether efforts aimed at change might result in deterioration of one or more of the family members. In some families, members are psychologically so delicately balanced that they cannot tolerate family meetings or might decompensate during intensive family therapy.

6. A Family Member Is Extremely Defensive or Anxious Some clients are simply too uncomfortable to benefit from family therapy, even if in all other respects it might be considered the treatment of choice. Of course, many clients will become apprehensive when family meetings are suggested. But, just as a worker treating an individual must be careful not to press hard for material that will stimulate immobilizing discomfort, so the family therapist must be able to assess a particular client's level of anxiety about family meetings before strongly encouraging them. The work with Jed Cooper (Chapter 20) illustrates this type of situation, in which family therapy was contraindicated even though this client's difficulties were complexly intertwined with his relationships with his parents.

7. Family Relationships Are "Dead" Under these circumstances, family members cannot mobilize the energy to work on them. ("Dead" relationships are very different from "cutoffs" or estrangements; the latter lack resolution, are highly charged, and extract an emotional toll.) Even though the relationships have been terminated, divorcing or divorced couples sometimes work together effectively to separate, to sort out for each spouse the issues that led to the breakdown of the marriage, or to work out problems relating to children.

8. A Client Is Strongly Motivated for Individual Treatment Some clients choose one-to-one treatment and make progress without suffering setbacks resulting from counterpressures from the family process. Individuals who have established living arrangements and lives separate from their families, including many single young adults, often fall into this category. Frequently, one member of a family may have personal issues or particular problems to resolve that do not require the ongoing participation of the others. The large bulk of some clinical caseloads is comprised of such individuals. Nevertheless, occasional or intermittent joint and family meetings may be arranged to facilitate a particular piece of work with an individual client. Sometimes, as we have mentioned, family sessions may lead to individual treatment for one or more members who are motivated to continue. When the entire family is in treatment, each individual is an equal participant in the therapy. When an individual is in treatment and the family is invited for sessions, the worker still observes the family system, but the family members are viewed as part of the individual's environment; they are related to as collaterals—unless they are engaged subsequently in ongoing family treatment. (See Chapter 8 for a discussion of the use of family sessions in the service of individual treatment.)

In our experience, the feasibility of family therapy is often best tested during exploratory sessions. Sometimes the most unwieldy, disorganized, or uncommunicative families respond surprisingly well. In very difficult situations it may be wise to involve a co-therapist. Not only can two heads be better than one, but also the dangers of being hopelessly "inducted" by the family pathology may be averted. The "blind spot" of one therapist may turn out to be readily discerned by the other. If they work well together, co-therapists can supplement each other as they address the multifarious and perplexing issues that can spring up in family meetings.

Finally, we share Wynne's view that it is easy to exaggerate the possible dangers of embarking on family treatment: "The likelihood of bringing about drastic or precipitous changes unintentionally is extremely low."[9] As he goes on to say, helping families to make real and enduring changes is a formidable task. We are less likely to contribute to unwanted change than we are to discover that the family system is so intransigent that it is difficult for new patterns to evolve, as hard as the family may try to make changes.

ADVANTAGES OF FAMILY THERAPY

In cases where conditions favor seeing the family as a unit, we have found this approach to have distinct advantages over individual treatment:

1. Direct Observation Aids Understanding Observing family interaction affords the worker, and ultimately the clients, a more complete understanding of the complex situations of individual members. Direct observation is worth a thousand descriptive words. Reports from individual clients, however conscientiously rendered, are necessarily limited to material that is conscious and reflects the perspective of one family member only. Much of the behavior and interpersonal transactions, verbal and nonverbal, that penetrate a family's system may be distorted or beyond the awareness of its members. Experience and assessment skills help the worker to make intelligent inferences about a family situation, even when only one member is seen. But by sitting with the family as a whole, worker and family together can learn firsthand about the interlocking "fits," the quality of individual and subsystem boundaries, alliances, and the repetitive circular patterns that perpetuate the difficulties. Data gathered in individual therapy rely heavily on the conjectures of the worker and client; in family sessions, many more facts can be witnessed and brought into focus.

2. Family Processes Can Be Exposed and Explored Assumptions, distortions, projections, myths, and family secrets that are burdening family members can be revealed and challenged. When timed appropriately, the worker can raise questions sensitively, such as: "Have you any idea what makes your son think you prefer his sister?" "Do you always act as though your feelings don't matter?" "When you tell Johnnie that you are going to call the policeman to take him away, do you really mean you would want him to go away for good? Johnnie seems to think you do." "Were you angry when you said that—as your husband assumes—or is that the way you act when you are frightened?" "Were you trying to protect your daughter by not telling her how sick your husband really is?" When they learn to speak directly, family members are far better equipped to shift from confusing and painful interactions and begin to communicate their thoughts, feelings, and visions more clearly and less hurtfully.

3. Dysfunctional Sequences Can Be Addressed or Interrupted When They Occur Bringing attention to these may have far more impact than talking about them in individual sessions where they can become intellectualized rather than experienced on the spot. For example, in a family meeting, a worker might inquire of a seemingly passive father, "Have you noticed that you often let others in the family answer questions for you?" Or, with a light touch, the family therapist might ask an angry adolescent girl, "What do you think would happen if you told your mother again how you feel about your early curfew, but this time without insulting her?"

4. Focus of Attention Can Be Expanded Family sessions can provide the opportunity to shift attention to the marital relationship when the problems of the children or adolescents appear to be a reflection of tensions between the parents. Similarly, because parent–child relationships can be heavily influenced by relational patterns that were established between the parents and *their* parents, family sessions provide an arena for exploring how introjects and intergenerational issues are manifested in the present family system. For example, the worker might ask a mother, "Do you notice that the things you hated most in your relationship with your mother seem to be occurring here between you and Susan?"

5. Family Members Can Make New and More Genuine Connections As discussed earlier, threats and fears of abandonment can stand in the way of family members accepting differences among them or of supporting each other's autonomy. When "I" statements rather than "you" or "we" statements are encouraged, individuation is enhanced. In enmeshed families (with diffuse boundaries), the lives of the members are complexly intertwined. Repeated experiences in conjoint meetings may be necessary to reassure family members that relationships need not be jeopardized when people speak for themselves; in fact, clients often learn that connections become more "real" and fulfilling when they dare to express their own thoughts and feelings. These opportunities to take risks and to allay anxieties cannot be provided in individual sessions.

6. Family Members Can Learn about and Empathize with Each Other Along similar lines, family meetings provide the climate for family members to share experiences, feelings, and past history. So often in family therapy we hear "I never knew you felt that way." Or, "Hey, Dad, you never told me that you played minor league baseball." Or, "Now that you have told me about your life as a child, I understand your stubbornness (or temper or reserve). Before this, I always took it personally." The fears about sharing vulnerable feelings or the belief that no one really cares can dissolve as families learn to talk together. In families with extremely rigid individual or subsystem boundaries, family members can be needlessly isolated from one another and deprived of support and affection that often become available when they begin to speak more personally with one another.

7. Family Sessions Can Reduce Suspicions Often family members are distrustful or worried about what the index client is doing or talking about in one-to-one therapy. Sometimes unconsciously, those who are not in treatment feel threatened about actual or potential changes in the family balance, and they interfere with or sabotage the efforts of those who are.

8. Addressing "Transferences" among Family Members Can Improve Relationships Whenever possible, it is more effective to work with "transferences" or projections—positive or negative—among family members than with those of an individual client toward a worker. *Relationships within the family are intrinsically far more important than the treatment relationship.* Moreover, transference to a therapist is not usually as intense, stable, or fully developed as it is with members of one's family, and hence it can be less accessible to interpretation or intervention. If a positive shift *within* the family system is achieved, resulting in a more nurturing family atmosphere, individuals can enjoy a "corrective" experience that potentially surpasses, and is more enduring than, one that derives from the worker–client relationship. This point as it relates to couple treatment will be discussed in greater detail in Chapter 17.

9. The Therapist's Style Facilitates a Healing Climate The way in which therapists use their personalities is important in every kind of treatment, but there is an added dimension to the impact they can have in family therapy. Workers not only encourage family exchanges along the lines mentioned above, by generating a climate of acceptance and trust, but also their tenderness, flexibility, ability to laugh at themselves, and willingness to take chances in relationship with the family provide a model that can lead members to risk new ways of relating to each other. *In many families that we see clinically, despair and low self-esteem cloak the many strengths and capacities that lie just below the surface.* The worker's leadership in promoting this special kind of "corrective" experience can facilitate greater intimacy and a sense of belonging among family members, as well as an opportunity for the healing of old wounds. Not only are family relationships improved, but also each individual may gain in confidence and self-reliance.

FAMILY THERAPY FOR THE RUSSO FAMILY

Making Decisions

Once the worker organized the data from her first interview with Mr. and Mrs. Russo, as outlined earlier, she considered treatment approaches to suggest to the family. She referred Mr. Russo, who had previously been on medication and wanted to try it again, for a psychopharmacological evaluation; a mild dosage of an antidepressant was prescribed.[10] She decided it would be premature to discuss the possibility of a referral to an employment service until she had more information about his job situation, what he wanted to do about it, and what opportunities might be available to him.

The immediate choice the worker had to make was whether to recommend to the Russos that they come to therapy as a family group. As she reviewed conditions for considering family therapy, the following indications (see pages 404–407) seemed relevant:

- Although the family was not requesting treatment for the entire group, Mrs. Russo had made the application and willingly participated in the interview with her husband. Furthermore, in the couple interview, particularly Mr. Russo expressed interest in having Angela attend meetings. (Indications 1 and 3)
- Marital difficulties were not the impetus for treatment, but the strains between the couple were immediately apparent. Mrs. Russo's anger and Mr. Russo's depression and withdrawal seemed linked to the marital interaction. The parents did not specifically complain about Angela, but difficulties in her relationship with her father were reported. (Indication 2)

- The worker believed that the mother and daughter were clinging to one another, to the detriment of the marriage. It also seemed possible that Angela would have difficulty separating. (Indication 5)
- Communication patterns were not yet fully understood by the worker, but she did note considerable restraint and indirectness. Mr. Russo did not reveal his feelings about his marriage or about Angela's attitudes toward him; instead he retreated into silence or self-blame. Mrs. Russo spoke on behalf of her husband and daughter but expressed little about her own feelings. (Indication 6)
- Mrs. Russo believed her husband's behavior and depression were the only family problems to which she and Angela were reacting. Relief of his symptoms, she assumed, would resolve any discomfort the others were experiencing. (Indication 8)
- The worker sensed that Mrs. Russo and Angela frequently teamed up against and scapegoated Mr. Russo. She further speculated that Mrs. Russo's mother might be part of the coalition that cast Mr. Russo into the role of outsider. (Indications 8 and 9)
- Mr. Russo's motivation for individual treatment seemed minimal. Apparently not given to reflection about his situation or his own dynamics, it seemed probable that he would be more amenable to group meetings. Should he (or any other family member) seek individual treatment in the future, there would be greater clarity about the family situation and all the family members would have had a therapeutic experience. (Indications 13 and 14)

Several conditions led the worker to favor the family therapy approach. In a telephone call to Mr. and Mrs. Russo, they both indicated a willingness to bring Angela to the next meeting. The worker could think of no contraindications, but any that might exist would be revealed in exploratory family sessions. A week after the intake interview, Angela had returned from her trip and accompanied her parents to the initial family meeting. An abbreviated summary of the first session (in sufficient detail for the reader to see the complex process) follows.

The Initial Interview

After the worker and Angela were introduced, there were friendly exchanges between the worker and each family member individually. The worker then briefly brought Angela up to date on the previous meeting with Mr. and Mrs. Russo. Angela said she saw no reason for her being present since the problem was her father's "bad mood." The worker said that in her experience, when one person in the family is unhappy, the entire household is often affected. Mrs. Russo agreed: "We all seem to be getting on each other's nerves lately." She added that she was particularly concerned about how her husband's depression was causing Angela to be "cranky." "Sometimes," she commented, "Angela stays with her grandmother to get away." The worker asked Mrs. Russo whether she was finding the going rough herself, to which she replied, "Not really." She said she would feel better when her husband and Angela got along better. The worker said she thought one purpose of family meetings would be to help everyone in the family to understand one another better, adding that perhaps ways of improving relationships among all of them could be found to make the family a happier place. Angela said she thought her father was acting like a baby and just feeling sorry for himself.

Up to this point, Mr. Russo said almost nothing. Turning to him, the worker said she wanted everyone's opinion about the problem. He answered that he thought the medication was helping him a little and he hoped soon he would be "out of the dumps."

He complained about his job change. Angela snapped at her father, saying, "You're stupid." She said the house was like a morgue lately, especially since her sister Linda, who used to visit frequently, had moved to Canada. She added that her father thought Linda was an "angel" and he was happy when *she* was there. Mrs. Russo smiled, apparently in appreciation of Angela's angry remarks. The worker asked the father how he accounted for Angela's sarcasm about him. Before he could answer, Angela blurted out, "You don't have to live with him!" Mrs. Russo began to make a comment supporting Angela. The worker interrupted by indicating that she wanted to hear from Mr. Russo, whose eyes had become watery. Angela sneered. The worker said to Mr. Russo that it looked like he was hurt by Angela's remarks. "I suppose I'm not much of a father to her," he replied. "That makes you sad, I imagine," the worker said. "Of course it does," murmured Mr. Russo. "She's my baby girl," he added almost inaudibly.

Then the worker addressed Angela: "Did you know it mattered to your father how you and he get on?" A little subdued, Angela replied, "He doesn't care." The worker asked Mr. Russo whether he ever let Angela know how disappointed he was about the way they get along. He said he supposed he hadn't but volunteered nothing further. Mrs. Russo began to explain Angela, saying that when Angela was young she "adored" her father, and she only turned on him this way when he started acting like a "zombie." Gently, the worker interrupted what she sensed would be a long defense of Angela, adding that she thought it would help more if each person spoke for himself or herself. The worker asked Angela what she thought. Angela said her mother was right. "Your mother understands you pretty well?" the worker offered. "She's the only one who does," Angela said, noting that she and her sister never got along because Linda was her father's "pet." "That must be hard to take," the worker said. Angela shrugged.

The worker then said to Mr. Russo that she gathered he had never gotten around to telling Angela how much she meant to him, and that perhaps it would be helpful if he did something about that. Mrs. Russo started to interject something when the worker said she thought that Dad and Angela had some things to straighten out with each other, reminding Mrs. Russo that she herself had said that their poor relationship bothered her. The worker added that there was no way Mrs. Russo could do their work for them. Mrs. Russo, a little uncomfortably silent now, glared at Mr. Russo. Angela laughed nervously. The worker turned to Mr. Russo, who said, tearfully, "I love both my daughters. One is miles away and the other one hates me." Angela said nothing but did not seem to be sneering; for just a moment, she looked more softly at her father. Mrs. Russo started to say, "Angela doesn't hate him but . . ." Good-humoredly, the worker cut in and reminded Mrs. Russo that it would be good if Angela spoke for herself. There followed some tentative but friendlier exchanges between Angela and her father. Shortly thereafter, characteristically, Mr. Russo withdrew in silence and Angela scoffed. Observing this interaction, the worker commented that she had some ideas about what often might happen between them: On the one hand, she pointed out, Mr. Russo seemed shy about telling Angela how much he cared about her, without putting himself down. On the other hand, Angela made it harder to find out her father's true feelings for her by sniping at him so regularly. Both mildly acknowledged the worker's remarks but said no more. The worker said she thought they could both learn to make their relationship a better one, but that it might take a little practice and willingness of both to stick their necks out.

Deciding to reinvolve Mrs. Russo in the interaction, on her own behalf rather than as a commentator, the worker told her she got the impression that she felt burdened sometimes by having to fix up the relationship between her husband and daughter and by looking after Mr. Russo when he was depressed. "What," the worker asked, "do you want for yourself from the family?" Mrs. Russo replied that her children had been her life, real joys to her. She said she was glad that Linda was happily married, but she missed her and wished she hadn't gone so far away. The worker commented that Angela was growing up too and recalled that college plans were in the offing. With feeling, Mrs. Russo said she hoped Angela would find a school nearby so she could live at home. "What would it be like if Angela moved away too?" the worker asked. Mrs. Russo became thoughtful and quiet, finally saying that she did not know what she would do. "Life would seem empty," she said. The worker spoke briefly about how difficult it is to make changes when one has been so devoted to one's children. Mrs. Russo cried.

Now including Mr. Russo, the worker said to them both that when children grow up and go away, the parents often have to find each other again and this can be a challenge. In a positive but not imposing or directive way, the worker asked whether they thought they would like to work on that. It seemed, she continued, that some of the pleasures of family life had gotten lost in the shuffle with all of the recent problems they had been facing. Mr. Russo nodded. Mrs. Russo said she thought everyone would feel a lot better if Mr. Russo got over his blues. Maybe, the worker said in a low-key tone, we can find some connection between the other family issues and Mr. Russo's unhappiness. Mrs. Russo indicated she understood and did not argue.

The worker suggested that the family meet together for six sessions (even though she suspected their work together might take longer) and then reevaluate the situation. Mrs. Russo asked whether she could call if Mr. Russo seemed very depressed. The worker told her that she certainly wanted to be available to them between sessions if absolutely necessary, but it would be preferable if they could bring the issues that concerned them into the family meetings. She further suggested that if Mr. Russo was depressed, he should be the one to call. In a matter-of-fact way, she added that she thought it would work best if any contacts made between sessions were shared at the next meeting so everyone could keep informed. Angela said she didn't want to come to every meeting because she had "better things to do." After giving Angela an opportunity to express her uneasiness about family sessions, the worker said she thought everyone's help would be needed, at least for the first six meetings. She added that she was impressed with the willingness and interest all of them had shown in talking about the family situation. It was a good sign, she told them. She thought they were the kind of people who would be able to work out some of their problems with each other. "He'll never change," Angela quipped, pointing to her father. "Don't be rude," the mother admonished. Mr. Russo seemed to brighten at this apparent show of support from his wife.

To the group, the worker said she was pleased that the family had asked questions about the meetings and that she wanted them to share their feelings about the therapy as it went along. Sometimes, the worker said, she might make a comment that they would find irritating or inaccurate. When this happened, she would like them to tell her about it. After arranging their meeting schedule, the worker added in passing that at some point they might want to invite Mrs. Russo's mother to join them since she was so close to the family. The worker shook hands with all three as they left.

THE INITIAL INTERVIEW: GUIDELINES AND "GROUND RULES"[11]

It is crucial for the family therapist to establish a tone and point of view that will help to engage the family in treatment. It is part of the "practice wisdom" of family work that the therapist moves back and forth between accommodating to the family style and taking positive leadership. As in any treatment situation, the worker must try not to "crash" family defenses by pressing for understanding or changes for which the family is not yet ready. Timing is of the utmost importance. In family therapy particularly, so much material is witnessed by the worker in such rapid-fire fashion that sometimes the temptation to interpret or intervene precipitously is difficult to resist. The discipline of the worker is strenuously tested as the family drama unfolds and reveals itself by way of the many-leveled verbal and nonverbal interactions that occur in the treatment session. The worker refrains from overzealous interventions, yet at the same time sets the stage for the therapy by defining its focus and by conveying leadership and expertise early in the relationship with the family. This often prevents escalation of negative interactions among family members.

In the initial Russo family interview described above, the worker carefully followed the cues of mood and the messages of the moment. She listened keenly and respected "where they were." For example, by accepting rather than interpreting Mr. Russo's

statement that he had not been "much of a father" to Angela, she recognized his sadness and gave him room to express it. Had the worker made a comment such as "Your wife and daughter seem to gang up on you often," or if she asked him why he thought he hadn't been a better father, the emotion of the event—which led to a fleeting but touching moment between Mr. Russo and Angela—might have been lost. Similarly, only gently, toward the end of the hour, did the worker touch on the marital problem that was so glaringly evident all along. The art and empathy necessary to family treatment have much in common with those needed for individual therapy, but the family process by its very nature calls for special care. If the worker prematurely or heavy-handedly reacts to the profound emotional charge and the large amount of dynamic material revealed by the family interactions, especially during the early stages of therapy, the family may defensively try to regain its equilibrium by closing ranks and even bolting from treatment.

The worker for the Russo family did not succumb to the pitfalls of the opposite extreme and allow the family to drift aimlessly. During the hour, she was able to weave into the process—usually explicitly, sometimes implicitly—a number of "ground rules." She thereby methodically paved the way for a working alliance with the family. Family therapy that lacks direction, focus, or structure can, at best, flounder and become chaotic. At worst, it can be so disenchanting to the family members that they terminate treatment.

In their chapter on family therapy outcome research, Gurman and Kniskern write:

> There exists an accumulating empirical literature supporting the relationship between treatment outcome and a therapist's relationship skills. This literature suggests that it is

generally important for the marital-family therapist to be active and to provide some structure to early interviews, but not to confront tenuous family defenses very early in treatment. Excesses in this direction are among the main contributors to premature termination and to negative outcomes.[12]

As we suggest the ground rules itemized below, we cannot caution the beginning family therapist enough about the importance of offering them to a family, as the worker for the Russos did, in a matter-of-fact yet easygoing and caring way that is in harmony with the process of the meeting. These can be effectively introduced *only* when they are relevant to the evolving interactions. *At no time should they be delivered as a series of pronouncements.* As the reader studies the following ground rules, it may be clarifying to refer to the Russo interview and to be cognizant of when and under what circumstances the worker used them to guide the treatment.

1. Telephone or interview contacts with one or more family members and the worker before the beginning of family therapy should be mentioned at least briefly to the entire group.*

2. The notion that unhappiness or pain in one family member usually involves everyone close to this member should be made explicit.

3. The purposes of family meetings should be defined as: (*a*) an effort to help everyone in the family to understand one another better; and (*b*) an attempt by the family and worker together to search for ways to improve family relationships so that family life can be more satisfying for all. Even when the initial problem appears to be the symptom of

one member, how this affects and is affected by other relationships should be explored with the family.

4. It should be made clear that if contacts between the worker and individual family members occur outside the regular meeting sessions, these should be shared or at least referred to at the next meeting.*

5. In words and actions, the worker must demonstrate an "involved impartiality." It should be made clear that the worker takes no one's side and is equally interested in each member. Family therapists must show that they are not concerned with "blame" or "fault," but with working together toward resolution of the difficulties. By giving support to each family member, and by directing questions and reflective or interpretive remarks to all members on a more or less equal basis, or to the family as a whole, a worker may quell concerns about partiality or about who will be "blamed."

6. At some point during the initial interview each family member's point of view if not volunteered, usually should be elicited with questions such as: "What do you think is wrong?" "What changes in the family would you like to see?" Or, "How are you hoping these family meetings will help? What do you envision?" Or, "Have you each got an idea of how you would like to bounce back? What have you tried?" Questions such as these convey more than the therapist's respect; they encourage family members to reflect on and articulate what matters to them. Family members may look to the therapist as an expert on family functioning, but when it comes to preferences, beliefs, decisions, and goals—the kinds of solutions they would like to see and the kinds of lives

they want to lead—these must ultimately be determined by them. Sometimes the therapist may offer guidance about how to get "there," but the clients will be expected to become empowered enough to determine where "there" is.[13]

7. Directly or indirectly, family members must be encouraged to speak for themselves rather than for others. "Mind reading" should be discouraged. Family members should be asked to put their assumptions in the form of questions to each other.

8. After a period when family members tend to talk directly to the worker, it is often best to encourage them to talk to one another. This shift must be carefully timed. Sometimes the members are too uncomfortable to do this in initial interviews. Occasionally, they talk or fight tenaciously with one another. In these cases, the worker may reverse the general rule and continue to engage each member in interaction.

9. When realistic, the family's ability and willingness to work on problems should be supported and optimism about possible improvement should be conveyed.

10. When a relative (or housekeeper, close family friend, etc.) appears to be important to the family situation, the worker should prepare the family for possibly including that person at future meetings on an as-needed basis.

11. Feedback from the family about the therapy and about the worker should be encouraged. This keeps the worker informed, demonstrates to the family ways of relating openly, and encourages the family to take its share of the responsibility for how the treatment progresses.

12. To reduce reluctance to attend family meetings, it is often important to establish a limited time structure that is definite, yet flexible enough to change later if necessary. A plan for evaluation, in which the family and the worker share reactions to the therapy, should be announced at the onset of treatment.

ASSESSMENT AND THE RUSSO FAMILY

Family Concepts

Many of the family concepts described in Chapter 14 are illustrated by the Russo family and were identified by the worker after the two interviews (one marital, one family) described earlier. *In nontechnical terms, the worker began to convey to family members some of the ways their patterns seemed to be contributing to Mr. Russo's depression (the presenting problem) and interfering with the comforts of family life.* A few examples of these follow:

Systems Concepts   These are illustrated by the changes that occurred in the family interactions when Linda left home, when Mr. Russo's job was less satisfying and supportive to him, and when the possibility that Angela might go away to college was considered. Every family member was affected. *Homeostasis* was evident in the family's initial reluctance to change, even though the present situation was unhappy for them all. The worker suggested including Angela in the treatment thinking that without her participation she might unconsciously impede positive changes made by her parents. Or her sense of responsibility for maintaining the family equilibrium, by being her mother's ally, might prevent her from individuating and going away to college.

Lack of Differentiation, Enmeshed Relationships, Diffuse Boundaries   When Mrs. Russo tended to speak for her husband and for Angela and not for herself, lack of differentiation became apparent. Angela, the worker surmised, voiced contemptuous feelings about Mr. Russo in part because Mrs. Russo was unwilling to express her disappointments directly. Mr. Russo allowed others to speak for and characterize him without correcting or commenting on what they said. *Individual boundaries,* then, tended to be unclear and diffuse.

Violation of Generational and Marital Boundaries Mr. and Mrs. Russo did not look to each other for refuge and primary support. Mr. Russo had gotten most of his comfort in the family from his daughter Linda, until she married and moved away. Mrs. Russo apparently looked to Angela to act out her own feelings of discontent. Currently, the relationship between Angela and her mother was closer and more mutually supportive than that between Mr. and Mrs. Russo. The worker guessed that the grandmother joined Mrs. Russo and Angela in criticism of Mr. Russo, thus intruding on marital and generational boundaries; this hunch was later substantiated. Neither spouse had made any concerted effort to protect or nurture the marital relationship.

Family Roles In the Russo case there were functional and dysfunctional roles. Mr. Russo worked and supported the family, Mrs. Russo ran the household, and Angela took her role as student seriously. On the other hand, Mr. Russo took on the *scapegoat* role. He became the symptomatic one, taking the blame and being blamed for the family's troubles. *Irrational role assignments* and dysfunctional role reciprocity were evident: Within the family, Mr. Russo behaved in some respects like the "helpless" one, requiring and supporting Mrs. Russo's tendency to be "overresponsible." Linda was the "angel" who could soothe Mr. Russo's

sadness. Angela was the "rude" one who "acted out" her mother's unstated negative feelings. Some of the *triangles* in the Russo family functioned to dilute and externalize tension and lack of resolution in the marital relationship. Dysfunctional *triangulation* was most evident in the fact that each parent was more allied with one of the children than with each other, negatively affecting each member.

Roles are assigned in every family; *members tend to rely on each other to balance or complement personality differences, to carry psychic functions for one another, to validate self-esteem or a sense of connection.* Assessments of families involve determinations of whether these tendencies are carried out in a *positive, flexible* or a *hurtful, rigid manner.* Although perhaps not immediately evident, the general sense of fairness and flexibility in the Russo family became apparent, with the result that more functional roles could evolve in family therapy; the major shift came when Angela was released from her role as Mrs. Russo's primary support.

Family Communication Compared with many other families, the Russo communication style was not as dysfunctional or entrenched. Yet patterns that created tension and interfered with their comfort as a family were apparent. A few comments in the sessions could be thought of as indirect, *mystifying messages.* Mrs. Russo and Angela each had the habit of defining Mr. Russo's thoughts, feelings, and motives rather than talking about what mattered to them. Mr. Russo did not protest the disdainful remarks his wife and daughter made about his inner experience. The most consistent and flagrant impediments to effective communication were observed when family members failed to make "I" statements about their own thoughts or feelings;

they were much more likely to speak for or about one another than for themselves.

Family Strengths

Several concepts describing dysfunctional patterns are illustrated in the Russo session, but others—such as the *double bind, pseudomutuality, myths,* and *secrets*—were *not* part of the family style.

The family clearly had many solid strengths. All three members were hard-working, conscientious, honest people with strong moral values. They were generous people who freely offered help to others: relatives and neighbors. Despite their present unhappiness, members of this family were loyal and had the capacity for caring. *But even the best—when stressed or frightened—can do harmful things:* Like the Russos, they can coerce or belittle one another; they can fail to listen; they can withdraw. In this family, as we said, *openness, fairness, flexibility,* and the *capacity for rebound* were also revealed early on. Many families who come for treatment are far more rigid and defensive than the Russos were. For example, Mr. Russo was able to move away from his role as "scapegoat" and speak for himself in the first family session. He was the first to express loving feelings and by doing so set a new tone; Mrs. Russo responded more kindly to him after this change. Briefly, Angela seemed to soften toward her father. Toward the end of the family session, the unhealthy alliance between Mrs. Russo and Angela was weakened when the mother rebuked her daughter for being "rude" to Mr. Russo. Since the negative patterns were not so firmly fixed, they were accessible to intervention. In the worker's opinion, the family members were very relieved when they began to find a way out of the painful interactions they had been engaged in; it became clear that they had wanted to

improve family relationships, but simply had not found the means to do so.

As this case illustrates, often our work involves *helping family members to uncover and strengthen loving connections that have been obscured through stress or neglect.* Family concepts help us to identify the factors that have contributed to the deterioration of relationships. As the Russo family case also demonstrates, when using family concepts to assess family functioning, one must evaluate the *severity* and *recalcitrance* as well as the *presence* of dysfunctional processes.

More family concepts are illustrated by the Russo family. By reviewing the case material presented earlier, the reader may be able to identify some of these.

ON DIAGNOSIS, GOALS, AND THE HEALTHY FAMILY

Assessing the Family

Over the years, attempts have been made to conceptualize family diagnosis by developing classifications of family dysfunction. For many reasons, no single satisfactory system has emerged.[14] Ideally, *if* the complexities and multiple dimensions of family processes could be classified by designating clusters of factors often found together, it would aid us in determining which strategies or procedures would be most effective in the treatment of particular types of dysfunction.

However, even without a satisfactory classification of family diagnoses, our own theoretical framework can guide us. As outlined in Chapter 11, the psychosocial approach to diagnosis scans the whole field and builds up a body of facts and hypotheses about the multiple aspects of the person–situation gestalt, including the interactional aspects. Choices about therapeutic interventions derive from an understanding of the *family's goals* and the clinician's assessment of those features of the situation that need to be *modified* or *strengthened* to achieve the objectives and improve family functioning.

Multilevel Assessment The family concepts discussed in the previous chapter, as illustrated above by the analysis of the Russo family interview, provide us with an outline for family evaluation. Again, from the psychosocial point of view, these concepts are useful when—and only when—they are combined with and adapted to the assessment processes detailed in earlier chapters; *personality assessment and an understanding of the larger systems with which the family interacts are part of the overall assessment.* In many cases, however, families provide the most significant context for personality growth, emotional fulfillment, and mutual support, even in the face of personal disabilities or failures in the social systems of which they are a part.

Common Assessment Questions When evaluating family functioning, some sample questions may guide the clinician in assessing and individualizing the *strengths* and *troubled areas* of a family's functioning:

What kinds of defenses or means does the family system employ to maintain the current equilibrium? If there are repetitive, destructive interactional patterns, what are the reactions to efforts to interrupt these? Is the index client's symptom a reflection of difficulties in the extended family or the marital relationship? How well differentiated are family members? Are individual and subsystem boundaries distinct, on the one hand, yet permeable, on the other? Are boundaries either overly rigid or dysfunctionally diffuse in various parts of the family system? What are the roles and role relationships? Are they appropriate to ages and generations? Is a child being "parenti-

fied"? Is the mother being infantalized as she and the grandmother cling together? Are family roles functional or dysfunctional? Who is scapegoated? Are family members taking turns as the symptomatic or scapegoated one? Who is triangulated, and how? Who teams up, defers, or speaks for whom? Is communication clear and direct? Or is it confused, amorphous, mystifying, or double-binding? What nonverbal communications should be explored? Do family members feel free to speak for themselves? Does the family tolerate differences of ideas and feelings among family members? What metacommunications qualify verbal statements?

Further areas the worker may explore concern the significance of introjects and projections of family members as they are played out in the interpersonal arena of the family. Can intergenerational processes be identified? Do family members cling to each other? Is there a pattern of estrangement or "cutoffs"? Are family supports consistent enough to promote growth and relatedness, yet allow for autonomy? Are there myths and secrets? How are family rules enforced and by whom? Of utmost importance: Are loyalties among family members apparent? Is loyalty to one family member seen as disloyalty by another? Are there indications of family patterns that have come down through the generations? Is a daughter paying an "emotional debt" to make up for mother's childhood deprivation? Can the family mobilize its resources to make a cooperative effort? What is the climate of emotional relationships among family members? Tender? Angry? Cold? Anxious? Even if not immediately apparent, do family relationships have potential for emotional availability? Is there flexibility or rigidity when ideas about change are discussed? How severe and/or pervasive are any dysfunctional processes that are observed?

These and many other diagnostic questions start to flow as the worker sits with a family in therapy. Understanding of the person-in-situation is supplemented if the worker is grounded in family theory. Diagnosis and treatment go hand and hand. The more the worker knows about a family, the clearer it will be which problems must be addressed. As the worker joins with the family to effect changes, more is learned about areas of strength, vulnerability, and accessibility, which influences further treatment strategies.

The Healthy Family

Framo is among a few others to suggest some principles that can be used to describe the well-functioning family. He makes the essential point that "nearly every person, family, and marriage, over the course of their lives, goes through periods of turmoil and disorganization that at the time appear pathological."[15] One can view his ideas as providing a framework against which current functioning of a family can be measured. Even though his notions were developed from observations of two-parent families, they can easily be adapted to single-parent or three-generational families. They might also be used to consider ideal goals toward which a family might want to move, an approach that is consistent with our efforts to help build on strengths, not just eliminate "pathological" processes. An abbreviated summary of principles of "normal" family functioning primarily developed by Framo, but slightly modified by us, follows:

1. Well-differentiated parents with a "sense of self" developed before separating from families of origin.
2. Clear generational boundaries, with children not expected to "save" parents or the marriage.

3. Realistic perceptions and expectations by parents of each other and the children.
4. Loyalty to family of procreation greater than to family of origin.
5. Spouses putting themselves and each other before others, but without excluding children.
6. Children not encouraged to feel that loyalty or closeness to one parent (or, for example, to a grandmother) means disloyalty to or alienation of another.
7. Identity development and autonomy encouraged for all family members.
8. Nonpossessive warmth and affection expressed among all family members.
9. Open, honest, and clear communication and ability to deal with issues directly.
10. Realistic, adult-to-adult relationship of parents with members of families of origin.
11. Involvement with others outside the family.
12. A sense of belonging or identity in the context of the culture or community of which the family is a part.[16]

THE HOLLIS TYPOLOGY AND FAMILY THERAPY

The Hollis classification of treatment procedures and worker–client communications (see Chapters 4 through 8 in this book) can be adapted to study family treatment.[17] Certainly, multiperson interviews are far more complex than one-to-one sessions, and the classification requires additional dimensions with which to analyze the interactional process. It is our hope that the dynamics of marital and family interviews will become an important subject for researchers. Among the many issues that could be studied are: Which treatment procedures and combinations of procedures prove most effective in family (or couple) therapy? Are therapists able to describe accurately which procedures they are using and toward what ends?

When evaluating their work, clinicians can apply Hollis's six major categories of worker and client communications to analyze a particular family session. For example, the first four casework procedures can be located at various points in the initial interview with the Russo family:

Sustainment The worker employed sustaining procedures, by conveying acceptance and encouragement, throughout the meeting. She used this procedure when she said to Angela, "That must be hard to take." When she praised the family as a whole for its interest and willingness to talk about the family situation, she was using sustaining techniques. In addition to the numerous verbal samples of sustainment there were the many unrecorded nods, smiles, and gestures that let the family members know of her interest, her wish to help, and her understanding. The worker's *involved impartiality* was sustaining on two counts: (1) It conveyed to each her intense concern for and ability to relate warmly to each family member while maintaining clear boundaries; and (2) By her actions, family members were notified that she was not blaming or taking sides with any member or faction, nor was she aligning herself with any individual's point of view; she was there to listen to each.

Direct Influence Directive procedures were important in this first meeting as the worker communicated the "ground rules" about the treatment process. When she interrupted Mrs. Russo or suggested that she step back so that Mr. Russo and Angela could work on their own relationship, the worker was giving direction to all three family members. On several occasions when she said that each person should speak for herself or himself, she was giving the Rus-

sos an important instruction about how to communicate more effectively. Experience leads us to believe that these procedures are more commonly employed in family sessions than in individual sessions because keeping discussions focused and handling the complex interactions usually requires more leadership and explanation. The psychosocial clinician is no more likely to give direct advice about *goals* to families than to individual clients.

Exploration, Description, and Ventilation These were evident in many worker and family communications in the Russo session. As Angela described the change in her father since Linda moved away, she also ventilated some bitterness about her sister's being an "angel" in her father's eyes. When the worker explored Mr. Russo's relationship with Angela, she opened the door for him to ventilate some of his sadness about it. The worker also paved the way for ventilation about the treatment process.

Person–Situation Reflection At several points this was encouraged by the worker and volunteered by family members. Examples of this category include: Mr. Russo saying about Angela, "I suppose I'm not much of a father to her"; the worker asking Mr. Russo how he accounted for Angela's sarcasm about him; and Mrs. Russo reflecting, in response to the worker's question, about how empty life would seem after both daughters left home.

Pattern-Dynamic and Developmental Reflections In the initial meeting, these procedures were not encouraged by the worker or volunteered by the Russo family members. They were sparingly employed by the worker in subsequent sessions in much the same way they would have been in individual interviews. The difference is that the other family members were privy to the process. For instance, with the worker's help, in one very moving interview, Mr. Russo reflected on how the early death of his mother and frequent changes of foster homes as a boy contributed to the sadness he felt when his daughter Linda moved. His recognition of this was touching to the rest of the family (including his mother-in-law, who was present). This helped to reduce the hostility of the others toward him and made the Russo family closer and more empathic toward one another. Use of these procedures in family treatment may be encouraging to those who are concerned that family therapy is not as "deep" as one-to-one treatment. In fact, as illustrated by this case, not only was Mr. Russo able to increase his own understanding, but also the family members were moved in ways that could not have occurred if Mr. Russo had gained the insight in an individual session. At other points in treatment, Mrs. Russo recognized that her patterned role as "manager" and "go-between" was a function of long-standing anxiety and was a disservice to herself and other family members. Here, too, her self-understanding was heard by the others, thereby enhancing changes in each member's way of interrelating.

Environmental Procedures These were considered by the worker primarily in connection with Mr. Russo's job situation. In some family therapy cases, environmental work is as important as any other intervention; in the Russo case, however, family members generally negotiated their way in other systems (community, school, employment) more successfully than they handled their intrafamily relationships.

Diverse Meanings of the Same Procedure Particularly exciting, although technically complicated for researchers, is the

potential for studying the diverse meanings to each family member of a single worker communication. In family practice, it is the worker's challenge to gauge the different meanings a particular comment may have. For example, as the worker explored Mr. Russo's positive feelings toward Angela in the initial interview, *his ventilation of sadness* about their relationship appeared to be *sustaining for Angela.* Similarly, when the worker spoke to Mrs. Russo *in a sustaining way* about the burden she carried by having to "fix up" the relationship between Mr. Russo and Angela and by looking after Mr. Russo when he was depressed, this very same communication suggested a *directive* (which the worker had already given more explicitly) to Mr. Russo and Angela: They would have to take more responsibility for their own relationship and problems. These examples only begin to touch on the many ways for researchers and clinicians to employ the Hollis classification to examine the multilevel dynamic events that occur in family interviews.

SPECIAL EMPHASES IN PSYCHOSOCIAL FAMILY THERAPY

Some family therapists declare that they discourage procedures that would lead to the following: the expression of emotion (*ventilation*); the development of self-awareness, or the understanding of the feelings and behaviors of others (*person–situation* and *pattern-dynamic reflection*), which they believe is unlikely to foster change and therefore is irrelevant to treatment; and the exploration of past history (*developmental reflection*); since they believe that the past is manifested in the present family relationships.[18]

Some of these same family therapists consider it unnecessary—or even detrimental to treatment—to make interpretations or to share with the families what they think about what they see. Certainly, as we demonstrated in our discussion of the Russo family interview, interpretations, observations, and interventions of all kinds should be measured and carefully timed. The therapist selects first for intervention those aspects of the family interaction that seem most accessible. As we pointed out earlier, in the first session with the Russos the worker chose to work very little with the marital relationship since the energy in the family could be directed most comfortably to the conflict between father and daughter and the mother's go-between role in it. Defenses against other explorations were respected for the time being. However, for both ethical *and* practical reasons, we strongly disagree with the point of view that admonishes against even well-timed interpretations and the sharing of observation and opinions by the therapist.

Our reason for taking this position is threefold: First, we believe that client family members have the right to know what the worker thinks and, on principle, should be privy to as much information as they can understand or tolerate.

Second, we believe that when the therapist consistently withholds impressions, the treatment relationship degenerates into an "expert–idiot" format in which the family is at the mercy of manipulations by the worker—which the worker never explains. In our experience most families are eager to know what the worker thinks. Interpretations or opinions openly shared give the family the opportunity to accept, reject, or modify them. Sometimes the therapist can be operating under a misapprehension that the family can correct. We advocate a treatment environment with as much equality as possible, in the sense that worker and family members, all fallible people, are sitting together, sharing thoughts and feelings and searching for solutions to the dilemmas

and aches in the family's life. Family therapists are experts, trained to understand family processes; they have developed methods and techniques, based on theory and experience, about how people change. Family members, however, are equally important experts on their own experience, on what their hopes and goals are, on what choices and changes they want to make, and on how they feel their therapy is progressing. A climate that promotes such mutual sharing between worker and family encourages the family members to take responsibility for their lives and for their work in therapy. If they are kept in the dark about the worker's maneuvers, their passivity and dependence are encouraged and their initiative is discouraged. Many clients we see in family and individual treatment who have problems involving differentiation have little confidence in their own abilities to make choices and changes. They have habitually given more value to the opinions of others than to their own. If the worker implies that he or she is in *total* charge of the therapeutic process, the tendency of some clients to give too much power away to others will be reinforced.

Third, in our view and experience, when people can understand and give meaning to their feelings and behavior they are in a far better position to use their intelligence to find their own solutions and to work toward change than when they submissively follow the leadership of the family therapist.

Few family therapists believe that *excessive* ventilation of negative or destructive feelings and so-called total frankness support the purposes of family meetings. There is legitimate concern about the dangers of "free-for-all" communications and "brutal honesty" that some fear are encouraged in family therapy.[19]

Caution is certainly essential. As indicated earlier, if negative interactions are too intense or destructive, and family members seem unwilling or unable to work together in a more positive fashion, it may be best to arrange individual interviews until a less vituperative climate can be promoted. In some families, however, the worker need not be too thin-skinned about insults and anger flying about in family meetings and can understand that in many instances these abuses are everyday occurrences. (In such families, the members are often more frightened by their own and each other's tender feelings than they are by the violence of affect to which they are so tragically accustomed.) If we keep in mind that beneath the bitter attacks and expressions of hostility there is often pain, disappointment, and sadness, the worker can encourage the expression of *these feelings,* which are frequently more "honest" than the anger that masks them.

Furthermore, the family therapist must develop a style with which to respond to ongoing abusiveness among family members. In the Russo family, for example, in essence the worker relabeled Angela's anger at her father as disappointment. Pittman, when confronted with a family of blaming attackers, remarked paradoxically in his low-key manner: "It seems kind of unpleasant to me, but I wouldn't want to change something y'all enjoy so much."[20] Any intervention or technique, consonant with worker style, that fosters reflection about the behavior that reinforces the problems the family wants to resolve can help us to avoid the trap some warn against.

"Brutal honesty" of other kinds—as in the case of the husband who enthusiastically describes his secretary's bust measurements to his jealous wife—must be explored to determine the underlying meaning of the communication. In this situation the worker would try to find out why the man wants to hurt his wife in this manner.

Some critics are concerned about negative effects of the exposure of differences among family members in conjoint sessions, fearing that conflict will be exacerbated rather than reduced. It is our opinion that the revealing of previously undisclosed disparate thoughts and feelings among family members can be helpful and, when handled skillfully by the family therapist, can actually reduce hostility. For example, in one case, the father who frequently expressed a lot of anger toward his children had never told his wife that he resented spending their precious time off in the summer at the beach. He wanted to visit the national parks, he said; "Why do you think I keep reading camping books?" The wife, startled by this news, had no objections to compromising over vacations. As it turned out, there were many unexpressed differences between husband and wife that had not been shared; once they talked about them more openly, there was much less hostility displaced onto their children. The purpose of family therapy is not to discourage differences, but to help family members to recognize that these need not be feared, and that relationships need not be lost because of them. In fact, when such fears are quelled, family members often find that diverse feelings, interests, and points of view are stimulating and enrich their relationships.

"Honest communication" also does not imply that the privacy of family members should be violated. Married couples share intimacies that need not be the property of their children or their parents. Adolescents, as they grow toward independence, are well known for their wish to conceal certain facets of their lives. In this connection, we refer the reader to the ground rules for family therapy suggested earlier in this chapter. Contacts between family members and the worker between family sessions should be shared with the entire group. This does not mean every aspect of the content need be revealed. For example, during one phase of treatment, Mr. and Mrs. Russo were seen in joint sessions, without Angela and the grandmother, to explore their marriage and sexual relationship. The *fact* that they met was revealed, and the couple and the worker indicated to the others that they were working on issues that were private to the marital relationship. Confidentiality was respected and marital boundaries were supported. On the other hand, when Mrs. Russo telephoned to report on her husband's depression, this information was part of the work of the whole family, and particularly of Mr. Russo. If the worker had concealed it, inadvertently she would have been inducted into a collusion with Mrs. Russo, thus reinforcing the latter's managerial tendencies and Mr. Russo's passivity. In short, outside of sessions, communication from a family member to the worker about *other* family members is discouraged and usually revealed. Under most circumstances, information that is personal to a family member or members is treated confidentially. Only under special conditions, such as the pregnancy of a 12-year-old daughter or a danger that a family member will attempt suicide, is confidentiality breached. In *every* instance, however, before revealing personal information, the worker should seek the consent of the individual and explain why it must be disclosed.

POSTSCRIPT: THE RUSSO FAMILY

Family therapy for the Russos lasted 10 months. In 6 of the 36 sessions, Mr. and Mrs. Russo met together, without any other family members, to work on their marital and sexual relationship. Of the remaining 30 sessions, Angela attended all except the last 2, which were scheduled after she left for college, several hundred miles away.

Linda, on a trip home, came to one session, eager to settle some misunderstandings that had developed between her and her mother.

The maternal grandmother attended three sessions. A deeply religious woman of middle-class, northern Italian background, Mrs. Russo's mother had been critical of Mr. Russo's occupational status and lack of interest in the church since the day she met him. Class and educational differences between Mr. and Mrs. Russo, influenced by Mrs. Russo's mother's attitude about these, played a role in the family conflicts. Mrs. Russo had attended college briefly, and Linda and Angela both aspired to professional careers that placed Mr. Russo, a high school dropout, in an inferior position in his eyes and the eyes of his family.

The worker's knowledge of cultural factors played only a small part in her work with this family. Both Mr. and Mrs. Russo were third-generation Italian Catholics and yet, even with the differences in their class backgrounds, as a family they were part of an upwardly mobile, lower-middle-class, heterogeneous community. In a minor way, the family members, particularly Mrs. Russo's mother, had a traditional reluctance about bringing their "dirty linen" to a stranger; she believed that if help was needed, the family should speak with a priest. Yet, as frequently occurs with Italian families, every member of the Russo family was quite expressive emotionally in therapy sessions. Mr. Russo was able to cry and to speak of tender and sentimental feelings; at the same time he berated himself for being less than a "man" as he compared himself unfavorably to his father, a domineering, occasionally violent person. The girls both attended parochial grammar schools, but went on to public high schools, which they preferred; only the grandmother had been disappointed by their choice. Although both parents were reluctant to see their daughters leave home, they did not—as some Italian parents do—resist these moves on the basis of concern about sexual behavior or vulnerability away from the family.

On balance, Angela probably benefited most from family treatment. Without guilt or fear, she was able to follow through on her wish to leave the household and prepare for her own life and career. Mrs. Russo became less intrusive in the relationship between Angela and Mr. Russo and, over the months of treatment, father and daughter enjoyed a warmer relationship than they had for years. During several sessions in the middle phase of therapy, Angela fought hard with her mother, as adolescents often do (but as Angela previously had not done), for the "right" to make her own decisions, large and small. Although reluctantly, Mrs. Russo was able to give her daughter some credit for being almost adult. In the last session before she left for college, Angela gave genuine thanks to her parents for their support and shared loving feelings with them both. Family therapy was clearly preventive for Angela, who, without it, might have given in to her mother's dependence on her and remained at home. Or she might have left defiantly for college, burdened with many unresolved feelings about her decision.

At the end of treatment, Mr. Russo was less depressed and was no longer taking medication. Periodically, he slipped back into "the dumps," but these episodes were less intense and of shorter duration than they had been. Without self-blame, he was able to announce to his family, including his mother-in-law, that he felt neither capable nor secure enough to face the "jungle" of the job market and seek employment with more prestige or personal reward. He had made peace, he said, with his current employment situation. The confidence with which he made this choice enhanced his self-respect and resulted in far less criti-

cism from his wife, his daughter, and even his mother-in-law. Involving Mrs. Russo's mother in the therapy exposed and diminished her contribution to the family alignment against Mr. Russo. A few weeks before termination, his mother-in-law broke her leg and Mr. Russo willingly gave her practical help he had never offered before.

Mrs. Russo, whose motivation was essential to the therapy, made more gains than she expected, since she had assumed that her husband would have to make all the changes. Of course, she did benefit from his progress and the greater family harmony achieved through treatment. But by being less intrusive and managerial—not easy for her—she also won appreciation from both her daughters and a new kind of closeness with them that was no longer primarily based on mutual dependency. Furthermore, it turned out, Mrs. Russo had many cultural and intellectual interests that her husband did not share. As she became less critical in general, she was able to stop complaining to Mr. Russo about his "narrow mind." Instead, she found friends to join her in activities she could enjoy apart from her husband.

The couple's sexual relationship, which had never been satisfactory, improved only slightly, if at all. However, the resentment they both felt about it was reduced, and neither was motivated to explore the matter further at the time of termination. On the whole, Mr. and Mrs. Russo were able to listen to each other better and to accept their differences more comfortably. Each made personal choices without resorting to self-blame or recriminations. They no longer clung to their daughters' love out of despair over their marriage. All family members expressed positive feelings about the treatment experience and wanted to make sure they could return should the need arise.

Would individual therapy for Mr. Russo have worked well? Medication and supportive casework might have relieved his depression. His improved self-esteem might have resulted in positive repercussions throughout the family. From the point of view of the worker, however, Mr. Russo could not have bucked the collusion of the other family members. Without the participation of them all, the worker believes, he would have retreated again into depression and self-blame. It also seems probable that Angela would not have made the gains she did without the support of family sessions.

Some families continue to grow and change after treatment ends. Others return during crises or setbacks or resume treatment to achieve further goals. In some cases, individual members continue in treatment after family meetings are terminated. Many families change more remarkably than the Russo family did. Others make far fewer gains. In families with limited intellectual and emotional resources, or with patterns of long-standing dependency and poor differentiation, change may be minimal. It is the task of the family therapist to travel with the family toward mutually agreed upon goals and to identify the point at which progress ceases. As in any casework treatment, the worker cannot expect more change for clients than they wish for themselves.

We move on from the Russo family now and turn to other subjects of importance to the clinical practice of social work with families. The remaining sections of this chapter will discuss transference and countertransference, resistance, single-parent families, and stepfamilies.

TRANSFERENCE AND COUNTERTRANSFERENCE IN FAMILY THERAPY

Much of the discussion in Chapter 9 about unrealistic reactions of the individual client and the worker toward one another applies to family work as well. But there are some real differences. In some instances, transference and countertransference reactions may be more diluted in family therapy than in individual treatment, where the emotional forces are concentrated on the one-to-one relationship. More often, however, the complexity of the family process intensifies, for both worker and family, the tendency to subjectify reactions. Patterns and defenses within any family group have been functioning for a long time, and the family has an established set of (often unrealistic) attitudes and responses with which to face any threat, including the intrusion of a family therapist! These reactions from the family can keenly affect the worker's perspective.

Transference

In any therapy situation, the person who applies for help feels vulnerable to some degree. Old childhood feelings, derived from relationships with parents, authority figures, and siblings, or feelings associated with later relationships can be reactivated as clients acknowledge to a professional that they cannot solve their problems by themselves. Fear of blame and disapproval, as well as hopes, warm feelings, awe, and longings for approval, are among the many "portable" reactions that people bring into treatment from other parts of their lives. In family group therapy, such transferences can become contagious and travel from one family member to another. Or they can be a function of the system as a whole, as may happen when, in a defensive effort to protect the homeostatic balance, family members band together to block the worker by assigning him or her a distorted negative role.

In a family of rigid, critical parents (who both had disapproving parents themselves) and two adolescent sons, the family reacted to the worker with suspicion.

As a group, family members falsely accused him of making judgmental statements about them all to the high school guidance counselor who had referred them for treatment. They joined together and displaced their negative experiences with their respective parents onto the worker. Only after many weeks, as greater trust was established, was the family able to risk exposure to the worker without the fear of his disapproval.

In other cases, deprived or dependent families may attribute to the worker the role of family "savior," a role impossible for anyone to fill.

To further complicate the picture, a family's unrealistic attitudes and responses may be divisive in the therapy situation. For example, the father who experienced himself as the "loser" in his original family may assume that his wife will get better attention than he will from the therapist (as perhaps his sister did from his mother). If the wife in this situation brings from *her* past a seductive or manipulative manner with which to curry favor from parental or authority figures, the husband's fears may be reinforced. On the basis of experiences in their family, children and adolescents, too, may bring various transference responses to the therapy, such as expectations of being favored, blamed, or required by the worker to try to rescue other family members. When family members have divergent responses to the therapist, angry or rivalrous feelings can be aroused within the family group. If there are co-therapists, the family may assign one the role of "good parent" and the other that of "bad" one. As unsettling as some family reactions may be, the worker who encourages open discussion and begins to challenge or interpret some of the distortions can use them to help family members learn more about themselves, each other, and the repetitive patterns that hamper the growth of the entire family. The focus of family treatment, as we have said, should be shifted as soon as possible to the complexities of "transferences" and projections *among* family members. Unrealistic responses to the therapist must be addressed, of course, but not induced. Ideally, the worker takes on the role of neutral "coach" or "facilitator," helping family members to recognize unrealistic attitudes that pervade and taint the family process. This issue will be discussed further in Chapters 16 and 17 on couple treatment.

Countertransference

The family caseworker, too, may displace early or unrealistic feelings or attitudes onto the family being treated. As important as it is for a worker interested in family work to master the theory and techniques of family therapy, it is equally essential that one be constantly alert to countertransference and countertherapeutic reactions. In individual treatment, when listening to descriptions of the family situation, the therapist can more often maintain an objectivity that may be elusive in the face of powerful family forces operating in vivo.

Induction   As we indicated earlier, when we speak of "induction" in family therapy, we usually mean that the worker is inadvertently pulled into the family system, on the side of its defenses and resistance.

A mother who was diabetic, arthritic, and had suffered a "nervous breakdown" many years earlier was seen by the father and by the children as fragile. The mother's demeanor invited this view. In frequent telephone conversations with the worker, the father expressed concern that family therapy would be detrimental to his wife's health. The worker allowed his own clinical judgment about the mother's very evident strengths to be discounted and was persuaded to treat her with "kid gloves" as the family did. Only after it was clear that therapy was at a standstill did the worker begin to challenge the family myth about the mother that, it turned out, was promoted by the father to shield himself from facing worries about his own emotional well-being. Had the worker allowed his induction to continue, the family resistance would have won out and treatment would have failed.

Such family forces can place extraordinary stresses on the most mature worker and thereby sap his or her effectiveness. It takes a secure therapist to feel comfortable in a family that pressures him as this one did. It is even harder, perhaps, to maintain one's perspective when faced with a family that closes ranks and isolates the worker as the worker begins to touch on patterns and interlocking defenses that have taken years to develop. Similarly, it can be difficult for the therapist to hold on to hope when meeting with a family immobilized by apathy or rigidity, or a family in which there has been violence, incest, or other kinds of abuse. In some instances, the therapist may be prompted to work too hard, too fast, or to attack the family.

There are other kinds of induction to be avoided. The worker may overidentify with a family member or subgroup or fail to empathize with others. The problem is compounded in a family that attempts to involve the worker in collusions or alignments with one member or subgroup against others within the family. Angry, competitive, or protective feelings may be stirred in the worker. For example, a particular worker may feel hostile toward the parents of an abused or scapegoated child and may want to prove she is a better "mother." Or another worker may be tempted to take the part of a "henpecked" husband against a controlling wife, if he loses sight of the hand-in-glove aspects of their relationship, which can be equally painful to both partners. Young workers may find it easy to identify with rebellious adolescents. Older workers, facing the trials of raising their own teenage children, may tend to feel partial to the beleaguered parents. A worker who has (or had) an angry or overly dependent relationship with either of his or her parents (or with a sibling, grandparent, etc.) may transfer feelings about that person to the relationship with the corresponding member of the client family. Finally, more often than we would wish, family therapists are tempted to repair the marriages of clients in ways that they have never been able to influence their own parent's relationships—or, for that matter, their own marriages. Countertransference problems can be provoked by patterns of family interaction as well as by the characteristics of an individual family member.

Involved Impartiality   The goal for workers who choose to treat families is to maintain "involved impartiality." Without involvement, there can be no working relationship. Without impartiality, the worker will be hopelessly inducted into the family system. If the worker consistently takes sides, sooner or later some or all of the family members are likely to refuse to continue in therapy. To be free to work for the benefit of the family, one must be as secure as possible about oneself and one's competence and must be ever alert to one's "Achilles' heel" or unresolved feelings about one's own family relationships. If the worker suspects that countertransference attitudes or responses are impeding progress with a family, supervision or consultation can be effective ways of regaining lost perspective. In many agencies, family therapists have made good use of one-way mirrors, videotape, "live supervision," and co-therapists as aids against slipping into unrealistic, countertherapeutic reactions. In attempting to help troubled families change, the worker is well advised to heed Whitaker's counsel that the therapist "must be available to each person of the family, yet belong to none; he must belong to himself."[21]

RESISTANCE AND FAMILY THERAPY

Much of what we said about resistance in Chapter 12 applies equally to family treatment. When we speak of resistance we must ask, resistance to what? Sometimes families resist ideas or suggestions of the worker because the worker has not explained them adequately. Perhaps the worker has explicit or implicit goals for the family that the family does not share. The worker with "hidden agendas" obstructs the work and also may stimulate hostility or premature terminations. So-called resistance is sometimes described pejoratively by workers: "She is resistant to separating from her alcoholic husband." Or, "The parents are resistant to sending their son to the day care center." In these cases, if these goals are the therapist's only, insufficient attention is being given to "where the client is."

Even though well-meaning, workers sometimes are dogmatic or rigid and try to convince clients of particular points of view. When families oppose such suggestions, the worker may respond with countertherapeutic reactions of anger or pessimism. These responses, in turn, often engender further reluctance in the family to engage in the difficult work of family treatment. The importance of mutuality has been mentioned several times in this book. When the therapist shares observations and opinions and attends closely to the family's priorities,

clients are then in the best position to make informed decisions. Resistance is inevitable, but therapists can intensify or diminish it on the basis of their respect for and their flexible responses to families and their situations. It is the worker's responsibility to explain the link between the family difficulties and the therapeutic suggestions and interventions. Basic concepts about family processes can be made clear in nontechnical terms. It is also the worker's responsibility to find out what family members think will help.

Family resistance often occurs immediately. During the intake telephone call, clients may oppose the idea of meeting conjointly. Sometimes such reactions have a cultural component. Clients may have concerns about privacy or about sharing of intimate family matters with outsiders. Some are concerned about secrets being uncovered in family meetings. Often family members fear they will be blamed for the problems by other family members or by the therapist. Initial reluctance may be dealt with in various ways. When speaking with a mother of a symptomatic child, for example, a worker might say, "If Peter is going to get the best help I can offer, it will be important for me to get to know the world he lives in, the people who matter the most to him." Or, "Although families can't be blamed for a problem like Peter's, they can usually be helpful in the solution." Or, "The work often goes faster when all who are involved put their heads to it." When resistance persists, the worker might suggest, "Why don't we get the whole family together for the first meeting and then decide on the best way to proceed after that?"

Some families want to exclude one or more family members from sessions. A mother may say the father is too busy or too critical of the child to be a helpful participant. Parents sometimes want to leave out the "well" siblings or other family members for fear of upsetting them. A few family therapists will not see families unless every member comes. In our opinion, this rigid stance can result in some families never getting much-needed treatment. When our best efforts to persuade the caller to bring the entire family to the first meeting fail, we may "join the resistance" and see whoever is willing or available. Occasionally, there may be good reasons, which the family understands better than the worker, for not meeting with the entire group. One can always try to expand the membership later, after family members have been given fuller explanations of the rationale for including the entire family and the worker has a better understanding of the reluctance to do so.

Forms resistance takes at any point during family treatment are too many to mention. Among common forms of resistance are lateness or missed sessions, missing members, complaints about lack of progress, hopelessness (i.e., denial of family strengths), refusal to discuss relevant issues, disruptive behavior by children or by fighting adults, persistent focus on one member (present or absent), constant blaming, unwillingness to talk, sessions monopolized by one member, intellectualization, and pseudomutuality (i.e., denial that there are problems). In every case, it is important to find ways to discuss evidence of possible resistance with family members without conveying the idea that they have been "caught" in something. Sometimes behaviors that seem resistant to the therapist have entirely different meanings to family members; they must be given the opportunity to explain *their* interpretations.

Resistance frequently derives from fear of change, of the family as a whole or of individuals within it. Homeostasis operates to counteract change. Moreover, family members who willingly come for family sessions, such as Mrs. Russo, often come with the idea of trying to change *other* family members, thus resisting the prospect of making changes themselves. Old patterns are hard to break. People often feel most comfortable carrying out familiar family roles and behaviors, even when these no longer work well for them. As Anderson and Stewart write in their useful book on resistance in family therapy:

> It is easy to understand why people resist changing their habits of relating, as the saying goes, "better a known devil than an unknown saint." The prospect of change in intimate personal relationships is more threatening to an individual's sense of emotional security than most other changes. It is not surprising that most people respond with fear and resistance. Change is frightening and could result in a situation that is worse than the current one. *Loss of one sort or another always accompanies change.* In order to change, individuals must give up something valued or thought to be essential, often giving up reality as they see it. [Emphasis ours][22]

When the worker understands the discomfort—at times the terror—induced in some clients by the prospect of change, it is easier to be empathic. The reality of some risks feared by clients must be acknowledged. If the family meets as a group, the members *may* face criticism. Dissatisfactions probably *will* be expressed. Unsettling secrets *may* be revealed. Feelings of uneasiness about these possibilities should be normalized. In a comfortable therapeutic climate the fear of change may be dissipated to some degree. Motivation—the wish for relief from pain, worry, and stress—counteracts some resistance. In every case, it is the worker's task to find the delicate balance between accommodating defensive resistance and providing leadership toward change.

SINGLE-PARENT FAMILIES

Early family research and theory usually described the "intact" family of procreation. The marital relationship, as we have said, was found to be an important key to modifying conditions for the entire family. In recent years, because of the dramatic increase in single-parent families in all walks of life, family therapists and theorists have turned their attention as well to special issues concerning this group. In contrast to earlier views and judgments about the negative consequences of "broken families," clinicians have come to recognize that these "nontraditional" families are *not necessarily more problem-prone than any other families.* There may be some differences in the ways single parents—over 90 percent of whom are women—adapt to their circumstances, depending in part on class or cultural factors, but many of the issues they have to deal with and the difficulties they encounter are similar to those faced by two-parent families. In recent years the literature has given more attention to fathers in general as well as to custodial and noncustodial fathers.[23]

Many single adults who are heads of households are not the parents of the children they are raising. Grandmothers, aunts, uncles, older siblings, or biologically unrelated adults have formally or informally become the caretakers of thousands of children who have been abandoned or orphaned by parents who died of AIDS or other illnesses and accidents. Some of the parents are drug or alcohol abusers, are chronically mentally ill, or have been incarcerated. The custodians of these children often have many of the same requirements as the single parents discussed in this section.

Assessment

Some of the principles we have discussed pertaining to "intact" families also apply to one-parent families. When a child becomes symptomatic, he or she is often sending out a signal that the family is troubled. A child's development may be distorted in an effort to diminish or absorb a parent's pain.[24] Children can be infantilized, parentified, presented as a parent's "best foot forward," neglected, or unduly criticized by a single parent as well as by parents living together. There *are* differences, however. Issues in the single-parent family can depend in part on how the parent became single. Some parents were never married. Others were separated, divorced, or abandoned. Some have spouses who have been incarcerated or mentally ill for many years. Still others lost husbands or wives through death. *Social attitudes and attitudes of the parents may vary according to whether the one-parent family derived from choice, rejection, a sudden loss, and so on. When treating any single-parent family, assessing these attitudes is essential.*

Other special issues are considered in the assessment of single-parent families coming for help. Some of the common ones follow. Generally they can apply to female or male parents.

1. Emotional Reliance on Children

When children are overly relied upon by a single parent, they may become symptomatic. Unfulfilled needs can lead a parent to seek major companionship from children or see them as the "reason for living." A parent who has been rejected, even the nonresident parent, may try to bolster self-esteem by proving adequacy as a parent at the child's expense or at the expense of the child's relationship with the other parent. Under these circumstances, a child may feel overly responsible for the parent's feelings or well-being. Some children do not develop age-appropriate peer relationships because of the intensity of the bond with a lonely parent. As a consequence of the extreme importance bestowed upon a child, problems around hierarchy and consistency may develop in single-parent homes. For example, one minute a child may be an intimate confidant to an unhappy parent, yet only a moment later be disciplined like a child. Adolescents acting out sexually or with drugs are sometimes protesting a parent's neediness. One-parent, one-child families can be particularly vulnerable to difficulties as they try to fill all of each other's relational needs. Encouragement of individuation in the children and social supports and networks for both children and parents may be sacrificed when generational boundaries are diffuse and family boundaries are closed to outsiders.

2. Parental Burdens Single parents can be enormously burdened. Most single parents work. Many do not have enough money and get little or no financial support or help with the children. Bitterness about responsibilities and about their lives and losses can induce feelings of resentment about children's needs. In some cases, the result may be neglect or apparent indifference. Negative feelings parents have about themselves—for example, when they feel they failed at marriage or have been rejected—can be projected onto children. When the noncustodial or absent parent is idealized by a child to compensate for disappointment in the overwhelmed or angry parent, bitterness may develop. Children of angry or distracted single parents may seek security (in healthy or destructive ways) elsewhere to feel less criticized or ignored. When they find teachers, families of friends, or others who show a genuine interest in them, some children are saved from serious damage or unhappiness.

3. Feelings toward the Absent Parent When one parent has disappeared or is dead, the custodial parent and child often have fantasies about the absent one. A parent, for example, may see the child as a "double" for the parent who is gone. In some such cases, when the marital relationship was positive, the child can "do no wrong"; when it was negative, the youngster may be unable to "do right." Both types of projections are unrealistic and destructive. Children in such situations may have secret longings for the absent parent, idealizing him or her to such an extent that the "in-house" parent can never match the fantasized image of the other one. Problems inevitably follow.

4. Parental Guilt Some single parents, whether custodial or noncustodial, are steeped in guilt because the child has been deprived of a two-parent home. There may be less money than there was, the child may be alone a lot, the parent may have less time or patience than previously. The initiator of a marital breakup often feels guilt most acutely. Self-esteem and confidence can be eroded by unnecessary self-criticism. Good judgment about what is best for children may be impaired by a parent's wish to reduce the guilt or to "make up" to the child for the sacrifices that resulted from the breakup of the marriage.

5. Unfinished Business Many single-parent familes are burdened by the effects of various kinds of unfinished business. Children may feel guilty, overresponsible, or heartbroken about the dissolved relationship. As can occur in intact homes, children of separated parents can become symptomatic, bringing the focus on themselves, hoping to unite their mother and father. Especially when the breakup is in some manner incomplete, children may be preoccupied with hopes of reconciliation. Parents whose feelings about the separation are unresolved often compete for the child's loyalty. A child may be coaxed to side with the parent who seems "pathetic" or "misused." Loyalty to one parent may be seen as disloyalty to the other. Many triangles and conflicts may emerge. A parent may say: "I'll send you to your father/mother if you don't behave." Or, "Why don't you go live with your father if you think he is so great?" Unhealthy polarizations and alliances often develop, with children caught in the middle.

6. Relationships with Families of Origin   Relatives are often *very* supportive to single-parent families, generously providing child care and emotional support. Sometimes, however, these relationships are stressful or complicated. Some parents of the single parent may have a "you made your bed, now you must sleep in it" or "I told you so" attitude. Others, going through changes in their own lives (e.g., widowhood or loneliness of the "empty nest"), may overtly or covertly welcome being needed by the grieving or overburdened single parent and the children. Sometimes hierarchical problems develop; grandparents may infantilize or demean the single parent and try to preempt major parental responsibilities. Single parents may depend too heavily on their families; they may take the help given for granted or they may reject offered assistance that they sorely need.

In some families, mothers had babies when they were very young and three generations live together, often in female-headed households. In addition to economic problems many such families face (in too many cases they live in poverty and must contend also with a capricious welfare system), the grandmothers bear enormous burdens; sometimes they are involved in raising their own children as well as those of their daughters (or sons). In these families, as we shall mention again shortly, it is often particularly important to help the young person (usually the mother) to assume her responsibility as parent without rejecting the needed help of the grandmother.[25]

Special Treatment Considerations

Systems issues can arise when treating single-parent families. Some single parents, for example, are eager to share parenting responsibilities with the worker. Those with meager support networks may especially look to the worker on an ongoing basis to share concerns about children, for help in disciplining them, or for adult companionship. One single parent said to her family therapist: "You are the first adult I have talked with since I saw you last week!" While the worker wants to be available to such a mother, it is equally important to help her to reflect on how to expand her support systems. If the worker continues to be a parent's *major* comfort, the parent may unconsciously encourage children's symptoms. Otherwise, there might be no need to keep coming to see the worker!

Conversely, some single parents feel rivalrous toward the family caseworker. In such cases, children may not relinquish symptoms, thereby saving the mother or father from humiliation: humiliation that the worker "succeeded" in helping after the parent had failed. It is with constant amazement that we witness the many and creative ways that children "tune in" to their parents' feelings and try to take care of them.

Worker overresponsibility can be a major pitfall when treating troubled single parents and their children. Sympathy and concern for these clients who are so often lonely or overwhelmed can induce workers to try to do more than they realistically can do. One can develop an "urge to rescue" when burdened parents feel helpless, when "latchkey" children seem to get little guidance or tender parenting, or when children are so involved in trying to take care of their parent(s) that they are not getting their own developmental needs met. As in all other kinds of casework, it is important for us to be realistic about what we can and cannot do. Otherwise we may find ourselves making promises we cannot keep.

Treatment Emphases

In our experience, working with troubled single-parent families often requires attention to the following areas:

1. Generational Boundaries, Privacy, and Detriangulation

When a parent and child are enmeshed and overly reliant on one another, when there is either infantilization or parentification of a child, firmer generational boundaries may be required. Children may have to be helped to understand that they cannot be privy to strictly adult concerns. Children in some single-parent families carry significant responsibilities for providing practical and even emotional assistance to parents; when these assignments are age-appropriate, self-reliance and competence are often better nurtured than in two-parent families. Nevertheless, generational distinctions are essential. Adolescents who have been close to their single parents and are striking out on their own may need special support when they explain that certain aspects of their lives are now "off limits." It is common for children to be triangulated in various ways by separated parents; frequently children burdened by being in this position need help to get out of the middle. Some single parents need help to differentiate their children's feelings toward absent spouses from their own attitudes; children's experiences with and feelings toward their parents are necessarily different from those between unhappy spouses.

In the three-generational family with a single parent, especially a young one, the family therapist may help a grandparent move into the position of *consultant* to the parent; this can discourage a wholesale appropriation of the parental role. In some cases, triangulation of the children by the grandparent can be avoided by clarification of role definitions. Under the best circumstances, inexperienced single parents can receive important guidance from their older family members without being stripped of their own status as parent.

2. Grief over Losses, Completion of Unfinished Business

Commonly, as we have said, single parents and their children coming for help have not completed their mourning or resolved problems in relationships. There is often reluctance to go over past painful experiences, even though the lack of resolution may be contributing to the difficulties that brought them to treatment. Parents may believe they are protecting their children, or vice versa, by never discussing sad experiences. In some families, deaths, divorces, desertions, and institutionalizations have never been mentioned, yet the effects of these continue to fester, sometimes preventing individuals from going on with their lives. Family meetings can provide an opportunity for sharing sorrow and uncovering the meanings of losses to each member.[26]

3. Reflection on Realistic Hardships; Reducing Conflict, Blame, and Self-Blame; Supporting Strengths and Resiliency

In the next chapter we will discuss in greater detail how, as a group, separated and divorced women are far worse off financially than their estranged husbands. As we said, in at least 9 out of 10 cases, women are the custodial parents, and child support payments from fathers are often meager or nonexistent. Working full-time and keeping a home for youngsters without assistance from a partner can be extremely grueling. When possible, family treatment should be stretched to try to help estranged parents resolve conflicts between them enough to enlist assistance from the noncustodial parent in child rearing; ideally, the result would be practical help and relief for the resident single parent and emotional support for the children.

Single parents often blame themselves for feeling burdened or for being less than perfect; depression and guilt are common. Sometimes single parents view themselves as "defective" for not having a "normal" family. Recognizing and normalizing ("depathologizing") their situations can be supportive and bolster flagging self-esteem. Frequently they need help in appreciating their strengths, abilities, and successes as parents; they often do not give themselves credit for managing so well under difficult circumstances. By the same token, children may blame themselves for the family breakup. Or they may blame their parents for their deprivations. In family treatment they can be helped to see their situations in perspective. They can be reassured that they are not at fault for their parents' problems. Parent–child relationships are enhanced when children realize that the reason they are doing without many (material or other) benefits is not because their mothers are withholding from or punishing them. Children, too, need recognition for the responsibilities they carry that help to keep the family functioning successfully.

4. Supportive Networks and Resources
Because of the countless needs and strains experienced by many single-parent families, the caseworker often can help locate opportunities for the adults and for the children. Legal assistance may be needed. Self-help support groups can be found in many communities or can be sponsored by agencies serving single-parent families; a sense of community can be very comforting to isolated and beleaguered parents. Women's centers often provide a multitude of services of interest to single mothers. Day care centers, camps, and after-school activities may make significant differences in the children's lives and bring needed relief to parents. Economic hardships experienced by many single parents may ultimately be relieved by referring them to job training programs or other educational opportunities. Self-esteem, too, may be bolstered when single parents who have no marketable skills are enabled to become independent and respected members of the workforce.

Expansion of networks for children and for single parents often leads to a healthy differentiation of needs and activities that are appropriate to their various ages; in a natural way generational boundaries are strengthened. Due to their heavy responsibilities, or out of a tendency to be inordinately child-focused for practical and/or emotional reasons, some single parents need "permission" to seek adult companions that are special to them. Children who feel responsible for their parents' happiness may need encouragement to seek peer relationships. Treatment of single-parent families, especially those that tend to be insular, is often heavily focused on exploring new opportunities for every member.[27]

STEPFAMILIES

Space constraints make it impossible to discuss in depth a complex lifestyle that is on the increase: the step, "blended," or "reconstituted" family. By the year 2000 the number of stepfamilies was expected to be greater than the number of traditional two-parent families.[28] For additional information on this diverse and growing group, and on treatment considerations, the reader is urged to turn to references supplied in the notes.[29] Here we will touch on only a few of the central issues confronted by these families and by the clinicians who are attempting to help them.

In this discussion, the terms *spouses* or *marriage* can often be applied to many partners and relationships that are committed on an ongoing basis, even if no legal bonds exist. Gay and lesbian couples, too, are raising children; many of our comments here can also apply to these families.

Although the discussion that follows describes some of the challenges and difficulties that stepfamilies may face, we want to emphasize that many families find creative adaptations to their new family lives. Often, however, those who seek help need support and encouragement to address the many issues that can arise.

Special Issues

Significant Adjustments Are Required
Whether one person without children is married to (or living on a consistent basis with) a person with a child or children, or whether both mates bring children to the relationship, major adjustments are required by everyone involved. Additional complications can arise when the couple subsequently has a child together. In many cases, the children have permanently lost a parent—through death or desertion. It is not uncommon for children to have never met their real parent. Sometimes babies were conceived when the mother was very young and the relationship with the father was a brief one; casual sexual encounters are responsible for some births. In some stepfamilies, the children's real parents are both very much a part of the children's lives. In others, the nonresident parent—usually the father—is only peripherally involved, if at all.

Compounding Factors Some of what we said about single-parent families applies to step or combined families. In most cases, these families are *born of loss and disappointment*—if not conflict or rejection—

of some sort. The loss of a "perfect" first marriage or family, the loss of a dream, is often deeply felt. Problems can arise because families are trying to adjust to the addition of a new member or new members under difficult conditions, such as financial pressures, children with special needs, or lack of extended family or social supports. Often, family members have to deal with moving to new homes and changing schools, friends, and jobs. The normal stresses associated with the creation of a step or blended family can be compounded by a number of factors:

1. If there is extreme sadness or bitterness about the first marriage on the part of either of the original partners and these feelings impede the bonding of the new relationship.
2. If the children profoundly long for or idealize their real father or mother, who is dead, absent, or neglectful.
3. If the children have not accepted the breakup of their parents.
4. If there is competition between stepchildren and a stepparent for the affections of a parent or spouse.
5. If the children are placed in the middle of a hostile relationship between their parents and are conflicted about their loyalties or feel guilty for having a loving relationship with a stepparent.
6. If a parent and the children have had such close relationships before the addition of the stepparent that the latter is hopelessly shut out.
7. If any of the adults involved feel resentment about financial or visitation arrangements.
8. If generational boundaries are not clearly established or are either too rigid or too diffuse.
9. If the couple relationship is not caring and cooperative or is diverted by the many factors involved in the formation of a new family.

Unrealistic Expectations The stepparent is often faced with enormous pressures. To be immediately successful, they sometimes set themselves up for difficulties, if not failure. Stepmothers, for example (perhaps especially those who never had children of their own), may bring excessive enthusiasm for mothering: to finally have a chance to be a parent, to replace the mother who died, to be a better mother than the real mother (whom the father may criticize), to win her new husband's approval, and so on. When there is an expectation—by the real parent or stepparent—that the child will feel "instant devotion" for the new family member and this does not occur, disappointment, anger, and self-criticism can sweep over the entire family.

Stepfathers, too, can have unrealistic expectations. They may have the urge to rescue a family that has been bereft. They may feel they have to be the "strong" one or the "disciplinarian" in the family, often making it harder for the children to accept the "intruder," especially if the mother is torn between the wishes of her new husband and the complaints of the youngsters.

Conflicts for Stepmothers Some stepmothers are conflicted about taking on the responsibilities of children. They may want to please the new husband, yet feel cheated of time for the marital relationship. This can be particularly problematic when the children were not originally part of the "package" but subsequently came to live with the father and his wife. When the stepmother brings children of her own to the marriage, competition among the children can create tensions, which, if either fostered or not handled competently and cooperatively by the adults, can create tremendous family tension. Stepmothers who do not live with their husbands' children also face some of the same demands as those who do, even if not on an everyday basis.

Conflicts for Stepfathers When the stepfather's children are not living with the blended family, the father can feel resentful and/or guilty that he is spending so much time and energy on his wife's children. Often the mother and children have developed patterns of doing things in the home, and they resent any interference with their established routines. Marital conflicts may result. When the children treat the stepfather like an interloper, he may either become harsh toward the youngsters or withdraw from them, which may add to tensions between the couple. Financial stresses may develop: If a stepfather has children of his own, his wife may begrudge the money he has to give to the other family; a man who has never been married before may resent sharing his paycheck with a spouse, to say nothing of with children.

Implications for Grandparents Grandparents often have complicated roles when a stepfamily is formed. In some cases, grandparents were heavily relied upon for babysitting or financial help when the family was a single-parent unit. Some grandparents are glad to be relieved of these responsibilities when their daughter or son remarries, but others can feel displaced and deserted. Grandparents, like some stepchildren, may resent or feel threatened by the new family member and actively denigrate him or her. The parent may be torn between his or her parents and the new spouse; children may be forced into complicated loyalty conflicts that involve three generations. Remarriages of both parents can result in the children having eight sets of grandparents, requiring adjustments to the suddenly expanded network for all involved.

Combining Unrelated Children This can be very difficult in some families. Territorial problems often develop if there is a new need to share living and sleeping space.

Rivalry between stepsiblings can develop out of fear of losing a sense of "specialness" in relationship to one's own parent. Different backgrounds, styles, interests, rules, and ways of doing things make it hard for some families to feel comfortable when trying to blend together. Because of this or because of unresolved feelings about the loss of the original parent or family, children often overtly or covertly do what they can to break up the new family, sometimes in hopes of getting the old one back.

Other Assessment Considerations Because of the changes required by all members of newly constituted families, those involved may react in numerous ways. In some families, there may be *loss of position or role* (favorite grandparent, oldest or smartest child, for example) or of self-esteem. There may be *worry about losing relationships:* Children may fear their father will withdraw because the stepfather is in the picture; as we said, grandparents may feel discarded. Some parents who left a spouse to enter into a new relationship may feel particularly *guilty or vulnerable:* as a result they may be distracted or defensive at the very time so many demands are being made of them. Others are still reeling under *feelings of rejection* by the former spouse with children caught in the middle; *divided loyalties, pressures to join alliances,* or *fears of losing allies* are often at the root of the trouble. *Antagonisms and rivalries* can occur among members of the family or extended family.

We have mentioned many difficulties that can arise when step or blended families are formed. We want to say again that *large numbers of such families find creative ways to overcome the problems of adjustment and adapt in positive and loving ways.* In some cases, families feel an immediate benefit from adding a new member or members and make changes fairly comfortably. As dis-

cussed in various ways in this book, the *assessment of strengths*—competence, values, capacity for relationships, past successes, among many others—is essential to work with stepfamilies that feel beleaguered by the pressures of their new circumstances.

The assessment of the many kinds and levels of reactions that occur in stepfamilies may be less complicated than it seems. When evaluating any stepfamily, we recommend that special attention be given to two fundamental issues from which many of the difficulties usually spring.

First, it is important to remember that *at the bottom of a great deal of the trouble are sadness, hidden grief, and fear.* More often than not, difficulties are not primarily related to the actual characteristics of the members of the blended family or even to their idiosyncratic reactions to the new situation so much as to unresolved feelings. The family and the clinician together may need to try to uncover underlying sources of sorrow and apprehension.

Second, as is true in all two-parent families, assessment of the *strength of the spousal relationship* and the *quality of generational boundaries* is key to treatment planning.

Treatment Considerations

When stepfamilies find themselves in trouble, their problems are manifested in various ways, so it is impossible to be very specific here about treatment goals. However, we offer the following general treatment suggestions that we have found apply to work with many blended families:

1. Keep Focus on Process and Underlying Issues As in many other family situations, with an eye to timing, it is usually important to try to *transcend the content and capture the spirit* of many specific complaints. It is important to determine what particular issues are creating pain. Children, for example, may grasp at concrete matters (such as "I hate the way my stepfather sits around in his bathrobe," or "My stepmother doesn't cook good meals") to explain their distress when, in fact, they are struggling with grief, rejection, or fear. In family meetings, these feelings can often be tapped when the children become comfortable enough to express themselves. Adults, too, may blame children's behavior or minor idiosyncrasies of others for their unhappiness or worry. They may try to feel better by castigating former spouses. It is the therapist's job to seek to understand the more basic issues, including the hidden feelings that foster violations of generational boundaries.

2. Support Strong Spousal Relationship

As is true in the treatment of many two-parent families, a major theme of therapy of stepfamilies often involves helping a couple work toward a solid, loving, cooperative relationship; when this is achieved, other issues almost always become more manageable.

3. Foster Understanding about Diverse Reactions

It is often very important to help family members feel *less threatened about differences* of feelings among them. Many variations are inevitable when new relationships form. For example, children often need permission to express sadness over losing their own mother, particularly when the stepmother is being very kind and unrealistically hopes to "make up" to the children for their loss and help them to forget it. In some cases, ex-spouses are very angry at one another and pressure the children to feel as they do. In family meetings adults can be helped to realize that the children's relationships to their parents are not the same as those of the disillusioned former mates; the children's adjustments will be far more comfortable if their feelings and experiences are respected rather than opposed.

To reduce conflict and rivalry and to bring a warmer climate to the complicated relationships, grandparents can be part of the treatment. When their importance is acknowledged and their feelings of loss understood, bitter feelings about being displaced can be eased; in turn, the grandparents will then be less likely to try to enter into dysfunctional alliances with their children or grandchildren. Stepparents, too, sometimes need special understanding; for example, many need to know that it is natural to have feelings for their own children that they do not have (and may never have) for their stepchildren.

Although *very* careful assessment is necessary, there are some situations when it is extremely helpful to bring the former spouses, at times with their new spouses, together to facilitate the resolution of "unfinished business" and to work out differences about handling of the children. There is plenty of evidence that children are more likely to thrive when the adults in their lives work out problems between them, including separation problems. The children are helped in this process, and the new spouses often feel less threatened when their mates are not so intensely preoccupied, negatively or positively, with their old relationships. Sometimes, again after careful assessment, family meetings with former spouses can include children who are caught in the middle or who need some relief from the trauma of the breakup. In these cases it is important to make it clear to the children that the parents are not seeking reconciliation, as the youngsters often unrealistically hope, but rather are interested in working together to make life better for them.

4. Expose Myths Often it is essential to help stepfamilies confront and dispel myths.[30] While most people operate on some myths that are idiosyncratic to them, many stepfamilies are burdened with specific and recurring demands. Perhaps the major expectation is that there will be "instant love" among all members of a newly constituted family. As unrealistic as it usually is, stepchildren and stepparents often feel compelled to try to feel close to each other from the start. Stepsiblings are admonished to get along with one another, often without recognizing the need for time to adjust to the changes that have been thrust upon them. It can be relieving for newly constituted families to know that it frequently takes as long as two years for the members to feel settled down and emotionally connected, and that blended family life simply cannot be "perfect" from the outset.

In some families, the myth of the "wicked stepmother" still prevails, although it is our impression that with the increasing number of blended families, this notion is losing ground. However, just as children are often scapegoated for the problems that arise, so are stepparents of either gender. Family meetings can provide an opportunity to support the spousal relationships and diffuse the tendency to blame the "intruder" for the adjustment problems.

Related Issues

In therapy with stepfamilies, it is not uncommon to meet with subgroups in addition to or instead of meeting with the family as a whole. The new couple may need sessions to cement and keep their focus on the relationship; they usually have decisions to make about how to handle situations involving the children. A displaced grandparent may meet with his or her son or daughter to mend hurt feelings stemming from the change in the family structure. Stepsiblings may have sessions without the adults. And, as we said, former spouses may need to resolve old or ongoing conflicts.

This section would not be complete without mentioning problems concerning sexuality that are particular to stepfamilies. The air is often sexually charged because the new couple is in a "honeymoon phase"; sometimes they can be careless about ensuring privacy for themselves and protecting the children from overstimulation. When stepsiblings, especially but not exclusively adolescents, are thrown together, sexual excitement often follows, even though it may not be acted upon. Stepfathers and stepdaughters, stepmothers and stepsons can feel sexual attractions toward one another. Many clinicians observe that when there has been no bonding between adult and child when the latter is very young, sexual feelings are less likely to be repressed. Under serious circumstances, this reality can lead to sexual abuse of children in stepfamilies. More frequently, jealousies between spouses evolve, or adults become overly strict with the children in an effort to contain the feelings and counteract their impulses.

We conclude by emphasizing that in stepfamilies, as in most families, the adults must take the leadership and bear the burden for making many of the changes, even though it often is the children's symptoms that bring the families into treatment. When the adults resolve their own conflicts and handle their own relationships, old and new, they not only provide a happier climate for the children, but they also are better able to help their youngsters go through the pains and adjustments that accompany the breakup of one family and the formation of another. When stepparents, who are taking on the responsibility of raising children that are not their own, do not have the support and nurturance of their spouses, the entire family is bound to suffer. Much of the family work, therefore, must be directed toward the relationship issues among the adults.

It has taken two long chapters to present some of the basic theoretical and practical concepts required for engaging, assessing, and treating families. Research on family practice may be relatively sparse, but there are indications that family therapy can bring positive results (and is cost effective). These findings are consistent with the experiences of many clinicians who regularly work with families. Reports that the family therapy field is losing ground, in agencies and in training programs, deeply concern us; we fervently hope any such trends will be resisted.[31]

While we strongly favor family group treatment when it is indicated and feasible, we also emphasize the importance of family and systems perspectives in our work with individuals. Individual and family dynamics interplay. In our view and that of many others, a family perspective is essential in preventing or effectively and humanely intervening in the physical and sexual abuse of children;[32] too often in the past we have tried to "rescue" the young victims without fully considering family influences and strengths. As we have said very often throughout this text, whatever affects one part of a system necessarily affects the other parts to some degree. Positive shifts in a family's structure or climate can result in profound personality modifications of individual members. Changes in an entire family can occur after one member has been in treatment and makes changes. Because of this, we need not despair if we cannot gather the entire family. When possible—whether we are seeing one family member, a subgroup, or an entire family—we search for the most accessible as-

pect of the system, the part that will be most responsive to intervention.[33]

In the two chapters that follow, some of the principles already discussed will be expanded upon as we direct our attention to the assessment and treatment of couples.

NOTES

1. See Wetzel (1984), especially Chapter 2. As indicated in previous chapters of this book, often the combination of individual or conjoint therapy *and* medication is more effective than just one treatment or the other; see note 10 to this chapter.
2. Gurman and Kniskern (1981), p. 750; see especially pp. 748–61 for a generally encouraging review of albeit very limited research on the outcome of family therapies. The difficulties of conducting studies of complex family treatment and the shortcomings of current research so far are discussed in Alexander, et al. (1994); although there certainly are indications from research and practice that family therapy is often associated with positive results, outcome studies of psychodynamic approaches are still "almost nonexistent" (p. 619). Family therapy process and outcome research are discussed in some detail by Goldenberg and Goldenberg (1991). See also Santa-Barbara, et al. (1979) for a report of one exploratory study of brief family therapy with a large sample size that showed positive outcome results for over three-fourths of the families treated. Wells and Dezen (1978) discuss some of the problems of research, one of the important ones deriving from the diversity of treatment methods and approaches in family work. Sandra Anderson (1995) also cites research that suggests that those receiving family treatment show positive results compared with control groups who receive other treatments or no treatment; furthermore, family therapy is more cost effective than individual therapy.
3. See Wynne (1965), Ackerman (1966), Offer and VanderStoep (1975), and Scherz (1966).

See also Leader's (1981) interesting article for a discussion of the importance of establishing connections between presenting problems and family conflicts and of determining how these connections guide the therapy.

4. Sherman (1966), p. 369. Zilversmit (1990) discusses the point that despite recognized benefits of young children attending family sessions, often they are excluded; she encourages including them and suggests approaches to engaging them. See also Frager (1985) for a discussion of acting out as a response to, and an attempt to repair, systemic dysfunction.

5. Mitchell (1968), p. 75. See also a pertinent article by Wechter (1983).

6. Minuchin, et al. (1967) described treatment of families of boys referred to a private residential treatment center (Wiltwyck School for Boys), most of whom lived a considerable distance from the institution. See also the volume edited by McFarlane (1983) for several very good articles on the involvement of families in the care and rehabilitation of mentally ill family members. Of interest, too, is Eda Goldstein's (1979) report of a study of young adult inpatients that strongly suggests the importance of parental involvement in the treatment process.

7. Sherman (1979), pp. 471–72.

8. Joseph Walsh (1989) discusses the fact that it can often be very effective to engage the family, in which there is often conflict among members, of a client who has recently had a schizophrenic break; support, assistance with relationship issues, and psychoeducation can make a difference to the family and help the client to restabilize. Of course, once the acute episode is over, the family and client may meet in sessions together. See also Walsh (1988) on the role of social workers in educating families about schizophrenia. See also Marley (1992).

9. Wynne (1965), pp. 321–22.

10. See Klerman, et al. (1994) whose review of research reports: "Interpersonal therapy is reported to be more effective for endogenous depression in combination with medication than is either treatment alone" (pp. 760–61). See

also the study by Weissman and Paykel (1974) in which all of the 150 moderately depressed women studied responded favorably (i.e., experienced some reduction of symptoms) to a period of four to six weeks of drug therapy; social adjustment (not affected by medication) was enhanced by those who received weekly psychotherapy in addition to drugs.

11. Many beginning family therapists have found very useful guidelines to conducting the initial interview provided by Haley (1987), Chapter 1. See also Patterson, et al. (1998), Chapter 3; and Stierlin, et al. (1980).

12. Gurman and Kniskern (1981), p. 751.

13. See Dyche and Zayas (1995). See also Chapter 1, notes 36, 37, and 38 for helpful references on constructivism, narrative therapy, the empowerment approach, and related perspectives.

14. For discussions of some of the attempts to develop classifications or nosologies of family disorders over the years, see Scherz (1966), Ackerman, et al. (1967), Wertheim (1975), and Greenberg (1977). See also Framo's (1982) informal scheme for classifying marriages, pp. 202–3. See also Chapter 14, note 17.

15. See Framo's (1982) chapter, "Marital Therapy and Family of Origin," p. 199.

16. Ibid., pp. 199–200.

17. An excellent beginning effort to use the Hollis typology was made by Ehrenkranz (1967) in her exploratory study of joint marital treatment. See Hollis (1968) who also studied joint interviews. The findings reported by both, however, were based on small samples and, as they indicated, further refinements of the typology would be required to study the many dimensions and complex interactions found in multiperson interviews.

18. See, for example, Haley (1987), pp. 125, 176, 198–99, and 228; and Minuchin (1974), p. 14.

19. See Briar and Miller (1971), pp. 191–92. We are often asked about the possibility of such dangers, but the literature does not seem to address the matter often.

20. Pittman (1977), p. 2.

21. Whitaker, et al. (1965), p. 335. See also Framo (1982), pp. 194–98, and Stierlin (1975).

By becoming more differentiated in their relations with their own families of origin, family therapists can learn to develop greater objectivity and less reactivity toward their clients. For readings on this, we recommend Carter and Orfanidis (1976), Rich (1980), and the very useful volume edited by Titelman (1987).

22. Anderson and Stewart (1983), pp. 25–26. Napier and Whitaker (1978) are among a few who have refused to see a family unless every member is present; Anderson and Stewart (1983), in a book we recommend, take a somewhat more flexible approach to addressing resistance on the one hand and accommodating the family's anxieties on the other.

23. For readings on single-parent families, see especially Morawetz and Walker (1984), Howard and Johnson (1985), and Kissman (1991).

    For readings on single fathers, see Greif (1987), Greif and Demaris (1990), and Nieto (1982). Greif and Bailey (1990) reviewed the major social work journals over a 27-year period and found very few articles on fathers; of those they found, many there viewed the fathers negatively. We recommend Cochran's (1997) review of the literature from 1986 to 1996 on African American fathers; in the same issue Greif updates the earlier review and indicates that more articles on fathers have appeared in the nine years since the 1990 report; see also Chapter 86 by Greif on lone fathers in Turner (1995). See Wade (1994) on African American men and their sons. See Kruk (1994) for a report of research on the disengaged father (half of noncustodial fathers gradually lose all contact with their children); implications for social work are discussed.

    For a good article on clinical practice with urban African American families with a case example of a single-parent family, see Wright and Anderson (1998). See Teyber (1992) on helping children cope with divorce.

24. See Satir (1983), especially Chapter 5.

25. For references on teenage pregnancy and parenthood, see Chapter 6, note 4.

26. See the very helpful volume edited by Walsh and McGoldrick (1991) on death in the family.

27. See a very interesting and positive report of a study by Olson and Haynes (1993) on the dynamics of successful single parenting. We recommend Chapter 7 of the excellent book by Walters, Carter, Papp, and Silverstein (1988) on single-parent, female-headed households.

28. Kheshgi-Genovese and Genovese (1997), p. 255; the authors review the literature on the spousal relationship within stepfamilies and underscore the importance of a strong couple relationship.

29. See especially the book by Visher and Visher (1988), which is extremely useful for clinicians working with stepfamilies. See also a good book by Wald (1981). See also Kent (1980) and Stanton (1986). Rosenberg and Hajal (1985) discuss stepsibling relationships. Kelley (1992) studied well-functioning stepfamilies and concludes in contrast to those in treatment, stepfamilies in general are not necessarily problematic; she discusses some characteristics of healthy functioning stepfamilies.

30. See an excellent article by Schulman (1972) on myths that intrude on stepfamilies.

31. See Sandra Anderson (1995). An editorial in the December 1997 issue of *Family Process* indicates that there is concern in some quarters that "the family therapy field is in danger of losing its vitality and excitement" (p. 323).

32. Selected references relevant to children who have endured physical and/or sexual abuse and to their families include: Kim Anderson (1997), Dietz and Craft (1980), Elbow and Mayfield (1991), Fatout (1990), McInnis-Dittrich (1996), Mennon and Meadow (1994), Ostbloom and Crase (1980), Pardeck (1990), Peck, et al. (1995), Roth (1975), Silvern and Kaersvang (1989), and Ronald Taylor (1984). See also John Taylor (1990) who discusses various underlying issues that may contribute to incestuous behavior. See Chapter 10, note 9 for readings related to family violence.

33. In addition to references cited in this chapter and in Chapter 14, readers may find the following readings relevant to the further study of the practice of family therapy. From various perspectives, the references address assessment, intervention, training and research, and an array of presenting issues.

We particularly recommend two volumes of special interest to family therapists: Minuchin, Colapinto, and Minuchin (1998) on working with families of the poor, including families in which children are or may be placed in foster care, residential centers, and psychiatric facilities. The volume edited by McGoldrick, et al. (1989) on women in families; among other issues, several chapters address gender issues in family therapy, including hidden attitudes toward women's roles in traditional family theory.

See also: Abbott, et al. (1995), Anderson, et al. (1979), Aponte (1979 and 1986), Boszormenyi-Nagy and Spark (1973), Cates (1990), Farley (1990), Goldner (1985), Group for the Advancement of Psychiatry Committee on the Family (1996), Imber-Black (1988), Ingersoll-Dayton (1988), Jacobs (1990), Kagan and Schlosberg (1989), Kobat (1998), Kuhn (1990), Laird (1995 reprinted in Franklin and Nurius, 1998), Leader (1979

and 1983), Maluccio, et al. (1998), McGoldrick and Gerson (1985), McMillen and Rideout (1996), McPhatter (1991), Meezan and O'Keefe (1998); Minuchin, et al. (1978), Papp and Imber-Black (1996), Schibuck (1989), Shapiro (1994), Shernoff (1984), Sussal (1992), Taynor, et al. (1990), Unger and Levene (1994), Weick and Saleebey (1995), Weitzman (1985), Leonard Woods (1988), and Ziegler and Holder (1988).

For a practical guide to family therapy, with case illustrations and specific, detailed suggestions, see the book by Boyer and Jeffrey (1984).

We include here selected readings on cultural and class influences as they relate to family intervention. Of particular interest is Boyd-Franklin and Shenouda (1990) on a multisystems approach to treatment of an inner-city family. See also Boyd-Franklin (1989) on black families in therapy. See also Carter (1997), Falicov (1995), Hines and Boyd-Franklin (1996), Pearlmutter (1996), Robinson (1989), Shapiro (1996), Streier (1996), Weaver (1982), Zayas and Bryant (1984), and Zayas and Palleja (1988).

The reader is directed to two practical texts on family therapy techniques: Minuchin and Fishman (1981) and Griffin (1993).

CHAPTER 16

COUPLE TREATMENT: PROBLEMS IN RELATIONSHIPS

Joint interviewing of couples is an aspect of almost every clinical social worker's function. This chapter will discuss the psychosocial casework approach to marital therapy. It includes brief comments about the evolution of the psychosocial approach to marital therapy; some assessment and general treatment considerations; a typology of couple relationships and problems; and discussions of unique concerns of "nontraditional" couples, of women, and of marriages in which there have been extramarital affairs. Using case illustrations, Chapter 17 will address specific treatment issues and approaches. While the treatment of couples has been discussed in various places in this text, we include these two chapters to focus on additional intricacies of this modality.

It should not surprise us that at the very time the institution of marriage is believed to be in serious jeopardy (when approximately one-half of first marriages and over 40 percent of second marriages end in divorce),[1] more and more people are seeking professional help to understand and mend their marital relationships. Even though presenting complaints brought to family agencies, mental health clinics, and protective and other services have always included marital unhappiness, treatment of marital problems often evolved only *after* children's symptoms were explored. In recent years, however, parents seem to be more aware of the effects their marriages have on the emotional well-being of their children; as a result, children may not be required as frequently (as unconsciously they sometimes are) to be "passports" for troubled parents getting help. As we have illustrated many times, generally, when the adults take care of their relationships, life for all members of a family is enhanced.

Couples with or without children, separated and divorced couples concerned about the ongoing destructive effects of their conflictual relationships on their children, unmarried people of all ages who are living together, gay and lesbian pairs, couples interested in premarital counseling, others looking for "enrichment" and solutions to "midlife crises" or "empty-nest syndromes"—*all* are frequently seen by social workers in various kinds of agencies and clinics and in private practice. In these two chapters on couple treatment, even when we use terms such as *marriage, marital relationship,* and *spouse,* our discussions usually can apply to nontraditional as well as traditional couples.

THE EVOLUTION OF THE PSYCHOSOCIAL APPROACH TO MARITAL THERAPY

Like family therapy, couple therapy has roots in the casework tradition.[2] However, the emphasis on psychological matters in the 1920s, followed by the increasing influence of psychoanalytic ideas in the 1930s, tended to lead social work practitioners to work primarily with individuals and favor seeing marital spouses separately, even when marital difficulties were a major treatment focus.[3] In her book published in 1949, *Women in Marital Conflict,* Hollis wrote:

> If treatment is to go beyond environmental support and clarification, if it involves extensive use of psychological supportive processes, and particularly if insight development is contemplated, it is more economical and effective in the end *for each person to have his own worker* [emphasis ours]. Otherwise much time and effort will be dissipated in dealing with rivalry and misunderstanding created by attitudes toward the common worker, tremendous care will have to be taken to avoid and straighten out misquotations, and the worker will face a difficult task in establishing himself as both sympathetic and impartial in the minds of both clients.[4]

Some professionals, including social workers, still hold these notions today,

often for the same or similar reasons. However, it is now our opinion that for many, if not most, couple difficulties, joint interviewing proves to be the most effective approach. Many of the reasons we gave for conjoint interviewing in the chapters on family therapy (when the "indications" as summarized on pages 404–8 favor it) apply to work with couples. When spouses are seen separately, the complexities of the bond between them cannot be as effectively assessed or addressed as when it is *observed in vivo* by couple and worker together. We will say more about this later, especially in Chapter 17. As we shall also discuss there, joint interviewing requires the worker's *involved impartiality* (discussed in Chapter 15); we now believe this is not only possible, but also essential in couple and family therapy (and even in individual treatment).

Contraindications to conjoint couple therapy do exist, however, and are similar to those that apply to family sessions (see pages 408–10). There are situations in which separate interviews or different workers may seem to be the wisest approach for a particular couple. Also, as discussed in Chapter 15, when a member of a family or couple is unavailable or refuses to participate in treatment, shifts in the family or marital system can be fostered by changes and efforts made by one member in individual treatment.[5] Hollis made this point in her 1949 study on marital conflict, more than a decade before systems concepts as such were introduced into casework or mental health thinking:

> The writer . . . would definitely not agree with those who take the position that it is impossible to help in marriage conflict unless both partners are willing to participate in treatment. Many cases in this study demonstrate the opposite—that a change in one partner may in itself decrease the total con-

flict or even go further and *bring about a responding change in the other person involved.*
[Emphasis ours][6]

Over the years, our clinical experiences
have substantiated one of the basic premises
of current psychosocial and family therapy
practice: If one person changes, all others in
emotional relationships with him or her are
likely to make compensatory changes.

MULTILEVEL ASSESSMENT

In Chapters 2 and 14 we discussed our rationale for integrating systems and psychodynamic approaches in casework with individuals and families. Couple work represents a
subtype of family therapy, so, from the psychosocial point of view, the same reasoning
applies.[7] Familiarity with the basic psychodynamic and family concepts and approaches to assessment and treatment procedures covered in previous chapters will
provide the reader with a foundation for the
material presented in these two chapters on
couple treatment.

Framo, whose point of view is often consonant with ours, wrote: "In treating a couple one must consider that there are three
patients: the husband, the wife, and the relationship." Marriage therapy, he goes on,
"not only deals with the intrapsychic dynamics of each spouse but also examines
the interlocking nature of the marital bond."
[Emphasis ours][8]

Psychosocial therapy with couples considers the assessment of the *personality
characteristics of each partner* (including
personality development, ego functions,
strengths, and psychopathology) as described in previous chapters. Assessment is
made of the *quality of the relationship;* the
clinician seeks answers to questions such
as: What is the emotional climate or nature
of feelings between spouses? What projection processes are apparent? Is there coop-

eration or competition between spouses? Is
there a sense of fairness and equity or does
one partner seem to dominate another? Systems and family concepts discussed in detail in Chapter 14 (homeostasis, circular interactions, differentiation and enmeshment,
roles, communication patterns, secrets and
myths, and others) guide the assessment of
marital processes as well. Past and present
family-of-origin influences are often very
significant to couple interaction. As in every
kind of psychosocial practice, relevant cultural and environmental factors are evaluated. *Strengths and capacity for resilience of
the individuals and of the relationship are
assessed as carefully as are the problem
spots.* None of these areas is any more important than the others, even though interventions may focus on one level more than
another at a particular time.

The Power of the Marital Bond

Joan and Bill, married for 12 years, were
referred by Family Court for psychiatric
evaluations and social work treatment
following charges and countercharges of
physical and verbal abuse. Both had endured extraordinarily deprived child-
hoods. In addition to meeting DSM criteria for alcohol abuse, Bill was diagnosed
as having an antisocial personality disorder. Joan was believed to have a histrionic personality disorder with paranoid
feature. Seen first in individual and then
in couple treatment by a social worker in
a spouse abuse service, the interlocking
nature of the marital transactions became apparent. Briefly stated, when
Joan thought (often accurately) that Bill
was lying to her or seeing other women,
she would write letters to various members of his family accusing him of wanting to poison her. Particularly after bouts
of excessive drinking, Bill would respond

by assaulting her and they would engage in treacherous physical battles. The destructive pattern between them was so entrenched that they did not respond to casework efforts and the marital balance (or homeostasis) was maintained; the couple's children, who were constantly triangulated in the cross fire, were placed in foster care for their protection. Only after Bill was killed in an automobile accident a year later was Joan (who voluntarily returned to casework treatment) able to disentangle herself sufficiently from her enmeshment with Bill (as well as from members of her family of origin) to begin to embark on the work of self-differentiation. Even though the couple's motivation or capacity for change had not been sufficient before Bill's death, and the power of the marital bond had seemingly prevented movement on the part of either partner, subsequently Joan successfully built on the work involving her own issues that she had only just begun while Bill was alive.[9]

In this case, the caseworker assessed individual behavior and marital processes that were complexly intertwined. By the time Joan and Bill were married, each had already internalized many self-defeating behavioral and emotional patterns and poor self-esteem; ego capacities, including thought processes, judgment, and object relations, were unevenly developed. Subsequently, the marriage itself, with its own destructive patterns, blocked efforts either made to improve or to terminate their relationship.

When Joan's suspiciousness and Bill's defensive aggressiveness became part of the marriage, these along with other individual qualities interacted to form new and repetitive *marital* dynamics. *Interactional processes always go beyond the inner lives and behaviors of the individuals,* taking on a life of their own.

We emphasize the need for multilevel assessment and intervention because the power of the interactional phenomena is frequently overlooked, especially by practitioners and theoreticians primarily rooted in personality and intrapsychic theory. For example, to our amazement, Christopher Dare's search of the papers published in the three most influential and prestigious psychoanalytic journals found them "noticeably lacking in even passing references to marriage as an important feature of people's psychological life." Over a 10-year period, Dare found "no articles on marriage, although there are copious references to other family dyads; no extensive accounts of psychological features or causations of marital relations; and only passing references to the fact that many of the people represented in case histories, so extensively reported, are married."[10] How *troubled marriages derive from and yet also transcend the personalities of the individual partners* is a major emphasis of these chapters on couple treatment.

Enduring Personality Characteristics

While marital interactions have a powerful influence on the behaviors and emotions of individuals, enduring personality qualities also have a profound impact. As discussed more fully in Chapter 2, important influences on personality occur at very young ages. The nurturance of the relatively autonomous, self-reliant personality requires two basic conditions of "good enough parenting": (1) consistent parental availability, responsiveness, and support; and (2) age-appropriate encouragement of the child's independence and self-direction.

Absence of either of these can result in the child not internalizing an independent, stable concept of self, which can impair the capacity for relating to others. Many of the clients we see with personality disorders, including Joan and Bill, have come out of backgrounds of inconsistency, neglect, or overprotection. Mate selection is often made on the basis of a felt need to "complete" oneself and to bolster self-esteem.[11] Unfortunately, destructive marital patterns often emerge and further incapacitate rather than strengthen the individual personalities. When spouses look to one another to feel "whole," they usually place more of a burden on the relationship than it can handle.

On the other hand, marital dysfunction can be seen as a desperate attempt on the part of both partners to *solve* psychological conflicts. The couple's troubles or an individual's symptoms may call attention to marital disappointment or disillusionment. They may be viewed as a cry for help or drive for health, a constructive perspective that diminishes blame and offers hope. As we shall see, at its best, *the marital relationship can also become a force that heals,* a nurturing environment in which spouses can provide one another with "corrective" experiences.

SPECIAL ASSESSMENT CONCERNS

Marital and Individual Dynamics Interact

In couple treatment, understanding and intervening require attention to the following interpenetrating points:

1. Changes in Marriage Relationships Bring Changes in Individuals When shifts occur in the marital system, the behavior and inner lives of individuals also change. For example, when a man makes positive changes requested by his wife—such as spending more time at home, participating more with the children, becoming more interested in sexual relations, and so on—the wife actually may become indifferent or uncomfortable or may articulate a

new complaint (sometimes to the surprise of the inexperienced worker). Between spouses there is often an "agreement" about the degree of distance or intimacy to be maintained; thus, when one person makes a move, the other adjusts to maintain the accustomed balance. Along similar lines, when a partner who has had the role of "pursuer" withdraws, often the "distancer" begins to approach the former pursuer. When an alcoholic spouse stops drinking, it is not uncommon for the other one to become depressed. When the "weak" partner dies, we often find that the "strong" one breaks down. In a sense, the couple may become "one self," with each partner (whether apparently so or not) dependent on the other to feel "whole."

A spouse who takes on the role of "rescuer" usually requires a "helpless" mate to fend off fears of unworthiness, disapproval, or abandonment; the mate who "agrees" to be rescued, out of fear may disown his or her own strengths to assure the spouse's attachment and concern. In this case, if the "rescuer" begins to resent and resist the burden of taking care of his or her spouse, or the "rescuee" makes moves toward independence, one can expect a reaction on the part of the other to bring back the status quo. The actions of one spouse are both cause and effect of the behaviors and feelings of the other. Like the chicken and egg, cause and effect are inseparable.

2. Personality Features May Change According to Context Despite pressures to pinpoint clinical diagnoses, we must recognize the influence of the immediate social context as well as the abiding personality traits. Feelings, attitudes, and actions of each spouse (and even the quality of the marital dynamic itself) can be viewed as accommodations to the conditions under which they exist, within and outside the marriage. For example, in the case of Bill and Joan described above, Joan was unable to make moves toward self-improvement during her marriage; the marital interactions were greater than the personalities of both. Yet after Bill died she could develop new, more satisfying ways of leading her life by addressing long-standing personality issues of her own. A man may be labeled "impulse-ridden" or "aggressive" because of the manner in which he torments his wife but is described as "mild-mannered, well-disciplined, and hardworking" on his job. The wife in this marital situation may suffer from "depression," and it is only after she is working at a job in which she feels competent and valued that feelings of cheerfulness make her realize that her "depression" is situation-bound.[12] When the context changes, symptoms or certain so-called character traits may also change.[13]

3. Individual Change Alters the Marital Relationship

One spouse in therapy, without the participation of the other, can become a powerful intrusion on the marital system. When a relationship is faltering or even when there are no immediate complaints about the marriage, individual treatment may be an important contributing factor to its dissolution. The woman mentioned above learned that when at work and away from her husband, she did not feel depressed; without marital sessions she might have left her husband, never exploring the possibilities for change in their unhappy relationship. In another case, a woman who sought treatment for discontent with many aspects of her life developed a strong, positive transference to her male therapist, idealizing him to such an extent that her husband compared very unfavorably in her eyes. She ended her marriage. Had there been joint sessions, the transference to the therapist might not have emerged so powerfully and the issues *between the spouses* might have been addressed instead. In the next chapter we will discuss the issue of transference in couple therapy.

(We usually urge involvement of both spouses at the beginning of treatment, even in cases where the presenting complaint of an individual appears unrelated to the marriage. Alerting the couple that sometimes there are important repercussions on the relationship when only one partner makes changes may encourage both spouses to engage in the therapy. They are then in a better position to make informed choices.)

4. Individual Symptoms Often Interrelated with Marital Process

Taking the above points a step further, if an individual's symptoms are assessed as arising totally from intrapsychic issues, important opportunities for helping may be overlooked. Neurotic conflicts or developmental deficits may not explain a person's behavior, attitudes, or feelings that on first glance seem very personal. In our experience, most complaints presented by married clients are powerfully influenced by the marital relationship; the difficulties of one spouse, to some degree, are lived and acted out in combination with the other. It follows, then, that symptoms are often most effectively addressed in the context of the marriage.

An Analysis of Cases of Phobias

In this connection, Woods has studied in her own clinical practice more than 16 married women, from diverse racial, ethnic, and class backgrounds, suffering from phobias and anxiety attacks. In each situation the husband was asked to participate (sometimes puzzling or even annoying the wife who was usually sure that her marriage had no bearing on the problem). When the husband joined the treatment, each case experienced symptom relief for the wife and improved marital functioning. Before the husband's participation (or in rare instances when husband, wife, or both refused to be seen jointly), much less progress occurred.

The majority of these were marriages in which there was no threat of divorce and where there was mutual caring and general concern for one another. However, a common pattern was revealed: The husbands, while extremely concerned about their wives' welfare (often to the point of taking on the role of "rescuer"), tended to display little emotion and talked very little about themselves. The wives, particularly after becoming symptomatic, were often quite emotive: tearful, "hysterical," or angry. Yet, like their husbands, they seldom addressed their hopes or disappointments about their lives and marriages. Neither the husbands nor the wives seemed able to speak or make requests directly to their partners. In terms of intimacy, all led lonely lives. It can be speculated that the women's symptoms were, in part, communications, unconscious attempts to draw their husbands closer.

There were some dramatic moments when the men began to express themselves and take "I" positions in sessions; almost without exception the women showed signs of relaxation, some almost immediately, others eventually. Even when the men were expressing complaints or concerns about the relationship that they assumed their spouses would not want to hear, the wives soon were more gratified than threatened because they felt closer and less alone. In nearly all of these situations, the women indicated that they realized they had felt lonely (and sometimes "crazy" for being unhappy when they had such good mates). It was important to them to know what their husbands thought and felt. The men, most of whom had been trained to discount their inner lives, were amazed at how much more

they began to enjoy themselves and their marriages once they had their secret or disowned "real" selves revealed and understood by their wives. As Loewenstein said: "The need to be understood can be as urgent as the need for self-understanding."[14]

A Case Example: Phobic Symptoms and Couple Treatment

After an unsuccessful course of behavioral therapy, Barbara, age 33, came to a clinical social worker for help with anxiety and phobic symptoms that were seriously curtailing her activities. She was constantly terrified that she would have a panic attack; when one occurred, she had acute fears of death. For over a year she had been unable to drive a car or leave her house unless her husband, Al, was with her. She was so preoccupied that she could not give first-rate attention to her two young children.

Family-of-Origin Relationships As is often true of people with these symptoms, Barbara had not successfully separated from her family of origin. She came from an enmeshed family in which family members did not deal directly with one another and yet all were intricately intertwined. Barbara and her mother spoke on the telephone several times a day about how to help the father and younger sister with their problems. Barbara was the "good" girl, in contrast to her sister who was "bad," "difficult," and "selfish." She was very much involved in trying to mediate her parents' marital problems. It was also expected that she should take inordinate responsibility for the care of grandparents and for rescuing her sister from one predicament after another. Barbara did not protest her family's expectations and vehemently disagreed with the worker's suggestion that her symptoms might be a reaction to the heavy responsibilities she carried. It was almost impossible for her to claim, at least directly, any needs or wants of her own. She had a martyred demeanor, often self-righteously complaining that it is the "good" ones—of whom she saw herself as one—who suffer. Her sister, she grumbled, had no disabling symptoms despite her self-absorption. Barbara was extraordinarily sensitive to criticism, especially if she thought it challenged her selflessness. She saw herself and Al as among the very few who care about others.

Couple Treatment Begins   Only after several individual sessions was Barbara even willing to consider having Al join the treatment with her. She "owned" her own symptoms and resisted the notion that her husband had any part in them. She seemed to fear that she might "rock the boat" of her marriage, which she convincingly described as loyal and committed. Gently but repeatedly the worker suggested that solid relationships such as her's and Al's can have powerful healing powers; rather than emphasizing problems, the worker framed her recommendation in terms of the strengths of the marriage. Because of the acuteness of her symptoms, Barbara finally agreed to bring Al to sessions.

In his family of origin, as the oldest child, Al had the role of the "strong, silent" one. Apparently he had gotten the message from his parents that he would be most admired and loved if he was self-reliant and helpful to others. Rarely was he aware of his own wishes or feelings. Al's demeanor was matter-of-fact, not overtly warm, yet he was extremely helpful to Barbara and showed genuine concern for her, which, on the surface, she seemed to take for granted.

The therapeutic work was slow. Individual and interactional styles were firmly set. Barbara and Al were not open to the suggestion that—other than Barbara's symptoms—there were any individual,

marital, or family-of-origin concerns they needed to address. Meanwhile, Barbara's phobias were becoming more pervasive and paralyzing; they finally became serious enough to upset the delicate, yet heretofore stable, balance of the marriage.

A Breakthrough Comes   Al played an important role in the breakthrough that occurred. After many months, rather than just presenting himself as a helper to Barbara, he cautiously began to express some of his own feelings. At first he spoke of his resentment about the negative effect on their children for the entire focus of the family to be on Barbara's problems. Barbara, always verbose, began talking more and more rapidly, seemingly trying to drown out Al's remarks. For a brief period, Al retreated from speaking for himself. However, during one session Barbara, who habitually spoke for Al, mentioned that he did not mind how often she and her mother spoke on the telephone. Flushed and furious, Al uncharacteristically exclaimed, "I've had enough!" and stormed out of the office. The following week he dropped Barbara off but did not come in. He returned for the next appointment and was able to tell her how neglected he felt by all of the attention and caretaking she required. Furthermore, he told her that he thought he ranked fourth with her: after her family, the children, and her "damn fears." At first Barbara attacked Al and tried to discredit his complaints, but he doggedly persisted. He announced that he was "on a roll" and this time could not be stopped.

It took only a few weeks for Barbara to accept what Al was saying. She went on to admit for the first time that she had always feared that she was not "good enough" in his eyes, just as she never felt "good enough" to her family where so much attention went to her sister.

At last the work could begin. Both Barbara and Al realized that they had not paid much attention to their own feelings and needs. She was oppressed by the unending demands of her family of origin and her inability to be of any lasting help to them. He was constantly trying to come to the aid of Barbara, and though he kept doing more and more for her, her symptoms got worse. Barbara began to be less self-righteous, talking about herself instead of about others and what they needed or "should" do.

Barbara and Al Begin to Claim Their Own Feelings and Needs   As treatment continued, both Barbara and Al benefited tremendously from learning how to speak for themselves. They discovered that they would not be unloved or abandoned even if they spoke from the depth of their own (negative or positive) feelings. They recognized how, when both "sold their souls," they continually reinforced their loneliness and underrated the potentials in their relationship. They declared that they would not allow themselves to be "swallowed up" by external demands ever again and agreed that their marriage would become a primary priority. By the time treatment terminated, two years after it began, Barbara's symptoms (which may have had some physiological as well as psychosocial basis[15]) had greatly diminished and both were pleased with their enriched, more openly tender relationship in which there was genuine give-and-take between them for the first time.[16]

In *all* marriages, intense, interlocking dynamics transcend the inner lives of the individuals. But, beyond that, it is not uncommon for two (or more) people in close relationships to make often unconscious, unspoken "bargains" whereby they collusively carry out psychic functions for one another. By disowning his own needs, Al provided Barbara with attention she could never get from her family of origin. By becoming phobic, Barbara gave Al the opportunity to repeat the role he played with his parents, as

the helpful, self-reliant one who placed no demands on others. The whole *is* greater than the sum of its parts!

The results of spouses carrying psychic functions for each other, even unconsciously, often are relatively harmless and sometimes may even supply comfort to both partners; a benign "complementarity" may develop. For example, spouses may intuitively provide each other with the kind of affection that "makes up" for earlier emotional deprivation; under the best of circumstances, old sorrows are dissipated.

But it is a different matter when people discount their own needs to keep their part of the bargain. As illustrated in the case of Al and Barbara, trouble often develops when people believe, consciously or unconsciously, that they have to bury or disown important aspects of themselves: feelings, thoughts, values, or purposes. They can become symptomatic or unhappy, angry, confused, hopeless. Their marriages, at best, leave each wanting in some way. When we speak of facilitating autonomy or differentiation, we are talking about helping people to claim themselves and develop those hidden or unevolved parts that were compromised out of fear of losing love or of being overwhelmed. In couple therapy, therefore, not only is the opportunity for self-understanding offered, but also *being deeply understood by the people who count the most* (and this should not mean therapists!) can be one of the most meaningful outcomes. This potential is not intrinsic to individual treatment.

A TYPOLOGY OF COUPLE RELATIONSHIPS AND PROBLEMS

Some writers and practitioners have attempted to classify marital problems, but their emphases differ and they don't agree on a single typology.[17] However, some very distinct types of marital conditions that may significantly affect treatment goals and strategies have been identified. Some of these are revealed at the outset; others emerge as treatment evolves. The factors that influence the course a marriage takes are complex and not always clear, to the couple or the worker. In this section we will present an informal breakdown (or rough classification) of some types of dilemmas that frequently emerge when clients come to couple therapy; it is based on our experience, and its purpose is to provide possible guidelines for assessment and treatment.

Several factors should be kept in mind concerning the somewhat arbitrary divisions of our classification:

1. They frequently overlap. That is, a couple's situation may straddle two or more categories.
2. They may describe marital situations in which there has been *chronic* distress or dissatisfaction. Or, conversely, the marriage may be in *crisis,* mild or acute.
3. They are applicable whether a couple has sought treatment voluntarily, is in joint therapy because of concern about a symptomatic child, or has been mandated by the court or protective services to get help.
4. Consideration must be given to *strengths and healthy adaptive features* of the relationship as well as to dysfunctional and "pathological" aspects (intelligence, talents, emotionality, honesty, ability to empathize, flexibility, resiliency, lack of extreme defensiveness, etc.). Though not always specifically mentioned here, such positive qualities significantly affect treatment and must be assessed. As discussed several times previously, it is usually helpful to worker and clients to think in terms of building on strengths rather than eradicating pathology.[18]
5. In some instances a category may suggest the degree of severity of the prob-

lem, but usually is *not* a reliable predictor of the difficulty of the treatment or of the outcome; some troubles seem relatively minor and yet yield very little to therapeutic efforts; other serious relationship problems may be remarkably susceptible to changes.

6. Along similar lines, some individuals who seem deeply disturbed nevertheless have successful marriages, while others whom we would not diagnose as having significant psychological problems are involved in painfully destructive relationships.[19] In these latter situations, interactional patterns usually become the major focus of attention.

The categories of couples and their relationships seen in casework treatment include:

1. Essentially Solid, Committed Relationships with Minor Dysfunctions

Whether newly formed or long-standing, these usually require relatively small shifts or adjustments to alleviate the difficulties. In some instances, an educational approach brings significant relief. This may involve assistance with communication skills, universalization (helping the couple to realize that many others experience the same or similar difficulties), provision of information or guidance around crises or "expectable" life cycle transitions, and an examination of the stresses and tasks often associated with these. Many couples in this category are minimally defensive and are able to reflect on their situations and on their patterns of interaction, often making significant improvements quite quickly. When better understanding is achieved, empathy for one another may come naturally. It is not unusual for these couples, with the worker's help, to design "homework" derived from new perspectives and "tools" gained in treatment. Gains made between sessions can be rewarding and can reassure the couple that it is not the worker who is ultimately responsible for the improvement they are enjoying. Dick and Susan Jones's relationship, described in Chapter 3, belongs in this group.

There are couples in this category with rigid personality traits and/or interactional patterns, who make changes surprisingly slowly despite a high level of emotional differentiation and capacity for caring and understanding. The changes they *do* make usually "stick," but there may be many sessions in which nothing seems to happen. For other couples enrichment of the marriage is a primary goal. In our experience it is futile and antitherapeutic to insist on brief treatment or a fixed number of sessions just because the couple is essentially healthy and stable; if there is dissatisfaction with the status quo and motivation for change and growth, couples should not be penalized by impatient workers, unbending agency requirements, or managed care constraints because treatment is taking longer than someone thinks it should.

2. Couples Stressed by Life Cycle Transitions Difficulties may be associated with:

- The adjustment to a newly committed relationship.
- The shifts—in the couple relationship, and in job, financial, and other lifestyle arrangements—mandated by parenthood.
- The changes required, often by the mother, when the last child is ready to go to school.
- The tribulations induced by children moving into adolescence.
- The strains placed on the couple by the deterioration and death of aging parents.
- The change to being alone for the first time in many years after the "children" become young adults and leave home.
- The planning for retirement.

- The adjustments required by stresses imposed by the later years, including physical deterioration, concerns about illness, and death.

All these natural events in the couple's life require accommodations.[20]

Some major factors that influence the successful (or unsuccessful) adaptation of the couple to new life phases and circumstances are:

- The nature of social system supports such as socioeconomic status, employment and housing conditions, effects of social attitudes about sex roles and parenting, etc.
- Extended family relationships: the extent to which members of the couple differentiated from, or are severely enmeshed with, their families of origin. Are in-law relationships strained? (See category 7 for further discussion of extended family issues.) Along similar lines, are there culturally supported family attitudes that facilitate, retard, or distort life cycle transitions? For example, does closeness with families of origin (versus enmeshment), fostered by some cultural or family traditions, ease parents' burdens during difficult transitions of their children or does it contribute to conflict?
- Overall level of marital or couple functioning, such as stability of the relationship; competence at communication, negotiation, resolution of conflict; flexibility; level of differentiation; capacity for caring and empathy; degree of trust and intimacy.
- Personality qualities, such as ability and maturity, autonomy, resiliency, capacities for initiative, compromise, and optimism.

3. Couples in Which There Is One Symptomatic Partner When the symptom is of the "acting in" variety (energy is turned against the self), such as in depression, extreme "nervousness" or anxiety attacks,

phobias, compulsivity, and even in addictions, it is often the symptomatic one who seeks individual help. In these cases, the client's partner may willingly become involved. Some others do not want or see the need to participate in treatment. Still others volunteer as a collateral and try to help the spouse or the therapist.

When one spouse has symptoms, as we have said, it is usually most effective to have both partners join the treatment, at least in the beginning. Individual sessions can always be planned later. In the case of Al and Barbara, it became clear that Barbara's seemingly individual symptoms were significantly influenced by personality features of both partners and unrevealed strains in the relationship. Joint meetings became the most efficient treatment modality.

When the symptom is one of "acting out" or is in some way more conspicuously interactional in nature and consequence (sexual or physical abuse, violent rages) it is often the asymptomatic spouse or some outside agency worker who arranges for help.

In some situations, when spouses of individuals with acting-out symptoms apply for help, it may be difficult, although not impossible, to encourage couple sessions. Understandably, the symptomatic ones can feel defensive or assume they will be blamed by the worker as well as by their mates. While every effort should be made to include both partners, in severe situations of spouse abuse or other antisocial behaviors, the spouse may be too frightened to meet in joint sessions. (Each case of spousal abuse has to be individually assessed.) Also, the asymptomatic spouse may want help to become more self-directed and less reactive. Practical as well as psychological aid may be required for the spouse to get out of the "victim" position, with or without the relationship.

Couples with specific, sometimes severe, types of sexual dysfunction (e.g., premature ejaculation, inability to ejaculate, or so-called frigidity) belong to this group. Frequently the partner having the difficulty comes for help. Occasionally medical factors or truly functional disorders are involved; these should always be explored. Like phobias, symptoms often reflect overt or covert relationship issues and are diminished when the problems are exposed and addressed.

4. Chronically Conflictual Relationships   In these there is usually more bickering and disagreement than fulfillment. Quarrels are not necessarily limited to one issue. Usually, they address a wide range of topics, such as money, sex, child rearing, the sharing of responsibilities, how to deal with jobs, in-laws, and so on. Clinicians have come to realize that frequently the resolution of a presenting issue does not settle the marital distress (and, when it does, the relationship probably belongs to category 1). Settling one matter often uncovers another. In couple treatment, it becomes apparent that the dysfunctional interactional *process* is entrenched, and the function of particular, often interchangeable, *content* complaints is to maintain the status quo. Successful treatment requires attention to issues that are often concealed and reach beyond specific areas of discontent. Therefore, these often joyless—even if committed—relationships may be better understood and treated when viewed in the light of the categories that follow.

5. Relationships in Which Avoidance Is a Way of Life   When a spouse is "work-addicted," is a substance abuser, has an affair, or is so absorbed in the children, friends, family of origin, or outside activities, often there is little opportunity to nurture the relationship or to deal with dissatisfactions. Sometimes, bringing the feelings and attitudes of both spouses out in the open induces positive changes and reverses the pattern of avoidance. In other cases, as with conflictual relationships just discussed, the underlying problematic issues may be illuminated by referring to categories that follow. (Some couples *do* live comfortably when each spouse is deeply involved in individual activity and time together is limited. As we said in Chapter 14, families can fall within a wide range between the extremes of disengagement and closeness, or even enmeshment, without feeling distressed or being viewed as dysfunctional.)

6. Couples Strained by One or More Extraordinary External Pressures
War, unemployment, natural disasters, insufficient money, racism and all kinds of discrimination, unavailability of decent housing or safe living conditions, necessity of living with in-laws, chronic illness of one partner or other close family member, premature deaths: These are only a few of the many possible outside impingements that can seriously affect the quality of a love relationship.

Negative attitudes from society and/or extended family about intergroup marriage or homosexuality may also seriously strain a couple's relationship. (When such negative reactions reflect family emotional processes—such as lack of differentiation— instead of value differences, then category 7 may be more relevant. We shall also discuss these problems in more detail in a later section of this chapter: 'Nontraditional' Couples.")

Sometimes practical assistance and concrete services can alleviate difficulties flowing from external pressures; help with mourning may be required; or intergenerational sessions can address issues involving the extended family. In some situations, the caseworker may take on the role of advocate in some of the various ways described

in Chapter 8. In all cases, the chances for relief are best when spouses react to external pressures by working with rather than against one another.

7. Couples in Which There Are Dysfunctionally Enmeshed or Otherwise Disturbed Family-of-Origin Relationships
Many family therapists agree that when spouses have not successfully separated from their original families (that is, when they are unduly dependent or conflictual), they are usually not well differentiated in their nuclear families either.[21] In these cases, loyalties,[22] or attachments for whatever reasons, to extended family members may be more powerful and compelling than the bonds between the spouses. We often find that generational boundaries are blurred. As Framo commented, these spouses have "never really left home."[23] Complaints and jealousies about in-laws are common in these relationships.

Lack of differentiation from families of origin is a frequent treatment issue: Sometimes the ties binding the generations are complex, but sometimes rather easily resolved when the couple relationship is strengthened. In the Russo family (see Chapter 15), Mrs. Russo's relationship with her mother was one factor retarding the marital relationship; by the same token, Mr. Russo's sadness about his early family life diverted his energy from feelings toward his wife. When the couple worked on some of the difficulties between them, intergenerational difficulties diminished. Understandably, Mrs. Russo's mother's relationships with all members of the family subsequently improved; they were closer than ever, but not as enmeshed. When Al and Barbara, described earlier in this chapter, made improvements in their marriage, Barbara defined her relationships with members of her family of origin much more clearly. As discussed in the family therapy chapters, enmeshment is often accompanied by a high level of anxiety; when family members are poorly differentiated, they may fear engulfment or abandonment. Under these circumstances, triangulation is common; the Russo family included several examples of dyads that involved a third person in order to reduce stress and maintain the balance of the relationship.

Of course, "emotional cutoffs" (i.e., refusal to associate with some member or members of the families of origin) are as symptomatic of lack of differentiation as are overinvolvements; they are opposite sides of the same coin because they both arise from emotional intensity (rather than indifference) toward extended family members. Again, fears of rejection or fusion usually prompt the individual's efforts to avoid the interactions. Extreme reactivity reveals lack of individuation. In one case, a woman in her 60s had not spoken with her only sister, with whom she had been extremely close in childhood, for 40 years, purportedly because of a relatively minor misunderstanding at her own wedding. When she reflected on this in therapy, she began to realize that it had been "easier" for her to make a sharp break in anger than to bear the inevitable separation brought about by her marriage. Ironically, some of the marital problems she had had over the years arose in large part from unresolved feelings about her sister. (Some adults drift away from parents or siblings, having little contact with or connection to them; sometimes these individuals have come to peace with their vacuous or "dead" family-of-origin relationships, in which case they need not be thought of as "unresolved"; in these cases, they may find they are able to find greater fulfillment with other people.)

Unfinished business with families of origin can seriously impact a marital relationship in many ways. For example, a husband who has not separated comfortably may feel compelled to stop off at his mother's house for dinner before coming home to his increasingly angry wife. If a wife teams up with her mother (perhaps out of a need to please or appease her) to denigrate her husband, he will undoubtedly feel like an outsider and become more and more hurt, angry, or depressed. This was the situation in the Russo family. When husbands or wives have cut off or have been cut off by their parents, the unresolved grief, anger, and longing can overload the marital relationship. Often one spouse places unrealistic demands on the other in hopes of compensating for "lost" parents. The quality of the marital relationship of a spouse's parents—even if it is negative—can powerfully influence that person's expectations of marriage and ways of interacting, especially if there has not been much differentiation from the parents.[24]

As indicated in category 2 on page 459, important events in the lives of extended family members inevitably and naturally affect the marital relationship to an often considerable degree. A father's death, a mother's illness, a sister's divorce, a brother's alcoholism: all can negatively burden the marital system. On the other hand, couples sometimes are able to grow closer, on their own or in treatment, in the face of distress in extended families.

When there are identifiable complications arising from relationships with families of origin, we may recommend family-of-origin meetings.[25] And, as we shall soon see, sometimes these are suggested even when the intergenerational influences are not so immediately apparent. These sessions may be held with an individual and his or her original family, without the spouse attending. The presence of the "outsider" (the spouse) may constrain or distract the work, providing an opportunity to resist differentiation of relationships between the generations, a difficult enough task without the addition of inhibiting forces.

8. Couples in Which Projections and Irrational Role Assignments Are Negatively Affecting the Relationship

Dysfunctional roles, attitudes, emotional styles, and behaviors are expected and imposed on one another. (The reader may want to review pages 394–97, where introjection, family projection, intergenerational processes, and related concepts are discussed.) In an almost uncanny way, each spouse induces in the other behaviors and attitudes that correspond to introjects from the past, usually derived from perceptions of parent figures, but sometimes siblings or others. Repressed object relationships are re-created in the relationship with the marital partner. Experiences of roles, rules, and "programming" from the family of origin may be introduced into the marriage.[26] Clinical experience supports the conclusion that when individuals are insufficiently differentiated, they often want to avoid aloneness at all cost; they will, therefore, reproduce these emotionally familiar, sometimes hurtful, situations that connected them to their original families. For example, a woman who as a child felt criticized and undervalued by members of her original family may subtly invite negative judgments, contempt, or condescension from her husband. The man who felt overly depended on or suffocated by his overprotective mother may encourage his wife to pursue him, as his mother did, but if she does so he may push her away.

People often marry products of their fantasies, with little regard for the spouse's actual ability to meet demands placed on him or her to fulfill an idealized image. In such instances, disillusionment is bound to come.

People can marry their worst—rather than their ideal—fantasy or induce behaviors that guarantee their negative expectations will become self-fulfilling. In clinical practice and in life we have all encountered individuals who feel deprived or offended by circumstances others would consider trivial. In treatment it may be revealed that these people never had experience at defining what they want or negotiating for it, and thus they feel disappointed. Often these individuals seem almost driven to project their own negative expectations onto their marital relationship.

In some cases, mates have been chosen who have qualities that will be positively nurturing. Under the best of circumstances, as we have said, such marriages can provide each partner with a "*corrective*" experience. In various ways the relationship actually can "make up" for original parenting experiences, even in cases where the individuals have been emotionally deprived or abused. As many marital and family therapists know, good marriages sometimes provide the basis for a healing experience, introducing relationship gratifications never before experienced. However, when the mates are unconsciously locked into rigid, repetitive, collusive interactions based on negative introjects or unrealistic expectations, problems in the relationship are part of an *intergenerational transmission process* and are perpetuated by the projection of the internalized past onto the present.[27] The case of Al and Barbara illustrates this point.

In clinical practice we frequently see how spouses assume for themselves and imbue their mates with many kinds of roles in order to feel safe. For example, to carry on the role of "caretaker" or "hero," the spouse must try (often unconsciously) to induce dependency or neediness in the other and view him or her as "weak." If a woman learned to gain her parents' attention by acting "confused" or "hysterical" (albeit the attention was ridiculing and controlling), in her marriage she may repeat the same behavior and elicit the same results. For every "martyr" in a marriage, there must be a partner who is seen as abusive, irresponsible, uncooperative, or distant.

Similarly, it is not uncommon for couples to promote connections that are held together by the familiar "glue" derived from family-of-origin experience. Some families, and subsequently couples, maintain a sense of connection through worry (e.g., telephoning each other very frequently to make sure "everthing is all right"). Insults and teasing are often used by family members to touch base with one another and these behaviors may then be brought into marriages. Depression or pessimism sometimes becomes the predominant feature of a family's climate and, when transported to the couple's life, results in endless complaining, sullenness, perennial "victimization," or some other demoralizing behavior. Certainly angry interactions and even abuse, as painful as these are for the members, can become the "adhesive" for families and couples. These methods for maintaining relatedness are often passed down over many generations.

When losses in the original family have not been mourned and resolved,[28] not only is it difficult to bring full commitment and emotional energy to current relationships, but also introjects, either idealized or loathed, may be brought into the marriage. A woman, whose father deserted or died when she was young, may find ways in her marriage to reexperience the familiar feelings of longing, so familiar to her as a child; she may either encourage her husband to be distant or she may be so immersed in the old feelings that she cannot absorb his affections. The man whose mother cast him in the role of "stand-in" for his father (living and unavailable or dead) may be particularly anxious about marital intimacy, for fear of being smothered or overly relied upon once again.

It is fortunate when adult children have the opportunity to deal with introjects from the past by addressing their relationships with their parents in the present. Frequently, as we said, marital partners recognize that the difficulties between them are not as powerful as family-of-origin issues, however buried these latter may be. Often with the explanation and encouragement coming at first from the couple's therapist, enmeshment, "emotional cutoffs," unresolved losses, guilt and overresponsibility can be most effectively addressed directly with parents. When it is possible to have sessions with extended family members, the problems and the projections that have been transferred to the marriage can be dealt with in the relationships where they originated. In our experience this can bring immediate benefit to the marriage.[29] When such intergenerational work is not possible, couple treatment can still provide opportunities to understand families of origin in new ways, as will be demonstrated in the case of Tom and Kathy Brent discussed in Chapter 17.

9. Second Marriages that Introduce Special Difficulties for One or Both Partners If a previous spouse has died, there may be unresolved mourning, preventing a full commitment to the present relationship. Jealousies can be felt when the first relationship is unfinished for whatever reason. As discussed in the section on stepfamilies in Chapter 15, rivalries may arise when, for example, the biological father has continued involvement with his children living elsewhere, creating stress between the mother and stepfather. Situations involving stepchildren can strain new relationships. Second marriages follow failed or lost relationships and can be constant reminders of the precariousness of the marital union. In troubled second marriages, whatever the other problems, help is often needed to come to peace with the past, strengthen trust between partners, and solidify the new family relationships.[30]

10. A Variety of Couples Who Share What Some Clinicians Refer to as "Calcified" Marital Styles Generally, these do not bode well for successful marital treatment. In some instances, separation or divorce therapy may evolve as the agreed upon goal. In perhaps the majority of cases, even though deep unhappiness is felt by both partners and solutions seem to be out of reach, there is inability, reluctance, or refusal to consider separation. Often couples in this mixed group have attempted various kinds of treatment, all seemingly to no avail. Some have been referred as involuntary clients because of the repercussions their disastrous interactions have on other family members, particularly children. Relationships in this category may be distant and more or less "dead" on the one hand or chronically vituperative and vicious on the other, with the couple caught in repetitive, deeply destructive interactional cycles. Others can be loveless or "brother-sister" arrangements that disappoint one or both of the spouses. Although some of these marriages are long-standing, others may be relatively new but equally unmovable. When improvement seems impossible and separation is not seen as an option, sometimes the individuals can be helped to find satisfactions in other aspects of their lives—in their jobs, activities, friendships, etc.—with the added result that the disagreeable aspects of the marital relationship may be somewhat diminished.

11. Couples in Which One Spouse Wants to Leave the Relationship and the Other Wants to Save It Marital therapy is the effort of last resort. Sometimes joint meetings last a very short time, just long enough for the one who wants separation to get courage, "permission," or justification to go ahead with it. "Often," as Framo says, "the partner who is finished with the marriage would like to exit from the therapy and leave the partner with the therapist."[31] When one spouse has firmly closed the door on the marriage, frequently his or her affections have shifted to a new lover. Divorce therapy may follow the initial phase of treatment. Fairly often the rejected spouse continues in individual treatment to deal with the repercussions. Occasionally, the marriage gets a second wind and the relationship can be modified and enhanced.

Special caution on the worker's part may be required while working with couples in this category. When pained by the disappointment of the spurned spouse or when concerned about effects of a breakup on children, the worker may try too hard to help resurrect a marriage even when the spouse who wants to terminate it continues to show no motivation for working on it.

12. Marriages That Are Coming to an End by Mutual Agreement If casework help is sought, it is usually to address the problems involved in separating. Divorce therapy or mediation has gained prominence in recent years;[32] in some therapeutic circles it is viewed as a specialty requiring additional training and certification. Issues such as money, property, custody, and arrangements for the children are part of divorce. Some couples, concerned about escalating battles when lawyers become involved, prefer to try to negotiate these matters in a therapist's office. Such negotiations can be difficult because the problems of communication, negative and entrenched behaviors, projections, and individual personality problems that defeated the marriage in the first place may equally thwart the best-intentioned efforts to end it without rancor.

When it comes to difficulties in intimate relationships, too often history repeats itself. Individuals who blame the marriage or the other spouse for their unhappiness find the same distortions, projection processes, and negative behaviors recur in new contexts. In our experience, the most hopeful outcome for these couples occurs when both spouses are willing to examine the problems that destroyed the relationship; they are then better able to mourn their losses, let go of each other and of the dreams that brought them together, and go on to the next phase of their lives. If each partner is able to identify his or her particular contributions to the problems, future relationships and choices of mates may result in happier experiences. Even when it initially seems that interactional habits and feelings of hurt and anger would preclude serious work in therapy, sometimes spouses *are* able to find constructive ways to say farewell to each other and to begin to heal from disappointment.

"NONTRADITIONAL" COUPLES

Committed love relationships, regardless of lifestyle or sexual orientation, have more similarities than differences. Yet some do have special characteristics. The ones we shall mention here are premarital couples, unmarried pairs living together, cross-cultural relationships, and gay and lesbian couples. These categories may overlap: One could have as clients two lesbian lovers, from divergent cultural backgrounds, trying to determine if they want to live together.

Premarital Relationships

Customarily, two people planning to marry—equally committed to one another and experiencing no major difficulties in functioning or in the relationship—have sought "premarital counseling" (if they sought it at all) from pastoral advisors, family doctors, self-help groups, and the like. For the most part, they have not gone to marital therapists.[33] In the throes of anticipating marriage—with passion and optimism at a peak, when no distress or symptoms are apparent—preventive measures are not usually a high priority. Couples who do go to therapists for premarital counseling are often in their 30s, with one or both members having been married before.[34] With some notable exceptions, clinicians who do couple work have not developed interventive approaches to relationships *before* trouble comes. Certainly this is an area of *prevention* that requires more attention than it gets from clinical social workers.[35]

Premarital treatment usually covers particular areas. As is true of married couples, each pair is unique; each has special concerns and priorities. Repetitive patterns are usually not as entrenched as they are with couples who have been together a long time. Yet, whatever the presenting issues are, *person–situation reflection, pattern-dynamic reflection,* and even *developmental reflection* are often required; in premarital treatment, as well as marital therapy, enhancing awareness of self and other may be a major goal of the work.

Several overlapping areas commonly emphasized in premarital therapy include:

1. Communication and Interactional Styles and Skills   Learning early to make self-defined, clear "I" statements instead of "you" or "we" statements, especially during important discussions about the relationship

or in efforts to resolve conflicts, may avoid many later misunderstandings and disappointments. More open emotional expressiveness may be required to facilitate some significant communications. When each partner learns how his or her verbal or nonverbal behavior affects the relationship, positively or negatively, compatible styles of interacting can be established in the beginning, before dysfunctional patterns emerge.

2. Respect for Differences   Too often couples, especially those coming from enmeshed families or those who subscribe to the romantic notion that "togetherness" means that thoughts, opinions, and feelings are identical, are afraid to admit and accept dissimilarities.

3. Mutual Disclosure and Discussions Regarding Values, Attitudes, and Basic Emotional Requirements   This includes matters such as needs for distance and closeness, dependence and independence. Frankly shared statements from each can educate and prepare the other about important expectations. Becoming aware of and realistic about one's exaggerated visions of the role the other will play (e.g., "He will be able to save me from myself," or "She will be able to take care of me") is often an important focus of premarital treatment.

Encouragement from the couple therapist may be essential here. Many idealistic—often but not always young—people preparing for marriage underestimate the importance of their own individual views and, in their excitement, are all too willing to put them aside. Or else they are reluctant to be straightforward about some facets of themselves for fear that their future spouses will disapprove. Those with low self-esteem may be especially afraid that if they reveal too much about themselves they will no longer be loved. Couples will find that they must

learn to compromise on various issues; but negotiations cannot occur until they begin to speak honestly.

4. The Need to Develop Methods for Confronting Inevitable Changes, Crises, or Conflicts   There are no marriages without outside pressure and inner strife; when these occur, loving feelings can be overshadowed by anxiety or frustration. Evolving flexible means for coping with life's transitions and ordeals can help couples approach these events with more confidence and less fear.

5. Open Discussions about Sexuality in General and Expectations of Their Own Sexual Relationship in Particular   Obviously the direction this work takes will depend on whether or not the couple has been sexually active. How comfortable or sophisticated they are about sexual matters will also influence the premarital work. Some couples, even those married for many years, have never had *any* open talks together about sexual likes and dislikes, worries, difficulties, etc. The knowledge that such sharing is *normal* and *essential* can be preventive.

6. The Transition from Family of Origin to the Nuclear Family   Premarital treatment provides an opportunity to begin to cement the bond of the upcoming marriage while constructively separating from parents. At best, these shifts are lovingly achieved. When couples do not establish boundaries differentiating them from their extended families and defining what their relationships with the original families will be, the marriages may be plagued with conflict and stress. Couples from different backgrounds or with particular personal preferences will draw the limits differently; the critical point is that the boundaries should be unambiguously established, yet open enough to develop or maintain comfortable intergenerational relationships.

The areas described above often require intense attention from troubled couples who come for treatment later in the marriage. Optimally, many unhappy situations can be avoided through premarital exploration.

Unmarried Couples Living Together

This is a broad and varied group. It includes young premarital couples at one age extreme and on the other elderly companions who have reasons for not marrying, such as protection of social security or other benefits or fear of disapproving relatives (some adult children find it hard to believe that older people still desire sexual and romantic relationships!). Over the past 30 years there has been a dramatic increase in the number of unmarried couples living together.[36]

This divergent group brings to therapy many of the same dilemmas presented by married couples. Yet, there are some differences. Examples of unmarried couples seen by caseworkers include, among others:

1. Live-in Relationships That Are Truly Transitory These would include college students or people temporarily assigned to work in geographical areas away from home. Despite the absence of commitment, emotional involvements may lead to problems around unplanned pregnancy, dependency, or separation. Concern about AIDS and other sexually transmitted diseases has stimulated caution in many about casual sexual liaisons.

2. "Trial Marriages" to Determine Whether the Relationship Will Survive under One Roof According to some experts, there is no firm evidence that living together before marriage decreases the risk of divorce.[37] In these situations when discussions about marriage have reached a stalemate, on the part of one or both partners, or when problems similar to those found in married relationships arise, professional help often is sought.

3. Couples Unable to Marry Because One or Both of the Members Are Already Legally Married Divorce may be difficult or impossible because of financial reasons, the disappearance of a spouse, or a spouse's confinement in prison or a mental institution. Differential assessment is required in working with these couples. In some cases, the unmarried status is not a problem to either member; unrelated issues prompt them to seek treatment. In other instances, when legitimizing the relationship is a concern, the worker may help the couple to obtain legal help to learn about their rights and options. When it is compatible with the goals of the couple, the caseworker can assist in the resolution of practical and emotional issues needed to dissolve previous unions. (Along similar lines, because of immigrant status, marriage may not be possible; in these cases, too, the worker can try to help the couple find legal solutions.)

4. Couples to Whom Commitment Seems Risky Again, if neither member is uncomfortable about the legally uncommitted arrangement, this situation will not be the presenting problem. But sometimes couples come for help to overcome fears about marriage. Quite commonly a pair living together will seek therapy specifically because one member is beginning to press for marriage and the other is resisting it. If this is the true problem, brief treatment may resolve the matter. The reluctant one may be helped to overcome apprehensions, or the person seeking permanency may realize that he or she will have to look for it elsewhere.

In some cases, there is an unexpressed (often unconscious) pact between them: One "agrees" to express the ambivalence while the other claims to be ready to plunge into marriage. Yet, when one changes his or her position, the other will then take the opposite side. The work in therapy is for each partner to "own" his or her particular ambivalence, to resolve it, and then to decide for or against commitment. The importance of working through indecision is underscored by the repeated complaints of many married couples coming for help who feel that their relationships were far more satisfactory when they were living together than after they married. When fears of intimacy (of engulfment, entrapment, rejection, or abandonment) underlie ambivalence, defensiveness may significantly increase almost immediately after the wedding.

5. Couples Comfortable with Their Status but Pressured by Parents or Others to Marry Some parents are ashamed or morally offended; others are eager for grandchildren. Some may express simple disapproval, while others use punitive financial or emotional strategies to try to force marriage. Resolution requires differentiation from families of origin and a redefinition of the couple's relationships as adults to their parents. The couple may need help making independent decisions despite parental objections. The choice not to marry may be more related to leftover rebelliousness or reaction to parental control than to philosophical or emotional attitudes against getting married.

6. Couples in Which There Have Been Previous Marriages, Particularly Those with Children Too often, either because of the bitterness of the former spouse or attitudes of the children (possessiveness, loyalty to the other parent, or some combina-

tion of these) the new live-in relationship is scapegoated by the former family. Family meetings with the parent and children may provide an opportunity to resolve the difficulties so that the new love relationship is not destructively triangulated. Some of the difficulties encountered by stepfamilies (see Chapter 15) may apply here. Issues from previous marriages, intertwined with early family influences, can affect current relationship troubles.

7. Gay and Lesbian Couples So far, in the eyes of the law, these couples are unmarried and subject to particular pressures and conditions. These will be discussed later in this section.

Cross-Cultural Relationships

Over the years, much has been written in the literature of social work, sociology, and related fields about the stresses experienced by couples whose members have different ethnic, religious, or racial backgrounds. Failure to understand one another or to appreciate each other's values and lifestyle, identity struggles, disapproval of family and friends, and outright social discrimination are among difficulties some cross-cultural couples encounter.[38] Some research has suggested that ethnically mixed couples are more likely than others to get divorced, have personal problems, and experience difficulties with extended families and children.[39]

Increase in Cross-Cultural Relationships Nevertheless, the rate of intermarriage in the United States is triple the rate it was in the early 1970s. Until 1960, intermarriage by Jews was less than 10 percent, but estimates now range between 41 and 52 percent. Intermarriages by Hispanics have doubled since 1970.[40] Over 40 percent of all children born to an Asian or Pacific Island parent have a white parent. Even the least common and among the most stigmatized of intermarriages—those between people of color and whites—more than tripled over two decades from 1970 to 1991.[41] As Crohn says, "All of these transformations make it much more difficult to tease out the influence of an individual's cultural history."[42]

Marriages between Hispanics, or between Asians, or between African Americans, can bring two *very* disparate cultures together when the spouses come from different countries or from different parts of their country of origin: To the outsider, for example, an African American man from the rural South wedded to a woman born in Jamaica may not appear to have "married out," but the partners may find they have to accommodate many dissimilarities in culturally based attitudes and behaviors. Thus, the number of cross-cultural relationships is even greater than the statistics show.

Varied Degrees of Difficulty Encountered in Cross-Cultural Relationships

"Generally," write McGoldrick and Giordano, "the greater the difference between spouses in cultural background, the more difficulty they will have in adjusting to marriage."[43] In an article we highly recommend, McGoldrick and Preto[44] present several factors they believe influence the degree of adjustment required by cross-cultural marriages. They conclude that the more similar the values (e.g., between Puerto Rican and Italian mates in contrast to Irish and Italian), probably the less difficult the adjustment will be. Great differences between spouses in acculturation (such as between fourth- and first-generation immigrants from the same country) can lead to misunderstandings. When religious as well as cultural backgrounds are not alike, possibilities for disharmony

may be increased. Class differences, too, not uncommon in cross-cultural couples, add to the complexity of cross-cultural marriages.

Family-of-Origin Attitudes and Influences

Troubles experienced by cross-cultural couples are frequently believed to be strongly influenced by the negative reactions of families of origin, especially parents of the spouses.[45] Disapproval, refusal to "permit" the marriage or to attend the wedding, and "emotional cutoffs" (some of which last for years) can strain the relations. A son or daughter in an enmeshed, insular, or autocratic family may marry outside his or her culture to try to gain emotional distance or independence. The choice of spouse may serve as an expression of anger and defiance. The young person who has been "chosen" by the parents to be triangulated (or dysfunctionally overinvested in by one or both) may be the very one who intermarries as the route for confrontation or escape.

In an important—to some, controversial—article, Friedman, who has had extensive experience with intermarried couples, argues that cultural differences are often used as "cultural camouflage."[46] Parents may claim their objection to a mixed marriage is based on practical, philosophical, or religious concerns, when the disapproval actually represents an effort to avoid facing emotional processes in the family. At times of stress, differences—cultural or other kinds—can become the focal point and hide the true concerns in the family. For example, the young adult who has been important in maintaining the marital balance of his or her parents (usually, according to Friedman, the oldest or only child) is the one from whom the parents find it hardest to separate. Obviously, the greater the difficulties the parents have in letting go of the triangulated child, the more intense the pressure on him or her, and the harder it is for that child to leave home. Often, the more intensely entangled, the "further out" the young person will marry (e.g., interracially as well as interreligiously). As Friedman says: "More powerful circuits need more powerful circuit breakers."[47]

The Power of Social Attitudes The broader social context, in addition to the extended family context, in which the intermarried couple functions can tip the balance of the relationship. We suspect that the relationship between Susan and Dick Jones (see Chapter 3) would have been in much more trouble had they not had such supportive families or had lived in a less benign community. The interplay between the marital system and other systems can support or be devastatingly destructive to the fabric of the marriage. Ethnocentrism, racism, and other forms of bigotry in the community, in schools the children attend, or in the workplace can place heavy demands on the couple's emotional resources. When intolerance isolates the couple, realistic distrust of others can result and the spouses can begin to blame themselves or each other for their unhappiness. Self-esteem and the capacity for rebound can be severely battered.

Assessment and Treatment Issues As for every couple coming to the attention of the caseworker, appropriate intervention requires careful assessment. When therapists treat cross-cultural relationships specific issues must be taken into account.

Ultimately, *it is only the spouses who can construct the personal meanings of their cultural heritages and the influence the differences between them have had on their relationship*. The clinician cannot make that determination; however, he or she may enhance the clients' awareness of the power of ethnic factors by showing gen-

uine interest in their backgounds and by exploring and listening closely to the history of their relationship.

When differences are a problem within the relationship, we can often help couples understand and even value these instead of taking them personally. McGoldrick and Preto wrote: "Just as understanding family patterns, the role of sibling position, and life cycle stages is important for couples, so is understanding the impact of ethnic differences."[48] When those in a cross-cultural relationship recognize that difficulties between them—such as about how emotions are expressed, gender roles are defined, children are disciplined, extended family is involved—derive in large part from differences in tradition and background, they often begin to view their spouse's attitudes and behaviors less defensively and in a new light.

In cross-cultural unions, *it is important to determine whether cultural differences are contributing to relationship distress or whether exaggerated or inaccurate assumptions are being made by the worker and/or the clients*. Often, stresses within the relationship or pressures from outside have been major factors in their current circumstances; attributing them to cross-cultural influences may result in oversimplification or stereotyping. For example, destructive interactional cycles, one partner's phobia, a miscarriage, substance abuse, or employment problems may have profound effects on the relationship that cannot be accounted for primarily—if at all—by the intermarriage.

Along the same lines, *when a couple is troubled, the difficulties may be strongly, mildly, or not at all influenced by the varied backgrounds or by family and social reactions to the marriage*. In clinical practice we are less likely to see those intermarriages that are working successfully than those that are stressed or unhappy. In the case of

Dick and Susan Jones (Chapter 3), for example, racial differences played an insignificant part in their relatively minor difficulties; in-laws on both sides did not have intense negative reactions to the marriage and the couple's two children appeared to be unusually well adjusted. The family lived in a somewhat integrated rural area and reported that they had experienced very little discrimination in general and practically none in their immediate community, schools, and workplaces. From the couple's perspective, as well as the worker's, the issues that contributed to the crisis they faced were not basically attributable to cultural influences.

On the other hand, *many people who intermarry are placed under enormous stress because of family or social attitudes toward them.* In addition to helping such couples recognize what has happened, and *validating their sense that they have been victimized,* caseworkers often can provide encouragement and information about self-help groups and organizations in which mutual support and opportunities for socialization with others facing similar difficulties can be found. In some cases, meetings with a partner and his or her family of origin can foster new understandings and/or more loving connections. In other instances, *the worker can become an advocate* for the couple or family that has been discriminated against by employers, landlords, teachers, or others.

McGoldrick and Giordano are probably right when they say: "Intimate relationships of different ethnic, religious, and racial backgrounds offer convincing evidence that *Americans' tolerance of cultural differences may be much higher than most people think.*"[49] [Emphasis ours] Understanding of this by worker and couples may foster optimism about the ability to accommodate to differences between spouses, to improve family-of-origin relationships, or to locate social supports.

In our view, there is a *tendency to underemphasize the potential for stimulation, rich experiences, and opportunities for special kinds of complementarity in cross-cultural relationships.* The strengths that derive from diversity within a relationship can be underscored in therapy. Margaret Mead spoke to both sides of the issue: "If you are not going to marry the boy next door—and if you do you may die of boredom—then you are going to have to work much harder."[50]

Finally, sometimes we can *encourage couples to take one step further.* As McGoldrick and Preto write:

> Under the best of circumstances, the challenge of differences in a relationship may open the possibility for productive personal changes. For instance, a WASP female who has difficulty expressing anger for fear of losing control and who becomes instead depressed or symptomatic may learn to be more direct and comfortable with her anger by marrying an Italian male who tends to be confrontive and spontaneous with his feelings. Or a Jewish husband may teach his WASP wife a new repertoire of emotional expression, freeing her to experience her feelings more fully, while she may teach him that there is a time to stop analyzing feelings and to just get on with things.[51]

Gay and Lesbian Couples

The Inhospitable Social Climate Gays—singly or in pairs, men or women—have been consistently stigmatized in the United States.[52] Even in this era of heightened sexual enlightenment, gays are frequently viewed as morally or psychologically deviant. Fortunately, there is greater acceptance of same-sex relationships in some quarters. Advances in antidiscrimination legislation have also been made. Yet, at the time of this writing, there is no state that legitimizes same-sex marriage; and the "Moral Majority" and others who tout "family values" have become more outspoken than ever in their condemnation of homosexuality. Lesbians and gay men are still sometimes denied custody of children on the grounds of their sexual orientation. Gay males, perhaps always the target of special ridicule and ostracism, continue to endure violent reaction to their sexuality that was triggered by the advent of AIDS. Polls reveal significant numbers of radically hostile responses; some believe that AIDS is a just punishment for sinful behavior; others call for segregating homosexuals, an idea that actually preceded the AIDS panic.[53] Furthermore, gay males and females have been the subject of discrimination and disapproval—subtle and overt—by family, friends, co-workers, and employers as well as by the larger social systems.

Lesbians and gay men have responded to destructive attitudes in various ways. To minimize the effects of social disapproval and hatred, many have denied their sexual preferences (to others and/or to themselves), hidden and lied, developed "secret worlds" and "counterfeit relations" with associates, friends, and family.[54] As is true of any stigmatized group, gay men and women are vulnerable to low self-esteem and self-loathing. Feelings of personal alienation often bring gay men to treatment; *internalized homophobia* (defined broadly by Cornett as "the internalization of culture's virulent anti-homosexual bias") often accounts for much of the distress.[55] Prejudice and overt discrimination can take a toll on the hardiest personalities.

"Coming Out"   Those who have stayed "in the closet" often have borne the burden of deep feelings of shame about their differences; nevertheless, as Laird says, "many lesbians who do remain silent and secretive have unique ways of buffering and countering what we have seen as the insidious effects of secrecy."[56] There is evidence that when "coming out" is motivated by a grow-

ing sense of self-acceptance, it can foster pride and an enhanced sense of belonging. Laird also makes the point that " 'coming out' can clearly be a freeing, enriching, pride-making experience that can have enormous impact on both individual and couple narratives, as well as on the couple relationship."[57] One study of 124 gay women indicated that "lesbians . . . who disclosed their lesbianism, those who had a partner who was open about their relationship, and those who indicated that they were open about their relationship reported higher scores on relationship quality."[58] Gay support and action groups have provided gays with a sense of community and pride that was far less available even 30 years ago. Despite ongoing scapegoating of those with a same-sex orientation, political pressure from the gay community and its allies has contributed to increased enlightenment among heterosexuals.

Let us add a note of caution here. Sometimes as a result of pressure from peers who have "come out" and sometimes as a way of expressing pent-up rage about social and/or family biases against same-sex love relationships, gay clients feel compelled to enter into ill-considered confrontations—at work, with parents, or with friends—in a manner that will ensure hostile if not rejecting reactions. The approach taken may thus constrain resolution and actually contribute to further pain and isolation. Many clinicians working with gays have encouraged their clients to be open about their sexual orientation with the significant people in their life who are not gay. Cain, who conducted a study of 38 gay men on their attitudes and experiences about disclosure, writes that researchers as well as clinicians

> often view concealment in terms of self-acceptance, particular personality traits, levels of maturity, and social skills, rather than in terms of oppression or efforts to deal with

conflicting and often irreconcilable social demands. The absence of discussion of other factors that affect disclosure indicates that many professionals assume that identity development is *the* central element governing gays' decisions to reveal or conceal their homosexuality . . . this assumption draws attention from the range of other factors involved and obscures the fact that information management is not always related to self-acceptance. Furthermore, much of the current literature treats the various social relationships of gays in an undifferentiated fashion, as if disclosure to a parent entails the same considerations as does disclosure to a casual acquaintance.[59]

Although revealing one's sexual orientation may bring personal and political rewards in the long run,[60] the questions of how, when, where, and to whom (and, of course, whether) may take time and careful reflection.

Special Assessment and Treatment Considerations   For years, the mental health community labeled homosexuality as "abnormal" and "pathological"; only relatively recently has this view been modified somewhat, although social workers and others are hardly unanimous in their views on the matter. In one study on social workers' attitudes, 10 percent were found to be homophobic (defined as "fear, disgust, anger, aversion in dealing with gay people").[61] There are surprisingly few articles in mental health journals on gays and lesbians.[62] Yet, as Goldstein reports, "Results of several decades of research clearly show that homosexuals cannot be reliably differentiated from heterosexuals in their personality characteristics, family background, gender identity, defenses, ego strengths, object relations, psychopathology, problems in living, and social adjustment."[63]

When treating gay and lesbian clients, the worker brings the same respect, acceptance, humility, and sensitivity that one brings to all clients. A few additional comments on working with gay couples follow:

As is true of people from other oppressed groups, *resilience and the human capacity for adaptation have saved many from severe psychological damage and despair. Recognition of gay clients' strengths* in the face of alienation and abuse can be an important therapeutic function. *Validation of the reality of the injustice perpetrated by society's attitudes* can have meaning to those gay clients who have been blaming themselves for the prejudices they have experienced. Some clients, affected by prevailing negative opinions, need affirmation that homosexual relationships are viable and can be as fulfilling and productive as "straight" ones; they can benefit from a treatment relationship in which they are not viewed as "sick," "bad," or even as being in a "second best" kind of arrangement.

There are times, however, when clients and their caseworkers are inclined to dwell almost exclusively on the brutality of the "system," thereby neglecting the work that *can* be accomplished. As is true in all therapy, *it does not promote progress to ventilate endlessly about issues mostly outside of one's control.*

It is also true that *when those who are motivated (in this instance, the gay couples) make changes, corresponding changes in other parts of the larger system may occur,* especially in relationships with family, friends, and co-workers.

The importance of the *worker's self-awareness,* of one's own attitudes and countertransference reactions to gay clients, cannot be overstated. One must be particularly alert to any feelings that same-sex love is "unnatural" or "bad." Beyond that, it is important to pay close attention to an inclination to minimize the humiliation and shame many gays have experienced. Therapists who have had few personal or professional relationships with gays and lesbians are particularly vulnerable to stereotyping or misunderstanding. The worker's ongoing self-scrutiny is imperative.

When working with gay couples it is essential to know that, contrary to the notions some people have, *most partners in gay relationships do not take on roles that simulate stereotypical "male" and "female" roles.* A number of studies reveal that there are widely diverse behavioral and role patterns among both gay men and lesbians.[64] Furthermore, even though there are fewer established guidelines for defining roles within the gay relationship, many couples can grow to view positively the opportunity for flexibility and choice about distribution of functions.

As we have said about all clients, *it is only they who can arrive at the meanings of their lives and experiences.* They are the experts on how they view their sexual orientation, their relationships, and, as indicated earlier, their attitudes about disclosure. In this connection, it is important for the therapist to be keenly sensitive to the possibility that, for some clients, even *the best-planned "coming out" to family and friends may be met with painful hostility;* for this reason, it is important for the therapist to help the client reflect on the pros and cons of disclosure and to avoid encouraging clients to take steps that may be unwise or for which they are not ready.

In many respects, problems encountered by gay pairs, despite society's reluctance to accord them first-class status, are *remarkably similar to those for which other couples seek help:* difficulties dealing with various life transitions; symptomatic members who are depressed, anxious, sexually dysfunctional, and so forth; conflictual or disengaged relationships; troubled family-of-origin relationships; projections and irrational role assignments; unresolved former relationships,

including problems involving children from former marriages; and so on. *The typology of relationship problems discussed earlier in this chapter can apply to same-sex as well as to heterosexual relationships.* There can be confusion about role expectations in heterosexual relationships and these issues can cause difficulty for gay couples also.

There are also other issues that pertain specifically to gay couples and their families. For example, *parents can deny, sometimes even when they are clearly told, that their "child" is in a gay relationship;* this is not as likely when the relationship is a cross-cultural one.[65] Also, while parents of children who choose to intermarry may assume some guilt, parents of gay offspring seem to harass themselves more cruelly with self-blame (e.g.: "Where did we go wrong?"), inappropriately taking responsibility for their children's sexual orientation and measuring their own competency as parents or as people in relation to it. No wonder some parents, consciously or unconsciously, are inclined to refuse to believe even obvious facts about their child's sexual orientation. When invited to join their daughters and sons in treatment, they sometimes can get clarification and relief, thus improving intergenerational relationships.

Some of the comments we made above about the "camouflage" or "red herring" function of transcultural marriages vis-à-vis families of origin can apply to gay couples and their families. *Emotional problems can be masked by a fixed focus on the subject of sexual orientation* just as negative reactions to intermarriage can cloak family difficulties.

In enmeshed family systems, denial of gay relationships also can obstruct separation. Fears of differentiation can postpone, sometimes indefinitely, establishment of a distinct and committed gay couple relationship. If the original family sees their child's same-sex partner as only a "friend" or "roommate," and the couple does not draw clear boundaries around their relationship, both generations can perpetuate the notion that the younger person never really left home. In that sense, a gay "child" can protect the balance of such families in ways that the heterosexual cannot.

Even when there are only minimal negative or avoidance reactions, *the gay relationship is rarely viewed by families as having the same importance as the heterosexual marriage.* Denial and avoidance are not the only reasons. Gay relationships—even those that are stable, monogamous, and enduring—when contrasted with "straight" couples, do not have socially established role definitions, traditions, and powers to guide and protect them.

As discussed in the family chapters, the concepts of *"enmeshment" (or "fusion")* *should never be confused with even extreme closeness;* this is true for couples, gay or heterosexual. While some writers have described many lesbian couples as "fused" or "merged," in her excellent article on lesbian families Laird refers to Mencher who "argues that although mental health professionals, influenced by prevailing patriarchal norms for relationship and sexuality, tend to label fusion as problematical or pathological, *lesbian couples themselves see this same emotional connectedness as a central strength and source of satisfaction in their relationships.*"[66] [Emphasis ours] Our own clinical experience bears out this observation.

Clearly, *gay couples have to work harder than others to delimit the rules, roles, boundaries, and loyalties that give meaning and substance to their union:* this is particularly true when it comes to defining how it will function in the context of family and larger social systems. Ambiguity can result when outside expectations run counter to the spirit of their relationship: pressure to bring a "date" of the opposite sex to a function, for example, or invitations to go "home" as a single person for holidays, which could preclude the couple from spending special times together.

Whether or not they have supportive families and friends, the location of gay networks, social or action organizations—perhaps especially for young or newly "out" gay and lesbian couples—is often an important service for the worker to offer.

Finally, *there is no blueprint for working with gay and lesbian couples;* as with all clients, each situation is different and must be individualized. A major function of the therapist is to provide a safe and caring climate in which couples can be helped to arrive at their own solutions according to their own needs.

GENDER ISSUES: WOMEN IN COUPLES

Women's Roles and Denial of Self

Although times are changing, traditionally women have been expected to be selfless, nurturing, and focused on the needs of others rather than on their own. Even unmarried women of all classes have been guided by social role definitions into occupations of "service," as teachers, nurses, nurses' aides, domestic and child care workers, secretaries to men, and the like. Only relatively recently have substantial numbers of women, especially from the middle class, chosen formerly "masculine" careers in which money, status, and power constitute primary rewards. Others have sought fulfillment by putting creative or artistic careers ahead of traditional "women's work." Many have done so despite discouraging opposition, discrimination, and even ridicule. By describing "instrumental" (rational and task-oriented) roles of men in the work world, and "expressive" (emotional and nurturant) roles of women in the family, in 1955 Parsons and Bales endorsed these as "normal" and necessary to carrying out economic functions and family relationships.[67] Surprisingly, these fixed role definitions are still believed by large numbers of people to be fundamental to the well-being of all, even if the woman also has to supplement family income by going to work, which large numbers do. While there have always been role variations in some marriages, these tended to be, and sometimes still are, viewed as deviant.[68]

Married women's denial of self has been strongly reinforced by the larger social system: self-esteem and competence were to be achieved in the home—as comforter of hardworking husband, nurturer of children, mediator, and manager of household operations. Autonomous strivings that did not give top priority to caretaking functions were strongly discouraged. Although women are often the "hub" of the family, in charge of many of the interactions there (and, as we have seen in clinical practice, sometimes possessively so), this is often a thankless job. Family problems seem to be more consistently blamed (sometimes even by family therapists) on "overcontrolling" or "intrusive" wives and mothers than on "distant" or "ineffectual" husbands and fathers.[69]

Men's Roles

Men, too, have been expected to deny personal ambitions and fulfillments when these diverge from the norm; in particular, those who do not vigorously and successfully carry out the breadwinner role generally are not accorded full status as "men." Traditional roles can result in the denial of a "full life" to both sexes: Women often give up independence and personal fulfillment to be the "nurturer" and serve others'

needs; men frequently forfeit emotional closeness to live up to their economic responsibilities and "rational" self-image. It is important for the caseworker to recognize that men's as well as women's positions have been powerfully influenced by social values and expectations and to identify the ways in which this is so.

Gender Inequality

In couple treatment, although we may focus primarily on the processes *within* the confines of the marital system, the dynamics and influences of greater systems—even if these are not immediately open to change—must be acknowledged. As Goldner points out in her excellent article:

> Erecting a conceptual boundary around the family was clearly essential for the development of family systems theory, but it also deflected theoretical attention away from an encounter with the ways in which participation in family life is not merely an idiosyncratic accommodation to the "needs of the family system" but is regulated by social forces operating above and beyond the family's affective field.[70]

Systems far more powerful than the family impact the patterns, including gender patterns, of couple processes.

Gender roles are now less rigidly defined than they were (this varies in different cultural and economic groups and geographical areas). The trend toward egalitarian marriages—spearheaded in large part by the feminist movement—that began in the middle classes has spread to the working class in varying degrees. Nevertheless, the inequities continue. Despite equal opportunity laws, women are still paid less than men for doing the same work. In more than two-thirds of two-parent families with children both parents work, yet one study found that women who have jobs do more than five times as much housework as their husbands.[71] Although the number of working wives and mothers continues to increase, subsidized day care provisions are less available than they were a few years ago. Society's message is that even though women's earnings are often required to maintain a minimal standard of living for the family, it is still the woman's job to see to it that the children receive adequate supervison as well as other basic requirements.

Substantial research suggests that for various reasons wives as well as husbands are often reluctant to relinquish traditional roles. This is true even among those who subscribe to the idea of reciprocal sharing and support in job and family responsibilities.[72] Although less often than in previous years, in part because of the differential in earning power, women are still expected (and expect) to give up their jobs, their activities, and uproot themselves to adjust to their husbands' educational or occupational moves. Less commonly, the reverse can occur, especially when the woman's income exceeds her husband's.

Some of the most serious inequities become apparent when there is a separation or divorce. Men are not as socially stigmatized for leaving their spouses and children behind. Women, expected to "keep the home fires burning," are often subtly or not so subtly blamed for marital breakup, especially when it is their decision to end the marriage. And women who leave their children in the care of their husbands or others are viewed by most as having failed their responsibilities. (After divorce, only about 1 woman in 10 does not have full custody of the children.) Clinicians, hardly immune from traditional judgments, must be alert to the possibility of countertherapeutic reactions to such women.

The aftermath of divorce affects men and women very differently. Following divorce, a woman's standard of living is usually drastically reduced, while that of the man increases. Child support payments are received by fewer than half of female-headed families, and a large percentage receive very modest or only partial payments.[73] And, as Pittman points out:

> Gender relationships cannot be truly equal so long as the economy makes divorce more disadvantageous economically for women than for men, and fashion determines that middle-aged men are considered more desirable marriage partners than middle-aged women. Women may not be able to achieve equality within marriage, but they are even less able to do so outside marriage. Our current gender arrangements mean that women must value their marriages more than men do—an inherent inequality.[74]

Gender Issues and Couples of Color

Gender expectations of men and women in African American and other couples of color (especially non–middle class), and others who have been oppressed and discriminated against, can be quite different from those of white middle-class Americans. Of particular importance is the fact that men of color have been particularly discriminated against in the job market; women of color arouse less fear, apparently, and have been more successful in finding employment. It is, therefore, expected that women will work; in contrast to many white women, they have learned greater self-reliance because traditionally they have worked—albeit often in underpaid jobs—and raised children. Greater role flexibility is an advantage for some couples, but in other cases may result in overburdening one spouse; the woman may take on the major work and home responsibilities, or the man may work two jobs for inadequate pay to make ends meet. Too often, as a result of racism, men have been unable to pull their weight as providers, have been viewed with contempt by white society, and out of frustration or hopelessness become "absent" or "marginal" in the family; some succumb to drugs or alcohol or are incarcerated; as a result of homicide, dangerous job conditions, and other causes, African American men have life expectancies substantially lower than those of African American women who often find themselves having to shoulder major family responsibilities as single women. Boyd-Franklin and Franklin write:

> To this day, Black women are often received and treated better in the world of work than Black men are. Combined with their resourcefulness, this means that they sometimes gain more and fare better in a White-male-dominated work world than African American men . . . This has led to a gender power balance between African American men and women quite different from that of their White counterparts, wherein African American women's expectations of African American men as partners are compromised. As a result, great tension often exists in the relationship of Black women to Black men.[75]

Nevertheless, Hines and Boyd-Franklin remind us that Hill, "one of the most important researchers who has focused on adaptive strengths, attributed the group's [African American families'] survival to strong kinship bonds; flexibility of family roles; and high value placed on religion, education, and work."[76] It is important that therapists recognize and emphasize the remarkable resilience and capacity for survival in a group that has been so thoroughly and so long discriminated against and oppressed.

Special Treatment Emphases

Although couple treatment in general is the subject of this chapter and the next, a few suggestions that derive from knowledge of gender issues follow:

When we are treating couples, *differentials in the power of men and women, as these have been influenced by superordinate social forces, must be recognized by the worker and openly discussed with the couple.* One cannot assume, for example, that important decisions—whether the woman with children will take a job, whether the family will relocate to accommodate the husband's career, whether greater emotional closeness will become a goal, or whether the couple will separate—have equal implications for each spouse. Even though the couple has little control over society's expectations and norms, frank discussions about gender disparities permit more informed reflections and choices on the part of both partners. While it is not the job of workers to "impose" equality (as if they could!), it *is* their responsibility to raise the issues about gender influences so that the couple can consider these. With the worker's help, each couple has to arrive at its own definitions of equality, mutuality, or fairness in the marriage.[77]

When treating a couple in conflict, when it seems applicable, it can be helpful to *share with them that some research suggests that gender differences do sometimes exist in the manner in which couples communicate about problems to be solved.* One study, for example, found that women tended to be the ones to raise issues and draw men into discussions, but once problems were brought up, men "were dominant in defining and elaborating the problem, in limiting the emotional depth and substantive terrain in the discussion . . . [H]usbands were seen as having veto power over whether there would be a discussion at all, and whether a solution would be achieved . . . [B]oth men and women generally agreed that the men would have 'final say' over the outcome of the discussion."[78] Also, this same study found that fewer discrepancies between spouses in their perception of themselves and their marriage were associated with less conflict and greater marital satisfaction. "Objective" information about gender-linked power may make it possible to foster minimal blaming of each other by the partners (or by the therapist!). Above all, in this way the worker can invite the partners to begin to examine their own ways of communicating; the therapist is no longer the sole monitor of an imbalanced process that has been fostered in large part by the social context.

Finally, *it is important to individualize each couple.* For example, in the Russo family (Chapter 15), the "power" Mr. Russo wielded was the kind that is often attributed to women: He was seen as "pathetic," "depressed," "emotional," "whiny," and so on; in many respects, Mrs. Russo was more "task-oriented" than her husband. Dick and Susan Jones (Chapter 3) had arranged their relationship in a way that each seemed to have more or less equal status and power to influence role assignments, tasks, and so on. Despite the opinions of some, in our experience, *women are not always better than men at expressing vulnerabilities and feelings;* they are not necessarily more nurturing or more capable of intimacy. The reader may recall that Mr. Russo was the first family member to speak about tender and poignant feelings. By the same token, *men are not always as "rational" or practical as their wives;* nor are they inevitably focused on power and status. We need to be sure that when we seek to enhance communication between the genders, and when we fight for long overdue equality for women, that we do not do so by stereotyping or pitting one sex against the other.

EXTRAMARITAL RELATIONSHIPS

Chapters on marital treatment would not be complete without mentioning the common, yet culturally frowned upon, usually complicated, often heartbreaking extramarital relationship. While statistics on the frequency of sexual unfaithfulness in marriage differ, it seems safe to say that infidelity of some kind occurs in more than 50 percent (some say 70 percent) of marriages, with 30 to 60 percent of men and 25 to 40 percent of women unfaithful at some point during their married life. Traditionally men have been the "philanderers," but in recent years apparently more women are becoming involved in outside liaisons.[79]

Affairs can take various forms, including the single or occasional occurrence, recurrent extramarital activity, relationships in which the attraction is primarily or entirely sexual, deep friendships of long standing, and those in which there is a great deal of ongoing passion, often including strong feelings of being "in love." Some extramarital relationships are abruptly "confessed" to or discovered by the other spouse; others are known by the spouse but never discussed. Sometimes spouses will deny obvious evidence of their mates' affairs, consciously or unconsciously not wanting to know. And then there are situations in which the secret is very well kept and therefore never even suspected. (In Chapter 17, page 502, we discuss the importance of the therapist making clear at the outset how he or she will handle secrets that may be divulged by one spouse during an individual session or over the telephone, for example.)

Exposure of an affair may bring a couple to treatment (as in the case of Dick and Susan Jones, Chapter 3). In some cases, spouses may use couple sessions to admit unfaithfulness: sometimes to rid themselves of guilt, sometimes to rid themselves of the marriage. Extramarital relationships are frequently disclosed in individual therapy or in couple treatment in which individual sessions with the worker have been arranged or sought.

There is no single explanation for sexual unfaithfulness. Usually it is helpful to view it as a *symptom,* an indirect expression, of some intrapsychic or interactional process. In our view, it would be a mistake to assume that the affair derives solely from individual conflicts on the one hand or from failure of the marriage (or spouse) on the other. When interviewing a couple or an individual, disclosure of the past or current affair(s) requires careful assessment. In some situations, extramarital relations may be an expression of early developmental deficits and distortions or of other unresolved issues; in some families or cultures, men's sexual relationships outside of marriage are to some degree acceptable. There are those who have extramarital relationships to boost self-esteem, seeking constant reassurance of their sexual attractiveness. Affairs can arise in response to life-cycle transitions, such as those popularly referred to as "mid-life crises." There are also people who always want to feel the way they did when they were first married; usually the "high" of those days is not sustained in marriage and thus affairs can be the way to maintain the illusion of being perpetually "in love."

The marital relationship itself may be an important factor in the affair:

1. In some cases, the couple's need for distance—for protection against feeling engulfed or too dependent—may be accommodated by one or both spouses having an affair.
2. Infidelity can be a means for ventilating anger, disappointment, or despair about one's marriage.
3. The extramarital relationship may be a solution to serious deficits in the marriage or make an intolerable situation— a marriage that is dead, distant, or deeply irritating—tolerable. In clinical practice it is not uncommon to hear (sometimes as rationalization and sometimes not) that the affair allows spouses to be more considerate, patient, and in-

terested in their mates and families when they enjoy outside sexual and emotional replenishments not available within the marriage.
4. Sometimes, when a spouse cannot find the courage to terminate his or her marriage forthrightly, the discovery of infidelity may become the precipitant to its dissolution.
5. In some instances, the affair and its revelation can play a constructive function by provoking a marital crisis that ultimately may facilitate communication and resolution of long-standing marital conflicts. (This was true for Susan and Dick Jones.)

The treatment approach to a couple in which extramarital relations have played a part will depend on the assessment of the many factors mentioned above. It will be necessary to try to understand the individual and marital dynamics that influenced the situation. Some clinicians insist that there cannot be couple treatment if either spouse is actively involved in an outside relationship. In many cases, however, the couple may be coming to determine whether or not the marriage is viable. In most situations, whether the marriage continues or not, the one whose spouse has been extramaritally involved must deal with a broad range of feelings: anger, hurt, betrayal, rejection, fear of loss, and so on. The one who has had the affair may be ridden with guilt, self-doubt, or other feelings. Sometimes both spouses use treatment to mourn the end of an unhappy marriage. In most cases, even if the person involved in the affair is coming for individual treatment, it is our preference to encourage that person to bring in his or her spouse to confront the marital issues; often the impasse in the marriage (and in the treatment of the individual) can thereby be resolved. By the same token, when the one whose mate has been having the affair comes for help, participation of both spouses can be the most effective approach either to building a better relationship or to coming to decisions about the marriage that are as comfortable as possible for all concerned. Above all, it is important to determine what both spouses want to do about their relationship, why they are coming for treatment, and whether what they are hoping for is realistic in terms of the state of the marriage and the attitudes of their mates.[80]

In Chapter 17 we will discuss specific treatment issues and techniques in couple work.

NOTES

1. See Family Service America (1991) and Bronfenbrenner (1996).
2. In addition to references cited elsewhere, especially in Chapters 14 and 15, see Siporin (1980).
3. See, for example, Hamilton (1951) where no specific discussion of joint interviews can be found except in connection with home visits. See also Witmer (1942) who wrote (p. 94): "With respect to the institution of the family the function of social work is to facilitate the family's normal activities through counseling with individuals about the difficulties they encounter in family life."
4. Hollis (1949), p. 183.
   The reader may be interested in an article on marital therapy by Hefner and Prochaska (1984) who report results of a small study in which there were no significant differences in outcome between concurrent and conjoint treatments, although improvement occurred in both groups. See also Wells and Gianetti (1986) for a reappraisal of individual marital therapy, and "Commentary" by Gurman and Kniskern (1986).
5. See a chapter we recommend on coaching one individual to bring about changes in the marital or family system by Carter and Orfandis (1976). See also Bowen (1978).

6. Hollis (1949), p. 182.
7. See the very useful edited volume by Jacobson and Gurman (1986) for chapters on various, often overlapping, models of marital therapy.
8. We especially recommend Framo's (1982) Chapter 4 on "Marriage and Marital Therapy: Issues and Initial Interview Techniques."
9. For readings on spouse abuse and family violence see Chapter 10, note 9.
10. Dare (1986), p. 15.
11. Satir (1983), pp. 9–12. For good case illustrations, see Rice (1980).
12. See the excellent article by Vigilante (1982) on using the work situation in assessment and intervention.
13. See the very helpful article by Loewenstein (1979).
14. Ibid., p. 28.
15. American Psychiatric Association (1994); see the criteria for panic disorder with agoraphobia, pp. 402–3.
16. See Pittman (1987), especially p. 242. It is interesting that Pittman, in his work with families, also found a relationship between phobic symptoms and the "need for connectedness." See also Hafner (1986) on marital therapy for agoraphobia who also recommends couple interviews for women who present as agoraphobic. In their review of research, Alexander, et al. (1994, pp. 609–10) report that the data do seem to support the efficacy of spouse involvement in the treatment for agoraphobia.
    Marcus and Runge (1990) describe a community-based, successful pilot outreach program, staffed partly by volunteers, to provide in vivo desensitization to agoraphobic clients. Even though in our own experience we have independently come to appreciate the positive benefits of a couple approach to panic and agoraphobic symptoms, we certainly do not discredit other responsible approaches.
17. See, for example, Framo (1982), pp. 126–30; and Pittman (1987), Chapter 1.
18. See Framo (1982), p. 15.
19. See Solomon (1985) on treatment of narcissistic and borderline disorders in marital therapy. See also Wallace (1979, reprinted in

Turner's edited 1995 volume) on treatment of marital disorders, who suggests an approach to the synthesis of psychoanalytic and family systems concepts.

20. See Carter and McGoldrick (1988); Pittman (1987), Chapter 4; and Spitz and Evans (1981) on developmental phases of marriage and marital treatment.

21. See, for example, Bowen (1978); Friedman (1991); Framo's (1982) Chapter 8, "Family of Origin as a Therapeutic Resource for Adults in Marital Therapy: You Can and Should Go Home Again"; and the highly recommended book by Framo (1992) on the theory and practice of intergenerational therapy. See also Kerr (1985) and Hartman and Laird (1983), pp. 82–88.

22. See the well-known, important book by Boszormenyi-Nagy and Spark (1973) on invisible loyalties; see also Boszormenyi-Nagy, et al. (1991).

23. Framo (1982), p. 128.

24. See Fontane (1979) for a good discussion of this point.

25. See Framo (1982), Chapter 9; and Framo (1992), especially Chapter 3 on preparation for family-of-origin meetings and Chapter 4 on the use of techniques during such meetings.

26. See Scharff and Scharff (1987); Dicks (1967) is of interest as one of the early integrators of psychodynamic and relational concepts.

27. See Bowen (1978) and Framo's (1982) Chapter 2 on symptoms.

28. See the volume edited by Walsh and McGoldrick (1991) on living beyond loss for several excellent chapters on family deaths and mourning.

29. See Beck (1984) who reports on interviews with adults and their parents for a discussion pertinent to this point. See also Framo (1982), Chapter 9, and Framo (1992).

30. See Goldmeier (1980) for a useful discussion with case illustrations. See also Chapter 15 of this text, notes 29 and 30.

31. Framo (1982), p. 129.

32. On divorce mediation, see Barsky (1984), Milne (1986), and Weingarten (1986). See also Senger-Dickenson and Stewart (1987) for a useful discussion of the importance of clinical intervention during the separation phase of the divorce process. Rice and Rice (1986) have a helpful chapter on separation and divorce therapy. Bogolub (1991) discusses issues relevant to women and midlife divorce including dealing with loss, relationships with offspring, social life, and economic and vocational issues.

33. See Berman and Goldberg (1986) on therapy with unmarried couples and Markman, et al. (1986) on preventive work with couples planning to marry.

34. Berman and Goldberg (1986), p. 301.

35. Markman, et al. (1986, p. 173) cite references that indicate that "among marriages that do not end in divorce, 50 percent are not happy marriages and only 10 percent of all marriages reach their full potential."

36. Berman and Goldberg (1986), p. 301.

37. Ibid, pp. 305–6.

38. See John Brown (1987), Ursula Brown (1995), and Falicov (1986). See also McGoldrick and Giordano (1996), pp. 19–20.

39. McGoldrick and Preto (1984).

40. McGoldrick and Giordano (1996), p. 19.

41. Crohn (1998) and U.S. Bureau of Census (1993).

42. Crohn, p. 296.

43. McGoldrick and Giordano (1996), p. 19.

44. McGoldrick and Preto (1984).

45. Falicov (1986) and McGoldrick and Preto (1984).

46. Friedman (1982).

47. Ibid., p. 506.

48. McGoldrick and Preto (1984), p. 362.

49. McGoldrick and Giordano (1996).

50. Quoted by Falicov (1986), p. 429.

51. McGoldrick and Preto (1984), p. 349.

52. See, for example, Brown and Zimmer (1986) and Johnson and Keren (1998).

53. Warren (1980, p. 125) reported on a 1977 California poll, before the outbreak of AIDS, in which 5 percent of the respondents "said that homosexuals should be punished and kept away from 'normal' people," and 43 percent "said that homosexuals should be tolerated, but only if they do not publicly show their way of life."

A report of a June 1998 Gallup Poll in the *New York Times,* August 2, 1998 indicates that 84 percent of the respondents think homosexuals should have equal job opportunities (in contrast to 56 percent in 1977); nevertheless, 59 percent said they believe homosexuality is morally wrong.

Drawing on several polls, Yang (1997) reports that in 1994, 45 percent of 1,339 respondents thought that homosexual relations between consenting adults should be legal, but 46 percent thought they should not. In 1994, only 39 percent of 1,022 respondents favored extending civil rights to homosexuals while 58 percent were opposed. In 1994, 31 percent of 800 respondents thought marriages between homosexual men and between homosexual women should be recognized as legal by the law, but 64 percent thought they should not. When the same group was asked if homosexual couples should be legally permitted to adopt children, 28 percent thought they should be permitted, 65 percent thought they should not. In 1991, 60 percent of respondents indicated they had *not much* or had *no* sympathy for people who get AIDS from homosexual activity.

As Hartman and Laird (1998, p. 265) write, despite some advances (such as the fact that over 500 major corporations, universities, and municipalities have initiated domestic partners benefits, that 11 states have included sexual orientation in their antidiscrimination legislation, and that same-sex marriage in Hawaii will become a reality), we should not exaggerate the progress made or "underestimate the pervasive homophobia and heterosexism that continue to exist in our society" (p. 265). Surely the polls and the conservative right keep us informed of how far we have to go.

54. See, for example, Roth (1989) and Warren (1980).
55. Cornett (1997), p. 601.
56. Laird (1994), p. 280.
57. Ibid.
58. Caron and Ulin (1997), p. 417. Not surprisingly, they also conclude that support from family and other networks can positively influence satisfaction in lesbian love relationships.
59. Cain (1991), pp. 350–60; the author takes a balanced approach to the subject of disclosure and recommends a sensitive, individualized approach.
60. Roth and Murphy (1986). See also Laird (1994).
61. Berkman and Zinberg (1997) studied attitudes of 187 social workers and concluded that 10 percent were "homophobic"; additional results include their finding that the *majority* of social workers surveyed were "heterosexist" (defined on p. 320) which, among other attitudes, includes the notions that heterosexuality is superior to and more "natural" than nonheterosexuality. Eda Goldstein (1997, pp. 578–79) also discusses lingering homophobia among mental health professionals. Hartman and Laird (1998) address professional attitudes and the necessity of self-awareness. Long (1996) discusses the importance of helping supervisers challenge heterosexism in supervision.
62. See Green (1996) who challenges the subtle and unwritten but parallel unofficial policy about same-sex relationships in the field of family therapy with the official "Don't ask, don't tell" policy of the military.
63. Eda Goldstein (1997), p. 578. See also Laird (1994, p. 266) whose review of the research leads her to conclude that there are "no consistent differences between heterosexuals and homosexuals in degree of mental health or mental illness, in spite of the special environmental stresses experienced by gay men and lesbians"; she adds that "although there are certain kinds of important differences along various measures between homosexual and heterosexual couples as well as between gay and lesbian couples, my reading of the data suggests that, overall, *the similarities among these various kinds of couples far outweigh the differences."* [Emphasis ours]
64. Saghir and Robins (1980).
65. See Roth and Murphy (1980) and Krestan and Bepko (1980).
66. Laird (1994), p. 274.

In addition to references already cited, see Loewenstein (1980) for a helpful discussion on understanding lesbian women. The Hare (1994) study of lesbian mothers in committed relationships concluded, among other things, that the parents and co-parents are very committed to creating strong families; the couples in their sample appeared to identify more strongly with heterosexual families with children than with child-free lesbian families. See also Levy (1992) who interviewed 31 lesbian mothers; the author discusses implications for clinical practice derived from her findings that "coping patterns that emphasize social support, lesbian identity, and developing oneself are most helpful, whereas those that involved disclosure of lesbian identity to unsupportive people or social institutions were least helpful" (p. 23).

In a thought-provoking and interesting article, Slater and Mencher (1991) argue that Carter and McGoldrick's (1989) scheme about the changing life cycle is not applicable to lesbian life for several reasons; they write that "while lesbian families, like heterosexual ones, experience a need to know what is ahead over the family life cycle, neither popular culture nor family therapy provides a chart, nor do traditional rituals exist to light the way" (p. 375).

See also a very helpful paper by Van Voorhis and McClain (1997) on reactions, including feelings about loss of status, of children to mothers who shift from a heterosexual to a lesbian identity; the authors offer suggestions for helping mothers lovingly reach out to their children. In a recommended article, Faria (1994) discusses training for family preservation practice with lesbian families; she includes case illustrations. The June 1993 issue of *Smith College Studies in Social Work* is devoted to articles on

lesbians and lesbian families. Of particular interest is the Jones and Gabriel (1999) survey of the utilization of psychotherapy by lesbians, gay men, and bisexuals. See also Chapter 2 of this text, note 39.

67. Parsons and Bales (1955).
68. For very useful and thought-provoking articles about the general lack of recognition given to feminist ideology in family theory and practice, see Goldner (1985) and Hare-Mustin (1978). See several very good chapters in the volume edited by McGoldrick, et al. (1989) on women in families.
69. See the book by Walters, Carter, Papp, and Silverstein (1988), especially Chapter 1 in which, among other things, mother/wife blaming is discussed.
70. Goldner (1985), p. 33.
71. Ibid., p. 37. See also Smith (1980). See Bronfenbrenner (1996) and Family Service America (1991).
72. Smith and Reid (1986). As experience in clinical practice with families suggests, there are indications from reseach that both husbands and wives may be ambivalent about equal sharing of household and child care functions; the authors recommend helping couples clarify "covert contracts" that tend to be influenced by traditional roles.
73. See Haffey and Cohen (1992). See also Bogolub (1991).
74. Pittman (1987), p. 52.
75. Boyd-Franklin and Franklin (1998), p. 270.
76. Hines and Boyd-Franklin (1996), p. 68. For discussions of family resilience, see Froma Walsh (1996) and Hawley and Dehaan (1996).
77. See Knudson-Martin and Mahoney (1996).
78. Ball, et al. (1995), p. 316.
79. See Constantine (1986), p. 412.
80. For additional readings on extramarital affairs, see Pittman's (1987) "Infidelity" chapter, Rhodes (1995), and Taibbi (1983).

CHAPTER 17

COUPLE TREATMENT: CLINICAL ISSUES AND TECHNIQUES

In the previous three chapters, our discussions of family and marital treatment have been grounded in concepts that integrate intrapsychic and systems thinking. Understanding of the dynamics of individual personalities and of the interactions among or between them is required for effective treatment planning. We use these same concepts when working with individuals, but in family and couple therapy we observe and work with the relationship system in vivo. From the psychosocial point of view, behavior, emotions, and symptoms cannot be appraised apart from the systems in which they exist; often the marital relationship is the most salient and most accessible impinging system of all. As indicated in the last chapter, even when we use terms such as *marriage, marital relationship,* or *spouse,* our discussions here can apply to committed relationships of two people who are not legally married, to domestic partners, or to same-sex unions.

Even when severely stressed by negative socioeconomic conditions, an individual or couple has to decide how to circumvent or transcend them or how to try to join others to temper the noxious influences. When spouses are able to work *with* rather than *against* each other, when they are able to be gratified rather than deprived by their marriage, they have a far better chance at negotiating the other systems in their lives. Sometimes, a small tip in the balance of personality or marital systems or of living conditions can result in remarkable differences in couple functioning. In other cases, the work can be very slow or little progress seems possible, at least with the helping methods developed so far. Probably most cases, like the case of the Brent couple that follows, fall between these extremes.

Using the Brent case and other case vignettes, this chapter addresses specific treatment approaches and issues in couple treatment, including brief couple therapy in

487

diverse settings; a discussion of individual sessions with each spouse in conjunction with conjoint treatment; and transference and countertransference.

TOM AND KATHY BRENT

Some couples with difficulties, unable or unwilling to confront their own unhappiness, tenaciously cling to the notion that it is their child and the child only who needs therapy. Other parents present a child's problem, but very quickly the symptom diminishes or seems less important. In these situations, as was true in the Brent case, the child functions as a "passport" for marital treatment.

Tom and Kathy Brent (see genogram[1]) requested help from a family agency for their daughter Melissa, age 13, who was underachieving in school. Three family meetings were held with the parents, Melissa, and her brothers, Tommy, age 14, and Randy, age 12. It soon became apparent to the worker and to the parents that the core difficulties resided in the parental relationship; the children's issues were not critical and responded quickly to the brief family therapy. Tom and Kathy actually seemed relieved to have the opportunity to focus on their marital difficulties; with no apparent resistance, therefore, couple sessions were arranged. On the basis of information gathered from the Brents and from her own observations of family and marital interactions, the worker summarized Tom and Kathy's histories and their current relationship.

Tom's History

Tom, age 38, a meter reader for a utility company, was the oldest of four children, the only child of his mother's first marriage. His own father, who was Canadian-born, deserted the family when Tom was 10 months old and died of alcohol-related diseases when Tom was two. His mother, of English-Irish heritage, remarried when he was three and she and her second husband, Jim Cook, had three children, ages 30, 26, and 21 at the time of intake. From Tom's perspective, his stepfather had rejected and competed with him. When he paid Tom attention at all, it was critical or ridiculing. Jim seemed partial and more loving to his own children; they—Tom's half-siblings, whom he spoke of as his "sister" and "brothers"—admired their father and got along well with him. Tom said that his mother, probably to "keep the peace" with her husband, did not defend or protect him from his stepfather's abuse.

Tom's maternal grandparents, who lived with the family until Tom was 12, had strongly disapproved of his mother's first marriage. Apparently for this reason they never seemed fully able to accept Tom either. The effect of all this, Tom reported, was that he felt like an outsider in his own family. Furthermore, he described his mother, stepfather, and grandparents as frequently "deceitful." When Tom's siblings graduated from elementary school, for example, monies were deposited in a bank for their future use; but, when Tom inquired about this (no money had been given to him) he was told it was not true. Only later did his sister confirm his suspicions. In one of the first sessions, Tom readily admitted to having a quick temper, which he attributed to the anger he had felt toward his family all of his life. At the time he came into couple treatment, Tom's mother, stepfather, and siblings were alive and all resided within 100 miles of the Brent home.

Tom, a very serious man with a strong sense of responsibility, functioned well at work. In addition to his regular job, he sometimes worked at a gasoline station to make ends meet. The Brents had managed to save enough to buy a modest house in the small city in which they lived. Tom took

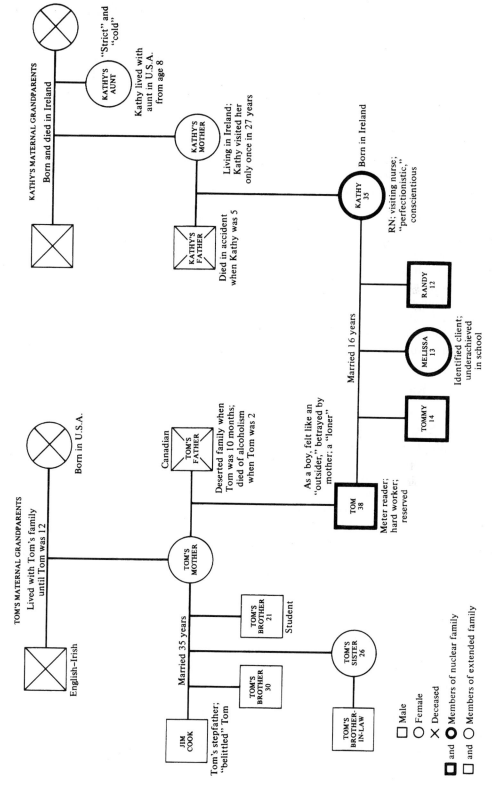

THE BRENT FAMILY
GENOGRAM

KATHY'S MATERNAL GRANDPARENTS
Born and died in Ireland

"Strict" and "cold"

KATHY'S AUNT

Kathy lived with aunt in U.S.A. from age 8

KATHY'S MOTHER

Living in Ireland; Kathy visited her only once in 27 years

KATHY'S FATHER

Died in accident when Kathy was 5

KATHY 35   Born in Ireland

RN; visiting nurse; "perfectionistic," conscientious

Married 16 years

RANDY 12

MELISSA 13

Identified client; underachieved in school

TOMMY 14

TOM'S MATERNAL GRANDPARENTS

Lived with Tom's family until Tom was 12

Born in U.S.A.

English–Irish

TOM'S FATHER   Canadian

Deserted family when Tom was 10 months; died of alcoholism when Tom was 2

TOM 38

As a boy, felt like an "outsider," betrayed by mother; a "loner"

Meter reader; hard worker; reserved

TOM'S MOTHER

Married 35 years

TOM'S BROTHER 21   Student

TOM'S BROTHER 30

TOM'S SISTER 26

TOM'S BROTHER-IN-LAW

JIM COOK

Tom's stepfather; "belittled" Tom

☐ Male
○ Female
✕ Deceased
☐ and ● Members of nuclear family
☐ and ○ Members of extended family

489

In the case of Tom and Kathy, from the worker's point of view, the obstacles to change included:

1. The Natural Tendency for Any System, Including a Marital System, to Maintain a Dynamic But Steady Balance (Homeostasis)   This concept was described in Chapter 14. Negative interactional patterns became entrenched and predictable. Irrational role assignments (the reciprocal projections of introjects) were firmly set. Demoralizing communication patterns were stabilized. Efforts to make changes that would extend beyond the range of their set patterns were met by counterforces that resisted those efforts, thereby maintaining the equilibrium of the marital system.

However, when the demand for change, whether from external events or inner motivation based on the intolerability of the present circumstances, upsets the balance sufficiently to *require* new adaptations, treatment usually progresses—sometimes rapidly. When couples seek help because inner and/or outer forces are demanding change, the resultant anxiety and need to find new ways of living facilitate treatment. But, like Tom and Kathy Brent, many couples are *not* totally desperate and therefore they resist disturbing the status quo. In the Brent case, had any of the children been severely symptomatic, the family might have been thrown into crisis, thus necessitating immediate and drastic changes.

2. The Attraction of the Familiar   In their marriage, Kathy and Tom actually recreated the circumstances and emotional climate that they experienced as children. Sometimes people tend to induce others to fulfull their negative expectations, not only to accommodate inner self-hate or self-doubt, but also to shape relationships similar to those to which they are accustomed.

In short, some kind of connection with others is better than none and, unless one has experienced a more gratifying kind, the tendency is to fall back on what is *known,* especially in the face of disappointments that *always* occur in intimate relationships.

3. Fear of the Pain of Losing Hope and Love Again   Tom and Kathy, like many other couples, were wary of bringing tender feelings back into their relationship. Often this fear is expressed explicitly. With sadness and resolution, one woman told her marital worker over and over, "My heart is closed." She was terrified to risk disappointment again after discovering that her husband had had an affair. When they married, Tom and Kathy believed that they had found in each other the answer to their deepest inner yearnings. But once disenchanted, neither felt strong enough to try again until their daughter led them to treatment.

HOW DO WE INTERVENE?

Responses to Treatment: The Question of Time

There are, as we have said, a significant number of couples in distress who can be helped with a little *environmental relief* (employment for one of the spouses, support groups, resources for the children or elderly relatives, etc.). In some cases, a comfortable state can be attained with a small tip in the balance of forces. A significant number of couples seen by caseworkers are naive about communication skills and interactional styles and require only brief *supportive* and *educational* treatment. Some *ventilation* often occurs as spouses share disappointments and resentments. Making a couple aware of interactional behavior and providing information and *suggestions* about *how* the partners might approach one another differently to achieve mutually established goals (usually a more gratifying relationship) are frequently the caseworker's functions. Even in brief couple treatment, *person–situation reflection* (see Chapter 6) is an important part of the work as partners consider the meanings of the behaviors of their spouses and the consequences of their own actions on the other and on the relationship. *Pattern-dynamic* and *developmental reflection* (see Chapter 7) are also often very important to marital therapy of every kind, as it was in the short-term case of Dick and Susan Jones (Chapter 3). There are examples of other brief couple treatment later in this chapter.

But when problems are more deeply entrenched, as they were with Tom and Kathy, positive changes do not usually come so quickly. How do we interrupt destructive interactional cycles? Before outlining some steps that frequently lead to success, we insert the following caveats:

Five Cautions

At the *beginning of treatment* when dysfunctional cycles resist the couple's or the worker's efforts to promote change:

1. We Do *Not* Encourage Ongoing, Freely Exchanged Ventilation of Current Negative Emotion Some disappointed spouses, especially at the beginning of treatment, unless guided otherwise by the clinician, will be unrestrained in expression of angry, blaming, hostile feelings about the other. It is important that the feelings be stated and understood, but in our view, repetitive venting is usually futile at best and dangerous to the relationship at worst. If it does not release inner pressure or help in mutual understanding very quickly, the likelihood is that this kind of exchange will become an acrimonious "free-for-all," escalat-

ing as it feeds on itself, thus alienating the spouses even more. Unbending expectations each partner has about how he or she will be treated in the marriage are further validated as distortions and dysfunctional patterns are reinforced. Moreover, in the minds of the spouses, the harrowing experience of reciprocal ventilation and blaming can become associated with therapy, discouraging them from continuing to come for help. Equally important is that most often negative emotion is a "cover" for the softer, more authentic and unexpressed feelings such as disappointment, hurt, sadness, loneliness, fear, inadequacy, and helplessness. Generally, it is more productive to create a climate in the sessions that will elicit *these* feelings than to facilitate the escalation of defensive attacks or complaints that make such sharing riskier.

2. We Do *Not* Promote Hand Holding, Hugs, or Other Kinds of Physical Closeness Some therapists try, and probably occasionally succeed, to break through negativity by urging exercises that include some sort of touching. From our point of view, such interventions should be very carefully considered because they may not be sensitive to "where the clients are": Clients can feel misunderstood and frightened if the worker pushes them into behaviors that feel unsafe. If the climate between the spouses warms up, there may be times when a worker gently suggests that they sit near to one another or reach out in some way, but we think it best to follow the couple's lead in this area. When they feel closer, they are likely to initiate affectionate moves *that suit them;* such voluntary moves are far better than those prompted by the worker.

3. We Do *Not* Suggest That Each Spouse Ask the Other for What He or She Wants or Claims to Need from the Other Exercises of this kind can be helpful when problems are not serious, or in "marriage enrichment" workshops and the like, or later in treatment when the climate of the marriage has improved. However, when difficulties are as entrenched as they were in Tom and Kathy's case, *the spouses are usually not yet ready to listen and do not feel like giving much to the other.* When requests partners make of each other are rejected, by words or actions, the upshot can be confirmation of the unlovability of self and/or of the intractability of the other.

4. We Do *Not* Urge Spouses to Listen Responsively and Creatively to One Another   Generally, we do not suggest that spouses try to put themselves in the other's shoes or to empathize with their spouse's feelings. When they first seek help, often couples are too angry to do this; even if the spouses are not inclined to be vicious or blaming, usually they are too stuck, self-absorbed, or frightened to react constructively to one another. Efforts to encourage such sensitivity are likely to lead to disappointment and reinforce the often considerable disillusionment in the marriage.

5. We Do *Not* Encourage Warming up a Fight or Disagreement That Occurred Some Days Ago   Couples usually want to go over such material, sometimes needing the opportunity to ventilate, and hence this kind of reporting will not be altogether prevented. But it is usually the worker's job to foster "here-and-now" communications during the session and respond most intensely to those. In this way, the quality of the couple relationship and reciprocal interactions can be addressed directly *as they are going on.* "Talking about" marital dynamics can lead to intellectual insight; we often see couples, including those who have been in therapy before, who are able to explain themselves and their relationships in very

enlightened terms but have failed to put their excellent understanding to use. When deeper (more emotionally resounding) insight is achieved *within* the session, in the interactive experience, it has a better chance of fostering awareness of previously unacknowledged emotion (e.g., "I feel lonely when you withdraw" in contrast to "You are so selfish"). This new self-understanding can lead to changes in behavior and very often evoke a different response from the other. Vulnerable feelings are more easily heard than blaming or angry ones. Occasionally, when couples battle viciously, it *can* be useful to help them examine what happened from a distance, at a time when they are less flooded by emotion and therefore can be more objective.

Some of the approaches described in the above "cautions" may be used to advantage as treatment progresses, when clients are less frightened and defensive and have more understanding of themselves, their spouses, and their relationships.

Treatment Steps

How, then, do we proceed? The following measures taken by the caseworker in couple sessions are recommended in cases, such as the Brents', in which there is serious marital distress. (These steps often require the entire range of worker–client communications described in Chapters 5 through 7: *sustainment, direct influence, exploration-description-ventilation, person–situation reflection,* and *reflective consideration of pattern-dynamic and developmental factors.*)

1. Set the Stage   It is usually effective to let couples know that there is nothing wrong with the fact that they are experiencing strong feelings about their relationship and its problems; this is often a good sign, a sign that the marriage is still alive. However, the worker can indicate, when the same arguments are repeated over and over, people stay "stuck" or become even more bitter and hopeless. It can be stated simply that most people want to feel a sense of closeness, belonging, understanding, and trust in their marriages; but, when disappointment sets in, people often start interacting in negative ways, making matters worse. "An important part of our work together, then," the therapist might add, "will probably be to try to help you to rediscover emotions that have been buried out of fear and hurt." The worker's *optimism* about the possibility of change can be enormously reassuring to embattled couples. As Greenberg and Johnson write: "It is not people's feelings and wants that cause problems in marriage . . . but the disowning or disallowing of these feelings and wants that leads to ineffective communication and escalating interactional cycles . . . intrapsychic fears of closeness and interactional patterns that prevent closeness are therefore the major targets of change."[3]

2. Convey through Action and Words the Worker's Warm Interest, Sensitivity, Trustworthiness, and "Involved Impartiality" (This last concept was described in the family chapters and will be discussed in greater detail later in this chapter.) Above all, for the work to be successful, the spouses must feel they are in a safe place and that the worker is fair and non-blaming. The worker must maintain a continuous balance between intense concern and detachment from judgment or partiality. *Therapeutic listening requires respect for and understanding of the couple's reality rather than the imposition of the caseworker's point of view.* On a regular basis, feedback about the couple's experience of the sessions and of the worker's approach should be solicited; the commitment

to *mutuality* is respectful to the clients and helpful to the worker and also may provide the spouses with an experience in teamwork, a model for their own conduct within the marital relationship. The Brents expressed their appreciation for the worker's ability to listen, understand, and avoid taking sides. They felt their own objectivity was enhanced by her example. Many couples may get the benefit of this attitude and yet not put it into words.

3. Seek Relevant History Usually, background information is required to help the worker and ultimately the spouses to identify and reflect upon the underlying bases for the repetitive projection of old introjects onto the current marital relationship. As was true in the case of Tom and Kathy, early family history can help to decipher the basis for expectations and reactivity between the spouses.

4. Help the Couple Become Aware of Individual and Joint Dysfunctional Behaviors and Cycles It is the caseworker's responsibility to assist each spouse in revealing and pinpointing vulnerable areas that contribute to the escalation of negative, disappointing reactions. Early in treatment, for example, Tom and Kathy were able to see how, when Kathy was afraid she would be criticized, she became evasive. And they learned how when Tom's anger and suspiciousness were triggered, Kathy withdrew even further. It is equally important to *support and facilitate the couple's positive patterns*. Both Tom and Kathy were very principled people with a well-developed social conscience; each had a solid sense of fairness. Hence, as treatment progressed, it became possible for the worker to bring attention to these qualities, as they were often revealed in relation to their children and other people in their

versa. For example, the worker might say to Tom: "Under stress, when you again have fears of being betrayed or of being an outsider, your impulse to attack and badger seems to crop up again. You can understand, though, that it is at those points that Kathy clams up." Or, to Kathy: "When you fear disapproval and rejection, you crawl right back inside of yourself again, don't you? Can you see, though, how this triggers Tom's feelings of being left out?"

As this phase of therapy progresses, it can become clearer to both spouses that they need not live reactively by giving up power to one another. *They need not assume that their behavior or feelings are "caused" by the other, but rather that they can take charge of their own conduct and communications, and even bring positive initiative to the relationship.* As Pittman describes, often both husband and wife "see the marriage as belonging to their spouse, who uses it as a form of tyranny over them, as if they are being held captive. They take little responsibility for making the marriage work. . . ."[4] When they are no longer so deeply entrenched in feeling like victims of one another, ideally each will learn to spot and interrupt the negative cycles, rather than waiting for a change of behavior from the spouse. Kathy learned not to withdraw automatically when she feared criticism. Tom almost ceased his verbally abusive behavior; instead he made a point of telling Kathy directly what was on his mind, including how frightened he became when he thought he might lose her.

During this final step, it is often necessary for the worker to continue to teach communication skills, helping the spouses to make "I" statements and to talk with one another in autonomous, emotionally meaningful terms. By now, if the treatment has been successful, both are in a much better position to hear and respond accurately. As

greater satisfactions arise, they give up negative, destructive, and lonely patterns. Ideally, they become better at delicately balancing intimacy and independence.[5]

RAPID ASSESSMENT, BRIEF TREATMENT, AND REFERRAL

In many agencies, both brief and extended couple treatment are provided by social workers according to the mutually agreed upon need. However, in a broad range of settings—including substance abuse programs, inpatient and outpatient hospital social services, hospices, prisons, employment assistance programs, agencies specializing in spouse abuse, and services to people with AIDS—casework is limited by the agency's functions and the clients' reasons for being involved with the setting. Those facilities unable to provide ongoing help to couples often have experienced workers who make rapid assessments, provide time-limited treatment, and, when needed, suggest referrals. Three illustrations of such brief treatment follow:

> Rita, a 17-year-old woman, was hospitalized for bulimia at a 21-day, experimental inpatient hospital service devoted to the evaluation and referral of adolescents with eating disorders. Two meetings with Rita's parents quickly revealed that, although rarely openly conflictual, both were depressed and unable to approach each other about the emptiness of their marriage. Financially pressured, the father had two almost full-time, low-paying jobs; when he was at home, he was usually sleeping. The mother devoted most of the hours during the day (she worked as a waitress in the evenings) visiting her recently widowed mother. Neither spouse knew how to bring closeness back to their drifting relationship. The skillful worker

aroused their interest in a referral to a family agency for couple therapy; she also arranged for Rita to join a group for teenagers with eating disorders. A follow-up call several weeks later revealed that Rita was doing well and that her parents had begun to communicate their disappointments and to clarify their misunderstandings; after only a few marital sessions, trust between them was beginning to be renewed.

In this case, the worker had to engage the couple's confidence quickly because she had only three weeks to prepare for a transfer to another service.

In a hospital counseling service for AIDS patients, John and his lover Arthur, with whom he had lived for seven years, were seen together for several months before John died. The social worker helped them both with their terrors about the illness; the men shared their outrage and sadness. From the worker's point of view, without her encouragement, John and Arthur would have been too frightened to mourn together; instead, they would have related superficially in the precious time they had left. In the process of saying good-bye, and as John got weaker and weaker, he found some peace and acceptance of his tragedy. Arthur's positive experience with the hospital social worker stimulated him to seek a referral for his own ongoing treatment. By being helped to grieve, he was released to begin to redefine his life and, ultimately, to seek new relationships.[6]

Because of the constraints of hospital policy, the worker could not continue with Arthur after John died; however, her strong relationship with him and her commitment to his welfare as well as to John's were central to the successful referral.

In preparation for his parole, Jim, a 30-year-old male prisoner, was seen by a social worker. Jim was becoming increasingly anxious; he worried especially about his jealous feelings toward his wife, Charlene. He had been arrested after severely assaulting a man whom he had believed was interested in her. Even though Charlene had visited him fairly regularly during his two-year incarceration, he was consumed by the fear that she would reject him now. Six weekly marital sessions held with the prison worker while Jim was still in prison brought some of Jim's worries out in the open; Charlene also had serious unexpressed concerns about the marriage. In the brief period of treatment it was established that the relationship was very important to them both and they wanted to protect and build on it. The couple was referred to a community mental health clinic to continue the work after Jim returned home.

By being responsive to Jim's apprehensions, the worker provided a service that was sufficiently helpful to both Jim and Charlene that they were willing to continue their couple treatment after Jim was released. Without the brief treatment, often not available to prisoners, it is probable that the marriage would have deteriorated and it is equally probable that Jim's jealous rage would have led to another arrest.

In each of the three cases just described, it was important that social workers were on the scene and saw beyond the immediate or practical concerns of their primary clients. Without the encouragement of the workers, not one of those who accepted referrals was likely to have sought help independently; yet, in all three situations, the referrals were successful and the clients were gratified by the opportunity to continue the work they began in the short-term services. As individual social workers and as members of agencies and of professional organizations, it is important that we register our concern about the current trend to reduce or eliminate social work staff in facilities such as those just mentioned. We need to demonstrate, through research and the publication of case material, the importance of brief preventive clinical intervention and referral.

Tipping the Balance: Brief Treatment of Multiple Problems in a Marriage

Helen and Juan (who preferred his nickname "Jake") Garcia and their four children living at home, who ranged in age from 19 to 5, were referred by Child Protective Services to a clinical social worker in private practice. The family had originally come to the attention of the protective agency because of allegations made by the 13-year-old daughter, Maria (the only girl), that her father had fondled her genitals on two occasions when he was intoxicated. A summary of the full investigation by the protective workers and the probation officer of family court where the case had been heard concluded that Jake was very remorseful about his behavior (he did not remember it, but he did not deny it) and had successfully abstained from alcohol for two months. He was attending Alcoholics Anonymous meetings and planned to continue. The family was being referred to the private practitioner, who worked closely with the protective services and the court, because of multiple problems. The child protective workers believed that if the problems were not alleviated, excessive drinking and sexual abuse could recur. Serious difficulties included the following: Jake, who had few work skills and spoke little English, through no fault of his own had recently lost his job as a chauffeur; the learning-disabled 11-year-old son

was truant from school; the 19-year-old son was not taking initiative to find work; Helen had never been employed outside of the home and for many reasons was reluctant to look for a job despite the current financial crisis.

After two meetings with the entire family, it became apparent that the most critical unresolved issues were within the parental relationship. Except for Maria, who had been "parentified" and was habitually protective of her mother, the children did not want to attend meetings. The worker offered resources for vocational counseling to the oldest son; she also contacted the teacher of the 11-year-old in hopes of getting him special remedial and supportive attention at school.

Some separate meetings were held with just the parents and Maria concerning the specific experiences she had with her father and her feelings of betrayal because she had not been protected by her mother (who at first did not believe the child's statements about the sexual abuse). Maria was also bitter because she felt that she had taken better care of her mother over the years than her mother had of her. In these meetings, Jake told Maria of his regret and shame. Although Helen was defensive at first, the worker was able to help her to *really* listen and respond to Maria's outlook on their relationship and the roles they had fallen into with each other.

Over four months, the worker held 12 marital sessions with Jake and Helen. In addition to the serious practical problems, it was soon revealed that unspoken resentments between them were quite close to the surface, even though each had a polite, almost deferential demeanor vis-à-vis one another as well as toward the outside world. As it turned out, Helen was harboring 20-year-old anger pertaining to their courtship; she felt that their first sexual experience had been forced upon her. Because of cultural and family beliefs, she had thought she had no choice but to marry Jake even though she did not respect him. Helen also blamed Jake for various actions that she felt had alienated her from her extended family.

Over the years, Jake had reacted to Helen's nonverbal sullen and critical attitudes toward him by becoming increasingly distant and morose; he began drinking heavily. Neither had directly discussed the unhappiness between them; therefore, neither understood the other and each experienced the other's behavior as attacking and rejecting. In couple therapy, the mutual disclosure of feelings and assumptions was intense and extremely difficult for both at first, but after only a few sessions each reported enormous relief, greater trust, and closeness. They reviewed scores of events in their lives that had led to pain and misunderstanding.

By the time the short-term treatment ended, the positive potential in the relationship had been uncovered. Once the grudges dissipated and there was greater fulfillment in the relationship, Jake and Helen were able to work together on other serious problems facing their family. Jake continued to go to AA, was not drinking, and was offered a secure job by a distant, well-to-do relative of Helen's from whom the Garcias had been estranged until Helen initiated a reconciliation during the treatment.

Treatment procedures employed by the worker included: a great deal of *sustainment,* in which the worker's warmth, nonjudgmental acceptance, and encouragement were conveyed, and *direct influence,* especially when the worker encouraged family members to communicate more openly. *Worker–client communications* involving *exploration-description-ventilation* were particularly important to the progress in this case, as Helen, Jake, and Maria shared their harbored resentments and sorrows—

some of years standing—with each other. There was *person–situation reflection* about many of the current dilemmas, but relatively little *intrareflection* as such; the relief was achieved in large part by the release of feeling and the correction of long-standing assumptions and distortions. *Pattern-dynamic* and *developmental reflection,* which involves introspection, was minimal. In this connection, it is important to distinguish the review of historical material from processes that lead to self-understanding; the Garcias shared many feelings about the past but, as indicated, these did not increase self-awareness as such; rather, they resulted in catharsis and increased understanding of one another. *Environmental help* was also given by the worker, especially to the two Garcia sons. This case illustrates the usefulness of the Hollis typology in analyzing couple treatment.

Certainly all the problems in this case were not settled, and they may never be. Enduring personality problems were only briefly addressed. However, *the balance of the marital system shifted, allowing the strengths of the partners and the relationship to emerge.* Helen and Jake were thereby freed to build on rather than to continue to obscure their capacities for affection and problem solving. Despite the many problems presented by the Garcia family members, they made changes more rapidly than Al and Barbara (see Chapter 16) who, on the surface or to the outsider, might have seemed to be much less troubled than the Garcias were.

At a follow-up family meeting six months after termination, it was apparent that the Garcia couple and the family continued to make progress. Communication among them all was vastly improved; the older son was working and the younger was getting better grades and enjoying school more. Maria seemed more relaxed and less involved in her parents' affairs. Jake and Helen worked together with less rancor and more mutual respect. Experience has taught us that if the couple relationship works well, parenting issues are usually vastly simplified. Even extremely destructive behaviors, such as incest and alcohol abuse, can be prevented or corrected when the marital relationship changes. In this case, as in many other intact families who come for family therapy, very soon after the initial explorations, the mutual decision is made to work mainly with the parents. And in some situations significant alleviation of long-standing dysfunction can occur in a short time.

COUPLE VERSUS CONCURRENT INDIVIDUAL SESSIONS

Many of the indications, contraindications, and advantages that pertain to family therapy, as discussed in Chapter 15, pertain also to conjoint couple treatment and need not be repeated here. However, we want to emphasize some specific issues relating to conjoint and concurrent individual sessions when marital matters are involved.

It is not uncommon for workers, even those who prefer conjoint to individual concurrent therapy of spouses with marital difficulties, to arrange a meeting or two with each spouse separately. Many therapists believe that rapport with each person is established more quickly by using this approach. It gives some spouses freedom to talk more easily about difficult material, including "secrets," such as extramarital affairs, and collusions of various sorts with other family members (often parents or children).[7] There is disagreement among clinicians about how such "classified" information should be handled. Some workers promise confidentiality, at times strongly encouraging that the information be revealed to the nonattending spouse, at other times dealing with the pros

and cons of keeping the material hidden. Many clinicians declare at the outset that they will not keep secrets. This approach has the advantage of protecting the therapist from collusion; it can also protect either spouse from feeling betrayed by the therapist who participated in withholding important information. Pittman describes his point of view: "I have found it helpful to offer one separate individual session for each marital partner. Most jump at this opportunity to charm me and tell me their secrets, even though I make clear I won't agree to keep the secrets. People just need to check out the safety of revealing things in their fragile marriage."[8]

As we said in our discussion of extramarital relationships in Chapter 16, it is our view that each situation has to be assessed individually. Understanding the function that the secret information plays in the relationship may be more important than sharing the details with the spouse. Whatever approach is taken, it is of utmost importance that the worker make his or her position about secrets and confidentiality clear *from the outset* to prevent later misunderstandings.

Whether or not there are occasional separate sessions with individual spouses, it is our general view that unless there are contraindications (such as those listed on pages 408–10), conjoint meetings are an easier, more direct and efficient approach to alleviating marital distress than concurrent individual sessions. Although we have mentioned some of our reasons for this point of view earlier, we summarize those that we think are most important here:

1. Observation of the Complexity of the Couple Bond Usually this cannot be as thoroughly understood or addressed when it is not seen in vivo. The energies involved in the interactional patterns—the emotional

and comp
her, maki
dividual :
The w
treatmei
focus on
Frequen
worker c(
aging it
achievec
marital :
neutral
"coache
spouses
get to ki
new wa}
each oth
and me:
ally, if t
it is to
grandpa
For the
not be p
require
volved i
further
ference.
for real
most al
commu
worker
Desp
there :
when t
require
times, (
or botl
rectly
worker
apy, la
ventec
quiries
her ap
partia
spouse

intensity of the interlocking process—go beyond the dynamics of each individual and take on a life of their own. Emotions, especially those connected to the marriage, will be talked about but rarely experienced as keenly by clients in individual sessions. Furthermore, people are not usually aware of the intricacy of their marital patterns and therefore cannot fully describe them.

2. Internalized Objects (Introjects) from the Past Can Often Be Corrected in the Context of Current Relationships
Experience has taught us that inner images of one's parents and corresponding self-images can change in the presence of the original object; however, it has also become apparent that close, meaningful relationships in the present can facilitate the revision of early internalizations. For example, when a spouse has projected an inner representation of a critical father onto his or her mate, it is still possible to amend it "second hand"; in other words, a positive marital relationship can provide a *corrective experience* and be instrumental in rectifying the old introjects, thereby freeing people to experience their mates and themselves as they actually are. Family-of-origin meetings with each spouse can be very valuable in remedying and/or updating internalized images of parents, but often this is not possible because the parents are not available or the clients refuse to involve them.

3. Transference to a Therapist Is Not Usually as Intense, Stable, or Fully Developed as It Is with a Spouse
It follows that it is therefore not as accessible to reflection and insight. Thus, it is usually far more effective to work on the transferences between the partners than those from spouses to the worker. We will be saying more about transference in the context of couple therapy in the next section.

4. The Interchangeability and Instability of Individual Symptomatology Become Much More Apparent to the Worker and to the Couple in Marital Sessions
As previously discussed, when one person's symptom diminishes, often that person's spouse may manifest some new problem. Along the same lines, the meanings behind the symptoms, such as the phobias described in the case of Barbara and Al (see Chapter 16), are frequently uncovered when the marital relationship is explored.

5. Each Spouse Has the Opportunity to Understand Qualities of the Other
When both spouses are present, it becomes more possible for each to understand the basis for the feelings and behavior of the other. Too often, each spouse takes the emotions and actions of the other personally, as rejections or attacks. It often becomes apparent that negative emotions expressed by a spouse are "covers" for other, usually softer, unacknowledged feelings. It can be extraordinarily relieving to learn that some unpleasant attitudes of one's partner derive from early childhood experiences and not primarily from the marriage. Obviously, when spouses are not defensive, they are much more likely to hear and to empathize with one another. We discussed these points in greater detail earlier in this chapter.

THE COUPLE–WORKER RELATIONSHIP

Much of what we said in Chapters 9 and 15 about realistic and unrealistic responses, transference, and countertransference applies to couple treatment as well as to individual and family therapy. However, there are some special issues, particularly in connection with transference and countertransference, that relate specifically to marital treatment and require mention here.

Wheneve
major foo
the tran:
toward
shall soo
titudes t
importan
by the sj
stances
ally best
deliber:
transfer

Intracc
in the c
jects roo
vealed
fenses, :
transfei
the spo
the mai
tive exp
far mor
apy ho
marita
intensi
to mak
strong
marita
(see Cl
the ot
origin
the int
couple
analys
betwee
can us
vidual
exami
lation:
Ou
they "
conne

thereby, much to the benefit of troubled couples who seek our professional help.[12]

POSTSCRIPT: KATHY AND TOM BRENT

Tom and Kathy were in marital treatment on a more or less weekly basis for just over two years. Toward the latter part of treatment, the three children attended four sessions with their parents. No other family members were invited to attend. Both Tom and Kathy were adamantly opposed to including any of them even though occasionally the worker suggested it, operating on the notion that many of their earlier unhappy experiences could be more deeply understood by them and perhaps modified in the present relationships.

During the first year the worker was extremely active and followed treatment steps described earlier in the chapter. Again and again, with acceptance and warmth, she helped both Tom and Kathy to understand themselves, in the past and present, so that they could begin to speak frankly about their own thoughts and feelings. Although the development of self-awareness and trust came slowly, after the first year—with only occasional setbacks under stress—they were able to talk to each other freely about heretofore hidden matters, with the result that each had increased appreciation of the other and listened more often without becoming defensive. Once self-awareness and communication were enhanced, focus on the problematic, dysfunctional aspects of their lives greatly diminished. By the end of the first year of therapy, the marital relationship was no longer the demoralizing, painful experience it had been when they first sought help.

The second year of therapy could be devoted to building on strengths and expanding potentials of the individuals and of the relationship. Tom and Kathy used their sessions to channel energies previously depleted by fear and self-doubt. They discussed vocational and educational plans: Tom decided to enroll in a technical school and prepare for a career as an electronics technician; Kathy contemplated an advanced degree in nursing, hoping eventually to become supervisor of her office at the visiting nurse association. Each felt supported by the other in these explorations and decisions. Because their families, both of which were experienced by them as emotionally barren, had provided them with few examples of creative and loving relationships, they had to learn how to bring tenderness and positive direction to their marriage. The worker's kind, honest, self-confident, but nonauthoritarian style offered a model that undoubtedly influenced this phase of treatment. Tom and Kathy were able to learn by example that their own energies and initiatives could enhance every aspect of their lives. Thus both the improved marriage and the "good aunt" transference to the worker provided a rich, reparative experience.

After years of silent dissatisfaction with their sexual life, Tom, with considerable difficulty but without blame, raised the subject in a session. They openly discussed how they felt about it and what they wanted. As often happens, outside the sessions rather than in the worker's presence, they began talking about some of the most intimate details. In a very short time they reported with delight renewed pleasure in their love life. For most of their lives they had been guided by what they thought were the expectations or attitudes of others or "rules" they had been raised by, with little sense that they could shape their own experiences in the ways *they* wanted. Whether in relation to sex or to a host of other matters, initially each had implicitly assumed that the fate of their marriage was determined by the other. Neither had confidence that his or her actions could influence the outcome of the relationship. During the second year of marital therapy, however, there were times of shared exhilaration as they enjoyed the rewards of the hard work both had put into the treatment.

Issues involving the children were discussed comfortably rather than defensively between them. The children came to four family sessions at the suggestion of Tom, not because there were any apparent difficulties, but rather so that they could participate with their parents in some of the changes that had been made. To the worker, they all seemed more relaxed and outgoing than they had when treatment began. Despite easier communication with each other and with the worker, Tom and Kathy's characteristic reserve at times still inhibited them from being as open with their children as they wanted to be. However, in the brief family therapy, they were more forthcoming than they had been, and there were several very touching moments in which all five members were able to share some feelings—primarily positive, often poignant—that had been "under cover" until then. Melissa, now almost 16, who was the "identified client" when the Brents first came for treatment, summed up the current family situation in the final family meeting: "We used to be more like an army troop than like a family. We all did everything we were supposed to do, on schedule, but it never seemed to matter how we felt about it. No one hardly ever laughed or cried except at the movies. But since Mom and Dad came for help, they both seem happier and have more patience about what concerns us. Dad's temper used to be very scary to me and he seemed so unapproachable; Mom was like a 'top sergeant,' keeping us in line. The difference is, now we can talk to them and they listen and really care about our feelings. Now, too, we can have fun as a family." Clearly, the improvement of the marital relationship yielded innumerable benefits for the children even though they were only peripherally involved in the actual therapeutic process. Successful marital treatment often has significantly preventive ramifications; dysfunctional family patterns handed down from generation to generation can be diminished, if not arrested, when parents interrupt the process by becoming self-defined and constructively taking charge of themselves and their relationships.

Couples of all ages,[13] walks of life, and lifestyles are seen by social workers in a broad range of contexts in brief and extended treatment. The Hollis typology of treatment procedures and worker–client communications can be adapted for conducting and studying conjoint interviews. Couple sessions provide the worker with opportunities for intervention not available in individual therapy. The intensity of marital interactions can make joint interviewing difficult and confusing; an attitude of neutrality takes practice to achieve, particularly with couples who activate intense responses. But the worker who strives for self-awareness and has seen couple after couple can become comfortable and skillful working with troubled marriages. Often one has the privilege of participating in a positive growth process that ultimately reaches many more people than the two who actually came for help.

NOTES

1. The genogram, which organizes useful information and provides a quick picture of a family tree and relationship patterns over generations, is valued by many individual, marital, and family therapists. For an excellent reference on how to construct and "read" genograms, see McGoldrick and Gerson (1985). See also Hartman and Laird (1983) and Guerin and Pendagast (1976).

2. For two special books that discuss illusions, myths, and disillusionments in intimate relationships, see: Lederer and Jackson (1968), written for professionals and nonprofessionals (in a marriage or contemplating marriage); and Shor and Sanville (1979).

3. Greenberg and Johnson (1986), p. 258; we highly recommend this article, which many experienced clinicians and students who see couples in treatment have found extremely helpful. We recommend the book by Greenberg and Johnson (1988), also on emotionally focused couples therapy. The volume edited by Johnson and Greenberg (1994) has several very useful chapters on the role of emotion in intimate relationships and how, in couples therapy, the experience and expression of authentic feelings can help to heal troubled marriages.

   Livingston (1998), from a self-psychological viewpoint, discusses how the expression of conflict and aggression can lead to uncovering underlying feelings of vulnerability.

4. Pittman (1987), p. 14; in addition to being a resource for family therapy, Pittman's book addresses problems in marriages and couple treatment.

5. For readings on couple treatment not cited in this chapter or in Chapter 16, we recommend Beck (1987) on redirecting blame in couples therapy, Larsen (1982) on improving marital communication, and Pugh (1986) on helping couples interact.

   We especially suggest an article by Greenspan (1993), with case illustrations, which discusses therapy with couples whose underdeveloped self-sustaining functions threaten their marriages.

   For a clear, informative description of three versions of the object relations approach to couple treatment, see Spaulding (1997). See an interesting article by Nelsen (1995) that describes the dynamics of two types of narcissistically vulnerable couples: "the narcissistic-overgiving couple and the borderline-codependent pair"; treatment implications are discussed.

   Mennen and Perlmutter (1993) raise clinicians' consciousness about the possibility of childhood sexual abuse as an influence on difficulties in current couple relationships; the authors suggest characteristics that may indicate early abuse in one or both partners and offer guidelines for introducing the issue.

   In a useful and interesting article, Mackay and O'Brien (1998) report on research on gender and ethnic differences in marital conflict management; it is important to point out that most research on couple treatment has studied white, middle-class, heterosexual couples.

   Jordan, et al. (1989) discuss the many issues faced by dual-career couples and how social workers may be able to help.

   See also two books on couple treatment: Guerin (1987) and Stuart (1980).

6. For references on bereavement, see Chapter 5, note 19. For references related to persons with HIV or AIDS, see Chapter 8, note 33.

7. See the chapter by Kayser (1997) on couples therapy, which discusses this point. References on extramarital affairs can be found in Chapter 16, notes 79 and 80.

8. Pittman (1987), p. 85.

9. Two good articles, Greenspan (1993) and Livingston (1995), discuss transference-like phenomena within couple relationships.

10. See especially Bowen (1978); however, from the psychosocial point of view, the clinician is not as apparently emotionally aloof as Bowenians sometimes seem to prefer to be.

11. We recommend the volume edited by Titelman (1987) with several very good chapters on the importance of therapists understanding processes of their families of origin; several authors discuss their efforts to strive for differentiation and self-definition.

12. Many of the forms countertransference can take in couple work are discussed in chapters in a recommended volume edited by Solomon and Siegel (1997).

13. For references on couple treatment of the elderly, see Getzel (1982) and Wolinsky (1986). Again, see Brown and Zimmer (1986) and Eda Goldstein (1997) on therapy with lesbian couples, Cornett (1997) on clinical practice with gay men, Boyd-Franklin and Franklin (1998) on African American couples, and Falicov (1986) on cross-cultural marriages; additional references can be found in previous chapters, especially Chapter 16.

CRISIS INTERVENTION AND BRIEF TREATMENT

Throughout this book there are discussions and case illustrations of brief treatment of individuals, couples, and families. This chapter summarizes some basic principles and approaches to crisis intervention and other brief therapies.

For years it was assumed by most caseworkers that a contact should be continued until the needed help was given, or the client withdrew, or the worker decided there was nothing more to be done. But many clients withdrew after only a few interviews. Others continued for many months, sometimes for several years. The "functional" school of social work, strongly influenced by Otto Rank's thinking, as early as the 1930s began advocating setting at the outset a limit on the length of contact.[1] Proponents of this approach believed the client worked best against such limits, that the will was mobilized and growth and individuation were fostered by establishing planned endings. Subse-

quently, for many reasons related to expediency and to clinical judgment, some of which we shall address in this chapter, caseworkers from all schools of thought began to assess when short-term treatment might be *as* effective as or even *more* effective than unlimited therapy. Various devices were tried to bring help more quickly, among them briefer services with more limited and specific goals.

CRISIS INTERVENTION

A major form of brief service is crisis treatment.[2] Originally seen only as an emergency measure, a holding operation until longer-term treatment could be arranged, crisis treatment, in which *help was offered immediately* and at the scene of the crisis when necessary, often proved effective in preventing long-range or devastating effects of traumatic events. A pioneer in crisis theory and intervention, Erich Lindemann, worked with the families of victims of the 1943 Boston Coconut Grove nightclub fire.[3] Finding remarkable uniformity in the "normal" grief reactions of the survivors, he described the "acute grief syndrome" and delineated phases of "grief work" through which the bereaved had to proceed to begin to free themselves from binding ties to the deceased, to readjust to life without that person, and to form new relationships. Lindemann's work led the way for others to outline predictable *phases* and *tasks,* typologies designed to guide interventions, associated with a broad range of hazardous events or developmental and transitional crises. We will say more about the benefits and limitations of these typologies shortly.

Categories of Crises

A crisis may be defined *as any major event or change that requires individuals or families to restructure their ways of viewing themselves, their world, and their plans for living in it.*[4] It may be precipitated by a specific trauma (or series of traumas) or a circumstance (or set of circumstances) that has been building over time. One may think of crises as *anticipated* or expectable or as *unanticipated.*

Anticipated Crises   These expectable events include *developmental* or maturational events, such as adolescence, midlife, and old age. Anticipated crises also embrace *transitional* points in the life of an individual or family such as starting a new job or school, moving to a new area, living in the "empty nest," or retiring.

Unanticipated Crises   These events include various kinds of *losses:* death of a family member or friend; desertion, separation, or divorce; a disabling accident; mental or physical illness of an individual or family member; loss of a job; a miscarriage

or stillbirth; and so on. Many changes can be experienced as *loss,* such as the behavior problem of a previously "model" child, the affair of a spouse, incest, alcoholism of a family member, or alienation among family members. *Additions,* too, may precipitate an unanticipated crisis: the birth of a new sibling, taking a foster child or elderly relative into the home, the merger of households required by shortage of housing, illness or death of a parent. And *external blows* and conditions create unanticipated crises: floods or droughts; earthquakes; fires; economic depression; war; and violence or rape perpetrated against an individual, family member, or associate are a few of many such hazardous events.

Although some events—anticipated or not—would be distressing to some degree to all people, *there are many variations in reactions to specific circumstances.* We all know people who have endured terrible tragedies or traumas yet are able to mourn very painful losses, regain their balance, and creatively call upon resources that help them develop new definitions of life situations and goals. For others, a disruption or change—even sending a young child to overnight camp for the first time or receiving a poor grade on an examination—can be perceived as being close to catastrophic from which rebound seems difficult. People who have experienced disasters or other crises are remarkably different in their vulnerability to stress and their capacities for problem solving, resilience, and creative adaptation to changes in circumstances. *Assessments of clients who have experienced disaster or are in a state of crisis must be individualized.*

The Crisis State

Whatever the precipitant, crisis upsets the equilibrium (the homeostatic balance) of the individual personality or family system.

Although the actual duration of the *acutely* disturbed state varies widely, it is time-limited. The tension and anxiety induced by the crisis mount until some resolution occurs (often during a period of up to six or eight weeks) with or without professional help. As described by Rapoport and by Galon, both of whom have studied and written extensively about crisis theory and treatment,[5] the individual or family may perceive the crisis and the subsequent circumstances as a *threat* to the sense of well-being (which stimulates anxiety), as a *loss* (which induces depression and grief), or as a *challenge* (which mobilizes positive energy and motivation for growth). Often people view their situations as a combination of these.

Depending on a number of factors we shall discuss shortly, including what coping mechanisms are activated, the resolution can result in a condition that is better than it was before the crisis, that returns to the previous state, or that deteriorates to dysfunctional patterns of living. *Once the crisis state subsides and some resolution occurs, individuals and families are far less likely to be accessible to outside intervention* than when they are feeling vulnerable, unsettled, or disorganized *immediately* following the crisis, when rapid change is possible within a short time.

Outcomes of Crisis

Tension induced by crisis calls for relief. When individuals and families are in an unsteady state, egos are fluid, defenses are shaken, emotions are at a peak; there is often a great deal of floundering and a search for comfort and answers. Thus action is taken that results in an outcome. Overlapping *positive* outcomes include (1) resolution, (2) redefinition of the problem or expectations, and (3) relinquishment of goals.

Resolution　This can be as specific as the location of a homemaker or the activation of a support network that comforts during a catastrophic or transitional time. A child may be encouraged to take a favorite doll to kindergarten until adjustment to school is achieved. A man who has lost his job may be retrained for another. Or resolution and the return to equilibrium may require that people go through a process, a series of stages, as they do in grief reactions.

Redefinition　This is often necessary to resolve the situation that brought on the crisis. For example, psychoeducation provides families of severely disturbed individuals with a realistic understanding of mental illness and attempts to diminish feelings of blame or failure.[6] Often when working with families with adolescents, an effort is made to help both the parents and the teenagers realize that the anger or behavior exhibited by either "side" is not intended to hurt, but rather arises from fear, frustration, self-doubt, or other negative emotions. Mr. Russo (see Chapter 15) reframed his employment situation; this capacity led to his decision to continue on in his familiar job rather than to seek work with more prestige.

Relinquishment　Moving beyond unavailable objectives and dreams often occurs through mourning and, ultimately, redirection of energies. Again and again, people must restructure their ways of looking at the world and their relation to it. Rejection from medical schools may lead a person to give up a life-long career ambition and consider another profession for which he or she is better qualified. A father may have to let go of hope that his son will join him in the family business. Parents who have fixed notions about how they want their children to lead their lives as adults find they must relinquish these when they realize that their son or daughter intends to remain single, is gay, or plans to intermarry. After his daughter moved out on her own, Mr. Kennedy (Chapter 3) had to resign himself to this fact and develop new strategies for living. Deaths and desertions that result in profound heartbreak and grief ultimately require new adaptations after the mourning phase. When a spouse has died, even when the relationship was close and interdependent, sometimes, to his or her surprise, the surviving spouse not only recovers from the devastating loss but also gets a "new lease" on life.

When positive solutions do *not* occur, however, greater—sometimes seemingly irreversible—disorganization may follow. When coping mechanisms habitually employed by individuals or families do not successfully resolve the current situation, maladaptive patterns often develop. *Chronic* grief and depression may set in after a loss. In clinical practice, for example, we often see people who have been widowed for years and continue to despair rather than redirecting their lives; some will repeatedly say something like: "I just don't want to go on without him (her)." (In some such cases, if treatment had been sought at the time of the loss, the unyielding, dysfunctional emotional response could have been prevented.) To handle painful events, people sometimes withdraw or refuse to associate with family members whom they blame for their troubles, thus intensifying feelings of anger or hurt. Others blame themselves so harshly for what has happened to them that problem-solving mechanisms are paralyzed.

Preventive Intervention

Everyone does not need or want professional help to go through a crisis and restore or improve previous emotional balance. However, in recent decades, social workers and other clinicians have become increasingly innovative in their approaches to victims of crisis and disaster and to populations "at risk." Mobile crisis units, telephone "hot lines" directing people to the help they need, special services providing assistance to victims of crime, mental health teams offering *immediate* attention to those who need it, and more have emerged in an effort to respond to people when they are most amenable to help and can best use it. These opportunities are designed to *prevent* disabling aftereffects. Brief help during this period, when people need to ventilate and are more open to reflection and advice, is usually far more effective than long-term treatment after the crisis is over. Clients in ongoing therapy often make the most rapid gains when a crisis arises. When stress following catastrophic or traumatic events (assault, rape, incest, and war, for example) is not treated quickly, posttraumatic stress disorder may follow, resulting in permanent emotional and/or cognitive impairment.[7] Evidence suggests that disasters inflicted or created by humans, in contrast to natural or accidental catastrophes (such as hurricanes, earthquakes, or airplane misfortunes), are often the most devastating because they assault a person's sense of trust and safety. Group "debriefing" interventions, conducted within 24 to 72 hours after exposure to a traumatic event, have been found to reduce symptoms of stress and accelerate the recovery process; social workers are believed to be particularly qualified to develop and lead these "debriefing" programs.[8]

Concerns about *prevention* have also been behind the development of other programs. These programs offer services *before* or *during* a crisis. Parents of children in day care are given an opportunity in groups to address issues such as child development, parenting, family relationships, and the like. "Rap groups" in schools and community centers offer support and direction to adolescents during an often tumultuous developmental phase. Relatives of cancer patients are sometimes seen in groups during the admission process at hospitals; not only are support and information supplied, but also social workers *screen* for individuals who need and want more extensive services. Under the best circumstances, family members are routinely seen by social workers in hospital emergency rooms, psychiatric facilities, nursing homes, and so on, not just to enlist help for the patients but also to determine who else may need assistance to prevent or minimize the effects of the crisis for everyone involved.[9]

(Unfortunately, as we said in Chapter 8, support for these preventive services often depends on the priorities of current political administrations or of private funding sources. Financial support that is inadequate, sporadic, or suddenly cut back interrupts the help, and some potential clients never receive assistance. The effectiveness of innovations in practice cannot always be properly evaluated because, as a result of the interruptions, they are too short-lived or fragmented.)

Generic Stages: Do They Occur in Reaction to Crisis? What about Time-Limited Tasks and Interventions?

Originally, crisis intervention was seen as relevant primarily to intact, well-functioning individuals who faced hazardous events or developmental transitions. Notions were then developed about predictable—so-called normative—reactions to a broad range of such situations. Kubler-Ross's typology of reactions to the diagnosis of terminal illness are well known: (1) denial and isolation, (2) anger, (3) bargaining, (4) depression, and (5) acceptance. It seems that there is hardly any maturational crisis, profound life change, or hazardous event that has not been studied and about which time-limited stages of reaction and tasks required for resolution have not been proposed.[10] These, in turn, have led clinicians to design interventive strategies. However, as Lukton points out, "Generally, proof is lacking that the coping tasks must be performed in a preordained sequence, or that being able to conceptualize the stages helps to perform the tasks." Generic interventive principles can be useful when flexibly applied, but they do not help workers differentiate one client from another. Lukton wrote: "When we fail to explore the unique experience of the crisis for each client, we may force the data into our own preconceived categories and *may miss discovering the meaning of the event for the individual*." [Emphasis ours] She adds, "We have been remarkably untroubled by the lack of agreement among the experts as to the nature of the normative tasks for various age groups." For example, some clinical writers view disengagement as one of the normative tasks of aging. Others take the opposite view that active interaction with the environment is normative. Lukton reminds us that we must think of older people and *all* people as diverse, with widely varying, sometimes unique needs that may conflict with rigid typologies of normative tasks and time frames.[11]

Taking Lukton's points a little further, on several grounds we believe it is misleading to design generic approaches to catastrophies or life stages for *intact and well-functioning people* on the assumption that they *react similarly to particular situations within a specific time frame*. First of all, people who are not so "intact" often creatively resolve crises and grow from the experience. Second, the generic approach tends to discount life experiences of clients in crisis that might influence the course re-actions and resolutions take. For example, some people who faced similar circumstances in the past may cope more easily as a result. On the other hand, previous, possibly unresolved, experiences can exaggerate current reactions, requiring attention to both past and present difficulties. Third, the environmental context in which the events are occurring can be of utmost importance to the outcome of the crisis. Available opportunities as well as the quality of support systems and living conditions may dramatically affect resolution. Fourth, the personalities of the people undergoing the crisis—their strengths and capacities, defense systems, and characteristic methods for handling problems and stress—are all very pertinent to crisis reactions and resolutions. Depending on a number of factors, then, crises that appear to be the same can have very different meanings and run very different courses. In crisis treatment, as in all other forms of psychosocial therapy, we need to think in systems terms rather than in linear terms.

We see the tendency to develop rigid typologies of interventive strategies designed for specific crises as unfortunate. It is equally unfortunate that crisis intervention is too often delegated to paraprofessionals or others with minimal training.

A woman who had recently been the victim of a vicious attempted rape was referred to a clinical social worker. She had first been seen individually and in a group by an earnest and caring woman police officer who headed a police department's Victims Assistance Service. Briefly trained in crisis techniques and operating on the notion that it was essential for this client to express her anger within a four-to-six-week period after the assault, the officer kindly but persistently prodded the woman to "get

in touch" with her rage. As it turned out, the woman characteristically had an extraordinarily peaceful, soft personality. She was numb and shocked, she was frightened by what had happened, she was having flashbacks of the terrible experience, but she had *no* awareness of anger. In her first visit with the social worker she asked, "Is there something wrong with me because I am not angry?" This woman's anger did not emerge until almost nine months after the incident, and her reaction to the crisis took well over a year to subside, in part because of the nature of her personality and in part because her assailant was out on bail (which terrified her) as the trial dragged on for 11 months. As a result of her minimal training, the police officer was not equipped to assess the fact that for these reasons this victim's fear transcended and blocked out her outrage for a far longer time than the generic approach suggested.

This case calls our attention to an important treatment consideration. If we always assume that crisis resolution must occur within a short time, we may find ourselves pushing clients too fast and too hard. In the case of Mr. Kennedy (Chapter 3), his daughter had moved away six months before intake; however, it was not until he had tried to work things out "his way" that he was willing to seek help. *Ideally,* interventions are made as soon as possible after the precipitating event. However, they may have to wait until the *cumulative* effects of the situation are so disturbing and efforts at problem solving so unproductive that the search for new solutions becomes essential. One researcher on trauma suggests, "The common belief that people recover after a few weeks from disaster is based on mistaking denial for recovery."[12] It sometimes takes months or even years for a person to assimilate fully the emotional impact of a catastrophic event. Again, *each situation has to be individually assessed.*

Crisis and the Assessment Process

It is essential to evaluate the *severity* of the crisis, the individuals going through it, the interplay with the environment, and the supports available. Fortunately, rapid diagnosis is often possible because the homeostatic balance has been upset. Among the interpenetrating areas to be assessed are the following.

The Meaning of the Crisis to the Individuals and Their Families In every situation, it is essential to evaluate the implications of the crisis to the people going through it. Although rape necessarily has a traumatic negative impact, a person who has never had sexual intercourse usually experiences the assault differently from one who does not have the added concern of loss of virginity. We mentioned previously the woman with several children whose husband had been killed in an accident a few years previously; when the worker expressed dismay about the tragedy, the woman replied: "Yes, it was terrible. But imagine how much worse it would have been if I had been in love with him!" Unemployment for an actor or actress may be less unexpected and less traumatic than for an assembly line worker thrown out of a job when the factory permanently closes. Some losses seem to be more symbolic than "real," yet are profoundly felt; for example, parents may need to be helped to take seriously their teenage son's reactions to a fender dent on the automobile he had saved for and pampered. As in all forms of psychosocial treatment, in crisis intervention it is clients who know best what their circumstances mean to them.

Current Adaptive Capacity Are the clients being assessed able to implement new methods of coping required by the present circumstances? How creative and flexible are they? Are functioning and problem-solving abilities impaired? In the case of Mr. Kennedy, for example, when he was first seen by the worker it was clear that there had been a significant loss of adaptive skills because he was so angry, depressed, and disorganized. In contrast, both Dick and Susan Jones (also Chapter 3) functioned almost as well as ever despite their acute distress. Esperanza Perez (also Chapter 3), who was having suicidal thoughts, quickly regained her balance once, with the help of her caseworker, she could normalize and put into perspective her feelings of distress in response to a series of upsetting events.

Pre-Crisis Personality Patterns and Level of Functioning As already suggested, an individual's or family's characteristic strengths, outlook, adaptational patterns, and defenses are often rapidly revealed when in crisis. In the Kennedy case, the worker quickly ascertained that Mr. Kennedy had been an active man with many interests who had relied heavily on his daughter for support; he had tried to adjust to his losses but simply could not achieve a comfortable balance in his life without help. When making an assessment, one may get some clues to personality functioning by comparing the client's reaction to a crisis to what might be an "expectable" reaction. One person may seem more thrown by a transient disappointment than another who has been given a diagnosis of cancer. It has been suggested that the more invulnerable one feels before a severe crisis and the more one views the world as benign, the more devastating the catastrophe will be.[13]

Relevant Prior Life Experiences Generally, in crisis treatment, we focus on present circumstances, coping mechanisms, adaptive capacities, and supports required for mastering the situation. History taking is generally limited to matters that are relevant to the current circumstances. Nevertheless, clients often spontaneously link previous events, feelings, or difficulties to their reactions to the crisis event. One woman who had been raised in a large and very poor family agonized when her apartment was burglarized: "I never, ever before had anything of my own." Poorly resolved old conflicts or losses may be revealed and reexamined while working on the crisis at hand. The woman described earlier who had endured an attempted rape was able to work on her difficult marital relationship while she was in treatment because her husband was more available to her than he had been in the past; the crisis had shifted the balance of the marital system. Adaptive capacities strengthened through resolution of a crisis frequently carry into the future, when new situations arise. Even though Mr. Kennedy spoke little about past history, his characteristic ways of handling loss and dependency were quickly revealed and modified. In the face of their current crisis, the Jones couple came to understand antecedents to maladaptive patterns and made changes that promised to be lasting. On the other hand, *positive* prior experiences, such as success in resolution of losses or traumas, with or without the worker's help, can be recalled by clients, reassuring them of their capacities for rebound and creative adaptation.

Family Circumstances and Attitudes When an individual is in a crisis, the approach taken by family members can make a big difference. Unintrusive but positive support provides the individual with the optimal context in which to go through and come to grips with the ordeal. When family members blame the victim, become dictatorial, or overprotect him or her, resolution may be diverted or distorted. Sometimes dysfunctional family patterns are intertwined in the crisis situation, as when, for example, a woman who has been extremely dependent on her grown children loses her husband and pressures at least one of them to return "home." When families as a whole are facing a crisis, it is important to assess the potential for mutual aid and support. In many crisis situations, family meetings or conjoint meetings with relatives and friends are helpful in arriving at accurate assessments and often can be crucial to a healthy outcome. The case of Mrs. Antonini (see page 212) illustrates how this approach can be useful in evaluating available supports and facilitating their involvement.

Support Systems: Needed Resources and Opportunities Each crisis event has its own requirements of the environment; these depend in part on the assessment of all the factors discussed above. For Mr. Kennedy, the location of a part-time job with a rent-free apartment was fortunate on both financial and emotional grounds. The crisis that occurred in the Carter family (Chapter 20), when the children were precipitously placed in foster care, could have escalated to a very serious situation if there had not been an experienced and caring clinical worker available to support and advocate for the parents and their children. Similarly, the crises faced by the Stones (Chapter 3) required the involvement of several collaterals and other environmental opportunities for the family to be able to achieve a more stable and comfortable way of life. First-rate medical evaluation for a baby with an organic brain defect, adequate educational facilities for extraordinary children of all kinds, a homemaker for an accident victim living alone can all provide an enormous amount of reassurance and practical help. Therapeutic and self-help groups sometimes are more effective than individual treatment in assisting people who have been victimized by catastrophic events.

Individualized Crisis Treatment

On the basis of the evaluation, crisis treatment usually includes the following.

Development of a Positive Therapeutic Relationship and Alliance that neither Overprotects nor Blames Victims of Abuse or Catastrophe   As is true in all brief therapies, effective crisis treatment requires early establishment of a comfortable, respectful worker–client relationship in which mutual agreement is reached about goals and tasks. The necessary components of the positive client–worker relationship discussed in Chapter 9 (which is directly associated with favorable outcomes) apply equally to crisis treatment.

When working with victims of every sort of disaster, it is particularly necessary to *avoid overidentifying* (in contrast to empathizing) with client pain. A common pitfall in treatment of clients who have been traumatized is to try to assuage their intense reactions with overreassurance when ventilation and an understanding listener are required. Because workers want their clients' anguish to end, they may introduce solutions before fully assessing what clients want and can do for themselves; overresponsibility or "too much" helpfulness can foster dependence, undermine strengths, and discourage self-direction. On the other hand, as we commented in Chapter 8 in the section on "Worker Burnout," when dealing with disaster victims (including those who have endured social oppression and injustice), work-

ers face potential countertransference reactions: To avoid feeling the intensity of their clients' suffering, workers sometimes withdraw emotionally; they may lose their interest and caring feelings or, even worse, begin to blame their clients ("Why can't he get over it and get on with his life?" "If she hadn't been associating with the 'wrong people,' she wouldn't have been raped.") To avoid countertherapeutic reactions, it may help to consult with a supervisor or colleague. Ideally, workers maintain consistent and accurate empathy and a sense of close connection with their clients yet protect their personal boundaries so they do not become overwhelmed by their clients' vulnerabilities and powerful emotions. In a highly recommended article, Gibbons and associates elaborate on some of these points as they apply to crisis intervention and other types of clinical work.[14]

Active, Decisive Intervention   During and after the rapid assessment, in many cases the worker is more direct than in long-term treatment, less often waiting for realizations to come from the client. To an overwhelmed woman with small children who has just learned that her husband has an inoperable brain tumor, the hospital social worker might say, "It's going to be essential that we make plans now for the care of the children when they arrive home from school." Or, after listening carefully to a distraught woman who is immobilized by news that her mother, from whom she has been estranged for many years, is critically ill, "It sounds like you won't forgive yourself if you don't make the trip to see her. Isn't that what you are really saying?" Frequently, we may state emphatically that to come to grips with the situation quickly, it will be important for family members to join in the treatment process. In short, people who are "swept away" by the immediate impact of a crisis often require a worker who presents as a confident, competent, and caring authority. Yet, to every extent possible, the clients' goals for treatment are quickly but fully explored and mutual agreement is sought.

Clear Explanations Offered by the Worker   On the basis of information gleaned from clients, including experiences with and observations of them, the worker often offers interpretations about reactions to the crisis. These must suit the individual and not simply follow an outline of "normative" stages of reaction. To the woman who was the victim of the attempted rape, the worker said, "It's perfectly normal to feel numb after such a shocking experience." To another woman who had had a very similar experience but had a different personality, "Of course you are angry." To a man who had experienced many losses but had trouble expressing the depth of his feelings about them, "One more deadly illness in the family is more than anyone would find bearable."

Encouragement of Cognitive Reflection and Prevention of Disabling Regression   To the extent possible, the worker attempts to enlist the client's thinking processes to understand the situation more clearly and to prevent emotional flooding. Although the *ventilation* of clients' feelings provoked by the crisis, and the sense that they are understood, is *critically* important to healthy resolution, it is equally important that a *balance between emotions and understanding* is maintained. Clients can be helped to realize personal meanings of traumatic experiences and to identify maladaptive coping skills interfering with recovery. *Pattern-dynamic* and *developmental reflection* may accompany *person–situation reflection.* A worker asked a man who had lost his mother when he was young and who had withdrawn from his wife after his teenage son's suicide, "Is it usual for you to isolate yourself when un-

speakable tragedy strikes?" A worker might observe to a woman railing at family members after a crisis, "It seems that when you feel frightened (sad, disappointed) you express it as anger." Again and again, when diagnostically indicated, we say to clients in the throes of crisis, "Even though you feel as though you can't bring yourself to take the actions you have to take and make the decisions you have to make, I'm certain you will find that you can. Would it help to begin by taking this (specific) step?" Throughout treatment, the worker endeavors to *support strengths,* to promote and restore hope, mastery, competence, and autonomy as quickly as possible. Often, after an initial interview, the client gains relief from the ventilation of feeling and from being understood. Security can be derived from setting realistic tasks. In the Stone case (Chapter 3), Mrs. Stone was helped to regain an active role in taking charge of her family and her situation, thereby preventing a decline into hopelessness; in the process, her increased capacity for mastery prepared her to feel more competent in the face of future vicissitudes and crises.

Involvement of Needed Supports and Resources   On an individualized basis, as suggested above, the worker either actively searches for or assists the client in locating networks, assistance, or opportunities that will be the right "fit" for that person. Again, accurate assessment makes the difference. There is no point in referring people to places they will not go or in offering opportunities they will not accept.

Goals   Lydia Rapoport, in her now classic article on crisis intervention, aptly summarizes general objectives that can lead to specific goals tailored to the individual client(s):

> The goals of crisis-oriented brief treatment can be . . . specified as follows: (1) relief of symptoms; (2) restoration to the optimal level

of functioning that existed before the present crisis; (3) understanding of the relevant precipitating events that contributed to the state of disequilibrium; (4) identification of remediable measures that can be taken by the client or family or that are available through community resources.

These are the minimum goals that should be achieved as part of crisis resolution. In addition, where the personality and social situation are favorable and the opportunity presents itself or can be created, work can be done to: (1) recognize the current stresses and their origins in past life experiences and conflicts; (2) initiate new modes of perceiving, thinking, and feeling and develop new adaptive and coping responses that will be useful beyond the immediate crisis resolution.[15]

Even after an initial interview, relief sometimes is promoted by setting specific goals and defining tasks required to achieve them.

Crisis Intervention: A Case Example

Mrs. Green, a 37-year-old African-American woman, shared an apartment with her only child, Linda, age 15, and her 58-year-old mother, Mrs. Cranston. On the way home from her home-health aide job, after dark, Mrs. Green was mugged, beaten, robbed, and apparently left for dead on the streets of an inner-city, drug-plagued neighborhood in which violence was rampant. She had been one block from her home when she was attacked. A witness to the assault, perpetrated by two African-American male teenagers, called for help and Mrs. Green was taken by ambulance to a large, metropolitan hospital. Although she survived, several ribs were broken and she suffered internal injuries; she lost the sight of one eye. Had she not gotten immediate medical attention, she would have bled to death. Before discharge from the hospital, an overworked but alert social service worker referred her to the Community Crisis Center;

the worker was concerned about Linda, in particular, who seemed withdrawn and angry. The center, funded by public and private sources, was primarily staffed by clinical social workers.

Mrs. Green, her daughter, and her mother came to the first session, two weeks after the assault, at the suggestion of the social worker who took the call from Mrs. Green. The worker was a white woman about Mrs. Cranston's age; she greeted all three warmly and personally. In response to the worker's question about what had happened, Mrs. Cranston spoke first; somewhat matter-of-factly she summarized the incident, saying that they were lucky her daughter was not killed. "That is so true," the worker replied with feeling, "but I imagine you have each gone through a lot in the two weeks since that terrible day." With the worker's encouragement, Mrs. Cranston then added several comments about her reactions, including, "I was worried sick." The worker directed questions to Mrs. Green, a somewhat self-effacing woman, who echoed her mother's sentiments: She was glad to be alive and glad that she would recover. As the worker showed ongoing sympathetic interest, verbally and nonverbally, Mrs. Green did go on to speak about how terrified she had been when her assailants approached her; she was unconscious soon after the assault began. After going over her experience, to her own surprise, Mrs. Green began to cry. "I guess I haven't had time to let down until now," she said. The worker commented, "It's natural to have a lot of feelings after such a frightening and outrageous experience." Mrs. Green spoke of her sadness and fear; at this point, she did not express anger. At some length Mrs. Cranston spoke about not knowing "what things are coming to when these boys go out beating up and shooting their neighbors." Linda sat in silence and volunteered nothing; her expressions seemed to convey bitterness. The worker did not press her, but after her mother and grandmother had spoken further, she asked, "How has this been for you?" "When blacks hurt blacks nobody cares," Linda said. Although her mother's assailants had been identified by the witness and arrested, "They'll be back on the street soon," Linda added. The worker spoke about how terrible it is (she did *not* say "must be") to be scared all the time about being attacked; the worker's understanding was conveyed by her warm and genuine manner and also by the fact that the center was in the same neighborhood in which the family lived. "My mother could be dead," Linda said emphatically. "But she's not," Mrs. Cranston interjected. So that Linda would not be cut off by Mrs. Cranston's tendency to try to see the positive side, the worker replied: "But I guess Linda is speaking out of anger and fear about the 'war zone' in this community." They talked about how much worse things had gotten, and how hard it is to lose trust in people and feel unsafe.

Following Linda's initiative, there was some further talk by all three about the way they had to live; each expressed resentment concerning general indifference about violence. As they continued on this subject, in this extended two-hour session, Mrs. Cranston exclaimed: "That settles it! I am going back to work full-time and we are going to move to that new housing complex in Greenville." If necessary, Mrs. Green said she would take a side job one day a week with a family for whom she occasionally worked. Linda would have a longer commute to school (where she was an honor student) but she said it would be worth it. All three were determined to find a better solution for themselves. Although there had been some thought about finding a new place to live after Mrs. Cranston recently moved in with her daughter and Linda, no steps had been taken. With obvious admiration, the worker said, "When the three of you talk things out you sure get on the move. How great you are at doing that!" Before this first session ended, the worker asked how they felt about the meeting. "It's good to talk things out," Mrs. Green said, using the same words the worker had. Mrs. Cranston and Linda nodded.

Immediately afterward, the worker said that they had gotten off to such a fast start that there had been no time to ask how they felt about talking with a white person about such personal matters. "No problem," Linda remarked. "You're really nice and understanding," Mrs. Green said. "You helped us already," Mrs. Cranston added. "I hope you will let me know if you ever think I don't 'get it,' " the worker said. "I really want to know." After such a terrible event, they had certainly bounced back, the worker added, but she asked if they wanted to return, perhaps once or twice again. Sometimes, she said, after blows like the one they had, more feelings come to the surface. Without hesitation, and rather to the worker's surprise, Linda declared, "I want to come back."

When they returned four days later, the worker learned that the application for a new apartment in Greenville had been filed. "You sure work fast," she commented. In response to questions about her recovery, Mrs. Green said she was feeling better all the time, but she would never see out of her left eye. "What a sorrow," the worker said, shaking her head. Mrs. Green, with more assertiveness than seemed characteristic of her, said, "They had no right to do that to me. I did nothing to them." Linda called the attackers strong names. Although Mrs. Cranston admonished Linda for her language, tears were rolling down her cheeks. "I feel so bad," she said. The various levels of their grief were even more fully expressed as they spoke further of Mrs. Green's loss.

In the same session, Linda, with tears in her eyes, turned to her mother and said angrily, "You never want to talk about daddy, but none of this would have happened if he had cared. And you know that. You and gramma always want to keep everything quiet and nice." Mrs. Green sighed and turned to the worker to say that Linda's father, her husband, who had abused alcohol and drugs, left home six years ago. He kept in touch occasionally but had not been heard from for over two years until his sister called to say that he had AIDS and was in the hospital. He died almost a year ago. Neither she nor Linda went to see him. Linda blurted out, "You never gave me the choice!"

Two more meetings were held in which Linda's anger and sorrow about her father were shared with her mother. In answer to the worker's question, Mrs. Green said she had no idea how hurt and angry and deeply affected Linda had been in relationship to her father. She spoke about her own disappointment in her husband; when they were first married they both had big plans. Linda was very interested in hearing, mostly for the first time, her mother's feelings about *her* loss. They exchanged a few memories, some about good times, but also about hurtful events. Mrs. Cranston, whose own marriage had failed years ago, said that Linda and her daughter deserved better. "So did you," Mrs. Green replied.

"There have been a lot of hard things to talk about," the worker suggested. "It seems to me, though, that the air is clearer and there is less tension among you when you speak straightforwardly to one another. Does it seem that way to you?" Linda answered by saying that she hoped her mother and grandmother would not go back to their old "sugar and honey" ways. The worker said to Linda, as she had at other points in their meetings, that Linda seemed very capable of reminding them to "talk straight," especially now that she was not so scared to do so. She gave Linda a lot of credit for how their conversations about important matters had progressed and deepened because of her initiative and willingness to take risks. "You have a lot to be proud of in Linda," the worker told the mother and grandmother. They agreed.

After four two-hour sessions, the family saw no need to return again, but were told by the worker that the door was wide open to them at any point should they want to do so. Together, at the worker's suggestion, they summarized the ground they had covered and the changes they had made. First, now they did not cover up feelings or avoid painful subjects as they had before, and they felt better and closer to each other as a result. Second, they had made a decision to change their surroundings; although it meant sacrifices, it also meant that they did not have to live with so much fear. While saying their good-byes, the worker asked them to let her know after they moved how things were going. Four months later Mrs. Green called to say that they were very happy in their new apartment and that they had followed the worker's suggestion to sit down together once a week and "talk straight." Linda didn't let them forget to do that, she said.

There is no "typical" crisis intervention case. As is apparent, this was a family with an abundance of strengths. Although the crisis was experienced by all three family members as a threat to their sense of safety and as a loss, they also viewed it as a challenge to mobilize resources and make changes. In the worker's opinion, and seemingly in the family's also, these four intense meetings were remarkably preventive. At a time when there had been such a vicious assault, all three were feeling shaken and vulnerable, leaving them far more accessible to intervention than they probably would have been at another time.

In her rapid assessment during the first session, the worker recognized and supported the family's strengths. She also knew very early on that Mrs. Green and Mrs. Cranston tended to "keep the lid" on feelings and painful matters; Linda, in her withdrawal, harbored a lot of unexpressed feelings and thoughts. It is unlikely that they would have made such positive changes on their own; once the shock was over, it is probable that they would have quickly reverted to their customary patterns of avoidance. But, with the worker's gentle encouragement, they shared feelings and thoughts that had never before been discussed. After they expressed and experienced reactions to the traumatic incident, the path was then cleared for Linda to initiate the conversation about her father that had previously felt "forbidden." As we said, it is not unusual for grief expressed about one painful event to stimulate pent-up emotions about another. Although crisis intervention, and brief treatment in general, is usually very focused, new material usually is introduced, as it fortunately was in this case. It is possible that Linda's sense of not being listened to, combined with pent-up feelings of resentment and abandonment in relationship to her father, would have led her to be untrusting and could have interfered with future relationships as well as with her personal growth and comfort.

As this case illlustrates, in brief and crisis treatment, the Hollis typology of worker–client communications is as applicable as in any other form of therapy. The worker's use of *sustaining procedures*—of acceptance, encouragement, reassurance, and keen interest—are apparent even in this abbreviated description of the treatment. *Direct influence* is more frequently employed in some crisis cases, but this family was able to summon its own initiative and sense of direction. Nevertheless, the worker used these procedures when she suggested that the family come together; when she suggested they return; when she recommended more open conversation and expression of feeling; and when she encouraged them to continue to "talk straight" after they terminated. Procedures of *exploration-description-ventilation,* always important in cases in which there has been trauma, gave these family members immediate relief, as the case summary describes. *Person–situation reflection,* encouraged by the worker, occurred at various points as the family members became aware of feelings that had been put aside and when they gained in self-awareness and in understanding of others. *Pattern-dynamic reflection* was apparent when all three family members identified their tendencies to minimize or cover up their feelings and, in Linda's case, to retreat. *Developmental reflection* was not prominent, although Linda commented that she thought she had kept her sadness about her father inside for a long time; she could see it had turned into bitterness.

This case demonstrates the importance of making a quick and strong connection to the family as a whole and to each member. The warm, attentive, straightforward manner of the worker, combined with the family's motivation, was critical to the success of this brief intervention. Added to many others, this case confirms our view that most potential problems related to worker–client differences in race, ethnicity, or class are avoidable. When clients feel truly valued and understood by a sensitive, skilled worker, they recognize it; when background issues influence clients' perspectives or approaches to treatment, more often than not they will gladly teach a worker who lets it be known that he or she wants to learn about these. This subject was covered in greater detail in Chapter 2.

Finally, this family case was selected in part because it illustrates a high-functioning family that has survived while living under demoralizing and life-threatening conditions. Too often, outsiders assume that most inner-city residents have succumbed to despair, drugs, or lawlessness. While these are all-too-common responses to noxious conditions, there are many families who cope remarkably well and have a strong sense of values and direction. *When* services are accessible, as they were in this case, individuals who might otherwise decline into hopelessness can be helped; it is the worker's opinion that despite Linda's intelligence and excellent school performance, if there had been no treatment, her bitterness and withdrawal could have escalated, profoundly interfering with her emotional development. Other illustrations of innovative preventive services can be found in Chapter 8.[16]

"Crisis-Prone" Clients

In direct contrast to the family just described, an initial assessment of individuals or families may quickly reveal that the clients characteristically experience small changes or simple problems as emergencies. Whether the recent precipitating event is serious or not, it sometimes becomes apparent that there has been a chronic pattern of self-defeating behaviors and attitudes that promote extreme anxiety, disorganization, failure, and inability to cope with life's minor vicissitudes, to say nothing of major disasters. In these cases, it is not very useful to think in terms of "restoration to a preexisting optimal level of functioning." One hopes to help clients *strengthen* capacities for coping.

When the precipitating event is truly minor, and there is evidence that panic and

confusion have been a way of life, clients are often reassured when the situation is put into perspective. Although we must be careful to acknowledge their feelings, relief may come when clients see the current situation is not an emergency but simply one that they can learn to handle differently. As with all crisis victims, we attempt to bolster cognitive functions and allay regressive tendencies, to do all we can to support self-esteem, mastery, and autonomy; but in contrast to most crisis situations, with these cases we usually do not encourage repetitive ventilation. Clients with such difficulties often need longer treatment than crisis intervention ordinarily requires; brief treatment may be a "Band-Aid," but it is almost inevitable that a new small occurrence will bring on another overwhelming response and, perhaps, another cry for professional help. In our experience, many crisis-prone clients are helped to recognize that ongoing treatment, in which they learn to build on their strengths, can help them to avoid recurrent and agonizing ups and downs. Principles that apply to the treatment of personality disorders are usually relevant; when there are no extenuating external circumstances to account for extreme reactions, clients with this chronic problem frequently have serious ego deficits.

OTHER BRIEF TREATMENTS

It is beyond the scope of this book to discuss the many variations of the brief treatment model that have come into being over the past 55 years.[17] From World War II on, caseworkers became increasingly concerned about long agency waiting lists, more and more applicants seeking help, budget cuts, demands for accountability, questions raised regarding casework effectiveness, and so on. Furthermore, many clients for whom long-term treatment was being planned chose not to continue after a few sessions. Scrutiny of casework and other kinds of treatment revealed that much, if not most, therapy was brief. Clients were feeling helped more quickly than their caseworkers had believed possible. These realities led practitioners from the mental health professions to develop treatment strategies for short-term services. Once viewed as superficial and expedient, brief services now are often *preferred* by clients and clinicians alike. Over the years, research has assured us that *for a wide range of problems and clients,* effective results can be achieved through a short period of treatment. Even people with severe and chronic problems can be helped by brief treatment methods if goals are reasonably set.[18] In general, caseworkers no longer simplistically assume that more treatment is better treatment.

The Advent of Managed Care

As already mentioned elsewhere in this book, the past decade or so has seen the burgeoning of managed care companies in the private and public sectors in which many millions of people are now enrolled. This development has had a profound effect on the mental health field; clinicians and agencies are challenged to devise brief, solution-oriented therapy methods that will help people quickly. Many agencies that offered long-term care for those clients who required it and wanted it, now feel compelled for fiscal reasons to provide brief services only. As discussed in Chapter 1, there is a growing array of specific, "empirically validated" treatment interventions (about which there are differences of opinion) designed to target particular symptoms or problems.[19] Often justified by positive findings of outcome studies of treatment of very

specific conditions, managed care companies specify the number of sessions they will approve for benefits on the belief these should be sufficient to modify manifest problems or restore individuals to previous levels of functioning.

Psychosocial clinicians have trouble with these trends. Individuals with similar presenting problems can require very different kinds of treatment and various lengths of time to resolve them. The exploration of *underlying* issues related to a difficulty or the client's need for a "corrective" experience in order to improve social functioning and emotional well-being, for example, may require more time than managed care would usually approve; furthermore, managed care companies often prefer, and sometimes insist on, behaviorally oriented treatment plans and approaches. Mrs. Stone and Mrs. Zimmer (Chapter 3) and the Stasio, Carter, and Cooper cases (Chapter 20) all required more time and more complicated treatment strategies than managed care would generally endorse.

At the very time we have expanded our knowledge and skills in the treatment of clients with personality disorders and developmental deficits (see Chapter 11), opportunities for long-term treatment may become increasingly unavailable. Requests for additional meetings can be made when the clinician deems them necessary but, as practitioners know, these requests are not always granted by third-party reviewers, even on appeal. Also, punitive actions are sometimes taken against practitioners or agencies (for example, by limiting referrals or even by dropping them from the plan) if there are "too many" such requests. Obviously, loyalty conflicts are encouraged when companies offer incentives to practitioners to limit care, regardless of their clinical judgment about a case. The pressure on the clinician for quick results can put an enormous strain on the therapeutic relationship. Because of managed care demands that DSM diagnoses be applied to clients, workers may exaggerate client pathology to be eligible for reimbursement. Preventive services, which have been demonstrated to be so important to avoiding problems, generally do not fit into managed care schemes. Often family and couple therapies are not covered unless they are in the service of the treatment of a symptomatic member. Also, too often the third-party reviewers recommend psychopharmacological treatment even when the clinician, who knows the client firsthand, firmly believes that casework therapy, with or without medication, is necessary. And the managed care practice of dictating fees that agencies or independent practitioners can charge has created additional difficulties.

As will become clear shortly, we believe there is a lot of merit to brief treatment approaches. However, for clients covered by managed care, the fact that the "contract" for treatment is no longer based on a mutual and private decision between client and worker, but instead is strongly influenced and periodically reviewed by managed care, alarms us. Required intrusions on confidentiality are troublesome. Also, the entire system results in discrimination against clients of modest or substandard means; well-to-do people can always pay for service, but those on limited budgets cannot. Depending on how the trends continue, people in poverty covered by Medicaid may increasingly be denied adequate mental health services. We do not believe it is ethical to passively buckle under and adapt to these developments; to do so compromises our standards of practice and our professional responsibility to our clients. Nor should we just stew in our anger and take no action. Strom-Gottfried, in an excellent article, writes:

Managed care, and the ethical and clinical problems that result, are artifacts of our society's mixed messages about health care and who should pay for it. Managed care replaces a system that was also characterized by inequity of access and uneven quality, and which fostered its own share of ethical breaches. Observing, describing, and critiquing the system's flaws are important first steps in resolving the problem, but they are not sufficient to remedy it. Outrage must be converted to social action and systemic change. To do so is not only wise; it is ethical.[20]

Our discussion of brief treatment will take the position that we have to do all we can to advocate for opportunities to make treatment decisions that we know are clinically sound, even while managed care prevails, as it does at the time of this writing. Therefore, we have *not* tailored our presentation in a way that compromises the psychosocial perspective on therapy. We are among those who believe that as clinicians we are ethically responsible to provide or arrange services when insurance benefits do not or cease to cover clients' treatment requirements.[21] In Chapter 8, we commented on how agencies and private practitioners sometimes find creative solutions to the constraints of managed care. It is our fervent hope that before this text requires another revision, major features of the current health care system will be overhauled in ways that will result in the ethical delivery of clinical services, based on the needs of individuals and families rather than on cost-saving strategies of profit-oriented insurance companies or on misguided public policy.

Basic Features of Short-Term Treatment

We have found the following steps to be fundamental to brief treatment. Each step requires *close collaboration between worker and client.* These guidelines apply to individual, couple, and family therapy.

1. Defining the Problem   As in crisis treatment, often but not always, the presenting problem in short-term therapy is identified as the problem to be addressed. It is critically important that the worker and client *mutually* understand the major difficulty the client seeks to change, with the worker following the client's lead; the worker usually brings focus, clarification, and sometimes suggestions to the formulation. Even when working with involuntary clients, some of whom may be relieved that time limits will be proposed, agreement must be sought. Sometimes a second difficulty will be identified. Rapid assessment is required, with history taking usually limited to areas relevant to the problem at hand. As in all initial interviews (see Chapter 10), questions should be asked about the duration of the problem(s) and what remedies have been tried or considered. Psychosocial workers, in contrast to some other clinicians, usually explain that the problem definition *may* shift as they proceed. Even in the crisis case of Mrs. Green, described in the last section, in four extended sessions the focus switched from the effects of the trauma and its meanings to family members to unresolved sorrows about Mr. Green's desertion and death; the identification and modification of dysfunctional communication patterns also became a central area of attention. In this case, crisis intervention evolved into brief therapy.

Obviously, there is a large overlap between short-term and crisis treatments. Often, people who are referred for or seek help feel they are in a crisis. However, many clients in short-term therapy deal with difficulties or dilemmas that are *not* catastrophic or even urgent; they are not necessarily overwhelmed. In crisis treatment, the initial objective is the restoration of equilibrium and relief of symptoms. In noncrisis brief treatment, the presenting problem may not be as specific or be felt so intensely and therefore may take more exploration and refinement to define precisely.

2. Setting Time Limits   Crisis intervention, by definition, tends to be self-limiting. In *planned time-limited treatment,* a specific or approximate time for ending is usually set at the beginning of the treatment relationship; most brief treatment approaches continue to recommend that the time contract be open to renegotiation if the problem takes more time to resolve or if help with additional problems is requested.[22] The length of the first contract for short-term treatment may vary from as few as two or three interviews to a period of three to four months. In psychosocial treatment, the worker usually suggests a specific time period, sometimes with a particular number of interviews closely spaced; in other cases, weekly sessions are planned. Thus the worker might say, "It seems to me that if we work hard on this together in the next four weeks, meeting twice weekly, we should be able to make progress quickly. Let's say we plan to have our last session on (specific date)." Or, "Let's plan (6, 8, 10) weekly sessions, with the final one planned for (date)." At no time should the clinician assure the client that the goals will *definitely* be achieved in the time period that is agreed upon; generally, it is understood that the worker and client will decide at that time whether to plan more sessions or to terminate. As important as the worker's realistic *optimism* is in all treatment, in brief therapy it is particularly important that the worker conveys the belief that significant changes can be made in a short time; if the worker does not have confidence that this is so, the treatment may fail.

In a few approaches to short-term therapy, the contract made about time arrangements is *nonnegotiable*. In our experience—and in that of many proponents of brief treatment—the decision about the actual number of sessions or months the work will require often cannot be determined immediately, even when it is agreed that the treatment will probably be short. For this reason, in the psychosocial approach, a time frame is often suggested by the worker and agreed upon by the client *with the understanding that there will be a reevaluation* at points along the way and when the period is up. (Sometimes the work is completed *before* the anticipated date.) The Jones couple in Chapter 3 "contracted" for 10 sessions but were clear that the therapy could be extended after an evaluation at that time; they chose to come for a final, 11th meeting in which they summarized and reinforced the work they had done. In the Russo case (Chapter 15), the worker suggested that the family meet together for six sessions and then evaluate the situation, even though she suspected the work would take longer. As it turned out, the family attended 36 sessions over 10 months. When client motivation and need are present, extending a contract for brief treatment can lead to productive and more intricate work than short-term therapy allows, as it did for the Russos. Various ways in which time can be set were discussed under "Deciding on Length of Treatment" in Chapter 10.

3. Decisively Intervening; Setting Attainable Goals and Realistic Tasks

As in crisis treatment, planned time-limited therapy often requires active interventions, concise interpretations, and direct advice when appropriate. Even though the pace can be quite fast, a positive therapeutic relationship is as important in brief treatments, even those that last only a few sessions, as it is in longer term or open-ended therapy. As in all treatment, attainable goals should be arrived at mutually; they should specifically pertain to the problem at hand, even though, as in the Green crisis case, goals may shift quickly. Or, as occurs fairly often, when a child's behavior is the presenting problem, it may soon be revealed that parents or co-caretakers (e.g., mother and grandmother) disagree on how to handle the situation, or they may have relationship difficulties that the child's troubles are reflecting; the conflict between adults may then be defined as the problem to be addressed. When certain problems are presented, often the worker's function is to "coach" or to teach communication, parenting, job interview, or other skills needed to achieve clients' objectives. Learning about developmental issues and needs, repetitive circular interactions, or basic systems concepts (discussed especially in family and couple chapters) often helps clients understand the difficulties they are experiencing, giving them a basis for considering new approaches to problem solving.

As goals are being set, the worker may need to help clients *partialize* their concerns and *prioritize* which of their needs seem to be the most *urgent* and/or *severe*. If, for example, a family is facing imminent eviction, housing will become *the* major priority, even if one of the children is manifesting behavior difficulties or there is marital conflict. When energies and attention are scattered, or when there are numerous difficulties that result in clients feeling overwhelmed, dividing the troubles into manageable parts and ranking them in terms of importance often enhances confidence and motivation. Otherwise, it may be impossible to bring enough concentration or hope to bear on the most immediate problem(s) to be solved.

Sometimes clients are very clear about what their difficulties are, but they are at a loss about how to proceed. In some brief treatment models, the clinician takes major responsibility for defining and assigning tasks. Sometimes the worker has definite ideas, based on knowledge and experience, about tasks or actions that might be effective in promoting change; however, as discussed in earlier chapters on treatment, we believe that the more involved clients are in formulating these, the more likely they will be to carry them out. Furthermore, their active involvement almost always enhances confidence and competence. Often, the worker's suggestions can be put in the form of a question ("Would it help to make a chart or start a journal to help you keep track of your alcohol intake?" "What if you took your mother to lunch before our next meeting, and you initiated conversations that may start to heal the rift between you? Do you think that would be more effective than just waiting for her to apologize? Together we can 'rehearse' how it might be best to approach her." "Would you think it would get you going if you decided that, no matter what, this week you will answer three newspaper ads for jobs?") The client may come up with a better idea or modify the worker's suggestion. The collaboration between client and worker should result in a plan of action—tasks or "homework" assignments—that make sense to the client and seem realistic to both client and worker. The identification of tasks often helps to make it clear to clients that their participation in bringing about change will be necessary and that generally goals are actually achieved in the "real world" (not in the clinician's office or by the clinician).[23]

4. Renegotiating or Terminating; Following Up In all psychosocial treatment, including short-term contacts, the worker initiates periodic discussions with the client to evaluate the progress that has (or has not)

been made. The client's reactions to treatment and to the worker are also elicited. If one approach to change has not been successful, worker and client consider alternative avenues. If the treatment is going well, often at least two sessions before the agreed upon target date, the worker reminds the client that there are two more meetings left. Specific objectives may be set for the remaining meetings. At the last session, if the goals have not been achieved or if new issues seem pressing to the client, worker and client may decide to recontract for additional sessions; at this point it may become clear that longer-term treatment is indicated and the second contract may or not be time-limited. If the work has been satisfactory to the client, then the termination process begins (see Chapter 19). Ideally, the clients are told that they can return, to the same worker if they wish, should the need arise. As we shall discuss shortly, when the service is not designed to accommodate clients' ongoing or future needs, information about suitable resources should be provided if the client wants it. It is often helpful to plan a follow-up meeting or at least a telephone call (as the worker suggested in the Green crisis case) to determine the degree to which changes proved helpful in the long run. Clients often feel very supported to know that the worker's interest and caring continue. Also, clients' feedback about treatment and its benefits or disappointments is invaluable to expanding the worker's body of knowledge about what has been helpful and what has not. We often learn that progress continued after the contact ended, especially when clients have made changes during treatment.

Selection of Clients

Which clients are most suitable for short-term work? Some clinicians recommend brief therapy for all clients or patients seeking help. If no improvement occurs, then long-term treatment might be suggested. In our view, we do not yet have adequate or firm knowledge of diagnostic indicators that determine for whom brief services are *definitely* indicated. Some who seem to have complex problems make large, satisfying gains very quickly. Sometimes, as we said, brief help with communication skills can vastly improve the quality of family relationships; this was true for the Green family. Or, as in the Garcia brief treatment case (pages 500–02), a relatively small change in one part of a family, even one with multiple problems, can have significant effects on every family member, including those who do not participate in the treatment. On the other hand, there are clients whose requirements for help initially appear to be quite circumscribed, yet change comes slowly or else they subsequently decide to explore additional issues.

Clients Often Suited for Short-Term Treatment Nevertheless, a broad range of criteria for selecting those believed to be best suited for brief therapy has been suggested by clinicians and researchers:[24]

1. Those whose difficulties began recently and whose concerns relate primarily to current matters.
2. Those who view or can be helped to view their problems as specific and concrete rather than diffuse and abstract.
3. Those whose previous level of functioning has been satisfactory.
4. Those who have a rapid ability to relate realistically, flexibly, and honestly to the therapist.
5. Those whose relationships, past or present, demonstrate a capacity for depth and reciprocity.
6. Those who are able to experience and express feelings fairly easily and freely.

7. Those who have high initial motivation for change and will make the necessary sacrifices to achieve it.
8. Those willing and able to participate *actively* in working on problems and tasks.
9. Those who are "psychologically minded," who have the capacity for introspection and for emotional as well as intellectual insight.
10. Those who are initially reluctant to accept any help but are reassured by the suggestion of time limits.

Clients Less Likely to Be Suited for Short-Term Therapy It is generally believed that those unlikely to benefit from brief therapy include people who have serious personality disorders or deficits and who both *need and want extensive personality change* or reconstruction to live more satisfying lives. Many clients with psychotic disorders, even those whose most severe symptoms are managed by medications, often cannot benefit from brief service, but can be helped with distortions of perception or with communication skills and relationship difficulties, for example, over a longer period. Severe dependency, anxiety, and antisocial or "acting out" behaviors usually cannot be reversed in a short time. Clients with deep-seated narcissistic, borderline, passive-dependent, masochistic, or self-destructive traits rarely make basic changes quickly. Extreme rigidity and negativism do not easily yield to even the most skillful therapeutic intervention; change usually requires extended treatment. In short, individuals and families who seek help for problems deriving from *chronic, recalcitrant personal and relationship problems* often are not appreciably helped in brief treatment.

However, some clients with these difficulties or disorders sometimes *can* make changes in a brief time. As discussed many times in this book, a small tip of the balance in the family or personality system can result in significant and gratifying progress. Because of her strengths and motivation, Mrs. Barry (Chapter 20), diagnosed as having a paranoid schizophrenic disorder, made impressive changes within herself and her marriage in less than a month once antipsychotic medication treatment was resumed.

William J. Reid, who has been studying and developing a special form of short-term treatment since the 1960s, has identified types of clients for whom his brief *task-centered* approach is usually *not* indicated: (1) those not interested in taking action to solve specific problems but who want an understanding person with whom to explore "existential" issues, such as concerns about life goals, identity, stresses, and losses; (2) those who for various reasons are unwilling or unable to isolate precise problems and carry out the relevant tasks; (3) those who wish to alter conditions, such as certain psychogenic or motor difficulties, for which problem-solving tasks cannot be identified; and (4) those who do not want help but are being seen for "protective" reasons.[25]

Characteristics and Benefits of Brief Therapies

Under what circumstances would we consider time-limited service the treatment of choice? What are some of its common characteristics? How does it compare with extended therapies? What special advantages may it have? While there are no definitive answers, we offer comments here that relate to these often-posed questions:

1. Circumscribed Problems When the client and worker define a problem or problems that are precise and have specific solutions, time limits are often appropriate. In *task-centered* and many other brief treatments, as we said, client and worker together identify specific difficulties, goals, and tasks, and decide upon the duration of the treatment. The agreement on these makes up the contract for treatment. In general, but not always, the issues addressed and the tasks agreed upon are not only precise but also concerned with the "here and now." Although there may be some discussion of early history, dreams, transference, and so on, *extensive* exploration of these is less common than in some forms of long-term therapy. To maintain the limited focus, some practitioners conducting brief psychotherapy will not respond to material raised by the client that is not related to the agreed-upon problems and tasks. When successful, this exercise is believed not only to achieve the immediate goal but also to enhance confidence and competence. The expectation is that because the client's problem-solving capacities and autonomous functioning are strengthened through the treatment process, ability to handle difficulties that arise in the future will be maximized. Generally, this approach would not suit psychosocial therapists who would view it as mechanistic and rigid; in our experience, as described in the Green case for example, exploration of one area is often naturally followed by another related or underlying concern that is not initially presented.

Therapy of any length is not a "cure". Rather, it provides a foundation for self-awareness and continued growth. Clients may come to recognize self-defeating patterns and devise ways to avoid them. Ideally, during treatment clients adopt "tools" for coping and problem solving, which they continue to use and build upon as new situations arise. Clearly, the Green family did this. Individuals, couples, and families are encouraged to continue to work on themselves after treatment ends. Thus, particularly in brief treatment, immediate accomplishments may be modest, but over time, as many have reported, continued application of methods learned during treatment will help bring about ongoing changes.[26]

2. A Wide Range of Presenting Difficulties

Much of brief treatment involves *pattern-dynamic* and *developmental reflection,* as well as *person–situation reflection* and the other treatment procedures described in this text; the entire Hollis typology of techniques is applicable to treatments of all lengths. Short-term treatment definitely *does not address just concrete matters,* even though they may be circumscribed, as many illustrations throughout this book demonstrate. In still another example, a woman concerned about her relationship with her seven-year-old daughter realized very quickly that she had transferred old anger at her now-deceased mother onto her child. On the basis of this developmental understanding, she reflected on possibilities for modifying her behavior; she set tasks for herself, implementing them between sessions, to deal differently with her daughter. In just a few weeks the relationship between mother and daughter improved remarkably.

3. Modification of the Balance of Forces

Most of us with clinical practice in family therapy and with a systems orientation have seen dramatic and rapid changes occur when one member of a family changes an attitude or behavior. For instance, one seemingly small piece of initiative taken by a heretofore "distant" father and husband sometimes has immediate and lasting repercussions on the relationships and inner lives of all family members. (See an example of this on pages 74–75.) As we have said many times in this book, seemingly small accomplishments can result in

very meaningful changes. When a mother gives up the "go-between" role, other changes in the family system often follow quickly, as was true in the Russo case (Chapter 15), even though treatment of this family was extended to deal with additional issues. When adults are helped to work out long-standing conflicts or "cut-offs" with members of their family of origin (and sometimes this can happen surprisingly quickly), there are often immediate and positive effects on their own emotional and/or family lives.

4. Support of Clients' Strengths and Progress

Sometimes clients are urged to remain in treatment even though they express satisfaction with their accomplishments. By recognizing the value of short-term contacts, caseworkers can avoid the implication that people choosing to terminate "prematurely" are leaving in an "impaired" or unfinished condition. Even a subtle message of this sort can demoralize clients; it tends to dampen confidence in the progress achieved and may foster dependency. Mutuality is certainly better served when we support clients in what they have done rather than judge them for what they choose not to do.

5. A Minimum of Drifting or Regression

When time limits are established—and workers and clients are focused on achievements, tasks, and goals—there is usually less meandering or aimless exploration. Many clinicians believe that "regressive," open-ended treatment can be a disservice to clients who, before development of the problem that led them to seek help, were satisfied with their lives and functioning.

In long-term, unfocused treatment, clients may cease growing or may even regress, as they increasingly rest on a comfortable, dependent treatment relationship rather than seek meaningful companionship in their "real" lives. It was Mann's view[27] that open-ended therapy stimulates the unconscious longing for fusion, while time-limited treatment provides an opportunity for a maturational event, a leap toward autonomy, an opportunity to resolve difficulties surrounding separation and individuation.

6. Mobilization of Strengths and Motivation

As the "functionalists" asserted over a half century ago, time limits and the dynamic use of time as a variable in treatment can mobilize clients' strengths and foster motivation; there can be greater incentive to work more quickly and productively than when the contact is open-ended. Workers, too, may concentrate their efforts more consistently when they know that time is not unlimited. Deadlines, even if they can be renegotiated, often goad us to muster our best energies. When (even flexible) time limits are *not* set, the treatment misses out on this important advantage. Although two very different case situations, Mrs. Barry and Mrs. Stasio (Chapter 20) were both working against time, a factor that helped them accomplish a lot in a short period.

7. Advantages for Reluctant or Involuntary Clients

We mentioned earlier that when the problem at hand appears to be one that can be resolved quickly, clients who might otherwise resist treatment may agree to a brief contact. Concern about being trapped in an endless process may be allayed when a time frame for the contact is suggested. Similarly, those who have been pressured or mandated to have therapy are much more likely to find a goal to work on if time limits are suggested. For example, in the Carter case (Chapter 20), the initial short-term goal agreed upon was to work toward the release of the children from foster care; as it turned out, the Carter couple

asked for further help with other matters after the original objective was achieved.

8. Agency Function and Other Variables May Limit Contact

The function of the agency or service and other factors beyond the control of workers and clients are very relevant to the duration of treatment. Social workers attached to inpatient services in hospitals, crisis teams, residential treatment centers, prisons, or day care centers, for example, remain active with individuals and families only as long as these clients are directly involved with the service or facility. (Examples of short-term work with couples in settings in which contact is limited by agency function can be found on pages 498–500.) Similarly, when social work interns or staff members will soon be leaving their agencies, or clients plan to move to another locale, the therapy is necessarily time-limited. If the contact has been a positive experience for clients, and further treatment is wanted and needed, abbreviated treatment can be a springboard for future service elsewhere. When treatment is ended by circumstances rather than by clients' choices or requirements, it is important that social workers utilize special skills necessary for effecting successful referrals. It is essential that *appropriate resources* are located that are a good "fit" for the people involved. It is equally important that workers share with clients all the information they have about the resource. Clients' feelings and attitudes about the transfer must be discussed with sensitivity and in detail. Chapter 19 addresses termination issues.

9. Advantages for Research

We note an important additional benefit: Because of its structure and often clearer focus, planned brief treatment is especially suited to research, providing excellent opportunities for measuring treatment effectiveness and for studying and improving our methods of helping clients in need.

Further Comments on Brief and Extended Treatment

What are the limitations of brief treatment? We have outlined above some client characteristics and problems that are usually not amenable to abbreviated therapies. We believe that we do not yet have reliable guidelines to inform us just when time-limited treatment is preferable and when longer help is needed. Even though there is considerable evidence that short-term approaches can be extremely effective and well-received by clients, and in many cases result in greater gains for clients than open-ended therapies, research findings are nevertheless contradictory and inconclusive when it comes to comparing long-term and brief treatments. Generally, the data confirm the usefulness of brief therapy for some problems, but cast doubt on its value for other difficulties.[28] In our experience, benefits often accrue in unlimited treatment that may not be measured by research methods, particularly those that do not solicit the reactions of clients themselves. As Henry and associates state in their summary of research studies on psychodynamic approaches to treatment, "Psychodynamic research tends to be more difficult than research on some of the other therapeutic approaches (such as behavioral or cognitive-behavioral) to translate directly into improved practice." They urge further research of widely practiced psychodynamic therapies. They see it as a possible way "to realize the long-sought tie between psychotherapy research and practice."[29]

Since, as we have said, it is usually not possible to predict at the beginning of treatment just how many sessions, weeks, months, or even years will be required to achieve clients' goals, it certainly seems reasonable, when a limit is set, to keep the option open for reconsideration in case further treatment seems desirable as the work proceeds. In some cases, the worker and client may discuss intermitting and make plans for another stint of treatment in the future. Studies have demonstrated that as many as *60 percent of brief-treatment patients return for additional therapy.*[30] When clients aspire to extensive understanding of self and of relationships in order to bring about changes in feelings, attitudes, and ways of living, therapy often takes a long time or requires a series of contacts.

Without a doubt, brief treatment approaches have alerted us to the need to *maintain focus,* to *avoid drifting,* and to *guard against regressive client dependency* in all of our work. We have also become acutely aware that when time limits are too flexible, reactions that naturally accompany termination may be evaded. However, workers aware of these hazards can pay attention to conducting well-focused sessions; they can indicate to clients their reluctance to continue along the same path if, over a significant period, no movement is occurring; and they can guard against dependency by supporting clients' strengths, competence, and autonomy. By the same token, the consolidation and reinforcement of gains made and the expression of joys, sorrows, and disappointments that are part of many terminations need not be lost if, when treatment goals have been reached, there is a *planned* process for evaluation and ending.

When psychosocial casework is extended, it involves either contact over a lengthy period or intermittent contacts of varying duration and intensity, sometimes over years. The latter requires *continuity* of understanding and of the treatment process, even though there may be long or short intervals in which contact is not needed. It is often well to prepare the client for the possibility of return and, when feasible, for the client to be seen each time by the same worker. Work with children, the elderly, the handicapped, deinstitutionalized mental patients, adolescent mothers, and many others often benefit from the "open-door" approach. When people's circumstances or aspirations change, or old dysfunctional coping patterns revive under stress, or unanticipated catastrophic events occur, it is humane and gratifying to be available to help returning clients regain equilibrium or advance to new levels of functioning.[31]

As important as brief treatment methods and research have been to the advancement of casework practice, we do not want to overestimate the usefulness of the short-term approach, as managed care companies do, or as administrators sometimes do as a way of solving fiscal or other problems. There is no way to measure the value of personal development in quantitative terms. *One can waste money, time, and human potential by giving too little service and by encouraging inappropriate long-term treatment.* Mrs. Zimmer (Chapter 3) provides a case in point: We are convinced that little or nothing would have been accomplished by her within a three- or six-month time limit. If this client had been forced to terminate, she might have mustered the motivation at some point to start all over again elsewhere, but we believe the first stint of treatment probably would have been a virtual waste; she simply would not have been able to sustain the benefits of the rudimentary gains achieved in a few months.

Along similar lines, we *caution against stereotyping "lower-class" clients* who are presumed to prefer and benefit more from time-limited therapies than from open-ended treatment.[32] Even if this is *statisti-*

cally accurate, if we act arbitrarily and make policy decisions on the basis of this information, services will be withheld from those who do not fit the generalization. Our years of practice and those of our colleagues convince us that *many* lower socioeconomic clients make *excellent* use of long-term treatment. It is our responsibility to advocate for services for low-income clients; they should not be denied such opportunities for treatment to save costs or because of biases promoted by statistics! The case of Mrs. Stone (Chapter 3) illustrates this point.

The use of brief treatment is expanding; it is employed in more and more settings with an increasing number of clients and presenting problems. It is our opinion that some special training is required for the successful practice of time-limited therapy. Like conjoint treatment, crisis and brief therapies rest comfortably on the psychosocial theoretical base, but additional knowledge and skill are required to develop expertise in these demanding and complex modalities. The need for active engagement and a direct approach, rapid assessment and intervention, task-assignment and implementation, all require a pace, focus, and knowledge that are not always seen as essential to open-ended treatment. Yet we firmly believe these special skills are useful to *all* clinicians for several reasons: First, until treatment is in progress, we usually cannot be sure how long it will take. Second, most treatments can benefit from these methods at various junctures: Long-term clients may face catastrophic events; task-centered activities can help *any* client convert understanding into goal-oriented behaviors. We therefore strongly recommend that clinical social workers read about various brief treatments and attend courses, workshops, or seminars on crisis intervention and time-limited approaches and techniques. Third, in the opinion of many researchers and clinicians, brief treatment is the preferred modality in a large variety of cases and situations.

Writing about his carefully researched time-limited, task-centered social work model, Reid affirms that "a practitioner might use task-centered methods during the course of long-term psychosocial treatment to help the client translate into action some aspect of insight into his or her problems." Furthermore, in his opinion, "When the task-centered system is used in full as the sole or primary method of treatment, its range of application, while narrower, is still broad enough to serve as a basic approach for the majority of clients seen by clinical social workers."[33] Although we believe there are many situations in which brief methods are not sufficient, we thoroughly endorse the notion that all clinicians should be solidly grounded in the concepts and practices that have emerged from over 50 years of studying short-term approaches.

NOTES

1. See Dunlap (1996), Lemon (1983), and Smalley (1970) for discussions of the functional approach to time limits and time phases.

    Readers are also referred to Presley (1987) and Toseland (1987). Both articles report on studies that find that many discontinuing clients, even those who drop out after one session, report benefit from the treatment.
2. A great deal has been written on crisis theory and practice by and for social workers. Special mention is made of the early compilation edited by Parad (1965) that is still in wide use and provides very valuable reading. See also Caplan (1964) who was also among the major developers of crisis theory which was based, in part on his studies at the Family Guidance Center, Harvard School of Public Health, in 1954.

For other readings on crisis theory and intervention, see Bell (1995), Dixon and Sands (1983), Ell (1996), Golan's classic book (1978), Goldring (1980), the classic by Rapoport (1970), and Schwartz-Borden (1986). The reader may want to look at the volume edited by Roberts (1995) who recommends time-limited cognitive therapy; his book reviews the history and theoretical base of crisis intervention and there are chapters that cover an array of personal and social crises.
3. Lindemann (1965).
4. See Lemon (1983), pp. 404–06.

    See Herman (1992) whose excellent book covers traumas from domestic abuse to political terror. Her definition of trauma is an experience that "overwhelms the ordinary human adaptation to life," disrupting the sense of control, connection, and meaning; leaving people with a sense of helplessness and terror; creating "lasting changes in physiological arousal, emotion, cognition, and memory."
5. Rapoport (1970) and Golan (1978).
6. See Bernhein and Lehman (1985) and Joseph Walsh (1988 and 1989).
7. See American Psychiatric Association (1994), pp. 424–29 for diagnostic criteria of posttraumatic stress disorder. See also McNew and Abell (1995) on posttraumatic stress disorder and sexual abuse; their study found more similarities than differences in symptomatology between Vietnam veterans and adult survivors of childhood sexual abuse. Stone (1992) discusses the role of shame in posttraumatic stress disorder. Silvern and Kaersvang (1989) urge immediate intervention for children traumatized by family violence. See also a recommended book Ochberg (1988) on posttraumatic therapy for victims of various kinds of violence; the author favors an empowerment approach. We also recommend the two-part article on self-injury by trauma survivors by Connors (1996). See Patten et al. (1989) on sexual abuse and the treatment of posttraumatic disorder. We recommend an exceptionally interesting article by McInnis-Dittrich (1996) on "life-review" therapy for elderly female survivors of childhood sexual abuse; case illustrations are included.

For further references on adult survivors of childhood sexual abuse, see Chapter 7, note 2.

8. See Bell (1995).

9. See the volume edited by Jacobson (1980) for relevant readings. See also Anderson and Stark (1988) on strategies for reducing job relocation stress, Bernier (1990) on a caring approach to parents on the birth of a disabled child with case examples, Borden (1992) on narrative perspectives on interventions following adverse life events, Garvin, et al. (1991) on preventive intervention for children of divorce, Gibbons, et al. (1997) on being empathic helpers to victims, a helpful article by Kuhn (1990) on helping family members with the crisis of dementia, and Zayas, et al.(1997) on cultural-competency training for staff serving Hispanic families with children in psychiatric crisis. King (1993) discusses the impact on families of the disproportionate percentage of African Americans who are incarcerated; he advocates more social services for inmates and their families.

10. Elizabeth Kubler-Ross (1969).

See Golan (1979) for a discussion of the broad range of events and a rich bibliography on transitional events and processes that are now included under the rubric of "crisis." See also Golan (1980) for a very useful discussion on treatment of "normal people with normal troubles."

11. See the excellent and highly recommended article on myths and realities of crisis intervention by Lukton (1982).

12. The *New York Times,* November 26, 1985, p. C1. See also The *New York Times,* August 8, 1989, p. C1: "Research suggests normal range of reactions to grave loss is wider than thought."

13. Ibid., p. C1.

14. Gibbons, et al. (1994).

15. Rapoport (1970), pp. 297–98.

16. See a relevant article by Temple (1997) on treating inner-city families of homicide victims; even though Mrs. Green survived, her life was threatened; there were powerful repercussions, including loss of a sense of control and the physical loss of sight in one

of Mrs. Green's eyes. For references on bereavement, see Chapter 5, note 19.

17. There is a wealth of current literature on brief and time-limited treatments. See, for example, Budman and Gurman (1988), Epstein (1976) on brief therapy with children and parents, Fontane (1979), Fox (1987) on short-term family therapy, Goldstein and Noonan (1999) for a book by and for social workers, Morawetz and Walker (1984) on brief therapy with single-parent families, Norman (1980) on short-term treatment with the adolescent, Reid (1992 and 1996) on task-centered social work, Wells (1994), and a book edited by Wells and Giannetti (1990) on various approaches to brief treatment. Other references on brief therapies include: Sifneos (1987), Singh (1982), Wolberg (1980) and a volume edited by Zeig et al. (1990).

See also Goldie Kadushin (1998) for a useful article on adapting the traditional interview to a brief treatment approach.

18. See Koss and Butcher (1986) and Koss and Shiang (1994).

19. See Araoz and Carrese (1995) whose book on solution-oriented brief therapy for adjustment disorders discusses the requirements of managed care organizations. See Chapter 1, especially note 57.

20. Strom-Gottfried (1998), p. 306.

21. See Reamer (1997). For other readings on issues related to managed care, see Alperin (1994), Corcoran and Vandiver (1996), Grossberg and Brandell (1997), Strom (1992), and Shapiro (1995). See Meyer (1993) who, in his defense of long-term treatment, reminds us that by tradition social workers have provided services for the most troubled.

22. The volume edited by Wells and Giannetti (1990) and the book by Wells (1994) are excellent resources on brief psychotherapy.

23. See Reid (1992 and 1996).

24. Reid (1992) and Wells (1994).

25. Reid (1996), p. 634.

26. See, for example, Wolberg (1980) and Wells (1994).

27. Mann (1973).

28. In their chapter reviewing research on brief psychotherapy, Koss and Shiang (1994) con-

clude that there "is now compelling empirical evidence that brief psychotherapy is effective with specific populations . . . including: (1) patients with less severe problems, such as job-related stress, anxiety disorders, mild depression, and grief reactions; (2) patients who have experienced unusual stress situations, such as those with PTSD [posttraumatic stress disorder], earthquake experience, and rape" (p. 681). "On the other hand, brief therapy has been found to be less effective for patients with more severe disorders such as those of personality, substance abuse, and psychosis" (p. 681). See also Lambert and Bergin (1994) in the same volume, especially pp. 180–81.

An interesting study by Holmes (1995) found that "a history of childhood abuse divided those who responded favorably to short-term treatment and those who did not respond favorably . . . Duration of therapy may need to be extended for clients who have a history of abuse or specialized short-term treatment methods may need to be developed for this population" (p. 355).

29. Henry et al. (1994), p. 503.
30. See Orlinsky et al. (1994), especially p. 282, who say that "patients who agree to a specific time-limited term often end up having longer treatments in time-limited than in nominally unlimited therapy . . . Given the fact that longer treatment durations tend to be associated with better outcomes, comparisons between time-limited and open-ended therapies need to control for this factor."
31. See Budman and Gurman (1988), especially Chapter 9.
32. Garfield (1994), p. 192.
33. Reid (1996), p. 634.

CHAPTER 19

TERMINATION

It may seem paradoxical that successful treatment leads to separation from the very relationship that nurtured the progress.[1] Yet, as we well know, when children and adolescents move from one developmental phase to another, they must forgo certain aspects of dependency to achieve greater growth and autonomy. In therapy, too, where a feeling of childlike dependency and many other feelings can be present, the attainment of mutually agreed upon goals is often, sometimes painfully, "rewarded" by loss. There are clients for whom the loss is profound because treatment has provided an extraordinary opportunity to be accepted, listened to, encouraged to grow, and to learn to take fuller charge of their lives. Grief and mourning, expressed in stages that include denial, anger, sadness, and acceptance, can be at the core of the termination process for some (but not most) clients. Sometimes anxiety stems from a conflict between dependence and independence ("Will I be able to make it on my own?"). Feelings of disappointment may arise when treatment expectations could not be fully realized.

In recent years, the previous notion that most terminations evoked grief reactions from clients has been challenged by research.[2] For many, perhaps most, clients who are terminating a successful and satisfying course of treatment, *excitement* about gains that have been made and goals that have been achieved may be the prominent response, outweighing mournful emotions, if these are present at all. Improvement in feelings of well-being, in relationships, or in environmental conditions often results in *optimism.* Successful treatment often bolsters clients' feelings of pride, competence, and mastery. Termination is usually a time to consider the positive changes that have been made and how these can be consolidated and built upon after treatment is over.

An examination of the therapeutic alliance can also lead clients to reflect on ways they handle other important relationships. When relevant, transfer to another worker or agency may be part of the ending phase. For the benefit of workers and agencies, as well as for clients, feedback about the treatment experience is essential.

In both brief and long-term contacts, the way the termination process is managed can have significant implications for clients, sometimes long after treatment ends. The worker's role can be critical. This chapter will discuss some basic principles, gleaned from practice experience and the literature, involved in an *individualized* approach to termination.

SPECIAL FEATURES OF TERMINATION

Although careful handling of the *beginning* phase of treatment can be extremely important, the process of *ending* a therapeutic relationship often requires even greater skill, sensitivity, and self-awareness. This is true for many reasons.

First, when clients initially come to see a worker, they are usually feeling pressured by the difficulties that led them to seek help and, often with very little encouragement, they become involved in the treatment process if they feel the worker is interested and accepting. During termination, however, even when complex issues about the therapy and the therapeutic relationship are involved, there may be more reluctance to address them because they can be difficult, sometimes painful, and more easily denied or shelved than those that surround presenting problems. Thus, the process may require far more persistence on the worker's part to promote a therapeutic climate that fosters openness and honesty between client and worker.

Second, especially when treatment is going well, there may be a minimum of discussion about the feelings *between* clients and worker. In many cases of individual and conjoint therapy, much more emphasis is placed on internal concerns or family relationships or on matters outside the interviewing room. Termination generally requires some acknowledgment by clients of the meaning of the therapy and of their feelings toward the worker.

Third, many practitioners agree that when termination is inaccurately or carelessly handled, gains made in treatment may be interfered with or even reversed. Growth that is expected to continue after treatment is over may be stunted. If the ending is experienced negatively by clients, even if earlier phases seemed productive, there may be reluctance to become involved with social or therapeutic services again should the need arise. Because time is short, mistakes made by the worker at the conclusion of the contact are less likely to be processed and corrected than at any other point.

Fourth, as we shall discuss further, termination is complicated by special factors, including whether the termination is planned or unplanned, who initiates the ending, and whether it is mutually agreed upon.

Finally, an issue we shall also expand upon is that terminations are sometimes difficult for the worker. Ambivalence is more likely to be present around endings than beginnings. The worker's feelings toward the client and the treatment experience, the worker's general way of handling separations, the worker's current emotional and relational situation can all profoundly influence the course termination takes. Sometimes a worker simply does not want to let go. When workers are disappointed in the outcomes of treatment (whether the clients are or not), they may have negative thoughts about their own skills or feel resentment toward the client. Obviously, for workers as well as for clients, experiences with previous losses may critically affect how separation is handled. Difficulties around intimacy also may inhibit the worker's awareness of feelings aroused during the final phase of treatment. On the other hand, there is evidence that among clinicians' strongest reactions during this period may be feelings of pleasure in the client's success, of pride in their ability to be helpful, and of confidence in their therapeutic skills.[3]

ASSESSMENT OF CLIENT REACTIONS TO TERMINATION

Ideally, in every case, there will be time to address relevant issues around the ending of treatment, time to say a good-bye that is appropriate to the client's feelings about the experience and the relationship with the worker. To do so, one has to assess, *with the client's active participation,* the factors that will influence the ending of treatment and of the therapeutic relationship. *The worker must not try to guide the ending process according to preconceived notions about the course termination should take. Termination of therapy must be tailored to follow the clients' lead; only they can know the meaning treatment has had to them and how they feel about saying good-bye to the worker. This requires very careful listening.*

Intensity of the Relationship

The intensity of the treatment relationship, or the emotional investment clients have in their workers, is a critical factor. Strong involvement often entails an abundance of positive feelings. Ambivalent relationships can also stimulate powerful emotions. Generally, the more intense the involvement of clients with their workers, the more acute the response to ending will be. Clients have very diverse reactions to

the treatment relationship, ranging from profound attachment to little awareness of feelings toward the worker, with many falling somewhere between the extremes. These reactions to the worker significantly affect termination experiences.

The differences in the quality and intensity of worker–client relationships may be based on several factors, including:

The Meaning of the Relationship For some clients, the relationship with the worker is the first one ever experienced in which full attention is paid, unconditional acceptance is given, and little is asked in return. It is easy to understand how deeply tied to their workers they sometimes feel and how reluctant they can be to give them up. On the other hand, there are clients who have or have had close, nurturing relationships and who therefore are not so profoundly touched by or dependent upon the worker–client connection.

Idiosyncratic and Cultural Factors On the basis of idiosyncratic personal style or cultural tradition, some clients are effusive while others maintain a formal reserve from beginning to end, even in long-term treatment; many fall in a middle range between the two. Sometimes Latino or Italian clients, for example, may be very expressive and Irish Catholics may show considerable emotional restraint; of course, generalizations about people belonging to a specific group often do not apply to the particular clients we are seeing.

Diagnostic and Personality Factors Clients who function relatively autonomously often do not feel shaken by termination. Dick and Susan Jones (Chapter 3), for example, clearly respected and appreciated the worker and her help, but they had turned to her primarily as an expert in marital relationships and expected little nurturance beyond that; in their case, separation was not laced with complex reactions. They used their final session to review the changes they made, to reinforce the skills they had developed, and to express pleasure in their greatly improved relationships. In contrast, for Mrs. Zimmer (also Chapter 3), whose capacity for autonomous functioning and for object relations was unevenly developed, treatment and—to a lesser degree—termination were tempestuous, fraught with separation-individuation conflicts; alternately she clung to or angrily lashed out at the worker, blaming her for her distress. Nevertheless, during the planned termination phase, she *was* able to express satisfaction in her achievements and discuss plans for maintaining and building upon them. Clients with prominent schizoid features generally prefer to be "loners" and often seem indifferent to personal relationships; if they do have contact with caseworkers, they are not likely to have significant emotional reactions during treatment or at termination. The degree to which clients have mastered separation-individuation crises and the manner in which they have characteristically coped with conflicts around dependence and independence can influence responses to termination for better or worse.

The nature and depth of transference involvement during the treatment process can significantly influence the separation process. Dependent therapeutic attachments often resemble early relationships, or longed-for relationships, with parents; thus, the positive and negative aspects of these attachments can arouse sadness and anxiety when it is time to leave the relationship that fostered growth during the treatment. *Equally important* are the exhilaration and pride that usually accompany the realization that one has achieved one's objectives,

has become independent, and can now carry on without the worker's help. It is Palumbo's view that when treatment has been successful for clients with personality disorders, grief and mourning are not always present during the termination phase because the client has internalized the functions of the therapist and therefore no longer requires the fused relationship that was present during earlier phases.[4] It is our experience, too, that by the time such treatments end, the extreme intensity of the attachment has often diminished considerably; termination often represents a maturational event, a giant step toward autonomy. However, we also agree with Webb who writes: "The fact that one is happy and exhilarated about the prospect of being on one's own does not negate the possibility of some anxiety about the prospect, nor the feeling of some loss connected to missing the person who helped make the independence possible."[5]

Other kinds of transference responses to the worker may also shift during the final phase. For example, those clients who incorrectly tend to feel that people either want to cling to or get rid of them may use termination with the worker as an opportunity to correct these distorted expectations. Clients who have customarily related to others either deferentially or arrogantly may become able to say good-bye to the worker as one equal to another. People who sought help during treatment to reduce self-centeredness may use termination to focus on reciprocity in the therapeutic relationship.

Whether Crises Were Experienced During Treatment Individuals and families who have shared catastrophic or other extraordinary emotional experiences with their workers are far more likely to be invested in the treatment relationship than others whose lives were less turbulent during or immediately before therapy. Just as people may feel more grateful to surgeons who have saved their lives than to allergists who give weekly shots, so even brief casework treatment during an acute crisis may lead to stronger client–worker attachment than some less eventful long-term treatments.

Whether Treatment Is Individual or Conjoint In our experience and that of others, therapeutic relationships are often more profound in intensive individual therapy than in equally intensive conjoint treatment. Complex dependency and transference relationships, whether encouraged or not, are more likely to occur in the exclusivity of one-to-one treatment. As we have pointed out in the chapters on family and couple treatments, the focus of these therapies is usually less on the worker–client interaction and more on the relationships among family members. It stands to reason, then, that often there will be less mourning by couples and families when they terminate than when individuals leave treatment. Of course, each member will have his or her particular responses to ending therapy. Nevertheless, when couples and families do experience a deep sense of loss, this can be shared among themselves; clients in individual therapy may find it harder to find others who can understand what the meaning of the client–worker relationship has been. Of course, termination of positive treatment experiences can be as exhilarating to family members seen in therapy as to individual clients.

Client Satisfaction

The degree of *satisfaction* or *dissatisfaction* with the worker and with the treatment can significantly influence termination. If clients feel the worker was either incompetent or unable to offer the right kind of help, leaving that worker will usually be ac-companied by few positive feelings. More likely, there will be anger or indifference; some clients may get some relief and strength from taking the initiative to terminate and seek help elsewhere.

It is not uncommon for people to have exaggerated expectations of what treatment or the worker can provide; if, during treatment, there has been no resolution of these unrealistic hopes, disappointment is bound to emerge at termination time. Similarly, there are clients who desperately want to change, but because of lack of capacity or opportunity simply cannot; in these cases, too, there are bound to be regrets.

On the other hand, when clients have had a positive treatment experience, they likely will be proud of their successes, often grateful for the worker's help, but focused more on going on with their own lives than immersed in complex, ambivalent, or sorrowful feelings.

Experiences with Loss

Previous experiences with loss and characteristic ways of handling it can have enormous influence on client responses to termination. Some people confront loss of an important relationship by distancing from it, by maintaining a "stiff upper lip," or by hastily expressing farewells. Others become overwhelmed by sorrow or fear and want to prolong the contact. Many of our clients have been traumatized by early separations or emotional abandonment, and reactions to termination often mirror responses to previous losses.

Sanville writes:

> Most of our patients would probably subscribe to the old French proverb, "to part is to die a little," for they often experience separation or impending aloneness as threatening psychic extinction, if not as stirring up actual suicidal impulses. These are frequently persons who

have had too early and too often to face the trauma both of miserable relationships and of unchosen breakings up. Most tend to react by a desperate search for new ties, and their very urgency makes for a tendency to repeat past patterns. Others resolve, "Never again" and rigidly avoid commitments. Neither is left with a sense of free choice.[6]

In our experience, the majority of clients seen by clinical social workers are not as fragile or as "stuck" as those Sanville so movingly describes; yet certainly some are. When these reactions emerge at the end of treatment, if dealt with at the time, they can provide important opportunities for growth, for modifying old reactions, and for developing new patterns. Again, if the client's separation from the worker can be experienced as a *challenge,* as an opportunity to *deal with loss in new ways,* and as a way to *affirm strengths* that will support a stronger sense of self, then the work done during the termination can be reassuring and rewarding.

Current Life Circumstances

Current issues in clients' lives and their situations can shape emotional reactions to termination. If there are no extraordinary external pressures and clients feel competent and confident about handling themselves and their circumstances, termination may feel less problematic than when they are in a state of distress. But when clients are in the midst of change or turmoil or problems have not been comfortably resolved, anxious or painful feelings may emerge when the conclusion of treatment draws near.

Social Supports

The state of clients' *social network* is often very relevant to how termination is experienced. Because of personality idiosyn-

crasies, illness, advanced age, or various situational factors, some people have meager social connections. When relationships are impoverished and supports are sparse, the ending process with the worker may be keenly felt. Environmental interventions during treatment or at the time of termination can make an enormous difference. In many cases, creative thinking on the part of the worker and the client can result in the location of social opportunities that suit the client's personality and situation; often isolation need not be viewed as a "given." The more familiar the worker is with resources in the community, the more likely, for example, an appropriate group can be located or a volunteer who visits the homebound can be found.

CONDITIONS OF ENDINGS: ASSESSMENT AND TREATMENT IMPLICATIONS

Client reactions can be affected by whether termination is *planned* or *unplanned,* by *who* terminates, and by whether termination is *permanent* or an *open-door* arrangement is possible.

When Endings Are Forced   Extraordinary circumstances, such as a worker's disabling accident, illness, or even death, may force an abrupt ending to a treatment relationship. In these cases of unplanned and traumatic discontinuance, there is no opportunity to review the treatment process or to resolve feelings—such as anger, abandonment, sorrow, worry—stirred by termination, at least with the original worker. In these cases, it is *preventive* and humane for colleagues or supervisors of the clinicians to *reach out* to clients who have lost their workers through unfortunate circumstances; opportunities for crisis intervention or transfer should be made readily available.

Usually less suddenly, a worker may decide to change careers, move to another area, or retire from practice. In these cases, or when a worker is leaving the service, or agency policy requires that treatment be discontinued, such endings may have very profound meanings to clients. There may be feelings of rejection, failure, and unworthiness; old losses may be reawakened. Every client will respond differently. The important point is that clients must be given every opportunity to react, in whatever ways or stages that they experience the forced decision. In our opinion, soon after the worker knows that an ending to the relationship is in sight for whatever reason, clients should be informed. We believe it is not only ethical for clients to have the same information that we do, but it is also therapeutic for them to have as much time as possible to process the information. As Siebold says, although loss (especially forced loss) may induce mourning, there may be a "prelude to mourning"—such as anxiety, avoidance, and/or denial—before clients become aware of grief reactions. When clients are given the facts—such as about why the worker is changing jobs or careers, where he or she is going, the reasons behind agency policy, and so on—the reality factors help to bring balance to the clients' reactions and understanding.[7] Also, from our point of view, when information that has so much bearing on clients' plans is withheld, the workers can come across as rigid, mean-spirited, or dismissive; psychosocial casework principles of mutuality and equality are not served by turning down clients who almost always want to know just why they are being terminated. The worker in the case of Mr. Kennedy (Chapter 3) was a graduate student of social work; early on, she let her client know when she would be leaving and why.

When Clients Terminate   When clients decide, for whatever reason, that they want to leave treatment, they can at least feel the satisfaction that accompanies making a choice. Even if the decision to leave is based on dissatisfaction with the treatment or, from the worker's view, is for the "wrong reasons," it is nevertheless a self-directed step; although possibly reactive, on some level it is positive. Or, if the clients are moving away, at least it is their choice or circumstance that accounts for the ending. Sometimes contacts are precipitously interrupted because clients withdraw and refuse to return. In these cases, unless the client is willing to offer some feedback, there is no way for the worker to know for certain what went wrong or how the client was affected by the hasty ending.

When Decisions Are Mutual   When the plan to discontinue is mutually arrived at, it is much more likely to be an organic choice, and any negative feelings of clients about termination have a better chance of resolution. In every case, effort should be made to take whatever time is required to discuss the treatment experience, the achievements or disappointments, and the meanings of ending it; sometimes treatment simply has not "worked," and this must be acknowledged and, if possible, understood. When therapy that clients and workers agree is successful is ending, time should be taken to review and consolidate the gains and discuss measures that can be taken to continue to build on these after treatment is over.

As indicated in Chapter 18, one advantage to planned brief treatment or therapy that is part of a limited service is that the idea of termination is built into the therapeutic process from the beginning.[8] Even when time limits are not set, it is possible and, from our point of view, necessary to keep treatment focused on goals; in this way, it is mutually understood that when objectives are reached, treatment will be ended.

When There Is an "Open Door" Many clinicians, and we are among them, endorse an "open-door" policy, which allows clients to return to see their worker on an "as-needed" basis, when possible. As we said in the previous chapter, some clients do their best work in spurts. Under these conditions, termination experiences are tempered by the realization that "good-bye" can actually mean "until we meet again." But, when students or other workers leave the agency, or the clients are no longer eligible for the service where the worker is employed, feelings around the loss of the relationship cannot be cushioned by thoughts of future meetings.

Whatever the conditions of termination are, how the worker handles this phase strongly influences clients' experiences of the separation. We now go on to discuss further the social worker's role and tasks.

TERMINATION AND THE TREATMENT PROCESS

The manner in which worker and client join to conclude treatment frequently determines the degree to which progress sustains and continues. *Termination—which sometimes can be compared to a crisis—is often a period of rapid growth.* An extra leap toward self-reliance may occur when the ending process is set in motion. Important features of successful termination include the following.

Anticipatory Preparation by the Worker

Whether treatment is time-limited by contract or not, the worker is often able to think ahead to the final phase of treatment.

With far greater accuracy than when preparing for the initial interview, client needs and reactions to termination can be anticipated. With the benefit of firsthand experience with clients, the worker can bring knowledge, sensitivity, and tentative planning to the work that will be required to make the ending as meaningful as possible. Cognitive and empathic anticipation of reactions to endings are only *tentative* and must be modified by paying close attention to how clients are responding rather than shaped by preconceived expectations of our own.

Eliciting and Dealing with Clients' Feelings

Just as there are no definite "normative" emotional responses or ordered tasks associated with particular crises, so individuals and families have their own unique ways of handling reactions to termination. As indicated above, *the range of responses is very broad and each client and family should be individualized.* The subphases of the final lap of treatment can vary greatly in emphasis. Euphoria, pride, gratitude for help given, shock, denial, anger, sadness, fear of aloneness, feelings of betrayal, disappointment, relief that a painful or inconvenient process is over, loving and/or hateful feelings toward the therapist: All can be included in the mix, in every possible sequence.

As indicated, in many cases, the predominant feeling for clients is pride in accomplishments and eagerness to get on with life with new means of handling themselves, their relationships, and their environment. But sometimes, even when treatment has been extremely successful, there may be moments of regression and discouragement, doubts that progress really occurred. Sometimes there *are* strong feelings of sadness and loss, even in the face of impressive achievements. Out of fear, perfectionism, or to forestall the ending of a meaningful relationship, clients may introduce new issues on which they want to work.[9] It is the worker's role to be available to and accepting of whatever combination of feelings the clients express, at the same time maintaining a realistic view of the clients' accomplishments and capacity for self-direction and ongoing growth.

It is necessary for the worker to be aware of two opposite risks when helping a client handle feelings about termination:

Overestimation of Client Reactions
The first is the risk of exaggerating or overestimating the importance the treatment or the relationship has had for the client. When a worker presses for positive feelings that are not there or are not expressed in the way the worker wants to hear them, clients may think the worker is self-involved or wants attention or praise; they may conclude that the worker does not want them to leave and thus they may feel guilty for doing so. Some people, as we have said, for various reasons do not become very attached to their workers even when they are very pleased with the outcome of treatment. While there are clients who are effusive in their gratitude and shower the worker with affection or even with farewell gifts, others express equal appreciation by shaking hands and saying, "Thank you for your help." We want to be careful not to induce feelings of guilt or inadequacy by attempting to elicit nonexistent or unavailable reactions. For some clients, termination can be a fairly brief, matter-of-fact process, while for others it requires many sessions to resolve deep, complex, or ambivalent feelings.

Even when the therapeutic relationship has been a very strong one, we must not assume that clients' excitement about ending represents denial of feelings of sadness and loss that should be elicited; such a message to a client can be demoralizing and dampen the clients' confidence in their achievements and competence. Again, overestimation of the depth of mournful feelings about separation can lead to the impression that the worker needs reassurance or wants to cling to the client. In most cases, therefore, if grief reactions are not forthcoming, it is far more helpful to rejoice with the client, underscore newfound confidence, and support future plans for continued growth and independence than to press hard for sad feelings.[10]

Underestimation of Client Reactions
On the other side of the coin, it is equally important not to underestimate the significance of the therapeutic experience to clients. Because of modesty, embarrassment, boredom, or unrealistic hopes for client change, workers may diminish client expressions of satisfaction, gratitude, warmth, and so on. Under these circumstances, clients may leave feeling misunderstood or disappointed in the worker's unwillingness to join in the sharing of good feelings. If clients do feel anxiety about separation, this should be explored and aired rather than handled with offhand reassurance. By the same token, when there are feelings of sorrow that the worker will no longer be part of the client's life, it is important to acknowledge and understand these. When *any* client response is underestimated or dismissed, it may seem that the worker thinks not enough was accomplished, that clients will not make it on their own, that their positive or affectionate feelings are somehow unacceptable, or that the relationship had no genuine meaning to the worker.

Evaluation of Progress

Consolidation of gains made by clients and preparation for ongoing growth require that during the final phase clients and worker

self-awareness that astonished the worker, that she felt she had never really been noticed, much less preferred, by her parents when she was growing up. Her older brother was her mother's favorite; her very "pretty" and "clever" younger sister, whom Mrs. Barry referred to as "spoiled," was her father's "pet." She, on the other hand, was the "plain" one who had gotten little encouragement or recognition. With feeling, she told the worker that she had developed a habit of pretending not to care whether she was noticed and to hide her feelings of resentment and sadness. With words and by her attitude, the worker gave recognition to Mrs. Barry for being able to understand herself so well.

The worker sensed that Mrs. Barry had truly begun to trust her. With her client's consent, she shared some of this information with the nurses to help them understand their patient better and feel less antagonistic. She also gave them suggestions about ways Mrs. Barry might be drawn out in patient therapy groups, since she tended to be reticent there and try to make herself "invisible."

The first task of individual treatment was to attempt to establish a solid relationship. Only when this was achieved, and after Mrs. Barry had become somewhat better organized with the help of medication, was the worker able to help her reflect on some of the issues and feelings she had never before shared in detail with anyone. Feelings of alienation, so pervasive in many disturbed clients, can often be alleviated when a warm and personal interest is taken in their private feelings and thoughts. The worker's next treatment objective was to help Mrs. Barry understand the importance of medication, without which it seemed probable that this client would periodically decompensate. In this setting, where patients were hospitalized

for a maximum of 60 days, it was important to help her with this quickly.

While eliciting Mrs. Barry's attitudes about antipsychotic medication, the worker looked for comments that might throw light on her refusal to take it before admission. Was there, the worker wondered, a connection between the medication and Mrs. Barry's notion that people were tampering with her brain or "wiring" her head wrong? Similarly, did Mrs. Barry's interest in electronics represent her way of attempting to gain control over her "brain"?

In one meeting, Mrs. Barry protested, "Why do *I* have to take medication and everybody else in the world doesn't?" When asked how she felt about that, she simply answered, "Crazy." The worker said that many other people *did* in fact take medication, for example, many diabetics use insulin, because body chemistry is different in everyone and does not always provide what is needed to stay well and feel good. The worker added that she herself also had to take medication regularly. Her approach was designed to help Mrs. Barry consider the reality of the situation; at this point, she did not pursue intrapsychic issues.

As they talked, however, Mrs. Barry admitted that, to her, being on medication meant she was not only "different" and "crazy" but "weak" as well. It made her feel she could not make it on her own, that she needed a "crutch"; and that this was why she had wanted to test herself by trying to get along without it from time to time. She said she had always been "disgusted" by her alcoholic father, whom her mother had belittled for needing drink to "lean on." The worker helped her to examine ways in which she might view her situation differently: In contrast to her father, who was incapacitated when he drank, she, Mrs. Barry, functioned well and felt better when she took medication. The need to make up for a biochemical deficit was quite different from the excessive use of alcohol.

During subsequent meetings, Mrs. Barry indicated she had given thought to these talks about medication. Until now, she had not looked at it in these ways. Probably never before had she linked her perception of herself to her father's "weakness." Since the issue of control is important to most patients with paranoid ideation and was clearly so to Mrs. Barry, the worker pointed out that when she was on medication she was able to control herself so that other people did not think she was sick and put her in the hospital against her will.

As Mrs. Barry became increasingly less confused, it seemed likely that some of her money *had* been stolen at the hospital, as she had suspected. Mr. Barry confirmed his wife's assertion that she always carried a 10-dollar bill pinned on her person. Although the money was not listed among her belongings in the property office, Mrs. Barry was convinced that it was being kept from her there. The worker took Mrs. Barry to the safe—other staff members had refused to do so on the grounds that she was delusional—and they looked for it together. It was not there, but the worker said that it was indeed very possible that her 10 dollars could have disappeared in the struggle on the day she was admitted. Together, they "mourned" the loss of the money. The worker said she knew how helpless and out of control one feels when carefully kept possessions disappear. Mrs. Barry spoke about an occasion when she found a wallet belonging to a co-worker and how "of course" she returned it, adding that she never did expect people would treat her as well as she treated them. To this, the worker responded that when these things happen, it certainly makes it harder to trust others.

In the session following her trip with the worker to check the safe, there was a marked change in Mrs. Barry. She greeted the worker with the statement that she felt she was "too suspicious"; she could not understand why she did not trust people and had to "see everything with my own eyes" before believing it. She had not believed the worker when she said the money was not there. The worker repeated that when people have been hurt or disappointed, it can be difficult to trust. At this, Mrs. Barry began talking about her husband and his early promises that he would give her everything when he became a successful musician. Now, not only were her husband's wages low but he also was a reckless spender. Moreover, in recent years he went out by himself much more often than he had in the early years. She felt lonely and often thought he must be seeing another woman. She believed her husband was sterile. He knew how much she wanted to have children, and she felt that if he truly cared he would have himself checked.

For the most part, the caseworker listened to Mrs. Barry and expressed her understanding of how disappointed she felt. She said she hoped they could arrange a session with her husband so they could talk over some of these matters. On speaking to the psychiatrist in charge of Mrs. Barry's case, however, the worker learned that the doctor disapproved of the idea of conjoint sessions; it was his belief that Mrs. Barry was trying to "control" the treatment and "manipulate" the worker. Tactfully, but with conviction, the worker shared her view that despite Mrs. Barry's illness and paranoia, there seemed to be some important reality aspects to the marital relationship that required Mr. Barry's participation. Reluctantly, the psychiatrist agreed to "go along" with the worker, who then scheduled a joint session.

During the third week of hospitalization, despite her improvement, Mrs. Barry was still periodically confused. But self-awareness was keener than it had been, and she often commented on how frustrated she became when she had difficulty expressing herself. The worker reassured her that she was sounding clearer than she had and encouraged her to take the time she needed to pull her thoughts together. When less pressured by others, she was often able to be more coherent and relaxed. Mrs. Barry acknowledged this and said she wished her husband would pressure her less about her high school equivalency test.

On the day before Mrs. Barry's 20-day commitment was to expire, and a few hours before the joint session with her husband was scheduled, the worker found her to be depressed, withdrawn, and uncommunicative. She was unresponsive to the worker's overtures. Returning an hour later, the worker asked Mrs. Barry whether she was apprehensive about going home or about the meeting planned with her husband. Mrs. Barry said she wanted to stay in the hospital to make sure she would feel well when she left. Moreover, she wanted to have more than one meeting with her husband; she did not want to go home until certain matters that she was afraid to bring up alone were discussed. She signed voluntary papers to remain another week, adding that this time she would be in the hospital "for myself, not for the court."

During this last week in the hospital, the three individual sessions turned out to be the most productive of all. It was Mrs. Barry who had chosen to extend her hospitalization, and she seemed determined to benefit from it. She was able to reflect further on her decision to stop medication that had resulted in her "going crazy." Aside from viewing medication as a hated "crutch," she had also been extremely fearful that she would not be "smart enough" to pass the high school equivalency examination.

Fearing that she would fail and prove to others, particularly her husband, who had such high expectations of her, that she was worthless and had "mixed-up brains," she supposed that she had played it "safe" by getting sick; she knew that if she discontinued medication she would be rehospitalized. Again, she related her fear of failure to having felt like the "plain" and "stupid" middle child. Once she was able to share her understanding and feelings with the worker, she also brought them up in the group therapy sessions where she got further support.

There were two conjoint meetings with Mr. and Mrs. Barry. Mrs. Barry told her husband that his encouragement about the test felt like pressure to her, and that his enthusiasm about her courses in electronics made her feel that she would disappoint him if she did not do well. She told him it angered her that he wanted her to work at the restaurant she despised. Mr. Barry had a tendency to evade, but he listened to her complaints and tried to understand them. He realized there might be some misunderstandings between them and made efforts to change. Even though he had little insight into his wife's problems or his contribution to them, he agreed to marital therapy, reassuring her that he loved her and did not want her to get sick again.

The worker had the impression that Mr. and Mrs. Barry were in competition with one another, that Mrs. Barry was trying to measure up to her husband, who was skilled in telephone repair, and that there were hidden mixed feelings below his overly determined interest in his wife's achievements. In these joint meetings, however, the focus was limited almost entirely to the problem of pressure. The worker chose not to open up other issues of the marriage, even though many of these seemed problematical, for fear of further upsetting the marital relationship. They had little time to work. Instead, before Mrs. Barry's discharge, a referral for marital therapy was arranged that the worker was not too optimistic about. First, Mr. Barry was resistant to it and, second, the choice of resources was limited. In the clinic near the Barry home, there was only one therapist, a pastoral counselor, who provided marital therapy, and it was the worker's hunch that he might not do well with this particular couple. Fortunately, Mrs. Barry was also interested in joining an outpatient group, in which the worker expected she would do well.

From time to time after she left the hospital, Mrs. Barry telephoned the worker. She said that they had gone only once for marital treatment and then discontinued, feeling they did not need it. She attended group therapy sessions regularly for four months until the group disbanded after a cut in funding to the clinic. A year and a half after Mrs. Barry's discharge, the worker made a follow-up telephone call to her. She learned that Mrs. Barry felt she was doing well. She had continued to take medication despite the fact that she was suffering side effects (constipation, blurred vision, dryness of the mouth, and so on). She kept her appointments at the medication clinic regularly. She also told the worker that when she left the hospital she had decided not to take the equivalency test. The following year, however—on her own and not because her husband expected it—she went back to study for it, took it, and failed by only a few points. She did not seem discouraged and said she would try again soon. Mrs. Barry also told the worker that if she felt further treatment was necessary she would definitely go for it. She wanted to stay as well as she was.

This case illustrates how diagnosis and treatment go hand in hand, and how even short-term treatment can be effective in laying the ground for more extended therapy when needed. It demonstrates how the often discouraging clinical diagnosis of "paranoid schizophrenia" need not lead to despair about a client's ability to grow and change to make more satisfactory adjustments to life. In this case, the worker's primary objective was to help Mrs. Barry recompensate with the help of medication and resume her previous adjustment. However, on the basis of her increased participation and initiative, within a short time further goals of awareness of self-defeating behavior and of improvement of the marital relationship seemed possible.

The worker's assessment evolved and changed as she learned more about her client. Similarly, her treatment approach shifted as Mrs. Barry began to be better related, to trust the worker, and to be ready for self-understanding. In the context of a great deal of support, Mrs. Barry was able to pour out many pent-up feelings and emotionally charged memories. Careful timing made it possible to help her gain understanding about her decision to stop taking medication, without which she might have discontinued it again after her discharge. Contrary to the view of those who believe that the mentally ill cannot benefit from procedures other than those that are *supportive* or *directive,* the work with Mrs. Barry demonstrates that she was able to think *reflectively* on several levels: about herself, her situation, and her patterns of thinking and behaving, and on influential aspects of her childhood experiences. All the Hollis treatment procedures were employed.

Effort was also made to improve the quality of service for Mrs. Barry by working closely with the nurses to help them treat their patient with greater understanding. Attuned to the client–situation interplay, the worker identified how certain features of the hospital milieu, such as the staff's refusal to allow Mrs. Barry to examine the safe, tended to exacerbate her delusions. Despite the pessimistic approach of the psychiatrist in charge, the worker was able to find a way of working with him without alienating him; she was able to persuade him to accept her plan for conjoint meetings, a plan that the worker believed was not only diagnostically sound but imperative to the success of Mrs. Barry's treatment. As a result, Mr. Barry was no longer viewed simply as a consultant about his wife's illness but also as an important participant in her environment.

This case also shows how important it is for clients, even those as disturbed as Mrs. Barry was, to take an active part in their own treatment. At several points, the work was guided by directions Mrs. Barry chose: The worker supported Mrs. Barry's wish to include her husband in treatment and helped to arrange it; she accepted Mrs. Barry's request to see for herself if the money was in the hospital safe. And, of utmost importance, Mrs. Barry worked most productively when *she* made the decision to remain in the hospital. In each instance, her autonomy and self-esteem were reinforced.

The handling of this case differed significantly from what it would have been three or four decades ago. Before the development of antipsychotic drugs, Mrs. Barry's future surely would have been less hopeful; it is possible that she would have become a chronic schizophrenic, hospitalized for years or for the rest of her life. Furthermore, deinstitutionalization has resulted in shorter periods of inpatient treatment and greater emphasis on outpatient services (which, as this case confirms, are still far from adequately financed or staffed in many areas). Happily, Mrs. Barry's chances for a relatively adequate adjustment, particularly if she returns for treatment when necessary,

are far greater than they would have been just a little more than a generation ago.

TERMINAL ILLNESS[3]

Anna Stasio, age 44, telephoned a mental health clinic asking for an appointment with a woman therapist as soon as possible, to discuss "serious personal problems." As it happened, the worker assigned to intake on the day she called was a man. He asked her if there were any particular reason why she thought he could not help her. She replied abruptly, "I haven't got time for that." She asserted that under no circumstances would she agree to see a man, adding that she needed someone mature and experienced. In response to her request, an experienced woman worker was assigned.

At the beginning of the first interview, with startling directness, Mrs. Stasio stated that a malignant tumor had been discovered on one of her lymph nodes several months previously. More recently, it was determined that the cancer had spread throughout her system. She was receiving chemotherapy. Although the doctors believed she was now in remission, she was, as she put it, "sitting with a time bomb." She had no idea how long she would live, having been given estimates ranging from six months to two years, but she knew her days were numbered and she wanted to have someone who was "dispassionate" to talk with on a regular basis. Her father was old, her mother had a serious heart condition, and she described her husband as "weak" and "neurotic." None of them were comforting to her, she said, because she felt *she* had to soothe *them* when she talked about her illness. She had insisted on a mature woman because she felt women were "stronger" than men. Furthermore, she did not want to see a social worker who was "wet behind the ears" or unduly frightened by a dying woman. The worker, a senior on staff with many years of experience, was genuinely moved by this woman's courage and determination to get what she needed for whatever time she had left to live. By gesture, tone of voice, and mood, she conveyed this. She agreed it was important for Mrs. Stasio to feel satisfied with the person she was seeing, urging her to tell her if she felt uncomfortable. Operating on Mrs. Stasio's clue that she was a person who tended to feel protective of the feelings of others, even at her own expense, the worker assured her that though she would be pleased to work with her, she would not feel hurt if Mrs. Stasio decided she was not the right therapist. At this, Mrs. Stasio visibly softened; her eyes filled and she said gently, "I liked you from the moment we met."

In taking this straightforward approach, the worker conveyed that she, too, was a strong person who could, in the interest of her client, tolerate a rejection. This was undoubtedly supportive to Mrs. Stasio, who seemed to need someone whom she felt was as fearless as she saw herself to be. As she sat with this remarkable woman, the worker considered how her own emotional resources were being put to the test. Paradoxically, Mrs. Stasio came across as attractive, vital, and colorful, yet she was dying. As the client talked about herself, she did so with a wide range of feeling: At times she was angry and impatient; at times she spoke with tenderness and sadness; despite everything, she had a sense of humor. In every instance, her emotions were expressed vividly. The worker realized she would have to prepare herself now to be intimately associated with the many physical and emotional processes associated with terminal illness.

In early interviews with Mrs. Stasio, the worker learned that she came from a middle-class, intellectual family; her mother had been a professional ballet dancer and her father a college professor of literature. Her father was English born, her mother of Italian origin. Both parents were of Protestant background but neither was religious; Mrs. Stasio described herself as an atheist. She was an only child and had always been thought of as "headstrong." In college, she majored in fine arts; at that time she married her first husband, an actor with whom she lived for five years. They had an exciting but stormy marriage that ended because they were both too "stubborn" and aggressive. Each fought to overpower the other. When she married again, she chose a man of the opposite extreme; she portrayed Mr. Stasio, an engineer who had worked at the same government job for 20 years, as insecure, passive, and dull, but very kind. He was not well paid but had not had the courage to get his master's degree or to seek more challenging work. They had two children, Roger, age 15, and Elizabeth, age 13. The marriage had never been a truly happy one for her, but she had resigned herself to it, knowing that her domineering qualities had led her to choose him. For the past few years, she and a woman friend (with whom she had had a brief sexual affair) had operated a small picture-framing business that had been fairly successful and important to the family income. Mrs. Stasio had had two years of intensive psychotherapy when her children were small; it had helped her to understand herself better and to feel less angry and disappointed about her husband.

In her characteristically definite way, Mrs. Stasio declared she did not want family therapy or joint meetings with her husband. The worker had not yet suggested these, but, once again, this client was taking charge of getting the kind of treatment she wanted. She would find her own way of saying good-bye to her family; she did not need help with this. What she did want, she said, was someone whom she could use as a sounding board, to help her think over how to plan the rest of her life. There were also certain aspects of her behavior she wanted to change, particularly toward her husband and her daughter. She did not want to continue to feel guilty, as she did, about the way she took out her anger over her illness on Mr. Stasio. She was falling into the pattern she had been in when she went into therapy the first time; she belittled her husband and raged at him over minor matters. After all, it was not his fault that she had "settled" for a marriage that bored her. When she learned that she would soon die, she realized she would never experience a better relationship, a fantasy that had kept her anger "in check" in recent years. She worried about the effect of her hostility on the children, who would have only their father when she died; she did not want to contaminate their future relationship by her actions toward her husband now.

She felt concern for both children. But Roger, she thought, would handle himself; she described him as an "all-American boy": a fine student, an athlete, with many friends. Elizabeth, however, who had been born with a cleft palate and had had many operations since infancy, was a withdrawn, immature girl who did not do well in school and had very few friends. Mrs. Stasio said that she tended to over protect her daughter and did not want to do this now that Elizabeth would have to learn to be self-reliant. The worker pointed out that, if it seemed indicated, the children—or at least Elizabeth—might benefit from individual sessions. Mrs. Stasio opposed this idea as strongly as she resisted family treatment; emphatically, she said that changes in her own behavior would be the most helpful thing for Elizabeth. Mrs. Stasio's characteristic need to control, undoubtedly reinforced by her illness, necessarily limited treatment options.

Very early in therapy, Mrs. Stasio said that she would like to meet twice weekly, if possible. She had a lot to talk about and very little time. Although it was a general rule at the clinic to make appointments with clients on a once-a-week basis, for two reasons the worker arranged to make an exception. First, she wanted to be responsive to this client's wishes, and, second, Mrs. Stasio did indeed have many issues to talk over. From the worker's knowledge of this kind of cancer (which she later verified with a medical consultant), it very often resulted in rapid decline and early death. For the next five months, except when Mrs. Stasio had to go into the hospital for treatment, they met twice weekly.

After the first month of therapy, Mrs. Stasio came in saying that her husband also wanted to see the worker, that he was "falling apart." She still did not want to have meetings with him, but said she had no objection to his seeing her worker on his own. In fact, she was urging him to come.

Mr. Stasio, although hardly "falling apart," did want someone to talk to, with whom he could share his very mixed emotions. He was frightened and grief-stricken; he both resented and admired his wife. He also wanted suggestions about ways the children should be handled during this time. An intelligent man, Mr. Stasio was not usually introspective, but he needed a great deal of support and an opportunity to ventilate and to discuss the practical problems he was facing. Occasionally, the worker offered *direct advice* about the children, but primarily she encouraged him to make his own decisions, helping him to *reflect* on and evaluate various options. During their work together, as his wife became weaker, Mr. Stasio took on more and more responsibility for the household and child care. He was concerned about money now that Mrs. Stasio was no longer working; he was having difficulty with Elizabeth, who was clinging to her mother and seemed irritable and sarcastic with him. Since he did not want to upset his wife, he preferred to share these worries with the worker. He, too, opposed family meetings, wanting to establish close relationships with his children on his own. In his view, to have a "mediator" would detract from his efforts to strengthen family bonds. For too long he had been in his wife's "shadow," and now he did not want to "hide behind" the worker.

Some clinicians might take the view that the worker should have pressed harder for family meetings (or for individual treatment for the children), particularly since Elizabeth appeared to be having difficulties. The worker believed that some avoidance was operating for both parents, but decided not to urge them to involve the children. She thought she could persuade Mr. Stasio to change his mind but was quite sure that any attempt to convince his wife could be deeply damaging to the therapeutic relationship. Furthermore, she believed it was important to respect Mrs. Stasio's method of handling her illness and her wish to do as much as she could herself. For Mr. Stasio, the decision not to urge family meetings may well have been one of the factors that encouraged him to function more independently with his children. It was he who would have to learn to take charge of the family and, if the worker conveyed the opinion that he could not do this without her direct help, she might have fostered his dependency. Under different circumstances, the worker might have pressed harder for family meetings. As it was, both Mr. and Mrs. Stasio discussed in detail their relationships with the children, reflecting on how they could be most helpful to them.

From meeting to meeting, Mr. Stasio would report on his increasingly effective efforts to get closer to the children. He was able to talk with them about the sadness they shared; he found he could enlist their help around the house in ways he never had before. They were showing him more respect than previously and this gratified him, but he regretted that he had waited until his wife was dying to change his "image." Mrs. Stasio also was no longer berating him frequently and he attributed this, in part, to the changes he had made. The worker was supportive of his new role but disagreed with him when he gave her more credit than he gave himself for the changes. She pointed out that he had worked hard and wondered why now he would want to downplay the importance of his own efforts and only recognize hers.

After three months, it became apparent to the worker that Mrs. Stasio's condition was rapidly deteriorating. Chemotherapy was no longer effective in forestalling the advance of the malignancy. Nevertheless, she remained mentally clear and actively engaged in all aspects of her life. She was grateful to her husband for taking more initiative at home; she spoke with appreciation of his good qualities and now found it comforting to view him as a "friend." She had neither the energy nor the inclination to belittle him now, and she was glad to achieve one of her major objectives: to behave differently toward him. By expressing her anger in the sessions, rather than directly at him, she had relieved the tension between them. She was also proud of the fact that she had been able to have loving talks about her condition with both children and had been able to listen to their concerns and questions. In a moving discussion with Elizabeth, which she had "rehearsed" with the worker beforehand, she told her daughter that she had probably "babied" her too much and that she regretted that, particularly now that Elizabeth would have to become increasingly independent. Mrs. Stasio spoke with compassion of her parents, now sick and old, who would have to face the loss of their only child; she gave a good deal of thought to how she could make it easier for them, fully aware that even now she was relating to them in a caretaking way, as had been her lifelong pattern.

Particularly after Mrs. Stasio had achieved the relationships she wanted with her family—or, perhaps, also because she knew she was close to death—she began to use her sessions to reflect spontaneously, sometimes in minute detail, on various periods of her life. She talked with regret about never having had a fulfilling marital relationship. Her most satisfying sexual experiences, she confided, had been with women; she was glad now that she had allowed these, although she had felt very guilty about them at the time. Sharing these confidences, she said, had a "cleansing" effect. She joked that even though she was not religious, she seemed to have the need to "confess." Her relationship with her parents, both of whom tended to be passive, indecisive people, interested her. In her view, she had become a "powerhouse" because they were so unassertive and needed her leadership, even when she was very young. If this situation had been a liability for Mrs. Stasio, she saw it now as an asset. From her standpoint, her aggressiveness had served her well. She had been part of life and had not simply watched from the sidelines as she felt her parents had.

As she spoke of her marriage, she said that her angry domination of her husband had, in some way, represented her effort to "make him over" into the strong man her father never was. As she saw it, she had taken on the role of the "man" in her parents' home and again in her current family. Her disappointment in her father had led

her to choose her first husband, whom she viewed as his opposite. Unable to tolerate the power struggles that ensued, she made sure her next husband would be easier to manage! Her occasional same-sex affairs, she assumed, were a response to frustrations with the men in her life.

It had always been Mrs. Stasio's inclination to be introspective; moreover, her two years of psychotherapy several years earlier had contributed to her sophisticated self-understanding. In contrast to many treatment situations in which change in emotional or behavioral patterns is a primary objective, for Mrs. Stasio this phase of treatment (which involved *dynamic and developmental reflection*) was important to her attempts to come to peace with or "make sense" out of her life. There was no attempt on her part or the worker's to help resolve long-standing conflicts or neurotic issues; reflections on these matters were important only to the degree that Mrs. Stasio was interested in them.

Since Mrs. Stasio could not control her disease, she was determined to manage its effects. She would take charge of her own dying. Unlike many terminally ill patients, at no point did she use the defense of denial against the *fact* of her impending premature death. If she exhibited any denial, as the worker believed she did, it was denial or repression of anxieties and helplessness naturally associated with terminal illness. She handled these through "counterphobic" behavior. In the face of death, she continued to orchestrate: how her therapy would be handled, how her husband would get treatment, and how she would say good-bye to her children. To one session she brought three long typewritten letters, one to her husband and one to each child, to be read after she died. In these she gave instructions about her funeral and made suggestions about the management of finances, detailing ideas for them all to follow in the future. Gently, the worker asked Mrs. Stasio if she thought the letters conveyed her doubts about whether the family would be able to manage without her. After thinking it over between sessions, Mrs. Stasio returned with a new set of letters, having discarded the first; in them she told each how much she cared, expressing confidence in them all. The only instructions included were those related to her funeral arrangements.

Diagnostically, Mrs. Stasio was seen as a woman who approached life intensely, even in the face of her debilitated physical condition. She had many well-developed ego functions that helped her master difficult situations in health and in illness. She had a clear sense of values and a capacity for self-criticism and change, even in the last months of her life. Her chief defenses, repression and some denial of her fear of imminent death, allowed her to function effectively, not only for her own benefit, but also for that of her family. She helped them prepare for the inevitable and offered them an opportunity to grieve with her while she still lived. Her characteristic mode of handling anxiety, as she often said, had been to "grab life by the tail," and this style served her through these days of illness. As already noted, there were character problems and neurotic patterns that Mrs. Stasio had never resolved, although she was aware of most of them. Her inordinate need to control undoubtedly masked a longstanding fear of dependency; she allowed herself to rely on the worker only after she was absolutely sure that the worker could "take it." Her ambivalence toward men and uncertain sexual identification were evident. The worker's diagnostic understanding was of utmost importance to the treatment. It was essential, for example, for the worker to respect Mrs. Stasio's need for

control and to recognize which defenses were necessary to protect her from overwhelming anxiety or despair. By getting to know her client as well as she did, the worker was also able to stay empathically attuned to the great vicissitudes of feeling Mrs. Stasio experienced during this final phase of her life.

Throughout the therapy, *sustaining procedures* were highly important. The worker used several forms of support. Mrs. Stasio needed the worker's strength, consistent interest, and encouragement. She enjoyed the worker's praise about the changes that led to warmer family relationships. A woman keenly connected to her emotions and experiences, Mrs. Stasio required an intense therapeutic relationship. She originally requested a worker who could be "dispassionate," but evidently she meant someone who did not need to be taken care of; she did not mean (and would not have tolerated!) a therapist who was emotionally unavailable. Following Mrs. Stasio's lead, the worker shared how genuinely privileged she felt to have gotten to know her; they spoke of their time together as a special kind of "journey." Empathically, the worker shared Mrs. Stasio's anger at the arbitrary way illness chooses its victims. She truly understood her client's tears of frustration and sadness: Mrs. Stasio had always wanted to live a long life; now she would never see her children become adults; now she would miss out on her grandchildren; now she would have no "third chance" at a better marriage. The worker refrained from offering false reassurances; Mrs. Stasio counted on her to share in the agony of accepting the inevitability of her early death.

With Mr. Stasio, the worker was also *supportive.* She reinforced his capacity for independent functioning and helped him to be aware of his strengths, which he generally underestimated. With the worker's encouragement, he was able to take more initiative with his children, particularly when not faced with his wife's extraordinary aggressiveness. As Mrs. Stasio related more softly with him, he, in turn, could be more confident and assertive. It proved important for Mr. Stasio to have someone to whom he could vent his long-standing resentments. He was then free to feel less conflicted in his loving feelings for his wife. He began truly to grieve for her and to face his fears about life without her. Like his wife, he never denied the reality of her condition, and this enabled them to share their pain. From his point of view, and Mrs. Stasio's as well, their times together became more tender and meaningful than ever.

In addition to *sustaining procedures* and those that fostered *ventilation,* the worker helped Mr. Stasio *reflect* on the many day-to-day difficulties and decisions that faced him. He became more aware of his pattern of either withdrawing or deferring to others, particularly his wife but at times the worker too. Occasionally, he mentioned his relationship with his domineering mother, to whom he was still close, and recognized some of the roots of his current behavior. But, in general, there was little emphasis on *developmental reflection;* he had no interest in concentrating on his early life. The most productive work seemed to come from the use of procedures that addressed his present feelings and behavior.

In what turned out to be her last office session, Mrs. Stasio looked very ill; she was failing quickly but, though subdued, remained mentally alert. She said she had talked over all the important matters that concerned her when she first came. She wanted the worker to know how much their meetings had meant. The following day she entered the hospital.

By telephone, a few days later, Mrs. Stasio asked the worker to visit. When she got there, she saw that Mrs. Stasio had many bruises, the result of falls when she tried to get out of bed. She said she did not want the worker to visit her again. She did not want anyone to see her in this weakened condition or to be remembered as a hospital patient. She knew she would die soon. She had said good-bye to her children, her parents, and a few close friends. She allowed only her husband to see her now; he was there many hours each day. She took the worker's hand, held it tightly for a minute, and then turned away. The worker touched Mrs. Stasio's shoulder, said good-bye, and left sadly, realizing that her client's battle for life was ending. She had turned over the controls: to her illness, to the doctors, to death itself.

Two weeks later, Mr. Stasio called to say that his wife had died. At the funeral, for the first time, the worker briefly met the children, who stayed close to their father throughout.

Mr. Stasio returned to therapy for a period of seven months. He expressed his grief and anger; he and the worker shared memories of Mrs. Stasio. The fact that the worker was unashamed of her own sadness helped Mr. Stasio to express his feelings of loss. He said it comforted him to speak with someone who had known his wife so well and who could understand the range of emotions he was experiencing. He was both consoled and frustrated as he reviewed the final weeks of his wife's life when they had become closer than ever before. He used his sessions to discuss issues related to the children who, on the whole, were relating well with each other. And they truly respected him now, too. He talked over practical plans and decided to move to another town, at some distance from the clinic, which would be closer to his mother, who could help with care of the children. Having a woman to lean on was still important to him, he said. Roger was doing well, but Elizabeth seemed unhappy and Mr. Stasio sought information, which the worker gave, about a mental health service in the area where they would be living. He was a lonely man now, but strikingly more confident about his ability to take charge of his family.

The process of dying is as individualized as the process of living. Similarly, the style of one's grief is idiosyncratic. Every adaptation, every expression of outrage and despair about death takes its own form, depending on the personalities of the dying patient and of those who are left behind. In contrast to the Stasios, the gravity of terminal illness is minimized by some patients and their families, who cling to hope for recovery long after the doctors have given up. Sometimes relatives feel they must "protect" patients by giving false reassurance to make their last days as untroubled as possible. In other situations, such avoidance is maintained to shield the family members themselves from anxiety and depression. Some doctors do not believe terminal patients should be given the whole truth about their condition, although this is less frequently so than it was only two decades ago. In every instance, the social worker has to take the lead from the client and family. One cannot recklessly intrude on defenses against death any more than one should push hard against any defense that has been erected to protect an individual from overwhelming emotion; otherwise, the psychological balance of some clients might be seriously endangered. On the other hand, there is increasing evidence that, when possible and diagnostically indicated, the opportunity for dying patients to share grief with those who will survive protects them from feelings of alienation and the sense that they are being dealt with dishonestly. Furthermore, often openness can provide a family with the op-

portunity to begin to face grief, to reduce potential guilt, and to prepare for adapting to life after the patient has died.

Almost two years after Mr. Stasio terminated treatment, he telephoned the worker asking for a joint session with a divorcée whom he planned to marry. For the most part, he and his family had done well since he last saw the worker. But he wanted help with problems related to tensions occurring between his and his fiancée's adolescent children. The worker met with the couple twice. However, Mr. Stasio's future wife, who appeared to have strong managerial tendencies and definite opinions, took a dark view of psychological help; she had always worked out difficult problems herself, she said. Efforts to explore this woman's adamance were met with unyielding resistance. Reluctantly, with only a token protest, Mr. Stasio acceded to her wishes not to meet again. The worker thought the children might be responding to unspoken struggles between the adults. But, under the circumstances, exploration was not possible. It seemed that once again Mr. Stasio was planning his life with a woman who, in a somewhat different manner from Anna Stasio, was, nevertheless, determined to take charge of situations her way.

In every treatment situation, the clinical social worker has to accept limitations imposed by the client. One can suggest other options, as the worker in this instance did, but the work can go on only to the extent that the client is willing to participate. Although she had been tremendously helpful to Mr. and Mrs. Stasio during the months before the latter died and to Mr. Stasio for a period thereafter, she saw no way to help forestall problems that might well ensue in this new family unless they were willing to examine the issues.

Only time would tell whether the couple, whom the worker was careful not to alienate, would return if difficulties did arise.

A FAMILY'S CRISIS: INVOLUNTARY CLIENTS ACCEPT HELP

It was almost three o'clock on a hot summer Friday afternoon when a case supervisor from Child Protective Services telephoned a very experienced senior worker at the Crisis Unit of the Family Guidance Center, whom she knew well. They had worked together on several cases. The supervisor briefly summarized her reason for calling: In her office at that moment were Lloyd and Sara Carter, an African-American couple, ages 47 and 34, respectively. Their two children, Robert, 11, and Denise, 8, had been placed in a foster home on an emergency basis on Monday. After an anonymous call, alleging child abuse and neglect, a child protective worker had gone to the home. The family lived in a large, well-kept apartment in a run-down building in "Southside" (the area where most blacks in the small city lived). When the protective worker arrived there in the afternoon, she found the children frightened by her visit and unwilling to answer her questions. At home with them was an elderly aunt of Mrs. Carter's, Mrs. Williams, who lived with the family; she said very little also but did admit that Robert had had several marks across his back and buttocks as the result of a beating his father had given him because the boy had taken money out of his sister's drawer. Robert nodded when the worker asked him whether all of this were true.

The protective worker contacted Mr. Carter at a local factory where he was employed loading tractor-trailers; Mrs. Carter, who worked nights for an office-cleaning service, could not be located. Reading from the worker's report, the supervisor said that

when Mr. Carter arrived home he was outraged at the worker's intrusion and launched into an intense argument with her, waving his arms and calling her names; he said that he had "whipped" Robert with a belt, that it was his right as a father to do so, that the boy deserved it and was not hurt, and that it was nobody's business but his and his wife's. He was not, he repeatedly insisted, a "child-beater." "Does this look like a house that doesn't take care of children?" he shouted, pointing to the neat, well-furnished apartment and the children's large rooms. Over and over he demanded, "Do these children look neglected?" directing the worker's attention to the children's healthy appearance. "I work two jobs and my wife works also to send these children to private [parochial] school." He either could not or would not say where Mrs. Carter was. "There's an adult here," he said, referring to Mrs. Williams. "That's all that should matter to you."

The worker, who reacted strongly to Mr. Carter's fury, was concerned that the children were not safe. She took steps the same day to have them declared "at risk" on an emergency basis; they were removed from the home that afternoon. Today, the supervisor said, the Family Court judge told Mr. and Mrs. Carter, who want the children returned to them, that they would have to accept a referral for counseling before he would release them. The supervisor said that they had spoken with the school principal, even though classes had ended; from their investigation, it appeared that there had *not* been a history of abuse. However, the principal thought that there might be marital difficulties. Something may be wrong, the supervisor said. Mrs. Carter seems uncommunicative; perhaps she has emotional problems, she speculated. The principal thought that Mrs. Carter was "strange" sometimes. Reluctantly, the parents accepted a referral to the Guidance Center, realizing that the children would remain in placement until they agreed to get help. Mr. Carter especially, the supervisor warned, was very, very angry: "a difficult man to deal with," she said. The supervisor concluded by saying that she had been out of town when the children were placed. Without exactly saying so, she left the impression that she thought the protective worker and substitute supervisor had acted too hastily.

The Guidance Center worker had to handle some misgivings about becoming involved immediately. She weighed in her own mind whether she should make the appointment for early next week or whether she should agree to see them right away, as the supervisor urged. She realized that if she had the meeting, she would have to put aside her own end-of-the-week fatigue; she would have to call home, as she had to fairly often, to say she would be late and then deal once again with her family's disappointment. Without doubt, the meeting would be a long and difficult one; she wondered to herself whether she had the energy for it. On the other hand, she had enough information to be able to empathize with the anger and desperation these parents must feel about the precipitous removal of their children. She thought she might be able to engage them most quickly if she could be available to them now, when they were so distraught. They were probably not feeling very trusting of "helping people," given the events of the week. Thinking through her own issues and negative feelings and taking a few moments for anticipatory preparation[4] helped to diminish her reluctance. She asked the supervisor to put one of the Carters on the telephone; in a controlled voice, Mr. Carter spoke with her and they arranged for an immediate appointment.

This initial appointment lasted almost two hours. The first hour was taken up with Mr. Carter's furious complaints about the way the protective services handled their investigation. The worker listened, expressing understanding and caring about how the couple must have experienced the entire episode, without presuming to judge the merits of every detail that Mr. Carter presented. The worker thought to herself that Mr. Carter seemed to be a very proud and private man who undoubtedly felt deeply humiliated by what had happened. When asked how it had been for her, Mrs. Carter said she felt that their case had been handled badly and that the worker had taken action without knowing the facts. "This would not have happened like this to a white family," she added. The protective services worker had a "mean way about her"; the supervisor they saw today was much more understanding. Mr. Carter agreed. Viewing it as a strength, the worker noted to herself that they were able to differentiate the personalities despite their distress; they were not indiscriminately blaming everybody equally. In a flat, phlegmatic tone Mrs. Carter added that neither her husband nor she physically abused the children; this was the worst physical punishment either Robert or Denise had ever received, and it had occurred after several warnings to Robert about taking money in the house. The worker believed her. If there were marital problems, they were not letting their conflicts interfere with their primary objectives: to have the children returned as soon as possible and to restore their reputation as conscientious, nonabusing parents. This, the worker thought, was another strength: When threatened, they stood together.

Both parents, but particularly Mrs. Carter, responded to questions about the children. Robert was sometimes difficult to manage; he got into minor difficulties in school fairly often. He did not get very good grades. But, the mother said, "He has a very sweet nature." Denise is "like a little old lady"; she gossips with adults and tries to boss other children, including her older brother. She loves school and does well there. Sometimes, when Mrs. Carter has to go to work early, Denise cooks supper for her father and brother. The worker had the impression that Denise was special to Mr. Carter and that Robert was closer to his mother than to his father. Mrs. Carter said that both children were very frightened by their sudden removal from the home and hate being away, even though the foster family is nice to them. Together and separately, the parents had visited the children several times since they were placed on Monday. Another strength, the worker noted.

Deliberately, the worker did not explore the marital relationship except to ask at one point, in a low-key way, whether they fought physically; they denied that they did. Her immediate goals were to encourage the couple to express their feelings about their situation and to enlist their trust. She wanted them to know that she would do whatever she could to help them, without reassuring them that she would use her influence to get the children home immediately. Although Mr. Carter was very angry at having to take time off from work, he was much calmer now and agreed to return with his wife on Monday so that they could "get all this over with."

As the worker drove home, she thought about the Carters. She had no difficulty understanding how desperate and misused they felt. She suspected that the child protective worker had been frightened by Mr. Carter's rage and, perhaps, this had provoked her to arrange for the emergency placement. Physical abuse, she thought to herself, is not the problem; she felt quite sure of this, and her impressions were supported by the protective services investigation. But *something* was wrong. Certainly,

Mr. Carter had quite a temper, yet apparently he usually controlled it. But was there anything beyond the immediate situation that accounted for Mr. Carter's anger? It was impossible to assess the quality of the couple's relationship; during the entire meeting there had been very little interaction between them. Except for Mr. Carter's anger, little emotion was expressed. Something about Mrs. Carter's listless manner and general demeanor was puzzling. Was there a drug or alcohol problem? Perhaps she could find a way to explore this, she thought, but first she needed to make sure she had their trust. And whatever the problem was, she believed it would be revealed only after the present crisis was resolved. She knew that the Carters would come to the Guidance Center for a few months at least, as long as the Family Court probation department remained active; they would do nothing to jeopardize their children. As she parked and prepared to make the most of the remainder of the evening with her family, the worker felt glad that she had decided to see this couple right away. Although she could not be sure, she thought that they had begun to have confidence in her.

The second meeting confirmed the worker's earlier impressions; she felt certain that the children were not at risk for physical abuse. The couple agreed to continue counseling, understanding that return of the children would be contingent upon this. The worker asked whether the Carters felt comfortable with her; counseling is a very personal experience, she said, and it was important that they see someone who feels right to them. She wondered whether they found it difficult to speak with a white worker. They could see another worker if they preferred. In a matter-of-fact way, both Carters said they wanted to stay with her. The protective services supervisor joined the Guidance Center worker in recommending to Family Court that the children be released. On Wednesday, they went home.

At the worker's request, Mr. and Mrs. Carter brought the children to the next meeting. They were pleasant but seemingly guarded; definitely on their best behavior, the worker thought. They did say that they had not been happy in the foster home. There was very little spontaneity during the entire session, except for Mr. Carter's continuing expressions of anger at the actions that had been taken against their family. Although indirectly he indicated that he appreciated the worker's help in getting the children returned, he made it very clear that he did not like to be forced to come for counseling. Mrs. Carter was quieter than ever. Although she had nothing concrete to base it on, intuitively, from some subtle cues in the woman's demeanor (such as tired-looking eyes, flat affect, and listlessness), the worker suspected there might be an alcohol problem. She knew, however, that if she were going to be helpful to this family, she would still have to wait for the opportunity to raise the question when she had the best chance of getting a nondefensive answer. The time was not now, she realized. This meeting was one in which everyone, including the worker, seemed to be treading water.

Less than an hour after the session ended, the worker received an agitated, almost unintelligible, call from Mr. Carter. "I need help," he said over and over again. Finally, the worker was able to make sense of what he was saying: When the family left the session, they had gone to a nearby shopping mall; Mrs. Carter went to the restroom, and when she returned Mr. Carter could tell ("I can always tell," he said) that she had been drinking. "She promised she wouldn't do this again," he said. "Can you

help?" Mr. Carter was calling from a phone booth. The worker made an appointment for Mr. Carter to return to the office with his wife the following day.

When the couple came in, both looked exhausted. They had been arguing bitterly since yesterday. Mr. Carter, close to tears now, kept asking his wife how she could have done this to him and to the children. Once he was a little calmer, the worker turned her attention to Mrs. Carter. The history of her alcoholism unfolded: She had had several bouts of heavy drinking over the years. Three years ago she attended AA meetings for a while but stopped going when her drinking seemed to be under control. Mr. Carter sometimes drank at home or with friends, occasionally to excess, but Mrs. Carter never openly drank. "You've tried to keep it a secret," the worker suggested. Mrs. Carter nodded. On a hunch, the worker gently inquired whether she also used pills. Mrs. Carter looked down and, after several moments, nodded. "Is it time to get help?" the worker asked. Mrs. Carter nodded again.

The worker did not get the details of when Mrs. Carter had begun drinking again or of what drugs she had been taking. Rather, she focused on her medical needs. She guessed that Mrs. Carter's drinking had not been immediately exposed, even to Mr. Carter despite his claims, because she was also taking pills; tremors and other telltale signs of alcohol abuse sometimes can be masked by drug use. When Mr. Carter raised the question of AA, the worker said that she thought Mrs. Carter needed attention from a doctor and suggested hospitalization at the detoxification unit of the local hospital. At first, Mr. Carter protested; he thought his wife could stay at home and get help. The worker looked at Mrs. Carter. "I'll go," she said. Arrangements were facilitated by the worker's call to social service at the hospital. Mr. Carter called later to say that his wife had been admitted.

Twice during her 21-day inpatient treatment Mrs. Carter telephoned the worker. The second time, when she was about to be released, the worker noted how vital her voice sounded, in contrast to her former flat way of speaking. Enthusiastically, she told the worker that the children had visited her several times and that she was looking forward to going home. She had attended AA meetings in the hospital and would continue in AA; the 12-step program made a lot of sense to her, she said.

Couple sessions began after Mrs. Carter returned home. Over an eight-month period, including three months after Family Court closed its case, there were 27 meetings; two of these were attended by the children. In a general sense, the worker was not surprised to learn that Mr. Carter had been the oldest of four children; his father deserted the family when he was 10, leaving him to be his mother's "right arm." She counted on him to help care for his siblings while she worked. By the time he was a young teenager, he had a full-time job; he left school after the eighth grade. His super-responsible role in his current family, his pride, his anger, his difficulty in asking for help, the worker thought, all were understandable in view of childhood circumstances that forced him to put his own needs aside and grow up quickly.

Mrs. Carter's early years were filled with deprivation and fear. Her mother, now dead for five years, had Mrs. Carter, her only child, when she was 16. She lived with several men during Mrs. Carter's childhood. Some of them were alcoholic; one of them sexually abused her when she was 12. She never thought her mother liked or wanted her; she tried desperately to please her but never thought she succeeded. Her brightest childhood memories were about summers spent with her maternal grandmother, who lived in the South. "I always knew she loved me, and that helped see me through the winter times," she told the worker.

Mr. and Mrs. Carter met when she was a teenager in the town where her grandmother lived and Mr. Carter was raised. At that time, Mr. Carter was married to someone else, with whom he had three children, who were now adults. It was not until after they met again at the grandmother's funeral, when Mrs. Carter was 22 and Mr. Carter was separated, that they became interested in one other. After a brief courtship, they decided to move north, where they lived together until Mr. Carter's divorce came through. Robert was born before their wedding.

Now that Mrs. Carter was not drinking and was regularly attending AA meetings, the couple and the worker discussed treatment goals. Although no longer resentful about the sessions, Mr. Carter did not see the need for them. He was coming because of the court requirement and, as it turned out, because Mrs. Carter found treatment helpful. She reviewed unhappy and terrifying childhood experiences; she was able to express anger and sadness when talking about her mother. As time went on, Mr. Carter said that he would do anything he could to help his wife stay sober; he participated in the treatment less reluctantly, as long as the focus remained on Mrs. Carter.

However, with the worker's well-timed encouragement, the marital relationship was explored. Predictably, Mr. Carter said that there were no problems as long as the drinking did not resume. Tentatively, Mrs. Carter began to talk about dissatisfactions. Her major complaint was that her husband always wanted to take charge: "His way is *the* way," she told the worker. When she was younger, she said, she needed a strong man—someone on whom she could depend, someone who would tell her and show her what to do—she had been very insecure as a result of the erratic circumstances of her childhood and her mother's rejection of her. But now she felt belittled and frustrated by his takeover style. Since she quit drinking, she had gotten very positive support from AA members; her sponsor, an older and kindly woman, "is like the mother I never had," Mrs. Carter said. Because she felt more confident, the very traits that attracted her to her husband now filled her with resentment.

For several sessions, Mr. Carter minimized his wife's complaints. When she persisted, he became belligerent, telling her she was just making excuses for her own shortcomings. As she grew stronger and more outspoken, his anger accelerated. The worker's countertransference reactions to his behavior were neutralized by her recognition of how threatened he was at having his authority challenged. In a sense, for many years, his "strength" was sustained by his wife's "weakness." If he no longer feels needed, the worker hypothesized to herself, he is afraid he will lose his wife. From his perspective, she surmised, his close relationship to his mother was based on the fact that he had taken care of her. Furthermore, his behavior was supported by traditional male–female relationships that had been highly valued in his family of origin. When irritated by Mr. Carter's bullying manner, the worker reminded herself of how frightening it is to shed familiar roles when there is no certainty that relationships will survive without them.

Mrs. Carter would not be intimidated. She had felt the relief and exhilaration of her newly found independence; she would not, could not, turn back. Tension mounted in the marital relationship. Concerned that Mr. Carter's anger might be displaced onto the children, the worker asked the parents to bring them to a few sessions. Issues involving Mrs. Carter's alcohol problem, of which the children were aware, were discussed. The worker articulated what the children also knew: that their parents were coming for sessions to work out some problems between them. The worker observed to herself, as she had previously, that Mr. Carter seemed to turn to Denise for comfort and that he and Robert were rather distant. Although the children were a little more relaxed than when she first met them, they were not very forthcoming in the two sessions they attended and had little interest in being there. The worker was reassured that they were not direct targets of Mr. Carter's perturbed state. She also believed that the children would become more expressive and more appropriately related to their parents only when the marital relationship was better resolved. After the next family session, she decided, she would recommend that they return to couple meetings.

As it turned out, Mr. and Mrs. Carter appeared alone for the next appointment. Mr. Carter looked shaken and disheveled. He told the worker that after an argument with his wife last night, he went out drinking, something he had not done since Mrs. Carter was hospitalized. When he got home, he accused his wife of having affairs. He told her that he had never believed that Robert was his son. Instead of his usual angry diatribes, however, he became what Mrs. Carter described as "hysterical." He "cried and cried," she said, until he finally fell asleep. Uncharacteristically (he rarely missed a day of work), he asked her to call his employer and say he was sick. "That's what I was and that's what I am," Mr. Carter groaned. "I need help," he added. When he said it this time, however, he knew it was for *him*. The worker did not have to reply. Mrs. Carter turned to her husband and said, "I'll help you."

This was the turning point. Very quickly, Mr. Carter realized how frightened he had been for his entire married life. He had never dared to lean on his wife. Most of the time he did not even know that he wanted or needed to. Mrs. Carter reassured him that Robert was his son and that she had never been unfaithful to him; she had no desire to leave him, unless he reverted to his domineering, stubborn ways. She told him that she felt much closer to him when he acted like a "normal" person, instead of a superman. She, too, liked to feel needed. She liked it when he talked *with* rather than *at* her; she had been very lonely before.

During the next to the last session, the couple and the worker all became tearful as Mr. Carter told a story of how frightened he had been at age 11 when he was sexually assaulted by a male friend of the family; he did not dare tell his mother, not because she would blame him but because she would feel sorry for him, a response that he would have found intolerable. He was only now allowing his wife's tenderness to touch him; in his mind it had always been mixed up with pity, he said.

The decision to terminate felt right to Mr. and Mrs. Carter and to the worker. "There will always be problems," Mrs. Carter said, "but we've got a hold on them now." Together they reviewed the many phases of their relatively short treatment. Mr. and Mrs. Carter each realized how when one made changes, the other grew too. The worker gave them a lot of credit for the courageous way they had tackled difficult issues. She also asked whether there was anything they wished she had done differently. Mr. Carter wondered whether the children should have been involved; he would have preferred to leave them out of it. His wife disagreed, saying that she thought it had helped them to know they were trying to make things better for the family. Mrs. Carter, who had been so listless when they first met, expressed her gratitude to the worker in almost flowery terms. She appreciated the worker's confidence in her and in their marriage; she said she never felt judged. "I'll never forget you," she added. Mr. Carter was less effusive than his wife, but when he left, he shook her hand, looked her in the eye, and said, "I thank you." As she watched them walk away from her, the worker thought: Now it is going to be *his* turn to learn from *her*.

A few months after they ended their sessions and again four years later, Mrs. Carter called to refer AA friends for therapy. She was proud of her sobriety; she continued to attend AA meetings regularly and still had the same caring sponsor. The children were doing well, although Robert was going through his "teenage ups and downs." As for the marriage, they had some "bumpy" times, she said, but nothing that compared to the way things used to be.

The success of this treatment relied heavily on strengths the couple brought with them and the worker's recognition of them. Throughout this text we have stressed the importance of focus on health as well as "pathology," of realistic optimism, of empathy, of warmth and genuineness. We have urged flexibility and have emphasized the importance of tailoring each piece of work to the needs and personalities of the clients being seen. Had the worker believed that involuntary clients are intractably "resistant" or that she had to confront Mrs. Carter's alcoholism before the timing was right, she would not have gained this couple's confidence. If she was convinced that lower-socioeconomic-class, relatively poorly educated black clients were unable to use casework assistance, her negative attitude probably would have stifled her best efforts. Fortunately, this worker preferred to make individualized assessments rather than to base her thinking on stereotypes that, as often as not, do not hold up in reality.

ANXIETY ATTACKS: THE ADULT CHILD OF AN ALCOHOLIC FATHER

At the suggestion of his sister, who worked in the mental health field, Jed Cooper, 22, made an appointment with a clinical social worker in private practice. In his first interview, he said he felt tongue-tied. He blushed frequently and shifted uneasily in his chair. When he tried to explain why he had come, he became flustered and inarticulate. In this session, therefore, the worker took a very active, supportive role; she told Jed that it was hard for most people to talk to a strange person about personal matters. She added that she thought it would become easier for him as they went along, saying too, that it can become more difficult if one tries too hard, before one feels more relaxed. Mostly, the worker asked factual questions, to which Jed responded fairly comfortably, postponing those related to his reasons for wanting help.

She learned that Jed was the youngest of four children; his three sisters were married and now only he lived at home with his parents. His father, a retired policeman, was working as a security guard. Recently, his mother had begun working part-time as a saleswoman in a department store. His mother was born in Ireland and his father was second-generation Irish; both were Catholic. At his mother's insistence, Jed had attended parochial schools. After graduating from high school, he had held various jobs and, for the past year, was learning woodworking skills by working as an assistant to a cabinetmaker. He seemed most at ease talking about his work and smiled for the first time when he answered questions about his job; he said he wanted to become an "A-1" craftsman. Speaking more spontaneously

now, Jed said that his employer was "like a father" to him. Rather than inquiring immediately about this, the worker waited a moment, at which point Jed volunteered that he hated his father, who was an alcoholic and had been for as long as he could remember. Once this was said, Jed's tension obviously mounted again and the worker, while demonstrating that she understood his strong feelings, did not explore the matter further. She simply agreed that it must feel good to have a boss he could really enjoy.

When the session ended, it was still unclear just what had precipitated Jed's request for help. Only in the last few minutes was he able to say that he tended to get "nervous" and his sister thought he should have "someone to talk to." At this point, the worker did not have enough information to assess the nature of Jed's difficulties. She *was* aware that his anxiety was high and that supportive measures designed to reduce it took precedence over getting more information. She considered cultural factors that might have contributed to his uneasiness. Clients with a strong especially Irish-Catholic background are sometimes loath to share personal material with outsiders, particularly those not connected with the church. As yet, she had no way of knowing whether some particular event had catalyzed Jed's acute state of anxiety and embarrassment. Some early childhood fears may have been activated. The possibility that Jed was severely disturbed could not be ruled out. But, seemingly well oriented, he functioned constructively on his job, and there was no apparent thought disorder. His affect was restricted, but when relaxed, he seemed emotionally responsive. To convey her caring and yet elicit Jed's motivation for and participation in treatment, the worker asked whether he wanted to meet again. When he nodded, she offered him three alternative dates for the next session, ranging from 3 to 10 days away from the first interview. Jed chose the nearest date and left, firmly shaking the worker's hand and thanking her.

The Course of Treatment

In the second meeting, again Jed was tense and constricted for the first few minutes but became calmer more quickly than in the initial session. Still blushing frequently, he was able to say fairly fluently that he had become worried when, two weeks before, he had been sitting in the living room with his father watching a ball game and suddenly became extremely "nervous" and dizzy. When he tried to get up, his knees buckled and he fell to the floor. The episode did not last long, but afterward he began to sob uncontrollably. He went to work the next day but could not concentrate. He was so frightened that he spoke with his oldest sister, who suggested that he see a doctor, who told him there seemed to be nothing physically wrong. Again, at the suggestion of his sister, he called the worker. He had come, he said, to find out what was wrong with him. When the worker said that the incident must have worried him, Jed asked, "Does it mean I'm crazy?" He did not seem "crazy" to her, she said, but it did sound as though something were frightening him a lot. Jed volunteered that he had a similar "spell" two years before, again when he was alone with his father. He asked the worker whether she had ever heard of anything like this before. He seemed to be asking to be reassured, either that the worker was competent to help him or that his situation was not unique or hopeless. She answered that she had known of other people who had responded to intense feeling or fear in similar ways, but that it might take a little time to find out why this had happened to him. "Is there a cure?" Jed asked. The worker, knowing that Jed was functioning normally in

his daily life, said that the worst of his "attack" seemed to be over, adding that she thought it was possible some of his nervousness may have come from fear that he was "crazy." Jed agreed but added that he tended to be a nervous person, especially when he was at home. The worker could not be totally reassuring, since she still did not fully understand the meanings of his symptoms, but she did say very positively that usually when people learn about themselves and their feelings they get considerable relief. Jed seemed encouraged.

For many meetings to come, Jed would arrive and say he did not know what he "should" talk about. His thoughts would block until he could find a comfortable subject—often his job, his car, the weather—from which he could then ease into more difficult material. In one session, after about two months of treatment, Jed asked the worker to come out to his car to see a bureau he had built and brought to show her. She was genuinely impressed with his work and freely told him so. Jed evidently needed support and encouragement, not only to reduce his anxiety but also to be reassured that the worker thought of him as a competent, worthwhile man.

Positive—as well as negative—countertransference is important for a worker to recognize. In this case, the worker was aware of very warm feelings for Jed; she saw him as an appealing, sensitive person who sparked in her a "motherly" response, a wish to look after him. She made a conscious effort to keep the expression of some of her strongest feelings in check and still provide the sustaining climate he required. Furthermore, since one's subjective reactions to a client can often be helpful in diagnosis, the worker was alerted to the possibility that Jed's manner might elicit overly protective responses from other people in his life, including perhaps his mother, about whom he had said very little.

Jed had particular difficulty talking about his feelings toward his parents. Although he discussed his woman friend Laura, of whom he was very fond, he also shied away from any discussion of their intimate relationship. When Jed became flustered, even by gently placed questions, the worker would make remarks such as "Perhaps you'll feel more like discussing that at another time," or, "Maybe you can let me know when you feel comfortable enough to tell me something about that." Of these troublesome subjects, Jed was least inhibited about his anger at his father, for being unavailable to and critical of him as a child, for being a "whiner," for his excessive drinking, and for the fact that he had let Jed's mother "wear the pants." He felt that his father had never liked him. His resentment was conscious and strong. Nevertheless, once he could *ventilate* it, he said it felt really good; in his family, people rarely shared deep feelings about anything. He said he usually did not confide in anyone, even his woman friend. Only when he became very frightened by his "attack" had he told his sister about it.

Aided by the worker's consistently calm, accepting, supportive approach, Jed slowly but surely took more initiative in starting sessions and in getting into the issues he had been side-stepping. He still needed sustainment, but to a far lesser degree. Having ventilated his anger at his father, he seemed relieved enough to begin to talk about his mother, whom he described as domineering and a "nag," although he knew she loved him. She had always catered to him, more than she did to his sisters and father. As he revealed more, it turned out that even when he was a small child his mother complained to him about his father, and this always made him feel very uncomfortable; it still did. His mother often asked him personal questions, about what he was doing and where he was going. She seemed hurt when he went out in the evenings. In the last year, since he had been dating Laura, his mother plied him with inquiries about her, giving him the impression that she was eager to find something to criticize. Mostly, he evaded her questions, but they annoyed him and made him "nervous." His mother, he complained, went through his bureau drawers, ostensibly searching for laundry. He never said anything to her about it but made sure he didn't keep anything private there. Jed also said he felt sorry for her because she had had "such a hard life," especially with his father.

By the time Jed had revealed this much, after about three months of therapy, he reported that on the whole he was feeling more relaxed than he had "for years." He was no longer afraid of "going crazy." Periodically, however, he felt guilty or, as he put it, "disloyal." He felt justified complaining about his father; but talking about his mother, he said, made him very uncomfortable. He felt he was hurting her, even though he knew she could not know what he was saying. He had not even told her he was in therapy.

Although initially it was difficult to evaluate the seriousness of Jed's problems, by this point in treatment the worker had formulated a fairly well-rounded diagnostic assessment. She viewed him as a man with intelligence, competence, and talents who functioned well in many areas. He had the capacity for good interpersonal relationships. Although shy and not given to sharing intimacies with others, he had several friends of long standing with whom he hunted and camped. When he spoke of his friend Laura, he did so with tenderness and sensitivity. He related warmly and positively to the worker. He had a clear sense of his own values and ethical standards. On the whole, ego and superego functions were well developed.

Although in early meetings Jed appeared quite disturbed, in time it appeared that some of his conflicts were centered in the psychosexual area. The worker surmised that his perception of his mother's intrusiveness, and perhaps actual seductiveness, influenced Jed to feel guilty and conflicted about his relationship with her. He loved her but feared her impingement on his life. Furthermore, his father's lack of assertiveness and degraded status in the family had deprived Jed of a strong male model to admire and emulate. From the psychoanalytic point of view, the worker thought, one could speculate that Jed's unconscious "castration fears" (believed to derive from repressed incestuous wishes and fears of father's retaliation), as well as his conscious anger at his father, were expressed through anxiety attacks, both of which had occurred in his father's presence. From this perspective, one could hypothesize that unresolved oedipal issues were related to his subtle doubts about his masculinity, evidenced by his strong need for confirmation as a "male" (for example, the manner in which he sought praise from the worker and his employer for his cabinetmaking skills). However, even if Jed's intense uneasiness could be explained by this frame of reference, the material as such would probably not be brought into consciousness; nevertheless, some related matters might come into focus. There also appeared to be some unfulfilled needs associated with having been either ignored or criticized by his often moody father and "babied" by his unhappy, apparently controlling, mother. The DSM diagnosis of "panic disorder" seemed to describe Jed's presenting problem, but did little to illuminate his underlying distress. Behavioral techniques, designed to reduce Jed's anxiety, the worker felt sure would not bring Jed the kind of sustained relief he wanted; *reflection* about emotional reactions to and meanings of his family experiences would undoubtedly be required.

There was still another perspective from which the worker could have assessed Jed's situation, had the information been available at the time treatment occurred. He was one of many adult children of alcoholic parents, a group that was not studied intensively until relatively recently. Jed and the Cooper family as a whole were obviously deeply affected by many of the problems that frequently develop around alcoholism. Jed's descriptions of his family suggested rigidity, a characteristic of many families with alcoholic members, rather than flexibility. Certainly Jed's inhibitions prevented much spontaneity. His difficulty talking about himself or his family was consistent with the spoken or unspoken rule in many families with members who have problems with alcohol: "Don't talk; don't feel; don't trust."[5] Children are often taught to hide the truth about the family situation from others. Families with alcoholic members may isolate themselves; the family system is often "closed," resistant to the involvement of "outsiders." When children are taught not to need others, it is hard (often impossible) for them, even when they are older, to ask for help. It was apparent that Jed had to struggle to reveal himself to the worker. Only when he was terrified by his symptoms did he talk to his sister about his concerns and seek treatment.

Thus, children of alcoholics often grow up learning not to talk about issues that really matter; to deny powerful emotions of terror, rage, and grief; to pretend to themselves and to others that problems in the family do not exist. Obviously, many of Jed's feelings were repressed and suppressed. The children may take on false roles ("hero," "scapegoat," "lost child," "mascot," "placater") that disguise and distract attention from the alcoholism and the feelings that derive from the family situation. We see such roles, efforts to adapt to and survive in the dysfunctional alcoholic system, assumed by children at a very young age. Although Jed was not as "lost" or as much of a "loner" as many of those who fall into the "lost child" category, to some degree he did share qualities of that role, such as his low profile, his choice of rather isolated vocational and recreational activities, his anxieties about intimacy, his tendency to seek or expect little help from others, and his subtle doubts about his sexual identity. On the other hand, Jed was not the "forgotten child" that some in this role are; his special relationship with his mother, for better and worse, probably prevented him from being as isolated as some "lost children" are. As inhibited and embarrassed by his feelings as he was, he was not as emotionally stunted as many "lost" people are. Jed was capable of warmth and sensitivity to others, including Laura. Just as all diagnostic categories must be used cautiously, without stereotyping and sacrificing the assessment of the individual, it is equally important to avoid pinning roles on adult children of alcoholics without careful evaluation of the unique qualities of the person in question.

Confusion naturally derives from the unpredictability and inconsistency that are almost always part of the experience of growing up in a house in which there is alcoholism. Particularly at the beginning of treatment, Jed seemed to be unsure of what kind of reactions he could expect from the worker. Personal and generational boundaries are often violated in alcoholic families. Certainly, Jed felt his privacy was invaded by his mother; his father's criticisms were probably mostly projections rather than related to actual qualities of Jed's and, as such, were intrusions. Because authentic interest in and affirmation of children of alcoholics is often uneven at best, self-esteem can be seriously flawed. Jed's parents were too self-involved to praise and validate him in his own right consistently; confidence was therefore not as well developed as it should have been. Yet, as the worker was aware, Jed's strengths were many and, despite his

uneasiness, he seemed motivated to continue coming to treatment until he felt better.

In the early months of Jed's therapy, the worker concentrated on procedures that were sustaining or that led to description and ventilation. *Reflective procedures* were limited to those related to current, practical matters. (For example, at one point Jed wondered whether he should consider moving out of his parents' home since he was so uncomfortable there. He decided that he was financially unprepared to make the change since he wanted to save money for the time when he would marry. He concluded that instead he would spend as little time at home as possible, a decision that may have contributed to his greater relaxation at this juncture.)

The worker made few interpretations except those that were reassuring. The *corrective relationship*—one that was consistent, accepting, and neither seductive, intrusive, nor possessive—was in contrast to the one he perceived he had with his mother. Although individual situations differ, in this case it was probably helpful that the worker was a woman roughly in his mother's age group who treated him with understanding and as an adult. It was also fortunate that concurrent with therapy he was benefiting from what might be called a corrective relationship with his employer, who, apparently unlike Jed's father, truly liked Jed, treated him "like a man," and admired his talents.

Throughout this early period, the worker refrained from encouraging reflection about issues close to Jed's psychosexual conflict, even though she suspected many of these were conscious or preconscious. Her reason for this was that trial questions, about Laura and their personal relationship or his parents, that could have tapped greater awareness in these areas were generally evaded by Jed. She knew it would not help to press him to the point that he would become blocked or immobilized by anxiety;

nor did she want to risk the possibility that he would bolt from therapy.

Gradually, after Jed had been in treatment close to six months, he began talking more about the discomfort he felt when he was around his parents. He wanted to understand it, realizing that his anxiety attack was related in some way. He also discussed some of his concerns about his relationship with Laura (heretofore he had only spoken of his pleasant, tender feelings for her), now confiding that he thought he had a "sexual hangup." He blushed when he said this but did not block or evade. He explained further that he would often spend the day excitedly thinking about Laura but, when they got together for intercourse, as often as not he lost his erection. Laura was very understanding, and he knew she loved him anyway, but he felt deeply humiliated.

Once he felt safe enough to approach these subjects, the worker began to elicit more and more relevant material. He could reflect now on how his anxiety when he was with his father related to unexpressed anger, but Jed could see that this was only a small part of a larger picture. He had known he was angry, and talking about it had brought relief, but he searched for more. He became interested in early memories. He recalled a frequent scene at home when he was young: His father would come from work, still wearing his gun and holster and he, Jed, would run in terror to his bedroom. On his day off, Jed's father would sit in the living room, drinking continuously, and Jed would imagine that as his father became increasingly intoxicated, he might grab him and beat him. In reality, his father never assaulted him, but the fear remained. Jed recalled recurrent childhood nightmares related to his fear of his father. As he reviewed these early events, he realized that his mother had wanted him as an ally against his father, frequently complaining about

what a "bum" the latter was and telling Jed that she hoped he would not grow up to be a "drunk." Evidently, she turned to him to try to make up for her disappointing marriage. The more he talked, the more he resented her for berating his father, who "didn't have a chance" in the face of her attacks.

Spontaneously, Jed recognized that there was something "sexy" about his mother's intrusiveness and overprotection of him. He remembered being uncomfortable at age five or six when his mother seemed "too eager" to help him with his bath. He once asked whether his father could bathe him instead, a request that insulted his mother. Jed was torn between wanting to "wriggle out" from her grip and wanting to please her. From a very young age he guarded his private thoughts and fantasies, knowing that by being secretive he was disappointing her. On the other hand, he helped her with her chores and would run all the way home to show her his good report card. Some of his happiest moments were when she told him he was the "nicest boy in the world." Much of this material was conscious; in fact, Jed said that he sometimes felt his head "swimming" with thoughts about his early years. Some of the memories were preconscious (such as those about his baths) but came to the surface during treatment. An important aspect of this phase of therapy was that Jed was able to see his anger at his parents in another perspective; he knew he resented his father, but he had never dared to feel more than mild annoyance toward his mother.

If Jed's intense uneasiness in the presence of his father derived from "castration anxiety" or if there had been incestuous wishes, these unconscious matters were never directly tapped. He reflected at some length, however, on the connections between his mother's need to intrude and his anger at his father for not taking charge of the situation and protecting him from her. The more he thought about it, the surer he was that what he had always believed was not true: his father *did* like him. He now saw him as a "coward" in the face of a domineering wife. Jed even remembered occasions when his father had invited him for a day of hunting and his mother said it was too dangerous and did not allow it. Instead of confronting her, Jed's father dropped the matter. One turning point in treatment came when Jed realized with sadness that his father was not anyone to fear at all, but a "pathetic" man. Thus, although possible oedipal issues were not discussed as such, related matters were, with the result that Jed no longer irrationally feared his father as he had; his anger and guilt were also greatly relieved.

Toward the latter phase of therapy, his anger at his father had dissipated and he was left primarily with the sadness that the older man's drinking and passivity had deprived them both of years that could never be recaptured. After the surge of resentment he felt toward his mother and the sense of guilt that accompanied it for being "disloyal," Jed realized too that she was a lonely woman who probably tried to control others because she felt so helpless herself. By the time treatment terminated, Jed's greater comfort with himself also led him to feel genuine sympathy for his parents' unhappiness.

After Jed revealed his sexual problem with Laura, there was very little further discussion about this. Intuitively, Jed seemed to know that it was related to experiences with and feelings about his parents. Undoubtedly, having grown up in an alcoholic family system affected Jed's capacity for intimacy and his self-esteem and interfered with confidence in his masculinity, as discussed earlier. One can only speculate about other connections. For example, were his fears about sexual intercourse related to his fear of his father's anger? to sexual anxiety stimulated by his mother's seductiveness? to guilt about betraying or being disloyal to his mother? to fear of losing his sense of privacy? to the fact that a parental model for adult love and intimacy was lacking? Most likely, some combination of all these was involved. As he was freed to express and work through some of his feelings about his childhood and the ways these related to his present situation, his sexual relationship with Laura markedly improved. He rarely had difficulty now maintaining an erection, and he felt more deeply satisfied than ever with their sexual life. By the time the treatment (which lasted a little over a year) ended, Jed was planning to share an apartment with Laura, whom, he assumed, he would eventually marry. After the final session, Jed asked the worker to come outside to meet Laura, who was waiting for him. As the worker recorded it, "It was hard to tell whether Jed was more proud of himself or of Laura."

To summarize, the complexity of diagnosis, the importance of the treatment relationship, and the selective, carefully timed use of treatment procedures are all well illustrated by this case. As is often true of clients with acute anxiety and strong inhibitions, at first Jed appeared to be more disturbed than he was. As his many strengths, including his capacity to engage in a warm relationship with the worker, became apparent, so did the assessment and treatment plan. Even though Jed was basically sound psychologically, the worker recognized he sorely needed a relationship he could trust without fear of being criticized or overwhelmed by the needs of another. He needed a caring, reliable, and "tuned in" person with clear personal boundaries who could help him to uncover the way he felt and to express his feelings without fear or guilt. The worker affirmed his achievements, his many fine personal qualities, and—of utmost importance—his right to feel "like a man."

The mutual long-range goals, explicitly shared by Jed and the worker, were to enable him to feel less anxious about himself and about "going crazy." As therapy progressed, he also wanted to improve his sexual functioning. Intermediate goals, primarily determined by the worker, were to provide a climate that would foster positive transference, necessary for providing the "corrective" experience and for helping him feel safe enough to be reflective. His anxiety and timidity, combined with his Catholic school and family training (where emotional expression was strongly discouraged), required an extended period of *sustainment*. When the diagnostic picture becomes clear, it is sometimes difficult to resist premature interpretations. However, it was fortunate that this worker was sufficiently empathic with the intensity of Jed's anxiety to wait. Once ready, he made good use of *reflective procedures*, including *person-situation*, *pattern-dynamic*, and *developmental reflection*, and was in large measure freed of burdensome inner pressures and confusions. The successful treatment was undoubtedly expedited by the reassuring, "man-to-man" relationship he had with his employer, a relationship he could never have with his father.

Readers may wonder why family therapy or family group meetings were not considered in this case, since Jed's difficulties were so intertwined with his relationships, past and present, with his parents. The worker was experienced in family therapy but did not view it as the treatment of choice. As discussed in Chapter 15, family treatment is contraindicated when a client's defenses or anxiety would be so intensified by group meetings that he could not benefit from them. Jed's inhibitions and anxiety were so marked, even when he was not in the presence of his parents, that the worker felt certain his blocking and discomfort would have presented insurmountable problems in family sessions. Only close to

the end of therapy, when Jed had resolved the major issues that handicapped him, would he have been able to relax enough to express himself meaningfully to his parents. Furthermore, Jed was able to make progress in individual treatment. Only if counterpressures from his family had prevented him from moving forward or had resulted in setbacks would family therapy have been indicated. In addition, the fact that Jed was in treatment on his own and taking charge of resolving his difficulties supported his wish to feel adult and self-reliant. And, as a result of the work he did on himself, his relationships with his parents felt much less threatening, more relaxed, although never truly close or comforting.

Attention that the helping professions are giving to the damaging consequences of growing up in an alcoholic family system has been enormously helpful to psychosocial assessment and treatment. According to the worker who treated Jed, this knowledge would have been extremely valuable had it been available at the time he was originally seen, even though both Jed and the worker felt the therapy had been very successful. Among many other benefits, it would have been reassuring to Jed to realize that his problems were common to many other adult children of alcoholics and that he was not a "freak" or "crazy." Nevertheless, the framework used by the worker was adequate to free Jed from most of his crippling inhibitions and to help him to lead a life free of many of the unresolved issues that had been signaled by the eruption of his anxiety attacks.

Postscript on Jed Cooper

Eight years after termination, Jed contacted the same worker and was seen for five sessions. He had been experiencing some anxiety—"not attacks like I had before"—and felt uncomfortable and worried that he might have similar episodes again. Jed had married Laura; their relationship had worked out very well, he reported. They had a five-year-old daughter, with whom he was obviously delighted. He had taken over his employer's small business after the latter retired and moved away; he still enjoyed his work but missed his friend and mentor. Six months before Jed called the worker, his father died; he had been severely disabled by emphysema and other complications for over two years but only stopped drinking and smoking a few months before his death. Jed said he "felt nothing" at the funeral and burial and still was mostly detached, although sad that his father had been "such a waste." For the first time in his life, after his father's death, Jed began drinking frequently—to excess, he feared. Realizing that he might be vulnerable to the addiction that destroyed his father, he gave up all alcohol "cold turkey." He did not and would not go to AA. It is hard enough to talk to one person, he said. Emphatically, he told the worker that "group conversations" held no interest for him. Characteristically, he had taken care of it himself and was proud that he had. Knowing Jed as she did, the worker did not suggest that he join a group for adult children of alcoholics. Again, individualized assessment is essential; although such groups are helpful to very many, others simply will not or cannot benefit from them. Nevertheless, Jed was very interested and reassured when the worker shared some of the insights that have come to light about common experiences of those who have grown up in an alcoholic family system.

Jed said that his mother seemed depressed and "lost" since his father's death. Although they had gotten along quite well, even if superficially, over the recent years, now he began to feel pressured by her again in a way he hadn't since terminating treatment the first time. Jed spent most of his therapy this time expressing feelings about both of his parents; he told the worker he re-

membered how helpful this had been before. After the second session, he was greatly relieved. He was able to be more compassionate toward his mother without feeling he should take care of her. He stayed for the three additional sessions for "insurance." At the suggestion of the worker, Laura attended the final session. This turned out to be particularly helpful because she felt that Jed had withdrawn from her in recent months. In the session, he shared with her the material and feelings about his parents he had discussed in treatment. With the worker's help, Jed could recognize that his anxieties, in part precipitated by the recent changes in his family of origin, were exacerbated because he had simultaneously retreated from his wife, from whom he could have received understanding and comfort (in which case he might never have had to return to see the worker!). Just as when he was a child, under stress, he "got lost." Once aware of how his old habits had reemerged, Jed vowed he would try not to let this happen again. The point was not lost on Laura either; by nature, she was a person who liked to reach out, especially when reassured that she was wanted, and Jed was able to respond. Both realized that they had to make a point of spending more "private time" together.

Interestingly, Jed's sister June, the sister who was seven years older than Jed and had originally urged him to seek help, came to see the worker shortly after Jed terminated for the second time. She had learned from her brother how helpful therapy had been for him. In contrast to Jed, she was overweight ("Food is my addiction," she announced), gregarious, and laughed and cried easily. When she came for treatment, she had just separated, painfully, from her alcoholic and verbally abusive husband. A social worker, working with disturbed children, June had many of the qualities of the "placater." She was the mediator and caretaker in her family; she recalled trying to break up fights between her parents when her father was drunk. She had tried to comfort her mother and felt responsible for her younger brother and sisters. She had repeatedly pleaded with her father to stop drinking. In large part, she had put aside her own needs, focusing mostly on trying to "fix" the problems and feelings of others. As treatment progressed, she began to realize how her marital relationship replicated many of her childhood experiences. June, an outgoing and friendly woman, became a member of an adult children of alcoholics group and found it extremely helpful. She was also in treatment working hard at trying to understand her own family experiences and to determine what *she* needed, wanted, and felt rather than being so preoccupied with rescuing and placating others. The rules, roles, and behaviors of families with alcoholic members tend to be transmitted down through the generations, but at least two of the Cooper children interrupted the process. Without doubt, they and their children will live far healthier and more autonomous and fulfilled lives as a result of having done so.

Successful treatment requires a worker with the personality, intuition, talent, and concern to do the work; it calls for enough personal security and flexibility to accept the pains and defeats as well as the pleasures and achievements of the clients we see. But as important as these worker characteristics are, they are not enough. A broad body of knowledge of people, their situations, and how these interact is required to individualize the particular client who asks for help. Responsible treatment rests on a theoretical framework, tested through practice and research, combined with a knowledge of the nature and effects of clinical methods and procedures.

The treatments described in this chapter clearly resulted in gratifying progress and changes for the clients, all of whom were able to find new ways of experiencing themselves, their relationships, and their situations. Except for Mrs. Barry, rigid time limits would not have been helpful to this particular group of clients; 10 or 15 sessions would not have sufficed. There are many others who require and deserve opportunities to have longer-term treatment available to them on the basis of need. We are hopeful that increased social action from clinicians will result in humane systemic changes in the current, often depriving, health care system.

The cases presented here are certainly not offered as "proof" either of theories or results but as demonstrations of the relationships among psychosocial study, assessment, and treatment presented in previous chapters. They are among the many cases on which the theories developed in this book are based.

NOTES

1. Laird (1998), p. 228.
2. See Chapter 11, note 25 for references on psychoses and schizophrenia.
3. See Chapter 5, note 19 for readings on loss and mourning.
4. On anticipatory preparation, see discussion in Chapter 10, pages 268–69; see Germain and Gitterman (1996) and Kadushin and Kadushin (1997).
5. Claudia Black (1982). In the 1980s rich material became available to professionals and to the general public on adult children of alcoholics, including the following references that continue to be helpful. One cannot generalize; each case must be individualized. See Robert Ackerman (1983), Kritsberg (1985), Robinson (1989), and Tainey (1998). See also the well-known book by Wegscheider (1981) on the "alcoholic family." See Chapter 10, note 12 for references relevant to the treatment of alcoholism.

CHAPTER 21

STUDYING AND WORKING WITH THE HOLLIS TYPOLOGY

Now that the reader has become familiar with the typology of treatment procedures and worker–client communications discussed and demonstrated throughout this text, our final chapter will describe the work that led up to the development of the Hollis classification and some of the studies of the casework process that were based upon it. As we indicated in Chapter 1, the study of outcome (change) combined with the study of the dynamics of worker–client communications (process) can give us information not only about *whether* clients are making progress but *what* actually is occurring between the worker and client during treatment. It should be noted that just as the single-subject design can be used by the individual clinician to track client progress, so, as will be discussed shortly, can the Hollis method of studying worker procedures and client communications provide a tool for the practitioner to use informally.

The groundbreaking and important clinical research initiated by Hollis sought to throw light on the actual nature of the psychosocial form of treatment as practiced by clinical social workers. What do we really do? What processes do we use? It was clear to her that not until this was definitively clarified could clinicians and researchers begin to study with precision such important questions as: What procedures are most useful in helping in one kind of problem or another? With one type of personality or another? Does a given procedure affect the client in the way we expect it to? What part does the client take in this process? We say this is a mutual undertaking. To what extent is it, and under what circumstances? Hollis knew that to answer such questions convincingly, detailed analyses of what actually occurs in interviews would be required and research tools with which to do this would be needed.

In an effort to develop such a tool and to answer the initial question of what procedures the psychosocial caseworker uses, the research that is the subject of this chapter was undertaken.[1] The studies were made possible by a five-year grant from the National Institute of Mental Health (NIMH). The first objective was to develop a typology or classification of casework processes that would describe all the procedures the worker uses in communicating with clients.

In Chapter 4 we described the early case studies, beginning in 1958, from which Hollis arrived at a classification that could be tested and experimented with in a larger, more rigorous study. In these studies, Hollis had set up the best classification she could devise on the basis of theory then current and tried to use it to sort out the interview content in a preliminary series of cases. When it was found that certain activities of the worker did not fit this classification, corrections were made in the typology to achieve a better "fit." This occurred again and again until the classification began to accommodate the data. Meanwhile, a logical organization began to emerge that made it possible to set up clear, mutually exclusive categories.

Concurrently with these studies, the classification was used in teaching and thus was exposed to the thinking and criticism of students in both master's and doctoral programs. Students were helpful in using the classification at its various stages in both master's theses and doctoral dissertations. Several of the most important features of the typology emerged from class discussion and student suggestions. One of these was the realization that the treatment process cannot be fully represented by classifying worker communications alone, since to varying degrees the client is self-propelling: that is, treats himself or herself. *To catch the full dynamics of what is going on, one must include what the client is doing as well as the* *worker's activity.* Interesting enough, we were unable to find at that time any other classification for content analysis in any of the therapeutic fields that had attempted this type of study of client activity. Most of the treatment categories developed for workers in our study could refer to client communications as well as to those of the worker. By including client communications in any study, one is recognizing that to a large degree treatment is something the client either does or fails to do for himself or herself. In the reflective categories, these codings also indicate to what extent the worker's intent of stimulating the client to reflection is followed by actual reflection by the client. A second major idea first suggested in class discussion was that work in the environment on the client's behalf basically involves many of the same forms of communication as those used in direct work with the client.

TESTING THE TYPOLOGY'S USABILITY

The next step taken by Hollis in the continuing study was to use the classification on new material to see to what degree independent coders could agree in classifying interview content. This was first undertaken by two groups of Smith College and New York School students in the studies referred to in Chapter 4. These studies located ambiguities in the typology and led to changes in several items. The NIMH grant was obtained after this, and larger studies were undertaken with the help of doctoral students. Fortunately a number of students with good backgrounds in casework practice were studying for their doctorates when this project was in its early stages and it was possible to enlist their interest. Francis Turner and Yetta Appel were the principal coders in the early stages and contributed a great deal to the clarification and application of the typology.

Appel searched the literature and organized it into comparative charts. Turner also used the typology in his dissertation and later in other studies. Shirley Ehrenkranz, in her dissertation, was the first to experiment with the typology in joint interviews. Others who worked with Hollis from time to time included Trudy Bradley, Shirley Hellenbrand, Edward Mullen, Ben Avis Orcutt, William Reid, and Fil Verdiani. Many of these associates are now well known in education, research, and practice.

A total of 123 interviews from 63 cases were used in these subsequent studies. The cases were carried by workers in six family service agencies in Cleveland, Cincinnati, Detroit, New York, and Philadelphia. The following criteria were set up:

1. The case be one in which at the end of the first interview the problem to be worked on was marital adjustment.
2. The case be new to the agency.
3. The case be the first of the above type assigned to the worker in the natural course of work, either after a given date or after completion of five interviews in a case previously assigned for study.
4. Participants be master's degree caseworkers.
5. The recording meet certain criteria discussed by the project director with the workers who volunteered to participate. Workers were asked to do very detailed "process recording," particularly indicating the interplay between client and worker in a way that would make clear which one initiated topics. Interviews were to be recorded not later than the second day after the interview was held. A minimum length was set at three single-spaced pages of typing.

Obviously, this was not verbatim reproduction but a detailed description of what transpired with considerable paraphrasing.

Although studies using both tape recording and process recording indicate that some skewing of material occurs in process recording, on the whole there is great similarity in the findings derived from these two kinds of recording. Excerpts from three of the interviews reproduced in Figures 1, 2, and 3 (pages 594, 596, and 598) illustrate the kind of detail secured. See page 603 for comments on some further differences found between tapes and process recording.*

This material was initially used to develop operational definitions for each category of the classifications and to clear up ambiguities in the typology. Where necessary, the definitions were modified and new categories were developed. Procedures were also worked out for coding in a way that would make it possible to handle the material quantitatively. This is not necessary for ordinary on-the-job use of the classification, but it is essential if it is to be used in research comparing groups of cases. For the purposes of the studies, it was decided to do line-by-line content analysis determining the proper coding by using the clause having its subject and predicate on the coded line.

The next step was a reliability study. A report of this is in the Appendix. The typology had by then appeared to accommodate over 95 percent of all casework communications between client and worker and could be used with reasonable reliability to make these communications accessible to quantitative research. The reliability study was followed first by a profile of the first five

*Four students, Marianne Buchenhorner, Robert Howell, Minna Koenigsberg, and Helen Sloss, made an exploratory study of this question in their master's thesis, "The Use of Content Analysis to Compare Three Types of Casework Recording" (Columbia University School of Social Work, 1966). The principal difference found was a smaller proportion of sustaining communication on the tapes than in the process recordings.

FIGURE 1
Record No. 18: Excerpt from a First Interview

15 but her husband would want to go home every other weekend. He would
16 leave her with his mother and then he would go out for the entire
17 weekend. Sometimes she would visit her mother on Sunday. If
18 they went there he would behave but if he stayed with his parents,
19 he didn't. With some anger in her voice she told me they
20 had bought furniture three times since they are here. Each time
21 he would want to go back home to live and actually they moved
22 back three times. However, when they went down there they wouldn't
23 have anything. In fact, she said there were times when they
24 didn't have enough to eat. I wondered how he always managed to
25 get jobs. She said one time he worked in a filling station;
26 another time he helped a man build a garage. I wondered what
27 he does up here and she said he works for the D. plant, and they
28 have taken him back each time that he returned. I said he must
29 be a good worker if they did this and she said he is and that is
30 the reason he has always gotten his job back. She said they
31 could have bought a home in the time they have been here if he
32 would only have stayed and acted like people should act. Now
33 he wants another baby. He told her when he came back last weekend
34 if she had another baby that would be all he wants. Their
35 youngest child is seven.
36   I asked how Mr. Z. was with the children. She said he is real
37 good with them. Makes over them and does like any normal father.
38 She feels the marital problem is hard on the children. The one
39 girl has dropped in her grades in school and while she isn't
40 certain it is because of the trouble at home, Mrs. Z. feels
41 there must be some connection. The older girl can cry but the

Source: Florence Hollis, *A Typology of Casework Treatment,* © 1967, 1968 by Family Service Association of America. Reprinted by permission of the publisher.

interviews, then by a study of continuers and discontinuers, and finally by studies of cases in which joint interviewing of married couples was the treatment mode.

The Coding

Three examples taken from interviews coded in the study show how case material was analyzed with this tool. See Figures 1, 2, and 3 and their accompanying codings in Charts 1, 2, and 3. The capital letters in the chart correspond to the major divisions of the classification discussed on pages 122 to 124 in Chapter 4. The numerals correspond to the subdivision of current person–situation reflective comments discussed on page 123. In these examples, the units coded were clauses. Each line was coded according to the clause having its subject and predicate on that line. When there were two such clauses, two codings were given. When there

CHART 1

	A	B	C	D	E	F	1	2	3	4	5	6	U	
15			X											15
16			X											16
17			X											17
18			X											18
19			X											19
20			X											20
21			X											21
22			X											22
23			X											23
24				O			O							24
25			X											25
26			X											26
27			OX											27
28			X											28
29				O			O							29
30				X			X							30
31			X											31
32			X											32
33			X											33
34			X											34
35			X											35
36			O											36
37			X											37
38			X											38
39			X											39
40			X											40
41			X											41

was no such communication, the line was placed in the "U" column.

The symbols used in the chart are as follows:

X = Client communication

O = Worker communication

A = Sustainment

B = Direct influence

C = Exploration-description-ventilation

D = Person–situation reflection

E = Pattern-dynamic reflection

F = Developmental reflection

U = Unclassified

Subdivisions of D are as follows:

1. Concerning others or any aspect of the outside world or of the client's physical health.
2. Concerning the effect or outcome of the client's own behavior.
3. Concerning the nature of the client's own behavior.

FIGURE 2

Record No. 27: Excerpt from a Third Interview

13   man should. I asked if she thought it was possible to force him

14   to marry her if he really did not want to, that many men do not

15   and of course many women do not care to marry either regardless

16   of pregnancy, by her own statements earlier his relatives tried

17   to influence him against marrying her, but he did anyway, and

18   from my impression of Mr. R. from the one interview, he did not

19   indicate any regrets about marrying her and does seem to care about

20   her. She answered that it is true, his uncles tried to persuade

21   him against marriage, but he could not have gotten away with it

22   anyway, because she was the "apple of my daddy's eye" and

23   her daddy made Mr. R. marry her, and Mr. R. knew her daddy would

24   not take any foolishness from him. Breaking down completely she

25   continued that she loved her daddy so much, and he her, and yet

26   she disgraced him and her mother, she disgraced her whole family,

27   when they had so much confidence in her and such high hopes for

28   her. They were shocked when she got pregnant and it was weeks

29   before they even spoke to her, and they forgave her but they have

30   not forgotten. I said it was rather cruel of them to stop speaking

31   to her for getting pregnant, but more importantly, since she

32   feels there is something to forgive she has not forgiven herself,

33   when everyone else has, and I thought perhaps her feeling against

34   herself for getting pregnant before marriage is causing her much

35   too much grief and other emotional problems, which is causing

36   herself and her whole family trouble. She continued crying, saying

37   "I know it is, I know it is, but I can't help it," to which I said

38   that we would continue to talk more about it and perhaps after

39   she will be able to feel differently about it. Eventually she

40   calmed down and meekly asked, "Do you really think I will?" to

41   which I said I thought she would if she really wanted to.

Source: Florence Hollis, *A Typology of Casework Treatment,* © 1967, 1968 by Family Service Association of America. Reprinted by permission of the publisher.

4. Concerning the provocation or current causation of his or her behavior.

5. Concerning evaluative aspects of his or her behavior.

6. Concerning treatment and the client–worker relationship.

The coded chart makes it easy to follow the flow of an interview. Did a worker's re-flective comment induce reflection for the client or did the client respond briefly and return to explanations and ventilation? To what extent does the client initiate reflective comments without needing stimulation by the worker? The charts give the answers. Note how clearly the contrast among the three interview samples shows up. Both client and worker in the first case stick

CHART 2

	A	B	C	D	E	F	1	2	3	4	5	6	U	
13				O			O							13
14				O			O							14
15				O			O							15
16				O			O							16
17				O			O							17
18				O			O							18
19				O			O							19
20				X			X							20
21				X			X							21
22				X			X							22
23				X			X							23
24				X			X							24
25				X			X		X					25
26				X							X			26
27				X							X			27
28			X											28
29			X											29
30	O													30
31	O													31
32				O							O			32
33				O							O			33
34					O									34
35					O									35
36				O				O						36
37				X	X				X					37
38		O												38
39	O													39
40				X					X					40
41	O													41

almost entirely to exploration-description-ventilation. In the second sample, communications are almost entirely in person–situation reflection, with the worker taking an active part in stimulating this and also offering sustainment. In the third interview, the worker's comment initiates the switch from the client's exploration-description-ventilation to reflection, but thereafter the worker is considerably less active than in the second excerpt.

Informal Use of Typology

When using the typology informally for study of one's own work or analysis of a single case, one can simply indicate the categories in pencil by code letter in the margins

FIGURE 3
Record No. 34: Excerpt from a Second Interview

1 I learned at this point that for five years during the marriage,
2 at the time when Mrs. Y. became involved with the other man, she had
3 worked as a doctor's assistant. Since then, she has on occasion done
4 fill in work for a doctor who has provided all kinds of free medical
5 services. This doctor recently called saying that one of his employees
6 was leaving, and asking if Mrs. Y. would work on Saturdays temporarily.
7 Her husband opposes this on the grounds that she should stay home
8 with the children. Mrs. Y. could not see this—he is at home on
9 Saturdays, can watch the children. Besides, they have their own
10 activities. She didn't see that it would hurt anyone for her to work
11 one day a week. I said perhaps her husband wants her to stay home
12 with him. She became a little thoughtful, saying that this might be
13 true, but when they are home together on Saturdays, he is out in the
14 barn working, she is running errands, etc., it is not that they are
15 sitting there kissing and holding hands.
16   At this, Mrs. Y. began to tell me that she is a very affectionate
17 person. But she can't show affection overtly to her children. This
18 sometimes bothers her—though she likes to cuddle "the baby in the
19 family." She guessed she felt this way about her oldest daughter
20 when she was born, but when the 2nd came along 2 years later she was
21 so overwhelmed with responsibility that she stopped being so affec-
22 tionate. She commented that neither of her parents had been people
23 who were affectionate with children. Maybe this explains the need she
24 has for affection. She commented here that her husband is not so af-
25 fectionate as she wished he was. When I asked about this, she said in
26 some ways they are very affectionate with each other, they always kiss
27 hello and goodby, she waves to him from the door, etc. Their friends
28 have commented on this. However, something is missing. I asked her
29 to think about what this was. She guessed she felt her husband's af-
30 fection was routine. She goes to him, hugs him, just on impulse,
31 but he never does this with her. I said this seemed to puzzle her,
32 and she believed it did. Went on to say that her husband doesn't like
33 her relationship with the children, her not being affectionate with
34 them. I said earlier she seemed to be connecting this with the fact
35 that her parents had not been affectionate with her. It might be
36 that because she hadn't received affection, it was hard to give it.
37 She couldn't understand this, though, because she can give it to her
38 husband. Maybe this seemed so important to him because his mother
39 was very affectionate with him. Even now, she kisses him when she
40 sees him. He has always been her favorite child. Perhaps he expects
41 that she be the same way with her children. She commented, as she

Source: Florence Hollis, *A Typology of Casework Treatment,* © 1967, 1968 by Family Service Association of America. Reprinted by permission of the publisher.

CHART 3

	A	B	C	D	E	F	1	2	3	4	5	6	U	
1													X	1
2			X											2
3			X											3
4			X											4
5			X											5
6			X											6
7			X											7
8			X											8
9			X											9
10			X											10
11				O			O							11
12				X			X							12
13				X			X							13
14				X			X							14
15													X	15
16				X					X					16
17				X					X					17
18				X					X					18
19				X					X					19
20				X						X				20
21				X						X				21
22						X								22
23						X								23
24				X					X					24
25				O					O					25
26				X					X					26
27				X					X					27
28				X					X					28
29				OX					OX					29
30				X					X					30
31				XO			XO							31
32		X		X			X							32
33			X											33
34						O								34
35						O								35
36						O								36
37						X								37
38				X			X							38
39				X			X							39
40				X			X							40
41				X			X							41
Total:														
X	0	0	11	21	0	3	9	0	10	2	0	0	2	X
O	0	0	0	4	0	3	2	0	2	0	0	0	0	O
T	0	0	11	25	0	6	11	0	12	2	0	0	2	T
	A	B	C	D	E	F	1	2	3	4	5	6	U	

of the record. This can give a quick picture of the type of intervention the worker is using and the nature of the client's participation in the treatment process. One can quickly spot, for instance, whether client or worker is entirely involved in description and ventilation or engaged in reflection. Having made this objective observation, the worker is then prompted to consider its significance: Has one perhaps not been sufficiently active in stimulating the client to reflection? On the other hand, perhaps at that particular stage it is necessary and important for a great deal of ventilation to occur.

It is possible to observe whether sustaining comments seem to have enabled a client to talk more freely or think more actively, or whether they have instead merely induced complacency or passivity. Or whether there has been an absence of sustainment where it could have been helpful. Similarly, many different questions concerning the nature of the worker's activities and the client's responses can be observed.

Analysis of a series of interviews of one's own with a number of clients enables a worker to spot personal idiosyncrasies. Do I tend toward activity or toward passivity? Am I too reassuring? How directive am I? In reflective communications, do I tend to stimulate the client to think or tend to give explanations or interpretations? To what extent are my procedures varied in accordance with the needs of different clients?

Employed in this way, the typology can be a most useful tool for analyzing general tendencies in one's own work and also in examining individual cases to determine exactly what both client and worker are doing. If one's main interest lies in self-study or in comparison of the treatment style of one worker with another, or even of one group of workers with another, it may be sufficient to analyze worker comments alone. This is far less time-consuming since,

the study found, in psychosocial work the client usually talks at least three times as much as the worker.

Study of Distribution of Procedures

The first study in which the classification was used in hypothesis testing attempted to answer such questions as "What are caseworkers really doing? What procedures do we use? Where do we put our emphasis?" The researcher's thinking at that time, 1960, was expressed in a series of hypotheses. It was predicted that communications (of both client and worker) would appear in the following order of frequency: first, exploration-description-ventilation; second, person–situation reflection; third, sustainment; fourth, developmental reflection; fifth and sixth, either pattern-dynamic reflection or direct influence. It was also predicted, seventh, that person–situation reflection would reach a maximum in the third interview and, eighth, remain steady from then on and that, ninth, pattern-dynamic reflection would be rare in the first and second interviews but more frequent in the third, fourth, and fifth. It was predicted, 10th, that early life reflection would be similar to pattern-dynamic reflection, though somewhat more frequent, and 11th, that direct influence would be rare throughout.

For this study, the first 5 interviews of 15 individual interview cases of marriage counseling were used. Seventy-five interviews were coded by two independent judges. When there was disagreement between judges, the material was reviewed by a third judge, the principal researcher, who entered a final rating in each instance. These codings then became the basis for establishing a "profile" of the distribution of communications.

Table 1 and Chart 4 show the results of this analysis. Table 1 gives the average per-

TABLE 1
Major Category Communications Expressed as Percentages of Total Communications (15 Cases)

Category	Client communications Interview					Worker communications Interview				
	1	2	3	4	5	1	2	3	4	5
A*	—	—	—	—	—	02.0	01.7	01.5	01.6	01.6
B*	—	—	—	—	—	00.6	00.8	00.7	01.3	00.7
C	78.3	62.4	60.8	60.8	56.4	08.4	07.0	06.9	06.0	06.7
D	05.7	14.4	17.3	17.1	18.7	04.8	10.8	11.7	12.1	14.6
E	—	00.4	00.3	00.2	00.1	—	00.2	00.5	00.5	00.6
F	00.1	01.8	00.2	00.2	00.2	00.1	00.5	00.1	00.2	00.3
Total	84.1	79.0	78.6	78.3	75.4	15.9	21.0	21.4	21.7	24.5

*Not applicable to client communications.
Source: Florence Hollis, *A Typology of Casework Treatment,* © 1967, 1968 by Family Service Association of America. Reprinted by permission of the publisher.

centage of all communications (i.e., client plus worker) in which each major type of procedure occurred in each of the five successive interviews. Chart 4 pictures this in graphic form for A, B, C, and D (E and F communications were so few they could not be charted).

One is at once struck by the extent to which client talk outweighs worker talk—three to five times as much—although the amount that the worker contributes increases as the interviews progress. This shift can be attributed to two major factors. First, the client's need for unburdening and the worker's need to learn as much as possible about the situation combine to put the emphasis on ventilation-description-exploration in the first interview. Usually, a brief inquiry from the worker touches off a fairly lengthy response from the client. Second, the worker's increased understanding of the situation, the client's desire for more definitive responses, and often the client's growing readiness for understanding lead to greater activity by the worker in subsequent interviews. Note that the proportion of both client and worker communications falling in reflective categories triples be-

tween the first and fifth interviews. Equally apparent is the important part played continuously by the client's descriptive communications and ventilation. A small part of this material relates to the client's early life, but predominantly it is related to current and recent events. Current person-situation reflection is clearly the second most important treatment process. Sustainment, although quantitatively small, is remarkably steady throughout the five interviews. Direct influence, pattern-dynamic reflection, and developmental reflection are all rare, with pattern-dynamic reflection, contrary to prediction, slightly more frequent than developmental reflection except in the second interview, where exploration of the past occasionally seems to lead to reflection about it. The fact that direct influence, contrary to prediction, is somewhat more frequent than developmental or pattern-dynamic reflection is accounted for by the number of comments made by the worker concerning how to use the interviews. That is, they pertain to the treatment process itself rather than to advice about the client's decisions or actions in outside life. Further analysis indicated that an average of only

CHART 4

Client and Worker Communications by Major Category:

Percentage of Total Interviews (15 cases)

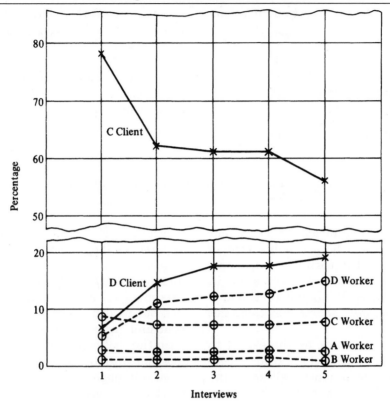

0.3 percent of the total content was of the latter type over the five interviews. Both client and worker person–situation reflection take their main jump in the second interview and increase slowly thereafter. The amount of developmental and pattern-dynamic reflection is so small that changes from one interview to another cannot be considered sufficient to indicate trends. Of the original hypotheses, the first, second, and third were fully supported by the study; the seventh and ninth were partially supported. Direct influence was somewhat more frequent than predicted; developmen-

tal reflection and pattern-dynamic reflection were both of low frequency, as predicted. Contrary to expectation, however, pattern-dynamic reflection was slightly more frequent than developmental.

What about variations between individual cases within these groups? Do they tend to be very much alike, or is there considerable variation in the work done with different families and individuals even when they seek help for the same problem? Uniformity is not the rule. On the contrary, there is great variation. Analysis revealed that over the first five interviews, total person–situation reflection varied from an average of 9 percent per interview in one case to 48 percent per interview in another. Over the third, fourth, and fifth interviews, one-third of the cases had less than 20 percent of their content in this category, one-third had between 20 and 39 percent, and one-third had 40 percent or over. Pattern-dynamic reflection varied from one case in which it did not appear in any interview to four cases in which it was touched on in three of the five interviews, although it never reached more than 4.2 percent of any one interview. Developmental reflection was absent in almost half the cases. Its maximum in a single interview was 9.4 percent.

This diversity is as we should expect it to be, for many factors influence the development of treatment: the nature of the problems the client is dealing with, the qualities and abilities of the client, the worker's preferences and skills, the time available, and other variables.

COMPARISON OF DATA FROM SEVERAL STUDIES

It is of value to compare these findings with those of three other researchers who have conducted similar studies. Mullen,[2] who used the Hollis instrument in a study of 87 taped interviews of marital and parent–child problems, included in his report a table combining four profiles: his own findings, the Hollis findings, the findings of a study of 121 taped interviews of marital and parent–child problems by Reid, and the findings of one by Pinkus consisting of 111 taped interviews from psychiatric clinics and family agencies. The last two studies used the Reid-Shyne reformulation of the Community Service Society classification[3] (see Table 2). Mullen was thoroughly familiar with both classifications and was able to

work out approximate equivalents between the two typologies.

In Table 2 worker communications only are used, and the percentages represent proportions of total worker communications rather than, as in the previous tables, percentages of the total of worker plus client communications. (For instance, total directive communications, which in the Hollis study constituted approximately 0.8 percent of all worker plus client communications, are 3.6 percent of worker communications.) Note that in all four studies more than 80 percent of the worker's part in the interview is devoted to exploration-description-ventilation and person–situation reflection. Pattern-dynamic reflection (which Mullen terms *personality reflection*) is 5 percent or less, developmental (which Mullen terms *early life reflection*) does not exceed 2 percent, direct influence is never more than 5.2 percent, and sustainment does not exceed 8.1 percent. As noted above, direct influence in the sense of advice or suggestions about matters outside the treatment situation itself is very small.

It is probable that more sustainment actually occurs in interviews than these studies reveal. Sustaining communications are very often of a nonverbal or paraverbal nature. Tape recordings do not reveal nonverbal communications, and the coding unit used did not provide for paraverbal phenomena from the tapes. Use of the typology on interviews recorded on videotape would probably reveal a far larger component of sustainment than has been noted in the studies so far reported. In the process recording, such communications were coded if they were described in the recording. This may account for the higher figure in the Hollis study. It is doubtful, however, that more than a very small proportion of the nonverbal and paraverbal sustaining communications were actually recorded even in the process material.

TABLE 2
A Comparison of Four Process Studies

Treatment procedure[a]	Proportion of worker communication			
	Mullen[b]	Hollis[c]	Reid-CSS[d]	Pinkus[e]
Sustainment (A)	.027	.081	.043	.050
Direct influence (B)	.052	.036	.040	.015
Exploration-description-ventilation (C)	.368	.398	.463	.508
Person–situation reflection (D)	.459	.457	.354	.313
Personality reflection (E)	.005	.013	.014	.050
Early life reflection (F)	.014	.015	.020	.016
Other[f]	.073	—	.066	.048
Total	.998	1.000	1.000	1.000

[a]Two classifications were used in these four studies, the Hollis and the Reid-CSS typologies. The figures are, therefore, approximations.
[b]Marital and parent–child problems. Hollis system. Continued-service client interviews 1 through 14, N = 87 taped interviews, 35 clients, 6 workers. See Edward J. Mullen, "Casework Treatment Procedures as a Function of Client Diagnostic Variables. A Study of Their Relationship in the Casework Interview" (doctoral dissertation, Columbia University School of Social Work, 1968), p. 119.
[c]Marital problems. Hollis system. Client interviews one through five. N = 75 process (written) interviews, 15 clients, 11 workers. See Florence Hollis, "A Profile of Early Interviews in Marital Counseling," *Social Casework*, 49 (January 1968), 39. (The figures are the means of the five groups of interviews reported by Hollis.)
[d]Marital and parent–child problems. Reid-CSS system. Short-term and continued-service client interviews one through five. N = 121 taped interviews, 30 cases, 7 workers. See William J. Reid, "Characteristics of Casework Intervention," *Welfare in Review*, 5 (October 1967), pp. 13–14.
[e]Psychiatric and family problems. Reid-CSS system. Primarily beyond client interview 15. N = 111 taped interviews, 59 workers. See Helen Pinkus, "Casework Techniques Related to Selected Characteristics of Clients and Workers" (doctoral dissertation, Columbia University School of Social Work, 1968), p. 176.
[f]Technical and inaudible.
Source: Edward J. Mullen, "Casework Communication," *Social Casework*, 49 (November 1968), p. 551. Copyright © 1967, 1968 by Family Service Association of America. Reprinted by permission of the publisher.

Note that in the relative proportion of C and D material, Mullen and Hollis find more D while Reid and Pinkus both find more C material. It is very likely that this is due to differences in the coding units used in the two systems. The units used by Reid and Pinkus did not give weighting to the length of a communication, whereas the Hollis system did. Since C-type comments by the worker tend to be shorter than D-type comments, which often include explanations and interpretations, this technical difference might explain the lighter weighting given C and the heavier weighting given D by the Hollis system.

These, then, are the central tendencies, the picture one gets by averaging the work done over many cases. Exploration-description-ventilation and person–situation reflection are clearly the central procedures, with the other four in a peripheral role.

Two important features of these studies must be kept in mind:

1. The first three studies used by Mullen in Table 2 consisted of cases in which *only* interpersonal adjustment problems were the focus of attention. The fourth study included was heavily weighted with such problems. In work with severely disorganized families, for instance, we should probably find more use of directive techniques and perhaps also more sustainment. Even so, the core treatment procedures would probably still be exploration-description-ventilation and person–situation reflection. Other types

of problems might produce somewhat different profiles. Further studies are needed to test these assumptions.

2. None of these studies included an analysis of environmental treatment. Undoubtedly, some direct work with factors in the environment was going on in many of these cases, even though the type of dysfunction involved called mainly for direct work with the individual. In other types of cases, in which the problem lies more in the social system than in interpersonal relationships, environmental work might assume major proportions.

A further word about pattern-dynamic and developmental reflection. The extremely small number of communications in these categories might lead one to think that forms of treatment leading to understanding in these areas are of little importance. This is not true. It used to be supposed that there were only a few cases in which this type of understanding was sought, and that in those cases a considerable portion of time was spent in talking directly about the dynamics of behavior and its development. It is now apparent that bits of such reflection are, not infrequently, embedded in a much larger matrix of understanding of current life events and responses, and that moments of such insight are followed by further person–situation content, which benefits from the insight gained. Such moments of insight are found in a wide range of cases. In a few cases, pattern-dynamic and developmental reflection become an extensive part of treatment.

Self-understanding is, of course, much broader than pattern-dynamic and developmental understanding. Readers will recall that the last four divisions of current person–situation understanding look at inward aspects of functioning. The second division looks both inwardly to what a person has done and outwardly to its effects or potential effects on others. So it can be said to be half inwardly directed and half outwardly. The first subdivision of person–situation reflection looks outward. By adding these communications to the outward-looking half of the second subdivision of person–situation reflection, one can arrive at an index of extrareflection. In contrast, by adding the inward facing D communications to E and F communications, one can secure an index of intrareflection. Examination of interviews 3, 4, and 5 of the profile study reveals that reflective comments are about evenly divided between intra- and extrareflection despite the very small amount of pattern-dynamic or developmental reflection.

A PROFILE OF THE CASEWORK PROCESS

Research inevitably deals in such abstractions that one tends to lose sight of the meaning and significance of the findings. What do these studies tell us about the nature of worker–client communications in psychosocial casework involving individual work with clients? Are they harmonious with the position set forth in earlier chapters?

The picture we get in these studies of clients having principally interpersonal relationship problems is of a reality-based treatment in which the individual is helped to learn about himself or herself primarily by learning to understand what is going on in the interactions—the transactions—of current life. On the one hand, it is a process of trying to understand other people with whom one has meaningful relationships, elements in one's practical life situation, sometimes one's physical condition and medical care. On the other hand, and intertwined with this, a person attempts to become more aware of reactions to specific people and, in specific circumstances, more aware of what touches off certain kinds of reactions. Sometimes one evaluates reactions; sometimes one looks at them in terms of their actual or possible consequences. To engage in these reflective processes, the client is encouraged to talk at length, descriptively, and often with emotion about the self, about associates, and about the situation, to a worker who listens with attention, understanding, and acceptance. The worker helps to focus the exploration-description-ventilation process on pertinent content and through sustaining expressions encourages the formation of the relationship of trust necessary for one person to use another's help. Directive techniques are used sparingly. Understanding of intrapsychic patterns and their development is by no means unimportant, although procedures dealing with them are used much less frequently than person–situation reflection. Procedures of pattern-dynamic and developmental reflection are used in highly varying degree. In many cases they do not appear at all, in others occasionally, and in some with fair regularity over a period of treatment. They usually rely for much of their impact on substantial prior and subsequent work on understanding the current person–situation gestalt. The picture is distinctly one of a blend of procedures, with the admixture of those procedures leading to intrapsychic understanding following the pattern of a continuum.

FURTHER STUDIES

This typology has been used as a research instrument in a number of other studies, as can be seen from the following partial list.

Boatman, Louise. "Caseworkers' Judgments of Clients' Hope."[4]

Chamberlain, Edna. "Testing with a Treatment Typology."[5]

Davis, Inger P. "Use of Influence Techniques in Casework with Parents."[6]

Ehrenkranz, Shirley M. "A Study of the Techniques and Procedures Used in Joint Interviewing in the Treatment of Marital Problems."[7]

Hollis, Florence. "Continuance and Discontinuance in Marital Counseling and Some Observations on Joint Interviews."[8]

Montgomery, Mitzie I. R. "Feedback Systems, Interaction Analysis, and Counseling Models in Professional Programmes."[9]

Mullen, Edward J. "Casework Treatment Procedures as a Function of Client Diagnostic Variables."[10]

Orcutt, Ben Avis. "Process Analysis in the First Phase of Treatment"—a part of a larger study, *Casework with Wives of Alcoholics.*[11]

Turner, Francis J. "Ethnic Differences and Client Performance"[12] and "Social Work Treatment and Value Differences."[13]

In most of these studies, groups of cases were compared to determine the extent to which procedures used in treatment vary in association with other variables. Each of the 10 studies produced important findings. Some of these findings support aspects of currently accepted theory. Some throw other aspects into question. Others that are primarily descriptive have brought previously unnoted or at least undemonstrated tendencies to light. One study (Montgomery) used the typology successfully in analyzing three different treatment approaches using interviews conducted by Fritz Perls, Carl Rogers, and Virginia Satir.

Sustainment and Countersustainment

The study by Boatman is of special interest here because it deals with an important aspect of sustainment. As we began using the typology, it became apparent that workers varied a great deal in the ways in which they chose and expressed communications designed primarily for other than direct sustainment. One has the impression that some workers seem to maintain a sustaining "atmosphere" and others do not. Others even seem to come close to a "countersustaining" climate. Boatman studied this phenomenon as part of a doctoral dissertation investigating correlates of various factors with caseworkers' judgment of client hopefulness.

She examined the possibility that sustainment is given not only by the directly sustaining communications coded A but also *indirectly* by the supportive quality of some communications whose primary dynamic is either reflection, exploration-ventilation, or direct influence. Indirectly sustaining communications were designated as those B, C, D, E, and F communications expressing "encouragement, approval, agreement, reassurance, or identification of the worker with the client's ideas, attitudes, feelings, or behavior." In contrast, B, C, D, E, and F communications expressing "discouragement, disapproval, disagreement, stimulation of anxiety, or identification of the worker with attitudes, ideas, feelings, or behavior contrary to those of the client were considered to be 'counter-sustaining.'" For instance:

> Indirect sustainment: To a wife who overreacts to her husband's anger and fears that he no longer loves her: "Do you think Ted may express anger pretty easily? You told me his family is much more spontaneous than yours. Lots of people can be angry and love very much at the same time, you know."
>
> Or, to a client with excessively high self-expectations: "Why are you so hard on yourself?"
>
> Countersustainment: A client who has told her worker she has a hard time get-

ting to work on time complains that her boss is "so irritable" in the mornings. Worker asks whether she thinks her late arrivals might have anything to do with it.

Boatman found that almost 8 percent of the "non-A" communications in her study were indirectly sustaining. This was more than two and a half times as much sustainment as was given in her sample by direct sustaining (A) comments. She also found that over 5 percent of the coded communications were *countersustaining*. The study went on to examine the extent to which workers differ from each other in their general supportiveness. Mullen had already shown that workers vary a great deal in the extent to which they use different procedures. Direct sustainment, however, he found to be an exception to this tendency. In contrast, Boatman's findings show that if one includes *indirect* sustainment, there is very great variation among workers. The extremes ran from one worker whose interviews showed sustainment and countersustainment in almost equal degrees to another whose sustainment/countersustainment ratio was eight to one.

Obviously, this area needs much further study. One could, for instance, examine relationships between total sustainment-countersustainment and client progress in either problem solving or general functioning, by combining a measurement of progress such as that developed by Dorothy Beck and Mary Ann Jones of the Family Service Association of America,[14] with measurements of sustainment-countersustainment. With the Beck and Jones technique, one could easily locate a small group of workers with high outcomes and another with low outcomes; analysis of each group over even a small sample of interviews might reveal highly significant differences in approach. A similar phenomenon exists in the measurement of directiveness. Undoubtedly, workers differ in the extent to which their reflective comments contain directive elements. This has not yet been studied but would be a very useful area of exploration.

Need for Further Research

Much interesting research lies ahead for skilled practitioners who are interested in strengthening the scientific foundation of clinical social work practice.

The typology itself needs further development. Work needs to be done on the unit to be coded. The small units used, although good from the point of view of precision, are expensive to use because the coding becomes very time-consuming. If a way can be found to code larger units reliably, the usefulness of the typology will be increased. It should be noted, however, that it is not necessary to use the entire typology in every study. If one is interested in directiveness, for example, it could be that only the B worker comments needed coding. Once located, each such unit could be studied for appropriateness, effect, differences between workers, and so on. It is also quite possible to add new categories, especially subcategories of the major six, when these are needed to study special questions. For instance, one might want to subdivide the C category by a time factor to see how much emphasis is placed on past history. Or one might look into the *content* of worker interpretations by devising suitable subcategories to the three reflective divisions.

The value of the typology in environmental or milieu treatment has not as yet been examined and this should be done. As for substantive studies, the questions that need examination are myriad. To name a few: Are certain "worker styles" associated with higher effectiveness of treatment with certain types of problems or certain types of personality? What are the components of these styles? What are the emphases within them? How do such factors as socioeconomic class or education relate to treatment procedures? In another type of study, one could take a series of person–situation reflection episodes or a series of pattern-dynamic or developmental episodes to examine what evidence there is that these did or did not affect the client's subsequent responses.

Caseworkers have long and inconclusively debated, on the basis of observed data, many issues that would lend themselves to more rigorous study. To move ahead in such studies, we must state our hypotheses in accurate terms based on the realities of casework practice, we must define our objectives far more precisely than heretofore, and we must continue to develop research instruments specifically designed for the examination and measurement of the phenomena to which they are to be applied.

NOTES

1. Readers interested in the full report on the research should turn to Hollis (1968), *A Typology of Casework Treatment.*
2. Mullen (1968).
3. Reid and Shyne (1969).
4. Boatman (1974).
5. Chamberlain (1969).
6. Davis (1969). See also her article on advice giving (1975).
7. See the Ehrenkranz doctoral dissertation (1967). Two articles based on the dissertation were published in *Social Casework* (1967).
8. See the article by Hollis (1968) published in *Social Casework.*
9. Montgomery (1973).
10. Mullen, doctoral dissertation (1968). Three articles based on the dissertation were published, one in 1968 and two in 1969.
11. Orcutt (1971).
12. Turner, doctoral dissertation (1963) and an article based on it (1964).
13. Turner (1970).
14. Beck and Jones (1973).

A NOTE ON THE RELIABILITY OF THE CLASSIFICATION*

Before using a research tool in formal study it is, of course, most important to know the degree of its reliability. Preliminary figures on the reliability of the classification when two judges are coding the same data are encouraging. Several reliability tests were run during the course of developing and experimenting with the typology. In the early stages a running record of agreement percentages was kept. There were times when we were greatly encouraged to find agreement rates in many of the categories that stayed above 80 percent and sometimes reached 90 percent or more for a series of three or four interviews. Then suddenly the agreement rate for an interview would drop to 70 percent, or even lower, either because the dictation was obscure or because it was particularly hard to decide whether the

client was really reflecting. Such sudden drops revealed several pitfalls in reliability testing into which it is easy to slip. If reliability had simply been checked until a desirable level was reached, as is sometimes done, a high agreement rate could have been reported fairly early. But this would really have meant that we had stopped playing when we were winning.

A high rate could also have been established, as is sometimes done, by setting up an experiment in which examples of the different types of material are typed on cards that are then coded. This is a useful device to show at least that the system is conceptually clear, but it tells nothing about the borderline instances that are the real cause of disagreement between coders. To avoid these pitfalls, in the two reliability tests 19 and 20 interviews were used, respectively, and coded over an arbitrarily selected time span.

The principal measure of reliability used in the tests was the Spearman Rank Order

* Taken by permission of *Social Casework* from "The Coding and Application of a Typology of Casework Treatment," *Social Casework,* 48 (October 1967).

Correlation Coefficient.[1] John Dollard and Frank Auld have pointed out the error introduced by relying, as is sometimes done, on a simple percentage agreement, the significance of which is so strongly influenced by the number of alternative choices available.[2] When only two choices are possible in a dimension, chance alone would yield 50 percent agreement even if the coding were completely unreliable. With each addition to the choices, however, the probability of chance agreement lessens. It is reduced to 33 percent when there are three possible choices, and to only 20 percent when there are five choices (assuming equal distribution over all alternatives). In other words, an agreement rate of 60 percent in the first instance would represent only 20 percent better than chance; in the second it would be almost twice as good as chance; and in the third three times as good.

With this in mind it was decided not to use percentage agreement but, instead, to use rank order correlations over a sample comparable in number of cases to the size of sample for which the classification was likely to be used. In this kind of test the number of alternatives available in a given dimension does not have a bearing on the significance of the score. If one assumes that errors are randomized, this test gives a guide to the extent to which, in an actual study of the same number of cases, errors of judges in a given category may obscure differences or similarities that can be located with a more exact research tool.

Reliability scores can be reported on the major means categories and on subject matter categories 1, 2, and 3 used in the exploratory–descriptive–ventilative material and on the change context categories.[3] For the most part, as the accompanying tables show, the Spearman test was used. Three of the major categories were used so rarely

TABLE I
Agreement between Judges as Measured by Spearman r

Category	Client	Worker
A	—	.83*
C	.82*	.87*
D	.76*	.75*
C1	.89*	.86*
C2	.78*	.74*
C3	.69†	.36
a[5]	.70†	.70†
b	.45	.65†
c	.73*	.84*
d	.56	.30

*Significance level ≤.001
†Significance level ≤.005

that they could not be tested by the Spearman formula. For these Fisher's Exact Probability Test was used, basing the test on the simple presence or absence of the given procedure in the respective interviews.[4]

The figures in Table I represent the average of the two reliability tests administered in the next to the last and the last year of the study. The figures in Table II were obtained in the later test. In some categories there was substantial progress in reliability between the first and second tests. For example, the analyses on the average score of .69 given for client C3 represent a rise from .60 to .79 between tests, the score of .36 for worker C3 represents a rise from .03 to .70, the .56 for client d represents a rise from .46 to .67.

The chief categories remaining in difficulty at the time of the second test were client b and worker d. These tables give a minimum estimate of the present reliability of the typology, however, since work was done subsequently to define the weaker categories further.

Though it is hoped that, eventually, all items can be brought up to a reliability score

TABLE II
Agreement between Judges as Measured by Fisher Exact Probability Test

Category	Agree Present	Agree Absent	Disagree	Sig. level
Client E	1	18	1	.10
Client F	5	13	2	.005
Worker B	4	11	5	.05
Worker E	0	18	2	N.S.
Worker F	2	16	2	.05

of .80, a score of .70 represents a substantial improvement not only over chance but also over judgments arrived at in a global way. For greatest reliability, two judges should be used on all material, the average of the two sets of coding being used in the analysis. When this averaging method is used, an agreement level of .80 between coders gives a reliability level of .88; agreement of .70, a reliability of .82; agreement of .65 a reliability of .79. (Using the Spearman-Brown formula,[6] inter-rater *r* is multiplied by 2 and divided by 1 + inter-rater *r*.)

NOTES

1. Hubert M. Blalock, Jr., *Social Statistics* (New York: McGraw-Hill, 1960), pp. 317–19.
2. John Dollard and Frank Auld, Jr., *Scoring Human Motives: A Manual* (New Haven, CT.: Yale University Press, 1959), p. 306.
3. Subject matter categories have not been useful and have since been dropped.
4. Blalock, *Social Statistics,* pp. 221–25.
5. Small letters correspond to arabic numerals, 1, 2, 3, and 4 in text.
6. J. P. Guilford, *Fundamental Statistics in Psychology and Education,* 4th ed. (New York: McGraw-Hill, 1965), pp. 457–58.

BIBLIOGRAPHY

Abbott, Douglas, et al. (April 1995). "Pathological Gambling and the Family: Practice Implications." *Families in Society* 76, pp. 213–19.

Abramson, Marcia (September 1985). "The Autonomy-Paternalism Dilemma in Social Work Practice." *Social Casework* 66, pp. 387–93.

_____ (February 1989). "Autonomy vs. Paternalistic Beneficence." *Social Casework* 70, pp. 101–5.

_____ (April 1996). "Reflections on Knowing Oneself Ethically: Toward a Working Framework for Social Work Practice." *Families in Society* 77, pp. 195–201.

Ackerman, Nathan W. (April 1954). "The Diagnosis of Neurotic Marital Interaction." *Social Casework* 35, pp. 139–47.

_____ (1972). "The Growing Edge of Family Therapy." In *Progress in Group and Family Therapy.* eds. Clifford J. Sagar and Helen Singer Kaplan. New York: Brunner/Mazel.

_____ (1969). "Prejudice and Scapegoating in the Family." In *Family Therapy and Disturbed Families.* eds. Gerald H. Zuk and Ivan Boszormenyi-Nagy. Palo Alto, CA: Science and Behavior Books, pp. 48–57.

_____ (1958). *The Psychodynamics of Family Life.* New York: Basic Books.

_____ (1966). *Treating the Troubled Family.* New York: Basic Books.

_____, et al. (1967). *Expanding Theory and Practice in Family Therapy.* New York: Family Service Association of America.

Ackerman, Robert J. (1983). *Children of Alcoholics: A Guidebook for Educators, Therapists and Parents.* Holmes Beach, FL: Learning Publications.

Agbayani-Siewert, Pauline (September 1994). "Filipino-American Culture and Family: Guidelines for Practitioners." *Families in Society* 75, pp. 429–38.

Ainsworth, Mary D. (1962). "The Effects of Maternal Deprivation: A Review of Findings and Controversy in the Context of Research Strategy." In *Deprivation of Maternal Care: A Reassessment of Its Effects.* Geneva: World Health Organization.

_____ and John Bowlby (1991). "An Ethological Approach to Personality Development." *American Psychologist* 46, pp. 331–41.

Alexander, James F., et al. (1994). "The Process and Outcome of Marital and Family Therapy." In *Handbook of Psychotherapy and Behavior Change.* eds. Allen E. Bergin and Sol L. Garfield. New York: Wiley & Sons.

Allen, David M. (1988). *Unifying Individual and Family Therapies.* San Francisco: Jossey-Bass.

Allen-Mears, Paula, and Bruce A. Lane (November 1987). "Grounding Social Work Practice in Theory: Ecosystems." *Social Casework* 68, pp. 515–21.

Alperin, Richard M. (Summer 1994). "Managed Care versus Psychoanalytic Psychotherapy: Conflicting Ideologies." *Clinical Social Work Journal* 22, pp. 137–48.

Ambrosino, Salvatore (December 1979). "Integrating Counseling, Family Life Education, and Family Advocacy." *Social Casework* 60, pp. 579–85.

American Psychiatric Association (1994). *Diagnostic and Statistical Manual of Mental Disorders.* 4th ed. Washington, DC: American Psychiatric Association.

Amodeo, Maryann, and L. Kay Jones. (May–June 1997). "Viewing Alcohol and Other Drug Use Cross Culturally: A Cultural Framework for Clinical Practice." *Families in Society* 78, pp. 240–54.

_____, and Joseph Liftik (March 1990). "Working Through Denial in Alcoholism." *Families in Society* 71, pp. 131–35.

Anderson, Carol M., and Susan Stewart (1983). *Mastering Resistance: A Practical Guide to Family Therapy.* New York: Guilford Press.

Anderson, Charlene, and Carolyn Stark (January–February 1988). "Psychosocial Problems of Job Relocation: Preventive Roles in Industry." *Social Work* 33, pp. 38–41.

Anderson, Kim M. (November–December 1997). "Uncovering Survival Abilities in Children Who Have Been Sexually Abused." *Families in Society* 78, pp. 592–99.

Anderson, Linda M., et al. (June 1979). "Training in Family Treatment: Needs and Objectives." *Social Casework* 60, pp. 323–29.

Anderson, Sandra C. (March 1995). "Education for Family-Centered Practice." *Families in Society* 76, pp. 173–81.

_____, and Deborah L. Mandell (May 1989). "The Use of Self-Disclosure by Professional Social Workers." *Social Casework* 70, pp. 259–67.

Andreae, Dan (1996). "Systems Theory and Social Work Treatment." In *Social Work Treatment: Interlocking Theoretical Approaches.* ed. Francis J. Turner. New York: Free Press, pp. 601–15.

Angell, Robert C. (1936). *The Family Encounters the Depression.* New York: Scribner's.

Anthony, Susan, and Gregory Pagano (Fall 1998). "The Therapeutic Potential for Growth During the Termination Process." *Clinical Social Work Journal* 26, pp. 281–96.

Aponte, Harry J. (1979). "Diagnosis in Family Therapy." In *Social Work Practice: People and Environments.* ed. Carel B. Germain. New York: Columbia University Press.

_____ (December 1986). "If I Don't Get Simple, I Cry." *Family Process* 25, pp. 531–48.

_____ (1976). "Underorganization in the Poor Family." In *Family Therapy.* ed. Philip J. Guerin. New York: Gardner Press, pp. 432–48.

Aptekar, Herbert H. (1955). *The Dynamics of Casework and Counseling.* Boston: Houghton Mifflin.

Araoz, Daniel L., and Marie A. Carrese (1995). *Solution-Oriented Brief Therapy for Adjustment Disorders: A Guide for Providers under Managed Care.* Newbury Park, CA: Sage.

Argles, Paul (December 1984). "The Threat of Separation in Family Conflict." *Social Casework* 65, pp. 610–14.

Arieti, Silvano (1974). *Interpretation of Schizophrenia.* 2nd ed. New York: Basic Books.

Atherton, Charles R. (December 1993). "Empiricists versus Social Constructionists: Time for a Cease-Fire." *Families in Society* 74, pp. 617–24.

Atwood, Nancy (March 1982). "Professional Prejudice and the Psychotic Client." *Social Work* 27, pp. 172–77.

Auslander, Gail K., and Howard Litwin (June 1987). "The Parameters of Network Intervention: A Social Work Application." *Social Service Review* 61, pp. 305–18.

_____ and _____ (May–June 1988). "Social Networks and the Poor: Toward Effective Policy and Practice." *Social Work* 33, pp. 234–38.

Austin, Carol D. (September 1990). "Case Management: Myths and Realities." *Families in Society* 71, pp. 398–407.

_____ (October 1993). "Case Management: A Systems Perspective." *Families in Society* 74, pp. 451–58.

_____, and Robert W. McClelland, eds. (1995). *Perspectives on Case Management Practice.* Milwaukee, WI: Families International.

Austin, Lucille N. (1956). "Qualifications for Psychotherapists, Social Caseworkers." *American Journal of Orthopsychiatry* 26, pp. 47–57.

_____ (June 1948). "Trends in Differential Treatment in Social Casework." *Journal of Social Casework* 29, pp. 203–11.

Baker, John E., et al. (January 1992). "Psychological Tasks for Bereaved Children." *American Journal of Orthopsychiatry* 62, pp. 105–16.

Balgopal, Pallassana R. (September 1989). "Occupational Social Work: An Expanded Clinical Perspective." *Social Work* 34, pp. 437–42.

Ball, F. L. Jessica, et al. (September 1995). "Who's Got the Power? Gender Differences in Partners' Perceptions of Influence During Marital Problem-Solving Discussions." *Family Process* 34, pp. 303–21.

Ballen, Bernice (Spring 1980). "The Growth of Psychoanalytic Developmental Psychology and the Application of Technique." *Clinical Social Work Journal* 8, pp. 28–37.

Barlam, Steven, and Harriet Hailparn Soares (1997). "Clinical Practice with the Elderly." In *Theory and Practice in Clinical Social Work.* ed. Jerrold R. Brandell. New York: Free Press, pp. 471–500.

Barry, Joan (September–October 1988). "Autobiographical Writing: An Effective Tool for Practice with the Oldest Old." *Social Work* 33, pp. 449–51.

Barsky, Morna (February 1984). "Strategies and Techniques of Divorce Mediation." *Social Casework* 65, pp. 102–8.

Bateson, Gregory, et al. (March 1963). "A Note on the Double Bind—1962." *Family Process* 2, pp. 154–61.

_____, Don D. Jackson, Jay Haley, and John Weakland (October 1956). "Toward a Theory of Schizophrenia." *Behavioral Science* 1, pp. 252–64.

Beck, Aaron T., and Arthur Freeman (1990). *Cognitive Therapy of Personality Disorders.* New York: Guilford Press.

Beck, Dorothy Fahs (January 1987). "Counselor Burnout in Family Service Agencies." *Social Casework* 68, pp. 3–15.

_____ (1988). *Counselor Characteristics: How They Affect Outcomes.* Milwaukee, WI: Family Service of America.

_____, and Mary Ann Jones (1973). *Progress on Family Problems.* New York: Family Service Association of America.

Beck, Robert L. (Spring 1984). "Beyond the Transference: Interviews with Adults and Their Parents in Psychotherapy." *Clinical Social Work Journal* 12, pp. 57–68.

_____ (Summer 1987). "Redirecting Blame in Marital Psychotherapy." *Clinical Social Work Journal* 15, pp. 148–58.

Beckett, Joyce O. (January–February 1988). "Plant Closings: How Older Workers Are Affected." *Social Work* 33, pp. 29–33.

Beder, Joan (September–October 1998). "The Home Visit, Revisited." *Families in Society* 79, pp. 514–22.

Bedrosian, Richard C., and George D. Bozicas (1994). *Treating Family of Origin Problems: A Cognitive Approach.* New York: Guilford Press.

Behrens, Marjorie, and Nathan Ackerman (January 1956). "The Home Visit as an Aid in Family Diagnosis and Therapy." *Social Casework* 37, pp. 11–19.

Bell, Janet L. (January 1995). "Traumatic Event Debriefing: Service Delivery Designs and the Role of Social Work." *Social Work* 40, pp. 36–43.

Bell, John E. (1961). *Family Group Therapy.* Public Monograph 64. Washington, DC: U.S. Government Printing Office.

Bellak, Leopold, et al. (1973). *Ego Functions in Schizophrenics, Neurotics, and Normals.* New York: John Wiley & Sons.

Ben-Ari, Adital (May 1995). "Coming Out: A Dialectic of Intimacy and Privacy." *Families in Society* 76, pp. 306–14.

Benatur, May (May 1995). "Running Away from Sexual Abuse: Denial Revisited." *Families in Society* 76, pp. 315–20.

Bender, Barbara (January 1976). "Management of Acute Hospitalization Anxiety." *Social Casework* 57, pp. 19–26.

Benedict, Ruth (1934). *Patterns of Culture.* New York: Houghton Mifflin.

Bentovim, Arnon, and Warren Kinston (1991). "Focal Family Therapy: Joining Systems Theory with Psychodynamic Understanding." In *Handbook of Family Therapy,* Vol. 2. eds. Alan S. Gurman and David P. Kniskern. New York: Brunner/Mazel, pp. 284–324.

Berger, David M. (1987). *Clinical Empathy.* Northvale, NJ: Jason Aronson.

Berger, Raymond M. (January 1986). "Social Work Practice Models: A Better Recipe." *Social Casework* 67, pp. 45–54.

Bergin, Allen E., and Sol L. Garfield, eds. (1994). *Handbook of Psychotherapy and Behavior Change.* 4th ed. New York: John Wiley & Sons.

Bergler, Edmund (1946). *Unhappy Marriage and Divorce.* New York: International Universities Press.

Berkman, Cathy S., and Gail Zinberg (July 1997). "Homophobia and Heterosexism in Social Workers." *Social Work* 42, pp. 319–32.

Berkowitz, Sidney (November 1955). "Some Specific Techniques of Psychosocial Diagnosis and Treatment in Family Casework." *Social Casework* 36, pp. 399–406.

Berlin, Sharon (Spring 1983). "Single Case Evaluation: Another Version." *Social Work Research and Abstracts* 19, pp. 3–11.

Berman, Ellen M., and Martin Goldberg (1986). "Therapy with Unmarried Couples." In *Clinical Handbook of Marital Therapy.* eds. Neil S. Jacobson and Alan S. Gurman. New York: Guilford Press, pp. 301–19.

Bernhein, Kayla F., and Anthony F. Lehman (1985). *Working with Families of the Mentally Ill.* New York: W. W. Norton.

Bernier, James C. (December 1990). "Parental Adjustment to a Disabled Child: A Family Systems Perspective." *Families in Society* 71, pp. 589–95.

Bertalanffy, Ludwig Von (1968). *General Systems Theory: Foundations, Development, Application.* New York: Braziller.

Beutler, Larry E., et al. (1994). "Therapist Variables." In *Handbook of Psychotherapy and Behavior Change.* eds. Allen E. Bergin and Sol L. Garfield. New York: John Wiley & Sons, pp. 229–69.

Bibring, Grete L. (June 1947). "Psychiatry and Social Work." *Journal of Social Casework* 28, pp. 203–11.

Biestek, Felix (1957). *The Casework Relationship.* Chicago: Loyola University Press.

Birdwhistell, Ray L. (1970). *Kinesics and Context.* Philadelphia: University of Pennsylvania Press.

Bitterman, Catherine M. (April 1968). "The Multimarriage Family." *Social Casework* 49, pp. 218–21.

Black, Claudia (1982). *It Will Never Happen to Me.* Denver: MAC Publications.

Blake-White, Jill, and Christine Madeline Kline (September 1985). "Treating the Dissociative Process in Adult Victims of Childhood Incest." *Social Casework* 66, pp. 394–402.

Blanck, Gertrude, and Rubin Blanck (1986). *Beyond Ego Psychology: Developmental Object Relations Theory.* New York: Columbia University Press.

———— and ———— (1974). *Ego Psychology: Theory and Practice.* New York: Columbia University Press.

———— and ———— (1979). *Ego Psychology II.* New York: Columbia University Press.

Blankertz, Laura E., et al. (September 1990). "Outreach Efforts with Dually Diagnosed Homeless Persons." *Families in Society* 71, pp. 387–95.

Blazyk, Stan, and Margaret M. Canavan (November–December 1985). "Therapeutic Aspects of Discharge Planning." *Social Work* 30, pp. 489–96.

Bloom, Martin, et al. (1995). *Evaluating Practice: Guidelines for the Accountable Professional.* Needham Heights, MA: Allyn and Bacon.

Blythe, Betty, et al. (1994). *Direct Practice Research in Human Services Agencies.* New York: Columbia University Press.

Boatman, Louise (1974). "Caseworkers' Judgments of Clients' Hope: Some Correlates among Client–Situation Characteristics and among Workers' Communication Patterns." Doctoral dissertation. Columbia University School of Social Work, New York.

Bogolub, Ellen B. (September 1991). "Women and Mid-Life Divorce: Some Practice Issues." *Social Work* 36, pp. 428–33.

Boie, Maurine (1937). "The Case Worker's Need for Orientation to the Culture of the Client." *Proceedings of the National Conference of Social Work.* Chicago: University of Chicago Press, pp. 112–23.

Bonnefil, Margaret C. (Spring 1979). "Therapist, Save My Child: A Family Crisis Case." *Clinical Social Work Journal* 7, pp. 6–14.

Bookin, Deborah, and Ruth E. Dunkle (January 1985). "Elder Abuse: Issues for the Practitioner." *Social Casework* 66, pp. 3–12.

Borden, William (March 1992). "Narrative Perspectives in Psychosocial Intervention Following Adverse Life Events." *Social Work* 37, pp. 135–41.

Boszormenyi-Nagy, Ivan, et al. (1991). "Contextual Therapy." In *Handbook of Family Therapy,* Vol. 2. eds. Alan S. Gurman and David P. Kniskern. New York: Brunner/Mazel, pp. 200–38.

———, and Geraldine Spark (1973). *Invisible Loyalties: Reciprocity in Intergenerational Family Therapy.* New York: Harper and Row.

Bowen, Murray (1978). *Family Therapy in Clinical Practice.* New York: James Aronson.

Bowlby, John (1980). *Attachment and Loss,* Vol. 3. New York: Basic Books.

——— (1952). *Maternal Care and Mental Health.* 2nd ed. Geneva: World Health Organization.

——— (1965). "Grief and Mourning in Infancy and Early Childhood." In *The Psychoanalytic Study of the Child,* Vol. 15. eds. Ruth S. Eissler et al. New York: International Universities Press.

——— (1988). *A Secure Base: Clinical Applications of Attachment Theory.* London: Routledge.

Boyd-Franklin, Nancy (1989). *Black Families in Therapy: A Multi Systems Approach.* New York: Guilford Press.

———, and Anderson J. Franklin (1998). "African American Couples in Therapy." In *Re-Visioning Family Therapy.* ed. Monica McGoldrick. New York: Guilford Press, pp. 268–81.

———, and Nivine T. Shenouda (April 1990). "A Multisystems Approach to the Treatment of a Black, Inner-City Family with a Schizophrenic Mother." *American Journal of Orthopsychiatry* 60, pp. 186–95.

Boyer, Patricia A., and Ronnald J. Jeffrey (1984). *A Guide for the Family Therapist.* New York: Jason Aronson.

Braverman, Lois (April 1986). "Social Casework and Strategic Therapy." *Social Casework* 67, pp. 234–39.

Brennan, Thomas P., et al. (June 1986). "Forensic Social Work: Practice and Vision." *Social Casework* 67, pp. 340–50.

Briar, Scott M., and Henry Miller (1971). *Problems and Issues in Social Casework.* New York: Columbia University Press.

Briere, John N. (1992). *Child Abuse Trauma: Theory and Treatment of the Lasting Effects.* Newbury Park, CA: Sage Publications.

Bronfenbrenner, Urie, et al. (1996). *The State of Americans.* New York: Free Press.

Brown, John A. (January 1987). "Casework Contacts with Black-White Couples." *Social Casework* 68, pp. 24–29.

Brown, Laura S., and Don Zimmer (1986). "An Introduction to Therapy Issues of Lesbian and Gay Male Couples." In *Clinical Handbook of Marital Therapy.* eds. Neil S. Jacobson and Alan S. Gurman. New York: Guilford Press, pp. 451–68.

Brown, Ursula M. (January 1995). "Black/White Interracial Young Adults. Quest for a Racial Identity." *American Journal of Orthopsychiatry* 65, pp. 125–30.

Browne, Colette V. (May 1995). "Empowerment in Social Work Practice with Older Women." *Social Work* 40, pp. 358–64.

———, and Alice Broderick (May 1994). "Asian and Pacific Island Elders: Issues for Social Work Practice and Education." *Social Work* 39, pp. 252–59.

Brunhofer, Margaret O'Kane (1997). "Mourning and Loss: A Life Cycle Perspective." In *Theory and Practice in Clinical Social Work*. ed. Jerrold R. Brandell. New York: Free Press, pp. 662–88.

Bruno, Frank J. (1957). *Trends in Social Work: 1874–1956*. New York: Columbia University Press.

Buckley, Peter, ed. (1986). *Essential Papers on Object Relations*. New York: New York University Press.

Budman, Simon H., and Alan S. Gurman (1988). *Theory and Practice of Brief Therapy*. New York: Guilford Press.

Burgess, Earnest W., and Leonard S. Cottrell, Jr. (1939). *Predicting Success or Failure in Marriage*. New York: Prentice Hall.

Burstein, Beth (October 1988). "Involuntary Aged Clients: Ethical and Treatment Issues." *Social Casework* 69, pp. 518–24.

Cain, Roy (June 1991). "Relational Contexts and Information Management among Gay Men." *Families in Society* 72, pp. 344–52.

Cancro, Robert (1974). "An Overview of the Schizophrenic Syndrome." In *Strategic Intervention in Schizophrenia*. eds. Cancro, et al. New York: Behavioral.

Caplan, Gerald (1964). *Principles of Preventive Psychiatry*. New York: Basic Books.

Caron, Sandra L., and Marjorie Ulin (July–August 1997). "Closeting and the Quality of Lesbian Relationships." *Families in Society* 78, pp. 413–19.

Carpenter, Donald (1996). "Constructivism and Social Work Treatment." In *Social Work Treatment: Interlocking Theoretical Approaches*. 4th ed. Francis J. Turner, ed. New York: Free Press, pp. 146–67.

Carter, Carolyn S. (September–October 1997). "Using African-Centered Principles in Family-Preservation Services." *Families in Society*. 78, pp. 531–38.

Carter, Elizabeth A., and Monica McGoldrick Orfanidis (1976). "Family Therapy with One Person and the Family Therapist's Own Family." In *Family Therapy*. ed. Philip J. Guerin. New York: Gardner Press, pp. 193–219.
_____, and Monica McGoldrick, eds. (1988). *The Changing Family Life Cycle*. 2nd ed. New York: Gardner Press.

Cascio, Toni (September–October 1998). "Incorporating Spirituality into Social Work Practice: A Review of What To Do." *Families in Society* 79, pp. 523–31.

Castex, Graciela M. (May 1994). "Providing Services to Hispanic/Latino Populations: Profiles in Diversity." *Social Work* 39, pp. 288–96.

Cates, Jim A., et al. (April 1990). "The Effect of AIDS on the Family System." *Families in Society* 71, pp. 95–201.

Cavan, Ruth Shonie, and Katherine Howland Ranck (1938). *The Family and the Depression*. Chicago: University of Chicago Press.

Cervera, Neil (January 1991). "Unwed Teenage Pregnancy: Family Relationships with the Father of the Baby." *Families in Society* 72, pp. 29–37.

Chamberlain, Edna (December 1969). "Testing with a Treatment Typology." *Australian Journal of Social Work* 22, pp. 3–8.

Chatters, Linda M., and Robert Joseph Taylor (July 1989). "Life Problems and Coping Strategies of Older Black Adults." *Social Work* 34, pp. 313–19.

Chernot, David K. (Fall 1998). "Mutual Values: Self Psychology, Intersubjectivity, and Social Work." *Clinical Social Work Journal* 26, pp. 297–311.

Chernus, Linde A. (February 1985). "Clinical Issues in Alcoholism Treatment." *Social Casework* 66, pp. 67–75.

Chescheir, Martha W. (Fall 1985). "Some Implications of Winnicott's Concepts for Clinical Practice." *Clinical Social Work Journal* 13, pp. 218–33.

Ching, June W. J., et al. (April 1995). "Perceptions of Family Values and Roles among Japanese Americans: Clinical Considerations." *American Journal of Orthopsychiatry* 65, pp. 216–24.

Christ, Grace H., et al. (April 1991). "A Preventive Intervention Program for Bereaved Children: Problems of Implementation." *American Journal of Orthopsychiatry* 61, pp. 168–78.

Cingolani, Judith (September–October 1984). "Social Conflict Perspective on Work with Involuntary Clients." *Social Work* 29, pp. 442–46.

Clark, Karla R. (Summer 1996). "The Nowhere (Wo)man: An Example of the Defensive Use of Emptiness in a Patient with a Schizoid Disorder of the Self." *Clinical Social Work Journal* 24, pp. 153–66.

Cloward, Richard A. (April 1959). "Illegitimate Means, Anomie and Deviant Behavior." *American Sociological Review* 24, pp. 164–76.

Coady, Nick F. (May 1993). "The Worker–Client Relationship Revisited." *Families in Society* 74, pp. 291–99.

_____, and Cyril S. Wolgien (Fall 1996). "Good Therapists' Views of How They Are Helpful." *Clinical Social Work Journal* 24, pp. 311–22.

Cochran, Donna L. (July–August 1997). "African American Fathers: A Decade Review of the Literature." *Families in Society* 78, pp. 340–51.

Cohen, Marcia B. (July–August 1998). "Perceptions of Power in Client/Worker Relationships." *Families in Society* 79, pp. 433–42.

Cohen, Nathan E., ed. (1964). *Social Work and Social Problems.* New York: National Association of Social Workers.

Cohen, Pauline C., and Merton S. Krause (1969). *Casework with Wives of Alcoholics.* New York: Family Service Association of America.

Cohen, Tamar (March 1983). "The Incestuous Family Revisited." *Social Casework* 64, pp. 154–61.

Coker, Kaye H., and Bruce A. Thyer (May 1990). "School- and Family-Based Treatment of Children with Attention Deficit Hyperactivity Disorder." *Families in Society* 71, pp. 276–82.

Cole, Elizabeth S. (March 1995). "Becoming Family Centered: Child Welfare's Challenge." *Families in Society* 76, pp. 163–72.

Coleman, Daniel (Winter 1996). "Positive Sibling Transference: Theoretical and Clinical Dimensions." *Clinical Social Work Journal* 24, pp. 377–87.

Collins, Barbara, and Thomas Collins (November 1990). "Parent–Professional Relationship in the Treatment of Seriously Emotionally Disturbed Children and Adolescents." *Social Work* 35, pp. 522–27.

Collins, John Stewart (1973). *The Vision of Glory.* New York: Braziller.

Comas-Diaz, Lillian (Spring 1992). "The Future of Psychotherapy with Ethnic Minorities." *Psychotherapy* 29, pp. 88–94.

_____, and Ezra E. H. Griffith, eds. (1988). *Clinical Guidelines in Cross-Cultural Mental Health.* New York: John Wiley & Sons.

_____, and Frederick M. Jacobsen (August 1987). "Ethnocultural Identification in Psychotherapy." *Psychiatry* 50, pp. 232–41.

_____, and _____ (July 1991). "Ethnocultural Transference and Countertransference in the Therapeutic Dyad." *American Journal of Orthopsychiatry* 61, pp. 392–402.

Compton, Beulah R., and Burt Galaway (1994). *Social Work Processes.* 5th ed. Pacific Grove, CA: Brooks Cole.

Congress, Elaine P. (November 1994). "The Use of Culturograms to Assess and Empower Culturally Diverse Families." *Families in Society* 75, pp. 531–39.

Connors, Kay Martel, et al. (1997). "Children's Treatment Groups." In *Theory and Practice in Clinical Social Work.* ed. Jerrold R. Brandell. New York: Free Press, pp. 288–314.

Connors, Robin (April 1996). "Self Injury in Trauma Survivors." *American Journal of Orthopsychiatry* 66, pp. 197–216.

Constantine, Larry L. (1986). "Jealousy and Extramarital Relations." In *Clinical Handbook of Marital Therapy.* eds. Neil S. Jacobson and Alan S. Gurman. New York: Guilford Press, pp. 407–27.

Consumer Reports (November 1995). "Does Therapy Help?" pp. 734–39.

Cook, Alicia S. (April 1980). "A Model for Working with the Elderly in Institutions." *Social Casework* 61, pp. 234–39.

Cooper, Marlene, and Joan Lesser (Fall 1997). "How Race Affects the Helping Process: A Case of Cross Racial Therapy." *Clinical Social Work Journal* 25, pp. 323–35.

Cooper, Shirley (1980). "The Master's and Beyond." In *Psychotherapy and Training in Clinical Social Work.* ed. Judith Mishne. New York: Gardner Press, pp. 19–35.

Corcoran, Kevin, and Vikki Vandiver (1996). *Maneuvering the Maze of Managed Care: Skills for Mental Health Practitioners.* New York: Free Press.

Cornell, William, and Karen A. Olio (January 1991). "Integrating Affect in Treatment with Adult Survivors of Physical and Sexual Abuse." *American Journal of Orthopsychiatry* 61, pp. 59–69.

Cornett, Carlton (1997). "Clinical Social Work Practice with Gay Men." In *Theory and Practice in Clinical Social Work.* ed. Jerrold R. Brandell. New York: Free Press, pp. 599–617.

Cornille, Thomas A., et al. (September 1996). "Dealing with Family Distress in Schools." *Families in Society* 77, pp. 435–45.

Corwin, Maria De Oca (January 1996). "Early Intervention Strategies with Borderline Clients." *Families in Society* 77, pp. 40–49.

Cournoyer, Barry R. (May 1988). "Personal and Professional Distress among Social Caseworkers." *Social Casework* 69, pp. 259–64.

Cowger, Charles D. (May 1994). "Assessing Client Strengths: Clinical Assessment for Client Empowerment." *Social Work* 39, pp. 262–68.

Crane, John A. (June 1976). "The Power of Social Intervention Experiments to Discriminate Differences between Experimental and Control Groups." *Social Service Review* 50, pp. 224–42.

Crohn, Joel (1998). "Intercultural Couples." In *Re-Visioning Family Therapy.* ed. Monica McGoldrick. New York: Guilford Press, pp. 295–308.

Crystal, David (September 1989). "Asian Americans and the Myth of the Model Minority." *Social Casework* 70, pp. 405–13.

Daly, Alfrieda, et al. (March 1995). "Effective Coping Strategies of African Americans." *Social Work* 40, pp. 240–48.

Dane, Barbara O., and Carol Levine, eds. (1994). *AIDS and the New Orphans: Coping with Death.* Westport, CT: Auburn House.

Dare, Christopher (1986). "Psychoanalytic Marital Therapy." In *Handbook of Marital Therapy.* eds. Neil S. Jacobson and Alan S. Gurman. New York: Guilford Press, pp. 13–28.

Davidson, Kay W. (May 1990). "Doubt as a Source of Innovation in Developing Effective Services to Families." *Families in Society* 71, pp. 296–302.

Davis, Diane Rae, and Golie G. Jansen (March 1998). "Making Meaning of Alcoholics Anonymous for Social Workers: Myths, Metaphors, and Realities." *Social Work* 43, pp. 169–82.

Davis, Inger P. (June 1975). "Advice-Giving in Parent Counselling." *Social Casework* 56, pp. 343–47.

———— (March 1969). "Use of Influence Techniques in Casework with Parents." Doctoral dissertation, University of Chicago.

Davis, Liane Vida (1996). "Role Theory and Social Work Treatment." In *Social Work Treatment: Interlocking Theoretical Approaches.* ed. Francis J. Turner. New York: Free Press, pp. 581–600.

Dean, Harvey (September 1994). "Social Work and the Concept of Individualism." *Families in Society* 75, pp. 423–28.

Dean, Ruth Grossman (March 1993). "Constructivism: An Approach to Clinical Practice." *Smith College Studies in Social Work* 63, pp. 127–46.

———— (Spring 1998). "A Narrative Approach to Groups." *Clinical Social Work Journal* 26, pp. 23–37.

————, and Helen Reinherz (Spring–Summer 1986). "Psychodynamic Practice and Single System Design: The Odd Couple." *Journal of Social Work Education* 22, pp. 71–81.

————, and ———— (March 1992). "Ethical-Clinical Tensions in Clinical Practice." *Social Work* 37, pp. 128–32.

————, and Margaret L. Rhodes (May–June 1998). "Social Constructionism and Ethics: What Makes a 'Better' Story?" *Families in Society* 79, pp. 254–62.

Dehoyos, Genevieve (March 1989). "Person-in-Environment: A Tri-Level Practice Model." *Social Casework* 70, pp. 131–38.

De Jong, Peter, and Scott D. Miller (November 1995). "How to Interview for Client Strengths." *Social Work* 40, pp. 729–36.

De La Fontaine, Elise (1940). "Cultural and Psychological Implications in Case Work Treatment with Irish Clients." In *Cultural Problems in Social Case Work.* New York: Family Welfare Association of America, pp. 21–37.

Dellmann-Jenkins, Mary, et al. (December 1993). "Adolescent Parenting: A Positive, Intergenerational Approach." *Families in Society* 74, pp. 590–601.

Denby, Ramona W., et al. (January–February 1998). "Family Preservation Services and Special Populations." *Families in Society* 79, pp. 3–14.

De Roos, Yosikazu S. (June 1990). "The Development of Practice Wisdom through Human Problem-Solving Processes." *Social Service Review* 64, pp. 276–87.

Dicks, Henry V. (1967). *Marital Tensions*. New York: Basic Books.

Dietz, Christine A., and John L. Craft (December 1980). "Family Dynamics of Incest: A New Perspective." *Social Casework* 61, pp. 602–9.

Dillon, Dennis (March–April 1994). "Understanding and Assessment of Intragroup Dynamics in Foster Family Care: African-American Families." *Child Welfare* 73, pp. 129–39.

Diorio, William D. (April 1992). "Parental Perceptions of the Authority of Public Child Welfare Caseworkers." *Families in Society* 73, pp. 222–35.

Dixon, Samuel L., and Roberta G. Sands (April 1983). "Identity and the Experience of Crisis." *Social Casework* 64, pp. 223–30.

Dolgoff, Ralph L. (May 1981). "Clinicians as Policymakers." *Social Casework* 62, pp. 284–92.

Donner, Susan (January 1988). "Self Psychology: Implications for Social Work." *Social Casework* 69, pp. 17–22.

Dougherty, Nora (May 1983). "The Holding Environment: Breaking the Cycle of Abuse." *Social Casework* 64, pp. 283–90.

Dore, Martha M. (September 1990). "Functional Theory: Its History and Influence on Contemporary Social Work Practice." *Social Service Review* 64, pp. 358–74.

_____, and Ana O. Dumois (February 1990). "Cultural Differences in the Meaning of Adolescent Pregnancy." *Families in Society* 71, pp. 93–101.

Dorfman, Rachelle A., ed. (1988). *Paradigms of Clinical Social Work*. New York: Brunner/Mazel.

Douglas, Harriet (November 1991). "Assessing Violent Couples." *Families in Society* 72, pp. 525–33.

Drachman, Diane, et al. (December 1996). "Migration and Resettlement Experiences of Dominican and Korean Families." *Families in Society* 77, pp. 627–38.

Drake, Robert E., et al. (January 1996). "The Course, Treatment, and Outcome of Substance Disorder in Persons with Severe Mental Illness." *American Journal of Orthopsychiatry* 66, pp. 42–51.

Du Bray, Wynne Hanson (January 1985). "American Indian Values: Critical Factor in Casework." *Social Casework* 66, pp. 30–37.

Duehn, Wayne D., and Nazneed Mayadas (February 1979). "Starting Where the Client Is: An Empirical Investigation." *Social Casework* 60, pp. 67–74.

Duncan, Barry L. (July–August 1997). "Stepping Off the Throne." *The Family Therapy Networker* 21, pp. 22–33.

Dungee-Anderson, Delores (Fall 1992). "Self-Nurturing: A Cognitive Behavioral Treatment Approach for the Borderline Client." *Clinical Social Work Journal* 20, pp. 295–312.

_____, and Joyce O. Beckett (October 1995). "A Process Model for Multicultural Social Work Practice." *Families in Society* 76, pp. 459–67.

Dunkel, Joan, and Shellie Hatfield (March–April 1986). "Counter transference Issues in Working with Persons with AIDS." *Social Work* 31, pp. 114–17.

Dunlap, Katherine M. (1996). "Functional Theory and Social Work Practice." In *Social Work Treatment: Interlocking Approaches*. 4th ed. ed. Francis J. Turner. New York: Free Press.

Dworkin, Joan (November 1990). "Political, Economic, and Social Aspects of Professional Authority." *Families in Society* 71, pp. 534–40.

Dwyer, Diane C., et al. (Summer 1995). "Domestic Violence Research: Theoretical and Practice Implications for Social Work." *Clinical Social Work Journal* 23, pp. 185–98.

Dyche, Larry, and Luis H. Zayas (December 1995). "The Value of Curiosity and Naivete for the Cross-Cultural Therapist." *Family Process* 34, pp. 389–99.

Eber, Lucille, and C. Michael Nelson (July 1997). "School-Based Wraparound Planning: Integrating Services for Students with Emotional and Behavioral Needs." *American Journal of Orthopsychiatry* 67, pp. 385–95.

Eckrich, Sherry (March–April 1985). "Identification and Treatment of Borderline Personality Disorder." *Social Work* 30, pp. 166–71.

Edward, Joyce, and Jean B. Sanville, eds. (1996). *Fostering Healing and Growth: A Psychoanalytic Social Work Approach.* Northvale, NJ: Jason Aronson.

Edwards, Jana K., and Jennifer M. Bess (Spring 1998). "Developing Effectiveness in the Therapeutic Use of Self." *Clinical Social Work Journal* 26, pp. 89–105.

Effron, Anne Kurtzman (May 1980). "Children and Divorce: Help from an Elementary School." *Social Casework* 61, pp. 305–12.

Ehline, David, and Peggy O'Dea Tigue (November 1977). "Alcoholism: Early Identification and Intervention in the Social Service Agency." *Child Welfare* 56, pp. 584–92.

Ehrenkranz, Shirley M. (October and November 1967). "A Study of Joint Interviewing in the Treatment of Marital Problems." *Social Casework* 48, pp. 498–502, 570–74.

———— (1967). "A Study of the Techniques and Procedures Used in Joint Interviewing in the Treatment of Marital Problems." Doctoral dissertation, Columbia University School of Social Work, New York.

Elbow, Margaret, and Judy Mayfield (February 1991). "Mothers of Incest Victims: Villains, Victims, or Protectors?" *Families in Society* 72, pp. 78–85.

Elkin, Irene, et al. (November 1989). "National Institute of Mental Health Treatment of Depression Collaborative Research Program." *Archives of General Psychiatry* 46, pp. 971–83.

Ell, Kathleen (1996). "Crisis Theory and Social Work Practice." In *Social Work Treatment: Interlocking Theoretical Approaches.* 4th ed. ed. Francis J. Turner. New York: Free Press, pp. 168–90.

Elliott, Martha W. (February 1984). "Hospitality as a Professional Virtue." *Social Casework* 65, pp. 109–12.

Elson, Miriam (1986). *Self Psychology in Clinical Social Work.* New York: W. W. Norton.

Epstein, Laura (June 1996). "The Trouble with the Researcher-Practitioner Idea." *Social Work Research* 20, pp. 113–17.

Epstein, Norman (May 1976). "Techniques of Brief Therapy with Children and Parents." *Social Casework* 57, pp. 317–24.

————, et al., eds. (1988). *Cognitive-Behavioral Therapy with Families.* New York: Brunner/Mazel.

Erikson, Erik (1950). *Childhood and Society.* New York: W. W. Norton.

———— (1959). *Identity and the Life Cycle.* New York: International Universities Press.

Ewalt, Patricia L., ed. (1980). "Toward a Definition of Clinical Social Work." *The National Association of Social Work Conference Proceedings.* Washington, DC: National Association of Social Workers.

————, and Noreen Mokuau (March 1995). "Self-Determination from a Pacific Perspective." *Social Work* 40, pp. 168–75.

Eysenck, Hans J. (1952). "The Effects of Psychotherapy: An Evaluation." *Journal of Consulting Psychology* 16, pp. 319–24.

Ezell, Mark (January 1994). "Advocacy Practice of Social Workers." *Families in Society* 75, pp. 36–46.

Fairbairn, W. R. D. (1954). *Object-Relations Theory of Personality.* New York: Basic Books.

Falicov, Celia Jaes (1986). "Cross-Cultural Marriages." In *Clinical Handbook of Marital Therapy.* ed. Neil S. Jacobson and Alan S. Gurman. New York: Guilford Press, pp. 429–50.

———— (1998). "The Cultural Meaning of Family Triangles." In *Re-Visioning Family Therapy.* ed. Monica McGoldrick. New York: Guilford Press, pp. 37–49.

———— (December 1995). "Training to Think Culturally: A Multidimensional Comparative Framework." *Family Process* 34, pp. 273–87.

Family Service America (1991). *The State of Families, 3.* Milwaukee, WI: Family Service America.

———— (1995). *The State of Families, 4.* Milwaukee, WI: Family Service America.

Family Service Association of America (1958). *Method and Process in Social Casework.* New York: Family Service Association of America.

_____ (1953). *Scope and Methods of the Family Service Agency.* New York: Family Service Association of America.

Fann, William E., et al., eds. (1979). *Phenomenology and Treatment of Anxiety.* New York: Spectrum.

Fanschel, David, and Eugene B. Shinn (1978). *Children in Foster Care: A Longitudinal Investigation.* New York: Columbia University Press.

Faria, Geraldine (September 1994). "Training for Family Preservation Practice with Lesbian Families." *Families in Society* 75, pp. 416–22.

Farley, Joan E. (Spring 1990). "Family Developmental Task Assessment." *Clinical Social Work Journal* 18, pp. 85–97.

Fatout, Marian F. (February 1990). "Consequences of Abuse on the Relationships of Children." *Families in Society* 71, pp. 76–81.

Feit, Marvin D., et al., eds. (1995). *Capturing the Power of Diversity.* New York: Haworth Press.

Ferman, Louis A., ed. (1965). *Poverty in America.* Ann Arbor: University of Michigan Press.

Ferreira, Antonio J. (July–December 1963). "Family Myths and Homeostasis." *Archives of General Psychiatry* 9, pp. 457–63.

Festinger, Trudy (1983). *No One Ever Asked Us . . . A Postscript to Foster Care.* New York: Columbia University Press.

Fink, Arthur E. (1942). *The Field of Social Work.* New York: Holt.

Finn, Jerry (June 1985). "The Stresses and Coping Behavior of Battered Women." *Social Casework* 66, pp. 341–49.

Fischer, Joel (January 1973). "Is Casework Effective? A Review." *Social Casework.* 18, pp. 5–20.

_____, and Kevin Corcoran (1994). *Measures for Clinical Practice: A Sourcebook.* 2nd ed. Vols 1 and 2. New York: Free Press.

_____, and Henry Miller (Summer 1973). "The Effect of Client Race and Social Class on Clinical Judgments." *Clinical Social Work Journal* 1, pp. 100–9.

Focht, Lynn, and William R. Beardsley, (December 1996). " 'Speech After Long Silence': The Use of Narrative Therapy in a Preventive Intervention for Children of Parents with Affective Disorder." *Family Process* 35, pp. 407–22.

Fontaine, Arlene S. (November 1979). "Using Family of Origin Material in Short-Term Marriage Counseling." *Social Casework* 60, pp. 529–37.

Fortune, Anne E. (Summer 1987). "Grief Only? Client and Social Worker Reactions to Termination." *Clinical Social Work Journal* 15, pp. 159–71.

_____, et al. (March 1992). "Reactions to Termination of Individual Treatment." *Social Work* 37, pp. 171–78.

Foster, Rose Marie Perez (Fall 1998). "The Clinician's Cultural Countertransference: The Psychodynamics of Culturally Competent Practice." *Clinical Social Work Journal* 26, pp. 253–70.

Fox, Evelyn, Marion Nelson, and William Bolman (October 1969). "The Termination Process." *Social Work* 14, pp. 53–63.

Fox, Raymond (1993). *Elements of the Helping Process: A Guide for Clinicians.* Binghamton, NY: Haworth Press.

_____ (October 1987). "Short-Term, Goal-Oriented Family Therapy." *Social Casework* 68, pp. 494–99.

Frager, Adena R. (March 1985). "A Family Systems Perspective on Acting-Out." *Social Casework* 66, pp. 167–76.

Fraiberg, Selma (1959). *The Magic Years.* New York: Scribner's.

Framo, James L. (1982). *Explorations in Marital and Family Therapy.* New York: Springer.

_____ (1992). *Family-of-Origin Therapy: An Intergenerational Approach.* New York: Brunner/Mazel.

Frank, Jerome D. (February 1959). "The Dynamics of the Psychotherapeutic Relationship." *Psychiatry* 22, pp. 17–39.

_____ (May 1968). "The Role of Hope in Psychotherapy." *International Journal of Psychiatry* 5, pp. 383–95.

Frankenstein, Renate (January 1982). "Agency and Client Resistance." *Social Casework* 63, pp. 24–28.

Franklin, Cynthia (September 1995). "Expanding the Vision of the Social Constructionist Debates: Creating Relevance for Practitioners." *Families in Society.* 76, pp. 395–406.

_____, and Cathleen Jordan (May 1995). "Qualitative Assessment: A Methodological Review." *Families in Society* 76, pp. 281–95.

_____, and Paula S. Nurius, eds. (1998). *Constructivism in Practice: Methods and Challenges.* Milwaukee, WI: Families International.

Franklin, Donna L. (September 1986). "Does Client Social Class Affect Clinical Judgment?" *Social Casework* 67, pp. 424–32.

Freed, Anne O. (November 1980). "The Borderline Personality." *Social Casework* 61, pp. 548–58.

_____ (October 1982). "Building Theory for Family Practice." *Social Casework* 63, pp. 472–81.

_____ (September 1984). "Differentiating between Borderline and Narcissistic Personalities." *Social Casework* 65, pp. 395–404.

_____ (July–August 1988). "Interviewing Through an Interpreter." *Social Work* 33, pp. 315–19.

_____ (April 1977). "Social Casework: More than a Modality." *Social Casework* 58, pp. 204–13.

Freeman, Arthur, et al., eds. (1989). *Comprehensive Handbook of Cognitive Therapy.* New York: Plenum Press.

_____, and David M. White (1989). "The Treatment of Suicidal Behavior." In *Comprehensive Handbook of Cognitive Therapy.* eds. Freeman, et al. New York: Plenum Press, pp. 321–46.

Freeman, David S. (1992). *Multigenerational Family Therapy.* New York: Haworth.

Freeman, Edith M. (May 1984). "Multiple Losses in the Elderly: An Ecological Approach." *Social Casework* 65, pp. 287–96.

_____, and Larry Dyer (September 1993). "High-Risk Children and Adolescents: Family and Community Environments." *Families in Society* 74, pp. 422–31.

Freud, Anna (1946). *The Ego and the Mechanisms of Defense.* New York: International Universities Press.

Freud, Sigmund (1964). "Analysis of Phobia in a Five-Year-Old Boy." In *The Complete Works of Sigmund Freud,* Vol. 10. ed. James Strachey. London: Hogarth, pp. 5–148.

Freud, Sophie (September–October 1998). "The Baby and the Bathwater: Some Thoughts on Freud as a Postmodernist." *Families in Society* 79, pp. 455–64.

Frey, Gerald A. (March 1990). "A Framework for Promoting Organizational Change." *Families in Society* 71, pp. 142–47.

Friedman, Donna Haig, and Steven Friedman (May 1982). "Day Care as a Setting for Intervention in Family Systems." *Social Casework* 63, pp. 291–95.

Friedman, Edwin H. (1991). "Bowen Theory and Therapy." In *Handbook of Family Therapy,* Vol. 2. eds. Alan S. Gurman and David P. Kniskern. New York: Brunner/Mazel, pp. 134–70.

_____ (1982). "The Myth of the Shiksa." In *Ethnicity and Family Therapy.* eds. Monica McGoldrick, et al. New York: Guilford Press, pp. 499–526.

Friedmann, Michael S., et al. (December 1997). "Family Functioning and Mental Illness: A Comparison of Psychiatric and Nonclinical Families." *Family Process* 36, pp. 357–67.

Furstenberg, Anne-Linda, and Kathleen A. Rounds (December 1995). "Self-Efficacy as a Target for Social Work Intervention." *Families in Society* 76, pp. 587–94.

Gabriel, Martha A. (Fall 1991). "Group Therapists' Countertransference Reactions to Multiple Deaths from AIDS." *Clinical Social Work Journal* 19, pp. 279–92.

Gardner, Howard (1983). *Frames of Mind: The Theory of Multiple Intelligences.* New York: Basic Books.

Garfield, Sol L. (1994). "Research on Client Variables in Psychotherapy." In *Handbook of Psychotherapy and Behavior Change.* eds. Allen E. Bergin and Sol Garfield. New York: John Wiley & Sons, pp. 190–228.

Garrett, Annette (1982). Revised by Margaret Mangold and Elinor P. Zaki. *Interviewing: Its Principles and Methods.* 3rd ed. New York: Family Service Association of America.

_____ (1958). "Modern Casework: The Contributions of Ego Psychology." In *Ego Psychology and Dynamic Casework.* ed. Howard J. Parad. New York: Family Service Association of America, pp. 38–52.

Garvin, Charles D. (1997). "Group Treatment with Adults." In *Theory and Practice in Clinical Social Work.* ed. Jerrold R. Brandell. New York: Free Press, pp. 315–42.

Garvin, Vicki, et al. (July 1991). "Children of Divorce: Predictors of Change Following Preventive Intervention." *American Journal of Orthopsychiatry* 61, pp. 438–47.

Geismer, Ludwig L. (1972). "Thirteen Evaluative Studies." In *Evaluation of Social Intervention.* eds. Edward J. Mullen, James R. Dumpson, et al. San Francisco: Jossey-Bass.

_____, and Katherine M. Wood (May 1982). "Evaluating Practice: Science as Faith." *Social Casework* 63, pp. 266–75.

_____, et al. (1972). *Early Supports for Family Life: A Social Work Experiment.* Metuchen, NJ: Scarecrow Press.

Geist, Joanne, and Norman Gerber (February 1960). "Joint Interviewing: A Treatment Technique with Marriage Partners." *Social Casework* 41, pp. 76–83.

Germain, Carel Bailey (1991). *Human Behavior and the Social Environment: An Ecological View.* New York: Columbia University Press.

_____, and Alex Gitterman (1996). *The Life Model of Social Work Practice: Advances in Theory and Practice.* New York: Columbia University Press.

Getzel, George S. (November 1982). "Helping Elderly Couples in Crisis." *Social Casework* 63, pp. 515–21.

Giancarlo, Thomas J. (February 1991). "Multiple Personality Disorder: A Challenge to Practitioners." *Families in Society* 72, pp. 95–105.

Gibbons, Dorothy, et al. (Summer 1994). "Working with Victims: Being Empathic Helpers." *Clinical Social Work Journal* 22, pp. 211–22.

Gibbs, Jewelle Taylor, and Gloria Moskowitz-Sweet (December 1991). "Clinical and Cultural Issues in the Treatment of Biracial and Bicultural Adolescents." *Families in Society* 72, pp. 579–91.

Gibelman, Margaret, and Harold W. Demone, Jr. (January 1989). "The Social Worker as Mediator in the Legal System." *Social Casework* 70, pp. 28–36.

_____, and Philip H. Schervish (February 1996). "Social Work and Public Social Services Practice: A Status Report." *Families in Society* 77, pp. 117–24.

_____, and _____ (Fall 1996). "The Private Practice of Social Work: Current Trends and Projected Scenarios in a Managed Care Environment." *Clinical Social Work Journal* 24, pp. 323–38.

Gilbert, Neil, and Harry Specht (July 1976). "Advocacy and Professional Ethics." *Social Work* 21, pp. 288–93.

Gilgun, Jane F. (July 1994). "A Case for Case Studies in Social Work Research." *Social Work* 39, pp. 371–80.

_____ (September and October 1996). "Human Development and Adversity in Ecological Perspective, Parts I and II." *Families in Society* 77, pp. 395–402, 459–76.

Gilligan, Stephen, and Reese Price, eds. (1993). *Therapeutic Conversations.* New York: W. W. Norton.

Gingerich, Wallace J., et al. (September 1982). "Name Calling in Social Work." *Social Service Review* 56, pp. 366–74.

Ginsberg, Leon H. (1983). *The Practice of Social Work in Social Welfare.* New York: Free Press.

Giovacchini, Peter L. (1986). *Developmental Disorders.* Northvale, NJ: Jason Aronson.

Gitterman, Alex (1991). *Handbook of Social Work Practice with Vulnerable Populations.* New York: Columbia University Press.

_____ (1996). "Life Model Theory and Social Work Treatment." In *Social Work Treatment: Interlocking Theoretical Approaches.* 4th ed. ed. Francis J. Turner. New York: Free Press, pp. 389–408.

_____ (March 1989). "Testing Professional Authority and Boundaries." *Social Casework* 70, pp. 165–71.

_____ (March–April 1983). "Uses of Resistance: A Transactional View." *Social Work* 28, pp. 127–31.

Goering, Paula N., and Stanley K. Stylianos (April 1988). "Exploring the Helping Relationship between the Schizophrenic Client and the Rehabilitation Therapist." *American Journal of Orthopsychiatry* 58, pp. 271–80.

Golan, Naomi (May 1980). "Intervention at Times of Transition: Sources and Forms of Help." *Social Casework* 61, pp. 259–66.

_____ (1978). *Treatment in Crisis Situations.* New York: Free Press.

Gold, Nora (January 1990). "Motivation: The Crucial but Unexplored Component of Social Work Practice." *Social Work* 35, pp. 49–56.

Goldberg, Gale (April 1975). "Breaking the Communication Barrier: The Initial Interview with an Abusing Parent." *Child Welfare* 54, pp. 274–82.

Goldenberg, Irene, and Herbert Goldenberg (1991). *Family Therapy: An Overview.* 3rd ed. Pacific Grove, CA: Brooks/Cole.

Goldmeier, John (June 1985). "Helping the Elderly in Times of Stress." *Social Casework* 66, pp. 323–32.

_____ (January 1980). "Intervention in the Continuum from Divorce to Family Reconstitution." *Social Casework* 61, pp. 39–47.

_____, and Donald V. Fandetti (April 1992). "Self Psychology in Clinical Intervention with the Elderly." *Families in Society* 73, pp. 214–21.

Goldner, Virginia (March 1985). "Feminism and Family Therapy." *Family Process* 24, pp. 31–47.

Goldring, Judith H. (1980). *Quick Response Therapy: A Time Limited Treatment Approach.* New York: Human Services Press.

Goldstein, Eda G. (1990). *Borderline Disorders: Clinical Models and Techniques.* New York: Guilford Press.

_____ (1997). "Clinical Practice with Lesbians." In *Theory and Practice in Clinical Social Work.* ed. Jerrold R. Brandell. New York: Free Press, pp. 578–98.

_____ (1995). *Ego Psychology and Social Work Practice.* 2nd ed. New York: Free Press.

_____ (June 1979). "The Influence of Parental Attitudes on Psychiatric Treatment Outcome." *Social Casework* 60, pp. 350–59.

_____ (Winter 1994). "Self-Disclosure in Treatment: What Therapists Do and Don't Talk About." *Clinical Social Work Journal* 22, pp. 417–33.

_____ (Spring 1997). "To Tell or Not to Tell." *Clinical Social Work Journal* 25, pp. 41–58.

_____ (Spring 1996). "What Is Clinical Social Work? Looking Back to Move Ahead." *Clinical Social Work Journal* 24, pp. 89–104.

_____ and Maryellen Noonan (1999). *Short-Term Treatment and Social Work Practice: An Integrative Approach.* New York: Free Press.

Goldstein, Howard (January 1986). "A Cognitive-Humanistic Approach to the Hard-to-Reach Client." *Social Casework* 67, pp. 27–36.

_____ (May–June 1998). "Education for Ethical Dilemmas in Social Work Practice." *Families in Society* 79, pp. 241–53.

_____ (January 1992). "Essay: If Social Work Hasn't Made Progress as a Science, Might It Be an Art?" *Families in Society* 73, pp. 48–55.

_____ (January 1990a). "The Knowledge Base of Social Work Practice: Theory, Wisdom, Analogue, or Art?" *Families in Society* 71, pp. 32–43.

_____ (May–June 1987). "The Neglected Moral Link in Social Work Practice." *Social Work* 32, pp. 181–86.

_____ (May 1983). "Starting Where the Client Is." *Social Casework* 64, pp. 267–75.

_____ (May 1990b). "Strength or Pathology: Ethical and Rhetorical Contrasts in Approaches to Practice." *Families in Society* 71, pp. 267–75.

_____ (September–October 1986). "Toward the Integration of Theory and Practice: A Humanistic Approach." *Social Work* 31, pp. 352–57.

Gondolf, Edward W. (June 1995). "Alcohol Abuse, Wife Assault, and Power Needs." *Social Service Review* 69, pp. 274–84.

Gorey, Kevin M. (June 1996). "Effectiveness of Social Work Intervention Research: Internal versus External Evaluations." *Social Work Research* 20, pp. 119–28.

Gorkin, Michael (1987). *The Uses of Countertransference.* Northvale, NJ: Jason Aronson.

Gourse, Judith E., and Martha W. Chescheir (February 1981). "Authority Issues in Treating Resistant Families." *Social Casework* 62, pp. 67–73.

Gray, Sylvia Sims, and Lynn M. Nybell (November–December 1990). "Issues in African-American Family Preservation." *Child Welfare* 69, pp. 513–23.

Grayer, Elinor Dunn, and Patricia R. Sax (Winter 1986). "A Model for the Diagnostic and Therapeutic Use of Countertransference." *Clinical Social Work Journal* 14, pp. 295–307.

Graziano, Roberta (Fall 1986). "Making the Most of Your Time: Clinical Social Work with a Borderline Patient." *Clinical Social Work Journal* 14, pp. 262–75.

Green, Robert-Jay (September 1996). "Why Ask, Why Tell? Teaching and Learning about Lesbians and Gays in Family Therapy." *Family Process* 35, pp. 389–400.

_____, and Paul D. Werner (June 1996). "Intrusiveness and Closeness-Caregiving: Rethinking the Concept of Family Enmeshment." *Family Process* 35, pp. 115–36.

Greenberg, George S. (December 1977). "The Family Interactional Perspective: A Study and Examination of the Work of Don D. Jackson." *Family Process* 16, pp. 385–412.

Greenberg, Leslie S., and Susan M. Johnson (1986). "Emotionally Focused Couples Therapy." In *Clinical Handbook of Marital Therapy.* eds. Neil S. Jacobson and Alan S. Gurman. New York: Guilford Press, pp. 253–76.

_____ and _____ (1988). *Emotionally Focused Therapy for Couples.* New York: Guilford Press.

Greenberg, Shirley (Spring 1986). "The Supportive Approach to Therapy." *Clinical Social Work Journal* 14, pp. 6–13.

Greene, Gilbert J. (1996). "Communication Theory and Social Work Treatment." In *Social Work Treatment: Interlocking Theoretical Approaches.* 4th ed. Francis J. Turner. New York: Free Press, pp. 116–45.

_____, et al. (March 1996). "A Constructivist Perspective on Clinical Social Work Practice with Ethnically Diverse Clients." *Social Work* 41, pp. 172–80.

Greene, Mary Jane, and Betty Orman (September 1981). "Nurturing the Unnurtured." *Social Casework* 62, pp. 398–404.

Greenspan, Rhoda (Winter 1993). "Marital Therapy with Couples Whose Lack of Self-Sustaining Function Threatens the Marriage." *Clinical Social Work Journal* 21, pp. 395–404.

Gregoire, Thomas K. (Fall 1995). "Alcoholism: The Quest for Transcendence and Meaning." *Clinical Social Work Journal* 23, pp. 339–59.

Greif, Geoffrey L. (Spring 1987). "Single Fathers and Noncustodial Mothers: The Social Worker's Helping Role." *Journal of Independent Social Work* 1, pp. 59–69.

_____, and Cynthia Bailey (February 1990). "Where Are the Fathers in Social Work Literature?" *Families in Society* 71, pp. 88–91.

_____, and Alfred DeMaris (May 1990). "Single Fathers with Custody." *Families in Society* 71, pp. 259–67.

Griffin, William A. (1993). *Family Therapy: Fundamentals of Theory and Practice.* New York: Brunner/Mazel.

Grinnell, Richard M., Jr., and Nancy S. Kyte (July 1975). "Environmental Modification: A Study." *Social Work* 20, pp. 313–18.

Grossberg, Sidney H., and Jerrold R. Brandell (1997). "Clinical Social Work in the Context of Managed Care." In *Theory and Practice in Clinical Social Work.* ed. Jerrold R. Brandell. New York: Free Press, pp. 404–22.

Group for the Advancement of Psychiatry Committee on the Family (June 1996). "Global Assessment of Relational Functioning Scale (GARF)." *Family Process* 35, pp. 155–89.

Guerin, Philip J., ed. (1976). *Family Therapy.* New York: Gardner Press.

_____, and Eileen G. Pendagast (1976). "Evaluation of Family System and Genogram." In *Family Therapy.* ed. Philip J. Guerin. New York: Gardner Press.

_____, et al. (1987). *The Evaluation and Treatment of Marital Conflict: A Four-Stage Approach.* New York: Basic Books.

Guidano, V. F., and G. Liotti (1983). *Cognitive Processes and Emotional Disorders.* New York: Guilford Press.

Guntrip, Harry (1961). *Personality Structure and Human Interaction.* London: Hogarth Press.

Gurman, Alan S., and David P. Kniskern (March 1986). "Commentary." *Family Process* 25, pp. 42–65.

_____, and _____ (1981). "Family Therapy Outcome Research: Knowns and Unknowns." In *Handbook of Family Therapy.* eds. Gurman and Kniskern. New York: Brunner/Mazel, pp. 742–75.

_____, and _____, eds. (1991). *Handbook of Family Therapy,* Vol. 2. New York: Brunner/Mazel.

Gutheil, Irene A. (September 1992). "Considering the Physical Environment: An Essential Component of Good Practice." *Social Work* 37, pp. 391–96.

Gutierrez, Lorraine (March 1990). "Working with Women of Color: An Empowerment Perspective." *Social Work* 35, pp. 149–53.

Gyarfas, Mary Gorman (1980). "A Systems Approach to Diagnosis." In *Psychotherapy and Training in Clinical Social Work.* ed. Judith Mischne. New York: Gardner Press, pp. 49–63.

Hadley, Trevor R., et al. (June 1974). "The Relationship between Family Developmental Crisis and the Appearance of Symptoms in a Family Member." *Family Process* 13, pp. 207–14.

Haffey, Martha, and Phyllis Malkin Cohen (March 1992). "Treatment Issues for Divorcing Women." *Families in Society* 73, pp. 142–48.

Hafner, Julian R. (1986). "Marital Therapy for Agoraphobia." In *Clinical Handbook of Marital Therapy.* eds. Neil S. Jacobson and Alan S. Gurman. New York: Guilford Press, pp. 471–93.

Haley, Jay (1987). *Problem Solving Therapy.* 2nd ed. San Francisco: Jossey-Bass.

Hamilton, Gordon (1937). "Basic Concepts upon Which Case Work Practice Is Formulated." *Proceedings of the National Conference of Social Work.* Chicago: University of Chicago Press.

_____ (1947). *Psychotherapy in Child Guidance.* New York: Columbia University Press.

_____ (1958). "A Theory of Personality: Freud's Contribution to Social Work." In *Ego Psychology and Dynamic Casework.* ed. Howard J. Parad. New York: Family Service Association of America, pp. 11–37.

_____ (1940). *Theory and Practice of Social Case Work.* New York: Columbia University Press.

_____ (1951). *Theory and Practice of Social Case Work.* 2nd ed. New York: Columbia University Press.

_____ (July 1941). "The Underlying Philosophy of Social Case Work." *The Family* 18, pp. 139–48.

Hammer, Emanuel F. (1968). "Interpretive Technique: A Primer." In *Use of Interpretation in Treatment: Technique and Art.* ed. Hammer. New York: Grune and Stratton, pp. 31–42.

Hancock, Betsy Ledbetter, and Leroy H. Pelton (January 1989). "Home Visits: History and Functions." *Social Casework* 70, pp. 21–27.

Hankins, Frank (1930). "Contributions of Sociology to Social Work." *Proceedings of the National Conference of Social Work.* Chicago: University of Chicago Press.

Hare, Jan (January 1994). "Concerns and Issues Faced by Families Headed by a Lesbian Couple." *Families in Society* 75, pp. 27–35.

Hare-Mustin, Rachel T. (June 1978). "A Feminist Approach to Family Therapy." *Family Process* 17, pp. 181–94.

Hartman, Ann (January 1990). "Education for Direct Practice." *Families in Society* 71, pp. 44–50.

_____ (March 1995). "Ideological Themes in Family Policy." *Families in Society* 75, pp. 182–92.

_____, and Joan Laird (1983). *Family-Centered Social Work Practice.* New York: Free Press.

_____, and _____ (May–June 1998). "Moral and Ethical Issues in Working with Lesbians and Gay Men." *Families in Society* 79, pp. 263–76.

Hartman, Carl, and Diane Reynolds (April 1987). "Resistant Clients: Confrontation, Interpretation, and Alliance." *Social Casework* 68, pp. 205–13.

Hartmann, Heinz (1958). *Ego Psychology and the Problem of Adaptation.* New York: International Universities Press.

_____, Ernst Kris, and R. Loewenstein (1946). "Comments on the Formation of Psychic Structure." In *The Psychoanalytic Study of the Child,* Vol. 2. eds. Ruth S. Eissler, et al., New York: International Universities Press, pp. 11–38.

Hartocollis, Lina (Summer 1998). "The Making of Multiple Personality Disorder: A Social Constructivist View." *Clinical Social Work Journal* 26, pp. 159–76.

Harvey, Aminifu R. (January 1995). "The Issue of Skin Color in Psychotherapy with African Americans." *Families in Society* 76, pp. 3–10.

Hashimi, Joan Kay (July 1981). "Environmental Modification: Teaching Social Coping Skills." *Social Work* 26, pp. 323–26.

Hawley, Dale R., and Laura DeHaan (September 1996). "Toward a Definition of Family Resilience: Integrating Life Span and Family Perspectives." *Family Process* 35, pp. 283–98.

Hefner, Charles W., and James O. Prochaska (May–June 1984). "Concurrent versus Conjoint Marital Therapy." *Social Work* 29, pp. 287–91.

Hegar, Rebecca L. (September 1989). "Empowerment-Based Practice with Children." *Social Service Review* 63, pp. 372–83.

Hellenbrand, Shirley (April 1961). "Client Value Orientations: Implications for Diagnosis and Treatment." *Social Casework* 42, pp. 163–69.

_____ (1965). "Main Currents in Social Casework, 1918–36." Doctoral dissertation. Columbia University School of Social Work, New York.

Heller, Nina R., and Terry B. Northcut (Summer 1996). "Utilizing Cognitive-Behavioral Techniques in Psychodynamic Practice with Clients Diagnosed as Borderline." *Clinical Social Work Journal* 24, pp. 203–20.

Hendricks-Matthews, Marybeth (March 1982). "The Battered Woman: Is She Ready for Help?" *Social Casework* 63, pp. 131–37.

Henry, William P., et al. (1994). "Psychodynamic Approaches." In *Handbook of Psychotherapy and Behavior Change*. eds. Allen E. Bergin and Sol L. Garfield. New York: John Wiley & Sons, pp. 467–508.

Hepworth, Dean H. (November 1993). "Managing Manipulative Behavior in the Helping Relationship." *Social Work* 38, pp. 674–82.

_____, et al. (1997). *Direct Social Work Practice: Theory and Skills*. 5th ed. Pacific Grove, CA: Brooks/Cole.

Herman, Judith Lewis (1992). *Trauma and Recovery: The Aftermath of Violence—From Domestic Abuse to Political Terror*. New York: Basic Books.

Hester, Reid K., and William R. Miller, eds. (1989). *Handbook for Alcoholism Treatment Approaches: Effective Alternatives*. New York: Pergamon Press.

Hines, Paulette Moore, and Nancy Boyd-Franklin (1996). "African American Families." In *Ethnicity and Family Therapy*. eds. Monica McGoldrick, et al. New York: Guilford Press, pp. 66–84.

Hodges, Vanessa G., and Betty J. Blythe (May 1992). "Improving Service Delivery to High-Risk Families: Home-Based Practice." *Families in Society* 73, pp. 259–65.

Holliday, Mindy, and Robin Cronin (May 1990). "Families First: A Significant Step toward Family Preservation." *Families in Society* 71, pp. 303–06.

Hollingshead, August B., and Frederick C. Redlich (1958). *Social Class and Mental Illness*. New York: John Wiley & Sons.

Hollis, Florence (1964). *Casework: A Psychosocial Therapy*. New York: Random House.

_____ (1947). "Casework in Marital Disharmony." Doctoral dissertation. Bryn Mawr College.

_____ (October 1965). "Casework and Social Class." *Social Casework* 46, pp. 463–71.

_____ (March 1968). "Continuance and Discontinuance in Marital Counseling and Some Observation on Joint Interviews." *Social Casework* 49, pp. 167–74.

_____ (1936). "Environmental (Indirect) Treatment as Determined by Client's Needs." In *Differential Approach in Casework Treatment*. New York: Family Welfare Association of America.

_____ (Fall 1976). "Evaluation: Clinical Results and Research Methodology." *Clinical Social Work Journal* 4, pp. 204–22.

_____ (Fall 1983). "How It Really Was." *Smith College School for Social Work Journal* 10, pp. 3–9.

_____ (January 1980). "On Revisiting Social Work." *Social Casework* 61, pp. 3–10.

_____ (1939). *Social Casework in Practice: Six Case Studies*. New York: Family Welfare Association of America, pp. 295–98.

_____ (June 1949). "The Techniques of Casework." *Journal of Social Casework* 30, pp. 235–44.

_____ (1968). *A Typology of Casework Treatment*. New York: Family Service Association of America.

_____ (1949). *Women in Marital Conflict.* New York: Family Service Association of America.

Holmes, Sally Ann (December 1981). "A Holistic Approach to the Treatment of Violent Families." *Social Casework* 62, pp. 594–600.

Holmes, Thomas R. (June 1995). "History of Child Abuse: A Key Variable in Client Response to Short-Term Treatment." *Families in Society* 76, pp. 349–59.

Hoorwitz, Aaron Noah (November 1983). "Guidelines for Treating Father–Daughter Incest." *Social Casework* 64, pp. 515–24.

Hopps, June Gary, et al. (1995). *The Power to Care: Clinical Practice Effectiveness with Overwhelmed Clients.* New York: Free Press.

Horejsi, Charles, et al. (July–August 1992). "Reactions by Native American Parents to Child Protection Agencies: Cultural and Community Factors." *Child Welfare* 71, pp. 329–42.

Horner, Elinor A. (Spring 1995). "The Meeting of Two Narratives." *Clinical Social Work Journal* 23, pp. 9–19.

Horton, Anne L., and Barry L. Johnson (October 1993). "Profile and Strategies of Women Who Have Ended Abuse." *Families in Society* 74, pp. 481–92.

Howard, Tina U., and Frank C. Johnson (October 1985). "An Ecological Approach to Practice with Single Families." *Social Casework* 66, pp. 482–89.

Hulewat, Phyllis (March 1996). "Resettlement: A Cultural and Psychological Crisis." *Social Work* 41, pp. 129–35.

Humphreys, Nancy A., et al. (March 1993). "Integrating Policy and Practice: The Contribution of Clinical Social Work." *Smith College Studies in Social Work* 63, pp. 177–85.

Hurst, Nancy C., D. Donald Sawatzky, and David P. Pare (November–December 1996). "Families with Multiple Problems through a Bowenian Lens." *Child Welfare* 75, pp. 693–708.

Hutchison, Elizabeth D. (December 1987). "Use of Authority in Direct Social Work Practice with Mandated Clients." *Social Service Review* 61, pp. 581–89.

Hwang, Sung-Chul, and Charles D. Cowger (January–February 1998). "Utilizing Strengths in Assessment." *Families in Society* 79, pp. 25–31.

Imber-Black, Evan (1988). *Families and Larger Systems: A Family Therapist's Guide through the Labyrinth.* New York: Guilford Press.

_____, ed. (1993). *Secrets in Families and Family Therapy.* New York: W. W. Norton.

Imre, Roberta Wells (January 1990). "Essay: Rationality *with* Feeling." *Families in Society* 71, pp. 57–62.

Ingersoll-Dayton, Berit et al. (May 1988). "Involving Grandparents in Family Therapy." *Social Casework* 69, pp. 280–89.

Innes, Max (December 1996). "Connecting Bowen Theory with Its Human Origins." *Family Process* 35, pp. 487–500.

Ivanoff, Andre M., et al. (1994). *Involuntary Clients in Social Work Practice: A Research-Based Approach.* Hawthorne, NY: Aldine de Gruyter.

_____, Betty J. Blythe, and Scott Briar (May 1987). "The Empirical Practice Debate." *Social Casework* 68, pp. 290–98.

Ivry, Joann (February 1995). "Aging in Place: The Role of Geriatric Social Work." *Families in Society* 75, pp. 76–85.

Jackson, Don D. (1968). "The Question of Family Homeostasis." In *Communication, Family and Marriage: Human Communication,* Vol. 1. ed. Don D. Jackson. Palo Alto, CA: Science and Behavior Books, pp. 1–11.

Jackson, Gerald F., ed. (1980). *Crisis Intervention in the 1980s.* San Francisco: Jossey-Bass.

Jackson, Helene, et al. (May 1995). "Preadolescent Suicide: How to Ask and How to Respond." *Families in Society* 76, pp. 267–79.

Jacobs, Judith Bula (September 1990). "Names, Naming and Name Calling in Practice with Families." *Families in Society* 71, pp. 415–21.

Jacobson, Neil S., and Alan S. Gurman, eds. (1986). *Clinical Handbook of Marital Therapy.* New York: Guilford Press.

_____, and John Gottman (1998). *When Men Batter Women.* New York: Simon and Schuster.

Jansson, Bruce S., and June Simmons (September–October 1984). "The Survival of Social Work Units in Host Organizations." *Social Work* 31, pp. 448–53.

Jayaratne, Srinika, and Wayne A. Chess (September–October 1984). "Job Satisfaction, Burnout, and Turnover: A National Study." *Social Work* 29, pp. 448–53.

Jiminez, Mary Ann (January 1990). "Historical Evolution and Future Challenges of the Human Services Profession." *Families in Society* 71, pp. 3–11.

Johnson, Harriette C. (1999). "Borderline Personality Disorders." In *Adult Psychopathology II*. ed. Francis J. Turner. New York: Free Press.

_____ (January 1996). "Violence and Biology: A Review of the Literature." *Families in Society* 77, pp. 3–18.

Johnson, Ida M. (March 1992). "Economic, Situational, and Psychological Correlates of the Decision-Making Process of Battered Women." *Families in Society* 73, pp. 168–76.

Johnson, Peter J., and Allen Rubin (January–February 1983). "Case Management in Mental Health: A Social Work Domain?" *Social Work* 28, pp. 49–55.

Johnson, Susan M., and Leslie S. Greenberg, eds. (1994). *The Heart of the Matter: Perspectives in Marital Therapy*. New York: Brunner/Mazel.

Johnson, Thomas W., and Michael S. Keren (1998). "The Families of Lesbian Women and Gay Men." In *Re-visioning Family Therapy*. ed. Monica McGoldrick. New York: Guilford Press, pp. 320–29.

Jolesch, Miriam (May 1962). "Casework Treatment of Young Married Couples." *Social Casework* 43, pp. 245–51.

Jones, Gwyn C., and Allie C. Kilpatrick (May 1996). "Wellness Theory: A Discussion and Application to Clients with Disabilities." *Families in Society* 77, pp. 259–67.

Jones, Mary Ann (1991). "Measuring Outcomes." In *Family Preservation Services: Research and Evaluation*. eds. Kathleen Wells and David E. Biegal. New York: Sage.

_____, and Martha A. Gabriel (April 1999). "Utilization of Psychotherapy by Lesbians, Gay Men, and Bisexuals: Findings from a Nationwide Survey." *American Journal of Orthopsychiatry* 69, pp. 209–19.

_____, Renee Neuman, and Ann W. Shyne (1976). *A Second Chance for Families*. New York: Child Welfare League of America.

Jordan, Cathleen, et al. (January 1989). "Clinical Issues of the Dual-Career Couple." *Social Work* 34, pp. 29–32.

Joyce, Patricia A. (Summer 1995). "Psychoanalytic Theory, Child Sexual Abuse and Clinical Social Work." *Clinical Social Work Journal* 23, pp. 199–214.

Jung, Marshall (June 1983). "Directions for Building Family Development Theory." *Social Casework* 64, pp. 363–70.

Jurkovic, Gregory J. (1997). *The Plight of the Parentified Child*. New York: Brunner/Mazel.

Kabat, Roberta (Fall 1996). "A Role-Reversal in the Mother–Daughter Relationship." *Clinical Social Work Journal* 24, pp. 255–69.

Kadushin, Alfred, and Goldie Kadushin (1997). *The Social Work Interview: A Guide for Human Services Professionals*. New York: Columbia University Press.

Kadushin, Goldie (July–August 1998). "Adaptations of the Traditional Interview to the Brief-Treatment Context." *Families in Society* 79, pp. 346–57.

Kagan, Richard, and Shirley Schlosberg (1989). *Families in Perpetual Crisis*. New York: W. W. Norton.

Kahn, Michael (1991). *Between Therapist and Client*. New York: W. H. Freeman.

Kaplan, Harold I., and Benjamin J. Sadock, eds. (1985). *Comprehensive Textbook of Psychiatry*. 4th ed. Baltimore, MD: Williams and Wilkens.

Kardiner, Abram (1939). *The Individual and His Society*. New York: Columbia University Press.

Kasius, Cora, ed. (1950). *Principles and Techniques in Social Casework: Selected Articles, 1940–1950*. New York: Family Service Association of America.

_____, ed. (1962). *Social Casework in the Fifties: Selected Articles, 1951–1960*. New York: Family Service Association of America.

Kassel, Suzanne D., and Rosalie A. Kane (Fall 1980). "Self-Determination Dissected." *Clinical Social Work Journal* 8, pp. 161–78.

Kates, Wendy Glockner, et al. (October 1991). "Whose Child Is This? Assessment and Treatment of Children in Foster Care." *American Journal of Orthopsychiatry* 61, pp. 584–91.

Kaufman, Edward (1994). *Psychotherapy of Addicted Persons*. New York: Guilford Press.

Kayser, Karen (1997). "Couples Therapy." In *Theory and Practice in Clinical Social Work.* ed. Jerrold R. Brandell. New York: Free Press, pp. 254–87.

Keefe, Thomas (March 1984). "Alienation and Social Work Practice." *Social Casework* 65, pp. 145–53.

_____ (September 1980). "Empathy Skill and Critical Consciousness." *Social Casework* 61, pp. 387–93.

Kelley, Patricia (December 1992). "Healthy Stepfamily Functioning." *Families in Society* 73, pp. 579–87.

_____ (1996). "Narrative Theory and Social Work Treatment." In *Social Work Treatment: Interlocking Theoretical Approaches.* 4th ed. ed. Francis J. Turner. New York: Free Press, pp. 461–79.

Kempe, Henry C., and Ray E. Helfer, eds. (1972). *Helping the Battered Child and His Family.* Philadelphia: Lippincott.

Kendall, Katherine A. (1982). "A Sixty-Year Perspective of Social Work." *Social Casework* 63, pp. 424–28.

Kent, Marilyn O. (March 1980). "Remarriage: A Family Systems Perspective." *Social Casework* 61, pp. 146–53.

Kerlin, Louise R., and Jerrold R. Brandell (1997). "Family Violence and Clinical Practice." In *Theory and Practice in Clinical Social Work.* ed. Jerrold R. Brandell. New York: Free Press, pp. 345–79.

Kernberg, Otto (1975). *Borderline Conditions and Pathological Narcissism.* New York: Jason Aronson.

_____ (1986). "Borderline Personality Organization." In *Essential Papers on Borderline Disorders.* ed. Michael H. Stone. New York: New York University Press.

_____ (1984). *Severe Personality Disorders.* New York: Yale University Press.

Kerr, Michael E. (1985). "Obstacles to Differentiation of Self." In *Casebook of Marital Therapy.* ed. Alan S. Gurman. New York: Guilford Press, pp. 111–53.

Kheshgi-Genovese, Zareena, and Thomas A. Genovese (May–June 1997). "Developing the Spousal Relationship within Stepfamilies." *Families in Society* 78, pp. 255–64.

King, Anthony E. O. (March 1993). "The Impact of Incarceration on African American Families: Implications for Practice." *Families in Society* 74, pp. 145–53.

Kirk, Stuart A., et al. (May 1989). "The Prognosis for Social Work Diagnosis." *Social Casework* 70, pp. 295–304.

Kissman, Kris (January 1991). "Feminist-Based Social Work with Single-Parent Families." *Families in Society* 72, pp. 23–28.

Kivowitz, Alexandra (Spring 1995). "Attending to Sibling Issues and Transferences in Psychodynamic Psychotherapy." *Clinical Social Work Journal* 23, pp. 37–46.

Klein, Amelia R., and Ram A. Cnaan (April 1995). "Practice with High-Risk Clients." *Families in Society* 76, pp. 203–11.

Klein, Emanuel (1945). "The Reluctance to Go to School." In *The Psychoanalytic Study of the Child,* Vol. 1. ed. Ruth S. Eissler, et al. New York: International Universities Press, pp. 263–79.

Klerman, Gerald L., et al. (1994). "Medication and Psychotherapy." In *Handbook of Psychotherapy and Behavior Change.* 4th eds. Allen E. Bergin and Sol L. Garfield. New York: John Wiley & Sons, pp. 734–82.

Klugman, David J., et al. (1995). "Suicide: Answering the Cry for Help." In *Differential Diagnosis and Treatment in Social Work.* 4th ed. Francis J. Turner. New York: Free Press, pp. 674–83.

Knapp, Mark (1980). *Essentials of Nonverbal Communication.* New York: Holt, Rinehart and Winston.

Knight, Carolyn (May 1990). "Use of Support Groups with Adult Female Survivors of Child Sexual Abuse." *Social Work* 35, pp. 202–6.

Knudson-Martin, Carmen, and Anne Rankin Mahoney (June 1996). "Gender Dilemmas and Myths in the Construction of Marital Bargains: Issues for Marital Therapy." *Family Process* 35, pp. 137–54.

Kobat, Roberta (Spring 1998). "The Conjoint Session as a Tool for the Resolution of Separation-Individuation in the Adult Mother–Daughter Relationship." *Clinical Social Work Journal* 26, pp. 73–88.

Kohut, Heinz (1977). *The Restoration of the Self.* New York: International Universities Press.

Komarovsky, Mirra (1940). *The Unemployed Man and His Family*. New York: Dryden Press.

Kondrat, Mary Ellen (September 1995). "Concept, Act, and Interest in Professional Practice: Implications of an Empowerment Perspective." *Social Service Review* 69, pp. 405–28.

Kopp, Judy (May 1989). "Self-Observation: An Empowerment Strategy on Assessment." *Social Casework* 70, pp. 276–84.

Koss, Mary P., and James N. Butcher (1986). "Research on Brief Psychotherapy." In *Handbook of Psychotherapy and Behavior Change*. 3rd eds. Sol L. Garfield and Allen E. Bergin. New York: John Wiley & Sons, pp. 627–70.

_____, and Julia Shiang (1994). "Research on Brief Psychotherapy." In *Handbook of Psychotherapy and Behavior Change*. 4th ed. Allen E. Bergin and Sol L. Garfield, eds. New York: John Wiley & Sons, pp. 664–700.

Kramer, Steven Aaron (1990). *Positive Endings in Psychotherapy*. San Francisco: Jossey-Bass.

Krestan, Jo-Ann, and Claudia S. Bepko (September 1980). "The Problem of Fusion in the Lesbian Relationship." *Family Process* 19, pp. 277–89.

Kris, Ernst (1950). "Notes on the Development and on Some Current Problems of Psychoanalytic Child Psychology." In *The Psychoanalytic Study of the Child,* Vol. 5. eds. Ruth S. Eissler, et al. New York: International Universities Press, pp. 24–46.

Kritsberg, Wayne (1985). *The Adult Children of Alcoholics Syndrome: From Discovery to Recovery*. Pompano Beach, FL: Health Communications.

Kruk, Edward (January 1994). "The Disengaged Non-Custodial Father: Implications for Social Work Practice with the Divorced Family." *Social Work* 39, pp. 15–25.

Krumer-Nevo, Michal (Summer 1998). "What's Your Story? Listening to the Stories of Mothers from Multi-Problem Families." *Clinical Social Work Journal* 26, pp. 177–94.

Krystal, Esther, et al. (February 1983). "Serving the Unemployed." *Social Casework* 64, pp. 67–76.

Kubler-Ross, Elisabeth (1969). *On Death and Dying*. New York: Macmillan.

Kuhn, Daniel R. (October 1990). "The Normative Crises of Families Confronting Dementia." *Families in Society* 71, pp. 451–59.

Kupers, Terry A. (1988). *Ending Therapy: The Meaning of Termination*. New York: New York University Press.

Kutchens, Herb, and Stuart A. Kirk (May–June 1988). "The Business of Diagnosis and Clinical Social Work." *Social Work* 33, pp. 215–20.

Laing, Ronald D. (1965). "Mystification, Confusion, and Conflict." In *Intensive Family Therapy*. eds. Ivan Boszormenyi-Nagy and James L. Framo. New York: Harper & Row, pp. 343–63.

_____, and A. Esterson (1971). *Sanity, Madness and the Family*. 2nd ed. New York: Basic Books.

Laird, Joan (1998). "Family-Centered Practice in the Post-Modern Era." In *Constructivism in Practice: Methods and Challenges*. eds. Cynthia Franklin and Paula S. Nurius. Milwaukee, WI: Families International, pp. 217–33. Reprinted from *Families in Society* 76 (March 1995), pp. 150–62.

_____ (June 1994). "Lesbian Families: A Cultural Perspective." *Smith College Studies in Social Work* 64, pp. 263–96.

_____, and Ann Hartman, eds. (1985). *A Handbook of Child Welfare: Context, Knowledge, and Practice*. New York: Free Press.

Lambert, Michael J. (1982). *The Effects of Psychotherapy.*, Vol. 2. New York: Human Sciences Press.

_____, and Allen E. Bergin (1994). "The Effectiveness of Psychotherapy." In *Handbook of Psychotherapy and Behavior Change*. 4th ed. Allen E. Bergin and Sol L. Garfield. New York: John Wiley & Sons, pp. 143–89.

Lammert, Marilyn (June 1986). "Experience as Knowing: Utilizing Therapist Self-Awareness." *Social Casework* 67, pp. 369–76.

Land, Helen, and George Harangody (October 1990). "A Support Group for Partners of Persons with AIDS." *Families in Society* 71, pp. 471–81.

Lantz, Jim (1996). "Cognitive Theory and Social Work Treatment." In *Social Work Treatment: Interlocking Theoretical Approaches*. 4th ed. Francis J. Turner. New York: Free Press, pp. 94–115.

Larner, Glenn (December 1996). "Narrative Child Family Therapy." *Family Process* 35, pp. 423–40.

Larsen, Jo Ann (January 1982). "Remedying Dysfunctional Marital Communication." *Social Casework* 63, pp. 15–23.

Lassers, Elizabeth, et al. (March 1973). "Steps in the Return to School of Children with School Phobia." *American Journal of Psychiatry* 130, pp. 265–68.

Lazlo, Ervin, ed. (1972). *The Relevance of General Systems Theory.* New York: Braziller.

Leader, Arthur L. (January 1969). "Current and Future Issues in Family Therapy." *Social Service Review* 43, pp. 1–11.

_____ (March 1978). "Intergenerational Separation Anxiety in Family Therapy." *Social Casework* 59, pp. 138–44.

_____ (March 1979). "The Notion of Responsibility in Family Therapy." *Social Casework* 60, pp. 131–37.

_____ (October 1981). "The Relationship of Presenting Problems to Family Conflicts." *Social Casework* 62, pp. 451–57.

_____ (Winter 1983). "Therapeutic Control in Family Therapy." *Clinical Social Work Journal* 11, pp. 351–61.

Lederer, William J., and Don D. Jackson (1968). *The Mirages of Marriage.* New York: W. W. Norton.

Lee, Evelyn (1995). "Chinese Families." In *Ethnicity and Family Therapy.* 2nd ed. eds. Monica McGoldrick, et al. New York: Free Press, pp. 249–67.

Lee, Judith A. B. (1994). *The Empowerment Approach to Social Work Practice.* New York: Columbia University Press.

_____ (1996). "The Empowerment Approach to Social Work Practice." In *Social Work Treatment: Interlocking Approaches.* 4th ed. ed. Francis J. Turner. New York: Free Press, pp. 218–49.

_____, and Susan J. Rosenthal (December 1983). "Working with Victims of Violent Assault." *Social Casework* 64, pp. 593–601.

Lee, Laura J. (July–August 1983). "The Social Worker in the Political Environment of a School System." *Social Work* 28, pp. 302–6.

Lee, Mo-Yee (Summer 1996). "A Constructivist Approach to the Help-Seeking Process of Clients: A Response to Cultural Diversity." *Clinical Social Work Journal* 24, pp. 187–202.

Lehman, Anthony F. (January 1996). "Heterogeneity of Person and Place: Assessing Co-Occuring Addictive and Mental Disorders." *American Journal of Orthopsychiatry* 66, pp. 32–41.

Leikin, Celia (February 1986). "Identifying and Treating the Alcoholic." *Social Casework* 67, pp. 67–73.

Lemon, Elizabeth C. (1983). "Planned Brief Treatment." In *Handbook of Clinical Social Work.* eds. Aaron Rosenblatt and Diana Waldfogel. San Francisco: Jossey-Bass, pp. 401–19.

Lerman, Robert I., and Theodora J. Ooms, eds. (1993). *Young Unwed Fathers: Changing Roles and Emerging Policies.* Philadelphia: Temple University Press.

Lesoff, Reeva (Spring 1977). "What to Say When . . . ." *Clinical Social Work Journal* 5, pp. 66–76.

Lester, Lois (October 1982). "The Special Needs of the Female Alcoholic." *Social Casework* 63, pp. 451–56.

Levin, Jerome D. (1987). *Treatment of Alcoholism and Other Addictions: A Self-Psychology Approach.* Northvale, NJ: Jason Aronson.

Levinson, Hilliard (October 1977). "Termination of Psychotherapy: Some Salient Issues." *Social Casework* 58, pp. 480–88.

Levy, Charles S. (March 1974). "Advocacy and the Injustice of Justice." *Social Service Review* 48, pp. 39–50.

_____ (June 1981). "Labeling: The Social Worker's Responsibility." *Social Casework* 62, pp. 332–42.

_____ (1979). *Values and Ethics for Social Work Practice.* Washington, DC: National Association of Social Workers.

Levy, Eileen F. (January 1992). "Strengthening the Coping Resources of Lesbian Families." *Families in Society* 73, pp. 23–31.

Lewis, Harold (Spring/Summer 1987). "Teaching Ethics Through Ethical Teaching." *Journal of Teaching in Social Work* 1, pp. 3–14.

_____ (1982). *The Intellectual Base of Social Work Practice: Tools for Thought in a Helping Profession.* New York: The Haworth Press.

Lewis, Hylan (1967). *Culture Class and Poverty.* Washington, DC: Cross Tell.

Lewis, Marian F. (April 1937). "Alcoholism and Family Casework." *The Family* 18, pp. 39–44.

Lewis, Michael (1992). *Shame: The Exposed Self.* New York: Free Press.

Libassi, Mary Frances (February 1988). "The Chronically Mentally Ill: A Practice Approach." *Social Casework* 69, pp. 88–96.

Lidz, Theodore (1968). *The Person: His Development Throughout the Life Cycle.* New York: Basic Books.

Lieberman, Florence (1979). *Social Work with Children.* New York: Human Services Press.

_____, ed. (1982). *Clinical Social Workers as Psychotherapists.* New York: Gardner Press.

Liebman, Janet (1994). *Victimized Daughters: Incest and the Development of the Female Self.* New York: Routledge.

Lightburn, Anita, and Susan P. Kemp (January 1994). "Family-Support Programs: Opportunities for Community-Based Practice." *Families in Society* 75, pp. 16–26.

Lindemann, Erich (1965). "Symptomatology and Management of Acute Grief." In *Crisis Intervention.* ed. Howard J. Parad. New York: Family Service Association of America, pp. 7–12.

Lindsey, Elizabeth W. (April 1996). "Mothers' Perceptions of Factors Influencing the Restabilization of Homeless Families." *Families in Society* 77, pp. 203–15.

_____, et al. (December 1987). "Evaluating Interpersonal Skills Training for Public Welfare Staff." *Social Service Review* 61, pp. 623–35.

Linzer, Norman (1984). *The Jewish Family.* New York: Human Sciences Press.

Livingston, Martin S. (Fall 1998). "Conflict and Aggression in Couples Therapy: A Self Psychological Vantage Point." *Family Process* 37, pp. 311–21.

_____ (December 1995). "A Self Psychologist in Couplesland: Multisubjective Approach to Transference and Countertransference-like Phenomena in Marital Relationships." *Family Process* 34, pp. 427–39.

Loewenstein, Sophie Freud (January 1979). "Inner and Outer Space in Social Casework." *Social Casework* 60, pp. 19–29.

_____ (March 1977). "An Overview of the Concept of Narcissism." *Social Casework* 58, pp. 136–42.

_____ (January 1980). "Understanding Lesbian Women." *Social Casework* 61, pp. 29–38.

Long, Janie K. (September 1996). "Working with Lesbians, Gays and Bisexuals: Addressing Heterosexism in Supervision." *Family Process* 35, pp. 377–88.

Lorion, Raymond P., and Robert D. Felner (1986). "Research on Mental Health Interventions with the Disadvantaged." In *Handbook of Psychotherapy and Behavior Change.* 3rd ed. Sol L. Garfield and Allen E. Bergin. New York: John Wiley & Sons, pp. 739–75.

Lowenstein, Liana (July–August 1995). "The Resolution Scrapbook as an Aid in the Treatment of Traumatized Children." *Child Welfare* 74, pp. 889–904.

Lucco, Alfred A. (September 1991). "Assessment of the School-Age Child." *Families in Society* 72, pp. 394–407.

Lukton, Rosemary Creed (May 1982). "Myths and Realities of Crisis Intervention." *Social Casework* 63, pp. 276–85.

_____, and Ruth Ehrlich Bro (Spring 1988). "An Alternative Model for Curriculum Building in Clinical Social Work Education: The California Institute for Clinical Social Work." *Clinical Social Work Journal* 16, pp. 8–21.

Lynn, Steven Jay, and Judith W. Rue, eds. (1992). *Dissociation: Clinical and Theoretical Perspectives.* New York: W. W. Norton.

Maas, Henry S. (February 1955). "Socio-cultural Factors in Psychiatric Clinic Services for Children." *Smith College Studies* 25, pp. 1–90.

Mac Eachron, Ann E., and Nora S. Gustavsson (November–December 1997). "Reframing Practitioner Research." *Families in Society* 78, pp. 651–56.

Mackey, Richard A., and Eileen F. Mackey (October 1994). "Personal Psychotherapy and the Development of a Professional Self." *Families in Society* 75, pp. 490–98.

_____, and _____ (Spring 1993). "The Value of Personal Psychotherapy to Clinical Practice." *Clinical Social Work Journal* 21, pp. 97–110.

_____, and Bernard A. O'Brien (March 1998). "Marital Conflict Management: Gender and Ethnic Differences." *Social Work* 43, pp. 128–41.

Madanes, Cloe, et al. (1995). *The Violence of Men.* San Francisco: Jossey-Bass.

Madden, Robert G., and Melissa Parody (Summer 1997). "Between a Legal Rock and a Practice Hard Place: Issues in 'Recovered Memory' Cases." *Clinical Social Work Journal* 25, pp. 223–47.

Magura, Stephen (November 1982). "Clients' View of Outcomes of Child Protective Services." *Social Casework* 63, pp. 522–31.

Mahler, Margaret S., et al. (1975). *The Psychological Birth of the Human Infant: Symbiosis and Individuation.* New York: Basic Books.

Mailick, Mildred D., and Florence W. Vigilante (July–August 1997). "The Family Assessment Wheel: A Social Constructionist Perspective." *Families in Society* 78, pp. 361–69.

Maltas, Carolynn, and Joseph Shay (October 1995). "Trauma Contagion in Partners of Survivors of Childhood Sexual Abuse." *American Journal of Orthopsychiatry* 65, pp. 529–39.

Maluccio, Anthony N. (1979). *Learning from Clients: Interpersonal Helping as Viewed by Clients and Social Workers.* New York: Free Press.

_____, and Wilma D. Marlow (January 1974). "The Case for the Contract." *Social Work* 19, pp. 28–36.

_____, et al. (1998, Numbers 1/2). "Teaching Family Preservation." *Journal of Teaching in Social Work* 16, pp. 3–17.

Mann, James (1973). *Time-Limited Psychotherapy.* Cambridge, MA: Harvard University Press.

Marcus, Hanna P., and Carol M. Runge (December 1990). "Community-Based Services for Agoraphobics." *Families in Society* 71, pp. 602–6.

Margulies, Alfred (1989). *The Empathic Imagination.* New York: W. W. Norton.

Markman, Howard J., et al. (1986). "Prevention." In *Clinical Handbook of Marital Therapy.* eds. Neil S. Jacobson and Alan S. Gurman. New York: Guilford Press, pp. 173–95.

Marley, James A. (September 1992). "Content and Context: Working with Mentally Ill People in Family Therapy." *Social Work* 37, pp. 412–17.

Marsella, Anthony J. (April 1993). "Counseling and Psychotherapy with Japanese Americans: Cross-Cultural Considerations." *American Journal of Orthopsychiatry* 63, pp. 200–8.

Martin, Jane Roland (1992). *The Schoolhome: Rethinking Schools for Changing Families.* Cambridge, MA: Harvard University Press.

Marziali, Elsa (January 1988). "The First Session: An Interpersonal Encounter." *Social Casework* 69, pp. 23–27.

_____, and Leslie Alexander (July 1991). "The Power of the Therapeutic Relationship." *American Journal of Orthopsychiatry* 61, pp. 383–91.

Masterson, James F. (1976). *Psychology of the Borderline Adult.* New York: Brunner/Mazel.

Mayer, John E., and Noel Timms (January 1969). "Clash in Perspective between Worker and Client." *Social Casework* 50, pp. 32–40.

_____, and _____ (1970). *The Client Speaks: Working Class Impressions of Casework.* New York: Atherton.

McDermott, F. E., ed. (1975). *Self Determination in Social Work.* London: Routledge and Kegan Paul.

McDonell, James R., et al. (January 1991). "Family Members' Willingness to Care for People with AIDS: A Psychosocial Assessment Model." *Social Work* 36, pp. 43–53.

McFarlane, William R., ed. (1983). *Family Therapy in Schizophrenia.* New York: Guilford Press.

McGoldrick, Monica, ed. (1998). *Re-Visioning Family Therapy: Race, Culture and Gender in Clinical Practice.* New York: Guilford Press.

_____, et al., eds. (1996). *Ethnicity and Family Therapy.* 2nd ed. New York: Guilford Press.

_____, et al., eds. (1989). *Women in Families: A Framework for Family Therapy.* New York: W. W. Norton.

_____, and Randy Gerson (1985). *Genograms in Family Assessment.* New York: W. W. Norton.

_____, and Joe Giordano (1996). "Overview: Ethnicity and Family Therapy." In *Ethnicity and Family Therapy.* eds. Monica McGoldrick, et al. New York: Guilford Press, pp. 1–27.

_____, and Nydia Garcia Preto (September 1984). "Ethnic Intermarriage: Implications for Therapy." *Family Process* 23, pp. 347–64.

McInnis-Dittrich, Kathleen (March 1996). "Adapting Life-Review Therapy for Elderly Female Survivors of Childhood Sexual Abuse." *Families in Society* 77, pp. 166–73.

———— (September 1996). "Violence Prevention: An Ecological Adaptation of Systemic Training for Effective Parenting." *Families in Society* 77, pp. 414–22.

McIntyre, Eilene L. G. (November–December 1986). "Social Networks: Potential for Practice." *Social Work* 31, pp. 421–26.

McMillen, J. Curtis (Summer 1992). "Attachment Theory and Clinical Social Work." *Clinical Social Work Journal* 20, pp. 205–18.

————, and Gregory B. Rideout (September 1996). "Breaking Intergenerational Cycles: Theoretical Tools for Social Workers." *Social Service Review* 70, pp. 378–99.

McNew, Judith, and Neil Abell (January 1995). "Posttraumatic Stress Symptomatology: Similarities and Differences between Vietnam Veterans and Adult Survivors of Childhood Sexual Abuse." *Social Work* 40, pp. 115–26.

McPhatter, Anna R. (January 1991). "Assessment Revisited: A Comprehensive Approach to Understanding Family Dynamics." *Families in Society* 72, pp. 11–20.

McQuaide, Sharon (September–October 1998). "Discontent at Midlife: Issues and Considerations in Working toward Women's Well Being." *Families in Society* 79, pp. 532–41.

————, and John H. Ehrenreich (March–April 1997). "Assessing Client Strengths." *Families in Society* 78, pp 201–12.

Mead, Margaret (1935). *Sex and Temperament in Three Primitive Societies*. New York: Morrow.

———— (1949). *Male and Female: A Study of the Sexes in a Changing World*. New York: Morrow.

Meezan, William, and Maura O'Keefe (January–February 1998). "Multifamily Group Therapy: Impact on Family Functioning and Child Behavior." *Families in Society* 79, pp. 32–44.

Meier, Elizabeth G. (July 1959). "Social and Cultural Factors in Casework Diagnosis." *Social Casework* 40, pp. 15–26.

Meissner, William W. (1985). "Theories of Personality and Psychopathology: Classical Psychoanalysis." In *Comprehensive Textbook of Psychiatry*. 4th ed. eds. Harold I. Kaplan and Benjamin J. Sadock. Baltimore, MD: Williams and Wilkens, pp. 337–418.

Mennen, Ferol, and Diane Meadow (February 1994). "Depression, Anxiety, and Self-Esteem in Sexually Abused Children." *Families in Society* 75, pp. 74–81.

————, and Lynn Perlmutter (February 1993). "Detecting Childhood Sexual Abuse in Couples Therapy." *Families in Society* 74, pp. 74–83.

Meyer, Carol H. (June 1996). "My Son the Scientist." *Social Work Research* 20, pp. 101–4.

Meyer, William S. (September 1993). "In Defense of Long-Term Treatment: On the Vanishing Holding Environment." *Social Work* 38, pp. 571–78.

Middleman, Ruth R., and Gale Goldberg Wood (March 1991). "Communicating by Doing." *Families in Society* 72, pp. 153–56.

Miller, Roger R. (Spring 1977). "Disappointment in Therapy." *Clinical Social Work Journal* 5, pp. 17–28.

Millon, Theodore (1996). *Disorders of Personality: DSM-IV and Beyond*. New York: John Wiley & Sons.

Milman, Donald S., and George D. Goldman, eds. (1987). *Techniques of Working with Resistance*. Northvale, NJ: Jason Aronson.

Milne, Ann L. (1986). "Divorce Mediation: A Process of Self-Definition and Self-Determination." In *Clinical Handbook of Marital Therapy*. eds. Neil S. Jacobson and Alan S. Gurman. New York: Guilford Press, pp. 197–216.

Minuchin, Patricia, Jorge Colapinto, and Salvador Minuchin (1998). *Working with Families of the Poor*. New York: Guilford Press.

Minuchin, Salvador (1974). *Families and Family Therapy*. Cambridge, MA: Harvard University Press.

————, et al. (1967). *Families of the Slums*. New York: Basic Books.

————, et al. (1978). *Psychosomatic Families: Anorexia Nervosa in Context*. Cambridge, MA: Harvard University Press.

_____, and H. Charles Fishman (1981). *Family Therapy Techniques*. Cambridge, MA: Harvard University Press.

Mirkin, Marsha Pravder, ed. (1985). *Handbook of Adolescents and Family Therapy*. New York: Gardner Press.

Mirowsky, John, and Catherine E. Ross (1989). *Social Causes of Psychological Distress*. New York: Aldine de Gruyter.

Mishne, Judith Marks (1986). *Clinical Work with Adolescents*. New York: Free Press.

_____ (1983). *Clinical Work with Children*. New York: Free Press.

_____ (Summer 1996). "Therapeutic Challenges in Clinical Work with Adolescents." *Clinical Social Work Journal* 24, pp. 137–52.

Mitchell, Celia (1968). "The Therapeutic Field in the Treatment of Families in Conflict: Recurrent Themes in Literature and Clinical Practice." In *New Directions in Mental Health.* ed. Bernard Reiss. New York: Grune & Stratton.

Mokuau, Noreen (December 1990). "A Family-Centered Approach in Native Hawaiian Culture." *Families in Society* 71, pp. 607–13.

_____, and Colette Browne (January 1994). "Life Themes of Native Hawaiian Female Elders: Resources for Cultural Preservation." *Social Work* 39, pp. 43–49.

Montalvo, Frank (Summer 1982). "The Third Dimension in Social Casework: Mary E. Richmond's Contribution to Family Treatment." *Clinical Social Work Journal* 10, pp. 103–12.

Montgomery, Mitzie I. R. (1973). "Feedback Systems, Interaction Analysis and Counseling Models in Professional Programs." Doctoral dissertation. University of Edinburgh.

Moore, Stephen (September 1992). "Case Management and the Integration of Services: How Service Delivery Systems Shape Case Management." *Social Work* 37, pp. 418–23.

Moore-Kirkland, Janet (1981). "Mobilizing Motivation: From Theory to Practice." In *Promoting Competence in Clients: A New / Old Approach to Social Work Practice*. ed. Anthony N. Maluccio. New York: Macmillan, pp. 27–54.

Morawetz, Anita, and Gillian Walker (1984). *Brief Therapy with Single-Parent Families.* New York: Brunner/Mazel.

Morrison, Andrew P. (1989). *Shame: The Underside of Narcissism*. Hillsdale, NJ: Analytic Press.

Morrow, Diane F. (November 1993). "Social Work with Gay and Lesbian Adolescents." *Social Work* 38, pp. 655–60.

Moultrup, David (Summer 1981). "Towards an Integrated Model of Family Therapy." *Clinical Social Work Journal* 9, pp. 111–25.

Moynihan, Rosemary, et al. (June 1988). "AIDS and Terminal Illness." *Social Casework* 69, pp. 380–87.

Mudd, Emily (1951). *The Practice of Marriage Counselling*. New York: Association Press.

Mufson, Laura, et al. (1993). *Interpersonal Psychotherapy for Depressed Adolescents*. New York: Guilford Press.

Muir, Elisabeth, and Eyglo Thorlaksdottir (January 1994). "Psychotherapeutic Intervention with Mothers and Children in Day Care." *American Journal of Orthopsychiatry* 64, pp. 60–67.

Mullen, Edward J. (November 1968). "Casework Communication." *Social Casework* 49, pp. 546–51.

_____ (1968). "Casework Treatment Procedures as a Function of Client Diagnostic Variables." Doctoral dissertation. Columbia University School of Social Work, New York.

_____ (June 1969). "Difference in Worker Style in Casework." *Social Casework* 50, pp. 347–53.

_____ (April 1969). "The Relation between Diagnosis and Treatment in Casework." *Social Casework* 50, pp. 218–26.

Murray, Henry A. (1938). *Explorations in Personality*. New York: Oxford University Press.

Myers, Laura L., and Bruce A. Thyer (May 1997). "Should Social Work Clients Have the Right to Effective Treatment?" *Social Work* 42, pp. 288–98.

Nace, Edgar P. (1987). *The Treatment of Alcoholism*. New York: Brunner/Mazel.

Napier, Augustus Y., and Carl A. Whitaker (1978). *The Family Crucible*. New York: Harper & Row.

Nathan, Peter E. (March 1998). "Practice Guidelines: Not Yet Ideal." *American Psychologist* 53, pp. 290–99.

Nathanson, Donald L., ed. (1987). *The Many Faces of Shame*. New York: Guilford Press.

National Association of Social Workers (1996). *Code of Ethics.* Washington, DC.

Neidig, Peter H., et al. (April 1985). "Domestic Conflict Containment: A Spouse Abuse Treatment Program." *Social Casework* 66, pp. 195–204.

Nelsen, Judith C. (1980). *Communication Theory and Social Work Practice.* Chicago: University of Chicago Press.

_____ (December 1975c). "Dealing with Resistance in Social Work Practice." *Social Casework* 56, pp. 587–92.

_____ (1990). "Single-Case Research and Traditional Practice." In *Advances in Clinical Social Work Research.* eds. Lynn Videka-Sherman and William J. Reid. Washington, DC: NASW Press.

_____ (March 1975b). "Treatment Issues in Schizophrenia." *Social Casework* 56, pp. 145–51.

_____ (February 1975a). "Treatment Planning for Schizophrenia." *Social Casework* 56, pp. 67–73.

_____ (Spring 1995). "Varieties of Narcissistically Vulnerable Couples: Dynamics and Practice Implications." *Clinical Social Work Journal* 23, pp. 59–70.

Nelson, Judith Kay (Spring 1998). "The Meaning of Crying Based on Attachment Theory." *Clinical Social Work Journal* 26, pp. 9–22.

Nelson, Mardell (December 1991). "Empowerment of Incest Survivors: Speaking Out." *Families in Society* 72, pp. 618–24.

Newhill, Christina E. (April 1990). "The Role of Culture in the Development of Paranoid Symptomatology." *American Journal of Orthopsychiatry* 60, pp. 176–85.

Nieto, Daniel S. (November 1982). "Aiding the Single Father." *Social Work* 27, pp. 473–78.

Noonan, Maryellen (Summer 1998). "Understanding the 'Difficult' Patient from a Dual Perspective." *Clinical Social Work Journal* 26, pp. 129–41.

Norman, Jennie Sage (February 1980). "Short-Term Treatment with the Adolescent Client." *Social Casework* 61, pp. 74–82.

Norris-Shortle, Carole, et al. (November 1993). "Understanding Death and Grief for Children Three and Younger." *Social Work* 38, pp. 736–42.

Northen, Helen (1995). *Clinical Social Work: Knowledge and Skills.* 2nd ed. New York: Columbia University Press.

_____ (1976). "Psychosocial Practice in Small Groups." In *Theories of Social Work with Groups.* eds. Robert W. Roberts and Helen Northen. New York: Columbia University Press, pp. 116–52.

Nye, Catherine H. (Spring 1994). "Narrative Interaction and the Development of Client Autonomy in Clinical Practice." *Clinical Social Work Journal* 22, pp. 43–57.

_____ (Fall 1998). "Power and Authority in Clinical Practice: A Discourse Analysis Approach to Narrative Process." *Clinical Social Work Journal* 26, pp. 271–80.

Ochberg, Frank M., M.D., ed. (1988). *Post-Traumatic Therapy and Victims of Violence.* New York: Brunner/Mazel.

O'Connor, Gerald O. (February 1988). "Case Management: System and Practice." *Social Casework* 69, pp. 97–106.

Offer, Daniel, and Evert VanderStoep (1975). "Indications and Contraindications for Family Therapy." In *The Adolescent in Group and Family Therapy.* ed. Max Sugar. New York: Brunner/Mazel, pp. 145–60.

Oktay, Julianne S. (September 1992). "Burnout in Hospital Social Workers Who Work with AIDS Patients." *Social Work* 37, pp. 432–39.

Olmstead, Kathleen A. (July–August 1983). "The Influence of Minority Social Work Students on an Agency's Service Methods." *Social Work* 28, pp. 308–12.

Olson, Myrna R., and Judith A. Haynes (May 1993). "Successful Single Parents." *Families in Society* 74, pp. 259–67.

Oquendo, Maria A. (January 1995). "Differential Diagnosis of Ataque de Nerviosa." *American Journal of Orthopsychiatry* 65, pp. 60–65.

Orcutt, Ben Avis (1971). "Process Analysis in the First Phase of Treatment." In *Casework with Wives of Alcoholics.* eds. Pauline Cohen and Merton Krause. New York: Family Service Association of America, pp. 147–64.

Orlinsky, David E., et al. (1994). "Process and Outcome in Psychotherapy—Noch Einmal." In *Handbook of Psychotherapy and Behavior Change.* 4th ed. eds. Allen E. Bergin and Sol L. Garfield. New York: John Wiley & Sons, pp. 270–376.

Ornstein, Anna (Spring 1986) "Supportive Psychotherapy: A Contemporary View." *Clinical Social Work Journal* 14, pp. 14–30.

Ostbloom, Norman, and Sedahlia Jasper Crase (March 1980). "A Model for Conceptualizing Child Abuse Causation and Intervention." *Social Casework* 61, pp. 164–72.

Oxley, Genevieve B. (December 1977). "Involuntary Clients' Responses to a Treatment Experience." *Social Casework* 58, pp. 607–14.

Ozawa, Martha N., and Simon Wai-On Law (September 1993). "Earnings History of Social Workers: A Comparison of Other Professional Groups." *Social Work* 38, pp. 542–51.

Padgett, Deborah K. (July 1998). "Does the Glove Really Fit? Qualitative Research on Clinical Social Work Practice." *Social Work* 43, pp. 373–81.

Padilla, Yolanda (November 1997). "Immigrant Policy: Issues for Social Work Practice." *Social Work* 42, pp. 595–606.

Palumbo, Joseph (Winter 1983). "Borderline Conditions: A Perspective from Self Psychology." *Clinical Social Work Journal* 11, pp. 323–38.

_____ (Spring 1979). "Perceptual Deficits and Self-Esteem in Adolescence." *Clinical Social Work Journal* 7, pp. 34–61.

_____ (Spring 1982). "The Psychology of Self and the Termination of Treatment." *Clinical Social Work Journal* 10, pp. 15–27.

_____ (Summer 1987). "Spontaneous Self Disclosures in Psychotherapy." *Clinical Social Work Journal* 15, pp. 107–20.

_____ (Fall 1976). "Theories of Narcissism and the Practice of Clinical Social Work." *Clinical Social Work Journal* 4, pp. 147–61.

Papp, Peggy (1983). *The Process of Change.* New York: Guilford Press.

_____, and Evan Imber-Black (March 1996). "Family Themes: Transmission and Transformation." *Family Process* 35, pp. 5–20.

Parad, Howard J., ed. (1965). *Crisis Intervention.* New York: Family Service Association of America.

_____, ed. (1958). *Ego Psychology and Dynamic Casework.* New York: Family Service Association of America.

_____, and Roger R. Miller, eds. (1963). *Ego-Oriented Casework: Problems and Perspectives.* New York: Family Service Association of America.

Pardeck, John T. (April 1990). "Bibliotherapy with Abused Children." *Families in Society* 71, pp. 229–35.

Paré, David A. (March 1996). "Culture and Meaning: Expanding the Metaphorical Repertoire of Family Therapy." *Family Process* 35, pp. 21–42.

Parsons, Ruth J., and Enid O. Cox (March 1989). "Family Mediation in Elder Caregiving Decisions: An Empowerment Intervention." *Social Work* 34, pp. 122–26.

_____, et al. (September–October 1988). "Integrated Practice: A Framework for Problem Solving." *Social Work* 33, pp. 417–21.

Parsons, Talcott, and R. F. Bales (1955). *Family, Socialization, and the Interaction Process.* New York: Free Press.

Patten, Sylvia B., et al. (May 1989). "Posttraumatic Stress Disorder and the Treatment of Sexual Abuse." *Social Work* 34, pp. 197–203.

Patterson, Jo Ellen, et al. (1998). *Essential Skills in Family Therapy: From the First Interview to Termination.* New York: Guilford Press.

Pearlman, Margaret H., and Mildred G. Edwards (November 1982). "Enabling in the Eighties: The Client Advocacy Group." *Social Casework* 63, pp. 532–39.

Pearlmutter, Lynn (Winter 1996). "Using Culture and the Intersubjective Perspective as a Resource: A Case Study of an African-American Couple." *Clinical Social Work Journal* 24, pp. 389–401.

Peck, Judith Stern, et al. (September 1995). "Forming a Consortium: A Design for Interagency Collaboration in the Delivery of Service Following the Disclosure of Incest." *Family Process* 34, pp. 287–302.

Perlman, Helen Harris (1957). *Social Casework: A Problem-Solving Process.* Chicago: University of Chicago Press.

_____ (1968). *Persona: Social Role and Personality.* Chicago: University of Chicago Press.

_____ (1979). *Relationship: The Heart of Helping People.* Chicago: University of Chicago Press.

Phillips, David G. (Fall 1993). "Integration and Alternatives: Some Current Issues in Psychoanalytic Theory." *Clinical Social Work Journal* 21, pp. 247–56.

Piaget, Jean, and Susan Isaacs (1937). *Social Development in Young Children.* New York: Harcourt, Brace.

Pill, Cynthia J., and Judith L. Zabin (Summer 1997). "Lifelong Legacy of Maternal Loss: A Women's Group." *Clinical Social Work Journal* 25, pp. 179–95.

Pilsecker, Carleton (September 1994). "Starting Where the Client Is." *Families in Society* 75, pp. 447–52.

Pinderhughes, Elaine (March 1995). "Empowering Diverse Populations: Family Practice in the 21st Century." *Families in Society* 76, pp. 131–40.

_____ (1989). *Understanding Race, Ethnicity, and Power.* New York: Free Press.

Pittman, Frank S., III. (1977). "The Family That Hides Together." In *Family Therapy: Full Length Case Studies.* ed. Peggy Papp. New York: Gardner Press.

_____ (1987). *Turning Points: Treating Families in Transition and Crisis.* New York: W. W. Norton.

_____, and Kalman Flomenhaft (June 1970). "Treating the Doll's House Marriage." *Family Process* 9, pp. 143–55.

Polansky, Norman A., et al. (January 1985). "Loneliness and Isolation in Child Neglect." *Social Casework* 66, pp. 38–47.

Powell, William E. (April 1994). "The Relationship between Feelings of Alienation and Burnout in Social Work." *Families in Society* 75, pp. 229–34.

Pozatek, Ellie (July 1994). "The Problem of Certainty: Clinical Social Work in the Postmodern Era." *Social Work* 39, pp. 396–403.

Pray, Jackie E. (January 1991). "Respecting the Uniqueness of the Individual: Social Work Practice within a Reflective Model." *Social Work* 36, pp. 80–85.

Presley, John H. (December 1987). "The Clinical Dropout: A View from the Client's Perspective." *Social Casework* 68, pp. 603–8.

Prichard, Elizabeth R., et al., eds. (1977). *Social Work with the Dying Patient and the Family.* New York: Columbia University Press.

Proctor, Enola (September 1982). "Defining the Worker–Client Relationships." *Social Work* 27, pp. 430–35.

Prodie, Richard D., Betty L. Singer, and Marian Winterbottom (June 1967). "Integration of Research Findings and Casework Techniques." *Social Casework* 48, pp. 360–66.

Pugh, Robert L. (Winter 1986). "Encouraging Interactional Processes with Couples in Therapy." *Clinical Social Work Journal* 14, pp. 321–34.

Raines, James C. (Spring 1990). "Empathy in Clinical Social Work." *Clinical Social Work Journal* 18, pp. 57–72.

_____ (Winter 1996). "Self-Disclosure in Clinical Social Work." *Clinical Social Work Journal* 24, pp. 357–75.

Rains, Prue, et al. (May–June 1998). "Taking Responsibility: An Insider View of Teen Motherhood." *Families in Society* 79, pp. 308–19.

Ranan, Wendy, and Andrea Blodgett (January 1983). "Using Telephone Therapy for 'Unreachable' Clients." *Social Casework* 64, pp. 39–44.

Rank, Otto (1936). *Will Therapy.* New York: Knopf.

Rapaport, David (1951). *Organization and Pathology of Thought.* New York: Columbia University Press.

Rapoport, Lydia (1970). "Crisis Intervention as a Mode of Brief Treatment." In *Theories of Social Casework.* eds. Robert W. Roberts and Robert H. Nee. Chicago: University of Chicago Press, pp. 265–311.

Ratliff, Nancy (March 1988). "Stress and Burnout in the Helping Professions." *Social Casework* 69, pp. 147–54.

Rauch, Julia B., et al. (December 1991). "Screening for Affective Disorders." *Families in Society* 72, pp. 602–7.

Raw, Saul D. (January 1998). "Who Is to Define Effective Treatment for Social Work Clients?" *Social Work* 43, pp. 81–86.

Reamer, Frederick G. (1990). *Ethical Dilemmas in Social Service.* New York: Columbia University Press.

_____ (January–February 1997). "Managing Ethics under Managed Care." *Families in Society* 78, pp. 224–36.

Reid, William J. (June 1994). "The Empirical Practice Movement." *Social Service Review* 68, pp. 165–84.

_____ (June 1997). "Long-Term Trends in Clinical Social Work." *Social Service Review* 71, pp. 200–13.

_____ (1996). "Task-Centered Social Work." In *Social Work Treatment.* 4th ed. ed. Francis J. Turner. New York: Free Press, pp. 617–640.

_____ (1992). *Task Strategies: An Empirical Approach to Clinical Social Work.* New York: Columbia University Press.

_____, and Barbara Shapiro (June 1969). "Client Reaction to Advice." *Social Service Review* 43, pp. 165–73.

_____, and Ann W. Shyne (1969). *Brief and Extended Casework.* New York: Columbia University Press.

Reiner, Beatrice Simcox (January 1979). "The Feelings of Irrelevance: The Effects of a Nonsupportive Society." *Social Casework* 60, pp. 3–10.

Reiter, Laura (Spring 1995). "The Client's Affective Impact on the Therapist: Implications for Therapist Responsiveness." *Clinical Social Work Journal* 23, pp. 21–35.

Resnick, Gary, and Martha R. Burt (April 1996). "Youth at Risk: Definitions and Implications for Service Delivery." *American Journal of Orthopsychiatry* 66, pp. 172–88.

Reynolds, Bertha Capen (September 1934). "A Study of Responsibility in Social Case Work." *Smith College Studies in Social Work* 5.

Reynolds, Rosemary, and Elsie Siegle (December 1959). "A Study of Casework with Sado-Masochistic Marriage Partners." *Social Casework* 40, pp. 545–51.

Rhodes, Margaret L. (January 1992). "Social Work Challenges: The Boundaries of Ethics." *Families in Society* 73, pp. 40–47.

Rhodes, Sonya L. (March 1977). "Contract Negotiation in the Initial Stage of Casework Service." *Social Service Review* 51, pp. 125–40.

_____ (1995). "Extramarital Affairs." In *Differential Diagnosis and Treatment in Social Work.* 4th ed. ed. Francis J. Turner. New York: Free Press, pp. 854–61.

_____ (May 1979). "The Personality of the Worker: An Unexplored Dimension in Treatment." *Social Casework* 60, pp. 259–64.

Rice, Celia F. (1980). "Marital Treatment with Narcissistic Character Disorders." In *Psychotherapy and Training in Clinical Social Work.* ed. Judith Mishne. New York: Gardner Press, pp. 261–73.

Rice, David G., and Joy K. Rice (1986). "Separation and Divorce Therapy." In *Handbook of Marital Therapy.* eds. Neil S. Jacobson and Alan S. Gurman. New York: Guilford Press, pp. 279–99.

Rich, Philip (September 1980). "Differentiation of Self in the Therapist's Family of Origin." *Social Casework* 61, pp. 394–99.

Richmond, Mary E. (1899). *Friendly Visiting among the Poor: A Handbook for Charity Workers.* New York: Macmillan.

_____ (1930). *The Long View.* New York: Russell Sage Foundation.

_____ (1917). *Social Diagnosis.* New York: Russell Sage Foundation.

_____ (1922). *What Is Social Casework? An Introductory Description.* New York: Russell Sage Foundation.

Ripple, Lillian, Ernestina Alexander, and Bernice Polemis (1964). *Motivation, Capacity and Opportunity.* Chicago: University of Chicago Press.

Robbins, Susan P. (October 1995). "Working through the Muddy Waters of Recovered Memory." *Families in Society* 76, pp. 478–89.

Roberts, Albert R., ed. (1995). *Crisis Intervention and Time-Limited Cognitive Treatment.* Thousand Oaks, CA: Sage Publications.

Roberts, Robert W., and Robert H. Nee, eds. (1970). *Theories of Social Casework.* Chicago: University of Chicago Press.

Robinson, Bryan E. (1989). *Working with Children of Alcoholics: The Practitioner's Handbook.* Lexington, MA: D.C. Heath.

Robinson, Jeanne B. (July 1989). "Clinical Treatment of Black Families: Issues and Strategies." *Social Work* 34, pp. 323–29.

Robinson, Virginia (July 1921). "An Analysis of Processes in the Records of Family Case Working Agencies." *The Family* 2, pp. 101–6.

_____ (1930). *A Changing Psychology in Social Case Work.* Chapel Hill: University of North Carolina Press.

Rogers, Carl R. (1961). *On Becoming a Person: A Therapist's View of Psychotherapy.* Boston: Houghton Mifflin.

_____ (1967). "The Therapeutic Relationship: Recent Theory and Research." In *The Human Dialogue.* eds. Floyd Matson and Ashley Montagu. New York: Free Press, pp. 246–59.

Rogler, Lloyd H., et al. (June 1987). "What Do Culturally Sensitive Mental Health Services Mean?" *American Psychologist* 42, pp. 565–70.

Rooney, Ronald H. (March 1988). "Socialization Strategies for Involuntary Clients." *Social Casework* 69, pp. 131–40.

_____ (1992). *Strategies for Working with Involuntary Clients.* New York: Columbia University Press.

Rose, Susan J., and William Meezan (March–April 1996). "Variations in Perceptions of Child Neglect." *Child Welfare* 75, pp. 139–60.

Rosen, Aaron, and Shula Livne (March 1992). "Personal versus Environmental Emphases in Social Workers' Perceptions of Client Problems." *Social Service Review* 66, pp. 85–96.

Rosen, Elliott J. (1990). *Families Facing Death.* San Francisco: Jossey-Bass.

Rosenberg, Elinor B., and Fady Hajal (May 1985). "Stepsibling Relationships in Remarried Families." *Social Casework* 66, pp. 287–92.

Rosenbloom, Maria (April 1983). "Implications of the Holocaust for Social Work." *Social Casework* 64, pp. 205–13.

Roth, Frederick (April 1975). "A Practice Regimen for Diagnosis and Treatment of Child Abuse." *Child Welfare* 54, pp. 268–73.

Roth, Sallyann (1989). "Psychotherapy with Lesbian Couples: Individual Issues, Female Socialization, and the Social Context." In *Women in Families: A Framework for Family Therapy.* eds. Monica McGoldrick, et al. New York: W. W. Norton.

_____, and Blanca Cody Murphy (1986). "Therapeutic Work with Lesbian Clients: A Systemic Therapy View." In *Women and Family Therapy.* ed. Marianne Ault-Riche. Rockville, MD. Aspen, pp. 78–89.

Rothery, Michael A. (Fall 1980). "Contracts and Contracting." *Clinical Social Work Journal* 8, pp. 179–85.

Rowe, Crayton E., and David S. MacIsaac, eds. (1989). *Empathic Attunement: The "Technique" of Psychoanalytic Self Psychology.* Northvale, NJ: Jason Aronson.

Rubenstein, Elaine (April 1991). "An Overview of Adolescent Development, Behavior, and Clinical Intervention." *Families in Society* 72, pp. 220–25.

_____, et al. (March 1990). "Peer Counseling with Adolescent Mothers: A Pilot Program." *Families in Society* 71, pp. 136–41.

Rueveni, Uri (1979). *Networking Families in Crisis.* New York: Human Services Press.

Rumelhart, Marilyn Austin (January 1984). "When Understanding the Situation Is the Real Problem." *Social Casework* 65, pp. 27–33.

Ryan, Angela Shen (June 1985). "Cultural Factors in Casework with Chinese-Americans." *Social Casework* 66, pp. 333–40.

Ryan-Wenger, Nancy M. (April 1992). "A Taxonomy of Children's Coping Strategies: A Step toward Theory Development." *American Journal of Orthopsychiatry* 62, pp. 256–63.

Sable, Pat (May 1992). "Attachment, Loss of Spouse, and Disordered Mourning." *Families in Society* 73, pp. 266–73.

_____ (Fall 1992). "Attachment Theory: Application to Clinical Practice with Adults." *Clinical Social Work Journal* 20, pp. 271–83.

_____ (May 1995). "Pets, Attachment, and Well-Being across the Life Cycle." *Social Work* 40, pp. 334–41.

_____ (Winter 1994). "Separation Anxiety, Attachment and Agoraphobia." *Clinical Social Work Journal* 22, pp. 369–83.

Safyer, Andrew W. (March 1994). "The Impact of Inner-City Life on Adolescent Development: Implications for Social Work." *Smith College Studies in Social Work* 64, pp. 153–67.

Saghir, Marcel T., and Eli Robins (1980). "Clinical Aspects of Female Homosexuality." In *Homosexual Behavior.* ed. Judd Marmor. New York: Basic Books, pp. 280–295.

Sakai, Caroline E. (November 1991). "Group Intervention Strategies with Domestic Abusers." *Families in Society* 72, pp. 536–42.

Saleebey, Dennis (March 1992). "Biology's Challenge to Social Work: Embodying the Person-in-Environment Perspective." *Social Work* 37, pp. 112–18.

_____ (July 1994). "Culture, Theory, and Narrative: The Intersection of Meaning in Practice." *Social Work* 39, pp. 351–59.

_____ (1996). *A Strengths Perspective in Social Work Practice.* 2nd ed. White Plains, NY: Longman.

_____ (May 1996). "The Strengths Perspective in Social Work Practice: Extensions and Cautions." *Social Work* 41, pp. 296–305.

Sands, Roberta G. (Summer 1996). "The Elusiveness of Identity in Social Work Practice with Women: A Postmodern Feminist Perspective." *Clinical Social Work Journal* 24, pp. 167–86.

_____ (March–April 1988). "Sociolinguistic Analysis of a Mental Health Interview." *Social Work* 33, pp. 148–54.

Santa-Barbara, Jack, et al. (Winter 1979). "The McMaster Family Therapy Outcome Study: An Overview of Methods and Results." *International Journal of Family Therapy* 1, pp. 304–23.

Sanville, Jean (Summer 1982). "Partings and Impartings: Toward a Nonmedical Approach to Interruptions and Terminations." *Clinical Social Work Journal* 10, pp. 123–31.

Satir, Virginia (1983). *Conjoint Family Therapy.* 3rd. ed. Palo Alto, CA: Science and Behavior Books.

Saunders, Daniel G. (April 1992). "A Typology of Men Who Batter: Three Types Derived from Cluster Analysis." *American Journal of Orthopsychiatry* 62, pp. 264–75.

Schamess, Gerald (Winter 1981). "Boundary Issues in Countertransference: A Developmental Perspective." *Clinical Social Work Journal* 9, pp. 244–57.

Scharff, David E., and Jill Savage Scharff (1987). *Object Relations Family Therapy.* Northvale, NJ: Jason Aronson.

Scharff, Jill Savage, ed. (1989). *Foundations of Object Relations Family Therapy.* Northvale, NJ: Jason Aronson.

Scherz, Frances H. (April 1966). "Family Treatment Concepts." *Social Casework* 47, pp. 234–40.

_____ (1970). "Theory and Practice in Family Therapy." In *Theories of Social Casework.* eds. Robert W. Roberts and Robert H. Nee. Chicago: University of Chicago Press, pp. 219–64.

Schibuck, Margaret (April 1989). "Treating the Sibling Subsystem: An Adjunct of Divorce Therapy." *American Journal of Orthopsychiatry* 59, pp. 226–37.

Schlosberg, Shirley B., and Richard M. Kagan (January 1988). "Practice Strategies for Engaging Chronic Multiproblem Families." *Social Casework* 69, pp. 3–9.

Schulman, Gerda L. (March 1972). "Myths that Intrude on the Adaptation of the Stepfamily." *Social Casework* 53, pp. 131–39.

_____ (October 1973). "Treatment of Intergenerational Pathology." *Social Casework* 54, pp. 462–72.

Schwartz-Borden, Gwen (October 1986). "Grief Work: Prevention and Intervention." *Social Casework* 67, pp. 499–505.

Seabury, Brett (January 1980). "Communication Problems in Social Work Practice." *Social Work* 25, pp. 40–44.

_____ (January 1976). "The Contract: Uses, Abuses and Limitations." *Social Work* 21, pp. 16–21.

Segal, Uma A. (April 1991). "Cultural Variables in Asian Indian Families." *Families in Society* 72, pp. 233–41.

Seligman, Martin E. P. (December 1995). "The Effectiveness of Psychotherapy: The *Consumer Reports* Study." *American Psychologist* 50, pp. 965–74.

Senger-Dickinson, Mary M., and Cyrus S. Stewart (September 1987). "Caseworker Recognition of Marital Separation." *Social Casework* 68, pp. 394–99.

Sewell-Coker, Beverly, Joyce Hamilton-Collins, and Edith Fein (November 1985). "Social Work Practice with West Indian Immigrants." *Social Casework* 66, pp. 563–68.

Shapiro, Ester R. (September 1996). "Family Bereavement and Cultural Diversity: A Social Developmental Perspective." *Family Process* 35, pp. 313–32.

_____ (1994). *Grief as a Family Process: A Developmental Approach to Clinical Practice.* New York: Guilford Press.

Shapiro, Joan (Winter 1995). "The Downside of Managed Mental Health Care." *Clinical Social Work Journal* 23, pp. 441–51.

Shepard, Melanie (November 1997). "Site-Based Services for Residents of Single-Room Occupancy Hotels." *Social Work* 42, pp. 585–92.

Sheridan, Michael J., et al. (September 1993). "Developing a Practice Model for the Homeless Mentally Ill." *Families in Society* 74, pp. 410–21.

Sherman, Sanford N. (1979). "Family Therapy." In *Social Work Treatment.* 2nd ed. ed. Francis J. Turner. New York: Free Press.

———— (June 1966). "Family Treatment: An Approach to Children's Problems." *Social Casework* 47, pp. 368–72.

———— (April 1967). "Intergenerational Discontinuity and Therapy of the Family." *Social Casework* 48, pp. 216–21.

Shernoff, Michael J. (July–August 1984). "Family Therapy for Lesbian and Gay Clients." *Social Casework* 29, pp. 393–96.

Shor, Joel, and Jean Sanville (1979). *Illusion in Loving: Balancing Intimacy and Independence.* New York: Penguin Books.

Shulamith, Lala Ashenberg Straussner, and Betsy Robin Spiegel (Fall 1996). "An Analysis of 12-Step Programs for Substance Abusers from a Developmental Perspective." *Clinical Social Work Journal* 24, pp. 299–309.

Shulman, Lawrence (1992). *The Skills of Helping Individuals, Families, and Groups.* 3rd ed. Itasca, IL: F. E. Peacock Publishers.

Siebold, Cathy (November 1992). "Forced Termination: Reconsidering Theory and Technique." *Smith College Studies in Social Work* 63, pp. 325–41.

———— (Summer 1991). "Termination: When the Therapist Leaves." *Clinical Social Work Journal* 19, pp. 191–204.

Siegel, Karolynn, et al. (April 1990). "A Prevention Program for Bereaved Children." *American Journal of Orthopsychiatry* 60, pp. 168–75.

Sifneos, Peter E. (1987). *Short-Term Dynamic Psychotherapy: Evaluation and Technique.* 2nd ed. New York: Plenum.

Silverman, Phyllis R. (December 1970). "A Reexamination of the Intake Procedure." *Social Casework* 51, pp. 625–34.

Silvern, Louise, and Lynn Kaersvang (July–August 1989). "The Traumatized Children of Violent Marriages." *Child Welfare* 68, pp. 421–36.

Simon, Bernice K. (1970). "Social Casework Theory: An Overview." In *Theories of Social Casework.* eds. Robert W. Roberts and Robert H. Nee. Chicago: University of Chicago Press, pp. 353–94.

Singer, Dorothy (1993). *Playing for Their Lives: Helping Troubled Children through Play Therapy.* New York: Free Press.

Singh, Ram Naresh (December 1982). "Brief Interviews: Approaches, Techniques, and Effectiveness." *Social Casework* 63, pp. 599–606.

Siporin, Max (March 1988). "Clinical Social Work as an Art Form." *Social Casework* 69, pp. 177–85.

———— (January 1980). "Marriage and Family Therapy in Social Work." *Social Casework* 61, pp. 11–21.

———— (Fall 1993). "The Social Worker's Style." *Clinical Social Work Journal* 21, pp. 257–70.

———— (May–June 1983). "The Therapeutic Process in Clinical Social Work." *Social Work* 28, pp. 193–98.

Sirles, Elizabeth A. (June 1982). "Client–Counselor Agreement on Problem and Change." *Social Casework* 63, pp. 348–53.

Skolnick, Arlene S., and Jerome H. Skolnick, eds. (1977). *Family in Transition.* 2nd ed. Boston: Little, Brown.

Slater, Suzanne, and Julie Mencher (July 1991). "The Lesbian Family Life Cycle: A Contextual Approach." *American Journal of Orthopsychiatry* 61, pp. 372–82.

Slonim-Nevo, Vared (May–June 1997). "Evaluating Practice: The Dual Roles of Clinician and Evaluator." *Families in Society* 78, pp. 228–38.

Smaldino, Angelo (July 1975). "The Importance of Hope in the Casework Relationship." *Social Casework* 56, pp. 328–33.

Smallen, Joanne M. (July 1995). "Social Timing, Life Continuity, and Life Coherence: Implications for Vocational Change." *Social Work* 40, pp. 533–41.

Smalley, Ruth E. (1970). "The Functional Approach to Casework Process." In *Theories of Social Casework*. eds. Robert E. Roberts and Robert H. Nee. Chicago: University of Chicago Press, pp. 79–128.

Smith, Audrey D. (May 1980). "Egalitarian Marriage: Implications for Practice and Policy." *Social Casework* 61, pp. 288–95.

———, and William J. Reid (September 1986). "Role Expectations and Attitudes in Dual-Earner Families." *Social Casework* 67, pp. 394–402.

Smith, Mary Lee, and Gene V. Glass (September 1977). "Meta-Analysis of Psychotherapy Outcome Studies." *American Psychologist,* pp. 752–60.

Smith, Priscilla (September–October 1998). "How Do We Understand Practice? A Qualitative Approach." *Families in Society* 79, pp. 543–50.

Smyth, Nancy J. (December 1996). "Motivating Persons with Dual Disorders." *Families in Society* 77, pp. 605–14.

Solomon, Marion F. (Summer 1985). "Treatment of Narcissistic and Borderline Disorders in Marital Therapy: Suggestions toward an Enhanced Therapeutic Approach." *Clinical Social Work Journal* 13, pp. 141–56.

———, and Judith P. Siegel, eds. (1997). *Countertransference in Couples Therapy.* New York: W. W. Norton.

Sosin, Michael R. (June 1987). "Delivering Services under Permanency Planning." *Social Service Review* 61, pp. 272–90.

———, and Sharon Caulum (January–February 1983). "Advocacy: A Conceptualization for Social Work Practice." *Social Work* 28, pp. 12–17.

Spalding, Elaine C. (Summer 1997). "Three Object Relations Models of Couples Treatment." *Clinical Social Work Journal* 25, pp. 137–61.

Specht, Harry, and Mark Courtney (1994). *Unfaithful Angels: How Social Work Has Abandoned Its Mission.* New York: Free Press.

———, and Riva Specht (November 1986). "Social Work Assessment: Route to Clienthood." *Social Casework* 67, pp. 525–32.

———, and John P. Spiegel (1968). "The Resolution of Role Conflict within the Family." In *Modern Introduction to the Family.* eds. Norman W. Bell and Ezra F. Vogel. New York: Free Press, pp. 391–411.

Spitz, Rene A. (1946). "Anaclitic Depression." *Psychoanalytic Study of the Child.* Vol. 2. New York: International Universities Press, pp. 313–42.

Sprung, Gloria M. (December 1989). "Transferential Issues in Working with Older Adults." *Social Casework* 70, pp. 597–602.

Stafford, Florence (January–February 1988). "Value of Gerontology for Occupational Social Work." *Social Work* 33, pp. 42–45.

Stamm, Isabel (1959). "Ego Psychology in the Emerging Theoretical Base of Casework." In *Issues in American Social Work.* ed. Alfred J. Kahn. New York: Columbia University Press, pp. 80–109.

Stanton, Greta W. (May–June 1986). "Preventive Intervention with Stepfamilies." *Social Work* 31, pp. 201–6.

Startz, Morton R., and Helen F. Cohen (September 1980). "The Impact of Social Change on the Practitioner." *Social Casework* 61, pp. 400–6.

———, and Claire W. Evans (June 1981). "Developmental Phases of Marriage and Marital Therapy." *Social Casework* 62, pp. 343–51.

Stevens, Ellen S. (November 1992). "Reciprocity in Social Support: An Advantage for the Aging Family." *Families in Society* 73, pp. 533–41.

Stierlin, Helm (1975). "Countertransference in Family Therapy with Adolescents." In *The Adolescent in Group and Family Therapy.* ed. Max Sugar. New York: Brunner/Mazel, pp. 161–77.

——— (June 1973). "Group Fantasies and Family Myths." *Family Process* 12, pp. 111–25.

———, et al. (1980). *The First Interview with the Family.* New York: Brunner/Mazel.

Stocks, J. T. (September 1998). "Recovered Memory Therapy: A Dubious Practice Technique." *Social Work* 43, pp. 423–36.

Stone, Andrew M. (January 1992). "The Role of Shame in Post-Traumatic Stress Disorder." *American Journal of Orthopsychiatry* 62, pp. 131–36.

Streepy, Joan (June 1981). "Direct-Service Providers and Burnout." *Social Casework* 62, pp. 352–61.

Streier, Dorit Roer (September 1996). "Coping Strategies of Immigrant Parents: Directions for Family Therapy." *Family Process* 35, pp. 363–76.

Strickland, Lee (Spring 1994). "Autobiographical Interviewing and Narrative Analysis: An Approach to Psychosocial Assessment." *Clinical Social Work Journal* 22, pp. 27–41.

Strom, Kimberly (October 1994). "Clinicians' Reasons for Rejecting Private Practice." *Families in Society* 75, pp. 499–508.

_____ (September 1992). "Reimbursement Demands and Treatment Decisions: A Growing Dilemma for Social Work." *Social Work* 37, pp. 398–402.

Strom-Gottfried, Kim (May–June 1998). "Is 'Ethical Managed Care' an Oxymoron?" *Families in Society* 79, pp. 297–307.

Stuart, Richard B. (1980). *Helping Couples Change.* New York: Guilford Press.

Sue, Stanley, et al. (1994). "Research on Psychotherapy with Culturally Diverse Populations." In *Handbook of Psychotherapy and Behavior Change.* 4th ed. eds. Allen E. Bergin and Sol L. Garfield. New York: John Wiley & Sons, pp. 783–817.

Sullivan, William Patrick, et al. (April 1992). "Case Management in Alcohol and Drug Treatment: Improving Client Outcomes." *Families in Society* 73, pp. 195–203.

Sunley, Robert (June 1970). "Family Advocacy from Case to Cause." *Social Casework* 51, pp. 347–57.

Super, Stacia I. (Summer 1982). "Successful Transition: Therapeutic Interventions with the Transferred Client." *Clinical Social Work Journal* 10, pp. 113–22.

Sussal, Carol M. (Fall 1992). "Object Relations Family Therapy as a Model for Practice." *Clinical Social Work Journal* 20, pp. 313–21.

Swigonski, Mary E. (March 1996). "Challenging Privilege through Africentric Social Work Practice." *Social Work* 41, pp. 153–60.

Taft, Jessie (1937). "The Relation of Function to Process in Social Casework." *Journal of Social Work Process* 1, pp. 1–18.

Taibbi, Robert (April 1983). "Handling Extramarital Affairs in Clinical Treatment." *Social Casework* 64, pp. 200–4.

Tainey, Phyllis (1988). *Adult Children of Alcoholics: Workshop Models for Family Life Education.* Milwaukee, WI: Family Service America.

Taylor, John W. (September 1990). "Incest Scenarios and Object-Relations Strivings: A Conceptual Framework." *Families in Society* 71, pp. 422–28.

_____ (January 1984). "Structured Conjoint Therapy for Spouse Abuse Cases." *Social Casework* 65, pp. 11–18.

Taylor, Robert Joseph, et al. (May 1989). "Evaluation by Black Americans of the Social Service Encounter during a Serious Personal Problem." *Social Work* 34, pp. 205–11.

Taylor, Ronald L. (April 1984). "Marital Therapy in the Treatment of Incest." *Social Casework* 65, pp. 195–202.

Taynor, Janet, et al. (April 1990). "The Family Intervention Scale: Assessing Treatment Outcome." *Families in Society* 71, pp. 202–10.

Teitelbaum, Sylvia (Fall 1991). "Countertransference and Its Potential for Abuse." *Clinical Social Work Journal* 19, pp. 267–77.

Temple, Scott (June 1997). "Treating Inner-City Families of Homicide Victims: A Contextually Oriented Approach." *Family Process* 36, pp. 133–49.

Terman, Lewis N. (1938). *Psychological Factors in Marital Happiness.* New York: McGraw-Hill.

Teyber, Edward (1992). *Helping Children Cope with Divorce.* New York: Lexington Books.

Thomlison, Ray J. (January–February 1984). "Something Works: Evidence from Practice Effectiveness Studies." *Social Work* 29, pp. 51–56.

Thrasher, Shirley, and Gary Anderson (March 1988). "The West Indian Family: Treatment Challenges." *Social Casework* 69, pp. 171–76.

Titelman, Peter, ed. (1987). *The Therapist's Own Family: Toward the Differentiation of Self.* Northvale, NJ: Jason Aronson.

Toseland, Ronald W. (April 1987). "Treatment Discontinuance." *Social Casework* 68, pp. 195–204.

Tower, Kristine D. (March 1994). "Consumer-Centered Social Work Practice: Restoring Client Self-Determination." *Social Work* 39, pp. 191–96.

Tracy, Elizabeth M., and James K. Whittaker (October 1990). "The Social Network Map: Assessing Social Support in Clinical Practice." *Families in Society* 71, pp. 461–70.

Truax, Charles B., and Robert R. Carkuff (1967). *Toward Effective Counseling and Psychotherapy: Training and Practice.* Chicago: Aldine.

Tung, May (April 1991). "Insight-Oriented Psychotherapy and the Chinese Patient." *American Journal of Orthopsychiatry* 61, pp. 186–94.

Turner, Francis J., ed. (1999). *Adult Psychopathology II.* New York: Free Press.

———— (May 1964). "A Comparison of Procedures in the Treatment of Clients with Two Different Value Orientations." *Social Casework* 45, pp. 273–77.

————, ed. (1995). *Differential Diagnosis and Treatment in Social Work.* 4th ed. New York: Free Press.

———— (March 1970). "Ethnic Difference and Client Performance." *Social Service Review* 44, pp. 1–10.

———— (1996). "An Interlocking Perspective for Treatment." In *Social Work Treatment: Interlocking Theoretical Approaches.* 4th ed. ed. Francis J. Turner. New York: Free Press, pp. 699–711.

———— (March 1994). "Reconsidering Diagnosis." *Families in Society* 75, pp. 168–71.

———— (1963). "Social Work Treatment and Value Differences." Doctoral dissertation. Columbia University School of Social Work, New York.

————, ed. (1996). *Social Work Treatment: Interlocking Theoretical Approaches.* 4th ed. New York: Free Press.

Unger, Michael T., and Judith E. Levene (Fall 1994). "Selfobject Functions of the Family: Implications for Family Therapy." *Clinical Social Work Journal* 22, pp. 303–16.

Valliant, George (1977). *Adaptation to Life.* New York: Little, Brown.

Van Lawick-Goodall, Jane (1971). *In the Shadow of Man.* Boston: Houghton-Mifflin.

Van Voorhis, Rebecca, and Linda McClain (November–December 1997). "Accepting a Lesbian Mother." *Families in Society* 78, pp. 642–50.

Videka-Sherman, Lynn (July–August 1988). "Metaanalysis of Research on Social Work Practice in Mental Health." *Social Work* 33, pp. 325–38.

Vigilante, Florence Wexler (May 1982). "Use of Work in the Assessment and Intervention Process." *Social Casework* 63, pp. 296–300.

————, and Mildred D. Mailick (March–April 1988). "Needs-Resource Evaluation in the Assessment Process." *Social Work* 33, pp. 101–4.

Vincentia, Sister M., and Sister Ann Patrick Conrad (September 1980). "A Parish Neighborhood Model for Social Work Practice." *Social Casework* 61, pp. 423–32.

Vinokur-Kaplan, Diane (June 1987). "A National Survey of In-Service Training Experiences of Child Welfare Supervisors and Workers." *Social Service Review* 61, pp. 291–304.

Visher, Emily B., and John S. Visher (1988). *Old Loyalties, New Ties: Therapeutic Strategies with Stepfamilies.* New York: Brunner/Mazel.

Vogel, Ezra F., and Norman W. Bell (1968). "The Emotionally Disturbed Child as the Family Scapegoat." In *Modern Introduction to the Family.* eds. Bell and Vogel. New York: Free Press, pp. 412–27.

Vosler, Nancy R. (1995). "Assessing Family Access to Basic Resources: An Essential Component of Social Work Practice." In *Differential Diagnosis and Treatment in Social Work.* 4th ed. ed. Francis J. Turner. New York: Free Press, pp. 1272–84.

Vourlekis, Betsy S., and Roberta R. Greene, eds. (1992). *Social Work Case Management.* Hawthorne, NY: Aldine de Gruyter.

Wachtel, Paul L. (1993). *Therapeutic Communication.* New York: Guilford Press.

Wade, Jay C. (November 1994). "African American Fathers and Sons: Social, Historical, and Psychological Considerations." *Families in Society* 75, pp. 561–70.

Wakefield, Jerome C., and Stuart A. Kirk (June 1996). "Unscientific Thinking about Scientific Practice: Evaluating the Scientist-Practitioner Model." *Social Work Research* 20, pp. 83–95.

Wald, Esther (1981). *The Remarried Family: Challenge and Promise.* New York: Family Service Association of America.

Wallace, Marquis Earl (July 1979). "A Focal Conflict Model of Marital Disorders." *Social Casework* 60, pp. 423–29.

Waller, Willard (1930). *The Old Love and the New.* New York: Liveright.

Wallerstein, Judith S. (October 1994). "The Early Psychological Tasks of Marriage: Part I." *American Journal of Orthopsychiatry* 64, pp. 640–50.

Walsh, M. Ellen (October 1981). "Rural Social Work Practice: Clinical Quality." *Social Casework* 62, pp. 458–64.

Walsh, Froma (1998). "Beliefs, Spirituality, and Transcendence." In *Re-visioning Family Therapy.* ed. Monica McGoldrick. New York: Guilford Press, pp. 62–77.

_____ (September 1996). "The Concept of Family Resilience: Crisis and Challenge." *Family Process* 35, pp. 261–81.

_____ (1997). "Family Therapy." In *Theory and Practice in Clinical Social Work.* ed. Jerrold R. Brandell. New York: Free Press, pp. 132–63.

_____, ed. (1993). *Normal Family Processes.* 2nd ed. New York: Guilford Press.

_____, and Carol Anderson (1988). *Chronic Disorders of the Family.* New York: Haworth.

_____, and Monica McGoldrick, eds. (1991). *Living beyond Loss: Death in the Family.* New York: W. W. Norton.

Walsh, Joseph A. (May 1987). "Burnout and Values in the Social Service Profession." *Social Casework* 68, pp. 279–83.

_____ (Spring 1995). "Clinical Relatedness with Persons Having Schizophrenia: A Symbolic Interactionist Perspective." *Clinical Social Work Journal* 23, pp. 71–85.

_____ (February 1989). "Engaging the Family of the Schizophrenic Client." *Social Casework* 70, pp. 106–13.

_____ (1999). "Schizophrenic Disorders." In *Adult Psychopathology II.* ed. Francis J. Turner. New York: Free Press.

_____ (March–April 1988). "Social Workers as Family Educators about Schizophrenia." *Social Work* 33, pp. 138–41.

Walters, Marianne, Betty Carter, Peggy Papp, and Olga Silverstein (1988). *The Invisible Web: Gender Patterns in Family Relationships.* New York: Guilford Press.

Warmbrod, Mary (June 1986). "Counseling Bereaved Children: Stages in the Process." *Social Casework* 67, pp. 351–58.

Warren, Carol (1980). "Homosexuality and Stigma." In *Homosexual Behavior.* ed. Judd Marmor. New York: Basic Books, pp. 123–41.

Wartel, Steven G. (March 1991). "Clinical Considerations for Adults Abused as Children." *Families in Society* 72, pp. 157–63.

Watkins, Sallie A. (March 1989). "Confidentiality and Privileged Communications: Legal Dilemma for Family Therapists." *Social Work* 34, pp. 133–36.

Watzlawick, Paul (1978). *The Language of Change: Elements of Therapeutic Communication.* New York: Basic Books.

_____, Janet Beaven, and Don D. Jackson (1967). *Pragmatics of Human Communication: A Study of Interactional Patterns, Pathologies and Paradoxes.* New York: W. W. Norton.

Weaver, Donna R. (February 1982). "Empowering Treatment Skills for Helping Black Families." *Social Casework* 63, pp. 100–5.

Webb, Nancy Boyd (October 1981). "Crisis Consultation: Preventive Implications." *Social Casework* 62, pp. 465–71.

_____ (Winter 1985). "A Crisis Intervention Perspective on the Termination Process." *Clinical Social Work Journal* 13, pp. 329–40.

_____, ed. (1991). *Play Therapy with Children in Crisis.* New York: Guilford Press.

Wechter, Sharon L. (February 1983). "Separation Difficulties between Parents and Young Adults." *Social Casework* 64, pp. 97–104.

Weeks, Gerald R., and Luciano L'Abate (1982). *Paradoxical Psychotherapy: Theory and Practice with Individuals, Couples, and Families.* New York: Brunner/Mazel.

Wegscheider, Sharon (1981). *Another Chance: Hope and Health for the Alcoholic Family.* Palo Alto, CA: Science and Behavior Books.

Weick, Ann (November 1986). "The Philosophical Context of a Health Model of Social Work." *Social Casework* 67, pp. 551–59.

_____, et al. (July 1989). "A Strengths Perspective for Social Work Practice." *Social Work* 34, pp. 350–54.

_____, and Loren Pope (January 1988). "Knowing What's Best: A New Look at Self Determination." *Social Casework* 69, pp. 10–16.

_____, and Dennis Saleebey (March 1995). "Supporting Family Strengths: Orienting Policy and Practice Toward the 21st Century." *Families in Society* 76, pp. 141–49.

Weidman, Arthur (April 1986). "Therapy with Violent Couples." *Social Casework* 67, pp. 211–18.

Weingarten, Helen R. (May–June 1986). "Strategic Planning for Divorce Mediation." *Social Work* 31, pp. 194–200.

Weingarten, Kathy (Spring 1998). "The Small and the Ordinary: The Daily Practice of a Postmodern Narrative Therapy." *Family Process* 37, pp. 3–15.

_____, and Sara Cobb (September 1995). "Timing Disclosure Sessions: Adding a Narrative Perspective to Clinical Work with Adult Survivors of Childhood Sexual Abuse." *Family Process* 34, pp. 257–69.

Weisberger, Eleanor B. (February 1967). "The Current Usefulness of Psychoanalytic Theory to Casework." *Smith College Studies in Social Work* 37, pp. 106–18.

Weissman, Myrna M., and Eugene S. Paykel (1974). *The Depressed Woman.* Chicago: University of Chicago Press.

Weitzman, Jack (December 1985). "Engaging the Severely Dysfunctional Family in Treatment: Basic Considerations." *Family Process* 24, pp. 473–85.

_____, and Karen Dreen (May 1982). "Wife Beating: A View of the Marital Dyad." *Social Casework* 63, pp. 259–65.

Wells, Richard A. (1994). *Planned Short-Term Treatment.* 2nd ed. New York: Free Press.

_____, and Alan E. Dezen (September 1978). "The Results of Family Therapy Revisited: The Nonbehavioral Methods." *Family Process* 17, pp. 251–74.

_____, and Vincent J. Giannetti (1990). *Handbook of the Brief Psychotherapies.* New York: Plenum Press.

_____, and _____ (March 1986). "Individual Marital Therapy: A Critical Reappraisal." *Family Process* 25, pp. 42–65.

Wertheim, Eleanor S. (September 1975). "Family Unit Therapy and the Science and Typology of Family Systems II." *Family Process* 14, pp. 285–309.

Wetzel, Janice Wood (1984). *Clinical Handbook of Depression.* New York: Gardner Press.

_____ (April 1980). "Interventions with the Depressed Elderly in Institutions." *Social Casework* 61, pp. 234–39.

Whitaker, Carl A., et al. (1965). "Countertransference in the Family Treatment of Schizophrenia." In *Intensive Family Therapy.* eds. Ivan Boszormenyi-Nagy and James L. Framo. New York: Harper & Row, pp. 323–41.

White, Robert W. (1963). *Ego and Reality and Psychoanalytic Theory.* New York: International Universities Press.

Whittaker, James K., and James Gargarino, eds. (1983). *Social Support Networks: Informal Helping in the Human Services.* Hawthorne, NY: Aldine Publishing.

_____, et al. (December 1986). "The Ecological Paradigm in Child, Youth, and Family Services: Implications for Policy and Practice." *Social Service Review* 60, pp. 483–503.

Williams, Betty L. (January 1994). "Essay: Reflections on Family Poverty." *Families in Society* 75, pp. 47–50.

Williams, Edith Ellison, and Florence Ellison (March 1996). "Culturally Informed Social Work Practice with American Indian Clients: Guidelines for Non-Indian Social Workers." *Social Work* 41, pp. 147–51.

Williams, Janet B. W. (March 1981). "DSM-III: A Comprehensive Approach to Diagnosis." *Social Work* 26, pp. 101–6.

Williams, Oliver J. (December 1992). "Ethnically Sensitive Practice to Enhance Treatment Participation of African American Men Who Batter." *Families in Society* 73, pp. 588–95.

Willinger, Barbara Halin (1997). "Psychopharmacology and Clinical Social Work Practice." In *Theory and Practice in Clinical Social Work*. ed. Jerrold R. Brandell. New York: Free Press, pp. 423–41.

Wilson, Suana J. (1978). *Confidentiality in Social Work: Issues and Principles*. New York: Free Press.

Winnicott, Donald W. (1958). *Collected Papers*. London: Tavistock.

———— (1986a). *Home Is Where We Start From*. New York: W. W. Norton.

———— (1986b). "Transitional Objects and Transitional Phenomena: A Study of the First Not-Me Possession." In *Essential Papers on Object Relations*. ed. Peter Buckley. New York: New York University Press.

Witkin, Stanley L. (September 1998b). "Mirror, Mirror on the Wall: Creative Tensions, the Academy, and the Field." *Social Work* 43, pp. 389–91.

———— (January 1998a). "The Right to Effective Treatment and the Effective Treatment of Rights: Rhetorical Empiricism and the Politics of Research." *Social Work* 43, pp 75–80.

Witmer, Helen Leland (1942). *Social Work*. New York: Rinehart.

Wolberg, Lewis (1980). *Handbook of Short-Term Psychotherapy*. New York: Thieme-Stratton.

Wolinsky, Mary Ann (October 1986). "Marital Therapy with Older Couples." *Social Casework*, pp. 475–83.

Wood, Katharine M. (November 1978). "Casework Effectiveness: A New Look at the Research Evidence." *Social Work* 23, pp. 437–58.

———— (1971). "The Contribution of Psychoanalysis and Ego Psychology to Social Casework." In *Social Casework*. ed. Herbert S. Strean. Metuchen, NJ: Scarecrow Press.

Woodroofe, Kathleen (1962). *From Charity to Social Work in England and in the United States*. Toronto: University of Toronto Press.

Woods, Leonard J. (May–June 1988). "Home-Based Family Therapy." *Social Work* 33, pp. 211–14.

Woods, Mary E. (1982). "Childhood Phobia and Family Therapy: A Case Illustration." In *Clinical Social Workers as Psychotherapists*. ed. Florence Lieberman. New York: Gardner, pp. 165–78.

———— (1983). "The Implications of Psychosocial Practice for Clinical Social Work Education." In *Education for Clinical Social Work Practice, Continuity and Change*. ed. Louise S. Bandler. New York: Pergamon Press, pp. 55–75.

———— (1999). "Personality Disorders." In *Adult Psychopathology II*. ed. Francis J. Turner. New York: Free Press, pp. 517–84.

————, and Howard Robinson (1996). "Psychosocial Theory and Social Work Treatment." In *Social Work Treatment: Interlocking Theoretical Approaches*. 4th ed. ed. Francis J. Turner. New York: Free Press, pp. 555–80.

Wright, Otha L., and Joseph P. Anderson (March–April 1998). "Clinical Social Work Practice with Urban African American Families. *Families in Society* 79, pp. 197–205.

Wynne, Lyman C. (1965). "Some Indications and Contraindications for Exploratory Family Therapy." In *Intensive Family Therapy*. eds. Ivan Boszormenyi-Nagy and James L. Framo. New York: Basic Books, pp. 289–322.

————, et al. (1968). "Pseudomutuality in the Family Relations of Schizophrenics." In *A Modern Introduction to the Family*. eds. Norman W. Bell and Ezra F. Vogel. New York: Free Press, pp. 628–49.

Yalom, Irving D. (1985). *The Theory and Practice of Group Psychotherapy*. New York: Basic Books.

Yamashiro, Greg, and Jon K. Matsuoka (March 1997). "Help-Seeking among Asian and Pacific Americans: A Multiperspective Analysis." *Social Work* 42, pp. 176–86.

Yang, Alan S. (1997). "Attitudes Toward Homosexuality." *Public Opinion Quarterly* 61, pp. 477–507.

Yapko, Michael D. (1994). *Suggestions of Abuse: True and False Memories of Childhood Sexual Trauma*. New York: Simon & Schuster.

Young, Leontine R. (1964). *Wednesday's Children: A Study of Child Neglect and Abuse*. New York: McGraw-Hill.

Young-Eisendrath, Pauline (June 1982). "Ego Development: Inferring the Client's

Frame of Reference." *Social Casework* 63, pp. 323–32.

Young, Thomas M. (June 1994). "Environmental Modification in Clinical Social Work: A Self-Psychological Perspective." *Social Service Review* 68, pp. 202–18.

Zayas, Luis H. (June 1995). "Family Functioning and Child Rearing in an Urban Environment." *Developmental and Behavioral Pediatrics* 16, pp. S21, S24.

———— (Fall 1994). "Hispanic Family Ecology and Early Childhood Socialization: Health Care Implications." *Family Systems Medicine* 12, pp. 315–25.

————, and Carl Bryant (Winter 1984). "Culturally Sensitive Treatment of Adolescent Puerto Rican Girls and Their Families." *Child and Adolescent Social Work Journal* 1, pp. 235–53.

————, and Nancy A. Busch-Rossnagel (November 1992). "Pregnant Hispanic Women: A Mental Health Study." *Families in Society* 73, pp. 515–21.

————, and Lawrence A. Dyche (1995). "Suicide Attempts in Puerto Rican Adolescent Females." In *Treatment Approaches with Suicidal Adolescents*. eds. J. K. Zimmerman and G. M. Asnis. New York: John Wiley & Sons.

————, and Michael Katch. (January 1989). "Contracting with Adolescents: An Ego-Psychological Approach." *Social Casework* 70, pp. 3–9.

————, and Josephine Palleja (July 1988). "Puerto Rican Familism: Consideration for Family Therapy." *Family Relations* 37, pp. 260–64.

————, and Kathleen Romano (1994). "Adolescents and Parental Death from AIDS." In *AIDS and the New Orphans: Coping with Death*. eds. Barbara O. Dane and Carol Levine. Westport, CT: Auburn House.

————, et al. (July–August 1997). "Cultural-Competency Training for Staff Serving Hispanic Families with a Child in Psychiatric Crisis." *Families in Society* 78, pp. 405–12.

Zeig, Jeffrey K., et al., eds. (1990). *Brief Therapy: Myths, Methods and Metaphors*. New York: Brunner/Mazel.

Zentner, Ervin, and Monna Zentner (May 1985). "The Psychomechanic, Non-chemical Management of Depression." *Social Casework* 66, pp. 275–86.

Zentner, Monna (March 1980). "The Paranoid Client." *Social Casework* 61, pp. 138–45.

Ziefert, Marjorie, and Kaaren Staunch Brown (April 1991). "Skill Building for Effective Intervention with Homeless Families." *Families in Society* 72, pp. 212–19.

Ziegler, Robert, and Lyn Holden (April 1988). "Family Therapy for Learning Disabled and Attention-Deficit Disordered Children." *American Journal of Orthopsychiatry* 58, pp. 196–210.

Zilversmit, Charlotte Perlman (April 1990). "Family Treatment with Families with Young Children." *Families in Society* 71, pp. 211–19.

Zimberg, Sheldon, et al., eds. (1978). *Practical Approaches to Alcoholism Psychotherapy*. New York: Plenum Press.

Zimmerman, Shirley L. (April 1980). "The Family-Building Block or Anachronism." *Social Casework* 61, pp. 195–204.

Zuk, Gerald H., and David Rubinstein (1965). "A Review of Concepts in the Study and Treatment of Families of Schizophrenics." In *Intensive Family Therapy*. eds. Ivan Boszormenyi-Nagy and James L. Framo. New York: Harper & Row, pp. 1–25.

INDEX